A History of Western Society

VALUE EDITION

D0162597

AVAILABLE VOLUMES

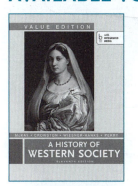

Combined Volume

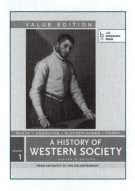

Volume 1
From Antiquity
to the Enlightenment

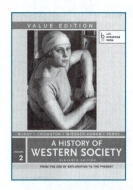

Volume 2
From the Age of
Exploration to the Present

ABOUT THE COVER ART

Raphael, *The Veiled Woman*

This portrait was painted in oil in about 1516 by the Italian Renaissance artist Raphael, the premier portrait painter of his era and one of the most influential artists of all time. The woman's identity is not known, but she may have been Raphael's mistress, Margarita Luti, who served as his model in other works, including several of his portraits of the Virgin Mary. Many stories about the two of them were invented after Raphael died at the relatively young age of 37, and their relationship became the subject of poems, paintings, drawings, operas, and a film. Whoever the woman is, Raphael portrays her here as beauty itself, in a magnificent white and gold satin dress, with a necklace of amber beads and a single pearl in her dark hair. The tiny lock of hair on her forehead that has escaped from her careful hair arrangement is a symbol of the Renaissance ideal of *sprezzatura,* an attitude of nonchalance in which difficult things are made to look easy, a quality that is found in many of Raphael's paintings.

VALUE EDITION

A History of Western Society

Eleventh Edition

John P. McKay
University of Illinois at Urbana-Champaign

Bennett D. Hill
Late of Georgetown University

John Buckler
Late of University of Illinois at Urbana-Champaign

Clare Haru Crowston
University of Illinois at Urbana-Champaign

Merry E. Wiesner-Hanks
University of Wisconsin–Milwaukee

Joe Perry
Georgia State University

BEDFORD/ST. MARTIN'S

Boston • New York

FOR BEDFORD/ST. MARTIN'S

Publisher for History: Mary V. Dougherty
Executive Editor for History: Traci M. Crowell
Director of Development for History: Jane Knetzger
Developmental Editor: Annette Fantasia
Senior Production Editor: Christina M. Horn
Senior Production Supervisor: Dennis J. Conroy
Executive Marketing Manager: Sandra McGuire
Editorial Assistant: Emily DiPietro
Production Assistant: Elise Keller
Copy Editor: Jennifer Brett Greenstein
Indexer: Leoni Z. McVey
Cartography: Mapping Specialists, Ltd.
Photo Researcher: Carole Frohlich and Elisa Gallagher, The Visual Connection Image Research, Inc.
Senior Art Director: Anna Palchik
Text Designer: Jonathon Nix
Cover Designer: Billy Boardman
Cover Art: Raphael (1483–1520), *The Veiled Woman (La Donna Velata)*, ca. 1516 (oil on canvas). Palazzo Pitti, Florence/Alinari/The Bridgeman Art Library.
Composition: Jouve
Printing and Binding: RR Donnelley and Sons

President, Bedford/St. Martin's: Denise B. Wydra
Director of Marketing: Karen R. Soeltz
Production Director: Susan W. Brown
Director of Rights and Permissions: Hilary Newman

Manufactured in the United States of America.

8   7   6   5   4   3
f   e   d   c   b   a

For information, write: Bedford/St. Martin's, 75 Arlington Street, Boston, MA 02116 (617-399-4000)

ISBN 978-1-4576-4849-6 (Combined Edition)
ISBN 978-1-4576-4850-2 (Volume 1)
ISBN 978-1-4576-4851-9 (Volume 2)

Preface
Why This Book This Way

A History of Western Society grew out of the initial three authors' desire to infuse new life into the study of Western Civilization. With this new edition, we three new authors, Clare Haru Crowston, Merry E. Wiesner-Hanks, and Joe Perry—who first used the book as students or teachers—have assumed full responsibility for the revision and continue to incorporate the latest and best scholarship in the field. We are now pleased to introduce *A History of Western Society*, Value Edition, which provides the same high-quality material included in the thoroughly revised eleventh edition—the full narrative and select images, maps, features, and pedagogical tools—in a two-color, trade-sized format at a low price.

We know that many of today's students are on a budget and that instructors desire greater flexibility and more digital options in their choice of course materials. We are proud to offer a low-cost text that not only offers the engaging and readable narrative infused with vivid details about life as it was lived—qualities that have long distinguished *A History of Western Society* and that make it an especially good fit for a trade-sized format—but also includes a rich abundance of print and digital tools designed to help students think historically and master the material. In response to the growing emphasis on historical thinking skills in the teaching of history at all levels, the Value Edition includes carefully chosen primary source excerpts as well as additional document sets online. Indeed, as the digital world continues to transform teaching and learning, this volume is integrated with exciting online resources—automatically available when students purchase a new copy of the book—consisting of **Online Document Assignments** tied closely to each chapter that allow students to practice analysis and synthesis of fascinating document sets, as well as **LearningCurve**, an adaptive learning tool that helps students master the content. Finally, this edition introduces **LaunchPad**, a robust new interactive e-book built into its own course space that makes customizing and assigning the book and its resources simpler than ever. To learn more about the benefits of LearningCurve and LaunchPad, see the "Versions and Supplements" section on page xiv.

The Story of *A History of Western Society*:
Bringing the Past to Life for Students

At the point when *A History of Western Society* was first conceptualized, social history was dramatically changing the ways we understood the past, and the original authors decided to create a book that would re-create the lives of ordinary people in appealing human terms, while also giving major economic, political, cultural, and intellectual developments the attention they unquestionably deserve. The three new authors remain committed to advancing this vision for today's classroom, with a broader definition of social history that brings the original idea into the twenty-first century.

History as a discipline never stands still, and over the last several decades cultural history has joined social history as a source of dynamism. Because of its emphasis on the ways people made sense of their lives, *A History of Western Society* has always included a large amount of cultural history, ranging from foundational works of philosophy and literature to popular songs and stories. The focus on cultural history highlights the interplay between men's and women's lived experiences and the ways men and women reflect on these experiences to create meaning. We know that engaging students' interest in the past is often a challenge, but we also know that the text's hallmark approach — the emphasis on daily life and individual experience in its social and cultural dimensions — connects with students and makes the past vivid and accessible.

Although social and cultural history can be found in every chapter, they are particularly emphasized in the acclaimed "Life" chapters that have always distinguished this book. In response to popular demand by reviewers of the previous edition of the parent text, these have been increased to five in this edition and now include Chapter 4: Life in the Hellenistic World, 336–30 B.C.E., and Chapter 30: Life in an Age of Globalization, 1990 to the Present, which join Chapter 10: Life in Villages and Cities of the High Middle Ages, 1000–1300; Chapter 18: Life in the Era of Expansion, 1650–1800; and Chapter 22: Life in the Emerging Urban Society, 1840–1914. We are delighted to incorporate additional "Life" chapters, as many instructors have told us that it is these distinctive chapters that spark student interest by making the past palpable and approachable in human terms. These "Life" chapters are also enhanced with **NEW Online Document Assignments**, rich and carefully crafted sets of primary sources that allow students to delve further into a key development from each chapter while they analyze and synthesize the evidence. See the "Primary Source Program" section below for more details.

Primary Source Program

To maintain students' interest and help them develop historical thinking skills, we are pleased to offer a selection of high-quality features both in the text and beyond the printed page. To give students many opportunities for analysis as well as a sense of the variety of sources on which historians rely, the Value Edition includes over **60 primary source boxes** that present a mix of canonical and lesser-known sources; a diversity of perspectives representing ordinary and prominent individuals alike; and a wide variety of source types, including tomb inscriptions, diaries, sermons, letters, poetry, and drama. In addition, we have quoted extensively from a wide range of primary sources in the narrative, demonstrating that such quotations are the "stuff" of history. We believe that our extensive use of primary source extracts as an integral part of the narrative as well as in extended form in the primary source boxes will give students ample practice in thinking critically and historically. Each source opens with a headnote and closes with questions for analysis that invite students to evaluate the evidence as historians would. Selected for their interest and carefully integrated into their historical context, these sources provide students with firsthand encounters with people of the past along with the means and tools for building historical skills.

This Value Edition also breaks new ground by offering additional document sets online — called **Online Document Assignments** — tied closely to each chapter of the text and available with the purchase of a new textbook via the code printed on the inside front cover. Each assignment, based on either the "Individuals in Society" feature or key developments from the "Life" chapters (Chapters 4, 10, 18, 22, and 30), prompts students to explore a key question through analysis of multiple sources. Chapter 14, for example, asks students to analyze documents on the complexities of race, identity, and slavery in the early modern era to shed light on the conditions that made Juan de Pareja's story possible. The assignments feature a wealth of textual and visual sources as well as video and audio. Assignments based on the "Individuals in Society" feature include three to four documents in each assignment, while those based on the "Life" chapters include six to eight documents. These Online Document Assignments provide instructors with a rich variety of assignment options that encourage students to draw their own conclusions, with the help of short-answer questions, multiple-choice questions that provide instant feedback, and a final essay assignment that asks students to use the sources in creative ways.

Finally, the thoroughly revised companion reader, *Sources for Western Society*, Third Edition, provides a rich selection of documents to complement each chapter of the text and is heavily discounted when packaged with the textbook.

"Individuals in Society"

To give students a chance to see the past through ordinary people's lives, each chapter includes one of the popular **"Individuals in Society" biographical essays**, which offer brief studies of individuals or groups, informing students about the societies in which they lived. We have found that readers empathize with these human beings as they themselves seek to define their own identities. The spotlighting of individuals, both famous and obscure, perpetuates the book's continued attention to cultural and intellectual developments, highlights human agency, and reflects changing interests within the historical profession as well as the development of "microhistory." The Value Edition includes essays on Cyrus the Great, who in the sixth century B.C.E. founded the Persian Empire; Rebecca Protten, a former slave and leader in the Moravian missionary movement; and Margaret Thatcher, the first woman elected to lead a major European state. As mentioned previously, the majority of these features are tied to **Online Document Assignments** that allow students to further explore the historical conditions in which these individuals lived.

Learning Aids

We know firsthand and take seriously the challenges students face in understanding, retaining, and mastering so much material that is often unfamiliar, and the Value Edition offers a number of pedagogical tools to help students grasp key concepts and get the most out of their reading. As mentioned earlier, the **LearningCurve online adaptive tool** allows students to rehearse the content and come to class prepared. In addition, to focus students' reading, each chapter includes **focus questions** keyed to the main chapter headings. These questions are repeated in the **Chapter Review** at the end of each chapter that provides helpful guidance for reviewing key topics. In addition, **"Make Connections" questions** in the Chapter Review prompt students to assess larger developments across chapters, thus allowing them to develop skills in evaluating change and continuity, making comparisons, and analyzing context and causation.

To promote clarity and comprehension, boldface **key terms** in the text are defined in the glossary and listed in the chapter review. **Phonetic spellings** are located directly after terms that readers are likely to find hard to pronounce. The **chapter chronologies**, which review major developments discussed in each chapter, mirror the key events of the chapter.

In this Value Edition, we made sure to include carefully selected illustrations and maps that complement and reinforce the narrative. The 150 **contemporaneous illustrations** — including paintings, photographs, and artifacts, make the past tangible and include captions that inform students while encouraging them to read the text more deeply. The high-quality **maps** illustrate major developments in the narrative.

The new directions taken in this Value format have not changed the central mission of the book, which is to introduce students to the broad sweep of Western Civilization in a fresh yet balanced manner. As we have made these changes, large and small, we have sought to give students and teachers an integrated perspective so that they could pursue — on their own or in the classroom — the historical questions that they find particularly exciting and significant.

Acknowledgments

It is a pleasure to thank the many instructors who read and critiqued the previous edition of *A History of Western Society* to make suggestions for the new edition of the parent text and this Value Edition:

William M. Abbott, Fairfield University
Joseph Avitable, Quinnipiac University
Dudley Belcher, Tri-County Technical College
Amy Bix, Iowa State University
Nancy Bjorklund, Fullerton College
Robert Blackey, California State University, San Bernardino
Stephen Blumm, Montgomery County Community College
Robert Brennan, Cape Fear Community College
Daniel Bubb, Gonzaga University
Jeff Burson, Georgia Southern University
George Carson, Central Bible College
Michael Cavey, Northern Virginia Community College
Marie Therese Champagne, University of West Florida
Mark W. Chavalas, University of Wisconsin–LaCrosse
David Cherry, Montana State University, Bozeman
Benzion Chinn, Ohio State University
Thomas Colbert, Marshalltown Community College
Elizabeth Collins, Triton College
Amy Colon, Sullivan County Community College
Kristen Cornelis, Community Colleges of Spokane, Institute for Extended
      Learning
Michael H. Creswell, Florida State University
Andrea DeKoter, State University of New York at Cortland

Donna Donald, Liberty University
Kurt J. Eberly, Tidewater Community College
John Ebley, Anne Arundel Community College
Christopher Ferguson, Auburn University
Robert Figueira, Lander University
Paula Findlen, Stanford University
Jennifer Foray, Purdue University
Laura Gathagan, State University of New York at Cortland
Stephen Gibson, Allegany College of Maryland
Gregory Golden, Rhode Island College
Jack Goldstone, George Mason University
Chuck Goodwin, Illinois Valley Community College
Dolores Grapsas, New River Community College
Robert Grasso, Monmouth University
Robert H. Greene, University of Montana
Edward Gutierrez, University of Hartford
David Halahmy, Cypress College
Michael Harkins, Harper College
David M. Head, John Tyler Community College
Jeff Horn, Manhattan College
Barry Jordan, Cape Fear Community College
Cheryl L. Kajs, Pellissippi State Community College
Michael Kennedy, High Point University
Michele Kinney, Strayer University
Willem Klooster, Clark University
Pamela Koenig, Seminole State College
Roy G. Koepp, University of Nebraska at Kearney
James Krapfl, McGill University
Andrew E. Larsen, Marquette University
Kenneth Loiselle, Rice University
Susan Mattern, The University of Georgia
Maureen A. McCormick, Florida State College at Jacksonville
James McIntyre, Moraine Valley Community College
Deena McKinney, East Georgia College
Linda A. McMillin, Susquehanna University
Jennifer McNabb, Western Illinois University
Michael Meng, Clemson University
Scott Merriman, Troy University
Ryan Messenger, Monroe Community College/Genesee Community College
Byron J. Nakamura, Southern Connecticut State University
Jeannine Olson, Rhode Island College
Lisa Ossian, Des Moines Area Community College
Jotham Parsons, Duquesne University
Margaret Peacock, The University of Alabama
Kathy L. Pearson, Old Dominion University
Amanda Podany, California State Polytechnic University, Pomona
Ann Pond, Bishop State Community College

Matthew Restall, Pennsylvania State University
Michael D. Richards, Northern Virginia Community College
Jason Ripper, Everett Community College
Russell J. Rockefeller, Anne Arundel Community College
Leonard N. Rosenband, Utah State University
Mark Edward Ruff, Saint Louis University
Ernest Rugenstein, Hudson Valley Community College
Anne Ruszkiewicz, Sullivan County Community College
Wendy A. Sarti, Oakton Community College
Linda Scherr, Mercer County Community College
Elise Shelton, Trident Technical College
Chris Shepard, Trident Technical College
Robert Shipley, Widener University
Sherri Singer, Alamance Community College
Daniel Snell, University of Oklahoma
Steven Soper, The University of Georgia
Susan Souza-Mort, Bristol Community College
James Taw, Valdosta State University
Alfred T. Terrell, Yuba College
Timothy Thibodeau, Nazareth College
Karl Valois, University of Connecticut, Torrington
Liana Vardi, University at Buffalo, The State University of New York
Joseph Villano, Indian River State College
Gregory Vitarbo, Meredith College
David Weiland, Collin County Community College
Scott White, Scottsdale Community College
Pamela Wolfe, Yeshiva of Greater Washington
James Wright, Triton College
Sergei Zhuk, Ball State University

It is also a pleasure to thank the many editors who have assisted us over the years, first at Houghton Mifflin and now at Bedford/St. Martin's. At Bedford/St. Martin's, these include development editor Annette Fantasia; freelance development editors Michelle McSweeney and Dale Anderson; associate editor Jack Cashman and editorial assistant Emily DiPietro; executive editor Traci Mueller Crowell; director of development Jane Knetzger; publisher for history Mary Dougherty; photo researcher Carole Frohlich; text permissions editor Eve Lehmann; and Christina Horn, senior production editor, with the assistance of Elise Keller and the guidance of managing editor Michael Granger and assistant managing editor John Amburg. Other key contributors were designer Jonathon Nix, page makeup artist Cia Boynton, copy editor Jennifer Brett Greenstein, proofreaders Angela Morrison and Susan Moore, indexer Leoni McVey, and cover designer Billy Boardman. We would also like to thank president Denise Wydra and co-president of Macmillan Higher Education Joan E. Feinberg.

Many of our colleagues at the University of Illinois, the University of Wisconsin–Milwaukee, and Georgia State University continue to provide information and stimulation, often without even knowing it. We thank them for it. We also thank the many students over the years with whom we have used earlier editions of this book. Their reactions and opinions helped shape the revisions to this edition, and we hope it remains worthy of the ultimate praise that they bestowed on it: that it's "not boring like most textbooks." Merry Wiesner-Hanks would, as always, also like to thank her husband, Neil, without whom work on this project would not be possible. Clare Haru Crowston thanks her husband, Ali, and her children, Lili, Reza, and Kian, who are a joyous reminder of the vitality of life that we try to showcase in this book. Joe Perry thanks his colleagues and students at Georgia State for their intellectual stimulation and is grateful to Joyce de Vries for her unstinting support and encouragement.

Each of us has benefited from the criticism of our coauthors, although each of us assumes responsibility for what he or she has written. Merry Wiesner-Hanks has intensively reworked and revised John Buckler's Chapters 1–6 and has revised Chapters 7–13; Clare Crowston has written and revised Chapters 14–19 and took responsibility for John McKay's Chapter 20; and Joe Perry took responsibility for John McKay's Chapters 21–24 and has written and revised Chapters 25–30.

We'd especially like to thank the founding authors, John P. McKay, Bennett D. Hill, and John Buckler, for their enduring contributions and for their faith in each of us to carry on their legacy.

Clare Haru Crowston
Merry E. Wiesner-Hanks
Joe Perry

Versions and Supplements

Adopters of the Value Edition of *A History of Western Society* and their students have access to abundant extra resources, including documents, presentation and testing materials, the acclaimed Bedford Series in History and Culture volumes, and much more. See below for more information, visit the book's catalog site at **bedfordstmartins.com /mckaywestvalue/catalog**, or contact your local Bedford/St. Martin's sales representative.

Get the Right Version for Your Class

To accommodate different course lengths and course budgets, the Value Edition of *A History of Western Society* is available in several different formats, including e-books, which are available at a substantial discount.

- Combined edition (Chapters 1–30): available in paperback and e-book formats
- Volume 1, From Antiquity to the Enlightenment (Chapters 1–16): available in paperback and e-book formats
- Volume 2, From the Age of Exploration to the Present (Chapters 14–30): available in paperback and e-book formats

Any of these volumes can be packaged with additional books for a discount. To get ISBNs for discount packages, see the online catalog at **bedfordstmartins.com/mckaywestvalue /catalog** or contact your Bedford/St. Martin's representative.

NEW Assign LaunchPad—the Online, Interactive e-Book in a Course Space Enriched with Integrated Assets

The new standard in digital history, LaunchPad course tools are so intuitive to use that online, hybrid, and face-to-face courses can be set up in minutes. Even novices will find it's easy to create assignments, track students' work, and access a wealth of relevant learning and teaching resources. It is the ideal learning environment for students to work with the text, maps, documents, and assessment. LaunchPad is loaded with the full interactive e-book and the *Sources for Western Society* documents collection—plus LearningCurve, the Online Document Assignments, additional primary sources, guided reading exercises designed to help students read actively for key concepts, boxed feature reading quizzes, chapter summative quizzes, and more. LaunchPad can be used as is or customized, and it easily integrates with course management systems. And with fast ways to build assignments, rearrange chapters, and add new pages, sections, or links, it lets teachers build the course materials they need and hold students accountable.

Let Students Choose Their e-Book Format. In addition to the LaunchPad e-book, students can purchase the downloadable *Bedford e-Book to Go for A History of Western Society* from our Web site or find other PDF versions of the e-book at our publishing partners' sites: CourseSmart, Barnes & Noble NookStudy, Kno, CafeScribe, or Chegg.

NEW Go Beyond the Printed Page with Bedford Integrated Media

As described in the preface and on the inside front cover, students purchasing new books receive access to LearningCurve and Online Document Assignments for *A History of Western Society*.

☑ **Assign LearningCurve so You Know What Your Students Know and They Come to Class Prepared.** Assigning LearningCurve in place of reading quizzes is easy for instructors, and the reporting features help instructors track overall class trends and spot topics that are giving students trouble so they can adjust their lectures and class activities. This online learning tool is popular with students because it was designed to help them rehearse content at their own pace in a nonthreatening, gamelike environment. The feedback for wrong answers provides instructional coaching and sends students back to the book for review. Students answer as many questions as necessary to reach a target score, with repeated chances to revisit material they haven't mastered. When LearningCurve is assigned, students come to class better prepared.

🄴 **Assign the Online Document Assignments so that Students Put Interpretation into Practice.** In addition to the primary sources embedded in each chapter, this text comes with brand-new, ready-made assignable document sets based either on the five "Life" chapters (Chapters 4, 10, 18, 22, and 30) or on the popular "Individuals in Society" feature. Callouts to these assignments appear in each chapter and prompt students to go online to explore a key question through analysis of the document set. The Online Document Assignments provide a helpful framework for working with the sources. Each assignment comes with an introduction that sets the specific context for the document set, as well as pre-reading questions that ask students to recall the related developments in the textbook. Individual documents are accompanied by a brief headnote and a set of questions. In addition, multiple-choice questions help students analyze the sources by providing instant feedback, and each assignment culminates in a one- to two-page essay prompt that encourages students to use the sources in creative ways. With Online Document Assignments, students draw their own conclusions about the past while practicing critical thinking and synthesis skills.

Send Students to Free Online Resources

The book's Student Site at **bedfordstmartins.com/mckaywestvalue** gives students a way to read, write, and study by providing plentiful quizzes and activities, study aids, and history research and writing help.

FREE Online Study Guide. Available at the Student Site, this popular resource provides students with quizzes and activities for each chapter, including multiple-choice self-tests that focus on important concepts; flash cards that test students' knowledge of key terms; timeline activities that emphasize causal relationships; and map quizzes intended to strengthen students' geography skills. Instructors can monitor students' progress through an online Quiz Gradebook or receive e-mail updates.

FREE Research, Writing, and Anti-plagiarism Advice. Available at the Student Site, Bedford's **History Research and Writing Help** includes **History Research and Reference**

Sources, with links to history-related databases, indexes, and journals; **Build a Bibliography**, a simple Web-based tool known as The Bedford Bibliographer that generates bibliographies in four commonly used documentation styles; and **Tips on Avoiding Plagiarism**, an online tutorial that reviews the consequences of plagiarism and features exercises to help students practice integrating sources and recognize acceptable summaries.

Take Advantage of Instructor Resources

Bedford/St. Martin's has developed a wide range of teaching resources for this book and for this course. They range from lecture and presentation materials and assessment tools to course management options. Most can be downloaded or ordered at bedfordstmartins.com/mckaywestvalue/catalog.

Instructor's Resource Manual. The instructor's manual offers both experienced and first-time instructors tools for preparing lectures and running discussions. It includes chapter-review material, teaching strategies, and a guide to chapter-specific supplements available for the text, plus suggestions on how to get the most out of LearningCurve and a survival guide for first-time teaching assistants.

Computerized Test Bank. The test bank includes a mix of fresh, carefully crafted multiple-choice, short-answer, and essay questions for each chapter. It also contains brand-new primary source and map-based questions. All questions appear in Microsoft Word format and in easy-to-use test bank software that allows instructors to add, edit, resequence, and print questions and answers. Instructors can also export questions into a variety of formats, including Blackboard, Desire2Learn, and Moodle.

The Bedford Lecture Kit: **PowerPoint Maps, Images, Lecture Outlines, and i>clicker Content.** Look good and save time with *The Bedford Lecture Kit*. These presentation materials are downloadable individually from the Instructor Resources tab at bedfordstmartins.com/mckaywestvalue/catalog and are available on *The Bedford Lecture Kit* **Instructor's Resource CD-ROM**. They provide ready-made and fully customizable PowerPoint multimedia presentations that include lecture outlines with embedded maps, figures, and selected images from the textbook and extra background for instructors. Also available are maps and selected images in JPEG and PowerPoint formats; content for i>clicker, a classroom response system, in Microsoft Word and PowerPoint formats; the Instructor's Resource Manual in Microsoft Word format; and outline maps in PDF format for quizzing or handing out. All files are suitable for copying onto transparency acetates.

Videos and Multimedia. A wide assortment of videos and multimedia CD-ROMs on various topics in Western Civilization is available to qualified adopters through your Bedford/St. Martin's sales representative.

Package and Save Your Students Money

For information on free packages and discounts up to 50 percent, visit bedfordstmartins.com/mckaywestvalue/catalog, or contact your local Bedford/St. Martin's sales representative. The products that follow all qualify for discount packaging.

Sources for Western Society, **Third Edition.** This primary source collection — available in Volume 1 and Volume 2 — provides a revised and expanded selection of sources to accompany *A History of Western Society.* Each chapter features five or six written and visual sources by well-known figures and ordinary individuals alike. With over fifty new selections — including a dozen new visual sources — and enhanced pedagogy throughout, students are given the tools to engage critically with canonical and lesser-known sources and prominent and ordinary voices. Each chapter includes a "Sources in Conversation" feature that presents differing views on key topics. This companion reader is an exceptional value for students and offers plenty of assignment options for instructors. Available at a deep discount when packaged with the print text and included in the LaunchPad e-book. Also available on its own as a downloadable PDF e-book or with the main text's e-Book to Go.

The Bedford Series in History and Culture. More than one hundred titles in this highly praised series combine first-rate scholarship, historical narrative, and important primary documents for undergraduate courses. Each book is brief, inexpensive, and focused on a specific topic or period. For a complete list of titles, visit bedfordstmartins .com/history/series. Package discounts are available.

Rand McNally Atlas of Western Civilization. This collection of over fifty full-color maps highlights social, political, and cross-cultural change and interaction from classical Greece and Rome to the postindustrial Western world. Each map is thoroughly indexed for fast reference. Available for $5.00 when packaged with the text.

The Bedford Glossary for European History. This handy supplement for the survey course gives students historically contextualized definitions for hundreds of terms — from *Abbasids* to *Zionism* — that they will encounter in lectures, reading, and exams. Available free when packaged with the text.

Trade Books. Titles published by sister companies Hill and Wang; Farrar, Straus and Giroux; Henry Holt and Company; St. Martin's Press; Picador; and Palgrave Macmillan are available at a 50 percent discount when packaged with Bedford/St. Martin's textbooks. For more information, visit bedfordstmartins.com/tradeup.

A Pocket Guide to Writing in History. This portable and affordable reference tool by Mary Lynn Rampolla provides reading, writing, and research advice useful to students in all history courses. Concise yet comprehensive advice on approaching typical history assignments, developing critical reading skills, writing effective history papers, conducting research, using and documenting sources, and avoiding plagiarism — enhanced by practical tips and examples throughout — have made this slim reference a bestseller. Package discounts are available.

A Student's Guide to History. This complete guide provides the practical help students need to be successful in any history course. In addition to introducing students to the nature of the discipline, author Jules Benjamin teaches a wide range of skills from preparing for exams to approaching common writing assignments and explains the research and documentation process with plentiful examples. Package discounts are available.

The Social Dimension of Western Civilization. Combining current scholarship with classic pieces, this reader's forty-eight secondary sources, compiled by Richard M. Golden, hook students with the fascinating and often surprising details of how everyday Western people worked, ate, played, celebrated, worshipped, married, procreated, fought, persecuted, and died. Package discounts are available.

The West in the Wider World: Sources and Perspectives. Edited by Richard Lim and David Kammerling Smith, the first college reader to focus on the central historical question "How did the West become the West?" offers a wealth of written and visual source materials that reveal the influence of non-European regions on the origins and development of Western Civilization. Package discounts are available.

Brief Contents

Contents

CHAPTER 1

Origins to 1200 B.C.E.   1

CHAPTER 8

Europe in the Early Middle Ages 600–1000   225

CHAPTER 9
State and Church in the High Middle Ages
1000–1300   259

CHAPTER 10
Life in Villages and Cities of the High Middle Ages
1000–1300   293

CHAPTER 11

The Later Middle Ages 1300–1450   331

CHAPTER 14

European Exploration and Conquest 1450–1650   438

CHAPTER 15

Absolutism and Constitutionalism ca. 1589–1725   476

CHAPTER 16

Toward a New Worldview 1540–1789   516

CHAPTER 20

The Revolution in Energy and Industry

ca. 1780–1850   654

CHAPTER 26

The Age of Anxiety 1880–1940   867

CHAPTER 27

Dictatorships and the Second World War

1919–1945   901

Maps, Figures, and Tables

Special Features

1

✔ LearningCurve
bedfordstmartins.com/mckaywestvalue
After reading the chapter, use
LearningCurve to retain what
you've read.

Origins

TO 1200 B.C.E.

WHAT IS HISTORY? THAT SEEMINGLY SIMPLE QUESTION HIDES GREAT
complexities. If history is the story of humans, what does it mean to be
human? As they have in the past, philosophers, religious leaders, politicians,
physicians, and others wrestle with this question every day, as do scientists
using technologies that were unavailable until very recently, such as DNA
analysis and radiocarbon dating. Is all of the human past "history"? Previous
generations of historians would generally have answered no, that history only
began when writing began and everything before that was "prehistory." This
leaves out most of the human story, however, and today historians no longer
see writing as such a sharp dividing line. They explore all eras of the human
past using many different types of sources, although they do still tend to pay
more attention to written sources.

For most of their history, humans were foragers moving through the landscape, inventing ever more specialized tools. About 11,000 years ago, people
in some places domesticated plants and animals, which many scholars describe
as the most significant change in human history. They began to live in permanent villages, some of which grew into cities. They created structures of governance to control their more complex societies, along with military forces and
taxation systems. Some invented writing to record taxes, inventories, and payments, and they later put writing to other uses, including the preservation of
stories, traditions, and history. The first places where these new technologies
and systems were introduced were the Tigris and Euphrates River Valleys of
southwest Asia and the Nile Valley of northeast Africa, areas whose history
became linked through trade connections, military conquests, and migrations.

Understanding Western History

What do we mean by "the West" and "Western civilization"?

Most human groups have left some record of themselves. Some left artifacts, others pictures or signs, and still others written documents. In many of these records, groups set up distinctions between themselves and others. Some of these distinctions are between small groups such as neighboring tribes, some between countries and civilizations, and some between vast parts of the world. Among the most enduring of the latter are the ideas of "the West" and "the East."

Describing the West

Ideas about the West and the distinction between West and East derived originally from the ancient Greeks. Greek civilization grew up in the shadow of earlier civilizations to the south and east of Greece, especially Egypt and Mesopotamia. Greeks defined themselves in relation to these more advanced cultures, which they saw as "Eastern." Greeks were also the first to use the word *Europe* for a geographic area, taking the word from the name of a minor goddess. They set Europe in opposition to "Asia" (also named for a minor goddess), by which they meant both what we now call western Asia and what we call Africa.

The Greeks passed this conceptualization on to the Romans, who saw themselves clearly as part of the West. For some Romans, Greece remained in the West, while other Romans came to view Greek traditions as vaguely "Eastern." To Romans, the East was more sophisticated and more advanced, but also decadent and somewhat immoral. Roman value judgments have continued to shape preconceptions, stereotypes, and views of differences between the West and the East—which in the past were also called the "Occident" and the "Orient"—to this day.

Greco-Roman ideas about the West were passed on to people who lived in western and northern Europe, who saw themselves as the inheritors of this classical tradition and thus as the West. When these Europeans established colonies outside of Europe beginning in the late fifteenth century, they regarded what they were doing as taking Western culture with them, even though many aspects of Western culture, such as Christianity, had actually originated in what Europeans by that point regarded as the East. With colonization, *Western* came to mean those cultures that included significant numbers of people of European ancestry, no matter where on the globe they were located.

In the early twentieth century educators and other leaders in the United States became worried that many people, especially young people, were becoming cut off from European intellectual and cultural traditions. They encouraged the establishment of college and university courses focusing on "Western civilization," the first of which was taught at Columbia University in 1919. In designing the course, the faculty included cultures that as far back as the ancient Greeks had been considered Eastern, such as Egypt and Mesopotamia. This conceptualization and the course spread to other colleges and universities, developing into what became known as the introductory Western civilization course, a staple of historical instruction for generations of college students.

After World War II divisions between the West and the East changed again. Now there was a new division between East and West within Europe, with *Western* coming to imply a capitalist economy and *Eastern* the Communist Eastern bloc. Thus, Japan was considered Western, and some Greek-speaking areas of Europe became Eastern. The collapse of communism in the Soviet Union and eastern Europe in the 1980s brought yet another refiguring, with much of eastern Europe joining the European Union, originally a Western organization.

At the beginning of the twenty-first century, *Western* still suggests a capitalist economy, but it also has certain cultural connotations, such as individualism and competition, which some see as negative and others as positive. Islamist radicals often describe their aims as an end to Western cultural, economic, and political influence, though Islam itself is generally described, along with Judaism and Christianity, as a Western monotheistic religion. Thus, throughout its long history, the meaning of "the West" has shifted, but in every era it has meant more than a geographical location.

What Is Civilization?

Just as the meaning of the word *Western* is shaped by culture, so is the meaning of the word *civilization*. In the ancient world, residents of cities generally viewed themselves as more advanced and sophisticated than rural folk—a judgment still made today. They saw themselves as more "civilized," a word that comes from the Latin adjective *civilis*, which refers to a citizen, either of a town or of a larger political unit such as an empire.

This depiction of people as either civilized or uncivilized was gradually extended to whole societies. Beginning in the eighteenth century, European scholars described any society in which political, economic, and social organizations operated on a large scale, not primarily through families and kin groups, as a **civilization**. Civilizations had cities; laws that governed human relationships; codes of manners and social conduct that regulated how people were to behave; and scientific, philosophical, and theological beliefs that explained the larger world. Civilizations also had some form of political organization, what political scientists call "the state," through which one group was able to coerce resources out of others to engage in group endeavors, such as building large structures or carrying out warfare. States established armies, bureaucracies, and taxation systems. Generally only societies that used writing were judged to be civilizations, because writing allowed more permanent expression of thoughts, ideas, and feelings. Human societies in which people were nomadic or lived in small villages without formal laws, and in which traditions were passed down orally, were not regarded as civilizations.

Until the middle of the twentieth century, historians often referred to the places where writing and cities developed as "cradles of civilization," proposing a model of development for all humanity patterned on that of an individual life span. However, the idea that all human societies developed (or should develop) on a uniform process from a "cradle" to a "mature" civilization has now been largely discredited, and some historians choose not to use the term *civilization* at all because it could imply that some societies are superior to others.

Just as the notion of "civilization" has been questioned, so has the notion of "Western civilization." Ever since the idea of "Western civilization" was first developed, people have debated what its geographical extent and core values are. Are there certain beliefs, customs, concepts, and institutions that set Western civilization apart from other civilizations, and if so, when and how did these originate? How were these values and practices transmitted over space and time, and how did they change? No civilization stands alone, and each is influenced by its neighbors. Whatever Western civilization was—and is—it has been shaped by interactions with other societies, cultures, and civilizations, but the idea that there are basic distinctions between the West and the rest of the world in terms of cultural values has been very powerful for thousands of years, and it still shapes the way many people, including people in power, view the world.

The Earliest Human Societies

How did early human societies develop and create new technologies and cultural forms?

Scientists who study the history of the earth use a variety of systems to classify and divide time. Geologists and paleontologists divide time into periods that last many millions of years, determined by the movements of continents and the evolution and extinction of plant and animal species. During the nineteenth century, archaeologists coined labels for eras of the human past according to the primary material out of which surviving tools had been made. Thus the earliest human era became the Stone Age, the next era the Bronze Age, and the next the Iron Age. They further divided the Stone Age into the **Paleolithic** (Old Stone) **era**, during which people used stone, bone, and other natural products to make tools and gained food largely by foraging—that is, by gathering plant products, trapping or catching small animals and birds, and hunting larger prey. This was followed by the **Neolithic** (New Stone) **era**, which saw the beginning of agricultural and animal domestication. People around the world adopted agriculture at various times, and some never did, but the transition between the Paleolithic and the Neolithic is usually set at about 9000 B.C.E., the point at which agriculture was first developed.

From the First Hominids to the Paleolithic Era

Using many different pieces of evidence from all over the world, archaeologists, paleontologists, and other scholars have developed a view of human evolution that has a widely shared basic outline, though there are disagreements about details. Sometime between 7 and 6 million years ago in southern and eastern Africa, groups of human ancestors (members of the biological "hominid" family) began to walk upright, which allowed them to carry things. About 3.4 million years ago some hominids began to use naturally occurring objects as tools, and around 2.5 million years ago, one group in East Africa began to make simple tools, a feat that was accompanied by, and may have spurred, brain development. Groups migrated into much of Africa, and then into Asia and Europe; by about 600,000 years ago there were hominids throughout much of Afroeurasia.

About 200,000 years ago, again in East Africa, some of these early humans evolved into *Homo sapiens* ("thinking humans"), which had still larger and more complex brains that allowed for symbolic language and better social skills. *Homo sapiens* invented highly specialized tools made out of a variety of materials: barbed fishhooks and harpoons, snares and traps for catching small animals, bone needles for sewing clothing, awls for punching holes in leather, sharpened flint pieces bound to wooden or bone handles for hunting and cutting, and slings for carrying infants. They made regular use of fire for heat, light, and cooking, increasing the range of foods that were easily digestible. They also migrated, first across Africa, and by 70,000 years ago out of Africa into Eurasia.

Eventually they traveled farther still, reaching Australia using rafts about 50,000 years ago and the Americas by about 15,000 years ago, or perhaps earlier. They moved into areas where other types of hominids lived, interacting with them and in some cases interbreeding with them. Gradually the other types of hominids became extinct, leaving *homo sapiens* as the only survivors and the ancestors of all modern humans.

In the Paleolithic period humans throughout the world lived in ways that were similar to one another. Archaeological evidence and studies of modern foragers suggest that people generally lived in small groups of related individuals and moved throughout the landscape in search of food. In areas where food resources were especially rich, such as along seacoasts, they settled more permanently in one place, living in caves or building structures. They ate mostly plants, and much of the animal protein in their diet came from foods gathered or scavenged, such as insects and bird's eggs, rather than hunted directly. Paleolithic peoples did, however, hunt large game. Groups working together forced animals over cliffs, threw spears, and, beginning about 15,000 B.C.E., used bows to shoot projectiles so that they could stand farther away from their prey while hunting.

Paleolithic people were not differentiated by wealth, because in a foraging society it was not advantageous to accumulate material goods. Most foraging societies that exist today, or did so until recently, have some type of division of labor by sex, and also by age. Men are more often responsible for hunting, through which they gain prestige as well as meat, and women for gathering plant and animal products. This may or may not have been the case in the Paleolithic era, or there may have been a diversity of patterns.

Early human societies are often described in terms of their tools, but this misses a large part of the story. Beginning in the Paleolithic era, human beings have expressed themselves through what we would now term the arts or culture: painting and decorating walls and objects, making music, telling stories, dancing alone or in groups. Paleolithic evidence, particularly from after about 50,000 years ago, includes flutes, carvings, jewelry, and amazing paintings done on cave walls and rock outcroppings that depict animals, people, and symbols. Burials, paintings, and objects also suggest that people may have developed ideas about supernatural forces that controlled some aspects of the natural world and the humans in it, what we now term spirituality or religion. Spiritually adept men and women communicated with that unseen world, and objects such as carvings or masks were probably thought to have special healing or protective powers. (See "Primary Source: Paleolithic Venus Figures," page 6.)

Total human population grew very slowly during the Paleolithic. One estimate proposes that there were perhaps 500,000 humans in the world about 30,000 years ago. By about 10,000 years ago, this number had grown to 5 million — ten times as many people. This was a significant increase, but it took twenty thousand years. The low population density meant that human impact on the environment was relatively small, although still significant.

Planting Crops

Foraging remained the basic way of life for most of human history, and for groups living in extreme environments, such as tundras or deserts, it was the only possible way to survive. In a few especially fertile areas, however, the natural environment provided

PRIMARY SOURCE   Paleolithic Venus Figures

Written sources provide evidence about the human past only after the development of writing, allowing us to read the words of people long dead. For most of human history, however, there were no written sources, so we "read" the past through objects. Interpreting written documents is difficult, and interpreting archaeological evidence is even more difficult and often contentious. For example, small stone statues of women with enlarged breasts and buttocks dating from the later Paleolithic period (roughly 33,000–9,000 B.C.E.) have been found in many parts of Europe. These were dubbed "Venus figures" by nineteenth-century archaeologists, who thought they represented Paleolithic standards of female beauty just as the goddess Venus represented classical standards. A reproduction of one of these statues, the six-inch-tall Venus of Lespugue made from a mammoth tusk about 25,000 years ago in southern France, is shown here.

(Ronald Sheridan/Ancient Art & Architecture Ltd.)

EVALUATE THE EVIDENCE

1. As you look at this statue, does it seem to link more closely with fertility or with sexuality? How might your own situation as a twenty-first-century person shape your answer to this question?

2. Some scholars see Venus figures as evidence that Paleolithic society was egalitarian or female dominated, but others point out that images of female deities or holy figures are often found in religions that deny women official authority. Can you think of examples of the latter? Which point of view seems most persuasive to you?

enough food that people could become more settled. About 15,000 years ago, the earth's climate entered a warming phase, and more parts of the world were able to support sedentary or semi-sedentary groups of foragers. In several of these places, foragers began planting seeds in the ground along with gathering wild grains, roots, and other foodstuffs. By observation, they learned the optimum times and places for planting. They removed unwanted plants through weeding and selected the seeds they planted in order to get crops that had favorable characteristics, such as larger edible parts. Through this human intervention, certain crops became domesticated, that is, modified by selective breeding so as to serve human needs.

Intentional crop planting first developed around 9000 B.C.E., in the area archaeologists call the **Fertile Crescent**, which runs from present-day Lebanon, Israel, and Jordan north to Turkey and then south and east to the Iran-Iraq border. In this area of mild climate, wild barley and wheat were abundant, along with fruit and nut trees, migrating ducks, and herds of gazelles and other animals. Over the next two millennia, intentional crop planting emerged for the most part independently in the Nile River Valley, western Africa, China, India, Papua New Guinea, Mesoamerica, and perhaps other places where the archaeological evidence has not survived.

Why, after living successfully as foragers for tens of thousands of years, did humans in so many parts of the world begin raising crops at about the same time? The answer to this question is not clear, but crop raising may have resulted from population pressures in those parts of the world where the warming climate provided more food through foraging. More food meant lower child mortality and longer life spans, which allowed populations to grow. People then had a choice: they could move to a new area—the solution that people had always relied on when faced with the problem of food scarcity—or they could develop ways to increase the food supply. They chose the latter and began to plant more intensively, beginning cycles of expanding population and intensification of land use that have continued to today.

A very recent archaeological find at Göbekli Tepe in present-day Turkey, at the northern edge of the Fertile Crescent, suggests that cultural factors may have played a role in the development of agriculture. Here, around 9000 B.C.E., hundreds of people came together to build rings of massive, multiton elaborately carved limestone pillars, and then covered them with dirt and built more. The people who created this site lived some distance away, where archaeological remains indicate that at the time they first carved the pillars, they ate wild game and plants, not crops. We can only speculate about why so many people expended the effort they did to carve these pillars and raise them into place, but the project may have unintentionally spurred the development of new methods of food production that would allow the many workers to be fed efficiently. Indeed, it is very near here that evidence of the world's oldest domesticated wheat has been discovered. Archaeologists speculate that, at least in this case, the symbolic, cultural, or perhaps religious importance of the structure can help explain why the people building it changed from foraging to agriculture.

Implications of Agriculture

Whatever the reasons for the move from foraging to agriculture, within several centuries of initial crop planting, people in the Fertile Crescent, parts of China, and the Nile Valley were relying primarily on domesticated food products. They built permanent houses near one another in villages and planted fields around the villages. In addition, they invented storage containers for food, such as pottery made from fired clay and woven baskets.

A field of planted and weeded crops yields ten to one hundred times as much food—measured in calories—as the same area of naturally occurring plants. It also requires much more labor, however, which was provided both by the greater number of people in the community and by those people working longer hours. In contrast to the twenty hours a week foragers spent on obtaining food, farming peoples were often in the fields from dawn to dusk. Early farmers were also less healthy than foragers were;

their narrower range of foodstuffs made them more susceptible to disease and nutritional deficiencies such as anemia, and also made them shorter. Still, farmers came to outnumber foragers, and slowly larger and larger parts of Europe, China, South and Southeast Asia, and Africa became home to farming villages, a dramatic human alteration of the environment.

At roughly the same time that they domesticated certain plants, people also domesticated animals. The earliest animal to be domesticated was the dog, which separated genetically as a subspecies from wolves at least 15,000 years ago and perhaps much earlier. In about 9000 B.C.E., at the same time they began to raise crops, people in the Fertile Crescent domesticated wild goats and sheep, probably using them first for meat, and then for milk, skins, and eventually fleece. They began to breed the goats and sheep selectively for qualities that they wanted, including larger size, greater strength, better coats, increased milk production, and more even temperaments. Sheep and goats allow themselves to be herded, and people developed a new form of living, **pastoralism**, based on herding and raising livestock; sometimes people trained dogs to assist them. Eventually other grazing animals, including cattle, camels, horses, yak, and reindeer, also became the basis of pastoral economies in central and western Asia, many parts of Africa, and far northern Europe.

Crop raising and pastoralism brought significant changes to human ways of life, but the domestication of certain large animals had an even bigger impact. Cattle and water buffalo were domesticated in some parts of Asia and North Africa, in which they occurred naturally, by at least 7000 B.C.E. Donkeys were domesticated by about 4000 B.C.E., and horses by about 2500 B.C.E. All these animals can be trained to carry people or burdens on their backs and pull against loads dragged behind them, two qualities that are rare among the world's animal species. The domestication of large animals dramatically increased the power available to humans to carry out their tasks, which had both an immediate effect in the societies in which this happened and a long-term effect when these societies later encountered other societies in which human labor remained the only source of power.

Sometime in the seventh millennium B.C.E., people attached wooden sticks to frames that animals dragged through the soil, thus breaking it up and allowing seeds to sprout more easily. These simple scratch plows, pulled by cattle and water buffalo, allowed Neolithic people to produce a significant amount of surplus food, which meant that some people in the community could spend their days performing other tasks, increasing the division of labor. Surplus food had to be stored, and some people began to specialize in making products for storage, such as pots, baskets, bags, bins, and other kinds of containers. Others specialized in making tools, houses, and other items needed in village life, or for producing specific types of food. Families and households became increasingly interdependent, trading food for other commodities or services.

The division of labor allowed by plow agriculture contributed to the creation of social hierarchies, that is, the divisions between rich and poor, elites and common people, that have been a central feature of human society since the Neolithic era. Although no written records were produced during this era, archaeological evidence provides some clues about how the hierarchies might have developed. Villagers needed more complex rules about how food was to be distributed and how different types of work were to be valued than did foragers. Certain individuals must have begun to specialize in the determination and enforcement of these rules, and informal structures of power gradually became more formalized. Religious specialists probably developed more elaborate ritu-als to celebrate life passages and to appeal to the gods for help in times of difficulty, such as illness.

Individuals who were the heads of large families or kin groups had control over the labor of others, and this power became more significant when that labor brought material goods that could be stored. The ability to control the labor of others could also come from physical strength, a charismatic personality, or leadership talents, and such traits may also have led to greater wealth. Material goods — plows, sheep, cattle, sheds, pots, carts — gave one the ability to amass still more material goods, and the gap between those who had them and those who did not widened. Social hierarchies were reinforced over generations as children inherited goods and status from their parents. By the time writing was invented, social distinctions between elites — rulers, nobles, hereditary priests, and other privileged groups — and the rest of the population were already in existence.

Along with hierarchies based on wealth and power, the development of agriculture was intertwined with a hierarchy based on gender. In many places, plow agriculture came to be a male task, perhaps because of men's upper-body strength or because plow agriculture was difficult to combine with care for infants and small children. Men's responsibility for plowing and other agricultural tasks took them outside the household more often than women's duties did, enlarging their opportunities for leadership. This role may have led to their being favored as inheritors of family land and the right to farm communally held land, because when inheritance systems were established in later millennia, they often favored sons when handing down land. Accordingly, over genera-tions, women's independent access to resources decreased.

The system in which men have more power and access to resources than women of the same social level, and in which some men are dominant over other men, is called **patriarchy** and is found in every society in the world with written records, although the level of inequality varies. Men's control of property was rarely absolute, because the desire to keep wealth and property within a family or kin group often resulted in women inheriting, owning, and in some cases managing significant amounts of wealth. Hierarchies of wealth and power thus intersected with hierarchies of gender in complex ways.

Trade and Cross-Cultural Connections

By 7000 B.C.E. or so, some agricultural villages in the Fertile Crescent may have had as many as ten thousand residents. One of the best known of these, Çatal Hüyük in what is now Turkey, shows evidence of trade as well as specialization of labor. Çatal Hüyük's residents lived in densely packed mud-brick houses with walls covered in white plaster that had been made with burned lime. The men and women of the town grew wheat, barley, peas, and almonds and raised sheep and perhaps cattle, though they also seem to have hunted. They made textiles, pots, figurines, baskets, carpets, copper and lead beads, and other goods, and decorated their houses with murals showing animal and human figures. They gathered, sharpened, and polished obsidian, a volcanic rock that could be used for knives, blades, and mirrors, and then traded it with neighboring towns, obtaining seashells and flint. From here the obsidian was exchanged still farther away, for Neolithic societies slowly developed local and then regional networks of exchange and communication.

Among the goods traded in some parts of the world was copper, which people hammered into shapes for jewelry and tools. Like most metals, in its natural state copper usually occurs mixed with other materials in a type of rock called ore, and by about 5500 B.C.E. people in the Balkans had learned that copper could be extracted from ore by heating it in a smelting process. Smelted copper was poured into molds and made into spear points, axes, chisels, beads, and other objects. Pure copper is soft, but through experimentation artisans learned that it would become harder if they mixed it with other metals such as zinc, tin, or arsenic during heating, creating an alloy called bronze.

Because it was stronger than copper, bronze had a far wider range of uses, so much so that later historians decided that its adoption marked a new period in human history: the **Bronze Age**. Like all new technologies, bronze arrived at different times in different places, so the dates of the Bronze Age vary. It began about 3000 B.C.E. in some places, and by about 2500 B.C.E. bronze technology was having an impact in many parts of the world. The end of the Bronze Age came with the adoption of iron technology, which also varied from 1200 B.C.E. to 300 B.C.E. (see Chapter 2). All metals were expensive and hard to obtain, however, so stone, wood, and bone remained important materials for tools and weapons long into the Bronze Age.

Objects were not the only things traded over increasingly long distances during the Neolithic period, for people also carried ideas as they traveled on foot, boats, or camels, and in wagons or carts. Knowledge about the seasons and the weather was vitally important for those who depended on crop raising, and agricultural peoples in many parts of the world began to calculate recurring patterns in the world around them, slowly developing calendars. Scholars have demonstrated that people built circular structures of mounded earth or huge upright stones to help them predict the movements of the sun and stars, including Nabta Playa, erected about 4500 B.C.E. in the desert west of the Nile Valley in Egypt, and Stonehenge, erected about 2500 B.C.E. in southern England.

The rhythms of the agricultural cycle and patterns of exchange also shaped religious beliefs and practices. Among foragers, human fertility is a mixed blessing, as too many children can overtax food supplies, but among crop raisers and pastoralists, fertility — of the land, animals, and people — is essential. Thus in many places multiple gods came to be associated with patterns of birth, growth, death, and regeneration in a system known as **polytheism**. Like humans, the gods came to have a division of labor and a social hierarchy. There were rain gods and sun gods, sky goddesses and moon goddesses, gods that assured the health of cattle or the growth of corn, goddesses of the hearth and home.

Civilization in Mesopotamia

What kind of civilization did the Sumerians develop in Mesopotamia?

The origins of Western civilization are generally traced to an area that is today not seen as part of the West: Mesopotamia (mehs-oh-puh-TAY-mee-uh), the Greek name for the land between the Euphrates (yoo-FRAY-teez) and Tigris (TIGH-grihs) Rivers (Map 1.1). The earliest agricultural villages in Mesopotamia were in the northern, hilly parts of the river valleys, where there is abundant rainfall for crops. Farmers had brought

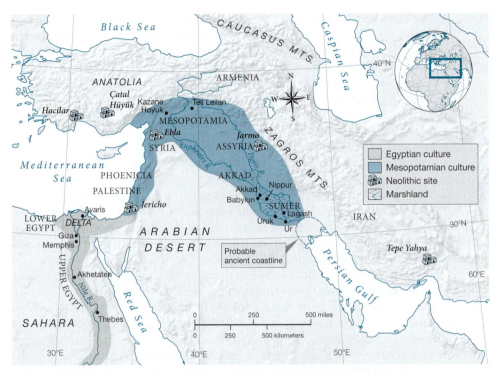

MAP 1.1 Spread of Cultures in the Ancient Near East, ca. 3000–1640 B.C.E.
This map illustrates the spread of the Mesopotamian and Egyptian cultures through the semi-circular stretch of land often called the Fertile Crescent. From this area, the knowledge and use of agriculture spread throughout western Asia, North Africa, and Europe.

techniques of crop raising southward by about 5000 B.C.E., to the southern part of Mesopotamia, called Sumer. In this arid climate farmers developed irrigation on a large scale, which demanded organized group effort, but allowed the population to grow. By about 3800 B.C.E., one of the agricultural villages, Uruk (OO-rook), had expanded significantly, becoming what many historians view as the world's first city, with a population that eventually numbered more than fifty thousand. People living in Uruk built large temples to honor their chief god and goddess, and also invented the world's first system of writing, through which they recorded information about their society. Over the next thousand years, other cities also grew in Sumer, trading with one another and adopting writing.

Environment and Mesopotamian Development

From the outset, geography had a profound effect on Mesopotamia, because here agriculture is possible only with irrigation. Consequently, the Sumerians and later civilizations built their cities along the Tigris and Euphrates Rivers and their branches. They used the rivers to carry agricultural and trade goods, and also to provide water for vast networks of irrigation channels.

The Tigris and Euphrates flow quickly at certain times of the year and carry silt down from the mountains and hills, causing floods. To prevent major floods, the Sumerians created massive hydraulic projects, including reservoirs, dams, and dikes as well as canals. In stories written later, they described their chief god, Enlil, as "the raging flood which has no rival," and believed that at one point there had been a massive flood, a tradition that also gave rise to the biblical story of Noah:

> A flood will sweep over the cult-centers;
> To destroy the seed of mankind . . .
> Is the decision, the word of the assembly of the gods.[1]

Judging by historical records, however, actual destructive floods were few.

In addition to water and transport, the rivers supplied fish, a major element of the Sumerian diet, and reeds, which were used for making baskets and writing implements. The rivers also provided clay, which was hardened to create bricks, the Sumerians' primary building material in a region with little stone. Clay was fired into pots, and inventive artisans developed the potter's wheel so that they could make pots that were stronger and more uniform than those made by earlier methods of coiling ropes of clay. The potter's wheel in turn appears to have led to the introduction of wheeled vehicles sometime in the fourth millennium B.C.E. Exactly where they were invented is hotly contested, but Sumer is one of the first locations in which they appeared. Wheeled vehicles, pulled by domesticated donkeys, led to road building, which facilitated settlement, trade, and conquest, although travel and transport by water remained far easier.

Cities and villages in Sumer and farther up the Tigris and Euphrates traded with one another, and even before the development of writing or kings, it appears that colonists sometimes set out from one city to travel hundreds of miles to the north or west to found a new city or to set up a community in an existing center. These colonies might well have provided the Sumerian cities with goods, such as timber and metal ores, that were not available locally. The cities of the Sumerian heartland continued to grow and to develop governments, and each one came to dominate the surrounding countryside, becoming city-states independent from one another, though not very far apart.

The city-states of Sumer continued to rely on irrigation systems that required co-operation and at least some level of social and political cohesion. The authority to run this system was, it seems, initially assumed by Sumerian priests. Encouraged and directed by their religious leaders, people built temples on tall platforms in the center of their cities. Temples grew into elaborate complexes of buildings with storage space for grain and other products and housing for animals. (Much later, by about 2100 B.C.E., some of the major temple complexes were embellished with a huge stepped pyramid, called a ziggurat, with a shrine on the top.) The Sumerians believed that humans had been created to serve the gods, who lived in the temples. The gods needed not only shelter but food, drink, and clothing. Surrounding the temple and other large buildings were the houses of ordinary citizens, each constructed around a central courtyard. To support the needs of the gods, including the temple constructions, and to support the religious leaders, temples owned large estates, including fields and orchards. Temple officials employed individuals to work the temple's land, paying the workers in rations of grain, oil, and wool.

By 2500 B.C.E. there were more than a dozen city-states in Sumer. Each city developed religious, political, and military institutions, and judging by the fact that people began to construct walls around the cities and other for- tifications, warfare between cities was quite common. Presumably their battles were sometimes sparked by disputes over water, as irrigation in one area reduced or altered the flow of rivers in other areas.

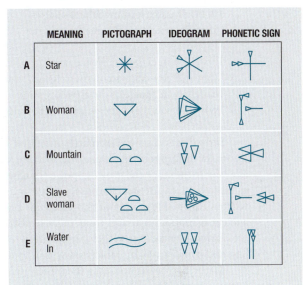

The Invention of Writing and the First Schools

The origins of writing probably go back to the ninth millennium B.C.E., when Near Eastern peoples used clay tokens as counters for record keeping. By the fourth millennium, people had realized that impressing the tokens on clay, or drawing pictures of the

FIGURE 1.1   Sumerian Writing

(Source: S. N. Kramer, *The Sumerians: Their History, Culture and Character.* Copyright © 1963 by The University of Chicago Press. All rights reserved. Used by permission of the publisher.)

tokens on clay, was simpler than making tokens. This breakthrough in turn suggested that more information could be conveyed by adding pictures of still other objects. The result was a complex system of pictographs in which each sign pictured an object, such as "star" (line A of Figure 1.1). These pictographs were the forerunners of the Sumerian form of writing known as **cuneiform** (kyou-NEE-uh-form), from the Latin term for "wedge shaped," used to describe the indentations made by a sharpened stylus in clay.

Scribes could combine pictographs to express meaning. For example, the sign for woman (line B) and the sign for mountain (line C) were combined, literally, into "mountain woman" (line D), which meant "slave woman" because the Sumerians regu- larly obtained their slave women from wars against enemies in the mountains. Pictographs were initially limited in that they could not represent abstract ideas, but the development of ideograms—signs that represented ideas—made writing more versatile. Thus the sign for star could also be used to indicate heaven, sky, or even god. The real breakthrough came when scribes started using signs to represent sounds. For instance, the symbol for "water" (two parallel wavy lines) could also be used to indicate "in," which sounded the same as the spoken word for "water" in Sumerian.

The development of the Sumerian system of writing was piecemeal, with scribes making changes and additions as they were needed. The system became so complicated that scribal schools were established, which by 2500 B.C.E. flourished throughout Sumer. Students at the schools were all male, and most came from families in the middle range of urban society. Each school had a master, teachers, and monitors. Discipline was strict, and students were caned for sloppy work and misbehavior. One graduate of a scribal school had few fond memories of the joy of learning:

My headmaster read my tablet, said:
"There is something missing," caned me.
. . .
The fellow in charge of silence said:
"Why did you talk without permission," caned me.
The fellow in charge of the assembly said:
"Why did you stand at ease without permission," caned me.[2]

Scribal schools were primarily intended to produce individuals who could keep records of the property of temple officials, kings, and nobles. Thus writing first developed as a way to enhance the growing power of elites, not to record speech, although it later came to be used for that purpose, and the stories of gods, kings, and heroes were also written down. Hundreds of thousands of hardened clay tablets have survived from ancient Mesopotamia, and from them historians have learned about many aspects of life, including taxes and wages. Sumerians wrote numbers as well as words on clay tablets, and some surviving tablets show multiplication and division problems.

Mathematics was not just a theoretical matter to the people living in Mesopotamia, because the building of cities, palaces, temples, and canals demanded practical knowledge of geometry and trigonometry.

Religion in Mesopotamia

To Sumerians, and to later peoples in Mesopotamia as well, the world was controlled by gods and goddesses, who represented cosmic forces such as the sun, moon, water, and storms. Each city generally had a chief god or goddess, or sometimes several, with a large temple built in his or her honor. In Uruk, for example, one of the central temples was dedicated to the goddess Inanna, the goddess of love and sexuality, who was also associated with the planet Venus. In one widely told myth, Inanna descends to the underworld, setting off a long struggle among her worshippers to find a replacement. Another deity is found to take her place, but then Inanna returns, just as Venus sets and rises. The king of the gods was Enlil, who was believed to rule over the gods just as the king of a city-state ruled his population. Almost as powerful were the gods of the sun, of storms, and of freshwater.

The gods judged good and evil and would punish humans who lied or cheated. Gods themselves suffered for their actions, and sometimes for no reason at all, just as humans did. People believed that humans had been created to serve the gods and generally anticipated being well treated by the gods if they served them well. The best way to honor the gods was to make the temple as grand and impressive as possible, because the temple's size demonstrated the strength of the community and the power of its chief deity. Once it was built, the temple itself, along with the shrine on the top of the ziggurat, was often off-limits to ordinary people, who did not worship there as a spiritual community. Instead the temple was staffed by priests and priestesses who carried out rituals to honor the god or goddess. Kings and other political leaders might also visit the temple and carry out religious ceremonies from time to time, particularly when they thought the assistance of the gods was especially needed.

The peoples of Mesopotamia had many myths to account for the creation of the universe. According to one told by the Babylonians, in the beginning was the primeval sea, known as the goddess Tiamat, who gave birth to the gods. When Tiamat tried to destroy the gods, Marduk, the chief god of the Babylonians, proceeded to kill her and divide her body and thus created the sky and earth. These myths are the earliest known attempts to answer the question, how did it all begin?

Stories about the gods traveled with people when they moved up and down the rivers, so that gods often acquired new names and new characteristics over the centuries. Myths and stories about them were not written down until long after they had first been told, and often had many variations. Written texts were not an important part of Sumerian religious life, nor were they central to the religious practices of most of the other peoples in this region.

In addition to stories about gods, the Sumerians also told stories about heroes and kings, many of which were eventually reworked into the world's first epic poem, the *Epic of Gilgamesh* (GIL-guh-mesh), which was later written down in Akkadian. An epic poem is a narration of the achievements, the labors, and sometimes the failures of heroes that embodies peoples' ideas about themselves. Historians can use epic poems to learn about various aspects of a society, and to that extent epics can be used as historical sources. The epic recounts the wanderings of Gilgamesh—the semihistorical king of Uruk—and his search for eternal life, and it grapples with enduring questions about life and death, friendship, humankind and deity, and immortality.

Sumerian Politics and Society

Exactly how kings emerged in Sumerian society is not clear. Scholars have suggested that during times of emergencies, a chief priest or perhaps a military leader assumed what was supposed to be temporary authority over a city. He established an army, trained it, and led it into battle. Temporary power gradually became permanent kingship, and sometime before 2450 B.C.E. kings in some Sumerian city-states began transferring their kingship to their sons, establishing patriarchal hereditary dynasties in which power was handed down through the male line. This is the point at which written records about kingship began to appear. The symbol of royal status was the palace, which came to rival the temple in grandeur.

Military leaders were sometimes able to conquer other cities, and in about 2350 B.C.E. Lugalzagesi, king of the city of Umma, conquered a number of other city-states and created a more unified state. Eventually he conquered Uruk as well, and declared in a long inscription that the god Enlil had given him a realm that extended from the Mediterranean to the Persian Gulf. Like many later rulers in all parts of the world, Lugalzagesi claimed territory far beyond what he actually held.

Kings made alliances with other powerful individuals, often through marriage. Royal family members were depended upon for many aspects of government. Kings worked closely with religious authorities and relied on ideas about the kings' connections with the gods, as well as the kings' military might, for their power. Royal children, both sons and daughters, were sometimes priests and priestesses in major temples. Acting together, priests, kings, and officials in Sumerian cities used force, persuasion, and taxation to maintain order, keep the irrigation systems working, and keep food and other goods flowing.

The king and his officials held extensive tracts of land, as did the temple; these lands were worked by the palace's or the temple's clients, free men and women who were dependent on the palace or the temple. They received crops and other goods in return for their labor. Although this arrangement assured the clients of a livelihood, the land they worked remained the possession of the palace or the temple. Some individuals and families owned land outright and paid their taxes in the form of agricultural products or items they made. At the bottom rung of society were slaves. Slavery predates written records, so like many other aspects of social hierarchies, we are not sure exactly how and when people first began to own other people. Like animals, slaves were a source of physical power for their owners, providing them an opportunity to amass more wealth and influence. Some Sumerian slaves were most likely prisoners of war and criminals who had lost their freedom as punishment for their crimes; others perhaps came into slavery to repay debts. Compared to many later societies, slaves were not widely used in Sumer, where most agricultural work was done by dependent clients. Slaves in Sumer also engaged in trade and made profits. They could borrow money, and many slaves were able to buy their freedom.

Each of the social categories included both men and women, but their experiences were not the same, for Sumerian society made distinctions based on gender. Most elite landowners were male, but women who held positions as priestesses or as queens ran their own estates, independently of their husbands and fathers. Some women owned businesses and took care of their own accounts. They could own property and distribute it to their offspring. Sons and daughters inherited from their parents, although a daughter received her inheritance in the form of a dowry, which technically remained hers but was managed by her husband or husband's family after marriage. The Sumerians established the basic social, economic, and intellectual patterns of Mesopotamia, and they influenced their neighbors to the north and east.

Empires in Mesopotamia

How did the Akkadian and Old Babylonian empires develop in Mesopotamia?

The wealth of Sumerian cities also attracted non-Sumerian conquerors from the north, beginning with the Akkadians and then the Babylonians. Both of these peoples created large states in the valley of the Tigris and Euphrates, and Hammurabi, one ruler of Babylon, proclaimed an extensive law code. Merchants traveled throughout the Fertile Crescent and beyond, carrying products and facilitating cultural exchange.

The Akkadians and the Babylonians

In 2331 B.C.E. Sargon, the king of a city to the north of Sumer, conquered a number of Sumerian cities with what was probably the world's first permanent army and created a large state. The symbol of his triumph was a new capital, the city of Akkad (AH-kahd). Sargon also expanded the Akkadian empire westward to North Syria, which became the breadbasket of the empire. He encouraged trading networks that brought in goods from as far away as the Indus River and what is now Turkey. Sargon spoke a different language than did the Sumerians, one of the many languages that scholars identify as belonging to the Semitic language family, which includes modern-day Hebrew and Arabic. However, Akkadians adapted cuneiform writing to their own language, and Akkadian became the diplomatic language used over a wide area.

Sargon of Akkad   This bronze head, with elaborately worked hair and beard, might portray the great conqueror Sargon of Akkad (though his name does not appear on it). The eyes were originally inlaid with jewels, which have since been gouged out. Produced around 2300 B.C.E., this head was found in the ruins of the Assyrian capital of Nineveh, where it had been taken as loot. (North Wind Pictures/Alamy)

Sargon tore down the defensive walls of Sumerian cities and appointed his own sons as their rulers to help him cement his power. He also appointed his daughter, Enheduana (2285–2250 B.C.E.), as high priestess in the city of Ur. Here she wrote a number of hymns, especially those in praise of the goddess Inanna, becoming the world's first author to put her name to a literary composition. For hundreds of years Enheduana's works were copied on clay tablets, which have been found in several cities in the area, indicating that people may have recited or read them.

Sargon's dynasty appears to have ruled Mesopotamia for about 150 years, during which time the Tigris and Euphrates Valleys attracted immigrants from many places. Then his empire collapsed, in part because of a period of extended drought, and the various city-states became independent again.

One significant city-state that arose in the wake of the Akkadian empire was settled by the Amorites (AM-uh-rites), who migrated in from the west, probably starting during the time of Sargon's empire. The Amorites were initially nomadic pastoralists, not agriculturalists, but they began to raise crops when they settled throughout Mesopotamia. One group of Amorites made their home in the city of Babylon along the middle Euphrates, where that river runs close to the Tigris. Positioned to dominate trade on both the Tigris and Euphrates Rivers, the city grew great because of its commercial importance and the sound leadership of a dynasty of Amorite rulers. Like other Amorite kingdoms of the time, Babylon was more than a city-state. It included smaller kingdoms whose rulers recognized the king of Babylon as their overlord.

Life Under Hammurabi

Hammurabi of Babylon (r. 1792–1750 B.C.E.) was initially a typical king of his era. As ruler of Babylon, he fought some of his neighbors, created treaties with others, taxed his people, expanded the city walls, and built temples. After he had ruled for thirty years, Babylon was attacked, and one of Hammurabi's allies did not provide the assistance he expected. Hammurabi defeated the attackers and also conquered his former ally and several other kingdoms, thus uniting most of Mesopotamia under his rule. The era from his reign to around 1595 B.C.E. is called the Old Babylonian period.

As had earlier rulers, Hammurabi linked his success with the will of the gods. He connected himself with the sun-god Shamash, the god of law and justice, and encouraged the spread of myths that explained how Marduk, the primary god of Babylon, had been elected king of the gods by the other deities in Mesopotamia. Marduk later became widely regarded as the chief god of Mesopotamia, absorbing the qualities and powers of other gods.

Hammurabi's most memorable accomplishment was the proclamation of an extensive law code, introduced about 1755 B.C.E. Hammurabi's was not the first law code in Mesopotamia; the earliest goes back to about 2100 B.C.E. Like the codes of the earlier lawgivers, **Hammurabi's law code** proclaimed that he issued his laws on divine authority "to establish law and justice in the language of the land, thereby promoting the welfare of the people." Hammurabi's code set a variety of punishments for breaking the law, including fines and physical punishment such as mutilation, whipping, and burning.

Hammurabi's code provides a wealth of information about daily life in Mesopotamia, although, like all law codes, it prescribes what the lawgivers hope will be the situation rather than providing a description of real life. We cannot know if its laws were enforced, but we can use it to see what was significant to people in Hammurabi's society. Because of farming's fundamental importance, the code dealt extensively with agriculture. Tenants faced severe penalties for neglecting the land or not working it at all. Since irrigation was essential to grow crops, tenants had to keep the canals and ditches in good repair. Anyone whose neglect of the canals resulted in damaged crops had to bear all the expense of the lost crops. Those tenants who could not pay the costs were forced into slavery.

Hammurabi gave careful attention to marriage and the family. As elsewhere in the Near East, marriage had aspects of a business agreement. The groom or his father offered the prospective bride's father a gift, and if this was acceptable, the bride's father provided his daughter with a dowry. As in Sumer, after marriage the dowry belonged to the woman (although the husband normally administered it) and was a means of protecting her rights and status. No marriage was considered legal without a contract, and although either party could break off the marriage, the cost was a stiff penalty. Fathers often contracted marriages while their children were still young, and once contracted, the children were considered to be wed even if they did not live together. Men were not allowed to take a second wife unless the first wife could not bear children or had a severe illness.

The penalty for adultery, defined as sex between a married woman and a man not her husband, was death. According to Hammurabi's code, "If the wife of a man has been caught while lying with another man, they shall bind them and throw them into the water."[3] A husband had the power to spare his wife by obtaining a pardon for her from the king. He could, however, accuse his wife of adultery even if he had not caught her in the act. In such a case she could try to clear herself, and if she was found innocent, she could take her dowry and leave her husband.

Law Code of Hammurabi   Hammurabi ordered his code to be inscribed on stone pillars and set up in public throughout the Babylonian empire. At the top of the pillar Hammurabi (left) is depicted receiving the rod and ring of authority from Shamash, the god of justice. (© www.BibleLandPictures.com/Alamy)

A father could not disinherit a son without just cause, and the code ordered the courts to forgive a son for his first offense. Men could adopt children into their families and include them in their wills, which artisans sometimes did to teach them the family trade, or wealthy landowners sometimes did to pass along land to able younger men, particularly if they had no children of their own.

The Code of Hammurabi demanded that the punishment fit the crime, calling for "an eye for an eye, and a tooth for a tooth," at least among equals. However, a higher-ranking man who physically hurt a commoner or slave, perhaps by breaking his arm or putting out his eye, could pay a fine to the victim instead of having his arm broken or losing his own eye. The fine for breaking an arm or otherwise hurting a commoner was huge—as much as five years' salary for a laborer—and commoners might have preferred to receive this rather than the less tangible recompense of seeing their assailant injured. As long as criminal and victim shared the same social status, however, the victim could demand exact vengeance.

Hammurabi's code began with legal procedure. There were no public prosecutors or district attorneys, so individuals brought their own complaints before the court. Each side had to produce witnesses to support its case. In cases of murder, the accuser had to prove the defendant guilty; any accuser who failed to do so was to be put to death. Another procedural regulation declared that once a judge had rendered a verdict, he could not change it. Anyone accused of witchcraft, even if the charges were not proved, underwent an ordeal by water. The defendant was thrown into the Euphrates, which was considered the instrument of the gods. A defendant who sank was guilty; a defendant who survived was innocent.

Consumer protection is not a modern idea; it goes back to Hammurabi's day. Merchants had to guarantee the quality of their goods and services. A boat builder who did sloppy work had to repair the boat at his own expense. House builders guaranteed their work with their lives. If inhabitants died when a house collapsed, the builder was put to death. A merchant who tried to increase the interest rate on a loan forfeited the entire amount. In these ways, Hammurabi's laws tried to ensure that consumers got what they paid for and paid a just price.

The practical impact of Hammurabi's code is much debated. There is disagreement about whether it recorded laws already established, promulgated new laws, recorded previous judicial decisions, or simply proclaimed what was just and proper. It is also unknown whether Hammurabi's proclamation was legally binding on the courts. Nevertheless, Hammurabi's code gives historians a valuable view into the lives of the Mesopotamians, and it influenced other law codes of the Near East, including those later written down in Hebrew scripture.

Cultural Exchange in the Fertile Crescent

Law codes, preoccupied as they are with the problems of society, provide a bleak view of things, but other Mesopotamian documents give a happier glimpse of life. Countless wills and testaments show that husbands habitually left their estates to their wives, who in turn willed the property to their children. Financial documents prove that many women engaged in business without hindrance.

Mesopotamians found their lives lightened by holidays and religious festivals. Traveling merchants brought news from far away and swapped marvelous tales. The

Mesopotamians enjoyed a vibrant and creative culture that left its mark on the entire Fertile Crescent. They made significant and sophisticated advances in mathematics using a numerical system based on units of sixty, ten, and six. They also developed the concept of place value—that the value of a number depends on where it stands in relation to other numbers.

Mesopotamian writing and merchandise, along with other aspects of the culture, spread far beyond the Tigris and Euphrates Valleys. Overland trade connected Sumer, Akkad, and Babylon with the eastern Mediterranean coast. Cities here were mercantile centers rich not only in manufactured goods but also in agricultural produce, textiles, and metals. The cities flourished under local rulers. People in Syria and elsewhere in the Middle East used Akkadian cuneiform to communicate in writing with their more distant neighbors. Cultural exchange remained a mixture of adoption and adaptation.

Southern and central Anatolia presented a similar picture of extensive contact between cultures. Major Anatolian cities with large local populations were also home to colonies of traders from Mesopotamia. Thousands of cuneiform tablets testify to centuries of commercial and cultural exchanges with Mesopotamia, and eventually with Egypt, which rose to power in the Nile Valley.

The Egyptians

How did the Egyptians create a prosperous and long-lasting society?

At about the same time that Sumerian city-states expanded and fought with one another in the Tigris and Euphrates Valleys, a more cohesive state under a single ruler grew in the valley of the Nile River in North Africa. This was Egypt, which for long stretches of history was prosperous and secure behind desert areas on both sides of the Nile Valley. At various times groups migrated into Egypt seeking better lives or invaded and conquered Egypt. Often these newcomers adopted aspects of Egyptian religion, art, and politics, and the Egyptians also carried their traditions with them when they established an empire and engaged in trade.

The Nile and the God-King

The Greek historian and traveler Herodotus (heh-RAHD-uh-tuhs) in the fifth century B.C.E. called Egypt the "gift of the Nile." No other single geographical factor had such a fundamental and profound impact on the shaping of Egyptian life, society, and history as this river. The Nile flooded once a year for a period of several months, bringing fertile soil and moisture for farming, and agricultural villages developed along its banks by at least 6000 B.C.E. Although the Egyptians worried at times that these floods would be too high or too low, they also praised the Nile as a creative and comforting force:

> Hail to thee, O Nile, that issues from the earth and comes to keep Egypt alive! . . .
> He that waters the meadows which Re [Ra] created,
> He that makes to drink the desert . . .
> He who makes barley and brings emmer [wheat] into being . . .
> He who brings grass into being for the cattle . . .
> He who makes every beloved tree to grow . . .
> O Nile, verdant art thou, who makest man and cattle to live.[4]

The Egyptians based their calendar on the Nile, dividing the year into three four-month periods: *akhet* (flooding), *peret* (growth), and *shemu* (harvest). Herodotus, accustomed to the rigors of Greek agriculture, was amazed by the ease with which the Egyptians seemed to raise crops. Egyptian texts, however, paint a different picture, recognizing the unrelenting work entailed in farming and the diseases from which people suffered. One of these was guinea worm disease, a parasite caused by drinking contaminated water, evidence of which has also been found in Egyptian mummies. Treatment for guinea worm today is exactly the same as that recommended in ancient Egyptian medical texts: when the head of the worm emerges from the large blister it causes, wrap the worm around a stick and gradually pull it out.

Through the fertility of the Nile and their own hard work, Egyptians produced an annual agricultural surplus, which in turn sustained a growing and prosperous population. The Nile also unified Egypt. The river was the region's principal highway, promoting communication and trade throughout the valley.

Egypt was fortunate in that it was nearly self-sufficient—it had most of the materials required to address its basic needs. Besides having fertile soil, Egypt possessed enormous quantities of stone, which served as the raw material of architecture and sculpture, and abundant clay for pottery. The raw materials that Egypt lacked were close at hand. The Egyptians could obtain copper from Sinai (SIGH-nigh) and timber from Lebanon, and they traded with peoples farther away to obtain other materials that they needed.

The political power structures that developed in Egypt came to be linked with the Nile. Somehow the idea developed that a single individual, a king, was responsible for the rise and fall of the Nile. This belief came about before the development of writing in Egypt, so, as with the growth of priestly and royal power in Sumer, the precise details of its origins have been lost. The king came to be viewed as a descendant of the gods, and thus as a god himself.

Political unification most likely proceeded slowly, but stories told about early kings highlighted one who had united Upper Egypt—the upstream valley in the south—and Lower Egypt—the delta area of the Nile that empties into the Mediterranean Sea—into a single kingdom around 3100 B.C.E. In some sources he is called Narmer and in other Menes, but his fame as a unifier is the same, whatever his name, and he is generally depicted in carvings and paintings wearing the symbols of the two kingdoms. Historians later divided Egyptian history into dynasties, or families of kings. For modern historical purposes, however, it is more useful to divide Egyptian history into periods. The political unification of Egypt in the Archaic Period (3100–2660 B.C.E.) ushered in the period known as the Old Kingdom (2660–2180 B.C.E.), an era remarkable for prosperity and artistic flowering.

The focal point of religious and political life in the Old Kingdom was the king, who commanded wealth, resources, and people. The king's surroundings had to be worthy of a god, and only a magnificent palace was suitable for his home; in fact, the word **pharaoh**, which during the New Kingdom came to be used for the king, originally meant "great house." Just as the kings occupied a great house in life, so they reposed in great pyramids after death. Built during the Old Kingdom, these massive stone tombs contained all the things needed by the king in his afterlife. The pyramid also symbolized the king's power and his connection with the sun-god. After burial the entrance was blocked and concealed to ensure the king's undisturbed peace, although grave robbers later actually found the tombs fairly easy to plunder.

To ancient Egyptians, the king embodied the concept of **ma'at**, a cosmic harmony that embraced truth, justice, and moral integrity. Ma'at gave the king the right, authority, and duty to govern. To the people, the king personified justice and order — harmony among themselves, nature, and the divine.

Kings did not always live up to this ideal, of course. The two parts of Egypt were difficult to hold together, and several times in Egypt's long history there were periods of disunity, civil war, and chaos. During the First Intermediate Period (2180–2080 B.C.E.), rulers of various provinces asserted their independence from the king and Upper and Lower Egypt were ruled by rival dynasties. There is evidence that the Nile's floods were unusually low during this period because of drought, which contributed to instability just as it helped bring down the Akkadian empire. Warrior-kings reunited Egypt in the Middle Kingdom (2080–1640 B.C.E.) and expanded Egyptian power southward into Nubia.

Egyptian Religion

Like the Mesopotamians, the Egyptians were polytheistic, worshipping many gods of all types, some mightier than others. They developed complex ideas of their gods that reflected the world around them, and these views changed over the many centuries of Egyptian history as gods took on new attributes and often merged with one another. During the Old Kingdom, Egyptians considered the sun-god Ra the creator of life. He commanded the sky, earth, and underworld. This giver of life could also take it away without warning. Ra was associated with the falcon-god Horus, the "lord of the sky," who served as the symbol of divine kingship.

Much later, during the New Kingdom (see page 27), the pharaohs of a new dynasty favored the worship of a different sun-god, Amon, whom they described as creating the entire cosmos by his thoughts. Amon brought life to the land and its people, they wrote, and he sustained both. Because he had helped them overthrow their enemies, Egyptians

Funeral Stele of a Wealthy Woman   This painted wooden stele shows Djed-amon-iu-ankh (right), a wealthy Egyptian woman who lived in the Third Intermediate Period, in a thin gown and with a cone of ointment on her head, and the sun-god Ra (left) in the form of Horus the falcon-god. Ra-Horus is holding a scepter in one hand and the ankh, the Egyptian symbol of life, in the other. Djed-amon-iu-ankh offers food and lotus flowers to the god, and the hieroglyphs above them describe the offering. Stelae were erected in Egypt for funeral purposes and depicted the person memorialized in an attitude of reverence. (Egyptian Museum, Cairo)

came to consider Amon the champion of fairness and justice, especially for the common people. Called the "vizier of the humble" and the "voice of the poor," Amon was also a magician and physician who cured ills, protected people from natural dangers, and watched over travelers. As his cult grew, Amon came to be identified with Ra, and eventually the Egyptians combined them into one sun-god, Amon-Ra.

The Egyptians likewise developed views of an afterlife that reflected the world around them and that changed over time. During the later part of the Old Kingdom, the walls of kings' tombs were carved with religious texts that provided spells that would bring the king back to life and help him ascend to Heaven, where he would join his divine father, Ra. Toward the end of the Old Kingdom, the tombs of powerful nobles also contained such inscriptions, an indication that more people expected to gain everlasting life, and a sign of the decentralization of power that would lead to the chaos of the First Intermediate Period. In the Middle Kingdom, new types of spells appeared on the coffins of even more people, a further expansion in admissions to the afterlife.

During the New Kingdom, a time when Egypt came into greater contact with the cultures of the Fertile Crescent, Egyptians developed more complex ideas about the afterlife, recording these in funerary manuscripts that have come to be known as the **Book of the Dead**, written to help guide the dead through the difficulties of the underworld. These texts explained that the soul left the body to become part of the divine after death and told of the god Osiris (oh-SIGH-ruhs), who died each year and was then brought back to life by his wife, Isis (IGH-suhs), when the Nile flooded. Osiris eventually became king of the dead, weighing dead humans' hearts to determine whether they had lived justly enough to deserve everlasting life. (See "Primary Source: Morality in the Egyptian *Book of the Dead*," page 24.) Egyptians also believed that proper funeral rituals, in which the physical body was mummified, were essential for life after death, so Osiris was assisted by Anubis, the jackal-headed god of mummification.

New Kingdom pharaohs came to associate themselves with both Horus and Osiris, and they were regarded as avatars of Horus in life and Osiris in death. The pharaoh's wife was associated with Isis, for both the queen and the goddess were regarded as protectors.

Egyptian Society and Work

Egyptian society reflected the pyramids that it built. At the top stood the king, who relied on a sizable circle of nobles, officials, and priests to administer his kingdom. All of them were assisted by scribes, who used a writing system perhaps adapted from Mesopotamia and perhaps developed independently. Egyptian scribes actually created two writing systems: one called hieroglyphic for engraving important religious or political texts on stone or writing them on papyrus made from reeds growing in the Nile Delta, and a much simpler system called hieratic that allowed scribes to write more quickly. Hieratic writing was used for the documents of daily life, such as letters, contracts, and accounts, and also for medical and literary works. Students learned hieratic first, and only those from well-off families or whose families had high aspirations took the time to learn hieroglyphics. In addition to scribes, the cities of the Nile Valley were home to artisans of all types, along with merchants and other tradespeople. A large group of farmers made up the broad base of the social pyramid.

PRIMARY SOURCE   Morality in the Egyptian *Book of the Dead*

During the New Kingdom, well-to-do Egyptians were buried with papyrus scrolls on which magical and religious texts were written that were to help the deceased make the crossing to the afterlife, which was viewed as more difficult in this era of insecurity than it had been earlier. Now known as the Book of the Dead, *these texts varied but increasingly included a description of the god Osiris weighing the person's heart to determine his or her fate. During this ritual, the deceased recited a standardized list of things he or she had not done during life, what modern scholars have called the "negative confession." A scribe writing this list to place in the coffin would have simply replaced the "N" in the first sentence with the name of the deceased.*

The Declaration of Innocence

To be said on reaching the Hall of the Two Truths so as to purge N of any sins committed and to see the face of every god:

Hail to you, great God, Lord of the Two Truths!
I have come to you, my Lord,
I was brought to see your beauty. . . .

I have not done crimes against people,
I have not mistreated cattle,
I have not sinned in the Place of Truth.
I have not known what should not be known,
I have not done any harm.
I did not begin a day by exacting more than my due,
My name did not reach the bark of the mighty ruler.
I have not blasphemed a god,
I have not robbed the poor.
I have not done what the god abhors,
I have not maligned a servant to his master.
I have not caused pain,
I have not caused tears.

For Egyptians, the Nile formed an essential part of daily life. During the season of its flooding, from June to October, farmers worked on the pharaoh's building programs and other tasks away from their fields. When the water began to recede, they diverted some of it into ponds for future irrigation and began planting wheat and barley for bread and beer, using plows pulled by oxen or people to part the soft mud. From October to February farmers planted and tended crops, and then from February until the next flood they harvested them. Reapers with wooden sickles fixed with flint teeth cut the grain high, leaving long stubble. Women with baskets followed behind to gather the cuttings. Last came the gleaners—poor women, children, and old men who gathered anything left behind.

I have not killed,
I have not ordered to kill,
I have not made anyone suffer.
I have not damaged the offerings in the temples,
I have not depleted the loaves of the gods,
I have not stolen the cakes of the dead [food left for the deceased].
I have not copulated nor defiled myself.
I have not increased nor reduced the measure,
I have not diminished the arura [arable land],
I have not cheated in the fields.
I have not added to the weight of the balance,
I have not falsified the plummet of the scales.
I have not taken milk from the mouth of children,
I have not deprived cattle of their pasture.
I have not snared birds in the reeds of the gods,
I have not caught fish in their ponds.
I have not held back water in its season,
I have not dammed a flowing stream,
I have not quenched a needed fire.
I have not neglected the days of meat offerings,
I have not detained cattle belonging to the god,
I have not stopped a god in his procession.
I am pure, I am pure, I am pure, I am pure!

EVALUATE THE EVIDENCE

1. What religious duties and personal actions does this ritualized statement suggest were important to New Kingdom Egyptians?

2. How do the various actions described here reflect the environment and economy of Egypt?

Source: *Ancient Egyptian Literature: Volume II, The New Kingdom*, by Miriam Lichtheim, pp. 124–126. © 2006 by the Regents of the University of California. Published by the University of California Press.

As in Mesopotamia, common people paid their obligations to their superiors in products and in labor, and many faced penalties if they did not meet their quota. One scribe described the scene at harvest time:

And now the scribe lands on the river bank and is about to register the harvest-tax. The janitors carry staves and the Nubians rods of palm, and they say, Hand over the grain, though there is none. The farmer is beaten all over, he is bound and thrown into a well, soused and dipped head downwards. His wife has been bound in his presence and his children are in fetters.[5]

Peoples' labor obligations in the Old Kingdom may have included forced work on the pyramids and canals, although recent research suggests that most people who built the pyramids were paid for their work. Some young men were drafted into the pharaoh's army, which served as both a fighting force and a labor corps.

Egyptian Family Life

The lives of all Egyptians centered around the family. Marriage was a business arrangement, just as in Mesopotamia, arranged by the couples' parents, and seems to have taken place at a young age. Once couples were married, having children, especially sons, was a high priority, as indicated by surviving charms to promote fertility and prayers for successful childbirth. Boys continued the family line, and only they could perform the proper burial rites for their father.

Wealthy Egyptians lived in spacious homes with attractive gardens and walls for privacy. Such a house had an ample living room and a comfortable master bedroom with an attached bathroom. Smaller rooms served other purposes, including housing family members and servants, and providing space for cows, poultry, and storage. Poorer people lived in cramped quarters. Excavations at a city now called Tell el Amarna show that residents' houses were about 16½ feet wide by 33 feet long. The family had narrow rooms for living, including two small rooms for sleeping and cooking. These small houses suggest that most Egyptians lived in small family groups, not as large extended families. The very poor lived in hovels with their animals.

Egyptian Home Life   This grave painting depicts an intimate moment in the life of an aristocratic family, with the father and mother in the center and their children around them. (Gianni Dagli Orti/The Art Archive at Art Resource, NY)

Life in Egypt began at dawn with a bath and clean clothes. The Egyptians bathed several times a day because of the heat and used soda ash for soap. Rich and poor alike used perfumes as deodorants. Egyptians generally wore linen clothes, made from fibers of the flax plant, because there were few sheep in Egypt, and during this period they did not grow cotton. Because of the heat, men often wore only a kilt and women a sheath.

Marriage was apparently not celebrated by any ritual or religious act; it seems to have been purely a legal contract in which a woman brought one-third of her family's property to the marriage. The property continued to belong to her, though her husband managed it. She could obtain a divorce simply because she wanted it. If she did, she took her marriage portion with her and could also claim a share of the profits made during her marriage. Most Egyptian men had only one wife, but among the wealthy some had several wives or concubines. One wife, however, remained primary among the others. A husband could order his wife to her quarters and even beat her, but if a man treated his wife too violently, she could take him to court. If she won, her husband received one hundred lashes from a whip and surrendered his portion of their joint property to her. A man could dispense with his wife for any reason, just as she could leave him.

Ordinary women were expected to obey their fathers, husbands, and other men, but they possessed considerable economic and legal rights. They could own land in their own names and operate businesses. They could testify in court and bring legal action against men. Information from literature and art depicts a world in which ordinary husbands and wives enjoyed each other's company alone, and together with family and friends. They held and attended parties together, and both participated in the festivities after dinner. Egyptian tomb monuments often show the couple happily standing together, arms around each other.

The Hyksos and New Kingdom Revival

While Egyptian civilization flourished in the Nile Valley, various groups migrated throughout the Fertile Crescent and then accommodated themselves to local cultures (Map 1.2). Some settled in the Nile Delta, including a group the Egyptians called Hyksos, which means "rulers of the uplands." Although they were later portrayed as a conquering horde, the Hyksos were actually migrants looking for good land, and their entry into the delta, which began around 1800 B.C.E., was probably gradual and generally peaceful.

The Hyksos brought with them the method of making bronze and casting it into tools and weapons that became standard in Egypt. They thereby brought Egypt fully into the Bronze Age culture of the Mediterranean world. Because bronze tools were sharper and more durable than the copper, stone, or bone tools they replaced, they made farming more efficient. The Hyksos also brought inventions that revolutionized Egyptian warfare, including bronze armor and weapons as well as horse-drawn chariots and the composite bow, made of laminated wood and horn, which was far more powerful than the simple wooden bow.

The migration of the Hyksos, combined with a series of famines and internal struggles for power, led Egypt to fragment politically in what later came to be known as the Second Intermediate Period (1640–1570 B.C.E.). During this time the Egyptians

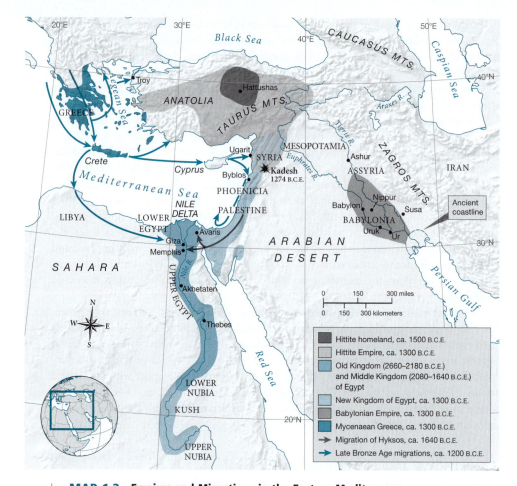

MAP 1.2 Empires and Migrations in the Eastern Mediterranean
The rise and fall of empires in the eastern Mediterranean were shaped by internal developments, military conflicts, and the migration of peoples to new areas.

adopted bronze technology and new forms of weaponry from the Hyksos, while the newcomers began to worship Egyptian deities and modeled their political structure on that of the Egyptians.

In about 1570 B.C.E. a new dynasty of pharaohs arose, pushing the Hyksos out of the delta, subduing Nubia in the south, and conquering parts of Canaan in the northeast. In this way, these Egyptian warrior-pharaohs inaugurated what scholars refer to as the New Kingdom—a period in Egyptian history characterized by not only enormous wealth and conscious imperialism but also a greater sense of insecurity because of new contacts and military engagements. By expanding Egyptian power beyond the Nile Valley, the pharaohs created the first Egyptian empire, and they celebrated their triumphs with monuments on a scale unparalleled since the pyramids of the Old Kingdom. Even today the colossal granite statues of these pharaohs and the rich tomb objects testify to the might and splendor of the New Kingdom. They might also be testimony to an expansion of imported slave labor, although recently some scholars are rethinking the extent of slave labor in the New Kingdom.

The New Kingdom pharaohs include a number of remarkable figures. Among these was Hatshepsut (r. ca. 1479–ca. 1458 B.C.E.), one of the few female pharaohs in Egypt's long history, who seized the throne for herself and used her reign to promote building and trade. Amenhotep III (r. ca. 1388–ca.1350 B.C.E.) corresponded with other powerful kings in Babylonia and other kingdoms in the Fertile Crescent, sending envoys, exchanging gifts, and in some cases marrying their daughters. The kings promised friendship and active cooperation, referring to each other as "brothers," using this familial term to indicate their connection. They made alliances for offensive and defensive protection and swore to uphold one another's authority. Hence, the greatest powers of the period maintained peace, which facilitated the movement of gifts between kings and trade between ordinary people. Along with his chief royal wife, Tiye, who is known for her correspondence with foreign queens, Amenhotep is depicted on hundreds of statues, vases, amulets, and other objects, including two sixty-foot-tall statues that stood at the gate of his huge mortuary temple.

Amenhotep III was succeeded by his son, who took the name Akhenaten (ah-keh-NAH-tuhn) (r. 1351–1334 B.C.E.). He renamed himself as a mark of his changing religious ideas. Egyptians had long worshipped various sun-gods and aspects of the sun—Ra, Amon, Amon-Ra—but instead Akhenaten favored the worship of the god Aten (also spelled Aton), the visible disk of the sun. He was not a monotheist (someone who worships only one god), but he did order the erasure of the names of other sun-gods from the walls of buildings, the transfer of taxes from the traditional priesthood of Amon-Ra, and the building of huge new temples to Aten, especially at his new capital in the area now known as Amarna. In these temples Aten was to be worshipped in bright sunlight. Akhenaten also had artists portray him in more realistic ways than they had portrayed earlier pharaohs; he is depicted interacting with his children and especially with his wife Nefertiti (nehf-uhr-TEE-tee), who supported his new religious ideas. (See "Individuals in Society: Hatshepsut and Nefertiti," page 30.)

Akhenaten's new religion, imposed from above, failed to find a place among the people, however. After his death, traditional religious practices returned and the capital was moved back to Thebes. The priests of Amon-Ra led this restoration, but it was also supported by Akhenaten's son, who rejected the name he had been given that honored Aten and instead chose one that honored the traditional sun-god Amon. This son was Tutankhamon (r. 1333–1323 B.C.E.), whose short reign was not particularly noteworthy, and whose name would probably not be remembered except for the fact that his was the only tomb of an Egyptian king to be discovered nearly intact. The wealth of "King Tut's tomb," assembled quickly for a boy-king who died unexpectedly at nineteen, can only suggest what must have originally been in the tomb of a truly powerful pharaoh.

The objects in the tomb have been studied intensively since it was first discovered in 1922 and have yielded much information about New Kingdom Egypt. In 2010 DNA analysis of Tutankhamon's mummy and other mummies from nearby tombs revealed, among other things, that he was the son of Akhenaten (there had been some doubt) and that his mother was probably one of Akhenaten's sisters. Brother-sister marriage was fairly common among Egyptian pharaohs, as it concentrated the family's power and connections with the gods. Marriage to close relatives can also cause genetic defects, however, and Tutankhamon seems to have suffered from several of these,

INDIVIDUALS IN SOCIETY • Hatshepsut and Nefertiti

Egyptians understood the pharaoh to be an avatar of the god Horus, the source of law and morality, and the mediator between gods and humans. The pharaoh's connection with the divine stretched to members of his family, so that his siblings and children were also viewed as divine in some ways. Because of this, a pharaoh often took his sister or half-sister as one of his wives. This concentrated divine blood set the pharaonic family apart from other Egyptians (who did not generally marry close relatives) and allowed the pharaohs to imitate the gods, who in Egyptian mythology often married their siblings. A pharaoh chose one of his wives, often a relative, to be the "Great Royal Wife," or principal queen.

The familial connection with the divine allowed a handful of women to rule in their own right in Egypt's long history. We know the names of four female pharaohs, of whom the most famous was Hatshepsut (r. 1479–1458 B.C.E.), the sister and wife of Thutmose II. After he died, she served as regent—adviser and co-ruler—for her young stepson Thutmose III. Hatshepsut sent trading expeditions and sponsored artists and architects, ushering in a period of artistic creativity and economic prosperity. She oversaw the building of one of the world's great buildings, an elaborate terraced temple at Deir el Bahri, which eventually served as her mortuary temple. Hatshepsut's status as a powerful female ruler was difficult for Egyptians to conceptualize, and she is often depicted in male dress or with a false beard, thus looking more like the male rulers who were the norm. After her death, Thutmose III tried to destroy all evidence that she had ever ruled, smashing statues and scratching her name off inscriptions, perhaps because of personal animosity and perhaps because he wanted to erase the fact that a woman had once been pharaoh. Only within recent decades have historians and archaeologists begun to (literally) piece together her story.

Though female pharaohs were very rare, many royal women had power through their position as "Great Royal Wives." The most famous was Nefertiti, the wife of Akhenaten. Her name means "the perfect (or beautiful) woman has come," and inscriptions also give her many other titles. Nefertiti used her position to spread the new religion of the sun-god Aten.

Together Nefertiti and Akhenaten built a new palace and capital city at Akhetaten, the present Amarna, away from the old centers of power. There they

including a malformed foot. It also revealed that he suffered from malaria and had broken his leg shortly before he died. His high status did not make him immune from physical ailments.

Tutankhamon's short reign was also marked by international problems, including warfare on several of the borders of the Egyptian empire. His grandfather and father had engaged in extensive diplomatic relations with rulers of states dependent on Egypt and with other powerful kings, but Tutankhamon was less successful at these. He also died childless. His successors were court officials, and in 1298 B.C.E. one of them established a new dynasty whose members would reassert Egypt's imperial power and respond to new challenges.

developed the cult of Aten to the exclusion of the traditional deities. Nearly the only literary survival of their religious belief is the "Hymn to Aten," which declares Aten to be the only god. It describes Nefertiti as "the great royal consort whom he, Akhenaten, loves. The mistress of the Two Lands, Upper and Lower Egypt."

Nefertiti is often shown as being the same size as her husband, and in some inscriptions she is performing religious rituals that would normally have been carried out only by the pharaoh. The exact details of her power are hard to determine, however. An older theory held that her husband removed her from power, though there is also speculation that after his death she may have ruled secretly in her own right under a different name. Her tomb has long since disappeared. In the last decade individual archaeologists have claimed that several different mummies were Nefertiti, but most scholars dismiss these claims. Because her parentage is not known for certain, DNA testing such as that done on Tutankhamon's corpse would not reveal whether any specific mummy was Nefertiti.

QUESTIONS FOR ANALYSIS

1. Why might it have been difficult for Egyptians to accept a female ruler?

2. What opportunities do hereditary monarchies such as that of ancient Egypt provide for women? How does this fit with gender hierarchies in which men are understood as superior?

ONLINE DOCUMENT ASSIGNMENT

Considering Egyptian views of gender roles, what complexities did Egyptian writers and artists face in depicting Hatshepsut? Analyze a range of written and visual representations of Hatshepsut, and then complete a writing assignment based on the evidence and details from this chapter.

bedfordstmartins.com/mckaywestvalue

Conflict and Cooperation with the Hittites

One of the key challenges facing the pharaohs after Tutankhamon was the expansion of the kingdom of the Hittites. At about the same time that the Sumerians were establishing city-states, speakers of Indo-European languages migrated into Anatolia. Indo-European is a large family of languages that includes English, most of the languages of modern Europe, Persian, and Sanskrit. It also includes Hittite, the language of a people who seem to have migrated into this area about 2300 B.C.E.

Information about the Hittites comes from archaeological sources, and also from written cuneiform tablets that provide details about politics and economic life. These records indicate that in the sixteenth century B.C.E. the Hittite king Hattusili I led his forces against neighboring kingdoms. Hattusili's grandson and successor, Mursili I, extended the Hittite conquests as far as Babylon. Upon his return home, the victorious Mursili was assassinated by members of his own family, which led to dynastic warfare. This pattern of expansion followed by internal conflict was repeated frequently, but when they were united behind a strong king, the Hittites were extremely powerful.

As the Hittites expanded southward, they came into conflict with the Egyptians, who were re-establishing their empire. The pharaoh Ramesses II engaged in numerous campaigns to retake Egyptian territory in Syria. He assembled a large well-equipped army with thousands of chariots and expected to defeat the Hittites easily, but was ambushed by them at the Battle of Kadesh in 1274 B.C.E. Returning to Egypt, Ramesses declared that he had won and had monuments carved commemorating his victory, including the giant temples at Abu Simbel in Nubia, which were also designed as a demonstration of Egypt's power over its southern neighbors. In reality, neither side gained much by the battle, though both sides seem to have recognized the impossibility of defeating the other.

In 1258 Ramesses II and the Hittite king Hattusili III concluded a peace treaty, which was recorded in both Egyptian hieroglyphics and Hittite cuneiform. Both of these have survived. Although peace treaties are known to have existed since the twenty-fourth century B.C.E., this is one of the best preserved. Returning to the language of cooperation established in earlier royal diplomacy, each side promised not to invade the other and to come to the other's aid if attacked. Each promised peace and brotherhood, and the treaty ended with a long oath to the gods, who would curse the one who broke the treaty and bless the one who kept it.

Notes

1. J. A. Black et al., *Electronic Text Corpus of Sumerian Literature* (http://etcsl.orinst.ox.ac.uk/), Oxford 1998–2006. Used by permission of Oxford University, ETCSL Project.
2. Quoted in S. N. Kramer, *The Sumerians: Their History, Culture, and Character*, p. 238. Copyright © 1963 by The University of Chicago. All rights reserved. Used by permission of the publisher.
3. James B. Pritchard (ed.), *Ancient Near Eastern Texts Relating to the Old Testament — Third Edition with Supplement*, p. 171. © 1950, 1955, 1969, renewed 1978 by Princeton University Press. Reprinted by permission of Princeton University Press.
4. Ibid., p. 372.
5. Quoted in A. H. Gardiner, "Ramesside Texts Relating to the Taxation and Transport of Corn," *Journal of Egyptian Archaeology* 27 (1941), pp. 19–20.

Chapter Review

MAKE IT STICK

LearningCurve
bedfordstmartins.com/mckaywestvalue
After reading the chapter, use LearningCurve to retain what you've read.

IDENTIFY KEY TERMS

Identify and explain the significance of each item below.

civilization (p. 3)   polytheism (p. 10)
Paleolithic era (p. 4)   cuneiform (p. 13)
Neolithic era (p. 4)   Hammurabi's law code (p. 18)
Fertile Crescent (p. 7)   pharaoh (p. 21)
pastoralism (p. 8)   ma'at (p. 22)
patriarchy (p. 9)   *Book of the Dead* (p. 23)
Bronze Age (p. 10)

REVIEW THE MAIN IDEAS

Answer the focus questions from each section of the chapter.

- What do we mean by "the West" and "Western civilization"? (p. 2)
- How did early human societies develop and create new technologies and cultural forms? (p. 4)
- What kind of civilization did the Sumerians develop in Mesopotamia? (p. 10)
- How did the Akkadian and Old Babylonian empires develop in Mesopotamia? (p. 16)
- How did the Egyptians create a prosperous and long-lasting society? (p. 20)

MAKE CONNECTIONS

Think about the larger developments and continuities within and across chapters.

1. What aspects of life in the Neolithic period continued with little change in the civilizations of Mesopotamia and Egypt? What key differences?

2. Looking at your answers to question 1, do you think the distinction between "civilizations" and human cultures that were not "civilizations" discussed in the first part of this chapter is a valid one? Why or why not?

3. How were the societies that developed in Mesopotamia and Egypt similar to one another? Which of the characteristics you have identified as a similarity do you predict will also be found in later societies, and why?

ONLINE DOCUMENT ASSIGNMENT

Hatshepsut and Nefertiti

Considering Egyptian views of gender roles, what complexities did Egyptian writers and artists face in depicting Hatshepsut?

You encountered Hatshepsut on page 30. Keeping the question above in mind, go online and analyze a range of written and visual representations of Hatshepsut. Then complete a writing assignment based on the evidence and details from this chapter.

bedfordstmartins.com/mckaywestvalue

CHRONOLOGY

ca. 250,000 B.C.E.	• *Homo sapiens* evolve in Africa
250,000–9,000 B.C.E.	• Paleolithic era
9000 B.C.E.	• Beginning of the Neolithic; crop raising; domestication of sheep and goats
ca. 7000 B.C.E.	• Domestication of cattle; plow agriculture
ca. 5500 B.C.E.	• Smelting of copper
ca. 3800 B.C.E.	• Establishment of first Mesopotamian cities
ca. 3200 B.C.E.	• Development of cuneiform and hieroglyphic writing
ca. 3100 B.C.E.	• Unification of Upper and Lower Egypt
ca. 3000 B.C.E.	• Development of wheeled transport; beginning of bronze technology
ca. 2500 B.C.E.	• Bronze technology becomes common in many areas
ca. 2300 B.C.E.	• Establishment of the Akkadian empire
ca. 1800 B.C.E.	• Hyksos people begin to settle in the Nile Delta
1792–1750 B.C.E.	• Hammurabi rules Babylon
1258 B.C.E.	• Peace treaty between Egyptian pharaoh Ramesses II and Hittite king Hattusuli III
ca. 1200 B.C.E.	• "Bronze Age Collapse"; destruction and drought

A note on dates: This book generally uses the terms B.C.E. (Before the Common Era) and C.E. (Common Era) when giving dates, a system of chronology based on the Christian calendar and now used widely around the world.

✓ **LearningCurve**
bedfordstmartins.com/mckaywestvalue
After reading the chapter, use
LearningCurve to retain what
you've read.

Small Kingdoms and Mighty Empires in the Near East

1200–510 B.C.E.

THE MIGRATIONS, DROUGHT, AND DESTRUCTION OF WHAT SCHOLARS call the "Bronze Age Collapse" in the late thirteenth century B.C.E. ended the Hittite Empire and weakened the Egyptians. Much was lost, but the old cultures of the ancient Near East survived to nurture new societies. The technology for smelting iron, which developed in Anatolia as well as other places in the world, improved and spread, with iron weapons and tools becoming stronger and thus more important by about 1000 B.C.E. In the absence of powerful empires, the Phoenicians, Kushites, Hebrews, and many other peoples carved out small independent kingdoms until the Near East was a patchwork of them. The Hebrews created a new form of religious belief with a single god and wrote down their religious ideas and traditions in what later became the most significant written document from this period.

In the tenth century B.C.E. this jumble of small states gave way to an empire that for the first time embraced the entire Near East: the empire of the Assyrians. They assembled a huge army that used sophisticated military technology and brutal tactics, and also developed effective administrative techniques and stunning artistic works. The Assyrian Empire lasted for about three hundred years and then broke apart with the rise of a new empire centered in Babylon. Beginning in 550 B.C.E. the Persians conquered the Medes—nomadic peoples who had settled in Iran—and then the Babylonians and Assyrians, creating the largest empire yet seen, stretching from Anatolia in the west to the Indus Valley in the east. The Persians established effective methods of governing their diverse subjects and built roads for conquest, trade, and communication.

Iron and the Emergence of New States

How did iron technology shape new states after 1200 B.C.E., including Kush and Phoenicia?

If the Bronze Age Collapse was a time of massive political and economic disruption, it was also a period of the spread of new technologies, especially iron. Even though empires shrank, many small kingdoms survived, each with cultures that combined elements shared across a wide area with local traditions. These states included several that developed on the borders of the shrinking Egyptian empire, including Kush and Phoenicia.

Iron Technology

Along with migration and drought, another significant development in the centuries around 1200 B.C.E. was the spread of iron tools and iron technology. Iron is the most common element in the earth, but most iron found on or near the earth's surface occurs in the form of ore, which must be smelted to extract the metal. This is also true of the copper and tin that are used to make bronze, but these can be smelted at much lower temperatures than iron. As artisans perfected bronze metalworking techniques, they also experimented with iron. They developed a long and difficult process for smelting iron, using charcoal and a bellows (which raised the temperature of the fire significantly) to extract the iron from the ore. This procedure was performed in an enclosed furnace, and the process was repeated a number of times as the ore was transformed into wrought iron, which could be hammered into shapes.

Exactly where and when the *first* smelted iron was produced is a matter of debate — many regions would like this honor — but it happened independently in several different places, including western Africa in what is now Nigeria, Anatolia (modern Turkey), and most likely India. In Anatolia, the earliest smelted weapon has been dated to about 2500 B.C.E., but there may have been some smelting earlier. Most of the iron produced was too brittle to be of much use until about 1100 B.C.E., however, when techniques improved and iron weapons gradually became stronger and cheaper than their bronze counterparts. Thus, in the schema of dividing history into periods according to the main material out of which tools are made (see Chapter 1), the **Iron Age** began in about 1100 B.C.E. Iron weapons became important items of trade around the Mediterranean and throughout the Tigris and Euphrates Valleys, and the technology for making them traveled as well. Iron appears to have been adopted more slowly in Egypt than in other parts of the Near East, so bronze remained important longer there. From Anatolia, iron objects were traded west into Greece and central Europe, and north into western Asia. By 500 B.C.E. knowledge of smelting had traveled these routes as well.

Ironworkers continued to experiment and improve their products. Somewhere in the Near East — again the exact location is disputed — ironworkers discovered that if the relatively brittle wrought iron objects were placed on a bed of burning charcoal and then cooled quickly, the outer layer would form into a layer of much harder material, steel. Goods made of cast or wrought iron were usually traded locally, but fine sword and knife blades of steel traveled long distances, and the knowledge of how to make them followed. Because it was fairly plentiful and relatively cheap when compared with bronze, iron has been called the "democratic metal." The transition from bronze to iron happened over many centuries, but iron (and even more so, steel) would be an important factor in history from this point on.

The Decline of Egypt and the Emergence of Kush

Although the treaty between the Egyptians and Hittites in 1258 B.C.E. seemed to indicate a future of peace and cooperation, this was not to be. Groups of seafaring peoples whom the Egyptians called "Sea Peoples" raided, migrated, and marauded in the eastern Mediterranean. Just who these people were and where they originated is much debated among scholars. They may have come from Greece, or islands in the Mediterranean such as Crete and Sardinia, or Anatolia (modern Turkey), or from all of these. Wherever they came from, their raids, combined with the expansion of the Assyrians (see page 47), led to the collapse of the Hittite Empire. The Hittite capital city of Hattusa was burned to the ground in 1180 B.C.E. by an army of many different peoples, and though small states re-emerged in Anatolia, these were very much under the influence of Assyria.

In Egypt, the pharaoh Ramesses III (r. 1186–1155 B.C.E.) defeated the Sea Peoples in both a land and sea battle, but these were costly, as were other military engagements. Ramesses appears to have also been the subject of an assassination plot, which he survived, but Egypt entered into a long period of political fragmentation and conquest by outsiders that scholars of Egypt refer to as the Third Intermediate Period (ca. 1070–712 B.C.E.). The long wars against invaders weakened and impoverished Egypt, causing political upheaval and economic decline. Scribes created somber portraits that no doubt exaggerated the negative, but were effective in capturing the mood:

> The land of Egypt was abandoned and every man was a law to himself. During many years there was no leader who could speak for others. Central government lapsed, small officials and headmen took over the whole land. Any man, great or small, might kill his neighbor. In the distress and vacuum that followed . . . men banded together to plunder one another. They treated the gods no better than men, and cut off the temple revenues.[1]

The decline of Egypt allowed new powers to emerge. South of Egypt was a region called Nubia, which as early as 2000 B.C.E. served as a conduit of trade through which ivory, gold, ebony, and other products flowed north from sub-Saharan Africa. Small kingdoms arose in this area, with large buildings and rich tombs. As Egypt expanded during the New Kingdom (see Chapter 1), it took over northern Nubia in what were sometimes brutal conquests, incorporating it into the

Nubian Cylinder Sheath   This small silver sheath made about 520 B.C.E., perhaps for a dagger, depicts a winged goddess and the Egyptian god Amon-Ra (not shown in photograph). It and others like it were found in the tombs of Kushite kings and suggest ways that Egyptian artistic styles and religious ideas influenced cultures farther up the Nile. (Nubian, Napatan Period, reign of King Amani-natakelebte, 538–519 B.C.E. Findspot: Sudan, Nubia, Nuri, Pyramid 10. Gilded silver, colored paste inclusions. Height × diameter: 12 × 3.1 cm [4¾ x 1¼ in.]. Museum of Fine Arts, Boston. Harvard University–Boston Museum of Fine Arts Expedition, 20.275)

PRIMARY SOURCE   The Report of Wenamun

This account describes the trip of the Egyptian official Wenamun to purchase Lebanese wood to make a large ceremonial boat named Amen-user-he for the god Amen-Ra. It is unknown whether this text describes a real mission, but the text reflects the political and economic situation in the decade from 1190 to 1180 B.C.E. Wenamun negotiated with the prince of Byblos, a Phoenician city-state in present-day Lebanon, for the timber, encountering great frustrations.

When morning came, he [the prince of Byblos] sent and brought me up. . . . Then he spoke to me, saying: "On what business have you come?" I said to him: "I have come in quest of timber for the great noble bark of Amen-Ra, King of Gods. What your father did, what the father of your father did, you too will do it." So I said to him. He said to me: "True, they did it. If you pay me for doing it, I will do it. My relations carried out this business after Pharaoh had sent six ships laden with the goods of Egypt, and they had been unloaded into their storehouses. You, what have you brought for me? . . . What are these foolish travels they made you do?"

I said to him: "Wrong! These are not foolish travels that I am doing. There is no ship on the river that does not belong to [the god] Amun. His is the sea and his the Lebanon of which you say, 'It is mine.' It is a growing ground for [the ceremonial ship called] *Amen-user-he*, the lord of every ship. . . . You are prepared to haggle over the Lebanon with Amun, its lord? As to your saying, the former kings sent silver and gold: If they had owned life and health, they would not have sent these things. It was in place of life and health that they sent these things to your fathers! But Amen-Ra, King of Gods, he is the lord of life and health, and he was the lord of your fathers! They passed their lifetimes [making] offering to Amun. You too, you are the servant of Amun! . . ."

growing Egyptian empire. The Nubians adopted many features of Egyptian culture, including Egyptian gods, the use of hieroglyphics, and the building of pyramids. Many Nubians became officials in the Egyptian bureaucracy and officers in the army, and there was significant intermarriage between the two groups.

With the contraction of the Egyptian empire in the Third Intermediate Period, an independent kingdom, **Kush**, rose in power in Nubia, with its capital at Napata in what is now Sudan. The Kushites conquered southern Egypt, and in 727 B.C.E. the Kushite king Piye (r. ca. 747–716 B.C.E.) swept through the Nile Valley to the delta in the north. United once again, Egypt enjoyed a brief period of peace during which the Egyptian culture continued to influence that of its conquerors. In the seventh century B.C.E. invading Assyrians (see page 47) pushed the Kushites out of Egypt, and the Kushite rulers moved their capital farther up the Nile to Meroë, where they built hundreds of pyramids. Meroë became a center for the production of iron, which was becoming the material of choice for weapons. Iron products from Meroë were the best in the world, smelted using wood from the vast forests in the area. They were traded to much of Africa and across the Red Sea and the Indian Ocean to India.

He placed my letter in the hand of his messenger; and he loaded the keel, the prow-piece, and the stern-piece, together with four other hewn logs, seven in all, and sent them to Egypt. His messenger who had gone to Egypt returned to me in Syria in the first month of winter, Smendes and Tentamun [the pharaoh and queen of the northern half of Egypt, Wenamun's employers] having sent: four jars and one *kakmen*-vessel of gold; five jars of silver; ten garments of royal linen; ten . . . garments of fine linen; five-hundred smooth linen mats; five-hundred ox-hides; five-hundred ropes; twenty sacks of lentils; and thirty baskets of fish. . . .

The prince rejoiced. He assigned three hundred men and three hundred oxen, and he set supervisors over them to have them fell the timbers. They were felled and they lay there during the winter. In the third month of summer they dragged them to the shore of the sea. The prince came out and stood by them, and he sent to me, saying: "Come!" . . . As I stood before him, he addressed me, saying: "Look, the business my fathers did in the past, I have done it, although you did not do for me what your fathers did for mine. Look, the last of your timber has arrived and is ready. Do as I wish, and come to load it."

EVALUATE THE EVIDENCE

1. How does Wenamun first attempt to get the prince of Byblos to give him the timber? What does the prince send in the first shipment? Why does he eventually provide more timber?

2. How does Wenamun's report reflect the decline of Egyptian power and wealth?

Source: Miriam Lichtheim, *Ancient Egyptian Literature: A Book of Readings*, vol. II, *The New Kingdom* (Berkeley: University of California Press, 1976), pp. 226–228. © 2006 by the Regents of the University of California. Published by the University of California Press.

The Rise of Phoenicia

While Kush expanded in the southern Nile Valley, another group rose to prominence along the Mediterranean coast of modern Lebanon, the northern part of the area called Canaan in ancient sources. These Canaanites established the prosperous commercial centers of Tyre, Sidon, and Byblos, all cities still thriving today, and were master ship-builders. With their stout ships, between about 1100 and 700 B.C.E. the residents of these cities became the seaborne merchants of the Mediterranean. (See "Primary Source: The Report of Wenamun," above.) Their most valued products were purple and blue textiles, from which originated their Greek name, **Phoenicians** (fih-NEE-shuhnz), meaning "Purple People."

The trading success of the Phoenicians brought them prosperity. In addition to textiles and purple dye, they began to manufacture goods for export, such as tools, weapons, and cookware. They worked bronze and iron, which they shipped processed or as ores, and made and traded glass products. Phoenician ships often carried hundreds of jars of wine, and the Phoenicians introduced grape growing to new regions around

Phoenician Coin This silver Phoenician coin shows an animal-headed ship containing soldiers with shields and helmets above the waves, and a hippocampus, a mythical beast, below. Phoenician gold and silver coins have been found throughout the Mediterranean, evidence of the Phoenicians' extensive trading network. This particular coin was most likely not used very often, as the images on it are still sharp; silver is soft, and frequent handling would have rubbed off the edges of the images. (Erich Lessing/Art Resource, NY)

the Mediterranean, dramatically increasing the wine available for consumption and trade. They imported rare goods and materials, including hunting dogs, gold, and ivory, from Persia in the east and their neighbors to the south. They also expanded their trade to Egypt, where they mingled with other local traders.

The variety and quality of the Phoenicians' trade goods generally made them welcome visitors. Moving beyond Egypt, they struck out along the coast of North Africa to establish new markets in places where they encountered little competition. In the ninth century B.C.E. they founded, in modern Tunisia, the city of Carthage (meaning "new city" in Phoenician), which prospered to become the leading city in the western Mediterranean, although it would one day struggle with Rome for domination of that region.

The Phoenicians planted trading posts and small farming communities along the coast, founding colonies in Spain and Sicily along with Carthage. Their trade routes eventually took them to the far western Mediterranean and beyond to the Atlantic coast of modern-day Portugal. The Phoenicians' voyages brought them into contact with the Greeks, to whom they introduced many aspects of the older and more urbanized cultures of Mesopotamia and Egypt.

The Phoenicians' overwhelming cultural achievement was the spread of a completely phonetic system of writing—that is, an alphabet. Writers of both cuneiform and hieroglyphics had developed signs that were used to represent sounds, but these were always used with a much larger number of ideograms. Sometime around 1800 B.C.E. workers in the Sinai Peninsula, which was under Egyptian control, began to write only with phonetic signs, with each sign designating one sound. This system vastly simplified writing and reading and spread among common people as a practical way to record things and communicate. Egyptian scribes and officials continued to use hieroglyphics, but the Phoenicians adopted the simpler system for their own language and spread it around the Mediterranean. The Greeks modified this alphabet and then used it to write their own language, and the Romans later based their alphabet—the script we use to write English today—on Greek. Alphabets based on the Phoenician alphabet were also created in the Persian Empire and formed the basis of Hebrew, Arabic, and various alphabets of South and Central Asia. The system invented by ordinary people and spread by Phoenician merchants is the origin of most of the world's phonetic alphabets today.

The Hebrews

How did the Hebrews create an enduring religious tradition?

The legacy of another people who took advantage of Egypt's collapse to found an independent state may have been even more far-reaching than that of the Phoenicians. For a period of several centuries, a people known as the Hebrews controlled first one and then two small states on the western end of the Fertile Crescent, Israel and Judah. Politically unimportant when compared with the Egyptians or Babylonians, the Hebrews created a new form of religious belief, a monotheism based on the worship of an all-powerful god they called **Yahweh** (YAH-way). Beginning in the late 600s B.C.E., they began to write down their religious ideas, traditions, laws, advice literature, prayers, hymns, history, and prophecies in a series of books. These were gathered together centuries later to form the Hebrew Bible, which Christians later adopted and termed the "Old Testament" to parallel specific Christian writings termed the "New Testament." These writings later became the core of the Hebrews' religion, Judaism, a word taken from the kingdom of Judah, the southern of the two Hebrew kingdoms and the one that was the primary force in developing religious traditions. (The word *Israelite*, often used as a synonym for *Hebrew*, refers to all people in this group, and not simply the residents of the northern kingdom of Israel.) Jews today revere these texts, as do many Christians, and Muslims respect them, all of which gives them particular importance.

The Hebrew State

Most of the information about the Hebrews comes from the Bible, which, like all ancient documents, must be used with care as a historical source. Archaeological evidence has supported many of its details, and because it records a living religious tradition, extensive textual and physical research into everything it records continues, with enormous controversies among scholars about how to interpret findings.

The Hebrews were nomadic pastoralists who may have migrated into the Nile Delta from the east, seeking good land for their herds of sheep and goats. According to the Hebrew Bible, they were enslaved by the Egyptians, but were led out of Egypt by a charismatic leader named Moses. The biblical account is very dramatic, and the events form a pivotal episode in the history of the Hebrews and the later religious practices of Judaism. Moses conveyed God's warning to the pharaoh that a series of plagues would strike Egypt, the last of which was the threat that all firstborn sons in Egypt would be killed. He instructed the Hebrews to prepare a hasty meal of a sacrificed lamb eaten with unleavened bread. The blood of the lamb was painted over the doors of Hebrew houses. At midnight Yahweh spread death over the land, but he passed over the Hebrew houses with the blood-painted doors. This event became known as the Passover, and later became a central religious holiday in Judaism. The next day a terrified pharaoh ordered the Hebrews out of Egypt. Moses then led them in search of what they understood to be the Promised Land, an event known as the Exodus, which was followed by forty years of wandering.

According to scripture, the Hebrews settled in the area between the Mediterranean and the Jordan River known as Canaan. They were organized into tribes, each tribe consisting of numerous families who thought of themselves as all related to one another and having a common ancestor. At first, good farmland, pastureland, and freshwater

A Golden Calf According to the Hebrew Bible, Moses descended from Mount Sinai, where he had received the Ten Commandments, to find the Hebrews worshipping a golden calf, which was against Yahweh's laws. In July 1990 an American archaeological team found this model of a gilded calf inside a pot. The figurine, which dates to about 1550 B.C.E., is strong evidence for the existence in Canaan of religious traditions that involved animals as divine symbols. (© www.BibleLandPictures.com/Alamy)

sources were held in common by each tribe. Common use of land was — and still is — characteristic of nomadic peoples. The Bible divides up the Hebrews at this point into twelve tribes, each named according to an ancestor.

In Canaan, the nomadic Hebrews encountered a variety of other peoples, whom they both learned from and fought. They slowly adopted agriculture, and not surprisingly, at times worshipped the agricultural gods of their neighbors, including Baal, an ancient fertility god represented as a golden calf. This was another example of the common historical pattern of newcomers adapting themselves to the culture of an older, well-established people.

The Bible reports that the greatest danger to the Hebrews came from a group known as the Philistines, who were most likely Greek-speaking people who had migrated to Canaan as part of the movement of the Sea Peoples and established a kingdom along the Mediterranean coast. The Philistines' superior technology and military organization at first made them invincible, but the Hebrews found a champion and a spirited leader in Saul. In the biblical account Saul and his men battled the Philistines for control of the land, often without success. In the meantime Saul established a monarchy over the twelve Hebrew tribes, becoming their king, an event conventionally dated to about 1025 B.C.E.

The Bible includes detailed discussion of the growth of the Hebrew kingdom. It relates that Saul's work was carried on by David of Bethlehem (r. ca. 1005–965 B.C.E.), who pushed back the Philistines and waged war against his other neighbors. To give his kingdom a capital, he captured the city of Jerusalem, which he enlarged, fortified, and made the religious and political center of his realm. David's military successes enlarged the kingdom and won the Hebrews unprecedented security, and his forty-year reign was a period of vitality and political consolidation.

David's son Solomon (r. ca. 965–925 B.C.E.) launched a building program that the biblical narrative describes as including cities, palaces, fortresses, and roads. The most symbolic of these projects was the Temple of Jerusalem, which became the home of the Ark of the Covenant, the chest that contained the holiest of Hebrew religious articles. The temple in Jerusalem was intended to be the religious heart of the kingdom, a symbol of Hebrew unity and Yahweh's approval of the kingdom built by Saul, David, and Solomon.

Evidence of this united kingdom may have come to light in August 1993 when an Israeli archaeologist found an inscribed stone slab that refers to a "king of Israel," and also to the "House of David." This discovery has been regarded by most scholars as the first mention of King David's dynasty outside of the Bible. The nature and extent of this kingdom continues to be disputed among archaeologists, who offer divergent datings and interpretations for the finds that are continuously brought to light.

Along with discussing expansion and success, the Bible also notes problems. Solomon's efforts were hampered by strife. The financial demands of his building program drained the resources of his people, and his use of forced labor for building projects further fanned popular resentment.

A united Hebrew kingdom did not last long. At Solomon's death his kingdom broke into political halves. The northern part became Israel, with its capital at Samaria, and the southern half became Judah, with Jerusalem remaining its center. War soon broke out between them, as recorded in the Bible, and the Assyrians wiped out the northern kingdom of Israel in 722 B.C.E. Judah survived numerous calamities until the Babylonians crushed it in 587 B.C.E. The survivors were forcibly relocated to Babylonia, a period commonly known as the Babylonian Captivity. In 538 B.C.E. the Persian king Cyrus the Great (see page 52) conquered the Babylonians and permitted some forty thousand exiles to return to Jerusalem. They rebuilt the temple, although politically the area was simply part of the Persian Empire.

The Jewish Religion

During and especially after the Babylonian Captivity, the most important legal and ethical Hebrew texts were edited and brought together in the **Torah**, the first five books of the Hebrew Bible. Here the exiles redefined their beliefs and practices, thereby establishing what they believed was the law of Yahweh. Fundamental to an understanding of the Jewish religion is the concept of the **Covenant**, an agreement that people believed to exist between themselves and Yahweh. According to the Bible, Yahweh appeared to the tribal leader Abraham, promising him that he would be blessed, as would his descendants, if they followed Yahweh. (Because Judaism, Christianity, and Islam all regard this event as foundational, they are referred to as the "Abrahamic religions.") Yahweh next appeared to Moses during the time he was leading the Hebrews out of Egypt, and Yahweh made a Covenant with the Hebrews: if they worshipped Yahweh as their only god, he would consider them his chosen people and protect them from their enemies. The Covenant was understood to be made with the whole people, not simply a king or elite, and was renewed again several times in the accounts of the Hebrew people in the Bible. Individuals such as Abraham and Moses who acted as intermediaries between Yahweh and the Hebrew people were known as "prophets"; much of the Hebrew Bible consists of writings in their voices, understood as messages from Yahweh to which the Hebrews were to listen.

Worship was embodied in a series of rules of behavior, the Ten Commandments, which Yahweh gave to Moses. These required certain kinds of religious observances and forbade the Hebrews to steal, kill, lie, or commit adultery, thus creating a system of ethical absolutes. From the Ten Commandments a complex system of rules of conduct was created and later written down as Hebrew law. The earliest part of this code, contained in the Torah, was most likely influenced by Hammurabi's code (see Chapter 1) and often called for harsh punishments. Later tradition, largely the work of the prophets who lived from the eighth to the fifth centuries B.C.E., put more emphasis on righteousness than on retribution.

Like the followers of other religions in the ancient Near East, Jews engaged in rituals through which they showed their devotion. They were also expected to please Yahweh by living up to high moral standards and by worshipping him above all other gods. The first of the Ten Commandments expresses this: "I am the Lord your God . . . you shall have no other gods besides me" (Exodus 20:23). Increasingly this was understood to be a commandment to worship Yahweh alone. The later prophets such as Isaiah created a system of ethical monotheism, in which goodness was understood to come from a single transcendent god, and in which religious obligations included fair and just behavior toward other people as well as rituals. They saw Yahweh as intervening directly in history and also working through individuals—both Hebrews and non-Hebrews—he had chosen to carry out his aims. (See "Individuals in Society: Cyrus the Great," page 54.) Judging by the many prophets (and a few prophetesses) in the Bible exhorting the Hebrews to listen to Yahweh, honor the Covenant, stop worshipping other gods, and behave properly, adherence to this system was a difficult challenge.

Like Mesopotamian deities, Yahweh punished people, but the Hebrews also believed he was a loving and forgiving god who would protect and reward all those who obeyed his commandments. A hymn recorded in the book of Psalms captures this idea:

> Blessed is every one who fears the Lord, who walks in his ways!
> You shall eat the fruit of the labor of your hands;
>   you shall be happy, and it shall be well with you.
> Your wife will be like a fruitful vine within your house;
>   your children will be like olive shoots around your table.
> Lo, thus shall the man be blessed who fears the Lord. (Psalms 128: 1–4)

The religion of the Hebrews was thus addressed to not only an elite but also the individual. Because kings or other political leaders were not essential to its practice, the rise or fall of a kingdom was not crucial to the religion's continued existence. Religious leaders were important in Judaism, but personally following the instructions of Yahweh was the central task for observant Jews in the ancient world.

Hebrew Family and Society

The Hebrews were originally nomadic, but they adopted settled agriculture in Canaan, and some lived in cities. The shift away from pastoralism affected more than just how people fed themselves. Communal use of land gave way to family or private ownership, and devotion to the traditions of Judaism came to replace tribal identity.

Family relationships reflected evolving circumstances. Marriage and the family were fundamentally important in Jewish life; celibacy was frowned upon and almost all major Jewish thinkers and priests were married. Polygamy was allowed, but the typical marriage was probably monogamous. In the codes of conduct written down in the Hebrew Bible, sex between a married woman and a man not her husband was an "abomination," as were incest and sex between men. Men were free to have sexual relations with concubines, servants, and slaves, however.

As in Mesopotamia and Egypt, marriage was a family matter, too important to be left to the whims of young people. (See "Primary Source: A Jewish Family Contract," page 46.) According to biblical rules, sexual relations were a source of impurity that needed to be cleansed with specific rituals, but sex itself was basically good because it was part of Yahweh's creation, and the bearing of children was seen in some ways as a religious function. Sons were especially desired because they maintained the family bloodline, while keeping ancestral property in the family. As in Mesopotamia, land was handed down within families, generally from father to son. A firstborn son became the head of the household at his father's death. Mothers oversaw the early education of the children, but as boys grew older, their fathers gave them more of their education. Both men and women were expected to know religious traditions so that they could teach their children and prepare for religious rituals and ceremonies. Women worked in the fields alongside their husbands in rural areas, and in shops in the cities. According to biblical codes, menstruation and childbirth made women ritually unpure, but the implications of this in ancient times is contested by scholars.

Children, according to the book of Psalms, "are a heritage of the lord, and the fruit of the womb is his reward" (Psalms 128:3), and newly married couples were expected to begin a family at once. The desire for children to perpetuate the family was so strong that if a man died before he could sire a son, his brother was legally obliged to marry the widow. The son born of the brother was thereafter considered the offspring of the dead man. If the brother refused, the widow had her revenge by denouncing him to the elders and publicly spitting in his face.

The development of urban life among the Jews created new economic opportunities, especially in crafts and trades. People specialized in certain occupations, such as milling flour, baking bread, making pottery, weaving, and carpentry. As in most ancient societies, these crafts were family trades. Sons worked with their father, daughters with their mother. If the business prospered, the family might be assisted by a few paid workers or slaves. The practitioners of a craft usually lived in a particular section of town, a custom still prevalent in the Near East today. Commerce and trade developed later than crafts. Trade with neighboring countries was handled by foreigners, usually Phoenicians. Jews dealt mainly in local trade, and in most instances craftsmen and farmers sold directly to their customers.

The Torah sets out rules about many aspects of life, including skin diseases, seminal emissions, childbirth, sexual actions, and animal sacrifices. Among these was the set of dietary laws known as *kashrut* (from which we derive the English word *kosher*, which means ritually pure and ready to be eaten), setting out what plants and animals Jews were forbidden to eat and how foods were to be prepared properly. Prohibited animals included pigs, rabbits, many birds, insects (except for locusts), and shellfish, as well as any animal not slaughtered in the proper way. Meat and dairy products were not to be eaten at the same meal or cooked in the same utensils. Later commentators sought to explain these laws as originating in concerns about health or hygiene, but the biblical text simply gives them as rules coming from Yahweh, sometimes expressed in terms of ritual purity or cleanliness. It is not clear how these rules were followed during the biblical period, because detailed interpretations were written down only much later, during the time of the Roman Empire, in the Talmud, a work that records civil and ceremonial law and Jewish traditions. Most scholars see the written laws as based on earlier oral traditions, but as with any law code, from Hammurabi's to contemporary

PRIMARY SOURCE   A Jewish Family Contract

During the time of Persian rule in Egypt, Jewish soldiers were stationed in Elephantine, a military post on the Nile. Historians have since recovered papyrus documents from that location, known as the Elephantine papyri, which provide information on all sorts of everyday social and economic matters, including marriage, divorce, property, slavery, and borrowing money. The text below is an agreement by a Jewish father regarding a house he had given to his daughter, probably as part of her dowry. It was written in Aramaic, the language of business in the Persian Empire.

On the 21st of Chisleu, that is the 1st of Mesore, year 6 of King Artaxerxes,* Mahseiah b. Yedoniah, a Jew of Elephantine, of the detachment of Haumadata, said to Jezaniah b. Uriah of the said detachment as follows: There is the site of 1 house belonging to me, west of the house belonging to you, which I have given to your wife, my daughter Mibtahiah, and in respect of which I have written her a deed. The measurements of the house in question are 8 cubits and a handbreadth by 11, *by the measuring-rod.*† Now do I, Mahseiah, say to you, Build and equip that site . . . and dwell thereon with your wife. But you may not sell that house or give it as a present to others; only your children by my daughter Mibtahiah shall have power over it after you two. If tomorrow or some other day you build upon this land, and then my daughter divorces you and leaves you, she shall have no power to take it or give it to others; only your children by Mibtahiah shall have power over it, in return for the work which you shall have done. If, on the other hand, she recovers from you [in other words, if Jezaniah divorces *her*], she [may] take half the house, and [the] othe[r] half shall be at your disposal in return for the building which you will have done on that house. And again as to that half, your children by Mibtahiah shall have power over it after you. If tomorrow or another day I should institute suit or process against you and say I did not give you this land to build on and did not draw up this deed for you, I shall give you a sum of 10 *karshin* by royal weight, at the rate of 2 *R* to the ten, and no suit or process shall lie. This deed was written by 'Atharshuri b. Nabuzeribni in the fortress of Syene at the dictation of Mahseiah.

Witnesses hereto (signatures)

EVALUATE THE EVIDENCE

1. How does Mahseiah seek to assist his daughter and his future grandchildren?

2. What does this contract reveal about the movement and mixtures of peoples in the Persian Empire, and about Persian methods of governing?

Source: James B. Pritchard, ed., *Ancient Near Eastern Texts Relating to the Old Testament: Third Edition with Supplement.* © 1950, 1955, 1969, renewed 1978 by Princeton University Press. Reprinted by permission of Princeton University Press.

*This is the date of the document. Chisleu was a month in the Hebrew calendar, Mesore a seasonal period in the Egyptian calendar. Artaxerxes is most likely Artaxerxes I, king of Persia from 465 to 424 B.C.E., which means the year this agreement was drafted was 459 B.C.E.

†A cubit was the length of a forearm, roughly 20 inches; the house site was thus about 15 by 18 feet.

ones, it is much easier to learn about what people were supposed to do according to the laws of the Torah than what they actually did.

Beliefs and practices that made Jews distinctive endured, but the Hebrew states did not. Small states like those of the Phoenicians and the Hebrews could exist only in the absence of a major power, and the beginning of the ninth century B.C.E. saw the rise of such a power: the Assyrians of northern Mesopotamia. They conquered the kingdom of Israel, the Phoenician cities, and eventually many other states as well.

Assyria, the Military Monarchy

What explains the rise and fall of the Assyrians?

The Assyrian kingdom originated in northern Mesopotamia. The Assyrians built up the military and conquered many of their neighbors, including Babylonia, and took over much of Syria all the way to the Mediterranean. The Assyrians then moved into Anatolia, where the pressure they put on the Hittite Empire was one factor in its collapse. Assyria's success allowed it to become the leading power in the Near East, with an army that at times numbered many tens of thousands.

Assyria's Long Road to Power

The Assyrians had inhabited northern Mesopotamia since the third millennium B.C.E., forming a kingdom that grew and shrank in size and power over the centuries. They had long pursued commerce with the Babylonians in the south, and the peoples of northern Syria and Anatolia in the north. During the time of Sargon of Akkad, they were part of the Akkadian empire, then independent, then part of the Babylonian empire under Hammurabi, then independent again (see Chapter 1). Warfare with the Babylonians and other Near Eastern states continued off and on, and in the thirteenth century B.C.E., under the leadership of a series of warrior kings, the Assyrians slowly began to create a larger state.

The eleventh century B.C.E.—the time of the Bronze Age Collapse—was a period of instability and retrenchment in the Near East. The Assyrians did not engage in any new wars of conquest, but remained fairly secure within their borders. Under the leadership of King Adad-nirari II (r. 911–892 B.C.E.), Assyria began a campaign of expansion and domination, creating what scholars have termed the Neo-Assyrian Empire. Assyrian armies pushed in all directions, conquering, exacting tribute, and building new fortified towns, palaces, and temples. King Shalmaneser III (shal-muh-NEE-zuhr) (r. 858–823 B.C.E.) conquered all of Babylonia, Syria, Phoenicia, and much of the northern half of the Arabian peninsula. The next several turbulent centuries were marked by Assyrian military campaigns, constant efforts by smaller states to maintain or recover their independence, and eventual further Assyrian conquest.

Assyrian history is often told as a story of one powerful king after another, but among the successful Assyrian rulers there was one queen, Shammuramat, whose name in Greek became Semiramis. She ruled with her husband and then as regent for her young son in 810–806 B.C.E. Although not much can be known for certain about the historical Queen Semiramis, many legends grew up about her, which were told throughout the ancient Near East, and later by Greek and Roman authors. Some emphasized her wisdom, beauty, and patronage of the arts, while others portrayed her as a sex-crazed

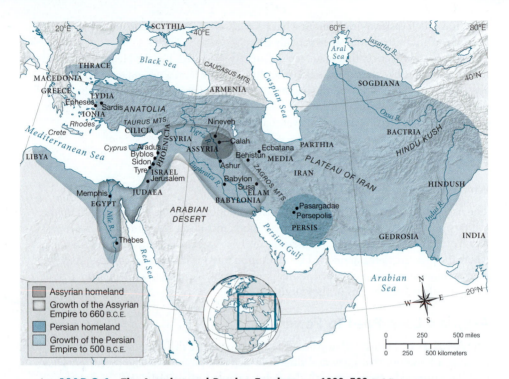

MAP 2.1   The Assyrian and Persian Empires, ca. 1000–500 B.C.E.
The Assyrian Empire at its height around 650 B.C.E. included almost all of the old centers of power in the ancient Near East. By 513 B.C.E., however, the Persian Empire was far larger.

sorceress. These stories cannot be used as evidence for the lives of women in the Assyrian Empire, but like the stories of Queen Cleopatra of Egypt (see Chapter 5), they can be used as evidence for the continuing fascination with the few women who held political power in the ancient world.

Eighth-century kings continued the expansion of Assyria, which established its capital at Nineveh (NIHN-uh-vuh) on the Tigris River. The kingdom of Israel and many other states fell; others, like the kingdom of Judah, became subservient to the warriors from the Tigris. In 717 B.C.E. Sargon II (r. 721–705 B.C.E.) led his army in a sweeping attack along the coast of the eastern Mediterranean south of Phoenicia, where he defeated the armies of the Egyptian pharaoh. Sargon also lashed out at Assyria's traditional enemies to the north and then turned south against a renewed threat in Babylonia. By means of almost constant warfare, the Assyrians created an empire that stretched from east and north of the Tigris River to central Egypt (Map 2.1). Revolt against the Assyrians inevitably promised the rebels bloody battles and cruel sieges followed by surrender, accompanied by systematic torture and slaughter, or by deportations. Like many conquerors, the Assyrians recognized that relocated peoples were less likely to rebel because they were forced to create new lives for themselves far from their original homelands, and that simply relocating leaders might be enough to destroy opposition.

Assyrian methods were certainly harsh, but in practical terms Assyria's success was actually due primarily to the size of its army and the army's sophisticated and effective military organization. By Sargon's time, the Assyrians had invented the mightiest military machine the ancient Near East had ever seen, with perhaps seventy thousand men in the field in an era that typically saw armies of under ten thousand. The mainstay of the Assyrian army was the infantryman armed with an iron spear and sword and protected by helmet and armor. The Assyrian army also featured archers, some on foot, others on horseback, and still others in chariots—the latter ready to wield lances once they had expended their supply of arrows. Some infantry archers wore heavy armor. These soldiers served as a primitive field artillery whose job was to sweep the enemy's walls of defenders so that others could storm the defenses. Slingers (warriors who used slingshots) also served as artillery in pitched battles. For mobility on the battlefield, the Assyrians organized a corps of chariots.

Assyrian military genius was remarkable for the development of a wide variety of siege machinery and techniques, including excavation to undermine city walls and battering rams to knock down walls and gates. Never before in the Near East had anyone applied such technical knowledge to warfare. The Assyrians even invented the concept of a corps of engineers, who bridged rivers with pontoons or provided soldiers with inflatable skins for swimming. And the Assyrians knew how to coordinate their efforts, both in open battle and in siege warfare. Assyrian king Sennacherib's (r. 705–681 B.C.E.) account of his attacks on the kingdom of Judah, which was under the leadership of King Hezekiah (r. ca. 715–686 B.C.E.) in 701 B.C.E., provides a vivid portrait of the Assyrian war machine:

> As to Hezekiah, the Jew, he did not submit to my yoke, I laid siege to 46 of his strong cities, walled forts and to the countless small villages in their vicinity, and conquered them by means of well-stamped earth-ramps, and battering rams brought thus near to the walls combined with the attack by foot soldiers, using mines, breaches as well as sapper work. . . . Himself I made prisoner in Jerusalem, his royal residence, like a bird in a cage. I surrounded him with earthwork in order to molest those who were leaving his city's gate.[2]

What Assyrian accounts do not mention is that the siege of Jerusalem was not successful. Although they had conquered many cities in Judah, the Assyrian armies gave up their attempts to conquer the entire kingdom and went home.

Sennacherib's campaign is also recorded several times in the Hebrew Bible, but there the point is very different. Instead of focusing on Assyrian might, the author stresses King Hezekiah's reliance on Yahweh. The biblical accounts attribute Judah's ability to withstand the Assyrian siege to an angel sent by Yahweh, but they also describe Hezekiah as taking practical measures to counter the Assyrian invasion. He "made weapons and shields in abundance," and also ordered the building of a tunnel that would divert water from the springs outside the walls of Jerusalem into the city, thus both limiting the water available for Assyrian troops and assuring the city of a steady supply:

> When Hezekiah saw that Sennacherib had come and intended to fight against Jerusalem, he planned with his officers and his mighty men to stop the water of the springs that were outside the city; and they helped him. A great many people were gathered, and they stopped all the springs and the brook that flowed through the land. (2 Chronicles 32: 2–4)

The tunnel was completed and functioned, and is now a major tourist attraction. An inscription that was originally on the wall recording the way in which it was built has been dated to the eighth century B.C.E., and chemical analysis confirms this dating.

Assyrian Rule and Culture

Although the Assyrians gave up on conquering Judah, they won most of their battles, and they also knew how to use their victories to consolidate their power. The key to success in all empires is to get cooperation from some people in the regions you wish to dominate, and the Assyrians did this well. As early as the reign of Tiglath-pileser III, the Assyrian kings began to organize their conquered territories into an empire. The lands closest to Assyria became provinces governed by Assyrian officials. Kingdoms beyond the provinces were not annexed but became dependent states that followed Assyria's lead and also paid Assyria a hefty tribute. The Assyrian king chose these states' rulers either by regulating the succession of native kings or by supporting native kings who appealed to him. Against more distant states the Assyrian kings waged frequent war in order to conquer them outright or make the dependent states secure.

In the seventh century B.C.E. Assyrian power seemed firmly established. Yet the downfall of Assyria was swift and complete. Babylon finally won its independence from Assyria in 626 B.C.E. and joined forces with the Medes, an Indo-European-speaking folk from Persia (modern Iran). Together the Babylonians and the Medes destroyed the Assyrian Empire in 612 B.C.E., paving the way for the rise of the Persians. The Hebrew prophet Nahum (NAY-uhm) spoke for many when he asked, "Nineveh is laid waste: who will bemoan her?" (Nahum 3:7). Their cities destroyed and their power shattered, the Assyrians disappeared from history, remembered only as a cruel people of the Old Testament who oppressed the Hebrews. Two hundred years later, when the Greek adventurer and historian Xenophon (ZEH-nuh-fuhn) passed by the ruins of Nineveh, he marveled at the extent of the former city but knew nothing of the Assyrians. The glory of their empire was forgotten.

Modern archaeology has brought the Assyrians out of obscurity. In 1839 the English archaeologist and traveler A. H. Layard began excavations at Nineveh. His findings electrified the world. Layard's workers unearthed masterpieces, including monumental sculpted figures—huge winged bulls, human-headed lions, and sphinxes—as well as brilliantly sculpted friezes. Among the most renowned of Layard's finds were the Assyrian palace reliefs, whose number has been increased by the discoveries of twentieth-century archaeologists. For the kings' palaces, Assyrian artists carved reliefs that showed scenes of war as a series of episodes that progressed from the time the army marched out until the enemy was conquered. In doing so, they created a visual narrative of events, a form still favored by comic-book artists and the authors of graphic novels.

Equally valuable were the numerous Assyrian cuneiform documents, which ranged from royal accounts of mighty military campaigns to simple letters by common people. The biggest find of these was the library of King Ashurbanipal (r. 668–627 B.C.E.), the last major Assyrian king, in the city of Nineveh. Like many Assyrian kings, Ashurbanipal was described as extremely cruel, but he was also well educated and deeply interested in literary and religious texts, especially those from what was already to him the ancient Mesopotamian past. Included in the tens of thousands of texts in his library were creation accounts from ancient Babylon (some most likely simply confiscated from the city of Babylon, which was part of the Assyrian Empire), the *Epic of Gilgamesh*, and many other mythological and religious texts, as well as word lists, chronicles, and royal documents. Some texts relate to medicine and astronomy, and others to foretelling the future or practicing magic. The clay tablets on which these were written are harder than normal, which many scholars think may have happened as a result of a fire that destroyed the city of Nineveh shortly after the end of Ashurbanipal's reign. Unfortunately the English archaeologists who dug up his library in the nineteenth century did not follow the standards of excavation that later archaeologists would, and they just shipped the tablets back to London all jumbled together without recording exactly where and how they had been found. Many broke and are still being pieced together more than a century after their discovery. Thus many questions that scholars have about the library are impossible to answer.

The Neo-Babylonian Empire

The decline of Assyria allowed another group of people, the Chaldeans, to create a new dynasty of kings and a somewhat smaller empire centered at Babylon. The Chaldeans were peoples that settled in southern Mesopotamia, where they established their rule, later extending it farther north. They grew strong enough to overthrow Assyrian rule in 626 B.C.E. with the help of another new people, the Medes, who had established themselves in modern western Iran (see page 52). The Neo- (or new) Babylonian empire they created was marked by an attempt at the restoration of past Babylonian greatness. Their most famous king, Nebuchadnezzar II (neh-buh-kuhd-NEH-zuhr) (r. 604–562 B.C.E.), thrust Babylonian power into Syria and Judah, destroying Jerusalem and forcibly deporting the residents to Babylonia.

The Chaldeans focused on solidifying their power and legitimizing their authority. Kings and priests consciously looked back to the great days of Hammurabi and other earlier kings. They instituted a religious revival that included restoring old temples and sanctuaries, as well as creating new ones in the same tradition. Part of their effort was commercial, as they sought to revive the economy in order to resurrect the image of Babylonian greatness. In their hands the city of Babylon grew and gained a reputation for magnificence and luxury. The city, it was said by later Greek and Roman writers, even housed hanging gardens, one of the "wonders of the ancient world." No contemporary written or archaeological sources confirm the existence of the hanging gardens, but they do confirm that Babylon was a bustling, thriving city.

The Neo-Babylonians preserved many basic aspects of older Babylonian law, literature, and government, yet they failed to bring peace and prosperity to Mesopotamia. Loss of important trade routes to the north and northeast reduced income, and additional misfortune came in the form of famine and plague. The Neo-Babylonian kingdom was weakened and ultimately conquered in 539 B.C.E. by their former allies the Medes, who had themselves found new allies, the Persians.

The Empire of the Persian Kings

How did the Persians consolidate their power and control and influence the subjects of their extensive empire?

The Assyrians rose to power from a base in the Tigris and Euphrates River Valleys of Mesopotamia, which had seen many earlier empires. They were defeated by a coalition that included a Mesopotamian power—Babylon—but also a people with a base of power in a part of the world that had not been the site of earlier urbanized states: Persia (modern-day Iran), a stark land of towering mountains and flaming deserts, with a broad central plateau in the heart of the country (see Map 2.1). The Persians created an even larger empire than the Assyrians did, and one that stretched far to the east. Though as conquerors they willingly used force to accomplish their ends, they also used diplomacy to consolidate their power and generally allowed the peoples that they conquered to practice their existing customs and religions. Thus the Persian Empire was one of political unity and cultural diversity.

Consolidation of the Persian Empire

Iran's geographical position and topography explain its traditional role as the highway between western and eastern Asia. Nomadic peoples migrating south from the broad steppes of Russia and Central Asia have streamed into Iran throughout much of history. Confronting the uncrossable salt deserts, most have turned either westward or eastward, moving on until they reached the advanced and wealthy urban centers of Mesopotamia and India. Cities did emerge along these routes, however, and Iran became the area where nomads met urban dwellers.

Among the nomadic groups were Indo-European-speaking peoples who migrated into this area about 1000 B.C.E. with their flocks and herds. They were also horse breeders, and the horse gave them a decisive military advantage over those who already lived in the area. One of the Indo-European groups was the Medes, who settled in northern Iran with their capital at Ecbatana, the modern Hamadan. The Medes united under one king and joined the Babylonians in overthrowing the Assyrian Empire. With the rise of the Medes, the balance of power in western Asia shifted for the first time to the area east of Mesopotamia.

In 550 B.C.E. Cyrus the Great (r. 559–530 B.C.E.), king of the Persians and one of the most remarkable statesmen of antiquity, conquered the Medes. (See "Individuals in Society: Cyrus the Great," page 54.) Cyrus's conquest of the Medes resulted not in slavery and slaughter but in the union of the two peoples. Having united Persia and Media, Cyrus set out to achieve two goals. First, he wanted to win control of the shore of the Mediterranean and thus of the terminal ports of the great trade routes that crossed Iran and Anatolia. Second, he strove to secure eastern Iran from the pressure of nomadic invaders.

In a series of major campaigns, Cyrus achieved his goals. He conquered the various kingdoms of the Tigris and Euphrates Valleys, including Babylon in 539 B.C.E. A text written in cuneiform on a sixth-century-B.C.E. Babylonian clay cylinder presents Cyrus describing the way in which the main Babylonian god Marduk selected him to conquer Babylon and restore proper government and worship:

> I am Cyrus, king of the universe, the great king, the powerful king, king of Babylon, king of Sumer and Akkad, king of the four quarters of the world. . . . When I went as harbinger of peace i[nt]o Babylon I founded my sovereign residence within the palace amid celebration and rejoicing. Marduk, the great lord, bestowed on me as my destiny the great magnanimity of one who loves Babylon, and I every day sought him out in awe. My vast troops marched peaceably in Babylon, and the whole of [Sumer]

and Akkad had nothing to fear. I sought the welfare of the city of Babylon and all its sanctuaries. As for the population of Babylon, . . . [w]ho as if without div[ine intention] had endured a yoke not decreed for them, I soothed their weariness, I freed them from their bonds. . . . Marduk, the great lord, rejoiced at [my good] deeds, and he pronounced a sweet blessing over me, Cyrus, the king who fears him, and over Cambyses, the son [my] issue, [and over] all my troops, that we might proceed further at his exalted command.[3]

We do not know who actually wrote this text, but whoever did made sure to portray Cyrus as someone who triumphed as the result of divine favor, not simply military conquest, and honored the gods of the regions he conquered.

Cyrus then swept into western Anatolia. Here his forces met those of the young kingdom of Lydia, a small state where gold may have first been minted into coins. Croesus (KREE-suhs), king of the Lydians, considered Cyrus an immediate threat and planned to attack his territory. Greek legends later related that Croesus consulted the oracle at Delphi, that is, the priestess of the temple to the god Apollo at Delphi, who was understood to convey the words of the god when she spoke. Speaking through the priestess, Apollo said of the invasion, "If you make war on the Persians, you will destroy a mighty empire" (Herodotus 1.53.3). Thinking that the oracle meant the Persian Empire, Croesus went ahead and was defeated; the oracle meant that he would destroy his own kingdom.

According to later Greek sources, Cyrus spared the life of Croesus, who then served him as an adviser. To the Greeks, Croesus became synonymous with enormous wealth, giving rise to the phrase "richer than Croesus." Recent scholarship has suggested that stories about Croesus's wealth were based primarily on the fact that Lydia was one of the earliest places where gold coins were minted. Historians studying Persian sources have also noted that the account of Croesus being spared and becoming an adviser to Cyrus might be an embellished story, yet another myth surrounding the kings of Lydia and Persia. The exact date and circumstances of Croesus's death have yet to be determined.

Whatever actually happened to Croesus, Cyrus's generals subdued the Greek cities along the coast of Anatolia, thus gaining him important ports on the Mediterranean. From Lydia, Cyrus marched to the far eastern corners of Iran and conquered the regions of Parthia and Bactria in Central Asia, though he ultimately died on the battlefield there.

Cyrus Cylinder
This sixth-century-B.C.E. clay cylinder, found in the temple of Marduk in Babylon, presents Cyrus defending his conquest as beneficial to the citizens of the city and pleasing to the god. (© The Trustees of the British Museum)

INDIVIDUALS IN SOCIETY • Cyrus the Great

Cyrus (r. 559–530 B.C.E.), known to history as "the Great" and the founder of the Persian Empire, began life as a subject of the Medes, an Iranian people very closely related to the Persians. There are few surviving sources describing his early life, and even the date of his birth is uncertain. There are many legends, however, some originating in Persia and others in Greece, as many later Greek leaders and authors admired Cyrus. The Greek historian Herodotus records the legend that Cyrus was the grandson of Astyages, king of the Medes, who ordered him killed to eliminate him as a future threat. Cyrus, like the biblical Moses, escaped the plot and went on to rule both his own Persians and the Medes.

Another story recounted by Herodotus tells how Cyrus's playmates chose him king. He assigned them specific duties, and when one aristocratic boy refused to obey his orders, Cyrus had him "arrested." The boy's father later demanded that Cyrus explain his haughty behavior. Cyrus replied that the other boys had chosen him king, and he did his duty justly, as a king should. He told the man that if he had done anything wrong, he was there to take his punishment. The man and the other boys admired his calm sense of duty and responsibility. Through this anecdote, the historian projected Cyrus's intelligence and good qualities, revealed later in life, back into his boyhood.

Astyages eventually marched against the grown Cyrus and was defeated. Instead of enslaving the Medes, Cyrus incorporated them into the new kingdom of Persia, thus demonstrating his inclusive concept of rule. This relatively mild rule continued with his later conquests. He won the admiration of many Greeks, whom he allowed to continue their religious rituals and intellectual pursuits.

After conquering Babylonia, Cyrus allowed the Jews who had been in forced exile there to return to Jerusalem. Hebrew scripture portrays Cyrus as divinely chosen, as evidenced by this biblical passage, probably written in the late sixth century B.C.E., shortly after the end of the Babylonian Captivity:

> Thus said the Lord to Cyrus, His anointed one—
> Whose right hand He has grasped,
> Treading down nations before him,
> Ungirding the loins of kings,
> Opening doors before him, and letting no gate stay shut:
> I will march before you, and level the hills that loom up;
> I will shatter doors of bronze
> And cut down iron bars.

After his victories, Cyrus made sure that the Persians were portrayed as liberators, and in some cases he was more benevolent than most conquerors were. According to his own account, he freed all of the captive peoples who were living in forced exile in Babylonia. This included the Hebrews. He returned their sacred objects to them and allowed those who wanted to do so to return to Jerusalem, where he paid for the rebuilding of their temple.

I will give you treasures concealed in the dark
And secret hoards—
So that you may know that it is I the Lord,
The God of Israel, who call you by name. . . .
It was I who roused him [Cyrus] for victory
And who level all roads for him.
He shall rebuild My city
And let My exiled people go
Without price and without payment
　—said the LORD of hosts. (Isaiah 45:1–3, 13)*

Cyrus died in 530 B.C.E. while campaigning in Central Asia. Though much of his life was spent at war, he knew how to govern conquered peoples effectively and acquired a reputation for benevolence and tolerance. Much about his life can never be known, but Cyrus appears to have been a practical man of sound judgment, keenly interested in foreign peoples and their ways of life.

QUESTIONS FOR ANALYSIS

1. How are the Greek stories, as told by Herodotus, and the biblical account similar in their portrayals of Cyrus? How are they different?

2. Herodotus, the Bible, and the inscription on the Cyrus cylinder discussed on page 53 have all been influential in establishing the largely positive historical view of Cyrus. What limitations might there be in using these as historical sources?

*Reprinted from the *Tanakh: The Holy Scriptures* by permission of the University of Nebraska Press. Copyright 1985 The Jewish Publication Society, Philadelphia.

ONLINE DOCUMENT ASSIGNMENT

What strategies did Persian rulers like Cyrus use to bind together far-flung and diverse peoples under their imperial rule? Examine sources that illuminate how the Persians saw their empire and how they ruled it, and then complete a writing assignment based on the evidence and details from this chapter.

bedfordstmartins.com/mckaywestvalue

Cyrus's successors continued Persian conquests, creating the largest empire the world had yet seen. In 525 B.C.E. Cyrus's son Cambyses (r. 530–522 B.C.E.) subdued the Egyptians and the Nubians. At Cambyses's death (the circumstances of which are disputed), Darius I (r. 521–486 B.C.E.) took over the throne and conquered Scythia in Central Asia, along with much of Thrace and Macedonia, areas north of the Aegean Sea. By 510 the Persians also ruled the western coast of Anatolia and many of the islands of the

Aegean. Thus, within forty years, the Persians had transformed themselves from a subject people to the rulers of a vast empire that included all of the oldest kingdoms and peoples of the region, as well as many outlying areas (see Map 2.1). Unsurprisingly, Darius began to call himself "King of Kings." Invasions of Greece by Darius and his son Xerxes were unsuccessful, but the Persian Empire lasted another two hundred years, until it became part of the empire of Alexander the Great (see Chapter 4).

The Persians also knew how to preserve the empire they had won on the battlefield. Learning from the Assyrians, they created an efficient administrative system to govern the empire based in their newly built capital city of Persepolis near modern Shiraz, Iran. Under Darius, they divided the empire into districts and appointed either Persian or local nobles as administrators called **satraps** to head each one. The satrap controlled local government, collected taxes, heard legal cases, and maintained order. He was assisted by a council, and also by officials and army leaders sent from Persepolis who made sure that the satrap knew the will of the king and that the king knew what was going on in the provinces. This system lessened opposition to Persian rule by making local elites part of the system of government, although sometimes satraps used their authority to build up independent power.

Communication and trade were eased by a sophisticated system of roads linking the empire from the coast of Asia Minor to the valley of the Indus River. On the roads were way stations where royal messengers could get food and horses, a system that allowed messages to be communicated quickly, much like the famed pony express in the American West. These roads meant that the king was usually in close touch with officials and subjects. The roads also simplified the defense of the empire by making it easier to move Persian armies. In addition the system allowed the easy flow of trade, which Persian rulers further encouraged by building canals, including one that linked the Red Sea and the Nile.

Persian Religion

Iranian religion was originally tied to nature. Ahuramazda (ah-HOOR-uh-MAZ-duh), the chief god, was the creator of all living creatures. Mithra, the sun-god whose cult would later spread throughout the Roman Empire, saw to justice and redemption. Fire was a particularly important god, and fire was often part of religious rituals. A priestly class, the Magi, developed among the Medes to officiate at sacrifices, chant prayers to the gods, and tend the sacred flame.

Around 600 B.C.E. the ideas of Zoroaster, a thinker and preacher whose dates are uncertain, began to gain prominence. Zoroaster is regarded as the author of key religious texts, later gathered together in a collection of sacred texts called the Avesta. He introduced new spiritual concepts to the Iranian people, stressing devotion to Ahuramazda alone and emphasizing the individual's responsibility to choose between the forces of creation, truth, and order and those of nothingness, chaos, falsehood, and disorder. Zoroaster taught that people possessed the free will to decide between these, and that they must rely on their own conscience to guide them through an active life in which they focused on "good thoughts, good words, and good deeds." Their decisions were crucial, he warned, for there would come a time of reckoning. At the end of time the forces of order would win, and the victorious Ahuramazda, like the Egyptian god Osiris

Gold Plaque from the Persian Empire
In the nineteenth century a huge collection of silver and gold objects from the fifth and fourth centuries B.C.E., including this gold plaque, was found on the banks of the Oxus River in what is now Tajikistan. Most likely, the spot had been a ferry crossing and the objects had been buried long ago. The plaque shows a man in the dress of the Medes with a short sword and a bundle of sticks called a *barsom*, which was used in religious ceremonies. Plaques such as this may have been offerings to a god. (© The Trustees of the British Museum)

(see Chapter 1), would preside over a last judgment to determine each person's eternal fate. Those who had lived according to good and truth would enter a divine kingdom. Liars and the wicked, denied this blessed immortality, would be condemned to eternal pain, darkness, and punishment. Thus Zoroaster preached a last judgment that led to a heaven or a hell.

Scholars—and contemporary Zoroastrians—debate whether Zoroaster saw the forces of disorder as a malevolent deity named Angra Mainyu who was co-eternal with and independent from Ahuramazda, or whether he was simply using this term to mean "evil thoughts" or "a destructive spirit." Later forms of **Zoroastrianism** followed each of these lines of understanding. Most Zoroastrians believed that the good Ahuramazda and the evil Angra Mainyu were locked together in a cosmic battle for the human race, a religious conceptualization that scholars call dualism, which was rejected in Judaism and Christianity. Some, however, had a more monotheistic interpretation and saw Ahuramazda as the only uncreated god.

Whenever he actually lived, Zoroaster's writings were spread by teachers, and King Darius began to use Zoroastrian language and images. Under the protection of the Persian kings, Zoroastrian ideas spread throughout Iran and the rest of the Persian Empire, and then beyond this into central China. It became the official religion of the later Persian Empire ruled by the Sassanid dynasty, and much later Zoroastrians migrated to western India, where they became known as Parsis and still live today. Zoroastrianism survived the fall of the Persian Empire to influence Christianity, Islam, and Buddhism, largely because of its belief in a just life on earth and a happy afterlife. Good behavior in the world, even though unrecognized at the time, would receive ample reward in the hereafter. Evil, no matter how powerful in life, would be punished after death. In some form or another, Zoroastrian concepts still pervade many modern religions and Zoroastrianism still exists as a religion.

Persian Art and Culture

The Persians made significant contributions to art and culture. They produced amazing works in gold and silver, often with inlaid jewels and semiprecious stones such as deep blue lapis lazuli. They transformed the Assyrian tradition of realistic monumental sculpture from one that celebrated gory details of slaughter to one that showed both the Persians and their subjects as dignified. They noted and carved the physical features of their subjects, the way they wore their hair, their clothing, their tools and weapons. Because they depicted both themselves and non-Persians realistically, Persian art serves as an excellent source for learning about the weapons, tools, clothing, and even hairstyles of many peoples of the area.

These carvings adorned temples and other large buildings in cities throughout the empire, and the Persians also built new cities from the ground up. The most spectacular of these was Persepolis, designed as a residence for the kings and an administrative and cultural center. The architecture of Persepolis combined elements found in many parts of the empire, including large, elegant columns topped by carvings of real and mythical animals. Underneath the city was a system of closed water pipes, drainage canals, and conduits that allowed water from nearby mountains to flow into the city without flooding it, provided water for households and plantings inside the city, and carried away sewage and waste from the city's many residents. The Persians thus further improved the technology for handling water that had been essential in this area since the time of the Sumerians.

The Persians allowed the peoples they conquered to maintain their own customs and beliefs, as long as they paid the proper amount of taxes and did not rebel. Their rule resulted in an empire that brought people together in a new political system, with a culture that blended older and newer religious traditions and ways of seeing the world. Even their opponents, including the Greeks who would stop their expansion and eventually conquer the Persian Empire, admired their art and institutions.

Notes

1. James H. Breasted, *Ancient Records of Egypt*, vol. 4 (Chicago: University of Chicago Press, 1907), para. 398.
2. James B. Pritchard (ed.), *Ancient Near Eastern Texts Relating to the Old Testament—Third Edition with Supplement*, p. 288. © 1950, 1955, 1969, renewed 1978 by Princeton University Press. Reprinted by permission of Princeton University Press.
3. Cylinder inscription translation by Irving Finkel, curator of the Cuneiform Collection at the British Museum, www.britishmuseum.org. © The Trustees of the British Museum. Used by permission of the British Museum.

Chapter Review

MAKE IT STICK

LearningCurve
bedfordstmartins.com/mckaywestvalue
After reading the chapter, use LearningCurve to retain what you've read.

IDENTIFY KEY TERMS

Identify and explain the significance of each item below.

Iron Age (p. 36)	**Torah** (p. 43)
Kush (p. 38)	**Covenant** (p. 43)
Phoenicians (p. 39)	**satraps** (p. 56)
Yahweh (p. 41)	**Zoroastrianism** (p. 57)

REVIEW THE MAIN IDEAS

Answer the focus questions from each section of the chapter.

- How did iron technology shape new states after 1200 B.C.E., including Kush and Phoenicia? (p. 36)
- How did the Hebrews create an enduring religious tradition? (p. 41)
- What explains the rise and fall of the Assyrians? (p. 47)
- How did the Persians consolidate their power and control and influence the subjects of their extensive empire? (p. 51)

MAKE CONNECTIONS

Think about the larger developments and continuities within and across chapters.

1. How were the Assyrian and Persian Empires similar to the earlier empires of the Near East (Chapter 1) in terms of their technology and political structure? How were they different? What might explain the pattern of similarities and differences?

2. Most peoples in the ancient world gained influence over others and became significant in history through military conquest and the establishment of empires. By contrast, how did the Phoenicians and the Hebrews shape the development of Western civilization?

ONLINE DOCUMENT ASSIGNMENT

Cyrus the Great

What strategies did Persian rulers like Cyrus use to bind together far-flung and diverse peoples under their imperial rule?

You encountered Cyrus the Great on page 54. Keeping the question above in mind, go online and explore sources that illuminate how Persian rulers saw their empire. Then complete a writing assignment based on the evidence and details from this chapter.

bedfordstmartins.com/mckaywestvalue

CHRONOLOGY

ca. 1200 B.C.E.	• "Bronze Age Collapse"; end of the Hittite Empire
ca. 1100 B.C.E.	• Beginning of the Iron Age; Phoenicians begin to trade in the Mediterranean
ca. 1070–712 B.C.E.	• Third Intermediate Period in Egypt
ca. 965–925 B.C.E.	• Hebrew kingdom ruled by Solomon
911–609 B.C.E.	• Neo-Assyrian Empire
727 B.C.E.	• Kushite Dynasty established in Egypt
722 B.C.E.	• Kingdom of Israel destroyed by the Assyrians
626–539 B.C.E.	• Neo-Babylonian empire
ca. 600 B.C.E.	• Ideas of Zoroaster gain prominence in Persia
587 B.C.E.	• Kingdom of Judah destroyed by the Neo-Babylonians
587–538 B.C.E.	• Babylonian Captivity of the Hebrews
550 B.C.E.	• Cyrus the Great conquers the Medes and consolidates the Persian Empire
539 B.C.E.	• Persians defeat the Neo-Babylonians
525 B.C.E.	• Persians defeat the Egyptians and Nubians

3

✓ LearningCurve
bedfordstmartins.com/mckaywestvalue
After reading the chapter, use
LearningCurve to retain what
you've read.

The Development of Greek Society and Culture

ca. 3000–338 B.C.E.

HUMANS CAME INTO GREECE OVER MANY THOUSANDS OF YEARS,
in waves of migrants whose place of origin and cultural characteristics have
been the source of much scholarly debate. The first to arrive were hunter-
gatherers, but techniques of agriculture and animal domestication had spread
into Greece from Turkey by about 6500 B.C.E., after which small farming communities worked much of the land. Early settlers to Greece brought skills in
making bronze weapons and tools, which became more common around
3000 B.C.E.

Although geographic conditions made farming difficult and limited the
growth of early kingdoms, the people of ancient Greece built on the traditions
and ideas of earlier societies to develop a culture that fundamentally shaped
the intellectual and cultural traditions of Western civilization. They were the
first to explore many of the questions about the world around them and the
place of humans in it that continue to concern thinkers today. Drawing on
their day-to-day experiences as well as logic and empirical observation, they
developed ways of understanding and explaining the world around them,
which grew into modern philosophy and science. They also created new
political forms and new types of literature and art.

The history of the Greeks is divided into three broad periods: the Helladic
period, which covered the Bronze Age, roughly 3000 B.C.E. to 1200 B.C.E.; the
Hellenic period, from the Bronze Age Collapse to the death in 323 B.C.E. of
Alexander the Great, the ruler of Macedonia, which by that point had conquered Greece; and the Hellenistic period, stretching from Alexander's death

to the Roman conquest in 30 B.C.E. of the kingdom established in Egypt by Alexander's successors. This chapter focuses on the Greeks in the Bronze (Helladic) Age and most of the Hellenic period, which is further divided into the Dark Age, the Archaic age, and the classical period. Alexander's brief reign and the Hellenistic world are the subject of Chapter 4.

Greece in the Bronze Age

How did the geography of Greece shape its earliest kingdoms, and what factors contributed to the decline of those kingdoms?

During the Bronze Age, which for Greek history is called the "Helladic period," early settlers in Greece began establishing small communities contoured by the mountains and small plains that shaped the land. These communities sometimes joined together to form kingdoms, most prominently the Minoan kingdom on the island of Crete and the Mycenaean kingdom on the mainland. The Minoan and Mycenaean societies flourished for centuries until the Bronze Age Collapse, when Greece entered a period of decline known as the Dark Age (ca. 1100–800 B.C.E.). Epic poems composed by Homer and Hesiod after the Dark Age provide the poets' versions of what life may have been like in these early Greek kingdoms.

Geography and Settlement

Hellas, as the Greeks still call their land, encompassed the Greek peninsula, the islands of the Aegean (ah-GEE-uhn) Sea, and the lands bordering the Aegean, an area known as the Aegean basin (Map 3.1). In ancient times this basin included the Greek settlements in Ionia, the western coast of the area known as Anatolia in modern western Turkey. Geography acts as an enormously divisive force in Greek life; mountains divide the land, and although there are good harbors on the sea, there are no navigable rivers. Much of the land is rocky and not very fertile, which meant that food availability was a constant concern.

The major regions of Greece were Thessaly and Macedonia in the north, and Boeotia (bee-OH-shuh) and the large island of Euboea (YOU-boh-ee-ah) in the center, lands marked by fertile plains that helped to sustain a strong population capable of serving as formidable cavalry and infantry. Immediately to the south of Boeotia was Attica, an area of thin soil in which olives and wine grapes flourished. Attica's harbors looked to the Aegean, which invited its inhabitants, the Athenians, to concentrate on maritime commerce. Still farther south, the Peloponnesus (peh-luh-puh-NEE-suhs), a large peninsula connected to the rest of mainland Greece by a very narrow isthmus at Corinth, was a patchwork of high mountains and small plains that divided the area into several regions. Beyond the coast, the islands of the Aegean served as stepping-stones to Anatolia.

The geographical fragmentation of Greece encouraged political fragmentation. Communications were poor, with rocky tracks far more common than roads. Early in Greek history several kingdoms did emerge, but the rugged terrain prohibited the growth of a great empire like those of Mesopotamia or Egypt. Instead tiny states became the most common form of government.

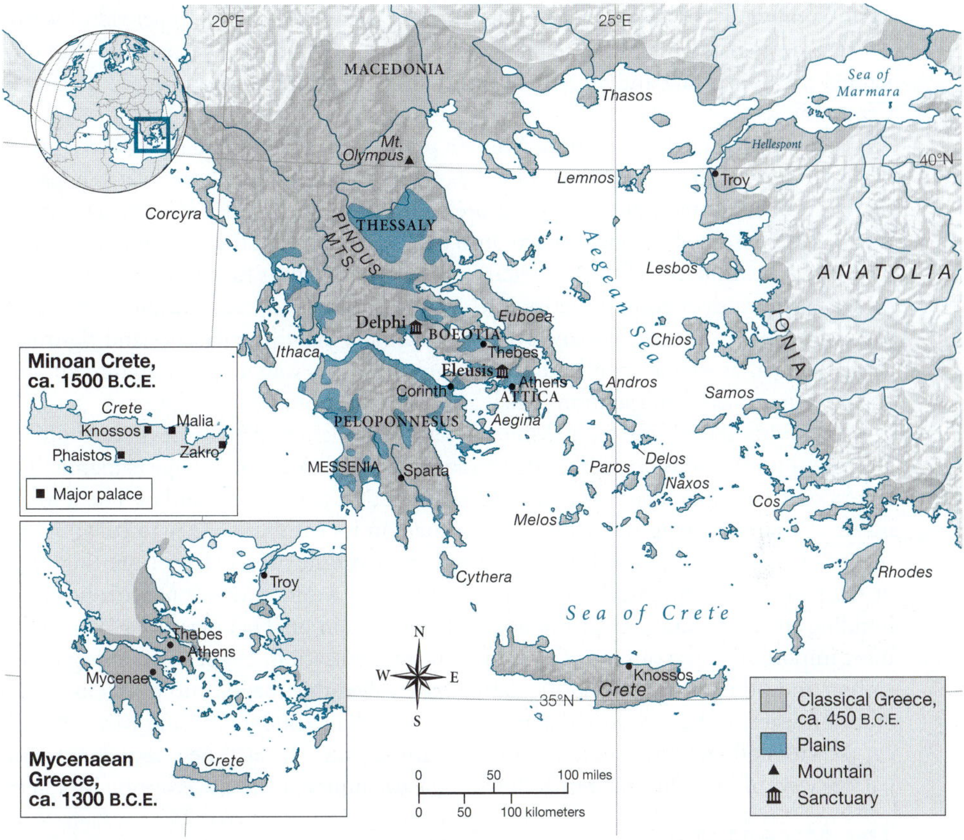
20°E
25°E
40°N
35°N
MACEDONIA
Mt. Olympus
PINDUS MTS.
THESSALY
Corcyra
Ithaca
Delphi
BOEOTIA
Thebes
Euboea
Eleusis
Athens
ATTICA
Corinth
Aegina
PELOPONNESUS
MESSENIA
Sparta
Cythera
Thasos
Lemnos
Sea of Marmara
Hellespont
Troy
Lesbos
ANATOLIA
IONIA
Chios
Samos
Andros
Aegean Sea
Delos
Paros
Naxos
Cos
Melos
Rhodes
Sea of Crete
Knossos
Crete
N
S
E
W
0
50
100 miles
0
50
100 kilometers
Classical Greece, ca. 450 B.C.E.
Plains
Mountain
Sanctuary
Minoan Crete, ca. 1500 B.C.E.
Crete
Knossos
Malia
Phaistos
Zakro
Major palace
Troy
Thebes
Athens
Mycenae
Crete
Mycenaean Greece, ca. 1300 B.C.E.

MAP 3.1 Classical Greece, 500–338 B.C.E.
In antiquity, the home of the Greeks included the islands of the Aegean and the western shore of Turkey as well as the Greek peninsula itself. Crete, the home of Minoan civilization, is the large island at the bottom of the map.

The Minoans

On the large island of Crete, Bronze Age farmers and fishermen began to trade their surpluses with their neighbors, and cities grew, housing artisans and merchants. Beginning about 2000 B.C.E. Cretans voyaged throughout the eastern Mediterranean and the Aegean, carrying the copper and tin needed for bronze and many other goods. Social hierarchies developed, and in many cities certain individuals came to hold power, although exactly how this happened is not clear. The Cretans began to use writing about 1900 B.C.E., in a form later scholars called Linear A. This has not been deciphered, but scholars know that the language of Crete was not related to Greek, so they do not consider the Cretans "Greek."

What we can know about the culture of Crete depends on archaeological and artistic evidence, and of this there is a great deal. At about the same time that writing began, rulers in several cities of Crete began to build large structures with hundreds of interconnected rooms. The largest of these, at Knossos (NOH-suhs), has over a thousand rooms along with pipes for bringing in drinking water and sewers to get rid of waste. The archaeologists who discovered these huge structures called them "palaces," and they named the flourishing and vibrant culture of this era **Minoan**, after a mythical king of Crete, Minos.

Few specifics are known about Minoan political life except that a king and a group of nobles stood at its head. Minoan life was long thought to have been relatively peaceful, but new excavations are revealing more and more walls around cities, which has called the peaceful nature of Minoan society into question, although there are no doubts that it was wealthy. In terms of their religious life, Minoans appear to have worshipped goddesses far more than gods. Whether this translated into more egalitarian gender roles for real people is unclear, but surviving Minoan art, including frescoes and figurines, shows women as well as men leading religious activities, watching entertainment, and engaging in athletic competitions, such as leaping over bulls.

Beginning about 1700 B.C.E. Minoan society was disrupted by a series of earthquakes and volcanic eruptions on nearby islands, some of which resulted in large tsunamis. The largest of these was a huge volcanic eruption that devastated the island of Thera to the north of Crete, burying the Minoan town there in lava and causing it to collapse into the sea. This eruption, one of the largest in recorded history, may have been the origin of the story of the mythical kingdom of Atlantis, a wealthy kingdom with beautiful buildings that had sunk under the ocean. The eruption on Thera was long seen as the most important cause of the collapse of Minoan civilization, but scholars using radiocarbon and other types of scientific dating have called this theory into question, as the eruption seems to have occurred somewhat earlier than 1600 B.C.E., and Minoan society did not collapse until more than two centuries later. In fact, new settlements and palaces were often built on Crete following the earthquakes and the eruption of Thera.

The Mycenaeans

As Minoan culture was flourishing on Crete, a different type of society developed on the mainland. This society was founded by groups who had migrated there during the period after 2000 B.C.E., and its members spoke an early form of Greek. By about 1650 B.C.E. one group of these immigrants had raised palaces and established cities at Thebes, Athens, Mycenae (migh-SEE-nee), and elsewhere. These palace-centers ruled by local kings formed a loose hegemony under the authority of the king of Mycenae, and the archaeologists who first discovered traces of this culture called it **Mycenaean** (migh-see-NEE-an).

As in Crete, the political unit in Mycenaean Greece was the kingdom, and the king and his warrior aristocracy stood at the top of society. The seat and symbol of the king's power was his palace, which was also the economic center of the kingdom. Within the palace's walls, royal artisans fashioned gold jewelry and rich ornaments, made and decorated fine pottery, forged weapons, prepared hides and wool for clothing, and manufactured the other goods needed by the king and his supporters. The Mycenaean economy was marked by an extensive division of labor, and at the bottom of the social scale were male and female slaves.

Palace scribes kept records with a script known as Linear B, which scholars realized was an early form of Greek and have learned to read. They thus consider the Mycenaeans the first truly "Greek" culture to emerge in this area. Information on Mycenaean culture comes through inscriptions and other forms of written records as well as buildings and

Mycenaean Dagger Blade This scene in gold and silver on the blade of an iron dagger depicts hunters armed with spears and protected by shields defending themselves against charging lions. Judging by the number of hunting scenes in surviving Mycenaean art, the Mycenaeans seemed to enjoy the thrill and the danger of hunting. (National Archaeological Museum, Athens, Ancient Art & Architecture Collection/The Bridgeman Art Library)

other objects. All of these point to a society in which war was common. Mycenaean cities were all fortified by thick stone walls, and graves contain bronze spears, javelins, swords, helmets, and the first examples of metal armor known in the world. Mycenaean kingdoms appear to have fought regularly with one another.

Contacts between the Minoans and Mycenaeans were originally peaceful, and Minoan culture and trade goods flooded the Greek mainland. But most scholars think that around 1450 B.C.E., possibly in the wake of an earthquake that left Crete vulnerable, the Mycenaeans attacked Crete, destroying many towns and occupying Knossos. For about the next fifty years, the Mycenaeans ruled much of the island. The palaces at Knossos and other cities of the Aegean became grander as wealth gained through trade and tribute flowed into the treasuries of various Mycenaean kings. Linear B replaced Linear A as a writing system, a further sign of Mycenaean domination.

Prosperity, however, did not bring peace, and between 1300 and 1100 B.C.E. various kingdoms in and beyond Greece ravaged one another in a savage series of wars that destroyed both the Minoan and Mycenaean civilizations. Among these wars was perhaps one that later became known as the Trojan War, fought by Greeks in Ionia (see page 66).

The fall of the Minoans and Mycenaeans was part of what scholars see as a general collapse of Bronze Age civilizations in the eastern Mediterranean, including the end of the Egyptian New Kingdom and the fall of the Hittite Empire (see Chapters 1 and 2). This collapse appears to have had a number of causes: internal economic and social problems, including perhaps slave revolts; invasions and migrations by outsiders, who destroyed cities and disrupted trade and production; changes in warfare and weaponry, particularly the adoption of iron weapons, which made foot soldiers the most important factor in battles and reduced the power of kings and wealthy nobles fighting from chariots; and natural disasters such as volcanic eruptions, earthquakes, and droughts, which reduced the amount of food and contributed to famines. Mycenaean Greeks joined the migrating Sea Peoples and probably settled in Canaan; here they became the group known in the Bible as Philistines (see Chapter 2).

These factors worked together to usher in a period of poverty and disruption that historians of Greece have traditionally called the Dark Age (ca. 1100–800 B.C.E.). Cities were destroyed, population declined, villages were abandoned, and trade decreased.

Migratory movements continued, including a group that later Greeks called the Dorians, who were originally thought to have been people speaking a language other than Greek invading from the north. Now the Dorians are generally regarded as Greek-speakers from the northern areas of the Greek mainland, and their movement is considered a combination of invasion and migration. Pottery became simpler, and jewelry and other grave goods became less ornate. Even writing, which had not been widespread previously, was a casualty of the chaos, and Linear A and B inscriptions were no longer produced.

The Bronze Age Collapse led to the widespread and prolonged movement of Greek peoples, both within Greece itself and beyond. They dispersed beyond mainland Greece farther south to the islands of the Aegean and in greater strength across the Aegean to the shores of Anatolia, arriving at a time when traditional states and empires had collapsed. By the conclusion of the Dark Age, the Greeks had spread their culture throughout the Aegean basin, and like many other cultures around the Mediterranean and the Near East, they had adopted iron.

Homer, Hesiod, and the Epic

Archaeological sources from the Dark Age are less rich than those from the periods that came after, and so they are often used in conjunction with literary sources written in later centuries to give us a more complete picture of the era. The Greeks, unlike the Hebrews, had no sacred book that chronicled their past. Instead they had epics, poetic tales of legendary heroes and of the times when people believed the gods still walked the earth. Of these, the *Iliad* and the *Odyssey* are the most important. Most scholars think they were composed in the eighth or seventh century B.C.E., with the *Iliad* appearing earlier than the *Odyssey.* By the fifth century B.C.E. they were attributed to a poet named Homer, though whether Homer was an actual historical individual is debated. Scholars also disagree about the ways in which the epics combine elements from the Bronze Age, the Dark Age, and the time in which they were written. What is not debated is their long-lasting impact, both on later Greek culture and on the Western world.

The *Iliad* recounts the tale of the Trojan War of the late Bronze Age. As Homer tells it, the Achaeans (uh-KEE-uhnz), the name he gives to the Mycenaeans, send an expedition to besiege the city of Troy to retrieve Helen, who was abducted by Paris, the Trojan king's son. The heart of the *Iliad*, however, concerns the quarrel between the Mycenaean king, Agamemnon, and the stormy hero of the poem, Achilles (uh-KIHL-eez), and how this brought suffering to the Achaeans. The first lines of the *Iliad* capture this well:

> Sing, O goddess, the anger of Achilles son of Peleus, that brought countless ills upon the Achaeans. Many a brave soul did it send hurrying down to Hades [underworld], and many a hero did it yield a prey to dogs and vultures.[1]

Ancient Greeks and Romans believed that the Trojan War was a real event embellished by poetic retelling, but by the modern era most people regarded it as a myth. Then in the late nineteenth century, the German businessman Heinrich Schliemann discovered and excavated the ruins of Troy. The city had actually been destroyed a number of times, including at least once in the late Mycenaean period, which provided evidence of the violence of this era, if not of the Trojan War itself. More recently, geologists studying the landscape features mentioned in the *Iliad* and historians examining written records from the Hittite and Egyptian Empires of the era have also confirmed the general picture portrayed in Homer's epic. Today most scholars think that the core of the story was a composite of many conflicts in Troy's past, although the characters are not historical.

Homer's *Odyssey* recounts the adventures of Odysseus (oh-DIH-see-uhs), a wise and fearless hero of the war at Troy, during his ten-year voyage home. He encounters many dangers, storms, and adventures, but he finally reaches his home and unites again with Penelope, the ideal wife, dedicated to her husband and family.

Both of Homer's epics portray engaging but flawed characters who are larger than life, yet human. The men and women at the center of the stories display the quality known as *arête* (ah-reh-TAY), that is, excellence and living up to one's fullest potential. Homer was also strikingly successful in depicting the great gods and goddesses, who generally sit on Mount Olympus in the north of Greece and watch the fighting at Troy like spectators at a baseball game, although they sometimes participate in the action.

Greeks also learned about the origin and descent of the gods and goddesses of their polytheistic system from another poet, Hesiod (HEH-see-uhd), who most scholars think lived sometime between 750 and 650 B.C.E. Hesiod made the gods the focus of his poem, the *Theogony*. By combining Mesopotamian myths, which the Hittites had adopted and spread to the Aegean, with a variety of Greek oral traditions, Hesiod forged a coherent story of the origin of the gods. At the beginning was "Chaos," the word Hesiod uses to describe the original dark emptiness. Then came several generations of deities, with the leader of each generation violently overthrowing his father to gain power. Despite this violence, Hesiod viewed the generation of gods who rule from Olympus as more just than those that came before. In another of Hesiod's poems, *Works and Days*, the gods watch over the earth, looking for justice and injustice, while leaving the great mass of men and women to live lives of hard work and endless toil. (See "Primary Source: Hesiod, *Works and Days*," page 68.)

The Development of the Polis in the Archaic Age

What was the role of the polis in Greek society?

Homer and Hesiod both lived in the era after the Dark Age, which later historians have termed the Archaic age (800–500 B.C.E.). The most important political change in this period was the development of the **polis** (PAH-luhs; plural *poleis*), a word generally translated as "city-state." With the polis, the Greeks established a new type of political structure. During the Archaic period, poleis established colonies throughout much of the Mediterranean, spreading Greek culture. Two particular poleis, each with a distinctive system of government, rose to prominence on the Greek mainland: Sparta and Athens.

Organization of the Polis

The Greek polis was not the first form of city-state to emerge. The earliest states in Sumer were also city-states, as were many of the small Mycenaean kingdoms. What differentiated the new Greek model from older city-states is the fact that the polis was

PRIMARY SOURCE   Hesiod, *Works and Days*

According to his description of himself in Works and Days *(ca. 700 B.C.E.), Hesiod was born in a small village he describes as "bad in winter, godawful in summer, nice never," with one brother, Perses, a lazy and irresponsible swindler who cheated him out of some of his inheritance but later came to him asking for money. Whether these details are true or not, they form the framework for the poem, a speech full of advice addressed to his brother, but designed for a larger audience.*

And here's a fable for kings, who'll not need it explained:

It's what the hawk said high in the clouds
As he carried off a speckle-throated nightingale
Skewered on his talons. She complained something pitiful,
And he made this high and mighty speech to her:
"No sense in your crying. You're in the grip of real strength now,
And you'll go where I take you, songbird or not.
I'll make a meal of you if I want, or I might let you go.
Only a fool struggles against his superiors.
He not only gets beat, but humiliated as well."

Thus spoke the hawk, the windlord, his long wings beating.

Justice

But you, Perses, you listen to Justice
And don't cultivate Violence.
                              Violent behavior is bad
For a poor man. Even a rich man can't afford it
But it's going to bog him down in Ruin some day.
There's a better road around the other way
Leading to what's right. When it comes down to it
Justice beats out Violence. A fool learns this the hard way.
Also, Oath, who's a god, keeps up with crooked verdicts,
And there's a ruckus when the Lady Justice
Gets dragged through the streets by corrupt judges
Who swallow bribes and pervert their verdicts.
Later, she finds her way back into town, weeping,

more than a political institution; it was a community of citizens with their own customs and laws. With one exception, the poleis that emerged after 800 did not have kings but instead were self-governing. The physical, religious, and political forms of the polis varied from place to place, but everywhere the polis was relatively small, reflecting the fragmented geography of Greece. The very smallness of the polis enabled Greeks to see how they fit individually into the overall system—and how the individual parts made up the social whole. This notion of community was fundamental to the polis and was the very badge of Greekness.

Wrapped in mist, and she gives grief to the men
Who drove her out and didn't do right by her.
. . .
Now I'm speaking sense to you, Perses you fool.
It's easy to get all of Wickedness you want.
She lives just down the road a piece, and it's a smooth road too.
But the gods put Goodness where we have to sweat
To get at her. It's a long, uphill pull
And rough going at first. But once you reach the top
She's as easy to have as she was hard at first.
. . .
Don't make dirty money; dirty money spells doomsday.
Return a friend's friendship and a visitor's visit.
Give gifts to the giver, give none to the non-giver.
The giver gets gifts, the non-giver gets naught.
And Give's a good girl, but Gimmee's a goblin.
The man who gives willingly, even if it costs him
Takes joy in his giving and is glad in his heart.

But let a man turn greedy and grab for himself
Even something small, it'll freeze his heart stiff.
. . .
And if the spirit within you moves you to get rich,
Do as follows:

> *Work*, *work*, and then *work* some more.

EVALUATE THE EVIDENCE

1. What does Hesiod's advice suggest about his notion of the role of humans in the world and their relationship with the gods?

2. Hesiod lived just after the period of the Greek Dark Age. How does his poem reflect the situation of his own society?

Source: Hesiod, *Works and Days and Theogony*, trans. Stanley Lombardo, pp. 29–30, 32, 34, 35. Copyright © 1993 by Hackett Publishing Company, Inc. Reprinted by permission of Hackett Publishing Company, Inc. All rights reserved.

Poleis developed from Dark Age towns, which were centers of administration, trade, and religion. When fully developed, each polis normally shared a surprisingly large number of features with other poleis. Physically a polis was a society of people who lived in a city (*asty*) and cultivated the surrounding countryside (*chora*). The countryside was essential to the economy of the polis and provided food to sustain the entire population. The city's water supply came from public fountains, springs, and cisterns. By the fifth century B.C.E. the city was generally surrounded by a wall. The city contained a point, usually elevated, called the acropolis, and a public square or marketplace called the agora (ah-guh-RAH). On the acropolis, which in the Dark Age was a place of refuge, people built temples, altars, public monuments, and various dedications to the gods of the polis. The agora was the political center of the polis. In the agora were shops, public buildings, and courts.

All poleis, with one exception, did not have standing armies. Instead they relied on their citizens for protection. Wealthy aristocrats often served as cavalry, which was never very important in military conflicts. The backbone of the army was the heavily armed infantry, or **hoplites**, ordinary citizens rather than members of the elite. Hoplites wore bronze helmets and leather and bronze body armor, which they purchased themselves. They carried heavy, round shields made of wood covered in bronze and armed themselves with iron-tipped spears and swords. They marched and fought in a close rectangular formation known as a phalanx, holding their shields together to form a solid wall, with the spears of the front row sticking out over the tops of the shields. As long as the phalanx stayed in formation, the hoplites presented an enemy with an impenetrable wall. This meant that commanders preferred to fight battles on open plains, where the hoplites could more easily maintain the phalanx, rather than in the narrow mountain passes that were common throughout much of Greece.

Governing Structures

Each Greek polis had one of several different types of government. Monarchy, rule by a king, had been prevalent during the Mycenaean period, but afterward declined. The polis of Sparta (see page 72) had a system with two kings, but they were part of a more broadly based constitution. Sporadic periods of violent political and social upheaval often led to the seizure of power by one man, a type of government the Greeks called **tyranny**. Tyrants generally came to power by using their wealth or by negotiating to win a political following that toppled the existing legal government. In contrast to its contemporary meaning, however, tyranny in ancient Greece did not necessarily mean oppressive rule. Some tyrants used their power to benefit average citizens by helping to limit the power of the landowning aristocracy, which made them popular.

Other types of government in the Archaic age were democracy and oligarchy. **Democracy** translates as "the power of the people" but was actually rule by citizens, not the people as a whole. Almost all Greek cities defined a citizen as an adult man with at least one or, at some times and places, two citizen parents. Thus citizens shared ancestry as well as a place of residence. Women were citizens for religious and reproductive purposes, but their citizenship did not give them the right to participate in government. Free men who were not children of a citizen, resident foreigners, and slaves were not citizens and had no political voice. Thus ancient Greek democracy did not reflect the modern concept that all people are created equal, but it did permit male citizens to share equally in determining the diplomatic and military policies of the polis, without respect to wealth. This comparatively broad basis of participation made Greek democracy an appealing model to some political thinkers across the ages, although others feared direct democracy and viewed it as "mob rule."

Oligarchy, which literally means "the rule of the few," was government by citizens who met a minimum property requirement. Many Greeks preferred oligarchy because it provided more political stability than democracy did. (Many of the Founding Fathers of the United States agreed, and they established a system in which the most important elections were indirect and only property owners had the right to vote.) Although oligarchy was the government of the prosperous, it left the door open to political and social advancement. If members of the polis obtained enough wealth to meet property or money qualifications, they could enter the governing circle.

Overseas Expansion

The development of the polis coincided with the growth of the Greek world in both wealth and numbers, bringing new problems. The increase in population created more demand for food than the land could supply. The resulting social and political tensions drove many people to seek new homes outside of Greece. In some cases the losers in a conflict within a polis were forced to leave. Other factors, largely intangible, played their part as well: the desire for a new start, a love of excitement and adventure, and curiosity about what lay beyond the horizon.

Greeks from the mainland and Ionia traveled throughout the Mediterranean, sailing in great numbers to Sicily and southern Italy, where there was ample space for expansion (Map 3.2). Here they established prosperous cities and often intermarried with local people. Some adventurous Greeks sailed farther west to Sardinia, France, Spain, and perhaps even the Canary Islands. In Sardinia they first established trading stations, and then permanent towns. From these new outposts Greek influence extended to southern France. The modern city of Marseilles, for example, began as a Greek colony and later sent settlers to southern Spain. In the far western Mediterranean the city of Carthage, established by the Phoenicians in the ninth century B.C.E., remained the dominant power. The Greeks traded with the Carthaginians but never conquered them.

Colonization changed the entire Greek world, both at home and abroad. In economic terms the expansion of the Greeks created a much larger market for agricultural and manufactured goods. From the east, especially from the northern coast of the Black Sea, came wheat. In return flowed Greek wine and olive oil, which could not be produced in the harsher climate of the north. Greek-manufactured goods, notably rich jewelry and fine pottery, circulated from southern Russia to Spain. During the same period the Greeks adopted the custom of minting coins from metal, first developed in the kingdom of Lydia in Anatolia. Coins provided many advantages over barter: they allowed merchants to set the value of goods in a determined system, they could be stored easily, and they allowed for more complex exchanges than did direct barter.

Golden Comb   This golden comb, produced about 400 B.C.E. in Scythia (see Map 3.2), shows a battle between three warriors, perhaps the three brothers who are the legendary founders of Scythia. Their dress shows a combination of Greek and Eastern details; the mounted horseman is clothed with largely Greek armor, while the warriors on foot are wearing Eastern dress. The comb may have been made by a Greek craftsman who had migrated to the Black Sea area, as the Greeks had established colonies there, but it was buried in a Scythian burial mound. (The State Hermitage Museum, St. Petersburg. © The State Hermitage Museum)

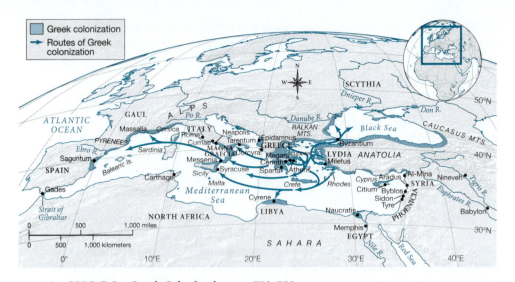

MAP 3.2   Greek Colonization, ca. 750–550 B.C.E.
The Greeks established colonies along the shores of the Mediterranean and the Black Sea, spreading Greek culture and creating a large trading network.

Colonization presented the polis with a huge challenge, for it required organization and planning on an unprecedented scale. The colonizing city, called the *metropolis,* or "mother city," first decided where to establish the colony, how to transport colonists to the site, and who would sail. Sometimes groups of people left willingly, and in other instances they left involuntarily after a civil war or other conflict. Then the metropolis collected and stored the supplies that the colonists would need both to feed themselves and to plant their first crop. All preparations ready, a leader, called an *oikist,* ordered the colonists to sail. Once the colonists landed, the oikist laid out the new polis, selected the sites of temples and public buildings, and established the government. Then he surrendered power to the new leaders. The colony was thereafter independent of the metropolis, a pattern that was quite different from most later systems of colonization. Colonization spread the polis and its values far beyond the shores of Greece.

The Growth of Sparta

Many different poleis developed during the Archaic period, but Sparta became the leading military power in Greece. To expand their polis, the Spartans did not establish colonies but set out in about 750 B.C.E. to conquer Messenia (muh-SEE-nee-uh), a rich, fertile region in the southwestern Peloponnesus. This conflict, called the First Messenian War by later Greek historians, lasted for twenty years and ended in a Spartan triumph. The Spartans appropriated Messenian land and turned the Messenians into **helots** (HEH-luhts), unfree residents forced to work state lands. Residents of coastal areas and the hills surrounding Messenia became a third group, known as *periokoi* (pehr-ee-OI-koi), who were free but had no political voice in the running of Sparta.

In about 650 B.C.E. Spartan exploitation and oppression of the Messenian helots, along with Sparta's defeat at the hands of a rival polis, led to a massive helot revolt that became known as the Second Messenian War. The Spartan poet Tyrtaeus, a contemporary of these events, vividly portrays the violence of the war:

> For it is a shameful thing indeed
> When with the foremost fighters
> An elder falling in front of the young men
> Lies outstretched,
> Having white hair and grey beard,
> Breathing forth his stout soul in the dust,
> Holding in his hands his genitals
> stained with blood.[2]

Finally, after some thirty years of fighting, the Spartans put down the revolt. Nevertheless, the political and social strain it caused led to a transformation of the Spartan polis. After the war, non-nobles who had shared in the fighting as hoplites appear to have demanded rights equal to those of the nobility and a voice in the government. (In more recent history, similar demands in the United States during the Vietnam War led to a lowering of the voting age to eighteen, to match the age at which soldiers were drafted.) It was under intense pressure that the aristocrats agreed to remodel the state into a new system.

The plan for the new system in Sparta was attributed to the lawgiver Lycurgus, who may or may not have been an actual person. According to later Greek sources, political distinctions among Spartan men were eliminated, and all citizens became legally equal. Governance of the polis was in the hands of two hereditary kings who were primarily military leaders. The kings were also part of the *Gerousia* (jeh-roo-SEE-ah), a council of men who had reached the age of sixty and thus retired from the Spartan army. The Gerousia deliberated on foreign and domestic matters and prepared legislation for the assembly, which consisted of all Spartan citizens. The real executive power of the polis was in the hands of five ephors (EH-fuhrs), or overseers, elected from and by all the citizens.

To provide for their economic needs, the Spartans divided the land of Messenia among all citizens. Helots worked the land, raised the crops, provided the Spartans with a certain percentage of their harvest, and occasionally served in the army. The Spartans kept the helots in line by means of systematic brutality and oppression.

In the system attributed to Lycurgus every citizen owed primary allegiance to Sparta. Suppression of the individual together with emphasis on military prowess led to a barracks state. Family life itself was sacrificed to the polis. Once Spartan boys reached the age of seven, they were enrolled in separate companies with other boys their age. They were required to live in the barracks and eat together in a common mess hall until age thirty. They slept outside on reed mats and underwent rugged physical and military training until they were ready to become frontline soldiers. For the rest of their lives, Spartan men kept themselves prepared for combat. Their military training never ceased, and the older men were expected to be models of endurance, frugality, and sturdiness. In battle Spartans were supposed to stand and die rather than retreat. Because men often

Spartan Hoplite   This bronze figurine portrays an armed foot soldier about to strike an enemy. His massive helmet with its full crest gives his head nearly complete protection, while a metal corselet covers his chest and back, and greaves (similar to today's shin guards) protect his lower legs. In his right hand he carries a thrusting spear (now broken off), and in his left a large, round shield. (Bildarchiv Preussischer Kulturbesitz/Art Resource, NY)

did not see their wives or other women for long periods, not only in times of war but also in peace, their most meaningful relations were same-sex ones. The Spartan military leaders may have viewed such relationships as militarily advantageous because they believed that men would fight even more fiercely for lovers and comrades.

Spartans expected women in citizen families to be good wives and strict mothers of future soldiers. They were prohibited from wearing jewelry or ornate clothes. They, too, were supposed to exercise strenuously in the belief that hard physical training promoted the birth of healthy children. Xenophon (ca. 430–354 B.C.E.), a later Athenian admirer of the Spartans, commented: "[Lycurgus had] insisted on the training of the body as incumbent no less on the female than the male; and in pursuit of the same idea instituted rival contests in running and feats of strength for women as for men. His belief was that where both parents were strong their progeny would be found to be more vigorous."[3]

An anecdote frequently repeated about one Spartan mother sums up Spartan military values. As her son was setting off to battle, the mother handed him his shield and advised him to come back either victorious, carrying the shield, or dead, being carried on it. Yet Spartan women were freer than many other Greek women. With men in military service much of their lives, women in citizen families owned land and ran the estates and were not physically restricted or secluded.

Along with the emphasis on military values for both sexes, the Spartan system served to instill in society the civic virtues of dedication to the state and a code of moral conduct. These aspects of Spartan society, along with Spartan military successes, were generally admired throughout the Greek world.

The Evolution of Athens

Like Sparta, Athens faced pressing social, economic, and political problems during the Archaic period, but the Athenian response was far different from that of the Spartans. Instead of creating a state devoted to the military, the Athenians created a state that became a democracy.

For Athens the late seventh century B.C.E. was a time of turmoil, the causes of which are unclear. In 621 B.C.E. Draco (DRAY-koh), an Athenian aristocrat, under pressure from small landholders and with the consent of the nobles, published the first law code of the Athenian polis. His code was harsh—and for this reason his name is the origin of the word *draconian*—but it embodied the ideal that the law belonged to all citizens.

Yet the aristocracy still governed Athens oppressively, and the social and economic situation remained dire. Despite Draco's code, noble landholders continued to force small farmers and artisans into economic dependence. Many families were sold into slavery because of debt; others were exiled, and their land was mortgaged to the rich.

One person who recognized these problems clearly was Solon (SOH-luhn), an aristocrat and poet. Reciting his poems in the Athenian agora, where anyone could hear his call for justice and fairness, Solon condemned his fellow aristocrats for their greed and dishonesty. According to later sources, Solon's sincerity and good sense convinced other aristocrats that he was no crazed revolutionary. Moreover, he gained the trust of the common people, whose problems provoked them to demand access to political life, much as commoners in Sparta had. Around 594 B.C.E. the nobles elected Solon chief *archon* (AHR-kahn), or magistrate of the Athenian polis, with authority over legal, civic, and military issues.

Solon immediately freed all people enslaved for debt, recalled all exiles, canceled all debts on land, and made enslavement for debt illegal. Solon allowed non-nobles into the old aristocratic assembly, where they could take part in the election of magistrates, including the annual election of the city's nine archons.

Although Solon's reforms solved some immediate problems, they did not satisfy either the aristocrats or the common people completely, and they did not bring peace to Athens. During the sixth century B.C.E. the successful general Pisistratus (pigh-SIHS-trah-tuhs) declared himself tyrant, developing a base of followers from among the common people. He was exiled several times, but returned to power each time. Under his rule Athens prospered, and his building program began to transform the city into one of the splendors of Greece. He raised the civic consciousness and prestige of the polis by instituting new cultural festivals that brought people together. Although he had taken over control of the city by force, his reign as tyrant weakened the power of aristocratic families and aroused rudimentary feelings of equality in many Athenian men.

Athens became more democratic under the leadership of Cleisthenes (KLIGHS-thuh-neez), a wealthy and prominent aristocrat who had won the support of lower-status men and became the leader of Athens in 508 B.C.E. Cleisthenes created the *deme* (deem), a unit of land that kept the roll of citizens, or *demos*, within its jurisdiction. Men enrolled as citizens through their deme—much as we would register to vote in the voting district in which we live—instead of through their family group, which brought people of different families together and promoted community and democracy. The demes were grouped into ten tribes, which thus formed the link between the demes and the central government. Each tribe elected a military leader, or *strategos* (plural *strategoi*).

The democracy functioned on the idea that all full citizens were sovereign. In 487 B.C.E. the election of the city's nine archons was replaced by reappointment by lot, which meant that any citizen with a certain amount of property had a chance of becoming an archon. This system gave citizens prestige, although the power of the archons gradually dwindled as the strategoi became the real military leaders of the city. Legislation was in the hands of two bodies, the *boule* (boo-LAY), or council, composed of five hundred members, and the *ecclesia* (ek-lay-SEE-yah), the assembly of all citizens. By supervising the various committees of government and proposing bills to the ecclesia, the boule guided Athenian political life. It received foreign envoys and forwarded treaties to the ecclesia for ratification. It oversaw the granting of state contracts and was responsible for receiving many revenues. It held the democracy together. Nonetheless, the ecclesia had the final word. Open to all male citizens over eighteen years of age, it met at a specific place to vote on matters presented to it.

War and Turmoil in the Classical Period

What were the major wars of the classical period, and how did they shape Greek history?

From the time of the Mycenaeans, violent conflict was common in Greek society, and this did not change in the fifth century B.C.E., the beginning of what scholars later called the classical period of Greek history, which they date from about 500 B.C.E. to the conquest of Greece by Philip of Macedon in 338 B.C.E. First, the Greeks beat back the armies of the Persian Empire. Then, turning their spears against one another, they destroyed their own political system in a century of warfare culminating in the Peloponnesian War. This war and its aftermath proved that the polis had reached the limits of its success as an effective political institution, with the attempts of various city-states to dominate the others leading only to incessant warfare. Many people went bankrupt, and the quality of life for most people changed for the worse. The Greeks' failure to unify against outsiders led to the rise of a dominant new power: the kingdom of Macedonia.

The Persian Wars

In 499 B.C.E. the Greeks who lived in Ionia unsuccessfully rebelled against the Persian Empire, which had ruled the area for fifty years (see Chapter 2). The Athenians had provided halfhearted help to the Ionians in this failed rebellion, and in 490 B.C.E. the Persians retaliated against Athens, only to be surprisingly defeated by the Athenian hoplites at the Battle of Marathon. (According to legend, a Greek runner carried the victory message to Athens. When the modern Olympic games were founded in 1896, they included a long-distance running race between Marathon and Athens, a distance of about twenty-five miles, designed to honor the ancient Greeks. The marathon was set at its current distance of 26.2 miles for the London Olympics of 1908, so that the finish would be in front of the royal box in the stadium.)

In 480 B.C.E. the Persian king Xerxes I (r. 485–465 B.C.E.) personally led a massive invasion of Greece. Under the leadership of Sparta, many Greek poleis, though not all, joined together to fight the Persians. The first confrontations between the Persians and the Greeks occurred at the pass of Thermopylae (thuhr-MAWP-uh-lee), where an outnumbered Greek army, including three hundred top Spartan warriors, held off a much larger Persian force for several days. Before the fighting began, a report came in that when the Persian archers shot their bows, the arrows darkened the sky. Herodotus (ca. 485–425 B.C.E.), a Greek historian born in the Persian-ruled city of Halicarnassus in Asia Minor, later wrote that one gruff Spartan, upon hearing this report, replied merely, "Fine, then we'll fight in the shade."[4] The Greeks at Thermopylae fought heroically, but the Persians won the battle after a local man showed them a hidden path over the mountains so that they could attack the Greeks from both sides. The victorious Persian army occupied and sacked Athens.

At the same time as the land battle of Thermopylae, Greeks and Persians fought one another in a naval battle at Artemisium off Boetia. The Athenians, led by the general Themistocles, provided the heart of the naval forces with their fleet of triremes, oar-propelled warships. Storms had wrecked many Persian ships, and neither side won a decisive victory. Only a month or so later, the Greek fleet met the Persian armada at Salamis, an island across from Athens. Though outnumbered, the Greek navy won an overwhelming victory by outmaneuvering the Persians. The remnants of the Persian fleet retired, and in 479 B.C.E. the Greeks overwhelmed the Persian army at Plataea.

The wars provided a brief glimpse of what the Greeks could accomplish when they worked together. By defeating the Persians, the Greeks ensured that they would not be ruled by a foreign power. The decisive victories meant that Greek political forms and intellectual concepts would be handed down to later societies. Among the thoughtful Greeks who felt prompted to record and analyze these events was Herodotus, who traveled the Greek world to piece together the rise and fall of the Persian Empire. Like many other authors and thinkers, he was born elsewhere but moved to Athens and lived there for a time.

Growth of the Athenian Empire

The defeat of the Persians created a power vacuum in the Aegean, and the Athenians took advantage of the situation. Led by Themistocles, the Athenians and their allies formed the **Delian League**, a military alliance aimed at protecting the Aegean Islands, liberating Ionia from Persian rule, and keeping the Persians out of Greece. The league took its name from the small island of Delos, on which stood a religious center sacred to all parties. The Delian (DEE-lee-uhn) League was intended to be a free alliance under the leadership of Athens, but as the Athenians drove the Persians out of the Aegean, they also became increasingly imperialistic. Athens began reducing its allies to the status of subjects. Tribute was often collected by force, and the Athenians placed the economic resources of the Delian League under tighter and tighter control. Major allies revolted, and were put down, for the Athenian ideas of freedom and democracy did not extend to the citizens of other cities.

The aggressiveness of Athenian rule also alarmed Sparta and its allies. Relations between Athens and Sparta grew more hostile, particularly when Pericles (PEHR-uh-kleez) (ca. 494–429 B.C.E.), an aristocrat of solid intellectual ability, became the leading statesman in Athens. Pericles gained support among the ordinary citizens of Athens by introducing measures that broadened democracy, such as lowering the property requirement for the position of archon. Like the democracy he led, Pericles was aggressive and imperialistic. In 459 B.C.E. Sparta and Athens went to war over conflicts between Athens and some of Sparta's allies. The war ended in 445 B.C.E. with a treaty promising thirty years of peace, and no serious damage to either side. The treaty divided the Greek world between the two great powers, with each agreeing to respect the other and its allies.

Peace lasted thirteen years instead of thirty. Athens continued its severe policies toward its subject allies and came into conflict with Corinth, one of Sparta's leading supporters. In this climate of anger and escalation, Pericles decided to punish the city of Megara, which had switched allegiance from Sparta to Athens and then back again. In 432 B.C.E. Pericles persuaded the Athenians to pass a law that excluded the Megarians from trading with Athens and its empire, a restriction that would have meant economic disaster for the Megarians. In response the Spartans and their allies declared war.

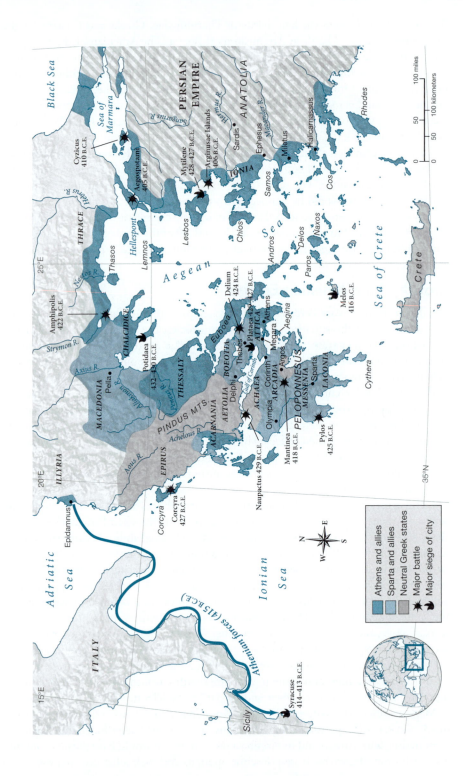

◄ **MAP 3.3   The Peloponnesian War, 431–404 B.C.E.**
This map shows the alignment of states on the sides of Sparta and Athens during the Peloponnesian War.

The Peloponnesian War

At the outbreak of the war, which became known as the Peloponnesian (puh-luh-puh-NEE-zhuhn) War, the Spartan ambassador Melesippus warned the Athenians: "This day will be the beginning of great evil for the Greeks." Few men have ever prophesied more accurately. The Peloponnesian War lasted a generation and brought in its wake disease, famine, civil wars, widespread destruction, and huge loss of life (Map 3.3). During the first Spartan invasion of Attica, which began in 431 B.C.E., cramped conditions within the walls of Athens nurtured a dreadful plague that killed huge numbers, eventually claiming Pericles himself. The death of Pericles opened the door to a new breed of politicians, men who were rash, ambitious, and more dedicated to themselves than to Athens. Under the non-aristocratic Cleon, the Athenians counterattacked and defeated the Spartans, though Cleon was killed. Recognizing that ten years of war had resulted only in death, destruction, and stalemate, Sparta and Athens concluded the Peace of Nicias (NIH-shee-uhs) in 421 B.C.E.

The Peace of Nicias resulted in a cold war. But even cold war can bring horror and misery. Such was the case when in 416 B.C.E. the Athenians sent a fleet to the largely neutral island of Melos with an ultimatum: the Melians could surrender or perish. The Melians resisted. The Athenians conquered them, killed the men of military age, and sold the women and children into slavery.

The cold war grew hotter, thanks to the ambitions of Alcibiades (al-suh-BIGH-uh-dees) (ca. 450–404 B.C.E.), an aristocrat, a kinsman of Pericles, and a student of the philosopher Socrates (see page 92). A shameless opportunist, Alcibiades widened the war to further his own career and increase the power of Athens. He convinced the Athenians to attack Syracuse, the leading polis in Sicily, which would cut off the grain supply from Sicily to Sparta and its allies, allowing Athens to end the war and become the greatest power in Greece. The undertaking was vast, requiring an enormous fleet and thousands of sailors and soldiers, and ended in disaster. The Athenian historian Thucydides (thoo-SIHD-ih-dees) (ca. 460–ca. 399 B.C.E.), who saw action in the war himself and later tried to understand its causes, wrote the epitaph for the Athenians: "infantry, fleet, and everything else were utterly destroyed, and out of many few returned home."[5]

The disaster in Sicily ushered in the final phase of the war, which was marked by three major developments: the renewal of war between Athens and Sparta, Persia's intervention in the war, and the revolt of many Athenian subjects. The year 413 B.C.E. saw Sparta's declaration of war against Athens and widespread revolt within the Athenian Empire, both supported by Alcibiades, who had defected to Sparta. The Persians threw their support behind Sparta and built a fleet of ships for them; in exchange they expected Ionia to be returned to them once the Spartans were successful. Now equipped with a fleet, the Spartans challenged the Athenians in the Aegean, and a long series of inconclusive naval battles followed.

The strain of war prompted the Athenians in 411 B.C.E. to recall Alcibiades from exile. He cheerfully double-crossed the Spartans and Persians, but even he could not restore Athenian fortunes. In 405 B.C.E. Spartan forces destroyed the last Athenian fleet at the Battle of Aegospotami, after which the Spartans blockaded Athens until it was starved into submission. In 404 B.C.E., after twenty-seven years of fighting, the Peloponnesian War was over, and the evils prophesied by the Spartan ambassador Melesippus in 431 B.C.E. had come true.

The Struggle for Dominance

The decades after the end of the Peloponnesian War were turbulent ones. The chief states—Sparta, Athens, and Thebes—each tried to create a political system in which it would dominate. When Athens surrendered to Sparta in 404 B.C.E., the Spartans used their victory to build an empire. Their decision brought them into conflict with Persia, which now demanded the return of Ionia to its control, as Sparta had promised earlier. From 400 to 386 B.C.E. the Spartans fought the Persians for Ionia, a conflict that eventually engulfed Greece itself. After years of stalemate the Spartans made peace with Persia and their own Greek enemies. The result was a treaty, the King's Peace of 386 B.C.E. in which the Greeks and Persians pledged themselves to live in harmony. This agreement cost Sparta its empire but not its position of dominance in Greece.

The Spartans were not long content with this situation, however, and decided to punish cities that had opposed Sparta during the war. They used naked force against old enemies even though they had formally agreed to peace. In 378 B.C.E. the Spartans launched an unprovoked attack on Athens. Together the Thebans and the Athenians created what was called the Second Athenian Confederacy, a federation of states to guarantee the terms of the peace treaty. The two fought Sparta until 371 B.C.E., when due to growing fear of Theban might, Athens made a separate peace with Sparta. Left alone, Thebes defended itself until later that year, when the brilliant Theban general Epaminondas (ih-pah-muh-NAHN-duhs) (ca. 418–362 B.C.E.) routed the Spartan army on the small plain of Leuctra and in a series of invasions eliminated Sparta as a major power.

The defeat of the once-invincible Spartans stunned the Greeks, who wondered how Thebes would use its victory. Epaminondas, also a gifted statesman, immediately grappled with the problem of how to translate military success into political reality. He concluded alliances with many Peloponnesian states but made no effort to dominate them, instead creating a federal league of cities in which people could marshal their resources, both human and material, to defend themselves from outside interference. Although he made Thebes the leader of this federation of cities, other city-states and leagues were bound to Thebes only by voluntary alliances. His premature death at the Battle of Mantinea in 362 B.C.E. put an end to his efforts, however.

Philip II and Macedonian Supremacy

While the Greek states exhausted themselves in endless conflicts, the new power of Macedonia arose in the north. The land, extensive and generally fertile, nurtured a large population. Whether the Macedonians should be considered Greeks is a controversial issue, among both scholars of the ancient world and Greeks and Macedonians living today. Macedonia had strong ties to the Greek poleis, but the government there developed as a kingdom, not a democracy or oligarchy.

The kings of Macedonia slowly built up their power over rival states, and in 359 B.C.E. the brilliant and cultured Philip II ascended to the throne. The young Philip had spent years in Thebes mastering diplomacy and warfare. With decades of effort he secured the borders of Macedonia against invaders from the north, and he then launched a series of military operations in the northwestern Aegean. By clever use of his wealth and superb army, he gained control of the area, and in 338 B.C.E. he won a decisive victory over Thebes and Athens that gave him command of Greece. Because the Greeks could not put aside their quarrels, they fell to an invader, and 338 B.C.E. is often seen as marking the end of the classical period.

After his victory, Philip led a combined army of soldiers from Macedonia and from many Greek states in an attempt to liberate the Ionian Greeks from Persian rule. Before he could launch this campaign, however, Philip fell to an assassin's dagger in 336 B.C.E. His young son Alexander vowed to carry on Philip's mission. He would succeed beyond all expectations.

Classical Greek Life and Culture

What were the lasting cultural and intellectual achievements of the classical period?

Despite the violence that dominated Greece for nearly two centuries beginning in 500 B.C.E., or to some degree because of it, playwrights and thinkers pondered the meaning of the universe and the role of humans in it, and artists and architects created new styles to celebrate Greek achievements. Thus, although warfare was one of the hallmarks of the classical period, intellectual and artistic accomplishments were as well.

Athenian Arts in the Age of Pericles

In the midst of the warfare of the fifth century B.C.E., Pericles turned Athens into the showplace of Greece. He appropriated Delian League funds to pay for a huge building program to rebuild the city that had been destroyed during the Persian occupation in 480 B.C.E., and to display to all Greeks the glory of the Athenian polis. Workers erected temples and other buildings as patriotic memorials housing statues and carvings, often painted in bright colors, showing the gods in human form and celebrating the Greek victory over the Persians. (The paint later washed away, leaving the generally white sculpture that we think of as "classical.") Many of the temples were built on the high, rocky Acropolis that stood in the center of the city, on top of the remains of temples that had been burned by the Persians, and sometimes incorporating these into their walls.

The Athenians normally hiked up the long approach to the Acropolis only for religious festivals, of which the most important and joyous was the Great Panathenaea, held every four years to honor the virgin goddess Athena and perhaps offer sacrifices to older deities as well. For this festival, Athenian citizens and legal noncitizen residents formed a huge procession to bring the statue of Athena in the Parthenon an exquisite robe, richly embroidered by the citizen women of Athens with mythological scenes. At the head of the procession walked an aristocratic young woman carrying an offering basket. She and other young unmarried women of the city had earlier left their toys and other marks of childhood in caves at the base of the Acropolis. Other richly dressed women followed her, most carrying gold and silver vessels containing wine and perfumes. Young men on horseback came next, followed by older men carrying staffs. Toward the rear came other young men carrying large pitchers of water and wine, or leading

The Discus Thrower   This marble statue shows an athlete in mid-throw, capturing the tension in the muscles and tendons. The original was made about 450 B.C.E., perhaps by the sculptor Myron of Athens. As is true of so much Greek statuary, the original is lost, and this is a Roman copy. Athletes in Greece regularly competed nude, including in the Olympic games. (Ancient Art and Architecture Collection Ltd./The Bridgeman Art Library)

the bulls to the sacrifice. After the religious ceremonies, all the people joined in a feast.

Once the procession began, the marchers first saw the Propylaea, the ceremonial gateway whose columns appeared to uphold the sky. On the right was the small temple of Athena Nike, built to commemorate the victory over the Persians. The broad band of sculpture above its columns depicted the struggle between the Greeks and the Persians. To the left of the visitors stood the Erechtheum, a temple that housed several ancient shrines. On its southern side was the famous Portico of the Caryatids, a porch whose roof was supported by huge statues of young women. As visitors walked on, they obtained a full view of the Parthenon, the chief temple dedicated to Athena at the center of the Acropolis, with a huge painted ivory and gold statue of the goddess inside.

The development of drama was tied to the religious festivals of the city, especially those to the god of wine, Dionysus (see page 91). Drama was as rooted in the life of the polis as were the architecture and sculpture of the Acropolis. The polis sponsored the production of plays and required wealthy citizens to pay the expenses of their production. At the beginning of the year, dramatists submitted their plays to the chief archon of the polis. He chose those he considered best and assigned a theatrical troupe to each playwright. Many plays were highly controversial, containing overt political and social commentary, but the archons neither suppressed nor censored them.

Not surprisingly, given the incessant warfare, conflict was a constant element in Athenian drama, and playwrights used their art in attempts to portray, understand, and resolve life's basic conflicts. The Athenian dramatists examined questions about the relationship between humans and the gods, the demands of society on the individual, and the nature of good and evil. Aeschylus (EHS-kuh-lihs) (525–456 B.C.E.), the first of the great Athenian dramatists, was also the first to express the agony of the individual caught in conflict. In his trilogy of plays, *The Oresteia* (ohr-eh-STEE-uh), Aeschylus deals with the themes of betrayal, murder, and reconciliation, urging that reason and justice be applied to reconcile fundamental conflicts. The final play concludes with a prayer that civil dissension never be allowed to destroy the city and that the life of the city be one of harmony and grace.

Sophocles (SOFF-uh-klees) (496–406 B.C.E.) also dealt with matters personal and political. Perhaps his most famous plays are *Oedipus* (EHD-uh-puhs) *the King* and its sequel, *Oedipus at Colonus*. *Oedipus the King* is the tragic story of a man doomed by the gods to kill his father and marry his mother. Try as he might to avoid his fate, his every action brings him closer to its fulfillment. When at last he realizes that he has unwittingly carried out the decree of the gods, Oedipus blinds himself and flees into exile. In *Oedipus at Colonus* Sophocles dramatizes the last days of the broken king, whose patient suffering and uncomplaining piety win him an exalted position. In the end the gods honor him for his virtue. The interpretation of these two plays has been hotly debated, but Sophocles seems to be saying that the gods only predict what is going to happen, not determine it. It is up to the individual, not the gods, to decide whether things turn out tragically or not. (See "Primary Source: Sophocles, *Antigone*," page 84.)

With Euripides (your-IHP-uh-dees) (ca. 480–406 B.C.E.) drama entered a new, and in many ways more personal, phase. To him the gods were far less important than human beings. The essence of Euripides's tragedy is the flawed character — men and women who bring disaster on themselves and their loved ones because their passions overwhelm reason. Although Euripides's plays were less popular in his lifetime than were those of Aeschylus and Sophocles, his work was to have a significant impact on Roman drama.

Writers of comedy treated the affairs of the polis and its politicians bawdily and often coarsely. Even so, their plays also were performed at religious festivals. Best known are the comedies of Aristophanes (eh-ruh-STAH-fuh-neez) (ca. 445–386 B.C.E.), an ardent lover of his city and a merciless critic of cranks and quacks. He lampooned eminent generals, at times depicting them as morons. He commented snidely on Cleon, poked fun at Socrates (see page 92), and hooted at Euripides. Like Aeschylus, Sophocles, and Euripides, Aristophanes used his art to dramatize his ideas on the right conduct of the citizen and the value of the polis.

Households and Work

In sharp contrast with the rich intellectual and cultural life of Periclean Athens stands the simplicity of its material life. The Athenians, like other Greeks, lived with comparatively few material possessions in houses that were rather simple. Well-to-do Athenians lived in houses consisting of a series of rooms opening onto a central courtyard, sometimes with bedrooms on an upper floor. Artisans often set aside a room to use as a shop or work area. Larger houses often had a dining room at the front where the men of the family ate and entertained guests at drinking parties called *symposia*, and a **gynaeceum** (also spelled *gynaikeion*), a room or section at the back where the women of the family and the female slaves worked, ate, and slept. Other rooms included the kitchen and bathroom. By modern standards there was not much furniture. In the men's dining room were couches, a sideboard, and small tables appropriate for social events. Cups and other pottery were often hung from pegs on the wall, as were hoplites' armor and, for aristocrats, the death masks of their relatives. In the courtyard were the well, a small altar, and a washbasin. If the family lived in the country, the stalls of the animals faced the courtyard. Country dwellers kept oxen for plowing, pigs for slaughtering, sheep for wool, goats for cheese, and mules and donkeys for transportation. Even in the city, chickens and perhaps a goat or two roamed the courtyard along with dogs and cats.

Cooking, done over a hearth in the house, provided welcome warmth in the winter. Baking and roasting were done in ovens. Meals consisted primarily of various grains, especially wheat and barley, as well as lentils, olives, figs, grapes, fish, and a little meat, foods that are now part of the highly touted "Mediterranean diet." The Greeks used olive oil for cooking, and also as an ointment and as lamp fuel.

PRIMARY SOURCE   Sophocles, *Antigone*

The plays of Sophocles concern matters personal, political, and divine. In Antigone *(an-TIH-guh-nee), produced in or before 441 B.C.E., Polyneices (pahl-eh-NIGH-sees) and Eteocles (eh-tee-OH-klees), the sons of King Oedipus of Thebes, have killed each other in a war over who would rule. Creon, the brother of Oedipus's wife, Jocasta (who is also Oedipus's mother, but that's the plot of another play; see page 82), is now king, and orders the body of Polyneices to be left to rot. Polyneices's sister (and Creon's niece) Antigone disobeys him, buries Polyneices, and carries out the proper funeral rituals. Creon condemns her to be walled up, so she hangs herself. Creon's son and Antigone's fiancé, Haemon, then kills himself, as does Creon's wife. The heart of the play is a series of confrontations between Creon and Antigone.*

Creon (to Antigone):
   You—tell me not at length but in a word.
   You knew the order not to do this thing?

Antigone:
   I knew, of course I knew. The word was plain.

Creon:
   And still you dared to overstep these laws?

Antigone:
   For me it was not Zeus who made that order.
   Nor did that Justice who lives with the gods below
   mark out such laws to hold among mankind.
   Nor did I think your orders were so strong
   that you, a mortal man, could over-run
   the gods' unwritten and unfailing laws.
   Not now, nor yesterday's, they always live,
   and no one knows their origin in time
   So not through fear of any man's proud spirit
   would I be likely to neglect these laws,
   draw on myself the gods' sure punishment.
   I knew that I must die; how could I not?
   even without your warning. If I die

The Greeks did not eat much meat. On special occasions, such as important religious festivals, the family ate the animal sacrificed to the god. The only Greeks who consistently ate meat were the Spartan warriors. They received a small portion of meat each day, together with the infamous Spartan black broth, a concoction of pork cooked in blood, vinegar, and salt. One Athenian, after tasting the broth, commented that he could easily understand why the Spartans were so willing to die.

In the city a man might support himself as a craftsman—a potter, bronze-smith, sailmaker, or tanner—or he could contract with the polis to work on public buildings. Certain crafts, including spinning and weaving, were generally done by women.

before my time, I say it is a gain.
Who lives in sorrows many as are mine
how shall he not be glad to gain his death?
And so, for me to meet this fate, no grief.
But if I left that corpse, my mother's son,
dead and unburied I'd have cause to grieve
as now I grieve not.
And if you think my acts are foolishness
The foolishness may be in a fool's eye.

. . .

I go, without a friend, struck down by fate,
live to the hollow chambers of the dead.
What divine justice have I disobeyed?
Why, in my misery, look to the gods for help?
Can I call any of them my ally?
I stand convicted of impiety,
the evidence my pious duty done.
Should the gods think that this is righteousness,
in suffering I'll see my error clear.
But if it is the others who are wrong
I wish them no greater punishment than mine.

. . .

Look what I suffer, at whose command,
Because I respected the right.

EVALUATE THE EVIDENCE

1. How does Antigone justify what she has done? How does she describe the relationship between divine law and political law?

2. Given what was going on in Athens at the time that this play was performed, how can Antigone's words be seen as political commentary?

Source: *Sophocles I: Antigone*, trans. Elizabeth Wyckoff, in *The Complete Greek Tragedies* (Chicago: Phoenix Books, 1954), pp. 173–174, 190, 191. Copyright © 1954 by The University of Chicago. All rights reserved. Used by permission of the publisher.

Men and women without skills worked as paid laborers but competed with slaves for work.

Slavery was commonplace in Greece, as it was throughout the ancient world. Slaves were usually foreigners and often "barbarians," people whose native language was not Greek. Most citizen households in Athens owned at least one slave. Slaves in Athens ranged widely in terms of their type of work and opportunities for escaping slavery. Some male slaves were skilled workers or well-educated teachers and tutors of writing, while others were unskilled laborers in the city, agricultural workers in the countryside, or laborers in mines, including the Athenian silver mines at Laurium. Female slaves worked in agriculture, or as domestic servants and nurses for children. Slaves received some protection under the law, and those who engaged in skilled labor for which they were paid could buy their freedom. A few ex-slaves even became Athenian citizens.

Gender and Sexuality

The social conditions of Athenian women have been the subject of much debate, in part because the sources are fragmentary. The available sources suggest that women rarely played notable roles in public affairs, and we know the names of no female poets, artists, or philosophers from classical Athens. However, we do know that the status of a free woman was strictly protected by law, and that only the sons of a citizen woman could be citizens. Only she was in charge of the household and the family's possessions, yet the law gave her these rights primarily to protect her husband's interests. Women in Athens and elsewhere in Greece, like those in Mesopotamia, brought dowries to their husbands upon marriage, which went back to their fathers in cases of divorce.

In ancient Athens the main function of women from citizen families was to bear and raise children. Childbirth could be dangerous for both mother and infant, so pregnant women usually made sacrifices or visited temples to ask help from the gods. Women relied on their relatives, on friends, and on midwives to assist in the delivery.

The ideal for Athenian citizen women was apparently a secluded life in which the only men they saw were relatives and tradesmen. In a treatise describing the ideal household, the writer Xenophon has a husband say to his wife: "It would be ridiculous if you were not here at home to take care of everything that I bring in from the outside."[6] The husband describes these gender roles as divinely created, "Now we know, dear, what duties have been assigned to us by God. We must try, each of us, to accomplish them as best as we can. The law approves of them, for it joins man and woman together. And God makes them partners in their children, and law likewise makes them partners in the home. The law also proclaims these duties to be noble."[7] The extent to which this ideal was actually a reality is impossible to know, but women in wealthier citizen families probably spent most of their time at home in the gynaeceum, leaving the house only to attend some religious festivals, and perhaps occasionally plays. (See "Individuals in Society: Aspasia," page 88.)

In the gynaeceum women oversaw domestic slaves and hired labor, and together with servants and friends worked wool into cloth. Women personally cared for slaves who became ill and nursed them back to health, and cared for the family's material possessions as well. Women from noncitizen families lived freer lives than citizen women, although they worked harder and had fewer material comforts. They performed manual labor in the fields or sold goods or services in the agora, going about their affairs much as men did.

Among the services that some women and men sold was sex. Women who sold sexual services ranged from poor streetwalkers known as *pornai* to middle-status hired mistresses known as *palakai* to sophisticated courtesans known as *hetaerae,* who added intellectual accomplishments to physical beauty. Hetaerae accompanied men at dinner parties and in public settings where their wives would not have been welcome, serving men as social as well as sexual partners.

Same-sex relations were generally accepted in all of ancient Greece, not simply in Sparta. In classical Athens part of a male adolescent citizen's training might entail a hierarchical sexual and tutorial relationship with an adult man, who most likely was

Young Man and Hetaera   In this scene painted on the inside of a drinking cup, a hetaera holds the head of a young man who has clearly had too much to drink. Sexual and comic scenes were common on Greek pottery, particularly on objects that would have been used at a private dinner party hosted by a citizen, known as a symposium. Wives did not attend symposia, but hetaerae and entertainers were often hired to perform for the male guests. (Martin von Wagner Museum der Universitat Wurzburg. Photo: Karl Oehrlein)

married and may have had female sexual partners as well. These relationships between young men and older men were often celebrated in literature and art, in part because Athenians regarded perfection as possible only in the male. Women were generally seen as inferior to men, dominated by their bodies rather than their minds. The perfect body was that of the young male, and perfect love was that between a young man and a slightly older man, not that between a man and a woman, who was marred by imperfection. The extent to which perfect love was sexual or spiritual was debated among the ancient Greeks. In one of his dialogues, the philosopher Plato (see page 93) argues that the best kind of love is one in which contemplation of the beloved leads to contemplation of the divine, an intellectualized love that came to be known as "platonic." Plato was suspicious of the power of sexual passion because it distracted men from reason and the search for knowledge.

Along with praise of intellectualized love, Greek authors also celebrated physical sex and desire. The soldier-poet Archilochus (d. 652 B.C.E.) preferred "to light upon the flesh of a maid and ram belly to belly and thigh to thigh."[8] The lyric poet Sappho, who lived on the island of Lesbos in the northern Aegean Sea in the sixth century B.C.E., wrote often of powerful desire. One of her poems describes her reaction on seeing her beloved talking to someone else:

> He appears to me, that one, equal to the gods,
> the man who, facing you,
> is seated and, up close, that sweet voice of yours
> he listens to
>
> And how you laugh your charming laugh. Why it
> makes my heart flutter within my breast,
> because the moment I look at you, right then, for me,
> to make any sound at all won't work any more.

INDIVIDUALS IN SOCIETY • Aspasia

"If it is necessary for me indeed to speak of female virtues, to those of you who have now become widows, I shall explain the entire situation briefly. It is in your hands whether you will not fall below your nature. The greatest glory to you is to be least talked about by men, either for excellence or blame" (Thucydides 2.46.1). These words were reportedly uttered by Pericles to the widows at a public funeral honoring those killed during the first year of the Peloponnesian War. We have no idea whether Pericles actually said something like this—Thucydides often inserted speeches to make his history more dramatic—but these words express the Athenian ideal of proper behavior for a citizen's wife: she should stay at home and limit her talents to her household. This ideal became the reality for most Athenian women, whose names and actions were not recorded and thus are lost to history.

One exception to this silence is Aspasia (as-PAY-zhuh), who was born in the Greek city of Miletus and came to Athens in about 445 B.C.E. Little is known for certain about her life—Thucydides never mentions her—but she appears to have played a role in Athenian society that was far different from that prescribed in Pericles's speech. Because she was not an Athenian, she could not marry an Athenian citizen. Instead of marrying another non-Athenian, she caught the eye of Pericles. After he had divorced his wife, Aspasia became his mistress and bore him a son, also named Pericles. She may have been a hetaera, one of the high-status courtesans in Athens who provided men with witty conversation at dinner parties as well as sexual services. The first person to mention her status as a hetaera was the comic playwright Aristophanes. Aristophanes was an opponent of Pericles, however, and he may have simply made this up. Other authors, including Plato, do discuss Aspasia, but they focus on her ability with words and her wit (which they see as good) and her influence over Pericles (which they generally see as bad). In one of Plato's dialogues, Socrates even says that Pericles learned his rhetoric from Aspasia, and that *she* wrote the famous funeral oration. Most scholars see this not as a statement of fact, but as an attempt by Socrates to ridicule Pericles and criticize his growing power in Athens.

Aspasia herself was accused by various Athenian authors of causing one or another of Athens's wars because of personal vendettas or perverse sexual desires.

My tongue has a breakdown and a delicate
—all of a sudden—fire rushes under my skin.
With my eyes I see not a thing, and there is a roar
that my ears make.
Sweat pours down me and a trembling
seizes all of me; paler than grass
am I, and a little short of death
do I appear to me.[9]

Pericles's death in 429 B.C.E. in the plague of Athens left Aspasia without a protector, and she disappears from the historical record shortly afterward. Ever more embellished stories about her continued to be told, however. By the time of the Roman biographer Plutarch in the first century C.E., it was said that she held public philosophical discussions, was put on trial for impiety, and became the mistress of another Athenian general after Pericles's death.

It is almost impossible to separate the historical Aspasia from the imaginary one, but what is clear is that her status was dependent on her personal relationships with prominent men. She may well have been a gifted and intelligent speaker, but her actions were severely limited because of her status as a noncitizen in a place where citizenship was essential, and even more, because of her status as a woman. Thanks largely to her enemies, we do know her name, but Aspasia lacked the honored social position of the anonymous Athenian citizen women her lover Pericles may have praised.

QUESTIONS FOR ANALYSIS

1. What allowed Aspasia to have a position quite different from that seen as ideal in Pericles's speech?
2. Why might Pericles's enemies have enhanced accounts about her talents and her influence over him? Can you think of more recent parallels?

ONLINE DOCUMENT ASSIGNMENT

What does Aspasia's story reveal about the expectations and ideals surrounding gender in classical Greek society? Analyze texts and images that testify to Greek attitudes about gender roles during Aspasia's time, and then complete a writing assignment based the evidence and details from this chapter.

bedfordstmartins.com/mckaywestvalue

Sappho's description of the physical reactions caused by love—and jealousy—reaches across the centuries. The Hellenic and even more the Hellenistic Greeks regarded her as a great lyric poet, although because some of her poetry is directed toward women, over the last century she has become better known for her sexuality than her writing. Today the English word *lesbian* is derived from Sappho's home island of Lesbos.

Same-sex relations did not mean that people did not marry, for Athenians saw the continuation of the family line as essential. Sappho, for example, appears to have been married and had a daughter. Sexual desire and procreation were both important aspects of life, but ancient Greeks did not necessarily link them.

Public and Personal Religion

Like most peoples of the ancient world, the Greeks were polytheists, worshipping a variety of gods and goddesses who were immortal but otherwise acted just like people. Migration, invasion, and colonization brought the Greeks into contact with other peoples and caused their religious beliefs to evolve. How much these contacts shaped Greek religion and other aspects of culture has been the subject of a fierce debate since the late 1980s, when in *Black Athena: The Afroasiatic Roots of Classical Civilization*, Martin Bernal proposed that the Greeks owed a great deal to the Egyptians and Phoenicians, and that scholars since the nineteenth century had purposely tried to cover this up to make the Greeks seem more European and less indebted to cultures in Africa and Asia.[10] Bernal's ideas are highly controversial, and most classicists do not accept his evidence, but they are part of a larger tendency among scholars in the last several decades — including those who vigorously oppose Bernal — to see the Greeks less in isolation from other groups and more in relation to the larger Mediterranean world.

Greek religion was primarily a matter of ritual, with rituals designed to appease the divinities believed to control the forces of the natural world. Processions, festivals, and sacrifices offered to the gods were frequently occasions for people to meet together socially, times of cheer or even drunken excess.

By the classical era the primary gods were understood to live metaphorically on Mount Olympus, the highest mountain in Greece. Zeus was the king of the gods and the most powerful of them, and he was married to Hera, who was also his sister (just as, in Egypt, Isis was Osiris's wife and sister; see Chapter 2). Zeus and Hera had several children, including Ares, the god of war. Zeus was also the father of the god Apollo, who represented the epitome of youth, beauty, and athletic skill, and who served as the patron god of music and poetry. Apollo's half-sister Athena was a warrior-goddess who had been born from the head of Zeus.

The Greeks also honored certain heroes. A hero was born of a union of a god or goddess and a mortal and was considered an intermediate between the divine and the human. A hero displayed his divine origins by performing deeds beyond the ability of human beings. Herakles (or Hercules, as the Romans called him), the son of Zeus and the mortal woman Alcmene, was the most popular of the Greek heroes, defeating mythical opponents and carrying out impossible (or "Herculean") tasks. Devotees to Hercules believed that he, like other heroes, protected mortals from supernatural dangers and provided an ideal of vigorous masculinity.

The polis administered cults and festivals, and everyone was expected to participate in what were events similar to today's patriotic parades or ceremonies. Much religion was local and domestic, and individual families honored various deities privately in their homes. Many people also believed that magic rituals and spells were effective and sought the assistance of individuals reputed to have special knowledge or powers to cure disease, drive away ghosts, bring good weather, or influence the actions of others. Even highly educated Greeks sought the assistance of fortune-tellers and soothsayers, from the oracle at Delphi to local figures who examined the flights of birds or the entrails of recently slaughtered chickens for clues about what was going to happen in the future.

Along with public and family forms of honoring the gods, some Greeks also participated in what later historians have termed **mystery religions**, in which participants underwent an initiation ritual and gained secret knowledge that they were forbidden to reveal to the uninitiated. The Eleusinian mysteries, held at Eleusis in Attica, are one of the oldest of these. They centered on Demeter, the goddess of the harvest, whose lovely daughter Persephone (Per-SEH-foh-nee), as the story goes, was taken by the god Hades to the underworld. In mourning, Demeter caused drought, and ultimately Zeus allowed Persephone to return to her, though she had to spend some months of the year in Hades. There is evidence of an agrarian ritual celebrating this mythological explanation for the cycle of the seasons as early as the Bronze Age, and in the sixth century B.C.E. the rulers of nearby Athens made the ritual open to all Greeks, women and slaves included. Many people flocked to the annual ceremonies and learned the mysteries, which by the fourth century B.C.E. appear to have promised life after death to those initiated into them.

Another somewhat secret religion was that of Dionysus (digh-uh-NIGH-suhs), the god of wine and powerful emotions. Dionysus appears to have been a god of non-Greek origin, though stories evolved to fit him into the Olympian system as a son of Zeus. He was killed and then reborn, which is why he, like Persephone, became the center of mystery religions offering rebirth. As the god of wine, he also represented freedom from the normal constraints of society, and his worshippers were reported to have danced ecstatically and even to have become a frenzied and uncontrolled mob. Whether or how often this actually happened is impossible to know, as contemporary Athenian writers who did not approve may have embellished their accounts of these wild rituals, and later scholars sometimes regarded them simply as fiction because chaotic orgies did not fit with their notions of the rational and orderly Greeks.

Greeks also shared some public Pan-Hellenic festivals, the chief of which were held at Olympia in honor of Zeus and at Delphi in honor of Apollo. The festivities at Olympia included athletic contests that have inspired the modern Olympic games. Held every four years, these games were for the glory of Zeus. They attracted visitors from all over the Greek world and lasted until the fourth century C.E., when they were banned by a Christian emperor because they were pagan. The Pythian (PIH-thee-uhn) games at Delphi were also held every four years and emphasized musical and literary contests as well as athletic prowess. Both the Olympic and the Pythian games were unifying factors in Greek life, bringing Greeks together culturally as well as religiously.

The Flowering of Philosophy

Just as the Greeks developed rituals to honor the gods, they spun myths and epics to explain the origin of the universe. Over time, however, as Greeks encountered other peoples with different beliefs, some of them began to question their old gods and myths, and they sought rational rather than supernatural explanations for natural phenomena. These Greek thinkers, based in Ionia, are called the Pre-Socratics because their rational efforts preceded those of the Athenian. They took individual facts and wove them into general theories that led them to conclude that, despite appearances, the universe is actually simple and subject to natural laws. Although they had little impact on the average Greek of their day, the Pre-Socratics began an intellectual revolution with their idea that nature was predictable, creating what we now call philosophy and science.

Drawing on their observations, the Pre-Socratics speculated about the basic building blocks of the universe. Thales (THAY-leez) (ca. 600 B.C.E.) thought the basic element of the universe was water, and Heraclitus (hehr-uh-KLIGH-tuhs) (ca. 500 B.C.E.) thought it was fire. Democritus (dih-MAW-kruh-tuhs) (ca. 460 B.C.E.) broke this down further and created the atomic theory, the idea that the universe is made up of invisible, inde-structible particles. The culmination of Pre-Socratic thought was the theory that four simple substances make up the universe: fire, air, earth, and water.

The stream of thought started by the Pre-Socratics branched into several directions. Hippocrates (hih-PAW-kruh-teez) (ca. 470–400 B.C.E.), who lived on the island of Kos near present-day Turkey, became the most prominent physician and teacher of medicine of his time. He appears to have written several works, and his followers wrote many more. These medical writings became known as the "Hippocratic corpus," although it is impossible to say who actually wrote any specific work. Hippocrates sought natural explanations for diseases and seems to have advocated letting nature take its course and not intervening too much. Illness was caused not by evil spirits, he asserted, but by physical problems in the body, particularly by imbalances in what he saw as four basic bodily fluids: blood, phlegm, black bile, and yellow bile. In a healthy body these fluids, called humors, were in perfect balance, and the goal of medical treatment of the ill was to help the body bring them back into balance.

The **Sophists** (SOFF-ihsts), a group of thinkers in fifth-century-B.C.E. Athens, applied philosophical speculation to politics and language, questioning the beliefs and laws of the polis to understand their origin. They believed that excellence in both politics and language could be taught, and they provided lessons for the young men of Athens who wished to learn how to persuade others in the often-tumultuous Athenian democracy. Their later opponents criticized them for charging fees and also accused them of using rhetoric to deceive people instead of presenting the truth. (Today the word *sophist* is usually used in this sense, describing someone who deceives people with clever-sounding but false arguments.)

Socrates (SOK-ruh-teez) (ca. 469–399 B.C.E.), whose ideas are known only through the works of others, also applied philosophy to politics and to people. He seemed to many Athenians to be a Sophist because he also questioned Athenian traditions, although he never charged fees. His approach when exploring ethical issues and defining concepts was to start with a general topic or problem and to narrow the matter to its essentials. He did so by continuously questioning participants in a discussion or argument through which they developed critical thinking skills, a process known as the **Socratic method**. Because he posed questions rather than giving answers, it is difficult to say exactly what Socrates thought about many things, although he does seem to have felt that through knowledge people could approach the supreme good and thus find happiness. He clearly thought that Athenian leaders were motivated more by greed and opportunism than by a desire for justice in the war with Sparta, and he criticized Athenian democracy openly.

Socrates was viewed with suspicion by many because he challenged the traditional beliefs and values of Athens. The playwright Aristophanes satirized him and his follow-ers in the riotously funny *The Clouds*, performed around 420 B.C.E. Twenty years later, after Athens's disastrous defeat at the hands of Sparta in the Peloponnesian War, Socrates came into serious conflict with the government. Charges were brought against him for corrupting the youth of the city, and for impiety, that is, for not believing in the gods honored in the city. Thus he was essentially charged with being unpatriotic because he criticized the traditions of the city and the decisions of government leaders. He was tried and imprisoned, and though he had several opportunities to escape, in 399 B.C.E. he drank the poison ordered as his method of execution, and died.

Most of what we know about Socrates, including the details of his trial and death, comes from his student Plato (427–347 B.C.E.), who wrote dialogues in which Socrates asks questions and who also founded the Academy, a school dedicated to philosophy. Plato developed the theory that there are two worlds: the impermanent, changing world that we know through our senses, and the eternal, unchanging realm of "forms" that constitute the essence of true reality. According to Plato, true knowledge and the possibility of living a virtuous life come from contemplating ideal forms—what later came to be called **Platonic ideals**—not from observing the visible world. Thus if you want to understand justice, asserted Plato, you should think about what would make perfect justice, not study the imperfect examples of justice around you. Plato believed that the ideal polis could exist only when its citizens were well educated. From education came the possibility of determining all of the virtues of life and combining them into a system that would lead to an intelligent, moral, and ethical life.

Plato's student Aristotle (384–322 B.C.E.) also thought that true knowledge was possible, but he believed that such knowledge came from observation of the world, analysis of natural phenomena, and logical reasoning, not contemplation. Aristotle thought that everything had a purpose, so that to know something, one also had to know its function. Excellence—*arête* in Greek—meant performing one's function to the best of one's ability, whether one was a horse or a person. To the qualities of courage and strength that Homer had seen as essential to arête in people (see page 67), Aristotle added justice, generosity, temperance, and other moral virtues. The range of Aristotle's thought is staggering. His interests embraced logic, ethics, natural science, physics, politics, poetry, and art. He studied the heavens as well as the earth and judged the earth to be the center of the universe, with the stars and planets revolving around it.

Plato's idealism profoundly shaped Western philosophy, but Aristotle came to have an even wider influence; for many centuries in Europe, the authority of Aristotle's ideas was second only to the Bible's. His works—which are actually a combination of his lecture notes and those of his students, copied and recopied many times—were used as the ultimate proof that something was true, even if closer observation of the phenomenon indicated that it was not. Thus, ironically, Aristotle's authority was sometimes invoked in a way that contradicted his own ideas. Despite these limitations, the broader examination of the universe and the place of humans in it that Socrates, Plato, and Aristotle engaged in is widely regarded as Greece's most important intellectual legacy.

Notes

1. Homer, *The Iliad*, trans. Samuel Butler (London: Longmans, Green, and Co., 1898), book 1, lines 1–5.
2. J. M. Edmonds, *Greek Elegy and Iambus* (Cambridge, Mass.: Harvard University Press, 1931), I.70, frag. 10.
3. *The Works of Xenophon*, trans. Henry G. Dakyns (London: Macmillan and Co., 1892), p. 296.
4. Herodotus, *Histories* 7.226.2. Works in Greek with no translator noted were translated by John Buckler.
5. Thucydides, *History of the Peloponnesian War* 7.87.6.
6. Xenophon, *Oeconomicus* 7.40.
7. Ibid., 7.29–30.
8. G. Tarditi, *Archilochus Fragmenta* (Rome: Edizioni dell'Ateno, 1968), frag. 112.
9. Sappho, fragment 31, trans. Gregory Nagy. Used by permission of Gregory Nagy, Center for Hellenic Studies.
10. Martin Bernal, *Black Athena: The Afroasiatic Roots of Classical Civilization* (New Brunswick, N.J.: Rutgers University Press, 1991). Essays by classical scholars refuting Bernal can be found in Mary R. Lefkowitz and Guy Maclean Rogers, *Black Athena Revisited* (Durham: University of North Carolina Press, 1996).

Chapter Review

MAKE IT STICK

LearningCurve
bedfordstmartins.com/mckaywestvalue

After reading the chapter, use LearningCurve to retain what you've read.

IDENTIFY KEY TERMS

Identify and explain the significance of each item below.

Minoan (p. 64)

Mycenaean (p. 64)

polis (p. 67)

hoplites (p. 70)

tyranny (p. 70)

democracy (p. 70)

oligarchy (p. 70)

helots (p. 72)

Delian League (p. 77)

gynaeceum (p. 83)

mystery religions (p. 90)

Sophists (p. 92)

Socratic method (p. 92)

Platonic ideals (p. 93)

REVIEW THE MAIN IDEAS

Answer the focus questions from each section of the chapter.

* How did the geography of Greece shape its earliest kingdoms, and what factors contributed to the decline of those kingdoms? (p. 62)

* What was the role of the polis in Greek society? (p. 67)

* What were the major wars of the classical period, and how did they shape Greek history? (p. 76)

* What were the lasting cultural and intellectual achievements of the classical period? (p. 81)

MAKE CONNECTIONS

Think about the larger developments and continuities within and across chapters.

1. What were the effects of the Bronze Age Collapse in Egypt, the Hittite Empire, Kush, Phoenicia, and Greece, and how did interactions among these societies change in this period of turmoil?

2. How were Greek understandings of the role of the gods in public and private life similar to those of the Egyptians and Sumerians? How were they different?

3. Looking at your own town or city, what evidence do you find of the cultural legacy of ancient Greece?

ONLINE DOCUMENT ASSIGNMENT

Aspasia

What does Aspasia's story reveal about the expectations and ideals surrounding gender in classical Greek society?

You encountered Aspasia on page 88. Keeping the question above in mind, go online and explore sources that testify to Greek attitudes about gender roles during Aspasia's time. Then complete a writing assignment based on the evidence and details from this chapter.

bedfordstmartins.com/mckaywestvalue

CHRONOLOGY

3000 B.C.E.	• Bronze tools and weapons become common in Greece
ca. 1900 B.C.E.	• Minoan culture begins to thrive on Crete
ca. 1650 B.C.E.	• Mycenaean culture develops in Greece
ca. 1300–1100 B.C.E.	• "Bronze Age Collapse"; migration, destruction
ca. 1100–800 B.C.E.	• Dark Age; population declines; trade decreases; writing disappears
ca. 800–500 B.C.E.	• Archaic age; rise of the polis; Greek colonization of the Mediterranean; Homer and Hesiod compose epics and poetry
ca. 750–500 B.C.E.	• Sparta expands and develops a military state
ca. 600–500 B.C.E.	• Political reforms in Archaic Athens
ca. 600–450 B.C.E.	• Pre-Socratics develop ideas about the nature of the universe
500–338 B.C.E.	• Classical period; development of drama, philosophy, and major building projects in Athens
499–479 B.C.E.	• Persian wars
431–404 B.C.E.	• Peloponnesian War
427–347 B.C.E.	• Life of Plato
384–322 B.C.E.	• Life of Aristotle
371–362 B.C.E.	• Thebes, with an alliance of city-states, rules Greece
338 B.C.E.	• Philip II of Macedonia gains control of Greece

4

LearningCurve
bedfordstmartins.com/mckaywestvalue
After reading the chapter, use
LearningCurve to retain what
you've read.

Life in the Hellenistic World

336–30 B.C.E.

WHEN HIS FATHER WAS ASSASSINATED IN 336 B.C.E., TWENTY-YEAR- old Alexander inherited not only Philip's crown but also his determination to lead a united Greek force in fighting Persia. Alexander's invasion of the Persian Empire led to its downfall, but he died while planning his next campaign, only a little more than a decade after he had started. He left behind an empire that quickly broke into smaller kingdoms, but more importantly, his death ushered in an era, the Hellenistic, in which Greek culture, the Greek language, and Greek thought spread as far as India, blending with local traditions. The end of the Hellenistic period is generally set at 30 B.C.E., the year of the death of Cleopatra VII—a Greek ruler—and the Roman conquest of her kingdom of Egypt. The Romans had conquered much of what had been Alexander's empire long before this, but many aspects of Hellenistic culture continued to flourish under Roman governance, adapting to Roman ways of life. Thus rather than coming to an abrupt end in one specific year, the Hellenistic world gradually evolved into the Roman.

ONLINE DOCUMENT ASSIGNMENT
Alexander the Great
What were the motives behind Alexander's conquests, and what were the consequences of Hellenization? Explore a variety of ancient perspectives on these questions, and then complete a writing assignment based on the evidence and details from this chapter.

bedfordstmartins.com/mckaywestvalue

In many ways, life in the Hellenistic world was not much different from life in Hellenic Greece or from that in any other Iron Age agricultural society: most people continued to be farmers, raising crops and animals for their own needs and for paying rents and taxes to their superiors. Those who lived in cities, however, often ate foods and drank wine that came from far away, did business with people who were quite unlike them, and adopted religious practices and ways of thinking unknown to their parents. Hellenistic cities thus offer striking parallels to those of today.

Alexander's Conquests and Their Political Legacy

How and why did Alexander the Great create an empire, and what was its political legacy?

Fully intending to carry out Philip's designs to lead the Greeks against the Persians, Alexander (r. 336–323 B.C.E.) proclaimed to the Greek world that the invasion of Persia was to be a mighty act of revenge for Xerxes's invasion of Greece in 480 B.C.E. (see Chapter 3) and more recent Persian interference in Greek affairs. Although he could not foresee this, Alexander's invasion ended up being much more. His campaign swept away the Persian Empire, which had ruled the area for over two hundred years. In its place Alexander established a Macedonian monarchy, and although his rule over these vast territories was never consolidated due to his premature death, he left behind a legacy of political and cultural influence, and a long period of war. Macedonian kings established dynasties and Greek culture spread in this **Hellenistic** era.

Military Campaigns

Despite his youth, Alexander was well prepared to invade Persia. Philip had groomed his son to become king and had given him the best education possible, hiring the Athenian philosopher Aristotle to be his tutor. In 334 B.C.E. Alexander led an army of Macedonians and Greeks into Persian territory in Asia Minor. With him went a staff of philosophers to study the people of these lands, poets to write verses praising Alexander's exploits, scientists to map the area and study strange animals and plants, and a historian to write an account of the campaign. Alexander intended not only a military campaign but also an expedition of discovery.

In the next three years Alexander moved east into the Persian Empire, winning major battles at the Granicus River and Issus (Map 4.1). He moved into Syria and took most of the cities of Phoenicia and the eastern coast of the Mediterranean without a fight. His army successfully besieged the cities that did oppose him, including Tyre and Gaza, executing the men of military age afterwards and enslaving the women and children. He then turned south toward Egypt, which had earlier been conquered by the Persians. The Egyptians saw Alexander as a liberator and he seized it without a battle. After honoring the priestly class, Alexander was proclaimed pharaoh, the legitimate ruler of the country. He founded a new capital, Alexandria, on the coast of the Mediterranean,

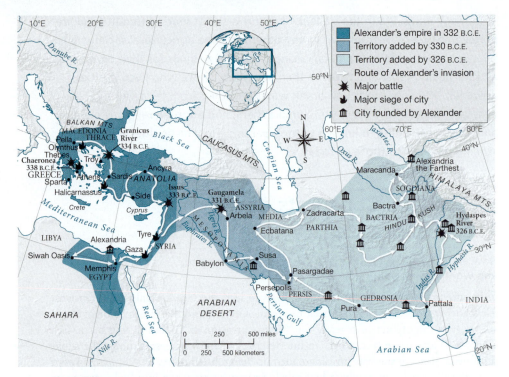

MAP 4.1   Alexander's Conquests, 334–324 B.C.E.
This map shows the course of Alexander's invasion of the Persian Empire. More important than
the great success of his military campaigns was the founding of new cities and expansion of
existing ones by Alexander and the Hellenistic rulers who followed him.

which would later grow into an enormous city. He next marched to the oasis of Siwah,
west of the Nile Valley, to consult the famous oracle of Zeus-Amon, a composite god
who combined qualities of the Greek Zeus and the Egyptian Amon (see Chapter 1). No
one will ever know what the priest told him, but henceforth Alexander called himself
the son of Zeus.

Alexander left Egypt after less than a year and marched into Assyria, where at
Gaugamela he defeated the Persian army. After this victory the principal Persian capital
of Persepolis fell to him in a bitterly fought battle. There he performed a symbolic act
of retribution by burning the royal buildings of King Xerxes, the invader of Greece
during the Persian wars 150 years earlier. In 330 B.C.E. he took Ecbatana, the last Persian
capital, and pursued the Persian king Darius III to his death.

The Persian Empire had fallen and the war of revenge was over, but Alexander had
no intention of stopping. Many of his troops had been supplied by Greek city-states
that had allied with him; he released these troops from their obligations of military
service, but then rehired them as mercenaries. Alexander then began his personal odyssey. With his Macedonian soldiers and Greek mercenaries, he set out to conquer more
of Asia. He plunged deeper into the East, into lands completely unknown to the Greek
world. It took his soldiers four additional years to conquer Bactria (in today's Afghanistan)

ONLINE DOCUMENT ASSIGNMENT

Alexander the Great

What were the motives behind Alexander's conquests, and what were the consequences of Hellenization? Explore a variety of ancient perspectives on these questions, and then complete a writing assignment based on the evidence and details from this chapter.

bedfordstmartins.com/mckaywestvalue

and the easternmost parts of the now-defunct Persian Empire, but still Alexander was determined to continue his march.

In 326 B.C.E. Alexander crossed the Indus River and entered India (in the area that is now Pakistan). There, too, he saw hard fighting, and finally at the Hyphasis (HIH-fuh-sihs) River his troops refused to go farther. Alexander was enraged by the mutiny, for he believed he was near the end of the world. Nonetheless, the army stood firm, and Alexander relented. Still eager to explore the limits of the world, Alexander turned south to the Arabian Sea, and he waged a bloody and ruthless war against the people of the area. After reaching the Arabian Sea and turning west, he led his army through the grim Gedrosian Desert (now part of Pakistan and Iran). The army and those who supported the troops with supplies suffered fearfully, and many soldiers died along the way. Nonetheless, in 324 B.C.E. Alexander returned to Susa in the Greek-controlled region of Assyria. His mission was over, but Alexander never returned to his homeland of Macedonia. He died the next year in Babylon from fever, wounds, and excessive drinking. He was only thirty-two, but in just thirteen years he had created an empire that stretched from his homeland of Macedonia to India, gaining the title "the Great" along the way.

Alexander so quickly became a legend that he still seems superhuman. That alone makes a reasoned interpretation of his goals and character very difficult. His contemporaries from the Greek city-states thought he was a bloody-minded tyrant, but later Greek and Roman writers and political leaders admired him and even regarded him as a philosopher interested in the common good. That view influenced many later European and American historians, but this idealistic interpretation has generally been rejected after a more thorough analysis of the sources. The most common view today is that Alexander was a brilliant leader who sought personal glory through conquest, and who tolerated no opposition. (See "Primary Source: Arrian on Alexander the Great," page 100.)

The Political Legacy

The main question at Alexander's death was whether his vast empire could be held together. Although he fathered a successor, the child was not yet born when Alexander died, and was thus too young to assume the duties of kingship. (Later he and his mother, Roxana, were murdered by one of Alexander's generals, who viewed him as a threat.) This meant that Alexander's empire was a prize for the taking. Several of the chief

PRIMARY SOURCE   Arrian on Alexander the Great

Arrian (ca. 86–160 C.E.) was a Greek military leader and historian who rose high in the ranks of the Roman army. He spent most of his career on the eastern border of the Roman Empire and thus lived in the heart of what had been Alexander's empire four hundred years earlier. He wrote a long history of Alexander's military campaigns based on accounts of Alexander's contemporaries, all of which are now lost, and modeled on the classical histories of war by Thucydides and Herodotus.

8. When [Alexander] arrived at Opis, he collected the Macedonians and announced that he intended to discharge from the army those who were useless for military service either from age or from being maimed in the limbs; and he said he would send them back to their own abodes. . . . [They were] offended by the speech which he delivered, thinking that now they were despised by him. . . . When Alexander heard this . . . , he ordered the most conspicuous of the men who had tried to stir up the multitude to sedition to be arrested. He himself pointed out with his hand to the shield-bearing guards those whom they were to arrest, to the number of thirteen; and he ordered these to be led away to execution. When the rest, stricken with terror, became silent, he mounted the platform again, and spoke as follows: . . .

10. ". . . Most of you have golden crowns, the eternal memorials of your valour and of the honour you receive from me. Whoever has been killed has met with a glorious end and has been honoured with a splendid burial. Brazen statues of most of the slain have been erected at home, and their parents are held in honour, being released from all public service and from taxation. But no one of you has ever been killed in flight under my leadership. And now I was intending to send back those of you who are unfit for service, objects of envy to those at home; but since you all wish to depart, depart all of you! Go back and report at home that your king Alexander, the conqueror of the Persians, Medes, Bactrians, and Sacians; . . . report that when you returned to Susa you deserted him and went away, handing him over to the protection of conquered foreigners. . . . Depart!"

Macedonian generals aspired to become sole ruler, which led to a civil war lasting for decades that tore Alexander's empire apart. By the end of this conflict, the most successful generals had carved out their own smaller monarchies, although these continued to be threatened by internal splits and external attacks.

Alexander's general Ptolemy (ca. 367–ca. 283 B.C.E.) was given authority over Egypt, and after fighting off rivals, established a kingdom and dynasty there, called the Ptolemaic (TAH-luh-MAY-ihk). In 304 B.C.E. he took the title of pharaoh, and by the end of his long life he had a relatively stable realm to pass on to his son. For these successes he was later called Ptolemy Soter, "Ptolemy the Savior." The Ptolemaic dynasty would rule Egypt for nearly three hundred years, until the death of the last Ptolemaic ruler, Cleopatra VII, in 30 B.C.E. (see Chapter 5). Seleucus (ca. 358–281 B.C.E.), another of Alexander's officers, carved out a large kingdom, the Seleucid (SUH-loo-suhd), that stretched from the coast of Asia Minor to India, for which he was later called Seleucus Nicator, "Seleucus the Victor." He was assassinated in 281 B.C.E. on the order of the

11. Having thus spoken, he leaped down quickly from the platform, and entered the palace, where . . . on the third day he summoned the select Persians within, and among them he distributed the commands of the brigades. . . . But the Macedonians who heard the speech were thoroughly astonished. . . . [T]hey were no longer able to restrain themselves; but running in a body to the palace, they cast their weapons there in front of the gates as signs of supplication to the king. Standing in front of the gates, they shouted, beseeching to be allowed to enter, and saying that they were willing to surrender the men who had been the instigators of the disturbance. . . . When he [Alexander] was informed of this, he came out without delay. . . . After this Alexander offered sacrifice to the gods to whom it was his custom to sacrifice, and gave a public banquet, over which he himself presided, with the Macedonians sitting around him; and next to them the Persians; after whom came the men of the other nations, preferred in honour for their personal rank or for some meritorious action.

EVALUATE THE EVIDENCE

1. According to Arrian, how does Alexander react when his Macedonian troops disagree with his decision about sending some of them home? How do they then respond to his actions?

2. Arrian is generally favorable toward Alexander. In your opinion, does the incident related here show Alexander in a good light? Why might he have done what Arrian describes?

Source: Arrian, *Anabasis of Alexander* 7.8.1–11.9, from *The Greek Historians*, by Francis R. B. Godolphin. Copyright 1942 and renewed 1970 by Random House, Inc. Used by permission of Random House, Inc. Any third-party use of this material, outside of this publication, is prohibited. Interested parties must apply directly to Random House, Inc., for permission.

---

ruler of the Ptolemaic kingdom, but his son succeeded him, founding a dynasty that also lasted for centuries, although the kingdom itself shrank as independent states broke off in Pergamum, Bactria, Parthia, and elsewhere. Antigonus I (382–301 B.C.E.), a third general, became king of Macedonia and established the Antigonid (an-TIH-guh-nuhd) dynasty, which lasted until it was overthrown by the Romans in 168 B.C.E. Rome would go on to conquer the Seleucid and Ptolemaic kingdoms as well (see Chapters 5 and 6).

Hellenistic rulers amassed an enormous amount of wealth from their large kingdoms, and royal patronage provided money for the production of literary works and the research and development that allowed discoveries in science and engineering. To encourage obedience, Hellenistic kings often created ruler cults that linked the king's authority with that of the gods, or they adopted ruler cults that already existed, as Alexander did in Egypt. These deified kings were not considered gods as mighty as Zeus or Apollo, and the new ruler cults probably had little religious impact on the people being ruled. The kingdoms never won the deep emotional loyalty that Greeks had once felt for the polis,

Royal Couple Cameo This Hellenistic cameo, designed to be worn as a necklace, probably portrays King Ptolemy II and his sister Arsinoe II, rulers of the Ptolemaic kingdom of Egypt. During the Hellenistic period portraits of queens became more common because of the increased importance of hereditary monarchies. (Erich Lessing/Art Resource, NY)

but the ruler cult was an easily understandable symbol of unity within the kingdom.

Hellenistic kingship was hereditary, which gave women who were members of royal families more power than any woman had in democracies such as Athens, where citizenship was limited to men. Wives and mothers of kings had influence over their husbands and sons, and a few women ruled in their own right when there was no male heir.

Greece itself changed politically during the Hellenistic period. To enhance their joint security, many poleis organized themselves into leagues of city-states, of which the two most extensive were the Aetolian (ee-TOH-lee-uhn) League in western and central Greece and the Achaean (uh-KEE-uhn) League in southern Greece. Until the arrival of the Romans in the eastern Mediterranean in the second century B.C.E. (see Chapter 5), the Hellenistic monarchies and Greek leagues of city-states waged frequent wars with one another that brought no lasting results. In terms of political stability and peace, these forms of government were no improvement on the Greek polis.

Building a Hellenized Society

How did Greek ideas and traditions spread across the eastern Mediterranean and Near East?

Alexander's most important legacy was clearly not political unity. Instead it was the spread of Greek ideas and traditions across a wide area, a process scholars later called **Hellenization**. To maintain contact with the Greek world as he moved farther eastward, he founded new cities and military colonies and expanded existing cities, settling Greek and Macedonian troops and veterans in them. Besides keeping the road back to Greece open, these settlements helped secure the countryside around them. This practice continued after his death, with more than 250 new cities founded in North Africa, West and Central Asia, and southeastern Europe. These cities and colonies became powerful instruments in the spread of Hellenism and in the blending of Greek and other cultures.

Urban Life

In many respects the Hellenistic city resembled a modern city. It was a cultural center with theaters, temples, and libraries. It was a seat of learning, a home of poets, writers, teachers, and artists. It was a place where people could find amusement through plays, musical performances, animal fights, and gambling. The Hellenistic city was also an economic center that provided a ready market for grain and produce raised in the surrounding countryside. In short, the Hellenistic city offered cultural and economic opportunities for rich and poor alike.

To the Greeks, civilized life was unthinkable outside of a city, and Hellenistic kings often gave cities all the external trappings of a polis. Each had an assembly of citizens, a council to prepare legislation, and a board of magistrates to conduct political business. Yet, however similar to the Greek polis it appeared, such a city could not engage in diplomatic dealings, make treaties, pursue its own foreign policy, or wage its own wars. The city was required to follow royal orders, and the king often placed his own officials in it to see that his decrees were followed.

A Hellenistic city differed from a Greek polis in other ways as well. The Greek polis had one body of law and one set of customs. In the Hellenistic city Greeks represented an elite class. Natives and non-Greek foreigners who lived in Hellenistic cities usually possessed lesser rights than Greeks and often had their own laws. In some instances this disparity spurred natives to assimilate Greek culture in order to rise politically and socially.

The city of Pergamum in northwestern Anatolia is a good example of an older city that underwent changes in the Hellenistic period. Previously an important strategic site, Pergamum was transformed by its new Greek rulers into a magnificent city complete with all the typical buildings of the polis, including gymnasia, baths, and one of the finest libraries in the entire Hellenistic world. The new rulers erected temples to the traditional Greek deities, but they also built imposing temples to other gods. There was a Jewish population in the city, who may have established a synagogue. Especially in

The Great Altar of Pergamum　　A new Hellenistic city needed splendid art and architecture to prove its worth in Greek eyes. The king of Pergamum ordered the construction of this huge monumental altar, which is now in a museum in Berlin. The scenes depict the mythical victory of the Greek Olympian gods over the Titans, who included their parents but who also symbolized barbarism. The altar served the propaganda purpose of celebrating the victory of Greeks over those they saw as less civilized. (Bildarchiv Preussischer Kulturbesitz/Art Resource, NY)

the agora, Greeks and indigenous people met to conduct business and exchange goods and ideas. Greeks felt as though they were at home, and the evolving culture mixed Greek and local elements.

The Bactrian city of Ay Khanoum on the Oxus River, on the border of modern Afghanistan, is a good example of a brand-new city where cultures met. Bactria and Parthia had been part of the Seleucid kingdom, but in the third century B.C.E., their governors overthrew the Seleucids and established independent kingdoms in today's Afghanistan and Turkmenistan (Map 4.2). Bactria became an outpost of Hellenism, from which the rulers of China and India learned of sophisticated societies other than their own. It had Greek temples and administration buildings, and on a public square was a long inscription in Greek verse carved in stone, erected by a man who may have been a student of Aristotle and taken from a saying of the Oracle at Delphi:

> In childhood, learn good manners
> In youth, control your passions
> In middle age, practice justice
> In old age, be of good counsel
> In death, have no regrets.[1]

Along with this very public display of Greek ideals, the city also had temples to local deities and artwork that blended Greek and local styles.

Greeks in Hellenistic Cities

The ruling dynasties of the Hellenistic world were Macedonian, and Macedonians and Greeks filled all the important political, military, and diplomatic positions. Besides building Greek cities, Hellenistic kings offered Greeks land and money as lures to further immigration.

The Hellenistic monarchy, unlike the Greek polis, did not depend solely on its citizens to fulfill its political needs, but instead relied on professionals. Talented Greek men had the opportunity to rise quickly in the government bureaucracy. Appointed by the king, these administrators did not have to stand for election each year, unlike many officials of Greek poleis. Since they held their jobs year after year, they had ample time to create new administrative techniques, and also time to develop ways to profit personally from their positions.

Greeks also found ready employment in the armies and navies of the Hellenistic monarchies. Alexander had proved the Greco-Macedonian style of warfare to be far superior to that of other peoples, and Alexander's successors, themselves experienced officers, realized the importance of trained soldiers. Hellenistic kings were reluctant to arm the local populations or to allow them to serve in the army, fearing military rebellions among their conquered subjects. The result was the emergence of professional armies and navies consisting primarily of Greeks, although drawn from many areas of Greece and Macedonia, not simply from one polis. Unlike the citizen hoplites of classical Greece, these men were full-time soldiers. Hellenistic kings paid them well, often giving them land or leasing it to them as an incentive to remain loyal.

Greeks were able to dominate other professions as well. Hellenistic kingdoms and cities recruited Greek writers and artists to create Greek literature, art, and culture. Greek

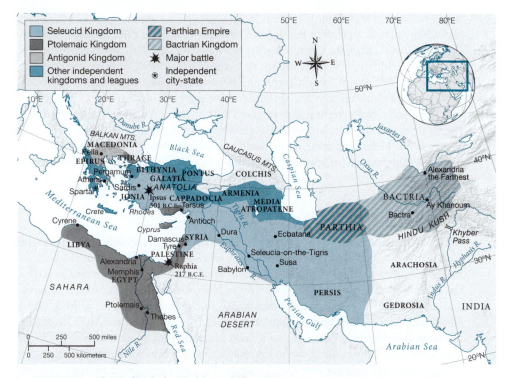

MAP 4.2 The Hellenistic World, ca. 263 B.C.E.
This map depicts the Hellenistic world after Alexander's death, when the areas he conquered had been divided into a number of kingdoms.

architects, engineers, and skilled craftsmen found themselves in great demand to produce the Greek-style buildings commissioned by the Hellenistic monarchs. Architects and engineers would sometimes design and build whole cities, which they laid out in check-erboard fashion and filled with typical Greek buildings. An enormous wave of construction took place during the Hellenistic period.

Increased physical and social mobility benefited some women as well as men. More women learned to read than before, and they engaged in occupations in which literacy was beneficial, including care of the sick. During the Hellenistic period women continued to be required to have male guardians to buy, sell, or lease land; to borrow money; and to represent them in other commercial transactions. (The requirement of a male guardian was later codified in Roman law and largely maintained in Europe into the nineteenth century.) Yet often such a guardian was present only to fulfill the letter of the law. The woman was the real agent and handled the business being transacted.

Because of the opportunities the Hellenistic monarchies offered, many people moved frequently. These were generally individual decisions, not part of organized colonization efforts such as those that had been common in Archaic Greece (see Chapter 3). Once a Greek man had left home to take service with, for instance, the army or the bureaucracy of the Ptolemies, he had no incentive beyond his pay and the comforts of life in Egypt to keep him there. If the Seleucid king offered him more money or a promotion, he might well accept it and take his talents to Asia Minor. Thus professional Greek soldiers and administrators were very mobile and were apt to look to their own interests, not their kingdom's. Linguistic changes further facilitated the ease with which people moved. Instead of the different dialects spoken in Greece itself, a new Greek dialect called the *koine* (koy-NAY), which means "common," became the spoken language of traders, the royal court, the bureaucracy, and the army across the Hellenistic world.

As long as Greeks continued to migrate, the kingdoms remained stable and strong. In the process they drew an immense amount of talent from the Greek peninsula. However, the Hellenistic monarchies could not keep recruiting Greeks forever, in spite of their wealth and willingness to spend lavishly. In time the huge surge of immigration slowed greatly.

Greeks and Non-Greeks

Across the Hellenistic world the prevailing institutions and laws became Greek. Everyone, Greek or non-Greek, who wanted to find an official position or compete in business had to learn Greek. Those who did gained an avenue of social mobility, and as early as the third century B.C.E. local people in some Hellenistic cities began to rise in power and prominence. They adopted a Greek name and, if they were male, went to Greek educational institutions or sent their sons there. Hoping to impress the Greek elite, priests in Babylon and Alexandria composed histories of their areas in Greek. Once a man knew Greek, he could move more easily to another area for better opportunities, and perhaps even hide his non-Greek origins. He could also join a military unit and perhaps be deployed far from his place of origin. Thus learning Greek was an avenue of geographic mobility as well.

Cities granted citizenship to Hellenized local people and sometimes to Greek-speaking migrants, although there were fewer political benefits of citizenship than there had been in the classical period, because real power was held by monarchs, not citizens. Even a few women received honorary citizenship in Hellenistic cities because of aid they had provided in times of crisis. Being Greek became to some degree a matter of culture, not bloodlines.

Cultural influences in the other direction occurred less frequently, because they brought fewer advantages. Few Greeks learned a non-Greek language, unless they were required to because of their official position. Greeks did begin to worship local deities, but often these were somewhat Hellenized and their qualities blended with those of an existing Greek god or goddess. Greeks living in Egypt generally cremated their dead while Egyptians continued to mummify them, although by the first century B.C.E. Greeks and Romans sometimes mummified their dead as well, attaching realistic portraits painted on wooden panels to the mummies that have served as important sources about clothing and hairstyles.

Yet the spread of Greek culture was wider than it was deep. Hellenistic kingdoms were never entirely unified in language, customs, and thought. The principal reason for this phenomenon is that Greek culture generally did not extend far beyond the reaches of the cities. Many urban residents adopted the aspects of Hellenism that they found useful, but people in the countryside generally did not embrace it, nor were they encouraged to.

Ptolemaic Egypt provides an excellent example of this situation. The indigenous people were the foundation of the kingdom: they fed it by their labor in the fields and financed its operations with their taxes. Because of this, the Ptolemies tied local people to the land more tightly than they had been before, making it nearly impossible for them to leave their villages. The Ptolemies maintained separate legal systems for Greeks and Egyptians. The bureaucracy of the Ptolemies was relatively efficient, and the indigenous population was viciously and cruelly exploited. Even in times of hardship, the king's taxes came first, although payment might mean starvation. The people's desperation was summed up by one Egyptian, who scrawled the warning, "We are worn out; we will run away."[2] To many Egyptians, revolt or a life of banditry was preferable to working the land under the harsh Ptolemies.

The situation was somewhat different in the booming city of Alexandria, founded by Alexander to be a new seaport, where there had been a small village earlier. Within a century of its founding, it was probably the largest city in the world, with a population numbering in the hundreds of thousands. The ruling elite was primarily Greek, and the Ptolemies tried to keep the Greek and Egyptian populations apart, but this was not always possible. Although the Ptolemies encouraged immigration from Greece, the number of immigrants was relatively low, so intermarriage increased. And the Ptolemies themselves gave privileges to local priests, building temples and sponsoring rituals honoring the local gods. Priestly families became owners of large landed estates and engaged in other sorts of business as well, becoming loyal supporters of the Ptolemaic regime. Even the processions honoring local gods still celebrated Greekness, however, and sometimes became a flash point sparking protests by Egyptians.

In about 280 B.C.E. the Ptolemies founded a library in Alexandria that both glorified Greek culture and sponsored new scholarship. It came to contain hundreds of thousands of papyrus scrolls of Greek writings, including copies of such classic works as the poems of Homer, the histories of Herodotus and Thucydides, and the philosophical works of Plato and Aristotle, as well as newer accounts of scientific discoveries. The Ptolemies sent representatives to Greece to buy books, paid for copies made of any Greek books that were brought to Alexandria, and supported scholars who edited multiple versions of older books into a single authoritative version. The library became one of the foremost intellectual centers of the ancient world, pulling in Greek-speaking writers, scholars, scientists, and thinkers from far away and preserving Greek writings.

Greek culture spread more deeply in the Seleucid kingdom than in Egypt, although this was not because the Seleucids had an organized plan for Hellenizing the local population. The primary problem for the Seleucids was holding on to the territory they had inherited. To do this, they established cities and military colonies throughout the region to nurture a vigorous and large Greek-speaking population and to defend the kingdom from their Persian neighbors. Seleucid military colonies were generally founded near existing villages, thus exposing even rural residents to all aspects of Greek life. Many local people found Greek political and cultural forms attractive and imitated them. In Asia Minor and Syria, for instance, numerous villages and towns developed along Greek lines, and some of them grew into Hellenized cities.

The kings of Bactria and Parthia spread Greek culture even further. Some of these rulers converted to Buddhism, and the Buddhist ruler of the Mauryan Empire in northern India, Asoka (ca. 269–233 B.C.E.), may have ordered translations of his laws into

Greek for the Greek-speaking residents of Bactria and Parthia. In the second century B.C.E., after the collapse of the Mauryan Empire, Bactrian armies conquered part of northern India, establishing several small Indo-Greek states where the mixing of religious and artistic traditions was particularly pronounced.

The Economy of the Hellenistic World

What new economic connections were created in the Hellenistic period?

Alexander's conquest of the Persian Empire not only changed the political face of the ancient world and led to a shared urban culture, but also brought the Near East and Egypt fully into the sphere of Greek economics. The Hellenistic period, however, did not see widespread improvements in the way people lived and worked. Cities flourished, but many people who lived in rural areas were actually worse off than they had been before, because of higher levels of rents and taxes. Alexander and his successors did link East and West in a broad commercial network, however. The spread of Greeks throughout the Near East and Egypt created new markets and stimulated trade.

Agriculture and Industry

Much of the revenue for the Hellenistic kingdoms was derived from agricultural products, rents paid by the tenants of royal land, and taxation of land. Trying to improve productivity, the rulers sponsored experiments on seed grain, selecting seeds that seemed the most hardy and productive. Egypt had a strong tradition of central authority dating back to the pharaohs, which the Ptolemies inherited and tightened. They had the power to mobilize local labor into the digging and maintenance of canals and ditches, and they even attempted to decree what crops Egyptian farmers would plant and what animals would be raised. Such centralized planning was difficult to enforce at the local level, however, especially because the officials appointed to do so switched positions frequently and concentrated most on extracting taxes. Thus despite royal interest in agriculture and a more studied approach to it in the Hellenistic period, there is no evidence that agricultural productivity increased or that practices changed. Technology was applied to military needs, but not to those of food production.

Diodorus Siculus, a Greek historian who apparently visited Ptolemaic Egypt around 60 B.C.E., was surprised that Egyptians could feed all their children instead of resorting to the selective exposure of infants practiced in Greece. He decided that this was because of their less formal child-rearing habits:

> They feed their children in a sort of happy-go-lucky fashion that in its inexpensiveness quite surpasses belief; for they serve them with stews made of any stuff that is ready to hand and cheap, and give them such stalks as the byblos plant [the reeds from which papyrus is made] as can be roasted in the coals and the roots and the stems of marsh plants, either raw or boiled or baked. And since most of the children are reared without shoes or clothing because of the mildness of the climate of the country, the entire expense incurred by the parents of a child until it comes to maturity is not more than twenty drachmas. These are the leading reasons why Egypt has such an extraordinarily large population.[3]

Egyptian parents would probably have given other reasons, such as rents and taxes, for why their children had simple food and no shoes.

As with agriculture, although demand for goods increased during the Hellenistic period, no new techniques of production appear to have developed. Manual labor, not machinery, continued to turn out the raw materials and manufactured goods the Hellenistic world used.

Diodorus gives a picture of this hard labor, commenting about life in the gold mines owned by the kings:

> At the end of Egypt is a region bearing many mines and abundant gold, which is extracted with great pain and expense. . . . For kings of Egypt condemn to the mines criminals and prisoners of war, those who were falsely accused and those who were put into jail because of royal anger, not only them but sometimes also all of their relatives. Rounding them up, they assign them to the gold mines, taking revenge on those who were condemned and through their labors gaining huge revenues. The condemned—and they are very many—all of them are put in chains; and they work persistently and continually, both by day and throughout the night, getting no rest and carefully cut off from escape. For the guards, who are barbarian soldiers and who speak a different language, stand watch over them so that no man can either by conversation or friendly contact corrupt any of them.[4]

Apart from gold and silver, which were used primarily for coins and jewelry, bronze continued to be used for shields. Iron was utilized for weapons and tools.

Pottery remained an important commodity, and most of it was produced locally. The coarse pottery used in the kitchen for plates and cups changed little. Fancier pots and bowls, decorated with a shiny black glaze, came into use during the Hellenistic period. This ware originated in Athens, but potters in other places began to imitate its style, heavily cutting into the Athenian market. In the second century B.C.E. a red-glazed ware, often called Samian, burst on the market and soon dominated it. Pottery was often decorated with patterns and scenes from mythology, legend, and daily life. Potters often portrayed heroic episodes, such as battles from the *Iliad*, or gods, such as Dionysus at sea. Pots journeyed with Greek merchants, armies, and travelers, so these images spread knowledge of Greek religion and stories west as far as Portugal and east as far as Southeast Asia. Pottery thus served as a means of cultural exchange—of ideas as well as goods—among people scattered across huge portions of the globe.

Commerce

Alexander's conquest of the Persian Empire had immediate effects on trade. In the conquered Persian capitals Alexander had found vast sums of gold, silver, and other treasure. This wealth financed the creation of new cities, the building of roads, and the development of harbors. It also provided the thousands who participated in his expeditions with booty, with which they could purchase commodities. Whole new fields lay open to Greek merchants, who eagerly took advantage of the new opportunities. Commerce itself was a leading area where Greeks and non-Greeks met on grounds of common interest.

Trade was facilitated by the coining of money. Most of the great monarchies coined their money according to a uniform system, which meant that much of the money used in Hellenistic kingdoms had the same value. Traders were less in need of money changers than in the days when each major power coined money on a different standard.

Overland trade was conducted by caravan, and the backbone of this caravan trade was the camel—a shaggy, ill-tempered, but durable animal ideally suited to the harsh climate of the caravan routes. Luxury goods that were light, rare, and expensive traveled over the caravan routes to Alexandria or to the harbors of Phoenicia and Syria, from which they were shipped to Greece, Italy, and Spain. In time these luxury items became more commonplace, in part as the result of an increased volume of trade. Due to the prosperity of the period, more people could afford to buy gold, silver, ivory, precious stones, spices, and a host of other easily transportable goods. Perhaps the most prominent good in terms of volume was silk, and the trade in silk later gave the major east-west route its name: the Great Silk Road. In return the Greeks and Macedonians sent east manufactured goods, especially metal weapons, cloth, wine, and olive oil. Although these caravan routes can trace their origins to earlier times, they became far more prominent in the Hellenistic period. Business customs and languages of trade developed and became standardized, so that merchants from different nationalities could communicate in a way understandable to all of them.

The durability and economic importance of the caravan routes are amply demonstrated by the fact that the death of Alexander, the ensuing wars of his successors, and later regional conflicts had little effect on trade. Numerous mercantile cities grew up along these routes, and commercial contacts brought people from far-flung regions together, even if sometimes indirectly. The merchants and the caravan cities were links in a chain that reached from the Mediterranean Sea to India and beyond to China, along which ideas as well as goods were passed.

More economically important than the trade in luxury goods were commercial dealings in essential commodities like raw materials and grain and such industrial products as pottery. The Hellenistic monarchies usually raised enough grain for their own needs as well as a surplus for export. This trade in grain was essential for the cities of Greece and the Aegean, many of which could not grow enough. Fortunately for them, abundant wheat supplies were available nearby in Egypt and in the area north of the Black Sea (see Map 4.2).

Most trade in bulk commodities was seaborne, and the Hellenistic merchant ship was the workhorse of the day. The merchant ship had a broad beam and relied on sails for propulsion. It was far more seaworthy than the contemporary warship, the trireme (see Chapter 3), which was long, narrow, and built for speed. A small crew of experienced sailors could handle the merchant vessel easily. Maritime trade provided opportunities for workers in other industries and trades: sailors, shipbuilders, dockworkers, accountants, teamsters, and pirates. Piracy was always a factor in the Hellenistic world, so ships' crews had to be ready to defend their cargoes as well as transport them.

Cities in Greece often paid for their grain by exporting olive oil and wine. When agriculture and oil production developed in Syria, Greek products began to encounter competition from the Seleucid monarchy. Later in the Hellenistic period, Greek oil and wine, shipped in mass-produced pottery jugs called amphoras, found a lucrative market in Italy and throughout the Mediterranean.

Another significant commodity was fish, which for export was salted, pickled, or dried. This trade was especially important because fish provided poor people with protein, an essential element of their diet. Salt, too, was often imported, and there was a very small trade in salted meat, which was a luxury item. Far more important was the trade in honey, dried fruit, nuts, and vegetables. Of raw materials, wood was high in demand, but little trade occurred in manufactured goods.

Slaves were a staple of Hellenistic trade, traveling in all directions on both land and sea routes. A few lists of slaves owned by a single individual have survived, and these indicate that slaves in one area often came from far away, and from many different regions. Ancient authors cautioned against having too many slaves from one area together, as this might encourage them to revolt. War provided prisoners for the slave market; to a lesser extent, so did kidnapping and capture by pirates, although the origins of most slaves are unknown. Both old Greek states and new Hellenistic kingdoms were ready slave markets, and throughout the Mediterranean world slaves were almost always in demand. Slaves were to be found in the cities and temples of the Hellenistic world; in the shops, fields, armies, and mines; and in the homes of wealthier people. Their price varied depending on their age, sex, health, and skill level, and also—as with any commodity—on market conditions. Large-scale warfare increased the number of slaves available, so the price went down; during periods of relative peace, fewer people were enslaved through conquest, so the price went up.

Religion and Philosophy in the Hellenistic World

How did religion and philosophy shape everyday life in the Hellenistic world?

The mixing of peoples in the Hellenistic era influenced religion and philosophy. The Hellenistic kings built temples to the old Olympian gods and promoted rituals and ceremonies like those in earlier Greek cities, but new deities also gained prominence. More people turned to mystery religions, which blended Greek and non-Greek elements. Others turned to practical philosophies that provided advice on how to live a good life.

Religion and Magic

When Hellenistic kings founded cities, they also built temples, staffed by priests and supported by taxes, for the Olympian gods of Greece. The transplanted religions, like those in Greece itself, sponsored literary, musical, and athletic contests, which were staged in beautiful surroundings among impressive new Greek-style buildings. These festivities offered bright and lively entertainment, both intellectual and physical. They fostered Greek culture and traditional sports and were attractive to socially aspiring individuals who adopted Greek culture.

Along with the traditional Olympian gods, Greeks and non-Greeks in the Hellenistic world also honored and worshipped deities that had not been important in the Hellenic period or that were a blend of imported Greek and indigenous gods and goddesses. Tyche (TIGH-kee), for example, was a new deity, the goddess and personification of luck, fate, chance, and fortune. Temples to her were built in major cities of the eastern Mediterranean, including Antioch and Alexandria, and her image was depicted on coins and bas-reliefs. Contemporaries commented that when no other cause could be found for an event, Tyche was responsible. Like the Olympians, she was unpredictable and sometimes malevolent.

Tyche could be blamed for bad things that happened, but Hellenistic people did not simply give in to fate. Instead they honored Tyche with public rituals and more-private ceremonies, and they also turned to professionals who offered spells for various purposes. We generally make a distinction between religion and magic, but for Greeks there was not a clear line. Thus these people would write spells using both ordinary Greek words and special "magical" language known only to the gods, often instructing those who purchased them to carry out specific actions to accompany their words. Thousands of such spells survive, many of which are curse tables, intended to bring bad luck to a political, business, or athletic rival; or binding spells, meant to force a person to do something against his or her will. These binding spells included hundreds intended to make another person love the petitioner. They often invoke a large number of deities to assist the petitioner, reflecting the mixture of gods that was common in Hellenistic society.

Hellenistic kings generally did not suppress indigenous religious practices. Some kings limited the power of existing priesthoods, but they also subsidized them with public money. Priests continued to carry out the rituals that they always had, perhaps now adding the name "Zeus" to that of the local deity or composing their hymns in Greek.

Some Hellenistic kings intentionally sponsored new deities that mixed Egyptian and Greek elements. When Ptolemy I Soter established the Ptolemaic dynasty in Egypt, he thought that a new god was needed who would appeal to both Greeks and Egyptians. Working together, an Egyptian priest and a Greek priest combined elements of the Egyptian god Osiris (god of the afterlife) with aspects of the Greek gods Zeus, Hades (god of the underworld), and Asclepius (god of medicine) to create a new god, Serapis. Like Osiris, Serapis came to be regarded as the judge of souls, who rewarded virtuous and righteous people with eternal life. Like Asclepius, he was also a god of healing. Ptolemy I's successors made Serapis the protector and patron of Alexandria and built a huge temple in the god's honor in the city. His worship spread as intentional government policy, and he was eventually adopted by Romans as well, who blended him with their own chief god, Jupiter.

Increasingly, many people were attracted to mystery religions, so called because at the center of each was an inexplicable event that brought union with a god and was not to be divulged to anyone not initiated into them. Early mystery religions in the Hellenic period, such as those of Eleusis, were linked to specific gods in particular places, which meant that people who wished to become members had to travel (see Chapter 3). But new mystery religions, like Hellenistic culture in general, were not tied to a particular place; instead they were spread throughout the Hellenistic world. People did not have to undertake long and expensive pilgrimages just to become members. In that sense the mystery religions came to the people, for temples of the new deities sprang up wherever Greeks lived.

Mystery religions incorporated aspects of both Greek and non-Greek religions and claimed to save their adherents from the worst that fate could do. Most taught that by the rites of initiation, in which the secrets of the religion were shared, devotees became united with a deity who had also died and risen from the dead. The sacrifice of the god and his victory over death saved the devotee from eternal death. Similarly, mystery religions demanded a period of preparation in which the converts strove to become pure and holy, that is, to live by the religion's precepts. Once aspirants had prepared

Isis and Horus   In this small statue from Egypt, the goddess Isis is shown suckling her son Horus. Worship of Isis spread throughout the Hellenistic world; her followers believed that Isis offered them life after death, just as she had brought Horus's father, Osiris, back to life. (Louvre, Paris, France/Peter Willi/The Bridgeman Art Library)

themselves, they went through the initiation, usually a ritual of great emotional intensity symbolizing the entry into a new life.

Among the mystery religions the Egyptian cult of Isis spread widely. In Egyptian mythology Isis brought her husband Osiris back to life (see Chapter 1), and during the Hellenistic era this power came to be understood by her followers as extending to them as well. She promised to save any mortal who came to her, and her priests asserted that she had bestowed on humanity the gift of civilization and founded law and literature. Isis was understood to be a devoted mother as well as a devoted wife, and she became the goddess of marriage, conception, and childbirth. She became the most important goddess of the Hellenistic world, where Serapis was often regarded as her consort instead of Osiris. Devotion to Isis, and to many other mystery religions, later spread to the Romans as well as to the Greeks and non-Greeks who lived in Hellenistic cities.

Hellenism and the Jews

Jews in Hellenistic cities were generally treated the same as any other non-Greek group. At first they were seen as resident aliens. As they grew more numerous, they received permission to form a political corporation, a *politeuma* (pah-lih-TOO-mah), which gave them a great deal of autonomy. The Jewish politeuma, like the rest of the Hellenistic city, was expected to obey the king's commands, but there was virtually no royal interference with the Jewish religion. The Seleucid king Antiochus III (ca. 242–187 B.C.E.), for instance, recognized that most Jews were loyal subjects, and in his efforts to solidify his empire he endorsed their religious customs and ensured their autonomy.

Antiochus IV Epiphanes (175–ca. 164 B.C.E.) broke with this pattern. He expanded the Seleucid kingdom and nearly conquered Egypt, but while he was there a revolt broke out in Judaea, led by Jews who opposed the Hellenized Jewish leader he had designated for them. Antiochus attacked Jerusalem, killing many, and restored his leader. According to Hebrew scripture, he then banned Jewish practices and worship, ordered copies of the Torah burned, and set up altars to the Greek gods in Jewish temples. This sparked a widespread Jewish revolt that began in 166 B.C.E., called the Revolt of the Maccabees after the name of one of its leaders. Using guerrilla tactics, the Maccabees fought Syrian troops who were fighting under Seleucid commanders, retook Jerusalem, and set up a semi-independent state in 164 B.C.E. This state lasted for about a century, until it was conquered by the Romans. (The rededication of the temple in Jerusalem after the Maccabee victory is celebrated in the Jewish holiday of Hanukkah.)

Jews living in Hellenistic cities often embraced many aspects of Hellenism. The Revolt of the Maccabees is seen by some historians, in fact, as primarily a dispute between Hellenized Jews and those who wanted to retain traditional practices. So many Jews learned Greek, especially in Alexandria, that the Hebrew Bible was translated into Greek and services in the synagogue there came to be conducted in Greek. Jews often took Greek names, used Greek political forms, adopted Greek practice by forming their own trade associations, and put inscriptions on graves as the Greeks did. Some Jews were given the right to become full citizens of Hellenistic cities, although relatively few appear to have exercised that right. Citizenship would have allowed them to vote in the assembly and serve as magistrates, but it would also have obliged them to worship the gods of the city—a practice few Jews chose to follow.

Philosophy and the People

Philosophy during the Hellenic period was the exclusive province of the wealthy and educated, for only they had leisure enough to pursue philosophical studies (see Chapter 3). During the Hellenistic period, however, although philosophy was still directed toward the educated elite, it came to touch the lives of more men and women than ever before. There were several reasons for this development. First, much of Hellenistic life, especially in the new cities of the East, seemed unstable and without venerable traditions. Greeks were far more mobile than they had ever been before, but their very mobility left them feeling uprooted. Second, traditional religions had declined and there was a growing belief that one could do relatively little to change one's fate. One could honor Tyche, the goddess of fortune, through rituals in the hope that she would be kind, but to protect against the worst that Tyche could do, many Greeks also looked to philosophy. Philosophers themselves became much more numerous, and several new schools of philosophical thought caught the minds and hearts of many contemporary Greeks and some non-Greeks.

One of these was **Epicureanism** (eh-pih-kyou-REE-uh-nih-zuhm), a practical philosophy of serenity in an often-tumultuous world. Epicurus (eh-pih-KYOUR-uhs) (340–270 B.C.E.) was influenced by the atomic theory developed by the Pre-Socratic philosopher Democritus (see Chapter 3). Like Democritus, he thought that the world was made up of small pieces of matter that move in space, which determine the events of the world. Although he did not deny the existence of the gods, Epicurus taught that they had no effect on human life. Epicurus used observation and logic to study the world, and also to examine the human condition. He decided that the principal goods of human life were contentment and pleasure, which he defined as the absence of pain, fear, and suffering. By encouraging the pursuit of pleasure, he was not advocating drunken revels or sexual excess, which he thought caused pain, but moderation in food, clothing, and shelter.

The writings of Epicurus survive only in fragments, but the third-century-C.E. biographer Diogenes Laertes quotes several of his letters. It is impossible to know if these are actual letters or not, but they express sentiments that fit with Epicurus's ideas, including these from a letter written at the end of his life, when he apparently suffered from kidney stones:

> I have written this letter to you on a happy day to me, which is also the last day of my life. For I have been attacked by a painful inability to urinate, and also dysentery, so violent that nothing can be added to the violence of my sufferings. But the cheerfulness of my mind, which comes from the recollection of all my philosophical contemplation, counterbalances all these afflictions. And I beg you to take care of the children of Metrodorus, in a manner worthy of the devotion shown by the young man to me, and to philosophy.[5]

Epicurus also taught that individuals could most easily attain peace and serenity by ignoring the outside world and looking into their personal feelings and reactions. This ideal was one to which anyone could aspire, no matter what their social standing. Epicurus is reported to have allowed slaves and even women to attend his school, a sharp contrast with the earlier philosopher Plato. Epicureanism taught its followers to ignore politics and issues, for politics led to tumult, which would disturb the soul. Although the Epicureans thought that the state originated through a social contract among individuals, they did not care about the political structure of the state. They were content to live under a democracy, oligarchy, monarchy, or any other form of government, and they never speculated about the ideal state.

Zeno (335–262 B.C.E.), a philosopher from Cyprus, advanced a different concept of human beings and the universe. Zeno first came to Athens to form his own school, the Stoa, named after the covered walkways where he preferred to teach, and his philosophy, **Stoicism** (STOH-uh-sih-zuhm), in turn, came to be named for his school. Zeno and his followers considered nature an expression of divine will; in their view people could be happy only when living in accordance with nature. They stressed the unity of humans and the universe, stating that all people were obliged to help one another.

Unlike the Epicureans, the Stoics taught that people should participate in politics and worldly affairs. Yet this idea never led to the belief that individuals should try to change the order of things. The Stoics used the image of an actor in a play: the Stoic plays an assigned part but never tries to change the play. Like the Epicureans, they were indifferent to specific political forms. They believed that people should do their duty to the state in which they found themselves. To the Stoics, the important question was not whether they achieved anything, but whether they lived virtuous lives. The patient self-control and fortitude that the Stoics advocated made this a popular philosophy among the Romans later, and gave rise to the modern adjective *stoic* to convey these virtues.

The Stoics' most significant practical achievement was the creation of the concept of **natural law**. They concluded that because all people were kindred, partook of divine reason, and were in harmony with the universe, one law governed them all. This law was a part of the natural order of life, not something created by individual states or rulers. Thus natural law was an abstract matter of ethics, and applicable everywhere, not something that applied to everyday political or social life.

Individualistic and individualized themes emerge in Hellenistic art and literature as well as in philosophy. Sculptors looked to the works of the classical period such as the reliefs and statuary on the Athenian Acropolis for their models in terms of composition, but then created works that show powerful emotions and straining muscles. In contrast to the classical preference for the perfect human form, the artists and the people who bought their works wanted art that showed real people, including those suffering from trauma, disease, and the physical problems that came with aging. Hellenistic art was more naturalistic than Hellenic art—portraying the poor, old, and ugly as well as the young and beautiful.

As had Athens in the classical period, Hellenistic cities offered theater performances to their residents, paid for by the government. People tended to prefer revivals of the tragedies of Aeschylus, Sophocles, and Euripides (see Chapter 3) over newly written tragic works, but in comedy they wanted new material. This was provided by Menander (ca. 342–291 B.C.E.), whose more than one hundred comedies poked fun at current philosophies and social trends, including love, luck, money, and marriage. Menander's comedies tended to be less political than those of Aristophanes, but they still commented on the ruler cults developed by Hellenistic kings, the dangers of the new professionalized mercenary armies to older values, and the conspicuous consumption of the newly rich.

Hellenistic Science and Medicine

How did science and medicine serve the needs of Hellenistic society?

In the scholarly realm, Hellenistic thinkers made advances in mathematics, astronomy, and mechanical design. Physicians used observation and dissection to better understand the way the human body works and to develop treatments for disease. Many of these developments occurred in Alexandria, where the Ptolemies did much to make the city an intellectual, cultural, and scientific center.

Science

The main advances in Hellenistic science came in astronomy, geography, and mechanics. The most notable of the Hellenistic astronomers was Aristarchus (a-ruh-STAHR-kuhs) of Samos (ca. 310–230 B.C.E.). Aristarchus concluded that the sun is far larger than the earth and that the stars are enormously distant from the earth. He argued against the common sense observation, which Aristotle had supported, that the earth was the center of the universe. Instead, Aristarchus developed the heliocentric theory—that the earth and planets revolve around the sun. His theory was discussed for several centuries, but was later forgotten when another astronomer working in Alexandria, Claudius Ptolemy (ca. 90–ca. 168 C.E.)—probably no relation to the ruling Ptolemies, as the name was a common one—returned to an earth-centered universe. Aristarchus's heliocentric theory was resurrected in the sixteenth century C.E. by the brilliant Polish astronomer Nicolaus Copernicus.

In geometry Hellenistic thinkers discovered little that was new, but Euclid (YOU-kluhd) (ca. 300 B.C.E.), a mathematician who lived in Alexandria, compiled a valuable textbook of existing knowledge. His *Elements of Geometry* rapidly became the standard introduction to geometry. Generations of students from the Hellenistic period to the twentieth century learned the essentials of geometry from it.

The greatest thinker of the Hellenistic period was Archimedes (ca. 287–212 B.C.E.), a native of Syracuse who was interested in nearly everything. A clever inventor, he devised new artillery for military purposes. In peacetime he perfected the water screw to draw water from a lower to a higher level. He also invented the compound pulley to lift heavy weights. His chief interest, however, lay in pure mathematics. He founded the science of hydrostatics (the study of fluids at rest) and discovered the principle that the volume of a solid floating in a liquid is equal to the volume of the liquid displaced by the solid. (See "Individuals in Society: Archimedes, Scientist and Inventor," page 118.)

Archimedes was willing to share his work with others, among them Eratosthenes (ehr-uh-TAHS-thuh-neez) (285–ca. 204 B.C.E.). Like Archimedes, he was a man of almost universal interests. From his native Cyrene in North Africa, Eratosthenes traveled to Athens, where he studied philosophy and mathematics. He refused to join any of the philosophical schools, for he was interested in too many things to follow any particular dogma. Around 245 B.C.E. King Ptolemy III invited Eratosthenes to Alexandria and made him the head of the library there. Eratosthenes continued his mathematical work and by letter struck up a friendship with Archimedes.

Eratosthenes used mathematics to further the geographical studies for which he is most famous. He concluded that the earth was a spherical globe and calculated the circumference of the earth geometrically, estimating it as about 24,675 miles. He was not wrong by much: the earth is actually 24,860 miles in circumference. He drew a map of the earth and discussed the shapes and sizes of land and ocean and the irregularities of the earth's surface. His idea that the earth was divided into large landmasses influenced other geographers and later shaped ordinary people's understanding of the world as well. Using geographical information gained by Alexander the Great's scientists, Eratosthenes declared that to get to India, a ship could sail around Africa or even sail directly westward, an idea that would not be tested until the end of the fifteenth century.

Other Greek geographers also turned their attention southward to Africa. During this period the people of the Mediterranean learned of the climate and customs of Ethiopia and gleaned some information about sub-Saharan Africa from Greek sailors and merchants who had traveled there. Geographers incorporated these travelers' reports into their more theoretical works.

As the new artillery devised by Archimedes indicates, Hellenistic science was used for purposes of war as well as peace. Theories of mechanics were used to build machines that revolutionized warfare. Fully realizing the practical possibilities of the first effective artillery in Western history, Philip of Macedonia had introduced the machines to the broader world in the middle of the fourth century B.C.E. The catapult became the first and most widely used artillery piece, shooting ever-larger projectiles. Generals soon realized that they could also hurl burning bundles over the walls to start fires in the city. As the Assyrians had earlier, engineers built siege towers, large wooden structures that served as artillery platforms, and put them on wheels so that soldiers could roll them up to a town's walls. Once there, archers stationed on top of the siege towers swept the enemy's ramparts with arrows, while other soldiers manning catapults added missile fire. As soon as the walls were cleared, soldiers from the siege towers swept over the enemy's ramparts and into the city. To augment the siege towers, generals added battering rams that consisted of long, stout shafts housed in reinforced shells. Inside the shell the crew pushed the ram up to the wall and then heaved the shaft against the wall. Rams proved even more effective than catapults in bringing down large portions of walls.

Diodorus provided a description of these machines in his discussion of Philip's attack on the city of Perinthos in 340 B.C.E.:

INDIVIDUALS IN SOCIETY • Archimedes, Scientist and Inventor

Archimedes (ca. 287–212 B.C.E.) was born in the Greek city of Syracuse in Sicily, an intellectual center where he pursued scientific interests. He was the most original thinker of his time and a practical inventor. In his book *On Plane Equilibriums* he dealt for the first time with the basic principles of mathematics, including the principle of the lever. He once said that if he were given a lever and a suitable place to stand, he could move the world. He also demonstrated how easily his compound pulley could move huge weights with little effort:

> A three-masted merchant ship of the royal fleet had been hauled on land by hard work and many hands. Archimedes put aboard her many men and the usual freight. He sat far away from her; and without haste, but gently working a compound pulley with his hand, he drew her towards him smoothly and without faltering, just as though she were running on the surface.*

He perfected what became known as the Archimedian screw, a pump to bring subterranean water up to irrigate fields, which he had observed in Egypt and which later came into wider use. He worked on issues involved with solid geometry, and in his treatise *On Floating Bodies* he founded the science of hydrostatics. He concluded that an object will float if it weighs less than the water it displaces, and that whenever a solid floats in a liquid, the volume of the solid equals the volume of the liquid displaced. The way he made his discovery has become famous:

> When he was devoting his attention to this problem, he happened to go to a public bath. When he climbed down into the bathtub there, he noticed that water in the tub equal to the bulk of his body flowed out. Thus, when he observed this method of solving the problem, he did not wait. Instead, moved with joy, he sprang out of the tub, and rushing home naked he kept indicating in a loud voice that he had indeed discovered what he was seeking. For while running he was shouting repeatedly in Greek, "Eureka, eureka" ("I have found it, I have found it").†

*Plutarch, *Life of Marcellus*.
†Vitruvius, *On Architecture*, 9 Preface, 10.

Philip launched a siege of Perinthos, advancing engines to the city and assaulting the walls in relays day after day. He built towers 120 feet tall that rose far above the towers of Perinthos. From their superior height he kept wearing down the besieged. He mined under the wall and also rocked it with battering-rams until he threw down a large section of it. The Perinthians fought stoutly and threw up a second wall. Philip rained down great destruction through his many and various arrow-shooting catapults. . . . Philip continually battered the walls with his rams and made breaches in them. With his arrow-firing catapults clearing the ramparts of defenders, he sent his soldiers in through the breaches in tight formation. He attacked with scaling-ladders the parts of the walls that had been cleared.[6]

War between Rome and Syracuse interrupted Archimedes's scientific life. In 213 B.C.E. during the Second Punic War, the Romans besieged the city. Hiero, its king and Archimedes's friend, asked the scientist for help in repulsing Roman attacks. Archimedes began to design and build remarkable devices that served as artillery. One weapon shot missiles to break up infantry attacks, and others threw huge masses of stones that fell on the enemy. For use against Roman warships, he is said to have designed a machine with beams from which large claws dropped onto the hulls of warships, hoisted them into the air, and dropped them back into the sea. Later Greek writers reported that he destroyed Roman ships with a series of polished mirrors that focused sunlight and caused the ships to catch fire. Modern experiments re-creating Archimedes's weapons have found that the claw might have been workable, but the mirrors probably were not, as they required a ship to remain stationary for the fire to ignite. It is not certain whether his war machines were actually effective, but later people recounted tales that the Romans became so fearful that whenever they saw a bit of rope or a stick of timber projecting over the wall, they shouted, "There it is—Archimedes is trying some engine on us," and fled. After many months the Roman siege was successful, however, and Archimedes was killed by a Roman soldier.

QUESTIONS FOR ANALYSIS

1. How did Archimedes combine theoretical mathematics and practical issues in his work?

2. What applications do you see in the world around you for the devices Archimedes improved or invented, such as the lever, the pulley, and artillery?

For the Perinthians this grim story had a happy ending when their allies arrived to lift the siege, but many cities were successfully besieged and conquered with the new machines. Over time, Hellenistic generals built larger, more complex, and more effective machines. The earliest catapults could shoot only large arrows and small stones. By the time Alexander the Great besieged Tyre in 332 B.C.E., his catapults could throw stones big enough to knock down city walls.

If these new engines made waging war more efficient, they also added to the misery of the people, as war often directly involved the populations of cities. As it had in Periclean Athens (see Chapter 3), war often contributed to the spread of disease, and battlefields gave surgeons and physicians plenty of opportunities to test their ideas about how the human body would best heal.

Physician with Young Patient   This plaster cast from about 350 B.C.E. shows a physician examining a child, while Asclepius, the god of healing, observes. Asclepius holds a staff with a snake coiled around it, which remains the symbol of medicine today. This cast was made through a process known as intaglio, in which the picture was carved onto a cylinder-shaped gemstone, then rolled across wet clay to produce the image. (Hulton Archive/Getty Images)

Medicine

Doctors as well as scientists combined observation with theory during the Hellenistic period. Herophilus, who lived in the first half of the third century B.C.E., worked at Alexandria and studied the writings attributed to Hippocrates (see Chapter 3). He accepted Hippocrates's theory of the four humors and approached the study of medicine in a systematic, scientific fashion: he dissected dead bodies and measured what he observed. He was the first to accurately describe the nervous system, and he differentiated between motor and sensory nerves. Herophilus also studied the brain, which he considered the center of intelligence, and discerned the cerebrum and cerebellum. His other work dealt with the liver, lungs, and uterus. His younger contemporary Erasistratus also conducted research on the brain and nervous system and improved on Herophilus's work. Erasistratus, too, followed in the tradition of Hippocrates and believed that the best way for the body to heal itself was through diet and air. To learn more about human anatomy, Herophilus and Erasistratus dissected corpses, and may even have dissected living criminals, provided for them by the Egyptian kings. They were probably the only scientists in antiquity to dissect human bodies, though animal dissection became very common in the Roman period.

Because Herophilus and Erasistratus followed the teachings of Hippocrates, later writers on medicine labeled them "Dogmatists" or the "Dogmatic school," from the Greek word *dogma*, or philosophical idea. Along with their hands-on study of the human body, the Dogmatists also speculated about the nature of disease and argued that there were sometimes hidden causes for illness. Opposing them was an "Empiric school" begun by a student of Herophilus, doctors who held observation and experiment to be the only way to advance medical knowledge and viewed the search for hidden causes as useless. Later Greek and Roman physicians sometimes identified themselves with one or the other of these ways of thinking, but the labels were also sometimes simply used as insults to dismiss the ideas of a rival.

Whether undertaken by Dogmatists or Empiricists, medical study did not lead to effective cures for the infectious diseases that were the leading cause of death for most people, however, and people used a variety of ways to attempt to combat illness. Medicines prescribed by physicians or prepared at home often included natural products blended with materials understood to work magically. One treatment for fever, for example, was the liver of a cat killed when the moon was waning and preserved in salt. People also invoked Asclepius, the god of medicine, in healing rituals, or focused on other deities who were understood to have power over specific illnesses. They paid specialists to devise spells that would cure them or prevent them from becoming ill in the first place (see page 112). Women in childbirth gathered their female friends and relatives around them, and in larger cities could also hire experienced midwives who knew how to decrease pain and assist in the birthing process if something went wrong. People in the Hellenistic world may have thought that fate determined what would happen, but they also actively sought to make their lives longer and healthier.

Notes

1. Ahmad Hasan Dani et al., *History of Civilizations of Central Asia* (Paris: UNESCO, 1992), p. 107.
2. Quoted in W. W. Tarn and G. T. Griffith, *Hellenistic Civilizations*, 3d ed. (Cleveland and New York: Meridian Books, 1961), p. 199.
3. All quotations from Diodorus are reprinted by permission of the publishers and the Trustees of the Loeb Classical Library from Diodorus of Sicily, *Biblioteca historica* 1.80–36, Loeb Classical Library Volume 279, with an English translation by C. H. Oldfather, pp. 275, 277. Cambridge, Mass.: Harvard University Press, Copyright © 1933 by the President and Fellows of Harvard College. Loeb Classical Library® is a registered trademark of the President and Fellows of Harvard College.
4. Ibid., 3.12.1–3.
5. Diogenes Laertius, *Lives of Eminent Philosophers* 10.22, trans. C. D. Yonge, at Attalus (http://www.attalus.org/old/diogenes10a.html#22).
6. Diodorus 3.12.2–3.

Chapter Review

MAKE IT STICK

LearningCurve
bedfordstmartins.com/mckaywestvalue

After reading the chapter, use LearningCurve to retain what you've read.

IDENTIFY KEY TERMS

Identify and explain the significance of each item below.

Hellenistic (p. 97)   Stoicism (p. 115)
Hellenization (p. 102)   natural law (p. 115)
Epicureanism (p. 114)

REVIEW THE MAIN IDEAS

Answer the focus questions from each section of the chapter.

* How and why did Alexander the Great create an empire, and what was its political legacy? (p. 97)
* How did Greek ideas and traditions spread across the eastern Mediterranean and Near East? (p. 102)
* What new economic connections were created in the Hellenistic period? (p. 108)
* How did religion and philosophy shape everyday life in the Hellenistic world? (p. 111)
* How did science and medicine serve the needs of Hellenistic society? (p. 116)

MAKE CONNECTIONS

Think about the larger developments and continuities within and across chapters.

1. How was Greek society in the Hellenistic era similar to that of the earlier Hellenic era examined in Chapter 3? How was it different? What would you judge to be more significant, the continuities or the changes?

2. Cities had existed in the Tigris and Euphrates Valleys and the Near East long before Alexander's conquests. What would residents of Sumer (Chapter 1), Babylon (Chapters 1 and 2), and Pergamum find unusual about one another's cities? What would seem familiar?

3. How would you compare religion in Egypt in the Old and New Kingdoms (Chapter 1) with religion in Hellenistic Egypt? What provides the best explanation for the differences you have identified?

ONLINE DOCUMENT ASSIGNMENT

Alexander the Great
What were the motives behind Alexander's conquests, and what were the consequences of Hellenization?

Keeping the question above in mind, go online and explore a variety of ancient perspectives on these questions. Then complete a writing assignment based on the evidence and details from this chapter.
bedfordstmartins.com/mckaywestvalue

CHRONOLOGY

ca. 342–291 B.C.E.	• Life of comedy writer Menander
340–270 B.C.E.	• Life of Epicurus, on whose ideas Epicureanism was based
335–262 B.C.E.	• Life of Zeno, on whose ideas Stoicism was based
334–324 B.C.E.	• Alexander the Great's military campaigns
ca. 330–200 B.C.E.	• Establishment of new Hellenistic cities
323 B.C.E.	• Alexander dies at age thirty-two
323–ca. 300 B.C.E.	• War of succession leads to the establishment of Antigonid, Ptolemaic, and Seleucid dynasties
ca. 287–212 B.C.E.	• Life of Archimedes
ca. 280 B.C.E.	• Founding of the library of Alexandria by the Ptolemies
168 B.C.E.	• Roman overthrow of the Antigonid dynasty
166–164 B.C.E.	• Revolt of the Maccabees in Judaea
30 B.C.E.	• Roman conquest of Egypt; end of the Ptolemaic dynasty

5

LearningCurve
bedfordstmartins.com/mckaywestvalue
After reading the chapter, use
LearningCurve to retain what
you've read.

The Rise of Rome

ca. 1000–27 B.C.E.

THE HELLENISTIC MONARCHIES THAT AROSE AFTER ALEXANDER'S
conquests extended eastward and southward from Greece. The Greek colonies that had been established in southern Italy were not part of these monarchies, but culturally they became part of the Hellenistic world. To the north of the Greek city-states in the Italian peninsula, other people built their own societies. Among these were the people who later became the Romans, who settled on hills along the Tiber River in central Italy. Beginning in the sixth century B.C.E., the Romans gradually took over more and more territory in Italy through conquest and annexation. At about the same time, a group of aristocrats revolted against the kings ruling Rome and established a republican government in which the main institution of power was a political assembly, the Senate. Under the direction of the Senate, the Romans continued their political and military expansion, first to all of Italy, then throughout the western Mediterranean basin, and then to areas in the east that had been part of Alexander's empire. As they did, they learned about and incorporated Greek art, literature, philosophy, and religion, but the wars of conquest also led to serious problems that the Senate proved unable to handle.

Roman history is generally divided into three periods: the monarchical period, traditionally dated from 753 B.C.E. to 509 B.C.E., in which the city of Rome was ruled by kings; the republic, traditionally dated from 509 B.C.E. to 27 B.C.E., in which it was ruled by the Senate and expanded its power first to all of Italy and then beyond; and the empire, from 27 B.C.E. to 476 C.E., in which the vast Roman territories were ruled by an emperor. This chapter covers the first two of these periods. The Roman Empire will be discussed in Chapters 6 and 7.

Rome's Rise to Power

How did the Romans become the dominant power in Italy?

The colonies established by Greek poleis (city-states) in the Hellenic era (see Chapter 3) included a number along the coast of southern Italy and Sicily, an area already populated by a variety of different groups that farmed, fished, and traded. So many Greek settlers came to this area and the Greek settlements there became so wealthy that it later became known as Magna Graecia—Greater Greece. Although Alexander the Great (see Chapter 4) created an empire that stretched from his homeland of Macedonia to India, his conquests did not reach as far as southern Italy and Sicily. Thus the Greek colonies there remained politically independent. They became part of the Hellenistic cultural world, however, and they transmitted much of that culture to people who lived farther north in the Italian peninsula. These included the Etruscans, who built the first cities north of Magna Graecia, and then the Romans, who eventually came to dominate the peninsula.

The Geography of Italy

The boot-shaped peninsula of Italy, with the island of Sicily at its toe, occupies the center of the Mediterranean basin (Map 5.1). To the south lies Africa; the distance between southwestern Sicily and the northern African coast is at one point only about a hundred miles. Italy and Sicily literally divide the Mediterranean into two basins and form the focal point between the two halves.

Like Greece and other Mediterranean lands, Italy enjoys a largely pleasant climate. The winters are rainy, but the summer months are dry. Because of the climate, the rivers of Italy usually carry little water during the summer, and some go entirely dry. Most of Italy's other rivers are unsuitable for regular large-scale shipping and never became major thoroughfares for commerce and communications. Yet the rivers nourished a bountiful agriculture that could produce enough crops for a growing population.

Geography encouraged Italy to look to the Mediterranean. In the north Italy is protected by the Alps, which form a natural barrier. The Alps retarded but did not prevent peoples from entering Italy by this route. From the north the Apennine Mountains run southward for the entire length of the Italian boot, cutting off access to the Adriatic Sea for those to their west. This barrier induced Italy to look west to Spain and Carthage rather than east to Greece, but it did not carve up the land in a way that would prevent the development of political unity.

In their southward course the Apennines leave two broad and fertile plains to their west: Latium and Campania. These plains attracted settlers and invaders from the time that peoples began to move into Italy. Among these peoples were those who would found Rome on the Tiber River in Latium.

This site enjoyed several advantages. The Tiber provided Rome with a constant source of water. Located at an easy crossing point on the Tiber, Rome thus stood astride the main avenue of communications between northern and southern Italy. Positioned amid seven hills, Rome was defensible and safe from the floods of the Tiber. It was also close to the sea through the port of Ostia. Thus Rome was in an excellent position to develop the resources of Latium and maintain contact with the rest of Italy.

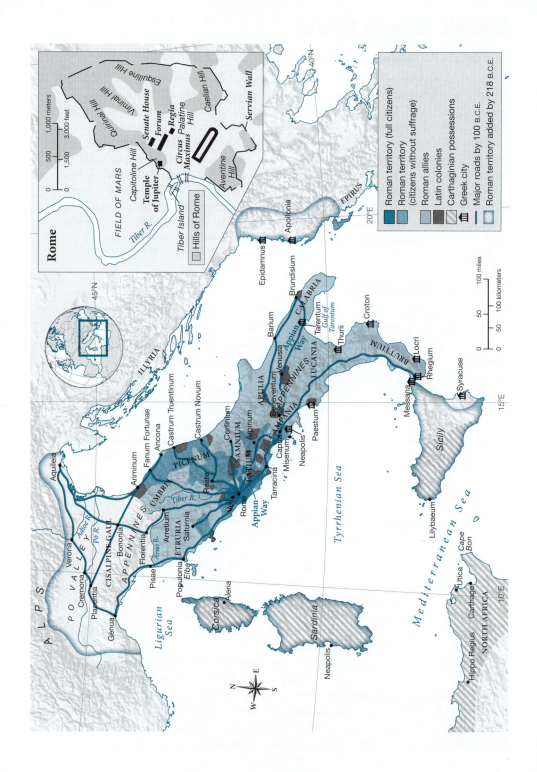

Rome

☐ Hills of Rome

Quirinal Hill
Viminal Hill
Esquiline Hill
Caelian Hill
Servian Wall
Senate House
Forum
Regia
Palatine Hill
Circus Maximus
Aventine Hill
Capitoline Hill
Temple of Jupiter
Tiber Island
FIELD OF MARS
Tiber R.

1,000 meters
500
0
3,000 feet
1,500
0

Legend:
- Roman territory (full citizens)
- Roman territory (citizens without suffrage)
- Roman allies
- Latin colonies
- Carthaginian possessions
- Greek city
- Major roads by 100 B.C.E.
- Roman territory added by 218 B.C.E.

ALPS
PO VALLEY
CISALPINE GAUL
Aquileia
Verona
Cremona
Placentia
Genua
Bononia
Florentia
Pisae
Populonia
Elba
Ariminum
Fanum Fortunae
Ancona
Castrum Truentinum
Castrum Novum
Corfinium
Reate
Veii
Rome
Saturnia
Arretium
PICENUM
UMBRIA
APENNINES
ETRURIA
LATIUM
SAMNIUM
Tiber R.
Appian Way
Tarracina
Aesernia
Capua
Misenum
Neapolis
Paestum
Beneventum
CAMPANIA
APULIA
Barium
Venusia
LUCANIA
Appian Way
APENNINES
Brundisium
CALABRIA
Tarentum
Gulf of Tarentum
Thurii
Croton
BRUTTIUM
Locri
Rhegium
Messana
Syracuse
Sicily
Lilybaeum
Mediterranean Sea
Tyrrhenian Sea
Ligurian Sea
Corsica
Aleria
Sardinia
Neapolis
Cape Bon
Utica
Carthage
Hippo Regius
NORTH AFRICA
ILLYRIA
EPIRUS
Apollonia
Epidamnus
Adige R.
Po R.
Arno R.

45°N
40°N
20°E
15°E
10°E

100 miles
100 kilometers
50
0

N E S W

◀ **MAP 5.1   Roman Italy and the City of Rome, ca. 218 B.C.E.**
As Rome expanded, it built roads linking major cities and offered various degrees of citizenship to the territories it conquered or with which it made alliances. The territories outlined in blue that are separate from the Italian peninsula were added by 218 B.C.E., largely as a result of the Punic Wars.

The Etruscans

The culture that is now called Etruscan developed in north-central Italy about 800 B.C.E. Recent studies of DNA evidence have indicated that the Etruscans most likely originated in Turkey or elsewhere in the Near East, although when they migrated to Italy is not clear. The Etruscans spoke a language that was very different from Greek and Latin, although they adopted the Greek alphabet to write it. We know they wrote letters, records, and literary works, but once the Romans conquered them, knowledge of how to read and write Etruscan died out. Also, the writings themselves largely disappeared because many were written on linen books that did not survive; what remain are inscriptions on stone or engravings in metal. Modern scholars have learned to read Etruscan to some degree, but most of what we know about their civilization comes from archaeological evidence and from the writings of other peoples who lived around them at the same time.

The Etruscans established permanent settlements that evolved into cities resembling the Greek city-states, and they thereby built a rich cultural life, full of art and music, that became the foundation of civilization in much of Italy. The Etruscans spread their influence over the surrounding countryside, which they farmed and mined for its rich mineral resources. They traded natural products, especially iron, with their Greek neighbors to the south and with other peoples throughout the Mediterranean, including the Phoenicians, in exchange for a variety of goods.

Etruscan cities appear to have been organized in leagues, and beginning about 750 B.C.E. the Etruscans expanded southward into central Italy through military actions on land and sea and through the establishment of colony cities. Written records of battles all come from the side of the Etruscans' opponents, but objects found in graves indicate that military values were important in their society, as wealthy men were buried with bronze armor and shields and iron weapons. In the process of expansion they encountered a small collection of villages subsequently called Rome.

The Founding of Rome

Archaeological evidence indicates that the ancestors of the Romans began to settle on the hills east of the Tiber during the early Iron Age, around 1000 to 800 B.C.E. Archaeological sources provide the most important information about this earliest period of Roman history, but later Romans told a number of stories about the founding of Rome. These mix legend and history, but they illustrate the traditional ethics, morals, and ideals of Rome.

The Romans' foundation myths were told in a number of different versions. In the most common of these, Romulus and Remus founded the city of Rome, an event later Roman authors dated precisely to 753 B.C.E. These twin brothers were the sons of the war god Mars, and their mother, Rhea Silvia, was a descendant of Aeneas, a brave and pious Trojan who left Troy after it was destroyed by the Greeks in the Trojan War (see

Chapter 3). The brothers, who were left to die by a jealous uncle, were raised by a female wolf. When they were grown they decided to build a city in the hills that became part of Rome, but they quarreled over which hill should be the site of the city. Romulus chose one hill and started to build a wall around it, and Remus chose another. After Remus jumped mockingly over Romulus's wall, Romulus killed him and named the city after himself. He also established a council of advisers later called the Senate, which means "council of old men."

Romulus and his mostly male followers expanded their power over the neighboring Sabine peoples, in part by abducting and marrying their women. The Sabine women then arranged a peace by throwing themselves between their brothers and their husbands, convincing them that killing kin would make the men cursed. The Romans, favored by the gods, continued their rise to power. Despite its tales of murder and kidnapping, this founding myth ascribes positive traits to the Romans: they are descended from gods and heroes, can thrive in wild and tough settings, will defend their boundaries at all costs, and mix with other peoples rather than simply conquering them. Also, the story portrays women who were ancestors of Rome as virtuous and brave.

Later Roman historians continued the story by describing a series of kings after Romulus—the traditional number is seven—each elected by the Senate. According to tradition, the last three kings were Etruscan, and another tale about female virtue was told to explain why the Etruscan kings were overthrown. In this story, of which there are several versions, the son of King Tarquin, the Etruscan king who ruled Rome, raped Lucretia, a virtuous Roman wife, in her own home. As related by the historian Livy (59 B.C.E.–17 C.E.) in his massive history of the Roman Republic, Lucretia summoned her husband and father to the house, told them what had happened, and demanded they seek vengeance:

> One after another they tried to comfort her. They told her she was helpless, and therefore innocent; that he alone was guilty. It was the mind, they said, that sinned, not the body: without intention there could never be guilt. "What is due to him," Lucretia said, "is for you to decide. As for me I am innocent of fault, but I will take my punishment. Never shall Lucretia provide a precedent for unchaste women to escape what they deserve." With these words she drew a knife from under her robe, drove it into her heart, and fell forward, dead.[1]

Her father and husband and the other Roman nobles, continued Livy, swore on the bloody knife to avenge Lucretia's death by throwing out the Etruscan kings, and they did. Whether any of this story was true can never be known, but Romans generally accepted it as history, and dated the expulsion of the Etruscan kings to 509 B.C.E. They thus saw this year as marking the end of the monarchical period and the dawn of the republic, which had come about because of a wronged woman and her demands.

Most historians today view the idea that Etruscan kings ruled the city of Rome as legendary, but they stress the influence of the Etruscans on Rome. The Etruscans transformed Rome from a relatively large town to a real city with walls, temples, a drainage system, and other urban structures. The Romans adopted the Etruscan alphabet, which the Etruscans themselves had adopted from the Greeks. Romans adopted the use of a bundle of rods tied together with an ax emerging from the center, which symbolized the Etruscan kings' power. This ceremonial object was called the fasces (FAS-eez), and was carried first by Etruscan officials and then by Romans. (In the twentieth century Mussolini would use the fasces as the symbol of his political party, the Fascists, and it is also used by many other governmental groups, including some in the United States.) Even the toga, the white woolen robe worn by citizens, came from the Etruscans, as did gladiatorial combat honoring the dead. In engineering and architecture the Romans adopted some design elements and the basic plan of their temples, along with paved roads, from the Etruscans.

In this early period the city of Rome does appear to have been ruled by kings, as were most territories in the ancient world. A hereditary aristocracy also developed — again, an almost universal phenomenon — which advised the kings and may have played a role in choosing them. And sometime in the sixth century B.C.E. a group of aristocrats revolted against these kings and established a government in which the main institution of power would be in the **Senate**, an assembly of aristocrats, rather than a single monarch. Executive power was in the hands of Senate leaders called **consuls**, but there were always two of them and they were elected for one-year terms only, not for life. Rome thereby became a republic, not a monarchy. Thus at the core of the myths was a bit of history.

Under kings and then the Senate, the villages along the Tiber gradually grew into a single city, whose residents enjoyed contacts with the larger Mediterranean world. Temples and public buildings began to grace Rome, and the Forum (see Map 5.1), a large plaza between two of Rome's hills, became a public meeting place similar to the Greek agora (see Chapter 3). The Capitoline Hill became the city's religious center when the temple of Jupiter Optimus Maximus (Jupiter the Best and Greatest) was built there. In addition, trade in metalwork became common, and wealthier Romans began to import fine Greek vases and other luxuries.

The Roman Conquest of Italy

In the years following the establishment of the republic, the Romans fought numerous wars with their neighbors on the Italian peninsula. The Roman army was made up primarily of citizens of Rome organized for military campaigns into legions; those who could afford it bought their own weapons and armor. War also involved diplomacy, at which the Romans became masters. At an early date they learned the value of alliances, which became a distinguishing feature of Roman expansion in Italy. Alliances with the towns around them in Latium provided a large population that could be tapped for military needs, organized into troops called auxiliaries who fought with the legions.

These wars of the early republic later became the source of legends that continued to express Roman values. One of these involved the aristocrat Cincinnatus, who had been expelled from the Senate and forced to pay a huge fine because of the actions of his son. As the story goes, in 458 B.C.E. he was plowing the fields of his small farm when the Senate asked him to return and assume the office of dictator. This position, which had been created very early in the republic, was one in which one man would be given ultimate powers for six months in order to handle a serious crisis such as an invasion or rebellion. (Like the word *tyrant* in ancient Greece, *dictator* did not have its current negative meaning in the early Roman Republic.) At this point the armies of the Aequi, a neighboring group, had surrounded Roman forces commanded by both consuls, and Rome was in imminent danger of catastrophe. Cincinnatus, wiping his sweat, listened to the appeal of his countrymen and led the Roman infantry in victory over the Aequi.

He then returned to his farm, becoming a legend among later Romans as a man of simplicity who put his civic duty to Rome before any consideration of personal interest or wealth, and who willingly gave up power for the greater good. The Roman Senate actually chose many more men as dictator in the centuries after Cincinnatus, and not until the first century B.C.E. would any try to abuse this position. No subsequent dictator achieved the legendary reputation of Cincinnatus, however. For George Washington and other leaders of the American War of Independence, he became the symbolic model of a leader who had performed selfless service but then stepped down from power. When in 1783 they decided to form a patriotic society, they named it after him: the Society of the Cincinnati (from which the Ohio city takes its name).

In 387 B.C.E. the Romans suffered a major setback when the Celts—or Gauls, as the Romans called them—invaded the Italian peninsula from the north, destroyed a Roman army, and sacked the city of Rome. (For more on the Gauls, see Chapter 7.) More intent on loot than on conquest, the Gauls agreed to abandon Rome in return for a thousand pounds of gold. As the story was later told, when the Gauls provided their own scale, the Romans howled in indignation. The Gallic chieftain Brennus then threw his sword on the scale, exclaiming "*Vae victis*" (woe to the conquered). These words, though legendary, were used by later Romans as an explanation for why they would not surrender, and the city of Rome was not sacked again until 410 C.E.

The Romans rebuilt their city and recouped their losses. They brought Latium and their Latin allies fully under their control and conquered Etruria (see Map 5.1). Starting in 343 B.C.E. they turned south and grappled with the Samnites in a series of bitter wars for the possession of Campania. The Samnites were a formidable enemy and inflicted serious losses on the Romans, and in response the Romans reorganized their army to create the mobile legion, a flexible unit of soldiers capable of fighting anywhere. The Romans won out in the end and continued their expansion southward.

In 280 B.C.E., alarmed by Roman expansion, the Greek city of Tarentum in southern Italy called for help from Pyrrhus (PIHR-uhs), king of Epirus in western Greece. A relative of Alexander the Great and an excellent general, Pyrrhus won two furious battles but suffered heavy casualties—thus the phrase "Pyrrhic victory" is still used today to describe a victory involving severe losses. According to the later historian Plutarch, Roman bravery and tenacity led Pyrrhus to comment: "If we win one more battle with the Romans, we'll be completely washed up."[2]

The Romans and the Carthaginians had made a series of treaties to help one another (see page 135), and the Carthaginians attacked Sicily, drawing the armies of Pyrrhus away from Italy for a while and relieving pressure on the Romans. The Romans threw new legions against Pyrrhus's army, which in the end left southern Italy. The Romans made formal alliances with many of the cities of Magna Graecia and then turned north again. Their superior military institutions, organization, and large supply of soldiers allowed them to conquer or take into their sphere of influence most of Italy by about 265 B.C.E.

As they expanded their territory, the Romans spread their religious traditions throughout Italy, blending them with local beliefs and practices. Religion for the Romans was largely a matter of honoring the state and the family. The main goal of religion was to secure the peace of the gods, what was termed *pax deorum*, and to harness divine power for public and private enterprises. Religious rituals were an important way of expressing common values, which for Romans meant those evident in their foundation

The Temple of Hercules Victor　This round temple, dating from the second century B.C.E., is the oldest surviving marble building in Rome and was imported from Greece. It once contained a statue of the mythical hero Hercules and was dedicated to him at this spot where legend told he killed a monster who had stolen some cattle. (© Justin Kase/Alamy)

myths: bravery, morality, seriousness, family, and home. The sacred fire at the shrine of the goddess Vesta in the city of Rome, for example, was attended by the vestal virgins, young women chosen from aristocratic families. Vesta was the goddess of hearth and home, whose protection was regarded as essential to Roman well-being. The vestal virgins were important figures at major public rituals, though at several times of military loss and political crisis they were also charged with negligence of duty or unchastity, another link between female honor and the Roman state. Along with the great gods, the Romans believed in spirits who inhabited fields, forests, crossroads, and even the home itself. These were to be honored with rituals and gifts so that they would remain favorable instead of becoming hostile.

Victorious generals made sure to honor the gods of people they had conquered and by doing so transformed them into gods they could also call on for assistance in their future campaigns. Greek deities and mythical heroes were absorbed into the Roman pantheon. Their names were changed to Roman names, so that Zeus (the king of the gods), for example, became Jupiter, and Herakles (the semidivine hero) became Hercules, but their personal qualities and powers were largely the same.

Once they had conquered an area, the Romans built roads, many of which continued to be used for centuries and can still be seen today. These roads provided an easy route for communication between the capital and outlying areas, allowed for the quick movement of armies, and offered an efficient means of trade. They were the tangible sinews of unity, and many were marvels of engineering, as were the stone bridges the Romans built over Italy's many rivers.

In politics the Romans shared full Roman citizenship with many of their oldest allies, particularly the inhabitants of the cities of Latium. In other instances they granted citizenship without the franchise, that is, without the right to vote or hold Roman office. These allies were subject to Roman taxes and calls for military service, but ran their own local affairs. The extension of Roman citizenship strengthened the state and increased its population and wealth, although limitations on this extension would eventually become a source of conflict (see page 150).

The Roman Republic

What were the key institutions of the Roman Republic?

Along with citizenship, the republican government was another important institution of Roman political life. Unlike the Greeks, the Romans rarely speculated on the ideal state or on political forms. Instead they created institutions, magistracies, and legal concepts to deal with practical problems and govern their ever-expanding state. These institutions were not static, but changed over time to allow a broader access to power and address new problems.

The Roman State

The Romans summed up their political existence in a single phrase: *senatus populusque Romanus*, "the Senate and the Roman people," which they abbreviated "SPQR." This sentiment reflects the republican ideal of shared government rather than power concentrated in a monarchy. It stands for the beliefs, customs, and laws of the republic—the unwritten constitution that evolved over two centuries to meet the demands of the governed. SPQR became a shorthand way of saying "Rome," just as U.S.A. says "the United States of America."

In the early republic social divisions determined the shape of politics. Political power was in the hands of a hereditary aristocracy—the **patricians**, whose privileged legal status was determined by their birth as members of certain families. Patrician men dominated the affairs of state, provided military leadership in time of war, and monopolized knowledge of law and legal procedure. The common people of Rome, the **plebeians** (plih-BEE-uhns), were free citizens with a voice in politics, but they had few of the patricians' political and social advantages. While some plebeian merchants increased their wealth in the course of Roman expansion and came to rival the patricians economically, most plebeians were poor artisans, small farmers, and landless urban dwellers.

The Romans created several assemblies through which men elected high officials and passed legislation. The earliest was the Centuriate Assembly, in which citizens were organized into groups called centuries, based loosely around their status in the military. Each citizen was assigned to a century depending on his status and amount of wealth, and the patricians possessed the majority of centuries. When an election was ordered, each century met separately and voted as a bloc, which meant that the patricians could easily outvote the plebeians. In 471 B.C.E. plebeian men won the right to meet in an assembly of their own, the *concilium plebis*, and to pass ordinances.

The highest officials of the republic were the two consuls, who were elected for one-year terms by the Centuriate Assembly. At a later time Romans believed that the consulship had initially been open only to patrician men, although surviving lists of consuls actually show that a few early consuls were plebeians. The consuls commanded the army in battle, administered state business, presided over the Senate and assemblies, and supervised financial affairs. In effect, they ran the state. The consuls appointed quaestors (KWEH-stuhrs) to assist them in their duties, and in 421 B.C.E. the quaestorship became an elective office open to plebeian men. The quaestors took charge of the public treasury and investigated crimes, reporting their findings to the consuls.

In 366 B.C.E. the Romans created a new office, that of praetor (PREE-tuhr). When the consuls were away from Rome, the praetors could act in their place; they could also command armies, be governors in the provinces, interpret law, and administer justice. Other officials included the powerful censors who had many responsibilities, the most important being supervision of public morals, the power to determine who lawfully could hold public office and sit in the Senate, the registration of citizens, the taking of a census, and the leasing of public contracts.

The most important institution of the republic was the Senate, a political assembly that by tradition was established by Romulus and in reality most likely originated in the monarchical period as a council of the heads of powerful families who advised the king. By the time written records begin for Roman history, the Senate was already in existence. During the republic the Senate grew to several hundred members, all of whom had previously been elected to one of the high positions, which automatically conferred Senate membership. Because the Senate sat year after year with the same members, while high officials changed annually, it provided stability and continuity. It passed formal decrees that were technically "advice" to the magistrates, who were not bound to obey them but usually did. It directed the magistrates on the conduct of war and had the power over the expenditure of public money. In times of emergency it could name a dictator. Technically the Senate could not pass binding legislation during the republican period. Its decisions had to be put to the Centuriate Assembly for a vote before they could become law, but patricians dominated both groups and generally agreed on legislative matters.

Within the city of Rome itself the Senate's powers were limited by laws and traditions, but as Rome expanded, the Senate had greater authority in the outlying territories. The Romans divided the lands that they conquered into provinces, and the Senate named the governors for these, most of whom were former consuls or praetors. Another responsibility of the Senate was to handle relations between Rome and other powers.

A lasting achievement of the Romans was their development of law. Roman civil law, the *ius civile*, consisted of statutes, customs, and forms of procedure that regulated the lives of citizens. As the Romans came into more frequent contact with foreigners, the consuls and praetors applied a broader *ius gentium*, the "law of the peoples," to such matters as peace treaties, the treatment of prisoners of war, and the exchange of diplomats. In the ius gentium all sides were to be treated the same regardless of their nationality. By the late republic Roman jurists had widened this principle still further into the concept of *ius naturale*, "natural law," based in part on Stoic beliefs (see Chapter 4). Natural law, according to these thinkers, is made up of rules that govern human behavior that come from applying reason rather than customs or traditions, and so apply to all societies. In reality, Roman officials generally interpreted the law to the advantage of Rome, of course, at least to the extent that the strength of Roman armies allowed them to enforce it. But Roman law came to be seen as one of the most important contributions Rome made to the development of Western civilization.

Social Conflict in Rome

Inequality between plebeians and patricians led to a conflict known as the **Struggle of the Orders**. In this conflict the plebeians sought to increase their power by taking advantage of the fact that Rome's survival depended on its army, which needed plebeians to fill the ranks of the infantry. According to tradition, in 494 B.C.E. the plebeians literally walked out of Rome and refused to serve in the army. Their general strike worked, and the patricians grudgingly made important concessions. They allowed the plebeians to elect their own officials, the **tribunes**, who presided over the concilium plebis, could bring plebeian grievances to the Senate for resolution, and could also veto the decisions of the consuls. Thus, as in Archaic age Greece (see Chapter 3), political rights were broadened because of military needs for foot soldiers.

The law itself was the plebeians' primary target. Only the patricians knew what the law was, and only they could argue cases in court. All too often they used the law for their own benefit. The plebeians wanted the law codified and published, but many patricians, including Cincinnatus and his son, vigorously opposed attempts by plebeians to gain legal rights. After much struggle, in 449 B.C.E. the patricians surrendered their legal monopoly and codified and published the Laws of the Twelve Tables, so called because they were inscribed on twelve bronze plaques. The Laws of the Twelve Tables covered many legal issues, including property ownership, guardianship, inheritance, procedure for trials, and punishments for various crimes. The penalty set for debt was strict:

> Unless they make a settlement [with their creditor], debtors shall be held in bonds for sixty days. During that time they shall be brought before the praetor's court in the meeting place on three successive market days, and the amount for which they are judged liable shall be announced; on the third market day they shall suffer capital punishment or be delivered for sale abroad, across the Tiber.[3]

Debtors no doubt made every effort to settle with their creditors. The patricians also made legal procedures public so that plebeians could argue cases in court. Later, in 445 B.C.E., the patricians passed a law, the *lex Canuleia*, that for the first time allowed patricians and plebeians to marry one another.

Licinius and Sextius were plebeian tribunes in the fourth century B.C.E. who mounted a sweeping assault on patrician privilege. Wealthy plebeians wanted the opportunity to provide political leadership for the state. After a ten-year battle the Licinian-Sextian laws passed in 367 B.C.E., giving wealthy plebeians access to all the offices of Rome, including the right to hold one of the two consulships. Once plebeians could hold the consulship, they could also sit in the Senate and advise on policy. They also gained such cosmetic privileges as wearing the purple-bordered toga, the symbol of aristocracy. Though decisive, this victory did not end the Struggle of the Orders. That happened only in 287 B.C.E. with the passage of the *lex Hortensia*, which gave the resolutions of the concilium plebis, the plebeian assembly, the force of law for patricians and plebeians alike.

The long Struggle of the Orders had resulted in an expansion of power to wealthy plebeians, but once certain plebeian families could hold the consulship and become members of the Senate, they became as guarded of their privileges and as uninterested in the problems of the average plebeian as the patricians had formerly been. Theoretically, all men could aspire to the highest political offices. In reality, political power had been expanded only slightly and still resided largely in a group of wealthy families, some of whom happened to be plebeian. Access to the highest political offices was still difficult for any plebeian, who often had to get the support of patrician families if he wanted a political career.

Networks of support were actually important for all Romans involved in public life, not simply aspiring plebeians. Roman politics operated primarily through a **patron-client system** whereby free men promised their votes to a more powerful man in exchange for his help in legal or other matters. The more powerful patron looked after his clients, and his clients' support helped the patron advance his career.

Roman Expansion

How did the Romans take control of the Mediterranean world?

As the republican government was developing, Roman territory continued to expand. Unlike Alexander the Great, the Romans did not map out grandiose strategies to conquer the world. Rather they responded to situations as they arose. This meant, however, that they sought to eliminate any state they saw as a military threat.

The Punic Wars

As they pushed southward, incorporating the southern Italian peninsula into their growing territory, the Romans confronted another great power in the western Mediterranean, the Carthaginians. The city of Carthage had been founded by Phoenicians as a trading colony in the eighth century B.C.E. (see Chapter 2). It commanded one of the best harbors on the northern African coast and was surrounded by fertile farmland. By the fourth century B.C.E. the Carthaginians began to expand their holdings, and they engaged in war with the Etruscans and with the Greek cities of southern Italy and Sicily. They had one of the largest navies in the Mediterranean and were wealthy enough to hire mercenaries to do much of their fighting. At the end of a long string of wars, the Carthaginians had created and defended a mercantile empire that stretched from western Sicily to the western end of the Mediterranean (see Map 5.1).

Beginning in the fifth century B.C.E. the Romans and the Carthaginians made a series of treaties with one another that defined their spheres of influence, and they worked together in the 270s B.C.E. to defeat Pyrrhus. But the Greek cities that became Roman allies in southern Italy and Sicily, including Syracuse, saw Carthage as a competitor in terms of trade. This competition led to the first of the three **Punic Wars** between Rome and Carthage. The First Punic War lasted for twenty-three years (264–241 B.C.E.). The Romans quickly learned that they could not hold Sicily unless they controlled the sea. Thus they hired Greeks from Syracuse to build and sail ships for them, engineering some of their vessels based on wrecked Carthaginian warships. The Romans adapted what they knew best, land warfare, to fighting at sea, rigging gangplanks to cross over to the Carthaginian ships and seize them. Of the seven major naval battles they fought with the Carthaginians, the Romans won six and finally wore their opponents down with superior resources and military might. In 241 B.C.E. the Romans took possession of Sicily, which became their first real province.

The peace treaty between Rome and Carthage brought no peace, as both powers had their sights set on dominating the western half of the Mediterranean. In 238 B.C.E.

Triumphal Column of Gaius Duilius   This is a replica of a monument celebrating Rome's first naval victory in the First Punic War in 260 B.C.E., a battle in which the admiral Gaius Duilius destroyed fifty Carthaginian ships. Models of the prows of the enemy ships are shown projecting from the column. The original was erected in the Roman Forum several centuries after the war to look back to earlier Roman glories, a common practice among Roman military and political leaders. (Museo della Civita Romana/Vanni/Art Resource, NY)

the Romans took advantage of Carthaginian weakness to seize Sardinia and Corsica. The Carthaginians responded by expanding their holdings in Spain, under the leadership of the commander Hamilcar Barca. With him he took his ten-year-old son, Hannibal, whom he had earlier led to an altar where he had made the boy swear to be an enemy to Rome forever. In the following years Hamilcar and his son-in-law Hasdrubal (HAHZ-droo-buhl) subjugated much of southern Spain and in the process rebuilt Carthaginian power. Rome first made a treaty with Hasdrubal setting the boundary between Carthaginian and Roman interests at the Ebro River, and then began to extend its own influence in Spain.

In 221 B.C.E. Hannibal became the Carthaginian commander in Spain and laid siege to Saguntum (suh-GUHN-tum), a Roman-allied city that lay within the sphere of Carthaginian interest and was making raids into Carthaginian territories. The Romans declared war, claiming that Carthage had attacked a friendly city. So began the Second Punic War, one of the most desperate wars ever fought by Rome. In 218 B.C.E. Hannibal marched an army of tens of thousands of troops—and, more famously, several dozen war elephants—from Spain across what is now France and over the Alps into Italy. Once there, he defeated one Roman army after another, and in 216 B.C.E. he won his greatest victory at the Battle of Cannae (KAH-nee). The exact number of Roman deaths is unknown, but ancient historians place it between fifty thousand and seventy thousand. Hannibal then spread devastation throughout the Italian peninsula, and a number of cities in central and southern Italy rebelled against Rome because it appeared to them that Hannibal would be victorious. Syracuse, Rome's ally during the First Punic War, also went over to the Carthaginians. Yet Hannibal was not able to win areas near Rome in central Italy, as Roman allies there, who had been extended citizenship rights, remained loyal. Hannibal's allies, who included Philip V, the Antigonid king of Macedonia (see Chapter 4), did not supply him with enough food and supplies to sustain his troops, and Rome fought back.

In 210 B.C.E. Rome found its answer to Hannibal in the young commander Scipio Africanus. Scipio copied Hannibal's methods of mobile warfare and using guerrilla tactics and made more extensive use of cavalry than had earlier Roman commanders. In the following years Scipio operated in Spain, which in 207 B.C.E. he wrested from the Carthaginians. That same year the Romans sealed Hannibal's fate in Italy. At the Battle of Metaurus the Romans destroyed a major Carthaginian army coming to rein-

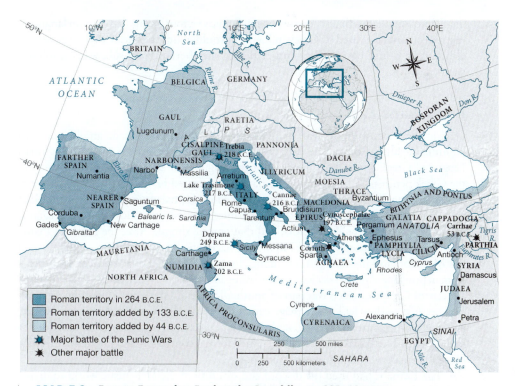

MAP 5.2 Roman Expansion During the Republic, ca. 282–44 B.C.E.
Rome expanded in all directions, first west and then east, eventually controlling every shore of the Mediterranean.

force Hannibal. Scipio then struck directly at Carthage itself, prompting the Carthaginians to recall Hannibal from Italy to defend their homeland.

In 202 B.C.E., at the town of Zama near Carthage (Map 5.2), Scipio defeated Hannibal in a decisive battle. The Carthaginians sued for peace and the Roman Senate agreed, on terms that were very favorable to the Romans. Hannibal himself later served as a military adviser at the Seleucid court in its battle with Rome, and then as an adviser to one of the small kingdoms in Anatolia.

The Second Punic War contained the seeds of still other wars. Unabated fear of Carthage combined with the encouragement of Cato the Elder (see page 144) led to the Third Punic War, a needless, unjust, and savage conflict that ended in 146 B.C.E. when Scipio Aemilianus, the grandson by adoption of Scipio Africanus, destroyed the hated rival and burned Carthage to the ground. Scipio's friend Polybius, a Greek historian and military leader, later reported that as the Roman conqueror watched the city burn, he said, "I fear and foresee that someday someone will give the same order about my fatherland."[4] It would, however, be centuries before an invader would stand before the gates of Rome.

During the war with Hannibal, the Romans had invaded the Iberian Peninsula, an area rich in material resources and the home of fierce warriors. They met with bloody and determined resistance. Not until 133 B.C.E., after years of brutal and ruthless warfare, did Scipio Aemilianus finally conquer Spain. Scipio's victory meant that Roman language, law, and culture, fertilized by Greek influences, would in time permeate this entire region, although it would be another century before the Iberian Peninsula was completely pacified.

Rome Turns East

During the Second Punic War, King Philip V of Macedonia made an alliance with Hannibal against Rome. The Romans, in turn, allied themselves with the Aetolian League of Greek city-states. The cities of the league bore the brunt of the fighting on the Greek peninsula until after the Romans had defeated Hannibal in 202 B.C.E. Then the Roman legions were deployed against Macedonian phalanxes, and the Macedonians were defeated in a series of wars. Roman armies also won significant victories against the forces of the Seleucid emperors, and that empire shrank. After the Battle of Pydna in 168, the Romans deported the important Macedonian leaders to Rome and reshaped the Macedonian kingdom to their liking. In 148 B.C.E. they made Macedonia into a Roman province. Another decisive victory came in 146 B.C.E., when the Romans attacked the city of Corinth, which was part of another league of Greek city-states, the Achaean League. Just as they had at Carthage earlier that year, the Romans destroyed the city, looting it for treasure. In 133 B.C.E. the king of Pergamum bequeathed his kingdom to the Romans. The Ptolemies of Egypt retained formal control of their kingdom, but they obeyed Roman wishes in terms of trade policy.

The Romans had used the discord and disunity of the Hellenistic world to divide and conquer it. Once they had done so, they faced the formidable challenge of governing it without further warfare, which they met by establishing the first Roman provinces in the East. Declaring the Mediterranean *mare nostrum*, "our sea," the Romans began to create political and administrative machinery to hold the Mediterranean together under a political system of provinces ruled by governors sent from Rome. Not all Romans were joyful over Rome's conquest of the Mediterranean world; some considered the victory a misfortune. The historian Sallust (86–34 B.C.E.), writing from hindsight, complained that the acquisition of an empire was the beginning of Rome's troubles:

> But when through labor and justice our Republic grew powerful, great kings defeated in war, fierce nations and mighty peoples subdued by force, when Carthage the rival of the Roman people was wiped out root and branch, all the seas and lands lay open, then fortune began to be harsh and to throw everything into confusion. The Romans had easily borne labor, danger, uncertainty, and hardship. To them leisure, riches — otherwise desirable — proved to be burdens and torments. So at first money, then desire for power grew great. These things were a sort of cause of all evils.[5]

Roman Society

How did expansion affect Roman society and culture?

Sallust was not alone in his feelings. By the second century B.C.E. the Romans ruled much of the Mediterranean world, and tremendous wealth poured into Rome. Roman institutions, social patterns, and ways of thinking changed to meet the new era. Some looked nostalgically back at what they fondly considered the good old days and idealized the traditional agrarian and family-centered way of life. Others embraced the new urban life and eagerly accepted Greek culture.

Roman Families

The core of traditional Roman society was the family, although the word "family" (*familia*) in ancient Rome actually meant all those under the authority of a male head of household, including nonrelated slaves and servants. In poor families this group might be very small, but among the wealthy it could include hundreds of slaves and servants.

The male head of household was called the **paterfamilias**. Just as slave owners held power over their slaves, fathers held great power over their children, which technically lasted for their children's whole lives. Initially this seems to have included power over life and death, but by the second century B.C.E. that had been limited by law and custom. Fathers continued to have the power to decide how family resources should be spent, however, and sons did not inherit until after their fathers had died.

In the early republic, legal authority over a woman generally passed from her father to her husband on marriage, but the Laws of the Twelve Tables allowed it to remain with her father even after a marriage. That was advantageous to the father, and could also be to the woman, for her father might be willing to take her side in a dispute with her husband, and she could return to her birth family if there was quarreling or abuse. By the late republic more and more marriages were of this type, and during the time of the empire (27 B.C.E. to 476 C.E.) almost all of them were.

In order to marry, both spouses had to be free Roman citizens. Most citizens did marry, with women of wealthy families marrying in their midteens and non-elite women in their late teens. Grooms were generally somewhat older than their brides. Marital agreements, especially among the well-to-do, were stipulated with contracts between the families involved. According to Roman law, marriage required a dowry, a payment of money, property, and/or goods that went from the bride's family to the groom. Roman law also prohibited marriages between slaves, between a slave and a free person, and initially between plebeians and patricians, although that changed in the fifth century B.C.E. (see page 134). If their owner allowed it, slaves could enter a marriage-like relationship called *contubernium*, which benefited their owner, as any children produced from it would be his. People who were not slaves or citizens certainly lived together in marriage-like relationships, but these had no standing before the law and their children could not legally inherit.

Weddings were central occasions in a family's life, with spouses chosen carefully by parents, other family members, or marriage brokers. Professional fortune-tellers were frequently consulted to determine whether a match was good or what day would be especially lucky or auspicious for a couple to marry. The ceremony typically began with the bride welcoming the groom and the wedding party to her home for a feast, and then later the whole group progressed with much noise to the groom's household. It would be very unlucky if the bride tripped while going into the house, so the groom often carried her across the doorstep. The bride's entrance into the groom's house marked the point at which the two were married. As elsewhere in the ancient world, no public officials or priests were involved.

Women could inherit and own property under Roman law, though they generally received a smaller portion of any family inheritance than their brothers did. A woman's

PRIMARY SOURCE   A Woman's Actions in the Turia Inscription

Because they were carved in stone, most funeral inscriptions from ancient Rome are very short. One of the few surviving long inscriptions about a woman is from a tombstone from the first century B.C.E. Neither she nor her husband—the speaker in the inscription—has been identified with certainty, though she is traditionally called "Turia," and he may have been a Roman official named Quintus Lucretius Vespillo. Both of them were caught up in the unrest of the civil wars of the late republic.

You became an orphan suddenly before the day of our wedding, when both your parents were murdered together in the solitude of the countryside. It was mainly due to your efforts that the death of your parents was not left unavenged. I had left for Macedonia, and your sister's husband Cluvius had gone to the Province of Africa.

So strenuously did you perform your filial duty by your persistent demands and your pursuit of justice that we could not have done more if we had been present. But these merits you have in common with that most virtuous lady your sister.

. . . Then pressure was brought to bear on you and your sister to accept the view that your father's will, by which you and I were heirs, had been invalidated by his having contracted a [fictitious purchase] with his wife. If that was the case, then you together with all your father's property would necessarily come under the guardianship of those who pursued the matter; your sister would be left without any share at all of that inheritance. . . .

You defended our common cause by asserting the truth, namely, that the will had not in fact been broken. . . .

They gave way before your firm resolution and did not pursue the matter any further. Thus you on your own brought to a successful conclusion the defence you took up of your duty to your father, your devotion to your sister, and your faithfulness towards me. . . .

inheritance usually came as her dowry on marriage. In the earliest Roman marriage laws, men could divorce their wives without any grounds while women could not divorce their husbands, but by the second century B.C.E. these laws had changed, and both men and women could initiate divorce. By then women had also gained greater control over their dowries and other family property, perhaps because Rome's military conquests meant that many husbands were away for long periods of time and women needed some say over family finances. (See "Primary Source: A Woman's Actions in the Turia Inscription," above.)

Although marriages were arranged by families primarily for the handing down of property to legitimate children, the Romans, somewhat contradictorily, viewed the model marriage as one in which husbands and wives were loyal to one another and shared interests and activities. The Romans praised women, like Lucretia of old, who were virtuous and loyal to their husbands and devoted to their children. Such praises emerge in literature, and also in epitaphs on tombstones, such as this one from around 130 B.C.E.:

You provided abundantly for my needs during my flight [into political exile] and gave me the means for a dignified manner of living, when you took all the gold and jewellery from your own body and sent it to me and over and over again enriched me in my absence with servants, money and provisions, showing great ingenuity in deceiving the guards posted by our adversaries.

You begged for my life when I was abroad—it was your courage that urged you to this step—and because of your entreaties I was shielded by the clemency of those against whom you marshalled your words. But whatever you said was always said with undaunted courage.

Meanwhile when a troop of men collected by Milo, whose house I had acquired by purchase when he was in exile, tried to profit by the opportunities provided by the civil war and break into our house to plunder, you beat them back successfully and were able to defend our home. . . .

EVALUATE THE EVIDENCE

1. What actions does the Roman woman in this tombstone inscription take to defend and support her family and husband?

2. How did the military campaigns and civil wars of the Roman Republic affect women's lives, and how did they shape what were regarded as admirable qualities in Roman women?

Source: Mary R. Lefkowitz and Maureen B. Fant, eds., *Women's Life in Greece and Rome: A Source Book in Translation*, Second Edition, pp. 135–137. Published by Johns Hopkins University Press, 1992, and Bristol Classical, an imprint of Bloomsbury Publishing, Plc. © 1982, 1992 M. B. Fant and M. R. Lefkowitz. Reprinted with permission of The Johns Hopkins University Press and Bloomsbury Publishing Plc.

Stranger, my message is short. Stand by and read it through. Here is the unlovely tomb of a lovely woman. Her parents called her Claudia by name. She loved her husband with all her heart. She bore two sons; of these she leaves one on earth; under the earth she has placed the other. She was charming in converse, yet gentle in bearing. She kept house, she made wool. That's my last word. Go your way.[6]

Traditionally minded Romans thought that mothers should nurse their own children and personally see to their welfare. Non-elite Roman women did nurse their own children, although wealthy women increasingly employed slaves as wet nurses and to help them raise the children. Very young children were under their mother's care, and most children learned the skills they needed from their own parents. For children from wealthier urban families, opportunities for formal education increased in the late republic. Boys and girls might be educated in their homes by tutors, who were often Greek slaves, and boys also might go to a school, paid for by their parents.

Roman School   In this carved stone relief from the second century C.E., a teacher makes a point to two older students who have scrolls in their hands, while a younger student enters. Roman methods of education developed in the late republic continued in the empire and spread to the provinces. This relief comes from Neumagen, a town in what is now Germany that was founded by the Romans. (Rheinisches Landesmuseum, Trier, Germany/Giraudon/The Bridgeman Art Library)

Most people in the expanding Roman Republic lived in the countryside. Farmers used oxen and donkeys to plow their fields, collecting the dung of the animals for fertilizer. Besides spreading manure, some farmers fertilized their fields by planting lupines and beans and plowing them under when they began to pod. Forage crops for animals to eat included clover, vetch, and alfalfa. Along with crops raised for local consumption and to pay their rents and taxes, many farmers raised crops to be sold. These included wheat, flax for making linen cloth, olives, and wine grapes.

Most Romans worked long days, and an influx of slaves from Rome's wars and conquests provided additional labor for the fields, mines, and cities. To the Romans, slavery was a misfortune that befell some people, but it did not entail any racial theories. Slave boys and girls were occasionally formally apprenticed in trades such as leatherworking, weaving, or metalworking. Well-educated slaves served as tutors or accountants, ran schools, and designed and made artwork and buildings. For loyal slaves the Romans always held out the possibility of freedom, and **manumission**, the freeing of individual slaves by their masters, was fairly common, especially for household slaves. Nonetheless, slaves rebelled from time to time, sometimes in large-scale revolts put down by Roman armies (see page 151).

Membership in a family did not end with death, as the spirits of the family's ancestors were understood to remain with the family. They and other gods regarded as protectors of the household—collectively these were called the *lares* and *penates*—were represented by small statues that stood in a special cupboard or a niche in the wall. The statues were taken out at meals and given small bits of food, or food was thrown into the household's hearth for them. The lares and penates represented the gods at family celebrations such as weddings, and families took the statues with them when they moved. They were honored in special rituals and ceremonies, although the later Roman poet Ovid (43 B.C.E.–17 C.E.) commented that these did not have to be elaborate:

The spirits of the dead ask for little.
They are more grateful for piety than for an expensive gift—
Not greedy are the gods who haunt the Styx [the river that bordered the
underworld] below.
A rooftile covered with a sacrificial crown,
Scattered kernels, a few grains of salt,
Bread dipped in wine, and loose violets—
These are enough.[7]

Greek Influence on Roman Culture

Many aspects of life did not change greatly during the Roman expansion. Most people continued to marry and form families, and to live in the countryside with the rhythm of their days and years determined by the needs of their crops. But with the conquest of the Mediterranean world, Rome became a great city, and many other cities emerged as well. The spoils of war went to build theaters, stadiums, and other places of amusement. Romans and Italian townspeople began to spend more of their time in leisure pursuits.

This new urban culture reflected Hellenistic influences. Romans developed a liking for Greek literature, and it became common for an educated Roman to speak both Latin and Greek. The poet Horace (64–8 B.C.E.) summed it up well: "Captive Greece captured her rough conqueror and introduced the arts into rustic Latium."[8]

The new Hellenism profoundly stimulated the growth and development of Roman art and literature. The Roman conquest of the Hellenistic East resulted in wholesale confiscation of Greek paintings and sculpture to grace Roman temples, public buildings, and private homes. Roman artists copied many aspects of Greek art, but used art, especially portraiture, to communicate Roman values. Portrait busts in stone were a favored art form. Those who commissioned them wanted to be portrayed as individuals, but also as representing certain admirable qualities, such as wisdom or dignity.

In literature the Greek influence was also strong. Roman authors sometimes wrote histories and poetry in Greek, or translated Greek classics into Latin. The poet Ennius (EHN-ee-uhs) (239–169 B.C.E.), the father of Latin poetry, studied Greek philosophy, wrote comedies in Latin, and adapted many of

African Acrobat   This marble statue, dating from the first century B.C.E. to the first century C.E., shows a young African acrobat balancing on the back of a crocodile. Conquest and prosperity brought entertainers of all sorts to Rome, as well as artwork depicting performers. (© The Trustees of the British Museum)

Euripides's tragedies for the Roman stage. Plautus (ca. 254–184 B.C.E.) brought a bawdy humor to his reworkings of Greek plays. The Roman dramatist Terence (ca. 195–159 B.C.E.), a follower of Scipio, wrote comedies of refinement and grace that owed their essentials to Greek models. All early Roman literature was derived from that of the Greeks, but it flourished because it also spoke to Roman ways of thinking.

The conquest of the Mediterranean world and the wealth it brought gave the Romans leisure, and Hellenism influenced how they spent their free time. Many rich urban dwellers changed their eating habits by consuming elaborate meals of exotic dishes. During the second century B.C.E. the Greek custom of bathing also gained popularity in the Roman world. In the early republic Romans had bathed infrequently, especially in the winter. Increasingly Romans built large public buildings containing pools and exercise rooms, and by the period of the early empire baths had become an essential part of any Roman city. Architects built intricate systems of aqueducts to supply the bathing establishments with water. The baths contained hot-air rooms to induce a good sweat and pools of hot and cold water to finish the actual bathing.

Conservative Romans railed against this Greek custom, calling it a waste of time and an encouragement to idleness and immorality. They were correct in that bathing establishments were more than just places to take a bath. They came to include gymnasia where men exercised and played ball, snack bars where people dined and chatted, and even libraries and lecture halls. Women also had opportunities to bathe, generally in separate facilities or at separate times.

The baths were socially important places where men and women went to see and be seen. Social climbers tried to talk to the right people and wangle invitations to dinner; politicians took advantage of the occasion to discuss the affairs of the day; marriages were negotiated by wealthy fathers. Baths were also places where people could buy sex, as the women and men who worked in bathhouses often made extra income through prostitution. Because of this, moralists portrayed them as dens of iniquity, but they were seen by most Romans as a normal part of urban life.

Opposing Views: Cato the Elder and Scipio Aemilianus

In addition to disagreeing over public baths, Romans differed greatly in their opinions about Hellenism and other new social customs. Two men, Marcus Cato (234–149 B.C.E.) and Scipio Aemilianus (185–129 B.C.E.), both of whom were military commanders and consuls, the highest office in the Roman Republic, can serve as representatives of these opposing views.

Marcus Cato, called Cato the Elder, was born a plebeian and owned a small rural estate, but his talent and energy caught the eye of high patrician officials and he became their client. He fought in the Second Punic War under Scipio Africanus and then returned to Rome, where he worked his way up through various offices. In 195 B.C.E. he was elected consul. A key issue facing Cato was the heated debate over the repeal of the Oppian Law, which had been passed twenty years earlier, right after Rome's disastrous loss to Carthage at the Battle of Cannae. Rome needed money to continue the war, and the law decreed that no woman was to own more than a small amount of gold, or wear clothing trimmed in purple, or drive a chariot in the city of Rome itself. These were all proclaimed to be luxuries that wasted money and undermined the war effort. The law was passed in part for financial reasons, but also had gendered social implications, as there was no corresponding law limiting men's conspicuous consumption. By 195 B.C.E. the war was over and this restriction on women's spending had lost its economic rationale. Roman women publicly protested against it, and Cato led the battle to prevent its repeal. He declared that women were like animals and would engage in an orgy of shopping if the law were lifted, and that Roman society would be destroyed by women's spending. The women's actions were more effective than Cato's speeches, however, and the law was lifted, although later in his political career Cato pushed for other laws forbidding women from wearing fancy clothing or owning property.

Women's spending was not the only problem destroying Roman society, according to Cato. Although he made certain his older son learned Greek as an essential tool in Roman society, he instructed the boy not to take Greek ideas too seriously and viewed the influx of Greek culture in general as dangerous. Cato set himself up as the defender of what he saw as traditional Roman values: discipline, order, morality, frugality, and an agrarian way of life. He even criticized his superior Scipio Africanus for being too lenient toward his troops and spending too much money. Cato proclaimed his views in speeches at the Senate, through his decisions when acting as a military commander, and also in his written works, which were all in Latin. His only work to survive in its entirety is a manual for running large agricultural estates written for the absentee landowners who were becoming more common. In this he advises the adoption of any measures that would increase efficiency and profitability, including selling off old or sickly slaves as soon as possible.

Cato held the office of censor, and he attempted to remove from the lists of possible officeholders anyone who did not live up to his standards. Late in life he was a diplomat to Carthage, and after seeing that the city had recovered economically from the war with Rome, he came home declaring, "Carthage must be destroyed." He repeated this often enough that shortly after his death the Romans decided to do just this in the Third Punic War.

Ironically, the mission to Carthage was led by Scipio Aemilianus, the grandson of Scipio Africanus and an avid devotee of Hellenism. Like his grandfather, Scipio believed that broader views had to replace the old Roman narrowness. Rome was no longer a small city on the Tiber; it was the capital of the world, and Romans had to adapt themselves to that fact. Scipio became an innovator in both politics and culture. He developed a more personal style of politics that looked unflinchingly at the broader problems that the success of Rome brought to its people. He embraced Hellenism wholeheartedly. Perhaps more than anyone else of his day, Scipio represented the new Roman—imperial, cultured, and independent.

In his education and interests, too, Scipio broke with the past. As a boy he had received the traditional Roman training, learning to read and write Latin and becoming acquainted with the law. He mastered the fundamentals of rhetoric and learned how to throw the javelin, fight in armor, and ride a horse. But as a young man he formed a lasting friendship with the historian Polybius, who after being brought to Rome as a war hostage was his tutor. Polybius actively encouraged him in his study of Greek and in his intellectual pursuits. In later life Scipio's love of Greek learning, rhetoric, and philosophy became legendary. Scipio also promoted the spread of Hellenism in Roman society, and his views became more widespread than those of Cato. In general, Rome absorbed and added what it found useful from Hellenism, just as earlier it had absorbed aspects of Etruscan culture.

The Late Republic

What led to the fall of the Roman Republic?

The wars of conquest created serious problems for the Romans. The republican constitution had suited the needs of a simple city-state but was inadequate to meet the requirements of Rome's new position in international affairs. New armies had to be provided for defense, and systems of administration and tax collection had to be created to support the republic. Moreover, the people of the Roman Republic came away from the war with differing needs and expectations. Roman generals, who had commanded huge numbers of troops for long periods of time, acquired great power and ambition and were becoming too mighty for the state to control. At the same time, non-Roman inhabitants of Italy who had fought in the wars of expansion began to agitate for full Roman citizenship, including the right to vote. Some individuals, including military contractors, profited greatly from the foreign wars, while average soldiers gained little.

These problems, complex and explosive, largely account for the turmoil of the late republic (133–27 B.C.E.). This era produced some of Rome's most famous figures: the Gracchi brothers, Marius, Sulla, Cicero, Crassus, Pompey, and Julius Caesar, among others.

Reforms for Poor and Landless Citizens

Hannibal's operations and the warfare in Italy had left the countryside a shambles. The prolonged fighting had also drawn untold numbers of Roman and Italian men away from their farms for long periods. Women often ran the farms in their absence, but with so many men away fighting they did not have enough workers to keep the land under full cultivation. When the legionaries returned to their farms in Italy, they encountered an appalling situation. All too often their farms looked like those they had destroyed in their wars of conquest: land was untilled, buildings were falling down, and animals were wandering.

The wars of conquest had also made some men astoundingly rich, and the newly wealthy invested their money in land. Land won by conquest was generally declared public land, and although officially there was a limit on how much public land one

Coin Showing a Voter This coin from 63 B.C.E. shows a citizen wearing a toga dropping a voting tablet into a voting urn, the Roman equivalent of today's ballot box. The tablet has a *V* on it, meaning a yes vote, and the coin has an inscription giving the name of the moneyer, the official who controlled the production of coins and decided what would be shown on them. Here the moneyer, Lucius Cassius Longinus, depicted a vote held fifty years earlier regarding whether an ancestor of his should be named prosecutor in a trial charging three vestal virgins with unchastity. As was common among moneyers, Longinus chose this image as a means to advance his political career, in this case by suggesting his family's long history of public office. (Snark/Art Resource, NY)

individual could hold, this law was often ignored. Wealthy people rented public land—though rents were frequently not collected—and bought up small farms, often at very low prices, to create huge estates, which the Romans called **latifundia** (lah-tuh-FUHN-dee-uh). The owners of the latifundia occasionally hired free men as day laborers, but they preferred to use slaves, who could not strike or be drafted into the army. Using slave labor, and farming on a large scale, owners of latifundia could raise crops at a lower cost than could small farmers.

Confronted by these conditions, veterans and their families took what they could get for their broken and bankrupt farms and tried their luck elsewhere. Sometimes large landowners simply appropriated public land and the small farms of former soldiers, and there was little that veterans could do about it. Gradually agriculture in Italy was transformed from subsistence farming to an important source of income for the Roman ruling class.

Most veterans migrated to the cities, especially to Rome. Although some found work, most did not. Industry and small manufacturing were generally in the hands of slaves, and even when work was available, slave labor kept the wages of free men low. Instead of a new start, veterans and their families encountered slum-like living conditions and continued dependency on others. If they were Roman citizens, they could vote in citizen's assemblies, however, and tended to back anyone who offered them better prospects.

Growing numbers of landless citizens held ominous consequences for the strength of Rome's armies. The Romans had always believed that only landowners should serve in the army, for only they had something to fight for. Landless men, even if they were Romans and lived in Rome, could not be conscripted into the army. These landless men may have been veterans of major battles and numerous campaigns, but once they lost their land, they became ineligible for further military service. The landless ex-legionaries wanted to be able to serve in the army again, and they were willing to support any leader who would allow them to.

One man who recognized the plight of Rome's peasant farmers and urban poor was an aristocrat, Tiberius Gracchus (tigh-BEER-ee-uhs GRAK-uhs) (163–133 B.C.E.). Appalled by what he saw, Tiberius warned his countrymen of the legionaries' plight:

> The wild beasts that roam over Italy have every one of them a cave or lair to lurk in. But the men who fight and die for Italy enjoy the common air and light, indeed, but nothing else. Houseless and homeless they wander about with their wives and children. And it is with lying lips that their generals exhort the soldiers in their battles to defend sepulchres and shrines from the enemy, for not a man of them has an hereditary altar, not one of all these many Romans an ancestral tomb, but they fight and die to support others in luxury, and though they are styled masters of the world, they have not a single clod of earth that is their own.[9]

After his election as tribune in 133 B.C.E., Tiberius proposed that Rome return to limiting the amount of public land one individual could farm and distribute the rest of the land to the poor in small lots. Although his reform enjoyed the support of some distinguished and popular members of the Senate, it angered those who had usurped large tracts of public land for their own use. They had no desire to give any of it back, so they bitterly resisted Tiberius's efforts. This was to be expected, yet he unquestionably made additional problems for himself. He introduced his land bill in the concilium

PRIMARY SOURCE   Plutarch on the Reforms of Gaius Gracchus

Plutarch (ca. 46–120 C.E.) was a Greek historian and biographer who became a Roman citizen. His most famous work was Parallel Lives, *a series of paired biographies of Greeks and Romans, designed to show the ways in which their characters influenced their lives. He drew information from the works of earlier historians—many of which are now lost—though he also altered biographical details in order to make his point. This is part of his portrait of tribune Gaius Gracchus, many of whose reforms Plutarch generally admired.*

Of the laws which he introduced to win the favor of the people and undermine the power of the Senate, the first concerned the public lands, which were to be divided among the poor citizens; another concerned the soldiers, who were to be clothed at public expense without any deductions from their pay, and no one was to be conscripted into the army who was under seventeen years old; another gave Italians the same voting rights as the citizens of Rome; a fourth related to the supply of grain and the lowering of its price to the poor; and a fifth regulated the courts of justice. This last law greatly reduced the power of the senators. Hitherto they alone sat as judges and were therefore much feared by the common people and the equestrian order [wealthy commoners]. Gaius added three hundred citizens of equestrian rank to the senators, who also numbered three hundred, and entrusted the judicial authority to the whole six hundred. . . .

After Gaius' return to Rome [from Carthage, where he supervised the founding of a colony], he gave up his house on the Palatine hill and went to live near the forum, which he thought more democratic since most of the poor and humble citizens lived there. He then announced the rest of his laws, intending to have them ratified by popular vote. A vast number of people gathered from all parts, but the

plebis without officially consulting the Senate. When King Attalus III of Pergamum died and left his wealth and kingdom to the Romans in his will, Tiberius had the money appropriated to finance his reforms—another slap at the Senate, which was responsible for managing the finances of the provinces. As tribune he acted totally within his rights, yet the way in which he proceeded was unprecedented.

Many powerful Romans became suspicious of Tiberius's growing influence with the people. Some considered him a tyrant, a concept that came from the Greeks for someone who gained power outside the normal structures and against the traditional ruling class. When he sought to be re-elected as tribune, riots erupted among his opponents and supporters, and a group of senators beat Tiberius to death in cold blood. Thus some of the very people who directed the affairs of state and administered the law had taken the law into their own hands. The death of Tiberius was the beginning of an era of political violence.

Although Tiberius was dead, his land bill became law. Furthermore, Tiberius's brother Gaius Gracchus (153–121 B.C.E.) took up the cause of reform. Gaius (GAY-uhs) was a veteran soldier with an enviable record, and when he became tribune he demanded even more extensive reform than had his brother. To help the urban poor, Gaius pushed

Senate persuaded the consul Fannius to order out of the city all who were not Romans. Accordingly a new and unusual proclamation was made, prohibiting any of the allies and friends of Rome to appear in the city during that time. Gaius published a counter-edict, denouncing the consul and promising the allies his support if they remained in Rome. . . . He had also, for the following reason, incurred the anger of his fellow tribunes. An exhibition of gladiators was to be held for the people in the forum, and most of the magistrates had erected seats round about with the intention of renting them. Gaius ordered them to dismantle the seats so the poor might see the show without cost. When no one obeyed this order, he collected a group of city employees and removed the seats the night before the spectacle. By the next morning the forum was clear, and in accomplishing this the common people thought he had acted the part of a man. But he had annoyed his colleagues, who regarded him as audacious and violent.

EVALUATE THE EVIDENCE

1. According to Plutarch, which of Gaius Gracchus's reforms made him especially popular with the people of Rome and its allies? Which ones made him especially unpopular with the Senate?

2. How did Gracchus's new laws address the social, economic, and political problems of second-century-B.C.E. Rome?

Source: Plutarch, *Parallel Lives*, "Gaius Gracchus," based on the translation by John Dryden and revised by Arthur H. Clough, in Nels M. Bailkey, *Readings in Ancient History: Thought and Experience from Gilgamesh to St. Augustine*, 3d ed. (Lexington, Mass.: D. C. Heath, 1987), pp. 302, 304–305.

legislation to provide them with cheap grain for bread. He defended his brother's land law and proposed that Rome send many of its poor and propertyless people out to form colonies, including one on the site where Carthage had once stood. The prospect of new homes, land, and a fresh start gave the urban poor new hope and made Gaius popular among them. (See "Primary Source: Plutarch on the Reforms of Gaius Gracchus," above.)

Like his brother Tiberius, Gaius aroused a great deal of personal and factional opposition. When Gaius failed in 121 B.C.E. to win the tribunate for the third time, he feared for his life. In desperation he armed his staunchest supporters, whereupon the Senate ordered the consul to restore order. Gaius was killed, and many of his supporters died in the turmoil.

Political Violence

The death of Gaius brought little peace, and trouble came from two sources: the outbreak of new wars in the Mediterranean basin and further political unrest in Rome. In 112 B.C.E. Rome declared war against the rebellious Jugurtha (joo-GUHR-thuh), king of Numidia in North Africa. Numidia had been one of Rome's client kingdoms, a kingdom still ruled by its own king but subject to Rome. Client kingdoms followed Rome's lead in foreign affairs but conducted their own internal business according to their own laws and customs. The benefits of these relationships were mutual, for the client kingdoms enjoyed the protection of Rome while defending Rome's borders, but they were not relationships between equals: Rome always remained the senior partner. In time many of these states became provinces of the Roman Empire (see Chapters 6 and 7).

The Roman legions made little headway against Jugurtha until 107 B.C.E., when Gaius Marius (MEHR-ee-uhs), a politician not from the traditional Roman aristocracy, became consul and led troops to Numidia. A man of fierce vigor and courage, Marius saw the army as the tool of his ambition. He took the unusual but not wholly unprecedented step of recruiting an army by permitting landless men to serve in the legions, thus tapping Rome's vast reservoir of poor citizens. Marius was unable to defeat Jugurtha directly, but his assistant, Sulla, bribed Jugurtha's father-in-law to betray him, and Jugurtha was captured and later executed in Rome. Marius later claimed this as a victory.

Fighting was also going on at Rome's northern border, where two German peoples, the Cimbri and Teutones, were moving into Gaul and later into northern Italy. After the Germans had defeated Roman armies sent to repel them, the Senate sent Marius to lead the campaign against them. Before engaging the Germans, Marius encouraged enlistments by promising his volunteers land after the war. Poor and landless citizens flocked to him. Marius and his army conquered the Germans, but when Marius proposed a bill to grant land to his troops once they had retired from military service, the Senate refused to act, in effect turning its back on the soldiers of Rome. It was a disastrous mistake. Henceforth the legionaries expected their commanders—not the Senate or the state—to protect their interests.

Rome was dividing into two political factions, both of whom wanted political power. The *populares* attempted to increase their power through the plebeian assembly and the power of the tribunes, while the *optimates* employed the traditional means of patron-client relationships and working primarily through the Senate. Both of these factions were represented in the Senate, and both had their favored general. Marius was the general backed by the populares, who from 104 to 100 B.C.E. elected him consul every year, although this was technically illegal and put unprecedented power into a Roman military commander's hands.

The favored general of the optimates was Sulla, who had earlier been Marius's assistant. In 90 B.C.E. many Roman allies in the Italian peninsula rose up against Rome because they were expected to pay taxes and serve in the army, but they had no voice in political decisions because they were not full citizens. This revolt became known as the Social War, so named from the Latin word *socius*, or "ally." Sulla's armies gained a number of victories over the Italian allies, and Sulla gained prestige through his success in fighting them. In the end, however, the Senate agreed to give many allies Roman citizenship in order to end the fighting.

Sulla's military victories led to his election as consul in 88 B.C.E., and he was given command of the Roman army in a campaign against Mithridates, the king of a state that had gained power and territory in what is now northern Turkey and was expanding into Greece. Before he could depart, however, the populares gained the upper hand in the assembly, revoked his consulship, and made Marius the commander of the troops against Mithridates. Riots broke out. Sulla fled the city and returned at the head of an army, an unprecedented move by a Roman general. He quelled the riots, put down his opponents, made some political changes that reduced the power of the assembly, and left again, this time to fight Mithridates.

Sulla's forces were relatively successful against Mithridates, but meanwhile Marius led his own troops into Rome in 86 B.C.E., undid Sulla's changes, and killed many of his supporters. Although Marius died shortly after his return to power, the populares who supported him continued to hold Rome. Sulla returned in 83 B.C.E., and after a brief but intense civil war he entered Rome and ordered a ruthless butchery of his opponents. He then attempted to turn back the clock, returning all power to the Senate and restoring the conservative constitution as it had been before the Gracchian reforms. In 81 B.C.E. he was granted the office of dictator, and in sharp contrast to Cincinnatus, used his position as a tool to gain personal power (see page 130). Dictators were supposed to step down after six months—and many had done so in Roman history—but Sulla held this position for two years. In 79 B.C.E. Sulla abdicated his dictatorship because he was ill and believed his policies would last. Yet civil war was to be the constant lot of Rome for the next forty-eight years, and Sulla's abuse of political office became the blueprint for later leaders.

Civil War

The history of the late republic is the story of power struggles among many famous Roman figures against a background of unrest at home and military campaigns abroad. This led to a series of bloody civil wars that raged from Spain across northern Africa to Egypt.

Sulla's political heirs were Pompey, Crassus, and Julius Caesar, all of them able military leaders and brilliant politicians. Pompey (106–48 B.C.E.) began a meteoric rise to power as a successful commander of troops for Sulla against Marius in Italy, Sicily, and Africa. He then suppressed a rebellion in Spain, led naval forces against pirates in the Mediterranean, and in 67 B.C.E. was sent by the Senate to command Roman forces in the East. He defeated Mithridates and the forces of other rulers as well, transforming their territories into Roman provinces.

Crassus (ca. 115–53 B.C.E.) also began his military career under Sulla and became the wealthiest man in Rome through buying and selling land. In 73 B.C.E. a major slave revolt broke out in Italy, led by Spartacus, a former gladiator. The slave armies, which eventually numbered in the tens of thousands, defeated several Roman units sent to quash them. Finally Crassus led a large army against them and put down the revolt. Spartacus was apparently killed on the battlefield, and the slaves who were captured were crucified, with thousands of crosses lining the main road to Rome.

Pompey and Crassus then made an informal agreement with the populares in the Senate. Both were elected consuls in 70 B.C.E. and began to dismantle Sulla's constitution and initiate economic and political reforms once again. They and the Senate moved too slowly for some people, however, who planned an uprising. This plot was discovered, and the forces of the rebels were put down in 63 B.C.E. by an army sent by Cicero

(106–43 B.C.E.), a leader of the optimates who was consul at the time. The rebellion and Cicero's skillful handling of it discredited the populares.

The man who cast the longest shadow over these troubled years was Julius Caesar (100–44 B.C.E.). Born of a noble family, he received an excellent education, which he furthered by studying in Greece with some of the most eminent teachers of the day. He had serious intellectual interests and immense literary ability. His account of his military operations in Gaul (present-day France), the *Commentaries on the Gallic Wars*, became a classic of Western literature. Caesar was a superb orator, and his personality and wit made him popular. Military service was an effective stepping-stone to politics, and Caesar was a military genius who knew how to win battles and turn victories into permanent gains. He was also a shrewd politician of unbridled ambition, who knew how to use the patron-client system to his advantage. He became a protégé of Crassus, who provided cash for Caesar's needs, and at the same time helped the careers of other politicians, who in turn looked to Caesar's interests in Rome when he was away from the city. Caesar launched his military career in Spain, where his courage won the respect and affection of his troops.

In 60 B.C.E. Caesar returned to Rome from Spain and Pompey returned from military victories in the east. Together with Crassus, the three concluded an informal political alliance later termed the **First Triumvirate** (trigh-UHM-veh-ruht), in which they agreed to advance one another's interests. Crassus's money helped Caesar be elected consul, and Pompey married Caesar's daughter Julia. Crassus was appointed governor of Syria, Pompey of Hispania (present-day Spain), and Caesar of Gaul.

Personal ambitions undermined the First Triumvirate. While Caesar was away from Rome fighting in Gaul, his supporters formed gangs that attacked the supporters of Pompey. These were countered by supporters of Pompey, and there were riots in the streets of Rome. The First Triumvirate disintegrated. Crassus died in battle while trying to conquer Parthia, and Caesar and Pompey accused each other of treachery. Fearful of Caesar's popularity and growing power, the Senate sided with Pompey and ordered Caesar to disband his army. He refused, and instead in 49 B.C.E. he crossed the Rubicon River in northern Italy — the boundary of his territorial command — with soldiers. ("Crossing the Rubicon" is still used as an expression for committing to an irreversible course of action.) Although their forces outnumbered Caesar's, Pompey and the Senate fled Rome, and Caesar entered the city without a fight.

Caesar then led his army against those loyal to Pompey and the Senate in Spain and Greece. In 48 B.C.E., despite being outnumbered, he defeated Pompey and his army at the Battle of Pharsalus in central Greece. Pompey fled to Egypt, which was embroiled in a battle for control not between two generals, but between a brother and sister, Ptolemy XIII and Cleopatra VII (69–30 B.C.E.). Caesar followed Pompey to Egypt, Cleopatra allied herself with Caesar, and Caesar's army defeated Ptolemy's army, ending the power struggle. Pompey was assassinated in Egypt, Cleopatra and Caesar became lovers, and Caesar brought Cleopatra to Rome. (See "Individuals in Society: Queen Cleopatra," page 154.) Caesar put down a revolt against Roman control by the king of Pontus in northern Turkey, then won a major victory over Pompey's army — now commanded by his sons — in Spain.

In the middle of defeating his enemies in battles all around the Mediterranean (see Map 5.2), Julius Caesar returned to Rome several times and was elected or appointed to various positions, including consul and dictator. He was acclaimed imperator, a title given to victorious military commanders and a term that later gave rise to the word *emperor*. Sometimes these elections happened when Caesar was away fighting; they were often arranged by his chief supporter and client in Rome, Mark Antony (83–30 B.C.E.), who was himself a military commander. Whatever Caesar's official position, after he crossed the Rubicon he simply made changes on his own authority, though often with the approval of the Senate, which he packed with his supporters. The Senate transformed his temporary positions as consul and dictator into ones he would hold for life.

Caesar began to make a number of legal and economic reforms. He issued laws about debt, the collection of taxes, and the distribution of grain and land. Families who had many children were to receive rewards, and Roman allies in Italy were to have full citizenship. He reformed the calendar, which had been based on the cycles of the moon, by replacing it with one based on the sun, adapted from the Egyptian calendar. He sponsored celebrations honoring his victories, had coins struck with his portrait, and founded new colonies, which were to be populated by veterans and the poor. He planned even more changes, including transforming elected positions such as consul, tribune, and provincial governor into ones that he appointed.

Caesar was wildly popular with most people in Rome, and even with many senators. Other senators, led by Brutus and Cassius, two patricians who favored the traditional republic, opposed his rise to what was becoming absolute power. In 44 B.C.E. they conspired to kill him and did so on March 15—a date called the "Ides of March" in the Roman calendar—stabbing him multiple times on the steps of the theatre of Pompey, where the Senate was meeting that day.

The conspiring senators called themselves the "Liberators" and said they were defending the liberties of the Roman Republic, but their support for the traditional power of the Senate could do little to save Rome from its pattern of misgovernment. The result of the assassination was another round of civil war. Caesar had named his eighteen-year-old grandnephew and adopted son, Octavian, as his heir. In 43 B.C.E. Octavian joined forces with Mark Antony and another of Caesar's lieutenants, Lepidus (LEH-puh-duhs), in a formal pact known later as the **Second Triumvirate**. Together they hunted down Caesar's killers and defeated the military forces loyal to Pompey's sons and to the conspirators. They agreed to divide the provinces into spheres of influence, with Octavian taking most of the west, Antony the east, and Lepidus the Iberian Peninsula and North Africa. The three came into conflict, and Lepidus was forced into exile by Octavian, leaving the other two to confront one another.

Both Octavian and Antony set their sights on gaining more territory. Cleopatra had returned to rule Egypt after Caesar's death, and supported Antony, who became her lover as well as her ally. In 31 B.C.E. Octavian's forces defeated the combined forces of Antony and Cleopatra at the Battle of Actium in Greece, but the two escaped. Octavian pursued them to Egypt, and they committed suicide rather than fall into his hands. Octavian's victory at Actium put an end to an age of civil war. For his success, the Senate in 27 B.C.E. gave Octavian the name Augustus, meaning "revered one." Although the Senate did not mean this to be a decisive break with tradition, that date is generally used to mark the end of the Roman Republic and the start of the Roman Empire.

INDIVIDUALS IN SOCIETY • Queen Cleopatra

C leopatra VII (69–30 B.C.E.) was a member of the Ptolemy dynasty, the Hellenistic rulers of Egypt who had established power in the third century B.C.E.
Although she was a Greek, she was passionately devoted to her Egyptian
subjects and was the first in her dynasty who could speak Egyptian in addition to
Greek. Just as ancient pharaohs had linked themselves with the gods, she had herself portrayed as the goddess Isis and may have seen herself as a reincarnation of
Isis (see Chapter 4).

At the time civil war was raging in the late Roman Republic, Cleopatra and her
brother Ptolemy XIII were in a dispute over who would be supreme ruler in Egypt.
Julius Caesar captured the Egyptian capital of Alexandria, Cleopatra arranged to
meet him, and the two became lovers, although Cleopatra was much younger and
Caesar was married. The two apparently had a son, Caesarion, and Caesar's army
defeated Ptolemy's army, ending the power struggle. In 46 B.C.E. Cleopatra arrived
in Rome, where Caesar put up a statue of her as Isis in one of the city's temples. The
Romans hated her because they saw her as a decadent Eastern queen and a threat
to what were considered traditional Roman values.

After Caesar's assassination, Cleopatra returned to Alexandria. There she became
involved in the continuing Roman civil war that now pitted Octavian, Caesar's grandnephew and heir, against Mark Antony, who commanded the Roman army in the
East. When Antony visited Alexandria in 41 B.C.E. he met Cleopatra, and though he
was already married to Octavian's sister, he became her lover. He abandoned (and
later divorced) his Roman wife, married Cleopatra in 37 B.C.E., and changed his will
to favor his children by Cleopatra. Antony's wedding present to Cleopatra was a
huge grant of territory, much of it Roman, that greatly increased her power and
that of all her children, including Caesarion. Antony also declared Caesarion to be
Julius Caesar's rightful heir.

Octavian used the wedding gift as the reason to declare Antony a traitor. He and
other Roman leaders described Antony as a romantic fool captivated by the seductive Cleopatra. Roman troops turned against Antony and joined with Octavian, and
at the Battle of Actium in 31 B.C.E. Octavian defeated the army and navy of Antony
and Cleopatra. Antony committed suicide, as did Cleopatra shortly afterward.
Octavian ordered the teenage Caesarion killed, but the young children of Antony

Notes

1. Aubrey de Sélincourt, trans., *Livy: The Early History of Rome, Books I–V of the History of Rome from Its Foundation* (Baltimore: Penguin Books, 1960), p. 58.
2. Plutarch, *Pyrrhos* 21.14. In this chapter, works in Latin with no translator noted were translated by John Buckler.
3. Naphtali Lewis and Meyer Reinhold, eds., *Roman Civilization: Sourcebook I: The Republic* (New York: Harper
Torchbooks, 1951), p. 104.
4. Polybius, *The Histories* 38.21.
5. Sallust, *War with Catiline* 10.1–3.
6. Lewis and Reinhold, *Roman Civilization*, p. 489.
7. Ovid, *Fasti* 2.535–539.
8. Horace, *Epistles* 2.1.156.
9. Plutarch, *Life of Tiberius Gracchus* 9.5.

and Cleopatra were allowed to go back to Rome, where they were raised by Antony's ex-wife. In another consequence of Octavian's victory, Egypt became a Roman province.

Roman sources are viciously hostile to Cleopatra, and she became the model of the alluring woman whose sexual attraction led men to their doom. Stories about her beauty, sophistication, lavish spending, desire for power, and ruthlessness abounded and were retold for centuries. The most dramatic story was that she committed suicide through the bite of a poisonous snake, which may have been true and which has been the subject of countless paintings. Her tumultuous relationships with Caesar and Antony have been portrayed in plays, novels, movies, and television programs.

QUESTIONS FOR ANALYSIS

1. How did Cleopatra benefit from her relationships with Caesar and Antony? How did they benefit from their relationships with her?

2. How did ideas about gender and Roman suspicion of the more sophisticated Greek culture combine to shape Cleopatra's fate and the way she is remembered?

3. In Chapter 1, "Individuals in Society: Hatshepsut and Nefertiti" (see page 30) also focuses on leading female figures in Egypt, but these two women lived more than a thousand years before Cleopatra. How would you compare their situation with hers?

ONLINE DOCUMENT ASSIGNMENT

What do Romans' negative depictions of Cleopatra tell us about the attitudes and values of her time? Explore Roman accounts and representations of Cleopatra to see what light they shed on political, social, and cultural values in the late republic and early empire, and then complete a writing assignment based on the evidence and details from the chapter.

bedfordstmartins.com/mckaywestvalue

Chapter Review

MAKE IT STICK

LearningCurve
bedfordstmartins.com/mckaywestvalue

After reading the chapter, use LearningCurve to retain what you've read.

IDENTIFY KEY TERMS

Identify and explain the significance of each item below.

Senate (p. 129)   Punic Wars (p. 135)
consuls (p. 129)   paterfamilias (p. 139)
patricians (p. 132)   manumission (p. 142)
plebeians (p. 132)   latifundia (p. 147)
Struggle of the Orders (p. 134)   First Triumvirate (p. 152)
tribunes (p. 134)   Second Triumvirate (p. 153)
patron-client system (p. 135)

REVIEW THE MAIN IDEAS

Answer the focus questions from each section of the chapter.

- How did the Romans become the dominant power in Italy? (p. 125)
- What were the key institutions of the Roman Republic? (p. 132)
- How did the Romans take control of the Mediterranean world? (p. 135)
- How did expansion affect Roman society and culture? (p. 138)
- What led to the fall of the Roman Republic? (p. 146)

MAKE CONNECTIONS

Think about the larger developments and continuities within and across chapters.

1. How would you compare ideals for male and female behavior in republican Rome with those of classical Sparta and classical Athens in Chapter 3? What are some possible reasons for the differences and similarities you have identified?

2. The Phoenicians, the Greeks, and the Romans all established colonies around the Mediterranean. How did these colonies differ, and how were they the same, in terms of their economic functions and political situation?

3. Looking over the long history of the Roman Republic, do interactions with non-Romans or conflicts among Romans themselves appear to be the most significant drivers of change? Why or why not?

ONLINE DOCUMENT ASSIGNMENT

Queen Cleopatra

What do Romans' negative depictions of Cleopatra tell us about the attitudes and values of her time?

You encountered Cleopatra's story on page 154. Keeping the question above in mind, go online and explore Roman accounts and representations of Cleopatra to see what light they shed on political, social, and cultural values in the late republic and early empire. Then complete a writing assignment based on the evidence and details from the chapter.

bedfordstmartins.com/mckaywestvalue

CHRONOLOGY

ca. 1000 B.C.E.	• Earliest settlements in the area that became the city of Rome
753 B.C.E.	• Traditional founding of the city of Rome
509 B.C.E.	• Traditional date of establishment of the Roman Republic
451–449 B.C.E.	• Laws of the Twelve Tables written and issued
387 B.C.E.	• Gauls sack Rome
367 B.C.E.	• Licinian-Sextian laws passed
ca. 265 B.C.E.	• Romans control most of Italy
264–201; 149–146 B.C.E.	• Punic Wars
133–121 B.C.E.	• Reforms of the Gracchi
107–31 B.C.E.	• Turmoil in the late republic
44 B.C.E.	• Julius Caesar assassinated
31 B.C.E.	• Octavian defeats Antony and Cleopatra at the Battle of Actium
27 B.C.E.	• Senate issues decrees giving Octavian great power

6

☑ LearningCurve
bedfordstmartins.com/mckaywestvalue
After reading the chapter, use
LearningCurve to retain what
you've read.

The Roman Empire

27 B.C.E.–284 C.E.

IN 27 B.C.E. THE CIVIL WARS WERE LARGELY OVER, AT LEAST FOR
a time. With peace came prosperity, stability, and a new vision of Rome's
destiny. In his epic poem the *Aeneid* celebrating the founding of Rome, the
Roman poet Virgil expressed this vision:

> You, Roman, remember—these are your arts:
> To rule nations, and to impose the ways of peace,
> To spare the humble and to conquer the proud.[1]

   This was an ideal, of course, but Augustus, now the ruler of Rome, recognized that ideals and traditions were important to Romans. Instead of creating a new form of government, he left the republic officially intact but held
all real power himself. The rulers that followed him continued to transform
Rome into an empire. The boundaries of the Roman Empire expanded in all
directions, and the army became an important means of Romanization through
its forts, camps, and cities. Gaul, Germany, Britain, and eastern Europe were
introduced to Greco-Roman culture. A new religion, Christianity, developed
in the eastern Roman province of Judaea, and spread on the roads and sea-
lanes used by Roman traders and troops. By the third century C.E. civil wars
had returned, however, and it seemed as if Augustus's creation would
collapse.

Augustus's Reign

How did Augustus create a foundation for the Roman Empire?

After Augustus (r. 27 B.C.E.–14 C.E.) ended the civil wars that had raged off and on for decades, he faced the monumental problems of reconstruction. He first had to reconstruct the constitution and the organs of government. Next he had to pay his armies for their services, and care for the welfare of the provinces. Then he had to address the danger of various groups on Rome's European frontiers.

Augustus was highly successful in meeting these challenges. The result of this work was a system of government in which the emperor held all executive power in both the civil government and the military. The Senate remained as a prestigious advisory body whose members functioned at the desire and request of the emperor.

The Principate

Augustus claimed that he was restoring the republic, but he actually transformed the government into one in which all real power was held by a single ruler. As he did this, however, he maintained the illusion that the republic still existed, and he linked his rule with the traditional idea of SPQR (see Chapter 5).

Augustus fit his own position into the republican constitution not by creating a new office for himself but by gradually taking over many of the offices that traditionally had been held by separate people. The Senate named him often as both consul and tribune. As consul, Augustus had the right to call the Senate into session and present legislation to the citizens' assemblies, and as tribune he presided over the *concilium plebis* (see Chapter 5). He was also named **imperator**, a title with which the Senate customarily honored a general after a major victory. He held control of the army, which he made a permanent standing organization. Furthermore, recognizing the importance of religion, he had himself named *pontifex maximus*, or chief priest.

An additional title that Augustus had the Senate bestow on him was *princeps civitatis* (prihn-KEHPS cih-vee-TAH-tees), "first citizen of the state." This title had no official powers attached to it and had been used as an honorific for centuries, so it was

Augustus as Imperator In this marble statue, found in the villa of Augustus's widow, Augustus is depicted in a military uniform and in a pose usually used to show leaders addressing their troops. This portrayal emphasizes his role as imperator, the head of the army. The figures on his breastplate show various peoples the Romans had defeated or with whom they had made treaties, along with assorted deities. Although Augustus did not declare himself a god—as later Roman emperors would—this statue shows him barefoot, just as gods and heroes were in classical Greek statuary, and accompanied by Cupid riding a dolphin, both symbols of the goddess Venus, whom he claimed as an ancestor. (Vatican Museums and Galleries, Vatican City/The Bridgeman Art Library)

inoffensive to Roman ears. One of Augustus's cleverest tactics was to use noninflammatory language for himself and the changes he was making. Only later would *princeps civitatis* become the basis of the word *prince*, meaning "sovereign ruler," although "prince" quite accurately describes what Augustus actually was.

Considering what had happened to Julius Caesar, Augustus wisely wielded all his power in the background, and the government he created is called the **principate**. Although principate leaders were said to be "first among equals," Augustus's tenure clearly marked the end of the republic. Still, for a generation that had known only civil war, the shift away from republican government may have seemed minor compared to the benefits brought by the stability of Augustus's rule.

Augustus curtailed the power of the Senate, but it continued to exist as the chief deliberative body of the state, and it continued to act as a court of law. Under Augustus and his successors, it provided officials to administer Rome and its provinces. The Senate's relations with particular emperors were often hostile, and senators were involved in plots to overthrow various emperors. In general, however, the Senate adapted itself to the new reality and cooperated in running the empire. Governors sent to the provinces were often members of the Senate, and they took the Roman legal system with them.

Without specifically saying so, Augustus created the office of emperor. The English word *emperor* is derived from the Latin word *imperator*, an origin that reflects the fact that Augustus's command of the army was the main source of his power. Augustus governed the provinces where troops were needed for defense and guarded the frontiers from attack. He could declare war, he controlled deployment of the Roman army, and he paid the soldiers' wages. He granted bonuses and gave veterans retirement benefits. Augustus never shared control of the army, and no Roman found it easy to defy him militarily.

Augustus professionalized the military even more than it had been in the late republic, and he made the army a recognized institution of government. Soldiers were generally volunteers; they received a salary and training under career officers who advanced in rank according to experience, ability, valor, and length of service. Soldiers served twenty-year terms, plus five in the reserves, and on retiring were to be given a discharge bonus of cash or a piece of land. To pay for this, Augustus ordered a tax on inheritance and on certain types of sales. Those soldiers who were Roman citizens were organized into legions, units of about five thousand men. The legions were backed up by auxiliaries, military forces of noncitizen volunteers or conscripts who also served twenty- or twenty-five-year terms. Auxiliaries were also paid—though at a lower rate than legionaries—and were granted Roman citizenship when they retired. Legions were often transferred from place to place as the need arose. Auxiliaries were more likely to stay near the area where they had been recruited, but sometimes they served far away from home as well.

Grants of land to veterans had originally been in Italy, but by Augustus's time there was not enough land for this. Instead he gave veterans land in the frontier provinces that had been taken from the people the Romans conquered, usually near camps with active army units. Some veterans objected, and at Augustus's death they briefly revolted, but these colonies of veterans continued to play an important role in securing the Roman Empire's boundaries and controlling its newly won provinces. Augustus's veterans took abroad with them their Latin language and Roman culture, becoming important agents of Romanization.

The army that Augustus developed was loyal to him as a person, not as the head of the Roman state. This would lead to trouble later, but the basics of the political and military system that Augustus created lasted fairly well for almost three centuries.

Roman Expansion

One of the most significant aspects of Augustus's reign was Roman expansion into northern and western Europe (Map 6.1). Augustus began his work in the west and north by completing the conquest of Spain begun by Scipio Africanus in the third century B.C.E. (see Chapter 5). In Gaul he founded twelve new towns, and the Roman road system linked new settlements with one another and with Italy. The German frontier along the Rhine River was the scene of hard fighting. In 12 B.C.E. Augustus ordered a major invasion of Germany beyond the Rhine. Roman legions advanced to the Elbe River, and the area north of the Main River and west of the Elbe was on the point of becoming Roman. But in 9 C.E. some twenty thousand Roman troops were annihilated at the Battle of the Teutoburg Forest and their general Varus was killed on the battlefield.

Meanwhile Roman troops penetrated the area of modern Austria, southern Bavaria, and western Hungary. Thereafter the Rhine and the Danube remained the Roman frontier in central Europe. The Romans began to build walls, forts, and watchtowers to firm up their defenses, especially in the area between the two rivers, where people could more easily enter Roman territory. The regions of modern Serbia, Bulgaria, and Romania in the Balkans fell, and the Romans created a land-based link between the eastern and western Mediterranean.

Within the area along the empire's northern border the legionaries and auxiliaries built fortified camps. Roads linked the camps with one another, and settlements grew up around the camps. Traders began to frequent the frontier and to do business with the people who lived there. Thus Roman culture—the rough-and-ready kind found in military camps—gradually spread into the north. As a result, for the first time central and northern Europe came into direct and continuous contact with Mediterranean culture. Many Roman camps grew into cities, transforming the economy of the area around them. Roman cities were the first urban developments in most parts of central and northern Europe.

As a political and religious bond between the provinces and Rome, Augustus encouraged the cult of **Roma et Augustus** (Rome and Augustus) as the guardians of the state and the source of all benefits to society. In praying for the good health and welfare of the emperor, Romans and provincials were praying for the empire itself. The cult spread rapidly, especially in the eastern Mediterranean, where it built on the ideas of divine kingship developed in the Hellenistic monarchies (see Chapter 4). Worshipping Roma et Augustus became a symbol of Roman unity, and Roman officials could often judge the degree of loyalty of a province by noting the extent of public temple activities.

To make his presence felt further, Augustus had himself portrayed on coins standing alongside the goddess Victory, and on celebratory stone arches built to commemorate military victories. In addition, he had temples, stadiums, marketplaces, and public buildings constructed in Rome and other cities. Later emperors expanded this imperial cult, erecting statues, triumphal arches, columns, temples, and other buildings to honor themselves, their family members, or their predecessors. Many of these were decorated with texts as well as images. Shortly after Augustus's death, for example, an inscription

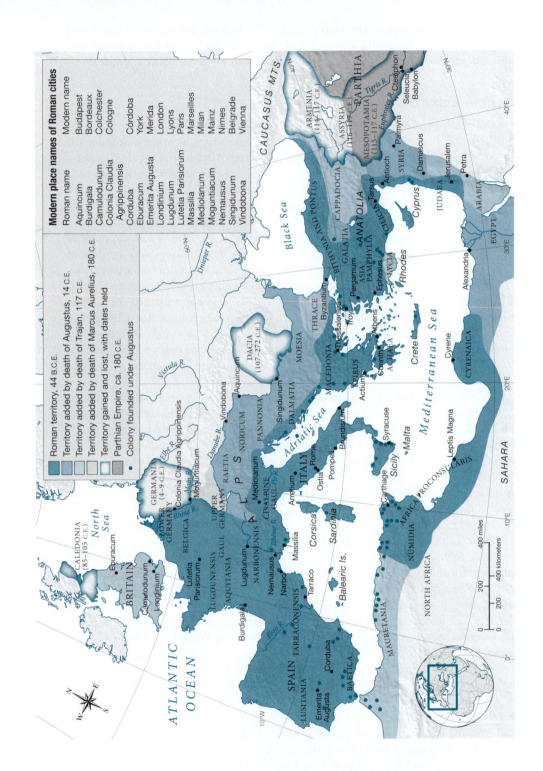

Modern place names of Roman cities

Roman name	Modern name
Aquincum	Budapest
Burdigala	Bordeaux
Camulodunum	Colchester
Colonia Claudia	Cologne
Agrippinensis	
Corduba	Cordoba
Eburacum	York
Emerita Augusta	Merida
Londinium	London
Lugdunum	Lyons
Lutetia Parisiorum	Paris
Massilia	Marseilles
Mediolanum	Milan
Moguntiacum	Mainz
Nemausus	Nimes
Singidunum	Belgrade
Vindobona	Vienna

Roman territory, 44 B.C.E.

Territory added by death of Augustus, 14 C.E.

Territory added by death of Trajan, 117 C.E.

Territory added by death of Marcus Aurelius, 180 C.E.

Territory gained and lost, with dates held

Parthian Empire, ca. 180 C.E.

Colony founded under Augustus

◀ **MAP 6.1**   **Roman Expansion Under the Empire, 44** B.C.E.**–180** C.E.
Following Roman expansion during the republic, Augustus added vast tracts of Europe to the
Roman Empire, which the emperor Trajan later enlarged by assuming control over parts of central
Europe, the Near East, and North Africa.

detailing his achievements, known as the *Res Gestae Divi Augusti* (The deeds of the divine
Augustus), was carved on monuments throughout the Roman Empire.

In the late eighteenth century the English historian Edward Gibbon dubbed the
stability and relative peace within the empire that Augustus created the **pax Romana**,
the "Roman peace," which he saw as lasting about two hundred years, until the end of
the reign of Marcus Aurelius in 180 C.E. Those outside the empire might not have agreed
that things were so peaceful. The Roman historian Tacitus wrote of a speech delivered
by the Scottish chieftain Calcagus before a battle with an invading Roman army in
which Calcagus says, "The Romans make a desert and call it peace." The speech may
be an invention by Tacitus—this was a common practice for ancient historians—but
it captures the idea that not everyone saw the Roman Empire as a positive force. Gibbon's
term has stuck, however, because, especially for those living away from contested frontier areas, this two-hundred-year stretch of Roman history was much more stable and
prosperous than what came before or after.

The pax Romana was enforced by troops who remained on active duty or as reserves
in the provinces and on the frontier, ready to respond to any resistance to Roman
dominance. In general, however, Augustus respected local customs and ordered his
governors to do the same. Roman governors applied Roman law to Romans living in
their territories, but they let local people retain their own laws. As long as they provided
taxes and did not rebel, they could continue to run their political and social lives as they
had before Roman conquest.

While Romans did not force their culture on local people in Roman territories,
local elites with aspirations knew that the best way to rise in stature and power was to
adopt aspects of Roman culture. Thus just as ambitious individuals in the Hellenistic
world embraced Greek culture and learned to speak Greek, those determined to get
ahead now learned Latin, and sometimes Greek as well if they wished to be truly well
educated.

Especially in cities, Roman culture blended with local traditions. The Roman city
of Lugdunum, modern Lyons in southern France, provides an example of this process.
The site was originally the capital of a state that had existed before the Roman conquest
of Gaul, named for the Gallic god Lug. Julius Caesar made it a Roman military settlement.
In 12 B.C.E. Augustus made it a political and religious center, with responsibilities for
administering the area and for honoring the gods of both the Romans and Gauls. Physical
symbols of this fusion of two cultures can still be seen today. The extensive remains of
the amphitheater and other buildings testify to the fact that the city was prosperous
enough to afford expensive Roman construction and the style of life that it represented.
Many such towns were eventually granted Roman citizenship due to their embrace of
Roman culture and government and their importance to the Roman economy. Ambitious
young men flocked to provincial capitals such as Lugdunum, for it was here, and not
in the countryside, that one could make one's mark.

The Flowering of Latin Literature

Many poets and prose writers were active in the late republic and the principate, and scholars of literature later judged their work to be of such high quality that they called the period from about 50 B.C.E. to 20 C.E. the "golden age" of Latin literature. Roman poets and prose writers celebrated the physical and emotional joys of a comfortable life. Their works were highly polished, elegant in style, and intellectual in conception. Roman poets referred to the gods often and treated mythological themes, but the core subject matter of their work was human, not divine.

Rome's greatest poet was Virgil (70–19 B.C.E.), who drew on earlier traditions, but gave them new twists. The *Georgics*, for example, is a poem about agriculture that used Hellenistic models to capture both the peaceful pleasures and the day-to-day violence of rural life. In vivid language Virgil depicts the death of one of the bulls pulling a plow and the farmer unyoking the remaining animal:

> Look, the bull, shining under the rough plough,
> falls to the ground
> and vomits from his mouth blood mixed with foam,
> and releases his dying groan.
> Sadly moves the ploughman, unharnessing the
> young steer grieving for the death of his brother
> and leaves in the middle of the job
> the plough stuck fast.[2]

Virgil's masterpiece is the *Aeneid* (uh-NEE-ihd), an epic poem that is the Latin equivalent of the Greek *Iliad* and *Odyssey* (see Chapter 3). Virgil's account of the founding of Rome and the early years of the city gave final form to the legend of Aeneas, the Trojan hero (and ancestor of Romulus and Remus) who escaped to Italy at the fall of Troy:

> Arms and the man I sing, who first made way,
> predestined exile, from the Trojan shore
> to Italy, the blest Lavinian strand.
> Smitten of storms he was on land and sea
> by violence of Heaven, to satisfy
> stern Juno's sleepless wrath; and much in war
> he suffered, seeking at the last to found
> the city, and bring o'er his fathers' gods
> to safe abode in Latium; whence arose
> the Latin race, old Alba's reverend lords,
> and from her hills wide-walled, imperial Rome.[3]

As Virgil told it, Aeneas became the lover of Dido, the widowed queen of Carthage, but left her because his destiny called him to found Rome. Swearing the destruction of Rome, Dido committed suicide, and according to Virgil, her enmity helped cause the Punic Wars. In leaving Dido, an "Eastern" queen, Aeneas put duty and the good of the state ahead of marriage or pleasure. The parallels between this story and the very recent real events involving Antony and Cleopatra were not lost on Virgil's audience. Making the public aware of these parallels, and of Virgil's description of Aeneas as an ancestor of Julius Caesar, fit well with Augustus's aims. Therefore, Augustus encouraged Virgil to write the *Aeneid* and made sure it was circulated widely immediately after Virgil died.

The poet Horace (65–8 B.C.E.) rose from humble beginnings to friendship with Augustus. The son of an ex-slave and tax collector, Horace nonetheless received an excellent education, which he finished in Athens. After Augustus's victory Horace returned to Rome and became Virgil's friend. His most important works are a series of odes, short lyric poems often focusing on a single individual or event. One of these commemorated Augustus's victory over Antony and Cleopatra at Actium in 31 B.C.E. Horace depicted Cleopatra as a frenzied queen, drunk with desire to destroy Rome, a view that has influenced opinions about Cleopatra until today.

The historian Livy (59 B.C.E.–17 C.E.) was a friend of Augustus and a supporter of the principate. He especially approved of Augustus's efforts to restore what he saw as republican virtues. Livy's history of Rome, titled simply *Ab Urbe Condita* (From the founding of the city), began with the legend of Aeneas and ended with the reign of Augustus. Livy used the works of earlier Greek and Roman writers, as well as his own experiences, as his source material.

Augustus actively encouraged poets and writers, but he could also turn against them. The poet Ovid (AH-vuhd) (43 B.C.E.–17 C.E.) wrote erotic poetry about absent lovers and the joys of seduction, as well as other works about religious festivals and mythology.

Ara Pacis   In the middle years of Augustus's reign, the Roman Senate ordered a huge altar, the Ara Pacis, built to honor him and the peace he had brought to the empire. This was decorated with life-size reliefs of Augustus and members of his family, prominent Romans, and other people and deities. One side, shown here, depicts a goddess figure, most likely the goddess Peace herself, with twin babies on her lap, flanked by nymphs representing land and sea, and surrounded by plants and animals. (De Agostini Picture Library/A. de Gregorio/The Bridgeman Art Library)

INDIVIDUALS IN SOCIETY • Ovid, *The Art of Love*

The Art of Love is a humorous guide for lovers written by the Roman poet Ovid. Ovid addresses the first two parts to men, instructing them on how to seduce and keep women—look good, give them compliments, don't be too obvious. The third part is his corresponding advice for women, which in its main points is the same. The section below comes from the beginning of part one, advising men on where and how to meet women.

While you are footloose and free to play the field at your pleasure,
    Watch for the one you can tell, "I want no other but you!"
She is not going to come to you floating down from the heavens:
    For the right kind of a girl you must keep using your eyes.
Hunters know where to spread their nets for the stag in his cover,
    Hunters know where the boar gnashes his teeth in the glade.
Fowlers know brier and bush, and fishermen study the waters
    Baiting the hook for the cast just where the fish may be found.
So you too, in your hunt for material worthy of loving,
    First will have to find out where the game usually goes.
. . .
. . . The theater's curve is a very good place for your hunting,
    More opportunity here, maybe, than anywhere else.
Here you may find one to love, or possibly only to have fun with,
    Someone to take for a night, someone to have and to hold.
. . .
Furthermore, don't overlook the meetings when horses are running;
    In the crowds at the track opportunity waits.
There is no need for a code of finger-signals or nodding,
    Sit as close as you like; no one will stop you at all.

His best-known work is *The Art of Love*, a satire of the serious instructional poetry that was common in Rome at the time. *The Art of Love* provides advice to men about how to get and keep women, and for women about how to get and keep men. (See "Primary Source: Ovid, *The Art of Love*," above.) This work was so popular, Ovid relates, that shortly afterward he felt compelled to write *The Cure for Love*, advising people how to fall out of love and forget their former lovers. Have lots of new lovers, it advises, and don't hang around places, eat foods, or listen to songs that will make you remember your former lover. In 8 B.C.E. Augustus banished Ovid to a city on the Black Sea far from Rome. Why he did so is a mystery, and Ovid himself states only that the reason was "a poem and a mistake." Some scholars argue that Augustus banished Ovid because his poetry celebrated adultery at a time when Augustus was promoting marriage and childbearing, and others say it was because the poet knew about political conspiracies. Whatever its causes, the exile of Ovid became a symbol of misunderstood poetic genius for many later writers.

In fact, you will have to sit close—that's one of the rules, at a race track.
    Whether she likes it or not, contact is part of the game.
Try to find something in common, to open the conversation;
    Don't care too much what you say, just so that every one hears
Ask her, "Whose colors are those?"—that's good for an opening gambit.
    Put your own bet down, fast, on whatever she plays.
. . .
Often it happens that dust may fall on the blouse of the lady.
    If such dust should fall, carefully brush it away.
Even if there's no dust, brush off whatever there isn't.
    Any excuse will do: why do you think you have hands?
. . .
    There is another good ground, the gladiatorial shows.
On that sorrowful sand Cupid has often contested,
    And the watcher of wounds often has had it himself.
While he is talking, or touching a hand, or studying entries,
    Asking which one is ahead after his bet has been laid,
Wounded himself, he groans to feel the shaft of the arrow;
    He is victim himself, no more spectator, but show.

EVALUATE THE EVIDENCE

1. What metaphors and symbols does Ovid use to describe finding a lover and falling in love?

2. What does this poem indicate about leisure activities in the Rome of Ovid?

Source: Ovid, *The Art of Love*, trans. Rolfe, pp. 106–110. Copyright © 1957 Indiana University Press. Reprinted with permission of Indiana University Press.

Marriage and Morality

Augustus's banishing of Ovid may have simply been an excuse to get rid of him, but concern with morality and with what were perceived as traditional Roman virtues was a matter not just for literature in Augustan Rome, but also for law. Augustus promoted marriage and childbearing through legal changes that released free women and freed-women (female slaves who had been freed) from male guardianship if they had given birth to a certain number of children. Men and women who were unmarried or had no children were restricted in the inheritance of property. Adultery, defined as sex with a married woman or with a woman under male guardianship, was made a crime, not simply the private family matter it had been.

In imperial propaganda, Augustus had his own family depicted as a model of traditional morality, with his wife Livia at his side and dressed in conservative and somewhat old-fashioned clothing rather than the more daring Greek styles that wealthy women were actually wearing in Rome at the time. In fact, Augustus's family did not live up to this ideal. Augustus had his daughter Julia arrested and exiled for adultery and treason. Although it is impossible to tell what actually happened, she seems to have had at least one affair after her father forced her to marry a second husband—her stepbrother Tiberius—whom she hated.

Same-sex relationships among men in Rome followed a variety of patterns: some were between social equals and others between men and their slaves. Moralists denounced sexual relationships in which men squandered family money or became subservient to those of lower social status, but no laws were passed against same-sex relationships. We do not know very much about same-sex relationships among women in Rome, though court gossip and criticism of powerful women, including the wives of Augustus's successors, sometimes included charges of such relationships, along with charges of heterosexual promiscuity and other sexual slander.

Augustus's Successors

How did the Roman state develop after Augustus?

Augustus's success in creating solid political institutions was tested by the dynasty he created, the Julio-Claudians, whose members schemed against one another trying to win and hold power. The incompetence of one of the Julio-Claudians, Nero, and his failure to deal with the army generals allowed a military commander, Vespasian (veh-SPAY-zhuhn), to claim the throne and establish a new dynasty, the Flavians. The Flavians were followed by the "five good emperors," who were relatively successful militarily and politically. Rome entered a period of political stability, prosperity, and relative peace that lasted until the end of the second century.

The Julio-Claudians and the Flavians

Because the principate was not technically an office, Augustus could not legally hand it to a successor. There were various plots surrounding the succession, including the one for which Ovid was banished. Augustus dealt firmly with plotters, sometimes having them executed, and he also found a way to solve the succession issue. Just as his great-uncle Julius Caesar had adopted him, he adopted his stepson Tiberius (who was also his son-in-law) as his son. Adoption of an heir was a common practice among members of the elite in Rome, who used this method to pass on property to a chosen younger man—often a relative—if they had no sons. Long before Augustus's death he shared his consular and tribunician powers with Tiberius, thus grooming him for the principate. In his will Augustus left most of his vast fortune to Tiberius, and the Senate formally requested Tiberius to assume the burdens of the principate. Formalities apart, by the time of his death in 14 C.E. Augustus had succeeded in creating a dynasty.

For fifty years after Augustus's death the dynasty that he established—known as the Julio-Claudians because all were members of the Julian and Claudian clans—provided the emperors of Rome. Two of the Julio-Claudians who followed Augustus, Tiberius and Claudius, were sound rulers and able administrators. The other two, Caligula and Nero, were weak and frivolous men who exercised their power poorly and to the detriment of the empire.

Augustus's creation of an imperial bodyguard known as the **Praetorians** (pree-TAWR-ee-uhnz) had repercussions for his successors. In 41 C.E. the Praetorians murdered Caligula and forced the Senate to ratify their choice of Claudius as emperor. The events were repeated frequently. During the first three centuries of the empire, the Praetorian Guard all too often murdered emperors they were supposed to protect, and raised to emperor men of their own choosing.

In his early years Nero ruled fairly well, but he became increasingly paranoid about the power of those around him. In 68 C.E. his erratic actions and his policies led to a revolt by several generals, which was supported by the Praetorian Guard and members of the Senate. He was declared an enemy of the people and committed suicide. This opened the way to widespread disruption and civil war. In 69 C.E., the "year of the four emperors," four men claimed the position of emperor in quick succession. Roman armies in Gaul, on the Rhine, and in the east marched on Rome to make their commanders emperor. The man who emerged triumphant was Vespasian, commander of the eastern armies.

Vespasian restored the discipline of the armies. To prevent others from claiming the throne, Vespasian designated his sons Titus and Domitian as his successors, thus establishing the Flavian dynasty. Although Roman policy was to rule by peaceful domination whenever possible, he used the army to suppress the rebellions that had begun erupting at the end of Nero's reign. The most famous of these was one that had burst out in Judaea in 66 C.E., sparked by long-standing popular unrest over taxes. Jewish rebels initially defeated the Roman troops stationed in Judaea, but a larger army under the leadership of Vespasian and his son Titus put down the revolt. They destroyed much of the city of Jerusalem, including the Jewish temple, in 70 C.E., and took thousands of Jews as military captives and slaves, dispersing them throughout the empire. The military conquest of Judaea represented a failure of official Roman policy, but it is a good example of the way in which the Romans maintained clear control over their subjects, a control backed by military force if initial attempts at negotiation failed.

The Flavians carried on Augustus's work in Italy and on the frontiers. During the brief reign of Vespasian's son Titus, Mount Vesuvius in southern Italy erupted, destroying Pompeii and other cities and killing thousands of people. Titus gave money and sent officials to organize the relief effort. His younger brother Domitian, who followed him as emperor, won additional territory in Germany, consolidating it into two new provinces. Later in life he became more autocratic, however, and he was killed in 96 C.E. in a plot that involved his own wife, ending the Flavian dynasty.

The Age of the "Five Good Emperors"

The Flavians were succeeded by a line of relatively competent emperors, whom the political philosopher Niccolò Machiavelli in the sixteenth century termed the **"five good emperors"** — Nerva, Trajan, Hadrian, Antoninus Pius, and Marcus Aurelius. Machiavelli praised them because they all adopted able men as their successors during their lifetimes instead of relying on birth to provide an heir, thus giving Rome stability. None except Marcus Aurelius had a legitimate son, however, so they actually had little choice. They were also following the pattern set by Julius Caesar and Augustus, not breaking new ground. The last four "good emperors" were, in fact, related members of the Antonine family. Historians since Machiavelli have also noted that in some cases their choices were the result of pressure by the army or members of their family, rather than their own political astuteness. Whatever the reasons for the pattern, however, because all of these emperors were experienced generals and members of the Senate, Rome was provided with a stable series of well-trained political and military leaders for nearly a century, from 96 C.E. to 180 C.E.

Augustus had claimed that his influence arose from the collection of offices the Senate had bestowed on him and that he was merely the first citizen. Already during his rule many recognized that this was a façade, but the Senate continued to exist as a deliberative body and Rome remained officially a republic. Gradually the rulers expanded their individual powers, however, and Rome became in fact an empire, in which increasing amounts of power were held by one man. Although they never adopted the title "king" — this would have been seen as too great a break with Roman traditions — the rulers of Rome are conventionally called emperors. And as emperors took on new tasks and functions, their influence was felt in more areas of life and government.

Hadrian is typical of the emperors of the second century. He received a solid education in Rome and became an ardent admirer of Greek culture. He caught the attention of his elder cousin Trajan, the future emperor, who started him on a military career. At age nineteen Hadrian served on the Danube frontier, where he learned the details of how the Roman army lived and fought and saw for himself the problems of defending the frontiers. When Trajan became emperor in 98 C.E., Hadrian was given important positions in which he learned how to defend and run the empire. Although Trajan did not officially declare Hadrian his successor, at Trajan's death in 117 Hadrian assumed power.

Hadrian built a number of buildings, including the circular Pantheon in Rome and new temples in Athens. He established more formal imperial administrative departments and separated civil service from military service. Men with little talent or taste for the army could instead serve the state as administrators. These innovations made for more efficient running of the empire and increased the authority of the emperor.

Under Trajan the boundaries of the Roman Empire were expanded to their farthest extent, and Hadrian worked to maintain most of these holdings, although he pulled back Roman armies from areas in the East he considered indefensible. No longer a conquering force, the army was expected to defend what had already been won. Forts and watch stations guarded the borders. Outside the forts the Romans built a system of roads that allowed the forts to be quickly supplied and reinforced in times of rebellion or unrest. Trouble for the Romans included two major revolts by Jews in the eastern part of the empire, which resulted in heavy losses on both sides and the exile of many Jews from Judaea.

Roman soldiers also built walls, of which the most famous was one across northern England built primarily during Hadrian's reign. Hadrian's Wall, as it became known, protected Romans from attacks from the north, and it also allowed them to regulate immigration and trade through the many gates along the wall. Like all walls around cities or across territory, it served as a symbol and means of power and control as well as a defensive strategy. The later emperor Antoninus Pius built a second wall one hundred miles north, but this was quickly abandoned. Thousands of troops patrolled Hadrian's Wall until the Romans pulled out of the area in the late fourth century.

As the empire expanded, the army grew larger, and more and more troops were auxiliary forces of noncitizens. Because army service could lead to citizenship, men from the provinces and even from beyond the borders of the Roman Empire joined the army willingly to gain this, receive a salary, and learn a trade. (See "Individuals in Society: Bithus, a Soldier in the Roman Army," page 172.) The army evolved into a garrison force, with troops guarding specific areas for long periods. Soldiers on active duty had originally been prohibited from marrying, but this restriction was increasingly ignored, and some troops brought their wives and families along on their assignments.

Rome and the Provinces

What was life like in the city of Rome, and what was it like in the provinces?

The expansion and stabilization of the empire brought changes to life in the city of Rome and also to life in the provinces in the first two centuries C.E. The city grew to a huge size, bringing the problems that plague any crowded urban area but also opportunities for work and leisure. Roads and secure sea-lanes linked the empire in one vast web, creating a network of commerce and communication. Trade and production flourished in the provinces, and Romans came into indirect contact with China.

Life in Imperial Rome

Rome was truly an extraordinary city, and with a population of over a million it may have been the largest city in the world. Although it boasted stately palaces and beautiful residential areas, most people lived in shoddily constructed houses. They took whatever work was available, producing food, clothing, construction materials, and the many other items needed by the city's residents, or selling these products from small shops or at the city's many marketplaces.

Many residents of the city of Rome were slaves, who ranged from highly educated household tutors or government officials and widely sought sculptors to workers who engaged in hard physical tasks. Slaves sometimes attempted to flee their masters, but those who failed in their escape attempts were returned to their masters and often branded on their foreheads. Others had metal collars fastened around their necks. One collar discovered near Rome read: "I have run away. Capture me. If you take me back to my master Zoninus, you will receive a gold coin."[4]

A story told about the author Plutarch reveals Roman attitudes toward slavery. One of Plutarch's educated slaves had read some of his master's philosophical writings and began to talk back to his master, for which Plutarch had him flogged. The slave accused his master of not acting very philosophically. Plutarch told the man with the whip to continue while he and the slave discussed philosophy. We have no idea whether this actually happened, but it demonstrates the reality of life for most slaves: lofty ideals did not interfere with their actual treatment.

Romans used the possibility of manumission as a means of controlling the behavior of their slaves, and individual Romans did sometimes free their slaves. Often these were house slaves who had virtually become members of the family and who often stayed with their former owner's family after being freed. The example of Helene, the slave of Marcus Aurelius Ammonio, is typical: the master "manumitted in the presence of friends his house-born female Helene, about 34 years old, and ordered her to be free."[5] Ammonio then gave her a gift of money. Manumission was limited by law, however, in part because freeing slaves made them citizens, allowing them to receive public grain and gifts of money, which some Romans thought debased pure Roman citizenship.

INDIVIDUALS IN SOCIETY • Bithus, a Soldier in the Roman Army

Citizenship and service in the military have long been linked. In classical Athens the hoplites, who were the backbone of Athenian armies, were all citizens (see Chapter 3). In the United States today, noncitizens serving on active duty in the armed forces may apply for citizenship immediately instead of having to wait the five years that are normally required for civilian noncitizen residents. Citizenship and army service were also connected in the Roman Empire. Only Roman citizens could be members of the Roman legions, but expanding and defending the empire required huge numbers of troops. These were provided by auxiliary units, open to all. Some men were drafted into the auxiliaries, but more joined voluntarily, attracted by the offer of pay and by the promise that if they survived, at the end of their service they would be awarded Roman citizenship, which would give them legal, social, and economic privileges.

A man's record of army service and his status as a citizen were recorded on what is known as a military diploma, two bronze sheets about the size of a paperback book wired together on which his military career was set out in an inscription. The names of witnesses were also inscribed on the diploma, and their seals attached, which made the document official. One copy of this diploma stayed in Rome, and one was sent to the soldier himself, much as members of the military today receive discharge papers. Most of these diplomas were melted down long ago and their metal was put to other uses, but about a thousand survive. They provide an exact date, which is very rare in ancient sources, so they can be used to trace the movements of units and many other aspects of the military. They also include details about the lives of ordinary soldiers unavailable in any other type of source.

One such soldier was the infantryman Bithus, who was born in Thrace in the northeastern region of modern Greece, a part of the empire that provided many troops. He joined an auxiliary unit of the Roman army in 63 C.E. and began with basic training, during which he learned to march and to use the standard weapons of a heavily armed infantryman. His training completed, Bithus was sent to Syria, where he spent most of his career. He was one of the thousands of soldiers sent to this area from all parts of the empire because of the revolt in Judaea. There he met others from as far west as Gaul and Spain, from northern Africa, and from other

---

A typical day for the Roman family began with a modest breakfast, as in the days of the republic. Afterward came a trip to the outdoor market for the day's provisions. Seafood was a favorite item, as the Romans normally ate meat only at festivals. While poor people ate salt fish, the more prosperous dined on rare fish, oysters, squid, and eels. Wine was the common drink, and the rich often enjoyed rare vintages imported from abroad. Rich or poor, Romans mixed their wine with water, because drinking wine straight was seen as vulgar.

As in the republic, children began their education at home, where parents emphasized moral conduct, especially reverence for the gods and the law and respect for elders. Daughters learned how to manage the house, and sons learned the basics of their future calling from their fathers, who also taught them the use of weapons for military service.

parts of Greece and the Balkans. Unlike many other units that were shifted periodically, his remained in the same area. While in the army, he raised a family, much like soldiers today. The sons of soldiers like Bithus often themselves joined the army, indicating that soldiers' families were a fruitful source for recruitment. After twenty-five years of duty, Bithus received his diploma on November 7, 88. Upon mustering out of the army, he received the grant of Roman citizenship for himself and his family, as his diploma attests. He apparently returned to Thrace, as that is where his diploma was found.

The example of Bithus is important not because he is unusual, but because he is typical. The might of the Roman Empire depended on hundreds of thousands of men just like him, who joined the army for the pay and the promise of a better life that it offered.

QUESTIONS FOR ANALYSIS

1. Why would it have been important for a soldier like Bithus to have a permanent record of his military career and status as a citizen?

2. Why did—and does—the promise of citizenship serve as an effective recruiting tool for the armed forces?

Source: *Corpus Inscriptionum Latinarum*, vol. 16, no. 35 (Berlin: G. Reimer, 1882).

ONLINE DOCUMENT ASSIGNMENT

How did the Roman Empire turn countless individuals like Bithus into the most powerful fighting machine the Mediterranean world had ever seen? Examine documents on the military's role in the empire's expansion, and then complete a writing assignment based on the evidence and details from this chapter.

bedfordstmartins.com/mckaywestvalue

Boys boxed, swam, and learned to ride when possible, all to increase their strength, while giving them basic skills. Wealthy boys gained formal education from tutors or schools, generally favoring rhetoric and law for a political career. Others entered the army, usually as cadets on the staffs of prominent officers.

Approaches to Urban Problems

Fire and crime were serious problems in the city, even after Augustus created urban fire and police forces. Streets were narrow, drainage was inadequate, and sanitation was poor. Numerous inscriptions record prohibitions against dumping human refuse and even

Roman Architecture The Pont du Gard at Nîmes in France is a bridge over a river carrying an aqueduct that supplied millions of gallons of water per day to the Roman city of Nîmes in Gaul; the water flowed in a channel at the very top. Although this bridge was built largely without mortar or concrete, many Roman aqueducts and bridges relied on concrete and sometimes iron rods for their strength. (© Masterfile Royalty Free)

cadavers on the grounds of sanctuaries and cemeteries. Private houses generally lacked toilets, so people used chamber pots.

In the second century urban planning and new construction improved the situation. For example, engineers built an elaborate system that collected sewage from public baths, the ground floors of buildings, and public latrines. They also built hundreds of miles of **aqueducts**, sophisticated systems of canals, channels, and pipes, most of them underground, that brought freshwater into the city from the surrounding hills. The aqueducts, powered entirely by gravity, required regular maintenance, but they were a great improvement and helped make Rome a very attractive place to live. Building aqueducts required thousands and sometimes tens of thousands of workers, who were generally paid out of the imperial treasury. Aqueducts became a feature of Roman cities in many parts of the empire.

Better disposal of sewage was one way that people living in Rome tried to maintain their health, and they also used a range of treatments to stay healthy and cure illness. This included treatments based on the ideas of the Greek physician Hippocrates; folk remedies; prayers and rituals at the temple of the god of medicine, Asclepius; surgery; and combinations of all of these.

The most important medical researcher and physician working in imperial Rome was Galen (ca. 129 C.E.–ca. 200 C.E.), a Greek born in modern-day Turkey. Like anyone hoping to rise in stature and wealth, he came to Rome. Building on the work of Hellenistic physicians (see Chapter 4), Galen wrote a huge number of treatises on anatomy and physiology, and became the personal physician of many prominent Romans, including several emperors. He promoted the idea that imbalances among various bodily fluids caused illness, and recommended bloodletting as a cure. This would remain a standard treatment in Western medicine until the eighteenth century. His research into the nervous system and the operation of muscles — most of which he conducted on animals, because the Romans forbade dissections of human cadavers — proved to be more accurate than did his ideas about the circulation of fluids. So did his practical advice on the treatment of wounds, much of which grew out of his and others' experiences with soldiers on the battlefield.

Neither Galen nor any other Roman physician could do much for infectious diseases, and in 165 troops returning from campaigns in the East brought a new disease with them, which spread quickly in the city and then beyond into other parts of the empire. Modern epidemiologists think this was most likely smallpox, but in the ancient world it became known simply as the Antonine plague, because it occurred during the reigns of emperors from the Antonine family. Whatever it was, it appears to have been extremely virulent in the city of Rome and among the Roman army for a decade or so.

Along with fire and disease, food was an issue in the ever more crowded city. Because of the danger of starvation, the emperor, following republican practice, provided the citizen population with free grain for bread and, later, oil and wine. By feeding the citizenry, the emperor prevented bread riots caused by shortages and high prices. For those who did not enjoy the rights of citizenship, the emperor provided grain at low prices. This measure was designed to prevent speculators from forcing up grain prices in times of crisis. By maintaining the grain supply, the emperor kept the favor of the people and ensured that Rome's poor did not starve.

Popular Entertainment

In addition to supplying grain, the emperor and other wealthy citizens also entertained the Roman populace, often at vast expense. This combination of material support and popular entertainment to keep the masses happy is often termed "bread and circuses." The most popular forms of public entertainment were gladiatorial contests and chariot racing. Gladiatorial combat had begun as a private event during the republic, sponsored by men seeking new ways to honor their ancestors. By the early empire it had grown into a major public spectacle, with sponsors sometimes offering hundreds of gladiator fights along with battles between animals or between animals and humans. Games were advertised on billboards, and spectators were given a program with the names and sometimes the fighting statistics of the pairs, so that they could bet more easily.

Men came to be gladiators through a variety of ways. Many were soldiers captured in war, sent to Rome or other large cities to be gladiators instead of being killed. Some were criminals, especially slaves found guilty of various crimes. By the imperial period increasing numbers were volunteers, often poor immigrants who saw gladiatorial combat as a way to support themselves. All gladiators were trained in gladiatorial schools and were legally slaves, although they could keep their winnings and a few became quite wealthy. The Hollywood portrayal of gladiatorial combat has men fighting to their death, but this was increasingly rare, as the owners of especially skilled fighters wanted them to continue to compete. Many — perhaps most — did die at a young age from their injuries or later infections, but some fought more than a hundred battles over long careers, retiring to become trainers in gladiatorial schools. Sponsors of matches sought to offer viewers ever more unusual spectacles: left-handed gladiators fighting right-handed ones, dwarf gladiators, and for a brief period even female gladiators. For a criminal

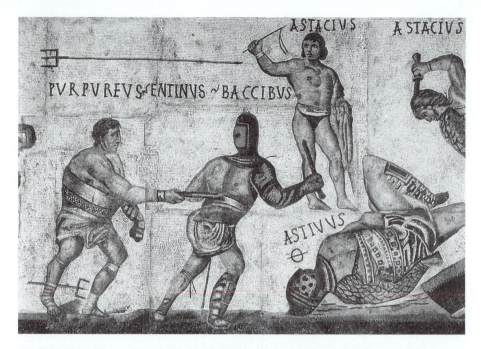

Gladiator Mosaic   Made in the first half of the fourth century, this mosaic from an estate outside Rome includes the name of each gladiator next to the figure. In the back a gladiator stands in a victory pose, while the fallen gladiator in the front is marked with the symbol Ø, indicating that he has died in combat. Many of the gladiators in this mosaic, such as those at the left, appear less fit and fearsome than the gladiators depicted in movies, more closely reflecting the reality that gladiatorial combat was a job undertaken by a variety of people. (Scala/Art Resource, NY)

condemned to die, the arena was preferable to the imperial mines, where convicts worked digging ore and died under wretched conditions. At least in the arena the gladiator might fight well enough to win freedom. Some Romans protested gladiatorial fighting, but the emperors recognized the political value of such spectacles, and most Romans enjoyed them.

The Romans were even more addicted to chariot racing than to gladiatorial shows. Under the empire four permanent teams competed against one another. Each had its own color — red, white, green, or blue. Two-horse and four-horse chariots ran a course of seven laps, about five miles. One charioteer, Gaius Appuleius Diocles, raced for twenty-four years, with over 4,000 starts and nearly 1,500 wins. His admirers honored him with an inscription that proclaimed him champion of all charioteers. Other winning charioteers were also idolized, just as sports stars are today.

Roman spectacles such as gladiator fights and chariot racing are fascinating subjects for movies and computer games, but they were not everyday activities for Romans. As is evident on tombstone inscriptions, ordinary Romans were proud of their work and accomplishments and affectionate toward their families and friends. An impression of them can be gained from their epitaphs.

Prosperity in the Roman Provinces

As the empire grew and stabilized, many Roman provinces grew prosperous. Peace and security opened Britain, Gaul, and the lands of the Danube to settlers from other parts of the Roman Empire (Map 6.2). Veterans were given small parcels of land in the provinces, becoming tenant farmers.

The rural population throughout the empire left few records, but the inscriptions that remain point to a melding of cultures. One sphere where this occurred was language. People used Latin for legal and state religious purposes, but gradually Latin blended with the original language of an area and with languages spoken by those who came into the area later. Slowly what would become the Romance languages of Spanish, Italian, French, Portuguese, and Romanian evolved. Religion was another site of cultural exchange and mixture. Romans moving into an area learned about and began to venerate local gods, and local people learned about Roman ones. Gradually hybrid deities and rituals developed. The process of cultural exchange was at first more urban than rural, but the importance of cities and towns to the life of the wider countryside ensured that its effects spread far afield.

The garrison towns that grew up around provincial military camps became the centers of organized political life, and some grew into major cities, including Eburacum (modern-day York), Lutetia Parisiorum (Paris), and Londinium (London). In order to supply these administrative centers with food, land around them was cultivated more intensively. Roman merchants became early bankers, loaning money to local people and often controlling them financially. Wealthy Roman officials also sometimes built country estates in rural areas near the city, where they did grow crops but also escaped from the stresses of city life.

During the first and second centuries, Roman Gaul became more prosperous than ever before, and prosperity attracted Roman settlers. Roman veterans mingled with the local population and sometimes married into local families. There was not much difference in many parts of the province between the original Celtic villages and their Roman successors.

In Britain, Roman influence was strongest in the south, where more towns developed. Archaeological evidence, such as coins and amphoras that held oil or wine, indicates healthy trading connections with the north, however, as Roman merchandise moved through the gates of Hadrian's Wall in exchange for food and other local products.

Across eastern Europe, Roman influence was weaker than it was in Gaul or southern Britain, and there appears to have been less intermarriage. In Illyria (ih-LIHR-ee-uh) and Dalmatia, regions of modern Albania, Croatia, and Montenegro, the local population never widely embraced either Roman culture or urban life. To a certain extent, however, Romanization occurred simply because the peoples lived in such close proximity.

The Romans were the first to build cities in northern Europe, but in the eastern Mediterranean they ruled cities that had existed before Rome itself was even a village. Here there was much continuity in urban life from the Hellenistic period. There was less construction than in the Roman cities of northern and western Europe because existing buildings could simply be put to new uses.

The well-preserved ruins of the ancient city of Aspendos, at the mouth of the Eurymedon (now Kopru) River on the south coast of modern Turkey (see Map 6.2), give a picture of life in one of these older Eastern cities. Built sometime before 500 B.C.E.,

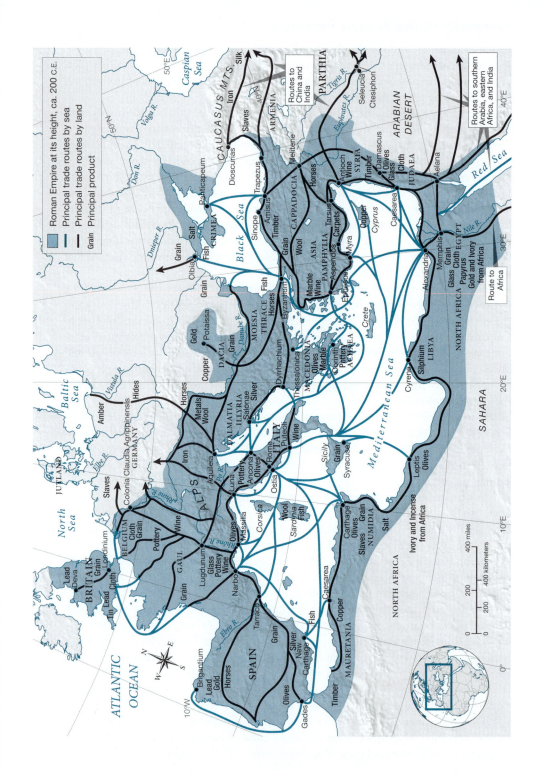

◀ **MAP 6.2** **Production and Trade in the Pax Romana, ca. 27** B.C.E.–**180** C.E.
This map gives a good idea of the principal products of various parts of the Roman Empire at its height and the trade routes connecting these regions.

the city was an important economic center in the Persian Empire and the site of a major battle in the wars between the Persian Empire and the Greek city-states. It sat among fertile fields, and the resources of the land provided raw materials for industry and trade. Trade along the river and in the port, especially salt, oil, horses, and wool, provided wealth to merchants. Aspendos was one of the earliest cities to mint coins. It was conquered by Alexander the Great and then by the Romans, but it remained prosperous. Romans and indigenous people mixed at the city's central marketplace and in temples and public buildings. The Romans built an aqueduct to bring water into the city, although this was later destroyed in an earthquake. Over the river they also built an arched stone bridge, about thirty feet wide so that carts and chariots could easily travel on it. This may have also collapsed in an earthquake, but its foundations were so sturdy that a thousand years later the area's Turkish rulers used them to build a new bridge, which still stands. In 155 C.E. a local architect built a magnificent theater that probably held seven thousand spectators, who sat under a retractable awning that provided shade. Here men and women enjoyed the great plays of the past and those popular in their own day. They also watched gladiatorial contests, for these were popular in Eastern cities, as was horse racing.

More than just places to live, cities like Aspendos were centers of intellectual and cultural life. Their residents were in touch with the ideas and events of the day, in a network that spanned the entire Mediterranean and reached as far north as Britain. As long as the empire prospered and the revenues reached the imperial coffers, life in provincial cities—at least for the wealthy—could be nearly as pleasant as that in Rome.

Trade and Commerce

The expansion of trade during the pax Romana made the Roman Empire an economic as well as a political force in the provinces (see Map 6.2). Britain and Belgium became prime grain producers, with much of their harvests going to the armies of the Rhine, and Britain's wool industry probably got its start under the Romans. Italy and southern Gaul produced huge quantities of wine, which was shipped in large pottery jugs wherever merchant vessels could carry it. Roman colonists introduced the olive to southern Spain and northern Africa, which soon produced most of the oil consumed in the western part of the empire. In the East the olive oil production of Syrian farmers reached an all-time high, and Egypt produced tons of wheat that fed the Roman populace.

The growth of industry in the provinces was another striking development of this period. Cities in Gaul and Germany eclipsed the old Mediterranean manufacturing centers. Lyons in Gaul and later Cologne in Germany became the new centers of the glassmaking industry, and the cities of Gaul were nearly unrivaled in the manufacture of bronze and brass. The Romans took the manufacture of pottery to an advanced stage by introducing a wider range of vessels and making some of these on an industrial scale in kilns that were large enough to fire tens of thousands of pots at once. The most prized pottery was *terra sigillata*, reddish decorated tableware with a glossy surface. Methods for making terra sigillata spread from Italy northwards into Europe, often introduced by soldiers in the Roman army who had been trained in potterymaking in Italy. These craftsmen set up facilities to make roof tiles, amphoras, and dishes for their units, and local potters began to copy their styles and methods of manufacturing. Terra sigillata often portrayed Greco-Roman gods and heroes, so this pottery spread Mediterranean myths and stories. Local artisans added their own distinctive flourishes and sometimes stamped their names on the pots; these individual touches have allowed archaeologists to trace the pottery trade throughout the Roman Empire in great detail. Aided by all this growth in trade and industry, Europe and western Asia were linked in ways they had not been before.

As the Romans drove farther eastward, they encountered the Parthians, who had established a kingdom in what is now Afghanistan and Iran in the Hellenistic period. In the second century the Romans tried unsuccessfully to drive out the Parthians, who came to act as a link between Roman and Chinese merchants. Chinese merchants sold their wares to the Parthians, who then carried the goods overland to Mesopotamia or Egypt, from which they were shipped throughout the Roman Empire. Silk was a major commodity traded from the East to the West, along with other luxury goods. In return the Romans traded glassware, precious gems, and slaves.

The pax Romana was also an era of maritime trade, and Roman ships sailed from Egyptian ports to the mouth of the Indus River, where they traded local merchandise and wares imported by the Parthians. In the late first century the Chinese emperor sent an ambassador, Gan Ying, to make contact with the Roman Empire. Gan Ying made it as far as the Persian Gulf ports, where he heard about the Romans from Parthian sailors and reported back to his emperor that the Romans were wealthy, tall, and strikingly similar to the Chinese. His report became part of a group of accounts about the Romans and other "Western" peoples that circulated widely among scholars and officials in Han China. Educated Romans did not have a corresponding interest in China. For them, China remained more of a mythical than a real place, and they never bothered to learn more about it.

The Coming of Christianity

How did Christianity grow into a major religious movement?

During the reign of the emperor Tiberius (r. 14–37 C.E.), in the Roman province of Judaea, which had been created out of the Jewish kingdom of Judah, a Jewish man named Jesus of Nazareth preached, attracted a following, and was executed on the order of the Roman prefect Pontius Pilate. At the time this was a minor event, but Christianity, the religion created by Jesus's followers, came to have an enormous impact first in the Roman Empire and later throughout the world.

Factors Behind the Rise of Christianity

The civil wars that destroyed the Roman Republic left their mark on Judaea, where Jewish leaders had taken sides in the conflict. The turmoil created a climate of violence throughout the area, and among the Jews movements in opposition to the Romans spread. Some of these, such as the Zealots, encouraged armed rebellion against Roman rule, which would, indeed, break out several times in the first and second centuries C.E.

(see page 169). Many Jews came to believe that a final struggle was near, and that it would lead to the coming of a savior, or **Messiah**, a descendant of King David who would destroy the Roman legions and inaugurate a period of peace, happiness, and prosperity for Jews. This apocalyptic belief was an old one among Jews, but by the first century C.E. it had become more widespread than ever, with many people prophesying the imminent coming of a Messiah and readying themselves for a cataclysmic battle.

The pagan world also played its part in the story of early Christianity. The term **pagan**, derived from a Latin word meaning "rural dweller," came to refer to those who practiced religions other than Judaism or Christianity. (Christianity was initially an urban religion, and those who lived in the countryside were less likely to be converts.) This included religions devoted to the traditional Roman gods of the hearth, home, and countryside; syncretistic religions that blended Roman and indigenous deities; the cult of the emperor spread through the erection of statues, temples, and monuments; and mystery religions that offered the promise of life after death (see Chapter 4). Many people in the Roman Empire practiced all of these, combining them in whatever way seemed most beneficial or satisfying to them.

The Life and Teachings of Jesus

Into this climate of Messianic hope and Roman religious blending came Jesus of Nazareth (ca. 3 B.C.E.–ca. 29 C.E.). According to Christian scripture, he was born to deeply religious Jewish parents and raised in Galilee, the stronghold of the Zealots and a trading center where Greeks and Romans interacted with Jews. His ministry began when he was about thirty, and he taught by preaching and telling stories.

Like Socrates, Jesus left no writings. Accounts of his sayings and teachings first circulated orally among his followers and were later written down. The principal evidence for his life and deeds are the four Gospels of the Bible (Matthew, Mark, Luke, John), books that are part of what Christians later termed the New Testament. These Gospels— the name means "good news"—are records of Jesus's teachings, written to build a community of faith sometime in the late first century. The Gospels were among the most widely copied and circulated early accounts of Jesus's life, and by the fourth century officials in the Christian Church decided that they, along with other types of writing such as letters and prophecies, would form Christian scripture. The four Gospels included in the Bible are called canonical, from the Greek word that means "the rule" or "the standard." Other early documents also circulated, some of which have been rediscovered in modern times, and their interpretation is often a source of controversy.

The Gospels include certain details of Jesus's life, but they were not meant to be biographies. Their authors had probably heard many different people talk about what Jesus said and did, and there are discrepancies among the four accounts. These differences indicate that early followers had a diversity of beliefs about Jesus's nature and purpose. This diversity of beliefs about Jesus continues today. Some see him as a moral teacher, some as a prophet, and many as the son of God who rose from the dead and is himself divine.

However, almost all the early sources agree on certain aspects of Jesus's teachings: He preached of a heavenly kingdom of eternal happiness in a life after death, and of the importance of devotion to God and love of others. His teachings were based on Hebrew scripture and reflected a conception of God and morality that came from Jewish tradition. Jesus's orthodoxy enabled him to preach in the synagogue and the temple, but he deviated from orthodoxy in insisting that he taught in his own name, not in the name of Yahweh (the Hebrew name for God). The Greek translation of the Hebrew word *Messiah* is *Christos*, the origin of the English word *Christ*. Was Jesus the Messiah, the Christ? A small band of followers thought so, and Jesus claimed that he was. Yet Jesus had his own conception of the Messiah. He would establish a spiritual kingdom, not an earthly one. As recounted in one of the Gospels, he commented:

> Do not lay up for yourselves treasures on earth, where moth and rust consume and where thieves break in and steal, but lay up for yourselves treasures in heaven, where neither moth nor rust consumes and where thieves do not break in and steal. For where your treasure is, there will your heart be also.[6]

The Roman official Pontius Pilate, who had authority over much of Judaea, knew little about Jesus's teachings. Like all Roman officials, he was concerned with maintaining peace and order, which was a difficult task in restive Judaea. According to the New Testament, crowds followed Jesus into Jerusalem at the time of Passover, a highly emotional time in the Jewish year that marked the Jewish people's departure from Egypt under the leadership of Moses (see Chapter 2). The prospect that these crowds would spark violence no doubt alarmed Pilate. Some Jews believed that Jesus was the long-awaited Messiah. Others hated and feared him because they thought him religiously dangerous. The four Gospels differ somewhat on exactly what actions Jesus took in the city and what Jesus and Pilate said to each other after Jesus was arrested. They agree that Pilate condemned Jesus to death by crucifixion, and his soldiers carried out the sentence. On the third day after Jesus's crucifixion, some of his followers claimed that he had risen from the dead. For his earliest followers and for generations to come, the resurrection of Jesus became a central element of faith.

The Spread of Christianity

The memory of Jesus and his teachings survived and flourished. Believers in his divinity met in small assemblies or congregations, often in one another's homes, to discuss the meaning of Jesus's message and to celebrate a ritual (later called the Eucharist or Lord's Supper) commemorating his last meal with his disciples before his arrest. Because they expected Jesus to return to the world very soon, they regarded earthly life and institutions as unimportant. Only later did these congregations evolve into what came to be called the religion of Christianity, with a formal organization and set of beliefs.

The catalyst in the spread of Jesus's teachings and the formation of the Christian Church was Paul of Tarsus, a well-educated Hellenized Jew who was comfortable in both the Roman and the Jewish worlds. The New Testament reports that at first he persecuted members of the new sect, but when on the road to the city of Damascus in Syria he was struck blind by a vision of light and heard Jesus's voice. He converted to belief in Jesus, regained his sight, and became a vigorous promoter of Jesus's ideas. Paul traveled all over the Roman Empire and wrote letters of advice to many groups. These letters were copied and widely circulated, transforming Jesus's ideas into more specific moral teachings. He recognized that Christianity would not grow if it remained within Judaism, and he connected it with the non-Jewish world. As a result of his efforts, Paul became the most important figure in changing Christianity from a Jewish sect into a separate religion, and many of his letters became part of Christian scripture.

The breadth of the Roman Empire was another factor behind the spread of Christianity. If all roads led to Rome, they also led outward to the provinces. This enabled early Christians to spread their faith easily throughout the known world, as Jesus had told his followers to do in the Gospels, thus making his teachings universal. The pagan Romans also considered their secular empire universal, and the early Christians combined the two concepts of universalism.

Though most of the earliest converts seem to have been Jews, or Greeks and Romans who were already interested in Jewish moral teachings, Paul urged that Gentiles, or non-Jews, be accepted on an equal basis. The earliest Christian converts included people from all social classes. These people were reached by missionaries and others who spread the Christian message through family contacts, friendships, and business networks. Many women were active in spreading Christianity. Paul greeted male and female converts by name in his letters and noted that women often provided financial support for his activities. The growing Christian communities differed about the extent to which women should participate in the workings of the religion; some favored giving women a larger role in church affairs, while others were more restrictive, urging women to be silent on religious matters.

People were attracted to Christian teachings for a variety of reasons. It was in many ways a mystery religion, offering its adherents special teachings that would give them immortality. But in contrast to traditional mystery religions, Christianity promised this immortality widely, not only to a select few.

Most early Christians believed that they would rise in body, not simply in spirit, after a final day of judgment, so they favored burial of the dead rather than the more common Roman practice of cremation. They retained the Roman belief that the dead were polluting and so had to be buried outside city walls, however, and in the second century began to dig tunnels in the soft rock around Rome for burials. The bodies were placed in niches along the walls of these underground chambers and then sealed up. Gradually huge complexes of burial passageways called catacombs were dug. Memorial services for martyrs were sometimes held in or near catacombs, but they were not regular places of worship. Many catacombs contain some of the earliest examples of Christian art, and others, dug by Jews or pagans who chose to bury rather than cremate their own dead, contain examples of Jewish and secular Roman art from this period.

Along with the possibility of life after death, Christianity also offered rewards in this world to adherents. One of these was the possibility of forgiveness, for believers accepted that human nature is weak and that even the best Christians could fall into sin. But Jesus loved sinners and forgave those who repented. Christianity was also attractive to many because it gave the Roman world a cause. Instead of passivity, Christians stressed the ideal of striving for a goal. By spreading the word of Christ, Christians played their part in God's plan for the triumph of Christianity on earth. Christianity likewise gave its devotees a sense of community, which was very welcome in the often highly mobile world of the Roman Empire. To stress the spiritual kinship of this new type of community, Christians often called one another brother and sister. Also, many Christians took Jesus's commandment to love one another as a guide and provided support for widows, orphans, and the poor, just as they did for family members. Such material support became increasingly attractive as Roman social welfare programs broke down in the third century.

The Growing Acceptance and Evolution of Christianity

At first most Roman officials largely ignored the followers of Jesus, viewing them simply as one of the many splinter groups within Judaism. Slowly some Roman officials and leaders came to oppose Christian practices and beliefs. They considered Christians to be subversive dissidents because they stopped practicing traditional rituals venerating the hearth and home and they objected—often publicly or in writing—to the cult of the emperor. Some Romans thought that Christianity was one of the worst of the mystery religions, with immoral and indecent rituals. For instance, they thought that the ritual of the Lord's Supper, at which Christians said that they ate and drank the body and blood of Jesus, was an act of cannibalism involving the ritual murder of Roman boys. Many in the Roman Empire also feared that the traditional gods would withdraw their favor from the Roman Empire because of the Christian insistence that these gods either did not exist or were evil spirits. The Christian refusal to worship Roman gods, in their opinion, endangered Roman lives and society. Others worried that Christians were trying to destroy the Roman family with their insistence on a new type of kinship, and they pointed to Jesus's words in the Gospels saying that salvation was far more important than family relationships. A woman who converted, thought many Romans, might use her new faith to oppose her father's choice of marital partner or even renounce marriage itself, an idea supported by the actions of a few female converts.

Persecutions of Christians, including torture and executions, were organized by governors of Roman provinces and sometimes by the emperor, beginning with Nero. Most persecutions were local and sporadic in nature, however, and some of the gory stories about the martyrs are later inventions, designed to strengthen believers with accounts of earlier heroes. Christians differed in their opinions about how to respond to persecution. Some sought out martyrdom, while others thought that doing so went against Christian teachings.

Responses to Christianity on the part of Roman emperors varied. The emperor Trajan forbade his governors to hunt down Christians. Though admitting that he considered Christianity an abomination, he decided it was better policy to leave Christians in peace. Later emperors, including Septimius Severus at the very end of the second century, Decius in the third century, and Diocletian in the fourth century, increased persecutions again, ordering Christians to sacrifice to the emperor and the Roman gods or risk death. Executions followed their edicts, although estimates of how many people were actually martyred in any of these persecutions vary widely.

Christian Oil Lamp   When Christianity spread in the Roman Empire, many believers purchased household goods with Christian symbols. This pottery lamp for an ordinary home, dating from the fourth century, is marked with a common symbol for Jesus, the letters *XP* (Chi Rho), the first two letters in Greek for *Christos*, "Christ." (Zev Radovan/www.BibleLandPictures.com)

By the second century C.E. Christianity was also changing. The belief that Jesus was soon coming again gradually waned, and as the number of converts increased, permanent institutions were established instead of simple house churches. These included buildings and a hierarchy of officials often modeled on those of the Roman Empire. **Bishops**, officials with jurisdiction over a certain area, became especially important. They began to assert that they had the right to determine the correct interpretation of Christian teachings and to choose their successors. Councils of bishops determined which writings would be considered canonical, and lines were increasingly drawn between what was considered correct teaching and what was considered incorrect, or **heresy**.

Christianity also began to attract more highly educated individuals, who developed complex theological interpretations of issues that were not clear in scripture. Often drawing on Greek philosophy and Roman legal traditions, they worked out understandings of such issues as how Jesus could be both divine and human, and how God could be both a father and a son (and later a spirit as well, a Christian doctrine known as the Trinity). Bishops and theologians often modified teachings that seemed upsetting to Romans, such as Jesus's harsh words about wealth and family ties. Given all these changes, Christianity became more formal in the second century, with power more centralized.

The Empire in Disarray

What explains the chaos of the third century C.E.?

The prosperity and political stability of the second century gave way to a period of domestic upheaval and foreign invasion. The third century saw a long series of able but ambitious military commanders who used their legions to make themselves emperors. Law yielded to the sword, and the office of the emperor lost legitimacy. The nature of the army changed, and the economy weakened because of unsound policies.

Civil Wars and Military Commanders

The reign of Marcus Aurelius (r. 161–180 C.E.), the last of the "five good emperors," was marked by problems. The Tiber River flooded in 162, destroying crops and killing animals, which led to famine. Soldiers returning from wars in the East brought the Antonine plague back to Rome (see page 175) and then carried it northward. Germanic-speaking groups attacked along the Rhine and Danube borders, and the emperor himself took over the campaign against them in 169. He spent most of the rest of his life in military camps along Rome's northern border, where in addition to leading troops he wrote a series of personal reflections in Greek. These *Meditations*, as they later came to be known, are advice to himself about doing one's duty and acting in accordance with nature, ideas that came from Stoic philosophy (see Chapter 4). He wrote:

> Do not act unwillingly nor selfishly nor without self-examination. . . . Take heed not to be transformed into a Caesar, not to be dipped in the purple dye [a color only the emperor could wear]. Keep yourself therefore simple, good, pure, grave, unaffected, the friend of justice, religious, kind, affectionate, strong for your proper work. Wrestle to continue to be the man Philosophy wished to make you. Reverence the gods, save men.[7]

The Emperor Marcus Aurelius
This larger-than-life bronze equestrian statue, sculpted to celebrate his military victories or shortly after his death in 180 C.E., shows the emperor holding up his hand in the conventional imperial greeting. More than twenty equestrian statues could be seen in late imperial Rome, but this is the only one to survive. In the sixteenth century Michelangelo built one of the major plazas of Rome around it, although now the original has been moved to a museum for better preservation and a copy stands outdoors. (Tibor Bognar/Alamy)

The *Meditations* are a good key to Marcus Aurelius's character, but they appear not to have circulated very much during the centuries immediately after they were written. Certainly very few later emperors took this advice to heart.

After the death of Marcus Aurelius, misrule by his successors led to a long and intense spasm of fighting. Marcus Aurelius's son Commodus was strangled by a conspiracy that included his wife, and in 193 five men claimed the throne in quick succession. Two of them were also assassinated, and Septimius Severus (r. 193–211) emerged as the victor. He restored order, expanded the borders of the Roman Empire in Africa and western Asia, and invaded Scotland. He increased the size of the army significantly and paid the soldiers better. This made him popular with soldiers, though it also increased the taxes on civilians. Some of his policies regarding the army created additional problems in the long run. Changes in recruiting practices that emphasized local recruiting of non-Romans created a Roman army that became less acculturated to Roman values. This army was no longer the vehicle for Romanization that it had been in earlier centuries. In part to increase the tax base, in 212 Septimius Severus's son Caracalla (r. 198–217) issued an edict making all free male residents of the Roman Empire citizens. This made them eligible to serve in the legions—which may have been why Caracalla did this—but also made army service less attractive, and reduced the number of men willing to join.

More than twenty different emperors seized power in the forty-nine years between 235 and 284, a period scholars call the "crisis of the third century." These emperors were generally military commanders from the border provinces, and there were so many that the middle of the third century has become known as the age of the **barracks emperors**. Almost all were either assassinated or died in civil wars, and their concentration on overthrowing the ruling emperor left the borders unguarded. Non-Roman groups on the frontiers took full advantage of the chaos to overrun vast areas. When they reached the Rhine and the Danube, they often found gaping holes in the Roman defenses.

Turmoil in Economic Life

This chaos also disrupted areas far away from the borders of the empire. Renegade soldiers and corrupt imperial officials, together with many greedy local agents, preyed on local people. In some places in the countryside, officials requisitioned villagers' livestock and compelled them to do forced labor. Farmers appealed to the government for protection so that they could cultivate the land. Although some of those in authority were unsympathetic and even violent to villagers, many others tried to maintain order. Yet even the best of them also suffered. If officials could not meet their tax quotas, which were rising to support the costs of civil war, they had to pay the deficits from their own pockets. Because the local officials were themselves so hard-pressed, they squeezed what they needed from rural families. Many farmers, unable to pay, were driven off their land, and those remaining faced ruin. As a result, agricultural productivity declined.

In response to the economic crisis, the emperors reduced the amount of silver used in coins, replacing it with less valuable metals such as copper, so that they could continue to pay their troops. This tactic, however, led to crippling inflation, which wiped out savings and sent prices soaring.

The Romans still controlled the Mediterranean, which nurtured commerce. The road system remained largely intact, though often roads were allowed to fall into disrepair. Trade still flowed, but with reduced efficiency and high costs.

By 284 C.E. the empire had reached a crisis that threatened its downfall. The position of emperor was gained no longer by lawful succession but rather by victory in civil war. The empire had failed at the top, and the repercussions of the disaster spread throughout the empire with dire effects.

Notes

1. Virgil, *Aeneid*, trans. Theodore C. Williams (Boston: Houghton Mifflin, 1910), 6.851–853.
2. Virgil, *Georgics* 3.515–519. In this chapter, works in Latin with no translator noted were translated by John Buckler.
3. Virgil, *Aeneid* 1.1–11.
4. Text in Mary Johnston, *Roman Life* (Chicago: Scott, Foresman, and Co., 1957), p. 172.
5. Napthali Lewis and Meyer Reinhold, *Roman Civilization*, vol. 2 (New York: Harper Torchbooks, 1955), p. 262.
6. Matthew 6:19–21.
7. Marcus Aurelius, *Meditations*, III, 5, VI, 30, trans. A. S. L. Farquharson (New York: Everyman's Library, 1961), pp. 12, 5.

Chapter Review

MAKE IT STICK

LearningCurve
bedfordstmartins.com/mckaywestvalue

After reading the chapter, use LearningCurve to retain what you've read.

IDENTIFY KEY TERMS

Identify and explain the significance of each item below.

imperator (p. 159)   aqueducts (p. 174)
principate (p. 160)   Messiah (p. 181)
Roma et Augustus (p. 161)   pagan (p. 181)
pax Romana (p. 163)   bishops (p. 185)
Praetorians (p. 169)   heresy (p. 185)
"five good emperors" (p. 169)   barracks emperors (p. 186)

REVIEW THE MAIN IDEAS

Answer the focus questions from each section of the chapter.

◆ How did Augustus create a foundation for the Roman Empire? (p. 159)

◆ How did the Roman state develop after Augustus? (p. 168)

◆ What was life like in the city of Rome, and what was it like in the provinces? (p. 171)

◆ How did Christianity grow into a major religious movement? (p. 180)

◆ What explains the chaos of the third century C.E.? (p. 185)

MAKE CONNECTIONS

Think about the larger developments and continuities within and across chapters.

1. What allowed large empires in the ancient world, including the Persians (Chapter 2) and the Romans, to govern vast territories and many different peoples successfully?

2. How was slavery in the Roman Empire different from that of earlier societies? How was it similar? What might account for the continuities and changes in slavery you have identified?

3. If a male resident of Athens during the time of Pericles (Chapter 3) had time-traveled to Rome during the time of Augustus, what might he have found familiar? What might have seemed strange? How might this differ if the time traveler were a female resident of Athens?

ONLINE DOCUMENT ASSIGNMENT

Bithus, a Soldier in the Roman Army

How did the Roman Empire turn countless individuals like Bithus into the most powerful fighting machine the Mediterranean world had ever seen?

You encountered Bithus's story on page 172. Keeping the question above in mind, go online and examine documents on the military's role in the empire's expansion. Then complete a writing assignment based on the evidence and details from this chapter.

bedfordstmartins.com/mckaywestvalue

CHRONOLOGY

27 B.C.E.–68 C.E.	• Julio-Claudian emperors; expansion into northern and western Europe
ca. 50 B.C.E.–20 C.E.	• "Golden age" of Latin literature
ca. 3 B.C.E.–ca. 29 C.E.	• Life of Jesus
69–96 C.E.	• Flavian emperors; restoration of order
70 C.E.	• Rebellion crushed in Judaea
96–180 C.E.	• Era of the "five good emperors," with relative peace and prosperity
193–211 C.E.	• Emperor Septimius Severus expands Rome's borders in Africa and western Asia
212 C.E.	• Edict of Caracalla makes all free males living in Roman Empire citizens
235–284 C.E.	• Barracks emperors; civil war; breakdown of the empire; economic decline

✔ LearningCurve
bedfordstmartins.com/mckaywestvalue
After reading the chapter, use
LearningCurve to retain what
you've read.

7

Late Antiquity

250–600

THE ROMAN EMPIRE, WITH ITS POWERFUL—AND SOMETIMES
bizarre—leaders, magnificent buildings, luxurious clothing, and bloody
amusements, has long fascinated people. Politicians and historians have
closely studied the reasons for its successes and have even more closely analyzed the weaknesses that led to its eventual collapse. From the third century
onward, the Western Roman Empire slowly disintegrated. Scholars have long
seen this era as one of the great turning points in Western history, a time
when the ancient world was transformed into the very different medieval
world. During the last several decades, however, focus has shifted to continuities as well as changes, and what is now usually termed "late antiquity"
has been recognized as a period of creativity and adaptation, not simply of
decline and fall.

The two main agents of continuity in late antiquity were the Christian
Church and the Byzantine or Eastern Roman Empire. Missionaries and church
officials spread Christianity within and far beyond the borders of the Roman
Empire, bringing with them the Latin language and institutions based on
Roman models. The Byzantine Empire lasted until 1453, a thousand years longer than the Western Roman Empire, and preserved and transmitted much
of ancient Greco-Roman law, philosophy, and institutions. The main agents of
change in late antiquity were groups the Romans labeled barbarians migrating
into the Roman Empire. They brought different social, political, and economic
structures with them, but as they encountered Roman culture and became
Christian, their own ways of doing things were also transformed.

Reconstruction Under Diocletian and Constantine

How did Diocletian and Constantine try to reform the empire?

In the middle of the third century, the Roman Empire faced internal turmoil and external attacks. Civil wars tore the empire apart as emperors rose and fell in quick succession, and barbarian groups migrated and marauded deep within the boundaries of the empire (see Chapter 6). Wars and invasions disrupted normal commerce and agriculture, the primary sources of tax revenues. The barracks emperors of the third century dealt with economic hardship by cutting the silver content of coins until money was virtually worthless. The immediate result was crippling inflation throughout the empire, made worse by the corruption of many officials. Many Romans had become Christian, but the followers of traditional Roman religion were divided in their views of what this meant for the empire. In the early fourth century, the emperor Diocletian (r. 284–305), who was born of low-status parents and had risen through the ranks of the military to become emperor, restored order, and the later emperor Constantine (r. 306–337) continued his work. How Diocletian, Constantine, and their successors responded to the problems facing the empire influenced later developments.

Political Measures

Under Diocletian, Augustus's polite fiction of the emperor as first among equals gave way to the emperor as absolute autocrat. The princeps became *dominus* (lord). The emperor claimed that he was "the elect of god" — that he ruled because of divine favor. To underline the emperor's exalted position, Diocletian and Constantine adopted the gaudy court ceremonies and trappings of the Persian Empire. People entering the emperor's presence prostrated themselves before him and kissed the hem of his robes.

Diocletian recognized that the empire had become too large for one man to handle and divided it into a western half and an eastern half. Diocletian assumed direct control of the eastern part; he gave the rule of the western part to a colleague, along with the title *augustus*. Around 293 Diocletian further delegated power by appointing two men to assist the augustus and him; each of the four men was given the title *caesar*, and the system was known as the **tetrarchy**

Diocletian's Tetrarchy   This sculpture represents the possibilities and problems of the tetrarchy established by the emperor Diocletian to rule the Roman Empire. Each of the four men has one hand on another's shoulder, a symbol of solidarity, but the other on his sword, a gesture that proved prophetic when the tetrarchy failed soon after Diocletian's death and another struggle for power began. (Alinari/Art Resource, NY)

PRIMARY SOURCE   Recruiting and Training Soldiers in the Roman Army

The Roman army in the late empire faced many challenges, and leaders attempted to make it stronger in a variety of ways. In De Re Militari *(On Military Matters), written about the year 500, the otherwise unknown author Vegetius sets out what he sees as ideal military recruitment and training, looking back somewhat nostalgically to the way he thought things were in the early days of the empire. The book was recopied many times over the centuries, was translated into other languages, and became a standard manual on warfare in the Middle Ages.*

The Proper Age for Recruits. If we follow the ancient practice, the proper time for enlisting youth into the army is at their entrance into the age of puberty. At this time instructions of every kind are more quickly imbibed and more lastingly imprinted on the mind. Besides this, the indispensable military exercises of running and leaping must be acquired before the limbs are too much stiffened by age. For it is activity, improved by continual practice, which forms the useful and good soldier. . . .

Signs of Desirable Qualities. Those employed to superintend new levies [groups of recruits] should be particularly careful in examining the features of their faces, their eyes, and the make of their limbs, to enable them to form a true judgment and choose such as are most likely to prove good soldiers. For experience assures us that there are in men, as well as in horses and dogs, certain signs by which their virtues may be discovered. The young soldier, therefore, ought to have a lively eye, should carry his head erect, his chest should be broad, his shoulders muscular and brawny, his fingers long, his arms strong, his waist small, his shape easy, his legs and feet rather nervous than fleshy. When all these marks are found in a recruit, a little height may be dispensed with, since it is of much more importance that a soldier should be strong than tall.

(TEH-trahr-kee), meaning "rule of four." He further divided each part of the empire into administrative units called **dioceses**, which were in turn subdivided into small provinces, all governed by an expanded bureaucracy. Although four men ruled the empire, Diocletian was clearly the senior partner and final source of authority.

Diocletian's political reforms were a momentous step. The reorganization made the empire easier to administer, and placed each of the four central military commands much closer to borders or other trouble spots, so that troops could be sent more quickly when needed. Diocletian hoped that the tetrarchy would supply a clearly defined order of succession and end struggles for power over the emperorship. That did not happen, but much of Diocletian's reorganization remained.

Like Diocletian, Constantine came up through the army, and took control after a series of civil wars. He eventually had authority over the entire empire, but ruled from the East, where he established a new capital for the empire at Byzantium, an old Greek city on the Bosporus, naming it "New Rome," though it was soon called Constantinople. Constantine sponsored a massive building program of palaces, warehouses, public buildings, and even a hippodrome for horse racing, modeling these on Roman

Trades Proper for New Levies. In choosing recruits regard should be given to their trade. Fishermen, fowlers, confectioners, weavers, and in general all whose professions more properly belong to women should, in my opinion, by no means be admitted into the service. On the contrary, smiths, carpenters, butchers, and huntsmen are the most proper to be taken into it. On the careful choice of soldiers depends the welfare of the Republic, and the very essence of the Roman Empire and its power is so inseparably connected with this charge, that it is of the highest importance not to be intrusted indiscriminately, but only to persons whose fidelity can be relied on.

Initial Training. The first thing the soldiers are to be taught is the military step, which can only be acquired by constant practice of marching quick and together. Nor is anything of more consequence either on the march or in the line than that they should keep their ranks with the greatest exactness. For troops who march in an irregular and disorderly manner are always in great danger of being defeated.

EVALUATE THE EVIDENCE

1. What does Vegetius see as the most important qualities of a soldier in the Roman army?

2. What military challenges facing the Roman Empire made the recruitment and training of soldiers essential?

Source: Flavius Vegetius Renatus, *The Military Institutions of the Romans* (*De Re Militari*), trans. Lieutenant John Clarke, 1767, http://www.pvv.ntnu.no/~madsb/home/war/vegetius/.

buildings. He built defensive works along the borders of the empire, trying hard to keep it together, and used various means to strengthen the army, as did his successors. (See "Primary Source: Recruiting and Training Soldiers in the Roman Army," above.) The emperors ruling from Constantinople could not provide enough military assistance to repel invaders in the western half of the Roman Empire, however, and Roman authority there slowly disintegrated.

Economic Issues

Diocletian and Constantine were faced with a number of economic problems, including inflation and declining tax revenues, and their attempts to solve them illustrate the methods and limitations of absolute monarchy. In a move unprecedented in Roman history, Diocletian issued an edict that fixed maximum prices and wages throughout the empire. He and his assistant emperors dealt with the tax system just as strictly and inflexibly. Taxes became payable in kind, that is, in goods such as grain, sheep, or cloth instead of money, which made them difficult to transport to central authorities. Constantine continued these measures and also made occupations more rigid: all people involved in the growing, preparation, and transportation of food and other essentials were locked into their professions. A baker, for example, could not go into any other business, and his son took up the trade at his death. In this period of severe depression many individuals and communities could not pay their taxes. In such cases local tax collectors, who were also bound to their occupations, had to make up the difference from their own funds. This system soon wiped out a whole class of moderately wealthy people and set the stage for the lack of social mobility that was a key characteristic of European society for many centuries to follow.

The emperors' measures did not really address Rome's central economic problems, however. Because of worsening conditions during the third and fourth centuries, many free farmers and their families were killed by invaders or renegade soldiers, fled the land to escape the barbarians, or abandoned farms ravaged in the fighting. Consequently, large tracts of land lay deserted. Landlords with ample resources began at once to reclaim as much of this land as they could, often hiring back the free farmers who had previously worked the land as paid labor or tenants. The huge villas that resulted were self-sufficient and became islands of stability in an unsettled world.

Free farmers who remained on the land were exposed to the raids of barbarians or robbers and to the tyranny of imperial officials. In return for the protection and security landlords could offer, small landholders gave over their lands and their freedom. To guarantee a supply of labor, landlords denied them freedom to move elsewhere. Henceforth they and their families worked their patrons' land, not their own. Free men and women were becoming tenant farmers bound to the land, what would later be called serfs.

The Acceptance of Christianity

The turmoil of the third century seemed to some emperors, including Diocletian, to be the punishment of the gods. Diocletian stepped up persecution of Christians who would not sacrifice to Rome's traditional deities, portraying them as disloyal to the empire in an attempt to wipe out the faith. These persecutions lasted only a few years, however. Increasing numbers of Romans, including members of prominent families, were converting to Christianity, and many who followed traditional Roman religions no longer saw Christianity as un-Roman (see Chapter 6). Constantine reversed Diocletian's policy and instead ordered toleration of all religions in the Edict of Milan, issued in 313. Whether Constantine was himself a Christian by this point is hotly debated. His later biographer, the Christian bishop Eusebius, reported that he had converted on a battlefield in 312 after seeing a vision, and other sources attribute his conversion to his Christian mother, Helena. On the other hand, he continued to worship the sun-god, and in 321 proclaimed that Sunday, "the Day of the Sun," would be the official day of rest. He was baptized only shortly before he died, although this was not uncommon for high officials. Whatever his personal beliefs at different stages of his life, there is no debate that he recognized the growing numbers of Christians in the empire and financially supported the church. He freed the clergy from imperial taxation and endowed the building of Christian churches. One of his gifts—the Lateran Palace in Rome—remained the official residence of the popes until the fourteenth century. He allowed others to make gifts to the church as well, decreeing in 321, "Every man, when dying, shall have the right to bequeath as much of his property as he desires to the holy and

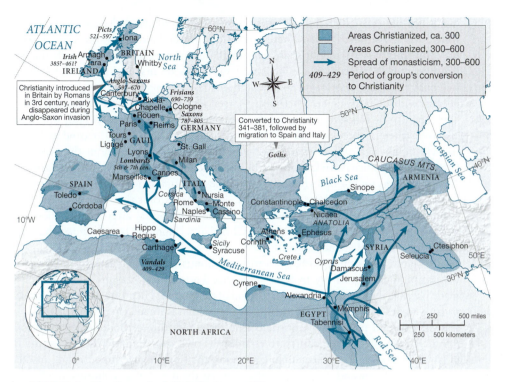

MAP 7.1   **The Spread of Christianity to 600**
Originating in Judaea, the southern part of modern Israel and Jordan, Christianity first spread throughout the Roman world and then beyond it in all directions.

venerable Catholic Church. And such wills are not to be broken."[1] In return for his support, Constantine expected the assistance of church officials in maintaining order. Helped in part by its favored position in the empire, Christianity slowly became the leading religion (Map 7.1).

Christians disagreed with one another about many issues, which led to schisms (SKIH-zuhms), denunciations, and sometimes violence. In the fourth and fifth centuries disputes arose over the nature of Christ. For example, **Arianism** (AI-ree-uh-nih-zuhm), developed by Arius (ca. 250–336), a priest of Alexandria, held that Jesus was created by the will of God the Father and thus was not co-eternal with him. Arian Christians reasoned that Jesus the Son must be inferior to God the Father because the Father was incapable of suffering and did not die. Arianism enjoyed such popularity and provoked such controversy that Constantine, to whom, as he put it, "internal strife within the Church of God is far more evil and dangerous than any kind of war and conflict," interceded. In 325 he summoned church leaders to a council in Nicaea (nigh-SEE-uh) in Asia Minor and presided over it personally "as your fellow servant of our common Lord and Savior."[2] The council produced the Nicene (nigh-SEEN) Creed, which defined the position that Christ is "eternally begotten of the Father" and of the same substance as the Father. Arius and those who refused to accept Nicene Christianity were banished. Their interpretation of the nature of Christ was declared a **heresy**, that is, a belief that contradicted the interpretation the church leaders declared was correct, which was termed orthodoxy. These actions did not end Arianism, however. Several later emperors were Arian Christians, and Arian missionaries converted many barbarian tribes, who were attracted by the idea that Jesus was God's first-in-command, which fit well with their own warrior hierarchies and was less complicated than the idea of two persons with one substance. The Nicene Creed says little specifically about the Holy Spirit, but in the following centuries the idea that the Father, Son, and Holy Spirit are "one substance in three persons"—the Trinity—became a central doctrine in Christianity, though again there were those who disagreed. Disputes about the nature of Christ also continued, with factions establishing themselves as separate Christian groups. The Nestorians, for example, regarded the divine and human natures in Jesus as distinct from one another, whereas the orthodox opinion was that they were united. The Nestorians split from the rest of the church in the fifth century after their position was outlawed, and settled in Persia. Nestorian Christian missionaries later founded churches in Central Asia, India, and China.

Religious and secular authorities tried in various ways to control this diversity as well as promote Christianity. In 380 the emperor Theodosius (thee-uh-DOH-shee-uhs) made Nicene Christianity the official religion of the empire. Theodosius stripped Roman pagan temples of statues, made the practice of the old Roman state religion a treasonable offense, and persecuted Christians who dissented from orthodox doctrine. Most significant, he allowed the church to establish its own courts and to use its own body of law, called canon law. The church courts, not the Roman government, had jurisdiction over the clergy and ecclesiastical disputes. At the death of Theodosius, the Christian Church was considerably independent of the Roman state. The foundation for later growth in church power had been laid.

Later emperors continued the pattern of active involvement in church affairs. They appointed the highest officials of the church hierarchy; the emperors or their representatives presided at ecumenical councils; and the emperors controlled some of the material resources of the church—land, rents, and dependent peasantry.

The Growth of the Christian Church

How did the Christian Church become a major force in Europe?

As the emperors changed their policies about Christianity from persecution to promotion, the church grew, gradually becoming the most important institution in Europe. The able administrators and creative thinkers of the church developed permanent institutions and complex philosophical concepts that drew on the Greco-Roman tradition, which attracted learned Romans.

The Church and Its Leaders

The early Christian Church benefited from the administrative abilities of church leaders. With the empire in decay, educated people joined and worked for the church in the belief that it was the one institution able to provide some stability. Bishop Ambrose of Milan (339–397) is typical of the Roman aristocrats who held high public office, were converted to Christianity, and subsequently became bishops. Like many bishops, Ambrose had a solid education in classical law and rhetoric, which he used to become an eloquent preacher. He had a strong sense of his authority and even stood up to Emperor Theodosius, who had ordered Ambrose to hand over his major church—called a basilica—to the emperor:

> At length came the command, "Deliver up the Basilica"; I reply, "It is not lawful for us to deliver it up, nor for your Majesty to receive it. By no law can you violate the house of a private man, and do you think that the house of God may be taken away? . . . But do not burden your conscience with the thought that you have any right as Emperor over sacred things. . . . It is written, God's to God and Caesar's to Caesar. The palace is the Emperor's, the churches are the Bishop's. To you is committed jurisdiction over public, not over sacred buildings."[3]

The emperor relented. Ambrose's assertion that the church was supreme in spiritual matters and the state in secular issues was to serve as the cornerstone of the church's position on church-state relations for centuries. Ambrose came to be regarded as one of the fathers of the church, that is, early Christian thinkers whose authority was seen as second only to the Bible in later centuries.

Gradually the church adapted the organizational structure of the Roman Empire begun during the reign of Diocletian. The territory under the authority of a bishop was also called a diocese, with its center a cathedral (from the Latin *cathedra*, meaning "chair"), the church that contained the bishop's official seat of power. A bishop's jurisdiction extended throughout the diocese, and he came to control a large amount of land that was given to or purchased by the church. Bishops generally came from prominent families and had both spiritual and political power; as the Roman Empire disintegrated, they became the most important local authority on many types of issues. They claimed to trace their spiritual ancestry back to Jesus's apostles, a doctrine called **apostolic succession**. Because of the special importance of their dioceses, five bishops—those of Antioch, Alexandria, Jerusalem, Constantinople, and Rome—gained the title of patriarch.

After the capital and the emperor moved to Constantinople, the power of the bishop of Rome grew because he was the only patriarch in the Western Roman Empire. The bishops of Rome stressed that Rome had special significance because of its history as the capital of a worldwide empire. More significantly, they asserted, Rome had a special place in Christian history. According to tradition, Saint Peter, chief of Jesus's disciples, had lived in Rome and been its first bishop. Thus as successors of Peter, the bishops of Rome—known as popes, from the Latin word *papa*, meaning "father"—claimed a privileged position in the church hierarchy, an idea called the **Petrine Doctrine** that built on the notion of apostolic succession. They stressed their supremacy over other Christian communities and urged other churches to appeal to Rome for the resolution of disputed doctrinal issues. Not surprisingly, the other patriarchs did not agree. They continued to exercise authority in their own regions, and local churches did as well, but the groundwork had been laid for later Roman predominance on religious matters.

In the fifth century the popes also expanded the church's secular authority. Pope Leo I (pontificate 440–461) made treaties with several barbarian leaders who threatened the city of Rome. Gregory I (pontificate 590–604), later called "the Great," made an agreement with the barbarian groups who had cut off Rome's food supply, reorganized church lands to increase production, and then distributed the additional food to the poor. He had been an official for the city of Rome before he became a church official, and his administrative and diplomatic talents helped the church expand. He sent missionaries to the British Isles (see page 214) and wrote letters and guides instructing bishops on practical and spiritual matters. He promoted the ideas of Augustine (see page 201), particularly those that defined church rituals as essential for salvation. The Western Christian Church headed by the pope in Rome would become the most enduring nongovernmental institution in world history.

The Development of Christian Monasticism

Christianity began and spread as a city religion. Since the first century, however, some especially pious Christians had felt that the only alternative to the decadence of urban life was complete separation from the world. They believed that the Christian life as set forth in the Gospel could not be lived in the midst of the immorality of Roman society.

This desire to withdraw from ordinary life led to the development of the monastic life. Monasticism began in third-century Egypt, where individuals like Saint Anthony (251?–356) and small groups first withdrew from cities and from organized society to seek God through prayer in desert or mountain caves and shelters, giving up all for Christ. Gradually large colonies of monks gathered in the deserts of Upper Egypt, and Christians came to believe that monks, like the early Christian martyrs executed by Roman authorities before them, could speak to God and that their prayers had special influence. These monks were called hermits, from the Greek word *eremos*, meaning "desert." Many devout women also were attracted to this eremitical (ehr-uh-MIH-tihk-uhl) type of monasticism.

The Egyptian ascetic Pachomius (puh-KOH-mee-uhs) (290–346?) drew thousands of men and women to the monastic life at Tabennisi on the Upper Nile. There were too many for them to live as hermits, so Pachomius organized communities of men and women, creating a new type of monasticism, known as cenobitic (seh-nuh-BIH-tik), that emphasized communal living. Saint Basil (329?–379), an influential bishop from Asia Minor and another of the fathers of the church, encouraged cenobitic monasticism. He and much of the church hierarchy thought that communal living provided an environment for training the aspirant in the virtues of charity, poverty, and freedom from self-deception.

Starting in the fourth century, information about Egyptian monasticism came to the West, and both men and women sought the monastic life. Because of the dangers of living alone in the forests of northern Europe, where wild animals, harsh climate, and barbarian tribes posed ongoing threats, the eremitical form of monasticism did not take root. Most of the monasticism that developed in Gaul, Italy, Spain, England, and Ireland was cenobitic.

Monastery Life

In 529 Benedict of Nursia (480–543), who had experimented with both eremitical and communal forms of monastic life, wrote a brief set of regulations for the monks who had gathered around him at Monte Cassino between Rome and Naples. Benedict's guide for monastic life, known as *The Rule of Saint Benedict*, came to influence all forms of organized religious life in the Western Christian Church. Men and women in monastic houses all followed sets of rules, first those of Benedict and later those written by other individuals. Because of this, men who lived a communal monastic life came to be called

regular clergy, from the Latin word *regulus* (rule). Priests and bishops who staffed churches in which people worshipped and who were not cut off from the world were called **secular clergy**. According to official church doctrine, women were not members of the clergy, but this distinction was not clear to most people.

The Rule of Saint Benedict outlined a monastic life of regularity, discipline, and moderation in an atmosphere of silence. Each monk had ample food and adequate sleep. The monk spent part of each day in formal prayer, which consisted of chanting psalms and other prayers from the Bible in the part of the monastery church called the choir. The rest of the day was passed in manual labor, study, and private prayer. The monastic life as conceived by Saint Benedict struck a balance between asceticism (extreme material sacrifice, including fasting and the renunciation of sex) and activity. It thus provided opportunities for men of entirely different abilities and talents—from mechanics to gardeners to literary scholars. The Benedictine form of religious life also appealed to women, because it allowed them to show their devotion and engage in study. Benedict's twin sister Scholastica (480–543) adapted the *Rule* for use by her community of nuns.

Benedictine monasticism also succeeded partly because it was so materially successful. In the seventh and eighth centuries monasteries pushed back forests and wastelands, drained swamps, and experimented with crop rotation. Benedictine houses thus made a significant contribution to the agricultural development of Europe.

Finally, monasteries conducted schools for local young people, and monks and nuns copied manuscripts, preserving classical as well as Christian literature. Local and royal governments drew on the services of the literate men and able administrators the monasteries produced. This was not what Saint Benedict had intended, but perhaps the effectiveness of the institution he designed made it inevitable.

Christianity and Classical Culture

The growth of Christianity was not simply a matter of institutions such as the papacy and monasteries, but also a matter of ideas. The earliest Christian thinkers sometimes rejected Greco-Roman culture, but as Christianity grew from a tiny persecuted group to the official religion of the Roman Empire, its leaders and thinkers gradually came to terms with classical culture (see Chapter 6). They incorporated elements of Greek and Roman philosophy and learning into Christian teachings, modifying them to fit with Christian notions.

Saint Jerome (340–419), for example, a distinguished theologian and linguist regarded as a father of the church, translated the Old and New Testaments from Hebrew and Greek into vernacular Latin. Called the Vulgate, his edition of the Bible served as the official translation until the sixteenth century, and scholars rely on it even today. Familiar with the writings of classical authors, Saint Jerome believed that Christians should study the best of ancient thought because it would direct their minds to God. He maintained that the best ancient literature should be interpreted in light of the Christian faith.

Christian Notions of Gender and Sexuality

Early Christians both adopted and adapted the then-contemporary views of women, marriage, and sexuality. In his plan of salvation, Jesus considered women the equal of men. Women were among the earliest converts to Christianity and took an active role

The Marys at Jesus's Tomb This late-fourth-century ivory panel tells the biblical story of Mary Magdalene and another Mary who went to Jesus's tomb to anoint the body (Matthew 28:1–7). At the top guards collapse when an angel descends from Heaven, and at the bottom the Marys listen to the angel telling them that Jesus has risen. Here the artist uses Roman artistic styles to convey Christian subject matter, synthesizing classical form and Christian teaching. (Castello Sforzesco/Scala/Art Resource, NY)

in its spread, preaching, acting as missionaries, being martyred alongside men, and perhaps even baptizing believers. Because early Christians believed that the Second Coming of Christ was imminent, they devoted their energies to their new spiritual family of co-believers. Early Christians often met in people's homes and called one another "brother" and "sister," a metaphorical use of family terms that was new to the Roman Empire. Women and men joyously accepted the ascetic life, renouncing marriage and procreation to use their bodies for a higher calling. Some women, either singly or in monastic communities, declared themselves "virgins in the service of Christ." All this initially made Christianity seem dangerous to many Romans, who viewed marriage as the foundation of society and the proper patriarchal order.

Not all Christian teachings about gender were radical, however. In the first century C.E. male church leaders began to place restrictions on female believers. Women were forbidden to preach and were gradually excluded from holding official positions in Christianity other than in women's monasteries. Women who chose lives of virginity in the service of God were to be praised; Saint Jerome commented that a woman "who wishes to serve Christ more than the world . . . will cease to be a woman and will be called man," the highest praise he could bestow.[4] Even such women were not to be too independent, however. Both Jewish and classical Mediterranean culture viewed women's subordination as natural and proper, so in limiting the activities of female believers the Christian Church was following well-established patterns, just as it did in modeling its official hierarchy after that of the Roman Empire.

Christian teachings about sexuality built on and challenged classical models. The rejection of sexual activity involved an affirmation of the importance of a spiritual life, but it also incorporated the hostility toward the body found in some Hellenistic philosophies and some of the other religions that had spread in the Roman Empire in this era, such as Manichaeism (MAN-ih-kee-ih-zuhm). Manichaeism, a dualistic religion based on the ideas of the third-century Persian thinker Mani, taught that the spiritual world was good and the material world was evil, so salvation came through education and self-denial. Christian teachings affirmed that God had created the material world and sanctioned marriage, but most Christian thinkers also taught that celibacy was the better life, and that anything that took one's attention from the spiritual world performed an evil function. For most clerical writers (who themselves were male) this temptation came from women, and in some of their writings women themselves are depicted as evil, the "devil's gateway." Thus the writings of many church fathers contain a strong streak of misogyny (hatred of women), which was passed down to later Christian thinkers.

Saint Augustine on Human Nature, Will, and Sin

The most influential church father in the West was Saint Augustine of Hippo (354–430). Saint Augustine was born into an urban family in what is now Algeria in North Africa. His father, a minor civil servant, was a pagan; his mother, Monica, a devout Christian. He gained an excellent classical education in philosophy and rhetoric and, as was normal for young Roman men, began relations with a concubine, who later had his son. Interested in new religious ideas, he became a Manichaean.

Augustine took teaching positions first in Rome and then in Milan, where he had frequent conversations with Bishop Ambrose. Through his discussions with Ambrose and his own reading, Augustine rejected his Manichaeism and became a Christian. He returned to Africa and later became bishop of the seacoast city of Hippo Regius. He was a renowned preacher to Christians there, a vigorous defender of orthodox Christianity, and the author of more than ninety-three books and treatises.

Augustine's autobiography, *The Confessions*, is a literary masterpiece and one of the most influential books in the history of Europe. Written in the rhetorical style and language of late Roman antiquity, it marks the synthesis of Greco-Roman forms and Christian thought. *The Confessions* describes Augustine's moral struggle, the conflict between his spiritual and intellectual aspirations and his sensual and material self. Many Greek and Roman philosophers had taught that knowledge would lead to virtue. Augustine came to reject this idea, claiming that people do not always act on the basis of rational knowledge. As he notes in *The Confessions*, even before he became a Christian he had decided that chastity was the best possible life, so he prayed to God for "chastity and continency," yet always added "but not yet." His education had not made him strong enough to avoid lust or any other evil; that would come only through God's power and grace.

Augustine's ideas on sin, grace, and redemption became the foundation of all subsequent Western Christian theology, Protestant as well as Catholic. He wrote that the basic force in any individual is the will, which he defined as "the power of the soul to hold on to or to obtain an object without constraint." The end or goal of the will determines the moral character of the individual. When Adam ate the fruit forbidden by God in the Garden of Eden (Genesis 3:6), he committed the "original sin" and corrupted the will. Adam's sin was not simply his own—it was passed on to all later humans through sexual intercourse; even infants were tainted. Original sin thus became a common social stain, in Augustine's opinion, transmitted by sexual desire. Coitus was theoretically good because it was created by God, but it had been corrupted by sin, so every act of intercourse was evil and every child was conceived through a sinful act. By viewing sexual desire as the result of Adam and Eve's disobedience to divine instructions, Augustine linked sexuality even more clearly with sin than had earlier church fathers. Because Adam disobeyed God and fell, all human beings have an innate tendency to sin: their will is weak. But according to Augustine, God restores the strength of the will through grace, which is transmitted in certain rituals that the church defined as **sacraments**. Grace results from God's decisions, not from any merit on the part of the individual.

When Visigothic forces captured the city of Rome in 410, horrified pagans blamed the disaster on the Christians. In response, Augustine wrote *City of God*. This original work contrasts Christianity with the secular society in which it exists. According to Augustine, history is the account of God acting in time. Human history reveals that there are two kinds of people: those who live the life of the flesh, and those who live the life of the spirit in what Augustine called the City of God. The former will endure eternal hellfire; the latter will enjoy eternal bliss.

Augustine maintained that states came into existence as the result of Adam's fall and people's inclination to sin. He believed that the state was a necessary evil with the power to do good by providing the peace, justice, and order that Christians need in order to pursue their pilgrimage to the City of God. States' legitimate power included the ability to wage war, and Augustine's ideas were later used to develop notions of just warfare.

Barbarian Society

What were the key characteristics of barbarian society?

Augustine's *City of God* was written in response to the conquest of Rome by an army of Visigoths, one of the many peoples the Romans—and later historians—labeled "barbarians." The word *barbarian* comes from the Greek *barbaros*, meaning someone who did not speak Greek. (To the Greeks, others seemed to be speaking nonsense syllables; *barbar* is the Greek equivalent of "blah-blah" or "yada-yada.") The Greeks used this word to include people such as the Egyptians, whom the Greeks respected. The Romans usually used the Latin version of *barbarian* to mean the peoples who lived beyond the northeastern boundary of Roman territory, whom they regarded as unruly, savage, and primitive. That value judgment is generally also present when we use "barbarian" in English, but there really is no other word to describe the many different peoples who lived to the north of the Roman Empire. Thus historians of late antiquity use the word *barbarian* to designate these peoples, who spoke a variety of languages but had similarities in their basic social, economic, and political structures. Many of these historians find much to admire in barbarian society.

Whalebone Chest   This eighth-century chest made of whalebone, depicting warriors, other human figures, and a horse, tells a story in both pictures and words. The runes along the border are one of the varieties from the British Isles. Contact with the Romans led to the increasing use of the Latin alphabet, though runes and Latin letters were used side by side in some parts of northern Europe for centuries. (Erich Lessing/Art Resource, NY)

Scholars have been hampered in investigating barbarian society because most groups did not write and thus kept no written records before Christian missionaries introduced writing. Greek and Roman authors did describe barbarian society, but they were not always objective observers, instead using barbarians to highlight what they thought was right or wrong about their own cultures. Thus written records must be combined with archaeological evidence to gain a more accurate picture. In addition, historians are increasingly deciphering and using the barbarians' own written records that do exist, especially inscriptions carved in stone, bone, and wood and written in the **runic alphabet**. Runic inscriptions come primarily from Scandinavia and the British Isles. Most are short and limited to names, such as inscriptions on tombstones, but some describe the actions of kings and other powerful individuals, and a few of them mention the activities of more ordinary people.

Barbarians included many different ethnic groups with social and political structures, languages, laws, and beliefs that developed in central and northern Europe over many centuries. Among the largest groups were Celts (whom the Romans called Gauls) and Germans; Germans were further subdivided into various groups, such as Ostrogoths, Visigoths, Burgundians, and Franks. *Celt* and *German* are often used as ethnic terms, but they are better understood as linguistic terms, a Celt being a person who spoke a Celtic language, an ancestor of the modern Gaelic or Breton language, and a German one who spoke a Germanic language, an ancestor of modern German, Dutch, Danish, Swedish, and Norwegian. Celts, Germans, and other barbarians brought their customs and traditions with them when they moved southward, and these gradually combined with classical and Christian patterns to form new types of societies.

PRIMARY SOURCE   Tacitus on Germanic Society

Toward the end of the first century, the Roman historian Tacitus wrote an account of Germanic society based on the works of earlier authors and most likely interviews with Romans who had traveled beyond the northern borders of the empire. His descriptions are not accurate in all respects, but evidence from other written sources and from archaeological excavations has supported a number of them.

Honor in battle; love of war and dislike of peace. When they have come into battle, it is shameful for the chieftain to be excelled in valor, shameful for the entourage not to match the valor of the chieftain. Furthermore, it is shocking and disgraceful for all of one's life to have survived one's chieftain and left the battle. . . .

The absence of cities; the German dwellings. It is common knowledge that the peoples of the Germans do not live in cities, and they do not even like their homes to be joined together. They live separated and scattered, as a spring or a field or a grove has attracted them. They do not plan their villages in our manner with buildings joined together and next to one another: each one has an open area around his home, whether as a protection against the disasters of fire or because of a lack of skill in building. They make no use at all of stones or tiles: they use unshaped timber for everything without regard to appearance or aesthetic pleasure. Certain parts they coat with greater care with an earth so pure and gleaming that it looks like painting and colored drawings. They are also accustomed to dig underground chambers and they cover them with a great deal of dung; these serve as a retreat against winter and a storage area for crops. . . .

The upbringing of the young. In every home the young, naked and dirty, grow to possess these limbs, these bodies, which we admire. His own mother nurses each one, and the children are not handed over to servants or nursemaids. You would not distinguish master and slave by any niceties of upbringing: they live amidst the

Village and Family Life

Barbarian groups usually resided in small villages, and climate and geography determined the basic patterns of how they lived off the land. Many groups lived in small settlements on the edges of clearings where they raised barley, wheat, oats, peas, and beans. Men and women tilled their fields with simple wooden plows and harvested their grains with small iron sickles. The vast majority of people's caloric intake came from grain in some form; the kernels of grain were eaten as porridge, ground up for flour, or fermented into strong, thick beer. (See "Primary Source: Tacitus on Germanic Society," above.)

Within the villages, there were great differences in wealth and status. Free men and their families constituted the largest class. The number of cattle a man possessed indicated his wealth and determined his social status. Free men also shared in tribal warfare. Slaves acquired through warfare worked as farm laborers, herdsmen, and household servants.

same animals and on the same ground until age sets the freeborn apart and valor recognizes them as her own. The young men experience love late, and for this reason their strength is not exhausted. Nor are the girls hurried into marriage; they have the same youthful vigor and similar stature: they are well matched in age and strength when they enter upon marriage, and the children reproduce the strength of the parents. . . .

Food and drink. The Germans' drunkenness. They have a beverage made from barley or wheat, fermented into something like wine [that is, beer]; those nearest the frontier also purchase wine. Their foods are simple, wild fruits, fresh game, or curdled milk: they satisfy their hunger without fancy preparation and without seasonings. They do not have the same moderation regarding thirst. If one would indulge their intoxication by furnishing as much drink as they long for, they will be conquered no less easily by their vices than by arms.

EVALUATE THE EVIDENCE

1. What does Tacitus praise, and what does he criticize, about Germanic warriors, food, houses, and child rearing?

2. Tacitus's work was written in part to criticize his fellow Romans, whom he saw as becoming weak from the influx of wealth into the empire. How does this inform his description of Germanic customs? How might such attitudes shape the way Romans responded to the barbarian migrations?

Source: Tacitus' *Agricola, Germany*, and *Dialogue on Orators*, rev. ed., trans. Herbert W. Benario (Norman: University of Oklahoma Press, 1991), pp. 70, 71, 73, 75. Copyright © 1967 by the Bobbs-Merrill Company, Inc. New edition copyright © 1991 by the University of Oklahoma Press, Norman, Publishing Division of the University. Reprinted by permission of Hackett Publishing Company, Inc. All rights reserved.

Ironworking represented the most advanced craft; much of northern Europe had iron deposits, and the dense forests provided wood for charcoal, which was used to provide the clean fire needed to make iron. The typical village had an oven and smiths who produced agricultural tools and instruments of war—one-edged swords, arrowheads, and shields. By the second century C.E. the swords produced by barbarian smiths were superior to the weapons of Roman troops.

In the first two centuries C.E. the quantity and quality of material goods increased dramatically. Goods were used locally and for gift giving, a major social custom. Gift giving conferred status on the giver, whose giving showed his higher (economic) status, cemented friendship, and placed the receiver in his debt. Goods were also traded, though commercial exchange was less important than in the Roman Empire.

Families and kin groups were the basic social units in barbarian society. Families were responsible for the debts and actions of their members and for keeping the peace in general. Barbarian law codes set strict rules of inheritance based on position in the family and often set aside a portion of land that could not be sold or given away by any family member so that the family always retained some land.

Barbarian society was patriarchal: within each household the father had authority over his wife, children, and slaves. Some wealthy and powerful men had more than one wife, a pattern that continued even after they became Christian, but polygamy was not widespread among ordinary people. Women worked alongside men in the fields and forests, and the Roman historian Tacitus reported that at times they joined men on the battlefield, urging them to fight harder. Once women were widowed, they sometimes assumed their husbands' rights over family property and held the guardianship of their children.

Tribes and Hierarchies

The basic social and political unit among barbarian groups was the tribe or confederation, a group whose members believed that they were all descended from a common ancestor and were thus kin. Tribes were led by chieftains. The chief was the member recognized as the strongest and bravest in battle and was elected from among the male members of the most powerful family. He led the group in war, settled disputes among its members, conducted negotiations with outside powers, and offered sacrifices to the gods. The period of migrations and conquests of the Western Roman Empire witnessed the strengthening of the power of chiefs, who often adopted the title of king, though this title implies broader power than they actually had.

Closely associated with the chief in some tribes was the **comitatus**, or war band. These warriors swore loyalty to the chief, fought with him in battle, and were not supposed to leave the battlefield without him; to do so implied cowardice, disloyalty, and social disgrace. These oaths of loyalty were later more formalized in the development of feudalism (see Chapter 8).

Although initially a social egalitarianism appears to have existed among members of the comitatus because they regarded each other as kin, during the migrations and warfare of the third and fourth centuries, the war band was transformed into a system of stratified ranks. Among the Ostrogoths, for example, a warrior nobility evolved. Contact with the Romans stimulated demand for goods such as metal armbands, which the Romans produced for trade with barbarian groups. Armbands were of different widths and value, and they became a symbol of hierarchy among warriors much as the insignia of military rank function today. During the Ostrogothic conquest of Italy, warrior-nobles also began to acquire land as both a mark of prestige and a means to power. As land and wealth came into the hands of a small elite class, social inequalities within the group emerged and gradually grew stronger. These inequalities help explain the origins of the European noble class.

Customary and Written Law

Early barbarian tribes had no written laws. Law was custom, but certain individuals were often given special training in remembering and retelling laws from generation to generation. Beginning in the late fifth century, however, some chieftains began to collect, write, and publish lists of their customs and laws.

The law code of the Salian Franks, one of the barbarian tribes, included a feature common to many barbarian codes. Any crime that involved a personal injury, such as assault, rape, and murder, was given a particular monetary value, called the **wergeld** (WUHR-gehld) (literally "man-money" or "money to buy off the spear"), that was to be paid by the perpetrator to the victim or the family. The Salic law lists many of these:

> If any person strike another on the head so that the brain appears, and the three bones which lie above the brain shall project, he shall be sentenced to 1200 denars, which make 300 shillings. . . .
>
> If any one have killed a free woman after she has begun bearing children, he shall be sentenced to 2400 denars, which make 600 shillings.[5]

The wergeld varied according to the severity of the crime and also the social status of the victim. The fine for the murder of a woman of childbearing years was the same value as that attached to military officers of the king, to priests, and to boys preparing to become warriors, which suggests the importance of women in Frankish society, at least for their childbearing capacity.

The wergeld system aimed to prevent or reduce violence. If a person accused of a crime agreed to pay the wergeld and if the victim and his or her family accepted the payment, there was peace. If the accused refused to pay the wergeld or if the victim's family refused to accept it, a blood feud ensued. At first, Romans had been subject to Roman law and barbarians to barbarian custom. As barbarian kings accepted Christianity and as Romans and barbarians increasingly intermarried and assimilated culturally, the distinction between the two sets of law blurred and, in the course of the seventh and eighth centuries, disappeared. The result would be the new feudal law, to which all who lived in certain areas were subject.

Celtic and Germanic Religion

Like Greeks and Romans, barbarians worshipped hundreds of gods and goddesses with specialized functions. They regarded certain mountains, lakes, rivers, or groves of trees as sacred because these were linked to deities. Rituals to honor the gods were held outdoors rather than in temples or churches, often at certain points in the yearly agricultural cycle. Presided over by a priest or priestess understood to have special abilities to call on the gods' powers, rituals sometimes involved animal (and perhaps human) sacrifice. Among the Celts, religious leaders called druids (DROO-ihds) had legal and educational as well as religious functions, orally passing down laws and traditions from generation to generation. Bards singing poems and ballads also passed down myths and stories of heroes and gods, which were written down much later.

The first written records of barbarian religion came from Greeks and Romans who encountered barbarians or spoke with those who had. They understood barbarian traditions through their own belief systems, often equating barbarian gods with Greco-Roman ones and adapting stories and rituals to blend the two. This assimilation appears to have gone both ways, at least judging by the names of the days of the week. In the Roman Empire the days took their names from Roman deities or astronomical bodies, and in the Germanic languages of central and northern Europe the days acquired the names of corresponding barbarian gods. Jupiter's day, for example, became Thor's day (Thursday); both of these powerful gods were associated with thunder.

Migration, Assimilation, and Conflict

What were some of the causes and consequences of the barbarian migrations?

Migrating groups that the Romans labeled barbarians had moved southward and eastward off and on since about 100 B.C.E. (see Chapters 5 and 6). As their movements became more organized in the third and fourth centuries C.E., Roman armies sought to defend the Rhine-Danube border of the Roman Empire, but with troop levels low because Italians were increasingly unwilling to serve in the army, generals were forced to recruit barbarians to fill the ranks. Barbarian refugees and enslaved prisoners of war joined Roman units, and free barbarian units, called *foederati*, allied themselves with Rome. Some barbarian leaders rose to the highest ranks of the Roman army and often assimilated into Roman culture, incorporating their own traditions and intermarrying with Roman families. By the fourth century barbarians made up the majority of those fighting both for and against Rome, and climbed higher and higher in the ranks of the Roman military. Toward the end of the fifth century this barbarian assumption of authority stretched all the way to the top, and the last person with the title of emperor in the Western Roman Empire was deposed by a Gothic general.

Why did the barbarians migrate? In part they were searching for more regular supplies of food, better farmland, and a warmer climate. In part they were pushed by groups living farther eastward, especially by the Huns from Central Asia in the fourth and fifth centuries. Conflicts within and among barbarian groups also led to war and disruption, which motivated groups to move (Map 7.2).

Celtic and Germanic People in Gaul and Britain

The Celts present a good example of both assimilation and conflict. Celtic-speaking peoples had lived in central Europe since at least the fifth century B.C.E. and spread out from there to the Iberian Peninsula in the west, Hungary in the east, and the British Isles in the north. As Julius Caesar advanced northward into what he termed Gaul (present-day France) between 58 and 50 B.C.E. (see Chapter 5), he defeated many Celtic tribes. Celtic peoples conquered by the Romans often assimilated Roman ways, adapting the Latin language and other aspects of Roman culture. In Roman Gaul and then in Roman Britain, towns were planned in the Roman fashion, with temples, public baths, theaters, and amphitheaters. In the countryside large manors controlled the surrounding lands. Roman merchants brought Eastern luxury goods and Eastern religions — including Christianity. The Romans suppressed the Celtic chieftains, and a military aristocracy made up of Romans — some of whom intermarried with Celtic families — governed. In the course of the second and third centuries, many Celts became Roman citizens and joined the Roman army. Celtic culture survived only in areas beyond the borders of the empire. (The modern Welsh, Bretons, Scots, and Irish are all peoples of Celtic descent.)

By the fourth century C.E. Gaul and Britain were under pressure from Germanic groups moving westward, and Rome itself was threatened (see Map 7.2). Imperial troops withdrew from Britain in order to defend Rome, and the Picts from Scotland and the Scots from Ireland (both Celtic-speaking peoples) invaded territory held by the Britons. According to the eighth-century historian Bede (beed), the Briton king Vortigern invited

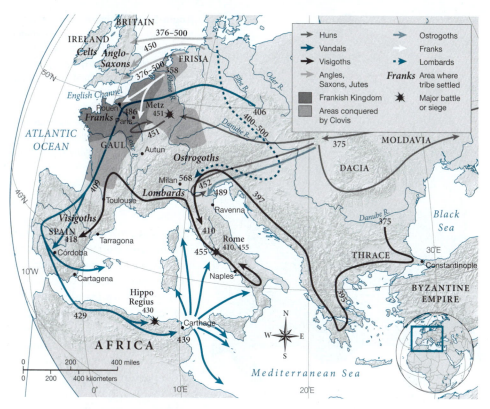

MAP 7.2   **The Barbarian Migrations, ca. 340–500**
This map shows the migrations of various barbarian groups in late antiquity.

the Saxons from Denmark to help him against his rivals. However, Saxons and other Germanic tribes from the area of modern-day Norway, Sweden, and Denmark turned from assistance to conquest. Their goal was plunder, and at first their invasions led to no permanent settlements. As more Germanic peoples arrived, however, they took over the best lands and eventually conquered most of Britain. Historians have labeled the years 500 to 1066 (the year of the Norman Conquest) the Anglo-Saxon period of English history, after the two largest Germanic groups in England, the Angles and the Saxons.

Anglo-Saxon England was divided along ethnic and political lines. The Germanic kingdoms in the south, east, and center were opposed by the Britons in the west, who wanted to get rid of the invaders. The Anglo-Saxon kingdoms also fought among themselves, causing boundaries to shift constantly. Finally, in the ninth century, under pressure from the Viking invasions, King Alfred of Wessex (r. 871–899) created a more unified state with a reorganized army and system of fortresses for defense.

The Anglo-Saxon invasion gave rise to a rich body of Celtic mythology, particularly legends about King Arthur, who first appeared in Welsh poetry in the sixth century and later in histories, epics, and saints' lives. Most scholars see Arthur as a composite

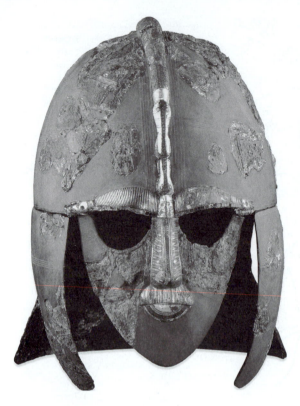

Anglo-Saxon Helmet   This ceremonial bronze helmet from seventh-century England was found inside a ship buried at Sutton Hoo. The nearly 100-foot-long ship was dragged overland before being buried completely. It held one body and many grave goods, including swords, gold buckles, and silver bowls made in Byzantium. The unidentified person who was buried here was clearly wealthy and powerful. (© Trustees of the British Museum)

figure that evolved over the centuries in songs and stories. In their earliest form as Welsh poems, the Arthurian legends may represent Celtic hostility to Anglo-Saxon invaders, but they later came to be more important as representations of the ideal of medieval knightly chivalry and as compelling stories whose retelling has continued to the present.

Visigoths and Huns

On the European continent, the Germanic peoples included a number of groups with very different cultural traditions. The largest Germanic group was the Goths, who were further subdivided by scholars into Ostrogoths (eastern Goths) and Visigoths (western Goths) based on their migration patterns. Both of these groups played important roles in the political developments of late antiquity.

Pressured by defeat in battle, starvation, and the movement of other groups, the Visigoths moved westward from their homeland north of the Black Sea, and in 376 they petitioned the Roman emperor Valens to admit them to the empire. They offered to fight for Rome in exchange for the province of Thrace in what is now Greece and Bulgaria. Seeing in the hordes of warriors the solution to his manpower problem, Valens agreed. However, the deal fell apart when crop failures led to famine and Roman authorities exploited the Visigoths' hunger by forcing them to sell their own people as slaves in exchange for dog flesh: "the going rate was one dog for one Goth." The Visigoths revolted, joined with other barbarian enemies of Rome, and defeated the Roman army at the Battle of Adrianople in 378, killing Valens and thousands of Roman soldiers in the process. This left a large barbarian army within the borders of the Roman Empire, and not that far from Constantinople.

Valens's successor made peace with the Visigoths, but relations worsened as the Visigoths continued migrating westward (see Map 7.2). The Visigothic king Alaric I, who had also been a general in one of the Roman armies in the east, invaded Italy and sacked Rome in 410. The Visigoths burned and looted the city for three days, which caused many Romans to wonder whether God had deserted them. Seeking to stabilize the situation at home, the imperial government pulled its troops from the British Isles and many areas north of the Alps, leaving these northern areas vulnerable to other migrating groups. A year later Alaric died, and his successor led his people into southwestern Gaul, where they established the Visigothic kingdom.

One significant factor in the migration of the Visigoths and other Germanic peoples was pressure from nomadic steppe peoples from Central Asia. They included the Alans, Avars, Bulgars, Khazars, and most prominently the Huns, who attacked the Black Sea area and the Byzantine Empire beginning in the fourth century. The Roman officer and historian Ammianus Marcellinus fought the Huns and later described them with both admiration and scorn:

> They are not at all adapted to battles on foot, but they are almost glued to their horses, which are hardy, it is true, but ugly. From their horses by night or day every one of the nation buys and sells, eats and drinks, and bowed over the narrow neck of the animal relaxes into a sleep so deep as to be accompanied by many dreams. . . . They are subject to no royal restraint, but they are content with the disorderly government of important men, and led by them they force their way through every obstacle. No one in their country ever plows a field or touches a plowhandle. They are all without fixed abode, without hearth, or law, or settled mode of life. . . . In wagons their wives weave for them their hideous garments, in wagons they cohabit with their husbands, bear children, and rear them. . . . Like unreasoning beasts, they are utterly ignorant of the difference between right and wrong.[6]

Under the leadership of their warrior-king Attila, the Huns attacked the Byzantine Empire in 447 and then turned westward. Several Germanic groups allied with them, as did the sister of the Roman emperor, who hoped to take over power from her brother. Their troops combined with those of the Huns, and a huge army took the city of Metz, now in eastern France. A combined army of Romans and Visigoths stopped the advance of the Huns at Châlons, and they retreated. The following year they moved into the Western Roman Empire again, crossing the Alps into Italy, and a papal delegation, including Pope Leo I himself, asked Attila not to attack Rome. Though papal diplomacy was later credited with stopping the advance of the Huns, their dwindling food supplies and a plague that spread among their troops were probably much more important. The Huns retreated from Italy, and within a year Attila was dead. Later leaders were not as effective, and the Huns were never again an important factor in European history. Their conquests had pushed many Germanic groups together, however, transforming smaller bands into larger, more unified peoples who could more easily pick the Roman Empire apart.

Germanic Kingdoms and the End of the Roman Empire

After they conquered an area, barbarians generally established states ruled by kings. However, the kingdoms did not have definite geographical borders, and their locations shifted as tribes moved. In the fifth century the Burgundians ruled over lands roughly circumscribed by the old Roman army camps in what is now central France and western Switzerland. The Visigoths exercised a weak domination over southern France and much of the Iberian Peninsula (modern Spain) until a Muslim victory at Guadalete in 711 ended Visigothic rule. The Vandals, another Germanic tribe whose destructive ways are commemorated in the word *vandal*, swept across Spain into North Africa in 429 and took over what had been Rome's breadbasket. They established a state that lasted about a century, raided many coastal cities, and even sacked the city of Rome itself in 455.

Barbarian states eventually came to include Italy itself. The Western Roman emperors were generally chosen by the more powerful successors of Constantine in the East, and they increasingly relied on barbarian commanders and their troops to maintain order. In the 470s a series of these commanders took over authority in name as well as in reality, deposing several Roman emperors. In 476 the barbarian chieftain Odoacer (OH-duh-way-suhr) deposed Romulus Augustus, the last person to have the title of Roman emperor in the West. Odoacer did not take on the title of emperor, calling himself instead the king of Italy, so that this date marks the official end of the Roman Empire in the West. Emperor Zeno, the Roman emperor in the East ruling from Constantinople, worried about Odoacer's growing power and promised Theoderic (r. 471–526), the leader of the Ostrogoths who had recently settled in the Balkans, the right to rule Italy if he defeated Odoacer. Theoderic's forces were successful, and in 493 Theoderic established an Ostrogothic state in Italy, with his capital at Ravenna.

For centuries, the end of the Roman Empire in the West was seen as a major turning point in history, the fall of the sophisticated and educated classical world to uncouth and illiterate tribes. This view was further promoted by the English historian and member of Parliament Edward Gibbon, whose six-volume *The History of the Decline and Fall of the Roman Empire*, published in 1776–1788, was required reading for university students well into the twentieth century. Over the last several decades, however, many historians have put greater stress on continuities. The Ostrogoths, for example, maintained many Roman ways. Old Roman families continued to run the law courts and the city governments, and well-educated Italians continued to study the Greek classics. Theoderic's adviser Boethius (ca. 480–524) translated Aristotle's works on logic from Greek into Latin. While imprisoned after falling out of royal favor, Boethius wrote *The Consolation of Philosophy*, which argued that philosophical inquiry was valuable for understanding God. This became one of the most widely read books in the Middle Ages, though its popularity did not prevent Boethius from being executed for treason.

In other barbarian states, as well, aspects of classical culture continued. Barbarian kings relied on officials trained in Roman law, and Latin remained the language of scholarly communication. Greco-Roman art and architecture still adorned the land, and people continued to use Roman roads, aqueducts, and buildings. The Christian Church in barbarian states modeled its organization on that of Rome, and many bishops were from upper-class families that had governed the empire.

Very recently some historians and archaeologists have returned to an emphasis on change. They note that people may have traveled on Roman roads, but the roads were rarely maintained, and travel itself was much less secure than during the Roman Empire. Merchants no longer traded over long distances, so people's access to goods produced outside their local area plummeted. Knowledge about technological processes such as the making of glass and roof tiles declined or disappeared. There was intermarriage and cultural assimilation among Romans and barbarians, but there was also violence and great physical destruction.

The kingdom established by the Franks is a good example of this combination of peaceful assimilation and violent conflict. The Franks were a confederation of Germanic peoples who originated in the marshy lowlands north and east of the northernmost part of the Roman Empire (see Map 7.2). In the fourth and fifth centuries they settled within the empire and allied with the Romans, some attaining high military and civil positions. The Franks believed that Merovech, a man of supernatural origins, founded their ruling dynasty, which was thus called Merovingian (mehr-uh-VIHN-jee-uhn).

The reign of Clovis (KLOH-vis) (ca. 481–511) marks the decisive period in the development of the Franks as a unified people. Through military campaigns, Clovis acquired the central provinces of Roman Gaul and began to conquer southern Gaul from the Burgundians and Visigoths. Clovis's conversion to Roman Christianity brought him the crucial support of the bishops of Gaul in his campaigns against tribes that were still pagan or had accepted the Arian version of Christianity. Along with brutal violence, however, the next two centuries witnessed the steady assimilation of Franks and Romans, as many Franks adopted the Latin language and Roman ways, and Romans copied Frankish customs and Frankish personal names.

From Constantinople, Eastern Roman emperors worked to hold the empire together and to reconquer at least some of the West from barbarian tribes. The emperor Justinian (r. 527–565) waged long and hard-fought wars against the Ostrogoths and temporarily regained Italy and North Africa, but his conquests had disastrous consequences. Justinian's wars exhausted the resources of the state, destroyed Italy's economy, and killed a large part of Italy's population. The wars also paved the way for the easy conquest of Italy by another Germanic tribe, the Lombards, shortly after Justinian's death. In the late sixth century the territory of the Western Roman Empire came once again under barbarian sway.

Christian Missionaries and Conversion

How did the church convert barbarian peoples to Christianity?

The Mediterranean served as the highway over which Christianity spread to the cities of the Roman Empire. Christian teachings were initially carried by all types of converts, but they were often spread into the countryside and into areas beyond the borders of the empire by those who had dedicated their lives to the church, such as monks. Such missionaries were often sent by popes specifically to convert certain groups. As they preached to barbarian peoples, the missionaries developed new techniques to convert them.

Throughout barbarian Europe, religion was not a private or individual matter; it was a social affair, and the religion of the chieftain or king determined the religion of the people. Thus missionaries concentrated their initial efforts not on ordinary people, but on kings or tribal chieftains and the members of their families, who then ordered their subjects to convert. Because they had more opportunity to spend time with missionaries, queens and other female members of the royal family were often the first converts in an area, and they influenced their husbands and brothers. Germanic kings sometimes accepted Christianity because they came to believe that the Christian God was more powerful than pagan gods and that the Christian God—in either its Arian or Roman version—would deliver victory in battle. They also appreciated that Christianity taught obedience to kingly as well as divine authority. Christian missionaries were generally literate, and they taught reading and writing to young men who became priests or officials in the royal household, a service that kings appreciated.

Missionaries' Actions

During the Roman occupation, small Christian communities were scattered throughout Gaul and Britain. The leaders of some of these, such as Bishop Martin of Tours (ca. 316–397), who founded a monastery and established a rudimentary parish system in his diocese, supported Nicene Christianity (see page 195). Other missionaries were Arian Christians, who also founded dioceses and converted many barbarian groups. Bishop Ulfilas (ca. 310–383), for example, an Ostrogoth himself, translated the Bible from the Greek in which it was normally written into the Gothic language, creating a new Gothic script in order to write it down. The Ostrogoths, Visigoths, Lombards, and Vandals were all originally Arian Christians, though over the sixth and seventh centuries most of them converted to Roman Christianity, sometimes peacefully and sometimes as a result of conquest.

Tradition identifies the conversion of Ireland with Saint Patrick (ca. 385–461). Born in England to a Christian family of Roman citizenship, Patrick was captured and enslaved by Irish raiders and taken to Ireland, where he worked as a herdsman for six years. He escaped and returned to England, where a vision urged him to Christianize Ireland. In preparation, Patrick studied in Gaul and was consecrated a bishop in 432. He returned to Ireland, where he converted the Irish tribe by tribe, first baptizing the chief of each tribe. By the time of Patrick's death, the majority of the Irish people had received Christian baptism.

In his missionary work, Patrick had the strong support of Bridget of Kildare (ca. 450–528), daughter of a wealthy chieftain. Bridget defied parental pressure to marry and became a nun. She and the other nuns at Kildare instructed relatives and friends in basic Christian doctrine, made religious vestments (clothing) for churches, copied books, taught children, and above all set a religious example by their lives of prayer. In this way, in Ireland and later in continental Europe, women like the nuns at Kildare shared in the process of conversion.

The Christianization of the English began in earnest in 597, when Pope Gregory I sent a delegation of monks under the Roman Augustine to Britain. Augustine's approach, like Patrick's, was to concentrate on converting those who held power. When he succeeded in converting Ethelbert, king of Kent, the baptism of Ethelbert's people took place as a matter of course. Augustine established his headquarters, or *see*, at Canterbury, the capital of Kent in southern England.

In the course of the seventh century, two Christian forces competed for the conversion of the pagan Anglo-Saxons: Roman-oriented missionaries traveling north from Canterbury, and Celtic monks from Ireland and northwestern Britain. The Roman and Celtic church organizations, types of monastic life, and methods of arriving at the date of the central feast of the Christian calendar, Easter, differed completely. Through the influence of King Oswiu of Northumbria and the dynamic abbess Hilda of Whitby, the Synod (ecclesiastical council) held at Hilda's convent of Whitby in 664 opted to follow the Roman practices. The conversion of the English and the close attachment of the English Church to Rome had far-reaching consequences because Britain later served as a base for the Christianization of the European continent (see Map 7.1), spreading Roman Christian teachings among both pagans and Arians.

The Process of Conversion

When a ruler marched his people to the waters of baptism, the work of Christianization had only begun. Christian kings could order their subjects to be baptized, married, and buried in Christian ceremonies, and people complied increasingly across Europe. Churches could be built, and people could be required to attend services and belong to parishes, but the process of conversion was a gradual one.

How did missionaries and priests get masses of pagan and illiterate peoples to understand Christian ideals and teachings? They did so through preaching, assimilation, the ritual of penance, and the veneration of saints. Missionaries preached the basic teachings of Christianity in simplified Latin or translated them into the local language. In monasteries and cathedrals, men — and a few women — wrote hymns, prayers, and stories about the lives of Christ and the saints. People heard these and slowly became familiar with Christian notions.

Deeply ingrained pagan customs and practices could not be stamped out by words alone, however, or even by royal edicts. Christian missionaries often pursued a policy of assimilation, easing the conversion of pagan men and women by stressing similarities between their customs and beliefs and those of Christianity. In the same way that classically trained scholars such as Jerome and Augustine blended Greco-Roman and Christian ideas, missionaries and converts mixed pagan ideas and practices with Christian ones. Bogs and lakes sacred to Germanic gods became associated with saints, as did various aspects of ordinary life, such as traveling, planting crops, and worrying about a sick child. Aspects of existing midwinter celebrations, which often centered on the return of the sun as the days became longer, were incorporated into celebrations of Christmas. Spring rituals involving eggs and rabbits (both symbols of fertility) were added to Easter.

The ritual of penance was also instrumental in teaching people Christian ideas. Christianity taught that certain actions and thoughts were sins, meaning that they were against God's commands. Only by confessing these sins and asking forgiveness could a sinning believer be reconciled with God. Confession was initially a public ritual, but by the fifth century individual confession to a parish priest was more common. The person knelt before the priest, who questioned him or her about sins he or she might have committed. The priest then set a penance such as fasting or saying specific prayers to allow the person to atone for the sin. The priest and penitent were guided by manuals known as penitentials (peh-nuh-TEHN-shuhlz), which included lists of sins and the appropriate penance. The seventh-century English penitential of Theodore, for example, stipulated that "if a lay Christian vomits because of drunkenness, he shall do penance for fifteen days," while drunken monks were to do penance for thirty days. Those who "commit fornication with a virgin" were to do penance for a year, as were those who perform "divinations according to the custom of the heathens." Penance for killing someone depended on the circumstances: usually it was seven years, but "in revenge for a brother" it was three years; if by accident, one year; and if "by command of his lord" or in "public war," only forty days.[7] Penance gave new Christians a sense of expected behavior, encouraged the private examination of conscience, and offered relief from the burden of sinful deeds.

Most religious observances continued to be community matters, as they had been in the ancient world. People joined with family members, friends, and neighbors at their parish church to attend baptisms, weddings, and funerals presided over by a priest. The parish church often housed the **relics** of a saint, that is, bones, articles of clothing, or other objects associated with a person who had lived (or died) in a way that was spiritually heroic or noteworthy. This patron saint was understood to provide protection and assistance for those who came to worship, and the relics served as a link between the material world and the spiritual.

Christians came to venerate the saints as powerful and holy. They prayed to saints or to the Virgin Mary to intercede with God, or they simply asked the saints to assist and bless them. The entire village participated in processions marking saints' days or points in the agricultural year, often carrying images of saints or their relics around the houses and fields. The decision to become Christian was often made first by an emperor or king, but actual conversion was a local matter, as people came to feel that the parish priest and the patron saint provided them with benefits in this world and the world to come.

The Byzantine Empire

How did the Byzantine Empire preserve the legacy of Rome?

Barbarian migrations and Christian conversions occurred throughout all of Europe in late antiquity, but their impact was not the same in the western and eastern halves of the Roman Empire. The Western Roman Empire gradually disintegrated, but the Roman Empire continued in the East. The Byzantine or Eastern Roman Empire preserved the forms, institutions, and traditions of the old Roman Empire, and its people even called themselves Romans. Byzantine emperors traced their lines back past Constantine to Augustus, and the Senate in Constantinople carried on the traditions of the old Roman Senate. Most important, however, is how Byzantium protected the intellectual heritage of Greco-Roman civilization and then passed it on to the rest of Europe.

Sources of Byzantine Strength

While the western parts of the Roman Empire gradually succumbed to barbarian invaders, the Byzantine Empire survived Germanic, Persian, and Arab attacks (Map 7.3). In 540 the Huns and Bulgars crossed the Danube and raided as far as southern Greece. In 559 a force of Huns and Slavs reached the gates of Constantinople. In 583 the Avars, a mounted Mongol people who had swept across Russia and southeastern Europe, seized Byzantine forts along the Danube and reached the walls of Constantinople. Between 572 and 630 the Sassanid Persians posed a formidable threat, and the Greeks were repeatedly at war with them. Beginning in 632 Muslim forces pressured the Byzantine Empire (see Chapter 8).

Why didn't one or a combination of these enemies capture Constantinople as the Ostrogoths had taken Rome? The answer lies in strong military leadership and even more in the city's location and its excellent fortifications. Justinian's generals were able to reconquer much of Italy and North Africa from barbarian groups, making them part of the Eastern Roman Empire. The Byzantines ruled most of Italy from 535 to 572 and the southern part of the peninsula until the eleventh century; they ruled North Africa until it was conquered by Muslim forces in the late seventh century. Under the skillful command of General Priskos (d. 612), Byzantine armies inflicted a severe defeat

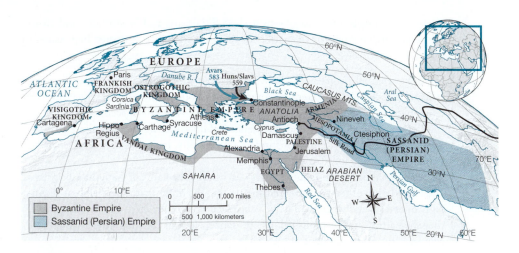

MAP 7.3   **The Byzantine Empire, ca. 600**
The strategic position of Constantinople on the waterway between the Black Sea and the Mediterranean was clear to Constantine when he chose the city as the capital of the Eastern Roman Empire. Byzantine territories in Italy were acquired in Emperor Justinian's sixth-century wars and were held for several centuries.

on the Avars in 601, and under Emperor Heraclius I (r. 610–641) they crushed the Persians at Nineveh in Iraq. Massive triple walls, built by the emperors Constantine and Theodosius II (408–450) and kept in good repair, protected Constantinople from sea invasion. Within the walls huge cisterns provided water, and vast gardens and grazing areas supplied vegetables and meat, so the defending people could hold out far longer than the besieging army. Attacking Constantinople by land posed greater geographical and logistical problems than a seventh- or eighth-century government could solve. The site was not absolutely impregnable — as the Venetians demonstrated in 1204 and the Ottoman Turks in 1453 — but it was almost so. For centuries, the Byzantine Empire served as a bulwark for the West, protecting it against invasions from the East.

The Law Code of Justinian

One of the most splendid achievements of the Byzantine emperors was the preservation of Roman law for the medieval and modern worlds. Roman law had developed from many sources — decisions by judges, edicts of the emperors, legislation passed by the Senate, and the opinions of jurists. By the fourth century it had become a huge, bewildering mass, and its sheer bulk made it almost unusable.

Sweeping and systematic codification took place under the emperor Justinian. He appointed a committee of eminent jurists to sort through and organize the laws. The result was the *Corpus Juris Civilis* (KAWR-puhs JOOR-uhs sih-VIH-luhs) (Body of Civil Law), a multipart collection of laws and legal commentary issued from 529 to 534. The first part of this work, the *Codex*, brought together all the existing imperial laws into a coherent whole, eliminated outmoded laws and contradictions, and clarified the law itself. It began with laws ordering the interpretation of Christian doctrine favored by the emperor in opposition to groups such as the Arians and Nestorians, and affirming the power of the emperor in matters of religion, such as this decree first issued by the emperor Theodosius:

> We desire that all peoples subject to Our benign Empire shall live under the same religion that the Divine Peter, the Apostle, gave to the Romans, and which the said religion declares was introduced by himself . . . that is to say, in accordance with the rules of apostolic discipline and the evangelical doctrine, we should believe that the Father, Son, and Holy Spirit constitute a single Deity, endowed with equal majesty, and united in the Holy Trinity.
>
>   We order all those who follow this law to assume the name of Catholic Christians, and considering others as demented and insane, We order that they shall bear the infamy of heresy; and when the Divine vengeance which they merit has been appeased, they shall afterwards be punished in accordance with our resentment, which we have acquired from the judgment of Heaven.[8]

The rest of the *Codex* was structured by topic and included provisions on every aspect of life, including economic issues, social concerns, and family life.

The second part of Justinian's compilation, the *Digest*, is a collection of the opinions of foremost Roman jurists on complex legal problems, and the third part, the *Institutes*, is a handbook of civil law designed for students and beginning jurists. All three parts were given the force of law and formed the backbone of Byzantine jurisprudence from that point on. Like so much of classical culture, the *Corpus Juris Civilis* was lost in western Europe with the end of the Roman Empire, but it was rediscovered in the eleventh century and came to form the foundation of law for nearly every modern European nation.

Byzantine Intellectual Life

The Byzantines prized education; because of them, many masterpieces of ancient Greek literature have survived to influence the intellectual life of the modern world. The literature of the Byzantine Empire was predominantly Greek, although politicians, scholars, and lawyers also spoke and used Latin. Justinian's *Codex* was first written in Latin. More people could read in Byzantium than anywhere else in Christian Europe at the time, and history was a favorite topic.

The most remarkable Byzantine historian was Procopius (ca. 500–562), who left a rousing account praising Justinian's reconquest of North Africa and Italy, but also wrote the *Secret History*, a vicious and uproarious attack on Justinian and his wife, the empress Theodora. (See "Individuals in Society: Theodora of Constantinople," page 220.)

Although the Byzantines discovered little that was new in mathematics and geometry, they made advances in terms of military applications. For example, they invented an explosive liquid that came to be known as "Greek fire." The liquid was heated and propelled by a pump through a bronze tube, and as the jet left the tube, it was ignited — somewhat like a modern flamethrower. Greek fire saved Constantinople from Arab assault in 678 and was used in both land and sea battles for centuries, although modern military experts still do not know the exact nature of the compound. In mechanics Byzantine scientists improved and modified artillery and siege machinery.

Greek Fire   In this illustration from a twelfth-century manuscript, sailors shoot Greek fire toward an attacking ship from a pressurized tube that looks strikingly similar to a modern flamethrower. The exact formula for Greek fire has been lost, but it was probably made from a petroleum product because it continued burning on water. Greek fire was particularly important in Byzantine defenses of Constantinople from Muslim forces in the late seventh century. (Prado, Madrid/The Bridgeman Art Library)

The Byzantines devoted a great deal of attention to medicine, and the general level of medical competence was far higher in the Byzantine Empire than in western Europe. Yet their physicians could not cope with the terrible disease, often called the "Justinian plague," that swept through the Byzantine Empire and parts of western Europe between 542 and about 560. Probably originating in northwestern India and carried to the Mediterranean region by ships, the disease was similar to what was later identified as the bubonic plague. Characterized by high fever, chills, delirium, and enlarged lymph nodes, or by inflammation of the lungs that caused hemorrhages of black blood, the Justinian plague claimed the lives of tens of thousands of people. The epidemic had profound political as well as social consequences: it weakened Justinian's military resources, thus hampering his efforts to restore unity to the Mediterranean world.

By the ninth or tenth century, most major Greek cities had hospitals for the care of the sick. The hospitals might be divided into wards for different illnesses, and hospital staff included surgeons, practitioners, and aids with specialized responsibilities. The imperial Byzantine government bore the costs of these medical facilities.

The Orthodox Church

The continuity of the Roman Empire in the East meant that Christianity developed differently there than it did in the West. The emperors in Constantinople were understood to be Christ's representative on earth; their palace was considered holy and was filled with relics and religious images, called icons. Emperors convened councils, appointed church officials, and regulated the income of the church. As in Rome, there

INDIVIDUALS IN SOCIETY • Theodora of Constantinople

The most powerful woman in Byzantine history was the daughter of a bear trainer for the circus. Theodora (ca. 497–548) grew up in what her contemporaries regarded as an undignified and morally suspect atmosphere, and she worked as a dancer and burlesque actress, both dishonorable occupations in the Roman world. Despite her background, she caught the eye of Justinian, who was then a military leader and whose uncle (and adoptive father) Justin had himself risen from obscurity to become the emperor of the Byzantine Empire. Under Justinian's influence, Justin changed the law to allow an actress who had left her disreputable life to marry whom she liked, and Justinian and Theodora married in 525. When Justinian was proclaimed co-emperor with his uncle Justin on April 1, 527, Theodora received the rare title of *augusta*, or empress. Thereafter her name was linked with Justinian's in the exercise of imperial power.

Most of our knowledge of Theodora's early life comes from the *Secret History*, a tell-all description of the vices of Justinian and his court written around 550 by Procopius (pruh-KOH-pee-uhs), who was the official court historian and thus spent his days praising those same people. In the *Secret History* he portrays Theodora and Justinian as demonic, greedy, and vicious, killing courtiers to steal their property. In scene after detailed scene, Procopius portrays Theodora as particularly evil, sexually insatiable, depraved, and cruel, a temptress who used sorcery to attract men, including the hapless Justinian.

In one of his official histories, *The History of the Wars of Justinian*, Procopius presents a very different Theodora. Riots between the supporters of two teams in chariot races—who formed associations somewhat like both street gangs and political parties—had turned deadly, and Justinian wavered in his handling of the perpetrators. Both sides turned against the emperor, besieging the palace while Justinian was inside it. Shouting "N-I-K-A" (victory), the rioters swept through the city, burning and looting, and destroyed half of Constantinople. Justinian's counselors urged flight, but, according to Procopius, Theodora rose and declared:

> For one who has reigned, it is intolerable to be an exile. . . . If you wish, O Emperor, to save yourself, there is no difficulty: we have ample funds and there are the ships. Yet reflect whether, when you have once escaped to a place of security, you will not prefer death to safety. I agree with an old saying that the purple [that is, the color worn only by emperors] is a fair winding sheet [to be buried in].

Justinian rallied, had the rioters driven into the hippodrome, and ordered between thirty thousand and thirty-five thousand men and women executed. The revolt was crushed and Justinian's authority was restored, an outcome approved by Procopius.

was a patriarch in Constantinople, but he did not develop the same powers that the pope did in the West because there was never a similar power vacuum into which he needed to step. The **Orthodox Church**, the name generally given to the Eastern Christian Church, was more subject to secular control than the Western Christian Church, although some churchmen did stand up to the emperor. Saint John Chrysostom (ca.

Other sources describe or suggest Theodora's influence on imperial policy. Justinian passed a number of laws that improved the legal status of women, such as allowing women to own property the same way that men could and to be guardians over their own children. Justinian is reputed to have consulted her every day about all aspects of state policy, including religious policy regarding the doctrinal disputes that continued throughout his reign. Theodora's influence over her husband and her power in the Byzantine state continued until she died, perhaps of cancer, twenty years before Justinian. Her influence may have even continued after death, for Justinian continued to pass reforms favoring women and, at the end of his life, accepted her interpretation of Christian doctrine. Institutions that she established, including hospitals, orphanages, houses for the rehabilitation of prostitutes, and churches, continued to be reminders of her charity and piety.

Theodora has been viewed as a symbol of the manipulation of beauty and cleverness to attain position and power, and also as a strong and capable co-ruler who held the empire together during riots, revolts, and deadly epidemics. Just as Procopius expressed both views, the debate has continued to today among writers of science fiction and fantasy as well as biographers and historians.

QUESTIONS FOR ANALYSIS

1. How would you assess the complex legacy of Theodora?
2. Since the official and unofficial views of Procopius are so different regarding the empress, should he be trusted at all as a historical source?

ONLINE DOCUMENT ASSIGNMENT

What do Procopius's descriptions of Theodora and Justinian tell us about the problems his society faced? Examine sources that reveal the connections Procopius saw between Byzantium's rulers and the rapid decline he perceived in Byzantine society, and then complete a writing assignment based on the evidence and details from this chapter.

bedfordstmartins.com/mckaywestvalue

347–407), for example, a bishop and one of the church fathers, thunderously preached against what he saw as the luxury and decadence of the emperor's court and its support of pagan practices, such as erecting statues of rulers. He was banished—twice—but his sermons calling for an ascetic life and support for the poor were copied and recopied for centuries.

Monasticism in the Orthodox world differed in fundamental ways from the monasticism that evolved in western Europe. First, while *The Rule of Saint Benedict* gradually became the universal guide for all western European monasteries, each individual house in the Byzantine world developed its own set of rules for organization and behavior. Second, education never became a central feature of Orthodox monasteries. Monks and nuns had to be literate to perform the appropriate rituals, but no Orthodox monastery assumed responsibility for the general training of the local young.

There were also similarities between Western and Eastern monasticism. As in the West, Eastern monasteries became wealthy property owners, with fields, pastures, livestock, and buildings. Since bishops and patriarchs of the Orthodox Church were recruited only from the monasteries, these religious leaders also exercised cultural influence.

Like their counterparts in the West, Byzantine missionaries traveled far beyond the boundaries of the empire in search of converts. In 863 the emperor Michael III sent the brothers Cyril (826–869) and Methodius (815–885) to preach Christianity in Moravia (a region in the modern Czech Republic). Other missionaries succeeded in converting the Russians in the tenth century. Cyril invented a Slavic alphabet using Greek characters, later termed the Cyrillic (suh-RIH-lihk) alphabet in his honor. In the tenth century other missionaries spread Christianity, the Cyrillic alphabet, and Byzantine art and architecture to Russia. The Byzantines were so successful that the Russians would later claim to be the successors of the Byzantine Empire. For a time Moscow was even known as the "Third Rome" (the second Rome being Constantinople).

Notes

1. Maude Aline Huttman, ed. and trans., *The Establishment of Christianity and the Proscription of Paganism* (New York: AMS Press, 1967), p. 164.
2. Eusebius, *Life of Constantine the Great*, trans. Ernest Cushing Richardson (Grand Rapids, Mich.: Eerdmans, 1979), p. 534.
3. R. C. Petry, ed., *A History of Christianity: Readings in the History of Early and Medieval Christianity* (Englewood Cliffs, N.J.: Prentice Hall, 1962), p. 70.
4. Saint Jerome, *Commentaries on the Letter to the Ephesians*, book 16, cited in Vern Bullough, *Sexual Variance in Society and History* (Chicago: University of Chicago Press, 1976), p. 365.
5. E. F. Henderson, ed., *Select Historical Documents of the Middle Ages* (London: G. Bell and Sons, 1912), pp. 176–189.
6. Reprinted by permission of the publishers and the Trustees of the Loeb Classical Library® from Ammianus Marcellinus, *The History*, vol. 1, Loeb Classical Library, trans. John C. Rolfe (Cambridge, Mass.: Harvard University Press, 1935), book 31, pt. 2, pp. 383, 385, 387. Copyright © 1935, 1950 by the President and Fellows of Harvard College. The Loeb Classical Library® is a registered trademark of the President and Fellows of Harvard College.
7. John McNeill and Helena M. Gamer, *Medieval Handbooks of Penance: A Translation of the Principal Libri Poenitentiales and Selections from Related Documents* (New York: Columbia University Press, 1938).
8. Justinian's Code, 1.1.1, in S. P. Scott, trans., *The Civil Law*, vol. 12 (Cincinnati: The Central Trust Company, 1932), p. 9.

Chapter Review

MAKE IT STICK

LearningCurve
bedfordstmartins.com/mckaywestvalue

After reading the chapter, use LearningCurve to retain what you've read.

IDENTIFY KEY TERMS

Identify and explain the significance of each item below.

tetrarchy (p. 191)
diocese (p. 192)
Arianism (p. 195)
heresy (p. 195)
apostolic succession (p. 197)
Petrine Doctrine (p. 197)
regular clergy (p. 199)

secular clergy (p. 199)
sacraments (p. 202)
runic alphabet (p. 203)
comitatus (p. 206)
wergeld (p. 207)
relics (p. 216)
Orthodox Church (p. 220)

REVIEW THE MAIN IDEAS

Answer the focus questions from each section of the chapter.

- How did Diocletian and Constantine try to reform the empire? (p. 191)
- How did the Christian Church become a major force in Europe? (p. 196)
- What were the key characteristics of barbarian society? (p. 202)
- What were some of the causes and consequences of the barbarian migrations? (p. 208)
- How did the church convert barbarian peoples to Christianity? (p. 213)
- How did the Byzantine Empire preserve the legacy of Rome? (p. 216)

MAKE CONNECTIONS

Think about the larger developments and continuities within and across chapters.

1. The end of the Roman Empire in the West in 476 has long been viewed as one of the most important turning points in history. Do you agree with this idea? Why or why not?

2. In what ways was the role of the family in barbarian society similar to that of the family in classical Athens (Chapter 3) and republican Rome (Chapter 5)? In what ways was it different? What might account for the similarities and differences that you identify?

3. How did the Christian Church adapt to Roman and barbarian society? How was it different in 600 from how it had been in 100?

ONLINE DOCUMENT ASSIGNMENT

Theodora of Constantinople

What do Procopius's descriptions of Theodora and Justinian tell us about the problems his society faced?

You encountered Theodora of Constantinople's story on page 220. Keeping the question above in mind, go online and examine sources that reveal the connections Procopius saw between Byzantium's rulers and the rapid decline he perceived in Byzantine society. Then complete a writing assignment based on the evidence and details from this chapter.

bedfordstmartins.com/mckaywestvalue

CHRONOLOGY

ca. 293	• Diocletian establishes the tetrarchy
313	• Edict of Milan, allowing practice of all religions in the Roman Empire
325	• Council of Nicaea
354–430	• Life of Saint Augustine
378	• Visigoths defeat the Roman army at Adrianople
380	• Theodosius makes Christianity the official religion of the Roman Empire
410	• Visigoths sack Rome
429	• Vandals begin their conquest of North Africa
476	• Odoacer deposes the last Roman emperor in the West
ca. 481–511	• Reign of Clovis
493	• Theoderic establishes an Ostrogothic state in Italy
527–565	• Reign of Justinian
529	• *The Rule of Saint Benedict*
535–572	• Byzantines reconquer and rule Italy
597	• Pope Gregory I sends missionaries to Britain

8

✓ LearningCurve
bedfordstmartins.com/mckaywestvalue
After reading the chapter, use
LearningCurve to retain what
you've read.

Europe in the Early Middle Ages

600–1000

BY THE FIFTEENTH CENTURY SCHOLARS IN THE GROWING CITIES OF
northern Italy began to think that they were living in a new era, one in which
the glories of ancient Greece and Rome were being reborn. What separated
their time from classical antiquity, in their opinion, was a long period of darkness, to which a seventeenth-century professor gave the name "Middle Ages."
In this conceptualization, Western history was divided into three periods—
ancient, medieval, and modern—an organization that is still in use today.

For a long time the end of the Roman Empire in the West was seen as the
division between the ancient period and the Middle Ages, but, as we saw in
the last chapter, there was continuity as well as change, and the transition
from ancient to medieval was a slow process, not a single event. The agents in
this process included not only the barbarian migrations that broke the Roman
Empire apart but also the new religion of Islam, Slavic and steppe peoples in
eastern Europe, and Christian officials and missionaries. The period from the
end of antiquity (ca. 600–1000), conventionally known as the "early Middle
Ages," was a time of disorder and destruction, but it also marked the creation
of a new type of society and a cultural revival that influenced later intellectual and literary traditions. While agrarian life continued to dominate Europe,
political and economic structures that would influence later European history
began to form, and Christianity continued to spread. People at the time did
not know that they were living in an era that would later be labeled "middle"
or sometimes even "dark," and we can wonder whether they would have
shared this negative view of their own times.

The Spread of Islam

What were the origins of Islam, and what impact did it have on Europe as it spread?

In the seventh century C.E. two empires dominated the area today called the Middle East: the Byzantine-Greek-Christian empire and the Sassanid-Persian-Zoroastrian empire. Between the two lay the Arabian peninsula, where a merchant called Muhammad began to have religious visions around 610. By the time he died in 632, all Arabia had accepted his creed of Islam. A century later his followers controlled what is now Syria, Palestine, Egypt, North Africa, Spain, and part of France. This Arabic expansion profoundly affected the development of Western civilization as well as the history of Africa and Asia.

The Arabs

In Muhammad's time Arabia was inhabited by various tribes, many of them Bedouins (BEH-duh-wuhnz). These nomadic peoples grazed goats and sheep on the sparse patches of grass that dotted the vast semiarid peninsula. The power of the Bedouins came from their fighting skills, toughness, ability to control trade, and possession of horses and camels. Other Arabs lived more settled lives in the southern valleys and coastal towns along the Red Sea, such as Yemen, Mecca, and Medina, supporting themselves by agriculture and trade. Caravan routes crisscrossed Arabia and carried goods to Byzantium, Persia, and Syria. The wealth produced by business transactions led to luxurious living for many residents in the towns.

For all Arabs, the basic social unit was the clan — a group of blood relations connected through the male line. Clans expected loyalty from their members and in turn provided support and protection. Although the nomadic Bedouins condemned the urbanized lifestyle of the cities as immoral and corrupt, Arabs of all types respected certain aspects of one another's customs and had some religious rules and rituals in common. For example, all Arabs kept three months of the year as sacred; during that time any fighting stopped so that everyone could attend holy ceremonies in peace. The city of Mecca was the major religious and economic center of western Arabia. For centuries before the rise of Islam, many Arabs prayed at the Ka'ba (KAH-buh), a temple in Mecca containing a black stone thought to be the dwelling place of a god as well as objects connected to other gods. Economic links also connected Arab peoples, but what eventually molded the diverse Arab tribes into a powerful political and social unity was a new religion based on the teachings of Muhammad.

The Prophet Muhammad

Except for a few vague remarks in the **Qur'an** (kuh-RAHN), the sacred book of Islam, Muhammad (ca. 571–632) left no account of his life. Arab tradition accepts some of the sacred stories that developed about him as historically true, but those accounts were not written down until about a century after his death. (Similarly, the earliest accounts of the life of Jesus, the Christian Gospels, were not written until forty to sixty years after his death.) Orphaned at the age of six, Muhammad was raised by his grandfather. As a young man he became a merchant in the caravan trade. Later he entered the service of a wealthy widow, and their subsequent marriage brought him financial independence.

The Qur'an reveals Muhammad to be an extremely devout man, ascetic, self-disciplined, and literate, but not formally educated. He prayed regularly, and when he was about forty he began to experience religious visions. Unsure for a time about what he should do, Muhammad discovered his mission after a vision in which the angel Gabriel instructed him to preach. Muhammad described his visions in a stylized and often rhyming prose and used this literary medium as his *Qur'an*, or "prayer recitation."

Muhammad's revelations were written down by his followers during his lifetime and organized into chapters, called *sura*, shortly after his death. In 651 Muhammad's third successor arranged to have an official version published. The Qur'an is regarded by Muslims as the direct words of God to his Prophet Muhammad and is therefore especially revered. (When Muslims around the world use translations of the Qur'an, they do so alongside the original Arabic, the language of Muhammad's revelations.) At the same time, other sayings and accounts of Muhammad, which gave advice on matters that went beyond the Qur'an, were collected into books termed *hadith* (huh-DEETH). Muslim tradition (*Sunna*) consists of both the Qur'an and the hadith.

Muhammad's visions ordered him to preach a message of a single God and to become God's prophet, which he began to do in his hometown of Mecca. He gathered followers slowly, but also provoked a great deal of resistance because he urged people to give up worship of the gods whose sacred objects were in the Ka'ba and also challenged the power of the local elite. In 622 he migrated with his followers to Medina, an event termed the *hijra* (hih-JIGH-ruh) that marks the beginning of the Muslim calendar. At Medina Muhammad was much more successful, gaining converts and working out the basic principles of the faith. That same year, through the Charter of Medina, Muhammad formed the first *umma*, a community that united his followers from different tribes and set religious ties above clan loyalty. The charter also extended rights to non-Muslims living in Medina, including Jews and Christians, which set a precedent for the later treatment of Jews and Christians under Islam.

In 630 Muhammad returned to Mecca at the head of a large army, and he soon united the nomads of the desert and the merchants of the cities into an even larger umma of Muslims, a word meaning "those who comply with God's will." The religion itself came to be called Islam, which means "submission to God." The Ka'ba was rededicated as a Muslim holy place, and Mecca became the most holy city in Islam. According to Muslim tradition, the Ka'ba predates the creation of the world and represents the earthly counterpart of God's heavenly throne, to which "pilgrims come dishevelled and dusty on every kind of camel."[1]

By the time Muhammad died in 632, the crescent of Islam, the Muslim symbol, prevailed throughout the Arabian peninsula. During the next century one rich province of the old Roman Empire after another came under Muslim domination — first Syria, then Egypt, and then all of North Africa (Map 8.1). Long and bitter wars (572–591, 606–630) between the Byzantine and Persian Empires left both so weak and exhausted that they easily fell to Muslim attack.

The Teachings and Expansion of Islam

Muhammad's religion eventually attracted great numbers of people, partly because of the straightforward nature of its doctrines. The strictly monotheistic theology outlined in the Qur'an has only a few central tenets: Allah, the Arabic word for God, is

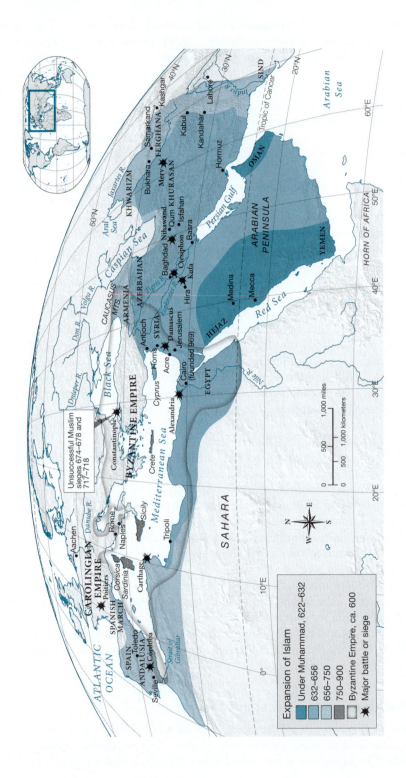

Unsuccessful Muslim sieges 674–678 and 717–718

Expansion of Islam

Under Muhammad, 622–632
632–656
656–750
750–900
Byzantine Empire, ca. 600
★ Major battle or siege

◄ **MAP 8.1   The Spread of Islam, 622–900**
The rapid expansion of Islam in a relatively short span of time testifies to the Arabs' superior fighting skills, religious zeal, and economic organization as well as to their enemies' weakness.

all-powerful and all-knowing. Muhammad, Allah's prophet, preached his word and carried his message. Muhammad described himself as the successor both of the Jewish patriarch Abraham and of Christ, and he claimed that his teachings replaced theirs. He invited and won converts from Judaism and Christianity.

Because Allah is all-powerful, believers must submit themselves to him. All Muslims have the obligation of the *jihad* (literally, "self-exertion") to strive or struggle to lead a virtuous life and to spread God's rule and law. In some cases striving is an individual struggle against sin; in others it is social and communal and could involve armed conflict, though this is not an essential part of jihad (jee-HAHD). The Islamic belief of "striving in the path of God" is closely related to the central feature of Muslim doctrine, the coming Day of Judgment. Muslims believe with conviction that the Day of Judgment will come; consequently, all of a Muslim's thoughts and actions should be oriented toward the Last Judgment and the rewards of Heaven.

To merit the rewards of Heaven, a person must follow the strict code of moral behavior that Muhammad prescribed. The Muslim must recite a profession of faith in

Dome of the Rock, Jerusalem   Completed in 691 and revered by Muslims as the site where Muhammad ascended to heaven, the Dome of the Rock is the third holiest place in Islam, after Mecca and Medina. Influenced by Byzantine and Persian architecture, it also has distinctly Arabic features, such as Qur'anic inscriptions. (imagebroker.net/SuperStock)

God and in Muhammad as God's prophet: "There is no god but God and Muhammad is his prophet." The believer must pray five times a day, fast and pray during the sacred month of Ramadan, and contribute alms to the poor and needy. If possible, the believer must make a pilgrimage to Mecca once during his or her lifetime. According to the Muslim *shari'a* (shuh-REE-uh), or sacred law, these five practices—the profession of faith, prayer, fasting, giving alms to the poor, and pilgrimage to Mecca—constitute the **Five Pillars of Islam**. The Muslim who faithfully observes the laws of the Qur'an can hope for salvation.

The Qur'an forbids alcoholic beverages and gambling, as well as a number of foods, such as pork, a dietary regulation adopted from the Mosaic law of the Hebrews. It condemns business usury—that is, lending money at interest rates or taking advantage of market demand for products by charging high prices for them.

Polygyny, the practice of men having more than one wife, was common in Arab society before Muhammad, though for economic reasons the custom was limited to the well-to-do. The Qur'an limited the number of wives a man could have, however: "[Of] women who seem good in your eyes, marry but two, three, or four; and if ye still fear that ye shall not act equitably then only one" (Sura 4:3).

The Qur'an sets forth a strict sexual morality and condemns immoral behavior on the part of men as well as women: "The whore and the fornicator: whip each of them a hundred times. . . . The fornicator shall not marry other than a whore; and the whore shall not marry other than a fornicator" (Sura 24:2–3).

The Qur'an also set out rules for inheritance:

> Men who die and leave wives behind shall bequeath to them a year's maintenance. . . . And your wives shall have a fourth part of what you leave, if you have no issue [offspring]; but if you have issue, then they shall have an eighth part. . . . With regard to your children, God commands you to give the male the portion of two females. (Sura 4:11–12)

With respect to matters of property, Muslim women of the early Middle Ages had more rights than Western women. For example, a Muslim woman retained complete jurisdiction over one-third of her property when she married and could dispose of it in any way she wished. Women in most European countries and the United States did not gain these rights until the nineteenth century.

Sunni and Shi'a Divisions

Every Muslim hoped that by observing the laws of the Qur'an, he or she could achieve salvation, and it was the tenets of Islam preached by Muhammad that bound all Arabs together. Despite the clarity and unifying force of Muslim doctrine, however, divisions developed within the Islamic faith within decades of Muhammad's death. Neither the Qur'an nor the hadith gave clear guidance about how successors to Muhammad were to be chosen, but, according to tradition, in 632 a group of Muhammad's closest followers chose Abu Bakr (uh-BOO BAH-kuhr), who was a close friend of the Prophet's and a member of a clan affiliated with the Prophet's clan, as **caliph** (KAY-luhf), a word meaning "successor." He was succeeded by two other caliphs, but these provoked opposition, which coalesced around Ali, Muhammad's cousin and son-in-law. Ali was chosen as the fourth caliph in 656, but he was assassinated only five years later by back-ers of the initial line of caliphs. Ali's supporters began to assert that the Prophet had designated Ali as *imam*, or leader, and that he should rightly have been the first caliph; thus, any caliph who was not a descendant of Ali was a usurper. These supporters of Ali—termed Shi'ites (SHEE-ights) or Shi'a (SHEE-ah) from Arabic terms meaning "supporters" or "partisans" of Ali—saw Ali and subsequent imams as the divinely inspired leaders of the community. The larger body of Muslims who accepted the first elections—termed Sunnis, a word derived from *Sunna*, the practices of the community derived from Muhammad's example—saw the caliphs as political leaders. Since Islam did not have an organized priesthood, the caliphs had an additional function of safeguarding and enforcing the religious law (shari'a) with the advice of scholars (*ulama*), particularly the jurists, judges, and scholastics who were knowledgeable about the Qur'an and hadith. Over the centuries enmity between Sunni and Shi'a Muslims has sometimes erupted into violence, and discord still exists today.

After the assassination of Ali, the caliphate passed to members of the Umayyad (oo-MIGH-uhd) clan, who asserted control and brought stability to the growing Muslim empire. They established their capital at Damascus in Syria, and the Muslim faith continued to expand eastward to India and westward across North Africa. That expansion was facilitated everywhere by three main factors: military strength, trade connections, and tolerance toward non-Muslims. By the early tenth century a Muslim proverb spoke of the Mediterranean Sea as a Muslim lake, though the Greeks at Constantinople contested that notion.

Life in Muslim Spain

In Europe, Muslim political and cultural influence was felt most strongly in the Iberian Peninsula. In 711 a Muslim force crossed the Strait of Gibraltar and easily defeated the weak Visigothic kingdom. (See "Primary Source: The Muslim Conquest of Spain," page 232.) A few Christian princes supported by the Frankish rulers held out in northern mountain fortresses, but by 720 the Muslims controlled most of Spain. A member of the Umayyad Dynasty, Abd al-Rahman (AHB-dal-ruh-MAHN) (r. 756–788) established a kingdom in Spain with its capital at Córdoba (KAWR-doh-buh).

Throughout the Islamic world, Muslims used the term **al-Andalus** to describe the part of the Iberian Peninsula under Muslim control. The name probably derives from the Arabic for "land of the Vandals," the Germanic people who swept across Spain in the fifth century (see Chapter 7). In the eighth century al-Andalus included the entire peninsula from Gibraltar in the south to the Cantabrian Mountains in the north (see Map 8.1). Today we often use the word *Andalusia* (an-duh-LOO-zhuh) to refer especially to southern Spain, but eighth-century Christians throughout Europe called the peninsula "Moorish Spain" because the Muslims who invaded and conquered it were Moors—Berbers from northwest Africa.

The ethnic term *Moorish* can be misleading, however, because the peninsula was home to sizable numbers of Jews and Christians as well as Muslim Moors. In business transactions and in much of daily life, all peoples used the Arabic language. With Muslims, Christians, and Jews trading with and learning from one another and occasionally intermarrying, Moorish Spain and Norman Sicily (see Chapter 9) were the only distinctly pluralistic societies in medieval Europe.

PRIMARY SOURCE   The Muslim Conquest of Spain

There are no contemporary descriptions from either Muslim or Christian authors of the Muslim conquest of the Iberian Peninsula that began in 711. One of the few existing documents is a treaty from 713 between 'Abd al-'Aziz, the son of the conquering Muslim governor and general Musa ibn Nusair, and Tudmir, the Visigothic Christian ruler of the city of Murcia in southern Spain. Treaties such as this, and military aspects of the conquest, were also described in the earliest surviving account, an anonymous Latin chronicle written by a Christian living in Muslim Spain in 754.

1. A Treaty from 713
In the name of God, the merciful and the compassionate.

This is a document [granted] by 'Abd al-'Aziz ibn Musa ibn Nusair to Tudmir, son of Ghabdush, establishing a treaty of peace and the promise and protection of God and his Prophet (may God bless him and grant him peace). We ['Abd al-'Aziz] will not set special conditions for him or for any among his men, nor harass him, nor remove him from power. His followers will not be killed or taken prisoner, nor will they be separated from their women and children. They will not be coerced in matters of religion, their churches will not be burned, nor will sacred objects be taken from the realm, [so long as] he [Tudmir] remains sincere and fulfills the [following] conditions that we have set for him. He has reached a settlement concerning seven towns: Orihuela, Valentilla, Alicante, Mula, Bigastro, Ello, and Lorca. He will not give shelter to fugitives, nor to our enemies, nor encourage any protected person to fear us, nor conceal news of our enemies. He and [each of] his men shall [also] pay one dinar every year, together with four measures of wheat, four measures of barley, four liquid measures of concentrated fruit juice, four liquid measures of vinegar, four of honey, and four of olive oil. Slaves must each pay half of this amount.

Some scholars believe that the eighth and ninth centuries in Andalusia were an era of remarkable interfaith harmony. Jews in Muslim Spain were generally treated well, and Córdoba became a center of Jewish as well as Muslim learning. Many Christians adopted Arabic patterns of speech and dress, gave up eating pork, and developed an appreciation for Arabic music and poetry. Some Christian women of elite status chose the Muslim practice of veiling their faces in public. Records describe Muslim and Christian youths joining in celebrations and merrymaking.

From the sophisticated centers of Muslim culture in Baghdad, Damascus, and Cairo, al-Andalus seemed a provincial backwater, a frontier outpost with little significance in the wider context of Islamic civilization. On the other hand, "northern barbarians," as Muslims called the European peoples, acknowledged the splendor of Spanish culture. The Saxon nun and writer Hroswitha of Gandersheim (roz-WEETH-uh of GAHN-duhr-shighm) called the city of Córdoba "the ornament of the world." By 950 the city had a population of about a half million, making it Europe's largest and most prosperous city. Many residents lived in large houses and easily purchased the silks and brocades made by the city's thousands of weavers. The streets were well paved and well lit—a

2. Chronicle of 754

In Justinian's time [711], . . . Musa . . . entered the long plundered and godlessly invaded Spain to destroy it. After forcing his way to Toledo, the royal city, he imposed on the adjacent regions an evil and fraudulent peace. He decapitated on a scaffold those noble lords who had remained, arresting them in their flight from Toledo with the help of Oppa, King Egica's son [a Visigothic Christian prince]. With Oppa's support, he killed them all with the sword. Thus he devastated not only [the former Roman province of] Hispania Ulterior, but [the former Roman province of] Hispania Citerior up to and beyond the ancient and once flourishing city of Zaragoza, now, by the judgment of God, openly exposed to the sword, famine, and captivity. He ruined beautiful cities, burning them with fire; condemned lords and powerful men to the cross; and butchered youths and infants with the sword. While he terrorized everyone in this way, some of the cities that remained sued for peace under duress and, after persuading and mocking them with a certain craftiness, the Saracens [Muslims] granted their requests without delay.

EVALUATE THE EVIDENCE

1. What conditions and guarantees are set for Christians living under Muslim rule in the treaty, and how does the author of the chronicle view treaties such as this?

2. What evidence do these documents provide for coexistence between Christians and Muslims in Spain and for hostility between the two groups?

Source: Olivia Remie Constable, ed. *Medieval Iberia: Readings from Christian, Muslim, and Jewish Sources* (Philadelphia: University of Pennsylvania Press, 1997), pp. 37–38, 30–31. Reprinted with permission of the University of Pennsylvania Press.

sharp contrast to the dark and muddy streets of other cities in Europe—and there was an abundance of freshwater for drinking and bathing. The largest library contained 400,000 volumes, a vast collection, particularly when compared with the largest library in northern Europe at the Benedictine abbey of St. Gall in Switzerland, which had only 600 books.

In Spain, as elsewhere in the Arab world, the Muslims had an enormous impact on agricultural development. They began the cultivation of rice, sugarcane, citrus fruits, dates, figs, eggplants, carrots, and, after the eleventh century, cotton. These crops, together with new methods of field irrigation, provided the population with food products unknown in the rest of Europe. Muslims also brought technological innovations westward, including new kinds of sails and navigational instruments, as well as paper.

Muslim-Christian Relations

What did early Muslims think of Jesus? Jesus is mentioned many times in the Qur'an, which affirms that he was born of Mary the Virgin. He is described as a righteous prophet chosen by God who performed miracles and continued the work of Abraham and Moses, and he was a sign of the coming Day of Judgment. But Muslims held that Jesus was an apostle only, not God, and that people (that is, Christians) who called Jesus divine committed blasphemy (showing contempt for God). The Christian doctrine of the Trinity—that there is one God in three persons (Father, Son, and Holy Spirit)—posed a powerful obstacle to Muslim-Christian understanding because of Islam's emphasis on the absolute oneness of God. Muslims esteemed the Judeo-Christian Scriptures as part of God's revelation, although they believed that the Qur'an superseded them.

Muslims call Jews and Christians *dhimmis*, or "protected people," because they were "people of the book," that is, the Hebrew Scriptures. Christians and Jews in the areas Muslims conquered were allowed to continue practicing their faith, although they did have to pay a special tax. This toleration was sometimes accompanied by suspicion, however. In Spain, Muslim teachers increasingly feared that close contact with Christians and Jews would lead to Muslim contamination and threaten the Islamic faith. Thus, beginning in the late tenth century, Muslim regulations began to officially prescribe what Christians, Jews, and Muslims could do. A Christian or Jew, however much assimilated, remained an **infidel**. An infidel was an unbeliever, and the word carried a pejorative or disparaging connotation.

By about 950 Caliph Abd al-Rahman III (912–961) of the Umayyad Dynasty of Córdoba ruled most of the Iberian Peninsula from the Mediterranean in the south to the Ebro River in the north. Christian Spain consisted of the tiny kingdoms of Castile, León, Catalonia, Aragon, Navarre, and Portugal. Civil wars among al-Rahman's descendants weakened the caliphate, and the small northern Christian kingdoms began to expand southward, sometimes working together. When Christian forces conquered Muslim territory, Christian rulers regarded their Muslim and Jewish subjects as infidels and enacted restrictive measures similar to those imposed on Christians in Muslim lands. Christian bishops worried that even a knowledge of Islam would lead to ignorance of essential Christian doctrines, and interfaith contacts declined. Christians' perception of Islam as a menace would help inspire the Crusades of the eleventh through thirteenth centuries (see Chapter 9).

Cross-Cultural Influences in Science and Medicine

Despite growing suspicions on both sides, the Islamic world profoundly shaped Christian European culture in Spain and elsewhere. Toledo, for example, became an important center of learning through which Arab intellectual achievements entered and influenced western Europe. Arabic knowledge of science and mathematics, derived from the Chinese, Greeks, and Hindus, was highly sophisticated. The Muslim mathematician al-Khwarizmi (al-KHWAHR-uhz-mee) (d. 830) wrote the important treatise *Algebra*, the first work in which the word *algebra* is used mathematically. Al-Khwarizmi adopted the Hindu system of numbers (1, 2, 3, 4), used it in his *Algebra*, and applied mathematics to problems of physics and astronomy. (Since our system of numbers is actually Hindu in origin, the term *Arabic numerals*, coined about 1847, is a misnomer.) Scholars in Baghdad translated Euclid's *Elements*, the basic text for plane and solid geometry (see Chapter 4). Muslims also instructed Westerners in the use of the zero, which permitted the execution of complicated problems of multiplication and long division.

Middle Eastern Arabs translated and codified the scientific and philosophical learning of Greek and Persian antiquity. In the ninth and tenth centuries that knowledge was brought to Spain, where between 1150 and 1250 it was translated into Latin. Europeans' knowledge of Aristotle (see Chapter 3) changed the entire direction of European philosophy and theology.

Muslim medical knowledge far surpassed that of the West. By the ninth century Arab physicians had translated most of the treatises of the ancient Greek physician Hippocrates and produced a number of important works of their own. Arabic science reached its peak in the physician, philologist, philosopher, poet, and scientist ibn-Sina of Bukhara (980–1037), known in the West as Avicenna (ah-vuh-SEH-nuh). His *Canon of Medicine* codified all Greco-Arabic medical thought, described the contagious nature of tuberculosis and the spreading of diseases, and listed 760 pharmaceutical drugs.

Unfortunately, many of these treatises came to the West as translations from Greek to Arabic and then to Latin and inevitably lost a great deal in translation. Nevertheless, in the ninth and tenth centuries Arabic knowledge and experience in anatomy and pharmaceutical prescriptions much enriched Western knowledge.

Frankish Rulers and Their Territories

How did the Franks build and govern a European empire?

Over two centuries before the Muslim conquest of Spain, the Frankish king Clovis converted to Roman Christianity and established a large kingdom in what had been Roman Gaul (see Chapter 7). Though at that time the Frankish kingdom was simply one barbarian kingdom among many, it grew to become the most important state in Europe, expanding to become an empire. Rulers after Clovis used a variety of tactics to enhance their authority and create a stable system. Charles the Great (r. 768–814), generally known by the French version of his name, Charlemagne (SHAHR-luh-mayne), built on the military and diplomatic foundations of his ancestors and on the administrative machinery of the Merovingian kings. He expanded the Frankish kingdom into what is now Germany and Italy and, late in his long reign, was crowned emperor by the pope.

The Merovingians

Clovis established the Merovingian dynasty in about 481 (see Chapter 7), and under him the Frankish kingdom included much of what is now France and a large section of southwestern Germany. Following Frankish traditions in which property was divided among male heirs, at Clovis's death the kingdom was divided among his four sons. Historians have long described Merovingian Gaul in the sixth and seventh centuries as wracked by civil wars, chronic violence, and political instability as Clovis's descendants fought among themselves. So brutal and destructive were these wars and so violent the conditions of daily life that the term "Dark Ages" was at one time used to designate the entire Merovingian period, although more recently historians have noted that the Merovingians also created new political institutions, so the era was not uniformly bleak.

Merovingian rulers also developed diverse sources of income. These included revenues from the royal estates and the "gifts" of subject peoples, such as plunder and tribute paid by peoples east of the Rhine River. New lands might be conquered and confiscated, and served to replace lands donated as monastic or religious endowments. All free landowners paid a land tax, although some landowners gradually gained immunity from doing so. Fines imposed for criminal offenses and tolls and customs duties on roads, bridges, and waterways (and the goods transported over them) also yielded income. As with the Romans, the minting of coins was a royal monopoly, with drastic penalties for counterfeiting.

The Franks also based some aspects of their government on Roman principles. For example, the basis of the administrative system in the Frankish kingdom was the **civitas** (SIH-vih-tahs) — Latin for a city and surrounding territory — similar to the political organization of the Roman Empire. A **comites** (KOH-meh-tehs) — a senior official or royal companion, later called a count — presided over the civitas, as had governors in Rome. He collected royal revenue, heard lawsuits, enforced justice, and raised troops. Many comites were not conquerors from outside, but came from families that had been administrators in Roman Gaul and were usually native to the regions they administered and knew their areas well. Frankish royal administration involved another official, the *dux* (dooks) or duke. He was a military leader, commanding troops in the territory of several civitas, and thus responsible for all defensive and offensive strategies. Clovis and

Saint Radegund and King Clotaire   This eleventh-century manuscript shows the Germanic princess Radegund (ca. 520–586) led before the Merovingian king Clotaire, who became her husband. They had no children, and after Clotaire had Radegund's brother killed, she left him and founded a convent, where she lived the rest of her life. Convents were islands of learning and safety in Merovingian society; from here Radegund corresponded with learned church officials and wrote Latin poems, a few of which have survived. (The Art Gallery Collection/Alamy)

his descendants also issued capitularies—Roman-style administrative and legislative orders—in an attempt to maintain order in Merovingian society. Some of these laws were designed to protect the clergy and church property from violence, others were meant to define ownership and inheritance, and still others set out to punish crimes such as drunkenness, robbery, arson, rape, and murder.

Within the royal household, Merovingian politics provided women with opportunities, and some queens not only influenced but occasionally also dominated events. Because the finances of the kingdom were merged with those of the royal family, queens often had control of the royal treasury just as more ordinary women controlled household expenditures. The status of a princess or queen also rested on her diplomatic importance, with her marriage sealing or her divorce breaking an alliance with a foreign kingdom or powerful noble family; on her personal relationship with her husband and her ability to give him sons and heirs; and on her role as the mother and guardian of princes who had not reached legal adulthood.

Queen Brunhilda (543?–613), for example, married first one Frankish king and at his death another. When her second husband died, Brunhilda overcame the objections of the nobles and became regent, ruling on behalf of her son until he came of age. Later she governed as regent for her grandsons and, when she was nearly seventy, for her great-grandson. Stories of her ruthlessness spread during her lifetime and were later much embellished by Frankish historians uncomfortable with such a powerful woman. The evil Brunhilda, they alleged, killed ten Frankish kings in pursuit of her political goals, and she was finally executed by being torn apart by horses while cheering crowds looked on. How much of this actually happened is impossible to say, but Brunhilda's legend became a model for the wicked queen in European folklore.

Merovingian rulers and their successors led peripatetic lives, traveling constantly to check up on local administrators and peoples. Merovingian kings also relied on the comites and bishops to gather and send local information to them. The court or household of Merovingian kings included scribes who kept records, legal officials who advised the king on matters of law, and treasury agents responsible for aspects of royal finance. These officials could all read and write Latin. Over them all presided the mayor of the palace, the most important secular figure after the king, who governed the palace and the kingdom in the king's absence. Mayors were usually from one of the great aristocratic families, which increasingly through intermarriage blended Frankish and Roman elites. These families possessed landed wealth—villas over which they exercised lordship, dispensing local customary, not royal, law—and they often had rich and lavish lifestyles.

The Rise of the Carolingians

From this aristocracy one family gradually emerged to replace the Merovingian dynasty. The rise of the Carolingians—whose name comes from the Latin *Carolus*, or Charles, the name of several important members of the family—rests on several factors. First, the Carolingian Pippin I (d. 640) acquired the powerful position of mayor of the palace and passed the title on to his heirs. As mayors of the palace and heads of the Frankish bureaucracy, Pippin I and his descendants were entrusted with extraordinary amounts of power and privilege by the Merovingian kings. Although the mayor of the palace was technically employed by the ruling family, the Carolingians would use their influential position to win support for themselves and eventually subvert Merovingian authority. Second, a series of advantageous marriage alliances brought the family estates and influence in different parts of the Frankish world, and provided the Carolingians with landed wealth and treasure with which to reward their allies and followers. Third, military victories over supporters of the Merovingians gave the Carolingians a reputation for strength and ensured their dominance. Pippin I's great-grandson, Charles Martel (r. 714–741), waged war successfully against the Saxons, Frisians, Alamanni, and Bavarians, which further enhanced the family's prestige. In 732 Charles Martel defeated a Muslim force near Poitiers (pwah-tee-AY) in central France. Muslims and Christians have interpreted the battle differently. To the Muslims it was a minor skirmish won by the Franks because of Muslim difficulties in maintaining supply lines over long distances and the distraction of ethnic conflicts and unrest in Islamic Spain. For Christians the Frankish victory was one of the great battles of history, halting Muslim expansion in Europe. Charles Martel and later Carolingians used it to enhance their reputation, portraying themselves as defenders of Christendom against the Muslims.

The Battle of Poitiers helped the Carolingians acquire the support of the church, perhaps their most important asset. Charles Martel and his son Pippin III (r. 751–768) further strengthened their ties to the church by supporting the work of Christian missionaries. The most important of these missionaries was the Englishman Boniface (BAH-nuh-fays) (680–754), who had close ties to the Roman pope. Boniface ordered the oak of Thor, a tree sacred to many pagans, cut down and used the wood to build a church. When the god Thor did not respond by killing him with his lightning bolts, Boniface won many converts. As missionaries preached, baptized, and established churches, they included the Christian duty to obey secular authorities as part of their message, thus extending to Frankish rulers the church's support of secular power that had begun with Constantine (see Chapter 7).

As mayor of the palace, Charles Martel had exercised the power of king of the Franks. His son Pippin III aspired to the title as well as the powers it entailed. Pippin's diplomats were able to convince an embattled Pope Zacharias to rule in his favor against the Merovingians in exchange for military support against the Lombards, who were threatening the papacy. Zacharias invoked his apostolic authority as pope, deposed the Merovingian ruler Chilperic in 752, and declared that Pippin should be king "in order to prevent provoking civil war [between the Merovingians and Carolingians] in Francia."[2] An assembly of Frankish magnates elected Pippin king, and Boniface anointed him. When in 754 Lombard expansion again threatened the papacy, Pope Stephen II journeyed to the Frankish kingdom seeking help. On this occasion, he personally anointed Pippin with the sacred oils and gave him the title "Patrician of the Romans," thus linking him symbolically with the ruling patrician class of ancient Rome. Pippin promised restitution of the papal lands and later made a gift of estates in central Italy.

Because of his anointment, Pippin's kingship took on a special spiritual and moral character. Prior to Pippin only priests and bishops had received anointment. Pippin became the first to be anointed with the sacred oils and acknowledged as *rex et sacerdos* (rehks eht SAHK-ehr-dohse), meaning king and priest. Anointment, not royal blood, set the Christian king apart. By having himself anointed, Pippin cleverly eliminated possible threats to the Frankish throne by other claimants, and the pope promised him support in the future. An important alliance had been struck between the papacy and the Frankish monarchs. When Pippin died, his son Charles, generally known as Charlemagne, succeeded him.

The Warrior-Ruler Charlemagne

Charlemagne's adviser and friend Alcuin (ca. 735–804; see page 244) wrote that "a king should be strong against his enemies, humble to Christians, feared by pagans, loved by the poor and judicious in counsel and maintaining justice."[3] Charlemagne worked to realize that ideal in all its aspects. Through brutal military expeditions that brought wealth — lands, booty, slaves, and tribute — and by peaceful travel, personal appearances, and the sheer force of his personality, Charlemagne sought to awe newly conquered peoples and rebellious domestic enemies.

If an ideal king was "strong against his enemies" and "feared by pagans," Charlemagne more than met the standard. In continuing the expansionist policies of his ancestors, his reign was characterized by constant warfare; according to the chroniclers of the time, only seven years between 714 and 814 were peaceful. Charlemagne fought more than fifty campaigns and became the greatest warrior of the early Middle Ages. He subdued all of the north of modern France, but his greatest successes were in today's Germany, where he fought battles he justified as spreading Christianity to pagan peoples. In the course of a bloody thirty-year war against the Saxons, he added most of the northwestern German peoples to the Frankish kingdom. In his biography of the ruler, Charlemagne's royal secretary Einhard reported that Charlemagne ordered more than four thousand Saxons killed on one day and deported thousands more. Those who surrendered were forced to become Christian, often in mass baptisms. He established bishoprics in areas he had conquered, so church officials and church institutions became important means of imposing Frankish rule.

Charlemagne also achieved spectacular results in the south, incorporating Lombardy into the Frankish kingdom. He ended Bavarian independence and defeated the nomadic Avars, opening eastern Germany for later settlement by Franks. He successfully fought the Byzantine Empire for Venetia, Istria, and Dalmatia and temporarily annexed those areas to his kingdom. Charlemagne's only defeat came at the hands of the Basques of northwestern Spain. By around 805 the Frankish kingdom included all of northwestern Europe except Scandinavia and Britain (Map 8.2). Not since the Roman emperors of the third century C.E. had any ruler controlled so much of the Western world. Other than brief periods under Napoleon and Hitler, Europe would never again see as large a unified state as it had under Charlemagne, which is one reason he has become an important symbol of European unity in the twenty-first century.

Carolingian Government and Society

Charlemagne's empire was not a state as people today understand that term; it was a collection of peoples and clans. For administrative purposes, Charlemagne divided his entire kingdom into counties based closely on the old Merovingian civitas. Each of the approximately six hundred counties was governed by a count (or in his absence by a viscount), who published royal orders, held courts and resolved legal cases, collected taxes and tolls, raised troops for the army, and supervised maintenance of roads and bridges. Counts were originally sent out from the royal court; later a person native to

MAP 8.2 Charlemagne's Conquests, ca. 768–814
Though Charlemagne's hold on much of his territory was relatively weak, the size of his empire was not equaled again until the nineteenth-century conquests of Napoleon.

the region was appointed. As a link between local authorities and the central government, Charlemagne appointed officials called *missi dominici* (mih-see doh-MEH-nee-chee), "agents of the lord king," who checked up on the counts and held courts to handle judicial and financial issues.

Considering the size of Charlemagne's empire, the counts and royal agents were few and far between, and the authority of the central government was weak. The abbots and bishops who served as Charlemagne's advisers envisioned a unified Christian society presided over by a king who was responsible for maintaining peace, law, and order and administering justice. This remained a vision, however, not reality. Instead, society was held together by alliances among powerful families, along with dependent relationships cemented by oaths promising faith and loyalty.

Family alliances were often cemented by sexual relations, including those of Charlemagne himself. Charlemagne had a total of four legal wives, most from other Frankish tribes, and six concubines. Charlemagne's personal desires certainly shaped his complicated relationships—even after the age of sixty-five he continued to sire children—but the security and continuation of his dynasty and the need for diplomatic alliances were also important motives. Despite all the women bearing his children, only three of Charlemagne's sons born in wedlock reached adulthood, and only one outlived him. Four surviving legitimate grandsons did ensure perpetuation of the family, however, and the marriages themselves linked Charlemagne with other powerful families even in the absence of sons. Several of his children born out of wedlock became abbots or abbesses of major monasteries, connecting his family with the church as well as the secular hierarchy.

In terms of social changes, the Carolingian period witnessed moderate population growth. The highest aristocrats and church officials lived well, with fine clothing and

Charlemagne and His Wife This illumination from a ninth-century manuscript portrays Charlemagne with one of his wives. Marriage was an important tool of diplomacy for Charlemagne, and he had a number of wives and concubines. (Erich Lessing/Art Resource, NY)

at least a few rooms heated by firewood. Male nobles hunted and managed their estates, while female nobles generally oversaw the education of their children and sometimes inherited and controlled land on their own. Craftsmen and craftswomen on manorial estates manufactured textiles, weapons, glass, and pottery, primarily for local consumption. Sometimes abbeys and manors served as markets; goods were shipped away to towns and fairs for sale; and a good deal of interregional commerce existed. In the towns, artisans and merchants produced and traded luxury goods for noble and clerical patrons. When compared with earlier Roman cities or with Muslim cities of the time, such as Córdoba and Baghdad, however, Carolingian cities were small; few north of the Alps had more than seven thousand people. Even in Charlemagne's main political center at Aachen, most buildings were made of wood and earth, streets were narrow and muddy, and beggars were a common sight.

The modest economic expansion benefited townspeople and nobles, but it did not significantly alter the lives of most people, who continued to live in a vast rural world dotted with isolated estates and small villages. Here life was precarious. Crops could easily be wiped out by hail, cold, or rain, and transporting food from other areas was impossible. People's diets centered on grain, which was baked into bread, brewed into beer, and especially cooked into gruel. To this were added seasonal vegetables such as peas, cabbage, and onions, and tiny amounts of animal protein, mostly cheese. Clothing and household goods were just as simple, and houses were drafty, smoky, and often shared with animals. Lice, fleas, and other vermin spread disease, and the poor diet led to frequent stomach disorders. Work varied by the season, but at all times of the year it was physically demanding and yielded relatively little. What little there was had to be shared with landowners, who demanded their taxes and rents in the form of crops, animals, or labor.

The Imperial Coronation of Charlemagne

In autumn of the year 800, Charlemagne paid a momentous visit to Rome. Einhard gives this account of what happened:

His last journey there [to Rome] was due to another factor, namely that the Romans, having inflicted many injuries on Pope Leo—plucking out his eyes and tearing out his tongue, he had been compelled to beg the assistance of the king. Accordingly, coming to Rome in order that he might set in order those things which had exceedingly disturbed the condition of the Church, he remained there the whole winter. It was at the time that he accepted the name of Emperor and Augustus. At first he was so much opposed to this that he insisted that although that day was a great [Christian] feast, he would not have entered the Church if he had known beforehand the pope's intention. But he bore very patiently the jealousy of the Roman Emperors [that is, the Byzantine rulers] who were indignant when he received these titles. He overcame their arrogant haughtiness with magnanimity, . . . by sending frequent ambassadors to them and in his letters addressing them as brothers.[4]

For centuries scholars have debated the reasons for the imperial coronation of Charlemagne. Did Charlemagne plan the ceremony in Saint Peter's on Christmas Day, or did he merely accept the title of emperor? What did he have to gain from it? If, as Einhard implies, the coronation displeased Charlemagne, was that because it put the pope in the superior position of conferring power on the emperor? What were Pope Leo's motives in arranging the coronation?

Though definitive answers will probably never be found, several things seem certain. First, after the coronation Charlemagne considered himself an emperor ruling a Christian people. Through his motto, *Renovatio romani imperi* (Revival of the Roman Empire), Charlemagne was consciously perpetuating old Roman imperial notions while at the same time identifying with the new Rome of the Christian Church. In this sense, Charlemagne might be considered a precursor of the eventual Holy Roman emperor, although that term didn't come into use for two more centuries. Second, Leo's ideas about gender and rule undoubtedly influenced his decision to crown Charlemagne. In 800 the ruler of the Byzantine Empire was the empress Irene, the first woman to rule Byzantium in her own name, but Leo did not regard her authority as legitimate because she was female. He thus claimed to be placing Charlemagne on a vacant throne. Third, both parties gained: the Carolingian family received official recognition from the leading spiritual power in Europe, and the papacy gained a military protector.

Not surprisingly, the Byzantines regarded the papal acts as rebellious and Charlemagne as a usurper. The imperial coronation thus marks a decisive break between Rome and Constantinople. From Baghdad, however, Harun-al-Rashid, caliph of the Abbasid (uh-BAH-suhd) Empire (786–809), congratulated the Frankish ruler with the gift of an elephant. It was named Abu'l Abbas after the founder of the Abbasid Dynasty and may have served as a symbol of the diplomatic link Harun-al-Rashid hoped to forge with the Franks against Byzantium. Having plodded its way to Charlemagne's court at Aachen, the elephant survived for nine years, and its death was considered important enough to be mentioned in the Frankish *Royal Annals*, the official chronological record of events, for the year 810. Like everyone else at Aachen, the elephant lived in a city that was far less sophisticated, healthy, and beautiful than the Baghdad of Harun-al-Rashid.

The coronation of Charlemagne, whether planned by the Carolingian court or by the papacy, was to have a profound effect on the course of German history and on the later history of Europe. In the centuries that followed, German rulers were eager to gain the imperial title and to associate themselves with the legends of Charlemagne and ancient Rome. Ecclesiastical authorities, on the other hand, continually cited the event as proof that the dignity of the imperial crown could be granted only by the pope.

Early Medieval Culture

What were the significant intellectual and cultural changes in Charlemagne's era?

As he built an empire through conquest and strategic alliances, Charlemagne also set in motion a cultural revival that had long-lasting consequences. The stimulus he gave to scholarship and learning may, in fact, be his most enduring legacy, although at the time most people continued to live in a world where knowledge was transmitted orally.

The Carolingian Renaissance

In Roman Gaul through the fifth century, the culture of members of the elite rested on an education that stressed grammar, Greco-Roman works of literature and history, and the legal and medical treatises of the Roman world. Beginning in the seventh and eighth centuries, a new cultural tradition common to Gaul, Italy, the British Isles, and to some extent Spain emerged. This culture was based primarily on Christian sources. Scholars have called the new Christian and ecclesiastical culture of the period from about 760 to 840, and the educational foundation on which it was based, the "Carolingian Renaissance" because Charlemagne was its major patron.

Charlemagne directed that every monastery in his kingdom should cultivate learning and educate the monks and secular clergy so that they would have a better understanding of the Christian writings. He also urged the establishment of cathedral and monastic schools where boys might learn to read and to pray properly. Thus the main purpose of this rebirth of learning was to promote an understanding of the Scriptures and of Christian writers and to instruct people to pray and praise God in the correct manner.

Women shared with men the work of evangelization and the new Christian learning. Rulers, noblemen, and noblewomen founded monasteries for nuns, each governed by an abbess. The abbess oversaw all aspects of life in the monastery. She handled the business affairs, supervised the copying of manuscripts, and directed the daily round of prayer and worship. Women's monasteries housed women who were unmarried, and also often widows, children being taught to read and recite prayers and chants, elderly people seeking a safe place to live, and travelers needing hospitality. Some female houses were, in fact, double monasteries in which the abbess governed two adjoining establishments, one for women and one for men. Monks provided protection from attack and did the heavy work on the land in double monasteries, but nuns handled everything else.

In monasteries and cathedral schools, monks, nuns, and scribes copied books and manuscripts and built up libraries. They developed the beautifully clear handwriting known as "Carolingian minuscule," with both uppercase and lowercase letters, from which modern Roman type is derived. In this era before printed books, works could survive only if they were copied. Almost all of the works of Roman authors that we are now able to read, both Christian and secular, were preserved by the efforts of Carolingian

Carolingian Minuscule In the Carolingian period books played a large role in the spread of Christianity and in the promotion of learning. The development of the clearer script known as Carolingian minuscule shown here made books more legible and copying more efficient because more words could fit on the page. (The Schoyen Collection MS 076, Schoyen Bede de Tabernaculo, Oslo and London. Photographer: Richard A. Linethal, London)

scribes. Some scholars went beyond copying to develop their own ideas, and by the middle years of the ninth century there was a great outpouring of more sophisticated original works. Ecclesiastical writers imbued with the legal ideas of ancient Rome and the theocratic ideals of Saint Augustine instructed the semibarbaric rulers of the West.

The most important scholar at Charlemagne's court was Alcuin (Al-KYOO-ihn), who came from Northumbria, one of the kingdoms in England. He was the leader of a palace school at Aachen, where Charlemagne assembled learned men from all over Europe. From 781 until his death, Alcuin was the emperor's chief adviser on religious and educational matters. Alcuin's letters to Charlemagne set forth political theories on the authority, power, and responsibilities of a Christian ruler.

Through monastic and cathedral schools, basic literacy in Latin was established among some of the clergy and even among some of the nobility, a change from Merovingian times. By the tenth century the patterns of thought and the lifestyles of educated western Europeans were those of Rome and Latin Christianity. Most people, however, continued to live in an oral world. They spoke local languages, which did not have a written form. Christian services continued to be conducted in Latin, but not all village priests were able to attend a school, and many simply learned the service by rote. Some Latin words and phrases gradually penetrated the various vernacular languages, but the Carolingian Renaissance did not trickle down to ordinary people.

This division between a learned culture of Latin that built on the knowledge of the ancient world and a vernacular culture of local traditions can also be seen in medicine. Christian teaching supported concern for the poor, sick, and downtrodden. Churchmen taught that all knowledge came from God, who had supplied it for people to use for their own benefit. The foundation of a medical school at Salerno in southern Italy in the ninth century gave a tremendous impetus to medical study. The school's location attracted Arabic, Greek, and Jewish physicians from all over the Mediterranean region. Students flocked there even from northern Europe.

Despite the advances at Salerno, however, physicians were few in the early Middle Ages, and only the rich could afford them. Local folk medicine practiced by nonprofessionals provided help for commoners, with treatments made from herbs, bark, and other natural ingredients. Infants and children were especially susceptible to a range of illnesses, and about half of the children born died before age five. Although a few people lived into their seventies, most did not, and a forty-year-old was considered old.

Northumbrian Learning and Writing

Charlemagne's court at Aachen was not the only center of learning in early medieval Christian Europe. Another was the Anglo-Saxon kingdom of Northumbria, situated at the northernmost tip of the old Roman world. Northumbrian creativity owed a great deal to the intellectual curiosity and collecting zeal of Saint Benet Biscop (ca. 628–689), who brought manuscripts and other treasures back from Italy. These formed the library on which much later study rested.

Northumbrian monasteries produced scores of books: missals (used for the celebration of the Mass); psalters (SAL-tuhrs), which contained the 150 psalms and other prayers used by the monks in their devotions; commentaries on the Scriptures; illuminated manuscripts; law codes; and collections of letters and sermons. (See "Individuals in Society: The Venerable Bede," on page 246.) The finest product of Northumbrian art is probably the Gospel book produced at Lindisfarne monastery around 700. The book was produced by a single scribe working steadily over a period of several years, with the expenses involved in the production of such a book—for vellum, coloring, and gold leaf—probably supplied by the monastery's aristocratic patrons.

As in Charlemagne's empire, women were important participants in Northumbrian Christian culture. Perhaps the most important abbess of the early medieval period anywhere in Europe was Saint Hilda (d. 680). A noblewoman of considerable learning and administrative ability, she ruled the double monastery of Whitby on the Northumbrian coast, advised kings and princes, and encouraged scholars and poets. Hilda played a key role in the adoption of Roman practices by Anglo-Saxon churches (see Chapter 7). At about the time the monks at Lindisfarne were producing their Gospel book, another author was probably at work on a nonreligious epic poem, *Beowulf* (BAY-uh-woolf). The poem tells the story of the hero Beowulf's progress from valiant warrior to wise ruler. (See "Primary Source: The Death of Beowulf," page 248.) In contrast to most writings of this era, which were in Latin, *Beowulf* was written in the vernacular Anglo-Saxon. The identity of its author (or authors) is unknown, and it survives only in a single copy. The poem includes descriptions of real historical events that took place in fifth- and sixth-century Denmark and Sweden, which have been confirmed by archaeological excavations. These are mixed in with legends, oral traditions, and material from the Bible; though it tells a story set in pagan Denmark and Sweden, it was written in Christian England sometime in the eighth to the tenth centuries. *Beowulf* provides evidence of the close relationship between England and the northern European continent in the early Middle Ages, for the North Sea was no barrier to regular contact and cultural exchange. The movements of people and ideas that allowed a work like *Beowulf* to be written only increased in the ninth century, when the North Sea became even more of a highway.

INDIVIDUALS IN SOCIETY • The Venerable Bede

The finest representative of Northumbrian, and indeed all Anglo-Saxon, scholarship is Bede (ca. 673–735). He was born into a noble family, and when he was seven his parents sent him to Benet Biscop's monastery at Wearmouth as a sign of their religious devotion. Later he was sent to the new monastery at Jarrow five miles away. Surrounded by the hundreds of pagan and Christian books Benet Biscop had brought from Italy, Bede spent the rest of his life there, studying and writing. He wrote textbooks on grammar and writing designed to help students master the intricacies of Latin, commentaries on the Old and New Testaments, historical works relating the lives of abbots and the development of the church, and scientific works on time. His biblical commentaries survive in hundreds of manuscripts, indicating that they were widely studied throughout the Middle Ages. His doctrinal works led him to be honored after his death with the title "Venerable," and centuries after his death to be named a "doctor of the church" by the pope.

Bede's religious writings were actually not that innovative, but his historical writings were, particularly his best-known work, the *Ecclesiastical History of the English People*, written about 720. As the title suggests, Bede's main topic is the growth of Christianity in England. The book begins with a short discussion of Christianity in Roman Britain, then skips to Augustine of Canterbury's mission to the Anglo-Saxons (see Chapter 7). Most of the book tells the story of Christianity's spread from one small kingdom in England to another, with missionaries and the kings who converted as its heroes, and the narrative ends with Bede's own day. Bede searched far and wide for his information, discussed the validity of his evidence, compared various sources, and exercised critical judgment. He includes accounts of miracles, but, like the stories of valiant missionaries, these are primarily related to provide moral lessons, which all medieval writers thought was the chief purpose of history.

One of the lessons that Bede sought to impart with his history is that Christianity should be unified, and one feature of the *Ecclesiastical History of the English People* inadvertently provided a powerful model for this. In his history, Bede adopted a way of reckoning time proposed by an earlier monk that would eventually provide a uniform chronology for all Christians. He dated events from the incarnation of Christ,

Invasions and Migrations

What were the consequences of the ninth-century invasions and migrations?

Charlemagne left his vast empire to his sole surviving son, Louis the Pious (r. 814–840), who attempted to keep the empire intact. This proved to be impossible. Members of the nobility engaged in plots and open warfare against the emperor, often allying themselves with one of Louis's three sons, who were in conflict with their father and with one another. In 843, shortly after Louis's death, his sons agreed to the **Treaty of Verdun** (vehr-DUHN), which divided the empire into three parts: Charles the Bald received the western part; Lothair the middle part and the title of emperor; and Louis the eastern

rather than from the foundation of the city of Rome, as the Romans had done, or from the regnal years of kings, as the Germans did. His history was recopied by monks in many parts of Europe, who used this dating method, *anno Domini*, "in the year of the Lord" (later abbreviated A.D.), for their own histories as well. (Though Bede does talk about "before the time of the incarnation of our Lord," the reverse dating system of B.C., "before Christ," does not seem to have been widely used before 1700.) Disputes about whether the year began with the incarnation (that is, the conception) of Christ or his birth, and whether these occurred in 1 B.C. or A.D. 1 (the Christian calendar does not have a year zero), continued after Bede, but his method prevailed.

QUESTIONS FOR ANALYSIS

1. How do the career and accomplishments of Bede fit with the notion of an early medieval "renaissance" of learning?

2. Does Bede's notion that history has a moral purpose still shape the writing of history? Do you agree with him?

3. The Christian calendar dates from a midpoint rather than from a starting point, the way many of the world's calendars do. What advantages does this create in reckoning time? What would you see as the primary reason that the Christian calendar has now been widely adopted worldwide?

ONLINE DOCUMENT ASSIGNMENT

What does Bede's life and work tell us about early medieval intellectual communities? Find out how knowledge was shared among scholars through excerpts from Bede's writings and those of other Carolingian Renaissance figures. Then complete a writing assignment based on the evidence and details from this chapter.

bedfordstmartins.com/mckaywestvalue

part, from which he acquired the title "the German." Though no one knew it at the time, this treaty set the pattern for political boundaries in Europe that has been maintained until today.

After the Treaty of Verdun, continental Europe was fractured politically. All three kingdoms controlled by the sons of Louis the Pious were torn by domestic dissension and disorder. The frontier and coastal defenses erected by Charlemagne and maintained by Louis the Pious were neglected. No European political power was strong enough to put up effective resistance to external attacks. Beginning around 850 three main groups began relentless attacks on Europe: Vikings from Scandinavia, representing the final wave of Germanic migrants; Muslims from the Mediterranean; and Magyars from central Europe forced westward by other peoples (Map 8.3).

PRIMARY SOURCE   The Death of Beowulf

In the long Anglo-Saxon epic poem that bears his name, the hero Beowulf fights and kills the monster Grendel and then Grendel's mother. He then becomes the king of the Geats, one of the Germanic groups that lived in western Sweden, and takes arms late in life against a dragon that was threatening his people.

He ruled it well for fifty winters—that was an aged king, a veteran guardian of his people,—until in the dark nights a certain one began to have power,—a dragon, who on an upland heath kept watch over a hoard. . . .

Then the fiend began to vomit forth flames, to burn the noble dwellings; the gleam of fire blazed forth, a terror to the sons of men; the hateful creature flying in the air would leave there no thing with life. . . .

Beowulf discoursed,—spoke a last time with words of boasting:—"I ventured on many battles in my younger days; once more will I, the aged guardian of the people, seek combat and get renown." . . .

Then rose the doughty champion by his shield; bold under his helmet, he went clad in his war-corslet to beneath the rock cliffs, and trusted in his own strength—not such is the coward's way. Then he who, excellent in virtues, had lived through many wars,—the tumult of battles, when armies dash together,—saw by the rampart a rocky arch whence burst a stream out from the mound; hot was the welling of the flood with deadly fire. He could not any while endure unscorched the hollow near the hoard, by reason of the dragon's flame. . . .

Never a whit [Not in the least] did his comrades, those sons of nobles, stand round him in a body, doing deeds of warlike prowess; but they shrank back into the wood and took care of their lives. . . . [One of Beowulf's warriors assists him, and together they kill the dragon, though Beowulf is mortally wounded in the fight.]

Vikings in Western Europe

From the moors of Scotland to the mountains of Sicily, there arose in the ninth century the prayer, "Save us, O God, from the violence of the Northmen." The feared Northmen were Germanic peoples from the area of modern-day Norway, Sweden, and Denmark who had remained beyond the sway of the Christianizing influences of the Carolingian Empire. They began to make overseas expeditions, which they themselves called *vikings*, a word that probably derives from a unit of maritime distance. *Viking* came to be used both for the activity ("to go a-viking") and for the people who went on such expeditions. Propelled either by oars or by sails, deckless, and about sixty-five feet long, a Viking ship could carry between forty and sixty men—enough to harass an isolated monastery or village. These ships, navigated by experienced and fearless sailors, moved through complicated rivers, estuaries, and waterways in Europe. The Carolingian Empire, with no navy, was helpless. The Vikings moved swiftly, attacked, and escaped to return again.

Scholars disagree about the reasons for Viking attacks and migrations. A very unstable Danish kingship and disputes over the succession led to civil war and disorder, which may have driven warriors abroad in search of booty and supporters. The population of Scandinavia may have grown too large for the available land to support, and

Then the chieftain wise in thought went on until he sat on a seat by the rampart. . . . Beowulf discoursed: despite his hurt, his grievous deadly wound, he spoke,—he knew full well that he had used up his time of earthly joy. . . . "I have ruled over this people fifty winters; there was not one of the kings of the neighbouring tribes who dared encounter me with weapons, or could weigh me down with fear. In my own home I awaited what the times destined for me, kept my own well, did not pick treacherous quarrels, nor have I sworn unjustly any oaths. In all this may I, sick with deadly wounds, have solace; because the Ruler of men may never charge me with the murder of kinsfolk, when my life parts from my body. . . .

"I utter in words my thanks to the Ruler of all, the King of Glory, the everlasting Lord. . . . Bid the war-veterans raise a splendid barrow [mound of earth] after the funeral fire, on a projection by the sea, which shall tower high on Hronesness as a memorial for my people, so that seafarers who urge their tall ships from afar over the spray of ocean shall thereafter call it Beowulf's barrow."

EVALUATE THE EVIDENCE

1. Based on Beowulf's actions and words, what were the qualities of an ideal leader in the early Middle Ages?

2. How do these sections of *Beowulf* provide evidence for the assimilation of Germanic and Christian values discussed in Chapter 7? For the distinctive aspects of early medieval culture discussed in this chapter?

Source: *Beowulf and the Finnesburg Fragment*, trans. John R. Clark Hall, rev. C. L. Wrenn (London: George Allen and Unwin, 1940), pp. 132, 137, 147, 148, 150, 156, 157, 160.

cities on the coasts of northern Europe offered targets for plunder. Goods plundered could then be sold, and looting raids turned into trading ventures. Some scholars assert that the Vikings were looking for trade and new commercial contacts from the beginning.

Whatever the motivations, Viking attacks were savage. The Vikings burned, looted, and did extensive property damage, although there is little evidence that they caused long-term physical destruction—perhaps because, arriving in small bands, they lacked the manpower to do so. They seized magnates and high churchmen and held them for ransom; they also demanded tribute from kings. In 844–845 Charles the Bald had to raise seven thousand pounds of silver, and across the English Channel Anglo-Saxon rulers collected a land tax, the *Danegeld*, to buy off the Vikings. In the Seine and Loire Valleys the frequent presence of Viking war bands seems to have had economic consequences, stimulating the production of food and wine and possibly the manufacture (for sale) of weapons and the breeding of horses.

The slave trade represented an important part of Viking plunder and commerce. Slaves, known as *thralls*, were common in Scandinavian society, and Vikings took people from the British Isles and territories along the Baltic Sea as part of their booty. They sold them as slaves in the markets of Magdeburg and Regensburg, at the fairs of Lyons,

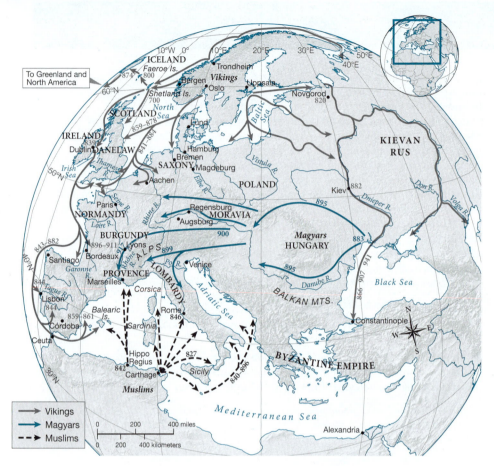

MAP 8.3 Invasions and Migrations of the Ninth and Tenth Centuries
This map shows the Viking, Magyar, and Arab invasions and migrations in the ninth and tenth centuries.

and in seaports of the Muslim world. Dublin became a center of the Viking slave trade, with hundreds and sometimes thousands of young men and women bought and sold there in any one year.

In the early tenth century Danish Vikings besieged Paris with fleets of more than a hundred highly maneuverable ships, and the Frankish king Charles the Simple bought them off in 911 by giving them a large part of northern France. There the Vikings established the province of "Northmanland," or Normandy as it was later known, intermarrying with the local population and creating a distinctive Norman culture. From there they sailed around Spain and into the Mediterranean, eventually seizing Sicily from the Muslim Arabs in 1060–1090, while other Normans crossed the English Channel, defeating Anglo-Saxon forces in 1066. Between 850 and 1000 Viking control of northern Europe reached its zenith. Norwegian Vikings moved farther west than any Europeans had before, establishing permanent settlements on Iceland and short-lived settlements in Greenland and Newfoundland in what is now Canada.

The Vikings made positive contributions to the areas they settled. They carried their unrivaled knowledge of shipbuilding and seamanship everywhere. The northeastern and central parts of England where the Vikings settled became known as the *Danelaw* because Danish, not English, laws and customs prevailed there. Scholars believe that some legal institutions, such as the ancestor of the modern grand jury, originated in the Danelaw. Exports from Ireland included iron tools and weapons manufactured there by Viking metal-smiths.

Slavs and Vikings in Eastern Europe

Vikings also brought change in eastern Europe, which was largely populated by Slavs. In antiquity the Slavs lived in central Europe, farming with iron technology, building fortified towns, and worshipping a variety of deities. With the start of the mass migrations of the late Roman Empire, the Slavs moved in different directions and split into what historians later identified as three groups: West, South, and East Slavs.

The group labeled the West Slavs included the Poles, Czechs, Slovaks, and Wends. The South Slavs, comprising peoples who became the Serbs, Croats, Slovenes, Macedonians, and Bosnians, migrated southward into the Balkans. In the seventh century Slavic peoples of the west and south created the state of Moravia along the banks of the Danube River. By the tenth century Moravia's residents were Roman Christian, along with most of the other West and South Slavs. The pattern of conversion was similar to that of the Germanic tribes: first the ruler was baptized, and then missionaries preached, built churches, and spread Christian teachings among the common people. The ruler of Poland was able to convince the pope to establish an independent archbishopric there in 1000, the beginning of a long-lasting connection between Poland and the Roman Church. In the Balkans the Serbs accepted Orthodox Christianity, while the Croats became Roman Christian, a division with a long-standing impact; it was one of the factors in the civil war in this area in the late twentieth century.

Between the fifth and ninth centuries the eastern Slavs moved into the vast areas of present-day European Russia and Ukraine. This enormous area consisted of an immense virgin forest to the north, where most of the eastern Slavs settled, and an endless prairie grassland to the south. In the tenth century Ibrahim Ibn Jakob, a learned Jew from the Muslim caliphate in Córdoba in Spain, traveled in Slavic areas. He found the Slavs to be "violent and inclined to aggression," but far cleaner than Christians in other parts of Europe in which he had traveled, "who wash only once or twice a year." Such filthy habits were unacceptable to someone raised in Muslim Spain, but the Slavs had an ingenious way of both getting clean and staying healthy: "They have no bathhouses as such, but they do make use of wooden huts [for bathing]. They build a stone stove, on which, when it is heated, they pour water. . . . They hold a bunch of grass in their hands, and waft the stream around. Then their pores open, and all excess matter escapes from their bodies."[5]

In the ninth century the Vikings appeared in the lands of the eastern Slavs. Called "Varangians" in the old Russian chronicles, the Vikings were interested primarily in gaining wealth through plunder and trade, and the opportunities were good. Moving up and down the rivers, they soon linked Scandinavia and northern Europe to the Black Sea and to the Byzantine Empire's capital at Constantinople. They raided and looted the cities along the Caspian Sea several times in the tenth century, taking booty and

Animal Headpost from Viking Ship   Skilled wood-carvers produced ornamental headposts for ships, sledges, wagons, and bedsteads. The fearsome quality of many carvings suggests that they were intended to ward off evil spirits and to terrify. (© University Museum of Cultural Heritage, Oslo. Photographer: Eirik Irgens Johnsen)

slaves, which they then sold elsewhere; thus raiding turned into trading, and the Scandinavians later established settlements, intermarried, and assimilated with Slavic peoples.

In order to increase and protect their international commerce and growing wealth, the Vikings declared themselves the rulers of the eastern Slavs. According to tradition, the semi-legendary chieftain Ruirik founded a princely dynasty about 860. In any event, the Varangian ruler Oleg (r. 878–912) established his residence at Kiev in modern-day Ukraine. He and his successors ruled over a loosely united confederation of Slavic territories known as Rus, with its capital at Kiev, until 1054. (The word *Russia* comes from *Rus*, though the origins of *Rus* are hotly debated, with some historians linking it with Swedish words and others with Slavic words.)

Oleg and his clansmen quickly became assimilated into the Slavic population, taking local wives and emerging as the noble class. Missionaries of the Byzantine Empire converted the Vikings and local Slavs to Eastern Orthodox Christianity, accelerating the unification of the two groups. Thus the rapidly Slavified Vikings left two important legacies for the future: in about 900 they created a loose unification of Slavic territories, **Kievan Rus**, under a single ruling prince and dynasty, and they imposed a basic religious unity by accepting Orthodox Christianity, as opposed to Roman Catholicism, for themselves and the eastern Slavs.

Even at its height under Great Prince Iaroslav (YAHR-uh-slahv) the Wise (r. 1019–1054), the unity of Kievan Rus was extremely tenuous. Trade, not government, was the main concern of the rulers. Moreover, the Slavified Vikings failed to find a way to peacefully transfer power from one generation to the next. In early Rus there were apparently no fixed rules, and much strife accompanied each succession. Possibly to avoid such chaos, Great Prince Iaroslav, before his death in 1054, divided Kievan Rus among his five sons, who in turn divided their properties when they died. Between 1054 and 1237, Kievan Rus disintegrated into more and more competing units, each ruled by a prince claiming to be a descendant of Ruirik. The princes divided their land like private property because they thought of it as private property. A prince owned a certain number of farms or landed estates and had them worked directly by his people, mainly slaves, called *kholops* in Russian. Outside of these estates, which constituted the princely domain, the prince exercised only limited authority in his principality. Excluding the clergy, two kinds of people lived there: the noble boyars and the commoner peasants.

The **boyars** were descendants of the original Viking warriors, and they also held their lands as free and clear private property. Although the boyars normally fought in princely armies, the customary law declared that they could serve any prince they wished. The ordinary peasants were also truly free. They could move at will wherever opportunities were greatest. In a touching phrase of the times, theirs was "a clean road, without boundaries."[6] In short, fragmented princely power, private property, and personal freedom all went hand in hand.

Magyars and Muslims

Groups of central European steppe peoples known as Magyars also raided villages in the late ninth century, taking plunder and captives, and forcing leaders to pay tribute in an effort to prevent further looting and destruction. Moving westward, small bands of Magyars on horseback reached as far as Spain and the Atlantic coast. They subdued northern Italy, compelled Bavaria and Saxony to pay tribute, and even penetrated into the Rhineland and Burgundy (see Map 8.3). Because of their skill with horses and their Eastern origins, the Magyars were often identified with the earlier Huns by those they conquered, though they are probably unrelated ethnically. This identification, however, may be the origin of the word *Hungarian*.

Magyar forces were defeated by a combined army of Frankish and other Germanic troops at the Battle of Lechfeld near Augsburg in southern Germany in 955, and the Magyars settled in the area that is now Hungary in eastern Europe. Much as Clovis had centuries earlier, the Magyar ruler Géza (GEE-zuh) (r. 970–997), who had been a pagan, became a Roman Christian. This gave him the support of the papacy and offered prospects for alliances with other Roman Christian rulers against the Byzantine Empire, Hungary's southern neighbor. Géza's son Stephen I (r. 997–1038) was officially crowned the king of Hungary by a papal representative on Christmas Day of 1000. He supported the building of churches and monasteries, increased royal power, and encouraged the use of Latin and the Roman alphabet. Hungary's alliance with the papacy shaped the later history of eastern Europe just as Charlemagne's alliance with the papacy shaped western European history. The Hungarians adopted settled agriculture, wrote law codes, and built towns, and Hungary became an important crossroads of trade for German and Muslim merchants.

The ninth century also saw invasions into Europe from the south. In many ways these were a continuation of the earlier Muslim conquests in the Iberian Peninsula, but now they focused on Sicily and mainland Italy. Muslim fleets had attacked Sicily, which was part of the Byzantine Empire, beginning in the seventh century, and by the end of the ninth century they controlled most of the island. The Muslims drove northward, reached Rome in 846 by sailing up the Tiber River and sacked the city, and captured towns along the Adriatic coast almost all the way to Venice. They attacked Mediterranean settlements along the coast of Provence and advanced on land as far as the Alps. In the tenth century Frankish, papal, and Byzantine forces were able to retake much territory, though the Muslims continued to hold Sicily. Under their rule, agricultural innovations from elsewhere in the Muslim world led to new crops such as cotton and sugar, and fortified cities became centers of Muslim learning. Disputes among the Muslim rulers on the island led one faction to ask the Normans for assistance, and between 1060 and 1090 the Normans gradually conquered all of Sicily.

What was the impact of these invasions? From the perspective of those living in what had been Charlemagne's empire, Viking, Magyar, and Muslim attacks contributed to increasing disorder and violence. Italian, French, and English sources often describe this period as one of terror and chaos: "Save us, O God," in the words of the prayer on page 248. People in other parts of Europe might have had a different opinion, however. In Muslim Spain scholars worked in thriving cities, and new crops such as rice enhanced ordinary people's lives. In eastern Europe, states such as Moravia and Hungary became strong kingdoms. A Viking point of view might be the most positive, for by 1100 descendants of the Vikings not only ruled their homelands in Denmark, Norway, and Sweden, but also ruled Normandy, England, Sicily, Iceland, and Kievan Rus, with an outpost in Greenland and occasional voyages to North America.

Political and Economic Decentralization

How did internal conflict and outside threats shape European political and economic development in this period?

The large-scale division of Charlemagne's empire into three parts in the ninth century led to a decentralization of power at the local level. Civil wars weakened the power and prestige of kings, who could do little about domestic violence. Likewise, the great invasions, especially those of the Vikings, weakened royal authority. The western Frankish kings were unable to halt the invaders, and the local aristocracy had to assume responsibility for defense. Thus, in the ninth and tenth centuries great aristocratic families increased their authority in the regions of their vested interests. They built private castles for defense and to live in, and they governed virtually independent territories in which distant and weak kings could not interfere. Common people turned for protection to the strongest power, the local counts, whom they considered their rightful rulers, and free peasants sank to the level of serfs.

Decentralization and the Origins of "Feudalism"

The political power of the Carolingian rulers had long rested on the cooperation of the dominant social class, the Frankish aristocracy. Charlemagne and his predecessors relied on the nobles to help wage wars of expansion and suppress rebellions, and in return these families were given a share of the lands and riches confiscated by the rulers. The most powerful nobles were those able to gain the allegiance of warriors, often symbolized in an oath-swearing ceremony of homage and fealty that grew out of earlier Germanic oaths of loyalty. In this ceremony a warrior (knight) swore his loyalty as a **vassal**—from a Celtic term meaning "servant"—to the more powerful individual, who became his lord. In return for the vassal's loyalty, aid, and military assistance, the lord promised him protection and material support. This support might be a place in the lord's household, but was more likely a piece of land called a *feudum* or **fief** (feef). In the Roman Empire, soldiers had been paid for their services with money, but in the cash-poor early Middle Ages, their reward was instead a piece of land. Most legal scholars and historians have seen these personal ties of loyalty cemented by grants of land rather than allegiance to an abstract state as a political and social system they term **feudalism**. They have traced its spread from Frankish areas to other parts of Europe.

In the last several decades, increasing numbers of medieval historians have found the idea of a "feudal system" problematic. They note that the word *feudalism* was a later invention, and that vassalage ceremonies, military obligations, and the ownership rights attached to fiefs differed widely from place to place and changed considerably in form and pattern over time. Thus, to these historians, "feudalism" is so varied that it doesn't really have a clear meaning, and it would be better not to use the term at all. The problem is that no one has come up with a better term for the loose arrangements of personal and property ties that developed in the ninth century.

Whether one chooses to use the word *feudalism* or not, these relationships provided some degree of cohesiveness in a society that lacked an adequate government bureaucracy or method of taxation. In fact, because vassals owed administrative as well as military service to their lords, vassalage actually functioned as a way to organize political authority. Vassals were expected to serve as advisers to their lord, and also to pay him fees for important family events, such as the marriage of the vassal's children.

Along with granting land to knights, lords gave land to the clergy for spiritual services or promises of allegiance. In addition, the church held its own lands, and bishops, archbishops, and abbots and abbesses of monasteries sometimes granted fiefs to their own knightly vassals. Thus the "lord" in a feudal relationship was sometimes an institution. Women other than abbesses were generally not granted fiefs, but in most parts of Europe daughters could inherit them if their fathers had no sons. Occasionally, women did go through ceremonies swearing homage and fealty and swore to send fighters when the lord demanded them. More commonly, women acted as surrogates when their husbands were away, defending the territory from attack and carrying out administrative duties.

Some of the problems associated with the word *feudal* come from the fact that it is sometimes used by nonhistorians as a synonym for "medieval," or to describe relations between landholders and the peasants who lived and worked on their estates. (The latter use comes from Karl Marx, who used "feudalism" to describe a stage of economic development between slavery and capitalism.) Medieval historians on all sides of the debate about feudalism agree, however, that peasants did not swear oaths of vassalage; if there was a feudal system, peasants were not part of it.

Manorialism, Serfdom, and the Slave Trade

In feudal relationships, the "lord" was the individual or institution that had authority over a vassal, but the word *lord* was also used to describe the person or institution that had economic and political authority over peasants who lived in villages and farmed the land. Thus a vassal in one relationship was a slightly different type of lord in another. Most European people in the early Middle Ages were peasants who lived in family groups in villages or small towns and made their living predominantly by raising crops and animals. The village and the land surrounding it were called a manor, from the Latin word for "dwelling" or "homestead." Some fiefs might include only one manor, while great lords or kings might have hundreds of manors under their direct control. Residents of manors worked for the lord in exchange for protection, a system that was later referred to as **manorialism**. Free peasants surrendered themselves and their lands to the lord's jurisdiction. The land was given back, but the peasants became tied to it by various kinds of payments and services. Thus like vassalage, manorialism involved an exchange. Because the economic power of the warring class rested on landed estates worked by peasants, feudalism and manorialism were linked, but they were not the same system.

Local custom determined precisely what services villagers would provide to their lord, but certain practices became common throughout Europe. The peasant was obliged to give the lord a percentage of the annual harvest, usually in produce, sometimes in cash. The peasant paid a fee to marry someone from outside the lord's estate. To inherit property, the peasant paid a fine, often the best beast the person owned. Above all, the peasant became part of the lord's permanent labor force. With vast stretches of uncultivated virgin land and a tiny labor population, manorial lords encouraged population growth and immigration. The most profitable form of capital was not land but laborers.

In entering into a relationship with a manorial lord, free farmers lost status. Their position became servile, and they became **serfs**. That is, they were bound to the land and could not leave it without the lord's permission. Serfdom was not the same as slavery in that lords did not own the person of the serf, but serfs were subject to the jurisdiction of the lord's court in any dispute over property and in any case of suspected criminal behavior.

The transition from freedom to serfdom was slow. In the late eighth century there were still many free peasants. And within the legal category of serfdom there were many economic levels, ranging from the highly prosperous to the desperately poor. Nevertheless, a social and legal revolution was taking place. By the year 800 perhaps 60 percent of the population of western Europe—completely free a century before—had been reduced to serfdom. The ninth-century Viking assaults on Europe created extremely unstable conditions and individual insecurity, increasing the need for protection, accelerating the transition to serfdom, and leading to additional loss of personal freedom.

Though serfdom was not slavery, the Carolingian trade in actual slaves was extensive, generally involving persons captured in war or raids. Merchants in early medieval towns used slaves to pay the suppliers of the luxury goods their noble and clerical customers desired, most of which came into Europe from the East. The Muslim conquest of Spain produced thousands of prisoner-slaves, as did Charlemagne's long wars and the Viking raids. When Frankish conquests declined in the tenth century, German and Viking merchants obtained people on the empire's eastern border who spoke Slavic languages, the origin of our word *slave*. Slaves sold across the Mediterranean fetched three or four times the amounts brought within the Carolingian Empire, so most slaves were sold to Muslims. For Europeans and Arabs alike, selling captives and other slaves was standard procedure. Christian moralists sometimes complained about the sale of Christians to non-Christians, but they did not object to slavery itself.

Notes

1. F. E. Peters, *A Reader on Classical Islam* (Princeton, N.J.: Princeton University Press, 1994), pp. 208–209.
2. Quoted in R. McKitterick, *The Frankish Kingdoms Under the Carolingians, 751–987* (New York: Longman, 1983), p. 34.
3. Quoted ibid., p. 77.
4. Quoted in B. D. Hill, ed., *Church and State in the Middle Ages* (New York: John Wiley & Sons, 1970), pp. 46–47.
5. From Charles Melville and Ahmad Ubaydli, eds. and trans., *Christians and Moors in Spain*, vol. 3 (New York: Oxbow Books, 1992), p. 54.
6. Quoted in R. Pipes, *Russia Under the Old Regime* (New York: Charles Scribner's Sons, 1974), p. 48.

Chapter Review

MAKE IT STICK

LearningCurve
bedfordstmartins.com/mckaywestvalue

After reading the chapter, use LearningCurve to retain what you've read.

IDENTIFY KEY TERMS

Identify and explain the significance of each item below.

Qur'an (p. 226)
Five Pillars of Islam (p. 230)
caliph (p. 230)
al-Andalus (p. 231)
infidel (p. 234)

civitas (p. 236)
comites (p. 236)
Treaty of Verdun (p. 246)
Kievan Rus (p. 252)
boyars (p. 253)

vassal (p. 254)
fief (p. 254)
feudalism (p. 255)
manorialism (p. 255)
serfs (p. 256)

REVIEW THE MAIN IDEAS

Answer the focus questions from each section of the chapter.

- What were the origins of Islam, and what impact did it have on Europe as it spread? (p. 226)

- How did the Franks build and govern a European empire? (p. 235)

- What were the significant intellectual and cultural changes in Charlemagne's era? (p. 243)

- What were the consequences of the ninth-century invasions and migrations? (p. 246)

- How did internal conflict and outside threats shape European political and economic development in this period? (p. 254)

MAKE CONNECTIONS

Think about the larger developments and continuities within and across chapters.

1. In both Christianity and Islam, political leaders played an important role in the expansion of the faith into new territory. How would you compare the actions of Constantine and Clovis (both in Chapter 7) with the Muslim caliphs and Charlemagne (in this chapter) in promoting, extending, and establishing their chosen religion?

2. How were the ninth-century migrations and invasions of the Vikings, Magyars, and Muslims similar to the earlier barbarian migrations discussed in Chapter 7? How were they different?

ONLINE DOCUMENT ASSIGNMENT

The Venerable Bede

What does Bede's life and work tell us about early medieval intellectual communities?

You encountered Bede's story on page 246. Keeping the question above in mind, go online and learn more about how knowledge was shared among scholars through excerpts from Bede's writings, as well as those from two other key figures of the Carolingian Renaissance, Alcuin of York and Einhard. Then complete a writing assignment based on the evidence and details from this chapter.

bedfordstmartins.com/mckaywestvalue

CHRONOLOGY

481–752	• Merovingian dynasty
ca. 571–632	• Life of the Prophet Muhammad
651	• Official version of the Qur'an published
711	• Muslim forces defeat Visigothic kingdom
711–720	• Muslim conquest of Spain
ca. 760–840	• Carolingian Renaissance
768–814	• Reign of Charlemagne
800	• Imperial coronation of Charlemagne
800–900	• Free peasants in western Europe increasingly tied to the land as serfs
843	• Treaty of Verdun divides Carolingian kingdom
850–1000	• Most extensive Viking voyages and conquests
ca. 900	• Establishment of Kievan Rus
911	• Vikings establish Normandy
950	• Muslim Córdoba is Europe's largest and most prosperous city
1000	• Stephen crowned first king of Hungary

9

✓ LearningCurve
bedfordstmartins.com/mckaywestvalue
After reading the chapter, use
LearningCurve to retain what
you've read.

State and Church in the High Middle Ages

1000–1300

THE CONCEPT OF THE STATE HAD BEEN ONE OF ROME'S GREAT
legacies to Western civilization, but for almost five hundred years after the
disintegration of the Roman Empire in the West, the state did not exist. Political authority was decentralized, with power spread among many lords, bishops, abbots, and other types of local rulers. The deeply fragmented political
units that covered the early medieval European continent did not have the
characteristics or provide the services of a modern state.

Beginning in the last half of the tenth century, the invasions and migrations
that had contributed to European fragmentation gradually ended, and domestic disorder slowly subsided. Rulers began to develop new institutions of law
and government that enabled them to assert their power over lesser lords and
the general population. Although nobles remained the dominant class, centralized states slowly crystallized, first in western Europe, and then in eastern and
northern Europe. At the same time, energetic popes built their power within
the Western Christian Church and tried to assert their superiority over kings
and emperors. Monks, nuns, and friars played significant roles in medieval
society, both as individuals and as members of institutions. A papal call to retake the holy city of Jerusalem led to nearly two centuries of warfare between
Christians and Muslims. Christian warriors, clergy, and settlers moved out from
western and central Europe in all directions, so that through conquest and colonization border regions were gradually incorporated into a more uniform
Christian realm.

Political Revival and the Origins of the Modern State

How did monarchs try to centralize political power?

The modern state is an organized territory with definite geographical boundaries, a body of law, and institutions of government. The modern national state provides its citizens with order and protection, supplies a currency that permits financial and commercial transactions, and conducts relations with foreign governments. To accomplish these functions, the state must have officials, bureaucracies, laws, courts of law, soldiers, information, and money. Early medieval governments had few of these elements, but beginning in the eleventh century rulers in some parts of Europe began to manipulate existing institutions to build up their power, becoming kings over growing and slowly centralizing states. As rulers expanded their territories and extended their authority, they developed larger bureaucracies, armies, judicial systems, and other institutions of state to maintain control and ensure order. Because these institutions cost money, rulers also initiated systems for generating revenue and handling financial matters. Some rulers were more successful than others, and the solutions they found to these problems laid the foundations for modern national states.

England

Throughout the ninth century the Vikings had made a concerted effort to conquer and rule all of Anglo-Saxon England. Because of its proximity to Scandinavia and its lack of unity under a single ruler, England probably suffered more from Viking invasions than any other part of Europe. In 878 Alfred, king of the West Saxons (or Wessex), defeated the Vikings, inaugurating a period of recovery and stability in England. Alfred and his immediate successors built a system of local defenses and slowly extended royal rule beyond Wessex to other Anglo-Saxon peoples until one law, royal law, took precedence over local custom. England was divided into local units called shires, or counties, each under the jurisdiction of a shire-reeve (a word that soon evolved into *sheriff*) appointed by the king. Sheriffs were unpaid officials from well-off families responsible for collecting taxes, catching and trying criminals, and raising infantry when the king required it.

The Viking invasions of England resumed, however, and the island eventually came under Viking rule. The Viking Canute (r. 1016–1035) made England the center of his empire while promoting a policy of assimilation and reconciliation between Anglo-Saxons and Vikings. When Canute's heir Edward died childless, there were three claimants to the throne of England—the Anglo-Saxon noble Harold Godwinson (ca. 1022–1066), who had been crowned by English nobles; the Norwegian king Harald III (r. 1045–1066), grandson of Canute; and Duke William of Normandy, who was the illegitimate son of Edward's cousin.

In 1066 the forces of Harold Godwinson crushed Harald's invading army in northern England, then quickly marched south when they heard that William had invaded England with his Norman vassals. Harold was decisively defeated by William at the Battle of Hastings—an event now known as the Norman conquest. In both England and Normandy, William the Conqueror limited the power of the nobles and church officials, and built a unified monarchy. In England he retained the office of sheriffs but named Normans to the posts. William wanted to determine how much wealth there was in his new kingdom and who held what land. Royal officials were sent to every part of the country, and in every village local men were put under oath to answer the questions of these officials. In the words of a contemporary chronicler:

> So very narrowly did he have it investigated, that there was no single hide [a hide was a measure of land large enough to support one family], nor yard of land, nor indeed . . . one ox nor one cow nor one pig was there left out, and not put down in his record: and all these records were brought to him afterwards.[1]

The resulting record, called the **Domesday Book** (DOOMZ-day) from the Anglo-Saxon word *doom*, meaning "judgment," helped William and his descendants tax land appropriately. The book still survives and is an invaluable source of social and economic information about medieval England. It also helped William and future English kings regard their country as one unit.

William's son Henry I (r. 1100–1135) established a bureau of finance called the Exchequer that became the first institution of the government bureaucracy of England. In addition to various taxes and annual gifts, Henry's income came from money paid to the Crown for settling disputes and as penalties for crimes, as well as money due to him in his private position as landowner and lord. Henry, like other medieval kings, made no distinction between his private income and state revenues, and the officials of the Exchequer began to keep careful records of all monies paid into and out of the royal treasury. (See "Primary Source: Marriage and Wardship in the Norman Exchequer," page 262.)

In 1128 Henry's daughter Matilda was married to Geoffrey of Anjou; their son became Henry II of England and inaugurated the Angevin (AN-juh-vuhn; from Anjou,

---

The Bayeux Tapestry   William's conquest of England was recorded in an embroidery panel measuring 231 feet by 19 inches. In this scene, two nobles (center left) and a bishop (center right) acclaim Harold Godwinson as king of England (center). Harold holds a scepter and an orb with a cross on top, symbolizing his secular and religious authority. The embroidery provides an important historical source for the clothing, armor, and lifestyles of the Norman and Anglo-Saxon warrior classes. It is now on display in Bayeux (bay-YUH), France, and is incorrectly called a "tapestry," a different kind of needlework. (By special permission of the City of Bayeux)

PRIMARY SOURCE   Marriage and Wardship in the Norman Exchequer

After the Norman conquest, the kings of England held the right to control the marriages of their vassals, and also held wardship over the widow and children of any vassal who had died. They often sold these rights for cash, which gave the buyer control of the marriage or control over the ward's lands until he or she came of age. The records of the Exchequer include many such payments.

Alice, countess of Warwick, renders account of £1000 and 10 palfreys [the type of horse ridden by women] to be allowed to remain a widow as long as she pleases, and not to be forced to marry by the king. And if perchance she should wish to marry, she shall not marry except with the assent and on the grant of the king, where the king shall be satisfied; and to have the custody of her sons whom she has from the earl of Warwick her late husband.

Hawisa, who was wife of William Fitz Robert renders account of 130 marks and 4 palfreys that she may have peace from Peter of Borough to whom the king has given permission to marry her; and that she may not be compelled to marry.

Geoffrey de Mandeville owes 20,000 marks to have as his wife Isabella, countess of Gloucester, with all the lands and tenements and fiefs which fall to her.

Thomas de Colville renders an account of 100 marks for having the custody of the sons of Roger Torpel and their land until they come of age.

William, bishop of Ely, owes 220 marks for having the custody of Stephen de Beauchamp with his inheritance and for marrying him where he wishes.

William of St. Mary's church renders an account of 500 marks for having the custody of the heir of Robert Young, son of Robert Fitzharding, with all his inheritance and all its appurtenances and franchises; that is to say with the services of knights and gifts of churches and marriages of women, and to be allowed to marry him to whatever one of his relatives he wishes; and that all his land is to revert to him freely when he comes of age.

Batholomew de Muleton renders an account of 100 marks for having the custody of the land and the heiress of Lambert of Ibtoft, and for marrying the wife of the same Lambert to whomsoever he wishes where she shall not be disparaged and that he may be able to confer her (the heiress) upon whom he wishes.

EVALUATE THE EVIDENCE

1. What types of individuals pay the king for power over marriage or wardship?
2. What do these payments reveal about marriage and family relationships among wealthier groups in medieval society?

Source: Edward P. Cheyney, ed., *Translations and Reprints from the Original Sources of European History*, vol. 4, part 3 (Philadelphia: The Department of History of the University of Pennsylvania, 1897), pp. 26–27.

his father's county) dynasty. Henry II inherited the French provinces of Anjou, Normandy, Maine, and Touraine in northwestern France, and in 1152 he married Eleanor of Aquitaine, who was heir to Aquitaine, Poitou (pwah-TOO), and Gascony in southwestern France. As a result, Henry claimed nearly half of today's France, and the histories of

England and France became closely intertwined, leading to disputes and conflicts down to the fifteenth century.

France

French kings overcame the Angevin threat to expand and increasingly unify their realm. Following the death of the last Carolingian ruler in 987, an assembly of nobles selected Hugh Capet (kah-PAY) as his successor. Soon after his own coronation, Hugh crowned his oldest surviving son Robert as king to ensure the succession and prevent disputes after his death. This broke with the earlier practices of elective kingship or dividing a kingdom among one's sons, establishing instead the principle of **primogeniture** (prigh-muh-JEH-nuh-choor), in which the king's eldest son received the Crown as his rightful inheritance. Primogeniture became the standard pattern of succession in medieval western Europe, and also became an increasingly common pattern of inheritance for noble titles as well as land and other forms of wealth among all social classes.

The Capetian (kuh-PEE-shuhn) kings were weak, but they laid the foundation for later political stability. This stability came slowly. In the early twelfth century France still consisted of a number of virtually independent provinces, and the king of France maintained clear jurisdiction over a relatively small area, the Île-de-France. Over time medieval French kings worked to increase the royal domain and extend their authority over the provinces.

The work of unifying France began under Louis VI's grandson Philip II (r. 1180–1223), also known as Philip Augustus. He took Normandy by force from King John of England in 1204 and gained other northern provinces as well. In the thirteenth century Philip Augustus's descendants acquired important holdings in the south. By the end of the thirteenth century most of the provinces of modern France had been added to the royal domain through diplomacy, marriage, war, and inheritance.

In addition to expanding the royal territory, Philip Augustus devised a method of governing the provinces and providing for communication between the central government in Paris and local communities. Each province retained its own institutions and laws, but royal agents were sent from Paris into the provinces as the king's official representatives with authority to act for him. These agents were never natives of the provinces to which they were assigned, and they could not own land there. This policy reflected the fundamental principle of French administration that officials should gain their power from their connection to the monarchy, not from their own wealth or local alliances.

Philip Augustus and his successors were slower and less effective than were English kings at setting up an efficient bureau of finance. There was no national survey of property like the *Domesday Book* to help determine equitable levels of taxation, and French nobles resisted paying any taxes or fees. Not until the fourteenth century, as a result of the Hundred Years' War, did a national financial bureau emerge—the Chamber of Accounts—and even after that French nobles continued to pay little or no taxes, a problem that would help spark the French Revolution centuries later.

Central Europe

In central Europe the German king Otto I (r. 936–973) defeated many other lords to build his power from his original base in Saxony. Some of our knowledge of Otto derives from *The Deeds of Otto*, a history of his reign in heroic verse written by a nun, Hroswitha

MAP 9.1   The Holy Roman Empire and the Kingdom of Sicily, ca. 1200
Frederick Barbarossa greatly expanded the size of the Holy Roman Empire, but it remained a loose collection of various types of governments. The Christian kingdom of Sicily was created when Norman knights overthrew the Muslim rulers, but was later ruled by Frederick II, who was also the Holy Roman emperor.

of Gandersheim (ca. 935–ca. 1003). Hroswitha viewed Otto's victories as part of God's plan: "As often as he set out for war, there was not a people, though haughty because of its strength, that could harm or conquer him, supported as he was by the consolation of the heavenly King."[2]

Otto garnered financial support from church leaders and also asserted the right to control ecclesiastical appointments. Before receiving religious consecration and being invested with the staff and ring symbolic of their offices, bishops and abbots had to perform feudal homage for the lands that accompanied the church office. This practice, later known as "lay investiture," created a grave crisis between the church and the monarchy in the eleventh century (see page 273).

In 955 Otto I inflicted a crushing defeat on the Magyars in the Battle of Lechfeld (see Chapter 8), which made Otto a great hero to the Germans. In 962 he used this victory to have himself crowned emperor by the pope in Aachen, which had been the capital of the Carolingian Empire. He chose this site to symbolize his intention to continue the tradition of Charlemagne and to demonstrate papal support for his rule. Though it was not exactly clear what Otto was the emperor of, by the eleventh century people were increasingly using the term **Holy Roman Empire** to refer to a loose confederation of principalities, duchies, cities, bishoprics, and other types of regional governments stretching from Denmark to Rome and from Burgundy to Poland (Map 9.1).

In this large area of central Europe and northern Italy, the Holy Roman emperors shared power with princes, dukes, archbishops, counts, bishops, abbots, and cities. The office of emperor remained an elected one, though the electors numbered seven — four secular rulers of large territories within the empire and three archbishops.

None of Otto's successors were as forceful as he had been, and by the first half of the twelfth century, civil wars wracked the empire. The electors decided the only alternative to continued chaos was the selection of a strong ruler. They chose Frederick Barbarossa of the house of Hohenstaufen (HOH-uhn-shtow-fuhn) (r. 1152–1190). Like William the Conqueror in England and Philip in France, Frederick required vassals to take an oath of allegiance to him as emperor and appointed officials to exercise full imperial authority over local communities. He forbade the regional rulers to engage in war with one another and established sworn peace associations with them. These peace associations punished criminals and those who breached the peace.

Between 1154 and 1188 Frederick made six military expeditions into Italy in an effort to assert his imperial rights over the increasingly wealthy towns of northern Italy. While he initially made significant conquests, the Italian cities formed leagues to oppose him, and also allied with the papacy. In 1176 Frederick suffered a crushing defeat at Legnano, where the league armies took massive amounts of booty and many prisoners (see Map 9.1). This battle marked the first time a cavalry of armed knights was decisively defeated by an army largely made of infantrymen from the cities. Frederick was forced to recognize the municipal autonomy of the northern Italian cities and the pope's sovereignty in central Italy. His campaigns in Italy took him away from the parts of the empire north of the Alps, and regional rulers there reasserted their authority toward the end of Frederick's reign and in the reigns of his successors. Thus in contrast to France and England, Germany did not become a unified state in the Middle Ages, and would not until the nineteenth century.

Italy

The emperor and the pope also came into conflict over Sicily and southern Italy, disputes that eventually involved the kings of France and Spain as well. Between 1061 and 1091 a bold Norman knight, Roger de Hauteville, with papal support and a small band of mercenaries, defeated the Muslims and Byzantines who controlled the island of Sicily. Roger then faced the problem of governing Sicily's heterogeneous population of native Sicilians, Italians, Greeks, Jews, Arabs, and Normans. Roger distributed scattered lands to his followers so no vassal would have a centralized power base. He took an inquest of royal property and forbade his followers to engage in war with one another. To these Norman practices, Roger fused Arabic and Greek institutions, such as the bureau for record keeping and administration that had been established by the previous Muslim rulers.

In 1137 Roger's son and heir, Count Roger II, took the city of Naples and much of the surrounding territory in southern Italy. The entire area came to be known as the Kingdom of Sicily (or sometimes the Kingdom of the Two Sicilies).

Roger II's grandson Frederick II (r. 1212–1250) was also the grandson of Frederick Barbarossa of Germany. He was crowned king of the Germans at Aachen (1216) and Holy Roman emperor at Rome (1220), but he concentrated all his attention on the southern parts of the empire. Frederick had grown up in multicultural Sicily, knew six languages, wrote poetry, and supported scientists, scholars, and artists, whatever their religion or background. In 1224 he founded the University of Naples to train officials for his growing bureaucracy, sending them out to govern the towns of the kingdom. He tried to administer justice fairly to all his subjects, declaring, "We cannot in the least permit Jews and Saracens [Muslims] to be defrauded of the power of our protection and to be deprived of all other help, just because the difference of their religious practices makes them hateful to Christians," implying a degree of toleration exceedingly rare at the time.[3]

Because of his broad interests and abilities, Frederick's contemporaries called him the "Wonder of the World." But Sicily required constant attention, and Frederick's absences on the Crusades—holy wars sponsored by the papacy for the recovery of Jerusalem from the Muslims (see page 284)—and on campaigns in mainland Italy took their toll. Shortly after he died, the unsupervised bureaucracy fell to pieces. The pope, worried about being encircled by imperial power, called in a French prince to rule the kingdom of Sicily. Like Germany, Italy would remain divided until the nineteenth century.

The Iberian Peninsula

From the eleventh to the thirteenth centuries, power in the Iberian Peninsula shifted from Muslim to Christian rulers. In the eleventh century divisions and civil war in the caliphate of Córdoba allowed Christian armies to conquer an increasingly large part of the Iberian Peninsula. Castile, in the north-central part of the peninsula, became the strongest of the growing Christian kingdoms, and Aragon, in the northeast, the second most powerful. In 1085 King Alfonso VI of Castile and León captured Toledo in central Spain. The following year forces of the Almoravid dynasty that ruled much of northwestern Africa defeated Christian armies, and halted Christian advances southward, though they did not retake Toledo. The Almoravids reunified and strengthened the Muslim state for several generations, but the Christians regrouped, and in their North African homeland the Almoravids were overthrown by a rival dynasty, the Almohads, who then laid claim to the remaining Muslim territories in southern Spain.

Alfonso VIII (1158–1214) of Castile, aided by the kings of Aragon, Navarre, and Portugal, crushed the Almohad-led Muslims in 1212, accelerating the Christian push southward. Over the next several centuries, successive popes gave Christian warriors in the Iberian Peninsula the same spiritual benefits that they gave those who traveled to Jerusalem, such as granting them forgiveness for their sins, transforming this advance into a crusade. Christian troops captured the great Muslim cities of Córdoba in 1236 and Seville in 1248. With this, Christians controlled nearly the entire Iberian Peninsula, save for the small state of Granada. The chief mosques in Muslim cities became cathedrals, and Christian rulers recruited immigrants from western and southern Europe. The cities quickly became overwhelmingly Christian, and gradually rural areas did as well. Fourteenth-century clerical writers would call the movement to expel the Muslims the **reconquista** (reconquest), a sacred and patriotic crusade to wrest the country from "alien" Muslim hands. This idea became part of Spanish political culture and of the national psychology.

Law and Justice

How did the administration of law evolve in this period?

In the early Middle Ages society perceived major crimes as acts against an individual, and such crimes were settled when the accused made a cash payment to the victim or his or her kindred. In the High Middle Ages suspects were pursued and criminals punished for acting against the public interest. Throughout Europe, however, the law was a hodgepodge of local customs and provincial practices. In this period national rulers tried to blend these elements into a uniform system of rules acceptable and applicable to all their peoples, though their success at doing so varied.

Local Laws and Royal Courts

In France, this effort to create a royal judicial system was launched by Louis IX (r. 1226–1270). Each French province, even after being made part of the kingdom of France, had retained its unique laws and procedures, but Louis IX published laws for the entire kingdom and sent royal judges to hear complaints of injustice. He established the Parlement of Paris, a kind of supreme court that heard appeals from local administrators and regional courts, and also registered (or announced) royal laws. By the very act of appealing the decisions of local courts to the Parlement of Paris, French people in far-flung provinces were recognizing the superiority of royal justice.

In the Holy Roman Empire, justice was administered at multiple levels. The manorial or seigneurial court, presided over by the local lay or ecclesiastical lord, dealt with such matters as damage to crops and fields, trespass, boundary disputes, and debt. Dukes, counts, bishops, and abbots possessed authority over larger regions, and they dispensed justice in serious criminal cases there. The Holy Roman emperors established a court of appeal similar to that of the French kings, but in their disunited empire it had little power.

England also had a variety of local laws with procedures and penalties that varied from one part of the country to another. Henry I occasionally sent out circuit judges, royal officials who traveled a given circuit or district, to hear civil and criminal cases. Henry II (r. 1154–1189) made this way of extending royal justice an annual practice. Every year royal judges left London and set up court in the counties. These courts regularized procedures in civil cases, gradually developing the idea of a **common law**, one that applied throughout the whole country. Over the next two or three centuries common law became a reality as well as a legal theory. Common law relied on precedent: a decision in an important case served as an authority for deciding similar cases. Thus written codes of law played a less important role in England than they did elsewhere. (This has continued to today; in contrast to the United States and most other countries, the United Kingdom does not have a written constitution.)

Henry also improved procedure in criminal justice. In 1166 he instructed the sheriffs to summon local juries to conduct inquests and draw up lists of known or suspected criminals. These lists, or indictments, sworn to by the juries, were to be presented to the royal judges when they arrived in the community. This accusing jury is the ancestor of the modern grand jury. Gradually, in the course of the thirteenth century, the king's judges adopted the practice of calling on twelve people (other than the accusing jury) to consider the question of innocence or guilt; this was the forerunner of the trial jury.

One aspect of Henry II's judicial reforms encountered stiff resistance from an unexpected source. In 1164 Henry insisted that everyone, including clerics, be subject to the royal courts. The archbishop of Canterbury Thomas Becket, who was Henry's friend and former chief adviser, vigorously protested that church law required clerics to be subject to church courts.

The disagreement between king and archbishop dragged on for years. Late in December 1170, in a fit of rage, Henry expressed the wish that Becket be destroyed. Four knights took the king at his word. They rode to Canterbury Cathedral and, as the archbishop was leaving evening services, murdered him, slashing off the crown of his head and scattering his brains on the floor of the cathedral. The assassination of an archbishop turned public opinion in England and throughout western Europe against the king, and Henry had to back down. He did public penance for the murder and gave up his attempts to bring clerics under the authority of the royal court. Miracles were recorded at Becket's tomb; Becket was made a saint; and in a short time Canterbury Cathedral became a major pilgrimage and tourist site.

The Magna Carta

In the later years of Henry's reign, his sons, spurred on by their mother, Eleanor of Aquitaine, fought against their father and one another for power and land. Richard I, known as the Lion-Hearted (r. 1189–1199), won this civil war and acceded to the throne on Henry's death. Soon after, however, he departed on one of the Crusades, and during his reign he spent only six months in England. Richard was captured on his way back from the Crusades and held by the Holy Roman emperor for a very high ransom, paid primarily through loans and high taxes on the English people.

John (r. 1199–1216) inherited his father's and brother's heavy debts, and his efforts to squeeze money out of his subjects created an atmosphere of resentment. In July 1214 John's cavalry suffered a severe defeat at the hands of Philip Augustus of France, which ended English hopes for the recovery of territories from France and strengthened the opposition to John back in England. A rebellion begun by northern barons eventually grew to involve many key members of the English nobility. After lengthy negotiations, John met the barons in 1215 at Runnymede and was forced to approve the charter of rights later called **Magna Carta**.

The charter was simply meant to assert traditional rights enjoyed by certain groups, including the barons, the clergy, and the merchants of London, and thus state limits on the king's power. In time, however, it came to signify the broader principle that everyone, including the king and the government, must obey the law. In the later Middle Ages references to Magna Carta underlined the Augustinian theory that a government, to be legitimate, must promote law, order, and justice (see Chapter 6). The Magna Carta also contains the germ of the idea of "due process of law," meaning that a person has the right to be heard and defended in court and is entitled to the protection of the law. Because later generations referred to Magna Carta as a written statement of English liberties, it gradually came to have an almost sacred symbolic importance.

Law in Everyday Life

Statements of legal principles such as the Magna Carta were not how most people experienced the law in medieval Europe. Instead they were involved in or witnessed something judged to be a crime, and then experienced or watched the determination of guilt and the punishment. Judges determined guilt or innocence in a number of ways. In some cases, particularly those in which there was little clear evidence, they ordered a trial by ordeal. An accused person could be tried by fire or water. In the latter case,

Punishment of Adulterers   A man and a woman found guilty of adultery are led naked through the streets in this thirteenth-century French manuscript, preceded by heralds blowing horns and followed by men carrying sticks. This procession may be driving the couple out of town; banishment was a very common punishment for a number of crimes, including theft and assault. (Bibliothèque municipale, Agen [Lot-et-Garonne]/The Bridgeman Art Library)

the accused was tied hand and foot and dropped in a lake or river. People believed that water was a pure substance and would reject anything foul or unclean. Thus a person who sank was considered innocent; a person who floated was found guilty. Trial by ordeal was a ritual that appealed to the supernatural for judgment.

Trials by ordeal are fascinating to modern audiences, but they were relatively rare, and their use declined over the High Middle Ages as judges and courts increasingly favored more rational procedures. Judges heard testimony, sought witnesses, and read written evidence if it was available. A London case in 1277 provides a good example of how law worked. Around Easter, a man was sent to clean a house that had been abandoned, "but when he came to a dark and narrow place where coals were usually kept, he there found [a] headless body; upon seeing which, he sent word to the chamberlain and sheriffs." These officials went to the house and interviewed the neighbors. The men who lived nearby said that the headless body belonged to Symon de Winten, a tavern owner, whom they had seen quarreling with his servant Roger in early December. That night Roger "seized a knife, and with it cut the throat of Symon quite through, so that the head was entirely severed from the body." He had stuffed the body in the coal room, stolen clothes and a silver cup, and disappeared.[4] The surviving records don't indicate whether Roger was ever caught, but they do indicate that the sheriffs took something as "surety" from the neighbors who testified, that is, cash or goods as a pledge that their testimony was true. Taking sureties from witnesses was a common practice, which may be why the neighbors had not come forward on their own even though they seemed to have detailed knowledge of the murder. People were supposed to report crimes, and they could be fined for not doing so, but it is clear from this case that such community involvement in crime fighting did not always happen.

Had Roger been caught and found guilty, his punishment would have been as public as the investigation. Murder was a capital crime, as were a number of other violent acts, and executions took place outdoors on a scaffold. Hanging was the most common method of execution, although nobles might be beheaded because hanging was seen as demeaning. Minor crimes were punished by fines, corporal punishments such as whipping, or banishment from the area.

Nobles

What were the roles of nobles, and how did they train for these?

The expansion of centralized royal power and law involved limiting the power of the nobility, but rulers also worked through nobles, who retained their privileged status and cultural importance. In fact, despite political, scientific, and industrial revolutions, the nobility continued to hold real political and social power in Europe into the nineteenth century. In order to account for this continuing influence, it is important to understand the development of the nobility in the High Middle Ages.

Origins and Status of the Nobility

In the early Middle Ages noble status was generally limited to a very few families who either were descended from officials at the Carolingian court or were leading families among Germanic tribes. Beginning in the eleventh century, knights in the service of higher nobles or kings began to claim noble status. Although nobles were only a small fraction of the total population, the noble class grew larger and more diverse, ranging from poor knights who held tiny pieces of land (or sometimes none at all) to dukes and counts with vast territories.

Originally, most knights focused solely on military skills, but around 1200 there emerged a different ideal of knighthood, usually termed **chivalry** (SHIH-vuhl-ree). Chivalry was a code of conduct in which fighting to defend the Christian faith and protecting one's countrymen were declared to have a sacred purpose. Other qualities gradually became part of chivalry: bravery, generosity, honor, graciousness, mercy, and eventually gallantry toward women, which came to be called "courtly love." The chivalric ideal created a new standard of masculinity for nobles, in which loyalty and honor remained the most important qualities, but graceful dancing and intelligent conversation were not considered unmanly.

Training, Marriage, and Inheritance

For children of aristocratic birth, the years from infancy to around the age of seven or eight were primarily years of play. At about the age of seven, a boy of the noble class who was not intended for the church was placed in the household of one of his father's friends or relatives. There he became a servant to the lord and received formal training in arms. The boy learned to ride and to manage a horse. He had to acquire skill in wielding a sword, hurling a lance, shooting with a bow and arrow, and caring for

Saint Maurice This sandstone statue from Magdeburg Cathedral, carved around 1250, shows the warrior Saint Maurice. Some of the individuals who were held up to young men as models of ideal chivalry were probably real, but their lives were embellished with many stories. One example was Saint Maurice (d. 287), a soldier apparently executed by the Romans for refusing to renounce his Christian faith. He first emerges in the Carolingian period, and later he was held up as a model knight and declared a patron of the Holy Roman Empire and protector of the imperial army in wars against the pagan Slavs. His image was used on coins, and his cult was promoted by the archbishops of Magdeburg, who moved his relics to their cathedral. Until 1240 he was portrayed as a white man, but after that he was usually represented as a black man, as in this statue. Historians have no idea why this change occurred. (Courtesy, The Menil Foundation, Houston)

armor and other equipment. Increasingly, noble youths learned to read and write some Latin. Formal training was concluded around the age of twenty-one, often with the ceremony of knighthood.

The ceremony of knighthood did not necessarily mean attainment of adulthood, power, and responsibility. Sons were completely dependent on their fathers for support. A young man remained a youth until he was in a financial position to marry—that is, until his father died. That might not happen until he was in his late thirties, and marriage at forty was not uncommon. Increasingly, families adopted primogeniture, with property passing to the oldest son. Younger sons might be forced into the clergy or simply forbidden to marry.

Once knighted, the young man traveled for two to three years. His father selected a group of friends to accompany, guide, and protect him. If the young knight and his companions did not depart on a crusade, they hunted, meddled in local conflicts, and did the tournament circuit. The tournament, in which a number of men competed from horseback (in contrast to the joust, which involved only two competitors), gave the young knight experience in pitched battle and a way to show off his masculinity before an audience. Since the horses and equipment of the vanquished were forfeited to the victors, the knight could also gain a profit. Everywhere they went, young knights stirred up trouble, for chivalric ideals of honorable valor and gallant masculinity rarely served as a check on actual behavior.

While noble girls were also trained in preparation for their future tasks, that training was quite different. They were often taught to read the local language and perhaps some Latin and to write and do enough arithmetic to keep household accounts. They also learned music, dancing, embroidery, and how to ride and hunt, both common noble pursuits. Much of this took place in the girl's own home, but, like boys, noble girls were often sent to the homes of relatives or higher nobles to act as servants or ladies in waiting or to learn how to run a household.

Parents often wanted to settle daughters' futures as soon as possible. Men tended to prefer young brides who would have more years to produce children. Therefore, aristocratic girls in the High Middle Ages were married at around the age of sixteen, often to much older men. In the early Middle Ages the custom was for the groom to present a dowry to the bride and her family, but by the late twelfth century the process was reversed because men were in greater demand. Thereafter, the sizes of dowries offered by brides and their families rose higher and higher.

Power and Responsibility

A male member of the nobility became fully adult when he came into the possession of property. He then acquired authority over lands and people, protecting them from attack, maintaining order, and settling disputes. With this authority went responsibility. In the words of Honorius of Autun:

> Soldiers: You are the arm of the Church, because you should defend it against its enemies. Your duty is to aid the oppressed, to restrain yourself from rapine and fornication, to repress those who impugn the Church with evil acts, and to resist those who are rebels against priests. Performing such a service, you will obtain the most splendid of benefices from the greatest of Kings.[5]

Nobles rarely lived up to this ideal, however, and there are countless examples of nobles stealing church lands instead of defending them, tyrannizing the oppressed rather than aiding them, and regularly engaging in "rapine and fornication" rather than resisting them.

Women played a large and important role in the functioning of the estate. They were responsible for the practical management of the household's "inner economy" — cooking, brewing, spinning, weaving, caring for yard animals. When the lord was away for long periods, the women frequently managed the herds, barns, granaries, and outlying fields as well. Often the responsibilities of the estate fell to them permanently, as the number of men slain in medieval warfare ran high.

Throughout the High Middle Ages, fighting remained the dominant feature of the noble lifestyle. The church's preaching and condemnations reduced but did not stop violence, and the military values of the nobles' social class encouraged petty warfare and disorder. The nobility thus represented a constant source of trouble for the monarchy.

The Papacy

How did the papacy reform the church, and what were the reactions to these efforts?

Kings and emperors were not the only rulers consolidating their power in the High Middle Ages; popes did so as well, through a series of measures that made the church more independent of secular control. In the ninth and tenth centuries secular lords like Otto I controlled the appointment of church officials. Popes and bishops were appointed to advance the political ambitions of their own families rather than for special spiritual qualifications. Under the leadership of a series of reforming popes in the eleventh century, the church tried to end this practice, but the popes' efforts were sometimes challenged by medieval kings and emperors, and the wealth of the church came under sharp criticism.

The Gregorian Reforms

During the ninth and tenth centuries the local church had come under the control of kings and feudal lords, who chose priests and bishops in their territories, granting them land and expecting loyalty and service in return. Church offices from village priest to pope were sources of income as well as positions of authority. Officeholders had the right to collect taxes and fees and often the profits from the land under their control. Church offices were thus sometimes sold outright—a practice called **simony** (SIGH-muh-nee). Not surprisingly, clergy at all levels who had bought their positions or had been granted them for political reasons provided little spiritual guidance, and their personal lives were rarely models of high moral standards. Although the Roman Church officially required men to be unmarried in order to be ordained, there were many married priests and others simply living with women. Popes were chosen by wealthy Roman families from among their members, and after gaining the papal office, they paid more attention to their families' political fortunes than to the health of the church.

Serious efforts to change all this began under Pope Leo IX (pontificate 1049–1054). Leo ordered clergy in Rome to dismiss their wives and invalidated the ordination of church officials who had purchased their offices. Pope Leo and several of his successors believed that secular or lay control over the church was largely responsible for its lack of moral leadership, so in a radical shift they proclaimed the church independent of secular rulers. The Lateran Council of 1059 decreed that the authority and power to elect the pope rested solely in the **college of cardinals**, a special group of priests from the major churches in and around Rome. The college retains that power today, though the membership has grown and become international.

Leo's successor Pope Gregory VII (pontificate 1073–1085) was even more vigorous in his championing of reform and expansion of papal power; for that reason, the eleventh-century movement is frequently called the "Gregorian reform movement." He denounced clerical marriage and simony in harsh language and ordered **excommunication** (being cut off from the sacraments and all Christian worship) for those who disagreed. He believed that the pope, as the successor of Saint Peter, was the vicar of God on earth and that papal orders were thus the orders of God. Gregory was particularly opposed to lay investiture—the selection and appointment of church officials by secular authority. In February 1075 he held a council at Rome that decreed that clerics who accepted investiture from laymen were to be deposed and laymen who invested clerics were to be excommunicated.

In the late eleventh century and throughout the twelfth and thirteenth, the papacy pressed Gregory's campaign for reform of the church. The popes held a series of councils, known as the Lateran Councils, that ratified decisions ending lay investiture, ordered bishops to live less extravagantly, and ordered married priests to give up their wives and children or face dismissal. Most church officials apparently obeyed, though we have little information on what happened to the families. In other reforms, marriage was defined as a sacrament — a ceremony that provided visible evidence of God's grace — and divorce was forbidden.

Gregory's reforms had a profound effect on nuns and other women in religious orders. The movement built a strict hierarchical church structure with bishops and priests higher in status than nuns, who could not be ordained. The double monasteries of the early Middle Ages were placed under the authority of male abbots. Church councils forbade monks and nuns to sing church services together and ordered priests to limit their visits to convents. The reformers' emphasis on clerical celibacy and chastity led them to portray women as impure and lustful. Thus in 1298 in the papal decree *Periculoso* Pope Boniface VIII ordered all nuns to be strictly cloistered, that is, to remain permanently inside the walls of the convent, and for visits with people from outside the house, including family members, to be limited. *Periculoso* was not enforced everywhere, but it did mean that convents became more cut off from medieval society than monasteries were.

Emperor Versus Pope

Gregory thought that the threat of excommunication would compel rulers to abide by his move against lay investiture. Immediately, however, Henry IV in the Holy Roman Empire, William the Conqueror in England, and Philip I in France protested, as the reform would deprive them not only of church income but also of the right to choose which monks and clerics would help them administer their kingdoms. The strongest reaction came from the Holy Roman Empire. Pope Gregory accused Henry IV of lack of respect for the papacy and insisted that disobedience to the pope was disobedience to God. Henry argued that Gregory's type of reform undermined royal authority. Within the empire, religious and secular leaders took sides to pursue their own advantage. In January 1076 many of the German bishops who had been invested by Henry withdrew their allegiance from the pope. Gregory promptly suspended them and excommunicated Henry. The pope told German nobles they no longer owed allegiance to Henry, which obviously delighted them. When powerful nobles invited the pope to come to Germany to settle their dispute with Henry, Gregory traveled to the north. Christmas of 1076 thus witnessed an ironic situation in Germany: the clergy supported the emperor while the great nobility favored the pope.

Henry managed to outwit the pope temporarily. In January 1077 he approached the castle of Countess Matilda of Tuscany (ca. 1046–1115) at Canossa in the Apennines (AH-puh-nighnz), where the pope was staying. According to a letter later sent by Gregory to his German noble allies, Henry stood for three days in the snow, imploring the pope to lift the excommunication. Henry's pleas for forgiveness won him public sympathy, and the pope readmitted the emperor to the Christian community. When the sentence of excommunication was lifted, however, Henry regained the emperorship and authority over his rebellious subjects, but continued his moves against papal power. In 1080 Gregory again excommunicated and deposed the emperor. In return, when Gregory died in 1085, Henry invaded Italy and captured Rome. But Henry won no lasting victory. Gregory's successors encouraged Henry's sons to revolt against their father.

Finally, in 1122 at a conference held at Worms, the issue was settled by compromise. Bishops were to be chosen by the clergy. But since lay rulers were permitted to be present at ecclesiastical elections and to accept or refuse homage from the new prelates, they still possessed an effective veto over ecclesiastical appointments. Papal power was enhanced, but neither side won a clear victory.

The long controversy over lay investiture had tremendous social and political consequences in Germany. The lengthy struggle between papacy and emperor allowed emerging noble dynasties to enhance their position. To control their lands, the great lords built castles, symbolizing their increased power and growing independence. When the papal-imperial conflict ended in 1122, the nobility held the balance of power in Germany, and later German kings, such as Frederick Barbarossa, would fail in their efforts to strengthen the monarchy. For these reasons, division and local independence characterized the Holy Roman Empire in the High Middle Ages.

Criticism and Heresy

The Gregorian reform movement contributed to dissatisfaction with the church among townspeople as well as monarchs. Papal moves against simony, for example, led to widespread concern about the role of money in the church just as papal tax collectors were becoming more efficient and sophisticated. Papal efforts to improve the sexual morality of the clergy led some laypersons to assume they could, and indeed should, remove priests for any type of immorality.

Criticism of the church emerged in many places but found its largest audience in the cities, where the contrast between wealth and poverty could be seen more acutely. In northern Italian towns, the monk Arnold of Brescia (BREH-shah) (ca. 1090–1155), a vigorous advocate of strict clerical poverty, denounced clerical wealth. In France, Peter Waldo (ca. 1140–ca. 1218), a rich merchant of the city of Lyons, gave his money to the poor and preached that only prayers, not sacraments, were needed for salvation. The Waldensians (wawl-DEHN-shuhnz) — as Peter's followers were called — bitterly attacked the sacraments and church hierarchy, and they carried these ideas across Europe. In the towns and cities of southern France, the Albigensians (al-buh-JEHN-see-uhns), also known as the Cathars, used the teachings of Jesus about the evils of material goods to call for the church to give up its property. They asserted that the material world was created not by the good God of the New Testament, but by a different evil God of the Old Testament. People who rejected worldly things, not wealthy bishops or the papacy, should be the religious leaders.

Critical of the clergy and spiritually unfulfilled, townspeople joined the Waldensians and the Albigensians. The papacy denounced supporters of both movements as heretics and began extensive campaigns to wipe them out. In 1208 Pope Innocent III proclaimed a crusade against the Albigensians, and the French monarchy and northern French knights willingly joined in, eager to gain the lands and wealth of southern French cities. After years of fighting, the leaders agreed to terms of peace, which left the French monarchy the primary beneficiary. Later popes sent inquisitors with the power to seek out and eliminate the remaining heretics.

The Popes and Church Law

Pope Urban II laid the foundations for the papal monarchy by reorganizing the papal *curia* (the central government of the Roman Church) and recognizing the college of cardinals as a definite consultative body. The papal curia had its greatest impact as a court of law. As the highest ecclesiastical tribunal, it formulated church law, termed **canon law**. The church developed a system of courts separate from those of secular rulers that handled disputes over church property and ecclesiastical elections and especially questions of marriage and annulment. Most of the popes in the twelfth and thirteenth centuries were canon lawyers who expanded the authority of church courts.

The most famous of the lawyer-popes was Innocent III (pontificate 1198–1216), who became the most powerful pope in history. During his pontificate the church in Rome declared itself to be supreme, united, and "catholic" (worldwide), responsible for the earthly well-being as well as the eternal salvation of Christians everywhere. Innocent pushed the kings of Europe to do his will, compelling King Philip Augustus of France to take back his wife, Ingeborg of Denmark, and King John of England to accept as archbishop of Canterbury a man John did not want.

Innocent called the Fourth Lateran Council in 1215, which affirmed the idea that ordained priests had the power to transform bread and wine during church ceremonies into the body and blood of Christ (a change termed transubstantiation). According to papal doctrine, priests now had the power to mediate for everyone with God, setting the spiritual hierarchy of the church above the secular hierarchies of kings and other rulers. The council affirmed that Christians should confess their sins to a priest at least once a year. It also ordered Jews and Muslims to wear special clothing that set them apart from Christians.

By the early thirteenth century papal efforts at reform begun more than a century earlier had attained phenomenal success, and the popes ruled a powerful, centralized institution. At the end of the century, however, the papacy again came into a violent dispute with secular rulers. Pope Boniface VIII (pontificate 1294–1303), arguing from precedent, insisted that King Edward I of England and Philip IV of France obtain his consent for taxes they had imposed on the clergy. Edward immediately denied the clergy the protection of the law, and Philip halted the shipment of all ecclesiastical revenue to Rome. Boniface had to back down.

The battle for power between the papacy and the French monarchy became a bitter war of propaganda, with Philip at one point calling the pope a heretic. Finally, in 1302, in a formal written statement known as a papal bull, Boniface insisted that all Christians—including kings—were subject to the pope. (See "Primary Source: Pope Boniface VIII, *Unam Sanctam*," page 277.) Philip maintained that he was completely sovereign in his kingdom and responsible to God alone. French mercenary troops assaulted and arrested the aged pope at Anagni in Italy. Although Boniface was soon freed, he died shortly afterward. The confrontation at Anagni foreshadowed further difficulties in the Christian Church in the fourteenth century.

Monks, Nuns, and Friars

What roles did monks, nuns, and friars play in medieval society?

While the reforming popes transformed the Christian Church into an institution free of lay control at the highest level, leaders of monasteries and convents asserted their independence from secular control on the local level as well. Monks, nuns, and friars played significant roles in medieval society, both as individuals and as members of institutions. Medieval people believed that monks and nuns performed an important

PRIMARY SOURCE   Pope Boniface VIII, *Unam Sanctam*

In late 1302, after several years of bitter conflict with King Philip IV of France over control and taxation of the clergy in France, Pope Boniface VIII issued a papal bull declaring the official church position on the proper relationships between church and state. Throughout, the pope uses the "royal we," that is, the plural "we" instead of "I" when talking about himself.

We are obliged by the faith to believe and hold—and we do firmly believe and sincerely confess—that there is one Holy Catholic and Apostolic Church, and that outside this Church there is neither salvation nor remission of sins. . . . In which Church there is "one Lord, one faith, one baptism." . . . Of this one and only Church there is one body and one head—not two heads, like a monster—namely Christ, and Christ's vicar is Peter, and Peter's successor, for the Lord said to Peter himself, "Feed my sheep." "My sheep" He said in general, not these or those sheep; wherefore He is understood to have committed them all to him. . . .

And we learn from the words of the Gospel that in this Church and in her power are two swords, the spiritual and the temporal. . . . Truly he who denies that the temporal sword is in the power of Peter, misunderstands the words of the Lord, "Put up thy sword into the sheath." Both are in the power of the Church, the spiritual sword and the material. But the latter is to be used for the Church, the former by her; the former by the priest, the latter by kings and captains but at the will and by the permission of the priest. The one sword, then, should be under the other, and temporal authority subject to spiritual. . . .

If, therefore, the earthly power err, it shall be judged by the spiritual power; and if a lesser power err, it shall be judged by a greater. But if the supreme power [the papacy] err, it can only be judged by God, not by man. . . . For this authority, although given to a man and exercised by a man, is not human, but rather divine, given at God's mouth to Peter and established on a rock for him and his successors in Him whom he confessed, the Lord saying to Peter himself, "Whatsoever thou shalt bind," etc. Whoever therefore resists this power thus ordained of God, resists the ordinance of God. . . . Furthermore, we declare, state, define, and pronounce that it is altogether necessary to salvation for every human creature to be subject to the Roman pontiff.

EVALUATE THE EVIDENCE

1. According to Pope Boniface, what is the proper relationship between the authority of the pope and the authority of earthly rulers? What is the basis for that relationship?

2. How might the earlier conflicts between popes and secular rulers traced in this chapter have influenced Boniface's declaration?

Source: Henry Bettenson, ed., *Documents of the Christian Church* (Oxford: Oxford University Press, 1963), pp. 115–116. Used by permission of Oxford University Press.

social service when they prayed, for their prayers and chants secured God's blessing for society. The friars worked in the cities, teaching and preaching Christian doctrine, but also investigating heretics.

Monastic Revival

In the early Middle Ages many religious houses followed the Benedictine *Rule*, while others developed their own patterns (see Chapter 7). In the High Middle Ages this diversity became more formalized, and **religious orders**, groups of monastic houses following a particular rule, were established. Historians term the foundation, strengthening, and reform of religious orders in the High Middle Ages the "monastic revival."

In Carolingian times, the best Benedictine monasteries had been centers of learning, copying and preserving manuscripts, maintaining schools, and setting high standards of monastic observance. In the period of political disorder that followed the disintegration of the Carolingian Empire, many religious houses fell under the control and domination of local lords. Powerful laymen appointed themselves or their relatives as abbots, took the lands and goods of monasteries, and seized monastic revenues. Accordingly, the level of spiritual observance and intellectual activity in monasteries and convents declined. The local lords also compelled abbots from time to time to provide contingents of soldiers, an obligation stemming from the abbots' judicial authority over knights and peasants on monastic lands. The conflict between an abbot's religious duties on the one hand and his judicial and military obligations on the other posed a serious dilemma.

The first sign of reform came in 909, when William the Pious, duke of Aquitaine, established the abbey of Cluny in Burgundy. Duke William declared that the monastery was to be free from any feudal responsibilities to him or any other lord, its members subordinate only to the pope. The monastery at Cluny, which initially held high standards of religious behavior, came to exert vast religious influence. In the eleventh century Cluny was fortunate in having a series of highly able abbots who ruled for a long time. In a disorderly world, Cluny gradually came to represent stability. Therefore, laypersons placed lands under its custody and monastic priories under its jurisdiction (a priory is a religious house, with generally fewer residents than an abbey, governed by a prior or prioress). In this way, hundreds of religious houses, primarily in France and Spain, came under Cluny's authority.

Deeply impressed laypeople showered gifts on monasteries with good reputations, such as Cluny and its many daughter houses. But as the monasteries became richer, the lifestyle of the monks grew increasingly luxurious. Monastic observance and spiritual fervor declined. Soon fresh demands for reform were heard, resulting in the founding of new religious orders in the late eleventh and early twelfth centuries.

The Cistercians (sihs-TUHR-shuhnz) best represent the new reforming spirit because of their phenomenal expansion and great economic, political, and spiritual influence. In 1098 a group of monks left the rich abbey of Molesmes in Burgundy and founded a new house in the swampy forest of Cîteaux (see-TOH). They planned to avoid all involvement with secular society and decided to accept only uncultivated lands far from regular habitation. The early Cistercians (the word is derived from Cîteaux) determined to keep their services simple and their lives austere, returning to work in the fields and other sorts of manual labor. As with Cluny, their high ideals made them a model, and 525 Cistercian monasteries were founded in the course of the twelfth century all over

Europe. The Cistercians' influence on European society was profound, for they used new agricultural methods and technology and spread them throughout Europe. Their improvements in farming and animal raising brought wealth, however, and wealth brought power. By the later twelfth century, as with Cluny earlier, economic prosperity and political power had begun to compromise the original Cistercian ideals.

Life in Convents and Monasteries

Medieval monasteries were religious institutions whose organization and structure fulfilled the social needs of the nobility. The monasteries provided noble boys with education and opportunities for ecclesiastical careers. Although a few men who rose in the ranks of church officials were of humble origins, most were from high-status families. Many had been given to the monastery by their parents. Beginning in the thirteenth century an increasing number of boys and men from professional and merchant families became monks, seeking to take advantage of the opportunities monasteries offered.

Throughout the Middle Ages social class also defined the kinds of religious life open to women. Kings and nobles usually established convents for their daughters, sisters, aunts, or aging mothers, and other women of their class. Like monks, many nuns came into the convent as children, and very often sisters, cousins, aunts, and nieces could all be found in the same place. Thus, though nuns were to some degree cut off from their families by being cloistered, family relationships were maintained within the convent.

The office of abbess or prioress was the most powerful position a woman could hold in medieval society. (See "Individuals in Society: Hildegard of Bingen," page 280.) Abbesses were part of the political structure in the same way that bishops and abbots were, with manors under their financial and legal control. They appointed tax collectors, bailiffs, judges, and often priests in their lands. Some abbesses in the Holy Roman Empire even had the right to name bishops and send representatives to imperial assemblies. Abbesses also opened and supported hospitals, orphanages, and schools, and they hired builders, sculptors, and painters to construct and decorate residences and churches.

Monasteries for men were headed by an abbot or prior, who was generally a member of a noble family, often a younger son in a family with several. The main body of monks, known as "choir monks" because one of their primary activities was reciting prayers and services while sitting in the part of the church called the choir, were largely of noble or middle-class background, and did not till the land themselves. Men from peasant families sometimes became choir monks, but more often they served as lay brothers, doing the manual labor essential to running the monastery. The novice master or novice mistress was responsible for the training of recruits. The efficient operation of a monastic house also required the services of cooks, laundresses, gardeners, seamstresses, mechanics, blacksmiths, pharmacists, and others whose essential work has left, unfortunately, little written trace.

The pattern of life within individual monasteries varied widely from house to house and from region to region. One central activity, however, was performed everywhere. Daily life centered on the liturgy or Divine Office, psalms and other prayers prescribed by Saint Benedict that monks and nuns prayed seven times a day and once during the night. Prayers were offered for peace, rain, good harvests, the civil authorities, and the monks' families and benefactors. Everything connected with prayer was understood as

INDIVIDUALS IN SOCIETY • Hildegard of Bingen

The tenth child of a lesser noble family, Hildegard (1098–1179) was given as a child to an abbey in the Rhineland when she was eight years old; there she learned Latin and received a good education. She spent most of her life in various women's religious communities, two of which she founded herself. When she was a child, she began having mystical visions, often of light in the sky, but told few people about them. In middle age, however, her visions became more dramatic: "And it came to pass . . . when I was 42 years and 7 months old, that the heavens were opened and a blinding light of exceptional brilliance flowed through my entire brain. And so it kindled my whole heart and breast like a flame, not burning but warming . . . and suddenly I understood of the meaning of expositions of the books."* She wanted the church to approve of her visions and wrote first to Bernard of Clairvaux, who answered her briefly and dismissively, and then to Pope Eugenius, who encouraged her to write them down. Her first work was *Scivias* (Know the Ways of the Lord), a record of her mystical visions that incorporates vast theological learning.

Possessed of leadership and administrative talents, Hildegard left her abbey in 1147 to found the convent of Rupertsberg near Bingen. There she produced *Physica* (On the Physical Elements) and *Causa et Curae* (Causes and Cures), scientific works on the curative properties of natural elements, as well as poems, a mystery play, and several more works of mysticism. She carried on a huge correspondence with scholars, prelates, and ordinary people. When she was over fifty, she left her community to preach to audiences of clergy and laity, and she was the only woman of her time whose opinions on religious matters were considered authoritative by the church.

*From *Scivias*, trans. Mother Columba Hart and Jane Bishop, *The Classics of Western Spirituality* (New York/Mahwah: Paulist Press, 1990), p. 65.

praise of God, so abbeys spent a large percentage of their income on splendid objects to enhance the service, including sacred vessels of embossed silver or gold, altar cloths of the finest silks or velvets, embroideries, and beautiful reliquaries to house the relics of the patron saint.

In some abbeys monks and nuns spent much of their time copying books and manuscripts and then illuminating them, decorating them with human and animal figures or elaborate designs, often painted in bright colors or gold. A few monasteries and convents became centers of learning where talented residents wrote their own works as well as copying those of others.

Monks and nuns also performed a variety of social services in an age when there was no state and no conception of social welfare as a public responsibility. Monasteries often ran schools that gave primary education to young boys; convents did the same for girls. Monasteries served as hotels and resting places for travelers, and frequently operated hospitals and leprosariums, which provided care and attention to the sick, the aged, and the afflicted.

Hildegard's visions have been explored by theologians and also by neurologists, who judge that they may have originated in migraine headaches, as she reports many of the same phenomena that migraine sufferers do: auras of light around objects, areas of blindness, feelings of intense doubt and intense euphoria. The interpretations that she develops come from her theological insight and learning, however, not illness. That same insight also emerges in her music, for which she is best known today. Eighty of her compositions survive—a huge number for a medieval composer—most of them written to be sung by the nuns in her convent, so they have strong lines for female voices. Many of her songs and chants have been recorded and are available on CD, as downloads, and on several Web sites.

QUESTIONS FOR ANALYSIS

1. Why do you think Hildegard sought church approval for her visions after keeping them secret for so many years?

2. In what ways is Hildegard's life representative of nuns' lives in the High Middle Ages? In what ways were her accomplishments extraordinary?

ONLINE DOCUMENT ASSIGNMENT

How did Hildegard of Bingen come to be seen as a worthy instrument for the transmission of God's word? Read excerpts from her correspondence and note the qualities that appealed to so many of her contemporaries. Then complete a writing assignment based on the evidence and details from this chapter.

bedfordstmartins.com/mckaywestvalue

The Friars

Monks and nuns carried out their spiritual and social services largely within the walls of their institutions, but in the thirteenth century new types of religious orders were founded whose members lived out in the world. Members of these new groups were friars, not monks. They thought that more contact with ordinary Christians, not less, was a better spiritual path. Friars stressed apostolic poverty, a life based on the teaching of the Gospels in which they would own no property and depend on Christian people for their material needs. Hence they were called mendicants, from the Latin word for begging. The friars' service to the towns and the poor, their ideal of poverty, and their compassion for the human condition made them popular.

One order of friars was started by Domingo de Gúzman (1170?–1221), born in Castile. Domingo (later called Dominic), a well-educated priest, accompanied his bishop in 1206 on an unsuccessful mission to win the Albigensians in southern France back to orthodox teaching. Determined to succeed through ardent preaching, he subsequently

Saint Francis Gives Up His Worldly Possessions   After Francis had given money to a church, his wealthy father ordered Francis to give him back the money. Francis instead took off all his clothes and returned them to his father, signifying his dependence on his father in Heaven rather than his earthly father. The fresco of this event, painted seventy years after Francis's death for the church erected in his honor in Assisi, captures the consternation of Francis's father and the confusion of the local bishop (holding the cloth in front of the naked Francis), who had told the young man to obey his earthly father. By the time the church was built, members of the Franciscan order were in violent disagreement over what Francis would have thought about a huge church built in his honor and other issues of clerical wealth. (San Francesco, Upper Church, Assisi/Giraudon/The Bridgeman Art Library)

returned to France with a few followers. In 1216 the group—officially known as the Preaching Friars, though often called Dominicans—won papal recognition as a new religious order.

Francesco di Bernardone (1181–1226), son of a wealthy Italian cloth merchant of Assisi, had a religious conversion and decided to live and preach the Gospel in absolute poverty. Francis of Assisi, as he came to be known, did not emphasize withdrawal from the world, but joyful devotion. In contrast to the Albigensians, who saw the material world as evil, Francis saw all creation as God-given and good. He was widely reported to perform miracles involving animals and birds, and wrote hymns to natural objects.

"Be praised, my Lord, through our sister Mother Earth" went one, "who feeds us and rules us and produces various fruits with colored flowers and herbs." This song also praises the sun, wind, air, water, and fire, and it was one of the first religious works ever written in a vernacular dialect. It also provides an example of how Franciscans and other friars used music to convey religious teachings.

The simplicity, humility, and joyful devotion with which Francis carried out his mission soon attracted others. Although he resisted pressure to establish an order, his followers became so numerous that he was obliged to develop some formal structure. In 1221 the papacy approved the Rule of the Little Brothers of Saint Francis, generally called the Franciscans (frahn-SIHS-kuhnz).

Friars worked among the poor, but also addressed the spiritual and intellectual needs of the middle classes and the wealthy. The Dominicans preferred that their friars be university graduates in order to better preach to a sophisticated urban society. Dominicans soon held professorial chairs at leading universities, and the Franciscans followed suit.

Beginning in 1231 the papacy also used friars to investigate heretics, sometimes under the auspices of a new ecclesiastical court, the Inquisition, in which accused people were subjected to lengthy interrogations and torture could be used to extract confessions. It is ironic that groups whose teachings were similar in so many ways to those of heretics were charged with rooting them out. That irony deepened in the case of the Spiritual Franciscans, a group that broke away from the main body of Franciscans to follow Francis's original ideals of absolute poverty. When they denied the pope's right to countermand that ideal, he ordered them tried as heretics.

Women sought to develop similar orders devoted to active service out in the world. Clare of Assisi (1193–1253) became a follower of Francis, who established a place for her to live in a church in Assisi. She was joined by other women, and they attempted to establish a rule that would follow Francis's ideals of absolute poverty and allow them to serve the poor. This rule was accepted by the papacy only after many decades, and then only because she agreed that the order, the Poor Clares, would be cloistered.

In the growing cities of Europe, especially in the Netherlands, groups of laywomen seeking to live religious lives came together as what later came to be known as Beguines (bay-GEENS). They lived communally in small houses called *beguinages*, combining lives of prayer with service to the needy. Beguine spirituality emphasized direct personal communication with God, sometimes through mystical experiences, rather than through the intercession of a saint or official church rituals. Initially some church officials gave guarded approval of the movement, but the church grew increasingly uncomfortable with women who were neither married nor cloistered nuns. By the fourteenth century beguines were declared heretical, and much of their property was confiscated.

The Crusades and the Expansion of Christianity

What were the causes, course, and consequences of both the Crusades and the broader expansion of Christianity?

The Crusades of the eleventh and twelfth centuries were the most obvious manifestation of the papal claim to the leadership of Christian society. The **Crusades** were wars sponsored by the papacy for the recovery of the holy city of Jerusalem from the Muslims.

The enormous popular response to papal calls for crusading reveals the influence of the reformed papacy and the depth of religious fervor among many different types of people. The Crusades also reflected the church's new understanding of the noble warrior class, for whom war against the church's enemies was understood as a religious duty. The word *crusade* was not actually used at the time and did not appear in English until the late sixteenth century. It means literally "taking the cross," from the cross that soldiers sewed on their garments as a Christian symbol. At the time people going off to fight simply said they were taking "the way of the cross" or "the road to Jerusalem."

Background and Motives of the Crusades

The medieval church's attitude toward violence was contradictory. On the one hand, church councils threatened excommunication for anyone who attacked peasants, clerics, or merchants or destroyed crops and unfortified places, a movement termed the Peace of God. Councils also tried to limit the number of days on which fighting was permitted, prohibiting it on Sundays, on special feast days, and in the seasons of Lent and Advent. On the other hand, popes supported armed conflict against kings and emperors if this worked to their advantage, thus encouraging warfare among Christians. After a serious theological disagreement in 1054 split the Orthodox Church of Byzantium and the Roman Church of the West, the pope also contemplated invading the Byzantine Empire, an idea that subsequent popes considered as well.

Although conflicts in which Christians fought Christians were troubling to many thinkers, war against non-Christians was another matter. By the ninth century popes and other church officials encouraged war in defense of Christianity, promising spiritual benefits to those who died fighting. By the eleventh century these benefits were extended to all those who simply joined a campaign: their sins would be remitted without having to do penance, that is, without having to confess to a priest and carry out some action to make up for the sins. Around this time, Christian thinkers were developing the concept of purgatory, a place where those on their way to Heaven stayed for a while to do any penance they had not completed while alive. (Those on their way to Hell went straight there.) Engaging in holy war could shorten one's time in purgatory, or, as many people understood the promise, allow one to head straight to paradise. Popes signified this by providing **indulgences**, grants with the pope's name on them that lessened earthly penance and postmortem purgatory. Popes promised these spiritual benefits, and also provided financial support, for Christian armies in the reconquista in Spain and the Norman campaign against the Muslims in Sicily. Preachers communicated these ideas widely and told stories about warrior-saints who slew hundreds of enemies.

Religious devotion had long been expressed through pilgrimages to holy places, and these were increasingly described in military terms, as battles against the hardships along the way. Pilgrims to Jerusalem were often armed, so the line between pilgrimage and holy war on this particular route was increasingly blurred.

In the midst of these developments came a change in possession of Jerusalem. The Arabic Muslims who had ruled Jerusalem and the surrounding territory for centuries had allowed Christian pilgrims to travel freely, but in the late eleventh century the Seljuk (SEHL-jook) Turks took over Palestine, defeating both Arabic and Byzantine armies (Map 9.2). The emperor at Constantinople appealed to the West for support, asserting that the Turks would make pilgrimages to holy places more dangerous, and that the

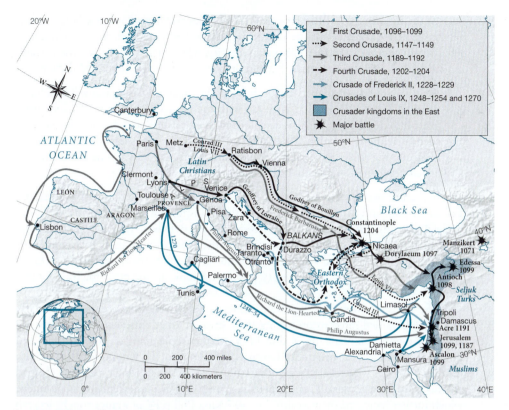

MAP 9.2 The Crusades
This map shows the many different routes that Western Christians took over the centuries to reach Jerusalem.

holy city of Jerusalem should be in Christian hands. The emperor's appeal fit well with papal aims, and in 1095 Pope Urban II called for a great Christian holy war against the infidels—a term Christians and Muslims both used to describe the other. Urban offered indulgences to those who would fight for and regain the holy city of Jerusalem.

The Course of the Crusades

Thousands of Western Christians of all classes joined the First Crusade, which began in 1096. Of all of the developments of the High Middle Ages, none better reveals Europeans' religious and emotional fervor and the influence of the reformed papacy than the extraordinary outpouring of support for the First Crusade.

The First Crusade was successful, mostly because of the dynamic enthusiasm of the participants. The Crusaders had little more than religious zeal. They knew nothing about the geography or climate of the Middle East. Although there were several nobles with military experience among them, the Crusaders could never agree on a leader, and the entire expedition was marked by disputes among the great lords. Lines of supply were never set up, and starvation and disease wracked the army. Nevertheless, the army pressed on, defeating the Turks in several land battles and besieging a few larger towns. Finally, in 1099, three years after departing Europe, the Crusaders reached Jerusalem. After a month-long siege they got inside the city, where they slaughtered the Muslim defenders. Fulcher of Chartres, a chaplain on the First Crusade, described the scene:

> Amid the sound of trumpets and with everything in an uproar they attacked boldly, shouting "God help us!" . . . They ran with the greatest exultation as fast as they could into the city and joined their companions in pursuing and slaying their wicked enemies without cessation. . . . If you had been there your feet would have been stained to the ankles in the blood of the slain. What shall I say? None of them were left alive. Neither women nor children were spared.[6]

In the aftermath of the First Crusade, four small "Crusader kingdoms" — Jerusalem, Edessa, Tripoli, and Antioch — were established. Castles and fortified towns were built to defend against Muslim reconquest (see Map 9.2). Between 1096 and 1270 the crusading ideal was expressed in eight papally approved expeditions, though none after the First Crusade accomplished very much. Despite this lack of success, members of European noble families from nearly every generation took up the cross for roughly two hundred years.

The Crusades inspired the establishment of new religious orders, particularly military orders dedicated to protecting the Christian kingdoms. The most important was the Knights Templars, founded in 1119. Many people going off to the Holy Land put their property in Europe under Templar protection, and by the end of the thirteenth century the order was extremely wealthy, with secret rituals in which members pledged obedience to their leaders. The Templars began serving as moneylenders and bankers, which further increased their wealth. In 1307 King Philip IV of France sought to grab that wealth for himself; he arrested many Templars, accusing them of heresy, blasphemy, and sodomy. They were tortured, a number were burned at the stake, Philip took much of their money, and the Templars were disbanded.

Women from all walks of life participated in the Crusades. When King Louis IX of France was captured on the Seventh Crusade (1248–1254), his wife Queen Marguerite negotiated the surrender of the Egyptian city of Damietta to the Muslims. Some women concealed their sex by donning chain mail and helmets and fought with the knights. Some joined in the besieging of towns and castles by assisting in filling the moats surrounding fortified places with earth so that ladders and war engines could be brought close. More typically, women provided water to fighting men, a service not to be underestimated in the hot, dry climate of the Middle East. They worked as washerwomen, foraged for food, and provided sexual services. There were many more European men than women, however, so marriage and sexual relations between Christian men and Muslim women were not unheard of, although marriages between Western Christian men and Orthodox Christian women who lived in the area were more common.

The Muslim states in the Middle East were politically fragmented when the Crusaders first came, and it took about a century for them to reorganize. They did so dramatically under Saladin (Salah al-Dihn), who first unified Egypt and Syria, and then retook Jerusalem in 1187. Christians immediately attempted to take it back in what was later called the Third Crusade (1189–1192). Frederick Barbarossa of the Holy Roman Empire, Richard the Lion-Hearted of England, and Philip Augustus of France participated, and the Third Crusade was better financed than the previous two. But disputes among the

The Capture of Jerusalem in 1099   In this illustration from a fourteenth-century French version of Archbishop William of Tyre's history of the First Crusade, Crusaders enter the city of Jerusalem on scaling ladders as engines hurl stones to breach the walls. (Bibliothèque nationale de France)

leaders and strategic problems prevented any lasting results. The Crusaders could not retake Jerusalem, though they did keep their hold on port towns, and Saladin allowed pilgrims safe passage to Jerusalem. He also made an agreement with Christian rulers for keeping the peace. From that point on, the Crusader states were more important economically than politically or religiously, giving Italian and French merchants direct access to Eastern products such as perfumes and silk.

     In 1202 Innocent III sent out preachers who called on Christian knights to retake Jerusalem. Those who responded — in what would become the Fourth Crusade — negotiated with the Venetians to take them by boat to Cairo, but Venetian interests combined with a succession struggle over the Byzantine throne led the fleet to go to Constantinople instead. Once there, the Crusaders decided to capture and sack Constantinople, destroying its magnificent library and seizing gold, silver, and relics to send home. The Byzantines reasserted their control over the empire in 1261, but it was much smaller and weaker and soon consisted of little more than the city of Constantinople. Moreover, the assault by one Christian people on another helped discredit the entire crusading movement and obviously had no effect on Muslim control of Jerusalem and other areas.

Nonetheless, there were a few more efforts. The Seventh Crusade in 1248, led by King Louis IX of France (r. 1223–1270), tried unsuccessfully to come in through Egypt. Louis also sent monks to the court of the Mongols in Central Asia, who were at this point led by Chinggis Khan, to forge an alliance that would encircle the Muslims. The monks were unsuccessful, but they brought back geographical knowledge of Asia and the peoples they had encountered. In the end, the Mamluk rulers of Egypt conquered the Crusader states, and in 1291 their last stronghold, the port of Acre, fell. Some knights continued their crusading efforts by joining the reconquista in Spain.

Consequences of the Crusades

The Crusades gave kings and the pope opportunities to expand their bureaucracies. They also provided kings with the perfect opportunity to get rid of troublemaking knights, particularly restless younger sons for whom the practice of primogeniture meant few prospects. Some of them were able to carve out lordships in Palestine, Syria, and Greece. Even some members of the middle class who stayed at home profited from the Crusades. Nobles often had to borrow money from city residents to pay for their expeditions, and they put up part of their land as security. If a noble did not return home or could not pay the interest on the loan, the middle-class creditor took over the land.

The Crusades introduced some Europeans to Eastern luxury goods, but their immediate cultural impact on the West remains debatable. Strong economic and intellectual ties with the East had already been developed by the late eleventh century. The Crusades did greatly benefit Italian merchants, who profited from outfitting military expeditions, the opening of new trade routes, and the establishment of trading communities in the Crusader states. Since commerce with the West benefited both Muslims and Europeans, it continued to flourish even after the Crusader states collapsed.

The Crusades proved to be a disaster for Jewish-Christian relations. In many parts of Europe, Jews lent money to peasants, townspeople, and nobles, and indebtedness bred resentment. Inspired by the ideology of holy war and resentment of Jewish economic activities, Christian armies on their way to Jerusalem on the First Crusade joined with local people to attack Jewish families and sometimes entire Jewish communities. In the German cities along the Rhine River, for example, an army of Crusaders under the leadership of a German noble forced Jews to convert through mass baptisms and killed those who resisted; more than eight hundred Jews were killed in Worms and more than a thousand in Mainz. Later Crusades brought similar violence, enhanced by rumors that Jews engaged in the ritual murder of Christians to use their blood in religious rites. As a result of growing hostility, legal restrictions on Jews gradually increased throughout Europe. In 1290 King Edward I of England expelled the Jews from England and confiscated their property and goods; it would be four centuries before they would be allowed back in. King Philip IV of France followed Edward's example in 1306. The Crusades also left a legacy of deep bitterness between Christians and Muslims. Each side dehumanized the other. Whereas Europeans perceived the Crusades as sacred religious movements, Muslims saw them as expansionist and imperialistic.

At the same time, the Crusades shaped the identity of the West. They represent the first great colonizing movement beyond the geographical boundaries of Europe. The ideal of a sacred mission to conquer or convert Muslim peoples entered Europeans' consciousness and became a continuing goal. When Christopher Columbus sailed west in 1492, he hoped to reach India in part to establish a Christian base from which a new crusade against Islam could be launched.

The Expansion of Christianity

The Crusades had a profound impact on both Europe and the Middle East, but they were not the only example of Christian expansion in the High Middle Ages. As we saw earlier, Christian kingdoms were established in the Iberian Peninsula through the reconquista. This gradual Christian advance was replicated in northern and eastern Europe in the centuries after 1000. People and ideas moved from western France and western Germany into Ireland, Scandinavia, the Baltic lands, and eastern Europe, with significant consequences for those territories. Wars of expansion, the establishment of new Christian bishoprics, and the vast migration of colonists, together with the papal emphasis on a unified Christian world, brought about the gradual Christianization of a larger area. By 1350 Roman Catholic Europe was double the size it had been in 950.

Ireland had been Christian since the days of Saint Patrick (see Chapter 7), but in the twelfth century Norman knights crossed from England, defeated Irish lords, and established bishoprics with defined territorial dioceses. Latin Christian influences also entered the Scandinavian and Baltic regions primarily through the erection of dioceses. Otto I established the first Scandinavian dioceses in Denmark. In Norway Christianity spread in coastal areas beginning in the tenth century, and King Olaf II (r. 1015–1028) brought in clergy and bishops from England and Germany to establish the church more firmly. From Norway Christianity spread to Iceland; from Denmark it spread to Sweden and Finland. In all of these areas, Christian missionaries preached, baptized, and built churches. Royal power advanced institutional Christianity, and traditional Norse religions practiced by the Vikings were outlawed.

In 1397 Queen Margrete I (1353–1412) united the crowns of Denmark, Sweden-Finland, and Norway in the Union of Kalmar. She continued royal support of bishops and worked toward creating a stronger state by checking the power of the nobility and creating a stronger financial base for the monarchy.

In eastern Europe, the German emperor Otto I planted a string of dioceses along his northern and eastern frontiers, hoping to pacify the newly conquered Slavs. German nobles built castles and ruthlessly crushed revolts by Slavic peoples, sometimes using the language of crusade to describe their actions. Albert the Bear, for example, a German noble, proclaimed a crusade against the Slavs and invited German knights to colonize conquered territories, just as earlier the French king had used French knights to crush the Albigensians. A military order of German knights founded in Palestine, the Teutonic (too-TAH-nihk) Knights, moved their operations to eastern Europe and waged wars against the pagan Prussians in the Baltic region, again terming these "crusades." After

1230, from a base in Poland, they established a new Christian territory, Prussia, and gradually the entire eastern shore of the Baltic came under their hegemony.

The church also moved into central Europe, first in Bohemia in the tenth century and from there into Poland and Hungary in the eleventh. In the twelfth and thirteenth centuries, thousands of settlers poured into eastern Europe. These immigrants were German in descent, name, language, and law. Larger towns such as Kraków and Riga engaged in long-distance trade and gradually grew into large urban centers.

Christendom

Through the actions of the Roman emperors Constantine and Theodosius (see Chapter 7), Christianity became in some ways a state as well as a religion. Early medieval writers began to use the word **Christendom** to refer to this Christian realm. Sometimes notions of Christendom were linked directly to specific states, such as Charlemagne's empire and the Holy Roman Empire. More often, however, Christendom was vague, a sort of loose sense of the body of all people who were Christian. When the pope called for holy war against the Muslims, for example, he spoke not only of the retaking of Jerusalem, but also of the defense of Christendom. When missionaries, officials, and soldiers took Christianity into the Iberian Peninsula, Scandinavia, or the Baltic region, they understood their actions as aimed at the expansion of Christendom.

From the point of view of popes such as Gregory VII and Innocent III, Christendom was a unified hierarchy with the papacy at the top. They pushed for uniformity of religious worship and campaigned continually for use of the same religious service, the Roman liturgy in Latin, in all countries and places. They forbade vernacular Christian rituals or those that differed in their pattern of worship. Under Innocent III papal directives and papal legates flowed to all parts of Europe. Twelve hundred church officials obediently came to Rome from the borderlands as well as the heartland for the Fourth Lateran Council of 1215.

As we have seen in this chapter, however, not everyone had the same view. Kings and emperors may have accepted the Roman liturgy in their lands, but they had their own ideas of the way power should operate in Christendom, even if this brought them into conflict with the papacy. They remained loyal to Christendom as a concept, but they had a profoundly different idea about how it should be structured and who could best defend it. The battles in the High Middle Ages between popes and kings and between Christians and Muslims were signs of how deeply religion had replaced tribal, political, and ethnic structures as the essence of Western culture.

Notes

1. D. C. Douglas and G. E. Greenaway, eds., *English Historical Documents*, vol. 2 (London: Eyre & Spottiswoode, 1961), p. 853.
2. *Hrosvithae Liber Tertius, a Text with Translation*, ed. and trans. Mary Bernardine Bergman (Covington, Ky.: The Sisters of Saint Benedict, 1943), p. 45.
3. J. Johns, *Arabic Administration in Norman Sicily: The Royal Dīwān* (New York: Cambridge University Press, 2002), p. 293.
4. H. T. Riley, ed., *Memorials of London* (London: Longmans Green, 1868).
5. Honorius of Autun, "Elucidarium sive Dialogus," vol. 172, col. 1148.
6. Fulcher of Chartres, *A History of the Expedition to Jerusalem, 1095–1127*, trans. Frances Rita Ryan, ed. Harold S. Fink (Knoxville: University of Tennessee Press, 1969), pp. 121–123.

Chapter Review

MAKE IT STICK

LearningCurve
bedfordstmartins.com/mckaywestvalue

After reading the chapter, use LearningCurve to retain what you've read.

IDENTIFY KEY TERMS

Identify and explain the significance of each item below.

Domesday Book (p. 261)   **college of cardinals** (p. 273)
primogeniture (p. 263)   **excommunication** (p. 273)
Holy Roman Empire (p. 264)   **canon law** (p. 276)
reconquista (p. 266)   **religious orders** (p. 278)
common law (p. 267)   **friars** (p. 281)
Magna Carta (p. 268)   **Crusades** (p. 283)
chivalry (p. 270)   **indulgences** (p. 284)
simony (p. 273)   **Christendom** (p. 290)

REVIEW THE MAIN IDEAS

Answer the focus questions from each section of the chapter.

- How did monarchs try to centralize political power? (p. 260)
- How did the administration of law evolve in this period? (p. 266)
- What were the roles of nobles, and how did they train for these? (p. 270)
- How did the papacy reform the church, and what were the reactions to these efforts? (p. 272)
- What roles did monks, nuns, and friars play in medieval society? (p. 276)
- What were the causes, course, and consequences of both the Crusades and the broader expansion of Christianity? (p. 283)

MAKE CONNECTIONS

Think about the larger developments and continuities within and across chapters.

1. What similarities and differences do you see between the institutions and laws established by medieval rulers and those of Roman and Byzantine emperors (Chapters 6 and 7)?

2. What factors over the centuries enabled the Christian Church to become the most powerful and wealthy institution in Europe, and what problems did this create?

ONLINE DOCUMENT ASSIGNMENT

Hildegard of Bingen

How did Hildegard of Bingen come to be seen as a worthy instrument for the transmission of God's word?

You encountered Hildegard of Bingen's story on page 280. Keeping the question above in mind, go online and read excerpts from her correspondence and note the qualities that appealed to so many of her contemporaries. Then complete a writing assignment based on the evidence and details from this chapter.

bedfordstmartins.com/mckaywestvalue

CHRONOLOGY

936–973	• Reign of Otto I in Germany; facilitates spread of Christianity in the Baltics and eastern Europe
1059	• Lateran Council restricts election of the pope to the college of cardinals
1061–1091	• Normans defeat Muslims and Byzantines in Sicily
1066	• Norman conquest of England
1073–1085	• Pontificate of Pope Gregory VII, proponent of Gregorian reforms
1095–1291	• Crusades
1098	• Cistercian order established
1100–1135	• Reign of Henry I of England; establishment of the Exchequer, England's bureau of finance
1100–1200	• Establishment of canon law
1154–1189	• Reign of Henry II of England; revision of legal procedure; beginnings of common law
1170	• Thomas Becket assassinated in England
1180–1223	• Reign of Philip II (Philip Augustus) in France; territory of France greatly expanded
1198–1216	• Innocent III; height of the medieval papacy
1215	• Magna Carta
1216	• Papal recognition of Dominican order
1221	• Papal recognition of Franciscan order
1290	• Jews expelled from England
1298	• Pope Boniface VIII orders all nuns to be cloistered
1302	• Pope Boniface VIII declares all Christians subject to the pope in *Unam Sanctam*
1306	• Jews expelled from France
1397	• Queen Margrete establishes Union of Kalmar

10

LearningCurve
bedfordstmartins.com/mckaywestvalue
After reading the chapter, use
LearningCurve to retain what
you've read.

Life in Villages and Cities of the High Middle Ages

1000–1300

KINGS, EMPERORS, NOBLES, AND THEIR OFFICIALS CREATED POLITICAL and legal institutions that structured many aspects of life in the High Middle Ages, but ordinary people typically worked and lived without paying much attention to the political developments that took place at faraway centers of power. Similarly, the conflicts between popes and secular leaders were dramatic, but for most people religion was primarily a matter of joining with neighbors and family members in rituals to express beliefs, thanks, and hopes.

While the routines of medieval life followed familiar rhythms for centuries, this does not mean that life in the High Middle Ages was unchanging. Agricultural improvements such as better plows and water mills increased the amount and quality of food, and the population grew. Relative security and the increasing food supply allowed for the growth and development of towns and a revival of long-distance trade. Some urban merchants and bankers became as wealthy as great nobles. Trade brought in new ideas as well as merchandise,

ONLINE DOCUMENT ASSIGNMENT
Life in Medieval Towns
How did merchant and craft guilds shape life in medieval towns? Examine primary texts and images that illuminate the role of guilds in medieval urban communities, and then complete a writing assignment based on the evidence and details from this chapter.

bedfordstmartins.com/mckaywestvalue

and cities developed into intellectual and cultural centers. The university, a new type of educational institution, came into being, providing advanced training in theology, medicine, and law. Traditions and values were spread orally and in written form through poems, stories, and songs. Gothic cathedrals, where people saw beautiful stained-glass windows and listened to complex music, were physical manifestations of medieval people's deep faith and pride in their own community.

Village Life

What was village life like in medieval Europe?

The vast majority of people in medieval Europe were peasants who lived in small villages and rarely traveled very far, but since villagers did not perform what were considered "noble" deeds, the aristocratic monks and clerics who wrote the records that serve as historical sources did not spend time or precious writing materials on the peasantry. When common people were mentioned, it was usually with contempt or in terms of the services and obligations they owed. There were exceptions. In the early twelfth century Honorius, a monk and teacher at the monastery of Autun, wrote: "What do you say about the agricultural classes? Most of them will be saved because they live simply and feed God's people by means of their sweat."[1] Today's scholars are far more interested than were their medieval predecessors in the lives of ordinary people, however, and are using archaeological, artistic, and material sources to fill in details that are rarely mentioned in written documents.

Slavery, Serfdom, and Upward Mobility

Honorius lumps together everyone who worked the land, but in fact there were many levels of peasants ranging from outright slaves to free but poor peasants to very rich farmers. The number of slaves who worked the land declined steadily in the High Middle Ages, and those who remained tended to live with wealthier peasant families or with lords. Most rural people in western Europe during this period were serfs rather than slaves, though the distinction between slave and serf was not always clear. Both lacked freedom and both were subject to the arbitrary will of one person, the manorial lord. Serfs remained bound to the land when their lords died, but unlike slaves they could not be bought and sold outright.

Most serfs worked small plots of land; in addition, all serfs were required to provide a certain number of days of labor a week — more in planting and harvest seasons — on a lord's land. Serfs were also often obliged to pay fees on common occurrences, such as marriage or the inheritance of land from one generation to the next.

Serfdom was a hereditary condition. A person born a serf was likely to die a serf, though many serfs did secure their freedom. As money became more widely available, some serfs bought their freedom. Some gained it when manorial lords organized groups of villagers to cut down forests or fill in swamps and marshes to make more land available for farming. A serf could clear a patch of fen or forestland, make it productive, and, through prudent saving, buy more land and eventually purchase freedom. Serfs who migrated longer distances, such as German peasants who moved eastward into Slavic lands, were often granted a reduction in labor services as a reward. Thus both internal and external frontier lands in the High Middle Ages provided some opportunities for upward mobility.

The Manor

Most peasants, free and serf, lived in family groups in small villages. One or more villages and the land surrounding them made up a manor controlled by a noble lord or a church official such as a bishop, abbot, or abbess. Peasant dwellings were clumped together, with the fields stretching out beyond. Most villages had a church. In some the lord's large residence was right next to the small peasant houses, while in others the lord lived in a castle or manor house separate from the village. Manors varied greatly in size; some contained a number of villages, and some were very small.

The arable land of the manor was divided between the lord and the peasantry, with the lord's portion known as the demesne (dih-MAYN), or home farm. The manor usually also held pasture or meadowland for the grazing of cattle, sheep, and sometimes goats and often had some forestland as well. Forests were valuable resources, providing wood, ash, and resin for a variety of purposes. Forests were also used for feeding pigs, cattle, and domestic animals on nuts, roots, and wild berries.

Lords generally appointed officials to oversee the legal and business operations of their manors, collect taxes and fees, and handle disputes. Villages in many parts of Europe also developed institutions of self-government to handle issues such as crop rotation, and villagers themselves chose additional officials such as constables and aletasters. Women had no official voice in running the village, but they did buy, sell, and hold land independently, especially as widows who headed households. In areas of Europe where men left seasonally or more permanently in search of work elsewhere, women played a larger decision-making role, though they generally did not hold official positions.

Manors did not represent the only form of medieval rural economy. In parts of Germany and the Netherlands and in much of southern France, free independent farmers owned land outright, free of rents and service obligations. In Scandinavia the soil was so poor and the climate so harsh that people tended to live on widely scattered farms rather than in villages.

Work

The peasants' work was typically divided according to gender. Men cleared new land, plowed, and cared for large animals; women cared for small animals, spun yarn, and prepared food. Both sexes planted and harvested, though often there were gender-specific tasks within these major undertakings.

Once children were able to walk, they helped their parents in the hundreds of chores that had to be done. Small children collected eggs if the family had chickens or gathered twigs and sticks for firewood. As they grew older, children had more responsible tasks, such as weeding the family's vegetable garden, milking the cows, and helping with the planting or harvesting.

In many parts of Europe, medieval farmers employed the **open-field system**, a pattern that differs sharply from modern farming practices. In the open-field system, the arable land of a manor was divided into two or three fields without hedges or fences to mark the individual holdings of the lord, serfs, and free men. The village as a whole decided what would be planted in each field, rotating the crops according to tradition and need. Some fields would be planted with crops such as wheat, rye, peas, or barley for human consumption, some with oats or other crops for both animals and humans, and some left unworked or fallow to allow the soil to rejuvenate. In addition, legume crops such as peas and beans helped the soil rebuild nutrients and also increased the villagers' protein consumption. In most areas with open-field agriculture the holdings farmed by any one family did not consist of a whole field but consisted, instead, of strips in many fields. If one strip held by a family yielded little, those in different fields might be more bountiful. Families worked their own land and the lord's, but also cooperated with other families if they needed help, particularly during harvest time. This meant that all shared in any disaster as well as in any large harvest.

Meteorologists think that a slow but steady retreat of polar ice occurred between the ninth and eleventh centuries, and Europe experienced a significant warming trend from 1050 to 1300. The mild winters and dry summers that resulted helped increase agricultural output throughout Europe, particularly in the north.

The tenth and eleventh centuries also witnessed a number of agricultural improvements, especially in the development of mechanisms that replaced or aided human labor. Mills driven by wind and water power dramatically reduced the time and labor required to grind grain, crush seeds for oil, and carry out other tasks. This change had a significant impact on women's productivity. In the ancient world, slaves had been responsible for grinding the grain for bread; as slavery was replaced by serfdom, grinding became women's work. When water- and wind-driven mills were introduced into an area, women were freed from the task of grinding grain and could turn to other tasks, such as raising animals, working in gardens or vineyards, and raising and preparing flax to make linen. They could also devote more time to spinning yarn, which was the bottleneck in cloth production, as each weaver needed at least six spinners. Thus the spread of wind and water power indirectly contributed to an increase in cloth production in medieval Europe.

Another change, which came in the early twelfth century, was a significant increase in the production of iron. Much of this was used for weapons and armor, but it also filled a growing demand in agriculture. Iron was first used for plowshares (the part of the plow that cuts a deep furrow), and then for pitchforks, spades, and axes. Harrows—cultivating instruments with heavy teeth that broke up and smoothed the soil after plowing—began to have iron instead of wooden teeth, making them more effective and less likely to break.

In central and northern Europe, peasants made increasing use of heavy wheeled iron plows pulled by teams of oxen to break up the rich, clay-filled soil common there, and agricultural productivity increased. Further technological improvements allowed horses to be used for plowing as well as oxen. The development of the padded horse collar that rested on the horse's shoulders and was attached to the load by shafts meant that the animal could put its entire weight into the task of pulling. Iron horseshoes prevented horses' hooves from splitting, and better harness systems allowed horses to be hitched together in teams. The use of horses spread in the twelfth century because their greater speed brought greater efficiency to farming and reduced the amount of human labor involved. Horses were also used to haul goods to markets, where peasants sold any excess vegetables, grain, and animals.

By modern standards, medieval agricultural yields were very low, but there was striking improvement between the fifth and the thirteenth centuries. Increased output had a profound impact on society, improving Europeans' health, commerce, industry, and general lifestyle. More food meant that fewer people suffered from hunger and malnourishment and that devastating famines were rarer. Higher yields brought more food for animals as well as people, and the amount of meat that people ate increased slightly. A better diet had an enormous impact on women's lives in particular. More food meant increased body fat, which increased fertility, and more meat—which provided iron—meant that women were less anemic and less subject to disease. Some researchers believe that it was during the High Middle Ages that Western women began to outlive men. Improved opportunities also encouraged people to marry somewhat earlier, which meant larger families and further population growth.

Home Life

In western and central Europe, villages were generally made up of small houses for individual families. Households consisted of a married couple, their children (including stepchildren), and perhaps one or two other relatives. Some homes contained only an unmarried person, a widow, or several unmarried people living together. In southern and eastern Europe, extended families were more likely to live in the same household.

The size and quality of peasants' houses varied according to their relative prosperity, which usually depended on the amount of land held. Poorer peasants lived in windowless cottages built of wood and clay or wattle (poles interwoven with branches or reeds) and thatched with straw. These cottages consisted of one large room that served as both kitchen and living quarters. A shed attached to the house provided storage for tools and shelter for animals. Prosperous peasants added rooms; some wealthy peasants in the early fourteenth century had two-story houses with separate bedrooms for parents and children. For most people, however, living space—especially living space close enough to a fire to feel some warmth in cold weather—was cramped, dark, smoky, and smelly, with animals and people both sharing tight quarters, sometimes with each other.

Every house had a small garden and an outbuilding. Onions, garlic, turnips, and carrots were grown and stored through the winter. Cabbage was shredded, salted, and turned into kraut for storage. The mainstay of the diet for peasants—and for all other classes—was bread. It was a hard, black substance made of barley, millet, and oats, rarely of expensive wheat, which they were more likely to use to pay their taxes and fees to the lord than for their own bread. Most households did not have ovens, which were expensive to build and posed a fire danger; their bread was baked in communal ovens or purchased from households that specialized in bread-baking. The main meal was often bread and a thick soup of vegetables and grains eaten around noon. Peasants ate vegetables not because they appreciated their importance for good health but because there was usually little else available. Animals were too valuable to be used for food on a regular basis, but weaker animals were often slaughtered in the fall so that they did not need to be fed through the winter. Their meat was salted for preservation and eaten on great feast days such as Christmas and Easter.

The diet of people with access to a river, lake, or stream would be supplemented with fish, which could be eaten fresh or preserved by salting. People living close to the sea gathered shellfish. Many places had severe laws against hunting and trapping in the forests. Deer, wild boars, and other game were reserved for the king and nobles. These laws were flagrantly violated, however, and rabbits and wild game often found their way to peasants' tables.

Medieval households were not self-sufficient but bought cloth, metal, leather goods, and even some food in village markets. They also bought ale, the universal drink of the common people in northern Europe. Women dominated in the production of ale. Ale not only provided needed calories but also provided some relief from the difficult, monotonous labor that filled people's lives. Medieval men and women often drank heavily. Brawls and violent fights were frequent at taverns, and English judicial records of the thirteenth century reveal a surprisingly large number of "accidental" deaths in which people drowned, got lost, or fell from horses, often, as the court records say, "coming from an ale," meaning that the victims were probably drunk.

The steady rise in population between the mid-eleventh and fourteenth centuries was primarily the result of warmer climate, increased food supply, and a reduction of violence with growing political stability, rather than dramatic changes in health care. Most treatment of illness was handled by home remedies handed down orally or perhaps through a cherished handwritten family herbal, cookbook, or household guide. Treatments were often mixtures of herbal remedies, sayings, specific foods, prayers, amulets, and ritual healing activities. People suffering from wounds, skin diseases, or broken bones sometimes turned to barber-surgeons. For internal ailments, people consulted apothecaries, who suggested and mixed compounds taken internally or applied orally as a salve or ointment; these were generally mixtures of plants, minerals, and other natural products.

Beginning in the twelfth century in England, France, and Italy, the clergy, noble men and women, and newly rich merchants also established institutions to care for the sick or for those who could not take care of themselves. Within city walls they built hospitals, where care was provided for those with chronic diseases that were not contagious, poor expectant mothers, the handicapped, people recovering from injuries, and foundling children. Outside city walls they built leprosariums or small hospices for people with leprosy and other contagious diseases. Such institutions might be staffed by members of religious orders or by laymen and laywomen who were paid for their work.

Childbirth and Child Abandonment

The most dangerous period of life for any person, peasant or noble, was infancy and early childhood. In normal years perhaps as many as one-third of all children died before age five from illness, malnutrition, and accidents, and this death rate climbed to more than half in years with plagues, droughts, or famines. However, once people reached adulthood, many lived well into their fifties and sixties.

Childbirth was dangerous for mothers as well as infants. Village women helped one another through childbirth, and women who were more capable acquired midwifery skills. In larger towns and cities, such women gradually developed into professional midwives who were paid for their services and who trained younger women as apprentices. For most women, however, childbirth was handled by female friends and family.

Many infants were abandoned by parents or guardians, who left their children somewhere, sold them, or legally gave authority over them to some other person or institution. Sometimes parents believed that someone of greater means or status might find the child and bring him or her up in better circumstances than they could provide. Christian parents gave their children to monasteries as religious acts, donating them to the service of God in the same way they might donate money.

Toward the end of his *Ecclesiastical History*, when he was well into his sixties, Orderic Vitalis (ca. 1075–ca. 1140), a monk of the Norman abbey of Saint Evroul, explained movingly how he became a monk:

> And so, O glorious God, you didst inspire my father Odeleric to renounce me utterly and submit me in all things to thy governance. So, weeping, he gave me, a weeping child, into the care of the monk Reginald, and sent me away into exile for love of thee, and never saw me again. . . . I crossed the English channel and came into Normandy as an exile, unknown to all, knowing no one. . . . But thou didst suffer me through thy grace to find nothing but kindness among strangers. . . . The name of Vitalis was given me in place of my English name, which sounded harsh to the Normans.[2]

Orderic had no doubt that God wanted him to be a monk, but even half a century later he still remembered his grief. Orderic's father was a Norman priest, and his Anglo-Saxon mother perhaps gave him his "English" name. Qualms of conscience over clerical celibacy may have led Orderic's father to place his son in a monastery.

Donating a child to a monastery was common among the poor until about the year 1000, but less common in the next three hundred years, which saw relative prosperity for peasants. On the other hand, the incidence of noble parents giving their younger sons and daughters to religious houses increased dramatically. This resulted from and also reinforced the system of primogeniture, in which estates were passed intact to the eldest son instead of being divided among heirs (see Chapter 9). Monasteries provided noble younger sons and daughters with career opportunities, and their being thus disposed of removed them as contenders for family land.

Popular Religion

How did religion shape everyday life in the High Middle Ages?

Apart from the land, the weather, and local legal and social conditions, religion had the greatest impact on the daily lives of ordinary people in the High Middle Ages. Religious practices varied widely from country to country and even from province to province. But nowhere was religion a one-hour-a-week affair. Most people in medieval Europe were Christian, but there were small Jewish communities scattered in many parts of Europe and Muslims lived in the Iberian Peninsula, Sicily, and other Mediterranean islands

Christian Life in Medieval Villages

For Christians the village church was the center of community life—social, political, and economic, as well as religious—with the parish priest in charge of a host of activities. From the side of the church, he read orders and messages from royal and ecclesiastical authorities to his parishioners. The front of the church, typically decorated with scenes of the Last Judgment, was the background against which royal judges traveling on circuit disposed of civil and criminal cases. In busy cities such as London, business agreements were made in the square in front of the church or even inside the church itself.

Although church law placed the priest under the bishop's authority, the manorial lord appointed the priest. Rural priests were peasants and often worked in the fields with the people during the week. On Sundays and holy days, they put on a robe and celebrated mass, or Eucharist, the ceremony in which the priest consecrated bread and wine and distributed it to believers, in a re-enactment of Jesus's Last Supper. They recited the mass in Latin, a language that few commoners, sometimes including the priest himself, could understand. At least once a year villagers were expected to take part in the ceremony and eat the consecrated bread. This usually happened at Easter, after they had confessed their sins to the priest and been assigned a penance.

In everyday life people engaged in rituals and used language heavy with religious symbolism. Before planting, the village priest customarily went out and sprinkled the fields with water, symbolizing refreshment and life. Everyone participated in village processions to honor the saints and ask their protection. The entire calendar was filled with reference to events in the life of Jesus and his disciples, such as Christmas, Easter, and Pentecost. Scriptural references and proverbs dotted everyone's language. The English *good-bye*, the French *adieu*, and the Spanish *adios* all derive from words meaning "God be with you." The signs and symbols of Christianity were visible everywhere, but so, people believed, was the Devil, who lured them to evil deeds. In some medieval images and literature, the Devil is portrayed as black, an identification that shaped Western racial attitudes.

Saints and Sacraments

Along with days marking events in the life of Jesus, the Christian calendar was filled with saints' days. Veneration of the saints had been an important tool of Christian conversion since late antiquity (see Chapter 7), and the cult of the saints was a central feature of popular culture in the Middle Ages. People believed that the saints possessed supernatural powers that enabled them to perform miracles, and the saint became the special property of the locality in which his or her relics rested. In return for the saint's healing and support, peasants offered the saint prayers, loyalty, and gifts.

In the later Middle Ages popular hagiographies (ha-gee-AH-gruh-fees)—biographies of saints based on myths, legends, and popular stories—attributed specialized functions to the saints. Saint Elmo (ca. 300), who supposedly had preached unharmed during a thunder and lightning storm, became the patron of sailors. Saint Agatha (third century), whose breasts were torn with shears because she rejected the attentions of a powerful suitor, became the patron of wet nurses, women with breast difficulties, and bell ringers (because of the resemblance of breasts to bells). Every occupation had a patron saint, as did cities and even realms.

How were saints chosen? Since the early days of Christianity, individuals whose exemplary virtue was proved by miracles had been venerated by laypeople. Church officials in Rome insisted that they had the exclusive right to determine sainthood, but ordinary people continued to declare people saints. Between 1185 and 1431 only seventy persons were declared saints at Rome, but hundreds of new saints were venerated across Europe. Some clergy preached against the veneration of saints' relics and called it idolatry, but their appeals had little effect.

Statue of Saint Anne, the Virgin Mary, and the Christ Child   Nearly every church had at least one image of the Virgin Mary, the most important figure of Christian devotion in medieval Europe. In this thirteenth-century wooden sculpture, she is shown holding the infant Jesus, and is herself sitting on the lap of her mother, Anne. Statues such as this reinforced people's sense that the heavenly family was much like theirs, with grandparents who some-times played important roles. (Scala/Art Resource, NY)

The Virgin Mary, Christ's mother, was the most important saint. In the eleventh century theologians began to emphasize Mary's spiritual motherhood of all Chris-tians. Special masses commemorated her, churches were built in her honor, and hymns and prayers to her multiplied. Villagers listened intently to sermons telling stories about her life and miracles. One favorite story told of a minstrel and acrobat inspired to perform tumbling feats in Mary's honor "until from head to heel sweat stood upon him, drop by drop, as blood falls from meat turning on a hearth . . . [then] there came down from the heavens a Dame so glorious, that certainly no man had seen one so precious, nor so richly crowned. . . . Then the sweet and courteous Queen her-self took a white napkin in her hand, and with it gently fanned her minstrel before the altar. . . . She blesses her minstrel with the sign of God."[3]

If Mary would even bless tumbling—a disreputable form of popular entertain-ment—as long as it was done with a reverent heart, people reasoned, how much more would she bless their lives of hard work and pious devotion.

Along with the veneration of saints, sacraments were an important part of reli-gious practice. Twelfth-century theologians expanded on Saint Augustine's understand-ing of sacraments (see Chapter 7) and created an entire sacramental system. In 1215 the Fourth Lateran Council formally accepted seven sacraments (baptism, penance, the Eucharist, confirmation, marriage, priestly ordination, anointment of the dying). Medi-eval Christians believed that these seven sacraments brought God's grace, the divine assistance or help needed to lead a good Christian life and to merit salvation. Most sacraments had to be dispensed by a priest, although spouses officially administered the sacrament of marriage to each other, and laypeople could baptize a dying infant or anoint a dying person if no priest could be found. The sacramental system enhanced the au-thority of priests over people's lives, but did not replace strong personal devotion to the saints.

Muslims and Jews

The centrality of Christian ceremonies to daily life for most Europeans meant that those who did not participate were clearly marked as outsiders. Many Muslims left Spain as the Christian "reconquest" proceeded and left Sicily when this became a Christian realm (see Chapter 9), but others converted. In more isolated villages, people simply continued their Muslim rituals and practices, including abstaining from pork, reciting verses from the Qur'an, praying at specified times of the day, and observing Muslim holy days, though they might hide this from the local priest or visiting officials.

Islam was geographically limited in medieval Europe, but by the late tenth century Jews could be found in many areas, often brought in from other areas as clients of rulers to help with finance. There were Jewish communities in Italian and French cities and in the cities along the Rhine. Jewish dietary laws require meat to be handled in a specific way, so Jews had their own butchers; there were Jewish artisans in many other trades as well. Jews held weekly religious services on Saturday, the Sabbath, and celebrated their own annual cycle of holidays. Each of these holidays involved special prayers, services, and often foods, and many of them commemorated events from Jewish history, including various times when Jews had been rescued from captivity.

Jews could supply other Jews with goods and services, but rulers and city leaders increasingly restricted their trade with Christians to banking and money-lending. This enhanced Christian resentment, as did the ideology of holy war that accompanied the Crusades (see Chapter 9). Violence against Jews and restrictions on their activities increased further in much of Europe. Jews were expelled from England and later from France. However, Jews continued to live in the independent cities of the Holy Roman Empire and Italy, and some migrated eastward into new towns that were being established in Slavic areas.

Rituals of Marriage and Birth

Increasing suspicion and hostility marked relations between religious groups throughout the Middle Ages, but there were also important similarities in the ways Christians, Jews, and Muslims understood and experienced their religions. In all three traditions, every major life transition was marked by a ceremony that included religious elements.

Christian weddings might be held in the village church or at the church door, though among well-to-do families the ceremony took place in the house of the bride or bridegroom. A priest's blessing was often sought, though it was not essential to the marriage. Muslim weddings were also finalized by a contract between the bride and groom and were often overseen by a wedding official. Jewish weddings were guided by statements in Talmudic law that weddings were complete when the bride had entered the *chuppah*, which medieval Jewish authorities interpreted to mean a room in the groom's house.

In all three faiths, the wedding ceremony was followed by a wedding party that often included secular rituals. Some rituals symbolized the proper hierarchical relations between the spouses — such as placing the husband's shoe on the bedstead over the couple, symbolizing his authority — or were meant to ensure the couple's fertility — such as untying all the knots in the household, for it was believed that people possessing magical powers could tie knots to inhibit a man's reproductive power. All this came together in what was often the final event of a wedding: the religious official blessed the couple in their marriage bed, often with family and friends standing around or banging on pans, yelling, or otherwise making as much noise as possible to make fun of the couple's first sexual encounter. (Tying cans on the back of the car in which a couple leaves the wedding is a modern remnant of such rituals.)

The friends and family members had generally been part of the discussions, negotiations, and activities leading up to the marriage; marriage united two families and was far too important to leave up to two people alone. Among serfs the manorial lord's permission was often required, with a special fee required to obtain it. (This permission did not, as often alleged, give the lord the right to deflower the bride. Though lords certainly forced sex on female serfs, there is no evidence in any legal sources that lords had the "right of first night," the *jus primae noctis*.) The involvement of family and friends in choosing one's spouse might lead to conflict, but more often the wishes of the couple and their parents, kin, and community were quite similar: all hoped for marriages that provided economic security, honorable standing, and a good number of healthy children. The best marriages offered companionship, emotional support, and even love, but these were understood to grow out of the marriage, not necessarily precede it. Breaking up a marriage meant breaking up the basic production and consumption unit, a very serious matter. The church forbade divorce, and even among non-Christians marital dissolution by any means other than the death of one spouse was rare.

Most brides hoped to be pregnant soon after the wedding. Christian women hoping for children said special prayers to the Virgin Mary or her mother, Anne. Some wore amulets of amber, bone, or mistletoe, thought to increase fertility. Others repeated charms and verses they had learned from other women, or, in desperate cases, went on pilgrimages to make special supplications. Muslim and Jewish women wore small cases with sacred verses or asked for blessings from religious leaders. Women continued these prayers and rituals throughout pregnancy and childbirth, often combining religious traditions with folk beliefs. Women in southern France, for example, offered prayers for easy childbirth and healthy children to Saint Guinefort, a greyhound who had been mistakenly killed by his owner after saving the owner's child from a poisonous snake. The fact that Guinefort was a dog meant he could never become an official saint, but women saw him as a powerful and martyred protector of children.

Judaism, Christianity, and Islam all required women to remain separate from the community for a short time after childbirth and often had special ceremonies welcoming them back once this period was over. These rituals often included prayers, such as this one from the Christian ritual of thanksgiving and purification, called churching, which a woman celebrated six weeks after giving birth: "Almighty and everlasting God, who has freed this woman from the danger of bearing a child, consider her to be strengthened from every pollution of the flesh so that with a clean heart and pure mind she may deserve to enter into the bosom of our mother, the church, and make her devoted to Your service."[4]

Religious ceremonies also welcomed children into the community. Among Christian families, infants were baptized soon after they were born to ensure that they could enter Heaven. Midwives who delivered children who looked especially weak and sickly often baptized them in an emergency service. In normal baptisms, the women who had assisted the mother in the birth often carried the baby to church, where godparents vowed their support. Godparents were often close friends or relatives, but parents might also choose prominent villagers or even the local lord in the hope that he might later look favorably on the child and provide for him or her in some way.

Within Judaism, a boy was circumcised by a religious official and given his name in a ceremony in his eighth day of life. This *brit milah*, or "covenant of circumcision," was viewed as a reminder of the covenant between God and Abraham described in Hebrew Scripture. Muslims also circumcised boys in a special ritual, though the timing varied from a few days after birth to adolescence.

Death and the Afterlife

Death was similarly marked by religious ceremonies, and among Europeans of all faiths, death did not sever family obligations and connections. Christians called for a priest to perform the sacrament of extreme unction when they thought the hour of death was near. The priest brought holy water, holy oil, a crucifix, and a censer with incense, all objects regarded as having power over death and the sin related to it.

Once the person had died, the body was washed and dressed in special clothing— or a sack of plain cloth—and buried within a day or two. Family and friends joined in a funeral procession, marked by the ringing of church bells; sometimes extra women were hired so that the mourning and wailing were especially loud and intense, a sign of the family's devotion. The wealthy were sometimes buried inside the church—in the walls, under the floor, or under the building itself in a crypt—but most people were buried in the churchyard or a cemetery close by. At the graveside, the priest asked for God's grace for the soul of the deceased and also asked that soul to "rest in peace." This final request was made not only for the benefit of the dead, but also for that of the living. The souls of the dead were widely believed to return to earth: mothers who had died in childbirth might come back seeking to take their children with them; executed criminals might return to gain revenge on those who had brought them to justice (to prevent that return, they were buried at crossroads, permanently under the sign of the cross, or under the gallows itself); ordinary people came seeking help from surviving family members in achieving their final salvation. Priests were hired to say memorial masses on anniversaries of family deaths, especially one week, one month, and one year afterward.

During the High Middle Ages, learned theologians increasingly emphasized the idea of purgatory, the place where souls on their way to Heaven went after death to make amends for their earthly sins. Souls in purgatory did not wander the earth, but they could still benefit from earthly activities; memorial masses, prayers, and donations made in their names could shorten their time in purgatory. So could indulgences (see Chapter 9), those papal grants that relieved a person from earthly penance. Indulgences were initially granted for performing meritorious acts, such as going on a pilgrimage or crusade, but later on they could be obtained by paying a small fee. (See "Primary Source: The Pilgrim's Guide to Santiago de Compostela," page 306.) With this development, their spiritual benefits became transferable, so indulgences could be purchased to shorten the stay in purgatory of one's deceased relatives, as well as to lessen one's own penance or time in purgatory.

The living also had obligations to the dead among Muslims and Jews. In both groups, deceased people were buried quickly, and special prayers were said by mourners and family members. Muslims fasted on behalf of the dead and maintained a brief period of official mourning. The Qur'an promises an eternal paradise with flowing rivers to "those who believe and do good deeds" (Qur'an, 4:57) and a Hell of eternal torment to those who do not.

Jews observed specified periods of mourning during which the normal activities of daily life were curtailed. Every day for eleven months after a death and every year after that on the anniversary of the death, a son of the deceased was to recite Kaddish, a special prayer of praise and glorification of God. Judaism emphasized life on earth more than an afterlife, so beliefs about what happens to the soul after death were more varied; the very righteous might go directly to a place of spiritual reward, but most souls went first to a place of punishment and purification generally referred to as *Gehinnom*. After a period that did not exceed twelve months, the soul ascended to the world to come. Those who were completely wicked during their lifetimes might simply go out of existence or continue in an eternal state of remorse.

Towns and Economic Revival

What led to Europe's economic growth and reurbanization?

Most people continued to live in villages in the High Middle Ages, but the rise of towns and the growth of a new business and commercial class was a central part of Europe's recovery after the disorders of the tenth century. The growth of towns was made possible by some of the changes already described: a rise in population; increased agricultural output, which provided an adequate food supply for town dwellers; and a degree of peace and political stability, which allowed merchants to transport and sell goods. As towns gained legal and political rights, merchant and craft guilds grew more powerful, and towns became centers of production as well as commerce.

The Rise of Towns

Medieval towns began in many different ways. Some were fortifications erected as a response to ninth-century invasions; the peasants from the surrounding countryside moved within the walls when their area was attacked. Other towns grew up around great cathedrals (see page 326) and monasteries whose schools drew students from distant areas. Many other towns grew from the sites of Roman army camps or cities, which had shrunk in the early Middle Ages but never entirely disappeared. Still others arose where a trade route crossed a river or a natural harbor allowed ships to moor easily.

ONLINE DOCUMENT ASSIGNMENT

Life in Medieval Towns

How did merchant and craft guilds shape life in medieval towns?
Examine primary texts and images that illuminate the role of guilds in medieval urban communities, and then complete a writing assignment based on the evidence and details from this chapter.

bedfordstmartins.com/mckaywestvalue

PRIMARY SOURCE   The Pilgrim's Guide to Santiago de Compostela

Making pilgrimages to holy shrines is a common practice in many religions. Medieval Christians of all social classes made pilgrimages, often to shrines understood to contain the body of a saint. The shrine of Santiago de Compostela (Saint James at Compostela) in the Kingdom of Galicia in the Iberian Peninsula, said to contain the bones of the biblical Saint James, was one of the most popular. In the twelfth century an unknown French author gathered many of the pilgrims' experiences and put these together in a sort of guidebook.

The church, however, was begun in the year 1116 of the Spanish era [1078 C.E.]. . . . From the time when it was begun up to the present day, this church is renewed by the light of the miracles of the blessed James. In it, indeed, health is given to the sick, sight restored to the blind, the tongue of the mute is loosened, hearing is given to the deaf, soundness of limb is granted to cripples, the possessed are delivered, and what is more, the prayers of the faithful are heard, their vows are accepted, the bonds of sin are broken, heaven is opened to those who knock, consolation is given to the grieving, and all the people of foreign nations, flocking from all parts of the world, come together here in crowds bearing with them gifts of praise to the Lord. . . .

    The land of Navarre . . . abounds in bread and wine, milk and cattle. . . . The Navarrese wear short black garments extending just down to the knee, like the Scots, and they wear sandals which they call *lavarcas* made of raw hide with the hair on and are bound around the foot with thongs, covering only the soles of the feet and leaving the upper foot bare. In truth, they wear black woollen hooded and fringed capes, reaching to their elbows, which they call *saias*. These people, in truth, are repulsively dressed, and they eat and drink repulsively. For in fact all those who dwell in the household of a Navarrese, servant as well as master, maid as well as

Regardless of their origins, medieval towns had a few common characteristics. Each town had a marketplace, and most had a mint for the coining of money. The town also had a court to settle disputes. In addition, medieval towns were enclosed by walls. The terms *burgher* (BUHR-guhr) and *bourgeois* derive from the Old English and Old German words *burg*, *burgh*, *borg*, and *borough* for "a walled or fortified place." Thus a burgher or bourgeois originally was a person who lived or worked inside the walls. Townspeople supported themselves primarily by exchanging goods and services with one another, becoming artisans, shopkeepers, and merchants. They bought their food from the surrounding countryside, and purchased goods from far away brought by traveling merchants.

    No matter where people congregated, they settled on someone's land and had to secure permission to live there from the king, count, abbot, or bishop. Aristocratic nobles and churchmen were sometimes hostile to the towns set up on their land, but they soon realized that these could be a source of profits and benefits.

    The growing towns of medieval Europe slowly gained legal and political rights, including the rights to hold municipal courts, select the mayor and other municipal officials, and tax residents and visitors. Lords were often reluctant to grant towns self-

mistress, are accustomed to eat all their food mixed together from one pot, not with spoons but with their own hands, and they drink with one cup. If you saw them eat you would think them dogs or pigs. If you heard them speak, you would be reminded of the barking of dogs. For their speech is utterly barbarous. . . .

Then comes Galicia . . . this is wooded and has rivers and is well-provided with meadows and excellent orchards, with equally good fruits and very clear springs; there are few cities, towns or cornfields. It is short of wheaten bread and wine, bountiful in rye bread and cider, well-stocked with cattle and horses, milk and honey, ocean fish both gigantic and small, and wealthy in gold, silver, fabrics, and furs of forest animals and other riches, as well as Saracen [Muslim] treasures. The Galicians, in truth, more than all the other uncultivated Spanish peoples, are those who most closely resemble our French race by their manners, but they are alleged to be irascible and very litigious.

EVALUATE THE EVIDENCE

1. How would you evaluate the author's opinion of the people of Navarre? Of Galicia? How does he compare these people to his own countrymen, the French?

2. Pilgrimages were in many ways the precursors of modern tourism. What similarities do you see between this guide and those for today's travelers?

Source: *The Pilgrim's Guide to Santiago de Compostela*, critical edition and annotated translation by Paula Gerson, Jeanne Krochalis, Annie Shaver-Crandell, and Alison Stones. Copyright © 1997. Reprinted by permission of the authors.

government, fearing loss of authority and revenue if they gave the residents full independence. When burghers bargained for a town's political independence, however, they offered sizable amounts of ready cash and sometimes promised payments for years to come. Consequently, lords ultimately agreed to self-government.

In addition to working for the independence of the towns, townspeople tried to acquire liberties for themselves. In the Middle Ages the word *liberties* meant special privileges. The most important privilege a medieval townsperson could gain was personal freedom. It gradually developed that an individual who fled his or her manor and lived in a town for a year and a day was free of servile obligations and status. Thus the growth of towns contributed to a slow decline of serfdom in western Europe, although this took centuries.

Towns developed throughout much of Europe, but the concentration of the textile industry led to the growth of many towns in the Low Countries (present-day Holland, Belgium, and French Flanders): Ghent with about 56,000 people, Bruges (broozh) with 27,000, and Tournai and Brussels with perhaps 20,000 each. In 1300 Paris was the largest city in western Christian Europe, with a population of about 200,000, and

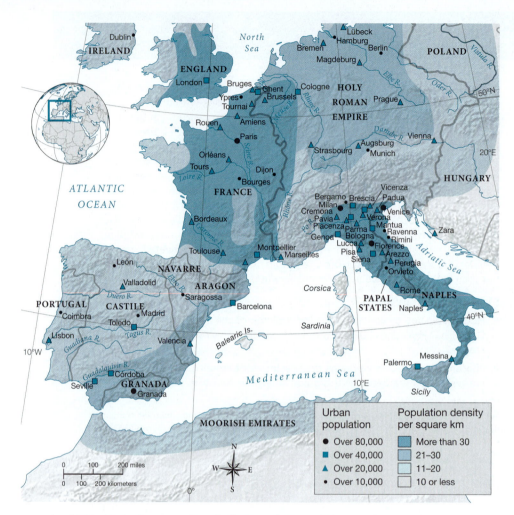

MAP 10.1   European Population Density, ca. 1300
The development of towns and the reinvigoration of trade were directly related in medieval Europe.

Venice, Florence, and Milan each had about 100,000 people (Map 10.1). Constantinople was larger still, with perhaps 300,000 people. Córdoba, the capital of Muslim Spain, may have been the largest city in the world, with a population that might have been nearly half a million, although this declined steeply when the city was conquered by Christian forces in 1236 and many people fled southward, swelling the population of Granada.

Merchant and Craft Guilds

The merchants, who were influential in winning towns' independence from feudal lords, also used their power and wealth to control life within the city walls. The merchants of a town joined together to form a **merchant guild** that prohibited nonmembers from trading in the town. Guild members often made up the earliest town government, serving as mayors and members of the city council, which meant that a town's economic policies were determined by its merchants' self-interest. By the late eleventh century, especially in the towns of the Low Countries and northern Italy, the leaders of the merchant guilds were rich and politically powerful.

While most towns were initially established as trading centers, they quickly became centers of production as well. Peasants looking for better opportunities moved to towns — either with their lord's approval or without it — providing both workers and mouths to feed. Some townspeople began to specialize in certain types of food and clothing production: they bought cloth and sewed it into clothing, or purchased and butchered cattle, selling the meat to others who made small meat pies and selling the leather to those who made shoes or bags. Over time some cities specialized in certain items, becoming known for their fine fabrics, their reliable arms and armor, or their elegant gold and silver work.

Like merchants, producers recognized that organizing would bring benefits, and beginning in the twelfth century in many cities they formed **craft guilds** that regulated most aspects of production. Guilds set quality standards for their particular product and regulated the size of workshops and the conduct of members. In most cities individual guilds, such as those of shoemakers or blacksmiths, achieved a monopoly in the production of one particular product, forbidding nonmembers to work. The craft guild then chose some of its members to act as inspectors and set up a court to hear disputes between members, though the city court remained the final arbiter.

Each guild set the pattern by which members were trained and the length of the training period. A boy who wanted to become a weaver, for instance, or whose parents wanted him to, spent four to seven years as an apprentice, often bound by a contract such as the following from thirteenth-century Marseilles in southern France:

> April the ninth. I, Peter Borre, in good faith and without guile, place with you, Peter Feissac, weaver, my son Stephen, for the purpose of learning the trade and craft of weaving, to live at your house, and to do work for you from the feast of Easter next for four continuous years, promising you by this agreement to take care that my son does the said work, and that he will be faithful and trustworthy in all that he does, and that he will neither steal nor take anything away from you, nor flee nor depart from you for any reason, until he had completed his apprenticeship.[5]

When the apprenticeship was finished, a young artisan spent several years as a journeyman, working in the shop of a master artisan. He then could make his "masterpiece" — in the case of weavers, a long piece of cloth. If the other masters judged the cloth acceptable, and if they thought the market in their town was large enough to support another weaver, the journeyman could then become a master and start a shop. If the guild decided there were already enough masters, he would need to leave that town and try elsewhere. Many guilds required masters to be married, as they recognized the vital role of the master's wife. She assisted in running the shop, often selling the goods her husband had produced. Their children, both male and female, also worked alongside the apprentices and journeymen. The sons were sometimes formally apprenticed, but the daughters were generally not apprenticed, because many guilds limited formal membership to males. Most guilds allowed a master's widow to continue operating a shop for a set period of time after her husband's death, for they recognized that she had the necessary skills and experience. Such widows paid all guild dues, but they were not considered full members and could not vote or hold office in the guild. In a handful of cities there were a few all-female guilds, especially in spinning gold thread or weaving silk ribbons for luxury clothing, trades in which girls were formally apprenticed in the same way boys were.

Both craft and merchant guilds were not only economic organizations, but also systems of social support. They took care of elderly masters who could no longer work, and they often supported masters' widows and orphans. They maintained an altar at a city church and provided for the funerals of members and baptisms of their children. Guild members marched together in city parades and reinforced their feelings of solidarity with one another by special ceremonies and distinctive dress. Merchant guilds in some parts of Europe, such as the German cities of Hamburg, Lübeck, and Bremen, had special buildings for celebrations and ceremonies.

The Revival of Long-Distance Trade

The growth of towns went hand in hand with a revival of trade as artisans and craftsmen manufactured goods for both local and foreign consumption. Most trade centered in towns and was controlled by professional traders. Long-distance trade was risky and required large investments of capital. Robbers and thieves roamed virtually all of the overland trade routes. Pirates infested the sea-lanes, and shipwrecks were common. Since the risks were so great, merchants preferred to share them. A group of people would thus pool their capital to finance an expedition to a distant place. When the ship or caravan returned and the cargo was sold, these investors would share the profits. If disaster struck the caravan, an investor's loss was limited to the amount of that individual's investment.

In the late eleventh century the Italian cities, especially Venice, led the West in trade in general and completely dominated trade with the East. Venetian ships carried salt from the city's own lagoon, pepper and other spices from India and North Africa, silks and carpets from Central Asia, and slaves from many places. In northern Europe, the towns of Bruges, Ghent, and Ypres (EE-pruh) in Flanders built a vast cloth industry, becoming leaders in both the manufacture and trade of textiles.

Two circumstances help explain the lead Venice and these Flemish towns gained in long-distance trade. Both areas enjoyed a high degree of peace and political stability. Geographical factors were equally, if not more, important. Venice, at the northwestern end of the Adriatic Sea, had easy access to transalpine land routes as well as the Adriatic and Mediterranean sea-lanes connected to the markets of North Africa, Byzantium, and Russia. Merchants from Venice and Genoa also seized the commercial opportunities offered by the great fairs (large periodic gatherings that attracted buyers, sellers, and goods) held in the county of Champagne in northern France. Champagne was on the main north-south trade routes, and the counts who ruled the area provided security and enforced contracts. Directly north of Champagne were the towns of Flanders, which also offered unusual possibilities for merchants: just across the Channel from England, Flanders had easy access to English wool. Because the weather in England was colder than in most of Europe, English sheep grew longer and denser wool than sheep elsewhere. With this wool, clothmakers could produce high-quality cloth, which was the most important manufactured product handled by merchants and one of the few European products for which there was a market in the East.

From the late eleventh through the thirteenth centuries, Europe enjoyed a steadily expanding volume of international trade. Trade surged markedly with demand for sugar from the Mediterranean islands to replace honey; spices from Asia to season a bland diet; and fine wines from the Rhineland, Burgundy, and Bordeaux to make life more pleasant. Other consumer goods included luxury woolens from Flanders and Tuscany, furs from Ireland and Russia, brocades and tapestries from Flanders, and silks from Constantinople and even China. Nobles prized fancy household furnishings such as silver plate, as well as swords and armor for their battles. As the trade volume expanded, the use of cash became more widespread. Beginning in the 1160s the opening of new silver mines in Germany, Bohemia, northern Italy, northern France, and western England led to the minting and circulation of vast quantities of silver coins.

Increased trade also led to a higher standard of living. Contact with Eastern civilizations introduced Europeans to eating utensils, and table manners improved. Nobles learned to eat with forks and knives instead of tearing the meat from a roast with their hands. They began to use napkins instead of wiping their greasy fingers on their clothes or on the dogs lying under the table.

Business Procedures

The economic surge of the High Middle Ages led merchants to invent new business procedures. Beginning in Italy, merchants formalized their agreements with new types of contracts, including temporary contracts for land and sea trading ventures and permanent partnerships termed *compagnie* (kahm-pah-NYEE; literally "bread together," that is, sharing bread; the root of the word *company*). Many of these agreements were initially between brothers or other relatives and in-laws, but they quickly grew to include people who were not family members. In addition, they began to involve individuals—including a few women—who invested only their money, leaving the actual running of the business to the active partners. Commercial correspondence, unnecessary when one businessperson oversaw everything and made direct bargains with buyers and sellers, proliferated. Accounting and record keeping became more sophisticated, and credit facilitated business expansion.

The ventures of the German Hanseatic League illustrate these new business procedures. The **Hanseatic League** (often called simply the Hansa) was a mercantile association of towns. It originated in agreements between merchants for mutual security and exclusive trading rights, and it gradually developed into agreements among towns themselves, often sealed with a contract. The first of these contracts was between the towns of Lübeck and Hamburg in 1241, and during the next century perhaps two hundred cities from Holland to Poland joined the league. From the fourteenth to the sixteenth centuries, the Hanseatic League controlled the trade of northern Europe. In cities such as Bruges and London, Hansa merchants secured special trading concessions, exempting them from all tolls and allowing them to trade at local fairs. These merchants established foreign trading centers, called "factories" because the commercial agents in them were called "factors."

The dramatic increase in trade ran into two serious difficulties in medieval Europe. One was the problem of minting money. Despite investment in mining operations to increase the production of metals, the amount of gold, silver, and copper available for coins was not adequate for the increased flow of commerce. Merchants developed paper

Lübeck   The dominant city in the Hanseatic League, Lübeck is portrayed in this woodcut as densely packed within its walls, with church steeples and the city hall dominating the skyline, and boats carrying goods and people moving swiftly along the river. Even in this stylized scene, the artist captures the key features of the "Queen of the Hansa": crowded, proud, and centered on commerce. (Private Collection/The Stapleton Collection/The Bridgeman Art Library)

bills of exchange, in which coins or goods in one location were exchanged for a sealed letter (much like a modern deposit statement), which could be used in place of metal coinage elsewhere. This made the long, slow, and very dangerous shipment of coins unnecessary, and facilitated the expansion of credit and commerce. By about 1300 the bill of exchange was the normal method of making commercial payments among the cities of western Europe, and it proved to be a decisive factor in their later economic development.

The second problem was a moral and theological one. Church doctrine frowned on lending money at interest, termed *usury* (YOO-zhuh-ree). This doctrine was developed in the early Middle Ages when loans were mainly for consumption, for instance, to tide a farmer over until the next harvest. Theologians reasoned that it was wrong for a Christian to take advantage of the bad luck or need of another Christian. This restriction on Christians charging interest is one reason why Jews were frequently the money-lenders in early medieval society; it was one of the few occupations not forbidden them. As money-lending became more important to commercial ventures, the church relaxed its position. It declared that some interest was legitimate as a payment for the risk the investor was taking, and that only interest above a certain level would be considered usury. (Even today, governments generally set limits on the rate businesses may charge for loaning money.) The church itself then got into the money-lending business, opening pawnshops in cities.

The stigma attached to lending money was in many ways attached to all the activities of a merchant. Medieval people were uneasy about a person making a profit merely from the investment of money rather than labor, skill, and time. Merchants themselves shared these ideas to some degree, so they gave generous donations to the church and to charities, and took pains not to flaunt their wealth through flashy dress and homes.

The Commercial Revolution

Changes in business procedures, combined with the growth in trade, led to a transformation of the European economy often called the **commercial revolution** by historians, who see it as the beginning of the modern capitalist economy. In using this label, historians point not only to increases in the sheer volume of trade and in the complexity and sophistication of business procedures, but also to the development of a new "capitalist spirit" in which making a profit is regarded as a good thing in itself, regardless of the uses to which that profit is put. (See "Individuals in Society: Francesco Datini," page 314.) Because capitalism in the Middle Ages primarily involved trade rather than production, it is referred to as mercantile capitalism.

Part of this capitalist spirit was a new attitude toward time. Country people needed only approximate times — dawn, noon, sunset — for their work. Monasteries needed more precise times to call monks together for the recitation of the Divine Office. In the early Middle Ages monks used a combination of hourglasses, sundials, and water-clocks to determine the time, and then rang bells by hand. In about 1280 new types of mechanical mechanisms seem to have been devised in which weights replaced falling water and bells were rung automatically. Records begin to use the word *clock* (from the Latin word for bell) for these machines, which sometimes indicated the movement of astronomical bodies as well as the hours. The merchants who ran city councils quickly saw clocks as useful, as these devices allowed the opening and closing of markets and shops to be set to certain hours. Through regulations that specified times and bells that marked the day, city people began to develop a mentality that conceived of the universe in quantitative terms. Clocks were also symbols of a city's prosperity. Beautiful and elaborate mechanical clocks, usually installed on the cathedral or town church, were in general use in Italy by the 1320s, in Germany by the 1330s, in England by the 1370s, and in France by the 1380s.

The commercial revolution created a great deal of new wealth, which did not escape the attention of kings and other rulers. Wealth could be taxed, and through taxation kings could create strong and centralized states. The commercial revolution also provided the opportunity for thousands of serfs to improve their social position. The slow but steady transformation of European society from almost completely rural and isolated to urban and relatively more sophisticated constituted the greatest effect of the commercial revolution that began in the eleventh century.

Even so, merchants and business people did not run medieval communities other than in central and northern Italy and in the county of Flanders. Kings and nobles maintained ultimate control over most European cities, such as Paris, London, and Córdoba. Most towns remained small, and urban residents never amounted to more than 10 percent of the total European population. The commercial changes of the eleventh through thirteenth centuries did, however, lay the economic foundations for the development of urban life and culture.

Urban Life

What was life like in medieval cities?

In their backgrounds and abilities, townspeople represented diversity and change. Their occupations and their preoccupations were different from those of nobles and peasants. Cities were crowded and polluted, though people flocked into them because they offered the possibility of economic advancement, social mobility, and improvement in legal status. Some urban residents grew spectacularly rich, but the numbers of poor swelled as well.

INDIVIDUALS IN SOCIETY • Francesco Datini

In 1348, when he was a young teenager, Francesco Datini (1335–1410) lost his father, his mother, a brother, and a sister to the Black Death epidemic that swept through Europe (see Chapter 11). Leaving his hometown of Prato in northern Italy, he apprenticed himself to merchants in nearby Florence for several years to learn accounting and other business skills. At fifteen, he moved to Avignon (ah-veen-YOHN) in southern France. The popes were at this point living in Avignon instead of Rome, and the city offered many opportunities for an energetic and enterprising young man. Datini first became involved in the weapons trade, which offered steady profits, and then became a merchant of spices, wool and silk cloth, and jewels. He was very successful, and when he was thirty-one he married the young daughter of another merchant in an elaborate wedding that was the talk of Avignon.

In 1378 the papacy returned to Italy, and Datini soon followed, setting up trading companies in Prato, Pisa, and Florence. He focused on cloth and leather and sought to control the trade in products used for the preparation of these materials as well, especially the rare dyes that created the brilliant colors favored by wealthy noblemen and townspeople. He eventually had offices all over Europe and became one of the richest men of his day, opening a mercantile bank and a company that produced cloth.

Datini was more successful than most businessmen, but what makes him particularly stand out was his record keeping. He kept careful account books and ledgers, all of them headed by the phrase "in the name of God and profit." He wrote to the managers of each of his offices every week, providing them with careful advice and blunt criticism: "You cannot see a crow in a bowl of milk." Taking on the son of a friend as an employee, he wrote to the young man: "Do your duty well, and you will acquire honor and profit, and you can count on me as if I were your own father. But if you do not, then do not count on me; it will be as if I had never known you."

When Datini was away from home, which was often, he wrote to his wife every day, and she sometimes responded in ways that were less deferential than we might

City Life

Walls surrounded almost all medieval towns and cities, and constant repair of these walls was usually the town's greatest expense. Gates pierced the walls, and visitors waited at the gates to gain entrance to the town. Most streets in a medieval town were marketplaces as much as passages for transit. Poor people selling soap, candles, wooden dishes, and similar cheap products stood next to farmers from the surrounding countryside selling eggs, chickens, or vegetables; people selling firewood or mushrooms they had gathered; and pawnbrokers selling used clothing and household goods. Because there was no way to preserve food easily, people—usually female family members or servants—had to shop every day, and the market was where they met their neighbors, exchanged information, and talked over recent events, as well as purchased needed supplies.

Some selling took place not in the open air but in the craftsman's home. A window or door in the home opened onto the street and displayed the finished products made

expect of a woman who was many years younger. "I think it is not necessary," she wrote at one point, "to send me a message every Wednesday to say that you will be here on Sunday, for it seems to me that on every Friday you change your mind."

Datini's obsessive record keeping lasted beyond his death, for someone saved all of his records—hundreds of ledgers and contracts, eleven thousand business letters, and over a hundred thousand personal letters—in sacks in his opulent house in Prato, where they were found in the nineteenth century. They provide a detailed picture of medieval business practices and also reveal much about Datini as a person. Ambitious, calculating, luxury loving, and a workaholic, Datini seems similar to a modern CEO. Like many of today's self-made billionaires, at the end of his life Datini began to think a bit more about God and less about profit. In his will, he set up a foundation for the poor in Prato and a home for orphans in Florence, both of which are still in operation. In 1967 scholars established an institute for economic history in Prato, naming it in Datini's honor; the institute now manages the collection of Datini's documents and gathers other relevant materials in its archives.

QUESTIONS FOR ANALYSIS

1. How would you evaluate Datini's motto, "In the name of God and profit"? Is it an honest statement of his aims, a hypocritical justification of greed, a blend of both, or something else?

2. Changes in business procedures in the Middle Ages have been described as a "commercial revolution." Do Datini's business ventures support this assessment? How?

Source: Iris Origo, *The Merchant of Prato: Francesco di Marco Datini, 1335–1410* (New York: Alfred A. Knopf, Inc., 1957).

within to attract passersby. The family lived above the business on the second or third floor. As the business and the family expanded, additional stories were added. Second and third stories jutted out over the ground floor and thus over the street. Since the streets were narrow to begin with, houses lacked fresh air and light. Initially, houses were made of wood and thatched with straw. Fire was a constant danger; because houses were built so close to one another, fires spread rapidly. Municipal governments consequently urged construction in stone or brick.

Most medieval cities developed with little planning. As the population increased, space became increasingly limited. Air and water pollution presented serious problems. Horses and oxen, the chief means of transportation and power, dropped tons of dung on the streets every year. It was universal practice in the early towns to dump household waste, both animal and human, into the road in front of one's house. The stench must have been abominable. In 1298 the citizens of the town of Boutham in Yorkshire, England, received the following order:

> To the bailiffs of the abbot of St. Mary's York, at Boutham. Whereas it is sufficiently evident that the pavement of the said town of Boutham is so very greatly broken up . . . , and in addition the air is so corrupted and infected by the pigsties situated in the king's highways and in the lanes of that town and by the swine feeding and frequently wandering about . . . and by dung and dunghills and many other foul things placed in the streets and lanes, that great repugnance overtakes the king's ministers staying in that town and also others there dwelling and passing through . . . : the king, being unwilling longer to tolerate such great and unbearable defects there, orders the bailiffs to cause the pavement to be suitably repaired . . . before All Saints next, and to cause the pigsties, aforesaid streets and lanes to be cleansed from all dung . . . and to cause them to be kept thus cleansed hereafter.[6]

People of all sorts, from beggars to wealthy merchants, regularly rubbed shoulders in the narrow streets and alleys of crowded medieval cities. This interaction did not mean that people were unaware of social differences, however, for clothing clearly indicated social standing and sometimes occupation. Friars wore black, white, or gray woolen clothing that marked them as members of a particular religious order, while priests and bishops wore layers of specialized clothing, especially when they were officiating at religious services. Military men and servants who lived in noble households dressed in the nobles' distinctive colors known as livery (LIH-vuh-ree). Wealthier urban residents wore bright colors, imported silk or fine woolen fabrics, and fancy headgear, while poorer ones wore darker clothing made of rough linen or linen and wool blends. In university towns, students wore clothing and headgear that marked their status. University graduates—lawyers, physicians, and professors—often wore dark robes, trimmed with fur if they could afford it.

In the later Middle Ages many cities attempted to make clothing distinctions a matter of law as well as of habit. City councils passed **sumptuary laws** that regulated the value of clothing and jewelry that people of different social groups could wear; only members of high social groups could wear velvet, satin, pearls, or fur, for example, or wear clothing embroidered with gold thread or dyed in colors that were especially expensive to produce, such as the purple dye that came from mollusk shells. Along with enforcing social differences, sumptuary laws also attempted to impose moral standards by prohibiting plunging necklines on women or doublets (fitted buttoned jackets) that were too short on men. Their limits on imported fabrics or other materials also served to protect local industries.

Some of these laws called for marking certain individuals as members of groups not fully acceptable in urban society. Many cities ordered prostitutes to wear red or yellow bands on their clothes that were supposed to represent the flames of Hell, and the Fourth Lateran Council required Jews and Muslims to dress in ways that distinguished them from their Christian neighbors. (Many Jewish communities also developed their own sumptuary laws prohibiting extravagant or ostentatious dress.) In some cities, sumptuary laws were expanded to include restrictions on expenditures for parties and family celebrations, again set by social class. Sumptuary laws were frequently broken and were difficult to enforce, but they provide evidence of the many material goods available to urban dwellers as well as the concern of city leaders about the social mobility and extravagance they saw all around them.

Servants and the Poor

Many urban houses were larger than the tiny village dwellings, so families took in domestic servants. A less wealthy household employed one woman who assisted in all aspects of running the household; a wealthier one employed a large staff of male and female servants with specific duties. When there was only one servant, she generally lived and ate with the family, for there was rarely enough space for separate quarters. Even in wealthier households that had many rooms, servants were rarely separated from their employers the way they would be in the nineteenth century, but instead lived on intimate terms with them. In Italian cities, household servants included slaves, usually young women brought in from areas outside of Western Christianity, such as the Balkans.

Along with live-in servants, many households hired outside workers to do specific tasks. These workers laundered clothing and household linens, cared for children or invalids, repaired houses and walls, and carried messages or packages around the city or the surrounding countryside. Urban workers had to buy all their food, so they felt any increase in the price of ale or bread immediately. Their wages were generally low, and children from such families sought work at very young ages.

Illegal activities offered another way for people to support themselves. They stole merchandise from houses, wagons, and storage facilities, fencing it to pawnbrokers or taking it to the next town to sell. They stole goods or money directly from people, cutting the strings of their bags or purses. They sold sex for money, standing on street corners or moving into houses that by the fifteenth century became official brothels. They made and sold mixtures of herbs and drugs claimed to heal all sorts of ailments, perhaps combining this with a puppet show, trained animals, magic tricks, or music to draw customers. Or they did all these things and also worked as laundresses, day laborers, porters, peddlers, or street vendors when they could. Cities also drew in orphans, blind people, and the elderly, who resorted to begging for food and money.

Popular Entertainment

Games and sports were common forms of entertainment and relaxation. There were wrestling matches and games akin to modern football, rugby, stickball, and soccer in which balls were kicked, hit, and thrown. People played card and board games of all types. They played with dice carved from stone or bone, or with the knucklebones of animals or wood carved in knucklebone shapes, somewhat like modern jacks. They trained dogs to fight each other or put them in an enclosure to fight a captured bear. In Spain, Muslim knights confronted and killed bulls from horseback as part of religious feast days, developing a highly ritualized ceremony that would later be further adapted by Spain's Christians. All these sports and games were occasions for wagering and gambling, which preachers sometimes condemned (especially when the games were attached to a holiday or saint's day celebration) but had little power to control.

Religious and family celebrations also meant dancing, which the church also had little success banning or regulating. Men and women danced in lines toward a specific object, such as a tree or a maypole, or in circles, groups, or pairs with specific step patterns. They were accompanied by a variety of instruments: reed pipes such as the chalumeau (an ancestor of the clarinet) and shawm (predecessor to the oboe); woodwinds such as flutes, panpipes, and recorders; stringed instruments including dulcimers, harps,

Young Men Playing Stickball   With their tunics hitched up in their belts so that they could move around more easily, young men play a game involving hitting a ball with a stick. Games involving bats and balls were popular, for the equipment needed was made from simple, inexpensive materials.

lyres, lutes, zithers, and mandolins; brass instruments such as horns and trumpets; and percussion instruments like drums and tambourines. Many of these instruments were simple and were made by their players. Musicians playing string or percussion instruments often sang as well, and people sang without instrumental accompaniment on festive occasions or while working.

Medieval Universities

How did universities serve the needs of medieval society?

Just as the first strong secular states emerged in the thirteenth century, so did the first universities. This was no coincidence. The new bureaucratic states and the church needed educated administrators, and universities were a response to this need.

Origins

In the early Middle Ages, monasteries and cathedral schools had offered most of the available formal instruction. Monastery schools were small, but cathedral schools, run by the bishop and his clergy in bustling cities, gradually grew larger. In the eleventh century in Italian cities like Bologna (boh-LOH-nyuh), wealthy businessmen established municipal schools. In the course of the twelfth century, cathedral schools in France and municipal schools in Italy developed into educational institutions that attracted students from a wide area (Map 10.2). These schools were often called *universitas magistrorum*

MAP 10.2   Intellectual Centers of Medieval Europe
Universities provided more sophisticated instruction than did monastery and cathedral schools, but all these institutions served to educate males who had the money to attend.

et scholarium (universal society of teachers and students), the origin of the English word *university*. The first European universities appeared in Italy in Bologna, where the specialty was law, and Salerno, where the specialty was medicine.

Legal and Medical Training

The growth of the University of Bologna coincided with a revival of interest in Roman law during the investiture controversy. The study of Roman law as embodied in the Justinian *Codex* (see Chapter 7) had never completely died out in the West, but in the late eleventh century a complete manuscript of the *Codex* was discovered in a library in Pisa. This discovery led scholars in nearby Bologna, beginning with Irnerius (ehr-NEH-ree-uhs) (ca. 1055–ca. 1130), to study and teach Roman law intently.

Irnerius and other teachers at Bologna taught law as an organic whole related to the society it regulated, an all-inclusive system based on logical principles that could be applied to difficult practical situations. Thus, as social and economic structures changed, law would change with them. Jurists educated at Bologna—and later at other universities—were hired by rulers and city councils to systematize their law codes and write legal treatises. In the 1260s the English jurist Henry Bracton wrote a comprehensive treatise bringing together the laws and customs of England, and King Alfonso X of Castile had scholars write the *Siete Partidas* (Book in Seven Parts), a detailed plan for administering his whole kingdom according to Roman legal principles.

Canon law (see Chapter 9) was also shaped by the reinvigoration of Roman law, and canon lawyers in ever-greater numbers were hired by church officials or became prominent church officials themselves. In about 1140 the Benedictine monk Gratian put together a collection of nearly 3,800 texts covering all areas of canon law. His collection, known as the *Decretum*, became the standard text on which teachers of canon law lectured and commented.

Jewish scholars also produced elaborate commentaries on law and religious tradition. Medieval universities were closed to Jews, but in some cities in the eleventh century special rabbinic academies opened that concentrated on the study of the Talmud, a compilation of legal arguments, proverbs, sayings, and folklore that had been produced in the fifth century in Babylon (present-day Iraq). Men seeking to become rabbis—highly respected figures within the Jewish community, with authority over economic and social as well as religious matters—spent long periods of time studying the Talmud, which served as the basis for their decisions affecting all areas of life.

Healthy Living   In this illustration from a very popular fourteenth-century Latin handbook on maintaining health and well-being, women with their sleeves rolled up prepare cloth for medical uses; the woman on the left is trimming small threads off with a one-bladed shear, and the woman on the right is boiling the cloth to bleach it. The men in the background eat a meal and drink wine. The text of this handbook was a translation of an Arabic medical treatise, made in the Kingdom of Sicily, the site of much cultural borrowing. (Austrian National Library, Vienna/The Bridgeman Art Library)

Professional medical training began at Salerno. Individuals there, such as Constantine the African (1020?–1087)—who was a convert from Islam and later a Benedictine monk—began to translate medical works out of Arabic. These translations included writings by the ancient Greek physicians and Muslim medical writers, a blending of knowledge that later occurred on the nearby island of Sicily as well. Students of medicine poured into the city.

Medical studies at Salerno were based on classical ideas, particularly those of Hippocrates and Aristotle (see Chapter 3). For the ancient Greeks, ideas about the human body were very closely linked to philosophy and to ideas about the natural world in general. Prime among these was the notion of the four bodily humors—blood, phlegm, black bile, and yellow bile—fluids in the body that influenced bodily health. Each individual was thought to have a characteristic temperament or complexion determined by the balance of these humors, just as today we might describe a person as having a "positive outlook" or a "type-A" personality. Disease was generally regarded as an imbalance of humors, which could be diagnosed by taking a patient's pulse or examining his or her urine. Treatment was thus an attempt to bring the humors back into balance, which might be accomplished through diet or drugs—mixtures of herbal or mineral substances—or by vomiting, emptying the bowels, or bloodletting. The bodily humors were somewhat gender related—women were regarded as tending toward cold and wet humors and men toward hot and dry—so therapies were also gender distinctive. Men's greater heat, scholars taught, created other gender differences: heat caused men's hair to burn internally so that they went bald, and their shoulders and brains to become larger than those of women (because heat rises and causes things to expand).

These ideas spread throughout Europe from Salerno and became the basis of training for physicians at other universities. University training gave physicians high social status and allowed them to charge high fees. They were generally hired directly by patients as needed, though some had more permanent positions as members of the household staffs of especially wealthy nobles or rulers.

Theology and Philosophy

Law and medicine were important academic disciplines in the Middle Ages, but theology was "the queen of sciences" because it involved the study of God, who made all knowledge possible. Paris became the place to study theology. In the first decades of the twelfth century, students from across Europe crowded into the cathedral school of Notre Dame (NOH-truh DAHM) in Paris.

University professors (a term first used in the fourteenth century) were known as "schoolmen" or **Scholastics**. They developed a method of thinking, reasoning, and writing in which questions were raised and authorities cited on both sides of a question. The goal of this method was to arrive at definitive answers and to provide rational explanations for what was believed on faith.

The Scholastic approach rested on the recovery of classical philosophical texts. Ancient Greek and Arabic texts entered Europe in the early twelfth century by way of Islamic intellectual centers at Baghdad, Córdoba, and Toledo (see Chapter 8). The major contribution of Arabic culture to the new currents of Western thought rested in the stimulus Arabic philosophers and commentators gave to Europeans' reflections on ancient Greek texts and the ways these texts fit with Christian teachings. One of the young men drawn to Paris was Peter Abelard (1079–1142), the son of a minor Breton knight. Abelard was fascinated by logic, which he believed could be used to solve most problems. He was one of the first Scholastics, and commented, "By doubting we come to questioning, and by questioning we perceive the truth." Abelard was severely censured by a church council, but his cleverness, boldness, and imagination made him a highly popular figure among students.

Abelard's reputation for brilliance drew the attention of one of the cathedral canons, Fulbert, who hired Abelard to tutor his intelligent niece Heloise. The relationship between teacher and pupil passed beyond the intellectual. Heloise became pregnant, and Fulbert pressured the couple to marry. The couple agreed, but wanted the marriage kept secret for the sake of Abelard's career. Furious at Abelard, Fulbert hired men to castrate him. Abelard persuaded Heloise to enter a convent, and he became a monk. Their baby, baptized Astrolabe for a recent Muslim navigational invention, was given to Heloise's family for adoption. The two became leaders of their communities—Abelard an abbot and Heloise a prioress—but they never saw each other again, though they wrote letters, which have become examples of the new self-awareness of the period.

In the thirteenth century Scholastics devoted an enormous amount of time to collecting and organizing knowledge on all topics. Such a collection was published as a *summa* (SOO-muh), or reference book. There were *summae* on law, philosophy, vegetation, animal life, and theology. Saint Thomas Aquinas (1225–1274), a Dominican friar and professor at Paris, produced the most famous of these collections, the *Summa Theologica*, a summation of Christian ideas on a vast number of theological questions, including the nature of God and Christ, moral principles, and the role of the sacraments. In this, and many of his other writings, Aquinas used arguments that drew from ancient Greek philosophers, especially Aristotle, as well as earlier Christian writers. Aquinas was both a theologian and a philosopher: he wrote sermons, prayers, commentaries on books of the Bible, and argumentative works on aspects of Christian theology such as the nature of evil and the power of God, but also commentaries on several of Aristotle's works.

In these, he investigated the branch of philosophy called epistemology, which is concerned with how a person knows something. Aquinas stated that first one knows through sensory perception of the physical world—seeing, hearing, touching, and so on. He maintained that there can be nothing in the mind that is not first in the senses. The second way knowledge comes is through reason, through the mind exercising its natural abilities.

In all these works, Aquinas stressed the power of human reason to demonstrate many basic Christian principles, including the existence of God. To obtain true Christian understanding, he wrote, one needed both reason and faith. (See "Primary Source: Thomas Aquinas on Reason and Faith," page 324.) His ideas have been extremely influential in both philosophy and theology: in the former through the philosophical school known as Thomism, and in the latter especially through the Catholic Church, which has affirmed many times that they are foundational to Roman Catholic doctrine.

University Students

The influx of students eager for learning, together with dedicated and imaginative teachers, created the atmosphere in which universities grew. By the end of the fifteenth century there were at least eighty universities in Europe. Some universities also offered younger students training in what were termed the seven liberal arts — grammar, rhetoric, logic, mathematics, geometry, music, and astronomy — that could serve as a foundation for more specialized study in all areas.

University students were generally considered to be lower-level members of the clergy — this was termed being in "minor orders" — so any students accused of legal infractions were tried in church courts, rather than in city courts. This clerical status, along with widely held ideas about women's lesser intellectual capabilities, meant that university education was restricted to men. Even more than feudal armies — which were often accompanied by women who did laundry, found provisions, cooked meals, and engaged in sex for money — universities were all-male communities. (Most European universities did not admit women until after World War I.)

Though university classes were not especially expensive, the many years that a university education required meant that the sons of peasants or artisans could rarely attend, unless they could find wealthy patrons who would pay their expenses. Most students were the sons of urban merchants or lower-level nobles, especially the younger sons who would not inherit family lands. University degrees were initially designed as licenses to teach at the university, but most students staffed the expanding diocesan, royal, and papal administrations as lawyers and officials.

Students did not spend all their time preparing for their degrees. Much information about medieval students concerns what we might call "extracurricular" activities: university regulations forbidding them to throw rocks at professors; sermons about breaking and entering, raping local women, attacking town residents, and disturbing church services; and court records discussing their drunken brawls, riots, and fights and duels. Students also delayed finishing their studies because life as a student could be pleasant, without the responsibilities that came with becoming fully adult. Student life was described by students in poems, usually anonymous, that celebrated the joys of Venus (the goddess of love) and other gods:

> When we are in the tavern,
> we do not think how we will go to dust,
> but we hurry to gamble,
> which always makes us sweat.
> . . .
> Here no-one fears death,
> but they throw the dice in the name of Bacchus.
> . . .
> To the Pope as to the king
> they all drink without restraint.[7]

Literature and Architecture

How did literature and architecture express medieval values?

The High Middle Ages saw the creation of new types of literature, architecture, and music. Technological advances in such areas as papermaking and stone masonry made some of these innovations possible, as did the growing wealth and sophistication of patrons. Artists and artisans flourished in the more secure environment of the High Middle Ages, producing works that celebrated the glories of love, war, and God.

PRIMARY SOURCE   Thomas Aquinas on Reason and Faith

In many of his writings, Thomas Aquinas discussed the role of human reason, a central issue for all Scholastic philosophers. In these brief selections from two of his long works, he examines the development of reason through time and its natural distribution among people and explores the relationship between reason and faith.

From *Summa Theologica*

Human reason naturally moves step by step from the imperfect to the perfect. Whence we see in the speculative sciences that those who first philosophized provided imperfect results which were afterwards made more perfect by their successors. Similarly in practical matters, those who first tried to find something useful for the human community, being unable to understand everything, introduced things in many ways deficient; but their successors replaced these with ones far less faulty. . . .

It may be said that a good proportionate to the ordinary state of nature is found in many and is lacking in few, but that a good that exceeds that ordinary state is discovered only in very few. It is evident that there are many who have knowledge sufficient for governing their own lives, and few, who are called fools or idiots, who lack this knowledge, but there are also very few who are able to attain a profound knowledge of intelligible things [that is, of philosophy]. Since, therefore, eternal blessedness, which consists in the vision of God, exceeds the ordinary state of nature (especially because grace has been weakened by the corruption of original sin), there are very few indeed who are saved.

Commentary on the book *On the Trinity*

[Philosophy] first proves things one needs to know in order to understand the faith . . . things proved by natural reason concerning God, namely, that He exists,

Vernacular Literature and Drama

Latin was the language used in university education, scholarly writing, and works of literature. By the High Middle Ages, however, no one spoke Latin as his or her original mother tongue. The barbarian invasions, the mixture of peoples, and the usual changes in language that occur over time had resulted in a variety of local dialects that blended words and linguistic forms in various ways. As kings increased the size of their holdings, they often ruled people who spoke many different dialects.

In the High Middle Ages, some authors departed from tradition and began to write in their local dialect, that is, in the everyday language of their region, which linguistic historians call the vernacular. This new **vernacular literature** gradually transformed some local dialects into literary languages, such as French, German, Italian, and English, while other local dialects, such as Breton and Bavarian, remained (and remain to this day) means of oral communication.

Facilitating this vernacular writing was a technological advance. By the thirteenth century techniques of making paper from old linen cloth and rags began to spread from

that He is one, or similar things concerning Him or his creatures. Second, to make known things of the faith by means of analogy, just as Augustine in his book *On the Trinity* used many analogies taken from philosophy in order to explain the Trinity. . . .

The gifts of grace are added to nature so that they do not do away with it, but instead perfect it. Hence the light of faith freely infused into us does not destroy the light of natural knowledge [reason] implanted in us naturally. Although the . . . human mind cannot show us things made manifest by faith, it is nonetheless impossible that that which faith gives is contrary to that implanted in us by nature. Were that the case, one or the other would be false, and, since God gave us both, He would be the author of untruth, which is impossible. . . . Just as sacred doctrine is founded on the light of faith, so is philosophy founded on the light of natural reason, and hence it is impossible that philosophical things are contrary to the things of faith.

EVALUATE THE EVIDENCE

1. According to Aquinas, what possibilities does human reason offer? What limitations are there to reason? What is the relationship between reason and faith?

2. Medieval universities developed in growing cities, and many students were from middle-status merchant families. What aspects of Aquinas's ideas might have been attractive to young men from this newly prominent class?

Source: Quoted in J. H. Mundy, *Europe in the High Middle Ages, 1150–1300*, 3d ed. (Harlow, U.K.: Pearson-Longman, 2000), pp. 296–297, 305, 312, 325. Copyright © Pearson Education Limited, 2000. Used by permission of Pearson Education.

Spain, where they had been developed by the Arabs, providing a much cheaper material on which to write than parchment or vellum (see Chapter 8). People started to write down things that were more mundane and less serious—personal letters, lists, songs, recipes, rules, instructions—in their dialects, using spellings that were often personal and idiosyncratic. These writings included fables, legends, stories, and myths that had circulated orally for generations, adding to the growing body of written vernacular literature.

Stories and songs in the vernacular were composed and performed at the courts of nobles and rulers. In Germany and most of northern Europe, the audiences favored stories and songs recounting the great deeds of warrior heroes. These epics, known as *chansons de geste* (SHAN-suhn duh JEHST; songs of great deeds), celebrate violence, slaughter, revenge, and physical power. In southern Europe, especially in Provence in southern France, poets who called themselves **troubadours** (TROO-buh-dorz) wrote and sang lyric verses celebrating love, desire, beauty, and gallantry. Troubadours included a few women, called *trobairitz*, most of whose exact identities are not known.

The songs of the troubadours were widely imitated in Italy, England, and Germany, so they spurred the development of vernacular literature there as well. At the court of his patron, Marie of Champagne, Chrétien de Troyes (ca. 1135–ca. 1190) used the legends of the fifth-century British king Arthur (see Chapter 7) as the basis for innovative tales of battle and forbidden love. His most popular story is that of the noble Lancelot, whose love for Guinevere, the wife of King Arthur, his lord, became physical as well as spiritual. Most of the troubadours came from and wrote for the aristocratic classes, and their poetry suggests the interests and values of noble culture. Their influence extended to all social groups, however, for people who could not read heard the poems and stories from people who could, so that what had originally come from oral culture was recycled back into it.

Drama, derived from the church's liturgy, emerged as a distinct art form during the High Middle Ages. Amateurs and later professional actors performed plays based on biblical themes and on the lives of the saints; these dramas were presented in the towns, first in churches and then at the marketplace. Members of the craft guilds performed "mystery" plays, so called because guilds were sometimes called "mysteries." By combining comical farce based on ordinary life with serious religious scenes, plays gave ordinary people an opportunity to identify with religious figures and think about their faith.

Churches and Cathedrals

The development of secular vernacular literature focusing on human concerns did not mean any lessening of the importance of religion in medieval people's lives. As we have seen, religious devotion was expressed through daily rituals, holiday ceremonies, and the creation of new institutions such as universities and religious orders. People also wanted permanent visible representations of their piety, and both church and city leaders wanted physical symbols of their wealth and power. These aims found their outlet in the building of tens of thousands of churches, chapels, abbeys, and, most spectacularly, **cathedrals** in the twelfth and thirteenth centuries. A cathedral is the church of a bishop and the administrative headquarters of a diocese. The word comes from the Greek word *kathedra*, meaning seat, because the bishop's throne, a symbol of the office, is located in the cathedral.

Most of the churches in the early Middle Ages had been built primarily of wood, which meant they were susceptible to fire. They were often small, with a flat roof, in a rectangular form with a central aisle; this structure, called a basilica, was based on earlier Roman public buildings. With the increasing political stability of the eleventh century, bishops and abbots supported the construction of larger and more fire-resistant churches made almost completely out of stone. As the size of the church grew horizontally, it also grew vertically. Builders adapted Roman-style rounded barrel vaults made of stone for the ceiling; this use of Roman forms led the style to be labeled **Romanesque**.

The next architectural style was **Gothic**, so named by later Renaissance architects who thought that only the uncouth Goths could have invented such a disunified style. In Gothic churches the solid stone barrel-vaulted roof was replaced by a roof made of stone ribs with plaster in between. Because this ceiling was much lighter, side pillars and walls did not need to carry as much weight. Exterior arched stone supports called flying buttresses also carried some of the weight of the roof, so solid walls could be replaced by windows, which let in great amounts of light. Originating in the Île-de-France in the twelfth century, Gothic architecture spread throughout France with the expansion of royal power. From France the new style spread to England, Germany, Italy, Spain, and eastern Europe.

Extraordinary amounts of money were needed to build these houses of worship. The economic growth of the period meant that merchants, nobles, and the church could afford the costs of this unparalleled building boom. Moreover, money was not the only need. A great number of artisans had to be assembled: quarrymen, sculptors, stonecutters, masons, mortar makers, carpenters, blacksmiths, glassmakers, roofers. Each master craftsman had apprentices, and unskilled laborers had to be recruited for the heavy work. Bishops and abbots sketched out what they wanted and set general guidelines, but they left practical needs and aesthetic considerations to the master mason. He held overall responsibility for supervision of the project.

Since cathedrals were symbols of civic pride, towns competed to build the largest and most splendid church. In 1163 the citizens of Paris began Notre Dame Cathedral, planning it to reach the height of 114 feet from the floor to the ceiling at the highest point inside. Many other cathedrals well over 100 feet tall on the inside were built as each bishop and town sought to outdo the neighbors. Towers and spires jutted up another several hundred feet. Medieval people built cathedrals to glorify God—and if mortals were impressed, all the better. The construction of a large cathedral was rarely

Notre Dame Cathedral, Paris   This view offers a fine example of the twin towers (left), the spire and great rose window over the south portal (center), and the flying buttresses that support the walls and the vaults. Like hundreds of other churches in medieval Europe, it was dedicated to the Virgin Mary. With a spire rising more than 300 feet, Notre Dame was the tallest building in Europe. (David R. Frazier/Photo Researchers)

completed in a lifetime; many were never finished at all. Because generation after generation added to the buildings, many of these churches show the architectural influences of two or even three centuries.

Stained glass beautifully reflects the creative energy of the High Middle Ages. It is both an integral part of Gothic architecture and a distinct form of visual art. From large sheets of colored glass made by glassblowers, artisans cut small pieces, linked them together with narrow strips of lead, and set them in an iron frame prepared to fit the window opening. Windows showed scenes from the Old and New Testaments and the lives of the saints, designed to teach people doctrines of the Christian faith visually. They also showed scenes from the lives of the artisans and merchants who paid for them.

Once at least part of a cathedral had been built, the building began to be used for religious services. Town residents gathered for masses, baptisms, funerals, and saint's day services, and also used it for guild meetings and other secular purposes. Services became increasingly complex to fit with their new surroundings. Originally, services were chanted by the clergy in unison, in a form of liturgical music termed plainsong or Gregorian chant, but by the eleventh century additional voices singing in different pitches were added, creating what is called polyphony. Church leaders sometimes fumed that polyphony made the text impossible to understand — Pope John XXII called this style an "avalanche of notes" in 1324 — but, along with incense, candles, stained-glass windows, statuary, tapestry wall hangings, and the building itself, music made services in a Gothic cathedral a rich experience.

The frenzy to create the most magnificent Gothic cathedrals eventually came to an end. Begun in 1247, the cathedral in Beauvais reached a height of 157 feet in the interior, exceeding all others. Unfortunately, the weight imposed on the vaults was too great, and the building collapsed in 1284. The collapse was viewed as an aberration, for countless other cathedrals were in various stages of completion at the same time, and none of them fell. In hindsight, however, it can be viewed as a harbinger. Very few cathedrals not yet completed at the time of its collapse were ever finished, and even fewer were started. In the fourteenth century the church itself splintered, and the cities that had so proudly built cathedrals were decimated by famine and disease.

Notes

1. Honorius of Autun, "Elucidarium sive Dialogus de Summa Totius Christianae Theologiae," in *Patrologia Latina*, ed. J. P. Migne (Paris: Garnier Brothers, 1854), vol. 172, col. 1149.
2. M. Chibnall, ed. and trans., *The Ecclesiastical History of Ordericus Vitalis* (Oxford: Oxford University Press, 1972), 2.xiii.
3. Thirteenth-century sermon story, in David Herlihy, ed., *Medieval Culture and Society* (New York: Harper and Row, 1968), pp. 295, 298.
4. Translated and quoted in Susan C. Karant-Nunn, *The Reformation of Ritual: An Interpretation of Early Modern Germany* (London: Routledge, 1997), p. 77.
5. Roy C. Cave and Hervet H. Coulson, *A Source Book for Medieval Economic History* (New York: Biblio and Tannen, 1965), p. 257.
6. H. Rothwell, ed., *English Historical Documents*, vol. 3 (London: Eyre & Spottiswoode, 1975), p. 854.
7. www.classical.net/music/comp.lst/works/orff-cb/carmlyr.php#track14. This verse is from one of the songs known as the Carmina Burana, which are widely available as recordings, downloadable files, and even cell phone ring tones.

Chapter Review

MAKE IT STICK

LearningCurve
bedfordstmartins.com/mckaywestvalue

After reading the chapter, use LearningCurve to retain what you've read.

IDENTIFY KEY TERMS

Identify and explain the significance of each item below.

open-field system (p. 295) **Scholastics** (p. 321)

merchant guild (p. 308) **vernacular literature** (p. 324)

craft guild (p. 309) **troubadours** (p. 325)

Hanseatic League (p. 311) **cathedral** (p. 326)

commercial revolution (p. 312) **Romanesque** (p. 326)

sumptuary laws (p. 316) **Gothic** (p. 326)

REVIEW THE MAIN IDEAS

Answer the focus questions from each section of the chapter.

- What was village life like in medieval Europe? (p. 294)
- How did religion shape everyday life in the High Middle Ages? (p. 299)
- What led to Europe's economic growth and reurbanization? (p. 305)
- What was life like in medieval cities? (p. 313)
- How did universities serve the needs of medieval society? (p. 318)
- How did literature and architecture express medieval values? (p. 323)

MAKE CONNECTIONS

Think about the larger developments and continuities within and across chapters.

1. How was life in a medieval city different from life in a Hellenistic city (Chapter 4), or life in Rome during the time of Augustus (Chapter 6)? In what ways was it similar? What problems did these cities confront that are still issues for cities today?

2. Chapter 4 and this chapter both examine ways in which religion and philosophy shaped life for ordinary people and for the educated elite. How would you compare Hellenistic religious practices with those of medieval Europe? How would you compare the ideas of Hellenistic philosophers such as Epicurus or Zeno with those of Scholastic philosophers such as Aquinas?

ONLINE DOCUMENT ASSIGNMENT

Life in Medieval Towns
How did merchant and craft guilds shape life in medieval towns?

Keeping the question above in mind, go online and examine primary texts and images that illuminate the role of guilds in medieval urban communities, and then complete a writing assignment based on the evidence and details from this chapter.

bedfordstmartins.com/mckaywestvalue

CHRONOLOGY

1050–1300	• Steady rise in population; period of milder climate
ca. 1100	• Merchant guilds become rich and powerful in many cities; artisans begin to found craft guilds
1100–1300	• Height of construction of cathedrals in Europe
1100s	• Hospitals and other homes for the sick begin appearing
1160s	• Silver mines opened in Germany, allowing for more coinage
ca. 1200	• Founding of first universities
1215	• Fourth Lateran Council orders Jews and Muslims to wear distinctive clothing
1225–1274	• Life of Thomas Aquinas; *Summa Theologica*
1241	• Contract between Lübeck and Hamburg, first in the Hanseatic League
ca. 1300	• Bill of exchange becomes most common method of commercial payment in western Europe
1300s	• Clocks in general use throughout Europe

11

LearningCurve
bedfordstmartins.com/mckaywestvalue
After reading the chapter, use
LearningCurve to retain what
you've read.

The Later Middle Ages

1300–1450

DURING THE LATER MIDDLE AGES THE LAST BOOK OF THE NEW
Testament, the Book of Revelation, inspired thousands of sermons and hundreds of religious tracts. The Book of Revelation deals with visions of the end of the world, with disease, war, famine, and death—often called the "Four Horsemen of the Apocalypse"—triumphing everywhere. It is no wonder this part of the Bible was so popular in this period, for between 1300 and 1450 Europeans experienced a frightful series of shocks. The climate turned colder and wetter, leading to poor harvests and famine. People weakened by hunger were more susceptible to disease, and in the middle of the fourteenth century a new disease, probably the bubonic plague, spread throughout Europe. With no effective treatment, the plague killed millions of people. War devastated the countryside, especially in France, leading to widespread discontent and peasant revolts. Workers in cities also revolted against dismal working conditions, and violent crime and ethnic tensions increased as well. Massive deaths and preoccupation with death make the fourteenth century one of the most wrenching periods of Western civilization. Yet, in spite of the pessimism and crises, important institutions and cultural forms, including representative assemblies and national literatures, emerged. Even institutions that experienced severe crisis, such as the Christian Church, saw new types of vitality.

Prelude to Disaster

How did climate change shape the late Middle Ages?

Toward the end of the thirteenth century the expanding European economy began to slow down, and in the first half of the fourteenth century Europe experienced ongoing climate change that led to lower levels of food production, which had dramatic and disastrous ripple effects. Rulers attempted to find solutions but were unable to deal with the economic and social problems that resulted.

Climate Change and Famine

The period from about 1000 to about 1300 saw a warmer-than-usual climate in Europe, which underlay all the changes and vitality of the High Middle Ages. Around 1300, however, the climate changed for the worse, becoming colder and wetter. Historical geographers refer to the period from 1300 to 1450 as a "little ice age," which they can trace through both natural and human records.

Evidence from nature emerges through the study of Alpine and polar glaciers, tree rings, and pollen left in bogs. Human-produced sources include written reports of rivers freezing and crops never ripening, as well as archaeological evidence such as the collapsed houses and emptied villages of Greenland, where ice floes cut off contact with the rest of the world and the harshening climate meant that the few hardy crops grown in earlier times could no longer survive. The Viking colony on Greenland died out completely, though Inuit people who relied on hunting sea mammals continued to live in the far north, as they had before the arrival of Viking colonists.

Across Europe, an unusual number of storms brought torrential rains, ruining the wheat, oat, and hay crops on which people and animals almost everywhere depended. Since long-distance transportation of food was expensive and difficult, most urban areas depended for grain, produce, and meat on areas no more than a day's journey away. Poor harvests—and one in four was likely to be poor—led to scarcity and starvation. Almost all of northern Europe suffered a **Great Famine** in the years 1315 to 1322, which contemporaries interpreted as a recurrence of the biblical "seven lean years" that afflicted Egypt.

Even in non-famine years, the cost of grain, livestock, and dairy products rose sharply, in part because diseases hit cattle and sheep. Increasing prices meant that fewer people could afford to buy food. Reduced caloric intake meant increased susceptibility to disease, especially for infants, children, and the elderly. Workers on reduced diets had less energy, which meant lower productivity, lower output, and higher grain prices.

Social Consequences

The changing climate and resulting agrarian crisis of the fourteenth century had grave social consequences. Poor harvests and famine led to the abandonment of homesteads. In parts of the Low Countries and in the Scottish-English borderlands, entire villages were deserted, and many people became vagabonds, wandering in search of food and work. In Flanders and eastern England, some peasants were forced to mortgage, sublease, or sell their holdings to richer farmers in order to buy food. Throughout the affected areas, young men and women sought work in the towns, delaying marriage.

Death from Famine In this fifteenth-century painting, dead bodies lie in the middle of a path, while a funeral procession at the right includes a man with an adult's coffin and a woman with the coffin of an infant under her arm. People did not simply allow the dead to lie in the street in medieval Europe, though during famines and epidemics it was sometimes difficult to maintain normal burial procedures. (Erich Lessing/Art Resource, NY)

Overall, the population declined because of the deaths caused by famine and disease, though the postponement of marriages and resulting decline in offspring may have also played a part.

As the subsistence crisis deepened, starving people focused their anger on the rich, speculators, and the Jews, who were often targeted as creditors fleecing the poor through pawnbroking. (As explained in Chapter 10, Jews often became moneylenders because Christian authorities restricted their ownership of land and opportunities to engage in other trades.) Rumors spread of a plot by Jews and their agents, the lepers, to kill Christians by poisoning wells. Based on "evidence" collected by torture, many lepers and Jews were killed, beaten, or heavily fined.

Meanwhile, the international character of trade and commerce meant that a disaster in one country had serious implications elsewhere. For example, the infection that attacked English sheep in 1318 caused a sharp decline in wool exports in the following years. Without wool, Flemish weavers could not work, and thousands were laid off. Without woolen cloth, the businesses of Flemish, Hanseatic, and Italian merchants suffered. Unemployment encouraged people to turn to crime.

Government responses to these crises were ineffectual. The three sons of Philip the Fair who sat on the French throne between 1314 and 1328 condemned speculators who held stocks of grain back until conditions were desperate and prices high, and they forbade the sale of grain abroad. These measures had few actual results, however. In England, Edward II (r. 1307–1327) also condemned speculators after his attempts to set price controls on livestock and ale proved futile. He did try to buy grain abroad, but little was available, and such grain as reached southern English ports was stolen by looters and sold on the black market. The king's efforts at famine relief failed.

The Black Death

How did the plague reshape European society?

Colder weather, failed harvests, and resulting malnourishment left Europe's population susceptible to disease, and unfortunately for the continent, a virulent one appeared in the mid-fourteenth century. Around 1300 improvements in ship design had allowed year-round shipping for the first time. European merchants took advantage of these advances, and ships continually at sea carried all types of cargo. They also carried vermin of all types, especially insects and rats, both of which often harbored pathogens. Rats, fleas, and cockroaches could live for months on the cargo carried along the coasts, disembarking at ports with the grain, cloth, or other merchandise. Just as modern air travel has allowed diseases such as AIDS and the H1N1 virus to spread quickly over very long distances, medieval shipping allowed the diseases of the time to do the same. The most frightful of these diseases, carried on Genoese ships, first emerged in western Europe in 1347; the disease was later called the **Black Death**.

Pathology

Most historians and microbiologists identify the disease that spread in the fourteenth century as the bubonic plague, which is caused by the bacillus *Yersinia pestis*. The disease normally afflicts rats. Fleas living on the infected rats drink their blood and then pass the bacteria that cause the plague on to the next rat they bite. Usually the disease is limited to rats and other rodents, but at certain points in history—perhaps when most rats have been killed off—the fleas have jumped from their rodent hosts to humans and other animals. One of these instances appears to have occurred in the Eastern Roman Empire in the sixth century, when a plague killed millions of people. Another was in China and India in the 1890s, when millions again died. Doctors and epidemiologists closely studied this outbreak, identified the bacillus as bubonic plague, and learned about the exact cycle of infection for the first time.

The fourteenth-century outbreak showed many similarities to the nineteenth-century one, but also some differences. There are no reports of massive rat die-offs in fourteenth-century records. The medieval plague was often transmitted directly from one person to another through coughing and sneezing (what epidemiologists term *pneumonic* transmission) as well as through fleabites. The fourteenth-century outbreak spread much faster than the nineteenth-century epidemic and was much more deadly, killing as much as one-third of the population when it first reached an area. These differences have led a few historians to question whether the Black Death was actually not the bubonic plague but a different disease, perhaps something like the Ebola virus. Other scholars counter that the differences could be explained by variant strains of the disease or improvements in sanitation and public health that would have significantly limited the mortality rate of later outbreaks, even in poor countries such as India. These debates fuel continued study of medical aspects of the plague, with scientists using innovative techniques such as studying the tooth pulp of bodies in medieval cemeteries to see if it contains DNA from plague-causing agents.

Though there is some disagreement about exactly what kind of disease the plague was, there is no dispute about its dreadful effects on the body. The classic symptom of the bubonic plague was a growth the size of a nut or an apple in the armpit, in the groin, or on the neck. This was the boil, or *bubo*, that gave the disease its name and caused agonizing pain. If the bubo was lanced and the pus thoroughly drained, the victim had a chance of recovery. If the boil was not lanced, however — and in the fourteenth century, it rarely was — the next stage was the appearance of black spots or blotches caused by bleeding under the skin. (This syndrome did not give the disease its common name; contemporaries did not call the plague the Black Death. Sometime in the fifteenth century the Latin phrase *atra mors*, meaning "dreadful death," was translated as "black death," and the phrase stuck.) Finally, the victim began to cough violently and spit blood. This stage, indicating the presence of millions of bacilli in the bloodstream, signaled the end, and death followed in two or three days. The coughing also released those pathogens into the air, infecting others when they were breathed in and beginning the deadly cycle again on new victims.

Spread of the Disease

Plague symptoms were first described in 1331 in southwestern China, then part of the Mongol Empire. Plague-infested rats accompanied Mongol armies and merchant caravans carrying silk, spices, and gold across Central Asia in the 1330s. The rats then stowed away on ships, carrying the disease to the ports of the Black Sea by the 1340s. One Italian chronicler told of more dramatic means of spreading the disease as well: Mongol armies besieging the city of Kaffa on the shores of the Black Sea catapulted plague-infected corpses over the walls to infect those inside. The city's residents dumped the corpses into the sea as fast as they could, but they were already infected.

In October 1347 Genoese ships brought the plague from Kaffa to Messina, from which it spread across Sicily. Venice and Genoa were hit in January 1348, and from the port of Pisa the disease spread south to Rome and east to Florence and all of Tuscany. By late spring southern Germany was attacked. Frightened French authorities chased a galley bearing plague victims away from the port of Marseilles, but not before plague had infected the city, from which it spread to southern France and Spain. In June 1348 two ships entered the Bristol Channel and introduced it into England, and from there it traveled northeast into Scandinavia. The plague seems to have entered Poland through the Baltic seaports and spread eastward from there (Map 11.1).

Medieval urban conditions were ideal for the spread of disease. Narrow streets were filled with refuse, human excrement, and dead animals. Houses whose upper stories projected over the lower ones blocked light and air. Houses were beginning to be constructed of brick, but many wood, clay, and mud houses remained. A determined rat had little trouble entering such a house. In addition, people were already weakened by famine, standards of personal hygiene remained frightfully low, and the urban populace was crowded together. Fleas and body lice were universal afflictions: everyone from peasants to archbishops had them. One more bite did not cause much alarm, and the

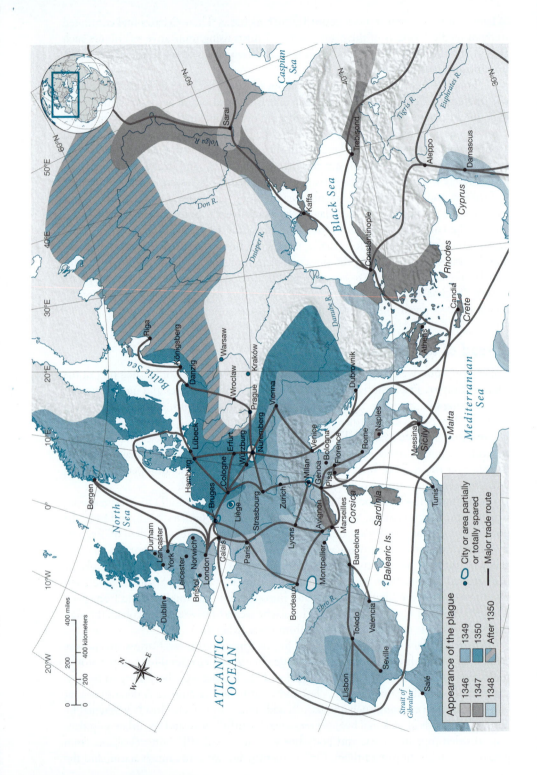

Caspian Sea

Sarai

Volga R.

Don R.

Dnieper R.

Kaffa

Black Sea

Trebisond

Tigris R.

Euphrates R.

Aleppo

Damascus

Constantinople

Cyprus

Rhodes

Candia
Crete

Athens

Dubrovnik

Mediterranean Sea

Malta

Naples

Messina
Sicily

Rome

Florence
Bologna
Pisa
Venice
Genoa
Milan

Avignon

Marseilles

Corsica

Sardinia

Balearic Is.

Tunis

Salé

Strait of Gibraltar

Lisbon

Seville

Valencia

Toledo

Barcelona

Montpellier

Ebro R.

Bordeaux

Lyons

Strasbourg

Zurich

Paris

Calais

Danube R.

Vienna

Prague

Kraków

Warsaw

Wrocław

Nuremberg
Würzburg
Erfurt

Cologne
Liège
Bruges

Lübeck

Hamburg

Danzig

Königsberg

Riga

Baltic Sea

Bergen

North Sea

London
Norwich
Bristol
Leicester
York
Lancaster
Durham
Dublin

ATLANTIC OCEAN

N
S
E
W

400 miles
200
0

400 kilometers
200
0

60°N
50°N
40°N
30°N

50°E
40°E
30°E
20°E
10°E
0°
10°W
20°W

Appearance of the plague

1346	1349
1347	1350
1348	After 1350

◦ City or area partially or totally spared

— Major trade route

◄ **MAP 11.1   The Course of the Black Death in Fourteenth-Century Europe**
The bubonic plague spread across Europe after beginning in the mid-1340s with the first cases of disease reported in Black Sea ports.

association between rats, fleas, and the plague was unknown. Mortality rates can be only educated guesses because population figures for the period before the arrival of the plague do not exist for most countries and cities. Of a total English population of perhaps 4.2 million, probably 1.4 million died of the Black Death. Densely populated Italian cities endured incredible losses. Florence lost between one-half and two-thirds of its population when the plague visited in 1348. Islamic parts of Europe were not spared, nor was the rest of the Muslim world. The most widely accepted estimate for western Europe and the Mediterranean is that the plague killed about one-third of the population in the first wave of infection. (Some areas, including such cities as Milan, Liege, and Nuremberg, were largely spared, primarily because city authorities closed the gates to all outsiders when plague was in the area, and enough food had been stored to sustain the city until the danger had passed.)

Nor did central and eastern Europe escape the ravages of the disease. One chronicler records that, in the summer and autumn of 1349, between five hundred and six hundred died every day in Vienna. As the Black Death took its toll on the Holy Roman Empire, waves of emigrants fled to Poland, Bohemia, and Hungary, taking the plague with them. In the Byzantine Empire the plague ravaged the population. The youngest son of Emperor John VI Kantakouzenos died just as his father took over the throne in 1347. "So incurable was the evil," wrote John later in his history of the Byzantine Empire, "that neither any regularity of life, nor any bodily strength could resist it. Strong and weak bodies were all similarly carried away, and those best cared for died in the same manner as the poor."[1]

Across Europe the Black Death recurred intermittently from the 1360s to 1400. It reappeared from time to time over the following centuries as well, though never with the same virulence because by then Europeans now had some resistance. Improved standards of hygiene and strictly enforced quarantine measures also lessened the plague's toll, but only in 1721 did it make its last appearance in Europe, in the French port of Marseilles. And only in 1947, six centuries after the arrival of the plague in Europe, did the American microbiologist Selman Waksman discover an effective treatment, streptomycin. Plague continues to infect rodent and human populations sporadically today.

Care of the Sick

Fourteenth-century medical literature indicates that physicians tried many different methods to prevent and treat the plague. People understood that plague and other diseases could be transmitted person to person, and they observed that crowded cities had high death rates, especially when the weather was warm and moist. We now understand that warm, moist conditions make it easier for germs to grow and spread, but fourteenth-century people thought in terms of "poisons" in the air or "corrupted air" coming from swamps, unburied animals, or the positions of the stars. Their treatments thus focused on ridding the air and the body of these poisons and on rebalancing bodily fluids.

People tried anything they thought might help. Perhaps loud sounds like ringing church bells or firing the newly invented cannon would clean poisoned air. Medicines made from plants that were bumpy or that oozed liquid might work, keeping the more dangerous swelling and oozing of the plague away. Magical letter and number combinations, called cryptograms, were especially popular in Muslim areas. They were often the first letters of words in prayers or religious sayings, and they gave people a sense of order when faced with the randomness with which the plague seemed to strike.

It is noteworthy that, in an age of mounting criticism of clerical wealth (see page 349), the behavior of the clergy during the plague was often exemplary. Priests, monks, and nuns cared for the sick and buried the dead. In places like Venice, from which even physicians fled, priests remained to give what ministrations they could. Consequently, their mortality rate was phenomenally high. The German clergy, especially, suffered a severe decline in personnel in the years after 1350.

There were limits to care, however. The Italian writer Giovanni Boccaccio (1313–1375), describing the course of the disease in Florence in the preface to his book of tales, *The Decameron*, identified what many knew—that the disease passed from person to person:

> This pestilence was so powerful that it was transmitted to the healthy by contact with the sick, the way a fire close to dry or oily things will set them aflame. And the evil of the plague went even further: not only did talking to or being around the sick bring infection and a common death, but also touching the clothes of the sick or anything touched or used by them seemed to communicate this very disease to the person involved.[2]

To avoid contagion, wealthier people often fled cities for the countryside, though sometimes this simply spread the plague faster. Some cities tried shutting their gates to prevent infected people and animals from coming in, which worked in a few cities. They also walled up houses in which there was plague, trying to isolate those who were sick from those who were still healthy. In Boccaccio's words, "Almost no one cared for his neighbor . . . brother abandoned brother . . . and—even worse, almost unbelievable—fathers and mothers neglected to tend and care for their children."[3]

Economic, Religious, and Cultural Effects

Economic historians and demographers sharply dispute the impact of the plague on the economy in the late fourteenth century. The traditional view that the plague had a disastrous effect has been greatly modified. By the mid-1300s the population of Europe had grown somewhat beyond what could easily be supported by available agricultural technology, and the dramatic drop in population allowed less fertile land to be abandoned. People turned to more specialized types of agriculture, such as raising sheep or wine grapes, which in the long run proved to be a better use of the land.

The Black Death did bring on a general European inflation. High mortality produced a fall in production, shortages of goods, and a general rise in prices. The price of wheat in most of Europe increased, as did the costs of meat, sausage, and cheese. This inflation continued to the end of the fourteenth century. But labor shortages resulting from the high mortality caused by the plague meant that workers could demand better wages, and the broad mass of people who survived enjoyed a higher standard of living. The greater demand for labor also meant greater mobility for peasants in rural areas and for artisans in towns and cities.

The plague also had effects on religious practices. Despite Boccaccio's comments about family members' coldness, people were saddened by the loss of their loved ones, especially their children. Not surprisingly, some people sought release from the devastating affliction in wild living, but more became more deeply pious. Rather than seeing the plague as a medical issue, they interpreted it as the result of an evil within themselves. God must be punishing them for terrible sins, they thought, so the best remedies were religious ones: asking for forgiveness, praying, trusting in God, making donations to churches, and trying to live better lives. John VI Kantakouzenos reported that in Constantinople, "many of the sick turned to better things in their minds . . . they abstained from all vice during that time and they lived virtuously; many divided their property among the poor, even before they were attacked by the disease."[4] In Muslim areas, religious leaders urged virtuous living in the face of death: give to the poor, reconcile with your enemies, free your slaves, and say a proper good-bye to your friends and family.

Believing that the Black Death was God's punishment for humanity's wickedness, some Christians turned to the severest forms of asceticism and frenzied religious fervor, joining groups of **flagellants** (FLA-juh-luhnts), who whipped and scourged themselves as penance for their and society's sins. Groups of flagellants traveled from town to town, often growing into unruly mobs. Officials worried that they would provoke violence and riots, and ordered groups to disband or forbade them to enter cities.

Along with seeing the plague as a call to reform their own behavior, however, people also searched for scapegoats, and savage cruelty sometimes resulted. As in the decades before the plague, many people believed that the Jews had poisoned the wells of Christian communities and thereby infected the drinking water. Others thought that killing Jews would prevent the plague from spreading to their town, a belief encouraged by flagellant groups. These charges led to the murder of thousands of Jews across Europe, especially in the cities of France and Germany. In Strasbourg, for example, several hundred Jews were publicly burned alive. Their houses were looted, their property was confiscated, and the remaining Jews were expelled from the city.

The literature and art of the late Middle Ages reveal a people gripped by morbid concern with death. One highly popular literary and artistic motif, the Dance of Death, depicted a dancing skeleton leading away living people, often in order of their rank. In the words of one early-fifteenth-century English poem:

> Death spareth not low nor high degree
> Popes, Kings, nor worthy Emperors
> When they shine most in felicity
> He can abate the freshness of their flowers
> Eclipse their bright suns with his showers . . .
> Sir Emperor, lord of all the ground,
> Sovereign Prince, and highest of nobles
> You must forsake your round apples of gold
> Leave behind your treasure and riches
> And with others to my dance obey.[5]

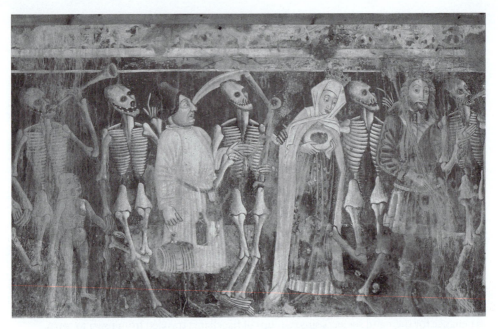

Dance of Death   In this fifteenth-century fresco from a tiny church in Croatia, skeletons lead people from all social classes in a procession. (Vladimir Bugarin, photographer)

The years of the Black Death witnessed the foundation of new colleges at old universities and of entirely new universities. The foundation charters explain the shortage of priests and the decay of learning as the reasons for their establishment. Whereas older universities such as those at Bologna and Paris had international student bodies, these new institutions established in the wake of the Black Death had more national or local constituencies. Thus the international character of medieval culture weakened, paving the way for schism (SKIH-zuhm) in the Catholic Church even before the Reformation.

As is often true with devastating events, the plague highlighted central qualities of medieval society: deep religious feeling, suspicion of those who were different, and a view of the world shaped largely by oral tradition, with a bit of classical knowledge mixed in among the educated elite.

The Hundred Years' War

What were the causes, course, and consequences of the Hundred Years' War?

The plague ravaged populations in Asia, North Africa, and Europe; in western Europe a long international war that began a decade or so before the plague struck and lasted well into the next century added further misery. England and France had engaged in sporadic military hostilities from the time of the Norman conquest in 1066, and in the middle of the fourteenth century these became more intense. From 1337 to 1453 the two countries intermittently fought one another in what was the longest war in European history, ultimately dubbed the **Hundred Years' War**, though it actually lasted 116 years.

Causes

The Hundred Years' War had a number of causes, including disagreements over rights to land, a dispute over the succession to the French throne, and economic conflicts. Many of these revolved around the duchy of Aquitaine, a province in southern France that became part of the holdings of the English crown when Eleanor of Aquitaine married King Henry II of England in 1152 (see Chapter 9; a duchy is a territory ruled by a duke). In 1259 Henry III of England had signed the Treaty of Paris with Louis IX of France, affirming English claims to Aquitaine in return for becoming a vassal of the French crown. French policy in the fourteenth century was strongly expansionist, however, and the French kings resolved to absorb the duchy into the kingdom of France. Aquitaine therefore became a disputed territory.

The immediate political cause of the war was a disagreement over who would inherit the French throne after Charles IV of France, the last surviving son of Philip the Fair, died childless in 1328. With him ended the Capetian dynasty of France. Charles IV had a sister — Isabella — but her son was Edward III, king of England. An assembly of French high nobles, meaning to exclude Isabella and Edward from the French throne, proclaimed that "no woman nor her son could succeed to the [French] monarchy." French lawyers defended the position with the claim that the exclusion of women from ruling or passing down the right to rule was part of Salic law, a sixth-century law code of the Franks (see Chapter 7), and that Salic law itself was part of the fundamental law of France. They used this invented tradition to argue that Edward should be barred from the French throne. (The ban on female succession became part of French legal tradition until the end of the monarchy in 1789.) The nobles passed the crown to Philip VI of Valois (r. 1328–1350), a nephew of Philip the Fair.

In 1329 Edward III formally recognized Philip VI's lordship over Aquitaine. Eight years later, Philip, eager to exercise full French jurisdiction there, confiscated the duchy. Edward III interpreted this action as a gross violation of the treaty of 1259 and as a cause for war. Moreover, Edward argued, as the eldest directly surviving male descendant of Philip the Fair, he deserved the title of king of France. Edward III's dynastic argument upset the feudal order in France: to increase their independent power, many French nobles abandoned Philip VI, using the excuse that they had to transfer their loyalty to a different overlord, Edward III. One reason the war lasted so long was that it became a French civil war, with some French nobles, most importantly the dukes of Burgundy, supporting English monarchs in order to thwart the centralizing goals of the French kings. On the other side, Scotland — resisting English efforts of assimilation — often allied with France; the French supported Scottish raids in northern England, and Scottish troops joined with French armies on the continent.

The governments of both England and France manipulated public opinion to support the war. The English public was convinced that the war was waged for one reason: to secure for King Edward the French crown he had been unjustly denied. Edward III issued letters to the sheriffs describing the evil deeds of the French in graphic terms and listing royal needs. Philip VI sent agents to warn communities about the dangers of invasion. Kings in both countries instructed the clergy to deliver sermons filled with patriotic sentiment. Royal propaganda on both sides fostered a kind of early nationalism, and both sides developed a deep hatred of the other.

Economic factors involving the wool trade and the control of Flemish towns were linked to these political issues. The wool trade between England and Flanders served as the cornerstone of both countries' economies; they were closely interdependent. Flanders technically belonged to the French crown, and the Flemish aristocracy was highly sympathetic to that monarchy. But the wealth of Flemish merchants and cloth manufacturers depended on English wool, and Flemish burghers strongly supported the claims of Edward III. The disruption of commerce with England threatened their prosperity.

The war also presented opportunities for wealth and advancement. Poor and idle knights were promised regular wages. Criminals who enlisted were granted pardons. The great nobles expected to be rewarded with estates. Royal exhortations to the troops before battles repeatedly stressed that, if victorious, the men might keep whatever they seized.

English Successes

The war began with a series of French sea raids on English coastal towns in 1337, but the French fleet was almost completely destroyed when it attempted to land soldiers on English soil, and from that point on the war was fought almost entirely in France and the Low Countries (Map 11.2). It consisted mainly of a series of random sieges and cavalry raids, fought in fits and starts, with treaties along the way to halt hostilities.

During the war's early stages, England was highly successful. At Crécy in northern France in 1346, English longbowmen scored a great victory over French knights and crossbowmen. Although the aim of longbowmen was not very accurate, the weapon

---

MAP 11.2 The Hundred Years' War, 1337–1453

These maps show the change in the land held by the English and French crowns over the course of the Hundred Years' War. Which year marked the greatest extent of English holdings in France?

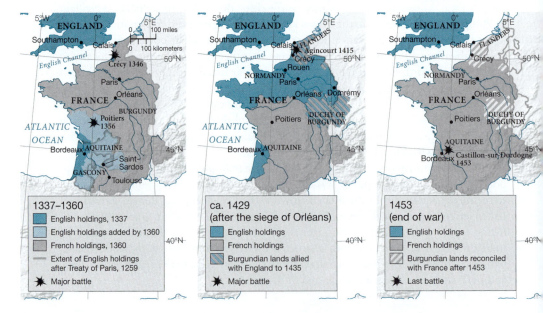

Suit of Armor   This fifteenth-century suit of Italian armor protected its wearer, but its weight made movement difficult. Both English and French mounted knights wore full armor at the beginning of the Hundred Years' War, but by the end they wore only breastplates and helmets, which protected their vital organs but allowed greater mobility. This particular suit has been so well preserved that it was most likely never used in battle; it may have been made for ceremonial purposes. (Image copyright © The Metropolitan Museum of Art/Art Resource, NY)

allowed for rapid reloading, and an English archer could send off three arrows to the French crossbowman's one. The result was a blinding shower of arrows that unhorsed the French knights and caused mass confusion. The roar of English cannon—probably the first use of artillery in the Western world—created further panic. This was not war according to the chivalric rules that Edward III would have preferred. Nevertheless, his son, Edward the Black Prince, used the same tactics ten years later to smash the French at Poitiers, where he captured the French king and held him for ransom. Edward was not able to take all of France, but the English held Aquitaine and other provinces, and allied themselves with many of France's nobles. After a brief peace, the French fought back and recovered some territory during the 1370s and 1380s, and then a treaty again halted hostilities as both sides concentrated on conflicts over power at home.

War began again in 1415 when the able English soldier-king Henry V (r. 1413–1422) invaded France. At Agincourt (AH-jihn-kort), Henry's army defeated a much larger French force, again primarily through the skill of English longbowmen. Henry followed up his triumph at Agincourt with the reconquest of Normandy, and by 1419 the English had advanced to the walls of Paris (see Map 11.2). Henry married the daughter of the French king, and a treaty made Henry and any sons the couple would have heir to the French throne. It appeared as if Henry would indeed rule both England and France, but he died unexpectedly in 1422, leaving an infant son as heir. The English continued their victories, however, and besieged the city of Orléans (or-lay-AHN), the only major city in northern France not under their control. But the French cause was not lost.

Joan of Arc and France's Victory

The ultimate French success rests heavily on the actions of Joan, an obscure French peasant girl whose vision and military leadership revived French fortunes and led to victory. (Over the centuries, she acquired the name "of Arc"—*d'Arc* in French—based on her father's name; she never used this name for herself, but called herself "the

PRIMARY SOURCE   The Trial of Joan of Arc

Joan's interrogation was organized and led by Bishop Pierre Cauchon, one of many French clergy who supported the English. In a number of sessions that took place over several months, she was repeatedly asked about her voices, her decision to wear men's clothing, and other issues. This extract is from the fourth session, on Tuesday, February 27, 1431; Joan is here referred to with the French spelling of her name, Jeanne.

In their presence Jeanne was required by my lord the Bishop of Beauvais to swear and take the oath concerning what touched her trial. To which she answered that she would willingly swear as to what touched her trial, but not as to everything she knew. . . .

Asked whether she had heard her voice since Saturday, she answered: "Yes, indeed, many times." . . . Asked what it said to her when she was back in her room, she replied: "That I should answer you boldly." . . . Questioned as to whether it were the voice of an angel, or of a saint, or directly from God, she answered that the voices were those of Saint Catherine and of Saint Margaret. And their heads are crowned with beautiful crowns, most richly and preciously. And [she said] for [telling you] this I have leave from our Lord. . . .

Asked if the voice ordered her to wear a man's dress, she answered that the dress is but a small matter; and that she had not taken it by the advice of any living man; and that she did not take this dress nor do anything at all save by the command of Our Lord and the angels.

Questioned as to whether it seemed to her that this command to take male dress was a lawful one, she answered that everything she had done was at Our Lord's command, and if He had ordered Jeanne to take a different dress, she would have done so, since it would have been at God's command. . . .

maiden" — *la Pucelle* in French.) Born in 1412 to well-to-do peasants in the village of Domrémy in Champagne, Joan grew up in a religious household. During adolescence she began to hear voices, which she later said belonged to Saint Michael, Saint Catherine, and Saint Margaret. In 1428 these voices spoke to her with great urgency, telling her that the dauphin (DOH-fuhn), the uncrowned King Charles VII, had to be crowned and the English expelled from France. Joan traveled to the French court wearing male clothing. She had an audience with Charles, who had her questioned about her angelic visions and examined to make sure she was the virgin she said she was. She secured his support to travel with the French army to Orléans dressed as a knight — with borrowed armor and sword. There she dictated a letter to the English ordering them to surrender:

King of England . . . , do right in the King of Heaven's sight. Surrender to The Maid sent hither by God the King of Heaven, the keys of all the good towns you have taken and laid waste in France. She comes in God's name to establish the Blood Royal, ready to make peace if you agree to abandon France and repay what you have taken. And you, archers, comrades in arms, gentles and others, who are before the town of Orléans, retire in God's name to your own country.[6]

Asked if she had her sword when she was taken prisoner, she said no, but that she had one which was taken from a Burgundian. . . . Asked whether, when she was before the city of Orleans, she had a standard, and of what colour it was, she replied that it had a field sown with fleurs-de-lis, and showed a world with an angel on either side, white in colour, of linen or *boucassin* [a type of fabric], and she thought that the names JESUS MARIA were written on it; and it had a silk fringe. . . . Asked which she preferred, her sword or her standard, she replied that she was forty times fonder of her standard than she was of her sword. . . . She said moreover that she herself bore her standard during an attack, in order to avoid killing anyone. And she added that she had never killed anyone at all. . . .

She also said that during the attack on the fort at the bridge she was wounded in the neck by an arrow, but she was greatly comforted by Saint Catherine, and was well again in a fortnight. . . . Asked whether she knew beforehand that she would be wounded, she said that she well knew it, and had informed her king of it; but that notwithstanding she would not give up her work.

EVALUATE THE EVIDENCE

1. How does Joan explain the way that she chose to answer the interrogators' questions, and her decisions about clothing and actions in battle?

2. Thinking about the structures of power and authority in fifteenth-century France, how do you believe the interrogators would have regarded Joan's answers?

Source: *The Trial of Joan of Arc*, translated with an introduction by W. S. Scott (Westport, Conn.: Associated Booksellers, 1956), 76, 77, 79–80, 82, 83. © 1956, The Folio Society.

Such words coming from a teenage girl — even one inspired by God — were laughable given the recent course of the conflict, but Joan was amazingly successful. She inspired and led French attacks, forcing the English to retreat from Orléans. The king made Joan co-commander of the entire army, and she led it to a string of victories; other cities simply surrendered without a fight and returned their allegiance to France. In July 1429, two months after the end of the siege of Orléans, Charles VII was crowned king at Reims.

Joan and the French army continued their fight against the English and their Burgundian allies. In 1430 the Burgundians captured Joan. Charles refused to ransom her, and she was sold to the English. A church court headed by a pro-English bishop tried her for heresy, and though nothing she had done was heretical by church doctrine, she was found guilty and burned at the stake in the marketplace at Rouen. (See "Primary Source: The Trial of Joan of Arc," above.)

The French army continued its victories without her. Sensing a shift in the balance of power, the Burgundians switched their allegiance to the French, who reconquered Normandy and, finally, ejected the English from Aquitaine in the 1440s. As the war dragged on, loss of life mounted, and money appeared to be flowing into a bottomless pit, demands for an end increased in England. Parliamentary opposition to additional war grants stiffened, fewer soldiers were sent, and more territory passed into French hands. At the war's end in 1453, only the town of Calais (KA-lay) remained in English hands.

What of Joan? A new trial in 1456—requested by Charles VII, who either had second thoughts about his abandonment of Joan or did not wish to be associated with a condemned heretic—was held by the pope. It cleared her of all charges and declared her a martyr. She became a political symbol of France from that point on, and sometimes also a symbol of the Catholic Church in opposition to the government of France. In 1920, for example, she was canonized as a saint shortly after the French government declared separation of church and state in France. Similarly, Joan has been (and continues to be) a symbol of deep religious piety to some, of conservative nationalism to others, and of gender-bending cross-dressing to others. Beneath the pious and popular legends is a teenage girl who saved the French monarchy, the embodiment of France.

Aftermath

In France thousands of soldiers and civilians had been slaughtered and hundreds of thousands of acres of rich farmland ruined, leaving the rural economy of many areas a shambles. These losses exacerbated the dreadful losses caused by the plague. The war had disrupted trade and the great trade fairs, resulting in the drastic reduction of French participation in international commerce. Defeat in battle and heavy taxation contributed to widespread dissatisfaction and aggravated peasant grievances.

The war had wreaked havoc in England as well, even though only the southern coastal ports saw actual battle. England spent the huge sum of over £5 million on the war effort, and despite the money raised by some victories, the net result was an enormous financial loss. The government attempted to finance the war by raising taxes on the wool crop, which priced wool out of the export market.

In both England and France, men of all social classes had volunteered to serve in the war in the hope of acquiring booty and becoming rich, and some were successful in the early years of the war. As time went on, however, most fortunes seem to have been squandered as fast as they were made. In addition, the social order was disrupted because the knights who ordinarily served as sheriffs, coroners, jurymen, and justices of the peace were abroad.

The war stimulated technological experimentation, especially with artillery. Cannon revolutionized warfare, making the stone castle no longer impregnable. Because only central governments, not private nobles, could afford cannon, their use strengthened the military power of national states.

The long war also had a profound impact on the political and cultural lives of the two countries. Most notably, it stimulated the development of the English Parliament. Between 1250 and 1450 **representative assemblies** flourished in many European countries. In the English Parliament, German *diets*, and Spanish *cortes*, deliberative practices developed that laid the foundations for the representative institutions of modern democratic nations. While representative assemblies declined in most countries after the fifteenth century, the English Parliament endured. Edward III's constant need for money to pay for the war compelled him to summon not only the great barons and bishops, but knights of the shires and citizens from the towns as well. Parliament met in thirty-seven of the fifty years of Edward's reign.

The frequency of the meetings is significant. Representative assemblies were becoming a habit. Knights and wealthy urban residents—or the "Commons," as they came to be called—recognized their mutual interests and began to meet apart from the great lords. The Commons gradually realized that they held the country's purse strings, and a parliamentary statute of 1341 required parliamentary approval of most new taxes. By signing the law, Edward III acknowledged that the king of England could not tax without Parliament's consent.

In England, theoretical consent to taxation and legislation was given in one assembly for the entire country. France had no such single assembly; instead, there were many regional or provincial assemblies. Why did a national representative assembly fail to develop in France? Linguistic, geographical, economic, legal, and political differences remained very strong. People tended to think of themselves as Breton, Norman, Burgundian, and so on, rather than French. In addition, provincial assemblies, highly jealous of their independence, did not want a national assembly. The costs of sending delegates to it would be high, and the result was likely to be increased taxation and a lessening of their own power. Finally, the initiative for convening assemblies rested with the king, but some monarchs lacked the power to call them, and others, including Charles VII, found the very idea of representative assemblies thoroughly distasteful.

In both countries, however, the war did promote the growth of nationalism—the feeling of unity and identity that binds together a people. After victories, each country experienced a surge of pride in its military strength. Just as English patriotism ran strong after Crécy and Poitiers, so French national confidence rose after Orléans. French national feeling demanded the expulsion of the enemy not merely from Normandy and Aquitaine but from all French soil. Perhaps no one expressed this national consciousness better than Joan when she exulted that the enemy had been "driven out of *France*."

Challenges to the Church

Why did the church come under increasing criticism?

In times of crisis or disaster, people of all faiths have sought the consolation of religion. In the fourteenth century, however, the official Christian Church offered little solace. Many priests and friars helped the sick and the hungry, but others paid more attention to worldly matters, and the leaders of the church added to the sorrow and misery of the times. In response to this lack of leadership, members of the clergy challenged the power of the pope, and laypeople challenged the authority of the church itself. Women and men increasingly relied on direct approaches to God, often through mystical encounters, rather than on the institutional church.

The Babylonian Captivity and Great Schism

Conflicts between the secular rulers of Europe and the popes were common throughout the High Middle Ages, and in the early fourteenth century the dispute between King Philip the Fair of France and Pope Boniface VIII became particularly bitter (see Chapter 9). After Boniface's death, in order to control the church and its policies, Philip pressured the new pope, Clement V, to settle permanently in Avignon in southeastern France. The popes lived in Avignon from 1309 to 1376, a period in church history often called the **Babylonian Captivity** (referring to the seventy years the ancient Hebrews were held captive in Mesopotamian Babylon).

The Babylonian Captivity badly damaged papal prestige. The seven popes at Avignon concentrated on bureaucratic and financial matters to the exclusion of spiritual objectives, and the general atmosphere was one of luxury and extravagance, which was also the case at many bishops' courts. The leadership of the church was cut off from its historic roots and the source of its ancient authority, the city of Rome. In 1377 Pope Gregory XI brought the papal court back to Rome but died shortly afterward. Roman citizens pressured the cardinals to elect an Italian, and they chose a distinguished administrator, the archbishop of Bari, Bartolomeo Prignano, who took the name Urban VI.

Urban VI (pontificate 1378–1389) had excellent intentions for church reform, but he went about it in a tactless manner. He attacked clerical luxury, denouncing individual cardinals and bishops by name, and even threatened to excommunicate some of them. The cardinals slipped away from Rome and met at Anagni. They declared Urban's election invalid because it had come about under threats from the Roman mob, and excommunicated the pope. The cardinals then elected Cardinal Robert of Geneva, the cousin of King Charles V of France, as pope. Cardinal Robert took the name Clement VII. There were thus two popes in 1378—Urban at Rome and Clement VII (pontificate 1378–1394) at Avignon. So began the **Great Schism**, which divided Western Christendom until 1417.

The powers of Europe aligned themselves with Urban or Clement along strictly political lines. France naturally recognized the French pope, Clement. England, France's long-time enemy, recognized the Italian pope, Urban. Scotland, an ally of France, supported Clement. Aragon, Castile, and Portugal hesitated before deciding for Clement as well. The German emperor, hostile to France, recognized Urban. At first the Italian city-states recognized Urban; later they opted for Clement.

John of Spoleto, a professor at the law school at Bologna, eloquently summed up intellectual opinion of the schism: "The longer this schism lasts, the more it appears to be costing, and the more harm it does; scandal, massacres, ruination, agitations, troubles and disturbances."[7] The schism weakened the religious faith of many Christians and brought church leadership into serious disrepute.

Critiques, Divisions, and Councils

Criticism of the church during the Avignon papacy and the Great Schism often came from the ranks of highly learned clergy and lay professionals. One of these was William of Occam (1289?–1347?), a Franciscan friar and philosopher who predated the Great Schism but saw the papal court at Avignon during the Babylonian Captivity. Occam argued vigorously against the papacy and also wrote philosophical works in which he questioned the connection between reason and faith that had been developed by Thomas Aquinas (see Chapter 10). All governments should have limited powers and be accountable to those they govern, according to Occam, and church and state should be separate.

The Italian lawyer and university official Marsiglio of Padua (ca. 1275–1342) agreed with Occam. In his *Defensor Pacis* (The Defender of the Peace), Marsiglio argued against the medieval idea of a society governed by both church and state, with church supreme. Instead, Marsiglio claimed, the state was the great unifying power in society, and the church should be subordinate to it. Church leadership should rest in a general council made up of laymen as well as priests and superior to the pope. Marsiglio was excommunicated for these radical ideas, and his work was condemned as heresy — as was Occam's — but in the later part of the fourteenth century many thinkers agreed with these two critics of the papacy. They believed that reform of the church could best be achieved through periodic assemblies, or councils, representing all the Christian people. Those who argued this position were called **conciliarists**.

The English scholar and theologian John Wyclif (WIH-klihf) (ca. 1330–1384) went further than the conciliarists in his argument against medieval church structure. He wrote that Scripture alone should be the standard of Christian belief and practice and that papal claims of secular power had no foundation in the Scriptures. He urged that the church be stripped of its property. He also wanted Christians to read the Bible for themselves and produced the first complete translation of the Bible into English. Wyclif's followers, dubbed Lollards, from a Dutch word for "mumble" by those who ridiculed them, spread his ideas and made many copies of his Bible. Lollard teaching allowed women to preach, and women played a significant role in the movement. Lollards were persecuted in the fifteenth century; some were executed, some recanted, and others continued to meet secretly in houses, barns, and fields to read and discuss the Bible and other religious texts in English. Bohemian students returning from study at the University of Oxford around 1400 brought Wyclif's ideas with them to Prague, the capital of what was then Bohemia and is now the Czech Republic. There another university theologian, Jan Hus (ca. 1372–1415), built on them. He also denied papal authority, called for translations of the Bible into the local Czech language, and declared indulgences — papal offers of remission of penance — useless. Hus gained many followers, who linked his theological ideas with their opposition to the church's wealth and power and with a growing sense of Czech nationalism in opposition to the pope's international power. Hus's followers were successful at defeating the combined armies of the pope and the emperor many times. In the 1430s the emperor finally agreed to recognize the Hussite Church in Bohemia, which survived into the Reformation and then merged with other Protestant churches.

The ongoing schism threatened the church, and in response to continued calls throughout Europe for a council, the cardinals of Rome and Avignon summoned a council at Pisa in 1409. That gathering of prelates and theologians deposed both popes and selected another. Neither the Avignon pope nor the Roman pope would resign, however, and the appalling result was the creation of a threefold schism.

Finally, under pressure from the German emperor Sigismund, a great council met at the imperial city of Constance (1414–1418). It had three objectives: to wipe out heresy, to end the schism, and to reform the church. Members included cardinals, bishops, abbots, and professors of theology and canon law from across Europe. The council moved first on the last point: despite being granted a safe-conduct to go to Constance by the emperor, Jan Hus was tried, condemned, and burned at the stake as a heretic in 1415. The council also eventually healed the schism. It deposed both the Roman pope and the successor of the pope chosen at Pisa, and it isolated the Avignon pope. A conclave elected a new leader, the Roman cardinal Colonna, who took the name Martin V (pontificate 1417–1431).

The Execution of Jan Hus   This fifteenth-century manuscript illustration shows men placing logs around Hus at the Council of Constance, while soldiers, officials, a priest, and a cardinal look on. Hus became an important symbol of Czech independence, and in 1990 the Czech Republic declared July 6, the date of his execution in 1415, a national holiday. (The Art Archive at Art Resource)

Martin proceeded to dissolve the council. Nothing was done about reform, the third objective of the council. In the later part of the fifteenth century the papacy concentrated on Italian problems to the exclusion of universal Christian interests. But the schism and the conciliar movement had exposed the crying need for ecclesiastical reform, thus laying the foundation for the great reform efforts of the sixteenth century.

Lay Piety and Mysticism

The failings of the Avignon papacy followed by the scandal of the Great Schism did much to weaken the spiritual mystique of the clergy in the popular mind. Laypeople had already begun to develop their own forms of piety somewhat separate from the authority of priests and bishops, and these forms of piety became more prominent in the fourteenth century.

In the thirteenth century lay Christian men and women had formed **confraternities**, voluntary lay groups organized by occupation, devotional preference, neighborhood, or charitable activity. Some confraternities specialized in praying for souls in purgatory, either for specific individuals or for the anonymous mass of all souls. In England they held dances, church festivals, and collections to raise money to clean and repair church buildings and to supply churches with candles and other liturgical objects. Like craft guilds, most confraternities were groups of men, but separate women's confraternities were formed in some towns, often to oversee the production of vestments, altar cloths, and other items made of fabric. All confraternities carried out special devotional practices such as prayers or processions, often without the leadership of a priest. Famine, plague, war, and other crises led to an expansion of confraternities in larger cities and many villages.

In Holland beginning in the late fourteenth century, a group of pious laypeople called the Brethren and Sisters of the Common Life lived in stark simplicity while daily carrying out the Gospel teaching of feeding the hungry, clothing the naked, and visiting the sick. They sought to both ease social problems and make religion a personal inner experience. The spirituality of the Brethren and Sisters of the Common Life found its finest expression in the classic *The Imitation of Christ* by the Dutch monk Thomas à Kempis (1380?–1471), which gained wide appeal among laypeople. It urges Christians to take Christ as their model, seek perfection in a simple way of life, and look to the Scriptures for guidance in living a spiritual life. In the mid-fifteenth century the movement had founded houses in the Netherlands, in central Germany, and in the Rhineland.

For some individuals, both laypeople and clerics, religious devotion included mystical experiences. (See "Individuals in Society: Meister Eckhart," page 352.) Bridget of Sweden (1303–1373) was a noblewoman who journeyed to Rome after her husband's death. She began to see visions and gave advice based on these visions to both laypeople and church officials. At the end of her life Bridget made a pilgrimage to Jerusalem, where she saw visions of the Virgin Mary, who described to her exactly how she was standing "with my knees bent" when she gave birth to Jesus, and how she "showed to the shepherds the nature and male sex of the child."[8] Bridget's visions provide evidence of the ways in which laypeople used their own experiences to enhance their religious understanding; Bridget's own experiences of childbirth shaped the way she viewed the birth of Jesus, and she related to the Virgin Mary in part as one mother to another.

The confraternities and mystics were generally not considered heretical unless they began to challenge the authority of the papacy the way Wyclif, Hus, and some conciliarists did. However, the movement of lay piety did alter many people's perceptions of their own spiritual power.

Social Unrest in a Changing Society

What explains the social unrest of the late Middle Ages?

At the beginning of the fourteenth century famine and disease profoundly affected the lives of European peoples. As the century wore on, decades of slaughter and destruction, punctuated by the decimating visits of the Black Death, added further woes. In many parts of France and the Low Countries, fields lay in ruin or untilled for lack of labor. In England, as taxes increased, criticisms of government policy and mismanagement multiplied. Crime and new forms of business organization aggravated economic troubles, and throughout Europe the frustrations of the common people erupted into widespread revolts.

INDIVIDUALS IN SOCIETY • Meister Eckhart

Mysticism—the direct experience of the divine—is an aspect of many world religions and has been part of Christianity throughout its history. During the late Middle Ages, however, the pursuit of mystical union became an important part of the piety of many laypeople, especially in the Rhineland area of Germany. In this they were guided by the sermons of the churchman generally known as Meister Eckhart. Born into a German noble family, Eckhart (1260–1329?) joined the Dominican order and studied theology at Paris and Cologne, attaining the academic title of "master" (*Meister* in German). The leaders of the Dominican order appointed him to a series of administrative and teaching positions, and he wrote learned treatises in Latin that reflected his Scholastic training and deep understanding of classical philosophy.

He also began to preach in German, attracting many listeners through his beautiful language and mystical insights. God, he said, was "an oversoaring being and an overbeing nothingness," whose essence was beyond the ability of humans to express: "if the soul is to know God, it must know Him outside time and place, since God is neither in this or that, but One and above them." Only through "unknowing," emptying oneself, could one come to experience the divine. Yet God was also present in individual human souls, and to a degree in every creature, all of which God had called into being before the beginning of time. Within each human soul there was what Eckhart called a "little spark," an innermost essence that allows the soul—with God's grace and Christ's redemptive action—to come to God. "Our salvation depends upon our knowing and recognizing the Chief Good which is God Himself," preached Eckhart; "the Eye with which I see God is the same Eye with which God sees me." "I have a capacity in my soul for taking in God entirely," he went on, a capacity that was shared by all humans, not only members of the clergy or those with special spiritual gifts. Although Eckhart did not reject church sacraments or the hierarchy, he frequently stressed that union with God was best accomplished through quiet detachment and simple prayer rather than pilgrimages, extensive fasts, or other activities:

Peasant Revolts

Nobles and clergy lived on the food produced by peasant labor, thinking little of adding taxes to the burden of peasant life. While peasants had endured centuries of exploitation, the difficult conditions of the fourteenth and fifteenth centuries spurred a wave of peasant revolts across Europe. Peasants were sometimes joined by those low on the urban social ladder, resulting in a wider revolution of poor against rich.

The first large-scale rebellion was in the Flanders region of present-day Belgium in the 1320s (Map 11.3). In order to satisfy peace agreements, Flemish peasants were forced to pay taxes to the French, who claimed fiscal rights over the county of Flanders. Monasteries also pressed peasants for additional money above their customary tithes. In retaliation, peasants burned and pillaged castles and aristocratic country houses. A

"If the only prayer you said in your whole life was 'thank you,' that would suffice."*

Eckhart's unusual teachings led to charges of heresy in 1327, which he denied. The pope—who was at this point in Avignon—presided over a trial condemning him, but Eckhart appears to have died during the course of the proceedings or shortly thereafter. His writings were ordered destroyed, but his followers preserved many and spread his teachings.

In the last few decades, Meister Eckhart's ideas have been explored and utilized by philosophers and mystics in Buddhism, Hinduism, and neo-paganism, as well as by Christians. His writings sell widely for their spiritual insights, and quotations from them—including the one above about thank-you prayers—can be found on coffee mugs, tote bags, and T-shirts.

QUESTIONS FOR ANALYSIS

1. Why might Meister Eckhart's preaching have been viewed as threatening by the leaders of the church?

2. Given the situation of the church in the late Middle Ages, why might mysticism have been attractive to pious Christians?

*Meister Eckhart's Sermons, trans. Claud Field (London: n.p., 1909).

ONLINE DOCUMENT ASSIGNMENT

What does Meister Eckhart's life tell us about the religious climate of the early fourteenth century? Through his own words and those of his critics, examine how he might have appealed to lay audiences and what compelled church leaders to condemn his teachings, and then complete a writing assignment based on the evidence and details from this chapter.

bedfordstmartins.com/mckaywestvalue

French army crushed the peasant forces, however, and savage repression and the confiscation of peasant property followed in the 1330s.

In the following decades, revolts broke out in many other places. In 1358, when French taxation for the Hundred Years' War fell heavily on the poor, the frustrations of the French peasantry exploded in a massive uprising called the **Jacquerie** (zhah-kuh-REE), after a mythical agricultural laborer, Jacques Bonhomme (Good Fellow). Peasants blamed the nobility for oppressive taxes, for the criminal banditry of the countryside, for losses on the battlefield, and for the general misery. Crowds swept through the countryside, slashing the throats of nobles, burning their castles, raping their wives and daughters, and killing or maiming their horses and cattle. Artisans and small merchants in cities and parish priests joined the peasants. Rebels committed terrible destruction, and for several weeks the nobles were on the defensive. Then the upper class united to

MAP 11.3 **Fourteenth-Century Revolts**
In the later Middle Ages, peasant and urban uprisings were endemic, as common as factory strikes in the industrial world. The threat of insurrection served to check unlimited exploitation.

repress the revolt with merciless ferocity. Thousands of the "Jacques," innocent as well as guilty, were cut down. That forcible suppression of social rebellion, without any effort to alleviate its underlying causes, served to drive protest underground.

In England the Black Death drastically cut the labor supply, and as a result peasants demanded higher wages and fewer manorial obligations. Their lords countered in 1351 with the Statute of Laborers, a law issued by the king that froze wages and bound workers to their manors. (See "Primary Source: The Statute of Laborers," page 355.) This attempt to freeze wages could not be enforced, but a huge gap remained between peasants and their lords, and the peasants sought release for their economic frustrations in revolt. Other factors combined with these economic grievances to fuel the rebellion. The south of England, where the revolt broke out, had been subjected to destructive

PRIMARY SOURCE   The Statute of Laborers

The English population had declined by about one-third because of the Black Death, and rural and urban workers responded by demanding higher wages. In 1351 the English Parliament and King Edward III passed a law ordering wages to be set at their pre-plague levels, and attempting to force people to work.

Because a great part of the people and especially of the workmen and servants has now died in that pestilence, some, seeing the straights of the masters and the scarcity of servants, are not willing to serve unless they receive excessive wages, and others, rather than through labour to gain their living, prefer to beg in idleness: We, considering the grave inconveniences which might come from the lack especially of ploughmen and such labourers . . . have seen fit to ordain: that every man and woman of our kingdom of England, of whatever condition, whether bond or free, who is able bodied and below the age of sixty years, . . . if he, considering his station, be sought after to serve in a suitable service, he shall be bound to serve him who has seen fit so to seek after him; and he shall take only the wages . . . or salary which, in the places where he sought to serve, were accustomed to be paid in the twentieth year of our reign of England [1346], . . . and if any man or woman, being thus sought after in service, will not do this, the fact being proven by two faithful men before the sheriffs or the bailiffs of our lord the king, or the constables of the town where this happens to be done,—straightway through them, or some one of them, he shall be taken and sent to the next jail, and there he shall remain in strict custody until he shall find surety for serving in the aforesaid form.

And if a reaper or mower, or other workman or servant, of whatever standing or condition he be, who is retained in the service of any one, do depart from the said service before the end of the term agreed, without permission or reasonable cause, he shall undergo the penalty of imprisonment. . . .

Likewise saddlers, skinners, white-tawers, cordwainers, tailors, smiths, carpenters, masons, tilers, shipwrights, carters and all other artisans and labourers shall not take for their labour and handiwork more than what, in the places where they happen to labour, was customarily paid to such persons in [1346]; and if any man take more, he shall be committed to the nearest jail in the manner aforesaid. . . .

And because many sound beggars do refuse to labour so long as they can live from begging alms, giving themselves up to idleness and sins, and, at times, to robbery and other crimes—let no one, under the aforesaid pain of imprisonment presume, under colour of piety or alms to give anything to such as can very well labour, or to cherish them in their sloth,—so that thus they may be compelled to labour for the necessaries of life.

EVALUATE THE EVIDENCE

1. What does the law require rural laborers, urban artisans, and the poor to do, and what penalties does it provide if they do not?

2. Why were measures such as this most likely ineffective, and how did they contribute to growing social tensions?

Source: Ernest F. Henderson, trans. and ed., *Select Historical Documents of the Middle Ages* (London: George Bell and Sons, 1892).

French raids during the Hundred Years' War. The English government did little to protect the region, and villagers grew increasingly frightened and insecure. Moreover, decades of aristocratic violence against the weak peasantry had bred hostility and bitterness. Social and religious agitation by the popular preacher John Ball fanned the embers of discontent. Ball's famous couplet calling for a return to the social equality that had existed in the Garden of Eden ("When Adam delved and Eve span; / Who was then the gentleman?") reflected real revolutionary sentiment.

The English revolt was ignited by the reimposition of a tax on all adult males. Despite widespread opposition to the tax in 1380, the royal council ordered the sheriffs to collect it again in 1381. This led to a major uprising known as the **English Peasants' Revolt**, which involved thousands of people. Beginning with assaults on the tax collectors, the revolt in England followed a course similar to that of the Jacquerie in France. Castles and manors were sacked. Manorial records were destroyed. Many nobles, including the archbishop of Canterbury who had ordered the collection of the tax, were murdered. The center of the revolt lay in the highly populated and economically advanced south and east, but sections of the north also witnessed rebellions (see Map 11.3).

The boy-king Richard II (r. 1377–1399) met the leaders of the revolt, agreed to charters ensuring peasants' freedom, tricked them with false promises, and then crushed the uprising with terrible ferocity. In the aftermath of the revolt, the nobility tried to restore the labor obligations of serfdom, but they were not successful, and the conversion to money rents continued. The English Peasants' Revolt did not bring social equality to England, but rural serfdom continued to decline, disappearing in England by 1550.

Urban Conflicts

In Flanders, France, and England, peasant revolts often blended with conflicts involving workers in cities. Unrest also occurred in Italian, Spanish, and German cities. The urban revolts had their roots in the changing conditions of work. In the thirteenth century craft guilds had organized the production of most goods, with masters, journeymen, and apprentices working side by side. In the fourteenth century a new system evolved to make products on a larger scale. Capitalist investors hired many households, with each household performing only one step of the process. Initially these investors were wealthy bankers and merchants, but eventually shop masters themselves embraced the system. This promoted a greater division within guilds between wealthier masters and the poorer masters and journeymen they hired. Some masters became so wealthy from the profits of their workers that they no longer had to work in a shop themselves, nor did their wives and family members, though they still generally belonged to the craft guild.

While capitalism provided opportunities for some artisans to become investors and entrepreneurs, especially in cloth production, for many it led to a decrease in income and status. Guilds sometimes responded to crises by opening up membership, as they did in some places immediately after the Black Death, but they more often responded to competition by limiting membership to existing guild families, which meant that journeymen who were not master's sons or who could not find a master's widow or daughter to marry could never become masters themselves. Remaining journeymen their entire lives, they lost their sense of solidarity with the masters of their craft. Resentment led to rebellion.

Urban uprisings were also sparked by issues involving honor, such as employers' requiring workers to do tasks they regarded as beneath them. As their actual status and economic prospects declined and their work became basically wage labor, journeymen and poorer masters emphasized skill and honor as qualities that set them apart from less-skilled workers.

Guilds increasingly came to view the honor of their work as tied to an all-male workplace. When urban economies were expanding in the High Middle Ages, the master's wife and daughters worked alongside him, and female domestic servants also carried out productive tasks. Masters' widows ran shops after the death of their husbands. But in the fourteenth century women's participation in guilds declined, despite labor shortages caused by the plague. First, masters' widows were limited in the amount of time they could keep operating a shop or were prohibited from hiring journeymen; later, female domestic servants were excluded from any productive tasks; finally, the number of daughters a master craftsman could employ was limited. When women were allowed to work, it was viewed as a substitute for charity.

Sex in the City

Peasant and urban revolts and riots had clear economic bases, but some historians have suggested that late medieval marital patterns may have also played a role. In northwestern Europe, people believed that couples should be economically independent before they married. Thus not only during times of crisis such as the Great Famine, but also in more general circumstances, men and women spent long periods as servants or workers in other households, saving money for married life and learning skills, or they waited until their own parents had died and the family property was distributed.

The most unusual feature of this pattern was the late age of marriage for women. Unlike in earlier time periods and in most other parts of the world, a woman in late medieval northern and western Europe generally entered marriage as an adult in her twenties and took charge of running a household immediately. She was thus not as dependent on her husband or mother-in-law as was a woman who married at a younger age. She also had fewer pregnancies than a woman who married earlier, though not necessarily fewer surviving children.

Men of all social groups had long tended to be older than women when they married. In general, men were in their middle or late twenties at first marriage, with wealthier urban merchants often much older. Journeymen and apprentices were often explicitly prohibited from marrying, as were the students at universities, who were understood to be in "minor orders" and thus like clergy, even if they were not intending to have careers in the church.

The prohibitions on marriage for certain groups of men and the late age of marriage for most men meant that cities and villages were filled with large numbers of young adult men with no family responsibilities who often formed the core of riots and unrest. Not surprisingly, this situation also contributed to a steady market for sexual services outside of marriage, services that in later centuries were termed prostitution. Research on the southern French province of Languedoc in the fourteenth and fifteenth centuries

City Brothel   In this rather fanciful scene of a medieval brothel, two couples share baths and wine, while a third is in bed in the back, and two nobles peer in from a window across the street. Most brothels were not this elaborate, although some did have baths. Many cities also had commercial bathhouses where people paid a small fee to take a hot bath, a luxury otherwise unavailable. Bathhouses did sometimes offer sex, but their main attraction was hot water. (Bibliothèque nationale de France)

has revealed the establishment of legal houses of prostitution in many cities. Municipal authorities set up houses or districts for prostitution either outside the city walls or away from respectable neighborhoods. For example, authorities in Montpellier set aside Hot Street for prostitution, required women who sold sex to live there, and forbade anyone to molest them. Prostitution thus passed from being a private concern to a social matter requiring public supervision. The towns of Languedoc were not unique. Public authorities in Amiens, Dijon, Paris, Venice, Genoa, London, Florence, Rome, most of the larger German towns, and the English port of Sandwich set up brothels.

Young men associated visiting brothels with achieving manhood; for the women themselves, of course, their activities were work. Some women had no choice, for they had been traded to the brothel manager by their parents or some other person as payment for debt, or had quickly become indebted to the manager (most of whom were men) for the clothes and other finery regarded as essential to their occupation. The small amount they received from their customers did not equal what they had to pay for their upkeep in a brothel. Poor women — and men — also sold sex illegally outside of city brothels, combining this with other sorts of part-time work such as laundering or sewing. Prostitution was an urban phenomenon because only populous towns had large numbers of unmarried young men, communities of transient merchants, and a culture accustomed to a cash exchange.

Though selling sex for money was legal in the Middle Ages, the position of women who did so was always marginal. In the late fifteenth century cities began to limit brothel residents' freedom of movement and choice of clothing, requiring them to wear distinctive head coverings or bands on their clothing so that they would not be mistaken for "honorable" women. Cities also began to impose harsher penalties on women who did not live in the designated house or section of town. A few women who sold sex did earn enough to donate money to charity or buy property, but most were very poor.

Along with buying sex, young men also took it by force. Unmarried women often found it difficult to avoid sexual contact. Many worked as domestic servants, where their employers or employers' sons or male relatives could easily coerce them, or they worked in proximity to men. Notions of female honor kept upper-class women secluded in their homes, particularly in southern and eastern Europe, but there was little attempt anywhere to protect female servants or day laborers from the risk of seduction or rape. Rape was a capital crime in many parts of Europe, but the actual sentences handed out were more likely to be fines and brief imprisonment, with the severity of the sentence dependent on the social status of the victim and the perpetrator.

According to laws regarding rape in most parts of Europe, the victim had to prove that she had cried out and had attempted to repel the attacker, and she had to bring the charge within a short period of time after the attack had happened. Women bringing rape charges were often more interested in getting their own honorable reputations back than in punishing the perpetrators. For this reason, they sometimes asked the judge to force their rapists to marry them.

Same-sex relations — what in the late nineteenth century would be termed "homosexuality" — were another feature of medieval urban life (and of village life, though there are very few sources relating to sexual relations of any type in the rural context). Same-sex relations were of relatively little concern to church or state authorities in the early Middle Ages, but this attitude changed beginning in the late twelfth century. By 1300 most areas had defined such actions as "crimes against nature," with authorities seeing them as particularly reprehensible because they thought they did not occur anywhere else in creation. Same-sex relations, usually termed "sodomy," became a capital crime in most of Europe, with adult offenders threatened with execution by fire. The Italian cities of Venice, Florence, and Lucca created special courts to deal with sodomy, which saw thousands of investigations.

How prevalent were same-sex relations? This is difficult to answer, even in modern society, but the city of Florence provides a provocative case study. In 1432 Florence set up a special board of adult men, the Office of the Night, to "root out . . . the abominable vice of sodomy."[9] Between 1432 and the abolition of the board in 1502, about seventeen thousand men came to its attention, which, even over a seventy-year period, represents a great number in a population of about forty thousand. The men came from all classes of society, but almost all cases involved an adult man and an adolescent boy; they ranged from sex exchanged for money or gifts to long-term affectionate relationships. Florentines believed in a generational model in which different roles were appropriate to different stages in life. In a socially and sexually hierarchical world, the boy in the passive role was identified as subordinate, dependent, and mercenary, words usually applied to women. Florentines, however, never described the dominant partner in feminine terms, for he had not compromised his masculine identity or violated a gender ideal; in fact, the adult partner might be married or have female sexual partners as well as male. Only if an adult male assumed the passive role was his masculinity jeopardized.

Thus in Florence, and no doubt elsewhere in Europe, sodomy was not a marginal practice, which may account for the fact that, despite harsh laws and special courts, actual executions for sodomy were rare. Same-sex relations often developed within the context of all-male environments, such as the army, the craft shop, and the artistic workshop, and were part of the collective male experience. Homoerotic relationships played important roles in defining stages of life, expressing distinctions of status, and shaping masculine gender identity. Same-sex relations involving women almost never came to the attention of legal authorities, so it is difficult to find out how common they were. However, female-female desire was expressed in songs, plays, and stories, as was male-male desire, offering evidence of the way people understood same-sex relations.

Fur-Collar Crime

The Hundred Years' War had provided employment and opportunity for thousands of idle and fortune-seeking knights. But during periods of truce and after the war finally ended, many nobles once again had little to do. Inflation hurt them. Although many were living on fixed incomes, their chivalric code demanded lavish generosity and an aristocratic lifestyle. Many nobles thus turned to crime as a way of raising money. The fourteenth and fifteenth centuries witnessed a great deal of what we might term "fur-collar crime," a medieval version of today's white-collar crime in which those higher up the social scale prey on those who are less well-off.

This "fur-collar crime" involved both violence and fraud. Groups of noble bandits roamed the English countryside, stealing from both rich and poor. Operating like modern urban racketeers, knightly gangs demanded that peasants pay protection money or else have their hovels burned and their fields destroyed. They seized wealthy travelers and held them for ransom. Corrupt landowners, including some churchmen, pushed peasants to pay higher taxes and extra fees. When accused of wrongdoing, fur-collar criminals intimidated witnesses, threatened jurors, and used their influence to persuade judges to support them—or used cash to bribe them outright.

Aristocratic violence led to revolt, and it also shaped popular culture. The ballads of Robin Hood, a collection of folk legends from late medieval England, describe the adventures of the outlaw hero and his merry men as they avenge the common people against fur-collar criminals—grasping landlords, wicked sheriffs, and mercenary churchmen. Robin Hood was a popular figure because he symbolized the deep resentment of aristocratic corruption and abuse; he represented the struggle against tyranny and oppression.

Ethnic Tensions and Restrictions

Large numbers of people in the twelfth and thirteenth centuries migrated from one part of Europe to another in search of land, food, and work: the English into Scotland and Ireland; Germans, French, and Flemings into Poland, Bohemia, and Hungary; Christians into Muslim Spain. Everywhere in Europe, towns recruited people from the countryside as well (see Chapter 10). In frontier regions, townspeople were usually long-distance immigrants and, in eastern Europe, Ireland, and Scotland, ethnically different from the surrounding rural population. In eastern Europe, German was the language of the towns; in Irish towns, French, the tongue of Norman or English settlers, predominated. As a result of this colonization and movement to towns, peoples of different ethnic backgrounds lived side by side.

In the early periods of conquest and colonization, and in all regions with extensive migrations, a legal dualism existed: native peoples remained subject to their traditional laws; newcomers brought and were subject to the laws of the countries from which they came. On the Prussian and Polish frontier, for example, the law was that "men who come there . . . should be judged on account of any crime or contract engaged in there according to Polish custom if they are Poles and according to German custom if they are Germans."[10] Likewise, the conquered Muslim subjects of Christian kings in Spain had the right to be judged under Muslim law by Muslim judges.

The great exception to this broad pattern of legal pluralism was Ireland. From the start, the English practiced an extreme form of discrimination toward the native Irish. The English distinguished between the free and the unfree, and the entire Irish population, simply by the fact of Irish birth, was unfree. When English legal structures were established beginning in 1210, the Irish were denied access to the common-law courts. In civil (property) disputes, an English defendant did not need to respond to an Irish plaintiff; no Irish person could make a will. In criminal procedures, the murder of an Irishman was not considered a felony. Other than in Ireland, although native peoples commonly held humbler positions, both immigrant and native townspeople prospered during the expanding economy of the thirteenth century. But with the economic turmoil of the fourteenth century, ethnic tensions multiplied.

The later Middle Ages witnessed a movement away from legal pluralism or dualism and toward legal homogeneity and an emphasis on blood descent. The dominant ethnic group in an area tried to bar others from positions of church leadership and guild membership. Marriage laws were instituted that attempted to maintain ethnic purity by prohibiting intermarriage, and some church leaders actively promoted ethnic discrimination. As Germans moved eastward, for example, German bishops refused to appoint non-Germans to any church office, while Czech bishops closed monasteries to Germans.

The most extensive attempt to prevent intermarriage and protect ethnic purity is embodied in the **Statute of Kilkenny** (1366), a law the ruling English imposed on Ireland, which states that "there were to be no marriages between those of immigrant and native stock; that the English inhabitants of Ireland must employ the English language and bear English names; that they must ride in the English way [that is, with saddles] and have English apparel; that no Irishmen were to be granted ecclesiastical benefices or admitted to monasteries in the English parts of Ireland."[11]

Late medieval chroniclers used words such as *gens* (race or clan) and *natio* (NAH-tee-oh; species, stock, or kind) to refer to different groups. They held that peoples differed according to language, traditions, customs, and laws. None of these were unchangeable, however, and commentators increasingly also described ethnic differences in terms of "blood," which made ethnicity heritable. As national consciousness grew with the Hundred Years' War, for example, people began to speak of "French blood" and "English blood." Religious beliefs came to be conceptualized in terms of blood as well, with people regarded as having Jewish blood, Muslim blood, or Christian blood. The most dramatic expression of this was in Spain, where "purity of blood"—having no Muslim or Jewish ancestors—became an obsession. Blood also came to be used as a way to talk about social differences, especially for nobles. Just as the Irish and English were prohibited from marrying each other, those of "noble blood" were prohibited from marrying commoners in many parts of Europe. As Europeans increasingly came into contact with people from Africa and Asia, and particularly as they developed colonial empires, these notions of blood also became a way of conceptualizing racial categories.

Literacy and Vernacular Literature

The development of ethnic identities had many negative consequences, but a more positive effect was the increasing use of the vernacular, that is, the local language that people actually spoke, rather than Latin (see Chapter 10). Two masterpieces of European culture, Dante's *Divine Comedy* (1310–1320) and Chaucer's *Canterbury Tales* (1387–1400), illustrate a sophisticated use of the rhythms and rhymes of the vernacular.

The *Divine Comedy* of Dante Alighieri (DAHN-tay ah-luh-GYEHR-ee) (1265–1321) is an epic poem of one hundred cantos (verses), each of whose three equal parts describes one of the realms of the next world: Hell, Purgatory, and Paradise. The Roman poet Virgil, representing reason, leads Dante through Hell, where Dante observes the torments of the damned and denounces the disorders of his own time. Passing up into Purgatory, Virgil shows the poet how souls are purified of their disordered inclinations. From Purgatory, Beatrice, a woman Dante once loved and who serves as the symbol of divine revelation in the poem, leads him to Paradise.

The *Divine Comedy* portrays contemporary and historical figures, comments on secular and ecclesiastical affairs, and draws on the Scholastic philosophy of uniting faith and reason. Within the framework of a symbolic pilgrimage, the *Divine Comedy* embodies the psychological tensions of the age. A profoundly Christian poem, it also contains bitter criticism of some church authorities. In its symmetrical structure and use of figures from the ancient world such as Virgil, the poem perpetuates the classical tradition, but as the first major work of literature in the Italian vernacular, it is distinctly modern.

Geoffrey Chaucer (1342–1400) was an official in the administrations of the English kings Edward III and Richard II and wrote poetry as an avocation. His *Canterbury Tales* is a collection of stories in lengthy rhymed narrative. On a pilgrimage to the shrine of Saint Thomas Becket at Canterbury (see Chapter 9), thirty people of various social backgrounds tell tales. In depicting the interests and behavior of all types of people, Chaucer presents a rich panorama of English social life in the fourteenth century. Like the *Divine Comedy*, the *Canterbury Tales* reflects the cultural tensions of the times. Ostensibly Christian, many of the pilgrims are also materialistic, sensual, and worldly, suggesting the ambivalence of the broader society's concern for the next world and frank enjoyment of this one.

Beginning in the fourteenth century, a variety of evidence attests to the increasing literacy of laypeople. Wills and inventories reveal that many people, not just nobles, possessed books — mainly devotional texts, but also romances, manuals on manners and etiquette, histories, and sometimes legal and philosophical texts. In England the number of schools in the diocese of York quadrupled between 1350 and 1500. Information from Flemish and German towns is similar: children were sent to schools and were taught the fundamentals of reading, writing, and arithmetic. Laymen increasingly served as managers or stewards of estates and as clerks to guilds and town governments; such positions obviously required the ability to keep administrative and financial records.

The penetration of laymen into the higher positions of governmental administration, long the preserve of clerics, also illustrates rising lay literacy. With growing frequency, the upper classes sent their daughters to convent schools, where, in addition to instruction in singing, religion, needlework, deportment, and household management, they gained the rudiments of reading and sometimes writing.

The spread of literacy represents a response to the needs of an increasingly complex society. Trade, commerce, and expanding government bureaucracies required an increasing number of literate people. Late medieval culture remained a decidedly oral culture. But by the fifteenth century the evolution toward a more literate culture was already perceptible, and craftsmen would develop the new technology of the printing press in response to the increased demand for reading materials.

Notes

1. Christos S. Bartsocas, "Two Fourteenth Century Descriptions of the 'Black Death,'" *Journal of the History of Medicine* (October 1966): 395.
2. Giovanni Boccaccio, *The Decameron*, trans. Mark Musa and Peter Bondanella (New York: W. W. Norton, 1982), p. 7.
3. Ibid., p. 9.
4. Bartsocas, "Two Fourteenth Century Descriptions," p. 397.
5. Florence Warren, ed., *The Dance of Death* (Oxford: Early English Text Society, 1931), 10 lines from p. 8. Spelling modernized. Used by permission of Oxford University Press and the Council of the Early English Text Society.
6. W. P. Barrett, trans., *The Trial of Jeanne d'Arc* (London: George Routledge, 1931), pp. 165–166.
7. Quoted in J. H. Smith, *The Great Schism, 1378: The Disintegration of the Medieval Papacy* (New York: Weybright & Talley, 1970), p. 15.
8. Quoted in Katharina M. Wilson, ed., *Medieval Women Writers* (Athens: University of Georgia Press, 1984), p. 245.
9. Michael Rocke, *Forbidden Friendships: Homosexuality and Male Culture in Renaissance Florence* (New York: Oxford University Press, 1996), p. 45.
10. Quoted in R. Bartlett, *The Making of Europe: Conquest, Colonization and Cultural Change, 950–1350* (Princeton, N.J.: Princeton University Press, 1993), p. 205.
11. Quoted ibid., p. 239.

Chapter Review

MAKE IT STICK

LearningCurve
bedfordstmartins.com/mckaywestvalue

After reading the chapter, use LearningCurve to retain what you've read.

IDENTIFY KEY TERMS

Identify and explain the significance of each item below.

Great Famine (p. 332)

Black Death (p. 334)

flagellants (p. 339)

Hundred Years' War (p. 340)

representative assemblies (p. 346)

Babylonian Captivity (p. 348)

Great Schism (p. 348)

conciliarists (p. 349)

confraternities (p. 350)

Jacquerie (p. 353)

English Peasants' Revolt (p. 356)

Statute of Kilkenny (p. 361)

REVIEW THE MAIN IDEAS

Answer the focus questions from each section of the chapter.

* How did climate change shape the late Middle Ages? (p. 332)
* How did the plague reshape European society? (p. 334)
* What were the causes, course, and consequences of the Hundred Years' War? (p. 340)
* Why did the church come under increasing criticism? (p. 347)
* What explains the social unrest of the late Middle Ages? (p. 351)

MAKE CONNECTIONS

Think about the larger developments and continuities within and across chapters.

1. The Black Death has often been compared with later pandemics, including the global spread of HIV/AIDS, which began in the 1980s. What similarities do you see in the course of the two diseases and their social and cultural consequences?

2. Beginning with Chapter 7, every chapter in this book has discussed the development of the papacy and relations between popes and secular rulers. How were the problems facing the papacy in the fourteenth century the outgrowth of long-term issues? Why had attempts to solve these issues not been successful?

3. In Chapter 3 you learned about the Bronze Age Collapse, and in Chapter 7 about the end of the Roman Empire in the West, both of which have also been seen as "calamitous." What similarities and differences do you see in these earlier times of turmoil and those of the late Middle Ages?

ONLINE DOCUMENT ASSIGNMENT

Meister Eckhart

What does Meister Eckhart's life tell us about the religious climate of the early fourteenth century?

You encountered Meister Eckhart's story on page 352. Keeping the question above in mind, go online and examine Eckhart's own words and those of his critics. Think about why he appealed to lay audiences and what compelled church leaders to condemn his teachings. Then complete a writing assignment based on the evidence and details from this chapter.

bedfordstmartins.com/mckaywestvalue

CHRONOLOGY

1300–1450	• Little ice age
1309–1376	• Babylonian Captivity; papacy in Avignon
1310–1320	• Dante writes *Divine Comedy*
1315–1322	• Great Famine in northern Europe
1320s	• First large-scale peasant rebellion in Flanders
1337–1453	• Hundred Years' War
1347	• Black Death arrives in Europe
1358	• Jacquerie peasant uprising in France
1366	• Statute of Kilkenny
1378–1417	• Great Schism
1381	• English Peasants' Revolt
1387–1400	• Chaucer writes *Canterbury Tales*

12

☑ LearningCurve
bedfordstmartins.com/mckaywestvalue
After reading the chapter, use
LearningCurve to retain what
you've read.

European Society in the Age of the Renaissance

1350–1550

WHILE THE HUNDRED YEARS' WAR GRIPPED NORTHERN EUROPE, A
new culture emerged in southern Europe. The fourteenth century witnessed
remarkable changes in Italian intellectual, artistic, and cultural life. Artists
and writers thought that they were living in a new golden age, but not until
the sixteenth century was this change given the label we use today—the
Renaissance, derived from the French word for "rebirth." That word was first
used by art historian Giorgio Vasari (1511–1574) to describe the art of "rare
men of genius" such as his contemporary Michelangelo. Through their works,
Vasari judged, the glory of the classical past had been reborn after centuries
of darkness. Over time, the word's meaning was broadened to include many
aspects of life during that period. The new attitude had a slow diffusion out
of Italy, so that the Renaissance "happened" at different times in different
parts of Europe. The Renaissance was a movement, not a time period.

Later scholars increasingly saw the cultural and political changes of the Renaissance, along with the religious changes of the Reformation (see Chapter 13)
and the European voyages of exploration (see Chapter 14), as ushering in the
"modern" world. Some historians view the Renaissance as a bridge between
the medieval and modern eras because it corresponded chronologically with
the late medieval period and because there were many continuities with that
period along with the changes that suggested aspects of the modern world.
Others have questioned whether the word *Renaissance* should be used at all to
describe an era in which many social groups saw decline rather than advance.
The debates remind us that these labels—medieval, Renaissance, modern—are
intellectual constructs devised after the fact, and all contain value judgments.

Wealth and Power in Renaissance Italy

How did politics and economics shape the Renaissance?

The magnificent art and new ways of thinking in the **Renaissance** rested on economic and political developments in the city-states of northern Italy. Economic growth laid the material basis for the Italian Renaissance, and ambitious merchants gained political power to match their economic power. They then used their money and power to buy luxuries and hire talent in a system of **patronage**, through which cities, groups, and individuals commissioned writers and artists to produce specific works. Political leaders in Italian cities admired the traditions and power of ancient Rome, and this esteem shaped their commissions. Thus economics, politics, and culture were interconnected. .

Trade and Prosperity

Northern Italian cities led the way in the great commercial revival of the eleventh century (see Chapter 10). By the middle of the twelfth century Venice, supported by a huge merchant marine, had grown enormously rich through overseas trade, as had Genoa and Milan, which had their own sizable fleets. These cities made important strides in shipbuilding that allowed their ships to sail all year long at accelerated speeds and carrying ever more merchandise.

Another commercial leader, and the city where the Renaissance began, was Florence, situated on fertile soil along the Arno River. Its favorable location on the main road northward from Rome made Florence a commercial hub, and the city grew wealthy buying and selling all types of goods throughout Europe and the Mediterranean — grain, cloth, wool, weapons, armor, spices, glass, and wine.

A Florentine Bank Scene Originally a "bank" was just a counter; money changers who sat behind the counter became "bankers," exchanging different currencies and holding deposits for merchants and business people. In this scene from fifteenth-century Florence, the bank is covered with an imported Ottoman geometric rug, one of many imported luxury items handled by Florentine merchants. (Prato, San Francesco/ Scala/Art Resource, NY)

Florentine merchants also loaned and invested money, and they acquired control of papal banking toward the end of the thirteenth century. Florentine mercantile families began to dominate European banking on both sides of the Alps, setting up offices in major European and North African cities. The profits from loans, investments, and money exchanges that poured back to Florence were pumped into urban industries such as clothmaking, and by the early fourteenth century the city had about eighty thousand people, about twice the population of London at that time. Profits contributed to the city's economic vitality and allowed banking families to control the city's politics and culture.

By the first quarter of the fourteenth century, the economic foundations of Florence were so strong that even severe crises could not destroy the city. In 1344 King Edward III of England repudiated his huge debts to Florentine bankers, forcing some of them into bankruptcy. Soon after, Florence suffered frightfully from the Black Death, losing at least half its population, and serious labor unrest shook the political establishment (see Chapter 11). Nevertheless, the basic Florentine economic structure remained stable, and the city grew again. In the fifteenth century the Florentine merchant and historian Benedetto Dei (DAY-ee) boasted proudly of his city in a letter to an acquaintance from Venice:

> Our beautiful Florence contains within the city in this present year two hundred seventy shops belonging to the wool merchants' guild . . . eighty-three rich and splendid warehouses of the silk merchants' guild. . . . The number of banks amounts to thirty-three; the shops of the cabinet-makers, whose business is carving and inlaid work, to eighty-four . . . there are forty-four goldsmiths' and jewellers' shops.[1]

In Florence and other thriving Italian cities, wealth allowed many people greater material pleasures, a more comfortable life, and leisure time to appreciate and patronize the arts. Merchants and bankers commissioned public and private buildings from architects, and hired sculptors and painters to decorate their homes and churches. The rich, social-climbing residents of Venice, Florence, Genoa, and Rome came to see life more as an opportunity to be enjoyed than as a painful pilgrimage to the City of God.

Communes and Republics of Northern Italy

The northern Italian cities were **communes**, sworn associations of free men who, like other town residents, began in the twelfth century to seek political and economic independence from local nobles. The merchant guilds that formed the communes built and maintained the city walls and regulated trade, collected taxes, and kept civil order within them. The local nobles frequently moved into the cities, marrying the daughters of rich commercial families and starting their own businesses, often with money they had gained through the dowries provided by their wives. This merger of the northern Italian nobility and the commercial elite created a powerful oligarchy, a small group that ruled the city and surrounding countryside. Yet because of rivalries among competing powerful families within this oligarchy, Italian communes were often politically unstable.

Unrest from below exacerbated the instability. Merchant elites made citizenship in the communes dependent on a property qualification, years of residence within the city, and social connections. Only a tiny percentage of the male population possessed these qualifications and thus could hold political office. The common people, called the **popolo**, were disenfranchised and heavily taxed, and they bitterly resented their exclusion from power. Throughout most of the thirteenth century, in city after city, the popolo used armed force to take over the city governments. At times republican government — in which political power theoretically resides in the people and is exercised by their chosen representatives — was established in numerous Italian cities, including Bologna, Siena, Parma, Florence, Genoa, and other cities. These victories of the popolo proved temporary, however, because they could not establish civil order within their cities. Merchant oligarchies reasserted their power and sometimes brought in powerful military leaders to establish order. These military leaders, called *condottieri* (kahn-duh-TYER-ee; singular *condottiero*), had their own mercenary armies, and in many cities they took over political power once they had supplanted the existing government.

Many cities in Italy became **signori** (seen-YOHR-ee), in which one man — whether condottiero, merchant, or noble — ruled and handed down the right to rule to his son. Some signori (the word is plural in Italian and is used for both persons and forms of government) kept the institutions of communal government in place, but these had no actual power. As a practical matter, there wasn't much difference between oligarchic regimes and signori. Oligarchies maintained a façade of republican government, but the judicial, executive, and legislative functions of government were restricted to a small class of wealthy merchants.

In the fifteenth and sixteenth centuries the signori in many cities and the most powerful merchant oligarchs in others transformed their households into **courts**. Courtly culture afforded signori and oligarchs the opportunity to display and assert their wealth and power. They built magnificent palaces in the centers of cities and required all political business to be done there. Ceremonies connected with family births, baptisms, marriages, and funerals offered occasions for magnificent pageantry and elaborate ritual. Cities welcomed rulers who were visiting with magnificent entrance parades that often included fireworks, colorful banners, mock naval battles, decorated wagons filled with people in costume, and temporary triumphal arches modeled on those of ancient Rome. Rulers of nation-states later copied and adapted all these aspects of Italian courts.

City-States and the Balance of Power

Renaissance Italians had a passionate attachment to their individual city-states: political loyalty and feeling centered on the city. This intensity of local feeling perpetuated the dozens of small states and hindered the development of one unified state.

In the fifteenth century five powers dominated the Italian peninsula: Venice, Milan, Florence, the Papal States, and the kingdom of Naples (Map 12.1). The major Italian powers controlled the smaller city-states, such as Siena, Mantua, Ferrara, and Modena, and competed furiously among themselves for territory. While the states of northern Europe were moving toward centralization and consolidation, the world of Italian politics resembled a jungle where the powerful dominated the weak. Venice, with its enormous trade empire, ranked as an international power. Though Venice was a republic in name, an oligarchy of merchant-aristocrats actually ran the city. Milan was also called a republic, but the condottieri-turned-signori of the Sforza (SFORT-sah) family

MAP 12.1   The Italian City-States, ca. 1494
In the fifteenth century the Italian city-states represented great wealth and cultural sophistication, though the many political divisions throughout the peninsula invited foreign intervention.

ruled harshly and dominated Milan and several smaller cities in the north from 1447
to 1535. Likewise, in Florence the form of government was republican, with authority
vested in several councils of state, but the city was effectively ruled by the great Medici
(MEH-duh-chee) banking family for three centuries, beginning in 1434. Though not
public officials, Cosimo, his son Piero, and his grandson Lorenzo ruled from behind
the scenes from 1434 to 1492. The Medici were then in and out of power for several
decades, and in 1569 Florence became no longer a republic, but the hereditary Grand

Duchy of Tuscany, with the Medici as the Grand Dukes until 1737. The Medici family produced three popes, and most other Renaissance popes were also members of powerful Italian families, selected for their political skills, not their piety. Along with the Italians was one Spaniard, Pope Alexander VI (pontificate 1492–1503), who was the most ruthless; aided militarily and politically by his illegitimate son Cesare Borgia, he reasserted papal authority in the papal lands. South of the Papal States, the kingdom of Naples was under the control of the king of Aragon.

In one significant respect, however, the Italian city-states anticipated future relations among competing European states after 1500. Whenever one Italian state appeared to gain a predominant position within the peninsula, other states combined against it to establish a balance of power. In the formation of these alliances, Renaissance Italians invented the machinery of modern diplomacy: permanent embassies with resident ambassadors in capitals where political relations and commercial ties needed continual monitoring. The resident ambassador was one of the great political achievements of the Italian Renaissance.

At the end of the fifteenth century Venice, Florence, Milan, and the papacy possessed great wealth and represented high cultural achievement. Wealthy and divided, however, they were also an inviting target for invasion. When Florence and Naples entered into an agreement to acquire Milanese territories, Milan called on France for support, and the French king Charles VIII (r. 1483–1498) invaded Italy in 1494.

Prior to this invasion, the Dominican friar Girolamo Savonarola (1452–1498) had preached in Florence a number of fiery sermons attended by large crowds predicting that God would punish Italy for its moral vice and corrupt leadership. Florentines interpreted the French invasion as the fulfillment of this prophecy and expelled the Medici dynasty. Savonarola became the political and religious leader of a new Florentine republic and promised Florentines even greater glory in the future if they would reform their ways. (See "Primary Source: A Sermon of Savonarola," page 372.) He reorganized the government; convinced it to pass laws against same-sex relations, adultery, and drunkenness; and organized groups of young men to patrol the streets looking for immoral dress and behavior. He held religious processions and what became known as "bonfires of the vanities," huge fires on the main square of Florence in which fancy clothing, cosmetics, pagan books, musical instruments, paintings, and poetry that celebrated human beauty were gathered together and burned.

For a time Savonarola was wildly popular, but eventually people tired of his moral denunciations, and he was excommunicated by the pope, tortured, and burned at the very spot where he had overseen the bonfires. The Medici returned as the rulers of Florence.

The French invasion inaugurated a new period in Italian and European power politics. Italy became the focus of international ambitions and the battleground of foreign armies, particularly those of the Holy Roman Empire and France in a series of conflicts called the Habsburg-Valois wars (named for the German and French dynasties). The Italian cities suffered severely from continual warfare, especially in the frightful sack of Rome in 1527 by imperial forces under the emperor Charles V. Thus the failure of the city-states to consolidate, or at least to establish a common foreign policy, led to centuries of subjection by outside invaders. Italy was not to achieve unification until 1870.

PRIMARY SOURCE A Sermon of Savonarola

In the autumn of 1494 French armies under Charles VIII surrounded Florence. The Dominican friar Girolamo Savonarola met with the French king and convinced him to spare the city and keep moving his huge army southward. He preached a series of sermons that winter saying that God had chosen Florence to achieve even greater heights under his leadership than it had in the past, provided that it followed his instructions.

O Florence . . . I tell you, do first those two things I told you another time, that is, that everyone go to confession and be purified of sins, and let everyone attend to the common good of the city; and if you will do this, your city will be glorious because in this way she will be reformed spiritually as well as temporally, that is, with regard to her people, and from you will issue the reform of all Italy. Florence will become richer and more powerful than she has ever been, and her empire will expand into many places. But if you will not do what I tell you, God will elect those who, as I said, want to see you divided, and this will be your final destruction. If you would do what I have told you, here is the fire and here is the water: now do it! . . .

But, Florence, if you want your government to be stable and strong and to endure a long time, you must return to God and to living uprightly; otherwise, you will come to ruin. . . . *Furthermore*, it is necessary that the Magnificent Signory [the government of the city] ordain that all those things contrary to godly religion be removed from the city, and in the first place, to act and ordain that the clergy must be good, because priests have to be a mirror to the people wherein everyone beholds and learns righteous living. But let the bad priests and religious be expelled. . . . They should not puff themselves up with so much material wealth, but give it to the very poor for God's sake. . . .

Intellectual Change

What new ideas were associated with the Renaissance?

The Renaissance was characterized by self-conscious conviction among educated Italians that they were living in a new era. Somewhat ironically, this idea rested on a deep interest in ancient Latin and Greek literature and philosophy. Through reflecting on the classics, Renaissance thinkers developed new notions of human nature, new plans for education, and new concepts of political rule. The advent of the printing press with movable type would greatly accelerate the spread of these ideas throughout Europe.

Humanism

Giorgio Vasari was the first to use the word *Renaissance* in print, but he was not the first to feel that something was being reborn. Two centuries earlier the Florentine poet and scholar Francesco Petrarch (1304–1374) spent long hours searching for classical Latin manuscripts in dusty monastery libraries and wandering around the many ruins of the Roman Empire remaining in Italy. He became obsessed with the classical past and felt

It is necessary that the Signory pass laws against that accursed vice of sodomy [same-sex relations], for which you know that Florence is infamous throughout the whole of Italy; this infamy arises perhaps from your talking and chattering about it so much, so that there is not so much in deeds, perhaps, as in words. Pass a law, I say, and let it be without mercy; that is, let these people be stoned and burned. On the other hand, it is necessary that you remove from among yourselves these poems and games and taverns and the evil fashion of women's clothes, and, likewise, we must throw out everything that is noxious to the health of the soul. Let everyone live for God and not for the world. . . .

The second [resolution]: attend to the common good. O citizens, if you band together and with a good will attend to the common welfare, each shall have more temporal and spiritual goods than if he alone attended to his own particular case. Attend, I say, to the common good of the city, and if anyone would elevate himself, let him be deprived of all his goods.

EVALUATE THE EVIDENCE

1. What does Savonarola tell Florentines they must do, and what will be their reward if they follow his instructions?

2. Savonarola initially had many followers, including well-known writers and artists. Why might his words have found such a ready audience in Florence at that time?

Source: *Selected Writings of Girolamo Savonarola: Religion and Politics, 1490–1498*, trans. and ed. Anne Borelli and Maria Pastore Passaro (New Haven: Yale University Press, 2006), pp. 153, 157, 158. Copyright © 2006 Yale University. All rights reserved. Used by permission of Yale University Press.

that the writers and artists of ancient Rome had reached a level of perfection in their work that had not since been duplicated. Writers of his own day should follow these ancient models, thought Petrarch, and ignore the thousand-year period between his own time and that of Rome, which he called the "dark ages" ushered in by the barbarian invasions. Petrarch believed that the recovery of classical texts would bring about a new golden age of intellectual achievement, an idea that many others came to share.

Petrarch clearly thought he was witnessing the dawning of a new era in which writers and artists would recapture the glory of the Roman Republic. Around 1350 he proposed a new kind of education to help them do this, in which young men would study the works of ancient Roman authors, using them as models of how to write clearly, argue effectively, and speak persuasively. The study of Latin classics became known as the *studia humanitates* (STOO-dee-uh oo-mahn-ee-TAH-tayz), usually translated as "liberal studies" or the "liberal arts." People who advocated it were known as *humanists* and their program as **humanism**. Humanism was the main intellectual component of the Renaissance. Like all programs of study, humanism contained an implicit philosophy: that human nature and achievements, evident in the classics, were worthy of contemplation. (See "Primary Source: Cassandra Fedele on Humanist Learning," page 374.)

PRIMARY SOURCE   Cassandra Fedele on Humanist Learning

Italian humanists detailed the type of education that they regarded as ideal and promoted its value to society and the individual. Several women from the bustling cities of northern Italy became excited by the new style of learning and through tutors or self-study became extremely well educated. One of these was the Venetian Cassandra Fedele (1465–1558), who became the best-known female scholar in her time, corresponding with humanist writers, church officials, university professors, nobles, and even the rulers of Europe. She gave this oration in Latin at the University of Padua in honor of her (male) cousin's graduation.

I shall speak very briefly on the study of the liberal arts, which for humans is useful and honorable, pleasurable and enlightening since everyone, not only philosophers but also the most ignorant man, knows and admits that it is by reason that man is separated from beasts. For what is it that so greatly helps both the learned and the ignorant? What so enlarges and enlightens men's minds the way that an education in and knowledge of literature and the liberal arts do? . . . But erudite men who are filled with the knowledge of divine and human things turn all their thoughts and considerations toward reason as though toward a target, and free their minds from all pain, though plagued by many anxieties. These men are scarcely subjected to fortune's innumerable arrows and they prepare themselves to live well and in happiness. They follow reason as their leader in all things; nor do they consider themselves only, but they are also accustomed to assisting others with their energy and advice in matters public and private.

And so Plato, a man almost divine, wrote that those states would be fortunate in which the men who were heads of state were philosophers or in which philosophers took on the duty of administration. . . . The study of literature refines men's minds, forms and makes bright the power of reason, and washes away all stains

---

The glory of Rome had been brightest, in the opinion of the humanists, in the works of the Roman author and statesman Cicero (106–43 B.C.E.). Cicero had lived during the turbulent era when Julius Caesar and other powerful generals transformed the Roman Republic into an empire (see Chapter 5). In forceful and elegantly worded speeches, letters, and treatises, Cicero supported a return to republican government. Petrarch and other humanists admired Cicero's use of language, literary style, and political ideas. Many humanists saw Caesar's transformation of Rome as a betrayal of the great society, marking the beginning of a long period of decay that the barbarian migrations then accelerated. In his history of Florence written in 1436, the humanist historian and Florentine city official Leonardo Bruni (1374–1444) closely linked the decline of the Latin language after the death of Cicero to the decline of the Roman Republic: "After the liberty of the Roman people had been lost through the rule of the emperors . . . the flourishing condition of studies and of letters perished, together with the welfare of the city of Rome."[2] In this same book, Bruni was also very clear that by the time of his writing, the period of decay had ended and a new era had begun. He was the first to

from the mind, or at any rate, greatly cleanses it. It perfects the gifts and adds much beauty and elegance to the physical and material advantages that one has received by nature. States, however, and their princes who foster and cultivate these studies become more humane, more gracious, and more noble. For this reason, these studies have won for themselves the sweet appellation, "humanities." . . . Just as places that lie unused and uncultivated become fertile and rich in fruits and vegetables with men's labor and hard work and are always made beautiful, so are our natures cultivated, enhanced, and enlightened by the liberal arts. . . .

But enough on the utility of literature since it produces not only an outcome that is rich, precious, and sublime, but also provides one with advantages that are extremely pleasurable, fruitful, and lasting—benefits that I myself have enjoyed. And when I meditate on the idea of marching forth in life with the lowly and execrable weapons of the little woman—the needle and the distaff [the rod onto which yarn is wound after spinning]—even if the study of literature offers women no rewards or honors, I believe women must nonetheless pursue and embrace such studies alone for the pleasure and enjoyment they contain.

EVALUATE THE EVIDENCE

1. What does Fedele see as the best course of study and the purposes of study?

2. In what ways does gender appear to shape ideas about humanist learning?

Source: Excerpt from Cassandra Fedele, *Letters and Orations*, pp. 159–162, ed. and trans. Diana Robin. Copyright © 2000 by The University of Chicago Press. Used with permission of the publisher.

divide history into three eras—ancient, medieval, and modern—though it was another humanist historian who actually invented the term "Middle Ages."

In the fifteenth century Florentine humanists became increasingly interested in Greek philosophy as well as Roman literature, especially in the ideas of Plato. Under the patronage of Cosimo de' Medici (1389–1464), the scholar Marsilio Ficino (1433–1499) began to lecture to an informal group of Florence's cultural elite; his lectures became known as the Platonic Academy, but they were not really a school. Ficino regarded Plato as a divinely inspired precursor to Christ. He translated Plato's dialogues into Latin and wrote commentaries attempting to synthesize Christian and Platonic teachings. Plato's emphasis on the spiritual and eternal over the material and transient fit well with Christian teachings about the immortality of the soul. The Platonic idea that the highest form of love was spiritual desire for pure, perfect beauty uncorrupted by bodily desires could easily be interpreted as Christian desire for the perfection of God.

For Ficino and his most gifted student, Giovanni Pico della Mirandola (1463–1494), both Christian and classical texts taught that the universe was a hierarchy of beings from

INDIVIDUALS IN SOCIETY • Leonardo da Vinci

What makes a genius? A deep curiosity about an extensive variety of subjects? A divine spark that emerges in talents that far exceed the norm? Or is it just "one percent inspiration and ninety-nine percent perspiration," as Thomas Edison said? However it is defined, Leonardo da Vinci counts as a genius. In fact, Leonardo was one of the individuals whom the Renaissance label "genius" was designed to describe: a special kind of human being with exceptional creative powers. Leonardo (who, despite the title of a popular novel and film, is always called by his first name) was born in Vinci, near Florence, the illegitimate son of Caterina, a local peasant girl, and Ser Piero da Vinci, a notary public. When Ser Piero's marriage to Donna Albrussia produced no children, he and his wife took in Leonardo, whose mother had married another man. Ser Piero secured Leonardo an apprenticeship with the painter and sculptor Andrea del Verrocchio in Florence. In 1472, when Leonardo was just twenty years old, he was already listed as a master in Florence's "Company of Artists."

Leonardo's most famous portrait, *Mona Lisa*, shows a woman with an enigmatic smile that Giorgio Vasari described as "so pleasing that it seemed divine rather than human." The portrait, probably of the young wife of a rich Florentine merchant (her exact identity is hotly debated), may be the best-known painting in the history of art. One of its competitors for that designation would be another work of Leonardo, *The Last Supper*, which has been called "the most revered painting in the world."

Leonardo's reputation as a genius does not rest on his paintings, however, which are actually few in number, but rather on the breadth of his abilities and interests. He is considered by many the first "Renaissance man," a phrase still used for a multi-talented individual. Hoping to reproduce what the eye can see, he drew everything he saw around him, including executed criminals hanging on gallows as well as the beauties of nature. Trying to understand how the human body worked, Leonardo studied live and dead bodies, doing autopsies and dissections to investigate muscles and circulation. He carefully analyzed the effects of light, and he experimented with perspective.

Leonardo used his drawings not only as the basis for his paintings but also as a tool of scientific investigation. He drew plans for hundreds of inventions, many of which would become reality centuries later, such as the helicopter, tank, machine gun, and parachute. He was hired by one of the powerful new rulers in Italy, Duke

God down through spiritual beings to material beings, with humanity, right in the middle, as the crucial link that possessed both material and spiritual natures.

Man's divinely bestowed nature meant there were no limits to what he could accomplish. Families, religious brotherhoods, neighborhoods, workers' organizations, and other groups continued to have meaning in peoples' lives, but Renaissance thinkers increasingly viewed these groups as springboards to far greater individual achievement. They were especially interested in individuals who had risen above their background to become brilliant, powerful, or unique. (See "Individuals in Society: Leonardo da Vinci," above.) Such individuals had the admirable quality of **virtù** (vihr-TOO),

Ludovico Sforza of Milan, to design weapons, fortresses, and water systems, as well as to produce works of art. Leonardo left Milan when Sforza was overthrown, and spent the last years of his life painting, drawing, and designing for the pope and the French king.

Leonardo experimented with new materials for painting and sculpture, not all of which worked. The experimental method he used to paint *The Last Supper* caused the picture to deteriorate rapidly, and it began to flake off the wall as soon as it was finished. Leonardo regarded it as never quite completed, for he could not find a model for the face of Christ who would evoke the spiritual depth he felt the figure deserved. His gigantic equestrian statue in honor of Ludovico's father, Duke Francesco Sforza, was never made, and the clay model collapsed. He planned to write books on many subjects but never finished any of them, leaving only notebooks. Leonardo once said that "a painter is not admirable unless he is universal." The patrons who supported him—and he was supported very well—perhaps wished that his inspirations would have been a bit less universal in scope, or at least accompanied by more perspiration.

QUESTIONS FOR ANALYSIS

1. In what ways do the notions of a "genius" and of a "Renaissance man" both support and contradict each other? Which better fits Leonardo?
2. Has the idea of artistic genius changed since the Renaissance? How?

Sources: Giorgio Vasari, *Lives of the Artists*, vol. 1, trans. G. Bull (London: Penguin Books, 1965); S. B. Nuland, *Leonardo da Vinci* (New York: Lipper/Viking, 2000).

ONLINE DOCUMENT ASSIGNMENT

How did the needs and desires of Leonardo's patrons influence his work? Examine letters written by Leonardo to his patrons as well as other written and visual evidence that sheds light on the dynamic between the artist and his employers, and then complete a writing assignment based on the evidence and details from this chapter.

bedfordstmartins.com/mckaywestvalue

which is not virtue in the sense of moral goodness, but their ability to shape the world around them according to their will. Bruni and other historians included biographies of individuals with virtù in their histories of cities and nations, describing ways in which these people had affected the course of history. Through the quality of their works and their influence on others, artists could also exhibit virtù, an idea that Vasari captures in the title of his major work, *The Lives of the Most Excellent Painters, Sculptors, and Architects*. His subjects had achieved not simply excellence but the pinnacle of excellence.

The last artist included in Vasari's book is Vasari himself, for Renaissance thinkers did not exclude themselves when they searched for models of talent and achievement.

Vasari begins his discussion of his own works modestly, saying that these might "not lay claim to excellence and perfection" when compared with those of other artists, but he then goes on for more than thirty pages, clearly feeling he has achieved some level of excellence.

Leon Battista Alberti (1404–1472) had similar views of his own achievements. He had much to be proud of: he wrote novels, plays, legal treatises, a study of the family, and the first scientific analysis of perspective; he designed churches, palaces, and fortifications effective against cannon; he invented codes for sending messages secretly and a machine that could cipher and decipher them. In his autobiography—written late in his life, and in the third person, so that he calls himself "he" instead of "I"—Alberti described his personal qualities and accomplishments:

> Assiduous in the science and skill of dealing with arms and horses and musical instruments, as well as in the pursuit of letters and the fine arts, he was devoted to the knowledge of the most strange and difficult things. . . . He played ball, hurled the javelin, ran, leaped, wrestled. . . . He learned music without teachers . . . and then turned to physics and the mathematical arts. . . . Ambition was alien to him. . . . When his favorite dog died he wrote a funeral oration for him.[3]

His achievements in many fields did make Alberti a "Renaissance man," as we use the term, though it may be hard to believe his assertion that "ambition was alien to him."

Biographies and autobiographies presented individuals that humanist authors thought were worthy models, but sometimes people needed more direct instruction. The ancient Greek philosopher Plato, whom humanists greatly admired, taught that the best way to learn something was to think about its perfect, ideal form. If you wanted to learn about justice, for example, you should imagine what ideal justice would be, rather than look at actual examples of justice in the world around you, for these would never be perfect. Following Plato's ideas, Renaissance authors speculated about perfect examples of many things. Alberti wrote about the ideal country house, which was to be useful, convenient, and elegant. The English humanist Thomas More described a perfect society, which he called *Utopia* (see page 381).

Education

Humanists thought that their recommended course of study in the classics would provide essential skills for future politicians, diplomats, lawyers, military leaders, and businessmen, as well as writers and artists. It would provide a much broader and more practical type of training than that offered at universities, which at the time focused on theology and philosophy or on theoretical training for lawyers and physicians. Humanists poured out treatises, often in the form of letters, on the structure and goals of education and the training of rulers and leaders. They taught that a life active in the world should be the aim of all educated individuals and that education was not simply for private or religious purposes but also for the public good.

Humanists put their ideas into practice. Beginning in the early fifteenth century, they opened schools and academies in Italian cities and courts in which pupils began with Latin grammar and rhetoric, went on to study Roman history and political philosophy, and then learned Greek in order to study Greek literature and philosophy. Gradually, humanist education became the basis for intermediate and advanced education for well-to-do urban boys and men. Humanist schools were established in Florence, Venice, and other Italian cities, and by the early sixteenth century across the Alps in Germany, France, and England.

Humanists disagreed about education for women. Many saw the value of exposing women to classical models of moral behavior and reasoning, but they also wondered whether a program of study that emphasized eloquence and action was proper for women, whose sphere was generally understood to be private and domestic. In his book on the family, Alberti stressed that a wife's role should be restricted to the orderliness of the household, food preparation and the serving of meals, the education of children, and the supervision of servants. (Alberti never married, so he never put his ideas into practice in his own household.) Women themselves were bolder in their claims about the value of the new learning. Although humanist academies were not open to women, a few women did become educated in the classics. They argued in letters and published writings that reason was not limited to men and that learning was compatible with virtue for women as well as men. (See "Primary Source: Cassandra Fedele on Humanist Learning," page 374.)

No book on education had broader influence than Baldassare Castiglione's *The Courtier* (1528). This treatise sought to train, discipline, and fashion the young man into the courtly ideal, the gentleman. According to Castiglione (kahs-teel-YOH-nay), himself a courtier serving several different rulers, the educated man should have a broad background in many academic subjects, and should train his spiritual and physical faculties as well as intellect. Castiglione envisioned a man who could compose a sonnet, wrestle, sing a song while accompanying himself on an instrument, ride expertly, solve difficult mathematical problems, and, above all, speak and write eloquently. Castiglione also included discussion of the perfect court lady, who, like the courtier, was to be well educated and able to play a musical instrument, to paint, and to dance. Physical beauty, delicacy, affability, and modesty were also important qualities for court ladies.

In the sixteenth and seventeenth centuries *The Courtier* was translated into most European languages and widely read. It influenced the social mores and patterns of conduct of elite groups in Renaissance and early modern Europe and became a how-to manual for people seeking to improve themselves and rise in the social hierarchy as well. Echoes of its ideal for women have perhaps had an even longer life.

Political Thought

Ideal courtiers should preferably serve an ideal ruler, and biographies written by humanists often described rulers who were just, wise, pious, dignified, learned, brave, kind, and distinguished. In return for such flattering portraits of living rulers or their ancestors, authors sometimes received positions at court, or at least substantial payments. Particularly in Italian cities, however, which often were divided by political factions, taken over by homegrown or regional despots, and attacked by foreign armies, such ideal rulers were hard to find. Humanists thus looked to the classical past for their models. Some, such as Bruni, argued that republicanism was the best form of government. Others used the model of Plato's philosopher-king in the *Republic* to argue that rule by an enlightened individual might be best. Both sides agreed that educated men should be active in the political affairs of their city, a position historians have since termed "civic humanism."

The most famous (or infamous) civic humanist, and ultimately the best-known political theorist of this era, was Niccolò Machiavelli (1469–1527). After the ouster of the Medici with the French invasion of 1494, Machiavelli was secretary to one of the governing bodies in the city of Florence; he was responsible for diplomatic missions and organizing a citizen army. Almost two decades later, power struggles in Florence between rival factions brought the Medici family back to power, and Machiavelli was arrested, tortured, and imprisoned on suspicion of plotting against them. He was released but had no government position, and he spent the rest of his life writing—political theory, poetry, prose works, plays, and a multivolume history of Florence—and making fruitless attempts to regain employment.

The first work Machiavelli finished—though not the first to be published—is his most famous: *The Prince* (1513), which uses the examples of classical and contemporary rulers to argue that the function of a ruler (or any government) is to preserve order and security. Weakness only leads to disorder, which might end in civil war or conquest by an outsider, situations clearly detrimental to any people's well-being. To preserve the state, a ruler should use whatever means he needs—brutality, lying, manipulation—but should not do anything that would make the populace turn against him; stealing or cruel actions done for a ruler's own pleasure would lead to resentment and destroy the popular support needed for a strong, stable realm. "It is much safer for the prince to be feared than loved," Machiavelli advised, "but he ought to avoid making himself hated."[4]

Like the good humanist he was, Machiavelli knew that effective rulers exhibited the quality of virtù. He presented examples from the classical past of just the type of ruler he was describing, but also wrote about contemporary leaders. Cesare Borgia (1475?–1507), Machiavelli's primary example, was the son of Rodrigo Borgia, a Spanish nobleman who later became Pope Alexander VI. Cesare Borgia combined his father's power and his own ruthlessness to build up a state of his own in central Italy. He made good use of new military equipment and tactics, hiring Leonardo da Vinci (1452–1519) as a military engineer, and murdered his political enemies, including the second husband of his sister, Lucrezia. Despite Borgia's efforts, his state fell apart after his father's death, which Machiavelli ascribed not to weakness, but to the operations of fate (*fortuna*, for-TOO-nah, in Italian), whose power even the best-prepared and most merciless ruler could not fully escape, though he should try. Fortuna was personified and portrayed as a goddess in ancient Rome and Renaissance Italy, and Machiavelli's last words about fortune are expressed in gendered terms: "It is better to be impetuous than cautious, for fortune is a woman, and if one wishes to keep her down, it is necessary to beat her and knock her down."[5]

The Prince is often seen as the first modern guide to politics, though Machiavelli was denounced for writing it, and people later came to use the word *Machiavellian* to mean cunning and ruthless. Medieval political philosophers had debated the proper relation between church and state, but they regarded the standards by which all governments were to be judged as emanating from moral principles established by God. Machiavelli argued that governments should instead be judged by how well they provided security, order, and safety to their populace. A ruler's moral code in maintaining these was not the same as a private individual's, for a leader could—indeed, should—use any means necessary. Machiavelli put a new spin on the Renaissance search for perfection, arguing that ideals needed to be measured in the cold light of the real world. This more pragmatic view of the purposes of government, along with Machiavelli's discussion of the role of force and cruelty, was unacceptable to many.

Even today, when Machiavelli's more secular view of the purposes of government is widely shared, scholars debate whether Machiavelli actually meant what he wrote. Most regard him as realistic or even cynical, but some suggest that he was being ironic or satirical, showing princely government in the worst possible light to contrast it with republicanism. He dedicated *The Prince* to the new Medici ruler of Florence, however, so any criticism was deeply buried within what was, in that era of patronage, essentially a job application.

Christian Humanism

In the last quarter of the fifteenth century, students from the Low Countries, France, Germany, and England flocked to Italy, absorbed the "new learning," and carried it back to their own countries. Northern humanists shared the ideas of Ficino and Pico about the wisdom of ancient texts, but they went beyond Italian efforts to synthesize the Christian and classical traditions to see humanist learning as a way to bring about reform of the church and deepen people's spiritual lives. These **Christian humanists**, as they were later called, thought that the best elements of classical and Christian cultures should be combined. For example, the classical ideals of calmness, stoical patience, and broad-mindedness should be joined in human conduct with the Christian virtues of love, faith, and hope.

The English humanist Thomas More (1478–1535) began life as a lawyer, studied the classics, and entered government service. Despite his official duties, he had time to write, and he became most famous for his controversial dialogue *Utopia* (1516), a word More invented from the Greek words for "nowhere." *Utopia* describes a community on an island somewhere beyond Europe where all children receive a good education, primarily in the Greco-Roman classics, and adults divide their days between manual labor or business pursuits and intellectual activities. The problems that plagued More's fellow citizens, such as poverty and hunger, have been solved by a beneficent government. There is religious toleration, and order and reason prevail. Because Utopian institutions are perfect, however, dissent and disagreement are not acceptable.

More's purposes in writing *Utopia* have been debated just as much as have Machiavelli's in penning *The Prince*. Some view it as a revolutionary critique of More's own hierarchical and violent society, some as a call for an even firmer hierarchy, and others as part of the humanist tradition of satire. It was widely read by learned Europeans in the Latin in which More wrote it, and later in vernacular translations, and its title quickly became the standard word for any imaginary society.

Better known by contemporaries than Thomas More was the Dutch humanist Desiderius Erasmus (dehz-ih-DARE-ee-us ih-RAZ-muhs) (1466?–1536) of Rotterdam. His fame rested on both scholarly editions and translations, and popular works. Erasmus's long list of publications includes *The Education of a Christian Prince* (1504), a book combining idealistic and practical suggestions for the formation of a ruler's character through the careful study of the Bible and classical authors; *The Praise of Folly* (1509), a witty satire poking fun at political, social, and especially religious institutions; and, most important, a new Latin translation of the New Testament alongside the first printed edition of the Greek text (1516). In the preface to the New Testament, Erasmus expressed his ideas about Bible translations: "I wish that even the weakest woman should read the Gospel — should read the epistles of Paul. And I wish these were translated into all

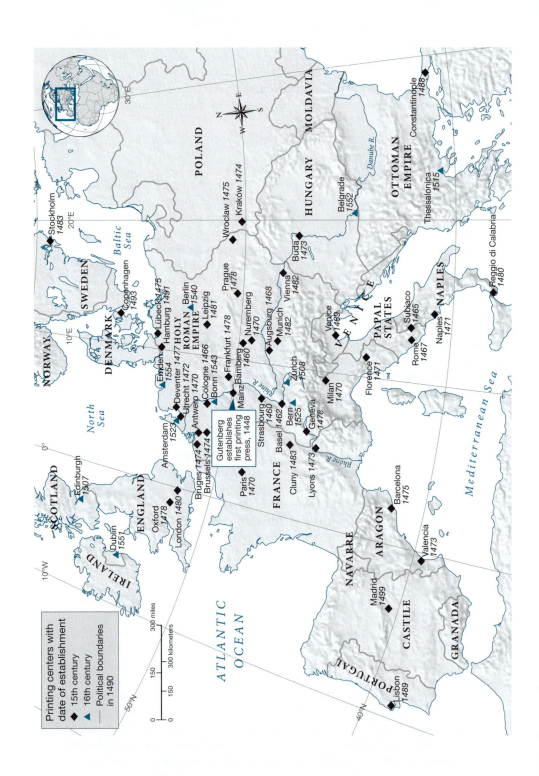

Printing centers with date of establishment
◆ 15th century
▲ 16th century
— Political boundaries in 1490

300 miles
300 kilometers

Gutenberg establishes first printing press, 1448

Stockholm 1483
Copenhagen 1493
Lübeck 1475
Hamburg 1491
Berlin 1540
Leipzig 1481
Emden 1554
Deventer 1477
Utrecht 1472
Cologne 1466
Bonn 1543
Bruges 1474
Brussels 1474
Antwerp 1470
Amsterdam 1523
Edinburgh 1507
Dublin 1551
Oxford 1478
London 1480
Paris 1470
Strasbourg 1460
Basel 1462
Cluny 1483
Bern 1525
Geneva 1478
Lyons 1473
Mainz
Bamberg 1460
Frankfurt 1478
Nuremberg 1470
Munich 1482
Augsburg 1468
Vienna 1482
Zürich 1508
Prague 1478
Wrocław 1475
Kraków 1474
Buda 1473
Belgrade 1552
Venice 1469
Milan 1470
Florence 1471
Rome 1467
Subiaco 1465
Naples 1471
Reggio di Calabria 1480
Thessalonica 1515
Constantinople 1488
Barcelona 1475
Valencia 1473
Madrid 1499
Lisbon 1489

NORWAY
SWEDEN
DENMARK
SCOTLAND
IRELAND
ENGLAND
FRANCE
HOLY ROMAN EMPIRE
POLAND
HUNGARY
MOLDAVIA
OTTOMAN EMPIRE
VENICE
PAPAL STATES
NAPLES
NAVARRE
ARAGON
CASTILE
GRANADA
PORTUGAL

North Sea
Baltic Sea
Mediterranean Sea
ATLANTIC OCEAN
Rhine R.
Rhône R.
Danube R.

30°E
20°E
10°E
0°
10°W
60°N
40°N

◀ **MAP 12.2**   **The Growth of Printing in Europe, 1448–1552**
The speed with which artisans spread printing technology across Europe provides strong evidence for the growing demand for reading material. Presses in the Ottoman Empire were first established by Jewish immigrants who printed works in Hebrew, Greek, and Spanish.

languages, so that they might be read and understood, not only by Scots and Irishmen, but also by Turks and Saracens."[6]

Two fundamental themes run through all of Erasmus's work. First, education in the Bible and the classics is the means to reform, the key to moral and intellectual improvement. Erasmus called for a renaissance of the ideals of the early church to accompany the renaissance in classical education that was already going on, and criticized the church of his day for having strayed from these ideals. Second, renewal should be based on what he termed "the philosophy of Christ," an emphasis on inner spirituality and personal morality rather than Scholastic theology or outward observances such as pilgrimages or venerating relics. His ideas, and Christian humanism in general, were important roots of the Protestant Reformation, although Erasmus himself denied this and never became a follower of Luther (see Chapter 13).

The Printed Word

The fourteenth-century humanist Petrarch and the sixteenth-century humanist Erasmus had similar ideas on many topics, but the immediate impact of their ideas was very different because of one thing: the invention of the printing press with movable metal type. The ideas of Petrarch were spread slowly from person to person by hand copying. The ideas of Erasmus were spread quickly through print, allowing hundreds or thousands of identical copies to be made in a short time.

Printing with movable metal type developed in Germany in the 1440s as a combination of existing technologies. Several metal-smiths, most prominently Johann Gutenberg, recognized that the metal stamps used to mark signs on jewelry could be covered with ink and used to mark symbols onto a surface in the same way that other craftsmen were using carved wood stamps to print books. (This woodblock printing technique originated in China and Korea centuries earlier.) Gutenberg and his assistants made metal stamps — later called *type* — for every letter of the alphabet and built racks that held the type in rows. This type could be rearranged for every page and so used over and over.

The printing revolution was also made possible by the ready availability of paper, which was also produced using techniques that had originated in China, though, unlike the printing press, this technology had been brought into Europe through Muslim Spain rather than developing independently.

By the fifteenth century the increase in urban literacy, the development of primary schools, and the opening of more universities had created an expanding market for reading materials (see Chapter 11). When Gutenberg developed what he saw at first as a faster way to copy, professional copyists writing by hand and block-book makers, along with monks and nuns, were already churning out reading materials on paper as fast as they could for the growing number of people who could read.

Gutenberg was not the only one to recognize the huge market for books, and his invention was quickly copied. Other craftsmen made their own type, built their own presses, and bought their own paper, setting themselves up in business (Map 12.2).

Historians estimate that, within a half century of the publication of Gutenberg's Bible in 1456, somewhere between 8 million and 20 million books were printed in Europe. Whatever the actual figure, the number is far greater than the number of books produced in all of Western history up to that point.

The effects of the invention of movable-type printing were not felt overnight. Nevertheless, movable type radically transformed both the private and the public lives of Europeans by the dawn of the sixteenth century. Print shops became gathering places for people interested in new ideas. Though printers were trained through apprenticeships just like blacksmiths or butchers were, they had connections to the world of politics, art, and scholarship that other craftsmen did not.

Printing gave hundreds or even thousands of people identical books, allowing them to more easily discuss the ideas that the books contained with one another in person or through letters. Printed materials reached an invisible public, allowing silent individuals to join causes and groups of individuals widely separated by geography to form a common identity; this new group consciousness could compete with and transcend older, localized loyalties.

Government and church leaders both used and worried about printing. They printed laws, declarations of war, battle accounts, and propaganda, and they also attempted to censor books and authors whose ideas they thought challenged their authority or were incorrect. Officials developed lists of prohibited books and authors, enforcing their prohibitions by confiscating books, arresting printers and booksellers, or destroying the presses of printers who disobeyed. None of this was very effective, and books were printed secretly, with fake title pages, authors, and places of publication, and smuggled all over Europe.

Printing also stimulated the literacy of laypeople and eventually came to have a deep effect on their private lives. Although most of the earliest books and pamphlets dealt with religious subjects, printers produced anything that would sell. They printed professional reference sets for lawyers, doctors, and students, and historical romances, biographies, and how-to manuals for the general public. They discovered that illustrations increased a book's sales, so they published books on a wide range of topics—from history to pornography—full of woodcuts and engravings. Single-page broadsides and fly sheets allowed great public events and "wonders" such as comets and two-headed calves to be experienced vicariously by a stay-at-home readership. Since books and other printed materials were read aloud to illiterate listeners, print bridged the gap between the written and oral cultures.

Art and the Artist

How did art reflect new Renaissance ideals?

No feature of the Renaissance evokes greater admiration than its artistic masterpieces. The 1400s (*quattrocento*) and 1500s (*cinquecento*) bore witness to dazzling creativity in painting, architecture, and sculpture. In all the arts, the city of Florence led the way. But Florence was not the only artistic center, for Rome and Venice also became important, and northern Europeans perfected their own styles.

Patronage and Power

In early Renaissance Italy, powerful urban groups often flaunted their wealth by commissioning works of art. The Florentine cloth merchants, for example, delegated Filippo

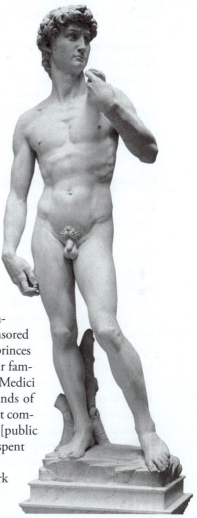

Michelangelo's *David* (1501–1504) Like all Renaissance artists, Michelangelo worked largely on commissions from patrons. Officials of the city of Florence contracted the young sculptor to produce a statue of the Old Testament hero David to be displayed on the city's main square. Michelangelo portrayed David anticipating his fight against the giant Goliath, and the statue came to symbolize the republic of Florence standing up to its larger and more powerful enemies. The *David* captures ideals of human perfection and has come to be an iconic symbol of Renaissance artistic brilliance. (Scala/Ministero per i Beni e le Attività Culturali/Art Resource, NY)

Brunelleschi (broo-nayl-LAYS-kee) to build the magnificent dome on the cathedral of Florence and selected Lorenzo Ghiberti (gee-BEHR-tee) to design the bronze doors of the adjacent Baptistery, a separate building in which baptisms were performed. These works represented the merchants' dominant influence in the community.

Increasingly in the late fifteenth century, wealthy individuals and rulers, rather than corporate groups, sponsored works of art. Patrician merchants and bankers, popes, and princes spent vast sums on the arts to glorify themselves and their families. Writing in about 1470, Florentine ruler Lorenzo de' Medici declared that his family had spent hundreds of thousands of gold florins for artistic and architectural commissions, but commented, "I think it casts a brilliant light on our estate [public reputation] and it seems to me that the monies were well spent and I am very pleased with this."[7]

Patrons varied in their level of involvement as a work progressed; some simply ordered a specific subject or scene, while others oversaw the work of the artist or architect very closely, suggesting themes and styles and demanding changes while the work was in progress. For example, Pope Julius II (pontificate 1503–1513), who commissioned Michelangelo to paint the ceiling of the Vatican's Sistine Chapel in 1508, demanded that the artist work as fast as he could and frequently visited him at his work with suggestions and criticisms. Michelangelo, a Florentine who had spent his young adulthood at the court of Lorenzo de' Medici, complained in person and by letter about the pope's meddling, but his reputation did not match the power of the pope, and he kept working until the chapel was finished in 1512.

In addition to power, art reveals changing patterns of consumption among the wealthy elite in European society. In the rural world of the Middle Ages, society had been organized for war, and men of wealth spent their money on military gear. As Italian nobles settled in towns (see Chapter 10), they adjusted to an urban culture. Rather than employing knights for warfare, cities hired mercenaries. Accordingly, expenditures on military hardware by nobles declined. For the noble recently arrived from the countryside or the rich merchant of the city, a grand urban palace represented the greatest outlay of cash. Wealthy individuals and families ordered gold dishes, embroidered table-cloths, wall tapestries, paintings on canvas (an innovation), and sculptural decorations to adorn these homes. By the late sixteenth century the Strozzi banking family of Florence spent more on household goods than they did on clothing, jewelry, or food, though these were increasingly elaborate as well.

After the palace itself, the private chapel within the palace symbolized the largest expenditure for the wealthy of the sixteenth century. Decorated with religious scenes and equipped with ecclesiastical furniture, the chapel served as the center of the household's religious life and its cult of remembrance of the dead.

Changing Artistic Styles

The content and style of Renaissance art both often differed from those of the Middle Ages. Religious topics, such as the Annunciation of the Virgin and the Nativity, remained popular among both patrons and artists, but frequently the patron had himself and his family portrayed in the scene. As the fifteenth century advanced and humanist ideas spread more widely, classical themes and motifs, such as the lives and loves of pagan gods and goddesses, figured increasingly in painting and sculpture, with the facial features of the gods sometimes modeled on living people.

The individual portrait emerged as a distinct artistic genre in this movement. Rather than reflecting a spiritual ideal, as medieval painting and sculpture tended to do, Renaissance portraits showed human ideals, often portrayed in the more realistic style increasingly favored by both artists and patrons. The Florentine painter Giotto (JAH-toh) (1276–1337) led the way in the use of realism; his treatment of the human body and face replaced the formal stiffness and artificiality that had long characterized representation of the human body. Piero della Francesca (frahn-CHAY-skah) (1420–1492) and Andrea Mantegna (mahn-TEHN-yuh) (1430/31–1506) pioneered perspective, the linear representation of distance and space on a flat surface, which enhanced the realism of paintings and differentiated them from the flatter and more stylized images of medieval art. The sculptor Donatello (1386–1466) revived the classical figure, with its balance and self-awareness. In architecture, Filippo Brunelleschi (1377–1446) looked to the classical past for inspiration, designing a hospital for orphans and foundlings in which all proportions—of the windows, height, floor plan, and covered walkway with a series of rounded arches—were carefully thought out to achieve a sense of balance and harmony.

Art produced in northern Europe tended to be more religious in orientation than that produced in Italy. Some Flemish painters, notably Rogier van der Weyden (1399/1400–1464) and Jan van Eyck (1366–1441), were considered the artistic equals of Italian painters and were much admired in Italy. Van Eyck was one of the earliest artists to use oil-based paints successfully, and his religious scenes and portraits all show great realism and remarkable attention to human personality. Albrecht Dürer (1471–1528), from the German city of Nuremberg, studied with artists in Italy, and produced woodcuts, engravings, and etchings that rendered the human form and the natural world in amazing detail. He was fascinated with the theoretical and practical problems of perspective, and designed mechanical devices that could assist artists in solving these. Late in his life he saw the first pieces of Aztec art shipped back to Europe from the New World and commented in his diary about how amazing they were.

In the early sixteenth century the center of the new art shifted from Florence to Rome, where wealthy cardinals and popes wanted visual expression of the church's and their own families' power and piety. Renaissance popes expended enormous enthusiasm and huge sums of money to beautify the city. Pope Julius II tore down the old Saint Peter's Basilica and began work on the present structure in 1506. Michelangelo went to Rome from Florence in about 1500 and began the series of statues, paintings, and architectural projects from which he gained an international reputation: the *Pietà*, *Moses*, the redesigning of the plaza and surrounding palaces on the Capitoline Hill in central Rome, and, most famously, the dome for Saint Peter's and the ceiling and altar wall of the nearby Sistine Chapel.

Raphael Sanzio (1483–1520), another Florentine, got the commission for frescoes in the papal apartments, and in his relatively short life he painted hundreds of portraits and devotional images, becoming the most sought-after artist in Europe. Raphael also oversaw a large workshop with many collaborators and apprentices—who assisted on the less difficult sections of some paintings—and wrote treatises on his philosophy of art in which he emphasized the importance of imitating nature and developing an orderly sequence of design and proportion.

Venice became another artistic center in the sixteenth century. Titian (TIH-shuhn) (1490–1576) produced portraits, religious subjects, and mythological scenes, developing techniques of painting in oil without doing elaborate drawings first, which speeded up the process and pleased patrons eager to display their acquisitions. Titian and other sixteenth-century painters developed an artistic style known in English as "mannerism" (from *maniera* or "style" in Italian) in which artists sometimes distorted figures, exaggerated musculature, and heightened color to express emotion and drama more intently.

The Renaissance Artist

Some patrons rewarded certain artists very well, and some artists gained great public acclaim as, in Vasari's words, "rare men of genius." This adulation of the artist has led many historians to view the Renaissance as the beginning of the concept of the artist as having a special talent. In the Middle Ages people believed that only God created, albeit through individuals; the medieval conception recognized no particular value in artistic originality. Renaissance artists and humanists came to think that a work of art was the deliberate creation of a unique personality who transcended traditions, rules, and theories. A genius had a peculiar gift, which ordinary laws should not inhibit. Michelangelo and Leonardo da Vinci perhaps best embody the new concept of the Renaissance artist as genius. (See "Individuals in Society: Leonardo da Vinci," page 376.)

It is important not to overemphasize the Renaissance notion of genius. As certain artists became popular and well known, they could assert their own artistic styles and pay less attention to the wishes of patrons, but even major artists like Raphael generally worked according to the patron's specific guidelines. Whether in Italy or northern Europe, most Renaissance artists trained in the workshops of older artists; Botticelli, Raphael, Titian, and at times even Michelangelo were known for their large, well-run, and prolific workshops. Though they might be men of genius, artists were still expected to be well trained in proper artistic techniques and stylistic conventions; the notion that artistic genius could show up in the work of an untrained artist did not emerge until the twentieth century. Beginning artists spent years mastering their craft by copying

Botticelli, *Primavera* (Spring), ca. 1482   Framed by a grove of orange trees, Venus, goddess of love, is flanked on the right by Flora, goddess of flowers and fertility, and on the left by the Three Graces, goddesses of banquets, dance, and social occasions. Above, Venus's son Cupid, the god of love, shoots darts of desire, while at the far right the wind god Zephyrus chases the nymph Chloris. The entire scene rests on classical mythology, though some art historians claim that Venus is an allegory for the Virgin Mary. Botticelli captured the ideal for female beauty in the Renaissance: slender, with pale skin, a high forehead, red-blond hair, and sloping shoulders. (Galleria degli Uffizi, Florence, Italy/The Bridgeman Art Library)

drawings and paintings; learning how to prepare paint and other artistic materials; and, by the sixteenth century, reading books about design and composition. Younger artists gathered together in the evenings for further drawing practice; by the later sixteenth century some of these informal groups had turned into more formal artistic "academies," the first of which was begun in 1563 in Florence by Vasari under the patronage of the Medici.

As Vasari's phrase indicates, the notion of artistic genius that developed in the Renaissance was gendered. All the most famous and most prolific Renaissance artists were male. The types of art in which more women were active, such as textiles, needlework, and painting on porcelain, were not regarded as "major arts," but only as "minor" or "decorative" arts. (The division between "major" and "minor" arts begun in the Renaissance continues to influence the way museums and collections are organized today.) Like painting, embroidery changed in the Renaissance to become more naturalistic, more visually complex, and more classical in its subject matter. Embroiderers were not trained to view their work as products of individual genius, however, so they rarely included their names on the works, and there is no way to discover their identities.

There are no female architects whose names are known and only one female sculptor, though several women did become well known as painters in their day. Stylistically, their works are different from one another, but their careers show many similarities. The majority of female painters were the daughters of painters or of minor noblemen with ties to artistic circles. Many were eldest daughters or came from families in which there were no sons, so their fathers took unusual interest in their careers. Many women painters began their careers before they were twenty and either produced far fewer paintings after they married or stopped painting entirely. Women were not allowed to study the male nude, a study that was viewed as essential if one wanted to paint large history or biblical paintings with many figures. Women also could not learn the technique of fresco, in which colors are applied directly to wet plaster walls, because such work had to be done in public, which was judged inappropriate for women. Joining a group of male artists for informal practice was also seen as improper, so women had no access to the newly established artistic academies. Like universities, humanist academies, and most craft guild shops, artistic workshops were male-only settings in which men of different ages came together for training and created bonds of friendship, influence, patronage, and sometimes intimacy.

Women were not alone in being excluded from the institutions of Renaissance culture. Though a few rare men of genius such as Leonardo and Michelangelo emerged from artisanal backgrounds, most scholars and artists came from families with at least some money. The ideas of the highly educated humanists did not influence the lives of most people in cities and did not affect life in the villages at all. For rural people and for less well-off town residents, work and play continued much as they had in the High Middle Ages: religious festivals and family celebrations provided people's main amusements, and learning came from one's parents, not through formal schooling (see Chapter 10).

Social Hierarchies

What were the key social hierarchies in Renaissance Europe?

The division between educated and uneducated people was only one of many social hierarchies evident in the Renaissance. Every society has social hierarchies; in ancient Rome, for example, there were patricians and plebeians (see Chapter 5). Such hierarchies are to some degree descriptions of social reality, but they are also idealizations — that is, they describe how people imagined their society to be, without all the messy reality of social-climbing plebeians or groups that did not fit the standard categories. Social hierarchies in the Renaissance were built on those of the Middle Ages that divided nobles from commoners, but they also developed new concepts that contributed to modern social hierarchies, such as those of race, class, and gender.

Race and Slavery

Renaissance people did not use the word *race* the way we do, but often used *race, people,* and *nation* interchangeably for ethnic, national, religious, or other groups — the French race, the Jewish nation, the Irish people, "the race of learned gentlemen," and so on. They did make distinctions based on skin color that provide some of the background for later conceptualizations of race, but these distinctions were interwoven with other characteristics when people thought about human differences.

Ever since the time of the Roman Republic, a small number of black Africans had lived in western Europe. They had come, along with white slaves, as the spoils of war. Even after the collapse of the Roman Empire, Muslim and Christian merchants continued to import them. Unstable political conditions in many parts of Africa enabled enterprising merchants to seize people and sell them into slavery. Local authorities afforded these Africans no protection. Long tradition, moreover, sanctioned the practice of slavery. The evidence of medieval art attests to the continued presence of Africans in Europe throughout the Middle Ages and to Europeans' awareness of them.

Beginning in the fifteenth century sizable numbers of black slaves entered Europe. Portuguese sailors brought perhaps a thousand Africans a year to the markets of Seville, Barcelona, Marseilles, and Genoa. In the late fifteenth century this flow increased, with thousands of people taken from the west coast of Africa. By 1530 between four thousand and five thousand were sold to the Portuguese each year. By the mid-sixteenth century blacks, both slave and free, constituted about 10 percent of the population of the Portuguese cities of Lisbon and Évora and roughly 3 percent of the Portuguese population overall. Cities such as Lisbon also had significant numbers of people of mixed African and European descent, as African slaves intermingled with the people they lived among and sometimes intermarried.

Although blacks were concentrated in the Iberian Peninsula, some Africans must have lived in northern Europe as well. In the 1580s, for example, Queen Elizabeth I of England complained that there were too many "blackamoores" competing with needy English people for places as domestic servants. Black servants were much sought after; the medieval interest in curiosities, the exotic, and the marvelous continued in the Renaissance. Italian aristocrats had their portraits painted with their black page boys to indicate their wealth. Blacks were so greatly in demand at the Renaissance courts of northern Italy, in fact, that the Venetians defied papal threats of excommunication to secure them. In 1491 Isabella d'Este, the duchess of Mantua and a major patron of the arts, instructed her agent to secure a black girl between four and eight years old, "shapely and as black as possible." She hoped the girl would become "the best buffoon in the world," noting that "we shall make her very happy and shall have great fun with her."[8] The girl would join musicians, acrobats, and dancers at Isabella's court as a source of entertainment, her status similar to that of the dwarves who could be found at many Renaissance courts.

Africans were not simply amusements at court. In Portugal, Spain, and Italy slaves supplemented the labor force in virtually all occupations — as servants, agricultural laborers, craftsmen, and seamen on ships going to Lisbon and Africa. Agriculture in Europe did not involve large plantations, so large-scale agricultural slavery did not develop there as it would in the late fifteenth century in the New World.

Until the voyages down the African coast in the late fifteenth century, Europeans had little concrete knowledge of Africans and their cultures. They perceived Africa as a remote place, the home of strange people isolated by heresy and Islam from superior European civilization. Africans' contact, even as slaves, with Christian Europeans could only "improve" the blacks, they thought. The expanding slave trade reinforced negative preconceptions about the inferiority of black Africans.

Wealth and the Nobility

The word *class*—as in working class, middle class, and upper class—was not used in the Renaissance to describe social divisions, but by the thirteenth century, and even more so by the fifteenth, the idea of a hierarchy based on wealth was emerging. This was particularly true in cities, where wealthy merchants who oversaw vast trading empires lived in splendor that rivaled the richest nobles. As we saw earlier, in many cities these merchants had gained political power to match their economic might, becoming merchant oligarchs who ruled through city councils. This hierarchy of wealth was more fluid than the older divisions into noble and commoner, allowing individuals and families to rise—and fall—within one generation.

The development of a hierarchy of wealth did not mean an end to the prominence of nobles, however, and even poorer nobility still had higher status than wealthy commoners. Thus wealthy Italian merchants enthusiastically bought noble titles and country villas in the fifteenth century, and wealthy English or Spanish merchants eagerly married their daughters and sons into often-impoverished noble families. The nobility maintained its status in most parts of Europe not by maintaining rigid boundaries, but by taking in and integrating the new social elite of wealth.

Along with being tied to hierarchies of wealth and family standing, social status was linked to considerations of honor. Among the nobility, for example, certain weapons and battle tactics were favored because they were viewed as more honorable. Among urban dwellers, certain occupations, such as city executioner or manager of the municipal brothel, might be well paid but were understood to be dishonorable and so of low status. In cities, sumptuary laws reflected both wealth and honor (see Chapter 10); merchants were specifically allowed fur and jewels, while prostitutes were ordered to wear yellow bands that would remind potential customers of the flames of Hell.

Gender Roles

Renaissance people would not have understood the word *gender* to refer to categories of people, but they would have easily grasped the concept. Toward the end of the fourteenth century, learned men (and a few women) began what was termed the **debate about women** (*querelle des femmes*), a debate about women's character and nature that would last for centuries. Misogynist (muh-SAH-juh-nihst) critiques of women from both clerical and secular authors denounced females as devious, domineering, and demanding. In answer, several authors compiled long lists of famous and praiseworthy women exemplary for their loyalty, bravery, and morality. Christine de Pizan was among the writers who were interested not only in defending women, but also in exploring the reasons behind women's secondary status—that is, why the great philosophers, statesmen, and poets had generally been men. In this they were anticipating discussions about the "social construction of gender" by six hundred years. (See "Primary Source: Cassandra Fedele on Humanist Learning," page 374.)

With the development of the printing press, popular interest in the debate about women grew, and works were translated, reprinted, and shared around Europe. Prints that juxtaposed female virtues and vices were also very popular, with the virtuous women depicted as those of the classical or biblical past and the vice-ridden dressed in contemporary clothes. The favorite metaphor for the virtuous wife was either the snail or the

Phyllis Riding Aristotle   Among the many scenes that expressed the debate about women visually were woodcuts, engravings, paintings, and even cups and plates that showed the classical philosopher Aristotle as an old man being ridden by the young, beautiful Phyllis (shown here in a German woodcut). The origins of the story are uncertain, but in the Renaissance everyone knew the tale of how Aristotle's infatuation with Phyllis led to his ridicule. Male moralists used it as a warning about the power of women's sexual allure, though women may have interpreted it differently. (Réunion des Musées Nationaux/Art Resource, NY)

tortoise, both animals that never leave their "houses" and are totally silent, although such images were never as widespread as those depicting wives beating their husbands or hiding their lovers from them.

Beginning in the sixteenth century, the debate about women also became a debate about female rulers, sparked primarily by dynastic accidents in many countries, including Spain, England, Scotland, and France, which led to women ruling in their own right or serving as advisers to child kings. The questions were vigorously and at times viciously argued. They directly concerned the social construction of gender: could a woman's being born into a royal family and educated to rule allow her to overcome the limitations of her sex? Should it? Or stated another way: which was (or should be) the stronger determinant of character and social role, gender or rank? Despite a prevailing sentiment that women were not as fit to rule as men, there were no successful rebellions against female rulers simply because they were women, but in part this was because female rulers, especially Queen Elizabeth I of England, emphasized qualities regarded as masculine—physical bravery, stamina, wisdom, duty—whenever they appeared in public.

Ideas about women's and men's proper roles determined the actions of ordinary men and women even more forcefully. The dominant notion of the "true" man was that of the married head of household, so men whose social status and age would have normally conferred political power but who remained unmarried did not participate in politics to the same level as their married brothers. Unmarried men in Venice, for example, could not be part of the ruling council.

Women were also understood as either "married or to be married," even if the actual marriage patterns in Europe left many women (and men) unmarried until quite late in life (see Chapter 11). This meant that women's work was not viewed as financially supporting a family—even if it did—and was valued less than men's. If they worked for wages, and many women did, women earned about half to two-thirds of what men did, even for the same work. Regulations for vineyard workers in the early sixteenth century, for example, specified:

> Men who work in the vineyards, doing work that is skilled, are to be paid 16 pence per day; in addition, they are to receive soup and wine in the morning, at midday beer, vegetables and meat, and in the evening soup, vegetables and wine. Young boys are to be paid 10 pence per day. Women who work as haymakers are to be given 6 pence a day. If the employer wants to have them doing other work, he may make an agreement with them to pay them 7 or 8 pence. He may also give them soup and vegetables to eat in the morning—but no wine—milk and bread at midday, but nothing in the evening.[9]

The maintenance of appropriate power relationships between men and women, with men dominant and women subordinate, served as a symbol of the proper functioning of society as a whole. Disorder in the proper gender hierarchy was linked with social upheaval and was viewed as threatening. Of all the ways in which Renaissance society was hierarchically arranged—social rank, age, level of education, race, occupation—gender was regarded as the most "natural" and therefore the most important to defend.

Politics and the State in Western Europe

How did nation-states develop in this period?

The High Middle Ages had witnessed the origins of many of the basic institutions of the modern state. Sheriffs, inquests, juries, circuit judges, professional bureaucracies, and representative assemblies all trace their origins to the twelfth and thirteenth centuries. The linchpin for the development of states, however, was strong monarchy, and during the period of the Hundred Years' War, no ruler in western Europe was able to provide effective leadership. The resurgent power of feudal nobilities weakened the centralizing work begun earlier.

Beginning in the fifteenth century, however, rulers utilized aggressive methods to rebuild their governments. First in the regional states of Italy, then in the expanding monarchies of France, England, and Spain, rulers began the work of reducing violence, curbing unruly nobles, and establishing domestic order. They attempted to secure their borders and enhanced methods of raising revenue. The monarchs of western Europe emphasized royal majesty and royal sovereignty and insisted on the respect and loyalty of all subjects, including the nobility. In central Europe the Holy Roman emperors attempted to do the same, but they were not able to overcome the power of local interests to create a unified state (see Chapter 13).

France

The Black Death and the Hundred Years' War left France drastically depopulated, commercially ruined, and agriculturally weak. Nonetheless, the ruler whom Joan of Arc had seen crowned at Reims, Charles VII (r. 1422–1461), revived the monarchy and France. He seemed an unlikely person to do so. Frail, indecisive, and burdened with questions about his paternity (his father had been deranged; his mother, notoriously promiscuous), Charles VII nevertheless began France's long recovery.

Charles reconciled the Burgundians and Armagnacs (ahr-muhn-YAKZ), who had been waging civil war for thirty years. By 1453 French armies had expelled the English from French soil except in Calais. Charles reorganized the royal council, giving increased influence to lawyers and bankers, and strengthened royal finances through taxes on certain products and on land, which remained the Crown's chief sources of income until the Revolution of 1789.

By establishing regular companies of cavalry and archers — recruited, paid, and inspected by the state — Charles created the first permanent royal army anywhere in Europe. His son Louis XI (r. 1461–1483), called the "Spider King" because of his treacherous character, improved upon Charles's army and used it to control the nobles' separate militias and to curb urban independence. The army was also employed in 1477 when Louis conquered Burgundy upon the death of its ruler Charles the Bold. Three years later, the extinction of the house of Anjou with the death of its last legitimate male heir brought Louis the counties of Anjou, Bar, Maine, and Provence.

Two further developments strengthened the French monarchy. The marriage of Louis XII (r. 1498–1515) and Anne of Brittany added the large western duchy of Brittany to the state. Then King Francis I and Pope Leo X reached a mutually satisfactory agreement about church and state powers in 1516. The new treaty, the Concordat of Bologna, approved the pope's right to receive the first year's income of newly named bishops and abbots in France. In return, Leo X recognized the French ruler's right to select French bishops and abbots. French kings thereafter effectively controlled the appointment and thus the policies of church officials in the kingdom.

England

English society also suffered severely from the disorders of the fifteenth century. The aristocracy dominated the government of Henry IV (r. 1399–1413) and indulged in disruptive violence at the local level, fighting each other, seizing wealthy travelers for ransom, and plundering merchant caravans (see Chapter 11). Population continued to decline. Between 1455 and 1471 adherents of the ducal houses of York and Lancaster contended for control of the Crown in a civil war, commonly called the Wars of the Roses because the symbol of the Yorkists was a white rose and that of the Lancastrians a red one. The chronic disorder hurt trade, agriculture, and domestic industry. Under the pious but mentally disturbed Henry VI (r. 1422–1461), the authority of the monarchy sank lower than it had been in centuries.

The Yorkist Edward IV (r. 1461–1483) began establishing domestic tranquillity. He succeeded in defeating the Lancastrian forces and after 1471 began to reconstruct the monarchy. Edward, his brother Richard III (r. 1483–1485), and Henry VII (r. 1485–1509) of the Welsh house of Tudor worked to restore royal prestige, to crush the power of the nobility, and to establish order and law at the local level. All three rulers used methods that Machiavelli himself would have praised — ruthlessness, efficiency, and secrecy.

Edward IV and subsequently the Tudors, except Henry VIII, conducted foreign policy on the basis of diplomacy, avoiding expensive wars. Thus the English monarchy did not have to depend on Parliament for money, and the Crown undercut that source of aristocratic influence.

Henry VII did summon several meetings of Parliament in the early years of his reign, primarily to confirm laws, but the center of royal authority was the royal council, which governed at the national level. There Henry VII revealed his distrust of the nobility: though not completely excluded, very few great lords were among the king's closest advisers. Instead he chose men from among the smaller landowners and urban residents trained in law. The council conducted negotiations with foreign governments and secured international recognition of the Tudor dynasty through the marriage in 1501 of Henry VII's eldest son, Arthur, to Catherine of Aragon, the daughter of Ferdinand and Isabella of Spain. The council dealt with real or potential aristocratic threats through a judicial offshoot, the Court of Star Chamber, so called because of the stars painted on the ceiling of the room. The court applied methods that were sometimes terrifying: accused persons were not entitled to see evidence against them; sessions were secret; juries were not called; and torture could be applied to extract confessions. These procedures ran directly counter to English common-law precedents, but they effectively reduced aristocratic troublemaking.

When Henry VII died in 1509, he left a country at peace both domestically and internationally, a substantially augmented treasury, an expanding wool trade, and a crown with its dignity and role much enhanced. He was greatly missed after he died "by all his subjects," wrote the historian Polydore Vergil, "who had been able to conduct their lives peaceably, far removed from the assaults and evildoings of scoundrels."[10]

Spain

While England and France laid the foundations of unified nation-states during the Middle Ages, Spain remained a conglomerate of independent kingdoms. By the middle of the fifteenth century, the kingdoms of Castile and Aragon dominated the weaker Navarre, Portugal, and Granada; and the Iberian Peninsula, with the exception of Granada, had been won for Christianity (Map 12.3). But even the wedding in 1469 of the dynamic and aggressive Isabella of Castile and the crafty and persistent Ferdinand of Aragon did not bring about administrative unity. Rather, their marriage constituted a dynastic union of two royal houses, not the political union of two peoples. Although Ferdinand and Isabella (r. 1474–1516) pursued a common foreign policy, until about 1700 Spain existed as a loose confederation of separate kingdoms, each maintaining its own cortes (parliament), laws, courts, and systems of coinage and taxation.

Ferdinand and Isabella were able to exert their authority in ways similar to the rulers of France and England, however. They curbed aristocratic power by excluding high nobles from the royal council, which had full executive, judicial, and legislative powers under the monarchy, instead appointing lesser landowners. The council and various government boards recruited men trained in Roman law, which exalted the power of the Crown. They also secured from the Spanish Borgia pope Alexander VI — Cesare Borgia's father — the right to appoint bishops in Spain and in the Hispanic territories in America, enabling them to establish the equivalent of a national church. With the revenues from ecclesiastical estates, they were able to expand their territories to include the remaining land held by Arabs in southern Spain. The victorious entry of Ferdinand

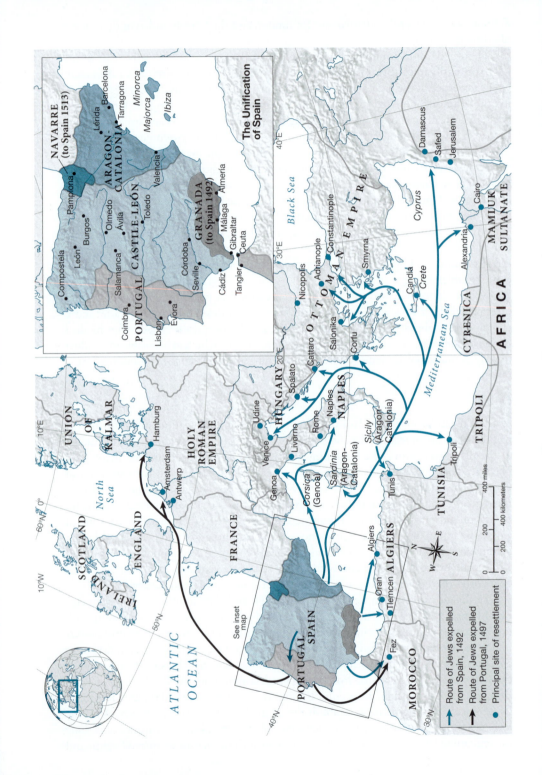

The Unification of Spain

NAVARRE (to Spain 1513)

ARAGON-CATALONIA

Barcelona
Lérida
Tarragona
Minorca
Majorca
Ibiza
Pamplona
Valencia

CASTILE-LEÓN

Compostela
León
Burgos
Olmedo
Ávila
Salamanca
Toledo
Almería
Málaga
GRANADA (to Spain 1492)
Córdoba
Gibraltar
Ceuta
Seville
Cádiz
Tangier

PORTUGAL
Coimbra
Lisbon
Évora

Damascus
Safed
Jerusalem

MAMLUK SULTANATE

Black Sea

Constantinople
Adrianople
Smyrna
Cyprus
Cairo
Alexandria

O T T O M A N   E M P I R E

Nicopolis
Candia
Crete
Salonika
Corfu

CYRENICA

AFRICA

Mediterranean Sea

UNION OF KALMAR

Hamburg

HOLY ROMAN EMPIRE

Udine
HUNGARY
Spalato
Cattaro
Venice
Amsterdam
Antwerp

North Sea

SCOTLAND
IRELAND
ENGLAND

FRANCE

Genoa
Livorno
Rome
Naples
NAPLES
Sicily (Aragon-Catalonia)
Sardinia (Aragon-Catalonia)
Corsica (Genoa)

Tunis
TUNISIA
TRIPOLI
Tripoli

See inset map

ATLANTIC OCEAN

PORTUGAL
SPAIN

Algiers
ALGIERS
Oran
Tlemcen
Fez
MOROCCO

400 miles
400 kilometers
200
200
0

Route of Jews expelled from Spain, 1492
Route of Jews expelled from Portugal, 1497
Principal site of resettlement

◀ **MAP 12.3**   **The Unification of Spain and the Expulsion of the Jews, Fifteenth Century**
The marriage of Ferdinand of Aragon and Isabella of Castile in 1469 brought most of the Iberian Peninsula under one monarchy, although different parts of Spain retained distinct cultures, languages, and legal systems. In 1492 Ferdinand and Isabella conquered Granada, where most people were Muslim, and expelled the Jews from all of Spain. Spanish Jews resettled in cities of Europe and the Mediterranean that allowed them in, including Muslim states such as the Ottoman Empire. Muslims were also expelled from Spain over the course of the sixteenth and early seventeenth centuries.

and Isabella into Granada on January 6, 1492, signaled the conclusion of the reconquista. Granada was incorporated into the Spanish kingdom, and in 1512 Ferdinand conquered Navarre in the north.

There still remained a sizable and, in the view of the majority of the Spanish people, potentially dangerous minority, the Jews. When the kings of France and England had expelled the Jews from their kingdoms (see Chapter 9), many had sought refuge in Spain. During the long centuries of the reconquista, Christian kings had recognized Jewish rights and privileges; in fact, Jewish industry, intelligence, and money had supported royal power. While Christians borrowed from Jewish moneylenders and while all who could afford them sought Jewish physicians, a strong undercurrent of resentment of Jewish influence and wealth festered.

In the fourteenth century anti-Semitism in Spain was aggravated by fiery anti-Jewish preaching, by economic dislocation, and by the search for a scapegoat during the Black Death. Anti-Semitic pogroms swept the towns of Spain, and perhaps 40 percent of the Jewish population was killed or forced to convert. Those converted were called *conversos* or **New Christians**. Conversos were often well educated and held prominent positions in government, the church, medicine, law, and business. Numbering perhaps two hundred thousand in a total Spanish population of about 7.5 million, New Christians and Jews in fifteenth-century Spain exercised influence disproportionate to their numbers.

Such successes bred resentment. Aristocratic grandees resented the conversos' financial dependence; the poor hated the converso tax collectors; and churchmen doubted the sincerity of their conversions. Queen Isabella shared these suspicions, and she and Ferdinand had received permission from Pope Sixtus IV in 1478 to establish their own Inquisition to "search out and punish converts from Judaism who had transgressed against Christianity by secretly adhering to Jewish beliefs and performing rites of the Jews."[11] Investigations and trials began immediately, as officials of the Inquisition looked for conversos who showed any sign of incomplete conversion, such as not eating pork.

Recent scholarship has carefully analyzed documents of the Inquisition. Most conversos identified themselves as sincere Christians; many came from families that had received baptism generations before. In response to conversos' statements, officials of the Inquisition developed a new type of anti-Semitism. A person's status as a Jew, they argued, could not be changed by religious conversion, but was in the person's blood and was heritable, so Jews could never be true Christians. In what were known as "purity of blood" laws, having pure Christian blood became a requirement for noble status. Ideas about Jews developed in Spain were important components in European concepts of race, and discussions of "Jewish blood" later expanded into notions of the "Jewish race."

Tax Collectors New types of taxes and more effective methods of tax collection were essential to the growth of Renaissance states, but both were often highly unpopular. In this painting from about 1540 the Dutch artist Marinus van Reymerswaele depicts two tax collectors as they count their take and record it in a ledger. Tax collectors were men of middling status, but these wear clothing more appropriate for nobles. (Erich Lessing/Art Resource, NY)

In 1492, shortly after the conquest of Granada, Isabella and Ferdinand issued an edict expelling all practicing Jews from Spain. Of the community of perhaps 200,000 Jews, 150,000 fled. Many Muslims in Granada were forcibly baptized and became another type of New Christian investigated by the Inquisition. Absolute religious orthodoxy and purity of blood served as the theoretical foundation of the Spanish national state.

The Spanish national state rested on marital politics as well as military victories and religious courts. In 1496 Ferdinand and Isabella married their second daughter, Joanna, heiress to Castile, to the archduke Philip, heir to the Burgundian Netherlands and the Holy Roman Empire. Philip and Joanna's son Charles V (r. 1519–1556) thus succeeded to a vast inheritance. When Charles's son Philip II joined Portugal to the Spanish crown in 1580, the Iberian Peninsula was at last politically united.

Notes

1. In Gertrude R. B. Richards, *Florentine Merchants in the Age of the Medici* (Cambridge: Harvard University Press, 1932).
2. From *The Portable Renaissance Reader*, p. 27, by James B. Ross and Mary Martin McLaughlin, editors, copyright 1953, renewed © 1981 by Viking Penguin Inc. Used by permission of Viking Penguin, a division of Penguin Group (USA) Inc.
3. Ibid., pp. 480–481, 482, 492.
4. Niccolò Machiavelli, *The Prince*, trans. Leo Paul S. de Alvarez (Prospect Heights, Ill.: Waveland Press, 1980), p. 101.
5. Ibid., p. 149.
6. Quoted in F. Seebohm, *The Oxford Reformers* (London: J. M. Dent & Sons, 1867), p. 256.
7. Quoted in Lauro Martines, *Power and Imagination: City-States in Renaissance Italy* (New York: Vintage Books, 1980), p. 253.
8. Quoted in J. Devisse and M. Mollat, *The Image of the Black in Western Art*, vol. 2, trans. W. G. Ryan (New York: William Morrow, 1979), pt. 2, pp. 187–188.
9. Stuttgart, Württembergische Hauptstaatsarchiv, Generalreskripta, A38, Bü. 2, 1550; trans. Merry Wiesner-Hanks.
10. Denys Hay, ed. and trans., *The Anglia Historia of Polydore Vergil, AD 1485–1537*, book 74 (London: Camden Society, 1950), p. 147.
11. Quoted in Benzion Netanyahu, *The Origins of the Inquisition in Fifteenth Century Spain* (New York: Random House, 1995), p. 921.

Chapter Review

MAKE IT STICK

LearningCurve
bedfordstmartins.com/mckaywestvalue
After reading the chapter, use LearningCurve to retain what you've read.

IDENTIFY KEY TERMS

Identify and explain the significance of each item below.

Renaissance (p. 367)   courts (p. 369)   debate about women
patronage (p. 367)   humanism (p. 373)   (p. 391)
communes (p. 368)   virtù (p. 376)   New Christians (p. 397)
popolo (p. 369)   Christian humanists
signori (p. 369)   (p. 381)

REVIEW THE MAIN IDEAS

Answer the focus questions from each section of the chapter.

- How did politics and economics shape the Renaissance? (p. 367)
- What new ideas were associated with the Renaissance? (p. 372)
- How did art reflect new Renaissance ideals? (p. 384)
- What were the key social hierarchies in Renaissance Europe? (p. 389)
- How did nation-states develop in this period? (p. 393)

MAKE CONNECTIONS

Think about the larger developments and continuities within and across chapters.

1. The word *Renaissance*, invented to describe the cultural flowering in Italy that began in the fifteenth century, has often been used for other periods of advance in learning and the arts, such as the "Carolingian Renaissance" that you read about in Chapter 8. Can you think of other, more recent "Renaissances"? How else is the word used today?

2. The Renaissance was clearly a period of cultural change for educated men. Given what you have read about women's lives and ideas about women in this and earlier chapters, did women have a Renaissance? (This question was posed first by the historian Joan Kelly in 1977 and remains a topic of great debate.) Why or why not?

ONLINE DOCUMENT ASSIGNMENT

Leonardo da Vinci

How did the needs and desires of Leonardo's patrons influence his work?

You encountered Leonardo da Vinci's story on page 376. Keeping the question above in mind, go online and examine letters written by Leonardo to his patrons as well as other written and visual evidence that sheds light on the dynamic between the artist and his employers. Then complete a writing assignment based on the evidence and details from this chapter.

bedfordstmartins.com/mckaywestvalue

CHRONOLOGY

ca. 1350	• Petrarch develops ideas of humanism
1434–1737	• Medici family in power in Florence
1440s	• Invention of movable metal type
1447–1535	• Sforza family in power in Milan
1455–1471	• Wars of the Roses in England
1469	• Marriage of Isabella of Castile and Ferdinand of Aragon
1477	• Louis XI conquers Burgundy
1478	• Establishment of the Inquisition in Spain
1492	• Spain conquers Granada, ending reconquista; practicing Jews expelled from Spain
1494	• Invasion of Italy by Charles VIII of France
1508–1512	• Michelangelo paints ceiling of Sistine Chapel
1513	• Machiavelli writes *The Prince*
1563	• Establishment of first formal academy for artistic training in Florence

13

Reformations and Religious Wars

1500–1600

CALLS FOR REFORM OF THE CHRISTIAN CHURCH BEGAN VERY EARLY
in its history. Throughout the centuries, many Christians believed that the
early Christian Church represented a golden age, akin to the golden age of
the classical past celebrated by Renaissance humanists. When Christianity
became the official religion of the Roman Empire in the fourth century,
many believers thought that the church had abandoned its original mission,
and they called for a return to a church that was not linked to the state.
Throughout the Middle Ages, individuals and groups argued that the church
had become too wealthy and powerful and urged monasteries, convents,
bishoprics, and the papacy to give up their property and focus on service to
the poor. Some asserted that basic teachings of the church were not truly
Christian and that changes were needed in theology as well as in institutional
structures and practices. The Christian humanists of the late fifteenth and
early sixteenth centuries such as Erasmus urged reform, primarily through
educational and social change. What was new in the sixteenth century was
the breadth of acceptance and the ultimate impact of the calls for reform.
This acceptance was due not only to religious issues and problems within the
church, but also to political and social factors. In 1500 there was one Christian
Church in western Europe to which all Christians at least nominally belonged.
One hundred years later there were many, a situation that continues today.

The Early Reformation

What were the central ideas of the reformers, and why were they appealing to different social groups?

In early-sixteenth-century Europe a wide range of people had grievances with the church. Educated laypeople such as Christian humanists and urban residents, villagers and artisans, and church officials themselves called for reform. This widespread dissatisfaction helps explain why the ideas of Martin Luther, an obscure professor from a new and not very prestigious German university, found a ready audience. Within a decade of his first publishing his ideas (using the new technology of the printing press), much of central Europe and Scandinavia had broken with the Catholic Church, and even more radical concepts of the Christian message were being developed and linked to calls for social change.

The Christian Church in the Early Sixteenth Century

If external religious observances are an indication of conviction, Europeans in the early sixteenth century were deeply pious. Villagers participated in processions honoring the local saints. Merchants and guild members made pilgrimages to the great shrines, such as Saint Peter's in Rome, and paid for altars in local churches. Men and women continued to remember the church in their wills. People of all social groups devoted an enormous amount of their time and income to religious causes and foundations.

Despite—or perhaps because of—the depth of their piety, many people were also highly critical of the Roman Catholic Church and its clergy. The papal conflict with the German emperor Frederick II in the thirteenth century, followed by the Babylonian Captivity and the Great Schism, badly damaged the prestige of church leaders, and the fifteenth-century popes' concentration on artistic patronage and building up family power did not help matters. Papal tax collection methods were attacked orally and in print. Some criticized the papacy itself as an institution, and even the great wealth and powerful courts of the entire church hierarchy. Some groups and individuals argued that certain doctrines taught by the church, such as the veneration of saints and the centrality of the sacraments, were incorrect. They suggested measures to reform institutions, improve clerical education and behavior, and alter basic doctrines. Occasionally these reform efforts had some success, and in at least one area, Bohemia (the modern-day Czech Republic), they led to the formation of a church independent of Rome a century before Luther (see Chapter 11).

In the early sixteenth century, court records, bishops' visitations of parishes, and popular songs and printed images show widespread **anticlericalism**, or opposition to the clergy. The critics concentrated primarily on three problems: clerical immorality, clerical ignorance, and clerical pluralism (the practice of holding more than one church office at a time), with the related problem of absenteeism. Charges of clerical immorality were aimed at a number of priests who were drunkards, neglected the rule of celibacy, gambled, or indulged in fancy dress. Charges of clerical ignorance were motivated by barely literate priests who simply mumbled the Latin words of the Mass by rote without understanding their meaning. Many priests, monks, and nuns lived pious lives of devotion, learning, and service and had strong support from the laypeople in their areas, but everyone also knew (and repeated) stories about lecherous monks, lustful nuns, and greedy priests.

In regard to absenteeism and pluralism, many clerics held several benefices, or offices, simultaneously, but they seldom visited the benefices, let alone performed the spiritual responsibilities those offices entailed. Instead, they collected revenues from all of them and hired a poor priest, paying him just a fraction of the income to fulfill the spiritual duties of a particular local church. Many Italian officials in the papal curia, the pope's court in Rome, held benefices in England, Spain, and Germany. Revenues from those countries paid the Italian clerics' salaries, provoking not only charges of absenteeism but also nationalistic resentment aimed at the upper levels of the church hierarchy, which was increasingly viewed as foreign. This was particularly the case in Germany, where the lack of a strong central government to negotiate with the papacy meant that demands for revenue were especially high.

There was also local resentment of clerical privileges and immunities. Priests, monks, and nuns were exempt from civic responsibilities, such as defending the city and paying taxes. Yet religious orders frequently held large amounts of urban property, in some cities as much as one-third. City governments were increasingly determined to integrate the clergy into civic life by reducing their privileges and giving them public responsibilities. Urban leaders wanted some say in who would be appointed to high church offices, rather than having this decided far away in Rome. This brought city leaders into opposition with bishops and the papacy, which for centuries had stressed the independence of the church from lay control and the distinction between members of the clergy and laypeople.

Martin Luther

By itself, widespread criticism of the church did not lead to the dramatic changes of the sixteenth century. Instead, the personal religious struggle of a German university professor and priest, Martin Luther (1483–1546), propelled the wave of movements we now call the Reformation. Luther was born at Eisleben in Saxony. At considerable sacrifice, his father sent him to school and then to the University of Erfurt, where he earned a master's degree with distinction. Luther was to proceed to the study of law and a legal career, which for centuries had been the stepping-stone to public office and material success. Instead, however, a sense of religious calling led him to join the Augustinian friars, a religious order whose members often preached to, taught, and assisted the poor. (Religious orders were groups whose members took vows and followed a particular set of rules.) Luther was ordained a priest in 1507 and after additional study earned a doctorate of theology. From 1512 until his death in 1546, he served as professor of the Scriptures at the new University of Wittenberg. Throughout his life, he frequently cited his professorship as justification for his reforming work.

Martin Luther was a very conscientious friar, but his scrupulous observance of religious routine, frequent confessions, and fasting gave him only temporary relief from anxieties about sin and his ability to meet God's demands. Through his study of Saint Paul's letters in the New Testament, he gradually arrived at a new understanding of Christian doctrine. His understanding is often summarized as "faith alone, grace alone, Scripture alone." He believed that salvation and justification come through faith. Faith is a free gift of God's grace, not the result of human effort. God's word is revealed only in Scripture, not in the traditions of the church.

Selling Indulgences   A German single-page pamphlet shows a monk offering an indulgence, with the official seals of the pope attached, as people run to put their money in the box in exchange for his promise of heavenly bliss, symbolized by the dove above his head. Indulgences were sold widely in Germany and became the first Catholic practice that Luther criticized openly. This pamphlet also attacks the sale of indulgences, calling this practice devilish and deceitful. Indulgences were often printed fill-in-the-blank forms. (akg-images)

At the same time that Luther was engaged in scholarly reflections and professorial lecturing, Pope Leo X authorized the sale of a special Saint Peter's indulgence to finance his building plans in Rome. The archbishop who controlled the area in which Wittenberg was located, Albert of Mainz, was an enthusiastic promoter of this indulgence sale. For his efforts, he received a share of the profits so that he could pay off a debt he had incurred in order to purchase a papal dispensation allowing him to become the bishop of several other territories as well.

What exactly was an **indulgence**? According to Catholic theology, individuals who sin could be reconciled to God by confessing their sins to a priest and by doing an assigned penance, such as praying or fasting. But beginning in the twelfth century learned theologians increasingly emphasized the idea of purgatory, a place where souls on their way to Heaven went to make further amends for their earthly sins. Both earthly penance and time in purgatory could be shortened by drawing on what was termed the "treasury of merits." This was a collection of all the virtuous acts that Christ, the apostles, and the saints had done during their lives. People thought of it as a sort of strongbox, like those in which merchants carried coins. An indulgence was a piece of parchment (later, paper), signed by the pope or another church official, that substituted a virtuous act from the treasury of merits for penance or time in purgatory. The papacy and bishops had given Crusaders such indulgences, and by the later Middle Ages they were offered for making pilgrimages or other pious activities and also sold outright (see Chapter 9).

Archbishop Albert's indulgence sale, run by a Dominican friar named Johann Tetzel who mounted an advertising blitz, promised that the purchase of indulgences would bring full forgiveness for one's own sins or release from purgatory for a loved one. One of the slogans—"As soon as coin in coffer rings, the soul from purgatory springs"— brought phenomenal success, and people traveled from miles around to buy indulgences.

Luther was severely troubled that many people believed they had no further need for repentance once they had purchased indulgences. In 1517 he wrote a letter to Archbishop Albert on the subject and enclosed in Latin his "Ninety-five Theses on the Power of Indulgences." His argument was that indulgences undermined the seriousness of the sacrament of penance, competed with the preaching of the Gospel, and down-played the importance of charity in Christian life. After Luther's death, biographies reported that the theses were also nailed to the door of the church at Wittenberg Castle on October 31, 1517. Such an act would have been very strange—they were in Latin and written for those learned in theology, not for ordinary churchgoers—but it has become a standard part of Luther lore.

Whether the theses were posted or not, they were quickly printed, first in Latin and then in German translation. Luther was ordered to come to Rome, although because of the political situation in the empire, he was able instead to engage in formal scholarly debate with a representative of the church, Johann Eck, at Leipzig in 1519. He refused to take back his ideas and continued to develop his calls for reform, publicizing them in a series of pamphlets in which he moved further and further away from Catholic theology. Both popes and church councils could err, he wrote, and secular leaders should reform the church if the pope and clerical hierarchy did not. There was no distinction between clergy and laypeople, and requiring clergy to be celibate was a fruitless attempt to control a natural human drive. Luther clearly understood the power of the new medium of print, so he authorized the publication of his works.

The papacy responded with a letter condemning some of Luther's propositions, ordering that his books be burned, and giving him two months to recant or be excom-municated. Luther retaliated by publicly burning the letter. By 1521, when the excom-munication was supposed to become final, Luther's theological issues had become interwoven with public controversies about the church's wealth, power, and basic structure. The papal legate wrote of the growing furor, "All Germany is in revolution. Nine-tenths shout 'Luther' as their war cry; and the other tenth cares nothing about Luther, and cries 'Death to the court of Rome.'"[1] In this highly charged atmosphere, the twenty-one-year-old emperor Charles V held his first diet (assembly of the nobility, clergy, and cities of the Holy Roman Empire) in the German city of Worms and sum-moned Luther to appear. Luther refused to give in to demands that he take back his ideas. "Unless I am convinced by the evidence of Scripture or by plain reason," he said, "I cannot and will not recant anything, for it is neither safe nor right to go against conscience."[2] His appearance at the Diet of Worms in 1521 created an even broader audience for reform ideas, and throughout central Europe other individuals began to preach and publish against the existing doctrines and practices of the church, drawing on the long tradition of calls for change as well as on Luther.

Protestant Thought

The most important early reformer other than Luther was the Swiss humanist, priest, and admirer of Erasmus, Ulrich Zwingli (ZWIHNG-lee) (1484–1531). Zwingli announced in 1519 that he would not preach from the church's prescribed readings but, relying on Erasmus's New Testament, go right through the New Testament "from A to Z," that is, from Matthew to Revelation. Zwingli was convinced that Christian life rested on the Scriptures, which were the pure words of God and the sole basis of religious truth. He went on to attack indulgences, the Mass, the institution of monasticism, and clerical celibacy. In his gradual reform of the church in Zurich, he had the strong support of the city authorities, who had long resented the privileges of the clergy.

The followers of Luther, Zwingli, and others who called for a break with Rome came to be called Protestants. The word **Protestant** derives from the protest drawn up by a small group of reforming German princes at the Diet of Speyer in 1529. The princes "protested" the decisions of the Catholic majority, and the word gradually became a general term applied to all non-Catholic western European Christians.

Luther, Zwingli, and other early Protestants agreed on many things. First, how is a person to be saved? Traditional Catholic teaching held that salvation is achieved by both faith and good works. Protestants held that salvation comes by faith alone, irrespective of good works or the sacraments. God, not people, initiates salvation. Second, where does religious authority reside? Christian doctrine had long maintained that authority rests both in the Bible and in the traditional teaching of the church. For Protestants, authority rested in the Bible alone. For a doctrine or issue to be valid, it had to have a scriptural basis. Because of this, most Protestants rejected Catholic teachings about the sacraments — the rituals that the church had defined as imparting God's benefits on the believer (see Chapter 10) — holding that only baptism and the Eucharist have scriptural support.

Third, what is the church? Protestants held that the church is a spiritual priesthood of all believers, an invisible fellowship not fixed in any place or person, which differed markedly from the Roman Catholic practice of a hierarchical clerical institution headed by the pope in Rome. Fourth, what is the highest form of Christian life? The medieval church had stressed the superiority of the monastic and religious life over the secular. Protestants disagreed and argued that every person should serve God in his or her individual calling.

Protestants did not agree on everything, and one important area of dispute was the ritual of the Eucharist (also called communion, the Lord's Supper, and, in Catholicism, the Mass). Catholicism holds the dogma of transubstantiation: by the consecrating words of the priest during the Mass, the bread and wine become the actual body and blood of Christ. In opposition, Luther believed that Christ is really present in the consecrated bread and wine, but this is the result of God's mystery, not the actions of a priest. Zwingli understood the Eucharist as a memorial in which Christ was present in spirit among the faithful, but not in the bread and wine. The Colloquy of Marburg, summoned in 1529 to unite Protestants, failed to resolve these differences, though Protestants reached agreement on almost everything else.

The Appeal of Protestant Ideas

Pulpits and printing presses spread the Protestant message all over Germany, and by the middle of the sixteenth century people of all social classes had rejected Catholic teachings and had become Protestant. What was the immense appeal of Luther's religious ideas and those of other Protestants?

Educated people and many humanists were much attracted by Luther's teachings. He advocated a simpler personal religion based on faith, a return to the spirit of the early church, the centrality of the Scriptures in the liturgy and in Christian life, and the abolition of elaborate ceremonies—precisely the reforms the Christian humanists had been calling for. The Protestant insistence that everyone should read and reflect on the Scriptures attracted literate and thoughtful city residents. This included many priests and monks who left the Catholic Church to become clergy in the new Protestant churches. In addition, townspeople who envied the church's wealth and resented paying for it were attracted by the notion that the clergy should also pay taxes and should not have special legal privileges. After Zurich became Protestant, the city council taxed the clergy and placed them under the jurisdiction of civil courts.

Scholars in many disciplines have attributed Luther's fame and success to the invention of the printing press, which rapidly reproduced and made known his ideas. Many printed works included woodcuts and other illustrations, so that even those who could not read could grasp the main ideas. Equally important was Luther's incredible skill with language, as seen in his two catechisms (compendiums of basic religious knowledge) and in hymns that he wrote for congregations to sing. Luther's linguistic skill, together with his translation of the New Testament into German in 1523, led to the acceptance of his dialect of German as the standard written version of the German language.

Both Luther and Zwingli recognized that for reforms to be permanent, political authorities as well as concerned individuals and religious leaders would have to accept them. Zwingli worked closely with the city council of Zurich, and city councils themselves took the lead in other cities and towns of Switzerland and south Germany. They appointed pastors who they knew had accepted Protestant ideas, required them to swear an oath of loyalty to the council, and oversaw their preaching and teaching.

Luther lived in a territory ruled by a noble—the elector of Saxony—and he also worked closely with political authorities, viewing them as fully justified in asserting control over the church in their territories. Indeed, he demanded that German rulers reform the papacy and its institutions, and he instructed all Christians to obey their secular rulers, whom he saw as divinely ordained to maintain order. Individuals may have been convinced of the truth of Protestant teachings by hearing sermons, listening to hymns, or reading pamphlets, but a territory became Protestant when its ruler, whether a noble or a city council, brought in a reformer or two to re-educate the territory's clergy, sponsored public sermons, and confiscated church property. This happened in many of the states of the Holy Roman Empire during the 1520s.

The Radical Reformation and the German Peasants' War

While Luther and Zwingli worked with political authorities, some individuals and groups rejected the idea that church and state needed to be united. Beginning in the 1520s groups in Switzerland, Germany, and the Netherlands sought instead to create a voluntary community of believers separate from the state, as they understood it to have existed in New Testament times. In terms of theology and spiritual practices, these individuals and groups varied widely, though they are generally termed "radicals" for their insistence on a more extensive break with prevailing ideas. Some adopted the baptism of adult believers, for which they were called by their enemies "Anabaptists," which means "re-baptizers." (Early Christians had practiced adult baptism, but infant baptism became the norm, which meant that adults undergoing baptism were repeating the ritual.) Some groups attempted communal ownership of property, living very simply and rejecting anything they thought unbiblical. Some reacted harshly to members who deviated, but others argued for complete religious toleration and individualism.

Some religious radicals thought the end of the world was coming soon, and in the 1530s a group took over the German city of Münster, which they predicted would be the site of a New Jerusalem that would survive God's final judgment. They called for communal ownership of property and expelled those who refused to be rebaptized. Combined armies of Catholics and Protestants besieged the city and executed its leaders. The insurrection at Münster and the radicals' unwillingness to accept a state church marked them as societal outcasts and invited hatred and persecution, for both Protestant and Catholic authorities saw a state church as key to maintaining order. Anabaptists and other radicals were banished or cruelly executed by burning, beating, or drowning. (See "Individuals in Society: Anna Jansz of Rotterdam," page 410.) Their community spirit and heroism in the face of martyrdom, however, contributed to the survival of radical ideas. Later, the Quakers, with their pacifism; the Baptists, with their emphasis on inner spiritual light; the Congregationalists, with their democratic church organization; and in 1787 the authors of the U.S. Constitution, with their opposition to the "establishment of religion" (state churches), would all trace their origins, in part, to the radicals of the sixteenth century.

Radical reformers sometimes called for social as well as religious change, a message that resonated with the increasingly struggling German peasantry. In the early sixteenth century the economic condition of the peasantry varied from place to place but was generally worse than it had been in the fifteenth century and was deteriorating. Crop failures in 1523 and 1524 aggravated an explosive situation. Nobles had aggrieved peasants by seizing village common lands, by imposing new rents and requiring additional services, and by taking the peasants' best horses or cows whenever a head of household died. The peasants made demands that they believed conformed to the Scriptures, and they cited radical thinkers as well as Luther as proof that they did.

Luther wanted to prevent rebellion. Initially he sided with the peasants, blasting the lords for robbing their subjects. But when rebellion broke out, peasants who expected Luther's support were soon disillusioned. Freedom for Luther meant independence from the authority of the Roman Church; it did not mean opposition to legally established secular powers. As for biblical support for the peasants' demands, he maintained that Scripture had nothing to do with earthly justice or material gain, a position that Zwingli supported. Firmly convinced that rebellion would hasten the end of civilized society, Luther wrote the tract *Against the Murderous, Thieving Hordes of the Peasants:* "Let everyone who can smite, slay, and stab [the peasants], secretly and openly, remembering that nothing can be more poisonous, hurtful or devilish than a rebel."[3] The nobility ferociously crushed the revolt. Historians estimate that more than seventy-five thousand peasants were killed in 1525.

The German Peasants' War of 1525 greatly strengthened the authority of lay rulers. Not surprisingly, the Reformation lost much of its popular appeal after 1525, though peasants and urban rebels sometimes found a place for their social and religious ideas in radical groups. Peasants' economic conditions did moderately improve, however. For example, in many parts of Germany, enclosed fields, meadows, and forests were returned to common use.

Marriage, Sexuality, and the Role of Women

Luther and Zwingli both believed that a priest's or nun's vows of celibacy went against human nature and God's commandments, and that marriage brought spiritual advantages and so was the ideal state for nearly all human beings. Luther married a former nun, Katharina von Bora (1499–1532), and Zwingli married a Zurich widow, Anna Reinhart (1491–1538). Both women quickly had several children. Most other Protestant reformers also married, and their wives had to create a new and respectable role for themselves — pastor's wife — to overcome being viewed as simply a new type of priest's

Martin Luther and Katharina von Bora   Lucas Cranach the Elder painted this double marriage portrait to celebrate Luther's wedding in 1525 to Katharina von Bora, a former nun. The artist was one of the witnesses at the wedding and, in fact, had presented Luther's marriage proposal to Katharina. Using a go-between for proposals was very common, as was having a double wedding portrait painted. This particular couple quickly became a model of the ideal marriage, and many churches wanted their portraits. More than sixty similar paintings, with slight variations, were produced by Cranach's workshop and hung in churches and wealthy homes. (Galleria degli Uffizi, Florence, Italy/Alinari/The Bridgeman Art Library)

INDIVIDUALS IN SOCIETY • Anna Jansz of Rotterdam

Anna Jansz (1509–1539) was born into a well-to-do family in the small city of Briel in the Netherlands. She married, and when she was in her early twenties she and her husband came to accept Anabaptism after listening to a traveling preacher. They were baptized in 1534 and became part of a group who believed that God would soon come to bring judgment on the wicked and deliver his true followers. Jansz wrote a hymn conveying these apocalyptic beliefs and foretelling vengeance on those who persecuted Anabaptists: "I hear the Trumpet sounding, From far off I hear her blast! . . . O murderous seed, what will you do? Offspring of Cain, you put to death The lambs of the Lord, without just cause—It will be doubly repaid to you! Death now comes riding on horseback, We have seen your fate! The sword is passing over the land, With which you will be killed and slain, And you will not escape from Hell!"

Jansz and her husband traveled to England, where she had a child, but in November 1538 she and her infant son, Isaiah, returned to the Netherlands, along with another woman. As the story was later told, the two women were recognized as Anabaptists by another traveler because of songs they were singing, perhaps her "Trumpet Song" among them. They were arrested and interrogated in the city of Rotterdam, and sentenced to death by drowning. The day she was executed— January 24, 1539—Anna Jansz wrote a long testament to her son, providing him with spiritual advice: "My son, hear the instruction of your mother, and open your ears to hear the words of my mouth. Watch, today I am travelling the path of the Prophets, Apostles, and Martyrs, and drink from the cup from which they have all tasted. . . . But if you hear of the existence of a poor, lowly, cast-out little company, that has been despised and rejected by the World, go join it. . . . Honor the Lord through the works of your hands. Let the light of Scripture shine in you. Love your Neighbor; with an effusive, passionate heart deal your bread to the hungry."

Anabaptists later compiled accounts of trials and executions, along with letters and other records, into martyrologies designed to inspire deeper faith. One of the most widely read of these describes Jansz on her way to the execution. She offered a certain amount of money to anyone who would care for her son; a poor baker with six children agreed, and she passed the child to him. The martyrology reports that the baker later became quite wealthy, and that her son, Isaiah, became mayor of the city of Rotterdam. As such, he would have easily been able to read the court records of his mother's trial.

concubine. They were living demonstrations of their husband's convictions about the superiority of marriage to celibacy, and they were expected to be models of wifely obedience and Christian charity.

Though they denied that marriage was a sacrament, Protestant reformers stressed that it had been ordained by God when he presented Eve to Adam, served as a "remedy" for the unavoidable sin of lust, provided a site for the pious rearing of the next generation of God-fearing Christians, and offered husbands and wives companionship and conso-

Anna Jansz was one of thousands of people executed for their religious beliefs in sixteenth-century Europe. A few of these were high-profile individuals
such as Thomas More, the Catholic former chancellor of England executed by
King Henry VIII, but most were quite ordinary people. Many were women.
Women's and men's experiences of martyrdom were similar in many ways, but
women also confronted additional challenges. Some were pregnant while in
prison—execution was delayed until the baby was born—or, like Jansz, had infants with them. They faced procedures of questioning, torture, and execution
that brought dishonor as well as pain. Eventually many Anabaptists, as well as
others whose religion put them in opposition to their rulers, migrated to parts
of Europe that were more tolerant. By the seventeenth century the Netherlands
had become one of the most tolerant places in Europe, and Rotterdam was no
longer the site of executions for religious reasons.

QUESTIONS FOR ANALYSIS

1. How did religion, gender, and social class all shape Jansz's experiences and
   the writings that she left behind?

2. Why might Jansz's hymn and her Anabaptist beliefs have seemed threatening
   to those who did not share her beliefs?

Source: Quotations are from *Elisabeth's Manly Courage: Testimonials and Songs of Martyred Anabaptist Women in the Low Countries*, ed. and trans. Hermina Joldersma and Louis Peter Grijp (Milwaukee: Marquette University Press, 2001).

ONLINE DOCUMENT ASSIGNMENT

**What might have led Jansz and thousands like her to die for their
religious convictions?** Learn more about Anna Jansz and other
Anabaptist martyrs by analyzing images and hymns, and then
complete a writing assignment based on the evidence and details
from this chapter.

bedfordstmartins.com/mckaywestvalue

lation. A proper marriage was one that reflected both the spiritual equality of men and
women and the proper social hierarchy of husbandly authority and wifely obedience.

Protestants did not break with medieval scholastic theologians in their idea that
women were to be subject to men. Women were advised to be cheerful rather than
grudging in their obedience, for in doing so they demonstrated their willingness to
follow God's plan. Men were urged to treat their wives kindly and considerately, but
also to enforce their authority, through physical coercion if necessary. European marriage

Domestic Scene   The Protestant notion that the best form of Christian life was marriage and a family helps explain the appeal of Protestantism to middle-class urban men and women, such as those shown in this domestic scene. The engraving, titled "Concordia" (harmony), includes the biblical inscription of what Jesus called the greatest commandment—"You shall love the Lord your God with all your heart and all your soul and your neighbor as yourself" (Deuteronomy 6; Matthew 22)—on tablets at the back. The large covered bed at the back was both a standard piece of furniture in urban homes and a symbol of proper marital sexual relations. (Mary Evans Picture Library/The Image Works)

manuals used the metaphor of breaking a horse for teaching a wife obedience, though laws did set limits on the husband's power to do so.

Protestants saw marriage as a contract in which each partner promised the other support, companionship, and the sharing of mutual goods. Because, in Protestant eyes, marriage was created by God as a remedy for human weakness, marriages in which spouses did not comfort or support one another physically, materially, or emotionally endangered their own souls and the surrounding community. The only solution might be divorce and remarriage, which most Protestants came to allow. Protestant allowance of divorce differed markedly from Catholic doctrine, which viewed marriage as a sacramental union that, if validly entered into, could not be dissolved (Catholic canon law allowed only separation with no remarriage). Although permitting divorce was a dramatic legal change, it did not have a dramatic impact on newly Protestant areas. Because marriage was the cornerstone of society socially and economically, divorce was a desperate last resort. In many Protestant jurisdictions the annual divorce rate hovered around 0.02

to 0.06 per thousand people. (By contrast, in 2010 the U.S. divorce rate was 3.6 per thousand people.)

As Protestants believed marriage was the only proper remedy for lust, they uniformly condemned prostitution. The licensed brothels that were a common feature of late medieval urban life (see Chapter 11) were closed in Protestant cities, and harsh punishments were set for prostitution. Many Catholic cities soon closed their brothels as well, although Italian cities favored stricter regulations rather than closure. Selling sex was couched in moral rather than economic terms, as simply one type of "whoredom," a term that also included premarital sex, adultery, and other unacceptable sexual activities. "Whore" was also a term that reformers used for their theological opponents; Protestants compared the pope to the biblical whore of Babylon, a symbol of the end of the world, while Catholics called Luther's wife a whore because she had first been married to Christ as a nun before her marriage to Luther. Closing brothels did not end the exchange of sex for money, of course, but simply reshaped it. Smaller illegal brothels were established, or women selling sex moved to areas right outside city walls.

The Protestant Reformation clearly had a positive impact on marriage, but its impact on women was more mixed. Many nuns were in convents not out of a strong sense of religious calling, but because their parents placed them there. Convents nevertheless provided women of the upper classes with an opportunity to use their literary, artistic, medical, or administrative talents if they could not or would not marry. The Reformation generally brought the closing of monasteries and convents, and marriage became virtually the only occupation for upper-class Protestant women. Women in some convents recognized this and fought the Reformation, or argued that they could still be pious Protestants within convent walls. Most nuns left, however, and we do not know what happened to them. The Protestant emphasis on marriage made unmarried women (and men) suspect, for they did not belong to the type of household regarded as the cornerstone of a proper, godly society.

A few women took Luther's idea about the priesthood of all believers to heart and wrote religious works. Argula von Grumbach, a German noblewoman, supported Protestant ideas in print, asserting, "I am not unfamiliar with Paul's words that women should be silent in church but when I see that no man will or can speak, I am driven by the word of God when he said, he who confesses me on earth, him will I confess, and he who denies me, him will I deny."[4] No sixteenth-century Protestants allowed women to be members of the clergy, however, though monarchs such as Elizabeth I of England and female territorial rulers of the states of the Holy Roman Empire did determine religious policies just as male rulers did.

The Reformation and German Politics

How did the political situation in Germany shape the course of the Reformation?

Although criticism of the church was widespread in Europe in the early sixteenth century, reform movements could be more easily squelched by the strong central governments that had evolved in Spain and France. England, too, had a strong monarchy, but the king broke from the Catholic Church for other reasons (see page 417). The Holy Roman Empire, in contrast, included hundreds of largely independent states. Against this

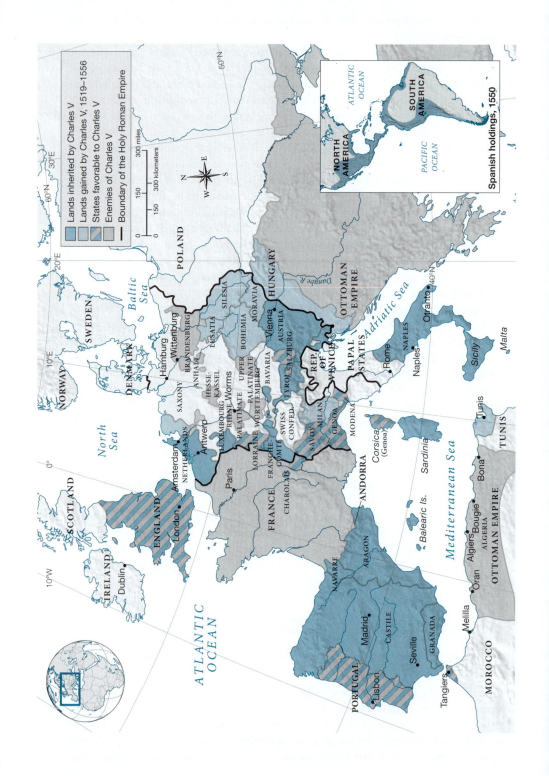

Lands inherited by Charles V
Lands gained by Charles V, 1519–1556
States favorable to Charles V
Enemies of Charles V
Boundary of the Holy Roman Empire

300 miles
300 kilometers
150
150
0
0

Spanish holdings, 1550

ATLANTIC OCEAN

NORTH AMERICA

SOUTH AMERICA

PACIFIC OCEAN

50°N

60°N

40°N

30°E

20°E

10°E

0°

10°W

POLAND

SWEDEN

NORWAY

DENMARK

Baltic Sea

North Sea

SCOTLAND

IRELAND
Dublin

ENGLAND
London

NETHERLANDS
Amsterdam
Antwerp

Hamburg
Wittenburg
BRANDENBURG
ANHALT
SAXONY
HESSE-
KASSEL
Worms
RHINE
PALATINATE
LUXEMBOURG

LUSATIA
SILESIA
BOHEMIA
MORAVIA
UPPER
PALATINATE
BAVARIA

HUNGARY

Vienna
AUSTRIA
Danube R.

OTTOMAN EMPIRE

Adriatic Sea

WÜRTTEMBERG
LORRAINE
FRANCHE-
COMTÉ
SWISS
CONFED.
TYROL
SALZBURG
REP. of VENICE
PAPAL STATES
Rome

MILAN
SAVOY
GENOA
MODENA

Otranto
NAPLES
Naples
Sicily
Malta

FRANCE
Paris
CHAROLAIS

ANDORRA
Corsica (Genoa)
Sardinia

Balearic Is.
Mediterranean Sea

Tunis
TUNIS

OTTOMAN EMPIRE
Bona
Bougie
Algiers
ALGERIA
Oran

NAVARRE
ARAGON

PORTUGAL
Lisbon
Madrid
CASTILE
Seville
GRANADA
Tangiers
Melilla
MOROCCO

ATLANTIC OCEAN

◄ **MAP 13.1**   **The Global Empire of Charles V, ca. 1556**

Charles V exercised theoretical jurisdiction over more European territory than anyone since Charlemagne. He also claimed authority over large parts of North and South America (see Map 14.2, page 448), though actual Spanish control was weak in much of the area.

background of decentralization and strong local power, Martin Luther had launched a movement to reform the church. Two years after he published the "Ninety-five Theses," the electors of the Holy Roman Empire chose as emperor a nineteen-year-old Habsburg prince who ruled as Charles V (r. 1519–1556). The course of the Reformation was shaped by this election and by the political relationships surrounding it.

The Rise of the Habsburg Dynasty

War and diplomacy were important ways that states increased their power in sixteenth-century Europe, but so was marriage. Royal and noble sons and daughters were important tools of state policy. The benefits of an advantageous marriage stretched across generations, a process that can be seen most dramatically with the Habsburgs. The Holy Roman emperor Frederick III, a Habsburg who was the ruler of most of Austria, acquired only a small amount of territory—but a great deal of money—with his marriage to Princess Eleonore of Portugal in 1452. He arranged for his son Maximilian to marry Europe's most prominent heiress, Mary of Burgundy, in 1477; she inherited the Netherlands, Luxembourg, and the County of Burgundy in what is now eastern France. Through this union with the rich and powerful duchy of Burgundy, the Austrian house of Habsburg, already the strongest ruling family in the empire, became an international power. The marriage of Maximilian and Mary angered the French, however, who considered Burgundy French territory, and inaugurated centuries of conflict between the Austrian house of Habsburg and the kings of France.

Maximilian learned the lesson of marital politics well, marrying his son and daughter to the children of Ferdinand and Isabella, the rulers of Spain, much of southern Italy, and eventually the Spanish New World empire. His grandson Charles V (1500–1558) fell heir to a vast and incredibly diverse collection of states and peoples, each governed in a different manner and held together only by the person of the emperor (Map 13.1). Charles's Italian adviser, the grand chancellor Gattinara, told the young ruler, "God has set you on the path toward world monarchy." Charles, a Catholic, not only believed this but also was convinced that it was his duty to maintain the political and religious unity of Western Christendom.

Religious Wars in Switzerland and Germany

In the sixteenth century the practice of religion remained a public matter. The ruler determined the official form of religious practice in his (or occasionally her) jurisdiction. Almost everyone believed that the presence of a faith different from that of the majority represented a political threat to the security of the state, and few believed in religious liberty.

Luther's ideas appealed to German rulers for a variety of reasons. Though Germany was not a nation, people did have an understanding of being German because of their language and traditions. Luther frequently used the phrase "we Germans" in his attacks on the papacy. Luther's appeal to national feeling influenced many rulers otherwise confused by or indifferent to the complexities of the religious matters of the time. Some German rulers were sincerely attracted to Lutheran ideas, but material considerations swayed many others to embrace the new faith. The rejection of Roman Catholicism and adoption of Protestantism would mean the legal confiscation of lush farmlands, rich monasteries, and wealthy shrines. Thus many political authorities in the empire became Protestant in part to extend their financial and political power and to enhance their independence from the emperor.

Charles V was a vigorous defender of Catholicism, so it is not surprising that the Reformation led to religious wars. The first battleground was Switzerland, which was officially part of the Holy Roman Empire, though it was really a loose confederation of thirteen largely autonomous territories called cantons. Some cantons remained Catholic, and some became Protestant, and in the late 1520s the two sides went to war. Zwingli was killed on the battlefield in 1531, and both sides quickly decided that a treaty was preferable to further fighting. The treaty basically allowed each canton to determine its own religion and ordered each side to give up its foreign alliances, a policy of neutrality that has been characteristic of modern Switzerland.

Trying to halt the spread of religious division, Charles V called an Imperial Diet in 1530, to meet at Augsburg. The Lutherans developed a statement of faith, later called the Augsburg Confession, and the Protestant princes presented this to the emperor. (The Augsburg Confession remains an authoritative statement of belief for many Lutheran churches.) Charles refused to accept it and ordered all Protestants to return to the Catholic Church and give up any confiscated church property. This demand backfired, and Protestant territories in the empire—mostly northern German principalities and southern German cities—formed a military alliance. The emperor could not respond militarily, as he was in the midst of a series of wars with the French: the Habsburg-Valois wars (1521–1559), fought in Italy along the eastern and southern borders of France and eventually in Germany. The Ottoman Turks had also taken much of Hungary and in 1529 were besieging Vienna.

The 1530s and early 1540s saw complicated political maneuvering among many of the powers of Europe. Various attempts were made to heal the religious split with a church council, but stubbornness on both sides made it increasingly clear that this would not be possible and that war was inevitable. Charles V realized that he was fighting not only for religious unity, but also for a more unified state, against territorial rulers who wanted to maintain their independence. He was thus defending both church and empire.

Fighting began in 1546, and initially the emperor was very successful. This success alarmed both France and the pope, however, who did not want Charles to become even more powerful. The pope withdrew papal troops, and the Catholic king of France sent money and troops to the Lutheran princes. Finally, in 1555 Charles agreed to the Peace of Augsburg, which, "in order to bring peace into the holy empire," officially recognized Lutheranism. The political authority in each territory was permitted to decide whether the territory would be Catholic or Lutheran and was ordered to let other territories "enjoy their religious beliefs, liturgy, and ceremonies as well as their estates in peace." Most of northern and central Germany became Lutheran, while the south remained Roman Catholic. There was no freedom of religion within the territories, however. Princes or town councils established state churches to which all subjects of the area had to belong. Dissidents had to convert or leave, although the treaty did order that "they shall neither be hindered in the sale of their estates after due payment of the local taxes nor injured in their honor."[5] Religious refugees became a common feature on the roads of the empire, though rulers did not always let their subjects leave as easily as the treaty stipulated.

The Peace of Augsburg ended religious war in Germany for many decades. His hope of uniting his empire under a single church dashed, Charles V abdicated in 1556 and moved to a monastery, transferring power over his holdings in Spain and the Netherlands to his son Philip and his imperial power to his brother Ferdinand.

The Spread of Protestant Ideas

How did Protestant ideas and institutions spread beyond German-speaking lands?

States within the Holy Roman Empire were the earliest territories to accept the Protestant Reformation, but by the later 1520s and 1530s religious change came to Denmark-Norway, Sweden, England, France, and eastern Europe. In most of these areas, a second generation of reformers built on Lutheran and Zwinglian ideas to develop their own theology and plans for institutional change. The most important of the second-generation reformers was John Calvin, whose ideas would profoundly influence the social thought and attitudes of European peoples and their descendants all over the world.

Scandinavia

The first area outside the empire to officially accept the Reformation was the kingdom of Denmark-Norway under King Christian III (r. 1536–1559). Danish scholars studied at the University of Wittenberg, and Lutheran ideas spread into Denmark very quickly. In the 1530s the king officially broke with the Catholic Church, and most clergy followed. The process went smoothly in Denmark, but in northern Norway and Iceland (which Christian also ruled) there were violent reactions, and Lutheranism was only gradually imposed on a largely unwilling populace.

In Sweden, Gustavus Vasa (r. 1523–1560), who came to the throne during a civil war with Denmark, also took over control of church personnel and income. Protestant ideas spread, though the Swedish Church did not officially accept Lutheran theology until later in the century.

Henry VIII and the Reformation in England

As on the continent, the Reformation in England had economic and political as well as religious causes. The impetus for England's break with Rome was the desire of King Henry VIII (r. 1509–1547) for a new wife, though his own motives also included political, social, and economic elements.

Henry VIII was married to Catherine of Aragon, the daughter of Ferdinand and Isabella and widow of Henry's older brother, Arthur. Marriage to a brother's widow went against canon law, and Henry had been required to obtain a special papal dispensation to marry Catherine. The marriage had produced only one living heir, a daughter, Mary. By 1527 Henry decided that God was showing his displeasure with the marriage by denying him a son, and he appealed to the pope to have the marriage annulled. He was also in love with a court lady in waiting, Anne Boleyn, and assumed that she would give him the son he wanted. Normally an annulment would not have been a problem, but the troops of Emperor Charles V were in Rome at that point, and Pope Clement VII was essentially their prisoner. Charles V was the nephew of Catherine of Aragon and thus was vigorously opposed to an annulment, which would have declared his aunt a fornicator and his cousin Mary a bastard. The pope stalled.

With Rome thwarting his matrimonial plans, Henry decided to remove the English Church from papal jurisdiction. In a series of measures during the 1530s, Henry used Parliament to end the authority of the pope and make himself the supreme head of the church in England. Some opposed the king and were beheaded, among them Thomas More, the king's chancellor and author of *Utopia* (see Chapter 12). When Anne Boleyn failed twice to produce a male child, Henry VIII charged her with adulterous incest and in 1536 had her beheaded. His third wife, Jane Seymour, gave Henry the desired son, Edward, but she died in childbirth. Henry went on to three more wives.

Theologically, Henry was conservative, and the English Church retained such traditional Catholic practices and doctrines as confession, clerical celibacy, and transubstantiation. Under the influence of his chief minister, Thomas Cromwell, and the man he had appointed archbishop of Canterbury, Thomas Cranmer, he did agree to place an English Bible in every church. He also decided to dissolve the English monasteries, primarily because he wanted their wealth. Working through Parliament, between 1535 and 1539 the king ended nine hundred years of English monastic life, dispersing the monks and nuns and confiscating their lands. Their proceeds enriched the royal treasury, and hundreds of properties were sold to the middle and upper classes, the very groups represented in Parliament. The dissolution of the monasteries did not achieve a more equitable distribution of land and wealth; rather, the redistribution of land strengthened the upper classes and tied them to both the Tudor dynasty and the new Protestant Church.

The nationalization of the church and the dissolution of the monasteries led to important changes in government administration. Vast tracts of formerly monastic land came temporarily under the Crown's jurisdiction, and new bureaucratic machinery had to be developed to manage those properties. Cromwell reformed and centralized the king's household, the council, the secretariats, and the Exchequer. New departments of state were set up. Surplus funds from all departments went into a liquid fund to be applied to areas where there were deficits. This balancing resulted in greater efficiency and economy, and Henry VIII's reign saw the growth of the modern centralized bureaucratic state.

Did the religious changes under Henry VIII have broad popular support? Historians disagree about this. Some English people had been dissatisfied with the existing Christian Church before Henry's measures, and Protestant literature circulated. Traditional Catholicism exerted an enormously strong and vigorous hold over the imagination and loyalty of the people, however. Most clergy and officials accepted Henry's moves, but all did not quietly acquiesce. In 1536 popular opposition in the north to the religious changes led to the Pilgrimage of Grace, a massive rebellion that proved the largest in English history. The "pilgrims" accepted a truce, but their leaders were arrested, tried, and executed. Recent scholarship points out that people rarely "converted" from Catholicism to Protestantism overnight. People responded to an action of the Crown that was played out in their own neighborhood—the closing of a monastery, the ending of Masses for the dead—with a combination of resistance, acceptance, and collaboration. Some enthusiastically changed to Protestant forms of prayer, for example, while others recited Protestant prayers in church while keeping pictures of the Catholic saints at home.

Loyalty to the Catholic Church was particularly strong in Ireland. Ireland had been claimed by English kings since the twelfth century, but in reality the English had firm control of only the area around Dublin, known as the Pale. In 1536, on orders from London, the Irish parliament, which represented only the English landlords and the people of the Pale, approved the English laws severing the church from Rome. The Church of Ireland was established on the English pattern, and the (English) ruling class adopted the new reformed faith. Most of the Irish people remained Roman Catholic, thus adding religious antagonism to the ethnic hostility that had been a feature of English policy toward Ireland for centuries (see Chapter 11). Irish armed opposition to the Reformation led to harsh repression by the English. Catholic property was confiscated and sold, and the profits were shipped to England. The Roman Church was essentially driven underground, and the Catholic clergy acted as national as well as religious leaders.

Upholding Protestantism in England

In the short reign of Henry's sickly son, Edward VI (r. 1547–1553), Protestant ideas exerted a significant influence on the religious life of the country. Archbishop Thomas Cranmer simplified the liturgy, invited Protestant theologians to England, and prepared the first *Book of Common Prayer* (1549), which was later approved by Parliament. In stately and dignified English, the *Book of Common Prayer* included the order for all services and prayers of the Church of England.

The equally brief reign of Mary Tudor (r. 1553–1558) witnessed a sharp move back to Catholicism. The devoutly Catholic daughter of Catherine of Aragon, Mary rescinded the Reformation legislation of her father's reign and restored Roman Catholicism. Mary's marriage to her cousin Philip II of Spain (r. 1556–1598), son of the emperor Charles V, proved highly unpopular in England, and her execution of several hundred Protestants further alienated her subjects. During her reign, about a thousand Protestants fled to the continent. Mary's death raised to the throne her half-sister Elizabeth, Henry's daughter with Anne Boleyn, who had been raised a Protestant. Elizabeth's reign from 1558 to 1603 inaugurated the beginnings of religious stability.

At the start of Elizabeth's reign, sharp differences existed in England. On the one hand, Catholics wanted a Roman Catholic ruler. On the other hand, a vocal number of returning exiles wanted all Catholic elements in the Church of England eliminated. The latter, because they wanted to "purify" the church, were called "Puritans."

Shrewdly, Elizabeth chose a middle course between Catholic and Puritan extremes. Working through Parliament, she ordered church and government officials to swear that she was supreme in matters of religion as well as politics, required her subjects to attend services in the Church of England or risk a fine, and called for frequent preaching of Protestant ideas. (See "Primary Source: Elizabethan Injunctions About Religion," page 420.) She did not interfere with people's privately held beliefs, however. As she put it, she did not "want to make windows into men's souls." The Anglican Church, as the Church of England was called, moved in a moderately Protestant direction. Services were conducted in English, monasteries were not re-established, and clergymen were allowed

PRIMARY SOURCE   Elizabethan Injunctions About Religion

In 1559, acting through Parliament, Queen Elizabeth issued a series of rules governing many aspects of religious life. These prohibited clergy and laypeople from engaging in certain religious practices, and required them to do others.

The first is that all deans, archdeacons, parsons, vicars, and other ecclesiastical persons shall faithfully keep and observe, and as far as in them may be, shall cause to be observed and kept of others, all and singular laws and statutes made for the restoring to the crown the ancient jurisdiction over the state ecclesiastical, and abolishing of all foreign power repugnant to the same. And furthermore, all ecclesiastical persons having cure of soul [that is, clergy who preach], shall to the uttermost of their wit, knowledge, and learning, purely and sincerely, and without any color or dissimulation, declare, manifest and open, four times every year at the least, in their sermons and other collations, that all usurped and foreign power, having no establishment nor ground by the law of God, was of most just causes taken away and abolished, and that therefore no manner of obedience or subjection within her Highness's realms and dominions is due unto any such foreign power. And that the queen's power within her realms and dominions is the highest power under God, to whom all men within the same realms and dominions, by God's laws owe most loyalty and obedience, afore and above all other powers and potentates in earth. . . .

That they, the persons above rehearsed, shall preach in their churches, and every other cure they have, one sermon, every quarter of the year at the least, wherein they shall purely and sincerely declare the Word of God, and in the same, exhort their hearers to the works of faith, mercy, and charity specially prescribed and commanded in Scripture, and that works devised by men's fantasies, besides Scripture, as wandering to pilgrimages, offering of money, candles, or tapers to relics or images, or kissing and licking of the same, praying upon beads, or such like

to marry. But the church remained hierarchical, with archbishops and bishops, and services continued to be elaborate, with the clergy in distinctive robes, in contrast to the simpler services favored by many continental Protestants.

Toward the end of the sixteenth century Elizabeth's reign was threatened by European powers attempting to re-establish Catholicism. Philip II of Spain had hoped that his marriage to Mary Tudor would reunite England with Catholic Europe, but Mary's death ended those plans. Another Mary — Mary, Queen of Scots (r. 1560–1567) — provided a new opportunity. Mary was Elizabeth's cousin, but she was Catholic. Mary was next in line to the English throne, and Elizabeth imprisoned her because she worried — quite rightly — that Mary would become the center of Catholic plots to overthrow her. In 1587 Mary became implicated in a plot to assassinate Elizabeth, a conspiracy that had Philip II's full backing. When the English executed Mary, the Catholic pope urged Philip to retaliate.

Philip prepared a vast fleet to sail from Lisbon to Flanders, where a large army of Spanish troops was stationed because of religious wars in the Netherlands (see page 432). The Spanish ships were to escort barges carrying some of the troops across the

superstition, have not only no promise of reward in Scripture, for doing of them, but contrariwise, great threats and malediction of God, for that they be things tending to idolatry and superstition, which of all other offenses God almighty doth most detest and abhor, for that the same diminish his honor and glory. . . .

Every parson, vicar, and curate shall upon every holy day and every second Sunday in the year, hear and instruct all the youth of the parish for half an hour at the least, before Evening Prayer, in the Ten Commandments, the Articles of the Belief, and in the Lord's Prayer. . . .

Because in all alterations and specially in rites and ceremonies, there happeneth discord among the people, and thereupon slanderous words and railings whereby charity, the knot of all Christian society, is loosed. The queen's Majesty being most desirous of all other earthly things, that her people should live in charity both towards God and man, and therein abound in good works, willeth and straightly commandeth all manner of her subjects to forbear all vain and contentious disputations in matters of religion.

EVALUATE THE EVIDENCE

1. Whose authority in matters of religion do these rules reject, and whose do they declare to be supreme? What religious activities are required, and what religious activities are prohibited?

2. Given what you have read in this chapter, would you expect that the queen's order to end "disputations in matters of religion" was followed?

Source: Denis R. Janz, ed., *A Reformation Reader: Primary Texts with Introductions* (Minneapolis: Fortress Press, 1999), pp. 315, 316.

English Channel to attack England. On May 9, 1588, *la felícissima armada*—"the most fortunate fleet," as it was ironically called in official documents—composed of more than 130 vessels, sailed from Lisbon harbor. The **Spanish Armada** met an English fleet in the Channel before it reached Flanders. The English ships were smaller, faster, and more maneuverable, and many of them had greater firing power than their Spanish counterparts. A combination of storms and squalls, spoiled food and rank water, inadequate Spanish ammunition, and, to a lesser extent, English fire ships that caused the Spanish to scatter gave England the victory. On the journey home many Spanish ships went down in the rough seas around Ireland; perhaps sixty-five ships managed to reach home ports.

The battle in the English Channel has frequently been described as one of the decisive battles in world history. In fact, it had mixed consequences. Spain soon rebuilt its navy, and after 1588 the quality of the Spanish fleet improved. The war between England and Spain dragged on for years. Yet the defeat of the Spanish Armada prevented Philip II from reimposing Catholicism on England by force. In England the victory contributed to a David and Goliath legend that enhanced English national sentiment.

Calvinism

In 1509, while Luther was preparing for a doctorate at Wittenberg, John Calvin (1509–1564) was born in Noyon in northwestern France. As a young man he studied law, which had a decisive impact on his mind and later his thought. In 1533 he experienced a religious crisis, as a result of which he converted to Protestantism.

Calvin believed that God had specifically selected him to reform the church. Accordingly, he accepted an invitation to assist in the reformation of the city of Geneva. There, beginning in 1541, Calvin worked assiduously to establish a well-disciplined Christian society in which church and state acted together.

To understand Calvin's Geneva, it is necessary to understand Calvin's ideas. These he embodied in *The Institutes of the Christian Religion*, published first in 1536 and in its final form in 1559. The cornerstone of Calvin's theology was his belief in the absolute sovereignty and omnipotence of God and the total weakness of humanity. Before the infinite power of God, he asserted, men and women are as insignificant as grains of sand.

Calvin did not ascribe free will to human beings because that would detract from the sovereignty of God. Men and women cannot actively work to achieve salvation; rather, God in his infinite wisdom decided at the beginning of time who would be saved and who damned. This viewpoint constitutes the theological principle called **predestination**. Calvin explained his view:

> Predestination we call the eternal decree of God, by which he has determined in himself, what he would have become of every individual. . . . For they are not all created with a similar destiny; but eternal life is foreordained for some, and eternal damnation for others. . . . To those whom he devotes to condemnation, the gate of life is closed by a just and irreprehensible, but incomprehensible, judgment. How exceedingly presumptuous it is only to inquire into the causes of the Divine will; which is in fact, and is justly entitled to be, the cause of everything that exists. . . . For the will of God is the highest justice; so that what he wills must be considered just, for this very reason, because he wills it.[6]

Many people consider the doctrine of predestination, which dates back to Saint Augustine and Saint Paul, to be a pessimistic view of the nature of God. But "this terrible decree," as even Calvin called it, did not lead to pessimism or fatalism. Instead, many Calvinists came to believe that although one's own actions could do nothing to change one's fate, hard work, thrift, and proper moral conduct could serve as signs that one was among the "elect" chosen for salvation.

Calvin transformed Geneva into a community based on his religious principles. The most powerful organization in the city became the Consistory, a group of laymen and pastors charged with investigating and disciplining deviations from proper doctrine and conduct. (See "Primary Source: 1547 Ordinances in Calvin's Geneva," page 424.)

Serious crimes and heresy were handled by the civil authorities, which, with the Consistory's approval, sometimes used torture to extract confessions. Between 1542 and 1546 alone seventy-six persons were banished from Geneva, and fifty-eight were executed for heresy, adultery, blasphemy, and witchcraft (see page 432). Among them was the Spanish humanist and refugee Michael Servetus, who was burned at the stake for denying the scriptural basis for the Trinity, rejecting child baptism, and insisting that a person under twenty cannot commit a mortal sin, all of which were viewed as threats to society.

Geneva became the model of a Christian community for many Protestant reformers. Religious refugees from France, England, Spain, Scotland, and Italy visited Calvin's Geneva, and many of the most prominent exiles from Mary Tudor's England stayed. Subsequently, the church of Calvin — often termed "Reformed" — served as the model for the Presbyterian Church in Scotland, the Huguenot Church in France (see page 430), and the Puritan Churches in England and New England.

Calvinism became the compelling force in international Protestantism. Calvinists believed that any occupation could be a God-given "calling," and should be carried out with diligence and dedication. This doctrine encouraged an aggressive, vigorous activism in both work and religious life, and Calvinism became the most dynamic force in sixteenth- and seventeenth-century Protestantism.

Calvinism spread on the continent of Europe, and also found a ready audience in Scotland. There, as elsewhere, political authority was the decisive influence in reform. The monarchy was weak, and factions of virtually independent nobles competed for power. King James V and his daughter Mary, Queen of Scots, staunch Catholics and close allies of Catholic France, opposed reform, but the Scottish nobles supported it. One man, John Knox (1505?–1572), dominated the reform movement, which led to the establishment of a state church.

Knox was determined to structure the Scottish Church after the model of Geneva, where he had studied and worked with Calvin. In 1560 Knox persuaded the Scottish parliament, which was dominated by reform-minded barons, to end papal authority and rule by bishops, substituting governance by presbyters, or councils of ministers. The Presbyterian Church of Scotland was strictly Calvinist in doctrine, adopted a simple and dignified service of worship, and laid great emphasis on preaching.

The Reformation in Eastern Europe

While political and economic issues determined the course of the Reformation in western and northern Europe, ethnic factors often proved decisive in eastern Europe, where people of diverse backgrounds had settled in the later Middle Ages. In Bohemia in the fifteenth century, a Czech majority was ruled by Germans. Most Czechs had adopted the ideas of Jan Hus, and the emperor had been forced to recognize a separate Hussite Church (see Chapter 11). Yet Lutheranism appealed to Germans in Bohemia in the 1520s and 1530s, and the nobility embraced Lutheranism in opposition to the Catholic Habsburgs. The forces of the Catholic Reformation (see page 427) promoted a Catholic spiritual revival in Bohemia, and some areas reconverted. This complicated situation would be one of the causes of the Thirty Years' War in the early seventeenth century.

By 1500 Poland and the Grand Duchy of Lithuania were jointly governed by king, senate, and diet (parliament), but the two territories retained separate officials, judicial systems, armies, and forms of citizenship. The combined realms covered almost five hundred thousand square miles, making Poland-Lithuania the largest European polity, but a population of only about 7.5 million people was very thinly scattered over that land.

The population of Poland-Lithuania was also very diverse; Germans, Italians, Tartars, and Jews lived among Poles and Lithuanians. Such peoples had come as merchants, invited by medieval rulers because of their wealth or to make agricultural improvements.

PRIMARY SOURCE   1547 Ordinances in Calvin's Geneva

John Calvin thought that a well-disciplined city, like a well-disciplined individual, might be seen as evidence of God's election. He put his ideas into action in Geneva, encouraging city leaders to issue ordinances that regulated many aspects of life, and establishing the Consistory to enforce them. The following ordinances also applied to the villages that the city controlled in the surrounding territory.

Concerning the Times of Assembling at Church

That the temples [the churches] be closed for the rest of the time [when services are not in session], in order that no one shall enter therein out of hours, impelled thereto by superstition; and if anyone be found engaged in any special act of devotion therein or near by he shall be admonished for it: if it be found to be of a superstitious nature for which simple correction is inadequate then he shall be chastised.

Blasphemy

Whoever shall have blasphemed, swearing by the body or by the blood of our Lord, or in similar manner, he shall be made to kiss the earth for the first offence; for the second to pay 5 sous, and for the third 6 sous, and for the last offence be put in the pillory [a wooden frame set up in a public place, in which a person's head and hands could be locked] for one hour.

Drunkenness

1. That no one shall invite another to drink under penalty of 3 sous.
2. That taverns shall be closed during the sermon, under penalty that the tavern-keeper shall pay 3 sous, and whoever may be found therein shall pay the same amount.
3. If anyone be found intoxicated he shall pay for the first offence 3 sous and shall be remanded to the consistory; for the second offence he shall be held to pay the sum of 6 sous, and for the third 10 sous and be put in prison.

Each group spoke its native language, though all educated people spoke Latin. Luther's ideas took root in Germanized towns but were opposed by King Sigismund I (r. 1506–1548) as well as by ordinary Poles, who held strong anti-German feeling. The Reformed tradition of John Calvin, with its stress on the power of church elders, appealed to the Polish nobility, however. The fact that Calvinism originated in France, not in Germany, also made it more attractive than Lutheranism. But doctrinal differences among Calvinists, Lutherans, and other groups prevented united opposition to Catholicism, and a Counter-Reformation gained momentum. By 1650, due largely to the efforts of the Jesuits (see page 429), Poland was again staunchly Roman Catholic.

Hungary's experience with the Reformation was even more complex. Lutheranism was spread by Hungarian students who had studied at Wittenberg, and sympathy for it developed at the royal court of King Louis II in Buda. But concern about "the German heresy" by the Catholic hierarchy and among the high nobles found expression in a decree of the Hungarian diet in 1523 that "all Lutherans and those favoring them . . . should have their property confiscated and themselves punished with death as heretics."[7]

Songs and Dances

If anyone sing immoral, dissolute or outrageous songs, or dance the *virollet* or other dance, he shall be put in prison for three days and then sent to the consistory.

Usury

That no one shall take upon interest or profit [on a loan] more than five percent, upon penalty of confiscation of the principal and of being condemned to make restitution as the case may demand.

Games

That no one shall play at any dissolute game or at any game whatsoever it may be, neither for gold nor silver nor for any excessive stake, upon penalty of 5 sous and forfeiture of stake played for.

EVALUATE THE EVIDENCE

1. Given the actions prohibited in these ordinances, how would you describe ideal Christian behavior, in Calvin's eyes?

2. Other than the punishments set for disobeying these ordinances, what might have motivated Genevans to obey them, particularly given Calvinist beliefs that a person's own behavior had no effect on whether he or she would achieve salvation?

Source: Merrick Whitcomb, ed., *Translations and Reprints from the Original Sources of European History*, vol. 3 (Philadelphia: University of Pennsylvania, 1897), no. 3, pp. 10–11.

Before such measures could be acted on, a military event on August 26, 1526, had profound consequences for both the Hungarian state and the Protestant Reformation there. On the plain of Mohács in southern Hungary, the Ottoman sultan Suleiman the Magnificent inflicted a crushing defeat on the Hungarians, killing King Louis II, many of the nobles, and more than sixteen thousand ordinary soldiers. The Hungarian kingdom was then divided into three parts: the Ottoman Turks absorbed the great plains, including the capital, Buda; the Habsburgs ruled the north and west; and Ottoman-supported Janos Zapolya held eastern Hungary and Transylvania.

The Turks were indifferent to the religious conflicts of Christians, whom they regarded as infidels. Christians of all types paid extra taxes to the sultan, but kept their faith. Many Magyar (Hungarian) nobles accepted Lutheranism; Lutheran schools and parishes headed by men educated at Wittenberg multiplied; and peasants welcomed the new faith. The majority of Hungarian people were Protestant until the late seventeenth century, when Hungarian nobles recognized Habsburg (Catholic) rule and Ottoman Turkish withdrawal in 1699 led to Catholic restoration.

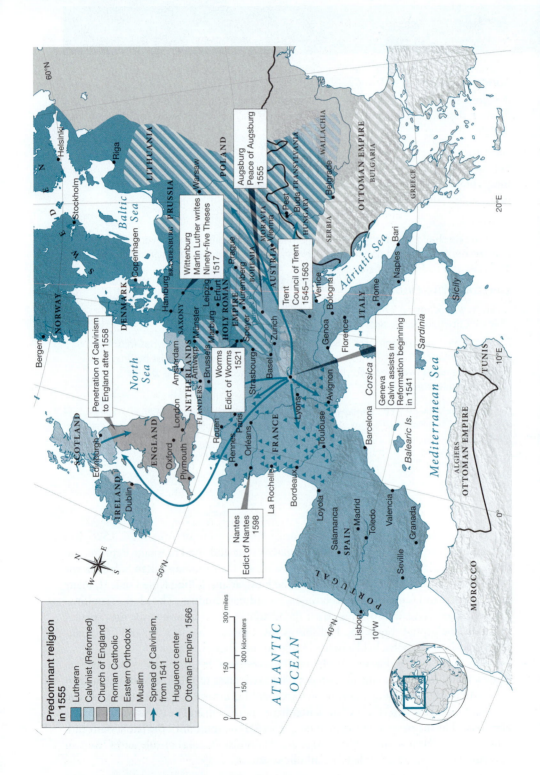

Predominant religion
in 1555
- Lutheran
- Calvinist (Reformed)
- Church of England
- Roman Catholic
- Eastern Orthodox
- Muslim
- ▲ Spread of Calvinism, from 1541
- ◄ Huguenot center
- — Ottoman Empire, 1566

Augsburg
Peace of Augsburg
1555

Wittenburg
Martin Luther writes
Ninety-five Theses
1517

Trent
Council of Trent
1545–1563

Geneva
Calvin assists in
Reformation beginning
in 1541

Worms
Edict of Worms
1521

Penetration of Calvinism
to England after 1558

Nantes
Edict of Nantes
1598

◀ **MAP 13.2   Religious Divisions in Europe, ca. 1555**
The Reformations shattered the religious unity of Western Christendom. The situation was even
more complicated than a map of this scale can show. Many cities within the Holy Roman Empire,
for example, accepted a different faith than the surrounding countryside; Augsburg, Basel, and
Strasbourg were all Protestant, though surrounded by territory ruled by Catholic nobles.

The Catholic Reformation

**What reforms did the Catholic Church make, and how did it respond to
Protestant reform movements?**

Between 1517 and 1547 Protestantism made remarkable advances. Nevertheless, the
Roman Catholic Church made a significant comeback. After about 1540 no new large
areas of Europe, other than the Netherlands, accepted Protestant beliefs (Map 13.2).
Many historians see the developments within the Catholic Church after the Protestant
Reformation as two interrelated movements, one a drive for internal reform linked to
earlier reform efforts, and the other a Counter-Reformation that opposed Protestants
intellectually, politically, militarily, and institutionally. In both movements, the papacy,
new religious orders, and the Council of Trent that met from 1545 to 1563 were important agents.

Papal Reform and the Council of Trent

Renaissance popes and their advisers were not blind to the need for church reforms, but
they resisted calls for a general council representing the entire church, and feared that
any transformation would mean a loss of power, revenue, and prestige. This changed
beginning with Pope Paul III (pontificate 1534–1549), when the papal court became
the center of the reform movement rather than its chief opponent. The lives of the pope
and his reform-minded cardinals, abbots, and bishops were models of decorum and
piety, in contrast to Renaissance popes who concentrated on building churches and
enhancing the power of their own families. Paul III and his successors supported improvements in education for the clergy, the end of simony (the selling of church offices),
and stricter control of clerical life.

In 1542 Pope Paul III established the Supreme Sacred Congregation of the Roman
and Universal Inquisition, often called the **Holy Office**, with jurisdiction over the Roman
Inquisition, a powerful instrument of the Catholic Reformation. The Roman Inquisition
was a committee of six cardinals with judicial authority over all Catholics and the power
to arrest, imprison, and execute suspected heretics. The Holy Office published the *Index
of Prohibited Books*, a catalogue of forbidden reading that included works by Christian
humanists such as Erasmus as well as by Protestants. Within the Papal States, the
Inquisition effectively destroyed heresy, but outside the papal territories, its influence
was slight.

Pope Paul III also called a general council, which met intermittently from 1545 to
1563 at Trent, an imperial city close to Italy. It was called not only to reform the Catholic Church but also to secure reconciliation with the Protestants. Lutherans and Calvinists were invited to participate, but their insistence that the Scriptures be the sole
basis for discussion made reconciliation impossible. In addition, the political objectives

of Charles V and France both worked against reconciliation: Charles wanted to avoid alienating the Lutheran nobility in the empire, and France wanted the Catholics and Lutherans to remain divided in order to keep Germany decentralized and weak.

Nonetheless, the decrees of the Council of Trent laid a solid basis for the spiritual renewal of the Catholic Church. It gave equal validity to the Scriptures and to tradition as sources of religious truth and authority. It reaffirmed the seven sacraments and the traditional Catholic teaching on transubstantiation. It tackled the disciplinary matters that had disillusioned the faithful, requiring bishops to reside in their own dioceses, suppressing pluralism and simony, and forbidding the sale of indulgences. Clerics who kept concubines were to give them up, and bishops were given greater authority. The council required every diocese to establish a seminary for the education and training of the clergy. Seminary professors were to determine whether candidates for ordination had vocations, genuine callings to the priesthood. This was a novel idea, since from the time of the early church, parents had determined their sons' (and daughters') religious careers. For the first time, great emphasis was laid on preaching and instructing the laity, especially the uneducated.

One decision had especially important social consequences for laypeople. The Council of Trent stipulated that for a marriage to be valid, the marriage vows had to be made publicly before a priest and witnesses. Trent thereby ended the widespread practice of private marriages in Catholic countries, curtailing the number of denials and conflicts that inevitably resulted from marriages that took place in secret.

Although it did not achieve all of its goals, the Council of Trent composed decrees that laid a solid basis for the spiritual renewal of the church. The doctrinal and disciplinary legislation of Trent served as the basis for Roman Catholic faith, organization, and practice through the middle of the twentieth century.

New and Reformed Religious Orders

Just as seminaries provided education, so did religious orders, which aimed at raising the moral and intellectual level of the clergy and people. The monasteries and convents of many existing religious orders were reformed so that they followed more rigorous standards. In Spain, for example, the Carmelite nun Teresa of Ávila (1515–1582) founded new convents and reformed her Carmelite order to bring it back to stricter standards of asceticism and poverty, a task she understood God had set for her in mystical visions. Some officials in the Spanish Church thought the life she proposed was too strict for women, and at one point she was even investigated by the Spanish Inquisition in an effort to make sure her inspiration came from God and not the Devil. The process was dropped, and she founded many new convents, which she saw as answers to the Protestant takeover of Catholic churches elsewhere in Europe.

New religious orders were founded, some of which focused on education. The Ursuline order of nuns, for example, founded by Angela Merici (1474–1540), focused on the education of women. The daughter of a country gentleman, Angela Merici worked for many years among the poor, sick, and uneducated around her native Brescia in northern Italy. In 1535 she established the first women's religious order concentrating exclusively on teaching young girls, with the goal of re-Christianizing society by training future wives and mothers. After receiving papal approval in 1565, the Ursulines rapidly spread to France and the New World.

The most significant new order was the Society of Jesus, or **Jesuits**. Founded by Ignatius Loyola (1491–1556), the Jesuits played a powerful international role in strengthening Catholicism in Europe and spreading the faith around the world. While recuperating from a severe battle wound in his legs, Loyola studied books about Christ and the saints and decided to give up his military career and become a soldier of Christ. During a year spent in seclusion, prayer, and asceticism, he gained insights that went into his great classic, *Spiritual Exercises* (1548). This work, intended for study during a four-week period of retreat, set out a training program of structured meditation designed to develop spiritual discipline and allow one to meld one's will with that of God. Loyola introduces his program by noting:

> By the term "Spiritual Exercises" is meant every method of examination of conscience, of meditation, of contemplation, of vocal and mental prayer, and of other spiritual activities. For just as taking a walk, journeying on foot, and running are bodily exercises, so we call Spiritual Exercises every way of preparing and disposing the soul to rid itself of all inordinate attachments, and, after their removal, of seeking and finding the will of God in the disposition of our life for the salvation of our soul.[8]

Just like today's physical trainers, Loyola provides daily exercises that build in intensity over the four weeks of the program, and charts on which the exerciser can track his progress.

Loyola was a man of considerable personal magnetism. After study at universities in Salamanca and Paris, he gathered a group of six companions and in 1540 secured papal approval of the new Society of Jesus. The first Jesuits, recruited primarily from wealthy merchant and professional families, saw their mission as improving people's spiritual condition rather than altering doctrine. Their goal was not to reform the church, but "to help souls."

The Society of Jesus developed into a highly centralized, tightly knit organization. In addition to the traditional vows of poverty, chastity, and obedience, professed members vowed special obedience to the pope. Flexibility and the willingness to respond to the needs of time and circumstance formed the Jesuit tradition, which proved attractive to many young men. The Jesuits achieved phenomenal success for the papacy and the reformed Catholic Church, carrying Christianity to India and Japan before 1550 and to Brazil, North America, and the Congo in the seventeenth century. Within Europe the Jesuits brought southern Germany and much of eastern Europe back to Catholicism. Jesuit schools adopted the modern humanist curricula and methods, educating the sons of the nobility as well as the poor. As confessors and spiritual directors to kings, Jesuits exerted great political influence.

Religious Violence

What were the causes and consequences of religious violence, including riots, wars, and witch-hunts?

In 1559 France and Spain signed the Treaty of Cateau-Cambrésis (CAH-toh kam-BRAY-sees), which ended the long conflict known as the Habsburg-Valois wars. Spain was the victor. France, exhausted by the struggle, had to acknowledge Spanish dominance in Italy, where much of the fighting had taken place. However, true peace was elusive, and over the next century religious differences led to riots, civil wars, and international conflicts. Especially in France and the Netherlands, Protestants and Catholics used violent actions as well as preaching and teaching against each other, for each side regarded the other as a poison in the community that would provoke the wrath of God. Catholics continued to believe that Calvinists and Lutherans could be reconverted; Protestants persisted in thinking that the Roman Church should be destroyed. Catholics and Protestants alike feared people of other faiths, whom they often saw as agents of Satan. Even more, they feared those who were explicitly identified with Satan: witches living in their midst. This era was the time of the most virulent witch persecutions in European history, as both Protestants and Catholics tried to make their cities and states more godly.

French Religious Wars

The costs of the Habsburg-Valois wars, waged intermittently through the first half of the sixteenth century, forced the French to increase taxes and borrow heavily. King Francis I (r. 1515–1547) also tried two new devices to raise revenue: the sale of public offices and a treaty with the papacy. The former proved to be only a temporary source of money: once a man bought an office, he and his heirs were exempt from taxation. But the latter, known as the Concordat of Bologna (see Chapter 12), gave the French crown the right to appoint all French bishops and abbots, ensuring a rich supplement of money and offices. Because French rulers possessed control over appointments and had a vested financial interest in Catholicism, they had no need to revolt against Rome.

Significant numbers of those ruled, however, were attracted to the Reformed religion of Calvinism. Initially, Calvinism drew converts from among reform-minded members of the Catholic clergy, industrious city dwellers, and artisan groups. Most French Calvinists, called **Huguenots**, lived in major cities, such as Paris, Lyon, and Rouen. By the time King Henry II (r. 1547–1559) died in 1559—accidentally shot in the face at a tournament celebrating the Treaty of Cateau-Cambrésis—perhaps one-tenth of the population had become Calvinist.

The feebleness of the French monarchy was the seed from which the weeds of civil violence sprang. The three weak sons of Henry II who occupied the throne could not provide the necessary leadership, and they were often dominated by their mother, Catherine de' Medici. The French nobility took advantage of this monarchical weakness. Just as German princes in the Holy Roman Empire had adopted Lutheranism as a means of opposition to Emperor Charles V, so French nobles frequently adopted Protestantism as a religious cloak for their independence. Armed clashes between Catholic royalist lords and Calvinist antimonarchical lords occurred in many parts of France. Both Calvinists and Catholics believed that the others' books, services, and ministers polluted the community. Preachers incited violence, and religious ceremonies such as baptisms, marriages, and funerals triggered it.

Calvinist teachings called the power of sacred images into question, and mobs in many cities took down and smashed statues, stained-glass windows, and paintings, viewing this as a way to purify the church. Though it was often inspired by fiery Protestant sermons, this iconoclasm, or destruction of religious images, is an example of ordinary men and women carrying out the Reformation themselves. Catholic mobs responded by defending images, and crowds on both sides killed their opponents, often in gruesome ways.

Iconoclasm in the Netherlands Calvinist men and women break stained-glass windows, remove statues, and carry off devotional altarpieces. Iconoclasm, or the destruction of religious images, is often described as a "riot," but here the participants seem very purposeful. Calvinist Protestants regarded pictures and statues as sacrilegious and saw removing them as a way to purify the church. (The Fotomas Index/The Bridgeman Art Library)

A savage Catholic attack on Calvinists in Paris on Saint Bartholomew's Day, August 24, 1572, followed the usual pattern. The occasion was the wedding of the king's sister Margaret of Valois to the Protestant Henry of Navarre, which was intended to help reconcile Catholics and Huguenots. Instead, Huguenot wedding guests in Paris were massacred, and other Protestants were slaughtered by mobs. Religious violence spread to the provinces, where thousands were killed. This Saint Bartholomew's Day massacre led to a civil war that dragged on for fifteen years. Agriculture in many areas was destroyed; commercial life declined severely; and starvation and death haunted the land.

What ultimately saved France was a small group of moderates of both faiths, called **politiques**, who believed that only the restoration of strong monarchy could reverse the trend toward collapse. The politiques also favored accepting the Huguenots as an officially recognized and organized group. The death of Catherine de' Medici, followed by the assassination of King Henry III, paved the way for the accession of Henry of Navarre (the unfortunate bridegroom of the Saint Bartholomew's Day massacre), a politique who became Henry IV (r. 1589–1610).

Henry's willingness to sacrifice religious principles to political necessity saved France. He converted to Catholicism but also issued the **Edict of Nantes** in 1598, which granted liberty of conscience and liberty of public worship to Huguenots in 150 fortified towns. The reign of Henry IV and the Edict of Nantes prepared the way for French absolutism in the seventeenth century by helping restore internal peace in France.

The Netherlands Under Charles V

In the Netherlands, what began as a movement for the reformation of the church developed into a struggle for Dutch independence. Emperor Charles V had inherited the seventeen provinces that compose present-day Belgium and the Netherlands (see page 415). Each was self-governing and enjoyed the right to make its own laws and collect its own taxes. The provinces were united politically only in recognition of a common ruler, the emperor. The cities of the Netherlands made their living by trade and industry.

In the Low Countries as elsewhere, corruption in the Roman Church and the critical spirit of the Renaissance provoked pressure for reform, and Lutheran ideas took root. Charles V had grown up in the Netherlands, however, and he was able to limit their impact. But Charles V abdicated in 1556 and transferred power over the Netherlands to his son Philip II, who had grown up in Spain. Protestant ideas spread.

By the 1560s Protestants in the Netherlands were primarily Calvinists. Calvinism's intellectual seriousness, moral gravity, and emphasis on any form of labor well done appealed to urban merchants, financiers, and artisans. Whereas Lutherans taught respect for the powers that be, Calvinism tended to encourage opposition to political authorities who were judged to be ungodly.

When Spanish authorities attempted to suppress Calvinist worship and raised taxes in the 1560s, rioting ensued. Calvinists sacked thirty Catholic churches in Antwerp, destroying the religious images in them in a wave of iconoclasm. From Antwerp the destruction spread. Philip II sent twenty thousand Spanish troops under the duke of Alva to pacify the Low Countries. Alva interpreted "pacification" to mean ruthless extermination of religious and political dissidents. On top of the Inquisition, he opened his own tribunal, soon called the "Council of Blood." On March 3, 1568, fifteen hundred men were executed. To Calvinists, all this was clear indication that Spanish rule was ungodly and should be overthrown.

Between 1568 and 1578 civil war raged in the Netherlands between Catholics and Protestants and between the seventeen provinces and Spain. Eventually the ten southern provinces, the Spanish Netherlands (the future Belgium), came under the control of the Spanish Habsburg forces. The seven northern provinces, led by Holland, formed the **Union of Utrecht** and in 1581 declared their independence from Spain. The north was Protestant; the south remained Catholic. Philip did not accept this, and war continued. England was even drawn into the conflict, supplying money and troops to the northern United Provinces. (Spain launched an unsuccessful invasion of England in response; see page 420.) Hostilities ended in 1609 when Spain agreed to a truce that recognized the independence of the United Provinces.

The Great European Witch-Hunt

The relationship between the Reformation and the upsurge in trials for witchcraft that occurred at roughly the same time is complex. Increasing persecution for witchcraft actually began before the Reformation in the 1480s, but it became especially common about 1560, and the mania continued until roughly 1660. Religious reformers' extreme notions of the Devil's powers and the insecurity created by the religious wars contributed to this increase. Both Protestants and Catholics tried and executed witches, with church officials and secular authorities acting together.

The heightened sense of God's power and divine wrath in the Reformation era was an important factor in the witch-hunts, but so was a change in the idea of what a witch was. Nearly all premodern societies believe in witchcraft and make some attempts to control witches, who are understood to be people who use magical forces. In the later

Middle Ages, however, many educated Christian theologians, canon lawyers, and officials added a demonological component to this notion of what a witch was. For them, the essence of witchcraft was making a pact with the Devil. Witches were no longer simply people who used magical power to get what they wanted, but rather people used by the Devil to do what he wanted. Witches were thought to engage in wild sexual orgies with the Devil, fly through the night to meetings called sabbats that parodied Christian services, and steal communion wafers and unbaptized babies to use in their rituals. Some demonological theorists also claimed that witches were organized in an international conspiracy to overthrow Christianity. Witchcraft was thus spiritualized, and witches became the ultimate heretics, enemies of God.

Trials involving this new notion of witchcraft as diabolical heresy began in Switzerland and southern Germany in the late fifteenth century, became less numerous in the early decades of the Reformation when Protestants and Catholics were busy fighting each other, and then picked up again in about 1560. Scholars estimate that during the sixteenth and seventeenth centuries between 100,000 and 200,000 people were officially tried for witchcraft and between 40,000 and 60,000 were executed.

Though the gender balance varied widely in different parts of Europe, between 75 and 85 percent of those tried and executed were women. Ideas about women and the roles women actually played in society were thus important factors shaping the witch-hunts. Some demonologists expressed virulent misogyny, or hatred of women, and particularly emphasized women's powerful sexual desire, which could be satisfied only by a demonic lover. Most people viewed women as weaker and so more likely to give in to an offer by the Devil. In both classical and Christian traditions, women were associated with nature, disorder, and the body, all of which were linked with the demonic. Women's actual lack of power in society and gender norms about the use of violence meant that they were more likely to use scolding and cursing to get what they wanted instead of taking people to court or beating them up. Curses were generally expressed (as they often are today) in religious terms; "go to Hell" was calling on the powers of Satan.

Legal changes also played a role in causing, or at least allowing for, massive witch trials. One of these was a change from an accusatorial legal procedure to an inquisitorial procedure. In the former, a suspect knew the accusers and the charges they had brought, and an accuser could in turn be liable for trial if the charges were not proven. In the latter, legal authorities themselves brought the case. This change made people much more willing to accuse others, for they never had to take personal responsibility for the accusation or face the accused person's relatives. Areas in Europe that did not make this legal change saw very few trials. Inquisitorial procedure involved intense questioning of the suspect, often with torture. Torture was also used to get the names of additional suspects, as most lawyers firmly believed that no witch could act alone.

The use of inquisitorial procedure did not always lead to witch-hunts. The most famous inquisitions in early modern Europe, those in Spain, Portugal, and Italy, were in fact very lenient in their treatment of people accused of witchcraft. The Inquisition in Spain executed only a handful of witches, the Portuguese Inquisition only one, and the Roman Inquisition none, though in each of these there were hundreds of cases. Inquisitors believed in the power of the Devil and were no less misogynist than other judges, but they doubted very much whether the people accused of witchcraft had actually made pacts with the Devil that gave them special powers. They viewed such people not as diabolical Devil worshippers but as superstitious and ignorant peasants who should be educated rather than executed. Thus most people brought up before the Inquisition for witchcraft were sent home with a warning and a penance.

Most witch trials began with a single accusation in a village or town. Individuals accused someone they knew of using magic to spoil food, make children ill, kill animals, raise a hailstorm, or do other types of harm. Tensions within families, households, and neighborhoods often played a role in these accusations. Women number very prominently among accusers and witnesses as well as among those accused of witchcraft because the actions witches were initially charged with, such as harming children or curdling milk, were generally part of women's sphere. A woman also gained economic and social security by conforming to the standard of the good wife and mother and by confronting women who deviated from it.

Once a charge was made, the suspect was brought in for questioning. One German witch pamphlet from 1587 described a typical case:

> Walpurga Hausmännin . . . upon kindly questioning and also torture . . . confessed . . . that the Evil One indulged in fornication with her . . . and made her many promises to help her in her poverty and need. . . . She promised herself body and soul to him and disowned God in heaven. . . . She destroyed a number of cattle, pigs, and geese . . . and dug up [the bodies] of one or two innocent children. With her devil-paramour and other playfellows she has eaten these and used their hair and their little bones for witchcraft.

Confession was generally followed by execution. In this case, Hausmännin was "dispatched from life to death by burning at the stake . . . her body first to be torn five times with red-hot irons."[9]

Detailed records of witch trials survive for many parts of Europe. They have been used by historians to study many aspects of witchcraft, but they cannot directly answer what seems to us an important question: did people really practice witchcraft and think they were witches? They certainly confessed to evil deeds and demonic practices, sometimes without torture, but where would we draw the line between reality and fantasy? Clearly people were not riding through the air on pitchforks, but did they think they did? Did they actually invoke the Devil when they were angry at a neighbor, or was this simply in the minds of their accusers? Trial records cannot tell us, and historians have answered these questions very differently, often using insights from psychoanalysis or the study of more recent victims of torture in their explanations.

After the initial suspect had been questioned, and particularly if he or she had been tortured, the people who had been implicated were brought in for questioning. This might lead to a small hunt, involving from five to ten suspects, and it sometimes grew into a much larger hunt, which historians have called a "witch panic." Panics were most common in the part of Europe that saw the most witch accusations in general: the Holy Roman Empire, Switzerland, and parts of France. Most of this area consisted of very small governmental units that were jealous of each other and, after the Reformation, were divided by religion. The rulers of these small territories often felt more threatened than did the monarchs of western Europe, and they saw persecuting witches as a way to demonstrate their piety and concern for order. Moreover, witch panics often occurred after some type of climatic disaster, such as an unusually cold and wet summer, and they came in waves.

Witch Pamphlet   This printed pamphlet presents the confession of "Mother Waterhouse," a woman convicted of witchcraft in England in 1566, who describes her "many abominable deeds" and "execrable sorcery" committed over fifteen years, and asks for forgiveness right before her execution. Enterprising printers often produced cheap, short pamphlets during witch trials, knowing they would sell, sometimes based on the actual trial proceedings and sometimes just made up. They both reflected and helped create stereotypes about what witches were and did. (The Granger Collection, New York)

In large-scale panics a wider variety of suspects were taken in — wealthier people, children, a greater proportion of men. Mass panics tended to end when it became clear to legal authorities, or to the community itself, that the people being questioned or executed were not what they understood witches to be, or that the scope of accusations was beyond belief.

As the seventeenth century ushered in new ideas about science and reason, many began to question whether witches could make pacts with the Devil or engage in the wild activities attributed to them. Doubts about whether secret denunciations were valid or whether torture would ever yield truthful confessions gradually spread among the same type of religious and legal authorities who had so vigorously persecuted witches. Prosecutions for witchcraft became less common and were gradually outlawed. The last official execution for witchcraft in England was in 1682, though the last one in the Holy Roman Empire was not until 1775.

Notes

1. Quoted in Owen Chadwick, *The Reformation* (Baltimore: Penguin Books, 1976), p. 55.
2. Quoted in E. H. Harbison, *The Age of Reformation* (Ithaca, N.Y.: Cornell University Press, 1963), p. 52.
3. Quoted in S. E. Ozment, *The Age of Reform, 1250–1550: An Intellectual and Religious History of Late Medieval and Reformation Europe* (New Haven, Conn.: Yale University Press, 1980), p. 284.
4. Ludwig Rabus, *Historien der heyligen Außerwolten Gottes Zeugen, Bekennern und Martyrern* (n.p., 1557), fol. 41. Trans. Merry Wiesner-Hanks.
5. From Henry Bettenson, ed., *Documents of the Christian Church*, 2d ed. (London: Oxford University Press, 1963), pp. 301–302. Used by permission of Oxford University Press.
6. J. Allen, trans., *John Calvin: The Institutes of the Christian Religion* (Philadelphia: Westminster Press, 1930), bk. 3, chap. 21, para. 5, 7.
7. Quoted in David P. Daniel, "Hungary," in *The Oxford Encyclopedia of the Reformation*, vol. 2, ed. H. J. Hillerbrand (New York: Oxford University Press, 1996), p. 273.
8. *The Spiritual Exercises of St. Ignatius of Loyola*, trans. Louis J. Puhl, S.J. (Chicago: Loyola University, 1951), p. 1.
9. From *The Fugger News-Letters*, ed. Victor von Klarwell, trans. P. de Chary (London: John Lane, The Bodley Head Ltd., 1924), quoted in James Bruce Ross and Mary Martin McLaughlin, *The Portable Renaissance Reader* (New York: Penguin, 1968), pp. 258, 260, 262.

Chapter Review

MAKE IT STICK

LearningCurve
bedfordstmartins.com/mckaywestvalue

After reading the chapter, use LearningCurve to retain what you've read.

IDENTIFY KEY TERMS

Identify and explain the significance of each item below.

anticlericalism (p. 402)

indulgence (p. 404)

Protestant (p. 406)

Spanish Armada
(p. 421)

*The Institutes of the
Christian Religion*
(p. 422)

predestination (p. 422)

Holy Office (p. 427)

Jesuits (p. 429)

Huguenots (p. 430)

politiques (p. 431)

Edict of Nantes (p. 431)

Union of Utrecht (p. 432)

REVIEW THE MAIN IDEAS

Answer the focus questions from each section of the chapter.

◆ What were the central ideas of the reformers, and why were they appealing to different social groups? (p. 402)

◆ How did the political situation in Germany shape the course of the Reformation? (p. 413)

◆ How did Protestant ideas and institutions spread beyond German-speaking lands? (p. 417)

◆ What reforms did the Catholic Church make, and how did it respond to Protestant reform movements? (p. 427)

◆ What were the causes and consequences of religious violence, including riots, wars, and witch-hunts? (p. 429)

MAKE CONNECTIONS

Think about the larger developments and continuities within and across chapters.

1. How did Protestant ideas about gender, marriage, and the role of women break with those developed earlier in the history of the Christian Church (Chapters 6, 7, 9)? What continuities do you see? What factors account for the pattern?

2. In what ways was the Catholic Reformation of the sixteeenth century similar to earlier efforts to reform the church, including the Gregorian reforms of the twelfth century (Chapter 9) and late medieval reform efforts (Chapter 11)? In what ways was it different?

ONLINE DOCUMENT ASSIGNMENT

Anna Jansz of Rotterdam

What might have led Jansz and thousands like her to die for their religious convictions?

You encountered Anna Jansz's story on page 410. Learn more about Jansz and other Anabaptist martyrs by analyzing images and hymns, and then complete a writing assignment based on the evidence and details from this chapter.

bedfordstmartins.com/mckaywestvalue

CHRONOLOGY

1517	• Martin Luther writes "Ninety-five Theses on the Power of Indulgences"
1521	• Diet of Worms
1521–1559	• Habsburg-Valois wars
1525	• German Peasants' War
1526	• Turkish victory at Mohács, which allows spread of Protestantism in Hungary
1530s	• Henry VIII ends the authority of the pope in England
1535	• Angela Merici establishes the Ursulines as first women's teaching order
1536	• John Calvin publishes *The Institutes of the Christian Religion*
1540	• Papal approval of Society of Jesus (Jesuits)
1542	• Pope Paul III establishes the Supreme Sacred Congregation of the Roman and Universal Inquisition
1545–1563	• Council of Trent
1553–1558	• Reign of Mary Tudor and temporary restoration of Catholicism in England
1555	• Peace of Augsburg; official recognition of Lutheranism
1558–1603	• Reign of Elizabeth in England
1560–1660	• Height of the European witch-hunt
1568–1578	• Civil war in the Netherlands
1572	• Saint Bartholomew's Day massacre
1588	• England defeats Spanish Armada
1598	• Edict of Nantes

14

✓ **LearningCurve**
bedfordstmartins.com/mckaywestvalue
After reading the chapter, use
LearningCurve to retain what
you've read.

European Exploration and Conquest

1450–1650

BEFORE 1450 EUROPEANS WERE RELATIVELY MARGINAL PLAYERS IN A centuries-old trading system that linked Africa, Asia, and Europe. Elites everywhere prized Chinese porcelains and silks, while wealthy members of the Celestial Kingdom, as China called itself, wanted ivory and black slaves from Africa, and exotic goods and peacocks from India. African people wanted textiles from India and cowrie shells from the Maldives in the Indian Ocean. Europeans craved Asian silks and spices, but they had few desirable goods to offer their trading partners.

Europeans' search for better access to Asian trade led to a new empire in the Indian Ocean and the accidental discovery of the Western Hemisphere. Within a few decades European colonies in South and North America would join this worldwide web of commerce. Capitalizing on the goods and riches they found in the Americas, Europeans came to dominate trading networks and built political empires of truly global proportions. The era of globalization had begun.

Global contacts created new forms of cultural exchange, assimilation, conversion, and resistance. Europeans struggled to comprehend the peoples and societies they encountered and sought to impose European cultural values on them. New forms of racial prejudice emerged, but so did new openness and curiosity about different ways of life. Together with the developments of the Renaissance and the Reformation, the Age of Discovery—as the period of European exploration and conquest from 1450 to 1650 is known—laid the foundations for the modern world.

World Contacts Before Columbus

What was the Afroeurasian trading world before Columbus?

Columbus did not sail west on a whim. To understand his and other Europeans' explorations, we must first understand late medieval trade networks. Historians now recognize that a type of world economy, known as the Afroeurasian trade world, linked the products and people of Asia, Africa, and Europe in the fifteenth century. The West was not the dominant player before Columbus, and the European voyages derived from a desire to share in and control the wealth coming from the Indian Ocean.

The Trade World of the Indian Ocean

The Indian Ocean was the center of the Afroeurasian trade world. Its location made it a crossroads for exchange among China, India, the Middle East, Africa, and Europe (Map 14.1). From the seventh through the fourteenth centuries, the volume of this trade steadily increased, declining only during the years of the Black Death.

Merchants congregated in a series of cosmopolitan port cities strung around the Indian Ocean. Most of these cities had some form of autonomous self-government. Mutual self-interest had largely limited violence and attempts to monopolize trade. The most developed area of this commercial web was in the South China Sea. In the fifteenth century the port of Malacca became a great commercial entrepôt (AHN-truh-poh), a trading post to which goods were shipped for storage while awaiting redistribution. To Malacca came Chinese porcelains, silks, and camphor (used in the manufacture of many medications); pepper, cloves, nutmeg, and raw materials such as sandalwood from the Moluccas; sugar from the Philippines; and Indian textiles, copper weapons, incense, dyes, and opium.

The Mongol emperors opened the doors of China to the West, encouraging Europeans like the Venetian trader and explorer Marco Polo to do business there. Marco Polo's tales of his travels from 1271 to 1295 and his encounter with the Great Khan fueled Western fantasies about the exotic Orient. Polo vividly recounted the splendors of the Khan's court and the city of Hangzhou, which he described as "the finest and noblest in the world" in which "the number and wealth of the merchants, and the amount of goods that passed through their hands, was so enormous that no man could form a just estimate thereof."[1] After the Mongols fell to the Ming Dynasty in 1368, China entered a period of economic expansion, population growth, and urbanization. By the end of the dynasty in 1644, the Chinese population had tripled to between 150 million and 200 million. The city of Nanjing had 1 million inhabitants, making it the largest city in the world, while the new capital, Beijing, had more than 600,000 inhabitants, larger than any European city. Historians agree that China had the most advanced economy in the world until at least the start of the eighteenth century.

China also took the lead in exploration, sending Admiral Zheng He's fleet along the trade web as far west as Egypt. From 1405 to 1433, each of his seven expeditions involved hundreds of ships and tens of thousands of men. In one voyage alone, Zheng He (JEHNG HUH) sailed more than 12,000 miles, compared to Columbus's 2,400 miles on his first voyage some sixty years later.[2] Court conflicts and the need to defend against renewed Mongol encroachment led to the abandonment of the maritime expeditions after the

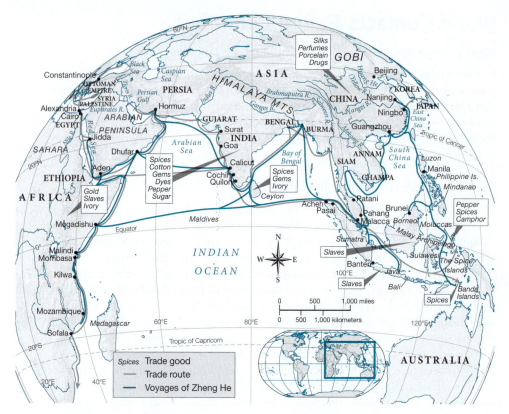

MAP 14.1   The Fifteenth-Century Afroeurasian Trading World

After a period of decline following the Black Death and the Mongol invasions, trade revived in the fifteenth century. Muslim merchants dominated trade, linking ports in East Africa and the Red Sea with those in India and the Malay Archipelago. Chinese admiral Zheng He's voyages (1405–1433) followed the most important Indian Ocean trade routes, in the hope of imposing Ming dominance of trade and tribute.

deaths of Zheng He and the emperor. China's turning away from external trade opened new opportunities for European states to claim a decisive role in world trade.

Another center of trade in the Indian Ocean was India. The subcontinent had ancient links with its neighbors to the northwest: trade between South Asia and Mesopotamia dates back to the origins of human civilization. Romans had acquired cotton textiles, exotic animals, and other luxury goods from India. Arab merchants who circumnavigated India on their way to trade in the South China Sea established trading posts along the southern coast of India, where the cities of Calicut and Quilon became thriving commercial centers. India was an important contributor of goods to the world trading system; much of the world's pepper was grown there, and Indian cotton textiles were highly prized.

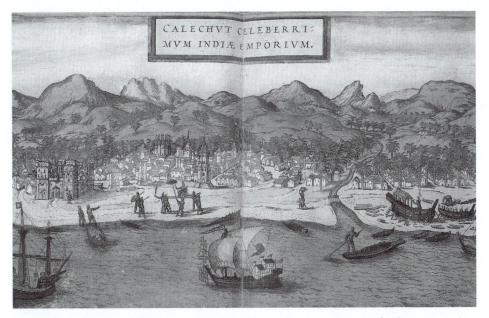

CALECHVT CELEBERRI-
MVM INDIÆ EMPORIVM.

The Port of Calicut in India   The port of Calicut, located on the west coast of India, was a center of the Indian Ocean spice trade during the Middle Ages. Vasco da Gama arrived in Calicut in 1498 and obtained permission to trade there, leading to hostilities between the Portuguese and the Arab traders who had previously dominated the port. (Private Collection/The Stapleton Collection/ The Bridgeman Art Library)

The Trading States of Africa

By 1450 Africa had a few large empires along with hundreds of smaller states. From 1250 until its defeat by the Ottomans in 1517, the Mamluk Egyptian empire was one of the most powerful on the continent. Its capital, Cairo, was a center of Islamic learning and religious authority as well as a hub for Indian Ocean trade goods. Sharing in Cairo's prosperity was the African highland state of Ethiopia, a Christian kingdom with scattered contacts with European rulers. On the east coast of Africa, Swahili-speaking city-states engaged in the Indian Ocean trade, exchanging ivory, rhinoceros horn, tortoise shells, and slaves for textiles, spices, cowrie shells, porcelain, and other goods. Peopled by confident and urbane merchants, cities like Kilwa, Malindi, Mogadishu, and Mombasa were known for their prosperity and culture.

In the fifteenth century most of the gold that reached Europe came from the western part of the Sudan region in West Africa and from the Akan (AH-kahn) peoples living near present-day Ghana. Transported across the Sahara by Arab and African traders on camels, the gold was sold in the ports of North Africa. Other trading routes led to the Egyptian cities of Alexandria and Cairo, where the Venetians held commercial privileges.

Nations inland that sat astride the north-south caravan routes grew wealthy from this trade. In the mid-thirteenth century the kingdom of Mali emerged as an important player on the overland trade route, gaining prestige from its ruler Mansa Musa's fabulous pilgrimage to Mecca in 1324/25. Mansa Musa reportedly came to the throne after the previous king failed to return from a naval expedition he led to explore the Atlantic Ocean. A document by a contemporary scholar, al-Umari, quoted Mansa Musa's description of his predecessor as a man who "did not believe that the ocean was impossible to cross. He wished to reach the other side and was passionately interested in doing so."[3] After only one ship returned from an earlier expedition, the king set out himself at the head of a fleet of two thousand vessels, a voyage from which no one returned. Corroboration of these early expeditions is lacking, but this report underlines the wealth and ambition of Mali in this period. In later centuries the diversion of gold away from the trans-Sahara routes would weaken the inland states of Africa politically and economically.

Gold was one important object of trade; slaves were another. Slavery was practiced in Africa, as it was virtually everywhere else in the world, before the arrival of Europeans. Arabic and African merchants took West African slaves to the Mediterranean to be sold in European, Egyptian, and Middle Eastern markets and also brought eastern Europeans— a major element of European slavery—to West Africa as slaves. In addition, Indian and Arabic merchants traded slaves in the coastal regions of East Africa.

Legends about Africa played an important role in Europeans' imagination of the outside world. They long cherished the belief in a Christian nation in Africa ruled by a mythical king, Prester John, who was believed to be a descendant of one of the three kings who visited Jesus after his birth.

The Ottoman and Persian Empires

The Middle East served as an intermediary for trade between Asia, Africa, and Europe and was also an important supplier of goods for foreign exchange, especially silk and cotton. Two great rival empires, the Persian Safavids (sah-FAH-vidz) and the Turkish Ottomans, dominated the region. Persian merchants could be found in trading communities as far away as the Indian Ocean. Persia was also a major producer and exporter of silk.

The Persians' Shi'ite Muslim faith clashed with the Ottomans' adherence to Sunnism. Economically, the two competed for control over western trade routes to the East. Under Sultan Mohammed II (r. 1451–1481), the Ottomans captured Europe's largest city, Constantinople, in May 1453. Renamed Istanbul, the city became the capital of the Ottoman Empire. By the mid-sixteenth century the Ottomans controlled the sea trade in the eastern Mediterranean, Syria, Palestine, Egypt, and the rest of North Africa, and their power extended into Europe as far west as Vienna.

Ottoman expansion frightened Europeans. The Ottoman armies seemed invincible and the empire's desire for expansion limitless. In France in the sixteenth century, only forty books were published on the American discoveries compared to eighty on Turkey and the Turks.[4] The strength of the Ottomans helps explain some of the missionary fervor Christians brought to new territories. It also raised economic concerns. With trade routes to the East dominated by the Ottomans, Europeans wished to find new trade routes free of Ottoman control.

Genoese and Venetian Middlemen

Compared to the riches and vibrancy of the East, Europe constituted a minor outpost of the world trading system. European craftsmen produced few products to rival the fine wares and coveted spices of Asia. In the late Middle Ages, the Italian city-states of Venice and Genoa controlled the European luxury trade with the East.

In 1304 Venice established formal relations with the sultan of Mamluk Egypt, opening operations in Cairo, the gateway to Asian trade. Venetian merchants specialized in goods like spices, silks, and carpets, which they obtained from middlemen in the eastern Mediterranean and Asia Minor. A little went a long way. Venetians purchased no more than five hundred tons of spices a year around 1400, with a profit of about 40 percent. The most important spice was pepper, grown in India and Indonesia, which composed 60 percent of the spices they purchased in 1400.[5]

The Venetians exchanged Eastern luxury goods for European products they could trade abroad, including Spanish and English wool, German metal goods, Flemish textiles, and silk cloth made in their own manufactures with imported raw materials. Eastern demand for such items, however, was low. To make up the difference, the Venetians earned currency in the shipping industry and through trade in firearms and slaves. At least half of what they traded with the East took the form of precious metal, much of it acquired in Egypt and North Africa. When the Portuguese arrived in Asia in the late fifteenth century, they found Venetian coins everywhere.

Venice's ancient rival was Genoa. In the wake of the Crusades, Genoa dominated the northern route to Asia through the Black Sea. Expansion in the thirteenth and fourteenth centuries took the Genoese as far as Persia and the Far East. In 1291 they sponsored an expedition into the Atlantic in search of India. The ships were lost, and their exact destination and motivations remain unknown. This voyage reveals the long roots of Genoese interest in Atlantic exploration.

In the fifteenth century, with Venice claiming victory in the spice trade, the Genoese shifted focus from trade to finance and from the Black Sea to the western Mediterranean. Located on the northwestern coast of Italy, Genoa had always been active in the western Mediterranean, trading with North African ports, southern France, Spain, and even England and Flanders through the Strait of Gibraltar. When Spanish and Portuguese voyages began to explore the western Atlantic (see pages 447–452), Genoese merchants, navigators, and financiers provided their skills to the Iberian monarchs, whose own subjects had much less commercial experience. The Genoese, for example, ran many of the sugar plantations established on the Atlantic islands colonized by the Portuguese. Genoese merchants would eventually help finance Spanish colonization of the New World.

A major element of Italian trade was slavery. Merchants purchased slaves, many of whom were fellow Christians, in the Balkans. The men were sold to Egypt for the sultan's army or sent to work as agricultural laborers in the Mediterranean. Young girls, who constituted the majority of the trade, were sold in western Mediterranean ports as servants or concubines. After the loss of the Black Sea — and thus the source of slaves — to the Ottomans, the Genoese sought new supplies of slaves in the West, taking the Guanches (indigenous peoples from the Canary Islands), Muslim prisoners and Jewish refugees from Spain, and by the early 1500s both black and Berber Africans. With the growth of Spanish colonies in the New World, Genoese and Venetian merchants would become important players in the Atlantic slave trade.

Italian experience in colonial administration, slaving, and international trade served as a model for the Iberian states as they pushed European expansion to new heights. Mariners, merchants, and financiers from Venice and Genoa — most notably Christopher Columbus — played a crucial role in bringing the fruits of this experience to the Iberian Peninsula and to the New World.

The European Voyages of Discovery

How and why did Europeans undertake ambitious voyages of expansion?

As we have seen, Europe was by no means isolated before the voyages of exploration and its "discovery" of the New World. But because they did not produce many products desired by Eastern elites, Europeans played only a small role in the Indian Ocean trading world. As Europe recovered after the Black Death, new European players entered the scene with novel technology, eager to spread Christianity and to undo Italian and Ottoman domination of trade with the East. A century after the plague, Iberian explorers began the overseas voyages that helped create the modern world, with staggering consequences for their own continent and the rest of the planet.

Causes of European Expansion

European expansion had multiple causes. By the middle of the fifteenth century, Europe was experiencing a revival of population and economic activity after the lows of the Black Death. This revival created demand for luxuries, especially spices, from the East. The fall of Constantinople and subsequent Ottoman control of trade routes created obstacles to fulfilling these demands. Europeans needed to find new sources of precious metal to trade with the Ottomans or trade routes that bypassed the Ottomans.

Why were spices so desirable? Introduced into western Europe by the Crusaders in the twelfth century, pepper, nutmeg, ginger, mace, cinnamon, and cloves added flavor and variety to the monotonous European diet. Not only did spices serve as flavorings for food, but they were also used in anointing oil and as incense for religious rituals, and as perfumes, medicines, and dyes in daily life. Take, for example, cloves, for which Europeans found many uses. If picked green and sugared, the buds could be transformed into jam; if salted and pickled, cloves became a flavoring for vinegar. Cloves sweetened the breath. When added to food or drink, they were thought to stimulate the appetite and clear the intestines and bladder. When crushed and powdered, they were a medicine rubbed on the forehead to relieve head colds and applied to the eyes to strengthen vision. Taken with milk, they were believed to enhance sexual pleasure.

Religious fervor was another important catalyst for expansion. The passion and energy ignited by the Christian reconquista (reconquest) of the Iberian Peninsula encouraged the Portuguese and Spanish to continue the Christian crusade. Just seven months separated Isabella and Ferdinand's conquest of the emirate of Granada, the last remaining Muslim state on the Iberian Peninsula, and Columbus's departure across the Atlantic. Overseas exploration was in some ways a transfer of the crusading spirit to new non-Christian territories. Since the remaining Muslim states, such as the mighty Ottoman Empire, were too strong to defeat, Iberians turned their attention elsewhere.

Combined with eagerness to earn profits and to spread Christianity was the desire for glory and the urge to chart new waters. Scholars have frequently described the European discoveries as a manifestation of Renaissance curiosity about the physical universe—the desire to know more about the geography and peoples of the world. The detailed journals many voyagers kept attest to their wonder and fascination with the new peoples and places they visited.

Individual explorers combined these motivations in unique ways. Christopher Columbus was a devout Christian who was increasingly haunted by messianic obsessions in the last years of his life. As Portuguese explorer Bartholomew Diaz put it, his own motives were "to serve God and His Majesty, to give light to those who were in darkness and to grow rich as all men desire to do." When the Portuguese explorer Vasco da Gama reached the port of Calicut, India, in 1498 and a native asked what he wanted, he replied, "Christians and spices."[6] The bluntest of the Spanish **conquistadors** (kohn-KEES-tuh-dorz), Hernando Cortés, announced as he prepared to conquer Mexico, "I have come to win gold, not to plow the fields like a peasant."[7]

Eagerness for exploration was heightened by a lack of opportunity at home. After the reconquista, young men of the Spanish upper classes found their economic and political opportunities greatly limited. The ambitious turned to the sea to seek their fortunes.

Their voyages were made possible by the growth of government power. The Spanish monarchy was stronger than before and in a position to support foreign ventures. In Portugal explorers also looked to the monarchy, to Prince Henry the Navigator in particular (page 447), for financial support and encouragement. Like voyagers, monarchs shared a mix of motivations, from the desire to please God to the desire to win glory and profit from trade. Competition among European monarchs and between Protestant and Catholic states was an important factor in encouraging the steady stream of expeditions that began in the late fifteenth century.

Ordinary sailors were ill paid, and life at sea meant danger, overcrowding, and hunger. For months at a time, 100 to 120 people lived and worked in a space of 1,600 to 2,000 square feet. A lucky sailor would find enough space on deck to unroll his sleeping mat. Horses, cows, pigs, chickens, rats, and lice accompanied sailors on the voyages. As one scholar concluded, "traveling on a ship must have been one of the most uncomfortable and oppressive experiences in the world."[8]

Men chose to join these miserable crews to escape poverty at home, to continue a family trade, or to find better lives as illegal immigrants in the colonies. Many orphans and poor boys were placed on board as young pages and had little say in the decision. Women also paid a price for the voyages of exploration. Left alone for months or years at a time, and frequently widowed, sailors' wives struggled to feed their families. The widow of a sailor lost on a voyage in 1519 had to wait almost thirty years to collect her husband's salary from the Spanish crown.[9]

The people who stayed at home had a powerful impact on the process. Royal ministers and factions at court influenced monarchs to provide or deny support for exploration. The small number of people who could read served as a rapt audience for tales of fantastic places and unknown peoples. Cosmography, natural history, and geography aroused enormous interest among educated people in the fifteenth and sixteenth centuries. One of the most popular books of the time was the fourteenth-century text *The Travels of Sir John Mandeville*, which purported to be a firsthand account of the author's travels in the Holy Land, Egypt, Ethiopia, the Middle East, and India and his service to the Mamluk sultan of Egypt and the Mongol Great Khan of China. Although we now know the stories were fictional, these fantastic tales of cannibals, one-eyed giants, men with the heads of dogs, and other marvels convinced audiences through their vividly and persuasively described details. Christopher Columbus took a copy of Mandeville and the equally popular and more reliable *The Travels of Marco Polo* on his voyage in 1492.

Technology and the Rise of Exploration

Technological developments in shipbuilding, weaponry, and navigation also paved the way for European expansion. Since ancient times, most seagoing vessels had been narrow, open boats called galleys, propelled largely by slaves or convicts manning the oars. Though well suited to the placid waters of the Mediterranean, galleys could not withstand the rough winds and uncharted shoals of the Atlantic. The need for sturdier craft, as well as population losses caused by the Black Death, forced the development of a new style of ship that would not require much manpower to sail. In the course of the fifteenth century, the Portuguese developed the **caravel**, a small, light, three-mast sailing ship. Though somewhat slower than the galley, the caravel held more cargo. Its triangular lateen sails and sternpost rudder also made the caravel a much more maneuverable vessel. When fitted with cannon, it could dominate larger vessels.

Great strides in cartography and navigational aids were also made during this period. Around 1410 Arab scholars reintroduced Europeans to **Ptolemy's *Geography***. Written in the second century C.E. by a Hellenized Egyptian, the work synthesized the geographical knowledge of the classical world. Ptolemy's work provided significant improvements over medieval cartography, clearly depicting the world as round and introducing the idea of latitude and longitude to plot position accurately. It also contained crucial errors. Unaware of the Americas, Ptolemy showed the world as much smaller than it is, so that Asia appeared not very distant from Europe to the west. Based on this work, cartographers fashioned new maps that combined classical knowledge with the latest information from mariners. First the Genoese and Venetians, and then the Portuguese and Spanish, took the lead in these advances.

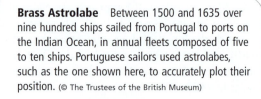

The magnetic compass enabled sailors to determine their direction and position at sea. The astrolabe, an instrument invented by the ancient Greeks and perfected by Muslim navigators, was used to determine the altitude of the sun and other celestial bodies. It permitted mariners to plot their latitude, that is, their precise position north or south of the equator.

Like the astrolabe, much of the new technology that Europeans used on their voyages was borrowed from the East. Gunpowder, the compass, and the sternpost rudder were Chinese inventions. The lateen sail, which allowed European ships to tack against the wind, was a product of the Indian Ocean trade world. Advances in cartography drew on the rich tradition of Judeo-Arabic mathematical and astronomical learning

Brass Astrolabe Between 1500 and 1635 over nine hundred ships sailed from Portugal to ports on the Indian Ocean, in annual fleets composed of five to ten ships. Portuguese sailors used astrolabes, such as the one shown here, to accurately plot their position. (© The Trustees of the British Museum)

in Iberia. Sometimes assistance to Europeans came from humans rather than instruments. The famed explorer Vasco da Gama employed a local Indian pilot to guide his expedition from the East African coast to India. In exploring new territories, European sailors thus called on techniques and knowledge developed over centuries in China, the Muslim world, and the Indian Ocean.

The Portuguese Overseas Empire

For centuries Portugal was a small, poor nation on the margins of European life whose principal activities were fishing and subsistence farming. It would have been hard for a European to predict Portugal's phenomenal success overseas after 1450. Yet Portugal had a long history of seafaring and navigation. Blocked from access to western Europe by Spain, the Portuguese turned to the Atlantic and North Africa, whose waters they knew better than other Europeans. Nature favored the Portuguese: winds blowing along their coast offered passage to Africa, its Atlantic islands, and, ultimately, Brazil.

In the early phases of Portuguese exploration, Prince Henry (1394–1460), a younger son of the king, played a leading role. A nineteenth-century scholar dubbed Henry "the Navigator" because of his support for the study of geography and navigation and for the annual expeditions he sponsored down the western coast of Africa. Although he never personally participated in voyages of exploration, Henry's involvement ensured that Portugal did not abandon the effort despite early disappointments.

The objectives of Portuguese exploration policy included military glory; the conversion of Muslims; and a quest to find gold, slaves, and an overseas route to the spice markets of India. Portugal's conquest of Ceuta, an Arab city in northern Morocco, in 1415 marked the beginning of European overseas expansion. In the 1420s, under Henry's direction, the Portuguese began to settle the Atlantic islands of Madeira (ca. 1420) and the Azores (1427). In 1443 they founded their first African commercial settlement at Arguin in North Africa. By the time of Henry's death in 1460, his support for exploration was vindicated by thriving sugar plantations on the Atlantic islands, the first arrival of enslaved Africans in Portugal (see page 463), and new access to African gold.

The Portuguese next established trading posts and forts on the gold-rich Guinea coast and penetrated into the African continent all the way to Timbuktu (Map 14.2). By 1500 Portugal controlled the flow of African gold to Europe. The golden century of Portuguese prosperity had begun.

The Portuguese then pushed farther south down the west coast of Africa. In 1487 Bartholomew Diaz rounded the Cape of Good Hope at the southern tip, but storms and a threatened mutiny forced him to turn back. A decade later Vasco da Gama succeeded in rounding the Cape while commanding a fleet of four ships in search of a sea route to India. With the help of an Indian guide, da Gama reached the port of Calicut in India. Overcoming local hostility, he returned to Lisbon loaded with spices and samples of Indian cloth. He had failed to forge any trading alliances with local powers, and Portuguese arrogance ensured the future hostility of Muslim merchants who dominated the trading system. Nonetheless, da Gama proved the possibility of lucrative trade with the East via the Cape route. Thereafter, a Portuguese convoy set out for passage around the Cape every March.

Lisbon became the entrance port for Asian goods into Europe, but this was not accomplished without a fight. Muslim-controlled port city-states had long controlled

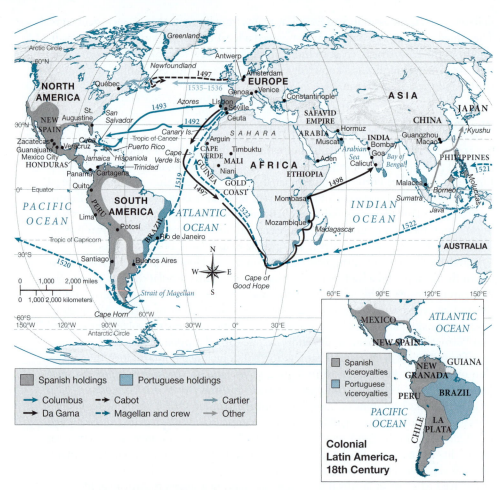

MAP 14.2   Overseas Exploration and Conquest in the Fifteenth and Sixteenth Centuries

The voyages of discovery marked a dramatic new phase in the centuries-old migrations of European peoples. This world map depicts the voyages of the most significant explorers of this period, while the inset map shows Spanish and Portuguese colonies of the eighteenth century.

the rich spice trade of the Indian Ocean, and they did not surrender their dominance willingly. From 1500 to 1511 the Portuguese used a combination of bombardment and diplomatic treaties to establish trading forts at Calicut, Malacca, Hormuz, and Goa, thereby laying the foundation for Portuguese imperialism in the sixteenth and seventeenth centuries. (See "Primary Source: A Portuguese Traveler Describes Swahili City-States of East Africa," page 450.)

In March 1493, between the voyages of Diaz and da Gama, Spanish ships under a triumphant Genoese mariner named Christopher Columbus (1451–1506), in the service of the Spanish crown, entered Lisbon harbor. Spain also had begun the quest for an empire.

The Problem of Christopher Columbus

Christopher Columbus is a controversial figure in history—glorified by some as a courageous explorer, vilified by others as a cruel exploiter of Native Americans. Many have questioned how he could "discover" the Americas, given the millennia of indigenous population prior to his arrival and earlier transatlantic crossings of the Vikings. Rather than judging Columbus by debates and standards of our time, it is more important to understand him in the context of his own time. First, what kind of man was Columbus, and what forces or influences shaped him? Second, in sailing westward from Europe, what were his goals? Third, did he achieve his goals, and what did he make of his discoveries?

In his dream of a westward passage to the Indies, Columbus embodied a long-standing Genoese ambition to circumvent Venetian domination of eastward trade, which was now being claimed by the Portuguese. Columbus was very knowledgeable about the sea. He had worked as a mapmaker, and he was familiar with fifteenth-century Portuguese navigational developments and the use of the compass as a nautical instrument. As he asserted in his journal: "I have spent twenty-three years at sea and have not left it for any length of time worth mentioning, and I have seen every thing from east to west [meaning he had been to England] and I have been to Guinea [North and West Africa]."[10] His successful thirty-three-day voyage to the Caribbean owed a great deal to his seamanship.

Columbus was also a deeply religious man. He had witnessed the Spanish conquest of Granada and shared fully in the religious and nationalistic fervor surrounding that event. Like the Spanish rulers and most Europeans of his age, Columbus understood Christianity as a missionary religion that should be carried to all places of the earth. He viewed himself as a divine agent: "God made me the messenger of the new heaven and the new earth of which he spoke in the Apocalypse of St. John . . . and he showed me the post where to find it."[11]

What was the object of this first voyage? Columbus gave the answer in the very title of the expedition, "The Enterprise of the Indies." He wanted to find a direct ocean trading route to Asia. Rejected for funding by the Portuguese in 1483 and by Ferdinand and Isabella in 1486, the project finally won the backing of the Spanish monarchy in 1492. The Spanish crown named Columbus viceroy over any territory he might discover and promised him one-tenth of the material rewards of the journey. Inspired by the stories of Mandeville and Marco Polo, Columbus dreamed of reaching the court of the Mongol emperor, the Great Khan (not realizing that the Ming Dynasty had overthrown the Mongols in 1368). Based on Ptolemy's *Geography* and other texts, he expected to pass the islands of Japan and then land on the east coast of China.

How did Columbus interpret what he had found, and in his mind did he achieve what he had set out to do? Columbus's small fleet left Spain on August 3, 1492. He landed in the Bahamas, which he christened San Salvador, on October 12, 1492. Columbus believed he had found some small islands off the east coast of Japan. On encountering natives of the islands, he gave them some beads and "many other trifles of small value," pronouncing them delighted with these gifts and eager to trade. In a letter he wrote to Ferdinand and Isabella on his return to Spain, Columbus described the natives as handsome, peaceful, and primitive people whose body painting reminded him of that of the Canary Islands natives. Believing he was in the Indies, he called them

PRIMARY SOURCE   A Portuguese Traveler Describes Swahili City-States of East Africa

Duarte Barbosa traveled to India as an interpreter and scribe for the Portuguese government and ultimately perished as a member of Magellan's expedition in 1521. Before embarking with Magellan, he published a book of his observations of the people, lands, and commerce of the Indian Ocean trade world, from which the excerpt below is taken.

Going along the coast from this town of Mozambique, there is an island hard by the mainland which is called Kilwa, in which is a Moorish [Muslim] town with many fair houses of stone and mortar, with many windows after our fashion, very well arranged in streets, with many flat roofs. . . . From this place they trade with Sofala, whence they bring back gold, and from here they spread all over . . . the sea-coast [which] is well-peopled with villages and abodes of Moors. Before the King our Lord [the Portuguese king] sent out his expedition to discover India the Moors of Sofala, Cuama, Angoya and Mozambique were all subject to the King of Kilwa, who was the most mighty king among them. And in this town was great plenty of gold, as no ships passed towards Sofala without first coming to this island. Of the Moors there are some fair and some black, they are finely clad in many rich garments of gold and silk and cotton, and the women as well. . . .

This town was taken by force from its king by the Portuguese, as, moved by arrogance, he refused to obey the King our Lord. There they took many prisoners and the king fled from the island, and His Highness [the Portuguese king] ordered that a fort should be built there, and kept it under his rule and governance. . . .

Journeying along the coast towards India, there is a fair town on the mainland lying along a strand, which is named Malindi. It pertains to the Moors and has a Moorish king over it; the which place has many fair stone and mortar houses of many storeys, with great plenty of windows and flat roofs, after our fashion. The place is well laid out in streets. The folk are both black and white; they go naked,

"Indians," a name later applied to all inhabitants of the Americas. Columbus concluded that they would make good slaves and could easily be converted to Christianity.

Scholars have identified the inhabitants of the islands as the Taino people, speakers of the Arawak language, who inhabited Hispaniola (modern-day Haiti and Dominican Republic) and other islands in the Caribbean. Columbus received reassuring reports from Taino villagers—via hand gestures and mime—of the presence of gold and of a great king in the vicinity. From San Salvador, Columbus sailed southwest, believing that this course would take him to Japan or the coast of China. He landed instead on Cuba on October 28. Deciding that he must be on the mainland near the coastal city of Quinsay (now Hangzhou), he sent a small embassy inland with letters from Ferdinand and Isabella and instructions to locate the grand city.

The landing party found only small villages. Confronted with this disappointment, Columbus apparently gave up on his aim to meet the Great Khan. Instead, he focused on trying to find gold or other valuables among the peoples he had discovered. The sight of Taino people wearing gold ornaments on Hispaniola seemed to prove that gold was

covering only their private parts with cotton and silk cloths. Others of them wear cloths folded like cloaks and waist-bands, and turbans of many rich stuffs on their heads.

They are great barterers, and deal in cloth, gold, ivory, and divers other wares with the Moors and Heathen of the great kingdom of Cambaya; and to their haven come every year many ships with cargoes of merchandise, from which they get great store of gold, ivory and wax. In this traffic the Cambay merchants make great profits, and thus, on one side and the other, they earn much money. There is great plenty of food in this city (rice, millet and some wheat which they bring from Cambaya), and divers sorts of fruit, inasmuch as there is here abundance of fruit-gardens and orchards. Here too are plenty of round-tailed sheep, cows and other cattle and great store of oranges, also of hens.

The king and people of this place ever were and are friends of the King of Portugal, and the Portuguese always find in them great comfort and friendship and perfect peace.

EVALUATE THE EVIDENCE

1. What impressed Barbosa in the city-states he visited? What was his attitude toward the various peoples and places he saw? Do you detect any Portuguese or Western prejudices?

2. How does this document help explain Portuguese ambitions in the Indian Ocean trade world and the relationship between the Portuguese and the Swahili city-states at the time Duarte Barbosa visited them?

Source: Mansel Longworth Dames, trans., *The Book of Duarte Barbosa*, vol. 1 (London: Bedford Press, 1918), 17–18, 22–23.

available in the region. In January, confident that its source would soon be found, he headed back to Spain to report on his discovery. News of his voyage spread rapidly across Europe.[12]

Over the next decades, the Spanish would follow a policy of conquest and colonization in the New World, rather than one of exchange with equals (as envisaged for the Mongol khan). On his second voyage, Columbus forcibly subjugated the island of Hispaniola and enslaved its indigenous peoples. On this and subsequent voyages, Columbus brought with him settlers for the new Spanish territories, along with agricultural seed and livestock. Columbus himself, however, had limited skills in governing. Revolt soon broke out against him and his brother on Hispaniola. A royal expedition sent to investigate returned the brothers to Spain in chains. Columbus was cleared of wrongdoing, but the territories remained under royal control.

Columbus was very much a man of his times. To the end of his life in 1506, he believed that he had found small islands off the coast of Asia. He never realized the scope of his achievement: to have found a vast continent unknown to Europeans, except for a fleeting Viking presence centuries earlier. He could not know that the scale of his discoveries would revolutionize world power, raising issues of trade, settlement, government bureaucracy, and the rights of native and African peoples.

Later Explorers

The Florentine navigator Amerigo Vespucci (veh-SPOO-chee) (1454–1512) realized what Columbus had not. Writing about his discoveries on the coast of modern-day Venezuela, Vespucci stated: "Those new regions which we found and explored with the fleet . . . we may rightly call a New World." This letter, titled *Mundus Novus* (The New World), was the first document to describe America as a continent separate from Asia. In recognition of Amerigo's bold claim, the continent was named for him.

To settle competing claims to the Atlantic discoveries, Spain and Portugal turned to Pope Alexander VI. The resulting **Treaty of Tordesillas** (tor-duh-SEE-yuhs) in 1494 gave Spain everything to the west of an imaginary line drawn down the Atlantic and Portugal everything to the east. This arbitrary division worked in Portugal's favor when in 1500 an expedition led by Pedro Alvares Cabral, en route to India, landed on the coast of Brazil, which Cabral claimed as Portuguese territory.

The search for profits determined the direction of Spanish exploration. With insignificant profits from the Caribbean compared to the enormous riches that the Portuguese were reaping in Asia, Spain renewed the search for a western passage to Asia. In 1519 Charles V of Spain sent the Portuguese mariner Ferdinand Magellan (1480–1521) to find a sea route to the spices of the Moluccas off the southeast coast of Asia. Magellan sailed southwest across the Atlantic to Brazil, and after a long search along the coast he located the treacherous straits that now bear his name (see Map 14.2). The new ocean he sailed into after a rough passage through the straits seemed so calm that Magellan dubbed it the Pacific, from the Latin word for peaceful. He soon realized his mistake. His fleet sailed north up the west coast of South America and then headed west into the immense expanse of the Pacific toward the Malay Archipelago. (Some of these islands were conquered later, in the 1560s, and named the "Philippines" for Philip II of Spain.)

Terrible storms, disease, starvation, and violence devastated the expedition. Magellan had set out with a fleet of five ships and around 270 men. Sailors on two of the ships attempted mutiny on the South American coast; one ship was lost, and another ship deserted and returned to Spain before even traversing the straits. The trip across the Pacific took ninety-eight days, and the men survived on rats and sawdust. Magellan himself died in a skirmish in the islands known today as the Philippines. Only one ship, with eighteen men aboard, returned to Spain from the east by way of the Indian Ocean, the Cape of Good Hope, and the Atlantic in 1522. The voyage — the first to circumnavigate the globe — had taken close to three years.

This voyage revolutionized Europeans' understanding of the world by demonstrating the vastness of the Pacific. The earth was clearly much larger than Columbus had believed. Although the voyage made a small profit in spices, it also demonstrated that the westward passage to the Indies was too long and dangerous for commercial purposes. Spain soon abandoned the attempt to oust Portugal from the Eastern spice trade and concentrated on exploiting her New World territories.

Spain's European rivals also set sail across the Atlantic during the early days of exploration in search of a northwest passage to the Indies. In 1497 John Cabot, a Genoese merchant living in London, undertook a voyage to Brazil, but discovered Newfoundland instead. The next year he returned and reconnoitered the New England coast. These forays proved futile, and the English established no permanent colonies in the territories they explored. News of the riches of Mexico and Peru later inspired the English to renew their efforts, this time in the extreme north. Between 1576 and 1578 Martin Frobisher made three voyages in and around the Canadian bay that now bears his name. Frobisher hopefully brought a quantity of ore back to England with him, but it proved to be worthless.

Early French exploration of the Atlantic was equally frustrating. Between 1534 and 1541 Frenchman Jacques Cartier made several voyages and explored the St. Lawrence region of Canada, searching for a passage to the wealth of Asia. His exploration of the St. Lawrence was halted at the great rapids west of the present-day island of Montreal; he named the rapids "La Chine" in the optimistic belief that China lay just beyond. When this hope proved vain, the French turned to a new source of profit within Canada itself: trade in beavers and other furs. As had the Portuguese in Asia, French traders bartered with local peoples, who maintained control over their trade goods. French fishermen also competed with Spanish and English ships for the teeming schools of cod they found in the Atlantic waters around Newfoundland. Fishing vessels salted the catch on board and brought it back to Europe, where a thriving market for fish was created by the Catholic prohibition on eating meat on Fridays and during Lent.

Spanish Conquest in the New World

In 1519, the year Magellan departed on his worldwide expedition, the Spanish sent an exploratory expedition from their post in Cuba to the mainland under the command of the brash and determined conquistador Hernando Cortés (1485–1547). Accompanied by six hundred men, sixteen horses, and ten cannon, Cortés was to launch the conquest of the **Mexica Empire**. Its people were later called the Aztecs, but now most scholars prefer to use the term *Mexica* to refer to them and their empire.

The Mexica Empire was ruled by Montezuma II (r. 1502–1520) from his capital at Tenochtitlán (tay-nawch-teet-LAHN), now Mexico City. Larger than any European city of the time, it was the heart of a sophisticated civilization with advanced mathematics, astronomy, and engineering; a complex social system; and oral poetry and historical traditions.

Cortés landed on the coast of the Gulf of Mexico on April 21, 1519. The Spanish camp was soon visited by delegations of unarmed Mexica leaders bearing lavish gifts and news of their great emperor. Impressed with the wealth of the local people, Cortés soon began to exploit internal dissension within the empire to his own advantage. The Mexica state religion necessitated constant warfare against neighboring peoples to secure captives for religious sacrifices and laborers for agricultural and building projects. Conquered peoples were required to relinquish products of their agriculture and craftsmanship to pay tribute to the Mexica state through their local chiefs.

Cortés quickly forged an alliance with the Tlaxcalas (Tlah-scalas) and other subject kingdoms, which chafed under the tribute demanded by the Mexica. In October a combined Spanish-Tlaxcalan force occupied the city of Cholula, the second largest in the empire and its religious capital, and massacred many thousands of inhabitants. Strengthened by this display of power, Cortés made alliances with other native kingdoms.

Doña Marina and Cortés   In April 1519 Doña Marina (or La Malinche as she is known in Mexico) was among twenty women given to the Spanish as slaves. Fluent in Nahuatl (NAH-wah-tuhl) and Yucatec Mayan (spoken by a Spanish priest accompanying Cortés), she acted as an interpreter and diplomatic guide for the Spanish. She had a close relationship with Cortés and bore his son, Don Martín Cortés, in 1522. This image was created by Tlaxcalan artists shortly after the conquest of Mexico and represents one indigenous perspective on the events. (The Granger Collection, New York)

In November 1519, with a few hundred Spanish men and some six thousand indigenous warriors, Cortés marched on Tenochtitlán.

Montezuma refrained from attacking the Spaniards as they advanced toward his capital and welcomed Cortés and his men into Tenochtitlán. Historians have often condemned the Mexica ruler for vacillation and weakness. Certainly other native leaders did attack the Spanish. But Montezuma relied on the advice of his state council, itself divided, and on the dubious loyalty of tributary communities. Historians have questioned one long-standing explanation, that he feared the Spaniards as living gods. This idea is mostly found in texts written after the fact by Spanish missionaries and their converts, who used it to justify and explain the conquest. Montezuma's hesitation proved disastrous. When Cortés took Montezuma hostage and tried to rule the Mexica through the emperor's authority, Montezuma's influence over his people crumbled.

In May 1520 Spanish forces massacred Mexica warriors dancing at an indigenous festival. This act provoked an uprising within Tenochtitlán, during which Montezuma was killed. The Spaniards and their allies escaped from the city and began gathering forces against the Mexica. One year later, in May 1521, Cortés laid siege to Tenochtitlán at the head of an army of approximately 1,000 Spanish and 75,000 native warriors.[13] Spanish victory in August 1521 resulted from its superior technology and the effects of the siege and smallpox. After the defeat of Tenochtitlán, Cortés and other conquistadors began the systematic conquest of Mexico. Over time, a series of indigenous kingdoms gradually fell under Spanish domination, although not without decades of resistance.

More surprising than the defeat of the Mexica was the fall of the remote **Inca Empire**. Perched more than 9,800 feet above sea level, the Incas were isolated from North American indigenous cultures and knew nothing of the Mexica civilization or its collapse. Like the Mexica, the Incas had created a civilization that rivaled that of the Europeans in population and complexity. To unite their vast and well-fortified empire, the Incas built an extensive network of roads, along which traveled a highly efficient postal service. The imperial government, with its capital in the city of Cuzco, taxed, fed, and protected its subjects.

At the time of the Spanish invasion the Inca Empire had been weakened by an epidemic of disease, possibly smallpox. Even worse, the empire had been embroiled in a civil war over succession. Francisco Pizarro (ca. 1475–1541), a conquistador of modest Spanish origins, landed on the northern coast of Peru on May 13, 1532, the very day Atahualpa (ah-tuh-WAHL-puh) won control of the empire after five years of fighting. As Pizarro advanced across the steep Andes toward Cuzco, Atahualpa was proceeding to the capital for his coronation.

Like Montezuma in Mexico, Atahualpa was aware of the Spaniards' movements. He sent envoys to invite the Spanish to meet him in the provincial town of Cajamarca. His plan was to lure the Spanish into a trap, seize their horses and ablest men for his army, and execute the rest. With an army of some forty thousand men stationed nearby, Atahualpa felt he had little to fear. Instead, the Spaniards ambushed and captured him, collected an enormous ransom in gold, and then executed him in 1533 on trumped-up charges. The Spanish now marched on the capital of the empire itself, profiting once again from internal conflicts to form alliances with local peoples. When Cuzco fell in 1533, the Spanish plundered immense riches in gold and silver.

As with the Mexica, decades of violence and resistance followed the defeat of the Incan capital. Struggles also broke out among the Spanish for the spoils of empire. Nevertheless, Spanish conquest opened a new chapter in European relations with the New World. It was not long before rival European nations attempted to forge their own overseas empires.

Early French and English Settlement in the New World

For over a hundred years, the Spanish and the Portuguese dominated settlement in the New World. The first English colony was founded at Roanoke (in what is now North Carolina) in 1585. After a three-year loss of contact with England, the settlers were found to have disappeared; their fate remains a mystery. The colony of Virginia, founded by a private company of investors at Jamestown in 1607, also struggled in its first years and relied on food from the Powhatan Confederacy. Over time, the colony gained a steady hold by producing tobacco for a growing European market.

Settlement on the coast of New England was undertaken for different reasons. There, radical Protestants sought to escape Anglican repression in England and begin new lives. The small and struggling outpost of Plymouth (1620), founded by the Pilgrims who arrived on the *Mayflower*, was followed by Massachusetts (1630), a colony of Puritans that grew into a prosperous settlement. Religious disputes in Massachusetts itself led to the dispersion of settlers into the new communities of Providence, Connecticut, Rhode Island, and New Haven. Catholics acquired their own settlement in Maryland (1632) and Quakers in Pennsylvania (1681).

Whereas the Spanish conquered indigenous empires and established large-scale dominance over Mexico and Peru, English settlements merely hugged the Atlantic coastline. This did not prevent conflict with the indigenous inhabitants over land and resources, however. At Jamestown, for example, English expansion undermined prior cooperation with the Powhatan Confederacy; disease and warfare with the English led to drastic population losses among the Powhatans. The haphazard nature of English colonization also led to conflicts of authority within the colonies. As the English crown grew more interested in colonial expansion, efforts were made to acquire the territory between New England in the north and Virginia in the south. This would allow the English to unify their holdings and overcome French and Dutch competition on the North American mainland.

French navigator and explorer Samuel de Champlain founded the first permanent French settlement, at Quebec, in 1608, a year after the English founding of Jamestown. Ville-Marie, latter-day Montreal, was founded in 1642. Although the population of New France was small compared to that of the English and Spanish colonies, the French were energetic traders and explorers. Following the waterways of the St. Lawrence, the Great Lakes, and the Mississippi, they ventured into much of modern-day Canada and at least thirty-five of the fifty states of the United States. French traders forged relations with the Huron Confederacy, a league of four indigenous nations that dominated a large region north of Lake Erie, as a means of gaining access to hunting grounds and trade routes for beaver and other animals. In 1682 French explorer René-Robert Cavelier LaSalle descended the Mississippi to the Gulf of Mexico, opening the way for French occupation of Louisiana.

While establishing their foothold in the north, the French slowly acquired new territories in the West Indies, including Cayenne (1604), St. Christophe (1625), Martinique, Guadeloupe, and Saint-Domingue (1697) on the western side of the island of Hispaniola. These islands became centers of tobacco and then sugar production. French ambitions on the mainland and in the Caribbean sparked a century-long competition with the English.

European involvement in the Americas led to profound transformation of pre-existing indigenous societies and the rise of a transatlantic slave trade. It also led to an acceleration of global trade and cultural exchange. Over time, the combination of indigenous, European, and African cultures gave birth to new societies in the New World. In turn, the profits of trade and the impact of cultural exchange greatly influenced European society.

The Impact of Conquest

What was the impact of European conquest on the peoples and ecologies of the New World?

The growing European presence in the New World transformed its land and its peoples forever. Violence and disease wrought devastating losses, while surviving peoples encountered new political, social, and economic organizations imposed by Europeans. The Columbian exchange brought infectious diseases to the Americas, but also gave new crops to the Old World that altered consumption patterns in Europe and across the globe (see page 462).

Colonial Administration

Spanish conquistadors had claimed the lands they had "discovered" for the Spanish crown. As the wealth of the new territories became apparent, the Spanish government acted to impose its authority and remove that of the original conquerors. The House of Trade, located in Seville, controlled the flow of goods and people to and from the colonies, while the Council of the Indies guided royal policy and served as the highest court for colonial affairs.

The crown divided its New World possessions into two **viceroyalties**, or administrative divisions: New Spain, with the capital at Mexico City, and Peru, with the capital at Lima. Two new viceroyalties added in the eighteenth century were New Granada, with Bogotá as its administrative center, and La Plata, with Buenos Aires as the capital (see Map 14.2).

Within each territory, the viceroy, or imperial governor, exercised broad military and civil authority as the direct representative of Spain. The viceroy presided over the *audiencia* (ow-dee-EHN-see-ah), a board of twelve to fifteen judges that served as his advisory council and court of appeal. At the local level, officials called *corregidores* (kuh-REH-gih-dawr-ays) held judicial and administrative powers.

The Portuguese adopted similar patterns of rule, with India House in Lisbon functioning much like the Spanish House of Trade and royal representatives overseeing its possessions in West Africa and Asia. To secure the vast expanse of Brazil, the Portuguese implemented the system of captaincies, hereditary grants of land given to nobles and loyal officials who bore the costs of settling and administering their territories. Over time, the Crown secured greater power over the captaincies, appointing royal governors to act as administrators. The captaincy of Bahia was the site of the capital, Salvador, home to the governor general and other royal officials.

Like their European neighbors, France and England initially entrusted their overseas colonies to individual explorers and monopoly trading companies. By the end of the seventeenth century, the French crown had successfully imposed direct rule over New France and other colonies. The king appointed military governors to rule alongside intendants, royal officials possessed of broad administrative and financial authority within their intendancies. In the mid-eighteenth century, reform-minded Spanish king Charles III (r. 1759–1788) adopted the intendant system for the Spanish colonies.

England's colonies followed a distinctive path. Drawing on English traditions of representative government (see Chapter 15), its colonists established their own proudly autonomous assemblies to regulate local affairs. Wealthy merchants and landowners dominated the assemblies, although even common men had more say in politics than was the case in England. Up to the mid-eighteenth century, the Crown found little reason to dispute colonial liberties in the north, but it did acquire greater control over the wealthy plantation colonies of the Caribbean and tobacco-rich Virginia.

Impact of European Settlement on Indigenous Peoples

Before Columbus's arrival, the Americas were inhabited by thousands of groups of indigenous peoples, each with distinct cultures and languages. Their patterns of life varied widely, from hunter-gatherer tribes organized into tribal confederations on the North American plains to two large-scale agriculture-based empires connecting bustling cities and towns, the Mexica (Aztec) Empire centered in modern-day Mexico and the Inca Empire in the Andean highlands. The history of human settlement in the Americas was so long and complex that many cultures had risen and fallen by the time of Columbus's voyage. These included the abandoned city of Cahokia (near modern-day St. Louis, Missouri) that at its peak in the twelfth century held a population of up to 10,000 people and the palaces and cities of ancestors of the Maya in the Yucatán peninsula, whose regional capital of Chichén Itzá thrived around the same period. Although historians continue to debate the numbers, the best estimate is that in 1492 the peoples of the Americas numbered around 50 million.

Their lives were radically transformed by the arrival of Europeans. In the sixteenth century perhaps two hundred thousand Spaniards immigrated to the New World. After assisting in the conquest of the Mexica and the Incas, these men carved out vast estates called haciendas in temperate grazing areas and imported Spanish livestock. In coastal tropical areas, the Spanish erected huge plantations to supply sugar to the European market. Around 1550 silver was discovered in present-day Bolivia and Mexico. To work the cattle ranches, sugar plantations, and silver mines, the conquistadors first turned to the indigenous peoples.

The Spanish quickly established the **encomienda system**, in which the Crown granted the conquerors the right to employ groups of Native Americans as laborers or to demand tribute from them in exchange for providing food and shelter. Theoretically, the Spanish were supposed to care for the indigenous people under their command and teach them Christianity; in actuality, the system was a brutal form of exploitation only one level removed from slavery.

The new conditions and hardships imposed by conquest and colonization resulted in enormous native population losses. The major cause of death was disease. Having little or no resistance to diseases brought from the Old World, the inhabitants of the New World fell victim to smallpox, typhus, influenza, and other illnesses. Another factor was overwork. Unaccustomed to forced labor, especially in the blistering heat of tropical cane fields or in dank and dangerous mines, native workers died in staggering numbers. Moreover, forced labor diverted local people from agricultural work, leading to malnutrition, reduced fertility rates, and starvation. Women forced to work were separated from their infants, leading to high infant mortality rates in a population with no livestock to supply alternatives to breast milk. Malnutrition and hunger in turn lowered resistance to disease. Finally, many indigenous peoples also died through outright violence in warfare.[14]

The Franciscan Bartolomé de Las Casas (1474–1566) was one of the most outspoken critics of Spanish brutality against indigenous peoples. Las Casas documented their treatment at the hands of the Spanish:

> To these quiet Lambs . . . came the Spaniards like most c(r)uel Tygres, Wolves and Lions, enrag'd with a sharp and tedious hunger; for these forty years past, minding nothing else but the slaughter of these unfortunate wretches, whom with divers kinds of torments neither seen nor heard of before, they have so cruelly and inhumanely butchered, that of three millions of people which Hispaniola itself did contain, there are left remaining alive scarce three hundred persons.[15]

Las Casas and other missionaries asserted that the Indians had human rights, and through their persistent pressure the Spanish emperor Charles V abolished the worst abuses of the encomienda system in 1531.

Franciscan, Dominican, and Jesuit missionaries who accompanied the conquistadors and other European settlers played an important role in converting indigenous peoples to Christianity, teaching them European methods of agriculture, and instilling loyalty to their colonial masters. In areas with small Spanish populations, the friars set up missions for a period of ten years, after which established churches and priests would take over and they could move on to new areas. Jesuits in New France also established missions far distant from the centers of French settlement. Behind its wooden palisades, a mission might contain a chapel, a hospital, a mill, stables, barns, workshops, and residences from which the Jesuits traveled to spread the word of God.

Missionaries' success in conversion varied over time and space. In Central and South America, large-scale conversion forged enduring Catholic cultures in Portuguese and Spanish colonies. One Franciscan missionary estimated that he and his colleagues had baptized between 4 and 9 million indigenous people in New Spain by 1536. Although these figures must be significantly inflated (both by the exaggeration of zealous missionaries and by multiple baptism of the same individuals), they suggest the extensive Christianization under way among the native population. Galvanized by their opposition to Catholicism and fueled by their own religious fervor, English colonizers also made efforts to convert indigenous peoples. On the whole, however, these attempts were less successful, in part because the English did not establish wholesale dominance over large native populations as did the Spanish.

Rather than a straightforward imposition of Christianity, conversion entailed a complex process of cultural exchange. (See "Primary Source: Tenochtitlán Leaders Respond to Spanish Missionaries," page 460.) Catholic friars were among the first Europeans to seek understanding of native cultures and languages as part of their effort to render Christianity comprehensible to indigenous people. In turn, Christian ideas and practices in the New World took on a distinctive character. For example, a sixteenth-century apparition of the Virgin Mary in Mexico City, known as the Virgin of Guadalupe, became a central icon of Spanish-American Catholicism.

The pattern of devastating disease and population loss occurred everywhere Europeans settled. The best estimate of native population loss is a decline from roughly 50 million people in 1492 to around 9 million by 1700. It is important to note, however, that native populations and cultures did survive the conquest period, sometimes by blending with European incomers and sometimes by maintaining cultural autonomy.

PRIMARY SOURCE   Tenochtitlán Leaders Respond to Spanish Missionaries

For the conquered peoples of the New World, the imposition of Christianity and re-pression of their pre-existing religions represented yet another form of loss. This document describes the response of the vanquished leaders of Tenochtitlán to Franciscan missionaries seeking to convert them in 1524. The account was written down in the 1560s by or for Bernardino de Sahagún, a Franciscan missionary. Sahagún is well known for his General History of the Things of New Spain *(also known as the* Florentine Codex*), a multivolume account of Mexica history, culture, and society he produced in collabo-ration with indigenous artists and informants.*

You have told us that we do not know the One who gives us life and being, who is Lord of the heavens and of the earth. You also say that those we worship are not gods. This way of speaking is entirely new to us, and very scandalous. We are fright-ened by this way of speaking because our forebears who engendered and governed us never said anything like this. On the contrary, they left us this our custom of wor-shiping our gods, in which they believed and which they worshiped all the time that they lived here on earth. They taught us how to honor them. And they taught us all the ceremonies and sacrifices that we make. They told us that through them [our gods] we live and are, and that we were beholden to them, to be theirs and to serve countless centuries before the sun began to shine and before there was daytime. They said that these gods that we worship give us everything we need for our physi-cal existence: maize, beans, chia seeds, etc. We appeal to them for the rain to make the things of the earth grow.

These our gods are the source of great riches and delights, all of which belong to them. They live in very delightful places where there are always flowers, vegeta-tion, and great freshness, a place unknown to mere mortals, called Tlalocan, where there is never hunger, poverty, or illness. It is they who bestow honors, property, titles, and kingdoms, gold and silver, precious feathers, and gemstones.

There has never been a time remembered when they were not worshiped, honored, and esteemed. Perhaps it is a century or two since this began; it is a time beyond counting. . . .

It is best, our lords, to act on this matter very slowly, with great deliberation. We are not satisfied or convinced by what you have told us, nor do we understand or give credit to what has been said of our gods. . . . All of us together feel that it is enough to have lost, enough that the power and royal jurisdiction have been taken from us. As for our gods, we will die before giving up serving and worshiping them.

EVALUATE THE EVIDENCE

1. What reasons do the leaders of Tenochtitlán offer for rejecting the missionaries' teachings? In their view, what elements of their lives will be affected by aban-doning the worship of their gods?

2. What insight does this document provide into the mind-set of Mexica people shortly following conquest?

Source: *Coloquios y doctrina Cristiana*, ed. Miguel León-Portilla, in *Colonial Spanish America: A Documentary History*, ed. Kenneth Mills and William B. Taylor (Wilmington, Del.: SR Books, 1998), pp. 21–22. Used by permission of Rowan & Littlefield.

For colonial administrators, the main problem posed by the astronomically high death rate was the loss of a subjugated labor force to work the mines and sugar plantations. As early as 1511 King Ferdinand of Spain observed that the Indians seemed to be "very frail" and that "one black could do the work of four Indians."[16] Thus was born an absurd myth, and the new tragedy of the transatlantic slave trade would soon follow (see pages 464–465).

Life in the Colonies

Many factors helped to shape life in European colonies, including geographical location, religion, indigenous cultures and practices, patterns of European settlement, and the cultural attitudes and official policies of the European nations that claimed them as empire. Throughout the New World, colonial settlements were hedged by immense borderlands where European power was weak and Europeans and non-Europeans interacted on a more equal basis.

Women played a crucial role in the creation of new identities and the continuation of old ones. The first explorers formed unions with native women, through coercion or choice, and relied on them as translators and guides and to form alliances with indigenous powers. As settlement developed, the character of each colony was influenced by the presence or absence of European women. Where women and children accompanied men, as in the British colonies and the Spanish mainland colonies, new settlements took on European languages, religion, and ways of life that have endured, with input from local cultures, to this day. Where European women did not accompany men, as on the west coast of Africa and most European outposts in Asia, local populations largely retained their own cultures, to which male Europeans acclimatized themselves. The scarcity of women in all colonies, at least initially, opened up opportunities for those who did arrive, leading one cynic to comment that even "a whore, if handsome, makes a wife for some rich planter."[17]

It was not just the availability of Englishwomen that prevented Englishmen from forming unions with indigenous women. English cultural attitudes drew strict boundaries between "civilized" and "savage," and even settlements of Christianized native peoples were segregated from the English. This was in strong contrast with the situation in New France, where royal officials initially encouraged French traders to form ties with indigenous people, including marrying local women. Assimilation of the native population was seen as one solution to the low levels of immigration from France.

Most women who crossed the Atlantic were Africans, constituting four-fifths of the female newcomers before 1800.[18] Wherever slavery existed, masters profited from their power to engage in sexual relations with enslaved women. One important difference among European colonies was in the status of children born from such unions. In some colonies, mostly those dominated by the Portuguese, Spanish, or French, substantial populations of free blacks descended from the freed children of such unions. In English colonies, masters were less likely to free children they fathered with female slaves.

The mixing of indigenous peoples with Europeans and Africans created whole new populations and ethnicities and complex self-identities. In Spanish America the word *mestizo* — *métis* in French — described people of mixed Native American and European descent. The blanket terms "mulatto" and "people of color" were used for those of mixed African and European origin. With its immense slave-based plantation agriculture system, large indigenous population, and relatively low Portuguese immigration, Brazil developed a particularly complex racial and ethnic mosaic.

The Columbian Exchange

The migration of peoples to the New World led to an exchange of animals, plants, and disease, a complex process known as the **Columbian exchange**. European immigrants to the Americas wanted a familiar diet, so they searched for climatic zones favorable to those crops. Columbus had brought sugar plants on his second voyage; Spaniards also introduced rice and bananas from the Canary Islands, and the Portuguese carried these items to Brazil. Everywhere they settled, the Spanish and Portuguese brought and raised wheat with labor provided by the encomienda system. Grapes and olives brought over from Spain did well in parts of Peru and Chile. Not all plants arrived intentionally. In clumps of mud on shoes and in the folds of textiles came the seeds of immigrant grasses, including the common dandelion.

Apart from wild turkeys and game, Native Americans had no animals for food. Moreover, they did not domesticate animals for travel or use as beasts of burden, except for alpacas and llamas in the Inca Empire. On his second voyage in 1493 Columbus introduced horses, cattle, sheep, dogs, pigs, chickens, and goats. The multiplication of these animals proved spectacular. The horse enabled the Spanish conquerors and native populations to travel faster and farther and to transport heavy loads. In turn, Europeans returned home with many food crops that became central elements of their diet.

Disease brought by European people and animals was perhaps the most important form of exchange. The wave of catastrophic epidemic disease that swept the Western Hemisphere after 1492 can be seen as an extension of the swath of devastation wreaked by the Black Death in the 1300s, first on Asia and then on Europe. The world after Columbus was thus unified by disease as well as by trade and colonization.

Europe and the World After Columbus

How was the era of global contact shaped by new commodities, commercial empires, and forced migrations?

The centuries-old Afroeurasian trade world was forever changed by the European voyages of discovery and their aftermath. For the first time, a truly global economy emerged in the sixteenth and seventeenth centuries, and it forged new links among far-flung peoples, cultures, and societies. The ancient civilizations of Europe, Africa, the Americas, and Asia confronted one another in new and rapidly evolving ways. Those confrontations often led to conquest and exploitation, but they also contributed to cultural exchange and renewal.

Sugar and Slavery

Throughout the Middle Ages slavery was deeply entrenched in the Mediterranean, but it was not based on race; many slaves were white. How, then, did black African slavery enter the European picture and take root in the Americas? In 1453 the Ottoman capture of Constantinople halted the flow of white slaves from the eastern Mediterranean to western Europe. The successes of the Iberian reconquista also meant that the supply of Muslim captives had drastically diminished. Cut off from its traditional sources of slaves, Mediterranean Europe then turned to sub-Saharan Africa, which had a long history of internal slave trading. (See "Individuals in Society: Juan de Pareja," page 464.) As Portuguese explorers began their voyages along the western coast of Africa, one of the first commodities they sought was slaves. In 1444 the first ship returned to Lisbon with a cargo of enslaved Africans; the Crown was delighted, and more shipments followed.

While the first slaves were simply seized by small raiding parties, Portuguese merchants soon found that it was easier to trade with local leaders, who were accustomed to dealing in slaves captured through warfare with neighboring powers. From 1490 to 1530 Portuguese traders brought hundreds of enslaved Africans to Lisbon each year (Map 14.3), where they eventually constituted 10 percent of the city's population.

In this stage of European expansion, the history of slavery became intertwined with the history of sugar. Originally sugar was an expensive luxury that only the very affluent could afford, but population increases and monetary expansion in the fifteenth century led to increasing demand. Native to the South Pacific, sugar was taken in ancient times to India, where farmers learned to preserve cane juice as granules that could be stored and shipped. From there, sugar crops traveled to China and the Mediterranean, where islands like Crete and Sicily had the warm and wet climate needed for growing sugarcane. When Genoese and other Italians colonized the Canary Islands and the Portuguese settled on the Madeira Islands, sugar plantations came to the Atlantic.

A New World Sugar Refinery, Brazil Sugar was the most important and most profitable plantation crop in the New World. This image shows the processing and refinement of sugar on a Brazilian plantation. Sugarcane was grown, harvested, and processed by African slaves who labored under brutal and ruthless conditions to generate enormous profits for plantation owners. (The Bridgeman Art Library/Getty Images)

INDIVIDUALS IN SOCIETY • Juan de Pareja

During the long wars of the reconquista, Muslims and Christians captured each other in battle and used the defeated as slaves. As the Muslims were gradually eliminated from Iberia in the fifteenth and sixteenth centuries, the Spanish and Portuguese turned to the west coast of Africa for a new supply of slaves. Most slaves worked as domestic servants, rather than in the fields. Some received specialized training as artisans.

Not all people of African descent were slaves, and some experienced both freedom and slavery in a single lifetime. The life and career of Juan de Pareja (pah-REH-huh) illustrates the complexities of the Iberian slave system and the heights of achievement possible for those who gained freedom.

Pareja was born in Antequera, an agricultural region and the old center of Muslim culture near Seville in southern Spain. Of his parents we know nothing. Because a rare surviving document calls him a "mulatto," one of his parents must have been white and the other must have had some African blood. In 1630 Pareja applied to the mayor of Seville for permission to travel to Madrid to visit his brother and "to perfect his art." The document lists his occupation as "a painter in Seville." Since it mentions no other name, it is reasonable to assume that Pareja arrived in Madrid a free man. Sometime between 1630 and 1648, however, he came into the possession of the artist Diego Velázquez (1599–1660); Pareja became a slave.

How did Velázquez acquire Pareja? By purchase? As a gift? Had Pareja fallen into debt or committed some crime and thereby lost his freedom? We do not know. Velázquez, the greatest Spanish painter of the seventeenth century, had a large studio with many assistants. Pareja was set to grinding powders to make colors and to preparing canvases. He must have demonstrated ability because when Velázquez went to Rome in 1648, he chose Pareja to accompany him.

In 1650, as practice for a portrait of Pope Innocent X, Velázquez painted Pareja. The portrait shows Pareja dressed in fine clothing and gazing self-confidently at the viewer. Displayed in Rome in a public exhibition of Velázquez's work, the painting won acclaim from his contemporaries. That same year, Velázquez signed the docu-

---

Sugar was a particularly difficult and demanding crop to produce for profit. Seed-stems were planted by hand, thousands to the acre. When mature, the cane had to be harvested and processed rapidly to avoid spoiling, requiring days and nights of work with little rest. Moreover, sugar's growing season is virtually constant, meaning that there is no fallow period when workers could recuperate from the arduous labor. The demands of sugar production only increased with the invention of roller mills to crush the cane more efficiently. Yields could be augmented, but only if a sufficient labor force was found to supply the mills. Europeans solved the labor problem by forcing first native islanders and then enslaved Africans to provide the backbreaking work.

Sugar gave New World slavery its distinctive shape. Columbus himself, who spent a decade in Madeira, brought the first sugar plants to the New World. The transatlantic slave trade began in 1518 when the Spanish emperor Charles V authorized traders

ment that gave Pareja his freedom, to become effective in 1654. Pareja lived out the rest of his life as an independent painter.

What does the public career of Pareja tell us about the man and his world? Pareja's career suggests that a person of African descent might fall into slavery and yet still acquire professional training and work alongside his master in a position of confidence. Moreover, if lucky enough to be freed, a former slave could exercise a profession and live his own life in Madrid. Pareja's experience was far from typical for a slave in the seventeenth century, but it reminds us of the myriad forms that slavery took in this period.

QUESTIONS FOR ANALYSIS

1. Since slavery was an established institution in Spain, speculate on Velázquez's possible reasons for giving Pareja his freedom.

2. In what ways does Pareja represent Europe's increasing participation in global commerce and exploration?

Sources: Jonathan Brown, *Velázquez: Painter and Courtier* (New Haven, Conn.: Yale University Press, 1986); *Grove Dictionary of Art* (New York: Macmillan, 2000); Sister Wendy Beckett, *Sister Wendy's American Collection* (New York: Harper Collins Publishers, 2000), p. 15.

ONLINE DOCUMENT ASSIGNMENT

How could an individual like Pareja experience both slavery and freedom in a single lifetime? Analyze sources from Pareja's contemporaries that reflect changing ideas about racial identity and slavery, and then complete a writing assignment based on the evidence and details from this chapter.

bedfordstmartins.com/mckaywestvalue

to bring enslaved Africans to the Americas. The Portuguese brought slaves to Brazil around 1550; by 1600 four thousand were being imported annually. After its founding in 1621, the Dutch West India Company, with the full support of the United Provinces, transported thousands of Africans to Brazil and the Caribbean, mostly to work on sugar plantations. In the mid-seventeenth century the English got involved. From 1660 to 1698 the Royal African Company held a monopoly over the slave trade from the English crown.

European sailors found the Atlantic passage cramped and uncomfortable, but conditions for enslaved Africans were lethal. Before 1700, when slavers decided it was better business to improve conditions, some 20 percent of slaves died on the voyage.[19] The most common cause of death was from dysentery induced by poor-quality food and water, crowding, and lack of sanitation. Men were often kept in irons during the

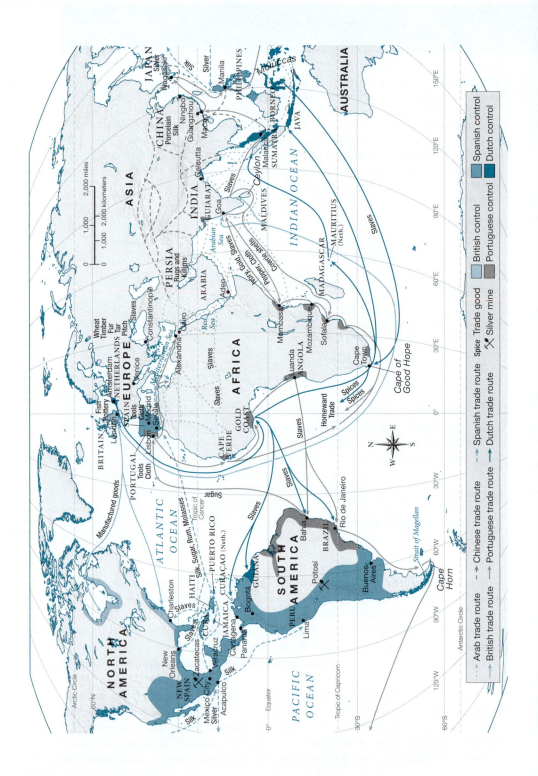

◄ **MAP 14.3**   **Seaborne Trading Empires in the Sixteenth and Seventeenth Centuries**
By the mid-seventeenth century, trade linked all parts of the world except for Australia. Notice that trade in slaves was not confined to the Atlantic but involved almost all parts of the world.

passage, while women and girls were considered fair game for sailors. To increase profits, slave traders packed several hundred captives on each ship. One slaver explained that he removed his boots before entering the slave hold because he had to crawl over the slaves' packed bodies.[20] On sugar plantations, death rates from the brutal pace of labor were extremely high, leading to a constant stream of new shipments of slaves from Africa.

In total, scholars estimate that European traders embarked over 10 million enslaved Africans across the Atlantic from 1518 to 1800 (of whom roughly 8.5 million disembarked), with the peak of the trade occurring in the eighteenth century.[21] By comparison, only 2 to 2.5 million Europeans migrated to the New World during the same period. Slaves worked in an infinite variety of occupations: as miners, soldiers, sailors, servants, and artisans and in the production of sugar, cotton, rum, indigo, tobacco, wheat, and corn.

Spanish Silver and Its Economic Effects

The sixteenth century has often been called Spain's golden century, but silver mined in the Americas was the true source of Spain's wealth. In 1545, at an altitude of fifteen thousand feet, the Spanish discovered an extraordinary source of silver at Potosí (poh-toh-SEE) (in present-day Bolivia) in territory conquered from the Inca Empire. The frigid place where nothing grew had been unsettled. A half century later 160,000 people lived there, making it about as populous as the city of London. By 1550 Potosí yielded perhaps 60 percent of all the silver mined in the world. From Potosí and the mines at Zacatecas (za-kuh-TAY-kuhhs) and Guanajuato (gwah-nah-HWAH-toh) in Mexico, huge quantities of precious metals poured forth. To protect this treasure from French and English pirates, armed convoys transported it to Spain each year. Between 1503 and 1650, 35 million pounds of silver and over 600,000 pounds of gold entered Seville's port. Spanish predominance, however, proved temporary.

In the sixteenth century Spain experienced a steady population increase, creating a sharp rise in the demand for food and goods. Spanish colonies in the Americas also demanded consumer goods, such as cloth and luxury goods. Since Spain had expelled some of its best farmers and businessmen — the Muslims and Jews — in the fifteenth century, the Spanish economy was suffering and could not meet the new demands. The excess of demand over supply led to widespread inflation. The result was a rise in production costs and a further decline in Spain's productive capacity.

Did the flood of silver bullion from America cause the inflation? Prices rose most steeply before 1565, but bullion imports reached their peak between 1580 and 1620. Thus silver did not cause the initial inflation. It did, however, exacerbate the situation, and, along with the ensuing rise in population, the influx of silver significantly contributed to the upward spiral of prices. Inflation severely strained government budgets. Several times between 1557 and 1647, Spain's King Philip II and his successors wrote off the state debt, thereby undermining confidence in the government and leaving the

Philip II, ca. 1533   This portrait of Philip II as a young man and crown prince of Spain is by the celebrated artist Titian, court painter to Philip's father, Charles V. After taking the throne, Philip became another great patron of the artist. (Palazzo Pitti, Florence, Italy/The Bridgeman Art Library)

economy in shambles. After 1600, when the population declined, prices gradually stabilized.

As Philip II paid his armies and foreign debts with silver bullion, Spanish inflation was transmitted to the rest of Europe. Between 1560 and 1600 much of Europe experienced large price increases. Prices doubled and in some cases quadrupled. Spain suffered most severely, but all European countries were affected. Because money bought less, people who lived on fixed incomes, such as nobles, were badly hurt. Those who owed fixed sums of money, such as the middle class, prospered because in a time of rising prices, debts lessened in value each year. Food costs rose most sharply, and the poor fared worst of all.

In many ways, though, it was not Spain but China that controlled the world trade in silver. The Chinese demanded silver for their products and for the payment of imperial taxes. China was thus the main buyer of world silver, absorbing half the world's production. The silver market drove world trade, with New Spain and Japan being mainstays on the supply side and China dominating the demand side. The world trade in silver is one of the best examples of the new global economy that emerged in this period.

The Birth of the Global Economy

With the Europeans' discovery of the Americas and their exploration of the Pacific, the entire world was linked for the first time in history by seaborne trade. The opening of that trade brought into being three successive commercial empires: the Portuguese, the Spanish, and the Dutch.

The Portuguese were the first worldwide traders. In the sixteenth century they controlled the sea route to India (see Map 14.3). From their fortified bases at Goa on the Arabian Sea and at Malacca on the Malay Peninsula, ships carried goods to the Portuguese settlement at Macao in the South China Sea. From Macao Portuguese ships loaded with Chinese silks and porcelains sailed to the Japanese port of Nagasaki and to the Philippine port of Manila, where Chinese goods were exchanged for Spanish silver from New Spain. Throughout Asia the Portuguese traded in slaves — sub-Saharan Africans, Chinese, and Japanese. The Portuguese exported horses from Mesopotamia and copper from Arabia to India; from India they exported hawks and peacocks for the Chinese and Japanese markets. Back to Portugal they brought Asian spices that had been purchased with textiles produced in India and with gold and ivory from East Africa. They also shipped back sugar from their colony in Brazil, produced by enslaved Africans whom they had transported across the Atlantic.

Coming to empire a few decades later than the Portuguese, the Spanish were determined to claim their place in world trade. The Spanish Empire in the New World was basically a land empire, but across the Pacific the Spaniards built a seaborne empire centered at Manila in the Philippines. The city of Manila served as the transpacific bridge between Spanish America and China. In Manila, Spanish traders used silver from American mines to purchase Chinese silk for European markets. The European demand for silk was so huge that in 1597, for example, 12 million pesos of silver, almost the total value of the transatlantic trade, moved from Acapulco in New Spain to Manila (see Map 14.3). After 1640 the Spanish silk trade declined in the face of stiff competition from Dutch imports.

In the late sixteenth century the Protestant Dutch were engaged in a long war of independence from their Spanish Catholic overlords (see Chapter 15). The joining of the Portuguese crown to Spain in 1580 gave the Dutch a strategic incentive to attack Portugal, a major economic competitor for the Dutch. Drawing on their commercial wealth and determined use of force, the Dutch emerged by the end of the seventeenth century as both a free nation and a worldwide seaborne trading power. The Dutch Empire was initially built on spices. In 1599 a Dutch fleet returned to Amsterdam carrying 600,000 pounds of pepper and 250,000 pounds of cloves and nutmeg. Those who had invested in the expedition received a 100 percent profit. The voyage led to the establishment in 1602 of the Dutch East India Company, founded with the stated intention of capturing the spice trade from the Portuguese.

The Dutch set their sights on gaining direct access to and control of the Indonesian sources of spices. The Dutch fleet sailed from the Dutch Republic to the Cape of Good Hope in Africa and, avoiding the Portuguese forts in India, steered directly for the Sunda Strait in Indonesia (see Map 14.3). In return for assisting Indonesian princes in local squabbles and disputes with the Portuguese, the Dutch won broad commercial concessions. Through agreements, seizures, and outright military aggression, they gained control of the western access to the Indonesian archipelago in the first half of the seventeenth century. Gradually, they acquired political domination over the archipelago itself. By the 1660s the Dutch had managed to expel the Portuguese from Ceylon and other East Indian islands, thereby establishing control of the lucrative spice trade.

Not content with challenging the Portuguese in the Indian Ocean, the Dutch also aspired to a role in the Americas. Founded in 1621, when the Dutch were at war with the Spanish, the Dutch West India Company aggressively sought to open trade with North and South America and capture Spanish territories there. The company captured or destroyed hundreds of Spanish ships, seized the Spanish silver fleet in 1628, and captured portions of Brazil and the Caribbean. The Dutch also successfully interceded in the transatlantic slave trade, establishing a large number of trading stations on the west coast of Africa. Ironically, the nation that was known throughout Europe as a bastion of tolerance and freedom came to be one of the principal operators of the slave trade starting in the 1640s.

Dutch efforts to colonize North America were less successful. The colony of New Netherland, governed from New Amsterdam (modern-day New York City), was hampered by lack of settlement and weak governance and was easily captured by the British in 1664.

Changing Attitudes and Beliefs

How did new ideas about race and the works of Montaigne and Shakespeare reflect the encounter with new peoples and places?

The age of overseas expansion heightened Europeans' contacts with the rest of the world. These contacts gave birth to new ideas about the inherent superiority or inferiority of different races, in part to justify European participation in the slave trade. Cultural encounters also inspired more positive views. The essays of Michel de Montaigne epitomized a new spirit of skepticism and cultural relativism, while the plays of William Shakespeare reflected the efforts of one great writer to come to terms with the cultural complexity of his day.

New Ideas About Race

At the beginning of the transatlantic slave trade, most Europeans would have thought of Africans, if they thought of them at all, as savages because of their eating habits, morals, clothing, and social customs and as barbarians because of their language and methods of war. Despite lingering belief in a Christian Ethiopia under the legendary Prester John, they grouped Africans into the despised categories of pagan heathens and Muslim infidels. Africans were certainly not the only peoples subject to such dehumanizing attitudes. Jews were also viewed as alien people who, like Africans, were naturally sinful and depraved. More generally, elite Europeans were accustomed to viewing the peasant masses as a lower form of humanity. They scornfully compared rustic peasants to dogs, pigs, and donkeys and even reviled the dark skin color peasants acquired while laboring in the sun.[22]

As Europeans turned to Africa for new sources of slaves, they drew on and developed ideas about Africans' primitiveness and barbarity to defend slavery and even argue that enslavement benefited Africans by bringing the light of Christianity to heathen peoples. In 1444 an observer defended the enslavement of the first Africans by Portuguese explorers as necessary for their salvation "because they lived like beasts, without any of the customs of rational creatures, since they did not even know what were bread and wine, nor garments of cloth, nor life in the shelter of a house; and worse still was their ignorance, which deprived them of knowledge of good, and permitted them only a life of brutish idleness."[23] Compare this with an early-seventeenth-century Englishman's complaint that the Irish "be so beastly that they are better like beasts than Christians."[24]

Over time, the institution of slavery fostered a new level of racial inequality. In contrast to peasants, Jews, and the Irish, Africans gradually became seen as utterly distinct from and wholly inferior to Europeans. From rather vague assumptions about non-Christian religious beliefs and a general lack of civilization, Europeans developed increasingly rigid ideas of racial superiority and inferiority to safeguard the growing profits gained from plantation slavery. Black skin became equated with slavery itself as Europeans at home and in the colonies convinced themselves that blacks were destined by God to serve them as slaves in perpetuity.

Support for this belief went back to the Greek philosopher Aristotle's argument that some people are naturally destined for slavery and to biblical associations between darkness and sin. A more explicit justification was found in the story of Noah's curse upon Canaan, the son of his own son Ham. According to the Bible, Ham defied Noah's ban on sexual relations on the ark and further enraged his father by entering his tent and viewing him unclothed. To punish Ham, Noah cursed his son Canaan and all his descendants to be the "servant of servants." Biblical genealogies listing Ham's sons as those who peopled North Africa and Cush were read to mean that all inhabitants of those regions bore Noah's curse. From the sixteenth century onward, defenders of slavery often cited this story as justification for their actions.

After 1700 the emergence of new methods of observing and describing nature led to the use of science to define race. Although the term originally referred to a nation or an ethnic group, henceforth "race" would mean biologically distinct groups of people, whose physical differences produced differences in culture, character, and intelligence. Biblical justifications for inequality thereby gave way to supposedly scientific ones.

Michel de Montaigne and Cultural Curiosity

Racism was not the only possible reaction to the new worlds emerging in the sixteenth century. Decades of religious fanaticism, bringing civil anarchy and war, led some Catholics and Protestants to doubt that any one faith contained absolute truth. Added to these doubts was the discovery of peoples in the New World who had radically different ways of life. These shocks helped produce ideas of skepticism and cultural relativism. Skepticism is a school of thought founded on doubt that total certainty or definitive knowledge is ever attainable. The skeptic is cautious and critical and suspends judgment. Cultural relativism suggests that one culture is not necessarily superior to another, just different. Both notions found expression in the work of Frenchman Michel de Montaigne (duh mahn-TAYN) (1533–1592).

Montaigne developed a new literary genre, the essay—from the French *essayer*, meaning "to test or try"—to express his ideas. Published in 1580, Montaigne's *Essays* consisted of short reflections drawing on his extensive reading in ancient texts, his experience as a government official, and his own moral judgment. Intending his works to be accessible to ordinary people, Montaigne wrote in French rather than Latin and in an engaging conversational style. His essays were quickly translated into other European languages and became some of the most widely read texts of the early modern period.

Montaigne's essay "Of Cannibals" reveals the impact of overseas discoveries on one thoughtful European. In contrast to the prevailing views of his day, he rejected the notion that one culture is superior to another. Speaking of native Brazilians, he wrote:

> I find that there is nothing barbarous and savage in this nation [Brazil], . . . except, that everyone gives the title of barbarism to everything that is not according to his usage; as, indeed, we have no other criterion of truth and reason, than the example and pattern of the opinions and customs of the place wherein we live. . . . They are

> savages in the same way that we say fruits are wild, which nature produces of herself and by her ordinary course; whereas, in truth, we ought rather to call those wild whose natures we have changed by our artifice and diverted from the common order.[25]

In his own time, few would have agreed with Montaigne's challenge to ideas of European superiority or his even more radical questioning of the superiority of humans over animals. Nevertheless, his popular essays contributed to a basic shift in attitudes. "Wonder," he said, "is the foundation of all philosophy, research is the means of all learning, and ignorance is the end."[26] Montaigne thus inaugurated an era of doubt.

William Shakespeare and His Influence

In addition to the essay as a literary genre, the period fostered remarkable creativity in other branches of literature. England—especially in the latter part of Queen Elizabeth I's reign and in the first years of her successor, James I (r. 1603–1625)—witnessed remarkable literary expression. The undisputed master of the period was the dramatist William Shakespeare, whose genius lay in the originality of his characterizations, the diversity of his plots, his understanding of human psychology, and his unsurpassed gift for language. Born in 1564 to a successful glove manufacturer in Stratford-upon-Avon, Shakespeare grew into a Renaissance man with a deep appreciation of classical culture, individualism, and humanism. Although he wrote sparkling comedies and stirring historical plays, his greatest masterpieces were his later tragedies, including *Hamlet*, *Othello*, and *Macbeth*, which explore an enormous range of human problems and are open to an almost infinite variety of interpretations.

Like Montaigne's essays, Shakespeare's work reveals the impact of the new discoveries and contacts of his day. The title character of *Othello* is described as a "Moor of Venice." In Shakespeare's day, the term "Moor" referred to Muslims of North African origin, including those who had migrated to the Iberian Peninsula. It could also be applied, though, to natives of the Iberian Peninsula who converted to Islam or to non-Muslim Berbers in North Africa. To complicate things even more, references in the play to Othello as "black" in skin color have led many to believe that Shakespeare intended him to be a sub-Saharan African. This confusion in the play aptly reflects the uncertainty in Shakespeare's own time about racial and religious classifications. In contrast to the prevailing view of Moors as inferior, Shakespeare presents Othello as a complex human figure, whose only crime is to have "loved [his wife] not wisely, but too well."

Shakespeare's last play, *The Tempest*, also highlights the issue of race and race relations. The plot involves the stranding on an island of sorcerer Prospero and his daughter Miranda. There Prospero finds and raises Caliban, a native of the island, whom he instructs in his own language and religion. After Caliban's attempted rape of Miranda, Prospero enslaves him, earning the hatred of his erstwhile pupil. Modern scholars often note the echoes between this play and the realities of imperial conquest and settlement in Shakespeare's day. It is no accident, they argue, that the poet portrayed Caliban as a monstrous dark-skinned island native who was best suited for slavery. Shakespeare himself borrows words from Montaigne's essay "Of Cannibals," suggesting that he may have intended to criticize, rather than endorse, racial intolerance. Shakespeare's work shows us one of the finest minds of the age grasping to come to terms with the racial and religious complexities around him.

Notes

1. Marco Polo, *The Book of Ser Marco Polo, the Venetian: Concerning the Kingdoms and Marvels of the East*, vol. 2, trans. and ed. Colonel Sir Henry Yule (London: John Murray, 1903), pp. 185–186.
2. Thomas Benjamin, *The Atlantic World: Europeans, Africans, Indians and Their Shared History, 1400–1900* (Cambridge, U.K.: Cambridge University Press, 2009), p. 56.
3. Quoted in J. Devisse, "Africa in Inter-Continental Relations," in *General History of Africa*, vol. 4., *Africa from the Twelfth to the Sixteenth Century*, ed. D. T. Niane (Berkeley, Calif.: Heinemann Educational Books, 1984), p. 664.
4. Geoffrey Atkinson, *Les nouveaux horizons de la Renaissance française* (Paris: Droz, 1935), pp. 10–12.
5. G. V. Scammell, *The World Encompassed: The First European Maritime Empires, c. 800–1650* (Berkeley: University of California Press, 1981), pp. 101, 104.
6. Quoted in C. M. Cipolla, *Guns, Sails, and Empires: Technological Innovation and the Early Phases of European Expansion, 1400–1700* (New York: Minerva Press, 1965), p. 132.
7. Quoted in F. H. Littell, *The Macmillan Atlas: History of Christianity* (New York: Macmillan, 1976), p. 75.
8. Pablo E. Pérez-Mallaína, *Spain's Men of the Sea: Daily Life on the Indies Fleet in the Sixteenth Century* (Baltimore: Johns Hopkins University Press, 1998), p. 133.
9. Ibid., p. 19.
10. Quoted in F. Maddison, "Tradition and Innovation: Columbus' First Voyage and Portuguese Navigation in the Fifteenth Century," in *Circa 1492: Art in the Age of Exploration*, ed. J. A. Levenson (Washington, D.C.: National Gallery of Art, 1991), p. 69.
11. Quoted in R. L. Kagan, "The Spain of Ferdinand and Isabella," in *Circa 1492: Art in the Age of Exploration*, ed. J. A. Levenson (Washington, D.C.: National Gallery of Art, 1991), p. 60.
12. Peter Hulme, *Colonial Encounters: Europe and the Native Caribbean, 1492–1797* (London: Methuen, 1986), pp. 22–31.
13. Benjamin, *The Atlantic World*, p. 141.
14. Ibid., pp. 35–59.
15. Quoted in C. Gibson, ed., *The Black Legend: Anti-Spanish Attitudes in the Old World and the New* (New York: Knopf, 1971), pp. 74–75.
16. Quoted in L. B. Rout, Jr., *The African Experience in Spanish America* (New York: Cambridge University Press, 1976), p. 23.
17. Cited in Geoffrey Vaughn Scammell, *The First Imperial Age: European Overseas Expansion, c. 1400–1715* (London: Routledge, 2002), p. 62.
18. Ibid., p. 432.
19. Herbert S. Klein, "Profits and the Causes of Mortality," in David Northrup, ed., *The Atlantic Slave Trade* (Lexington, Mass.: D. C. Heath and Co., 1994), p. 116.
20. Malcolm Cowley and Daniel P. Mannix, "The Middle Passage," in David Northrup, ed., *The Atlantic Slave Trade* (Lexington, Mass.: D. C. Heath and Co., 1994), p. 101.
21. Voyages: The Trans-Atlantic Slave Trade Database, http://www.slavevoyages.org/tast/assessment/estimates .faces.
22. Paul Freedman, *Images of the Medieval Peasant* (Stanford, Calif.: Stanford University Press, 1999).
23. Quoted in James H. Sweet, "The Iberian Roots of American Racist Thought," *The William and Mary Quarterly* 54 (1997): 155.
24. Quoted in Sean J. Connolly, *Contested Island: Ireland, 1460–1630* (Oxford: Oxford University Press, 2007), p. 397.
25. C. Cotton, trans., *The Essays of Michel de Montaigne* (New York: A. L. Burt, 1893), pp. 207, 210.
26. Ibid., p. 523.

Chapter Review

MAKE IT STICK

LearningCurve
bedfordstmartins.com/mckaywestvalue

After reading the chapter, use LearningCurve to retain what you've read.

IDENTIFY KEY TERMS

Identify and explain the significance of each item below.

conquistadors (p. 445)

caravel (p. 446)

Ptolemy's *Geography* (p. 446)

Treaty of Tordesillas (p. 452)

Mexica Empire (p. 453)

Inca Empire (p. 455)

viceroyalties (p. 457)

encomienda system (p. 458)

Columbian exchange (p. 462)

REVIEW THE MAIN IDEAS

Answer the focus questions from each section of the chapter.

* What was the Afroeurasian trading world before Columbus? (p. 439)

* How and why did Europeans undertake ambitious voyages of expansion? (p. 444)

* What was the impact of European conquest on the peoples and ecologies of the New World? (p. 457)

* How was the era of global contact shaped by new commodities, commercial empires, and forced migrations? (p. 462)

* How did new ideas about race and the works of Montaigne and Shakespeare reflect the encounter with new peoples and places? (p. 470)

MAKE CONNECTIONS

Think about the larger developments and continuities within and across chapters.

1. Michel de Montaigne argued that people's assessments of what was "barbaric" merely drew on their own habits and customs; based on the earlier sections of this chapter, how widespread was this openness to cultural difference? Was he alone or did others share this view?

2. To what extent did the European voyages of expansion and conquest inaugurate an era of global history? Is it correct to date the beginning of "globalization" from the late fifteenth century? Why or why not?

ONLINE DOCUMENT ASSIGNMENT

Juan de Pareja

How could an individual like Pareja experience both slavery and freedom in a single lifetime?

You encountered Juan de Pareja's story on page 464. Keeping the question above in mind, go online and examine primary sources from Pareja's time—including visual art, drama, and legal excerpts—to draw your own conclusions. Then complete a writing assignment based on the evidence and details from this chapter.

bedfordstmartins.com/mckaywestvalue

CHRONOLOGY

1271–1295	• Marco Polo travels to China
1443	• Portuguese establish first African trading post at Arguin
1492	• Columbus lands in the Americas
1511	• Portuguese capture Malacca from Muslims
1518	• Spanish king authorizes slave trade to New World colonies
1519–1522	• Magellan's expedition circumnavigates the world
1521	• Cortés conquers the Mexica Empire
1533	• Pizarro conquers the Inca Empire
1602	• Dutch East India Company established

15

LearningCurve
bedfordstmartins.com/mckaywestvalue
After reading the chapter, use
LearningCurve to retain what
you've read.

Absolutism and Constitutionalism

ca. 1589–1725

DESPITE THE LAVISH LIFESTYLES OF WEALTHY NOBLES AND ROYALS,
the seventeenth century was a period of crisis and transformation in Europe.
Agricultural and manufacturing slumps led to food shortages and shrinking
population rates. Religious and dynastic conflicts led to almost constant war,
visiting violence and destruction on ordinary people and reshaping European
states. With Louis XIV of France taking the lead, armies grew larger than they
had been since the time of the Roman Empire, resulting in new government
bureaucracies and higher taxes. Yet even with these obstacles, European
states succeeded in gathering more power, and by 1680 much of the unrest
that originated with the Reformation was resolved.

These crises were not limited to western Europe. Central and eastern
Europe experienced even more catastrophic dislocation, with German lands
serving as the battleground of the Thirty Years' War and borders constantly
vulnerable to attack from the east. In Prussia and in Habsburg Austria absolutist states emerged in the aftermath of this conflict. Russia and the Ottoman
Turks also experienced turmoil in the mid-seventeenth century, but maintained
their distinctive styles of absolutist government. The Russian and Ottoman
Empires seemed foreign and exotic to western Europeans, who saw them as
the antithesis of their political, religious, and cultural values.

While absolutism emerged as the solution to crisis in many European states,
a small minority adopted a different path, placing sovereignty in the hands of
privileged groups rather than the Crown. Historians refer to states where power
was limited by law as "constitutional." The two most important seventeenth-

century constitutionalist states were England and the Dutch Republic. Constitutionalism should not be confused with democracy. The elite rulers of England and the Dutch Republic pursued familiar policies of increased taxation, government authority, and social control. Nonetheless, they served as influential models to onlookers across Europe as a form of government that checked the power of a single ruler.

Seventeenth-Century Crisis and Rebuilding

What were the common crises and achievements of seventeenth-century European states?

Historians often refer to the seventeenth century as an "age of crisis." After the economic and demographic growth of the sixteenth century, Europe faltered into stagnation and retrenchment. This was partially due to climate changes beyond anyone's control, but it also resulted from bitter religious divides, increased governmental pressures, and war. These challenges overwhelmed the fragile balance of rural villages, leading to hunger and population loss. Overburdened peasants and city dwellers took action to defend themselves from high prices and overtaxation, sometimes profiting from conflicts to obtain relief. In the long run, however, governments proved increasingly able to impose their will on the populace. With France under Louis XIV commanding European leadership, the period witnessed spectacular growth in army size as well as new forms of taxation, government bureaucracies, and increased state sovereignty.

The Social Order and Peasant Life

Peasants occupied the lower tiers of a society organized in hierarchical levels. At the top, the monarch was celebrated as a semidivine being, chosen by God to embody the state. In Catholic countries, the clergy occupied the second level, due to their sacred role interceding with God and the saints on behalf of their flocks. Next came nobles, whose privileged status derived from their ancient bloodlines and centuries of sacrifice on the battlefield. Christian prejudices against commerce and money meant that merchants could never lay claim to the highest honors. However, many prosperous mercantile families had bought their way into the nobility through service to the rising monarchies of the fifteenth and sixteenth centuries and constituted a second tier of nobles. Those lower on the social scale, the peasants and artisans who constituted the vast majority of the population, were expected to defer to their betters with humble obedience. This was the "Great Chain of Being" that linked God to his creation in a series of ranked social groups.

In addition to being rigidly hierarchical, European societies were patriarchal in nature, with men assuming authority over women as a God-given prerogative. The family thus represented a microcosm of this social order. The father ruled his family like a king ruled his domains. Religious and secular law commanded a man's wife, children, servants, and apprentices to defer to his will. Fathers did not possess the power of life and death, like Roman patriarchs, but they were entitled to use physical violence, imprisonment, and other forceful measures to impose their authority. These powers were balanced by expectations that a good father would provide and care for his dependents.

Estonian Serfs in the 1660s
The Estonians were conquered by German military nobility in the Middle Ages and reduced to serfdom. The German-speaking nobles ruled the Estonian peasants with an iron hand, and Peter the Great reaffirmed their domination when Russia annexed Estonia. (Mansell Collection/Time Life Pictures/Getty Images)

In the seventeenth century most Europeans lived in the countryside. The hub of the rural world was the small peasant village centered on a church and a manor. Life was in many ways circumscribed by the village, although we should not underestimate the mobility induced by war, food shortage, and the desire to seek one's fortune or embark on a religious pilgrimage.

In western Europe, a small number of peasants in each village owned enough land to feed themselves and had the livestock and plows necessary to work their land. These independent farmers were leaders of the peasant village. They employed the landless poor, rented out livestock and tools, and served as agents for the noble lord. Below them were small landowners and tenant farmers who did not have enough land to be self-sufficient. These families sold their best produce on the market to earn cash for taxes, rent, and food. At the bottom were villagers who worked as dependent laborers and servants. In eastern Europe, the vast majority of peasants toiled as serfs for noble landowners and did not own land in their own right (see page 492).

Rich or poor, east or west, bread was the primary element of the diet. The richest ate a white loaf, leaving brown bread to those who could not afford better. Peasants paid stiff fees to the local miller for grinding grain into flour and sometimes to the lord for the right to bake bread in his oven. Bread was most often accompanied by a soup made of roots, herbs, beans, and perhaps a small piece of salt pork. An important annual festival in many villages was the killing of the family pig. The whole family gathered to help, sharing a rare abundance of meat with neighbors and carefully salting the extra and putting down the lard. In some areas, menstruating women were careful to stay away from the kitchen for fear they might cause the lard to spoil.

Famine and Economic Crisis

European rural society lived on the edge of subsistence. Because of the crude technology and low crop yield, peasants were constantly threatened by scarcity and famine. In the seventeenth century a period of colder and wetter climate throughout Europe, dubbed the "little ice age" by historians, meant a shorter farming season with lower yields. A bad harvest created food shortages; a series of bad harvests could lead to famine. Recurrent famines significantly reduced the population of early modern Europe. Most people did not die of outright starvation, but through the spread of diseases like smallpox and typhoid, which were facilitated by malnutrition and exhaustion. Outbreaks of bubonic plague continued in Europe until the 1720s.

The Estates of Normandy, a provincial assembly, reported on the dire conditions in northern France during an outbreak of plague:

> Of the 450 sick persons whom the inhabitants were unable to relieve, 200 were turned out, and these we saw die one by one as they lay on the roadside. A large number still remain, and to each of them it is only possible to dole out the least scrap of bread. We only give bread to those who would otherwise die. The staple dish here consists of mice, which the inhabitants hunt, so desperate are they from hunger. They devour roots which the animals cannot eat; one can, in fact, not put into words the things one sees. . . . We certify to having ourselves seen herds, not of cattle, but of men and women, wandering about the fields between Rheims and Rhétel, turning up the earth like pigs to find a few roots; and as they can only find rotten ones, and not half enough of them, they become so weak that they have not strength left to seek food.[1]

Given the harsh conditions of life, industry also suffered. The output of woolen textiles, one of the most important European manufactures, declined sharply in the first half of the seventeenth century. Food prices were high, wages stagnated, and unemployment soared. This economic crisis was not universal: it struck various regions at different times and to different degrees. In the middle decades of the century, for example, Spain, France, Germany, and England all experienced great economic difficulties, but these years were the golden age of the Netherlands.

The urban poor and peasants were the hardest hit. When the price of bread rose beyond their capacity to pay, they frequently expressed their anger by rioting. In towns they invaded bakers' shops to seize bread and resell it at a "just price." In rural areas they attacked convoys taking grain to the cities. Women often led these actions, since their role as mothers gave them some impunity in authorities' eyes. Historians have used the term "moral economy" for this vision of a world in which community needs predominate over competition and profit.

The Thirty Years' War

In the first half of the seventeenth century, the fragile balance of life was violently upturned by the ravages of the Thirty Years' War (1618–1648). The Holy Roman Empire was a confederation of hundreds of principalities, independent cities, duchies, and other polities loosely united under an elected emperor. The uneasy truce between Catholics and Protestants created by the Peace of Augsburg in 1555 deteriorated as the faiths of various areas shifted. Lutheran princes felt compelled to form the Protestant Union (1608), and Catholics retaliated with the Catholic League (1609). Each alliance was determined that the other should make no religious or territorial advance. Dynastic interests were also involved; the Spanish Habsburgs strongly supported the goals of their Austrian relatives: the unity of the empire and the preservation of Catholicism within it.

The war is traditionally divided into four phases. The first, or Bohemian, phase (1618–1625) was characterized by civil war in Bohemia between the Catholic League and the Protestant Union. In 1620 Catholic forces defeated Protestants at the Battle of the White Mountain. The second, or Danish, phase of the war (1625–1629) — so called because of the leadership of the Protestant king Christian IV of Denmark (r. 1588–1648) — witnessed additional Catholic victories. The Catholic imperial army led by Albert of Wallenstein swept through Silesia, north to the Baltic, and east into Pomerania, scoring smashing victories. Under Charles I, England briefly and unsuccessfully intervened in this phase of the conflict by entering alliances against France and Spain. Habsburg power peaked in 1629. The emperor issued the Edict of Restitution, whereby all Catholic properties lost to Protestantism since 1552 were restored, and only Catholics and Lutherans were allowed to practice their faiths.

The third, or Swedish, phase of the war (1630–1635) began with the arrival in Germany of the Swedish king Gustavus Adolphus (r. 1594–1632) and his army. The ablest administrator of his day and a devout Lutheran, he intervened to support the empire's Protestants. The French chief minister, Cardinal Richelieu, subsidized the Swedes, hoping to weaken Habsburg power in Europe. Gustavus Adolphus won two important battles but was fatally wounded in combat. The final, or French, phase of the war (1635–1648) was prompted by Richelieu's concern that the Habsburgs would rebound after the death of Gustavus Adolphus. Richelieu declared war on Spain and sent military as well as financial assistance. Finally, in October 1648 peace was achieved.

The 1648 **Peace of Westphalia** that ended the Thirty Years' War marked a turning point in European history. For the most part, conflicts fought over religious faith receded. The treaties recognized the independent authority of more than three hundred German princes, reconfirming the emperor's severely limited authority. The Augsburg agreement of 1555 became permanent, adding Calvinism to Catholicism and Lutheranism as legally permissible creeds. The north German states remained Protestant; the south German states, Catholic.

The Thirty Years' War was the most destructive event for the central European economy and society prior to the world wars of the twentieth century. Perhaps one-third of urban residents and two-fifths of the rural population died, leaving entire areas depopulated. Trade in southern German cities, such as Augsburg, was virtually destroyed. Agricultural areas suffered catastrophically. Many small farmers lost their land, allowing nobles to enlarge their estates and consolidate their control.[2]

Achievements in State-Building

In the context of war and economic depression, seventeenth-century monarchs began to make new demands on their people. Traditionally, historians have distinguished between the "absolutist" governments of France, Spain, central Europe, and Russia and the constitutionalist governments of England and the Dutch Republic. Whereas absolutist monarchs gathered all power under their personal control, English and Dutch rulers were obliged to respect laws passed by representative institutions. More recently, historians have emphasized commonalities among these powers. Despite their political differences, all these states shared common projects of protecting and expanding their frontiers, raising new taxes, consolidating central control, and competing for the new colonies opening up in the New and Old Worlds.

Rulers encountered formidable obstacles in achieving these goals. Some were purely material. Without paved roads, telephones, or other modern technology, it took weeks to convey orders from the central government to the provinces. Rulers also suffered from lack of information about their realms, making it impossible to police and tax the population effectively. Local power structures presented another serious obstacle. Nobles, the church, provincial and national assemblies, town councils, guilds, and other bodies held legal privileges, which could not easily be rescinded. In some kingdoms many people spoke a language different from that of the Crown, further diminishing their willingness to obey its commands.

Nonetheless, over the course of the seventeenth century both absolutist and constitutional governments achieved new levels of central control. This increased authority focused on four areas in particular: greater taxation, growth in armed forces, larger and more efficient bureaucracies, and the increased ability to compel obedience from subjects. To meet the demands of running their expanding governments, rulers turned to trusted ministers. Cardinal Richelieu in France and Count-Duke Olivares in Spain each played the role of chief adviser to his king and enabler of state power. Royal favorites acquired power and fortune from their position; however, they were vulnerable to distrust and hostility from others at court. Olivares ended his career in disgrace, while the duke of Buckingham, favorite to James I and Charles I of England, was assassinated.

Over time, centralized power added up to something close to sovereignty. A state may be termed sovereign when it possesses a monopoly over the instruments of justice and the use of force within clearly defined boundaries. In a sovereign state, no system of courts, such as church tribunals, competes with state courts in the dispensation of justice; and private armies, such as those of feudal lords, present no threat to central authority. While seventeenth-century states did not acquire total sovereignty, they made important strides toward that goal.

Warfare and the Growth of Army Size

The driving force of seventeenth-century state-building was warfare. In medieval times, feudal lords had raised armies only for particular wars or campaigns; now monarchs began to recruit their own forces and maintain permanent standing armies. Instead of serving their own interests, army officers were required to be loyal and obedient to those who commanded them. New techniques for training and deploying soldiers meant a rise in the professional standards of the army.

Along with professionalization came an explosive growth in army size. The French took the lead, with the army growing from roughly 125,000 men in the Thirty Years' War to 340,000 at the end of the seventeenth century.[3] Changes in the style of armies encouraged this growth. Mustering a royal army took longer than simply hiring a mercenary band, giving enemies time to form coalitions. For example, the large coalitions Louis XIV confronted (see page 489) required him to fight on multiple fronts with huge armies. In turn, the relative size and wealth of France among European nations allowed Louis to field enormous armies and thereby to pursue the ambitious foreign policies that caused his alarmed neighbors to form coalitions against him.

Noble values of glory and honor outshone concerns for safety or material benefit. Because they personally led their men in battle, noble officers experienced high death rates on the battlefield. Nobles also fell into debt because they had to purchase their positions in the army and the units they commanded, which meant that they were obliged to assume many of the costs involved in creating and maintaining their units. It was not until the 1760s that the French government assumed the full cost of equipping troops.

Other European powers were quick to follow the French example. The rise of absolutism in central and eastern Europe led to a vast expansion in the size of armies. Great Britain followed a similar, albeit distinctive pattern. Instead of building a land army, the British focused on naval forces and eventually built the largest navy in the world.

Popular Political Action

As governments continuously raised taxes to meet the costs of war, neighborhood riots over the cost of bread turned into armed uprisings. Popular revolts were extremely common in England, France, Spain, Portugal, and Italy during the Thirty Years' War. In 1640 Philip IV of Spain faced revolt in Catalonia, the economic center of his realm. At the same time he struggled to put down uprisings in Portugal and in the northern provinces of the Netherlands. In 1647 the city of Palermo, in Spanish-occupied Sicily, exploded in protest over food shortages caused by a series of bad harvests. Fearing public unrest, the city government subsidized the price of bread, attracting even more starving peasants from the countryside. When Madrid ordered an end to subsidies, municipal leaders decided to lighten the loaf rather than raise prices. Not fooled by this change, local women led a bread riot, shouting "Long live the king and down with the taxes and the bad government!" Insurgency spread to the rest of the island and eventually to Naples on the mainland. Apart from affordable food, rebels demanded the suppression of extraordinary taxes and participation in municipal government. Some dreamed of a republic that would abolish noble tax exemptions. Despite initial successes, the revolt lacked unity and strong leadership and could not withstand the forces of the state.

In France urban uprisings became a frequent aspect of the social and political landscape. Beginning in 1630 and continuing on and off through the early 1700s, major insurrections occurred at Dijon, Bordeaux (bor-DOH), Montpellier, Lyons, and Amiens. All were characterized by deep popular anger and violence directed at outside officials sent to collect taxes. These officials were sometimes seized, beaten, and hacked to death. For example, in 1673 Louis XIV's imposition of new taxes on legal transactions, tobacco, and pewter ware provoked an uprising in Bordeaux.

Municipal and royal authorities often struggled to overcome popular revolt. They feared that stern repressive measures, such as sending in troops to fire on crowds, would create martyrs and further inflame the situation, while full-scale occupation of a city would be very expensive and detract from military efforts elsewhere. The limitations of royal authority gave some leverage to rebels. To quell riots, royal edicts were sometimes suspended, prisoners released, and discussions initiated.

By the beginning of the eighteenth century, this leverage had largely disappeared. Municipal governments were better integrated into the national structure, and local authorities had prompt military support from the central government. People who publicly opposed royal policies and taxes received swift and severe punishment.

Absolutism in France and Spain

What factors led to the rise of the French absolutist state under Louis XIV, and why did absolutist Spain experience decline in the same period?

In the Middle Ages jurists held that as a consequence of monarchs' coronation and anointment with sacred oil, they ruled "by the grace of God." Law was given by God; kings "found" the law and acknowledged that they must respect and obey it. Kings in absolutist states amplified these claims, asserting that they were responsible to God alone. They claimed exclusive power to make and enforce laws, denying any other institution or group the authority to check their power. In France the founder of the Bourbon monarchy, Henry IV, established foundations upon which his successors Louis XIII and Louis XIV built a stronger, more centralized French state. Louis XIV is often seen as the epitome of an "absolute" monarch, with his endless wars, increased taxes and economic regulation, and glorious palace at Versailles. In truth, his success relied on collaboration with nobles, and thus his example illustrates both the achievements and the compromises of absolutist rule.

As French power rose in the seventeenth century, the glory of Spain faded. Once the fabulous revenue from American silver declined, Spain's economic stagnation could no longer be disguised, and the country faltered under weak leadership.

The Foundations of Absolutism

Louis XIV's absolutism had long roots. In 1589 his grandfather Henry IV (r. 1589–1610), the founder of the Bourbon dynasty, acquired a devastated country. Civil wars between Protestants and Catholics had wracked France since 1561. Poor harvests had reduced peasants to starvation, and commercial activity had declined drastically. "Henri le Grand" (Henry the Great), as the king was called, promised "a chicken in every pot" and inaugurated a remarkable recovery.

He did so by keeping France at peace during most of his reign. Although he had converted to Catholicism, he issued the Edict of Nantes, allowing Protestants the right to worship in 150 traditionally Protestant towns throughout France. He sharply lowered taxes and instead charged royal officials an annual fee to guarantee the right to pass their positions down to their heirs. He also improved the infrastructure of the country, building new roads and canals and repairing the ravages of years of civil war. Despite his efforts at peace, Henry was murdered in 1610 by a Catholic zealot, setting off a national crisis.

After the death of Henry IV, his wife, the queen-regent Marie de' Medici, headed the government for the nine-year-old Louis XIII (r. 1610–1643). In 1628 Armand Jean du Plessis—Cardinal Richelieu (1585–1642)—became first minister of the French crown. Richelieu's maneuvers allowed the monarchy to maintain power within Europe and within its own borders despite the turmoil of the Thirty Years' War.

Cardinal Richelieu's political genius is best reflected in the administrative system he established to strengthen royal control. He extended the use of intendants, commissioners for each of France's thirty-two districts who were appointed directly by the monarch, to whom they were solely responsible. They recruited men for the army, supervised the collection of taxes, presided over the administration of local law, checked up on the local nobility, and regulated economic activities in their districts. As the intendants' power increased under Richelieu, so did the power of the centralized French state.

Under Richelieu, the French monarchy also acted to repress Protestantism. Louis personally supervised the siege of La Rochelle, an important port city and a major commercial center with strong ties to Protestant Holland and England. After the city fell in October 1628, its municipal government was suppressed. Protestants retained the right of public worship, but the Catholic liturgy was restored. The fall of La Rochelle was one step in the removal of Protestantism as a strong force in French life.

Richelieu did not aim to wipe out Protestantism in the rest of Europe, however. His main foreign policy goal was to destroy the Catholic Habsburgs' grip on territories that surrounded France. Consequently, Richelieu supported Habsburg enemies, including Protestants. In 1631 he signed a treaty with the Lutheran king Gustavus Adolphus promising French support against the Habsburgs in the Thirty Years' War. For the French cardinal, interests of state outweighed religious considerations.

Richelieu's successor as chief minister for the next child-king, the four-year-old Louis XIV, was Cardinal Jules Mazarin (1602–1661). Along with the regent, Queen Mother Anne of Austria, Mazarin continued Richelieu's centralizing policies. His struggle to increase royal revenues to meet the costs of war led to the uprisings of 1648–1653 known as the **Fronde**. A *frondeur* was originally a street urchin who threw mud at the passing carriages of the rich, but the word came to be applied to the many individuals and groups who opposed the policies of the government. In Paris, magistrates of the Parlement of Paris, the nation's most important court, were outraged by the Crown's autocratic measures. These so-called robe nobles (named for the robes they wore in court) encouraged violent protest by the common people. During the first of several riots, the queen mother fled Paris with Louis XIV. As rebellion spread outside Paris and to the sword nobles (the traditional warrior nobility), civil order broke down completely. In 1651 Anne's regency ended with the declaration of Louis as king in his own right. Much of the rebellion died away, and its leaders came to terms with the government.

The violence of the Fronde had significant results for the future. The twin evils of noble rebellion and popular riots left the French wishing for peace and for a strong monarch to reimpose order. This was the legacy that Louis XIV inherited in 1661 when he assumed personal rule of the largest and most populous country in western Europe at the age of twenty-three. Humiliated by his flight from Paris, he was determined to avoid any recurrence of rebellion.

Louis XIV and Absolutism

In the reign of Louis XIV (r. 1643–1715), the longest in European history, the French monarchy reached the peak of absolutist development. In the magnificence of his court and the brilliance of the culture that he presided over, Louis dominated his age. Religion, Anne, and Mazarin all taught Louis the doctrine of the divine right of kings: God had established kings as his rulers on earth, and they were answerable ultimately to him alone. Kings were divinely anointed and shared in the sacred nature of divinity, but they could not simply do as they pleased. They had to obey God's laws and rule for the good of the people. To symbolize his central role in the divine order, when he was fifteen years old Louis danced at a court ballet dressed as the sun, thereby acquiring the title of the "Sun King."

***Louis XIV, King of France and Navarre*, 1701** This was one of Louis XIV's favorite portraits of himself. He liked it so much that he had many copies of the portrait made, in full and half-size format. (Louvre, Paris, France/ Giraudon/The Bridgeman Art Library)

In addition to parading his power before the court, Louis worked very hard at the business of governing. He ruled his realm through several councils of state and insisted on taking a personal role in many of their decisions. He selected councilors from the recently ennobled or the upper middle class because he believed "that the public should know, from the rank of those whom I chose to serve me, that I had no intention of sharing power with them."[4] Despite increasing financial problems, Louis never called a meeting of the Estates General, thereby depriving nobles of united expression or action. Nor did Louis have a first minister. In this way he avoided the inordinate power of a Richelieu.

Although personally tolerant, Louis hated division within the realm and insisted that religious unity was essential to his royal dignity and to the security of the state. He thus pursued the policy of Protestant repression launched by Richelieu. In 1685 Louis revoked the Edict of Nantes. The new law ordered the Catholic baptism of Huguenots (French Calvinists), the destruction of Huguenot churches, the closing of schools, and the exile of Huguenot pastors who refused to renounce their faith. The result was the departure of some of the king's most loyal and industrially skilled subjects.

Despite his claims to absolute authority, multiple constraints existed on Louis's power. As a representative of divine power, he was obliged to rule in a manner consistent with virtue and benevolence. He had to uphold the laws issued by his royal predecessors. Moreover, he also relied on the collaboration of nobles, who maintained tremendous prestige and authority in their ancestral lands. Without their cooperation, it would have been impossible to extend his power throughout France or wage his many foreign wars. Louis's need to elicit noble cooperation led him to revolutionize court life at his spectacular palace at Versailles.

Life at Versailles

Through most of the seventeenth century, the French court had no fixed home, following the monarch to his numerous palaces and country residences. In 1682 Louis moved his court and government to the newly renovated palace at Versailles, a former hunting

PRIMARY SOURCE   Letter from Versailles

Born in 1652, the German princess Elisabeth-Charlotte was the daughter of the elector of the Palatinate, one of the many small states of the Holy Roman Empire. In 1671 she married the duke of Orléans, brother of Louis XIV. When Louis's wife died in 1683, Elisabeth-Charlotte became the highest-ranked woman at the French court. Despite the considerable pride she took in her position, her correspondence reveals her unhappiness and boredom with court life and her longing for home, as shown in the letter to her sister excerpted below.

I have nothing new to tell you; I walk and read and write; sometimes the king drives me to the hunt in his calèche. There are hunts every day; Sundays and Wednesdays are my son's days; the king hunts Mondays and Thursdays; Wednesdays and Saturdays Monseigneur [heir to the throne] hunts the wolf; M. le Comte de Toulouse, Mondays and Wednesdays; the Duc du Maine, Tuesdays; and M. le Duc, Fridays. They say if all the hunting kennels were united there would be from 900 to 1000 dogs. Twice a week there is a comedy. But you know, of course, that I go nowhere [due to mourning for her recently deceased husband]; which vexes me, for I must own that the theatre is the greatest amusement I have in the world, and the only pleasure that remains to me. . . .

    If the Court of France was what it used to be one might learn here how to behave in society; but—excepting the king and Monsieur [the king's brother, her deceased husband]—no one any longer knows what politeness is. The young men think only of horrible debauchery. I do not advise any one to send their children

lodge. The palace quickly became the center of political, social, and cultural life. The king required all great nobles to spend at least part of the year in attendance on him there, so he could keep an eye on their activities. Since he controlled the distribution of state power and wealth, nobles had no choice but to obey and compete with each other for his favor at Versailles.

The glorious palace, with its sumptuous interiors and extensive formal gardens, was a mirror to the world of French glory, soon copied by would-be absolutist monarchs across Europe. The reality of daily life in the palace was less glamorous. Versailles served as government offices for royal bureaucrats, as living quarters for the royal family and nobles, and as a place of work for hundreds of domestic servants. It was also open to the public at certain hours of the day. As a result, it was crowded with three thousand to ten thousand people every day. Even high nobles had to put up with cramped living space, and many visitors complained of the noise, smell, and crowds. (See "Primary Source: Letter from Versailles," above.)

Louis further revolutionized court life by establishing an elaborate set of etiquette rituals to mark every moment of his day, from waking up and dressing in the morning to removing his clothing and retiring at night. Courtiers vied for the honor of participating in these ceremonies, with the highest in rank claiming the privilege of handing the king his shirt. Endless squabbles broke out over what type of chair one could sit on at court and the order in which great nobles entered and were seated in the chapel for Mass.

here; for instead of learning good things, they will only take lessons in misconduct. You are right in blaming Germans who send their sons to France; how I wish that you and I were men and could go to the wars! — but that's a completely useless wish to have. . . . If I could with propriety return to Germany you would see me there quickly. I love that country; I think it more agreeable than all others, because there is less of luxury that I do not care for, and more of the frankness and integrity which I seek. But, be it said between ourselves, I was placed here against my will, and here I must stay till I die. There is no likelihood that we shall see each other again in this life; and what will become of us after that God only knows.

EVALUATE THE EVIDENCE

1. What are the principal amusements of court life, according to Elisabeth-Charlotte? What comparison does she draw between life in Germany and France?

2. How does the image of Versailles conveyed by Elisabeth-Charlotte contrast with the images of the palace found elsewhere in this chapter? How do you explain this contrast? If courtiers like her found life so dreary at court, why would they stay?

Source: *The Correspondence of Madame, Princess Palatine, Marie-Adélaïde de Savoie, and Madame de Maintenon*, ed. and trans. Katharine Prescott Wormeley (Boston: Hardy, Pratt, 1902), pp. 50–52.

These rituals may seem absurd, but they were far from trivial. The king controlled immense resources and privileges; access to him meant favored treatment for government offices, military and religious posts, state pensions, honorary titles, and a host of other benefits. The duke of Saint-Simon wrote of the king's power at court in his memoirs:

> No one understood better than Louis XIV the art of enhancing the value of a favour by his manner of bestowing it; he knew how to make the most of a word, a smile, even of a glance. If he addressed any one, were it but to ask a trifling question or make some commonplace remark, all eyes were turned on the person so honored; it was a mark of favour which always gave rise to comment.[5]

Courtiers sought these rewards for themselves and their family members and followers. A system of patronage — in which a higher-ranked individual protected a lower-ranked one in return for loyalty and services — flowed from the court to the provinces. Through this mechanism Louis gained cooperation from powerful nobles.

Although they could not hold public offices or posts, women played a central role in the patronage system. At court the king's wife, mistresses, and other female relatives recommended individuals for honors, advocated policy decisions, and brokered alliances between factions. Noblewomen played a similar role, bringing their family connections to marriage to form powerful social networks. Onlookers sometimes resented the influence of powerful women at court. The duke of Saint-Simon said of Madame de Maintenon,

Louis XIV's mistress and secret second wife, "Many people have been ruined by her, without having been able to discover the author of the ruin, search as they might."

Louis XIV was also an enthusiastic patron of the arts, commissioning many sculptures and paintings for Versailles as well as performances of dance and music. Scholars characterize the art and literature of the age of Louis XIV as French classicism. By this they mean that the artists and writers of the late seventeenth century imitated the subject matter and style of classical antiquity, that their work resembled that of Renaissance Italy, and that French art possessed the classical qualities of discipline, balance, and restraint. Louis XIV also loved the stage, and in the plays of Molière and Racine his court witnessed the finest achievements in the history of the French theater. In this period, aristocratic ladies wrote many genres of literature and held salons in their Parisian mansions where they engaged in witty and cultured discussions of poetry, art, theater, and the latest worldly events. Their refined conversational style led Molière and other observers to mock them as "*précieuses*" (PREH-see-ooz; literally "precious"), or affected and pretentious. Despite this mockery, the *précieuses* represented an important cultural force ruled by elite women.

With Versailles as the center of European politics, French culture grew in international prestige. French became the language of polite society and international diplomacy, gradually replacing Latin as the language of scholarship and learning. Royal courts across Europe spoke French, and the great aristocrats of Russia, Sweden, Germany, and elsewhere were often more fluent in French than in the tongues of their homelands. France inspired a cosmopolitan European culture in the late seventeenth century that looked to Versailles as its center.

French Financial Management Under Colbert

France's ability to build armies and fight wars depended on a strong economy. Fortunately for Louis, his controller general, Jean-Baptiste Colbert (1619–1683), proved to be a financial genius. Colbert's central principle was that the wealth and the economy of France should serve the state. To this end, from 1665 to his death in 1683, Colbert rigorously applied mercantilist policies to France.

Mercantilism is a collection of governmental policies for the regulation of economic activities by and for the state. It derives from the idea that a nation's international power is based on its wealth, specifically its supply of gold and silver. To accumulate wealth, a country always had to sell more goods abroad than it bought. To decrease the purchase of goods outside France, Colbert insisted that French industry should produce everything needed by the French people.

To increase exports, Colbert supported old industries and created new ones, focusing especially on textiles, which were the most important sector of the economy. Colbert enacted new production regulations, created guilds to boost quality standards, and encouraged foreign craftsmen to immigrate to France. To encourage the purchase of French goods, he abolished many domestic tariffs and raised tariffs on foreign products. In 1664 Colbert founded the Company of the East Indies with (unfulfilled) hopes of competing with the Dutch for Asian trade.

Colbert also hoped to make Canada — rich in untapped minerals and some of the best agricultural land in the world — part of a vast French empire. He sent four thousand colonists to Quebec, whose capital had been founded in 1608 under Henry IV.

Subsequently, the Jesuit Jacques Marquette and the merchant Louis Joliet sailed down the Mississippi River, which they named Colbert in honor of their sponsor (the name soon reverted to the original Native American one). Marquette and Joliet claimed possession of the land on both sides of the river as far south as present-day Arkansas. In 1684 French explorers continued down the Mississippi to its mouth and claimed vast territories for Louis XIV. The area was called, naturally, "Louisiana."

During Colbert's tenure as controller general, Louis was able to pursue his goals without massive tax increases and without creating a stream of new offices. The constant pressure of warfare after Colbert's death, however, undid many of his economic achievements.

Louis XIV's Wars

Louis XIV wrote that "the character of a conqueror is regarded as the noblest and highest of titles." In pursuit of the title of conqueror, he kept France at war for thirty-three of the fifty-four years of his personal rule. François le Tellier, marquis de Louvois, Louis's secretary of state for war, equaled Colbert's achievements in the economic realm. Louvois created a professional army in which the French state, rather than private nobles, employed the soldiers. Uniforms and weapons were standardized, and a rational system of training and promotion was devised. Many historians believe that the new loyalty, professionalism, and growth of the French army represented the peak of Louis's success in reforming government. As in so many other matters, his model was followed across Europe.

Louis's goal was to expand France to what he considered its natural borders. His armies managed to extend French borders to include important commercial centers in the Spanish Netherlands and Flanders as well as the entire province of Franche-Comté between 1667 and 1678. In 1681 Louis seized the city of Strasbourg, and three years later he sent his armies into the province of Lorraine. At that moment the king seemed invincible. In fact, Louis had reached the limit of his expansion. The wars of the 1680s and 1690s brought no additional territories but placed unbearable strains on French resources. Colbert's successors resorted to desperate measures to finance these wars, including devaluation of the currency and new taxes.

Louis's last war was endured by a French people suffering high taxes, crop failure, and widespread malnutrition and death. In 1700 the childless Spanish king Charles II (r. 1665–1700) died, opening a struggle for control of Spain and its colonies. His will bequeathed the Spanish crown and its empire to Philip of Anjou, Louis XIV's grandson (Louis's wife, Maria-Theresa, had been Charles's sister). The will violated a prior treaty by which the European powers had agreed to divide the Spanish possessions between the king of France and the Holy Roman emperor, both brothers-in-law of Charles II. Claiming that he was following both Spanish and French interests, Louis broke with the treaty and accepted the will, thereby triggering the War of the Spanish Succession (1701–1713).

In 1701 the English, Dutch, Austrians, and Prussians formed the Grand Alliance against Louis XIV. War dragged on until 1713. The **Peace of Utrecht**, which ended the war, allowed Louis's grandson Philip to remain king of Spain on the understanding that the French and Spanish crowns would never be united. France surrendered Newfoundland, Nova Scotia, and the Hudson Bay territory to England, which also acquired Gibraltar, Minorca, and control of the African slave trade from Spain (Map 15.1).

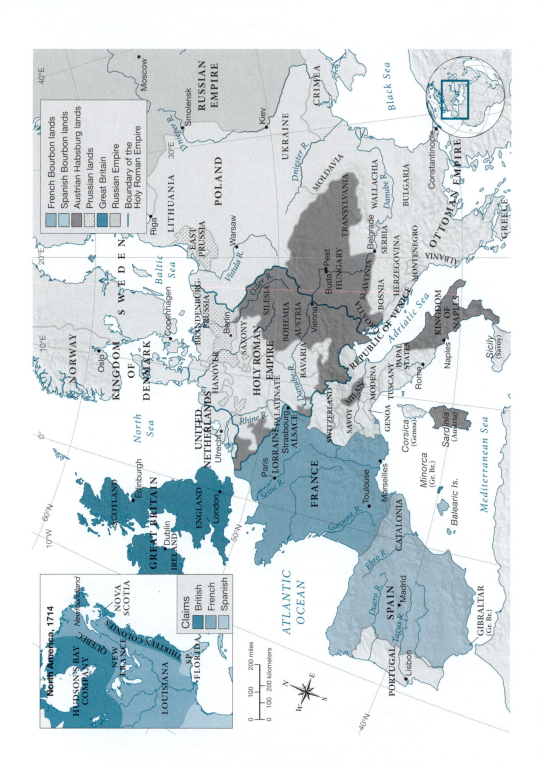

French Bourbon lands
Spanish Bourbon lands
Austrian Habsburg lands
Prussian lands
Great Britain
Russian Empire
Boundary of the Holy Roman Empire

North America, 1714

Claims
British
French
Spanish

◀ **MAP 15.1   Europe After the Peace of Utrecht, 1715**
The series of treaties commonly called the Peace of Utrecht ended the War of the Spanish Succession and redrew the map of Europe. A French Bourbon king succeeded to the Spanish throne. France surrendered the Spanish Netherlands (later Belgium), then in French hands, to Austria, and recognized the Hohenzollern rulers of Prussia. Spain ceded Gibraltar to Great Britain, for which it has been a strategic naval station ever since. Spain also granted Britain the *asiento*, the contract for supplying African slaves to the Americas.

The Peace of Utrecht represented the balance-of-power principle in operation, setting limits on the extent to which any one power — in this case, France — could expand. It also marked the end of French expansion. Thirty-five years of war had given France the rights to all of Alsace and some commercial centers in the north. But at what price? In 1714 an exhausted France hovered on the brink of bankruptcy. It is no wonder that when Louis XIV died on September 1, 1715, many subjects felt as much relief as they did sorrow.

The Decline of Absolutist Spain in the Seventeenth Century

At the beginning of the seventeenth century, France's position appeared extremely weak. Struggling to recover from decades of religious civil war that had destroyed its infrastructure and economy, France could not dare to compete with Spain's European and overseas empire or its mighty military. Yet by the end of the century their positions were reversed, and France had surpassed all expectations to attain European dominance.

By the early seventeenth century the seeds of Spanish disaster were sprouting. Between 1610 and 1650 Spanish trade with the colonies in the New World fell 60 percent due to competition from local industries in the colonies and from Dutch and English traders. At the same time, the native Indian and African slaves who toiled in the South American silver mines suffered frightful epidemics of disease. Ultimately, the mines that filled the empire's treasury started to run dry, and the quantity of metal produced steadily declined after 1620.

In Madrid, however, royal expenditures constantly exceeded income. To meet mountainous state debt, the Crown repeatedly devalued the coinage and declared bankruptcy, which resulted in the collapse of national credit. Meanwhile, manufacturing and commerce shrank. In contrast to the other countries of western Europe, Spain had a tiny middle class. The elite condemned moneymaking as vulgar and undignified. Thousands entered economically unproductive professions: there were said to be nine thousand monasteries in the province of Castile alone. To make matters worse, the Crown expelled some three hundred thousand *Moriscos*, or former Muslims, in 1609, significantly reducing the pool of skilled workers and merchants. Those working in the textile industry were forced out of business by steep inflation that pushed their production costs to the point where they could not compete in colonial and international markets.[6]

Spanish aristocrats, attempting to maintain an extravagant lifestyle they could no longer afford, increased the rents on their estates. High rents and heavy taxes in turn drove the peasants from the land, leading to a decline in agricultural productivity. In cities wages and production stagnated. Spain also ignored new scientific methods that might have improved agricultural or manufacturing techniques because they came from the heretical nations of Holland and England.

The Spanish crown had no solutions to these dire problems. Philip III (r. 1598–1621), a melancholy and deeply pious man, handed the running of the government over to the duke of Lerma, who used it to advance his personal and familial wealth. Philip IV (r. 1621–1665) left the management of his several kingdoms to Gaspar de Guzmán, Count-Duke of Olivares. Olivares was an able administrator who has often been compared to Richelieu. He did not lack energy and ideas, and he succeeded in devising new sources of revenue. But he clung to the grandiose belief that the solution to Spain's difficulties rested in a return to the imperial tradition of the sixteenth century. Unfortunately, the imperial tradition demanded the revival of war with the Dutch at the expiration of a twelve-year truce in 1622 and a long war with France over Mantua (1628–1659). Spain thus became embroiled in the Thirty Years' War. These conflicts, on top of an empty treasury, brought disaster.

Spain's situation worsened with internal conflicts and fresh military defeats through the remainder of the seventeenth century. In 1640 Spain faced serious revolts in Catalonia and Portugal. In 1643 the French inflicted a crushing defeat on a Spanish army at Rocroi in what is now Belgium. By the Treaty of the Pyrenees of 1659, which ended the French-Spanish conflict, Spain was compelled to surrender extensive territories to France. In 1688 the Spanish crown reluctantly recognized the independence of Portugal, almost a century after the two crowns were joined. The era of Spanish dominance in Europe had ended.

Absolutism in Austria and Prussia

What were the social conditions of eastern Europe, and how did the rulers of Austria and Prussia transform their nations into powerful absolutist monarchies?

The rulers of eastern Europe also labored to build strong absolutist states in the seventeenth century. But they built on social and economic foundations far different from those in western Europe, namely serfdom and the strong nobility who benefited from it. The endless wars of the seventeenth century allowed monarchs to increase their power by building large armies, increasing taxation, and suppressing representative institutions. In exchange for their growing political authority, monarchs allowed nobles to remain as unchallenged masters of their peasants, a deal that appeased both king and nobility, but left serfs at the mercy of the lords. The most successful states were Austria and Prussia, which witnessed the rise of absolutism between 1620 and 1740.

The Return of Serfdom in the East

While economic and social hardship was common across Europe, important differences existed between east and west. In the west the demographic losses of the Black Death allowed peasants to escape from serfdom as they acquired enough land to feed themselves. In eastern Europe seventeenth-century peasants had largely lost their ability to own land independently. Eastern lords dealt with the labor shortages caused by the Black Death by restricting the right of their peasants to move to take advantage of better opportunities elsewhere. In Prussian territories by 1500 the law required that runaway peasants be hunted down and returned to their lords. Moreover, lords steadily took more and more of their peasants' land and arbitrarily imposed heavier labor obligations. By the early 1500s lords in many eastern territories could command their peasants to work for them without pay for as many as six days a week.

The gradual erosion of the peasantry's economic position was bound up with manipulation of the legal system. The local lord was also the local prosecutor, judge, and jailer. There were no independent royal officials to provide justice or uphold the common law. The power of the lord reached far into serfs' everyday lives. Not only was their freedom of movement restricted, but they also required permission to marry or could be forced to marry. Lords could reallocate the lands worked by their serfs at will or sell serfs apart from their families. These conditions applied even on lands owned by the church.

Between 1500 and 1650 the consolidation of serfdom in eastern Europe was accompanied by the growth of commercial agriculture, particularly in Poland and eastern Germany. As economic expansion and population growth resumed after 1500, eastern lords increased the production of their estates by squeezing sizable surpluses out of the impoverished peasants. They then sold these surpluses to foreign merchants, who exported them to the growing cities of wealthier western Europe. The Netherlands and England benefited the most from inexpensive grain from the east.

It was not only the peasants who suffered in eastern Europe. With the approval of kings, landlords systematically undermined the medieval privileges of the towns and the power of the urban classes. Instead of selling products to local merchants, landlords sold directly to foreigners, bypassing local towns. Eastern towns also lost their medieval right of refuge and were compelled to return runaways to their lords. The population of the towns and the urban middle classes declined greatly. This development both reflected and promoted the supremacy of noble landlords in most of eastern Europe in the sixteenth century.

The Austrian Habsburgs

Like all of central Europe, the Habsburgs emerged from the Thirty Years' War impoverished and exhausted. Their efforts to destroy Protestantism in the German lands and to turn the weak Holy Roman Empire into a real state had failed. Although the Habsburgs remained the hereditary emperors, real power lay in the hands of a bewildering variety of separate political jurisdictions. Defeat in central Europe encouraged the Habsburgs to turn away from a quest for imperial dominance and to focus inward and eastward in an attempt to unify their diverse holdings. If they could not impose Catholicism in the empire, at least they could do so in their own domains.

Habsburg victory over Bohemia during the Thirty Years' War was an important step in this direction. Ferdinand II (r. 1619–1637) drastically reduced the power of the Bohemian Estates, the largely Protestant representative assembly. He also confiscated the landholdings of Protestant nobles and gave them to loyal Catholic nobles and to the foreign aristocratic mercenaries who led his armies. After 1650 a large portion of the Bohemian nobility was of recent origin and owed its success to the Habsburgs.

With the support of this new nobility, the Habsburgs established direct rule over Bohemia. Under their rule the condition of the enserfed peasantry worsened substantially: three days per week of unpaid labor became the norm. Protestantism was also stamped out. These changes were important steps in creating absolutist rule in Bohemia.

Ferdinand III (r. 1637–1657) continued to build state power. He centralized the government in the empire's German-speaking provinces, which formed the core Habsburg holdings. For the first time, a permanent standing army was ready to put down any internal opposition. The Habsburg monarchy then turned east toward the plains of Hungary, which had been divided between the Ottomans and the Habsburgs in the early sixteenth century. Between 1683 and 1699 the Habsburgs pushed the Ottomans from most of Hungary and Transylvania. The recovery of all the former kingdom of Hungary was completed in 1718.

The Hungarian nobility, despite its reduced strength, effectively thwarted the full development of Habsburg absolutism. Throughout the seventeenth century Hungarian nobles rose in revolt against attempts to impose absolute rule. They never triumphed decisively, but neither were they crushed the way the nobility in Bohemia had been in 1620. In 1703, with the Habsburgs bogged down in the War of the Spanish Succession, the Hungarians rose in one last patriotic rebellion under Prince Francis Rákóczy. The prince and his forces were eventually defeated, but the Habsburgs agreed to restore many of the traditional privileges of the aristocracy in return for Hungarian acceptance of hereditary Habsburg rule. Thus Hungary, unlike Austria and Bohemia, was never fully integrated into a centralized, absolute Habsburg state.

Despite checks on their ambitions in Hungary, the Habsburgs made significant achievements in state-building elsewhere by forging consensus with the church and the nobility. A sense of common identity and loyalty to the monarchy grew among elites in Habsburg lands, even to a certain extent in Hungary. German became the language of the state, and zealous Catholicism helped fuse a collective identity.

Vienna became the political and cultural center of the empire. By 1700 it was a thriving city with a population of one hundred thousand and its own version of Versailles, the royal palace of Schönbrunn.

Prussia in the Seventeenth Century

In the fifteenth and sixteenth centuries, the Hohenzollern family had ruled parts of eastern Germany as the imperial electors of Brandenburg and the dukes of Prussia. The title of "elector" gave its holder the privilege of being one of only seven princes or archbishops entitled to elect the Holy Roman emperor, but the electors had little real power. When he came to power in 1640, the twenty-year-old Frederick William, later known as the "Great Elector," was determined to unify his three provinces and enlarge his holdings. These provinces were Brandenburg; Prussia, inherited in 1618; and scattered territories along the Rhine inherited in 1614 (Map 15.2). Each was inhabited by German-speakers, but each had its own estates. Although the estates had not met regularly during the chaotic Thirty Years' War, taxes could not be levied without their consent. The estates of Brandenburg and Prussia were dominated by the nobility and the landowning classes, known as the **Junkers**.

Frederick William profited from ongoing European war and the threat of invasion from Russia when he argued for the need for a permanent standing army. In 1660 he persuaded Junkers in the estates to accept taxation without consent in order to fund an army. They agreed to do so in exchange for reconfirmation of their own privileges, including authority over the serfs. Having won over the Junkers, the king crushed poten-

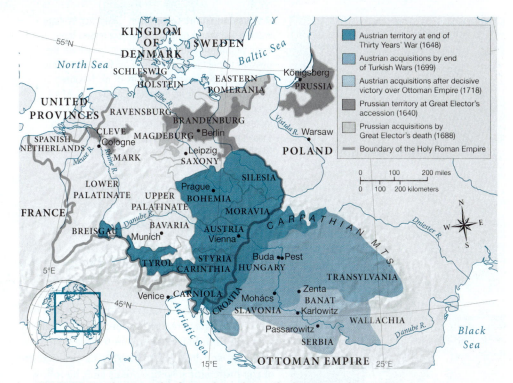

MAP 15.2   The Growth of Austria and Brandenburg-Prussia to 1748
Austria expanded to the southwest into Hungary and Transylvania at the expense of the Ottoman Empire. It was unable to hold the rich German province of Silesia, however, which was conquered by Brandenburg-Prussia.

tial opposition to his power from the towns. One by one, Prussian cities were eliminated from the estates and subjected to new taxes on goods and services.

Thereafter, the estates' power declined rapidly, for the Great Elector had both financial independence and superior force. He revealed his strategy toward managing the estates in the written instructions he left his son:

> Always regulate the expenditures according to the revenues, and have officials diligently render receipts every year. When the finances are in a good state again, then you will have enough means, and you will not have to request money from the estates or address them. Then it is also not necessary to hold the many and expensive parliaments, because the more parliaments you hold, the more authority is taken from you, because the estates always try something that is detrimental to the majesty of the ruler.[7]

By following his own sage advice, Frederick William tripled state revenue during his reign and expanded the army drastically. In 1688 a population of 1 million supported a peacetime standing army of 30,000. In 1701 the elector's son, Frederick I, received the elevated title of king of Prussia (instead of elector) as a reward for aiding the Holy Roman emperor in the War of the Spanish Succession.

A Prussian Giant Grenadier   Frederick William I wanted tall, handsome soldiers. He dressed them in tight, bright uniforms to distinguish them from the peasant population from which most soldiers came. He also ordered several portraits of his favorites, such as this one, from his court painter, J. C. Merk. Grenadiers (greh-nuh-DEERZ) wore the miter cap instead of an ordinary hat so that they could hurl their heavy grenades unimpeded by a broad brim. (The Royal Collection © 2013, Her Majesty Queen Elizabeth II)

The Consolidation of Prussian Absolutism

Frederick William I, "the Soldiers' King" (r. 1713–1740), completed his grandfather's work, eliminating the last traces of parliamentary estates and local self-government. It was he who truly established Prussian absolutism and transformed Prussia into a military state. Frederick William was intensely attached to military life. He always wore an army uniform, and he lived the highly disciplined life of the professional soldier. Years later he followed the family tradition by leaving his own written instructions to his son: "A formidable army and a war chest large enough to make this army mobile in times of need can create great respect for you in the world, so that you can speak a word like the other powers."[8]

Penny-pinching and hard-working, Frederick William achieved results. The king and his ministers built an exceptionally honest and conscientious bureaucracy to administer the country and foster economic development. Twelfth in Europe in population, Prussia had the fourth-largest army by 1740. The Prussian army was the best in Europe, astonishing foreign observers with its precision, skill, and discipline. As one Western traveler put it: "There is no theatre in Berlin whatsoever, diversion is understood to be the handsome troops who parade daily. A special attraction is the great Potsdam Grenadier Regiment . . . when they practice drill, when they fire and when they parade up and down, it is as if they form a single body."[9]

Nevertheless, Prussians paid a heavy and lasting price for the obsessions of their royal drillmaster. Army expansion was achieved in part through forced conscription, which was declared lifelong in 1713. Desperate draftees fled the country or injured themselves to avoid service. Finally, in 1733 Frederick William I ordered that all Prussian men would undergo military training and serve as reservists in the army, allowing him to preserve both agricultural production and army size. To appease the Junkers, the king enlisted them to lead his growing army. The proud nobility thus commanded the peasantry in the army as well as on the estates.

With all men harnessed to the war machine, Prussian civil society became rigid and highly disciplined. As a Prussian minister later summed up, "To keep quiet is the first civic duty."[10] Thus the policies of Frederick William I, combined with harsh peasant bondage and Junker tyranny, laid the foundations for a highly militaristic country.

The Development of Russia and the Ottoman Empire

What were the distinctive features of Russian and Ottoman absolutism?

A favorite parlor game of nineteenth-century intellectuals was debating whether Russia was a Western (European) or non-Western (Asian) society. This question was particularly fascinating because it was unanswerable. To this day, Russia differs from the West in some fundamental ways, though its history has paralleled that of the West in other aspects.

There was no question in the minds of Europeans, however, that the Ottomans were outsiders. Even absolutist rulers disdained Ottoman sultans as cruel and tyrannical despots. Despite stereotypes, however, the Ottoman Empire was in many ways more tolerant than its Western counterparts, providing protection and security to other religions while steadfastly maintaining the Muslim faith. The Ottoman state combined the Byzantine heritage of the territory it had conquered with Persian and Arab traditions. Flexibility and openness to other ideas and practices were sources of strength for the empire.

The Mongol Yoke and the Rise of Moscow

The two-hundred-year period of rule by the Mongol khan (king) set the stage for the rise of absolutist Russia. The Mongols, a group of nomadic tribes from present-day Mongolia, established an empire that, at its height, stretched from Korea to eastern Europe. In the thirteenth century the Mongols conquered the Slavic princes and forced them to render payments of goods, money, and slaves. The princes of Moscow became particularly adept at serving the Mongols and were awarded the title of "great prince." Ivan III (r. 1462–1505), known as Ivan the Great, successfully expanded the principality of Moscow toward the Baltic Sea.

By 1480 Ivan III was strong enough to defy Mongol control and declare the autonomy of Moscow. To legitimize their new position, the princes of Moscow modeled themselves on the Mongol khans. Like the khans, the Muscovite state forced weaker Slavic principalities to render tribute previously paid to Mongols and borrowed Mongol institutions such as the tax system, postal routes, and census. Loyalty from the highest-ranking nobles, or **boyars**, helped the Muscovite princes consolidate their power.

Another source of legitimacy for Moscow was its claim to the political and religious legacy of the Byzantine Empire. After the fall of Constantinople to the Turks in 1453, the princes of Moscow saw themselves as the heirs of both the caesars (or emperors) and Orthodox Christianity. The title "tsar," first taken by Ivan IV in 1547, is in fact a contraction of *caesar*. The tsars considered themselves rightful and holy rulers, an idea promoted by Orthodox churchmen who spoke of "holy Russia" as the "Third Rome." The marriage of Ivan III to the daughter of the last Byzantine emperor further enhanced Moscow's assertion of imperial authority.

The Tsar and His People

Developments in Russia took a chaotic turn with the reign of Ivan IV (r. 1533–1584), the famous "Ivan the Terrible," who ascended to the throne at age three. At age sixteen he pushed aside his advisers and in an awe-inspiring ceremony, complete with gold coins pouring down on his head, Ivan majestically crowned himself tsar.

Ivan's reign was successful in defeating the remnants of Mongol power, adding vast new territories to the realm, and laying the foundations for the huge, multiethnic Russian empire. After the sudden death of his wife, however, Ivan began a campaign of persecution against those he suspected of opposing him. He executed members of leading boyar families, along with their families, friends, servants, and peasants. To replace them, Ivan created a new service nobility, whose loyalty was guaranteed by their dependence on the state for land and titles.

As landlords demanded more from the serfs who survived the persecutions, growing numbers of peasants fled toward wild, recently conquered territories to the east and south. There they joined free groups and warrior bands known as **Cossacks**. Ivan responded by tying peasants ever more firmly to the land and to noble landholders. Simultaneously, he ordered that urban dwellers be bound to their towns and jobs so that he could tax them more heavily. The urban classes had no security in their property, and even the wealthiest merchants were dependent agents of the tsar. These restrictions checked the growth of the Russian middle classes and stood in sharp contrast to economic and social developments in western Europe.

After the death of Ivan and his successor, Russia entered a chaotic period known as the "Time of Troubles" (1598–1613). While Ivan's relatives struggled for power, ordinary people suffered drought, crop failure, and plague. The Cossacks and peasants rebelled against nobles and officials, demanding fairer treatment. This social explosion from below brought the nobles, big and small, together. They crushed the Cossack rebellion and brought Ivan's sixteen-year-old grandnephew, Michael Romanov, to the throne (r. 1613–1645).

Although the new tsar successfully reconsolidated central authority, he and his successors did not improve the lot of the common people. In 1649 a law extended serfdom to all peasants in the realm, giving lords unrestricted rights over their serfs and establishing penalties for harboring runaways. Social and religious uprisings among the poor and oppressed continued through the seventeenth century. One of the largest rebellions was led by the Cossack Stenka Razin, who in 1670 attracted a great army of urban poor and peasants. He and his followers killed landlords and government officials and proclaimed freedom from oppression, but their rebellion was defeated in 1671.

Despite the turbulence of the period, the Romanov tsars, like their Western counterparts, made several important achievements during the second half of the seventeenth century. After a long war, Russia gained land in Ukraine from Poland in 1667 and completed the conquest of Siberia by the end of the century. Territorial expansion was accompanied by growth of the bureaucracy and the army. The tsars employed foreign experts to reform the Russian army, and enlisted Cossack warriors to fight Siberian campaigns. The great profits from Siberia's natural resources, especially furs, funded the Romanovs' bid for Great Power status. Russian imperialist expansion to the east paralleled the Western powers' exploration and conquest of the Atlantic world in the same period.

The Reforms of Peter the Great

Heir to Romanov efforts at state-building, Peter the Great (r. 1682–1725) embarked on a tremendous campaign to accelerate and complete these processes. A giant for his time at six feet seven inches, and possessing enormous energy and willpower, Peter was determined to build the army and to continue Russian territorial expansion. Fascinated by weapons and foreign technology and eager to gain support against the powerful Ottoman Empire, the tsar led a group of 250 Russian officials and young nobles on an eighteen-month tour of western European capitals. Traveling unofficially to avoid lengthy diplomatic ceremonies, Peter met with foreign kings, toured the sites, and learned shipbuilding and other technical skills from local artisans and experts. He was particularly impressed with the growing economic power of the Dutch and the English, and he considered how Russia could profit from their example.

Returning to Russia, Peter entered into a secret alliance with Denmark and Poland to wage a sudden war of aggression against Sweden with the goal of securing access to the Baltic Sea and opportunities for westward expansion. Peter and his allies believed that their combined forces could win easy victories because Sweden was in the hands of a new and inexperienced king.

Eighteen-year-old Charles XII of Sweden (1697–1718) surprised Peter. He defeated Denmark quickly in 1700, then turned on Russia. In a blinding snowstorm, his well-trained professional army attacked and routed unsuspecting Russians besieging the Swedish fortress of Narva on the Baltic coast. It was, for the Russians, a grim beginning to the long and brutal Great Northern War, which lasted from 1700 to 1721.

Peter responded to this defeat with measures designed to increase state power, strengthen his armies, and gain victory. He required all nobles to serve in the army or in the civil administration—for life. Since a more modern army and government required skilled experts, Peter created new schools and universities and required every young nobleman to spend five years in education away from home. Peter established an interlocking military-civilian bureaucracy with fourteen ranks, and he decreed that all had

Peter the Great This compelling portrait by Grigory Musikiysky captures the strength and determination of the warrior-tsar in 1723, after more than three decades of personal rule. In his hand Peter holds the scepter, symbol of royal sovereignty, and across his breastplate is draped an ermine fur, a mark of honor. In the background are the battleships of Russia's new Baltic fleet and the famous St. Peter and St. Paul Fortress that Peter built in St. Petersburg. (Hermitage/St. Petersburg, Russia/The Bridgeman Art Library)

to start at the bottom and work toward the top. The system allowed some people of non-noble origins to rise to high positions, a rarity in Europe at the time. Drawing on his experience abroad, Peter sought talented foreigners and placed them in his service. These measures gradually combined to make the army and government more powerful and efficient.

Peter also greatly increased the service requirements of commoners. In the wake of the Narva disaster, he established a regular standing army of more than two hundred thousand peasant-soldiers, drafted for life and commanded by noble officers. He added an additional hundred thousand men in special regiments of Cossacks and foreign mercenaries. To fund the army, taxes on peasants increased threefold during Peter's reign. Serfs were also arbitrarily assigned to work in the growing number of factories and mines that supplied the military.

Peter's new war machine was able to crush the small army of Sweden in Ukraine at Poltava in 1709, one of the most significant battles in Russian history. Russia's victory against Sweden was conclusive in 1721, and Estonia and present-day Latvia came under Russian rule for the first time. After his victory at Poltava, Peter channeled enormous resources into building a new Western-style capital on the Baltic to rival the great cities of Europe. Originally a desolate and swampy Swedish outpost, the magnificent city of St. Petersburg was designed to reflect modern urban planning, with wide, straight avenues, buildings set in a uniform line, and large parks.

The government drafted twenty-five thousand to forty thousand men each summer to labor in St. Petersburg, many of whom died from hunger, sickness, and accidents. Nobles were ordered to build costly palaces in St. Petersburg and to live in them most of the year. Merchants and artisans were required to settle and build in the new capital. The building of St. Petersburg was, in truth, an enormous direct tax levied on the wealthy, with the peasantry forced to do the manual labor.

There were other important consequences of Peter's reign. For Peter, modernization meant westernization, and both Westerners and Western ideas flowed into Russia for the first time. He required nobles to shave their heavy beards and wear Western clothing, previously banned in Russia. He also ordered them to attend parties where young men and women would mix together and freely choose their own spouses. From these efforts a new elite class of Western-oriented Russians began to emerge.

Peter's reforms were unpopular with many Russians. For nobles, one of Peter's most detested reforms was the imposition of unigeniture — inheritance of land by one son alone — cutting daughters and other sons from family property. For peasants, the reign of the tsar saw a significant increase in the bonds of serfdom, and the gulf between the enserfed peasantry and the educated nobility increased. Despite the unpopularity of Peter's reforms, his modernizing and westernizing of Russia paved the way for it to move somewhat closer to the European mainstream in its thought and institutions during the Enlightenment, especially under Catherine the Great.

The Growth of the Ottoman Empire

Most Christian Europeans perceived the Ottomans as the antithesis of their own values and traditions and viewed the empire as driven by an insatiable lust for warfare and conquest. In their view the fall of Constantinople was a historic catastrophe and the taking of the Balkans a form of despotic imprisonment. To Ottoman eyes, the world

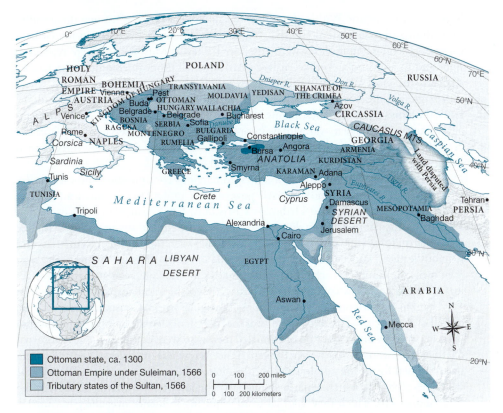

MAP 15.3   The Ottoman Empire at Its Height, 1566
The Ottomans, like their great rivals the Habsburgs, rose to rule a vast dynastic empire encompassing many different peoples and ethnic groups. The army and the bureaucracy served to unite the disparate territories into a single state under an absolutist ruler.

looked very different. The siege of Constantinople liberated a glorious city from its long decline under the Byzantines. Rather than being a despoiled captive, the Balkans became a haven for refugees fleeing the growing intolerance of Western Christian powers. The Ottoman Empire provided Jews, Muslims, and even some Christians safety from the Inquisition and religious war.

The Ottomans came out of Central Asia as conquering warriors, settled in Anatolia (present-day Turkey), and, at their peak in the mid-sixteenth century, ruled one of the most powerful empires in the world (see Chapter 14). Their possessions stretched from western Persia across North Africa and into the heart of central Europe (Map 15.3).

The Ottoman Empire was built on a unique model of state and society. Agricultural land was the personal hereditary property of the **sultan**, and peasants paid taxes to use the land. There was therefore an almost complete absence of private landed property and no hereditary nobility.

The Ottomans also employed a distinctive form of government administration. The top ranks of the bureaucracy were staffed by the sultan's slave corps. Because Muslim law prohibited enslaving other Muslims, the sultan's agents purchased slaves along the borders of the empire. Within the realm, the sultan levied a "tax" of one thousand to three thousand male children on the conquered Christian populations in the Balkans every year. These young slaves were raised in Turkey as Muslims and were trained to fight and to administer. Unlike enslaved Africans in European colonies, who faced a dire fate, the most talented Ottoman slaves rose to the top of the bureaucracy, where they might acquire wealth and power. The less fortunate formed the core of the sultan's army, the **janissary corps**. These highly organized and efficient troops gave the Ottomans a formidable advantage in war with western Europeans. By 1683 service in the janissary corps had become so prestigious that the sultan ceased recruitment by force, and it became a volunteer army open to Christians and Muslims.

The Ottomans divided their subjects into religious communities, and each *millet*, or "nation," enjoyed autonomous self-government under its religious leaders. The Ottoman Empire recognized Orthodox Christians, Jews, Armenian Christians, and Muslims as distinct millets, but despite its tolerance, the empire was an explicitly Islamic state. The **millet system** created a powerful bond between the Ottoman ruling class and religious leaders, who supported the sultan's rule in return for extensive authority over their own communities. Each millet collected taxes for the state, regulated group behavior, and maintained law courts, schools, houses of worship, and hospitals for its people.

Istanbul (known outside the empire by its original name, Constantinople) was the capital of the empire. The "old palace" was for the sultan's female family members, who lived in isolation under the care of eunuchs, men who were castrated to prevent sexual relations with women. The newer Topkapi palace was where officials worked and young slaves trained for future administrative or military careers. Sultans married women of the highest social standing, while keeping many concubines of low rank. To prevent the elite families into which they married from acquiring influence over the government, sultans procreated only with their concubines and not with official wives. They also adopted a policy of allowing each concubine to produce only one male heir. At a young age, each son went to govern a province of the empire accompanied by his mother. These practices were intended to stabilize power and prevent a recurrence of the civil wars of the late fourteenth and early fifteenth centuries.

Sultan Suleiman undid these policies when he boldly married his concubine, a former slave of Polish origin named Hürrem, and had several children with her. (See "Individuals in Society: Hürrem," page 504.) Starting with Suleiman, imperial wives began to take on more power. Marriages were arranged between sultans' daughters and high-ranking servants, creating powerful new members of the imperial household. Over time, the sultan's exclusive authority waned in favor of a more bureaucratic administration.

Alternatives to Absolutism in England and the Dutch Republic

How and why did the constitutional state triumph in the Dutch Republic and England?

While France, Prussia, Russia, and Austria developed the absolutist state, England and the Netherlands evolved toward **constitutionalism**, which is the limitation of government by law. Constitutionalism also implies a balance between the authority and power of the government, on the one hand, and the rights and liberties of the subjects, on the other. By definition, all constitutionalist governments have a constitution, be it written or unwritten. A nation's constitution may be embodied in one basic document and occasionally revised by amendment, like the Constitution of the United States. Or it may be only partly formalized and include parliamentary statutes, judicial decisions, and a body of traditional procedures and practices, like the English and Dutch constitutions.

Despite their common commitment to constitutional government, England and the Dutch Republic represented significantly different alternatives to absolute rule. After decades of civil war and an experiment with **republicanism**, the English opted for a constitutional monarchy in 1688. This settlement, which has endured to this day, retained a monarch as the titular head of government but vested sovereignty in an elected parliament. Upon gaining independence from Spain in 1648, the Dutch rejected monarchical rule, adopting a republican form of government in which elected estates held supreme power. Neither was democratic by any standard, but to other Europeans they were shining examples of the restraint of arbitrary power and the rule of law.

Absolutist Claims in England

In 1588 Queen Elizabeth I of England (r. 1558–1603) exercised very great personal power; by 1689 the English monarchy was severely circumscribed. A rare female monarch, Elizabeth was able to maintain control over her realm in part by refusing to marry and submit to a husband. She was immensely popular with her people, but left no immediate heir to continue her legacy.

In 1603 Elizabeth's Scottish cousin James Stuart succeeded her as James I (r. 1603–1625). King James was well educated and had thirty-five years' experience as king of Scotland. But he was not as interested in displaying the majesty of monarchy as Elizabeth had been. Urged to wave at the crowds who waited to greet their new ruler, James complained that he was tired and threatened to drop his breeches "so they can cheer at my arse."[11]

James's greatest problem, however, stemmed from his absolutist belief that a monarch has a divine right to his authority and is responsible only to God. James went so far as to lecture the House of Commons: "There are no privileges and immunities which can stand against a divinely appointed King." Such a view ran directly counter to English traditions that a person's property could not be taken away without due process of law. James I and his son Charles I (r. 1625–1649) considered such constraints intolerable and a threat to their divine-right prerogative. Consequently, bitter squabbles erupted between the Crown and the House of Commons. The expenses of England's intervention in the Thirty Years' War, through hostilities with Spain (1625–1630) and France (1627–1629), only exacerbated tensions. Charles I's response was to refuse to summon Parliament from 1629 onward.

Religious Divides and the English Civil War

Relations between the king and the House of Commons were also embittered by religious issues. In the early seventeenth century growing numbers of English people felt dissatisfied with the Church of England established by Henry VIII (r. 1509–1547). Many **Puritans** believed that the Protestant Reformation of the sixteenth century had not gone

INDIVIDUALS IN SOCIETY • Hürrem

In Muslim culture, *harem* means a sacred place or a sanctuary. The term was applied to the part of the household occupied by women and children and forbidden to men outside the family. The most famous harem member in the history of Ottoman sultans was Hürrem, wife of Suleiman the Magnificent.

Like many of the sultan's concubines, Hürrem (1505?–1558) was of foreign birth. Tradition holds that she was born Aleksandra Lisowska in the kingdom of Poland (present-day Ukraine). Captured during a Tartar raid and enslaved, she entered the imperial harem between 1517 and 1520, when she was about fifteen years old. Reports from Venetian visitors claimed that she was not outstandingly beautiful, but was possessed of wonderful grace, charm, and good humor, earning her the Turkish nickname Hürrem, or "joyful one." Soon after her arrival, Hürrem became the imperial favorite.

Suleiman's love for Hürrem led him to set aside all precedents for the role of a concubine, including the rule that concubines must cease having children once they gave birth to a male heir. By 1531 Hürrem had given Suleiman one daughter and five sons. In 1533 or 1534 Suleiman entered formal marriage with his consort—an unprecedented and scandalous honor for a concubine. Suleiman reportedly lavished attention on his wife and defied convention by allowing her to remain in the palace throughout her life instead of accompanying her son to a provincial governorship.

Contemporaries were shocked by Hürrem's influence over the sultan and resentful of the apparent role she played in politics and diplomacy. The Venetian ambassador Bassano wrote that "the Janissaries and the entire court hate her and her children likewise, but because the Sultan loves her, no one dares to speak."* Court rumors circulated that Hürrem used witchcraft to control the sultan and ordered the sultan's execution of his first-born son by another mother.

The correspondence between Suleiman and Hürrem, unavailable until the nineteenth century, along with Suleiman's own diaries, confirms her status as the sultan's most trusted confidant and adviser. During his frequent absences, the pair exchanged passionate love letters. Hürrem included political information and warned of potential uprisings. She also intervened in affairs between the empire and her former home, apparently helping Poland attain its privileged diplomatic status. She brought a feminine touch to diplomatic relations, sending personally embroidered articles to foreign leaders.

*Quoted in Galina Yermolenko, "Roxolana: The Greatest Empress of the East," *The Muslim World* 95 (2005): 235.

---

far enough. They wanted to "purify" the Anglican Church of lingering Roman Catholic elements—elaborate vestments and ceremonials, bishops, and even the giving and wearing of wedding rings.

James I responded to such ideas by declaring, "No bishop, no king." For James, bishops were among the chief supporters of the throne. His son and successor, Charles I, further antagonized religious sentiments. Not only did he marry a Catholic princess, but he also supported the heavy-handed policies of the archbishop of Canterbury William Laud (1573–1645). In 1637 Laud attempted to impose two new elements on church

Hürrem used her enormous pension to contribute a mosque, two schools, a hospital, a fountain, and two public baths to Istanbul. In Jerusalem, Mecca, and Istanbul, she provided soup kitchens and hospices for pilgrims and the poor. She died in 1558, eight years before her husband. Her son Selim II (r. 1566–1574) inherited the throne.

Relying on Western observers' reports, historians traditionally depicted Hürrem as a manipulative and power-hungry social climber. They portrayed her career as the beginning of a "sultanate of women" in which strong imperial leadership gave way to court intrigue and debauchery. More recent historians have emphasized the intelligence and courage Hürrem demonstrated in navigating the ruthlessly competitive world of the harem.

Hürrem's journey from Ukrainian maiden to concubine to sultan's wife captured enormous public attention. She is the subject of numerous paintings, plays, and novels, as well as an opera, a ballet, and a symphony by the composer Haydn. Interest in and suspicion of Hürrem continues. In 2003 a Turkish miniseries once more depicted her as a scheming intriguer.

QUESTIONS FOR ANALYSIS

1. What types of power did Hürrem exercise during her lifetime? How did her gender enable her to attain certain kinds of power and also constrain her ability to exercise it?

2. What can an exceptional woman like Hürrem reveal about the broader political and social world in which she lived?

Source: Leslie P. Pierce, *The Imperial Harem: Women and Sovereignty in the Ottoman Empire* (New York: Oxford University Press, 1993).

ONLINE DOCUMENT ASSIGNMENT

What forces shaped Western views of Hürrem? Examine characterizations of Hürrem as seen through the eyes of a Habsburg diplomat, and then complete a writing assignment based on the evidence and details from this chapter.

bedfordstmartins.com/mckaywestvalue

organization in Scotland: a new prayer book, modeled on the Anglican *Book of Common Prayer*, and bishoprics. The Presbyterian Scots rejected these elements and revolted. To finance an army to put down the Scots, King Charles was compelled to call a meeting of Parliament in November 1640.

Charles had ruled from 1629 to 1640 without Parliament, financing his government through extraordinary stopgap levies considered illegal by most English people. For example, the king revived a medieval law requiring coastal districts to help pay the cost of ships for defense, but he levied the tax, called "ship money," on inland as well as coastal counties. Most members of Parliament were not willing to trust such a despotic king with an army. Moreover, many supported the Scots' resistance to Charles's religious innovations. Accordingly, this Parliament, called the "Long Parliament" because it sat from 1640 to 1660, enacted legislation that limited the power of the monarch and made government without Parliament impossible.

In 1641 the Commons passed the Triennial Act, which compelled the king to summon Parliament every three years. The Commons impeached Archbishop Laud and then threatened to abolish bishops. King Charles, fearful of a Scottish invasion — the original reason for summoning Parliament — reluctantly accepted these measures.

The next act in the conflict was precipitated by the outbreak of rebellion in Ireland, where English governors and landlords had long exploited the people. In 1641 the Catholic gentry of Ireland led an uprising in response to a feared invasion by anti-Catholic forces of the British Long Parliament.

Without an army, Charles I could neither come to terms with the Scots nor respond to the Irish rebellion. After a failed attempt to arrest parliamentary leaders, Charles left London for the north of England. There, he recruited an army drawn from the nobility and its cavalry staff, the rural gentry, and mercenaries. In response, Parliament formed its own army, the New Model Army, composed of the militia of the city of London and country squires with business connections. During the spring of 1642 both sides prepared for war. In July a linen weaver became the first casualty of the civil war during a skirmish between royal and parliamentary forces in Manchester.

The English civil war (1642–1649) pitted the power of the king against that of the Parliament. After three years of fighting, Parliament's New Model Army defeated the king's armies at the Battles of Naseby and Langport in the summer of 1645. Charles, though, refused to concede defeat. Both sides jockeyed for position, waiting for a decisive event. This arrived in the form of the army under the leadership of Oliver Cromwell, a member of the House of Commons and a devout Puritan. In 1647 Cromwell's forces captured the king and dismissed anti-Cromwell members of the Parliament. In 1649 the remaining representatives, known as the "Rump Parliament," put Charles on trial for high treason. Charles was found guilty and beheaded on January 30, 1649, an act that sent shock waves around Europe.

Cromwell and Puritanical Absolutism in England

With the execution of Charles, kingship was abolished. The question remained of how the country would be governed. One answer was provided by philosopher Thomas Hobbes (1588–1679). Hobbes held a pessimistic view of human nature and believed that, left to themselves, humans would compete violently for power and wealth. The only solution, as he outlined in his 1651 treatise *Leviathan*, was a social contract in which all members of society placed themselves under the absolute rule of the sovereign, who would maintain peace and order. Hobbes imagined society as a human body in which the monarch served as head and individual subjects together made up the body. Just as the body cannot sever its own head, so Hobbes believed that society could not, having accepted the contract, rise up against its king.

Hobbes's longing for a benevolent absolute monarch was not widely shared in England. Instead, Oliver Cromwell and his supporters enshrined a commonwealth, or republican government, known as the **Protectorate**. Theoretically, legislative power rested in the surviving members of Parliament, and executive power was lodged in a council of state. In fact, the army controlled the government, and Oliver Cromwell controlled the army, ruling what was essentially a military dictatorship.

The army prepared a constitution, the Instrument of Government (1653), that invested executive power in a lord protector (Cromwell) and a council of state. It provided for triennial parliaments and gave Parliament the sole power to raise taxes. But after repeated disputes, Cromwell dismissed Parliament in 1655, and the instrument was never formally endorsed. Cromwell continued the standing army and proclaimed quasi-martial law. He divided England into twelve military districts, each governed by a major general. Reflecting Puritan ideas of morality, Cromwell's state forbade sports, closed the theaters, and rigorously censored the press.

On the issue of religion, Cromwell favored some degree of toleration, and the Instrument of Government gave all Christians except Roman Catholics the right to practice their faith. Cromwell had long associated Catholicism in Ireland with sedition and heresy, and led an army there to reconquer the country in August 1649. One month later, his forces crushed a rebellion at Drogheda and massacred the garrison. After Cromwell's departure for England, atrocities worsened. The English banned Catholicism in Ireland, executed priests, and confiscated land from Catholics for English and Scottish settlers. These brutal acts left a legacy of Irish hatred for England.

Cromwell adopted mercantilist policies similar to those of absolutist France. He enforced a Navigation Act (1651) requiring that English goods be transported on English ships. The act was a great boost to the development of an English merchant marine and brought about a short but successful war with the commercially threatened Dutch. While mercantilist legislation ultimately benefited English commerce, for ordinary people the turmoil of foreign war only added to the harsh conditions of life induced by years of civil war. Cromwell also welcomed the immigration of Jews because of their skills in business, and they began to return to England after four centuries of absence.

The Protectorate collapsed when Cromwell died in 1658 and his ineffectual son succeeded him. Fed up with military rule, the English longed for a return to civilian government and, with it, common law and social stability. By 1660 they were ready to restore the monarchy.

The Restoration of the English Monarchy

The Restoration of 1660 brought to the throne Charles II (r. 1660–1685), eldest son of Charles I, who had been living on the continent. Both houses of Parliament were also restored, together with the established Anglican Church. The Restoration failed to resolve two serious problems, however. What was to be the attitude of the state toward Puritans, Catholics, and dissenters from the established church? And what was to be the relationship between the king and Parliament?

To answer the first question, Parliament enacted the **Test Act** of 1673 against those outside the Church of England, denying them the right to vote, hold public office, preach, teach, attend the universities, or even assemble for meetings. But these restrictions could not be enforced. When the Quaker William Penn held a meeting of his Friends and was arrested, the jury refused to convict him.

In politics, Charles II's initial determination to work well with Parliament did not last long. Finding that Parliament did not grant him an adequate income, in 1670 Charles entered into a secret agreement with his cousin Louis XIV. The French king would give Charles £200,000 annually, and in return Charles would relax the laws against Catholics, gradually re-Catholicize England, and convert to Catholicism himself. When the details of this treaty leaked out, a great wave of anti-Catholic sentiment swept England.

When Charles died and his Catholic brother James became king, the worst English anti-Catholic fears were realized. In violation of the Test Act, James II (r. 1685–1688) appointed Roman Catholics to positions in the army, the universities, and local government. When these actions were challenged in the courts, the judges, whom James had appointed, decided in favor of the king. James and his supporters opened new Catholic churches and schools and issued tracts promoting Catholicism. Attempting to broaden his base of support with Protestant dissenters and nonconformists, James granted religious freedom to all.

James's opponents, a powerful coalition of eminent persons in Parliament and the Church of England, bitterly resisted James's ambitions. They offered the English throne to James's heir, his Protestant daughter Mary, and her Dutch husband, Prince William of Orange. In December 1688 James II, his queen, and their infant son fled to France and became pensioners of Louis XIV. Early in 1689 William and Mary were crowned king and queen of England.

Constitutional Monarchy and Cabinet Government

The English call the events of 1688 and 1689 the "Glorious Revolution" because they believe it replaced one king with another with barely any bloodshed. In truth, William's arrival sparked revolutionary riots and violence across the British Isles and in North American cities such as Boston and New York. Uprisings by supporters of James, known as Jacobites, occurred in 1689 in Scotland. In Ireland, the two sides waged outright war from 1689 to 1691. William's victory at the Battle of the Boyne (1690) and the subsequent Treaty of Limerick (1691) sealed his accession to power.

In England, the revolution represented the final destruction of the idea of divine-right monarchy. The men who brought about the revolution framed their intentions in the Bill of Rights, which was formulated in direct response to Stuart absolutism. Law was to be made in Parliament; once made, it could not be suspended by the Crown. Parliament had to be called at least once every three years. The independence of the judiciary was established, and there was to be no standing army in peacetime. Protestants could possess arms, but the Catholic minority could not. No Catholic could ever inherit the throne. Additional legislation granted freedom of worship to Protestant dissenters, but not to Catholics. William and Mary accepted these principles when they took the throne, and the House of Parliament passed the Bill of Rights in December 1689.

The Glorious Revolution and the concept of representative government found its best defense in political philosopher John Locke's *Second Treatise of Civil Government* (1690). Locke (1632–1704) maintained that a government that oversteps its proper function — protecting the natural rights of life, liberty, and property — becomes a tyranny. (See "Primary Source: John Locke, *Two Treatises of Government*," at right.) By

PRIMARY SOURCE   John Locke, *Two Treatises of Government*

In 1688 opponents of King James II invited his daughter Mary and her husband, the Dutch prince William of Orange, to take the throne of England. James fled for the safety of France. One of the most outspoken proponents of the "Glorious Revolution" that brought William and Mary to the throne was philosopher John Locke. In this passage, Locke argues that sovereign power resides in the people, who may reject a monarch who does not obey the law.

But government into whosesoever hands it is put, being as I have before shown, entrusted with this condition, and for this end, that men might have and secure their properties, the prince or senate, however it may have power to make laws for the regulation of property between the subjects one amongst another, yet can never have a power to take to themselves the whole, or any part of the subjects' property, without their own consent. For this would be in effect to leave them no property at all. . . .

'Tis true, governments cannot be supported without great charge, and 'tis fit every one who enjoys his share of the protection, should pay, out of this estate, his proportion for the maintenance of it. But still it must be with his own consent, i.e., the consent of the majority, giving it either by themselves, or their representatives chosen by them; for if any one shall claim a power to lay and levy taxes on the people, by his own authority, and without such consent of the people, he thereby invades the fundamental law of property, and subverts the end of government. For what property have I in that which another may be right to take when he pleases to himself. . . .

The constitution of the legislative is the first and fundamental act of society, whereby provision is made for the continuation of their union, under the direction of persons, and bonds of laws, made by persons authorized thereunto, by the consent and appointment of the people, without which no one man, or number of men, amongst them, can have authority of making laws that shall be binding to the rest. When any one, or more, shall take upon them to make laws, whom the people have not appointed so to do, they make laws without authority, which the people are not therefore bound to obey; by which means they come again to be out of subjection, and may constitute to themselves a new legislative, as they think best, being in full liberty to resist the force of those, who, without authority, would impose any thing upon them.

EVALUATE THE EVIDENCE

1. For what reason do people form a government, according to Locke? What would be the justification for disobeying laws and rejecting the authority of government?

2. In what ways does this document legitimize the events of the Glorious Revolution?

Source: John Locke, *Two Treatises of Government.* Reprinted in *England's Glorious Revolution, 1688–1689,* ed. Steven C. A. Pincus (Boston: Bedford/St. Martin's, 2006), pp. 161–162, 164.

"natural" rights Locke meant rights basic to all men because all have the ability to reason. Under a tyrannical government, the people have the natural right to rebellion. On the basis of this link, he justified limiting the vote to property owners. Locke's idea that there are natural or universal rights equally valid for all peoples and societies was especially popular in colonial America. American colonists also appreciated his arguments that Native Americans had no property rights since they did not cultivate the land and, by extension, no political rights because they possessed no property.

The events of 1688 and 1689 did not constitute a democratic revolution. The revolution placed sovereignty in Parliament, and Parliament represented the upper classes. The age of aristocratic government lasted at least until 1832 and in many ways until 1928, when women received full voting rights.

In the course of the eighteenth century, the cabinet system of government evolved. The term *cabinet* derives from the small private room in which English rulers consulted their chief ministers. In a cabinet system, the leading ministers, who must have seats in and the support of a majority of the House of Commons, formulate common policy and conduct the business of the country. During the administration of one royal minister, Sir Robert Walpole, who led the cabinet from 1721 to 1742, the idea developed that the cabinet was responsible to the House of Commons. The Hanoverian king George I (r. 1714–1727) normally presided at cabinet meetings throughout his reign, but his son and heir, George II (r. 1727–1760), discontinued the practice. The influence of the Crown in decision making accordingly declined. Walpole enjoyed the favor of the monarchy and of the House of Commons and came to be called the king's first, or "prime," minister. In the English cabinet system, both legislative power and executive power are held by the leading ministers, who form the government.

England's brief and chaotic experiment with republicanism under Oliver Cromwell convinced its people of the advantages of a monarchy, albeit with strong checks on royal authority. For supporters of Parliament, the tolerant and moderate Dutch Republic had provided a powerful counterexample to Louis XIV's absolutism.

The Dutch Republic in the Seventeenth Century

In the late sixteenth century the seven northern provinces of the Netherlands fought for and won their independence from Spain. The independence of the Republic of the United Provinces of the Netherlands was recognized in 1648 in the treaty that ended the Thirty Years' War. In this period, often called the "golden age of the Netherlands," Dutch ideas and attitudes played a profound role in shaping a new and modern worldview. At the same time, the United Provinces developed its own distinctive model of a constitutional state.

Rejecting the rule of a monarch, the Dutch established a republic, a state in which power rested in the hands of the people and was exercised through elected representatives. Other examples of republics in early modern Europe included the Swiss Confederation and several autonomous city-states of Italy and the Holy Roman Empire. Among the Dutch, an oligarchy of wealthy businessmen called regents handled domestic affairs in each province's Estates (assemblies). The provincial Estates held virtually all the power. A federal assembly, or States General, handled foreign affairs and war, but it did not possess sovereign authority. All issues had to be referred back to the local Estates for

Jan Steen, *The Merry Family*, 1668   In this painting from the Dutch golden age, a happy family enjoys a boisterous song while seated around the dining table. Despite its carefree appearance, the painting was intended to teach a moral lesson. The children are shown drinking wine and smoking, bad habits they have learned from their parents. The inscription hanging over the mantelpiece (upper right) spells out the message clearly: "As the Old Sing, so Pipe the Young." (Gianni Dagli Orti/The Art Archive)

approval, and each of the seven provinces could veto any proposed legislation. Holland, the province with the largest navy and the most wealth, usually dominated the republic and the States General.

In each province, the Estates appointed an executive officer, known as the **stad-holder**, who carried out ceremonial functions and was responsible for military defense. Although in theory freely chosen by the Estates and answerable to them, in practice the strong and influential House of Orange usually held the office of stadholder in several of the seven provinces of the republic. This meant that tensions always lingered between supporters of the House of Orange and those of the staunchly republican Estates, who suspected that the princes of Orange harbored monarchical ambitions. When one of them, William III, took the English throne in 1688 with his wife, Mary, the republic simply continued without stadholders for several decades.

The political success of the Dutch rested on their phenomenal commercial prosperity. The moral and ethical bases of that commercial wealth were thrift, frugality, and religious toleration. Although there is scattered evidence of anti-Semitism, Jews enjoyed a level of acceptance and assimilation in Dutch business and general culture unique in early modern Europe. In the Dutch Republic, toleration paid off: it attracted a great deal of foreign capital and investment.

The Dutch came to dominate the shipping business by putting profits from their original industry—herring fishing—into shipbuilding. They boasted the lowest shipping rates and largest merchant marine in Europe, allowing them to undersell foreign competitors (see Chapter 14).

Trade and commerce brought the Dutch the highest standard of living in Europe, perhaps in the world. Salaries were high, and all classes of society ate well. A scholar has described the Netherlands as "an island of plenty in a sea of want." Consequently, the Netherlands experienced very few of the food riots that characterized the rest of Europe.[12]

Baroque Art and Music

What was the baroque style in art and music, and where was it popular?

Throughout European history, the cultural tastes of one age have often seemed unsatisfactory to the next. So it was with the baroque. The term *baroque* may have come from the Portuguese word for an "odd-shaped, imperfect pearl" and was commonly used by late-eighteenth-century art critics as an expression of scorn for what they considered an overblown, unbalanced style. Specialists now agree that the baroque style marked one of the high points in the history of Western culture.

Rome and the revitalized Catholic Church of the late sixteenth century spurred the early development of the baroque. The papacy and the Jesuits encouraged the growth of an intensely emotional, exuberant art. These patrons wanted artists to go beyond the Renaissance focus on pleasing a small, wealthy cultural elite. They wanted artists to appeal to the senses and thereby touch the souls and kindle the faith of ordinary churchgoers while proclaiming the power and confidence of the reformed Catholic Church. In addition to this underlying religious emotionalism, the baroque drew its sense of drama, motion, and ceaseless striving from the Catholic Reformation. The interior of the famous Jesuit Church of Jesus in Rome—the Gesù—combined all these characteristics in its lavish, wildly active decorations and frescoes.

Taking definite shape in Italy after 1600, the baroque style in the visual arts developed with exceptional vigor in Catholic countries—in Spain and Latin America, Austria, southern Germany, and Poland. Yet baroque art was more than just "Catholic art" in the seventeenth century and the first half of the eighteenth. True, neither Protestant England nor the Netherlands ever came fully under the spell of the baroque, but neither did Catholic France. And Protestants accounted for some of the finest examples of baroque style, especially in music. The baroque style spread partly because its tension and bombast spoke to an agitated age that was experiencing great violence and controversy in politics and religion.

In painting, the baroque reached maturity early with Peter Paul Rubens (1577–1640), the most outstanding and most representative of baroque painters. Studying in his native

Flanders and in Italy, where he was influenced by masters of the High Renaissance such as Michelangelo, Rubens developed his own rich, sensuous, colorful style, which was characterized by animated figures, melodramatic contrasts, and monumental size. Rubens excelled in glorifying monarchs such as Queen Mother Marie de' Medici of France. He was also a devout Catholic; nearly half of his pictures treat Christian subjects. Yet one of Rubens's trademarks was the fleshy, sensual nudes who populate his canvases as Roman goddesses, water nymphs, and remarkably voluptuous saints and angels.

In music, the baroque style reached its culmination almost a century later in the dynamic, soaring lines of the endlessly inventive Johann Sebastian Bach (1685–1750). Organist and choirmaster of several Lutheran churches across Germany, Bach was equally at home writing secular concertos and sublime religious cantatas. Bach's organ music combined the baroque spirit of invention, tension, and emotion in an unforgettable striving toward the infinite. Unlike Rubens, Bach was not fully appreciated in his lifetime, but since the early nineteenth century his reputation has grown steadily.

Notes

1. Quoted in Cecile Hugon, *Social France in the XVII Century* (London: McMilland, 1911), p. 189.
2. H. Kamen, "The Economic and Social Consequences of the Thirty Years' War," *Past and Present* 39 (1968): 44–61.
3. John A. Lynn, "Recalculating French Army Growth," in *The Military Revolution Debate: Readings on the Military Transformation of Early Modern Europe*, ed. Clifford J. Rogers (Boulder, Colo.: Westview Press, 1995), p. 125.
4. Quoted in John A. Lynn, *Giant of the Grand Siècle: The French Army, 1610–1715* (Cambridge, U.K.: Cambridge University Press, 1997), p. 74.
5. F. Arkwright, ed., *The Memoirs of the Duke de Saint-Simon*, vol. 5 (New York: Brentano's, n.d.), p. 276.
6. J. H. Elliott, *Imperial Spain, 1469–1716* (New York: Mentor Books, 1963), pp. 306–308.
7. *German History Documents*, http://germanhistorydocs.ghidc.org/docpage.cfm?docpage_id=3734.
8. H. Rosenberg, *Bureaucracy, Aristocracy, and Autocracy: The Prussian Experience, 1660–1815* (Boston: Beacon Press, 1966), p. 43.
9. Cited in Giles MacDonogh, *Frederick the Great: A Life in Deed and Letters* (New York: St. Martin's, 2001), p. 23.
10. Rosenberg, *Bureaucracy, Aristocracy, and Autocracy*, p. 40.
11. For a revisionist interpretation, see J. Wormald, "James VI and I: Two Kings or One?" *History* 62 (1983): 187–209.
12. S. Schama, *The Embarrassment of Riches: An Interpretation of Dutch Culture in the Golden Age* (New York: Alfred A. Knopf, 1987), pp. 165–170; quotation is on p. 167.

Chapter Review

MAKE IT STICK

LearningCurve
bedfordstmartins.com/mckaywestvalue
After reading the chapter, use LearningCurve to retain what you've read.

IDENTIFY KEY TERMS

Identify and explain the significance of each item below.

Peace of Westphalia (p. 480)

Fronde (p. 484)

mercantilism (p. 488)

Peace of Utrecht (p. 489)

Junkers (p. 494)

boyars (p. 497)

Cossacks (p. 498)

sultan (p. 501)

janissary corps (p. 502)

millet system (p. 502)

constitutionalism (p. 502)

republicanism (p. 503)

Puritans (p. 503)

Protectorate (p. 507)

Test Act (p. 507)

stadholder (p. 511)

REVIEW THE MAIN IDEAS

Answer the focus questions from each section of the chapter.

- What were the common crises and achievements of seventeenth-century European states? (p. 477)

- What factors led to the rise of the French absolutist state under Louis XIV, and why did absolutist Spain experience decline in the same period? (p. 483)

- What were the social conditions of eastern Europe, and how did the rulers of Austria and Prussia transform their nations into powerful absolutist monarchies? (p. 492)

- What were the distinctive features of Russian and Ottoman absolutism? (p. 497)

- How and why did the constitutional state triumph in the Dutch Republic and England? (p. 502)

- What was the baroque style in art and music, and where was it popular? (p. 512)

MAKE CONNECTIONS

Think about the larger developments and continuities within and across chapters.

1. This chapter has argued that, despite their political differences, absolutist and constitutionalist rulers faced similar obstacles in the mid-seventeenth century and achieved many of the same goals. Do you agree? Why or why not?

2. Proponents of absolutism in western Europe believed their form of monarchical rule was fundamentally different from and superior to what they saw as Russian and Ottoman "despotism." Why did they believe this and was it accurate?

ONLINE DOCUMENT ASSIGNMENT

Hürrem
What forces shaped Western views of Hürrem?

You encountered Hürrem's story on page 504. Keeping the question above in mind, go online and examine characterizations of Hürrem as seen through the eyes of a Habsburg diplomat, and then complete a writing assignment based on the evidence and details from this chapter.

bedfordstmartins.com/mckaywestvalue

CHRONOLOGY

ca. 1500–1650	• Consolidation of serfdom in eastern Europe
1533–1584	• Reign of Ivan the Terrible in Russia
1589–1610	• Reign of Henry IV in France
1598–1613	• Time of Troubles in Russia
1620–1740	• Growth of absolutism in Austria and Prussia
1642–1649	• English civil war, which ends with execution of Charles I
1643–1715	• Reign of Louis XIV in France
1653–1658	• Military rule in England under Oliver Cromwell (the Protectorate)
1660	• Restoration of English monarchy under Charles II
1665–1683	• Jean-Baptiste Colbert applies mercantilism to France
1670	• Charles II agrees to re-Catholicize England in secret agreement with Louis XIV
1670–1671	• Cossack revolt led by Stenka Razin
ca. 1680–1750	• Construction of absolutist palaces
1682	• Louis XIV moves court to Versailles
1682–1725	• Reign of Peter the Great in Russia
1683–1718	• Habsburgs push the Ottoman Turks from Hungary
1685	• Edict of Nantes revoked in France
1688–1689	• Glorious Revolution in England
1701–1713	• War of the Spanish Succession

16

LearningCurve
bedfordstmartins.com/mckaywestvalue
After reading the chapter, use
LearningCurve to retain what
you've read.

Toward a New Worldview

1540–1789

THE INTELLECTUAL DEVELOPMENTS OF THE SIXTEENTH AND
seventeenth centuries created the modern worldview that the West continues to hold—and debate—to this day. In this period, fundamentally new ways of understanding the natural world emerged. Those leading the changes saw themselves as philosophers and referred to their field of study as "natural philosophy." Nineteenth-century scholars hailed these achievements as a "Scientific Revolution" that produced modern science as we know it. The new science entailed the search for precise knowledge of the physical world based on the union of experimental observations with sophisticated mathematics. Whereas medieval scholars looked to authoritative texts like the Bible or the classics, early modern natural philosophers performed experiments and relied on increasingly complex mathematical calculations. The resulting conception of the universe and its laws remained in force until Einstein's discoveries at the beginning of the twentieth century.

In the eighteenth century philosophers extended the use of reason from the study of nature to human society. They sought to bring the light of reason to bear on the darkness of prejudice, outmoded traditions, and ignorance. Self-proclaimed members of an "Enlightenment" movement, they wished to bring the same progress to human affairs as their predecessors had brought to the understanding of the natural world. While the Scientific Revolution ushered in modern science, the Enlightenment created concepts of human rights, equality, progress, universalism, and tolerance that still guide Western societies today. At the same time, some people used their new understanding of nature and reason to proclaim their own superiority, thus rationalizing such attitudes as racism and male chauvinism.

Major Breakthroughs of the Scientific Revolution

What revolutionary discoveries were made in the sixteenth and seventeenth centuries?

Until the middle of the sixteenth century, Europeans relied on an understanding of motion and matter drawn from the ancient Greek philosopher Aristotle and adapted to Christian theology. The rise of the university, along with the intellectual vitality of the Renaissance and technological advancements, inspired scholars to make closer observations and seek better explanations. From the sun-centered universe proposed by the Polish astronomer Nicolaus Copernicus to the great synthesis of physics and astronomy accomplished by the English scientist Isaac Newton, a revolutionary new understanding of the universe had emerged by the end of the seventeenth century. Hailed today as pioneers of a modern worldview, the major figures of the Scientific Revolution were for the most part devout Christians who saw their work as heralding the glory of creation and who combined older traditions of magic, astrology, and alchemy with their path-breaking experimentation.

Scientific Thought in 1500

The term "science" as we use it today came into use only in the nineteenth century. Prior to the Scientific Revolution, many different scholars and practitioners were involved in aspects of what came together to form science. One of the most important disciplines was **natural philosophy**, which focused on fundamental questions about the nature of the universe, its purpose, and how it functioned. In the early 1500s natural philosophy was still based primarily on the ideas of Aristotle, the great Greek philosopher of the fourth century B.C.E. Medieval theologians such as Thomas Aquinas brought Aristotelian philosophy into harmony with Christian doctrines. According to the revised Aristotelian view, a motionless earth was fixed at the center of the universe and was encompassed by ten separate concentric crystal spheres that revolved around it. In the first eight spheres were embedded, in turn, the moon, the sun, the five known planets, and the fixed stars. Then followed two spheres added during the Middle Ages to account for slight changes in the positions of the stars over the centuries. Beyond the tenth sphere was Heaven, with the throne of God and the souls of the saved. Angels kept the spheres moving in perfect circles.

Aristotle's cosmology made intellectual sense, but it could not account for the observed motions of the stars and planets and, in particular, provided no explanation for the apparent backward motion of the planets (which we now know occurs because planets closer to the sun periodically overtake the earth on their faster orbits). The great second-century scholar Ptolemy, a Hellenized Egyptian (see Chapter 14), offered a cunning solution to this dilemma. According to Ptolemy, the planets moved in small circles, called epicycles, each of which moved in turn along a larger circle, or deferent. Ptolemaic astronomy was less elegant than Aristotle's neat nested circles and required complex calculations, but it provided a surprisingly accurate model for predicting planetary motion.

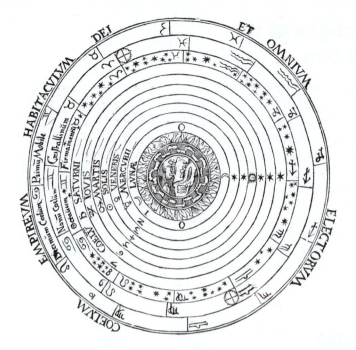

The Aristotelian Universe as Imagined in the Sixteenth Century
A round earth is at the center, surrounded by spheres of water, air, and fire. Beyond this small nucleus, the moon, the sun, and the five planets were embedded in their own rotating crystal spheres, with the stars sharing the surface of one enormous sphere. Beyond, the heavens were composed of unchanging ether. (Universal History Archive/ UIG/The Bridgeman Art Library)

Aristotle's views, revised by medieval philosophers, also dominated thinking about physics and motion on earth. Aristotle had distinguished sharply between the world of the celestial spheres and that of the earth — the sublunar world. The spheres consisted of a perfect, incorruptible "quintessence," or fifth essence. The sublunar world, however, was made up of four imperfect, changeable elements. The "light" elements (air and fire) naturally moved upward, while the "heavy" elements (water and earth) naturally moved downward. These natural directions of motion did not always prevail, however, for elements were often mixed together and could be affected by an outside force such as a human being. Aristotle and his followers also believed that a uniform force moved an object at a constant speed and that the object would stop as soon as that force was removed.

Natural philosophy was considered distinct from and superior to mathematics and mathematical disciplines like astronomy, optics, and mechanics, and Aristotle's ideas about the cosmos were accepted, with revisions, for two thousand years. His views offered a commonsense explanation for what the eye actually saw. Aristotle's science as interpreted by Christian theologians also fit neatly with Christian doctrines. It established a home for God and a place for Christian souls. It put human beings at the center of the universe and made them the critical link in a "great chain of being" that stretched from the throne of God to the lowliest insect on earth. This approach to the natural world was thus a branch of theology, and it reinforced religious thought.

Origins of the Scientific Revolution

Why did Aristotelian teachings give way to new views about the universe? The Scientific Revolution drew on long-term developments in European culture, as well as borrowings from Arabic scholars. The first important development was the medieval university. By the thirteenth century permanent universities had been established in western Europe to train the lawyers, doctors, and church leaders society required. By 1300 philosophy—including Aristotelian natural philosophy—had taken its place alongside law, medicine, and theology. Medieval philosophers acquired a limited but real independence from theologians and a sense of free inquiry.

Medieval universities drew on rich traditions of Islamic learning. With the expansion of Islam into lands of the Byzantine Empire in the seventh and eighth centuries, the Muslim world had inherited ancient Greek learning, to which Islamic scholars added their own commentaries and new discoveries. Many Greek texts, including many works of the philosopher Aristotle, which were lost to the West after the fall of the Western Roman Empire in the fifth century, re-entered circulation through translation from the Arabic in the twelfth century; these became the basis for the curriculum of the medieval universities. In the fourteenth and fifteenth centuries leading universities established new professorships of mathematics, astronomy, and optics within their faculties of philosophy. The prestige of the new fields was low, but the stage was set for the union of mathematics with natural philosophy that was to be a hallmark of the Scientific Revolution.

The Renaissance also stimulated scientific progress. Renaissance patrons played a role in funding scientific investigations, as they did for art and literature. Renaissance artists' turn toward realism and their use of geometry to convey three-dimensional perspective encouraged scholars to practice close observation and to use mathematics to describe the natural world. The quest to restore the glories of the ancient past led to the rediscovery of even more classical texts, such as Ptolemy's *Geography* (see Chapter 14), which had been preserved in the Byzantine Empire and was translated into Latin around 1410. The encyclopedic treatise on botany by the ancient Greek philosopher Theophrastus was rediscovered in the 1450s, moldering on the shelves of the Vatican library. The fall of Constantinople to the Muslim Ottomans in 1453 resulted in a great influx of little-known Greek works, as Christian scholars fled to Italy with their texts.

Developments in technology also encouraged the emergence of the Scientific Revolution. The rise of printing in the mid-fifteenth century provided a faster and less expensive way to circulate knowledge across Europe. Fascination with the new discoveries being made in Asia and the Americas greatly increased the demand for printed material. Publishers found an eager audience for the books and images they issued about unknown peoples, plants, animals, and other new findings.

The navigational problems of long sea voyages in the age of overseas expansion, along with the rise of trade and colonization, led to their own series of technological innovations. As early as 1484 the king of Portugal appointed a commission of mathematicians to perfect tables to help seamen find their latitude. Navigation and cartography were also critical in the development of many new scientific instruments, such as the telescope, barometer, thermometer, pendulum clock, microscope, and air pump. Better instruments, which permitted more accurate observations, enabled the rise of experimentation as a crucial method of the Scientific Revolution.

Recent historical research has also focused on the contribution to the Scientific Revolution of practices that no longer belong to the realm of science, such as astrology. For most of human history, interest in astronomy was inspired by the belief that the changing relationships between planets and stars influence events on earth. This belief was held in Europe up to and during the Scientific Revolution (and continues among some people today). Many of the most celebrated astronomers were also astrologers and spent much time devising horoscopes for their patrons. Used as a diagnostic tool in medicine, astrology formed a regular part of the curriculum of medical schools.

Centuries-old practices of magic and alchemy also remained important traditions for natural philosophers. Unlike modern-day conjurers, the practitioners of magic strove to understand and control hidden connections they perceived among different elements of the natural world, such as that between a magnet and iron. The idea that objects possessed invisible or "occult" qualities that allowed them to affect other objects through their innate "sympathy" with each other was a particularly important legacy of the magical tradition. Belief in occult qualities—or numerology or cosmic harmony—was not antithetical to belief in God. On the contrary, adherents believed that only a divine creator could infuse the universe with such meaningful mystery.

The Copernican Hypothesis

The desire to explain and thereby glorify God's handiwork led to the first great departure from the medieval system. This was the work of the Polish cleric Nicolaus Copernicus (1473–1543). As a young man Copernicus was drawn to the vitality of the Italian Renaissance. After studies at the university of Kraków, he departed for Italy, where he studied astronomy, medicine, and church law at the famed universities of Bologna, Padua, and Ferrara. Copernicus noted that astronomers still depended on the work of Ptolemy for their most accurate calculations, but he felt that Ptolemy's cumbersome and occasionally inaccurate rules detracted from the majesty of a perfect creator. He preferred an alternative ancient Greek idea: that the sun, rather than the earth, was at the center of the universe.

Finishing his university studies and returning to a position in church administration in East Prussia, Copernicus worked on his hypothesis from 1506 to 1530. Without questioning the Aristotelian belief in crystal spheres or the idea that circular motion was divine, Copernicus theorized that the stars and planets, including the earth, revolved around a fixed sun. Desiring to be certain of his shocking claims before revealing them to the world, Copernicus did not publish his *On the Revolutions of the Heavenly Spheres* until 1543, the year of his death.

The **Copernican hypothesis** had enormous scientific and religious implications, many of which the conservative Copernicus did not anticipate. First, it put the stars at rest, their apparent nightly movement simply a result of the earth's rotation. Thus it destroyed the main reason for believing in crystal spheres capable of moving the stars around the earth. Second, Copernicus's theory suggested a universe of staggering size. If in the course of a year the earth moved around the sun and yet the stars appeared to remain in the same place, then the universe was unthinkably large. Third, by using mathematics, instead of philosophy, to justify his theories, he challenged the traditional hierarchy of the disciplines. Finally, by characterizing the earth as just another planet, Copernicus destroyed the basic idea of Aristotelian physics—that the earthly sphere was quite different from the heavenly one. Where then were Heaven and the throne of God?

Religious leaders varied in their response to Copernicus's theories. A few Protestant scholars became avid Copernicans, while others accepted some elements of his criticism of Ptolemy, but firmly rejected the notion that the earth moved, a doctrine that contradicted the literal reading of some passages of the Bible. Among Catholics, Copernicus's ideas drew little attention prior to 1600. Because the Catholic Church had never held to literal interpretations of the Bible, it did not officially declare the Copernican hypothesis false until 1616.

Other events were almost as influential in creating doubts about traditional astronomy. In 1572 a new star appeared and shone very brightly for almost two years. The new star, which was actually a distant exploding star, made an enormous impression on people. It seemed to contradict the idea that the heavenly spheres were unchanging and therefore perfect. In 1577 a new comet suddenly moved through the sky, cutting a straight path across the supposedly impenetrable crystal spheres. It was time, as a sixteenth-century scientific writer put it, for "the radical renovation of astronomy."[1]

Brahe, Kepler, and Galileo: Proving Copernicus Right

One astronomer who agreed with Copernicus was Tycho Brahe (TEE-koh BRAH-hee) (1546–1601). Born into a Danish noble family, Brahe became passionately interested in astronomy as a young boy and spent many nights gazing at the skies. Completing his studies abroad and returning to Denmark, he established himself as Europe's leading astronomer with his detailed observations of the new star of 1572. Aided by generous grants from the king of Denmark, Brahe built the most sophisticated observatory of his day.

Upon the king's death, Brahe acquired a new patron in the Holy Roman emperor Rudolph II and built a new observatory in Prague. In return for the emperor's support, he pledged to create new and improved tables of planetary motions, dubbed the *Rudolphine Tables*. For twenty years Brahe meticulously observed the stars and planets with the naked eye, compiling much more complete and accurate data than ever before. His limited understanding of mathematics and his sudden death in 1601, however, prevented him from making much sense out of his mass of data. Part Ptolemaic, part Copernican, he believed that all the planets except the earth revolved around the sun and that the entire group of sun and planets revolved in turn around the earth-moon system.

It was left to Brahe's young assistant, Johannes Kepler (1571–1630), to rework Brahe's mountain of observations. From a minor German noble family, Kepler suffered a bout of smallpox as a small child, leaving him with permanently damaged hands and eyesight. A brilliant mathematician, Kepler was inspired by his belief that the universe was built on mystical mathematical relationships and a musical harmony of the heavenly bodies.

Kepler's examination of his predecessor's meticulously recorded findings convinced him that Ptolemy's astronomy could not explain them. Abandoning the notion of epicycles and deferents—which even Copernicus had retained in part—Kepler developed three new and revolutionary laws of planetary motion. First, largely through observations of the planet Mars, he demonstrated that the orbits of the planets around the sun are elliptical rather than circular. Second, he demonstrated that the planets do not move at a uniform speed in their orbits. When a planet is close to the sun it moves more rapidly, and it slows as it moves farther away from the sun. Kepler published the first two laws in his 1609 book, *The New Astronomy*, which heralded the arrival of an entirely new theory of the cosmos. In 1619 Kepler put forth his third law: the time a planet takes to make its complete orbit is precisely related to its distance from the sun.

Kepler's contribution was monumental. Whereas Copernicus had used mathematics to describe planetary movement, Kepler proved mathematically the precise relations of a sun-centered (solar) system. He thus united for the first time the theoretical cosmology of natural philosophy with mathematics. His work demolished the old system of Aristotle and Ptolemy, and with his third law he came close to formulating the idea of universal gravitation (see page 525). In 1627 he also fulfilled Brahe's pledge by completing the *Rudolphine Tables* begun so many years earlier. These tables were used by astronomers for many years.

Kepler was a genius with many talents. Beyond his great contribution to astronomy, he pioneered the field of optics. He was the first to explain the role of refraction within the eye in creating vision, and he invented an improved telescope. He was also a great mathematician whose work furnished the basis for integral calculus and advances in geometry.

Kepler was not, however, the consummate modern scientist that these achievements suggest. His duties as court mathematician included casting horoscopes, and he based his own daily life on astrological principles. He also wrote at length on cosmic harmonies and explained, for example, elliptical motion through ideas about the beautiful music created by the combined motion of the planets. Kepler's fictional account of travel to the moon, written partly to illustrate the idea of a non-earth-centered universe, caused controversy and may have contributed to the arrest and trial of his mother as a witch in 1620. Kepler also suffered deeply as a result of his unorthodox brand of Lutheranism, which led to his rejection by both Lutherans and Catholics. His career exemplifies the complex interweaving of ideas and beliefs in the emerging science of his day.

While Kepler was unraveling planetary motion, a young Florentine named Galileo Galilei (1564–1642) was challenging all the old ideas about motion. Like Kepler and so many early scientists, Galileo was a poor nobleman first marked for a religious career. Instead, his fascination with mathematics led to a professorship in which he examined motion and mechanics in a new way. His great achievement was the elaboration and consolidation of the **experimental method**. That is, rather than speculate about what might or should happen, Galileo conducted controlled experiments to find out what actually did happen.

In his early experiments, Galileo focused on deficiencies in Aristotle's theories of motion. He measured the movement of a rolling ball across a surface, repeating the action again and again to verify his results. In his famous acceleration experiment, he showed that a uniform force—in this case, gravity—produced a uniform acceleration. Through another experiment, he formulated the **law of inertia**. He found that rest was not the natural state of objects. Rather, an object continues in motion forever unless stopped by some external force. His discoveries proved Aristotelian physics wrong.

Galileo then applied the experimental method to astronomy. On hearing details about the invention of the telescope in Holland, Galileo made one for himself and trained it on the heavens. He quickly discovered the first four moons of Jupiter, which clearly suggested that Jupiter could not possibly be embedded in any impenetrable crystal sphere as Aristotle and Ptolemy maintained. This discovery provided new evidence for the Copernican theory, in which Galileo already believed. Galileo then pointed his telescope at the moon. He wrote in 1610 in *The Sidereal Messenger*: "By the aid of a telescope anyone may behold [the Milky Way] in a manner which so distinctly appeals to the senses that all the disputes which have tormented philosophers through so many ages are exploded by the irrefutable evidence of our eyes, and we are freed from wordy disputes upon the subject."[2] (See "Primary Source: Galileo Galilei, *The Sidereal Messenger*," at right.)

PRIMARY SOURCE   Galileo Galilei, *The Sidereal Messenger*

In this passage from The Sidereal Messenger *(1610), Galileo Galilei recounts his experiments to build a telescope and his observations of the moon. By discovering the irregularity of the moon's surface, Galileo disproved a central tenet of medieval cosmography: that the heavens were composed of perfect, unblemished spheres essentially different from the base matter of earth.*

About ten months ago a report reached my ears that a Dutchman had constructed a telescope, by the aid of which visible objects, although at a great distance from the eye of the observer, were seen distinctly as if near. . . . A few days after, I received confirmation of the report in a letter written from Paris . . . , which finally determined me to give myself up first to inquire into the principle of the telescope, and then to consider the means by which I might compass [achieve] the invention of a similar instrument, which a little while after I succeeded in doing, through deep study of the theory of refraction; and I prepared a tube, at first of lead, in the ends of which I fitted two glass lenses, both plane on one side, but on the other side one spherically convex, and the other concave. . . . At length, by sparing neither labour nor expense, I succeeded in constructing for myself an instrument so superior that objects seen through it appear magnified nearly a thousand times, and more than thirty times nearer than if viewed by the natural powers of sight alone. . . .

Let me speak first of the surface of the moon, which is turned towards us. For the sake of being understood more easily, I distinguish two parts in it, which I call respectively the brighter and the darker. The brighter part seems to surround and pervade the whole hemisphere, but the darker part, like a sort of cloud, discolours the moon's surface and makes it appear covered with spots. Now these spots . . . are plain to every one, and every age has seen them, wherefore I shall call them *great* or *ancient* spots, to distinguish them from other spots, smaller in size, but so thickly scattered that they sprinkle the whole surface of the moon, but especially the brighter portion of it. These spots have never been observed by any one before me, and from my observations of them, often repeated, I have been led to that opinion which I have expressed, namely, that I feel sure that the surface of the moon is not perfectly smooth, free from inequalities and exactly spherical, as a large school of philosophers considers with regard to the moon and the other heavenly bodies, but that, on the contrary, it is full of inequalities, uneven, full of hollows and protuberances, just like the surface of the earth itself, which is varied everywhere by lofty mountains and deep valleys.

EVALUATE THE EVIDENCE

1. What did the telescope permit Galileo to see on the moon that was not visible to the naked eye, and how did he interpret his observations?

2. Why were Galileo's observations so important to the destruction of the Ptolemaic universe?

Source: Galileo Galilei, *The Sidereal Messenger* (London: Rivingtons, 1880), pp. 10–11, 14–15.

Reading these famous lines, one feels a crucial corner in Western civilization being turned. No longer should one rely on established authority. A new method of learning and investigating was being developed, one that proved useful in any field of inquiry. A historian investigating documents of the past, for example, is not so different from a Galileo studying stars and rolling balls.

In 1597, when Johannes Kepler sent Galileo an early publication defending Copernicus, Galileo replied that it was too dangerous to express his support for heliocentrism publicly. The rising fervor of the Catholic Reformation increased the church's hostility to such radical ideas, and in 1616 the Holy Office placed the works of Copernicus and his supporters, including Kepler, on a list of books Catholics were forbidden to read. The accompanying decree declared that belief in a heliocentric world was "foolish and absurd, philosophically false and formally heretical."[3]

Galileo was a devout Catholic who sincerely believed that his theories did not detract from the perfection of God. Out of caution he silenced his beliefs for several years, until in 1623 he saw new hope with the ascension of Pope Urban VIII, a man sympathetic to developments in the new science. However, Galileo's 1632 *Dialogue on the Two Chief Systems of the World* went too far. Published in Italian and widely read, this work openly lampooned the traditional views of Aristotle and Ptolemy and defended those of Copernicus. The papal Inquisition placed Galileo on trial for heresy. Imprisoned and threatened with torture, the aging Galileo recanted, "renouncing and cursing" his Copernican errors.

Newton's Synthesis

Despite the efforts of the church, by about 1640 the work of Brahe, Kepler, and Galileo had been largely accepted by the scientific community. The old Aristotelian astronomy and physics were in ruins, and several fundamental breakthroughs had been made. But the new findings failed to explain what forces controlled the movement of the planets and objects on earth. That challenge was taken up by English scientist Isaac Newton (1642–1727).

Newton was born into the lower English gentry in 1642, and he enrolled at Cambridge University in 1661. A genius who spectacularly united the experimental and theoretical-mathematical sides of modern science, Newton was an intensely devout, albeit non-orthodox Christian, who privately rejected the doctrine of the Trinity. Newton was also fascinated by alchemy. He left behind thirty years' worth of encoded journals recording experiments to discover the elixir of life and a way to change base metals into gold and silver. He viewed alchemy as one path, alongside mathematics and astronomy, to the truth of God's creation. Like Kepler and other practitioners of the Scientific Revolution, he studied the natural world not for its own sake, but to understand the divine plan.

Newton arrived at some of his most basic ideas about physics between 1664 and 1666, during a break from studies at Cambridge caused by an outbreak of plague. As he later claimed, during this period he discovered his law of universal gravitation as well as the concepts of centripetal force and acceleration. Not realizing the significance of his findings, the young Newton did not publish them, and upon his return to Cambridge he took up the study of optics. It was in reference to his experiments in optics that Newton outlined his method of scientific inquiry most clearly, explaining the need for scientists "first to enquire diligently into the properties of things, and to establish these properties by experiment, and then to proceed more slowly to hypotheses for the explanation of them."[4]

In 1684 Newton returned to physics and the preparation of his ideas for publication. The result appeared three years later in *Philosophicae Naturalis Principia Mathematica* (Mathematical Principles of Natural Philosophy). Newton's towering accomplishment was a single explanatory system that could integrate the astronomy of Copernicus, as corrected by Kepler's laws, with the physics of Galileo and his predecessors. *Principia Mathematica* laid down Newton's three laws of motion, using a set of mathematical laws that explain motion and mechanics. These laws of dynamics are complex, and it took scientists and engineers two hundred years to work out all their implications.

The key feature of the Newtonian synthesis was the **law of universal gravitation**. According to this law, every body in the universe attracts every other body in the universe in a precise mathematical relationship, whereby the force of attraction is proportional to the quantity of matter of the objects and inversely proportional to the square of the distance between them. The whole universe—from Kepler's elliptical orbits to Galileo's rolling balls—was unified in one coherent system. The German mathematician and philosopher Gottfried von Leibniz, with whom Newton contested the invention of calculus, was outraged by Newton's claim that the "occult" force of gravity could allow bodies to affect one another at great distances. Newton's religious faith, as well as his alchemical belief in the innate powers of certain objects, allowed him to dismiss such criticism.

Newton's synthesis of mathematics with physics and astronomy prevailed until the twentieth century and established him as one of the most important figures in the history of science. Yet, near the end of his life, this acclaimed figure declared: "I do not know what I may appear to the world; but to myself I seem to have been only like a boy, playing on the seashore, and diverting myself, in now and then finding a smoother pebble or a prettier shell than ordinary, whilst the great ocean of truth lay all undiscovered before me."[5]

Important Changes in Scientific Thinking

What intellectual and social changes occurred as a result of the Scientific Revolution?

The creation of a new science was not accomplished by a handful of brilliant astronomers working alone. Scholars in many fields—medicine, chemistry, and botany, among others—used new methods to seek answers to long-standing problems, sharing their results in a community that spanned Europe. At the same time, monarchs and entrepreneurs launched explorations to uncover and understand the natural riches of newly conquered empires around the globe.

Bacon, Descartes, and the Scientific Method

One of the keys to the achievement of a new worldview in the seventeenth century was the development of better ways of obtaining knowledge about the world. Two important thinkers, Francis Bacon (1561–1626) and René Descartes (day-KAHRT) (1596–1650), were influential in describing and advocating for improved scientific methods based, respectively, on experimentation and mathematical reasoning.

English politician and writer Francis Bacon was the greatest early propagandist for the new experimental method. Rejecting the Aristotelian and medieval method of using speculative reasoning to build general theories, Bacon argued that new knowledge had to be pursued through empirical research. The researcher who wants to learn more about leaves or rocks, for example, should not speculate about the subject but should rather collect a multitude of specimens and then compare and analyze them to derive general principles. Bacon formalized the empirical method, which had already been used by Brahe and Galileo, into the general theory of inductive reasoning known as **empiricism**. Bacon's work, and his prestige as lord chancellor under James I, led to the widespread adoption of what was called "experimental philosophy" in England after his death. In 1660 followers of Bacon created the Royal Society (still in existence), which met weekly to conduct experiments and discuss the latest findings of scholars across Europe.

On the continent, more speculative methods retained support. The French philosopher René Descartes was a multitalented genius who made his first great discovery in mathematics. As a twenty-three-year-old soldier serving in the Thirty Years' War, he experienced a life-changing intellectual vision one night in 1619. Descartes saw that there was a perfect correspondence between geometry and algebra and that geometrical spatial figures could be expressed as algebraic equations and vice versa. A major step forward in the history of mathematics, Descartes's discovery of analytic geometry provided scientists with an important new tool.

Descartes used mathematics to elaborate a highly influential vision of the workings of the cosmos. Accepting Galileo's claim that all elements of the universe are composed of the same matter, Descartes began to investigate the basic nature of matter. Drawing on ancient Greek atomist philosophies, Descartes developed the idea that matter was made up of identical "corpuscules" that collided together in an endless series of motions. All occurrences in nature could be analyzed as matter in motion and, according to Descartes, the total "quantity of motion" in the universe was constant. Descartes's mechanistic view of the universe depended on the idea that a vacuum was impossible, which meant that every action had an equal reaction, continuing in an eternal chain reaction.

Although Descartes's hypothesis about the vacuum was proved wrong, his notion of a mechanistic universe intelligible through the physics of motion proved inspirational. Decades later, Newton rejected Descartes's idea of a full universe and several of his other ideas, but retained the notion of a mechanistic universe as a key element of his own system.

Descartes's greatest achievement was to develop his initial vision into a whole philosophy of knowledge and science. The Aristotelian cosmos was appealing in part because it corresponded with the evidence of the human senses. When the senses were proven to be wrong, Descartes decided it was necessary to doubt them and everything that could reasonably be doubted, and then, as in geometry, to use deductive reasoning from self-evident truths, which he called "first principles," to ascertain scientific laws. Descartes's reasoning ultimately reduced all substances to "matter" and "mind" — that is, to the physical and the spiritual. The devout Descartes believed that God had endowed man with reason for a purpose and that rational speculation could provide a path to the truths of creation. His view of the world as consisting of two fundamental entities is known as **Cartesian dualism**. Descartes's thought was highly influential in France and the Netherlands, but less so in England, where experimental philosophy won the day.

Both Bacon's inductive experimentalism and Descartes's deductive mathematical reasoning had their faults. Bacon's inability to appreciate the importance of mathematics and his obsession with practical results clearly showed the limitations of antitheoretical empiricism. Likewise, some of Descartes's positions demonstrated the inadequacy of rigid, dogmatic rationalism. For example, he believed that it was possible to deduce the whole science of medicine from first principles. Although insufficient on their own, Bacon's and Descartes's extreme approaches are combined in the modern scientific method, which began to crystallize in the late seventeenth century.

Medicine, the Body, and Chemistry

The Scientific Revolution soon inspired renewed study of the microcosm of the human body. For many centuries the ancient Greek physician Galen's explanation of the body carried the same authority as Aristotle's account of the universe. According to Galen, the body contained four humors: blood, phlegm, black bile, and yellow bile. Illness was believed to result from an imbalance of humors, which is why doctors frequently prescribed bloodletting to expel excess blood.

Swiss physician and alchemist Paracelsus (1493–1541) was an early proponent of the experimental method in medicine and pioneered the use of chemicals and drugs to address what he saw as chemical, rather than humoral, imbalances. Another experimentalist, Flemish physician Andreas Vesalius (1516–1564), studied anatomy by dissecting human bodies, often those of executed criminals. In 1543, the same year Copernicus published *On the Revolutions*, Vesalius issued his masterpiece, *On the Structure of the Human Body*. Its two hundred precise drawings revolutionized the understanding of human anatomy. The experimental approach also led English royal physician William Harvey (1578–1657) to discover the circulation of blood through the veins and arteries in 1628. Harvey was the first to explain that the heart worked like a pump and to explain the function of its muscles and valves.

Some decades later, Irishman Robert Boyle (1627–1691) helped found the modern science of chemistry. Following Paracelsus's lead, he undertook experiments to discover the basic elements of nature,

Frontispiece to *De Humani Corporis Fabrica* (On the Structure of the Human Body) The frontispiece to Vesalius's pioneering work, published in 1543, shows him dissecting a corpse before a crowd of students. This was a revolutionary new hands-on approach for physicians, who usually worked from a theoretical, rather than a practical, understanding of the body. Based on direct observation, Vesalius replaced ancient ideas drawn from Greek philosophy with a much more accurate account of the structure and function of the body. (© SSPL/Science Museum/The Image Works)

which he believed was composed of infinitely small atoms. Boyle was the first to create a vacuum, thus disproving Descartes's belief that a vacuum could not exist in nature, and he discovered Boyle's law (1662), which states that the pressure of a gas varies inversely with volume.

Empire and Natural History

While the traditional story of the Scientific Revolution focuses exclusively on developments within Europe itself, and in particular on achievements in mathematical astronomy, more recently scholars have emphasized the impact of Europe's overseas empires on the accumulation and transmission of knowledge about the natural world. Thus, moving beyond Ptolemy's *Geography* (see Chapter 14) was as important for the emergence of modern science as overturning his cosmography.

Building on the rediscovery of Theophrastus's botanical treatise (see page 519) and other classical texts, early modern scholars published new works cataloguing forms of life in northern Europe, Asia, and the Americas that were unknown to the ancients. These encyclopedias of natural history included realistic drawings and descriptions that emphasized the usefulness of animal and plant species for trade, medicine, food, and other practical concerns.

Much of the new knowledge contained in such works resulted from scientific expeditions, often sponsored by European governments eager to learn about and profit from their imperial holdings. Spain took an early lead in such voyages, given their early conquests in the Americas (see Chapter 14). The physician of King Philip II of Spain spent seven years in New Spain in the 1560s recording thousands of plant species and interviewing local healers about their medicinal properties. Other countries followed suit as their global empires expanded.

Audiences at home eagerly read the accounts of naturalists, who braved the heat, insects, and diseases of tropical jungles to bring home exotic animal, vegetable, and mineral specimens. They heard much less about the many indigenous guides, translators, and practitioners of medicine and science who made these expeditions possible and who contributed rich local knowledge about animal and plant species. In this period the craze for collecting natural history specimens in Europe extended from aristocratic lords to middle-class amateurs. Many public museums, like the British Museum in London, began with the donation of a large private collection.

Science and Society

The rise of modern science had many consequences, some of which are still unfolding. First, it went hand in hand with the rise of a new social group — the international scientific community. Members of this community were linked together by common interests and shared values as well as by journals and the learned scientific societies founded in many countries in the late seventeenth and the eighteenth centuries. The personal success of scientists and scholars depended on making new discoveries, and science became competitive. Second, as governments intervened to support and sometimes direct research, the new scientific community became closely tied to the state and its agendas, a development strongly endorsed by Francis Bacon in England. In addition to England's Royal Society, academies of science were created under state sponsorship in Paris in 1666, Berlin in 1700, and later across Europe. At the same time, scientists developed a critical attitude toward established authority that would inspire thinkers to question traditions in other domains as well.

It was long believed that the Scientific Revolution had little relationship to practical concerns and the life of the masses until the late-eighteenth-century Industrial Revolution (see Chapter 20). More recently, historians have emphasized the crossover between the work of artisans and the rise of science, particularly in the development of the experimental method. Many craftsmen developed strong interest in emerging scientific ideas and, in turn, the practice of science in the seventeenth century often relied on artisans' expertise in making instruments and conducting precise experiments.

Some things did not change in the Scientific Revolution. Scholars have noted that nature was often depicted as a female, whose veil of secrecy needed to be stripped away and penetrated by male experts. New "rational" methods for approaching nature did not question traditional inequalities between the sexes—and may have worsened them in some ways. For example, the rise of universities and other professional institutions for science raised new barriers because most of these organizations did not accept women.

There were, however, a number of noteworthy exceptions. In Italy, universities and academies did offer posts to women, attracting some foreigners spurned at home. Women across Europe worked as makers of wax anatomical models and as botanical and zoological illustrators, like Maria Sibylla Merian. They were also very much involved in informal scientific communities, attending salons (see page 538), participating in scientific experiments, and writing learned treatises. Some female intellectuals became full-fledged members of the philosophical dialogue. In England, Margaret Cavendish, Anne Conway, and Mary Astell all contributed to debates about Descartes's mind-body dualism, among other issues. Descartes himself conducted an intellectual correspondence with the princess Elizabeth of Bohemia, of whom he stated: "I attach more weight to her judgment than to those messieurs the Doctors, who take for a rule of truth the opinions of Aristotle rather than the evidence of reason."[6]

By the time Louis XIV died in 1715, many of the scientific ideas that would eventually coalesce into a new worldview had been assembled. Yet Christian Europe was still strongly attached to its established political and social structures and its traditional spiritual beliefs. By 1775, however, a large portion of western Europe's educated elite had embraced the new ideas. This was the work of many men and women across Europe who participated in the Enlightenment, either as publishers, writers and distributors of texts, or as members of the eager public that consumed them.

The Enlightenment

What new ideas about society and human relations emerged in the Enlightenment, and what new practices and institutions enabled these ideas to take hold?

The Scientific Revolution was a crucial factor in the creation of the new worldview of the eighteenth-century **Enlightenment**. This worldview, which has played a large role in shaping the modern mind, grew out of a rich mix of diverse and often conflicting ideas that were debated in international networks. Despite the diversity, three central concepts stand at the core of Enlightenment thinking. The first and foremost idea was that the methods of natural science could and should be used to examine and understand all aspects of life. This was what intellectuals meant by *reason*, a favorite word of

Enlightenment thinkers. Nothing was to be accepted on faith; everything was to be submitted to **rationalism**, a secular, critical way of thinking. A second important Enlightenment concept was that the scientific method was capable of discovering the laws of human society as well as those of nature. These tenets led to the third key idea, that of progress. Armed with the proper method of discovering the laws of human existence, Enlightenment thinkers believed, it was at least possible for human beings to create better societies and better people.

The Emergence of the Enlightenment

Loosely united by certain key ideas, the European Enlightenment (ca. 1690–1789) was a broad intellectual and cultural movement that gained strength gradually and did not reach its maturity until about 1750. Yet it was the generation that came of age between the publication of Newton's *Principia* in 1687 and the death of Louis XIV in 1715 that tied the crucial knot between the Scientific Revolution and a new outlook on life. Whereas medieval and Reformation thinkers had been concerned primarily with abstract concepts of sin and salvation, and Renaissance humanists had drawn their inspiration from the classical past, Enlightenment thinkers believed that their era had gone far beyond antiquity and that intellectual progress was very possible. Talented writers of that generation popularized hard-to-understand scientific achievements and set an agenda of human problems to be addressed through the methods of science.

Like the Scientific Revolution, the Enlightenment was also fueled by Europe's increased contacts with the wider world. In the wake of the great discoveries of the fifteenth and sixteenth centuries, the rapidly growing travel literature taught Europeans that the peoples of China, India, Africa, and the Americas all had their own very different beliefs and customs. Europeans shaved their faces and let their hair grow. Turks shaved their heads and let their beards grow. In Europe a man bowed before a woman to show respect. In Siam a man turned his back on a woman when he met her because it was disrespectful to look directly at her. Countless similar examples discussed in travel accounts helped change the perspective of educated Europeans. They began to look at truth and morality in relative, rather than absolute, terms. If anything was possible, who could say what was right or wrong?

The excitement of the Scientific Revolution also generated doubt and uncertainty, contributing to a widespread crisis in late-seventeenth-century European thought. In the wake of the devastation wrought by the Thirty Years' War, some people asked whether ideological conformity in religious matters was really necessary. Others skeptically asked if religious truth could ever be known with absolute certainty and concluded that it could not. The atmosphere of doubt spread from religious to political issues. This was a natural extension, since many rulers viewed religious dissent as a form of political opposition and took harsh measures to stifle unorthodox forms of worship. Thus, questioning religion inevitably led to confrontations with the state.

These concerns combined spectacularly in the career of Pierre Bayle (1647–1706), a French Protestant, or Huguenot, who took refuge from government persecution in the tolerant Dutch Republic. Bayle critically examined the religious beliefs and persecutions of the past in his *Historical and Critical Dictionary* (1697). Demonstrating that human beliefs had been extremely varied and very often mistaken, he concluded that nothing can ever be known beyond all doubt, a view known as skepticism. His very influential *Dictionary* was found in more private libraries of eighteenth-century France than any other book.

Like Bayle, many Huguenots fled France for the Dutch Republic, a center of early Enlightenment thought for people of many faiths. The Dutch Jewish philosopher Baruch Spinoza (1632–1677) borrowed Descartes's emphasis on rationalism and his methods of deductive reasoning, but rejected the French thinker's mind-body dualism. Instead, Spinoza came to believe that mind and body are united in one substance and that God and nature were merely two names for the same thing. He envisioned a deterministic universe in which good and evil were merely relative values and our actions were shaped by outside circumstances, not free will. Spinoza was excommunicated by the relatively large Jewish community of Amsterdam for his controversial religious ideas, but he was heralded by his Enlightenment successors as a model of personal virtue and courageous intellectual autonomy.

The German philosopher and mathematician Gottfried Wilhelm von Leibniz (1646–1716), who had developed calculus independently of Isaac Newton (see page 525), refuted both Cartesian dualism and Spinoza's monism (the idea that there is only one substance in the universe). Instead, he adopted the idea of an infinite number of substances or "monads" from which all matter is composed. His *Theodicy* (1710) declared that ours must be "the best of all possible worlds" because it was created by an omnipotent and benevolent God. Leibniz's optimism was later ridiculed by the French philosopher Voltaire in *Candide or Optimism* (1759).

Out of this period of intellectual turmoil came John Locke's *Essay Concerning Human Understanding* (1690). In this work Locke (1632–1704), a physician and member of the Royal Society, brilliantly set forth a new theory about how human beings learn and form their ideas. Whereas Descartes, Spinoza, and Leibniz based their philosophies on deductive logic, Locke insisted that all ideas are derived from experience. The human mind at birth is like a blank tablet, or tabula rasa, on which the environment writes the individual's understanding and beliefs. Human development is therefore determined by education and social institutions. Locke's essay contributed to the theory of sensationalism, the idea that all human ideas and thoughts are produced as a result of sensory impressions. With his emphasis on the role of perception in the acquisition of knowledge, Locke provided a systematic justification of Bacon's emphasis on the importance of observation and experimentation. The *Essay Concerning Human Understanding* passed through many editions and translations and, along with Newton's *Principia*, was one of the dominant intellectual inspirations of the Enlightenment. Locke's equally important contribution to political theory, *Two Treatises of Civil Government* (1690), insisted on the sovereignty of the elected Parliament against the authority of the Crown (see Chapter 15).

The Influence of the Philosophes

Divergences among the early thinkers of the Enlightenment show that, while they shared many of the same premises and questions, the answers they found differed widely. The spread of this spirit of inquiry and debate owed a great deal to the work of the **philosophes** (fee-luh-ZAWFZ), a group of intellectuals who proudly proclaimed that they, at long last, were bringing the light of reason to their ignorant fellow humans. *Philosophe* is the French word for "philosopher," and in the mid-eighteenth century France became a hub of Enlightenment thought. There were at least three reasons for this. First, French was the international language of the educated classes, and France was the wealthiest and most populous country in Europe. Second, the rising unpopularity of King Louis XV and his mistresses generated growing discontent and calls for reform among the educated elite. Third, the French philosophes made it their goal to reach a larger audience of elites, many of whom were joined together in a concept inherited from the Renaissance known as the Republic of Letters—an imaginary transnational realm of the well educated.

One of the greatest philosophes, the baron de Montesquieu (mahn-tuhs-KYOO) (1689–1755), brilliantly pioneered this approach in *The Persian Letters*, an extremely influential social satire published in 1721 and considered the first major work of the French Enlightenment. It consisted of amusing letters supposedly written by two Persian travelers who as outsiders saw European customs in unique ways, thereby allowing Montesquieu a vantage point for criticizing existing practices and beliefs.

Having gained fame by using wit as a weapon against cruelty and superstition, Montesquieu turned to the study of history and politics. His interest was partly personal, for, like many members of the French robe nobility, he was disturbed by the growth in absolutism under Louis XIV (see Chapter 15). But Montesquieu was also inspired by the example of the physical sciences, and he set out to apply the critical method to the problem of government in *The Spirit of Laws* (1748). The result was a complex, comparative study of republics, monarchies, and despotisms.

Showing that forms of government were shaped by history and geography, Montesquieu focused on the conditions that would promote liberty and prevent tyranny. He argued for a separation of powers, with political power divided and shared by a variety of classes and legal estates. Admiring greatly the English balance of power, Montesquieu believed that in France the thirteen high courts—the *parlements*—were frontline defenders of liberty against royal despotism. Apprehensive about the uneducated poor, Montesquieu was clearly no democrat, but his theory of separation of powers had a great impact on the constitutions of the young United States in 1789 and of France in 1791.

The most famous and perhaps most representative philosophe was François Marie Arouet, who was known by the pen name Voltaire (vohl-TAIR) (1694–1778). In his long career, this son of a comfortable middle-class family wrote more than seventy witty volumes, hobnobbed with royalty, and died a millionaire through shrewd speculations. His early career, however, was turbulent, and he was arrested on two occasions for insulting noblemen. Voltaire moved to England for three years in order to avoid a longer prison term in France, and there he came to share Montesquieu's enthusiasm for English liberties and institutions.

Returning to France, Voltaire had the great fortune of meeting Gabrielle-Emilie Le Tonnelier de Breteuil, marquise du Châtelet (SHAH-tuh-lay) (1706–1749), a noblewoman with a passion for science. Inviting Voltaire to live in her country house at Cirey in Lorraine and becoming his long-time companion (under the eyes of her tolerant husband), Madame du Châtelet studied physics and mathematics and published scientific articles and translations, including the first—and only—translation of Newton's *Principia* into French. (See "Primary Source: Du Châtelet, *Foundations of Physics*," page 534.) Excluded from the Royal Academy of Sciences because she was a woman, Madame du Châtelet had no doubt that women's limited role in science was due to their unequal education. Discussing what she would do if she were a ruler, she wrote, "I would reform an abuse which cuts off, so to speak, half the human race. I would make women par-

Madame du Châtelet The marquise du Châtelet was fascinated by the new world system of Isaac Newton. She helped spread Newton's ideas in France by translating his *Principia* and by influencing Voltaire, her companion for fifteen years until her death. (Private Collection/The Bridgeman Art Library)

ticipate in all the rights of humankind, and above all in those of the intellect."[7]

While living at Cirey, Voltaire wrote works praising England and popularizing English science. He had witnessed Newton's burial at Westminster Abbey in 1727, and he lauded Newton as history's greatest man, for he had used his genius for the benefit of humanity. In the true style of the Enlightenment, Voltaire mixed the glorification of science and reason with an appeal for better individuals and institutions.

Yet, like almost all of the philosophes, Voltaire was a reformer, not a revolutionary, in politics. He pessimistically concluded that the best one could hope for in the way of government was a good monarch, since human beings "are very rarely worthy to govern themselves." He lavishly praised Louis XIV and conducted an enthusiastic correspondence with King Frederick the Great of Prussia, whom he admired as an enlightened monarch (see page 541). Nor did Voltaire believe in social and economic equality, insisting that the idea of making servants equal to their masters was "absurd and impossible." The only realizable equality, Voltaire thought, was that "by which the citizen only depends on the laws which protect the freedom of the feeble against the ambitions of the strong."[8]

Voltaire's philosophical and religious positions were much more radical than his social and political beliefs. In the tradition of Bayle, his writings challenged the Catholic Church and Christian theology at almost every point. Voltaire clearly believed in God, but, like many eighteenth-century Enlightenment thinkers, he was a deist, envisioning God as akin to a clockmaker who set the universe in motion and then ceased to intervene in human affairs. Above all, Voltaire and most of the philosophes hated all forms of religious intolerance, which they believed led to fanaticism. Simple piety and human kindness—as embodied in Christ's commandments to "love God and your neighbor as yourself"—were religion enough.

The ultimate strength of the philosophes lay in their dedication and organization. The philosophes felt keenly that they were engaged in a common undertaking that transcended individuals. Their greatest and most representative intellectual achievement was, quite fittingly, a group effort—the seventeen-volume *Encyclopedia: The Rational Dictionary of the Sciences, the Arts, and the Crafts*, edited by Denis Diderot (DEE-duh-roh)

PRIMARY SOURCE   Du Châtelet, *Foundations of Physics*

Gabrielle-Emilie Le Tonnelier de Breteuil, marquise du Châtelet, was a French noble-woman. Frustrated by her limited education as a girl, she befriended philosophes, studied advanced calculus and analytic geometry, and assiduously read the latest scientific publications. Madame du Châtelet translated Newton's Principia *into French and offered her own commentary on his ideas. The passage below is from her* Foundations of Physics *(1740), an overview of natural philosophy that she wrote for her son's education. She died of complications of childbirth at the age of forty-two.*

Descartes appeared in that profound night like a star come to illuminate the universe. The revolution that this great man caused in the sciences is surely more useful, and perhaps even more memorable, than that of the greatest empires, one, it can be said, that human reason owes most to Descartes. For it is very much easier to find the truth, when once one is on the track of it, than to leave those of error. The geometry of this great man, his dioptrics, his method, are masterpieces of sagacity that will make his name immortal, and if he was wrong on some points of physics, that was because he was a man, and it is not given to a single man, nor to a single century, to know all.

We rise to the knowledge of the truth, like those giants who climbed up to the skies by standing on the shoulders of one another.* The Huygenses,† and the Leibnizes learned from Descartes and Galileo, these great men who, so far, are known to you only by name, and with whose works I hope soon to make you acquainted. It is by making the most of the works of Kepler, and using the theorems of Huygens, that M. Newton discovered this universal force spread throughout nature, which makes the planets circle around the Sun, and that operates as gravity on Earth. . . .

*Here, Madame du Châtelet echoes the famous statement of Newton from a 1676 letter to Robert Hooke, an English scientist.

†Christiaan Huygens (1629–1695) was a Dutch astronomer, physicist, and mathematician who observed the correct shape of the rings of Saturn and patented the first pendulum clock.

(1713–1784) and Jean le Rond d'Alembert (dah-luhm-BEHR) (1717–1783). From different circles and with different interests, the two men set out to find coauthors who would examine the rapidly expanding whole of human knowledge. Even more fundamentally, they set out to teach people how to think critically and objectively about all matters. As Diderot said, he wanted the *Encyclopedia* to "change the general way of thinking."[9]

The *Encyclopedia* survived initial resistance from the French government and the Catholic Church. Published between 1751 and 1772, it contained seventy-two thousand articles by leading scientists, writers, skilled workers, and progressive priests, and it treated every aspect of life and knowledge. Not every article was daring or original, but the overall effect was little short of revolutionary. Science and the industrial arts were exalted, religion and immortality questioned. Intolerance, legal injustice, and out-of-date social institutions were openly criticized. The encyclopedists were convinced that greater knowledge would result in greater human happiness, for knowledge was useful and made

Today the systems of Descartes and Newton divide the thinking world, so you should know the one and the other; but so many learned men have taken care to expound and to correct Descartes' system that it will be easy for you to learn from their works. One of my aims in the first part of this work is to put before your eyes the other part of this great process, to make you acquainted with the system of M. Newton, to show you how far making connections and determining probability are pushed, and how the phenomena are explained by the hypothesis of attraction. . . .

Guard yourself, my son, whichever side you take in this dispute among the philosophers, against the inevitable obstinacy to which the spirit of partisanship carries one: this frame of mind is dangerous on all occasions of life; but it is ridiculous in physics. The search for truth is the only thing in which the love of your country must not prevail, and it is surely very unfortunate that the opinions of Newton and of Descartes have become a sort of national affair. About a book of physics one must ask if it is good, not if the author is English, German, or French.

EVALUATE THE EVIDENCE

1. How does Madame du Châtelet explain progress in the physical sciences? What guidance does she offer her son in choosing between Descartes and Newton?

2. What support does this passage provide for the "international" character of the Scientific Revolution? Does this passage suggest any commonalities between the Scientific Revolution and the Enlightenment?

possible economic, social, and political progress. Summing up the new worldview of the Enlightenment, the *Encyclopedia* was widely read, especially in less-expensive reprint editions, and it was extremely influential.

Jean-Jacques Rousseau

In the early 1740s Jean-Jacques Rousseau (1712–1778), the son of a poor Swiss watchmaker, made his way into the Parisian Enlightenment through his brilliant intellect. He contributed articles on music to the *Encyclopedia* and became friends with its editors. Appealing but neurotic, Rousseau came to believe that the philosophes were plotting against him. In the mid-1750s he broke with them, living thereafter as a lonely outsider with his uneducated common-law wife and going in his own highly original direction.

Like other Enlightenment thinkers, Rousseau was passionately committed to individual freedom. Unlike them, however, he attacked rationalism and civilization as destroying, rather than liberating, the individual. Warm, spontaneous feeling had to complement and correct cold intellect. Moreover, the basic goodness of the individual and the unspoiled child had to be protected from the cruel refinements of civilization. Rousseau's ideals greatly influenced the early romantic movement, which rebelled against the culture of the Enlightenment in the late eighteenth century.

Rousseau also called for a rigid division of gender roles. According to Rousseau, women and men were radically different beings. Destined by nature to assume a passive role in sexual relations, women should also be subordinate in social life. Women's love for displaying themselves in public, attending social gatherings, and pulling the strings of power was unnatural and had a corrupting effect on both politics and society. Rousseau thus rejected the sophisticated way of life of Parisian elite women. His criticism led to calls for privileged women to renounce their frivolous ways and stay at home to care for their children.

Rousseau's contribution to political theory in *The Social Contract* (1762) was based on two fundamental concepts: the general will and popular sovereignty. According to Rousseau, the general will is sacred and absolute, reflecting the common interests of all the people, who have displaced the monarch as the holder of sovereign power. The general will is not necessarily the will of the majority, however. At times the general will may be the authentic, long-term needs of the people as correctly interpreted by a farsighted minority. Little noticed in its day, Rousseau's concept of the general will had a great impact on the political aspirations of the American and French Revolutions. Rousseau was both one of the most influential voices of the Enlightenment and, in his rejection of rationalism and social discourse, a harbinger of reaction against Enlightenment ideas.

The International Enlightenment

The Enlightenment was a movement of international dimensions, with thinkers traversing borders in a constant exchange of visits, letters, and printed materials. Voltaire alone wrote almost eighteen thousand letters to correspondents in France and across Europe. The Republic of Letters was a truly cosmopolitan set of networks stretching from western Europe to its colonies in the Americas, to Russia and eastern Europe, and along the routes of trade and empire to Africa and Asia.

Within this broad international conversation, scholars have identified regional and national particularities. Outside of France, many strains of Enlightenment — Protestant, Catholic, and Jewish — sought to reconcile reason with faith, rather than emphasizing the errors of religious fanaticism and intolerance. Some scholars point to a distinctive "Catholic Enlightenment" that aimed to renew and reform the church from within, looking to divine grace rather than human will as the source of progress.

The Scottish Enlightenment, centered in Edinburgh, was marked by an emphasis on common sense and scientific reasoning. After the Act of Union with England in 1707, Scotland was freed from political crisis to experience a vigorous period of intellectual growth. Scottish intellectual revival was also stimulated by the creation of the first public educational system in Europe.

A central figure in Edinburgh was David Hume (1711–1776), whose emphasis on civic morality and religious skepticism had a powerful impact at home and abroad. Building on Locke's teachings on learning, Hume argued that the human mind is really nothing but a bundle of impressions. These impressions originate only in sensory experiences and our habits of joining these experiences together. Since our ideas ultimately reflect only our sensory experiences, our reason cannot tell us anything about questions that cannot be verified by sensory experience (in the form of controlled experiments or mathematics), such as the origin of the universe or the existence of God. Paradoxically, Hume's rationalistic inquiry ended up undermining the Enlightenment's faith in the power of reason.

Another major figure of the Scottish Enlightenment was Adam Smith. His *Theory of Moral Sentiments* (1759) argued that the thriving commercial life of the eighteenth century produced civic virtue through the values of competition, fair play, and individual autonomy. In *An Inquiry into the Nature and Causes of the Wealth of Nations* (1776), Smith attacked the laws and regulations that, he argued, prevented commerce from reaching its full capacity (see Chapter 17).

The Enlightenment in British North America was heavily influenced by English and Scottish thinkers, especially John Locke, and by Montesquieu's arguments for checks and balances in government. Leaders of the American Enlightenment, including Benjamin Franklin and Thomas Jefferson, would play a leading role in the American Revolution (see Chapter 19).

After 1760 Enlightenment ideas were hotly debated in the German-speaking states, often in dialogue with Christian theology. Immanuel Kant (1724–1804), a professor in East Prussia, was the greatest German philosopher of his day. Kant posed the question of the age when he published a pamphlet in 1784 entitled *What Is Enlightenment?* He answered, "*Sapere Aude* [dare to know]! 'Have the courage to use your own understanding' is therefore the motto of enlightenment." He argued that if intellectuals were granted the freedom to exercise their reason publicly in print, enlightenment would almost surely follow. Kant was no revolutionary; he also insisted that in their private lives, individuals must obey all laws, no matter how unreasonable, and should be punished for "impertinent" criticism. Like other Enlightenment figures in central and east-central Europe, Kant thus tried to reconcile absolute monarchical authority and religious faith with a critical public sphere.

Northern Europeans often regarded the Italian states as culturally backward, yet important developments in Enlightenment thought took place in the Italian peninsula. After achieving independence from Habsburg rule (1734), the kingdom of Naples entered a period of intellectual expansion as reformers struggled to lift the heavy weight of church and noble power. In northern Italy a central figure was Cesare Beccaria (1738–1794), a nobleman educated at Jesuit schools and the University of Pavia. His *On Crimes and Punishments* (1764) was a passionate plea for reform of the penal system that decried the use of torture, arbitrary imprisonment, and capital punishment, and advocated the prevention of crime over the reliance on punishment. The text was quickly translated into French and English and made an impact throughout Europe.

Urban Culture and Life in the Public Sphere

Enlightenment ideas did not float on thin air. A series of new institutions and practices encouraged the spread of enlightened ideas in the late seventeenth and eighteenth centuries. First, the European production and consumption of books grew significantly. In Germany, for example, the number of new titles appearing annually rose from roughly six hundred in 1700 to twenty-six hundred in 1780. Moreover, the types of books people read changed dramatically. The proportion of religious and devotional books published in Paris declined after 1750; history and law held constant; the arts and sciences surged.

Reading more books on many more subjects, the educated public approached reading in a new way. The result was what some scholars have called a **reading revolution**. The old style of reading in Europe had been centered on a core of sacred texts that taught earthly duty and obedience to God. Reading had been patriarchal and communal, with the father slowly reading the text aloud to his assembled family. Now reading involved a broader field of books that constantly changed. Reading became individual and silent, and texts could be questioned. Subtle but profound, the reading revolution ushered in new ways of relating to the written word.

Conversation, discussion, and debate also played a critical role in the Enlightenment. Evolving from the gatherings presided over by the *précieuses* in the late seventeenth century (see Chapter 15), the **salon** was a regular meeting held in the elegant private drawing rooms (or salons) of talented, wealthy men and women. There they encouraged the exchange of witty observations on literature, science, and philosophy among great aristocrats, wealthy middle-class financiers, high-ranking officials, and noteworthy foreigners. Many of the most celebrated salons were hosted by women, known as *salonnières* (sah-lahn-ee-EHRZ), such as Madame du Deffand, whose weekly Parisian salon included such guests as Montesquieu, d'Alembert, and Benjamin Franklin, then serving as the first U.S. ambassador to France. Invitations to salons were highly coveted; introductions to the rich and powerful could make the career of an ambitious writer, and, in turn, the social elite found amusement and cultural prestige in their ties to up-and-coming artists and men of letters.

The salon thus represented an accommodation between the ruling classes and the leaders of Enlightenment thought. Salons were sites in which the philosophes, the French nobility, and the prosperous middle classes intermingled and influenced one another while maintaining due deference to social rank. Critical thought about almost any question became fashionable and flourished alongside hopes for human progress through greater knowledge and enlightened public opinion.

Elite women also exercised great influence on artistic taste. Soft pastels, ornate interiors, sentimental portraits, and starry-eyed lovers protected by hovering cupids were all hallmarks of the style they favored. This style, known as **rococo** (ruh-KOH-koh), was popular throughout Europe in the period from 1720 to 1780. It has been argued that feminine influence in the drawing room went hand in hand with the emergence of polite society and the general attempt to civilize a rough military nobility. Similarly, some philosophes championed greater rights and expanded education for women, claiming that the position and treatment of women were the best indicators of a society's level of civilization and decency.[10] For these male philosophes, greater rights for women did not mean equal rights, and the philosophes were not particularly disturbed by the fact that elite women remained legally subordinate to men in economic and political affairs. Elite women lacked many rights, but so did the majority of European men, who were poor.

While membership at the salons was restricted to the wellborn, the well connected, and the exceptionally talented, a number of institutions provided the rest of society with access to Enlightenment ideas. Lending libraries served an important function for people who could not afford their own books. The coffeehouses that first appeared in the late seventeenth century became meccas of philosophical discussion. In addition to these institutions, book clubs, debating societies, Masonic lodges (groups of Freemasons, a secret society that accepted craftsmen and shopkeepers as well as middle-class men and nobles), and newspapers all played roles in the creation of a new **public sphere** that celebrated open debate informed by critical reason. The public sphere was an idealized space where members of society came together as individuals to discuss issues relevant to the society, economics, and politics of the day.

What of the common people? Did they participate in the Enlightenment? Enlightenment philosophes did not direct their message to peasants or urban laborers. They believed that the masses had no time or talent for philosophical speculation and that elevating them would be a long and potentially dangerous process. Deluded by superstitions and driven by violent passions, the people, they thought, were like children in need of firm parental guidance. D'Alembert characteristically made a sharp distinction between "the truly enlightened public" and "the blind and noisy multitude."[11] Despite these prejudices, the ideas of the philosophes did find an audience among some members of the common people. At a time of rising literacy, book prices were dropping and many philosophical ideas were popularized in cheap pamphlets and through public reading. Although they were barred from salons and academies, ordinary people were not immune to the new ideas in circulation.

Race and the Enlightenment

If philosophers did not believe the lower classes qualified for enlightenment, how did they regard individuals of different races? In recent years, historians have found in the Scientific Revolution and the Enlightenment a crucial turning point in European ideas about race. A primary catalyst for new ideas about race was the urge to classify nature unleashed by the Scientific Revolution's insistence on careful empirical observation. In *The System of Nature* (1735), Swedish botanist Carl von Linné argued that nature was organized into a God-given hierarchy. As scientists developed taxonomies of plant and animal species, they also began to classify humans into hierarchically ordered "races" and to investigate the origins of race. The comte de Buffon (komt duh buh-FOHN) argued that humans originated with one species that then developed into distinct races due largely to climatic conditions.

Enlightenment thinkers such as David Hume and Immanuel Kant helped popularize these ideas. In *Of Natural Characters* (1748), Hume wrote:

> I am apt to suspect the negroes and in general all other species of men (for there are four or five different kinds) to be naturally inferior to the whites. There never was a civilized nation of any other complexion than white, nor even any individual eminent amongst them, no arts, no sciences. . . . Such a uniform and constant difference could not happen, in so many countries and ages if nature had not made an original distinction between these breeds of men.[12]

Kant taught and wrote as much about "anthropology" and "geography" as he did about standard philosophical themes such as logic, metaphysics, and moral philosophy. He elaborated his views about race in *On the Different Races of Man* (1775), claiming that there were four human races, each of which had derived from an original race. According to Kant, the closest descendants of the original race were the white inhabitants of northern Germany. (Scientists now believe the human race originated in Africa.)

Using the word *race* to designate biologically distinct groups of humans, akin to distinct animal species, was new. Previously, Europeans grouped other peoples into "nations" based on their historical, political, and cultural affiliations, rather than on supposedly innate physical differences. Unsurprisingly, when European thinkers drew up a hierarchical classification of human species, their own "race" was placed at the top. Europeans had long believed they were culturally superior to "barbaric" peoples in Africa and, since 1492, the New World. Now emerging ideas about racial difference taught them they were biologically superior as well. In turn, scientific racism helped legitimate and justify the tremendous growth of slavery that occurred during the eighteenth century. If one "race" of humans was fundamentally different and inferior, its members could be seen as particularly fit for enslavement and liable to benefit from tutelage by the superior race.

Racist ideas did not go unchallenged. The abbé Raynal's *History of the Two Indies* (1770) fiercely attacked slavery and the abuses of European colonization. *Encyclopedia* editor Denis Diderot adopted Montesquieu's technique of criticizing European attitudes through the voice of outsiders in his dialogue between Tahitian villagers and their European visitors. Scottish philosopher James Beattie (1735–1803) responded directly to claims of white superiority by pointing out that Europeans had started out as savage as nonwhites supposedly were and that many non-European peoples in the Americas,

Encyclopedia Image of the Cotton Industry   This romanticized image of slavery in the West Indies cotton industry was published in Diderot and d'Alembert's *Encyclopedia*. It shows enslaved men, at right, gathering and picking over cotton bolls, while the woman at left mills the bolls to remove their seeds. The *Encyclopedia* presented mixed views on slavery; one article described it as "indispensable" to economic development, while others argued passionately for the natural right to freedom of all mankind. (Courtesy, Dover Publications)

Asia, and Africa had achieved high levels of civilization. Former slaves, like Olaudah Equiano (see Chapter 17) and Ottobah Cugoana, published eloquent memoirs testifying to the horrors of slavery and the innate equality of all humans. These challenges to racism, however, were in the minority. Many other Enlightenment voices supporting racial inequality—Thomas Jefferson among them—may be found.

Scholars are only at the beginning of efforts to understand the links between Enlightenment thinkers' ideas about race and their notions of equality, progress, and reason. There are clear parallels, though, between the use of science to propagate racial hierarchies and its use to defend social inequalities between men and women. French philosopher Jean-Jacques Rousseau used women's "natural" passivity to argue for their subordinate role in society, just as other thinkers used non-Europeans' "natural" inferiority to defend slavery and colonial domination. The new powers of science and reason were thus marshaled to imbue traditional stereotypes with the force of natural law.

Enlightened Absolutism

What impact did new ways of thinking have on political developments and monarchical absolutism?

How did the Enlightenment influence political developments? To this important question there is no easy answer. Most Enlightenment thinkers outside of England and the Netherlands, especially in central and eastern Europe, believed that political change could best come from above—from the ruler—rather than from below. Royal absolutism was a fact of life, and the monarchs of Europe's leading states clearly had no intention of giving up their great power. Therefore, the philosophes and their sympathizers realistically concluded that a benevolent absolutism offered the best opportunities for improving society.

Many government officials were interested in philosophical ideas. They were among the best-educated members of society, and their daily involvement in complex affairs of state made them naturally attracted to ideas for improving human society. Encouraged and instructed by these officials, some absolutist rulers tried to reform their governments in accordance with Enlightenment ideals—what historians have called the **enlightened absolutism** of the later eighteenth century. In both Catholic and Protestant lands, rulers typically fused Enlightenment principles with religion, drawing support for their innovations from reform-minded religious thinkers. The most influential of the new-style monarchs were in Prussia, Russia, and Austria, and their example illustrates both the achievements and the great limitations of enlightened absolutism. France experienced its own brand of enlightened absolutism in the contentious decades prior to the French Revolution (see Chapter 19).

Frederick the Great of Prussia

Frederick II (r. 1740–1786), commonly known as Frederick the Great, built masterfully on the work of his father, Frederick William I (see Chapter 15). Although in his youth he embraced culture and literature rather than the militarism championed by his father, by the time he came to the throne Frederick was determined to use the splendid army he had inherited.

Therefore, when the young empress Maria Theresa of Austria inherited the Habsburg dominions upon the death of her father Charles VI, Frederick pounced. He invaded her rich province of Silesia (sigh-LEE-zhuh), defying solemn Prussian promises to respect the Pragmatic Sanction, a diplomatic agreement that had guaranteed Maria Theresa's succession. In 1742, as other greedy powers vied for her lands in the European War of the Austrian Succession (1740–1748), Maria Theresa was forced to cede almost all of Silesia to Prussia. In one stroke Prussia had doubled its population to 6 million people. Now Prussia unquestionably stood as a European Great Power.

Though successful in 1742, Frederick had to fight against great odds to save Prussia from total destruction after the ongoing competition between Britain and France for colonial empire brought another great conflict in 1756. Maria Theresa, seeking to regain Silesia, formed an alliance with the leaders of France and Russia. The aim of the alliance during the resulting Seven Years' War (1756–1763) was to conquer Prussia and divide up its territory. Despite invasions from all sides, Frederick fought on with stoic courage. In the end he was miraculously saved: Peter III came to the Russian throne in 1762 and called off the attack against Frederick, whom he greatly admired.

The terrible struggle of the Seven Years' War tempered Frederick's interest in territorial expansion and brought him to consider how more humane policies for his subjects might also strengthen the state. Thus Frederick went beyond a superficial commitment to Enlightenment culture for himself and his circle. He tolerantly allowed his subjects to believe as they wished in religious and philosophical matters. He promoted the advancement of knowledge, improving his country's schools and permitting scholars to publish their findings. Moreover, Frederick tried to improve the lives of his subjects more directly. As he wrote to his friend Voltaire, "I must enlighten my people, cultivate their manners and morals, and make them as happy as human beings can be, or as happy as the means at my disposal permit."

The legal system and the bureaucracy were Frederick's primary tools. Prussia's laws were simplified, torture was abolished, and judges decided cases quickly and impartially. Prussian officials became famous for their hard work and honesty. After the Seven Years' War ended in 1763, Frederick's government energetically promoted the reconstruction of agriculture and industry. Frederick himself set a good example. He worked hard and lived modestly, claiming that he was "only the first servant of the state." Thus Frederick justified monarchy in terms of practical results and said nothing of the divine right of kings.

Frederick's dedication to high-minded government went only so far, however. While he condemned serfdom in the abstract, he accepted it in practice and did not free the serfs on his own estates. He accepted and extended the privileges of the nobility, who remained the backbone of the army and the entire Prussian state.

In reforming Prussia's bureaucracy, Frederick drew on the principles of **cameralism**, the German science of public administration that emerged in the decades following the Thirty Years' War. Influential throughout the German lands, cameralism held that monarchy was the best of all forms of government, that all elements of society should be placed at the service of the state, and that, in turn, the state should make use of its resources and authority to improve society. Predating the Enlightenment, cameralist interest in the public good was usually inspired by the needs of war. Cameralism shared with the Enlightenment an emphasis on rationality, progress, and utilitarianism.

Catherine the Great of Russia

Catherine the Great of Russia (r. 1762–1796) was one of the most remarkable rulers of her age, and the French philosophes adored her. Catherine was a German princess from Anhalt-Zerbst, an insignificant principality sandwiched between Prussia and Saxony. Her father commanded a regiment of the Prussian army, but her mother was related to the Romanovs of Russia, and that proved to be Catherine's opening to power.

Catherine's Romanov connection made her a suitable bride at the age of fifteen for the heir to the Russian throne. It was a mismatch from the beginning, but her *Memoirs* made her ambitions clear: "I did not care about Peter, but I did care about the crown." When her husband, Peter III, came to power during the Seven Years' War, his decision to withdraw Russian troops from the coalition against Prussia alienated the army. Catherine profited from his unpopularity to form a conspiracy to depose her husband. In 1762 Catherine's lover Gregory Orlov and his three brothers, all army officers, murdered Peter, and the German princess became empress of Russia.

Catherine had drunk deeply at the Enlightenment well. Never questioning that absolute monarchy was the best form of government, she set out to rule in an enlightened manner. She had three main goals. First, she worked hard to continue Peter the Great's effort to bring the culture of western Europe to Russia (see Chapter 15). To do so, she imported Western architects, musicians, and intellectuals. She bought masterpieces of Western art and patronized the philosophes. An enthusiastic letter writer, she corresponded extensively with Voltaire and praised him as the "champion of the human race." When the French government banned the *Encyclopedia*, she offered to publish it in St. Petersburg, and she sent money to Diderot when he needed it. With these actions, Catherine won good press in the West for herself and for her country. Moreover, this intellectual ruler, who wrote plays and loved good talk, set the tone for the entire Russian nobility. Peter the Great westernized Russian armies, but it was Catherine who westernized the imagination of the Russian nobility.

Catherine's second goal was domestic reform, and she began her reign with sincere and ambitious projects. In 1767 she appointed a

Catherine the Great   Strongly influenced by the Enlightenment, Catherine the Great cultivated the French philosophes and instituted moderate reforms, only to reverse them in the aftermath of Pugachev's rebellion. This equestrian portrait now hangs above her throne in the palace throne room in St. Petersburg. (Musée des Beaux-Arts, Chartres/The Bridgeman Art Library)

legislative commission to prepare a new law code. This project was never completed, but Catherine did restrict the practice of torture and allowed limited religious toleration. She also tried to improve education and strengthen local government. The philosophes applauded these measures and hoped more would follow.

Such was not the case. In 1773 a common Cossack soldier named Emelian Pugachev sparked a gigantic uprising of serfs, very much as Stenka Razin had done a century earlier (see Chapter 15). Proclaiming himself the true tsar, Pugachev issued orders abolishing serfdom, taxes, and army service. Thousands joined his cause, slaughtering landlords and officials over a vast area of southwestern Russia. Pugachev's untrained forces eventually proved no match for Catherine's noble-led army. Betrayed by his own company, Pugachev was captured and savagely executed.

Pugachev's rebellion put an end to any intentions Catherine had about reforming the system. The peasants were clearly dangerous, and her empire rested on the support of the nobility. After 1775 Catherine gave the nobles absolute control of their serfs, and she extended serfdom into new areas, such as Ukraine. In 1785 she freed nobles forever from taxes and state service. Under Catherine the Russian nobility attained its most exalted position, and serfdom entered its most oppressive phase.

Catherine's third goal was territorial expansion, and in this respect she was extremely successful. Her armies subjugated the last descendants of the Mongols and the Crimean Tartars, and began the conquest of the Caucasus (KAW-kuh-suhs). Her greatest coup by far was the partition of Poland (Map 16.1). When, between 1768 and 1772, Catherine's armies scored unprecedented victories against the Ottomans and thereby threatened to disturb the balance of power between Russia and Austria in eastern Europe, Frederick of Prussia obligingly came forward with a deal. He proposed that Turkey be let off easily and that Prussia, Austria, and Russia each compensate itself by taking a gigantic slice of the weakly ruled Polish territory. Catherine jumped at the chance. The first partition of Poland took place in 1772. Subsequent partitions in 1793 and 1795 gave away the rest of Polish territory, and the ancient republic of Poland vanished from the map.

The Austrian Habsburgs

Another female monarch, Maria Theresa (r. 1740–1780) of Austria, set out to reform her nation, although traditional power politics was a more important motivation for her than were Enlightenment teachings. A devoutly Catholic mother and wife who inherited power from her father, Charles VI, Maria Theresa was a remarkable but old-fashioned absolutist. Her more radical son, Joseph II (r. 1780–1790), drew on Enlightenment ideals, earning the title of "revolutionary emperor."

Emerging from the long War of the Austrian Succession in 1748 with the serious loss of Silesia, Maria Theresa was determined to introduce reforms that would make the state stronger and more efficient. First, she initiated church reform, with measures aimed at limiting the papacy's influence, eliminating many religious holidays, and reducing the number of monasteries. Second, a whole series of administrative renovations strengthened the central bureaucracy, smoothed out some provincial differences, and revamped the tax system, taxing even the lands of nobles, previously exempt from taxation. Third, the government sought to improve the lot of the agricultural population, cautiously reducing the power of lords over their hereditary serfs and their partially free peasant tenants.

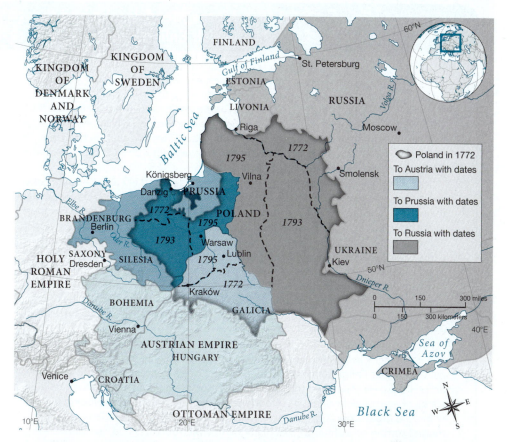

MAP 16.1   The Partition of Poland, 1772–1795

In 1772 war between Russia and Austria threatened over Russian gains from the Ottoman Empire. To satisfy desires for expansion without fighting, Prussia's Frederick the Great proposed that parts of Poland be divided among Austria, Prussia, and Russia. In 1793 and 1795 the three powers partitioned the remainder, and the republic of Poland ceased to exist.

Coregent with his mother from 1765 onward and a strong supporter of change from above, Joseph II moved forward rapidly when he came to the throne in 1780. Most notably, Joseph abolished serfdom in 1781, and in 1789 he decreed that peasants could pay landlords in cash rather than through labor on their land. This measure was violently rejected not only by the nobility but also by the peasants it was intended to help, because they lacked the necessary cash. When a disillusioned Joseph died prematurely at forty-nine, the entire Habsburg empire was in turmoil. His brother Leopold II (r. 1790–1792) canceled Joseph's radical edicts in order to re-establish order. Peasants once again were required to do forced labor for their lords.

Despite differences in their policies, Joseph II and the other absolutists of the later eighteenth century combined old-fashioned state-building with the culture and critical thinking of the Enlightenment. In doing so, they succeeded in expanding the role of the state in the life of society. They perfected bureaucratic machines that were to prove surprisingly adaptive and enduring. Their failure to implement policies we would

INDIVIDUALS IN SOCIETY • Moses Mendelssohn and the Jewish Enlightenment

In 1743 a small, humpbacked Jewish boy with a stammer left his poor parents in Dessau in central Germany and walked eighty miles to Berlin, the capital of Frederick the Great's Prussia. According to one story, when the boy reached the Rosenthaler (ROH-zuhn-taw-lehr) Gate, the only one through which Jews could pass, he told the inquiring watchman that his name was Moses and that he had come to Berlin "to learn." The watchman laughed and waved him through. "Go Moses, the sea has opened before you."*

In Berlin the young Mendelssohn studied Jewish law and eked out a living copying Hebrew manuscripts in a beautiful hand. But he was soon fascinated by an intellectual world that had been closed to him in the Dessau ghetto. There, like most Jews throughout central Europe, he had spoken Yiddish—a mixture of German, Polish, and Hebrew. Now, working mainly on his own, he mastered German; learned Latin, Greek, French, and English; and studied mathematics and Enlightenment philosophy. Word of his exceptional abilities spread in Berlin's Jewish community (the dwelling of 1,500 of the city's 100,000 inhabitants). He began tutoring the children of a wealthy Jewish silk merchant, and he soon became the merchant's clerk and later his partner. But his great passion remained the life of the mind and the spirit, which he avidly pursued in his off-hours.

Gentle and unassuming in his personal life, Mendelssohn was a bold thinker. Reading eagerly in Western philosophy since antiquity, he was, as a pious Jew, soon convinced that Enlightenment teachings need not be opposed to Jewish thought and religion. He concluded that reason could complement and strengthen religion, although each would retain its integrity as a separate sphere.† Developing his idea in his first great work, *On the Immortality of the Soul* (1767), Mendelssohn used the neutral setting of a philosophical dialogue between Socrates and his followers in ancient Greece to argue that the human soul lived forever. In refusing to bring religion and critical thinking into conflict, he was strongly influenced by contemporary

*H. Kupferberg, *The Mendelssohns: Three Generations of Genius* (New York: Charles Scribner's Sons, 1972), p. 3.
†David Sorkin, *Moses Mendelssohn and the Religious Enlightenment* (Berkeley: University of California Press, 1996), pp. 8ff.

recognize as humane and enlightened—such as abolishing serfdom—may reveal inherent limitations in Enlightenment thinking about equality and social justice, rather than deficiencies in their execution of Enlightenment programs. The fact that leading philosophes supported rather than criticized eastern rulers' policies exposes the blind spots of the era.

Jewish Life and the Limits of Enlightened Absolutism

Perhaps the best example of the limitations of enlightened absolutism are the debates surrounding the emancipation of the Jews. Europe's small Jewish populations lived under highly discriminatory laws. For the most part, Jews were confined to tiny, overcrowded

German philosophers who argued similarly on behalf of Christianity. He reflected the way the German Enlightenment generally supported established religion, in contrast to the French Enlightenment, which attacked it.

Mendelssohn's treatise on the human soul captivated the educated German public, which marveled that a Jew could have written a philosophical masterpiece. In the excitement, a Christian zealot named Lavater challenged Mendelssohn in a pamphlet to accept Christianity or to demonstrate how the Christian faith was not "reasonable." Replying politely but passionately, the Jewish philosopher affirmed that his studies had only strengthened him in his faith, although he did not seek to convert anyone not born into Judaism. Rather, he urged toleration in religious matters and spoke up courageously against Jewish oppression.

Orthodox Jew and German philosophe, Moses Mendelssohn serenely combined two very different worlds. He built a bridge from the ghetto to the dominant culture over which many Jews would pass, including his novelist daughter Dorothea and his famous grandson, the composer Felix Mendelssohn.

QUESTIONS FOR ANALYSIS

1. How did Mendelssohn seek to influence Jewish religious thought in his time?
2. How do Mendelssohn's ideas compare with those of the French Enlightenment?

ONLINE DOCUMENT ASSIGNMENT

How did Moses Mendelssohn fit into the larger Enlightenment debate about religious tolerance? Examine primary sources written by Mendelssohn and his contemporaries, and then complete a writing assignment based on the evidence and details from this chapter.

bedfordstmartins.com/mckaywestvalue

ghettos, were excluded by law from most professions, and could be ordered out of a kingdom at a moment's notice. Still, a very few did manage to succeed and to obtain the right of permanent settlement, usually by performing some special service for the state. Many rulers relied on Jewish bankers for loans to raise armies and run their kingdoms. Jewish merchants prospered in international trade because they could rely on contacts with colleagues in Jewish communities scattered across Europe.

In the eighteenth century an Enlightenment movement known as the **Haskalah** emerged from within the European Jewish community, led by the Prussian philosopher Moses Mendelssohn (1729–1786). (See "Individuals in Society: Moses Mendelssohn and the Jewish Enlightenment," above.) Christian and Jewish Enlightenment philosophers, including Mendelssohn, began to advocate for freedom and civil rights for European

Jews. In an era of reason and progress, they argued, restrictions on religious grounds could not stand. The Haskalah accompanied a period of controversial social change within Jewish communities, in which rabbinic controls loosened and heightened interaction with Christians took place.

Arguments for tolerance won some ground. The British Parliament passed a law allowing naturalization of Jews in 1753, but later repealed the law due to public outrage. The most progressive reforms took place under Austrian emperor Joseph II. Among his liberal edicts of the 1780s were measures intended to integrate Jews more fully into society, including eligibility for military service, admission to higher education and artisanal trades, and removal of requirements for special clothing or emblems. Welcomed by many Jews, these reforms raised fears among traditionalists of assimilation into the general population.

Many monarchs rejected all ideas of emancipation. Although he permitted freedom of religion to his Christian subjects, Frederick the Great of Prussia firmly opposed any general emancipation for the Jews, as he did for the serfs. Catherine the Great, who acquired most of Poland's large Jewish population when she annexed part of that country in the late eighteenth century, similarly refused. In 1791 she established the Pale of Settlement, a territory including parts of modern-day Poland, Latvia, Lithuania, Ukraine, and Belarus, in which most Jews were required to live. Jewish habitation was restricted to the Pale until the Russian Revolution in 1917.

The first European state to remove all restrictions on the Jews was France under the French Revolution. Over the next hundred years, Jews gradually won full legal and civil rights throughout the rest of western Europe. Emancipation in eastern Europe took even longer and aroused more conflict and violence.

Notes

1. Quoted in Butterfield, *The Origins of Modern Science*, p. 47.
2. Ibid., p. 120.
3. Quoted in John Freely, *Aladdin's Lamp: How Greek Science Came to Europe Through the Islamic World* (New York: Knopf, 2009), p. 206.
4. Ibid., p. 217.
5. Ibid., p. 225.
6. Jacqueline Broad, *Women Philosophers of the Seventeenth Century* (Cambridge, U.K.: Cambridge University Press, 2003), p. 17.
7. L. Schiebinger, *The Mind Has No Sex? Women in the Origins of Modern Science* (Cambridge, Mass.: Harvard University Press, 1989), p. 64.
8. Quoted in G. L. Mosse et al., eds., *Europe in Review* (Chicago: Rand McNally, 1964), p. 156.
9. Quoted in P. Gay, "The Unity of the Enlightenment," *History* 3 (1960): 25.
10. See E. Fox-Genovese, "Women in the Enlightenment," in *Becoming Visible: Women in European History*, 2d ed., ed. R. Bridenthal, C. Koonz, and S. Stuard (Boston: Houghton Mifflin, 1987), esp. pp. 252–259, 263–265.
11. Jean Le Rond d'Alembert, *Eloges lus dans les séances publiques de l'Académie française* (Paris, 1779), p. ix, quoted in Mona Ozouf, " 'Public Opinion' at the End of the Old Regime," *The Journal of Modern History* 60, Supplement: Rethinking French Politics in 1788 (September 1988): S9.
12. Quoted in Emmanuel Chukwudi Eze, ed., *Race and the Enlightenment: A Reader* (Oxford: Blackwell, 1997), p. 33.

Chapter Review

MAKE IT STICK

LearningCurve
bedfordstmartins.com/mckaywestvalue

After reading the chapter, use LearningCurve to retain what you've read.

IDENTIFY KEY TERMS

Identify and explain the significance of each item below.

natural philosophy (p. 517)

Copernican hypothesis (p. 520)

experimental method (p. 522)

law of inertia (p. 522)

law of universal gravitation (p. 525)

empiricism (p. 526)

Cartesian dualism (p. 526)

Enlightenment (p. 529)

rationalism (p. 530)

philosophes (p. 531)

reading revolution (p. 538)

salon (p. 538)

rococo (p. 538)

public sphere (p. 539)

enlightened absolutism (p. 541)

cameralism (p. 542)

Haskalah (p. 547)

REVIEW THE MAIN IDEAS

Answer the focus questions from each section of the chapter.

- What revolutionary discoveries were made in the sixteenth and seventeenth centuries? (p. 517)

- What intellectual and social changes occurred as a result of the Scientific Revolution? (p. 525)

- What new ideas about society and human relations emerged in the Enlightenment, and what new practices and institutions enabled these ideas to take hold? (p. 529)

- What impact did new ways of thinking have on political developments and monarchical absolutism? (p. 541)

MAKE CONNECTIONS

Think about the larger developments and continuities within and across chapters.

1. How did the era of European exploration (Chapter 14) impact the ideas of scientists and philosophers discussed in this chapter? How did contact with new peoples and places stimulate new forms of thought?

2. What was the relationship between the Scientific Revolution and the Enlightenment? How did new ways of understanding the natural world influence thinking about human society?

ONLINE DOCUMENT ASSIGNMENT

Moses Mendelssohn

How did Moses Mendelssohn fit into the larger Enlightenment debate about religious tolerance?

You encountered Moses Mendelssohn's story on page 546. Keeping the question above in mind, go online and examine primary sources from Mendelssohn's time—including a letter to a contemporary, an excerpt from a play, and a philosophical treatise. Then complete a writing assignment based on the evidence and details from this chapter.

bedfordstmartins.com/mckaywestvalue

CHRONOLOGY

ca. 1540–1700	• Scientific Revolution
ca. 1690–1789	• Enlightenment
ca. 1700–1800	• Growth of book publishing
1720–1780	• Rococo style in art and decoration
1740–1748	• War of the Austrian Succession
1740–1780	• Reign of the empress Maria Theresa of Austria
1740–1786	• Reign of Frederick the Great of Prussia
ca. 1740–1789	• Salons led by Parisian elites
1751–1772	• Philosophes publish *Encyclopedia: The Rational Dictionary of the Sciences, the Arts, and the Crafts*
1756–1763	• Seven Years' War
1762–1796	• Reign of Catherine the Great of Russia
1780–1790	• Reign of Joseph II of Austria
1791	• Establishment of the Pale of Settlement

17

✓ LearningCurve
bedfordstmartins.com/mckaywestvalue
After reading the chapter, use
LearningCurve to retain what
you've read.

The Expansion of Europe

1650–1800

ABSOLUTISM AND ARISTOCRACY, A COMBINATION OF RAW POWER and elegant refinement, were a world apart from the common people. For most people in the eighteenth century, life remained a struggle with poverty and uncertainty, with the landlord and the tax collector. In 1700 peasants on the land and artisans in their shops lived little better than had their ancestors in the Middle Ages, primarily because European societies still could not produce very much as measured by modern standards. Despite the hard work of ordinary men and women, there was seldom enough good food, warm clothing, and decent housing. The idea of progress, of substantial improvement in the lives of great numbers of people, was still the dream of only a small elite in fashionable salons.

Yet the economic basis of European life was beginning to change. In the course of the eighteenth century, the European economy emerged from the long crisis of the seventeenth century, responded to challenges, and began to expand once again. Population resumed its growth, while colonial empires extended and developed. Some areas were more fortunate than others. The rising Atlantic powers—the Dutch Republic, France, and above all England—and their colonies led the way. The expansion of agriculture, industry, trade, and population marked the beginning of a surge comparable to that of the eleventh- and twelfth-century springtime of European civilization. But this time, broadly based expansion was not cut short by plague and famine. This time the response to new challenges led toward one of the most influential developments in human history, the Industrial Revolution, considered in Chapter 20.

Working the Land

What important developments led to increased agricultural production, and how did these changes affect peasants?

At the end of the seventeenth century the economy of Europe was agrarian. With the exception of the Dutch Republic and England, at least 80 percent of the people of western Europe drew their livelihoods from agriculture. In eastern Europe the percentage was considerably higher. Men and women were tied to the land, plowing fields and sowing seed, reaping harvests and storing grain. Yet even in a rich agricultural region such as the Po Valley in northern Italy, every bushel of wheat seed sown yielded on average only five or six bushels of grain at harvest. By modern standards, output was distressingly low.

In most regions of Europe, climatic conditions produced poor or disastrous harvests every eight or nine years. In famine years the number of deaths soared far above normal. A third of a village's population might disappear in a year or two. But new developments in agricultural technology and methods gradually brought an end to the ravages of hunger in western Europe.

The Legacy of the Open-Field System

Why, in the late seventeenth century, did many areas of Europe produce barely enough food to survive? The answer lies in the pattern of farming that had developed in the Middle Ages, which sustained fairly large numbers of people, but did not produce material abundance. From the Middle Ages up to the seventeenth century, much of Europe was farmed through the open-field system. The land to be cultivated was divided into several large fields, which were in turn cut up into long, narrow strips. The fields were open, and the strips were not enclosed into small plots by fences or hedges. The whole peasant village followed the same pattern of plowing, sowing, and harvesting in accordance with long-standing traditions.

The ever-present problem was soil exhaustion. Wheat planted year after year in a field will deplete nitrogen in the soil. Since the supply of manure for fertilizer was limited, the only way for the land to recover was to lie fallow for a period of time. Clover and other annual grasses that sprang up in unplanted fields restored nutrients to the soil and also provided food for livestock. In the early Middle Ages a year of fallow was alternated with a year of cropping; then three-year rotations were introduced. On each strip of land, a year of wheat or rye was followed by a year of oats or beans and only then by a year of fallow. Peasants staggered the rotation of crops, so some wheat, legumes, and pastureland were always available. The three-year system was an important achievement because cash crops could be grown two years out of three, rather than only one year in two.

Traditional village rights reinforced communal patterns of farming. In addition to rotating field crops in a uniform way, villages maintained open meadows for hay and natural pasture. After the harvest villagers also pastured their animals on the wheat or rye stubble. In many places such pasturing followed a brief period, also established by tradition, for the gleaning of grain. In this process, poor women would go through the fields picking up the few single grains that had fallen to the ground in the course of the harvest. Many villages were surrounded by woodlands, also held in common, which provided essential firewood, building materials, and nutritional roots and berries.

The state and landlords continued to levy heavy taxes and high rents, thereby stripping peasants of much of their meager earnings. The level of exploitation varied. Generally speaking, the peasants of eastern Europe were worst off. As we saw in Chapter 15, they were serfs bound to their lords in hereditary service. In much of eastern Europe, working several days per week on the lord's land was not uncommon. Well into the nineteenth century, individual Russian serfs and serf families were regularly bought and sold.

Social conditions were better in western Europe, where peasants were generally free from serfdom. In France, western Germany, England, and the Low Countries (modern-day Belgium and the Netherlands), peasants could own land and could pass it on to their children. In years with normal harvests, most people had enough food to fill their bellies. Yet life in the village was hard, and poverty was the reality for most people.

New Methods of Agriculture

The seventeenth century saw important gains in productivity in some regions that would slowly extend to the rest of Europe. By 1700 less than half of the population of Britain and the Dutch Republic worked in agriculture, producing enough to feed the remainder of the population. Many elements combined in this production growth, but the key was new ways of rotating crops that allowed farmers to forgo the unproductive fallow period altogether and maintain their land in continuous cultivation. The secret to eliminating the fallow lay in deliberately alternating grain with crops that restored nutrients to the soil, such as peas and beans, root crops such as turnips and potatoes, and clover and other grasses.

Clover was one of the most important crops, because it restores nitrogen directly to the soil through its roots. Other crops produced additional benefits. Potatoes and many types of beans came to Europe as part of the sixteenth-century Columbian exchange between the New and the Old Worlds (see Chapter 14). Originally perceived by Europeans as fit only for animal feed, potatoes eventually made their way to the human table, where they provided a nutritious supplement to the peasant's meager diet. With more fodder, hay, and root vegetables for the winter months, peasants and larger farmers could build up their herds of cattle and sheep. More animals meant more manure to fertilize and restore the soil. More animals also meant more meat and dairy products as well as more power to pull ploughs in the fields and bring carts to market.

Over time, crop rotation spread to other parts of Europe, and farmers developed increasingly sophisticated patterns of crop rotation to suit different kinds of soils. For example, in the late eighteenth century farmers in French Flanders near Lille alternated a number of grain, root, and hay crops in a given field on a ten-year schedule. Ongoing experimentation, fueled by developments in the Scientific Revolution (see Chapter 16), led to more methodical farming.

Advocates of the new crop rotations, who included an emerging group of experimental scientists, some government officials, and a few big landowners, believed that new methods were scarcely possible within the traditional framework of open fields and common rights. A farmer who wanted to experiment with new methods would have to get all the landholders in the village to agree to the plan. Advocates of improvement argued that innovating agriculturalists needed to enclose and consolidate their scattered holdings into compact, fenced-in fields in order to farm more effectively. In doing so, the innovators also needed to enclose the village's natural pastureland, or common, into individual shares. According to proponents of this movement, known as **enclosure**, the upheaval of village life was the necessary price of technical progress.

That price seemed too high to many rural people who had small, inadequate holdings or very little land at all. Traditional rights were precious to these poor peasants, who used commonly held pastureland to graze livestock, and marshlands or forest outside the village as a source for foraged goods that could make the difference between survival and famine in harsh times. Thus, when the small landholders and the village poor could effectively oppose the enclosure of the open fields and the common lands, they did so. In many countries they found allies among the larger, predominantly noble landowners who were also wary of enclosure because it required large investments in purchasing and fencing land and thus posed risks for them as well.

The old system of unenclosed open fields and the new system of continuous rotation coexisted in Europe for a long time. Open fields could still be found in much of France and Germany as late as the nineteenth century because peasants there had successfully opposed eighteenth-century efforts to introduce the new techniques. Throughout the end of the eighteenth century, the new system of enclosure was extensively adopted only in the Low Countries and England.

The Leadership of the Low Countries and England

The seventeenth-century Dutch Republic, already the most advanced country in Europe in many areas of human endeavor (see Chapter 15), pioneered advancements in agriculture. By the middle of the seventeenth century intensive farming was well established, and the innovations of enclosed fields, continuous rotation, heavy manuring, and a wide variety of crops were all present. Agriculture was highly specialized and commercialized, especially in the province of Holland.

One reason for early Dutch leadership in farming was that the area was one of the most densely populated in Europe. In order to feed themselves and provide employment, the Dutch were forced at an early date to seek maximum yields from their land and to increase the cultivated area through the steady draining of marshes and swamps. The pressure of population was connected with the second cause: the growth of towns and cities. Stimulated by commerce and overseas trade, Amsterdam grew from thirty thousand to two hundred thousand inhabitants in its golden seventeenth century. The growing urban population provided Dutch peasants with markets for all they could produce and allowed each region to specialize in what it did best. Thus the Dutch could develop their potential, and the Low Countries became, as one historian wrote, "the Mecca of foreign agricultural experts who came . . . to see Flemish agriculture with their own eyes, to write about it and to propagate its methods in their home lands."[1]

The English were among their best students. In the mid-seventeenth century English farmers borrowed the system of continuous crop rotation from the Dutch. They also drew on Dutch expertise in drainage and water control. Large parts of seventeenth-century Holland had once been sea and sea marsh, and the efforts of centuries had made the Dutch the world's leaders in drainage. In the first half of the seventeenth century, Dutch experts made a great contribution to draining the extensive marshes, or fens, of wet and rainy England. The most famous of these Dutch engineers, Cornelius Vermuyden, directed one large drainage project in Yorkshire and another in Cambridgeshire. In the Cambridge fens, Vermuyden and his Dutch workers eventually reclaimed forty thousand

The Vegetable Market, 1662 The wealth and well-being of the industrious, capitalistic Dutch shine forth in this winsome market scene by Dutch artist Hendrick Sorgh. The market woman's baskets are filled with delicious fresh produce that ordinary citizens can afford—eloquent testimony to the responsive, enterprising character of Dutch agriculture. (Rijksmuseum, Amsterdam)

acres, which were then farmed intensively in the Dutch manner. Swampy wilderness was converted into thousands of acres of some of the best land in England.

Based on the seventeenth-century achievements, English agriculture continued to progress during the eighteenth century, growing enough food to satisfy a rapidly growing population. Jethro Tull (1674–1741), part crank and part genius, was an important English innovator. A true son of the early Enlightenment, Tull adopted a critical attitude toward accepted ideas about farming and tried to develop better methods through empirical research. He was especially enthusiastic about using horses, rather than slower-moving oxen, for plowing. He also advocated sowing seed with drilling equipment rather than scattering it by hand. Drilling distributed seed in an even manner and at the proper depth. There were also improvements in livestock, inspired in part by the earlier successes of English country gentlemen in breeding ever-faster horses for the races and fox hunts that were their passions. Selective breeding of ordinary livestock was a marked improvement over the haphazard breeding of the past.

One of the most important—and bitterly contested—aspects of agricultural development was the enclosure of open fields and commons. More than half the farmland in England was enclosed through private initiatives prior to 1700; Parliament completed this work in the eighteenth century. From the 1760s to 1815 a series of acts of Parliament enclosed most of the remaining common land. Arthur Young, another agricultural experimentalist, celebrated large-scale enclosure as a necessary means to achieve progress.

Many of his contemporaries, as well as the historians that followed him, echoed that conviction. More recent research, however, has shown that regions that maintained open-field farming were still able to adopt crop rotation and other innovations, suggesting that enclosures were not a prerequisite for increased production.

Many critics of Arthur Young's day emphasized the social upheaval caused by enclosure. By eliminating common rights and greatly reducing the access of poor men and women to the land, the eighteenth-century enclosure movement marked the completion of two major historical developments in England—the rise of market-oriented estate agriculture and the emergence of a landless rural proletariat. By the early nineteenth century a tiny minority of wealthy English and Scottish landowners held most of the land and pursued profits aggressively, leasing their holdings through agents at competitive prices to middle-size farmers, who relied on landless laborers for their workforce. These landless laborers worked very long hours, usually following a dawn-to-dusk schedule six days a week all year long. Not only was the small landholder deprived of his land, but improvements in technology meant that fewer laborers were needed to work the large farms, and unemployment spread throughout the countryside. As one observer commented:

> It is no uncommon thing for four or five wealthy graziers to engross a large inclosed lordship, which was before in the hands of twenty or thirty farmers, and as many smaller tenants or proprietors. All these are thereby thrown out of their livings, and many other families, who were chiefly employed and supported by them, such as blacksmiths, carpenters, wheelwrights and other artificers and tradesmen, besides their own labourers and servants.[2]

In no other European country had this **proletarianization**—this transformation of large numbers of small peasant farmers into landless rural wage earners—gone so far. England's village poor found the cost of change heavy and unjust.

The Beginning of the Population Explosion

Why did the European population rise dramatically in the eighteenth century?

Another factor that affected the existing order of life and forced economic changes in the eighteenth century was the beginning of the population explosion. Explosive growth continued in Europe until the twentieth century, by which time it was affecting non-Western areas of the globe. In this section we examine the background and causes of the population growth; the following section considers how the challenge of more mouths to feed and more hands to employ affected the European economy.

Long-Standing Obstacles to Population Growth

Until 1700 the total population of Europe grew slowly much of the time, and it followed an irregular cyclical pattern. This cyclical pattern had a great influence on many aspects of social and economic life. The terrible ravages of the Black Death of 1348–1350 caused a sharp drop in population and food prices after 1350 and also created a labor shortage throughout Europe. Some economic historians calculate that for those common people in western Europe who managed to steer clear of warfare and of power struggles within the ruling class, the later Middle Ages was an era of exceptional well-being.

By the mid-sixteenth century much of Europe had returned to its pre-plague population levels. In this buoyant period, farmers brought new land into cultivation and urban settlements grew significantly. But this well-being eroded in the course of the sixteenth century. The second great surge of population growth outstripped the growth of agricultural production after about 1500. There was less food per person, and food prices rose more rapidly than wages, a development intensified by the inflow of precious metals from the Americas (see Chapter 14) and a general, if uneven, European price revolution. The result was a substantial decline in living standards throughout Europe. By 1600 the pressure of population on resources was severe in much of Europe, and widespread poverty was an undeniable reality.

Births and deaths, fertility and mortality, were in a crude but effective balance. The population grew modestly in normal years at a rate of perhaps 0.5 to 1 percent, or enough to double the population in 70 to 140 years. This is, of course, a generalization encompassing many different patterns. In areas such as Russia and colonial New England, where there was a great deal of frontier to be settled, the annual rate of natural increase, not counting immigration, might well have exceeded 1 percent. In a country such as France, where the land had long been densely settled, the rate of increase might have been less than 0.5 percent.

Although population growth of even 1 percent per year seems fairly modest, it will produce a very large increase over a long period: in three hundred years it will result in sixteen times as many people. Yet such significant increases did not occur in agrarian Europe. In certain abnormal years and tragic periods — the Black Death was only the most extreme example — many more people died than were born, and total population fell sharply, even catastrophically. A number of years of modest growth would then be necessary to make up for those who had died in an abnormal year. Such savage increases in deaths occurred periodically in the seventeenth century on a local and regional scale, and these demographic crises combined to check the growth of population until after 1700.

The grim reapers of demographic crisis were famine, epidemic disease, and war. Episodes of famine were inevitable in all eras of premodern Europe, given low crop yields and unpredictable climatic conditions. In the seventeenth century much of Europe experienced unusually cold and wet weather, which produced even more severe harvest failures and food shortages than usual. Contagious diseases, like typhus, smallpox, syphilis, and the ever-recurring bubonic plague, also continued to ravage Europe's population on a periodic basis. War was another scourge, and its indirect effects were even more harmful than the purposeful killing during military campaigns. Soldiers and camp followers passed all manner of contagious diseases throughout the countryside. Armies requisitioned scarce food supplies and disrupted the agricultural cycle while battles destroyed precious crops, livestock, and farmlands. The Thirty Years' War (1618–1648) witnessed all possible combinations of distress (see Chapter 15). The number of inhabitants in the German states alone declined by more than two-thirds in some large areas and by at least one-third almost everywhere else.

The New Pattern of the Eighteenth Century

In the eighteenth century the population of Europe began to grow markedly. Growth took place unevenly, with Russia growing very quickly after 1700 and France much more slowly. Nonetheless, the explosion of population was a major phenomenon in all European countries. Europeans grew in numbers steadily from 1720 to 1789, with especially dramatic increases after about 1750. Between 1700 and 1835, the population of Europe doubled in size.

What caused this population growth? In some areas, especially England, women had more babies than before because new opportunities for employment in rural industry (see page 559) allowed them to marry at an earlier age. But the basic cause of European population increase as a whole was a decline in mortality—fewer deaths.

One of the primary reasons behind this decline was the mysterious disappearance of the bubonic plague. Following the Black Death in the fourteenth century, plagues had remained part of the European experience, striking again and again with savage force, particularly in towns. In 1720 a ship from Syria and the Levant brought the disease to Marseilles. As a contemporary account described it, "The Porters employ'd in unloading the Vessel, were immediately seiz'd with violent Pains in the Head . . . soon after they broke out in Blotches and Buboes, and died in three Days."[3] Plague quickly spread within and beyond Marseilles, killing up to one hundred thousand. By 1722 the epidemic had passed, and that was the last time plague fell on western and central Europe. Exactly why plague disappeared is unknown. Stricter measures of quarantine in Mediterranean ports and along the Austrian border with the Ottoman Empire helped by carefully isolating human carriers of plague. Chance and plain good luck were probably just as important.

Advances in medical knowledge did not contribute much to reducing the death rate in the eighteenth century. The most important advance in preventive medicine in this period was inoculation against smallpox, and this great improvement was long confined mainly to England, probably doing little to reduce deaths throughout Europe until the latter part of the century. However, improvements in the water supply and sewage, which were frequently promoted by strong absolutist monarchies, resulted in somewhat better public health and helped reduce such diseases as typhoid and typhus in some urban areas of western Europe. Improvements in water supply and the drainage of swamps also reduced Europe's large insect population. Flies and mosquitoes played a major role in spreading diseases, especially those striking children and young adults. Thus early public health measures helped the decline in mortality that began with the disappearance of plague and continued into the early nineteenth century.

Human beings also became more successful in their efforts to safeguard the supply of food. The eighteenth century was a time of considerable canal and road building in western Europe. These advances in transportation, which were also among the more positive aspects of strong absolutist states, lessened the impact of local crop failure and famine. Emergency supplies could be brought in, and localized starvation became less frequent. Wars became less destructive than in the seventeenth century and spread fewer epidemics. None of the population growth would have been possible if not for the advances in agricultural production in the seventeenth and eighteenth centuries, which increased the food supply and contributed nutritious new foods, particularly the potato from South America. In short, population grew in the eighteenth century primarily because years of higher-than-average death rates were less catastrophic. Famines, epidemics, and wars continued to occur and to affect population growth, but their severity moderated.

Population growth intensified the imbalance between the number of people and the economic opportunities available to them. Deprived of land by the enclosure movement, the rural poor were forced to look for new ways to make a living.

The Growth of Rural Industry

How and why did rural industry intensify in the eighteenth century?

The growth of population increased the number of rural workers with little or no land, and this in turn contributed to the development of industry in rural areas. The poor in the countryside increasingly needed to supplement their agricultural earnings with other types of work, and urban capitalists were eager to employ them, often at lower wages than urban workers received. **Cottage industry**, which consisted of manufacturing with hand tools in peasant cottages and work sheds, grew markedly in the eighteenth century and became a crucial feature of the European economy.

To be sure, peasant communities had always made clothing, processed food, and constructed housing for their own use. But medieval peasants did not produce manufactured goods on a large scale for sale in a market. By the eighteenth century, however, the pressures of rural poverty led many poor villagers to seek additional work, and far-reaching changes for daily rural life were set in motion.

The Putting-Out System

Cottage industry was often organized through the **putting-out system**. The two main participants in the putting-out system were the merchant capitalist and the rural worker. In this system, the merchant loaned, or "put out," raw materials to cottage workers, who processed the raw materials in their own homes and returned the finished products to the merchant. There were endless variations on this basic relationship. Sometimes rural workers bought their own raw materials and worked as independent producers before they sold to the merchant. Sometimes whole families were involved in domestic industry; at other times the tasks were closely associated with one gender. Sometimes several workers toiled together to perform a complicated process in a workshop outside the home. The relative importance of earnings from the land and from industry varied greatly for handicraft workers, although industrial wages usually became more important for a given family with time.

As industries grew in scale and complexity, production was often broken into many stages. For example, a merchant would provide raw wool to one group of workers for spinning into thread. He would then pass the thread to another group of workers to be bleached, to another for dyeing, and to another for weaving into cloth. The merchant paid outworkers by the piece and proceeded to sell the finished product to regional, national, or international markets.

The putting-out system grew because it had competitive advantages. Underemployed labor was abundant, and poor peasants and landless laborers would work for low wages. Since production in the countryside was unregulated, workers and merchants could change procedures and experiment as they saw fit. Because workers did not need to meet rigid guild standards, cottage industry became capable of producing many kinds of goods. Textiles; all manner of knives, forks, and housewares; buttons and gloves; and

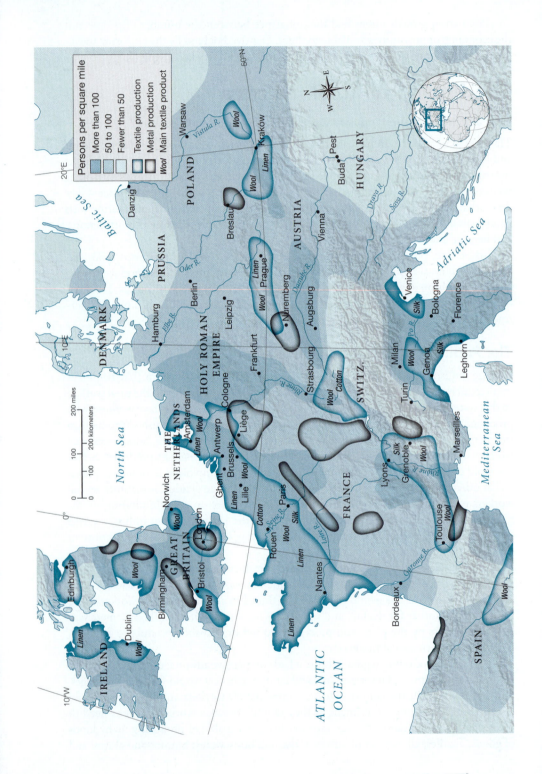

◄ **MAP 17.1   Industry and Population in Eighteenth-Century Europe**
The growth of cottage manufacturing in rural areas helped country people increase their income and contributed to population growth. The putting-out system began in England, and much of the work was in the textile industry. Cottage industry was also strong in the Low Countries—modern-day Belgium and the Netherlands.

clocks could be produced quite satisfactorily in the countryside. Although luxury goods for the rich, such as exquisite tapestries and fine porcelain, demanded special training, close supervision, and centralized workshops, the limited skills of rural industry were sufficient for everyday articles.

Rural manufacturing did not spread across Europe at an even rate. It developed most successfully in England, particularly for the spinning and weaving of woolen cloth. By 1500 half of England's textiles were being produced in the countryside. By 1700 English industry was generally more rural than urban and heavily reliant on the putting-out system. Most continental countries, with the exception of Flanders and the Dutch Republic, developed rural industry more slowly. The latter part of the eighteenth century witnessed a remarkable expansion of rural industry in certain densely populated regions of continental Europe (Map 17.1).

The Lives of Rural Textile Workers

Until the nineteenth century, the industry that employed the most people in Europe was textiles. The making of linen, woolen, and eventually cotton cloth was the typical activity of cottage workers engaged in the putting-out system. A look inside the cottage of the English weaver illustrates a way of life as well as an economic system. The rural worker lived in a small cottage with tiny windows and little space. The cottage was often a single room that served as workshop, kitchen, and bedroom. There were only a few pieces of furniture, of which the weaver's loom was by far the largest and most important. That loom changed somewhat in the early eighteenth century when John Kay's invention of the flying shuttle enabled the weaver to throw the shuttle back and forth between the threads with one hand. Aside from that improvement, however, the loom was as it had been for much of history and as it would remain until the arrival of mechanized looms in the first decades of the nineteenth century.

Handloom weaving was a family enterprise. All members of the family helped in the work, so that "every person from seven to eighty (who retained their sight and who could move their hands) could earn their bread," as one eighteenth-century English observer put it.[4] Operating the loom was usually considered a man's job, reserved for the male head of the family. Women and children worked at auxiliary tasks; they prepared the warp (vertical) threads and mounted them on the loom, wound threads on bobbins for the weft (horizontal) threads, and sometimes operated the warp frame while the father passed the shuttle.

The work of four or five spinners was needed to keep one weaver steadily employed. Since the weaver's family usually could not produce enough thread, merchants hired the wives and daughters of agricultural workers, who took on spinning work in their spare time. In England, many widows and single women also became "spinsters," so many in fact that the word became a synonym for an unmarried woman. In parts of Germany, spinning employed whole families and was not reserved for women.

The Linen Industry in Ireland
Many steps went into making textiles. Here the women are beating away the woody part of the flax plant so that the man can comb out the soft part. The combed fibers will then be spun into thread and woven into cloth by this family enterprise. The increased labor of women and girls from the late seventeenth century helped produce a significant expansion in the production of textiles in western Europe. (Private Collection/The Stapleton Collection/The Bridgeman Art Library)

Relations between workers and employers were often marked by sharp conflict. There were constant disputes over the weights of materials and the quality of finished work. Merchants accused workers of stealing raw materials, and weavers complained that merchants delivered underweight bales. Suspicion abounded.

Conditions were particularly hard for female workers. While men could earn decent wages through long hours of arduous labor, women's wages were usually much lower because they were not considered the family's primary wage earner. In England's Yorkshire wool industry, a male wool comber earned a good wage of 12 shillings or more a week, while a female spinner could hope for only 3½ shillings.[5] A single or widowed spinner faced a desperate struggle with poverty. Any period of illness or unemployment could spell disaster for her and any children she might have. In 1788 one English writer condemned the low wages of spinners in Norwich: "The suffering of thousands of wretched individuals, willing to work, but starving from their ill requited labour; of whole families of honest industrious children offering their little hands to the wheel, and asking bread of the helpless mother, unable through this well regulated manufacture to give it to them."[6]

From the merchant capitalist's point of view, the problem was not low wages but maintaining control over the labor force. Cottage workers were scattered across the countryside and their work depended on the agricultural calendar. In spring and late summer planting and haymaking occupied all hands in the rural village, leading to shortages in the supply of thread. Merchants bitterly resented their lack of control over rural labor because their own livelihood depended on their ability to meet orders on time. They accused workers — especially female spinners — of laziness, drunkenness, and immorality. If workers failed to produce enough thread, they reasoned, it must be because their wages were too high and they had little incentive to work.

Merchants thus insisted on maintaining the lowest possible wages to force the "idle" poor into productive labor. They also lobbied for, and obtained, new police powers over workers. Imprisonment and public whipping became common punishments for pilfering small amounts of yarn or cloth. For poor workers, their right to hold on to the bits and pieces left over in the production process was akin to the traditional peasant right of gleaning in common lands. With progress came the loss of traditional safeguards for the poor.

The Industrious Revolution

One scholar has used the term **industrious revolution** to summarize the social and economic changes taking place in northwestern Europe in the late seventeenth and early eighteenth centuries.[7] This occurred as households reduced leisure time, stepped up the pace of work, and, most important, redirected the labor of women and children away from the production of goods for household consumption and toward wage work. In the countryside, the spread of cottage industry can be seen as one manifestation of the industrious revolution, while in the cities there was a rise in female employment outside the home (see page 564). By working harder and increasing the number of wageworkers, rural and urban households could purchase more goods, even in a time of stagnant or falling wages.

The effect of these changes is still debated. While some scholars lament the encroachment of longer work hours and stricter discipline, others insist that poor families made decisions based on their own self-interests. With more finished goods becoming available at lower prices, households sought cash income to participate in an emerging consumer economy.

The role of women and girls in this new economy is particularly controversial. When women entered the labor market, they almost always worked at menial, tedious jobs for very low wages. Yet when women earned their own wages, they also seem to have taken on a greater role in household decision making. Most of their scant earnings went for household necessities, items of food and clothing they could no longer produce now that they worked full-time, but sometimes a few shillings were left for a ribbon or a new pair of stockings. Women's use of their surplus income thus helped spur the rapid growth of the textile industries in which they labored so hard.

These new sources and patterns of labor established important foundations for the Industrial Revolution of the late eighteenth and nineteenth centuries (see Chapter 20). They created households in which all members worked for wages rather than in a family business and in which consumption relied on market-produced rather than homemade goods. It was not until the mid-nineteenth century, with rising industrial wages, that a new model emerged in which the male "breadwinner" was expected to earn enough to support the whole family and women and children were relegated back to the domestic sphere. With women estimated to compose 40 percent of the global workforce, today's world is experiencing a second industrious revolution in a similar climate of stagnant wages and increased demand for consumer goods.[8]

The Debate over Urban Guilds

What were guilds, and why did they become controversial in the eighteenth century?

One consequence of the growth of rural industry was an undermining of the traditional **guild system** that protected urban artisans. Guilds continued to dominate production in towns and cities, providing their masters with economic privileges as well as a proud social identity, but they increasingly struggled against competition from rural workers.

Meanwhile, those excluded from guild membership—women, day laborers, Jews, and foreigners—worked on the margins of the urban economy.

In the second half of the eighteenth century, critics attacked the guilds as outmoded institutions that obstructed technical progress and innovation. Until recently, most historians repeated that view. An ongoing reassessment of guilds now emphasizes their ability to adapt to changing economic circumstances.

Urban Guilds

Originating around 1200 during the economic boom of the Middle Ages, the guild system reached its peak in most of Europe in the seventeenth and eighteenth centuries. During this period, urban guilds increased dramatically in cities and towns across Europe. In Louis XIV's France, for example, finance minister Jean-Baptiste Colbert revived the urban guilds and used them to encourage high-quality production and to collect taxes (see Chapter 15). The number of guilds in the city of Paris grew from 60 in 1672 to 129 in 1691.

Guild masters occupied the summit of the world of work. Each guild possessed a detailed set of privileges, including exclusive rights to produce and sell certain goods, access to restricted markets in raw materials, and the rights to train apprentices, hire workers, and open shops. Any individual who violated these monopolies could be prosecuted. Guilds also served social and religious functions, providing a locus of sociability and group identity to the middling classes of European cities.

To ensure there was enough work to go around, guilds jealously restricted their membership to local men who were good Christians, had several years of work experience, paid stiff membership fees, and completed a masterpiece. They also favored family connections. Masters' sons enjoyed automatic access to their fathers' guilds, while outsiders were often barred from entering. Most urban men and women worked in non-guild trades as domestic servants, as manual laborers, and as vendors of food, used clothing, and other goods.

The guilds' ability to enforce their rigid barriers varied a great deal across Europe. In England, national regulations superseded guild rules, sapping their importance. In France, the Crown developed an ambiguous attitude toward guilds, relying on them for taxes and enforcement of quality standards, yet allowing non-guild production to flourish in the countryside in the 1760s, and even in some urban neighborhoods. The German guilds were perhaps the most powerful in Europe, and the most conservative. Journeymen in German cities, with their masters' support, violently protested the encroachment of non-guild workers.

While most were hostile to women, a small number of guilds did accept women. Most involved needlework and textile production, occupations that were considered appropriate for women. In 1675 seamstresses gained a new all-female guild in Paris, and soon seamstresses joined tailors' guilds in parts of France, England, and the Dutch Republic. By the mid-eighteenth century male masters began to hire more female workers, often in defiance of their own guild statutes.

Adam Smith and Economic Liberalism

At the same time that cottage industry began to infringe on the livelihoods of urban artisans, new Enlightenment ideals called into question the very existence of the guild system. Eighteenth-century critics derided guilds as outmoded and exclusionary institutions that obstructed technical innovation and progress. One of the best-known critics of government regulation of trade and industry was Adam Smith (1723–1790), a leading figure of the Scottish Enlightenment (see Chapter 16). Smith developed the general idea of freedom of enterprise and established the basis for modern economics in his groundbreaking work *Inquiry into the Nature and Causes of the Wealth of Nations* (1776). Smith criticized guilds for their stifling and outmoded restrictions, a critique he extended to all state monopolies and privileged companies. Far preferable was free competition, which would best protect consumers from price gouging and give all citizens a fair and equal right to do what they did best. Smith advocated a more highly developed "division of labor," which entailed separating craft production into individual tasks to increase workers' speed and efficiency. (See "Primary Source: Adam Smith on the Division of Labor," page 566.)

In keeping with his deep-seated fear of political oppression and with the "system of natural liberty" that he championed, Smith argued that government should limit itself to "only three duties": it should provide a defense against foreign invasion, maintain civil order with courts and police protection, and sponsor certain indispensable public works and institutions that could never adequately profit private investors. He believed that the pursuit of self-interest in a competitive market would be sufficient to improve the living conditions of citizens, a view that quickly emerged as the classic argument for **economic liberalism**.

In the nineteenth and twentieth centuries Smith was often seen as an advocate of unbridled capitalism, but his ideas were considerably more complex. Unlike many disgruntled merchant capitalists, he applauded the modest rise in real wages of British workers in the eighteenth century, stating: "No society can surely be flourishing and happy, of which the far greater part of the members are poor and miserable." Smith also observed that employers were "always and everywhere in a sort of tacit, but constant and uniform combination, not to raise the wages of labor above their actual rate" and sometimes entered "into particular combinations to sink the wages even below this rate." While he celebrated the rise in productivity allowed by the division of labor, he also acknowledged its demoralizing effects on workers and called for government intervention to raise workers' living standards.[9]

Many educated people in France, including government officials, shared Smith's ideas. In 1776 the reform-minded economics minister Anne-Robert-Jacques Turgot issued a law abolishing all French guilds. The law stated:

> We wish to abolish these arbitrary institutions, which do not allow the poor man to earn his living; which reject a sex whose weakness has given it more needs and fewer resources . . . ; which destroy emulation and industry and nullify the talents of those whose circumstances have excluded them from membership of a guild; which deprive the state and the arts of all the knowledge brought to them by foreigners; which retard the progress of these arts . . . ; [and which] burden industry with an oppressive tax, which bears heavily on the people.[10]

Vociferous protests against this measure led to Turgot's disgrace shortly afterward, but the legislators of the French Revolution (see Chapter 19) were of the same liberal mind-set and disbanded the guilds again in 1791. Other European countries followed suit more slowly, with guilds surviving in central Europe and Italy into the second half of the nineteenth century.

PRIMARY SOURCE   Adam Smith on the Division of Labor

In An Inquiry into the Nature and Causes of the Wealth of Nations *(1776), Scottish philosopher Adam Smith argued that commercial society—his term for the early capitalism of his age—was finally freeing the individual from the constraints of tradition, superstition, and cumbersome regulations. The passage below contains Smith's famous description of the division of labor, which permits a small number of men to do the work of many more. Although Smith lauded the gains in efficiency, skilled artisans bitterly resented the loss of control and specialized knowledge imposed by dividing production into isolated, repetitive steps.*

To take an example, therefore, from a very trifling manufacture; but one in which the division of labor has been very often taken notice of, the trade of the pin-maker; a workman not educated to this business . . . nor acquainted with the use of the machinery employed in it . . . could scarce, perhaps, with his utmost industry, make one pin in a day, and certainly could not make twenty. But in the way in which this business is now carried on, not only the whole work is a peculiar trade, but it is divided into a number of branches, of which the greater part are likewise peculiar trades. One man draws out the wire, another straightens it, a third cuts it, a fourth points it, a fifth grinds it at the top for receiving the head; to make the head requires two or three distinct operations; to put it on, is a peculiar business, to whiten the pins is another; it is even a trade by itself to put them into the paper; and the important business of making a pin is, in this manner, divided into about eighteen distinct operations, which, in some manufactories, are all performed by distinct hands, though in others the same man will sometimes perform two or three of them. I have seen a small manufactory of this kind where ten men only were

Many artisans welcomed the economic liberalization espoused by Smith, but some continued to uphold the ideals of the guilds. In the late eighteenth and early nineteenth centuries, skilled artisans across Europe espoused the values of hand craftsmanship and limited competition in contrast to the proletarianization and loss of skills they endured in mechanized production. Recent scholarship has also challenged some of the criticism of the guilds, emphasizing the flexibility and adaptability of the guild system and the role it played in fostering confidence in quality standards. Nevertheless, by the middle of the nineteenth century economic deregulation was championed by most European governments and elites.

The Atlantic World and Global Trade

How did colonial markets boost Europe's economic and social development, and what conflicts and adversity did world trade entail?

In addition to agricultural improvement, population pressure, and growing cottage industry, the expansion of Europe in the eighteenth century was characterized by the increase of world trade. Adam Smith himself declared that "the discovery of America

employed, and where some of them consequently performed two or three distinct operations. But though they were very poor, and therefore but indifferently accommodated with the necessary machinery, they could, when they exerted themselves, make among them about twelve pounds of pins in a day. There are in a pound upward of four thousand pins of a middling size. Those ten persons, therefore, could make among them upward of forty-eight thousand pins in a day. Each person, therefore, making a tenth part of forty-eight thousand pins, might be considered as making four thousand eight hundred pins in a day. But if they had all wrought separately and independently, and without any of them having been educated to this peculiar business, they certainly could not each of them have made twenty, perhaps not one pin in a day; that is, certainly not the two hundred and fortieth, perhaps not the four thousand eight hundredth part of what they are at present capable of performing, in consequence of a proper division and combination of their different operations.

EVALUATE THE EVIDENCE

1. Into what steps—what Smith calls "peculiar trades"—is pin making divided? How do these steps make it possible for ten men to do the work of hundreds?

2. Why would skilled craftsmen oppose the division of labor described by Smith? What disadvantages did it create for them? For their guilds?

Source: Adam Smith, *The Wealth of Nations*, part 1 (New York: P. F. Collier & Son, 1902), pp. 44–45.

and that of a passage to the East Indies by the Cape of Good Hope, are the two greatest and most important events recorded in the history of mankind."[11] In the eighteenth century Spain and Portugal revitalized their empires and began drawing more wealth from renewed colonial development. Yet once again the countries of northwestern Europe—the Dutch Republic, France, and above all Great Britain—benefited most.

The Atlantic economy that these countries developed from 1650 to 1790 would prove crucial in the building of a global economy. Great Britain, which was formed in 1707 by the union of England and Scotland into a single kingdom, gradually became the leading maritime power. Thus the British played the critical role in building a fairly unified Atlantic economy that provided remarkable opportunities for them and their colonists. They also competed ruthlessly with France and the Netherlands for trade and territory in Asia.

Mercantilism and Colonial Competition

Britain's commercial leadership in the eighteenth century had its origins in the mercantilism of the seventeenth century (see Chapter 15). Eventually eliciting criticism from Enlightenment thinker Adam Smith and other proponents of free trade in the late

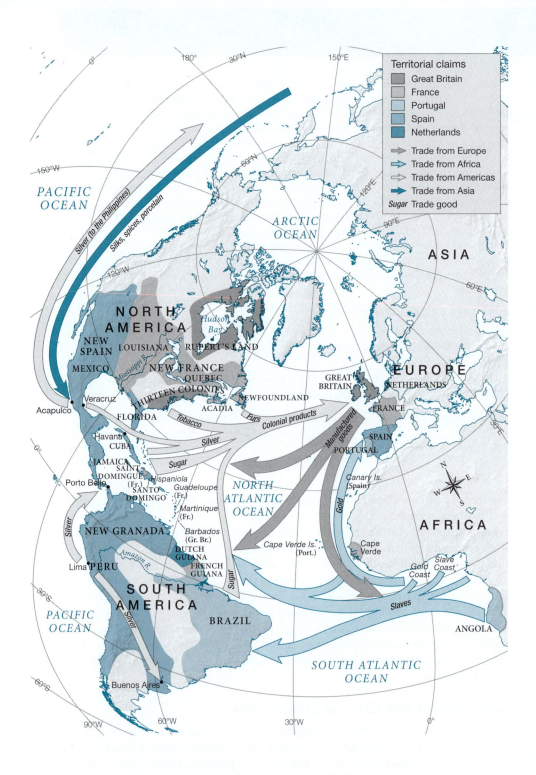

◀ **MAP 17.2**   **The Atlantic Economy in 1701**
The growth of trade encouraged both economic development and military conflict in the Atlantic basin. Four continents were linked together by the exchange of goods and slaves.

eighteenth century, European mercantilism was a system of economic regulations aimed at increasing the power of the state. As practiced by a leading advocate such as Colbert under Louis XIV, mercantilism aimed particularly at creating a favorable balance of foreign trade in order to increase a country's stock of gold. A country's gold holdings served as an all-important treasure chest that could be opened periodically to pay for war in a violent age.

In England, the desire to increase both military power and private wealth resulted in the mercantile system of the **Navigation Acts**. Oliver Cromwell established the first of these laws in 1651, and the restored monarchy of Charles II extended them in 1660 and 1663. The acts required that most goods imported from Europe into England and Scotland (Great Britain after 1707) be carried on British-owned ships with British crews or on ships of the country producing the article. Moreover, these laws gave British merchants and shipowners a virtual monopoly on trade with British colonies. The colonists were required to ship their products on British (or American) ships and to buy almost all European goods from Britain. It was believed that these economic regulations would eliminate foreign competition, thereby helping British merchants and workers as well as colonial plantation owners and farmers. It was hoped, too, that the emerging British Empire would develop a shipping industry with a large number of experienced seamen who could serve when necessary in the Royal Navy.

The Navigation Acts were a form of economic warfare. Their initial target was the Dutch, who were far ahead of the English in shipping and foreign trade in the mid-seventeenth century (see Chapter 15). In conjunction with three Anglo-Dutch wars between 1652 and 1674, the Navigation Acts seriously damaged Dutch shipping and commerce. The British seized the thriving Dutch colony of New Amsterdam in 1664 and renamed it New York. By the late seventeenth century the Dutch Republic was falling behind England in shipping, trade, and colonies.

Thereafter France stood clearly as England's most serious rival in the competition for overseas empire. Rich in natural resources, with a population three or four times that of England, and allied with Spain, continental Europe's leading military power was already building a powerful fleet and a worldwide system of rigidly monopolized colonial trade. Thus from 1701 to 1763 Britain and France were locked in a series of wars to decide, in part, which nation would become the leading maritime power and claim the profits of Europe's overseas expansion (Map 17.2).

The first round was the War of the Spanish Succession (see Chapter 15), which started in 1701 when Louis XIV accepted the Spanish crown willed to his grandson. Besides upsetting the continental balance of power, a union of France and Spain threatened to encircle and destroy the British colonies in North America (see Map 17.2). Defeated by a great coalition of states after twelve years of fighting, Louis XIV was forced in the Peace of Utrecht (YOO-trehkt) in 1713 to cede his North American holdings in Newfoundland, Nova Scotia, and the Hudson Bay territory to Britain. Spain was compelled to give Britain control of its West African slave trade — the so-called *asiento* (ah-SYEHN-toh)—and to let Britain send one ship of merchandise into the Spanish colonies annually.

Conflict continued among the European powers over both domestic and colonial affairs. The War of the Austrian Succession (1740–1748), which started when Frederick the Great of Prussia seized Silesia from Austria's Maria Theresa (see Chapter 16), gradually became a world war that included Anglo-French conflicts in India and North America. The war ended with no change in the territorial situation in North America. This inconclusive standoff helped set the stage for the Seven Years' War (1756–1763; see Chapter 19). In central Europe, France aided Austria's Maria Theresa in her quest to win back Silesia from the Prussians, who had formed an alliance with England. In North America, French and British settlers engaged in territorial skirmishes that eventually resulted in all-out war that drew in Native American allies on both sides of the conflict (see Map 19.1, page 622). By 1763 Prussia had held off the Austrians, and British victory on all colonial fronts was ratified in the **Treaty of Paris**. British naval power, built in large part on the rapid growth of the British shipping industry after the passage of the Navigation Acts, had triumphed decisively: Britain had realized its goal of monopolizing a vast trading and colonial empire.

The Atlantic Economy

As the volume of transatlantic trade increased, the regions bordering the ocean were increasingly drawn into an integrated economic system. Commercial exchange in the Atlantic has traditionally been referred to as the "triangle trade," designating a three-way transport of goods: European commodities, like guns and textiles, to Africa; enslaved Africans to the colonies; and colonial goods, such as cotton, tobacco, and sugar, back to Europe (see Map 17.2).

Across the eighteenth century the economies of European nations bordering the Atlantic Ocean, especially England, relied more and more on colonial exports. In England, sales to the mainland colonies of North America and the West Indian sugar islands—with an important assist from West Africa and Latin America—soared from £500,000 to £4 million. Exports to England's colonies in Ireland and India also rose substantially from 1700 to 1800. By 1800 sales to European countries—England's traditional trading partners—represented only half of exports, down from three-quarters a century earlier. England also benefited from importing colonial products. Colonial monopolies allowed the English to obtain a steady supply of such goods at beneficial prices and to re-export them to other nations at high profits. Moreover, many colonial goods, like sugar and tobacco, required processing before consumption and thus contributed new manufacturing jobs in England. In the eighteenth century, stimulated by trade and empire building, England's capital city, London, grew into the West's largest and richest city. Thus the mercantilist system achieved remarkable success for England, and by the 1770s the country stood on the threshold of the epoch-making changes that would become known as the Industrial Revolution (see Chapter 20).

Although they lost many possessions to the English in the Seven Years' War, the French still profited enormously from colonial trade. The colonies of Saint-Domingue (modern-day Haiti), Martinique, and Guadeloupe remained in French hands and provided immense fortunes in plantation agriculture and slave trading during the second half of the eighteenth century. By 1789 the population of Saint-Domingue included five hundred thousand slaves whose labor had allowed the colony to become the world's leading producer of coffee and sugar and the most profitable plantation colony in the New World.[12] The wealth generated from colonial trade fostered the confidence of the merchant classes in Paris, Bordeaux, and other large cities, and merchants soon joined other elite groups clamoring for political reforms.

The third major player in the Atlantic economy, Spain, also saw its colonial fortunes improve during the eighteenth century. Not only did it gain Louisiana from France in 1763, but its influence expanded westward all the way to northern California through the efforts of Spanish missionaries and ranchers. Its mercantilist goals were boosted by a recovery in silver production, which had dropped significantly in the seventeenth century.

Silver mining also stimulated food production for the mining camps, and wealthy Spanish landowners developed a system of **debt peonage** to keep indigenous workers on their estates. Under this system, which was similar to serfdom, a planter or rancher would keep workers in perpetual debt bondage by advancing them food, shelter, and a little money.

Although the "triangle trade" model highlights some of the most important flows of commerce across the Atlantic, it significantly oversimplifies the picture. For example, a brisk intercolonial trade also existed, with the Caribbean slave colonies importing food in the form of fish, flour, and livestock from the northern colonies and rice from the south, in exchange for sugar and slaves (see Map 17.2). Many colonial traders violated imperial monopolies to trade with the most profitable partners, regardless of nationality. Moreover, the Atlantic economy was inextricably linked to trade with the Indian and Pacific Oceans.

The Atlantic Slave Trade

At the core of the Atlantic world were the misery and profit of the **Atlantic slave trade**. The forced migration of millions of Africans—cruel, unjust, and tragic—was a key element in the Atlantic system and western European economic expansion throughout the eighteenth century. The brutal practice intensified dramatically after 1700 and especially after 1750 with the growth of trade and demand for slave-produced goods like sugar and cotton. According to the most authoritative source, European traders purchased and shipped 6.5 million enslaved Africans across the Atlantic between 1701 and 1800—more than half of the estimated total of 12.5 million Africans transported between 1450 and 1900, of whom 15 percent died in procurement and transit.[13] By the peak decade of the 1780s, shipments averaged about eighty thousand individuals per year in an attempt to satisfy the constantly rising demand for labor power—and also for slave owners' profits—in the Americas.

The rise of plantation agriculture was responsible for the tremendous growth of the slave trade. Among all European colonies, the plantations of Portuguese Brazil received by far the largest number of enslaved Africans over the entire period of the slave trade—45 percent of the total. Another 45 percent were divided among the many Caribbean colonies. The colonies of mainland North America took only 3 percent of slaves arriving from Africa, a little under four hundred thousand, relying mostly on natural growth of the enslaved population.

The Atlantic Slave Trade   This engraving from 1814 shows traders leading a group of slaves to the West African coast, where they will board ships to cross the Atlantic. Many slaves died en route or arrived greatly weakened and ill. The newspaper advertisement of the sale of a ship's cargo of slaves in Charleston, South Carolina, promises "fine, healthy negroes," testifying to the dangers of the crossing and to the frequency of epidemic diseases like smallpox. (engraving: Bibliothèque de l'Arsenal, Paris/Archives Charmet/The Bridgeman Art Library; advertisement: The Granger Collection, New York)

Eighteenth-century intensification of the slave trade resulted in fundamental changes in its organization. After 1700, as Britain became the undisputed leader in shipping slaves across the Atlantic, European governments and ship captains cut back on fighting among themselves and concentrated on commerce. They generally adopted the shore method of trading, which was less expensive than maintaining fortified trading posts. Under this system, European ships sent boats ashore or invited African dealers to bring traders and slaves out to their ships. This method allowed ships to move easily along the coast from market to market and to depart more quickly for the Americas.

Some African merchants and rulers who controlled exports profited from the greater demand for slaves. With their newfound wealth, some Africans gained access to European and colonial goods, including firearms. But generally such economic returns did not spread very far, and the negative consequences of the expanding slave trade predominated.

Wars among African states to obtain salable captives increased, and leaders used slave profits to purchase more arms than textiles and consumer goods. While the populations of Europe and Asia grew substantially in the eighteenth century, the population of Africa stagnated or possibly declined. As one contemporary critic observed:

> I do not know if coffee and sugar are essential to the happiness of Europe, but I know that these two products have accounted for the unhappiness of two great regions of the world: America has been depopulated so as to have land on which to plant them; Africa has been depopulated so as to have the people to cultivate them.[14]

Most Europeans did not personally witness the horrors of the slave trade between Africa and the Americas, and until the early part of the eighteenth century they considered the African slave trade a legitimate business. But as details of the plight of enslaved people became known, a campaign to abolish slavery developed in Britain. (See "Primary Source: Olaudah Equiano's Economic Arguments for Ending Slavery," page 574.) In the late 1780s the abolition campaign grew into a mass movement of public opinion, the first in British history. British women were prominent in this movement, denouncing the immorality of human bondage and stressing the cruel and sadistic treatment of enslaved women and families. These attacks put the defenders of slavery on the defensive. In 1807 Parliament abolished the British slave trade, although slavery continued in British colonies and the Americas for decades.

Identities and Communities of the Atlantic World

Not only slaves and commodities but also cultural ideas and values — as well as free people of European, African, and American descent — circulated through the eighteenth-century Atlantic world. As contacts between the Atlantic coasts of the Americas, Africa, and Europe became more frequent, and as European settlements grew into well-established colonies, new identities and communities emerged.

The term *Creole* referred to people of Spanish ancestry born in the Americas. Wealthy Creoles and their counterparts throughout the Atlantic colonies prided themselves on following European ways of life. In addition to their lavish plantation estates, they maintained townhouses in colonial cities built on the European model, with theaters, central squares, churches, and coffeehouses. They purchased luxury goods made in Europe, and their children were often sent to be educated in the home country.

Over time, however, the colonial elite came to feel that their circumstances gave them different interests and characteristics from those of their home population. As one observer explained, "A turn of mind peculiar to the planter, occasioned by a physical difference of constitution, climate, customs, and education, tends . . . to repress the remains of his former attachment to his native soil."[15] Creole traders and planters increasingly resented the regulations and taxes imposed by colonial bureaucrats, and such resentment would eventually lead to revolution against colonial powers (see Chapter 19).

Not all Europeans in the colonies were wealthy. Numerous poor or middling whites worked as clerks, shopkeepers, craftsmen, and plantation managers. With the exception of British North America, white Europeans made up a minority of the population. Since European migrants were disproportionately male, much of the population of the Atlantic world descended from unions — forced or through choice — of European men and indigenous or African women. Colonial attempts to classify and systematize racial

PRIMARY SOURCE   Olaudah Equiano's Economic Arguments
for Ending Slavery

*According to his autobiography, first published in 1789, Olaudah Equiano was born in
Benin (modern Nigeria) of Ibo ethnicity and was abducted and transported across the
Atlantic as a child. Equiano served a British Royal Navy officer, who educated the boy,
but then sold him to a Quaker merchant. Equiano eventually bought his freedom from
his master and returned to England, where he worked as a hairdresser and merchant
seaman. Having won fame by publishing his life story, Equiano campaigned ardently
to end slavery, as documented in the excerpt below.*

Tortures, murder, and every other imaginable barbarity and iniquity, are practised
upon the poor slaves with impunity. I hope the great slave trade will be abolished.
I pray it may be an event at hand. The great body of manufacturers, uniting in the
cause, will considerably facilitate and expedite it; and, as I have already stated, it
is most substantially their interest and advantage, and as such the nation's at large
(except those persons concerned in the manufacturing [of] neck-yokes, collars,
chains, hand-cuffs, leg-bolts, drags, thumbscrews, iron muzzles, and coffins; cats,
scourges, and other instruments of torture used in the slave trade). In a short time
one sentiment alone will prevail, from motives of interest as well as justice and
humanity. Europe contains one hundred and twenty million of inhabitants. Query—
How many millions doth Africa contain? Supposing the Africans, collectively and
individually, to expend 5£ a head in raiment and furniture yearly when civilized, &c.
an immensity beyond the reach of imagination!

    This I conceive to be a theory founded upon facts, and therefore an infallible
one. If the blacks were permitted to remain in their own country, they would double
themselves every fifteen years. In proportion to such increase will be the demand
for manufactures. Cotton and indigo grow spontaneously in most parts of Africa; a
consideration this of no small consequence to the manufacturing towns of Great
Britain. It opens a most immense, glorious, and happy prospect—the clothing, &c.
of a continent ten thousand miles in circumference, and immensely rich in produc-
tions of every denomination in return for manufactures.

EVALUATE THE EVIDENCE

1. Why does Equiano believe England will profit more by trading with free Africans
   than by enslaving them? Who do you think the audience for this document was,
   and how might the audience affect the message?

2. What broader economic and cultural developments in eighteenth-century
   England does Equiano's plea reflect?

Source: Olaudah Equiano, *The Interesting Narrative of the Life of Olaudah Equiano*, ed. Robert J. Allison,
2d ed. (Boston: Bedford/St. Martin's, 2007), p. 213.

categories greatly influenced developing Enlightenment thought on racial difference
(see Chapter 16).

    Mixed-race populations sometimes rose to the colonial elite. The Spanish conquis-
tadors often consolidated their power through marriage to the daughters of local rulers,
and their descendants were among the most powerful inhabitants of Spanish America.

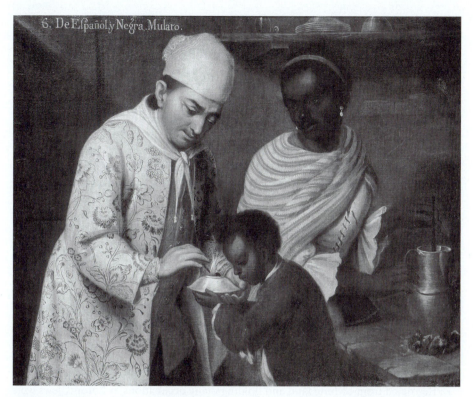

6. De Efpañol y Negra. Mulato.

Mulatto Painting   The caption in the upper left-hand corner of this mid-eighteenth-century painting identifies the family as being composed of a Spanish father and a black mother, whose child is described as "mulatto." The painting was number six in a series of sixteen images by the painter Jose de Alcibar, each showing a different racial and ethnic combination. The series belonged to a popular genre in the Spanish Americas known as *castas* paintings, which commonly depicted sixteen different forms of racial mixing. (Attrib. Jose de Alcibar, 6, De Espanol y Negra, Mulato, ca. 1760–1770. Denver Art Museum: Collection of Frederick and Jan Mayer. Photography provided by the Denver Art Museum)

In the Spanish and French Caribbean, as in Brazil, many masters acknowledged and freed their mixed-race children, leading to sizable populations of free people of color. Advantaged by their fathers, some became wealthy land and slave owners in their own right. In the second half of the eighteenth century, the prosperity of some free people of color brought a backlash from the white population of Saint-Domingue in the form of new race laws prohibiting nonwhites from marrying whites and forcing them to adopt distinctive attire.

British colonies followed a distinctive pattern. There, whole families, rather than individual men, migrated, resulting in a rapid increase in the white population. This development was favored by British colonial law, which forbade marriage between English men and women and Africans or Native Americans. In the British colonies of the Caribbean and the southern mainland, masters tended to leave their mixed-race progeny in slavery rather than freeing them, maintaining a stark discrepancy between free whites and enslaved people of color.[16] The identities inspired by racial and ethnic mixing were equally complex. Colonial elites became "Americanized" by adopting native foods, like chocolate and potatoes, and sought relief from tropical disease in native remedies. Some mixed-race people sought to enter Creole society and obtain its many official and unofficial privileges by passing as white. Where they existed in any number, though, free people of color established their own social hierarchies based on wealth, family connections, occupation, and skin color.

Converting indigenous people to Christianity was a key ambition for all European powers in the New World. Galvanized by the Protestant Reformation and the perceived need to protect and spread Catholicism, Catholic powers actively sponsored missionary efforts. Jesuits, Franciscans, Dominicans, and other religious orders established missions throughout Spanish, Portuguese, and French colonies (see Chapter 14). In Central and South America, large-scale conversion forged enduring Catholic cultures in Portuguese and Spanish colonies. Conversion efforts in North America were less effective because indigenous settlements were more scattered and native people were less integrated into colonial communities. On the whole, Protestants were less active as missionaries in this period, although some dissenters, like Moravians, Quakers, and Methodists, did seek converts among indigenous and enslaved people. (See "Individuals in Society: Rebecca Protten," page 578.)

The practice of slavery reveals important limitations on efforts to spread Christianity. Slave owners often refused to baptize their slaves, fearing that enslaved people would use their Christian status to claim additional rights. In some areas, particularly among the mostly African-born slaves of the Caribbean, elements of African religious belief and practice endured, often incorporated with Christian traditions.

Restricted from owning land and holding many occupations in Europe, Jews were eager participants in the new Atlantic economy and established a network of mercantile communities along its trade routes. As in the Old World, Jews in European colonies faced discrimination; for example, restrictions existed on the number of slaves they could own in Barbados in the early eighteenth century.[17] Jews were considered to be white Europeans and thus ineligible to be slaves, but they did not enjoy equal status with Christians. The status of Jews adds one more element to the complexity of Atlantic identities.

The Colonial Enlightenment

Enlightenment ideas thrived in the colonies, although with as much diversity and disagreement as in Europe (see Chapter 16). The colonies of British North America were deeply influenced by the Scottish Enlightenment, with its emphasis on pragmatic approaches to the problems of life. Following the Scottish model, leaders in the colonies adopted a moderate, "commonsense" version of the Enlightenment that emphasized self-improvement and ethical conduct. In most cases, this version of the Enlightenment was perfectly compatible with religion and was chiefly spread through the growing colleges and universities of the colonies, which remained church-based institutions.

Some thinkers went even further in their admiration for Enlightenment ideas. Benjamin Franklin's writings and political career provide an outstanding example of the combination of the pragmatism and economic interests of the Scottish Enlightenment with the constitutional theories of John Locke, Jean-Jacques Rousseau, and the baron de Montesquieu. Franklin was privately a lifelong deist, meaning that he believed in

God but not in organized religion. Nonetheless, he continued to attend church and respect religious proprieties, a cautious pattern followed by fellow deist Thomas Jefferson and other leading thinkers of the American Enlightenment.

Northern Enlightenment thinkers often depicted the Spanish American colonies as the epitome of the superstition and barbarity they contested. The Catholic Church strictly controlled the publication of books there, just as it did on the Iberian Peninsula. Nonetheless, educated elites were well aware of the new currents of thought, and the universities, newspapers, and salons of Spanish America produced their own reform ideas. The establishment of a mining school in Mexico City in 1792, the first in the Spanish colonies, illuminates the practical achievements of reformers. In all European colonies, one effect of Enlightenment thought was to encourage colonists to criticize the policies of the mother country and aspire toward greater autonomy.

Trade and Empire in Asia and the Pacific

As the Atlantic economy took shape, Europeans continued to vie for dominance in the Asian trade. Between 1500 and 1600 the Portuguese had become major players in the Indian Ocean trading world, eliminating Venice as Europe's chief supplier of spices and other Asian luxury goods. The Portuguese dominated but did not fundamentally alter the age-old pattern of Indian Ocean trade, which involved merchants from many areas as more or less autonomous players. This situation changed radically with the intervention of the Dutch and then the English (see Chapter 14).

Formed in 1602, the Dutch East India Company had taken control of the Portuguese spice trade in the Indian Ocean, with the port of Batavia (Jakarta) in Java as its center of operations. Within a few decades they had expelled the Portuguese from Ceylon and other East Indian islands. Unlike the Portuguese, the Dutch transformed the Indian Ocean trading world. Whereas East Indian states and peoples maintained independence under the Portuguese, who treated them as autonomous business partners, the Dutch established outright control and reduced them to dependents.

After these successes, the Dutch hold in Asia faltered in the eighteenth century due to the company's failure to diversify to meet changing consumption patterns. Spices continued to compose much of its shipping, despite their declining importance in the European diet, probably due to changing fashions in food and luxury consumption. Fierce competition from its main rival, the English East India Company (established 1600), also severely undercut Dutch trade.

Britain initially struggled for a foothold in Asia. With the Dutch monopolizing the Indian Ocean, the British turned to India, the source of lucrative trade in silks, textiles, and pepper. Throughout the seventeenth century the English East India Company relied on trade concessions from the powerful Mughal emperor, who granted only piecemeal access to the subcontinent. Finally, in 1716 the Mughals conceded empire-wide trading privileges. As Mughal power waned, British East India Company agents increasingly intervened in local affairs and made alliances or waged war against Indian princes.

Britain's great rival for influence in India was France. During the War of the Austrian Succession, British and French forces in India supported opposing rulers in local power struggles. In 1757 East India Company forces under Robert Clive conquered the rich northeastern province of Bengal at the Battle of Plassey. French-English rivalry was finally resolved by the Treaty of Paris, which granted all of France's possessions in India to the

INDIVIDUALS IN SOCIETY • Rebecca Protten

In the mid-1720s a young English-speaking girl who came to be known as Rebecca traveled by ship from Antigua to the small Danish sugar colony of St. Thomas, today part of the U.S. Virgin Islands. Eighty-five percent of St. Thomas's four thousand inhabitants were of African descent, almost all enslaved. Sugar plantations demanded backbreaking work, and slave owners used extremely brutal methods to maintain control, including amputations and beheadings for runaways.

Surviving documents refer to Rebecca as a "mulatto," indicating a mixed European and African ancestry. A wealthy Dutch-speaking planter named van Beverhout purchased the girl for his household staff, sparing her a position in the grueling and deadly sugar fields. Rebecca won the family's favor, and they taught her to read, write, and speak Dutch. They also shared with her their Protestant faith and took the unusual step of freeing her.

As a free woman, she continued to work as a servant for the van Beverhouts and to study the Bible and spread its message of spiritual freedom. In 1736 she met some missionaries for the Moravian Church, a German-Protestant sect that emphasized emotion and communal worship and devoted its mission work to the enslaved peoples of the Caribbean. The missionaries were struck by Rebecca's piety and her potential to assist their work. As one wrote: "She researches diligently in the Scriptures, loves the Savior, and does much good for other Negro women because she does not simply walk alone with her good ways but instructs them in the Scriptures as well." A letter Rebecca sent to Moravian women in Germany declared: "Oh how good is the Lord. My heart melts when I think of it. His name is wonderful. Oh! Help me to praise him, who has pulled me out of the darkness. I will take up his cross with all my heart and follow the example of his poor life."*

Rebecca soon took charge of the Moravians' female missionary work. Every Sunday and every evening after work, she would walk for miles to lead meetings with enslaved and free black women. The meetings consisted of reading and writing lessons, prayers, hymns, a sermon, and individual discussions in which she encouraged her new sisters in their spiritual growth.

In 1738 Rebecca married a German Moravian missionary, Matthaus Freundlich, a rare but not illegal case of mixed marriage. The same year, her husband bought a plantation, with slaves, to serve as the headquarters of their mission work. The Moravians—and presumably Rebecca herself—wished to spread Christian faith

*Quotations from Jon F. Sensbach, *Rebecca's Revival: Creating Black Christianity in the Atlantic World* (Cambridge, Mass.: Harvard University Press, 2006), pp. 61, 63.

British with the exception of Pondicherry, an Indian Ocean port city. With the elimination of their rival, British ascendancy in India accelerated. In 1765 the Mughal shah granted the East India Company *diwani*, the right to civil administration and tax collection, in Bengal and neighboring provinces. By the early nineteenth century the company had overcome vigorous Indian resistance to gain economic and political dominance

among slaves and improve their treatment, but did not oppose the institution of slavery itself.

Authorities nonetheless feared that baptized and literate slaves would agitate for freedom, and they imprisoned Rebecca and Matthaus and tried to shut down the mission. Only the unexpected arrival on St. Thomas of German aristocrat and Moravian leader Count Zinzendorf saved the couple. Exhausted by their ordeal, they left for Germany in 1741 accompanied by their small daughter, but both father and daughter died soon after their arrival.

In Marienborn, a German center of the Moravian faith, Rebecca encountered other black Moravians, who lived in equality alongside their European brethren. In 1746 she married another missionary, Christian Jacob Protten, son of a Danish sailor and, on his mother's side, grandson of a West African king. She and another female missionary from St. Thomas were ordained as deaconesses, probably making them the first women of color to be ordained in the Western Christian Church.

In 1763 Rebecca and her husband set out for her husband's birthplace, the Danish slave fort at Christiansborg (in what is now Accra, Ghana) to establish a school for mixed-race children. Her husband died in 1769, leaving Rebecca a widow once more. After declining the offer of passage back to the West Indies in 1776, she died in obscurity near Christiansborg in 1780.

QUESTIONS FOR ANALYSIS

1. Why did Moravian missionaries assign such an important leadership role to Rebecca? What particular attributes did she offer?

2. Why did Moravians, including Rebecca, accept the institution of slavery instead of fighting to end it?

3. What does Rebecca's story teach us about the Atlantic world of the mid-eighteenth century?

ONLINE DOCUMENT ASSIGNMENT

What does Rebecca Protten's story reveal about the complex relationship among between slavery, race, and religion in the eighteenth century? Examine primary sources concerning these interconnected issues, and then complete a writing assignment based on the evidence and details from this chapter.

bedfordstmartins.com/mckaywestvalue

of much of the subcontinent; direct administration by the British government replaced East India Company rule after a large-scale rebellion in 1857.

The late eighteenth century also witnessed the beginning of British settlement of the continent of Australia. The continent was first sighted by Europeans in the early seventeenth century, and thereafter parts of the coast were charted by European ships.

Captain James Cook claimed the east coast of Australia for England in 1770, naming it New South Wales. The first colony was established there in the late 1780s, relying on the labor of convicted prisoners forcibly transported from Britain. Settlement of the western portion of the continent followed in the 1790s. The first colonies struggled for survival and, after an initial period of friendly relations, soon aroused the hostility and resistance of aboriginal peoples. Cook himself was killed by islanders in Hawaii in 1779, having charted much of the Pacific Ocean for the first time.

The rising economic and political power of Europeans in this period drew on the connections they established between the Asian and Atlantic trade worlds. An outstanding example is the trade in cowrie shells. These seashells, originating in the Maldive Islands in the Indian Ocean, were used as a form of currency in West Africa. European traders obtained them in Asia, packing them alongside porcelains, spices, and silks for the journey home. The cowries were then brought from European ports to the West African coast to be traded for slaves. Indian textiles were also prized in Africa and played a similar role in exchange. Thus the trade of the Atlantic was inseparable from Asian commerce, and Europeans were increasingly found dominating commerce in both worlds.

Notes

1. B. H. Slicher van Bath, *The Agrarian History of Western Europe, A.D. 500–1850* (New York: St. Martin's Press, 1963), p. 240.
2. Cited in Paul Mantoux, *The Industrial Revolution in the Eighteenth Century: An Outline of the Beginnings of the Modern Factory System* (1961; Abingdon, U.K.: Routledge, 2005), p. 175.
3. Thomas Salmon, *Modern History: Or the Present State of All Nations* (London, 1730), p. 406.
4. Quoted in I. Pinchbeck, *Women Workers and the Industrial Revolution, 1750–1850* (New York: F. S. Crofts, 1930), p. 113.
5. Richard J. Soderlund, "'Intended as a Terror to the Idle and Profligate': Embezzlement and the Origins of Policing in the Yorkshire Worsted Industry, c. 1750–1777," *Journal of Social History* 31 (Spring 1998): 658.
6. Cited in Maxine Berg, *The Age of Manufactures, 1700–1820: Industry, Innovation, and Work in Britain* (London: Routledge, 1994), p. 124.
7. Jan de Vries, *The Industrious Revolution: Consumer Behavior and the Household Economy, 1650 to the Present* (Cambridge, U.K.: Cambridge University Press, 2008).
8. Jan de Vries, "The Industrial Revolution and the Industrious Revolution," *The Journal of Economic History* 54, no. 2 (June 1994): 249–270; discusses the industrious revolution of the second half of the twentieth century.
9. R. Heilbroner, *The Essential Adam Smith* (New York: W. W. Norton, 1986), p. 196.
10. S. Pollard and C. Holmes, eds., *Documents of European Economic History*, vol. 1, *The Process of Industrialization, 1750–1870* (New York: St. Martin's Press, 1968), p. 53.
11. Ibid., p. 281.
12. Laurent Dubois and John D. Garrigus, *Slave Revolution in the Caribbean, 1789–1904* (New York: Palgrave, 2006), p. 8.
13. Figures obtained from Voyages: The Trans-Atlantic Slave Trade Database, http://www.slavevoyages.org/tast/assessment/estimates.faces (accessed June 11, 2009).
14. Cited in Thomas Benjamin, *The Atlantic World: Europeans, Africans, Indians and Their Shared History, 1400–1900* (Cambridge, U.K.: Cambridge University Press, 2009), p. 211.
15. Pierre Marie François Paget, *Travels Round the World in the Years 1767, 1768, 1769, 1770, 1771*, vol. 1 (London, 1793), p. 262.
16. Orlando Patterson, *Slavery and Social Death* (Cambridge, Mass.: Harvard University Press, 1982), p. 255.
17. Erik R. Seeman, "Jews in the Early Modern Atlantic: Crossing Boundaries, Keeping Faith," in *The Atlantic in Global History, 1500–2000*, ed. Jorge Cañizares-Esguerra and Erik R. Seeman (Upper Saddle River, N.J.: Pearson Prentice Hall, 2007), p. 43.

Chapter Review

MAKE IT STICK

LearningCurve
bedfordstmartins.com/mckaywestvalue
After reading the chapter, use LearningCurve to retain what you've read.

IDENTIFY KEY TERMS

Identify and explain the significance of each item below.

enclosure (p. 554)   **economic liberalism** (p. 565)

proletarianization (p. 556)   **Navigation Acts** (p. 569)

cottage industry (p. 559)   **Treaty of Paris** (p. 570)

putting-out system (p. 559)   **debt peonage** (p. 571)

industrious revolution (p. 563)   **Atlantic slave trade** (p. 571)

guild system (p. 563)

REVIEW THE MAIN IDEAS

Answer the focus questions from each section of the chapter.

* What important developments led to increased agricultural production, and how did these changes affect peasants? (p. 552)

* Why did the European population rise dramatically in the eighteenth century? (p. 556)

* How and why did rural industry intensify in the eighteenth century? (p. 559)

* What were guilds, and why did they become controversial in the eighteenth century? (p. 563)

* How did colonial markets boost Europe's economic and social development, and what conflicts and adversity did world trade entail? (p. 566)

MAKE CONNECTIONS

Think about the larger developments and continuities within and across chapters.

1. What was the relationship among agriculture, industry, and population in the eighteenth century? How and why did developments in one area impact the others?

2. The eighteenth century was the period of the European Enlightenment, which celebrated tolerance and human liberty (Chapter 16). Paradoxically, it was also the era of a tremendous increase in slavery, which brought suffering and death to millions. How would you reconcile this paradox?

ONLINE DOCUMENT ASSIGNMENT

Rebecca Protten

What does Rebecca Protten's story reveal about the complex relationship among slavery, race, and religion in the eighteenth century?

You encountered Rebecca Protten's story on page 578. Keeping the question above in mind, go online and examine primary sources concerning these interconnected issues—including an account of early Moravian missionary activity in the West Indies, an essay on the conversion of slaves, and a pamphlet on the same topic. Then complete a writing assignment based on the evidence and details from this chapter.

bedfordstmartins.com/mckaywestvalue

CHRONOLOGY

1600–1850	• Growth in agriculture, pioneered by the Dutch Republic and England
1651–1663	• British Navigation Acts
1652–1674	• Anglo-Dutch wars
1700–1790	• Height of Atlantic slave trade; expansion of rural industry in Europe
1701–1763	• British and French mercantilist wars of empire
1720–1722	• Last outbreak of bubonic plague in Europe
1720–1789	• Growth of European population
1756–1763	• Seven Years' War
1760–1815	• Height of parliamentary enclosure in England
1763	• Treaty of Paris; France cedes its possessions in India and North America
1770	• James Cook claims the east coast of Australia for England
1776	• Adam Smith publishes *An Inquiry into the Nature and Causes of the Wealth of Nations*
1805	• British takeover of India complete
1807	• British slave trade abolished

18

LearningCurve
bedfordstmartins.com/mckaywestvalue
After reading the chapter, use
LearningCurve to retain what
you've read.

Life in the Era of Expansion

1650–1800

THE DISCUSSION OF AGRICULTURE AND INDUSTRY IN THE LAST chapter showed the common people at work, straining to make ends meet within the larger context of population growth, gradual economic expansion, and ferocious political competition at home and overseas. This chapter shows us how that world of work was embedded in a rich complex of family organization, community practices, everyday experiences, and collective attitudes. As with the economy, traditional habits and practices of daily life changed considerably over the eighteenth century. Change was particularly dramatic in the growing cities of northwestern Europe, where traditional social controls were undermined by the anonymity and increased social interaction of the urban setting.

Historians have intensively studied many aspects of popular life, including marriage patterns and family size, childhood and education, nutrition, health

ONLINE DOCUMENT ASSIGNMENT
The Inner Life of the Individual

How did the increasing emphasis on the inner life and development of the individual in the eighteenth century find expression in the art of the period? Analyze a series of paintings by Jean-Baptiste-Siméon Chardin that depict various aspects of daily life and reveal the era's increased attention to individual emotion and development. Then complete a writing assignment based on the evidence and details from this chapter.

bedfordstmartins.com/mckaywestvalue

care, and religious worship. Uncovering the life of the common people is a formidable challenge because they left few written records and regional variations abounded. Yet imaginative research has resulted in major findings and much greater knowledge. It is now possible to follow the common people into their homes, workshops, churches, and taverns and to ask, "What were the everyday experiences of ordinary people, and how did they change over the eighteenth century?"

Marriage and the Family

What changes occurred in marriage and the family in the course of the eighteenth century?

The basic unit of social organization is the family. Within the structure of the family human beings love, mate, and reproduce. It is primarily the family that teaches the child, imparting values and customs that condition an individual's behavior for a lifetime. The family is also an institution woven into the web of history. It evolves and changes, assuming different forms in different times and places. The eighteenth century witnessed such an evolution, as patterns of marriage shifted and individuals adapted and conformed to the new and changing realities of the family unit.

Late Marriage and Nuclear Families

Because census data before the modern period are rare, historians have turned to parish registers of births, deaths, and marriages to uncover details of European family life before the nineteenth century. These registers reveal that the three-generation extended family was a rarity in western and central Europe. When young European couples married, they normally established their own households and lived apart from their parents, much like the nuclear families (a family group consisting of parents and their children with no other relatives) common in America today. If a three-generation household came into existence, it was usually because a widowed parent moved into the home of a married child.

Most people did not marry young in the seventeenth and eighteenth centuries. The average person married surprisingly late, many years after reaching adulthood and many more after beginning to work. Studies of western Europe in the seventeenth and eighteenth centuries show that both men and women married for the first time at an average age of twenty-five to twenty-seven. Furthermore, 10 to 20 percent of men and women in western Europe never married at all. Matters were different in eastern Europe, where the multigeneration household was the norm, marriage occurred around age twenty, and permanent celibacy was much less common.

Why did young people in western Europe delay marriage? The main reason was that couples normally did not marry until they could start an independent household and support themselves and their future children. Peasants often needed to wait until their father's death to inherit land and marry. In the towns, men and women worked to accumulate enough savings to start a small business and establish their own home. As one father stated in an advice book written for his son: "Money is the sinew of love, as well as war; you can do nothing happily in wedlock without it; the other [virtue and beauty] are court-cards, but they are not of the trump-suit and are foiled by every sneaking misadventure."[1]

Laws and tradition also discouraged early marriage. In some areas couples needed permission from the local lord or landowner in order to marry. Poor couples had particular difficulty securing the approval of local officials, who believed that freedom to marry for the lower classes would result in more landless paupers, more abandoned children, and more money for welfare. Village elders often agreed.

The custom of late marriage combined with the nuclear-family household distinguished western European society from other areas of the world. Historians have argued that this late-marriage pattern was responsible for at least part of the economic advantage western Europeans acquired relative to other world regions. Late marriage joined a mature man and a mature woman — two adults who had already accumulated social and economic capital and could transmit self-reliance and skills to the next generation. This marriage pattern also favored a greater degree of equality between husband and wife.

Work Away from Home

Many young people worked within their families until they could start their own households. Boys plowed and wove; girls spun and tended the cows. Many others left home to work elsewhere. In the trades, a lad would enter apprenticeship around age fifteen and finish in his late teens or early twenties. During that time he would not be permitted to marry. An apprentice from a rural village would typically move to a city or town to learn a trade, earning little and working hard. If he was lucky and had connections, he might eventually be admitted to a guild and establish his economic independence. Many poor families could not afford apprenticeships for their sons. Without craft skills, these youths drifted from one tough job to another: hired hand for a small farmer, wage laborer on a new road, carrier of water or domestic servant in a nearby town.

Many adolescent girls also left their families to work. The range of opportunities open to them was more limited, however. Apprenticeship was sometimes available with mistresses in traditionally female occupations like seamstress, linen draper, or midwife. With the growth in production of finished goods for the emerging consumer economy during the eighteenth century (see Chapter 17), demand rose for skilled female labor and, with it, greater opportunities for women. Even male guildsmen hired girls and women, despite guild restrictions.

Service in another family's household was by far the most common job for girls, and even middle-class families often sent their daughters into service. The legions of young servant girls worked hard but had little independence. Constantly under the eye of her mistress, the servant girl had many tasks — cleaning, shopping, cooking, child care. Often the work was endless, for there were few laws to limit exploitation. Court records are full of servant girls' complaints of physical mistreatment by their mistresses. There were many like the fifteen-year-old English girl in the early eighteenth century who told the judge that her mistress had not only called her "very opprobrious names, as Bitch, Whore and the like," but also "beat her without provocation and beyond measure."[2]

Male apprentices told similar tales of abuse and they shared the legal status of "servants" with housemaids, but they were far less vulnerable to the sexual exploitation that threatened young girls. In theory, domestic service offered a girl protection and

Young Serving Girl Increased migration to urban areas in the eighteenth century contributed to a loosening of traditional morals and soaring illegitimacy rates. Young women who worked as servants or shopgirls could not be supervised as closely as those who lived at home. The themes of seduction, fallen virtue, and familial conflict were popular in eighteenth-century art, such as in this painting by Pietro Longhi (1702–1785). (akg-images/ Cameraphoto)

security in a new family. But in practice she was often the easy prey of a lecherous master or his sons or friends. If the girl became pregnant, she could be fired and thrown out in disgrace. Many families could not or would not accept such a girl back into the home. Forced to make their own way, these girls had no choice but to turn to a harsh life of prostitution and petty thievery (see page 588). "What are we?" exclaimed a bitter Parisian prostitute. "Most of us are unfortunate women, without origins, without education, servants and maids for the most part."[3] Adult women who remained in service, at least in large towns and cities, could gain more autonomy and distressed their employers by changing jobs frequently.

Premarital Sex and Community Controls

Ten years between puberty and marriage was a long time for sexually mature young people to wait. Many unmarried couples satisfied their sexual desires with fondling and petting. Others went further and engaged in premarital intercourse. Those who did so risked pregnancy and the stigma of illegitimate birth. Birth control was not unknown in Europe before the nineteenth century, but it was primitive and unreliable. Condoms, made from sheep intestines, became available in the mid-seventeenth century, replacing uncomfortable earlier versions made from cloth. They were expensive and mainly used by aristocratic libertines and prostitutes. The most common method of contraception was coitus interruptus — withdrawal by the male before ejaculation. The French, who were early leaders in contraception, were using this method extensively by the end of the eighteenth century.

Despite the lack of reliable contraception, premarital sex did not result in a large proportion of illegitimate births in most parts of Europe until 1750. English parish registers seldom listed more than one illegitimate child out of every twenty children baptized. Some French parishes in the seventeenth century had extraordinarily low rates of illegitimacy, with less than 1 percent of babies born out of wedlock. Illegitimate babies were apparently a rarity, at least as far as the official records are concerned.

Where collective control over sexual behavior among youths failed, community pressure to marry often prevailed. A study of seven representative parishes in seventeenth-century England shows that around 20 percent of children were conceived before the couple was married, while only 2 percent were born out of wedlock.[4] Figures for the French village of Auffay in Normandy in the eighteenth century were remarkably similar. No doubt many of these French and English couples were already engaged, or at least in a committed relationship, before they entered into intimate relations, and pregnancy simply set the marriage date once and for all.

The combination of low rates of illegitimate birth with large numbers of pregnant brides reflects the powerful **community controls** of the traditional village, particularly the open-field village, with its pattern of cooperation and common action. An unwed mother with an illegitimate child was inevitably viewed as a grave threat to the economic, social, and moral stability of the community. Irate parents, anxious village elders, indignant priests, and stern landlords all combined to pressure young people who wavered about marriage in the face of unexpected pregnancies. In the countryside these controls meant that premarital sex was not entered into lightly and that it was generally limited to those contemplating marriage.

The concerns of the village and the family weighed heavily on couples' lives after marriage as well. Whereas uninvolved individuals today try to stay out of the domestic disputes of their neighbors, the people in peasant communities gave such affairs loud and unfavorable publicity either at the time or during the carnival season (see page 598). Relying on degrading public rituals, known as **charivari**, the young men of the village would typically gang up on their victim and force him or her to sit astride a donkey facing backward and holding up the donkey's tail. They would parade the overly brutal spouse-beater or the adulterous couple around the village, loudly proclaiming the offenders' misdeeds. The donkey ride and other colorful humiliations ranging from rotten vegetables splattered on the doorstep to obscene and insulting midnight serenades were common punishments throughout much of Europe. They epitomized the community's effort to police personal behavior and maintain moral standards.

New Patterns of Marriage and Illegitimacy

In the second half of the eighteenth century, long-standing patterns of marriage and illegitimacy shifted dramatically. One important change was an increased ability for young people to choose partners for themselves, rather than following the interests of their families. This change occurred because social and economic transformations made it harder for families and communities to supervise their behavior. More youths in the countryside worked for their own wages, rather than on a family farm, and their economic autonomy translated into increased freedom of action. Moreover, many youths joined the flood of migrants to the cities, either with their families or in search of work on their own. Urban life provided young people with more social contacts and less social control.

A less positive outcome of loosening social control was an **illegitimacy explosion**, concentrated in England, France, Germany, and Scandinavia. In Frankfurt, Germany, for example, births out of wedlock rose steadily from about 2 percent of all births in the early 1700s to a peak of about 25 percent around 1850. In Bordeaux, France, 36 percent of all babies were being born out of wedlock by 1840. Small towns and villages experienced less startling climbs, but between 1750 and 1850 increases from a range of 1 to 3 percent initially and then 10 to 20 percent were commonplace. The rise in numbers did not alter social disapproval of single mothers and their offspring, leaving them in desperate circumstances.

Why did the number of illegitimate births skyrocket? One reason was a rise in sexual activity among young people. The loosened social controls that gave young people more choice in marriage also provided them with more opportunities to yield to the attraction of the opposite sex. As in previous generations, many of the young couples who engaged in sexual activity intended to marry. In one medium-size French city in 1787–1788, the great majority of unwed mothers stated that sexual intimacy had followed promises of marriage. Their sisters in rural Normandy frequently reported that they had been "seduced in anticipation of marriage."[5]

The problem for young women who became pregnant was that fewer men followed through on their promises. The second half of the eighteenth century witnessed sharply rising prices for food, homes, and other necessities of life. Many soldiers, day laborers, and male servants were no doubt sincere in their proposals, but their lives were insecure, and they hesitated to take on the burden of a wife and child.

Thus, while some happy couples benefited from matches of love rather than convenience, in many cases the intended marriage did not take place. The romantic yet practical dreams and aspirations of young people were frustrated by low wages, inequality, and changing economic and social conditions. Old patterns of marriage and family were breaking down. Only in the late nineteenth century would more stable patterns reappear.

Sex on the Margins of Society

Not all sex acts took place between men and women hopeful of marriage. Prostitution offered both single and married men an outlet for sexual desire. After a long period of relative tolerance, prostitutes encountered increasingly harsh and repressive laws in the sixteenth and early seventeenth centuries as officials across Europe closed licensed brothels and declared prostitution illegal.

Despite this repression, prostitution continued to flourish in the eighteenth century. Most prostitutes were working women who turned to the sex trade when confronted with unemployment. Such women did not become social pariahs, but retained ties with the communities of laboring poor to which they belonged. If caught by the police, however, they were liable to imprisonment or banishment. Venereal disease was also a constant threat. Prostitutes were subjected to humiliating police examinations for disease, although medical treatments were at best rudimentary. Farther up the social scale were courtesans whose wealthy protectors provided apartments, servants, fashionable clothing, and cash allowances. After a brilliant but brief career, an aging courtesan faced with the loss of her wealthy client could descend once more to streetwalking.

Relations between individuals of the same sex attracted even more condemnation than did prostitution, since they defied the Bible's limitation of sex to the purposes of procreation. Male same-sex relations, described as "sodomy" or "buggery," were prohibited by law in most European states, under pain of death. Such laws, however, were enforced unevenly, most strictly in Spain and far less so in the Scandinavian countries and Russia.[6]

Protected by their status, nobles and royals sometimes openly indulged their same-sex passions, which were accepted as long as they married and produced legitimate heirs. It was common knowledge that King James I, sponsor of the first translation of the Bible into English, had male lovers, but such relations did not prevent him from having seven children with his wife, Anne of Denmark. The duchess of Orléans, sister-in-law of French king Louis XIV, repeated rumors in her letters about the homosexual inclinations of King William of England, hero of the Glorious Revolution (see Chapter 15). She was hardly shocked by the news, given the fortune and favor her own husband lavished on his many *mignons*, as they were called.

In the late seventeenth century new homosexual subcultures began to emerge in Paris, Amsterdam, and London, with their own slang, meeting places, and styles of dress. Unlike the relations described above, which involved men who took both wives and male lovers, these groups included men exclusively oriented toward other men. In London, they called themselves "mollies," a term originally applied to prostitutes, and some began to wear women's clothing and act in effeminate ways. A new self-identity began to form among homosexual men: a belief that their same-sex desire made them fundamentally different from other men. As a character in one late-eighteenth-century fiction declared, he was in "a category of men different from the other, a class Nature has created in order to diminish or minimize propagation."[7]

Same-sex relations existed among women as well, but they attracted less anxiety and condemnation than those among men. Some women were prosecuted for "unnatural" relations; others attempted to escape the narrow confines imposed on them by dressing as men. Cross-dressing women occasionally snuck into the armed forces, such as Ulrika Elenora Stålhammar, who served as a man in the Swedish army for thirteen years and married a woman. After confessing her transgressions, she was sentenced to a lenient one-month imprisonment.[8] The beginnings of a distinctive lesbian subculture appeared in London at the end of the eighteenth century.

Across the early modern period, traditional tolerance for sexual activities outside of heterosexual marriage — be they sex with prostitutes or same-sex relations among male courtiers — faded. This process accelerated in the eighteenth century as Enlightenment critics attacked court immorality and preached virtue and morality for middle-class men, who were expected to prove their worthiness to claim the reins of political power.

Children and Education

What was life like for children, and how did attitudes toward childhood evolve?

On the whole, western European women married late, but then began bearing children rapidly. If a woman married before she was thirty, and if both she and her husband lived to fifty, she would most likely give birth to six or more children. Infant mortality varied across Europe, but was very high by modern standards, and many women died in childbirth due to limited medical knowledge.

For those children who did survive, new Enlightenment ideals in the latter half of the century stressed the importance of parental nurturing. New worldviews also led to an increase in elementary schools throughout Europe, but despite the efforts of enlightened absolutists and religious institutions, formal education reached only a minority of ordinary children.

Child Care and Nursing

Newborns entered a dangerous world. They were vulnerable to infectious diseases, and many babies died of dehydration brought about by bad bouts of ordinary diarrhea. Of those who survived infancy, many more died in childhood. Even in a rich family, little could be done for an ailing child. Childbirth was also dangerous. Women who bore six children faced a cumulative risk of dying in childbirth of 5 to 10 percent, a thousand times as great as the risk in Europe today.[9] They died from blood loss and shock during delivery and from infections caused by unsanitary conditions. The joy of pregnancy was thus shadowed by fear of loss of the mother or her child.

In the countryside, women of the lower classes generally breast-fed their infants for two years or more. Although not a foolproof means of birth control, breast-feeding decreases the likelihood of pregnancy by delaying the resumption of ovulation. By nursing their babies, women limited their fertility and spaced their children two or three years apart. Nursing also saved lives: breast-fed infants received precious immunity-producing substances and were more likely to survive than those who were fed other food.

Areas where babies were not breast-fed — typically in northern France, Scandinavia, and central and eastern Europe — experienced the highest infant mortality rates. In these areas, many people believed that breast-feeding was bad for a woman's health or appearance. Across Europe, women of the aristocracy and upper middle class seldom nursed their own children because they found breast-feeding undignified and it interfered with their social responsibilities. The alternatives to breast-feeding consisted of feeding babies cow's or goat's milk or paying lactating women to provide their milk.

Wealthy women hired live-in wet nurses to suckle their babies (which usually meant sending the nurse's own infant away to be nursed by someone else). Working women in the cities also relied on wet nurses because they needed to earn a living. Unable to afford live-in wet nurses, they often turned to the cheaper services of women in the countryside. Rural **wet-nursing** was a widespread business in the eighteenth century, conducted within the framework of the putting-out system. The traffic was in babies rather than in yarn or cloth, and two or three years often passed before the wet-nurse worker in the countryside finished her task.

Wet-nursing was particularly common in northern France. Toward the end of the century, roughly twenty thousand babies were born in Paris each year. Almost half were placed with rural wet nurses through a government-supervised distribution network; 20 to 25 percent were placed in the homes of Parisian nurses personally selected by their parents; and another 20 to 25 percent were abandoned to foundling hospitals, which would send them to wet nurses in the countryside. The remainder (perhaps 10 percent) were nursed at home by their mothers or live-in nurses.[10]

Reliance on wet nurses raised levels of infant mortality because of the dangers of travel, the lack of supervision of conditions in wet nurses' homes, and the need to share milk between a wet nurse's own baby and the one or more babies she was hired to feed.

A study of parish registers in northern France during the late seventeenth and early eighteenth centuries reveals that 35 percent of babies died before their first birthday, and another 20 percent before age ten.[11] In England, where more mothers nursed, only some 30 percent of children did not reach their tenth birthday.

Mortality rates were also higher in overcrowded and dirty cities; in low-lying, marshy regions; and during summer months when rural women were busy in agricultural work and had less time to tend to infants. The corollary of high infant mortality was high fertility. Women who did not breast-feed their babies or whose children died in infancy became pregnant more quickly and bore more children. Thus, on balance, the number of children who survived to adulthood tended to be the same across Europe, with higher births balancing the greater loss of life in areas that relied on wet-nursing.

In the second half of the eighteenth century, critics mounted a harsh attack against wet-nursing. Enlightenment thinkers proclaimed that wet-nursing was robbing European society of reaching its full potential. They were convinced, incorrectly, that the population was declining (in fact it was rising, but they lacked accurate population data) and blamed this decline on women's failure to nurture their children properly. Some also railed against practices of contraception and masturbation, which they believed were robbing their nations of potential children. Despite these complaints, many women continued to rely on wet nurses for convenience or from necessity.

Foundlings and Infanticide

The young woman who could not provide for an unwanted child had few choices, especially if she had no prospect of marriage. Abortions were illegal, dangerous, and apparently rare. In desperation, some women, particularly in the countryside, hid unwanted pregnancies, delivered in secret, and smothered their newborn infants. If discovered, infanticide was punishable by death.

Women in cities had more choices for disposing of babies they could not support. Foundling homes (orphanages) first took hold in Italy, Spain, and Portugal in the sixteenth century, spreading to France in 1670 and the rest of Europe thereafter. In eighteenth-century England the government acted on a petition calling for a foundling hospital "to prevent the frequent murders of poor, miserable infants at birth" and "to suppress the inhuman custom of exposing newborn children to perish in the streets." By the end of the eighteenth century, European foundling hospitals were admitting annually about one hundred thousand abandoned children, nearly all of them infants. At their best, foundling homes were a good example of Christian charity and social concern in an age of great poverty and inequality. Yet the foundling home was no panacea. By the 1770s one-third of all babies born in Paris were being immediately abandoned to foundling homes by their mothers. Many were the offspring of single women, the result of the illegitimacy explosion of the second half of the eighteenth century. But fully one-third of all the foundlings were abandoned by married couples too poor to feed another child.[12]

Millions of babies entered foundling homes, but few left. Even in the best of these homes, 50 percent of the babies normally died within a year. In the worst, fully 90 percent did not survive, falling victim to infectious disease, malnutrition, and neglect.[13] There appears to have been no differentiation by sex in the numbers of children sent to foundling hospitals.

Attitudes Toward Children

What were the typical circumstances of children's lives? Some scholars have claimed that high mortality rates prevented parents from forming emotional attachments to young children. With a reasonable expectation that a child might die, some scholars believe, parents maintained an attitude of indifference, if not downright negligence. Most historians now believe, however, that seventeenth- and eighteenth-century parents did love their children, suffered anxiously when they fell ill, and experienced extreme anguish when they died.

Parents were well aware of the dangers of infancy and childhood. The great eighteenth-century English historian Edward Gibbon (1737–1794) wrote, with some exaggeration, that "the death of a new born child before that of its parents may seem unnatural but it is a strictly probable event, since of any given number the greater part are extinguished before the ninth year, before they possess the faculties of the mind and the body." Gibbon's father named all his boys Edward after himself, hoping that at least one of them would survive to carry his name. His prudence was not misplaced. Edward the future historian and eldest survived. Five brothers and sisters who followed him all died in infancy.

Emotional prudence could lead to emotional distance. The French essayist Michel de Montaigne, who lost five of his six daughters in infancy, wrote, "I cannot abide that passion for caressing new-born children, which have neither mental activities nor recognisable bodily shape by which to make themselves loveable and I have never willingly suffered them to be fed in my presence."[14] In contrast to this harsh picture, however, historians have drawn ample evidence from diaries, letters, and family portraits that parents of all social classes did cherish their children. This was equally true of mothers and fathers and of attitudes toward sons and daughters. The English poet Ben Jonson wrote movingly in "On My First Son" of the death of his six-year-old son Benjamin, which occurred during a London plague outbreak in 1603:

> Farewell, thou child of my right hand, and joy;
> My sin was too much hope of thee, loved boy.
> Seven years thou wert lent to me, and I thee pay,
> Exacted by thy fate, on the just day.

In a society characterized by much violence and brutality, discipline of children was often severe. The axiom "Spare the rod and spoil the child" seems to have been coined in the mid-seventeenth century. Susannah Wesley (1669–1742), mother of John Wesley,

ONLINE DOCUMENT ASSIGNMENT

The Inner Life of the Individual

How did the increasing emphasis on the inner life and development of the individual in the eighteenth century find expression in the art of the period? Analyze a series of paintings by Jean-Baptiste-Siméon Chardin that depict various aspects of daily life and reveal the era's increased attention to individual emotion and development.

bedfordstmartins.com/mckaywestvalue

the founder of Methodism (see page 607), agreed. According to her, the first task of a parent toward her children was "to conquer the will, and bring them to an obedient temper." She reported that her babies were "taught to fear the rod, and to cry softly; by which means they escaped the abundance of correction they might otherwise have had, and that most odious noise of the crying of children was rarely heard in the house."[15] They were beaten for lying, stealing, disobeying, and quarreling, and forbidden from playing with other neighbor children. Susannah's methods of disciplining her children were probably extreme even in her own day, but they do reflect a broad consensus that children were born with an innately sinful will that parents must overcome. (See "Primary Source: Parisian Boyhood," page 594.)

The Enlightenment produced an enthusiastic new discourse about childhood and child rearing. Starting around 1760 critics called for greater tenderness toward children and proposed imaginative new teaching methods. In addition to supporting foundling homes and urging women to nurse their babies, these new voices ridiculed the practice of swaddling babies and using whaleboned corsets to mold children's bones. Instead of dressing children in miniature versions of adult clothing, critics called for comfortable

---

The First Step of Childhood   This tender snapshot of a baby's first steps toward an adoring mother exemplifies new attitudes toward children and raising them ushered in by the Enlightenment. Authors like Jean-Jacques Rousseau encouraged elite mothers like the one pictured here to take a more personal interest in raising their children, instead of leaving them in the hands of indifferent wet nurses and nannies. Many women responded eagerly to this call, and the period saw a more sentimentalized view of childhood and family life. (Erich Lessing/Art Resource, NY)

PRIMARY SOURCE   Parisian Boyhood

The life of Jacques-Louis Ménétra, a Parisian glazier, exemplified many of the social patterns of his day. He lost his mother in infancy, was educated at a parish school, married late, and had four children, two of whom died. Ménétra distinguished himself from other workingmen, however, by writing an autobiography describing his tumultuous childhood, his travels around France as a journeyman, and his settled life as a guild master. Ménétra's father was often violent, but he fiercely defended his son against rumored child abductions in Paris (in reality the police had overstepped orders to arrest children loitering in the streets).

I was born on 13 July 1738 a native of this great city. My father belonged to the class usually called artisans. His profession was that of glazier. Hence it is with him that I begin my family tree and I shall say nothing about my ancestors. My father married and set himself up at the same time and wed a virtuous girl who gave him four children, three daughters and one boy, myself, all of whose little pranks I'm going to write about.

My father became a widower when I was two years old. I had been put out to nurse. My grandmother who always loved me a great deal and even idolized me, knowing that the nurse I was with had her milk gone bad, came to get me and after curing me put me back out to nurse [where] I ended up with a pretty good woman who taught me early on the profession of begging. My [grand]mother and my godfather when they came to see me . . . found me in a church begging charity. They took me home and from then until the age of eleven I lived with my good grandmother. My father wanted me back, afraid that he would have to pay my board. He put me to work in his trade even though several people tried to talk him out of it [but] he wouldn't listen to them. . . .

When I felt a little better, I went back to my usual ways which is to say that my father was always angry with me. One night when I was lighting the way in a

clothing to allow freedom of movement. Rather than emphasizing original sin, these enlightened voices celebrated the child as an innocent product of nature. Since they viewed nature as inherently positive, Enlightenment educators advocated safeguarding and developing children's innate qualities rather than thwarting and suppressing them. Accordingly, they believed the best hopes for a new society, untrammeled by the prejudices of the past, lay in a radical reform of child-rearing techniques.

One of the century's most influential works on child rearing was Jean-Jacques Rousseau's *Emile, or On Education* (1762). Rousseau argued that boys' education should include plenty of fresh air and exercise and that they should be taught practical craft skills in addition to rote book learning. Reacting to what he perceived as the vanity and frivolity of upper-class Parisian women, Rousseau insisted that girls' education focus on their future domestic responsibilities. For Rousseau, women's "nature" destined them solely for a life of marriage and child rearing. The ideas of Rousseau and other reformers were enthusiastically adopted by elite women, some of whom began to nurse their own children.

staircase where he was installing a casement and not mounting it the way he wanted with an angry kick [he] knocked out all my teeth. When I got back home my (step)mother took me to a dentist by the name of Ricie who put back the teeth that weren't broken and I went three weeks eating nothing but bouillon and soup.

In those days it was rumored that they were taking young boys and bleeding them and that they were lost forever and that their blood was used to bathe a princess suffering from a disease that could only be cured with human blood. There was plenty of talk about that in Paris. My father came to get me at school as many other fathers did along with seven big coopers armed with crowbars. The rumor was so strong that the windows of the police station were broken and several poor guys were assaulted and one was even burned in the place de Grève because he looked like a police informer. Children weren't allowed to go outside; three poor wretches were hanged in the place de Grève to settle the matter and restore calm in Paris.

EVALUATE THE EVIDENCE

1. What hardships did the young Ménétra face in his childhood? What attitude did he display toward his childhood experiences?

2. What characteristic elements of eighteenth-century family life does Ménétra's childhood reflect? Does his story provide evidence for or against the thesis that parents deeply loved their children?

Source: Jacques-Louis Ménétra, *Journal of My Life*, ed. Daniel Roche, trans. Arthur Goldhammer, pp. 18, 21–22. Copyright © 1986 Columbia University Press. Reprinted with permission of the publisher.

For all his influence, Rousseau also reveals the occasional hypocrisy of Enlightenment thinkers. Although a passionate advocate for children's education, Rousseau abandoned the five children he fathered with his common-law wife in foundling hospitals despite their mother's protests. None are known to have survived. For Rousseau, popularizing the idea of creating a natural man was more important than raising real children.

The Spread of Elementary Schools

The availability of education outside the home gradually increased over the early modern period. The wealthy led the way in the sixteenth century with special colleges, often run by Jesuits in Catholic areas. Schools charged specifically with educating children of the common people began to appear in the second half of the seventeenth century. They taught six- to twelve-year-old children basic literacy, religion, and perhaps some arithmetic for the boys and needlework for the girls. The number of such schools expanded in the eighteenth century, although they were never sufficient to educate the majority of the population.

Religion played an important role in the spread of education. From the middle of the seventeenth century, Presbyterian Scotland was convinced that the path to salvation lay in careful study of the Scriptures, and it established an effective network of parish schools for rich and poor alike. The Church of England and the dissenting congregations—Puritans, Presbyterians, Quakers, and so on—established "charity schools" to instruct poor children. The first proponents of universal education, in Prussia, were inspired by the Protestant idea that every believer should be able to read the Bible and by the new idea of raising a population capable of effectively serving the state. As early as 1717 Prussia made attendance at elementary schools compulsory for boys and girls, albeit only in areas where schools already existed.[16] More Protestant German states, such as Saxony and Württemberg (VUHR-tuhm-burg), followed suit in the eighteenth century.

Catholic states pursued their own programs of popular education. In the 1660s France began setting up charity schools to teach poor children their catechism and prayers as well as reading and writing. These were run by parish priests or by new teaching orders created for this purpose. One of the most famous orders was Jean-Baptiste de la Salle's Brothers of the Christian Schools. Founded in 1684, the schools had thirty-five thousand students across France by the 1780s. Enthusiasm for popular education was even greater in the Habsburg empire. Inspired by the expansion of schools in rival Protestant German states, in 1774 Maria Theresa issued her own compulsory education edict, imposing five hours of school, five days a week, for all children aged six to twelve.[17] Across Europe some elementary education was becoming a reality, and schools became increasingly significant in the life of the child.

Popular Culture and Consumerism

How did increasing literacy and new patterns of consumption affect people's lives?

Because of the new efforts in education, basic literacy was expanding among the popular classes, whose reading habits centered primarily on religious material, but who also began to incorporate more practical and entertaining literature. In addition to reading, people of all classes enjoyed a range of leisure activities including storytelling, fairs, festivals, and sports.

One of the most important developments in European society in the eighteenth century was the emergence of a fledgling consumer culture. Much of the expansion took place among the upper and upper-middle classes, but a boom in cheap reproductions of luxury items also opened doors for people of modest means. From food to ribbons and from coal stoves to umbrellas, the material worlds of city dwellers grew richer and more diverse. This "consumer revolution," as it has been called, created new expectations for comfort, hygiene, and self-expression, thus dramatically changing European daily life in the eighteenth century.

Popular Literature

The surge in childhood education in the eighteenth century led to a remarkable growth in literacy between 1600 and 1800. Whereas in 1600 only one male in six was barely literate in France and Scotland, and one in four in England, by 1800 almost nine out of ten Scottish males, two out of three French males (Map 18.1), and more than half

MAP 18.1   Literacy in France, ca. 1789
Literacy rates increased but still varied widely between and within states in eighteenth-century Europe.

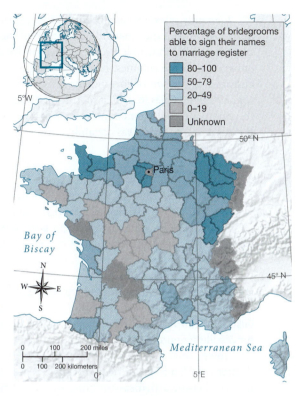

Percentage of bridegrooms able to sign their names to marriage register

- 80–100
- 50–79
- 20–49
- 0–19
- Unknown

of English males were literate. In all three countries, the bulk of the jump occurred in the eighteenth century. Women were also increasingly literate, although they lagged behind men.

The growth in literacy promoted growth in reading, and historians have carefully examined what the common people read. While the Bible remained the overwhelming favorite, especially in Protestant countries, short pamphlets known as chapbooks were the staple of popular literature. Printed on the cheapest paper, many chapbooks featured Bible stories, prayers, and the lives of saints and exemplary Christians. This pious literature gave believers moral teachings and a faith that helped them endure their daily struggles.

Entertaining, often humorous stories formed a second element of popular literature. Fairy tales, medieval romances, true crime stories, and fantastic adventures were some of the delights that filled the peddler's pack as he approached a village. These tales presented a world of danger and magic, of supernatural powers, fairy godmothers, and evil trolls, that provided a temporary flight from harsh everyday reality. They also contained nuggets of ancient folk wisdom, counseling prudence in a world full of danger and injustice, where wolves dress like grandmothers and eat Little Red Riding Hoods.

Finally, some popular literature was highly practical, dealing with rural crafts, household repairs, useful plants, and similar matters. Much lore was stored in almanacs, where calendars listing secular, religious, and astrological events were mixed with agricultural schedules, arcane facts, and jokes. The almanac was highly appreciated even by many in the comfortable classes. In this way, elites still shared some elements of a common culture with the masses.

While it is safe to say that the vast majority of ordinary people—particularly peasants in isolated villages—did not read the great works of the Enlightenment, they were not immune from the new ideas. Urban working people were exposed to Enlightenment thought through the rumors and gossip that spread across city streets, workshops, markets, and taverns. They also had access to cheap pamphlets that helped translate Enlightenment critiques into ordinary language. Servants, who usually came from rural areas and traveled home periodically, were well situated to transmit ideas from educated employers to the village.

Certainly some ordinary people did assimilate Enlightenment ideals. Thomas Paine, author of some of the most influential texts of the American Revolution, was an English corset-maker's son who left school at age twelve and carried on his father's trade before emigrating to the colonies. His 1776 pamphlet *Common Sense* attacked the weight of custom and the evils of government against the natural society of men. This text, which sold 120,000 copies in its first months of publication, is vivid proof of working people's reception of Enlightenment ideas. Paine's stirring mastery of them was perhaps unique, but his access to them was certainly not.

Leisure and Recreation

Despite the spread of literacy, the culture of the village remained largely oral rather than written. In the cold, dark winter months, peasant families gathered around the fireplace to sing, tell stories, do craftwork, and keep warm. In some parts of Europe, women would gather together in someone's cottage to chat, sew, spin, and laugh. Sometimes a few young men would be invited so that the daughters (and mothers) could size up potential suitors in a supervised atmosphere. A favorite recreation of men was drinking and talking with buddies in public places, and it was a sorry village that had no tavern. In addition to old favorites such as beer and wine, the common people turned with gusto to cheap and potent hard liquor, which fell in price because of improved techniques for distilling grain in the eighteenth century.

Towns and cities offered a wider range of amusements, including pleasure gardens, theaters, and lending libraries. Urban fairs featured prepared foods, acrobats, and conjuring acts. Leisure activities were another form of consumption marked by growing commercialization. For example, commercial, profit-making spectator sports emerged in this period, including horse races, boxing matches, and bullfights. Modern sports heroes, such as brain-bashing heavyweight champions and haughty bullfighting matadors, made their appearance on the historical scene.

Blood sports, such as bullbaiting and cockfighting, also remained popular with the masses. In bullbaiting, the bull, usually staked on a chain in the courtyard of an inn, was attacked by ferocious dogs for the amusement of the innkeeper's clients. Eventually the maimed and tortured animal was slaughtered by a butcher and sold as meat. In cockfighting, two roosters, carefully trained by their owners and armed with razor-sharp steel spurs, slashed and clawed each other in a small ring until the victor won — and the loser died. An added attraction of cockfighting was that the screaming spectators could bet on the lightning-fast combat.

Popular recreation merged with religious celebration in a variety of festivals and processions throughout the year. The most striking display of these religiously inspired events was **carnival**, a time of reveling and excess in Catholic Europe, especially in Mediterranean countries. Carnival preceded Lent — the forty days of fasting and penitence before Easter — and for a few exceptional days in February or March, a wild release of drinking, masquerading, and dancing reigned. Moreover, a combination of plays, processions, and raucous spectacles turned the established order upside down. Peasants dressed as nobles and men as women, and rich masters waited on their servants at the table. This annual holiday gave people a much-appreciated chance to release their pent-up frustrations and aggressions before life returned to the usual pattern of hierarchy and hard work.

In trying to place the vibrant popular culture of the common people in broad perspective, historians have stressed the growing criticism levied against it by the educated elites in the second half of the eighteenth century. These elites, who had previously shared the popular enthusiasm for religious festivals, carnival, drinking in taverns, blood sports, and the like, now tended to see superstition, sin, disorder, and vulgarity.[18] The resulting attack on popular culture, which was tied to the clergy's efforts to eliminate paganism and superstition, was intensified as an educated public embraced the critical worldview of the Enlightenment.

New Foods and Appetites

At the beginning of the eighteenth century, ordinary men and women depended on grain as fully as they had in the past. Bread was quite literally the staff of life. Peasants in the Beauvais region of France ate two pounds of bread a day, washing it down with water, wine, or beer. Their dark bread was made from roughly ground wheat and rye— the standard flour of the common people. Even peasants normally needed to buy some grain for food, and, in full accord with landless laborers and urban workers, they believed in the moral economy and the **just price**. That is, they believed that prices should be "fair," protecting both consumers and producers, and that just prices should be imposed by government decree if necessary. When prices rose above this level, they often took action in the form of bread riots (see Chapter 15).

The rural poor also ate a quantity of vegetables. Peas and beans were probably the most common. Grown as field crops in much of Europe since the Middle Ages, they were eaten fresh in late spring and summer. Dried, they became the basic ingredients in the soups and stews of the long winter months. In most regions other vegetables appeared on the tables of the poor in season, primarily cabbages, carrots, and wild greens. Fruit was mostly limited to the summer months. Too precious to drink, milk was used to make cheese and butter, which peasants sold in the market to earn cash for taxes and land rents.

The common people of Europe ate less meat in 1700 than in 1500 because their general standard of living had declined and meat was more expensive. Moreover, harsh laws in most European countries reserved the right to hunt and eat game, such as rabbits, deer, and partridges, to nobles and large landowners. Few laws were more bitterly resented—or more frequently broken—by ordinary people than those governing hunting.

The diet of small traders and artisans—the people of the towns and cities—was less monotonous than that of the peasantry. Bustling markets provided a substantial variety of meats, vegetables, and fruits, although bread and beans still formed the bulk of such families' diets. Not surprisingly, the diet of the rich was quite different from that of the poor. The upper classes were rapacious carnivores, and a truly elegant dinner consisted of an abundance of rich meat and fish dishes laced with piquant sauces and complemented with sweets, cheeses, and wine in great quantities. During such dinners, it was common to spend five or more hours at table, eating and drinking and enjoying the witty banter of polite society.

Patterns of food consumption changed markedly as the century progressed. Because of a growth of market gardening, a greater variety of vegetables appeared in towns and cities. This was particularly the case in the Low Countries and England, which pioneered

Parisian Street Scene   Here a milk seller doubles as a provider of news, reading a hand-printed news sheet to a small gathering. Gossip, rumor, and formal or informal newspapers, like the one pictured here, ensured that information traversed the city at astonishing speeds. (Musée de la Ville de Paris, Musée Carnavalet, Paris/Lauros/Giraudon/The Bridgeman Art Library)

new methods of farming. Introduced into Europe from the Americas — along with corn, squash, tomatoes, and many other useful plants — the humble potato provided an excellent new food source. Containing a good supply of carbohydrates, calories, and vitamins A and C, the potato offset the lack of vitamins in the poor person's winter and early-spring diet, and it provided a much higher caloric yield than grain for a given piece of land. After initial resistance, the potato became an important dietary supplement in much of Europe by the end of the century.

The most remarkable dietary change in the eighteenth century was in the consumption of commodities imported from abroad. Originally expensive and rare luxury items, goods like tea, sugar, coffee, chocolate, and tobacco became dietary staples for people of all social classes. With the exception of tea — which originated in China — most of the new consumables were produced in European colonies in the Americas. In many cases, the labor of enslaved peoples enabled the expansion in production and drop in prices that allowed such items to spread to the masses.

Why were colonial products so popular? Part of the motivation for consuming these products was a desire to emulate the luxurious lifestyles of the elite. Having seen pictures of or read about the fine lady's habit of "teatime" or the gentleman's appreciation for a pipe, common Europeans sought to experience these pleasures for themselves. Moreover, the quickened pace of work in the eighteenth century created new needs for stimulants among working people. Whereas the gentry took tea as a leisurely and genteel ritual, the lower classes drank tea or coffee at work to fight monotony and fatigue. With the widespread adoption of these products (which turned out to be mildly to extremely addictive), working people in Europe became increasingly dependent on faraway colonial economies and enslaved labor. Their understanding of daily necessities and how to procure those necessities shifted definitively, linking them to global trade networks they could not comprehend or control.

Toward a Consumer Society

Along with foodstuffs, all manner of other goods increased in variety and number in the eighteenth century. This proliferation led to a growth in consumption and new attitudes toward consumer goods so wide-ranging that some historians have referred to an eighteenth-century **consumer revolution**.[19] The result of this revolution was the birth of a new type of society in which people derived their self-identity as much from their consuming practices as from their working lives and place in the production process. As people gained the opportunity to pick and choose among a new variety of consumer goods, new notions of individuality and self-expression developed. A shopgirl could stand out from her peers by her choice of a striped jacket, a colored parasol, or simply a new ribbon for her hair. The full emergence of a consumer society did not take place until much later, but its roots lie in the eighteenth century.

Increased demand for consumer goods was not merely an innate response to increased supply. Eighteenth-century merchants cleverly pioneered new techniques to incite demand: they initiated marketing campaigns, opened fancy boutiques with large windows, and advertised the patronage of royal princes and princesses. By diversifying their product lines and greatly accelerating the turnover of styles, they seized the reins of fashion from the courtiers who had earlier controlled it. Instead of setting new styles, duchesses and marquises now bowed to the dictates of fashion merchants. (See "Individuals in Society: Rose Bertin, 'Minister of Fashion,'" page 602.) Fashion also extended beyond court circles to touch many more items and social groups.

Clothing was one of the chief indicators of the growth of consumerism. Shrewd entrepreneurs made fashionable clothing seem more desirable, while legions of women entering the textile and needle trades made it ever cheaper. As a result, eighteenth-century western Europe witnessed a dramatic rise in the consumption of clothing, particularly in large cities. One historian has documented an enormous growth in the size and value of Parisians' wardrobes from 1700 to 1789, as well as a new level of diversity in garments and accessories, colors, and fabrics.[20] Colonial economies again played an important role in lowering the cost of materials, such as cotton and vegetable dyes, largely due to the unpaid toil of enslaved Africans. Cheaper copies of elite styles made it possible for working people to aspire to follow fashion for the first time.

Elite onlookers were sometimes shocked by the sight of lower-class people in stylish outfits. In 1784 Mrs. Fanny Cradock described encountering her milkman during an evening stroll "dressed in a fashionable suit, with an embroidered waistcoat, silk knee-breeches and lace cuffs."[21] The spread of fashion challenged the traditional social order of Europe by blurring the boundaries between social groups and making it harder to distinguish between noble and commoner on the bustling city streets.

INDIVIDUALS IN SOCIETY • Rose Bertin, "Minister of Fashion"

One day in 1779, as the French royal family rode in a carriage through the streets of Paris, Queen Marie Antoinette noticed her fashion merchant, Rose Bertin, observing the royal procession. "Ah! there is mademoiselle Bertin," the queen exclaimed, waving her hand. Bertin responded with a curtsy. The king then stood and greeted Bertin, followed by the royal family and their entourage.* The incident shocked the public, for no common merchant had ever received such homage from royalty.

Bertin had come a long way from her humble beginnings. Born in 1747 to a poor family in northern France, she moved to Paris in the 1760s to work as a shop assistant. Bertin eventually opened her own boutique on the fashionable rue Saint-Honoré. In 1775 Bertin received the highest honor of her profession when she was selected by Marie Antoinette as one of her official purveyors.

Based on the queen's patronage, and riding the wave of the new consumer revolution, Bertin became one of the most successful entrepreneurs in Europe. Bertin established not only a large clientele, but also a reputation for pride and arrogance. She refused to work for non-noble customers, claiming that the orders of the queen and the court required all her attention. She astounded courtiers by referring to her "work" with the queen, as though the two were collaborators rather than absolute monarch and lowly subject. Bertin's close relationship with Marie Antoinette and the fortune the queen spent on her wardrobe hurt the royal family's image. One journalist derided Bertin as a "minister of fashion," whose influence outstripped that of all the others in royal government.

In January 1787 rumors spread through Paris that Bertin had filed for bankruptcy with debts of 2 to 3 million livres (a garment worker's annual salary was around 200

*Mémoires secrets pour servir à l'histoire de la république des lettres en France, vol. 13, 299, 5 mars 1779 (London: John Adamson, 1785).

Mrs. Cradock's milkman notwithstanding, women took the lead in the spread of fashion. Parisian women significantly out-consumed men, acquiring larger and more expensive wardrobes than those of their husbands, brothers, and fathers. This was true across the social spectrum; in ribbons, shoes, gloves, and lace, European working women reaped in the consumer revolution what they had sown in the industrious revolution (see Chapter 17). There were also new gender distinctions in dress. Previously, noblemen had vied with noblewomen in the magnificence of their apparel; by the end of the eighteenth century men had renounced brilliant colors and voluptuous fabrics to don early versions of the plain dark suit that remains standard male formal wear in the West. This was one more aspect of the increasingly rigid differences drawn between appropriate male and female behavior.

Changes in outward appearances were reflected in inner spaces, as new attitudes about privacy and intimate life also emerged. Historians have used notaries' probate inventories to peer into ordinary people's homes. In 1700 the cramped home of a mod-

livres). Despite her notoriously high prices and rich clients, this news did not shock Parisians, because the nobility's reluctance to pay its debts was equally well known. Bertin somehow held on to her business. Some said she had spread the bankruptcy rumors herself to shame the court into paying her bills.

Bertin remained loyal to the Crown during the tumult of the French Revolution (see Chapter 19) and sent dresses to the queen even after the arrest of the royal family. Fearing for her life, she left France for Germany in 1792 and continued to ply her profession in exile. She returned to France in 1800 and died in 1813, one year before the restoration of the Bourbon monarchy might have renewed her acclaim.†

Rose Bertin scandalized public opinion with her self-aggrandizement and ambition, yet history was on her side. She was the first celebrity fashion stylist and one of the first self-made career women to rise from obscurity to fame and fortune based on her talent, taste, and hard work. Her legacy remains in the exalted status of today's top fashion designers and in the dreams of small-town girls to make it in the big city.

QUESTIONS FOR ANALYSIS

1. Why was the relationship between Queen Marie Antoinette and Rose Bertin so troubling to public opinion? Why would relations between a queen and a fashion merchant have political implications?

2. Why would someone who sold fashionable clothing and accessories rise to such a prominent position in business and society? What makes fashion so important in the social world?

†On Rose Bertin, see Clare Haru Crowston, "The Queen and Her 'Minister of Fashion': Gender, Credit and Politics in Pre-Revolutionary France," *Gender and History* 14, 1 (April 2002): 92–116.

est family consisted of a few rooms, each of which had multiple functions. The same room was used for sleeping, receiving friends, and working. In the eighteenth century rents rose sharply, making it impossible to gain more space, but families began attributing specific functions to specific rooms. They also began to erect inner barriers within the home to provide small niches in which individuals could seek privacy.

New levels of comfort and convenience accompanied this trend toward more individualized ways of life. In 1700 a meal might be served in a common dish, with each person dipping his or her spoon into the pot. By the end of the eighteenth century even humble households contained a much greater variety of cutlery and dishes, making it possible for each person to eat from his or her own plate. More books and prints, which also proliferated at lower prices, decorated the shelves and walls. Improvements in glassmaking provided more transparent glass, which allowed daylight to penetrate into gloomy rooms. Cold and smoky hearths were increasingly replaced by more efficient and cleaner coal stoves, which also eliminated the backache of cooking over an open fire. Rooms were warmer, better lit, more comfortable, and more personalized, and the spread of street lighting made it safer to travel in cities at night.

Standards of bodily and public hygiene also improved. Public bathhouses, popular across Europe in the Middle Ages, had gradually closed in the early modern period due to concerns over sexual promiscuity and infectious disease. Many Europeans came to fear that immersing the body in hot water would allow harmful elements to enter the skin. Carefully watched by his physician, Louis XIII of France took his first bath at age seven, while James I of England refused to wash more than his hands. Personal cleanliness consisted of wearing fresh linen and using perfume to mask odors, both expensive practices that bespoke wealth and social status. From the mid-eighteenth century on, enlightened doctors revised their views and began to urge more frequent bathing. Spa towns, like Bath, England, became popular sites for the wealthy to see and be seen. Officials also took measures to improve the cleaning of city streets in which trash, human soil, and animal carcasses were often left to rot.

The scope of the new consumer economy should not be exaggerated. These developments were concentrated in large cities in northwestern Europe and North America. Even in these centers the elite benefited the most from new modes of life. This was not yet the society of mass consumption that emerged toward the end of the nineteenth century with the full expansion of the Industrial Revolution. The eighteenth century did, however, lay the foundations for one of the most distinctive features of modern Western life: societies based on the consumption of goods and services obtained through the market in which individuals form their identities and self-worth through the goods they consume.

Religious Authority and Beliefs

What were the patterns of popular religion, and how did they interact with the worldview of the educated public and their Enlightenment ideals?

Though the critical spirit of the Enlightenment made great inroads in the eighteenth century, the majority of ordinary men and women, especially those in rural areas, retained strong religious faith. The church promised salvation, and it gave comfort in the face of sorrow and death. Religion also remained strong because it was embedded in local traditions and everyday social experience.

Yet the popular religion of village Europe was also enmeshed in a larger world of church hierarchies and state power. These powerful outside forces sought to regulate religious life at the local level. Their efforts created tensions that helped set the scene for vigorous religious revivals in Protestant Germany and England as well as in Catholic France.

Church Hierarchy

In the eighteenth century religious faith not only endured, but grew in many parts of Europe. The local parish church remained the focal point of religious devotion and community cohesion. Congregants gossiped and swapped stories after services, and neighbors came together in church for baptisms, marriages, funerals, and special events. Priests and parsons kept the community records of births, deaths, and marriages; distributed charity; looked after orphans; and provided primary education to the common people. Thus the parish church was woven into the very fabric of community life.

While the parish church remained central to the community, it was also subject to greater control from the state. In Protestant areas, princes and monarchs headed the official church, and they regulated their "territorial churches" strictly, selecting personnel and imposing detailed rules. Clergy of the official church dominated education, and followers of other faiths suffered religious and civil discrimination. By the eighteenth century the radical ideas of the Reformation had resulted in another version of church bureaucracy.

Catholic monarchs in this period also took greater control of religious matters in their kingdoms, weakening papal authority. In both Spain and Portugal, the Catholic Church was closely associated with the state, a legacy of the long internal reconquista and sixteenth-century imperial conquests overseas. In the eighteenth century the Spanish crown took firm control of ecclesiastical appointments. Papal proclamations could not even be read in Spanish churches without prior approval from the government. In Portugal, religious enthusiasm led to a burst of new churches and monasteries in the early eighteenth century.

France went even further in establishing a national Catholic Church, known as the Gallican Church. Louis XIV's expulsion of Protestants in 1685 was accompanied by an insistence on the king's prerogative to choose and control bishops and issue laws regarding church affairs. Catholicism gained new ground in the Holy Roman Empire with the conversion of a number of Protestant princes and successful missionary work by Catholic orders among the populace. While it could not eradicate Protestantism altogether, the Habsburg monarchy successfully consolidated Catholicism as a pillar of its political control.

The Jesuit order played a key role in fostering the Catholic faith, providing extraordinary teachers, missionaries, and agents of the papacy. In many Catholic countries they exercised tremendous political influence, holding high government positions and educating the nobility in their colleges. By playing politics so effectively, however, the Jesuits elicited a broad coalition of enemies. Bitter controversies led Louis XV to order the Jesuits out of France in 1763 and to confiscate their property. France and Spain then pressured Rome to dissolve the Jesuits completely. In 1773 a reluctant pope caved in, although the order was revived after the French Revolution.

The Jesuit order was not the only Christian group to come under attack in the middle of the eighteenth century. The dominance of the larger Catholic Church and established Protestant churches was also challenged, both by enlightened reformers from above and by the faithful from below. Influenced by Enlightenment ideals, some Catholic rulers believed that the clergy in monasteries and convents should make a more practical contribution to social and religious life. Austria, a leader in controlling the church (see Chapter 16) and promoting primary education, showed how far the process could go. Maria Theresa began by sharply restricting entry into "unproductive" orders. In his Edict on Idle Institutions, her successor, Joseph II, abolished contemplative orders, henceforth permitting only orders that were engaged in teaching, nursing, or other practical work. The state expropriated the dissolved monasteries and used their wealth for charitable purposes and higher salaries for ordinary priests. Joseph II also issued edicts of religious tolerance, including for Jews, making Austria one of the first European states to lift centuries-old restrictions on its Jewish population.

Protestant Revival

Official efforts to reform state churches in the eighteenth century were confronted by a wave of religious enthusiasm from below. By the late seventeenth century the vast transformations of the Protestant Reformation were complete and had been widely adopted in most Protestant churches. Medieval practices of idolatry, saint worship, and pageantry were abolished; stained-glass windows were smashed and murals whitewashed. Yet many official Protestant churches had settled into a smug complacency. This, along with the growth of state power and bureaucracy in local parishes, threatened to eclipse one of the Reformation's main goals—to bring all believers closer to God.

In the Reformation heartland, one concerned German minister wrote that the Lutheran Church "had become paralyzed in forms of dead doctrinal conformity" and badly needed a return to its original inspiration.[22] His voice was one of many that prepared and then guided a Protestant revival that succeeded because it answered the intense but increasingly unsatisfied needs of common people.

The Protestant revival began in Germany in the late seventeenth century. It was known as **Pietism** (PIGH-uh-tih-zum), and three aspects helped explain its powerful appeal. First, Pietism called for a warm, emotional religion that everyone could experience. Enthusiasm—in prayer, in worship, in preaching, in life itself—was the key concept. "Just as a drunkard becomes full of wine, so must the congregation become filled with spirit," declared one exuberant writer.[23]

Second, Pietism reasserted the earlier radical stress on the priesthood of all believers, thereby reducing the gulf between official clergy and Lutheran laity. Bible reading and

Hogarth's Satirical View of the Church William Hogarth (1697–1764) was one of the foremost satirical artists of his day. This image mocks a London Methodist meeting, where the congregation swoons in enthusiasm over the preacher's sermon. The woman in the foreground giving birth to rabbits refers to a hoax perpetrated in 1726 by a servant named Mary Tofts; the gullibility of those who believed Tofts is likened to that of the Methodist congregation. (The Israel Museum, Jerusalem, Israel/ Vera & Arturo Schwarz Collection of Dada and Surrealist Art/The Bridgeman Art Library)

study were enthusiastically extended to all classes, and this provided a powerful spur for popular literacy as well as individual religious development. Pietists were largely responsible for the educational reforms implemented by Prussia in the early eighteenth century (see page 596). Finally, Pietists believed in the practical power of Christian rebirth in everyday affairs. Reborn Christians were expected to lead good, moral lives and to come from all social classes.

Pietism soon spread through the German-speaking lands and to Scandinavia. It also had a major impact on John Wesley (1703–1791), who served as the catalyst for popular religious revival in England. (See "Primary Source: Advice to Methodists," page 608.) Wesley came from a long line of ministers, and when he went to Oxford University to prepare for the clergy, he mapped a fanatically earnest "scheme of religion." After becoming a teaching fellow at Oxford, Wesley organized a Holy Club for similarly minded students, who were soon known contemptuously as **Methodists** because they were so methodical in their devotion. Yet like the young Martin Luther, Wesley remained intensely troubled about his own salvation even after his ordination as an Anglican priest in 1728.

Wesley's anxieties related to grave problems of the faith in England. The government shamelessly used the Church of England to provide favorites with high-paying jobs. Both church and state officials failed to respond to the spiritual needs of the people, and services and sermons had settled into an uninspiring routine. The separation of religion from local customs and social life was symbolized by church doors that were customarily locked on weekdays. Moreover, Enlightenment skepticism was making inroads among the educated classes, and deism—a belief in God but not in organized religion—was becoming popular. Some bishops and church leaders seemed to believe that doctrines such as the virgin birth were little more than elegant superstitions.

Wesley's inner search in the 1730s was deeply affected by his encounter with Moravian Pietists, whom he first met on a ship as he traveled across the Atlantic to take up a position in Savannah, Georgia. The small Moravian community in Georgia impressed him as a productive, peaceful, and pious world, reflecting the values of the first apostles. (For more on the Moravian Church, see Chapter 17, "Individuals in Society: Rebecca Protten," page 578.) After returning to London, following a disastrous failed engagement and the disappointment of his hopes to convert Native Americans, he sought spiritual counseling from a Pietist minister from Germany. Their conversations prepared Wesley for a mystical, emotional "conversion" in 1738. He described this critical turning point in his *Journal*:

> In the evening I went to a [Christian] society in Aldersgate Street where one was reading Luther's preface to the Epistle to the Romans. About a quarter before nine, while he was describing the change which God works in the heart through faith in Christ, I felt my heart strangely warmed. I felt I did trust in Christ, Christ alone for salvation; and an assurance was given me that he had taken away my sins, even mine, and saved me from the law of sin and death.[24]

Wesley's emotional experience resolved his intellectual doubts about the possibility of his own salvation. Moreover, he was convinced that any person, no matter how poor or uneducated, might have a similarly heartfelt conversion and gain the same blessed assurance. He took the good news to the people, traveling some 225,000 miles by horseback and preaching more than forty thousand sermons between 1750 and 1790. Since

PRIMARY SOURCE Advice to Methodists

John Wesley (1703–1791) was the fifteenth child of an Anglican rector and a strict mother. As a small child, he was rescued from certain death in a house fire; in later years, he saw this moment as a sign of providential grace. Along with his brother Charles, John Wesley is recognized as the founder of Methodism, an evangelical movement that began within the Church of England and was influenced by German Pietism. In the passage below, Wesley offers his advice to followers of the new religious movement he had inspired, who had been dubbed "Methodists" for their scrupulous and methodical approach to religious worship.

By *Methodists* I mean, a People who profess to pursue (in whatsoever Measure they have attained) Holiness of Heart and Life, inward and outward Conformity in all Things to the revealed Will of God: Who place Religion in an uniform Resemblance of the great Object of it; in a steady Imitation of Him they worship, in all his imitable Perfections; more particularly, in Justice, Mercy, and Truth, or universal Love filling the Heart, and governing the Life. . . .

  Your *Name* is new, (at least, as used in a religious Sense) not heard of, till a few Years ago, either in our own, or any other Nation. Your *Principles* are new, in this respect, That there is no other Set of People among us (and, possibly, not in the Christian World) who hold them all, in the same Degree and Connection; who so strenuously and continually insist on the absolute Necessity of universal Holiness both in Heart and Life; of a peaceful, joyous Love of God; of a supernatural Evidence of Things not seen; of an inward Witness that we are the Children of God, and of the Inspiration of the Holy Ghost, in order to any good Thought, or Word, or Work. And perhaps there is no other Set of People, (at least not visibly united together) who lay *so much*, and yet *no more* Stress than you do, on Rectitude of *Opinions*, on outward *Modes of Worship*, and the Use of those *Ordinances* which you acknowledge to be of God. . . .

  Your *Strictness* of Life, taking the whole of it together, may likewise be accounted new. I mean, your making it a Rule, to abstain from fashionable *Diversions*, from *reading* Plays, Romances, or Books of Humour, from *singing* innocent Songs, or *talking* in a merry, gay, diverting Manner; your *Plainness* of Dress; your *Manner of Dealing* in Trade; your Exactness in observing the *Lord's Day*; your Scrupulosity as to Things that have *not paid Custom*; your total Abstinence from *spirituous Liquors* (unless in Cases of Extreme Necessity;) your Rule, "not to mention the Fault of an absent Person, in Particular, of *Ministers*, or of *those in Authority*," may justly be termed new.

EVALUATE THE EVIDENCE

1. What elements of the Methodist faith does Wesley identify as "new" in this document? To what or whom is he comparing Methodists?

2. To what changes under way in English society does this document appear to be responding? What social practices do Methodists oppose according to Wesley?

Source: John Wesley, *Advice to the People Call'd Methodists* (Bristol: Felix Farley, 1745), 3, 5–6.

existing churches were often overcrowded and the church-state establishment was hostile, Wesley preached in open fields. People came in large numbers. Of critical importance was Wesley's rejection of Calvinist predestination—the doctrine of salvation granted to only a select few. Instead, he preached that all men and women who earnestly sought salvation might be saved. It was a message of hope and joy, of free will and universal salvation.

Wesley's ministry won converts, formed Methodist cells, and eventually resulted in a new denomination. And just as Wesley had been inspired by the Pietist revival in Germany, so evangelicals in the Church of England and the old dissenting groups now followed Wesley's example of preaching to all people, giving impetus to an even broader awakening among the lower classes. Thus in Protestant countries religion continued to be a vital force in the lives of the people.

Catholic Piety

Religion also flourished in Catholic Europe around 1700, but there were important differences from Protestant practice. First, the visual contrast was striking; baroque art still lavished rich and emotionally exhilarating figures and images on Catholic churches, just as most Protestants had removed theirs during the Reformation. Moreover, people in Catholic Europe on the whole participated more actively in formal worship than did Protestants. More than 95 percent of the population probably attended church for Easter communion, the climax of the religious year.

The tremendous popular strength of religion in Catholic countries can in part be explained by the church's integral role in community life and popular culture. Thus, although Catholics reluctantly confessed their sins to priests, they enthusiastically came together in religious festivals to celebrate the passage of the liturgical year. In addition to the great processional days—such as Palm Sunday, the joyful reenactment of Jesus's triumphal entry into Jerusalem—each parish had its own saints' days, processions, and pilgrimages. Led by its priest, a congregation might march around the village or across the countryside to a local shrine. Millions of Catholic men and women also joined religious associations, known as confraternities, where they participated in prayer and religious services and collected funds for poor relief and members' funerals. The Reformation had largely eliminated such festivities in Protestant areas.

Catholicism had its own version of the Pietist revivals that shook Protestant Europe. **Jansenism** has been described by one historian as the "illegitimate off-spring of the Protestant Reformation and the Catholic Counter-Reformation."[25] It originated with Cornelius Jansen (1585–1638), bishop of Ypres in the Spanish Netherlands, who called for a return to the austere early Christianity of Saint Augustine. In contrast to the worldly Jesuits, Jansen emphasized the heavy weight of original sin and accepted the doctrine of predestination. Although outlawed by papal and royal edicts as Calvinist heresy, Jansenism attracted Catholic followers eager for religious renewal, particularly among the French. Many members of France's urban elite, especially judicial nobles and some parish priests, became known for their Jansenist piety and spiritual devotion. Such stern religious values encouraged the judiciary's increasing opposition to the French monarchy in the second half of the eighteenth century.

Among the urban poor, a different strain of Jansenism took hold. Prayer meetings brought men and women together in ecstatic worship, and some participants fell into convulsions and spoke in tongues. The police of Paris posted spies to report on such gatherings and conducted mass raids and arrests.

Marginal Beliefs and Practices

In the countryside, many peasants continued to hold religious beliefs that were marginal to the Christian faith altogether, often of obscure or even pagan origin. On the Feast of Saint Anthony, for example, priests were expected to bless salt and bread for farm animals to protect them from disease. Catholics believed that saints' relics could bring fortune or attract lovers, and there were healing springs for many ailments. In 1796 the Lutheran villagers of Beutelsbach in southern Germany incurred the ire of local officials when they buried a live bull at a crossroads to ward off an epidemic of hoof-and-mouth disease.[26] The ordinary person combined strong Christian faith with a wealth of time-honored superstitions.

Inspired initially by the fervor of the Reformation era, then by the critical rationalism of the Enlightenment, religious and secular authorities sought increasingly to "purify" popular spirituality. Thus one parish priest in France lashed out at his parishioners, claiming that they were "more superstitious than devout . . . and sometimes appear as baptized idolators."[27] French priests particularly denounced the "various remnants of paganism" found in popular bonfire ceremonies during Lent, in which young men, "yelling and screaming like madmen," tried to jump over the bonfires in order to help the crops grow and protect themselves from illness. One priest saw rational Christians regressing into pagan animals — "the triumph of Hell and the shame of Christianity."[28]

The severity of the attack on popular belief varied widely by country and region. Where authorities pursued purification vigorously, as in Austria under Joseph II, pious peasants saw only an incomprehensible attack on age-old faith and drew back in anger. Their reaction dramatized the growing tension between the attitudes of educated elites and the common people.

It was in this era of growing intellectual disdain for popular beliefs that the persecution of witches slowly came to an end across Europe. Common people in the countryside continued to fear the Devil and his helpers, but the elite increasingly dismissed such fears and refused to prosecute suspected witches. The last witch was executed in England in 1682, the same year France prohibited witchcraft trials. By the late eighteenth century most European states and their colonies had followed suit.

Medical Practice

How did the practice of medicine evolve in the eighteenth century?

Although significant breakthroughs in medical science would not come until the middle and late nineteenth century, the Enlightenment's inherent optimism and its focus on improving human life through understanding of the laws of nature produced a great deal of research and experimentation in the 1700s. Medical practitioners greatly increased in number, although their techniques did not differ much from those of previous generations. Care of the sick in this era was the domain of several competing groups: traditional healers, apothecaries (pharmacists), physicians, surgeons, and midwives. From the Middle Ages through the seventeenth century, both men and women were medical practitioners. However, since women were generally denied admission to medical colleges and lacked the diplomas necessary to practice, the range of medical activities open to them was restricted. In the eighteenth century women's traditional roles as midwives and healers eroded even further.

Faith Healing and General Practice

In the course of the eighteenth century, traditional healers remained active, drawing on centuries of folk knowledge about the curative properties of roots, herbs, and other plants. Faith healing also remained popular, especially in the countryside. Faith healers and their patients believed that evil spirits caused illness by lodging in people and that the proper treatment was to exorcise, or drive out, the offending devil. Religious and secular officials did their best to stamp out such practices, but with little success.

In the larger towns and cities, apothecaries sold a vast number of herbs, drugs, and patent medicines for every conceivable "temperament and distemper." Some of the drugs and herbs undoubtedly worked. For example, strong laxatives were given to the rich for their constipated bowels, and regular purging of the bowels was considered essential for good health and the treatment of illness. Like all varieties of medical practitioners, apothecaries advertised their wares, their high-class customers, and their miraculous cures in newspapers and commercial circulars. Medicine, like food and fashionable clothing, thus joined the era's new and loosely regulated commercial culture.

Physicians, who were invariably men, were apprenticed in their teens to practicing physicians for several years of on-the-job training. This training was then rounded out with hospital work or some university courses. Seen as gentlemen who did not labor with their hands, many physicians diagnosed and treated patients by correspondence or through oral dialogue, without conducting a physical examination. Because their training was expensive, physicians came mainly from prosperous families and they usually concentrated on urban patients from similar social backgrounds. Nevertheless, even poor people spent hard-won resources to seek treatment for their loved ones.

Physicians in the eighteenth century were increasingly willing to experiment with new methods, but time-honored practices lay heavily on them. Like apothecaries, they laid great stress on purging, and bloodletting was still considered a medical cure-all. It was the way "bad blood," the cause of illness, was removed and the balance of humors necessary for good health was restored.

Improvements in Surgery

Long considered to be craftsmen comparable to butchers and barbers, surgeons began studying anatomy seriously and improved their art in the eighteenth century. With endless opportunities to practice, army surgeons on gory battlefields led the way. They learned that a soldier with an extensive wound, such as a shattered leg or arm, could perhaps be saved if the surgeon could obtain a flat surface above the wound that could be cauterized with fire. Thus if a soldier had a broken limb and the bone stuck out, the surgeon amputated so that the remaining stump could be cauterized and the likelihood of death reduced.

The eighteenth-century surgeon (and patient) labored in the face of incredible difficulties. Almost all operations were performed without painkillers, for the anesthesia of the day was hard to control and too dangerous for general use. Many patients died from the agony and shock of such operations. Surgery was also performed in utterly unsanitary conditions, for there was no knowledge of bacteriology and the nature of infection. The simplest wound treated by a surgeon could fester and lead to death.

Midwifery

Midwives continued to deliver the overwhelming majority of babies throughout the eighteenth century. Trained initially by another woman practitioner—and regulated by a guild in many cities—the midwife primarily assisted in labor and delivering babies. She also treated female problems, such as irregular menstrual cycles, breast-feeding difficulties, infertility, and venereal disease, and ministered to small children.

The midwife orchestrated labor and birth in a woman's world, where friends and relatives assisted the pregnant woman in the familiar surroundings of her own home. The male surgeon (and the husband) rarely entered this female world, because most births, then as now, were normal and spontaneous. After the invention of forceps became publicized in 1734, surgeon-physicians used their monopoly over this and other instruments to seek lucrative new business. Attacking midwives as ignorant and dangerous, they sought to undermine faith in midwives and persuaded growing numbers of wealthy women of the superiority of their services. As one male expert proclaimed:

> A midwife is usually a creature of the lowest class of human beings, and of course utterly destitute of education, who from indigence, and that she is incapable of everything else, has been compelled to follow, as the last and sole resources a profession which people fondly imagine no very difficult one, never dreaming that the least glimpse of previous instruction is required for that purpose. . . . Midwives are universally ignorant. For where or how should she come by any thing deserving the name of knowledge.[29]

Research suggests that women practitioners successfully defended much but not all of their practice in the eighteenth century. One enterprising French midwife, Madame du Coudray, wrote a widely used textbook, *Manual on the Art of Childbirth* (1757), in order to address complaints about incompetent midwives. She then secured royal financing for her campaign to teach birthing techniques. Du Coudray traveled all over France using a life-size model of the female torso and fetus to help teach illiterate women. Despite criticism, it appears that midwives generally lost no more babies than did male doctors, who were still summoned to treat non-elite women only when life-threatening situations required surgery.

Women also continued to perform almost all nursing. Female religious orders ran many hospitals, and at-home nursing was almost exclusively the province of women. Thus, although they were excluded from the growing ranks of formally trained and authorized practitioners, women continued to perform the bulk of informal medical care. Nursing as a secular profession did not emerge until the nineteenth century.

The Conquest of Smallpox

Experimentation and the intensified search for solutions to human problems led to some real advances in medicine after 1750. The eighteenth century's greatest medical triumph was the eradication of smallpox. With the progressive decline of bubonic plague, smallpox became the most terrible of the infectious diseases, and it is estimated that 60 million Europeans died of it in the eighteenth century.

The first step in the conquest of this killer in Europe came in the early eighteenth century. An English aristocrat whose beauty had been marred by the pox, Lady Mary Wortley Montagu, learned about the long-established practice of smallpox inoculation in the Muslim lands of western Asia while her husband was serving as British ambassador to the Ottoman Empire. She had her own son successfully inoculated with the pus from a smallpox victim and was instrumental in spreading the practice in England after her return in 1722. But inoculation was risky and was widely condemned because about one person in fifty died from it. In addition, people who had been inoculated were infectious and often spread the disease.

While the practice of inoculation with the smallpox virus was refined over the century, the crucial breakthrough was made by Edward Jenner (1749–1823), a talented country doctor. His starting point was the countryside belief that dairymaids who had contracted cowpox did not get smallpox. Cowpox produces sores that resemble those of smallpox, but the disease is mild and is not contagious.

For eighteen years Jenner practiced a kind of Baconian science, carefully collecting data. Finally, in 1796 he performed his first vaccination on a young boy using matter taken from a milkmaid with cowpox. After performing more successful vaccinations, Jenner published his findings in 1798. The new method of treatment spread rapidly, and smallpox soon declined to the point of disappearance in Europe and then throughout the world.

The Wonderful Effects of the New Inoculation!   The talented caricaturist James Gillray satirized widespread anxieties about the smallpox vaccination in this lively image. The discoveries of Edward Jenner a few years prior to Gillray's caricature had led to the adoption of a safer vaccine derived from cowpox. The artist mocks this breakthrough by showing cows bursting from the boils supposedly brought on by the vaccine. (Private Collection/The Bridgeman Art Library)

Notes

1. Archibald Campbell, Marquis of Argyll, *Instructions to a Son, Containing Rules of Conduct in Publick and Private Life* (Glasgow: E. Foulis, 1743), p. 33.
2. Quoted in J. M. Beattie, "The Criminality of Women in Eighteenth-Century England," *Journal of Social History* 8 (Summer 1975): 86.
3. Quoted in R. Cobb, *The Police and the People: French Popular Protest, 1789–1820* (Oxford, U.K.: Clarendon Press, 1970), p. 238.
4. Peter Laslett, *Family Life and Illicit Love: Essays in Historical Sociology* (Cambridge, U.K.: Cambridge University Press, 1977).
5. G. Gullickson, *Spinners and Weavers of Auffay: Rural Industry and the Sexual Division of Labor in a French Village, 1750–1850* (Cambridge, U.K.: Cambridge University Press, 1986), p. 186.
6. Louis Crompton, *Homosexuality and Civilization* (Cambridge, Mass.: Belknap Press, 2003), p. 321.
7. D. S. Neff, "Bitches, Mollies, and Tommies: Byron, Masculinity and the History of Sexualities," *Journal of the History of Sexuality* 11, 3 (July 2002): 404.
8. George E. Haggerty, ed., *Encyclopedia of Gay Histories and Cultures* (New York: Garland Publishing, 2000), pp. 1311–1312.
9. Pier Paolo Viazzo, "Mortality, Fertility, and Family," in *Family Life in Early Modern Times, 1500–1789*, ed. David I. Kertzer and Marzio Barbagli (New Haven, Conn.: Yale University Press, 2001), p. 180.
10. George Sussman, *Selling Mother's Milk: The Wet-Nursing Business in France, 1715–1914* (Urbana: University of Illinois Press, 1982), p. 22.
11. Robert Woods, "Did Montaigne Love His Children? Demography and the Hypothesis of Parental Indifference," *Journal of Interdisciplinary History* 33, 3 (2003): 426.
12. P. Viazzo, "Mortality, Fertility, and Family," in *The History of the European Family*, vol. 1, ed. D. Kertzer and M. Barbagli (New Haven, Conn.: Yale University Press, 2001), pp. 176–178.
13. Alysa Levene, "The Estimation of Mortality at the London Foundling Hospital, 1741–99," *Population Studies* 59, 1 (2005): 87–97.
14. Cited in Woods, "Did Montaigne Love His Children?" p. 421.
15. Ibid., pp. 13, 16.
16. James Van Horn Melton, *Absolutism and the Eighteenth-Century Origins of Compulsory Schooling in Prussia and Austria* (Cambridge, U.K.: Cambridge University Press, 2003), p. 46.
17. James Van Horn Melton, "The Theresian School Reform of 1774," in *Early Modern Europe*, ed. James B. Collins and Karen L. Taylor (Oxford, U.K.: Blackwell, 2006).
18. I. Woloch, *Eighteenth-Century Europe: Tradition and Progress, 1715–1789* (New York: W. W. Norton, 1982), pp. 220–221.
19. Neil McKendrik, John Brewer, and J. H. Plumb, *The Birth of a Consumer Society: The Commercialization of Eighteenth-Century England* (Bloomington: Indiana University Press, 1982).
20. Daniel Roche, *The Culture of Clothing: Dress and Fashion in the Ancien Regime*, trans. Jean Birrell (Cambridge, U.K.: Cambridge University Press, 1996).
21. Quoted in Cissie Fairchilds, "The Production and Marketing of Populuxe Goods in Eighteenth-Century Paris," in *Consumption and the World of Goods*, ed. John Brewer and Roy Porter (London: Routledge, 1993), p. 228.
22. Quoted in K. Pinson, *Pietism as a Factor in the Rise of German Nationalism* (New York: Columbia University Press, 1934), p. 13.
23. Ibid., pp. 43–44.
24. Quoted in S. Andrews, *Methodism and Society* (London: Longmans, Green, 1970), p. 327.
25. Dale Van Kley, "The Rejuvenation and Rejection of Jansenism in History and Historiography," *French Historical Studies* 29 (Fall 2006): 649–684.
26. David Sabean, *The Power in the Blood: Popular Culture and Village Discourse in Early Modern Germany* (Cambridge, U.K.: Cambridge University Press, 1984), p. 174.
27. Quoted in Woloch, *Eighteenth-Century Europe*, p. 292.
28. Quoted in T. Tackett, *Priest and Parish in Eighteenth-Century France* (Princeton, N.J.: Princeton University Press, 1977), p. 214.
29. Louis Lapeyre, *An Enquiry into the Merits of These Two Important Questions: I. Whether Women with Child Ought to Prefer the Assistance of Their Own Sex to That of Men-Midwives? II. Whether the Assistance of Men-Midwives Is Contrary to Decency?* (London: S. Bladon, 1772), p. 29.

Chapter Review

MAKE IT STICK

LearningCurve
bedfordstmartins.com/mckaywestvalue
After reading the chapter, use LearningCurve to retain what
you've read.

IDENTIFY KEY TERMS

Identify and explain the significance of each item below.

community controls (p. 587)   **just price** (p. 599)
charivari (p. 587)   **consumer revolution** (p. 601)
illegitimacy explosion (p. 587)   **Pietism** (p. 606)
wet-nursing (p. 590)   **Methodists** (p. 607)
blood sports (p. 598)   **Jansenism** (p. 609)
carnival (p. 598)

REVIEW THE MAIN IDEAS

Answer the focus questions from each section of the chapter.

◆ What changes occurred in marriage and the family in the course of the
eighteenth century? (p. 584)

◆ What was life like for children, and how did attitudes toward childhood
evolve? (p. 589)

◆ How did increasing literacy and new patterns of consumption affect
people's lives? (p. 596)

◆ What were the patterns of popular religion, and how did they interact
with the worldview of the educated public and their Enlightenment ideals?
(p. 604)

◆ How did the practice of medicine evolve in the eighteenth century? (p. 610)

MAKE CONNECTIONS

**Think about the larger developments and continuities within and
across chapters.**

1. How did the expansion of agriculture and trade (Chapter 17) contribute to
a new way of life in the eighteenth century?

2. What were the main areas of improvement in the lives of the common
people in the eighteenth century and what aspects of life remained
unchanged or even deteriorated?

3. How did Enlightenment thought (Chapter 16) impact education, child care,
medicine, and religion in the eighteenth century?

ONLINE DOCUMENT ASSIGNMENT

The Inner Life of the Individual

How did the increasing emphasis on the inner life and development of the individual in the eighteenth century find expression in the art of the period?

Keeping the question above in mind, go online and analyze a series of paintings by Jean-Baptiste-Siméon Chardin that depict various aspects of daily life and reveal the era's increased attention to individual emotion and development. Then complete a writing assignment based on the evidence and details from this chapter.

bedfordstmartins.com/mckaywestvalue

CHRONOLOGY

1684	• Jean-Baptiste de la Salle founds Brothers of the Christian Schools
1717	• Elementary school attendance mandatory in Prussia
1750–1790	• John Wesley preaches revival in England
1750–1850	• Illegitimacy explosion
1757	• Madame du Coudray publishes *Manual on the Art of Childbirth*
1762	• Jean-Jacques Rousseau advocates more attentive child care in *Emile*
1763	• Louis XV orders Jesuits out of France
1774	• Elementary school attendance mandatory in Austria
1776	• Thomas Paine publishes *Common Sense*
1796	• Edward Jenner performs first smallpox vaccination

19

Revolutions in Politics

1775–1815

A GREAT WAVE OF REVOLUTION ROCKED BOTH SIDES OF THE
Atlantic Ocean in the last decades of the eighteenth century. As trade goods,
individuals, and ideas circulated in ever-greater numbers across the Atlantic
Ocean, debates and events in one locale soon influenced those in another.
As changing social realities challenged the old order of life and Enlightenment ideals of freedom and equality flourished, reformers in many places
demanded fundamental changes in politics and government. At the same
time, wars fought for dominance of the Atlantic economy left European
states weakened by crushing debts, making them vulnerable to calls for
reform.

The revolutionary era began in North America in 1775. Then in 1789 France,
the most populous country in western Europe and a center of culture and
intellectual life, became the leading revolutionary nation. It established first
a constitutional monarchy, then a radical republic, and finally a new empire
under Napoleon that would last until 1815. During this period of constant
domestic turmoil, French armies violently exported revolution beyond the
nation's borders, eager to establish new governments throughout much of
Europe. Inspired both by the ideals of the Revolution on the continent and
by their own experiences and desires, the slaves of Saint-Domingue rose
up in 1791. Their rebellion would eventually lead to the creation of the new
independent nation of Haiti in 1804. In Europe and its colonies abroad, the
age of modern politics was born.

Background to Revolution

What were the factors behind the revolutions of the late eighteenth century?

The origins of the late-eighteenth-century revolutions in British North America, France, and Haiti were complex. No one cause lay behind them, nor was revolution inevitable or foreordained. However, certain important factors helped set the stage for reform. Among them were fundamental social and economic changes and political crises that eroded state authority. Another significant cause of revolutionary fervor was the impact of political ideas derived from the Enlightenment. Even though intellectuals of the Enlightenment were usually cautious about political reform themselves, their confidence in reason and progress helped inspire a new generation to fight for greater freedom from repressive governments. Perhaps most important, financial crises generated by war expenses brought European states to their knees and allowed abstract discussions of reform to become pressing realities.

Social Change

As in the Middle Ages, eighteenth-century European society was legally divided into groups with special privileges, such as the nobility and the clergy, and groups with special burdens, such as the peasantry. Nobles were the largest landowners, possessing one-quarter of the agricultural land of France, while constituting less than two percent of the population. They enjoyed exemption from direct taxation as well as exclusive rights to hunt game, bear swords, and wear gold ribbon in their clothing. In most countries, various middle-class groups—professionals, merchants, and guild masters—enjoyed privileges that allowed them to monopolize all sorts of economic activity. Poor peasants and urban laborers, who constituted the vast majority of the population, bore the brunt of taxation and were excluded from the world of privilege.

Traditional prerogatives for elite groups persisted in societies undergoing dramatic and destabilizing change. Europe's population rose rapidly after 1750, and its cities and towns swelled in size. Inflation kept pace with population growth, making it ever more difficult to find affordable food and living space. One way the poor kept up, and even managed to participate in the new consumer revolution (see Chapter 18), was by working harder and for longer hours. More women and children entered the paid labor force, challenging the traditional hierarchies and customs of village life.

Economic growth created new inequalities between rich and poor. While the poor struggled with rising prices, investors grew rich from the spread of manufacture in the countryside and overseas trade, including the trade in enslaved Africans and the products of slave labor. Old distinctions between landed aristocracy and city merchants began to fade as enterprising nobles put money into trade and rising middle-class bureaucrats and merchants purchased landed estates and noble titles. Marriages between proud nobles and wealthy, educated commoners (called the *bourgeoisie* [boor-ZHWAH-zee] in France) served both groups' interests, and a mixed-caste elite began to take shape. In the context of these changes, ancient privileges seemed to pose an intolerable burden to many observers.

Another social change involved the racial regimes established in European colonies to legitimize and protect slavery. By the late eighteenth century European law accepted that only Africans and people of African descent were subject to slavery. Even free people of color—a term for nonslaves of African or mixed African-European descent—were subject to special laws restricting the property they could own, whom they could marry, and what clothes they could wear. Racial privilege conferred a new dimension of entitlement on European settlers in the colonies, and they used extremely brutal methods to enforce it. The contradiction between slavery and the Enlightenment ideals of liberty and equality was all too evident to the enslaved and the free people of color.

Growing Demands for Liberty and Equality

In addition to destabilizing social changes, the ideals of liberty and equality helped fuel revolutions in the Atlantic world. What did these concepts mean to eighteenth-century politicians and other people, and why were they so radical and revolutionary in their day?

The call for liberty was first of all a call for individual human rights. Before the revolutionary period, even the most enlightened monarchs believed they needed to regulate what people wrote and believed. Opposing this long-standing practice, supporters of the cause of individual liberty (who became known as "liberals" in the early nineteenth century) demanded freedom to worship according to the dictates of their consciences, an end to censorship, and freedom from arbitrary laws and from judges who simply obeyed orders from the government. The Declaration of the Rights of Man and of the Citizen, issued at the beginning of the French Revolution, proclaimed that "liberty consists in being able to do anything that does not harm another person." In the context of the monarchical and absolutist forms of government then dominating Europe, this was a truly radical idea.

The call for liberty was also a call for a new kind of government. Reformers believed that the people had sovereignty—that is, that the people alone had the authority to make laws limiting an individual's freedom of action. In practice, this system of government meant choosing legislators who represented the people and were accountable to them. Monarchs might retain their thrones, but their rule should be constrained by the will of the people.

Equality was a more ambiguous idea. Eighteenth-century liberals argued that, in theory, all citizens should have identical rights and liberties and that the nobility had no right to special privileges based on birth. However, they accepted a number of distinctions. First, most eighteenth-century liberals were men of their times, and they generally believed that equality between men and women was neither practical nor desirable. Women played an important political role in the revolutionary movements at several points, but the men who wrote constitutions for the new republics limited formal political rights—the right to vote, to run for office, and to participate in government—to men. Second, few questioned the inequality between blacks and whites. Even those who believed that the slave trade was unjust and should be abolished usually felt that emancipation was so dangerous that it needed to be an extremely gradual process.

Finally, liberals never believed that everyone should be equal economically. Although Thomas Jefferson wrote in an early draft of the American Declaration of Independence that everyone was equal in "the pursuit of property," liberals certainly did not expect equal success in that pursuit. (Jefferson later changed "property" to the more noble-sounding "happiness.") Great differences in fortune between rich and poor were perfectly acceptable. The essential point was that every free white male should have a legally equal chance at economic gain. However limited they appear to modern eyes, these demands for liberty and equality were revolutionary, given that a privileged elite had long existed with little opposition.

The two most important Enlightenment references for late-eighteenth-century liberals were John Locke and the baron de Montesquieu (see Chapter 16). Locke maintained that England's long political tradition rested on "the rights of Englishmen" and on representative government through Parliament. He argued that if a government oversteps its proper function of protecting the natural rights of life, liberty, and private property, it becomes a tyranny. Montesquieu was also inspired by English constitutional history and the Glorious Revolution, which placed sovereignty in Parliament (see Chapter 15). He, too, believed that powerful "intermediary groups"—such as the judicial nobility of which he was a proud member—offered the best defense of liberty against despotism.

The belief that representative institutions could defend their liberty and interests appealed powerfully to the educated middle classes. Yet liberal ideas about individual rights and political freedom also appealed to members of the hereditary nobility, at least in western Europe and as formulated by Montesquieu. Representative government did not mean democracy, which liberal thinkers tended to equate with mob rule. Rather, they envisioned voting for representatives as being restricted to men who owned property—those with "a stake in society." The blurring of practical distinctions between landed aristocrats and wealthy commoners meant that there was no clear-cut opposition between nobles and non-nobles on political issues. The poor themselves usually had little time to plan for reform, given the challenges of earning their daily bread.

Revolutions thus began with aspirations for equality and liberty among the social elite. Soon, however, dissenting voices emerged as some revolutionaries became frustrated with the limitations of liberal notions of equality and liberty and clamored for a fuller realization of these concepts. Depending on location, their demands included political rights for women and free people of color, the emancipation of slaves, and government regulations to reduce economic inequality. The age of revolution was thus marked by sharp conflicts over how far reform should go once it was initiated.

The Seven Years' War

The roots of revolutionary ideas could be found in the writings of Locke or Montesquieu, but it was by no means inevitable that their ideas would result in revolution. Many members of the educated elite were satisfied with the status quo or too intimidated to challenge it. Instead, events—political, economic, and military—created crises that opened the door for radical action. One of the most important was the global conflict known as the Seven Years' War (1756–1763).

The war's battlefields stretched from central Europe to India to North America (where the conflict was known as the French and Indian War), pitting a new alliance of England and Prussia against the French and Austrians. Its origins were in conflicts left unresolved at the end of the War of the Austrian Succession in 1748 (see Chapter 16). In central Europe, Austria's Maria Theresa vowed to win back Silesia, which Prussia took in the war of succession, and to crush Prussia, thereby re-establishing the Habsburgs' traditional leadership in German affairs. By the end of the Seven Years' War, Maria Theresa had almost succeeded, but Prussia survived with its boundaries intact.

Unresolved tensions also lingered in North America, particularly regarding the border between the French and British colonies. The encroachment of English settlers into territory claimed by the French in the Ohio Valley resulted in skirmishes that soon became war. Although the inhabitants of New France were greatly outnumbered — Canada counted 55,000 inhabitants, compared to 1.2 million in the thirteen English colonies — French forces achieved major victories until 1758. Both sides relied on the participation of Native American tribes with whom they had long-standing trading contacts and actively sought new indigenous allies during the conflict. The tide of the conflict turned when the British diverted resources from the war in Europe, using superior sea power to destroy France's fleet and choke its commerce around the world. In 1759 the British laid siege to Quebec for four long months, finally defeating the French in a battle that sealed the nation's fate in North America.

British victory on all colonial fronts was ratified in the 1763 Treaty of Paris. Canada and all French territory east of the Mississippi River passed to Britain, and France ceded Louisiana to Spain as compensation for Spain's loss of Florida to Britain. France also gave up most of its holdings in India, opening the way to British dominance on the subcontinent (Map 19.1).

By 1763 Britain had become the leading European power in both trade and empire, but at a tremendous cost in war debt. France emerged from the conflict humiliated and broke, but with its profitable Caribbean colonies intact. In the aftermath of war, both British and French governments had to raise taxes to repay loans, raising a storm of protest and demands for fundamental reform. Since the Caribbean colony of Saint-Domingue remained French, political turmoil in the mother country would directly affect its population. The seeds of revolutionary conflict in the Atlantic world were thus sown.

The American Revolutionary Era, 1775–1789

Why and how did American colonists forge a new, independent nation?

Increased taxes were a crucial factor behind colonial protests in the New World, where the era of liberal political revolution began. After revolting against their home country, the thirteen mainland colonies of British North America succeeded in establishing a new unified government. Participants in the revolution believed they were demanding only the traditional rights of English men and women. But those traditional rights were liberal rights, and in the American context they had strong democratic and popular overtones. Thus the American Revolution was fought in the name of ideals that were still quite radical for their time. In founding a government based on liberal principles, the Americans set an example that would have a forceful impact on France and its colonies.

The Origins of the Revolution

The high cost of the Seven Years' War doubled the British national debt. Anticipating further expenses to defend newly conquered territories, the government in London imposed bold new administrative measures. Breaking with a tradition of loose colonial oversight, the British announced that they would maintain a large army in North America

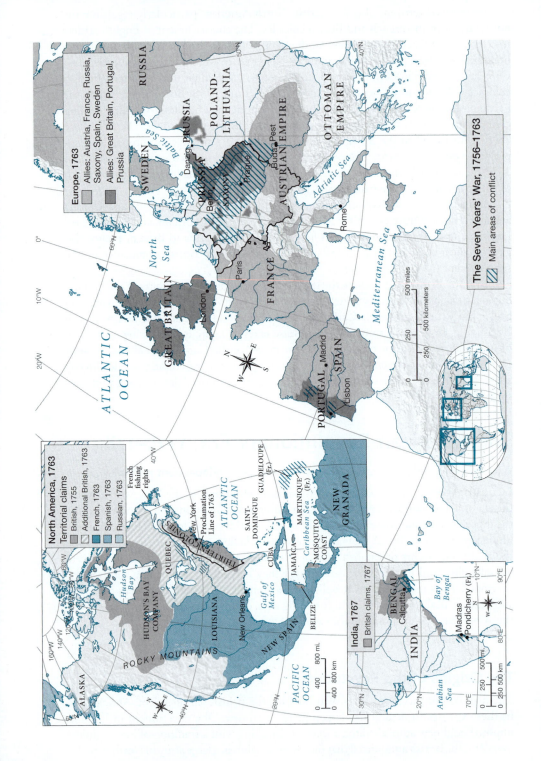

Europe, 1763
Allies: Austria, France, Russia, Saxony, Spain, Sweden
Allies: Great Britain, Portugal, Prussia

The Seven Years' War, 1756–1763
Main areas of conflict

North America, 1763
Territorial claims
British, 1755
Additional British, 1763
French, 1763
Spanish, 1763
Russian, 1763
French fishing rights

India, 1767
British claims, 1767

◀ **MAP 19.1** European Claims in North America and India Before and After the Seven Years' War, 1755–1763
As a result of the war, France lost its vast territories in North America and India. In an effort to avoid costly conflicts with Native Americans living in the newly conquered territory, the British government in 1763 prohibited colonists from settling west of the Appalachian Mountains. One of the few remaining French colonies in the Americas, Saint-Domingue (on the island of Hispaniola) was the most profitable plantation colony in the New World.

and tax the colonies directly. In 1765 Parliament passed the Stamp Act, which levied taxes on a long list of commercial and legal documents, diplomas, newspapers, almanacs, and playing cards. A stamp glued to each article indicated that the tax had been paid.

These measures seemed perfectly reasonable to the British, for a much heavier stamp tax already existed in Britain, and proceeds from the tax were to fund the defense of the colonies. Nonetheless, the colonists vigorously protested the Stamp Act by rioting and by boycotting British goods. Thus Parliament reluctantly repealed it.

This dispute raised important political questions. To what extent could the British government reassert its power while limiting the authority of elected colonial bodies? Who had the right to make laws for Americans? The British government replied that Americans were represented in Parliament, albeit indirectly (like most British people), and that Parliament ruled throughout the empire. Many Americans felt otherwise. In the words of John Adams, a major proponent of colonial independence, "A Parliament of Great Britain can have no more rights to tax the colonies than a Parliament of Paris." Thus British colonial administration and parliamentary supremacy came to appear as unacceptable threats to existing American liberties.

Americans' resistance to these threats was fed by the great degree of independence they had long enjoyed. In British North America, unlike in England and Europe, no powerful established church existed, and religious freedom was taken for granted. Colonial assemblies made the important laws, which were seldom overturned by the British government. Also, the right to vote was much more widespread than in England. In many parts of colonial Massachusetts, for example, as many as 95 percent of adult males could vote.

Moreover, greater political equality was matched by greater social and economic equality, at least for the free white population. No hereditary nobility exercised privileges over peasants and other social groups. Instead,

Commemorative Teapot Manufacturers were quick to bring products to the market celebrating weighty political events, like this British teapot heralding "Stamp Act Repeal'd." By purchasing such items, ordinary people could champion political causes of the day and bring public affairs into their private lives. (Peabody Essex Museum, Salem, Massachusetts)

independent farmers dominated colonial society. This was particularly true in the northern colonies, where the revolution originated.

In 1773 disputes over taxes and representation flared up again. Under the Tea Act of that year, the British government permitted the financially hard-pressed East India Company to ship tea from China directly to its agents in the colonies rather than through London middlemen, who sold to independent merchants in the colonies. Thus the company secured a profitable monopoly on the tea trade, and colonial merchants were excluded. The price on tea was actually lowered for colonists, but the act generated a great deal of opposition because it granted a monopoly to the East India Company.

In protest, Boston men disguised as Native Americans staged a rowdy protest (later called the "Tea Party") by boarding East India Company ships and throwing tea from them into the harbor. In response, the so-called Coercive Acts of 1774 closed the port of Boston, curtailed local elections, and expanded the royal governor's power. County conventions in Massachusetts urged that such measures be "rejected as the attempts of a wicked administration to enslave America." Other colonial assemblies joined in the denunciations. In September 1774 the First Continental Congress—consisting of colonial delegates who sought at first to peacefully resolve conflicts with Britain—met in Philadelphia. The more radical members of this assembly argued successfully against concessions to the English crown. The British Parliament also rejected compromise, and in April 1775 fighting between colonial and British troops began at Lexington and Concord.

Independence from Britain

As fighting spread, the colonists moved slowly toward open calls for independence. The uncompromising attitude of the British government and its use of German mercenaries did much to dissolve loyalties to the home country and to unite the separate colonies. *Common Sense* (1775), a brilliant attack by the recently arrived English radical Thomas Paine (1737–1809), also mobilized public opinion in favor of independence. A runaway bestseller with sales of 120,000 copies in a few months, Paine's tract ridiculed the idea of a small island ruling a great continent. In his call for freedom and republican government, Paine expressed Americans' growing sense of separateness and moral superiority.

On July 4, 1776, the Second Continental Congress adopted the Declaration of Independence. Written by Thomas Jefferson and others, this document boldly listed the tyrannical acts committed by George III (r. 1760–1820) and confidently proclaimed the natural rights of mankind and the sovereignty of the American states. The Declaration of Independence in effect universalized the traditional rights of English people and made them the rights of all mankind. It stated that "all Men are created equal, that they are endowed by their Creator with certain unalienable Rights, that among these are Life, Liberty, and the Pursuit of Happiness." No other American political document has ever caused such excitement, either at home or abroad.

After the Declaration of Independence, the conflict often took the form of a civil war pitting patriots against Loyalists, those who maintained an allegiance to the Crown. The Loyalists, who numbered up to 20 percent of the total white population, tended to be wealthy and politically moderate. They were small in number in New England and Virginia, but more common in the Deep South and on the western frontier. British commanders also recruited Loyalists from enslaved people by promising freedom to any slave who left his master to fight for the mother country.

Many wealthy patriots—such as John Hancock and George Washington—willingly allied themselves with farmers and artisans in a broad coalition. This coalition harassed the Loyalists and confiscated their property to help pay for the war, causing 60,000 to 80,000 of them to flee, mostly to Canada. The broad social base of the revolutionaries tended to make the revolution democratic. State governments extended the right to vote to many more men, including free African American men in many cases, but not to women.

On the international scene, the French wanted revenge against the British for the humiliating defeats of the Seven Years' War. Thus they sympathized with the rebels and supplied guns and gunpowder from the beginning of the conflict. By 1777 French volunteers were arriving in Virginia, and a dashing young nobleman, the marquis de Lafayette (1757–1834), quickly became one of the most trusted generals of George Washington, who was commanding American troops. In 1778 the French government offered a formal alliance to the American ambassador in Paris, Benjamin Franklin, and in 1779 and 1780 the Spanish and Dutch declared war on Britain. Catherine the Great of Russia helped organize the League of Armed Neutrality to protect neutral shipping rights and succeeded in hampering Britain's naval power.

Thus by 1780 Britain was engaged in a war against most of Europe as well as the thirteen colonies. In these circumstances, and in the face of severe reverses in India, in the West Indies, and at Yorktown in Virginia, a new British government decided to cut its losses and end the war. American officials in Paris were receptive to negotiating a deal with England alone, for they feared that France wanted a treaty that would bottle up the new nation east of the Allegheny Mountains and give British holdings west of the Alleghenies to France's ally, Spain. Thus the American negotiators deserted their French allies and accepted the extraordinarily favorable terms Britain offered.

Under the Treaty of Paris of 1783, Britain recognized the independence of the thirteen colonies and ceded all its territory between the Allegheny Mountains and the Mississippi River to the Americans. Out of the bitter rivalries of the Old World, the Americans snatched dominion over a vast territory.

Framing the Constitution

The liberal program of the American Revolution was consolidated by the federal Constitution, the Bill of Rights, and the creation of a national republic. Assembling in Philadelphia in the summer of 1787, the delegates to the Constitutional Convention were determined to end the period of economic depression, social uncertainty, and leadership under a weak central government that had followed independence. The delegates thus decided to grant the federal, or central, government important powers: regulation of domestic and foreign trade, the right to tax, and the means to enforce its laws.

Strong rule would be placed squarely in the context of representative self-government. Senators and congressmen would be the lawmaking delegates of the voters, and the president of the republic would be an elected official. The central government would operate in Montesquieu's framework of checks and balances, under which authority was distributed across three different branches—the executive, legislative, and judicial branches — that would systematically balance one another, preventing one interest from gaining too much power. The power of the federal government would in turn be checked by that of the individual states.

When the results of the secret deliberations of the Constitutional Convention were presented to the states for ratification, a great public debate began. The opponents of the proposed Constitution — the Antifederalists — charged that the framers of the new document had taken too much power from the individual states and made the federal government too strong. Moreover, many Antifederalists feared for the individual freedoms for which they had fought. To overcome these objections, the Federalists promised to spell out these basic freedoms as soon as the new Constitution was adopted. The result was the first ten amendments to the Constitution, which the first Congress passed shortly after it met in New York in March 1789. These amendments, ratified in 1791, formed an effective Bill of Rights to safeguard the individual. Most of them — trial by jury, due process of law, the right to assemble, freedom from unreasonable search — had their origins in English law and the English Bill of Rights of 1689. Other rights — the freedoms of speech, the press, and religion — reflected natural-law theory and the strong value colonists had placed on independence from the start.

Limitations of Liberty and Equality

The American Constitution and the Bill of Rights exemplified the strengths and the limits of what came to be called classical liberalism. Liberty meant individual freedoms and political safeguards. Liberty also meant representative government, but it did not mean democracy, with its principle of one person, one vote. Equality meant equality before the law, not equality of political participation or wealth. It did not mean equal rights for slaves, indigenous peoples, or women.

A vigorous abolitionist movement during the 1780s led to the passage of emancipation laws in all northern states, but slavery remained prevalent in the South, and discord between pro- and antislavery delegates roiled the Constitutional Convention of 1787. The result was a compromise stipulating that an enslaved person would count as three-fifths of a person in tallying population numbers for taxation and proportional representation in the House of Representatives. This solution levied higher taxes on the South, but also guaranteed slaveholding states greater representation in Congress, which they used to oppose emancipation.

The young republic also failed to protect the Native American tribes whose lands fell within or alongside the territory ceded by Britain to the United States at the Treaty of Paris. The 1787 Constitution promised protection to Native Americans and guaranteed that their land would not be taken without consent. Nonetheless, the federal government forced tribes to concede their land for meager returns; state governments and the rapidly expanding population paid even less heed to the Constitution and often simply seized Native American land for new settlements.

Although lacking the voting rights enjoyed by so many of their husbands and fathers in the relatively democratic colonial assemblies, women played a vital role in the American Revolution. As household provisioners, women were essential participants in boycotts of British goods, like tea, which squeezed profits from British merchants and fostered the revolutionary spirit. After the outbreak of war, women raised funds for the Continental Army and took care of homesteads, workshops, and other businesses when their men went off to fight. Yet despite Abigail Adams's plea to her husband, John Adams, that the framers of the Declaration of the Independence should "remember the ladies," women did not receive the right to vote in the new Constitution, an omission confirmed by a clause added in 1844. (See "Primary Source: Abigail Adams, 'Remember the Ladies,'" page 628.)

Revolution in France, 1789–1791

How did the events of 1789 result in a constitutional monarchy in France, and what were the consequences?

No country felt the consequences of the American Revolution more deeply than France. Hundreds of French officers served in America and were inspired by the experience. The most famous of these, the young and impressionable marquis de Lafayette, left home as a great aristocrat determined to fight France's traditional foe, England. He returned with a love of liberty and firm republican convictions. French intellectuals and publicists engaged in passionate analysis of the federal Constitution as well as the constitutions of the various states of the new United States. The American Revolution undeniably fueled dissatisfaction with the old monarchical order in France. Yet the French Revolution did not mirror the American example. It was more radical and more complex, more influential and more controversial, more loved and more hated. For Europeans and most of the rest of the world, it was the great revolution of the eighteenth century, the revolution that opened the modern era in politics.

Breakdown of the Old Order

As did the American Revolution, the French Revolution had its immediate origins in the government's financial difficulties. The efforts of the ministers of King Louis XV (r. 1715–1774) to raise taxes to meet the expenses of the War of the Austrian Succession and the Seven Years' War were thwarted by the high courts, known as the parlements. The noble judges of the parlements resented the Crown's threat to their exemption from taxation and decried the government's actions as a form of royal despotism.

When renewed efforts to reform the tax system met a similar fate in 1776, the government was forced to finance its enormous expenditures during the American war with borrowed money. As a result, the national debt soared. In 1786 the finance minister informed the timid king Louis XVI that the nation was on the verge of bankruptcy. Fully 50 percent of France's annual budget went to interest payments on the ever-increasing debt. Another 25 percent went to maintain the military, while 6 percent was absorbed by the royal family and the court at Versailles. Less than 20 percent of the national budget served the productive functions of the state, such as transportation and general administration.

Unlike England, which had a far larger national debt relative to its population, France had no central bank and no paper currency. Therefore, when a depressed economy and a lack of public confidence made it increasingly difficult for the government to obtain new loans, the government could not respond simply by printing more money. It had no alternative but to try increasing taxes. Because France's tax system was unfair and out-of-date, increased revenues were possible only through fundamental

PRIMARY SOURCE   Abigail Adams, "Remember the Ladies"

Abigail Adams wrote many letters to her husband, John Adams, during the long years of separation imposed by his political career. In March 1776 he was serving in the Continental Congress in Philadelphia as Abigail and their children experienced the British siege of Boston and a smallpox epidemic. This letter, written from the family farm in Braintree, Massachusetts, combines news from home with pressing questions about the military and political situation, and a call to "Remember the Ladies" when drafting a new constitution.

March 31, 1776

I wish you would ever write me a Letter half as long as I write you; and tell me if you may where your Fleet are gone? What sort of Defence Virginia can make against our common Enemy? Whether it is so situated as to make an able Defence? . . .

Do not you want to see Boston; I am fearful of the smallpox, or I should have been in before this time. I got Mr. Crane to go to our House and see what state it was in. I find it has been occupied by one of the Doctors of a Regiment, very dirty, but no other damage has been done to it. The few things which were left in it are all gone. . . .

I feel very differently at the approach of spring to what I did a month ago. We knew not then whether we could plant or sow with safety, whether when we had toiled we could reap the fruits of our own industry, whether we could rest in our own Cottages, or whether we should not be driven from the sea coasts to seek shelter in the wilderness, but now we feel as if we might sit under our own vine and eat the good of the land. . . .

I long to hear that you have declared an independency—and by the way in the new Code of Laws which I suppose it will be necessary for you to make I desire you

reforms. Such reforms, which would affect all groups in France's complex and fragmented society, were guaranteed to create social and political unrest.

These crises struck a monarchy that had lost much of its mantle of royal authority. Kings had always maintained mistresses, who were invariably chosen from the court nobility. Louis XV broke that pattern with Madame de Pompadour, daughter of a disgraced bourgeois financier. As the king's favorite mistress from 1745 to 1750, Pompadour exercised tremendous influence that continued even after their love affair ended. She played a key role, for example, in bringing about France's break with Prussia and its new alliance with Austria in the mid-1750s. Pompadour's low birth and political influence generated a stream of libelous pamphleteering. The king was being stripped of the sacred aura of God's anointed on earth (a process called desacralization) and was being reinvented in the popular imagination as a degenerate. Maneuverings among political factions at court further distracted the king and prevented decisive action from his government.

Despite the progressive desacralization of the monarchy, Louis XV would probably have prevailed had he lived longer, but he died in 1774. The new king, Louis XVI

would Remember the Ladies, and be more generous and favorable to them than your ancestors. Do not put such unlimited power in the hands of the Husbands. Remember all men would be tyrants if they could. If particular care and attention is not paid to the Ladies we are determined to foment a Rebellion, and will not hold ourselves bound by any Laws in which we have no voice, or Representation.

That your Sex are Naturally Tyrannical is a Truth so thoroughly established as to admit of no dispute, but such of you as wish to be happy willingly give up the harsh title of Master for the more tender and endearing one of Friend. Why then, not put it out of the power of the vicious and the Lawless to use us with cruelty and indignity with impunity. Men of Sense in all Ages abhor those customs which treat us only as the vassals of your Sex. Regard us then as beings placed by providence under your protection and in imitation of the Supreme Being make use of that power only for our happiness.

EVALUATE THE EVIDENCE

1. What does Adams's letter suggest about her relationship with her husband and the role of women in the family in this period?

2. What does Adams's letter tell us about what it was like to live through the American Revolution and how a woman might perceive the new liberties demanded by colonists?

Source: Letter from Abigail Adams to John Adams, 31 March–5 April 1776 (electronic edition), *Adams Family Papers: An Electronic Archive*, Massachusetts Historical Society, http://www.masshist.org /digitaladams/.

(r. 1774–1792), was a shy twenty-year-old with good intentions. Taking the throne, he is reported to have said, "What I should like most is to be loved."[1] The eager-to-please monarch Louis waffled on political reform and the economy, and he proved unable to quell the rising storm of opposition.

The Formation of the National Assembly

Spurred by a depressed economy and falling tax receipts, Louis XVI's minister of finance revived old proposals to impose a general tax on all landed property as well as to form provincial assemblies to help administer the tax, and he convinced the king to call an assembly of notables in 1787 to gain support for the idea. The assembled notables, mainly aristocrats and high-ranking clergy, declared that such sweeping tax changes required the approval of the **Estates General**, the representative body of all three estates, which had not met since 1614.

Facing imminent bankruptcy, the king tried to reassert his authority. He dismissed the notables and established new taxes by decree. The judges of the Parlement of Paris promptly declared the royal initiative null and void. When the king tried to exile the judges, a tremendous wave of protest swept the country. Frightened investors refused to advance more loans to the state. Finally in July 1788, a beaten Louis XVI bowed to public opinion and called for the Estates General. Absolute monarchy was collapsing.

As its name indicates, the Estates General was a legislative body with representatives from the three orders, or **estates**, of society: the clergy, nobility, and everyone else. Following centuries-old tradition, each estate met separately to elect delegates, first at a local and then at a regional level. Results of the elections reveal the mind-set of each estate on the eve of the Revolution. The local assemblies of the clergy, representing the first estate, elected mostly parish priests rather than church leaders, demonstrating their dissatisfaction with the church hierarchy. The nobility, or second estate, voted in a majority of conservatives, primarily from the provinces, where nobles were less wealthy and more numerous. Nonetheless, fully one-third of noble representatives were liberals committed to major changes. Commoners of the third estate, who constituted over 95 percent of the population, elected primarily lawyers and government officials to represent them, with few delegates representing business and the poor.

The petitions for change drafted by the assemblies showed a surprising degree of consensus about the key issues confronting the realm. In all three estates, voices spoke in favor of replacing absolutism with a constitutional monarchy in which laws and taxes would require the consent of the Estates General in regular meetings. There was also the strong feeling that individual liberties would have to be guaranteed by law and that economic regulations should be loosened.

On May 5, 1789, the twelve hundred delegates of the three estates gathered in Versailles for the opening session of the Estates General. Despite widespread hopes for serious reform, the Estates General quickly deadlocked over the issue of voting procedures. Controversy had begun during the electoral process itself, when the government confirmed that, following precedent, each estate should meet and vote separately. During the lead-up to the Estates General, critics had demanded a single assembly dominated by the third estate. In his famous pamphlet *What Is the Third Estate?* the abbé Emmanuel Joseph Sieyès (himself a member of the first estate) argued that the nobility was a tiny, overprivileged minority and that the third estate constituted the true strength of the French nation. The government conceded that the third estate should have as many delegates as the clergy and the nobility combined, but then upheld a system granting one vote per estate instead of one vote per person. This meant that the two privileged estates could always outvote the third.

In angry response, in June 1789 delegates of the third estate refused to meet until the king ordered the clergy and nobility to sit with them in a single body. On June 17 the third estate, which had been joined by a few parish priests, voted to call itself the **National Assembly**. On June 20, excluded from their hall because of "repairs," the delegates moved to a large indoor tennis court where they swore the famous Tennis Court Oath, pledging not to disband until they had been recognized as a national assembly and had written a new constitution.

The king's response was disastrously ambivalent. On June 23 he made a conciliatory speech urging reforms, and four days later he ordered the three estates to meet together. At the same time, Louis apparently followed the advice of relatives and court nobles who urged him to dissolve the Assembly by force. The king called an army of eighteen thousand troops toward the capital to bring the delegates under control, and on July 11 he dismissed his finance minister and other more liberal ministers. It appeared that the monarchy was prepared to use violence to restore its control.

Popular Uprising and the Rights of Man

While delegates at Versailles were pressing for political rights, economic hardship gripped the common people. Conditions were already tough, due to the disastrous financial situation of the Crown. A poor grain harvest in 1788 caused the price of bread to soar, and inflation spread quickly through the economy. As a result, demand for manufactured goods collapsed, and many artisans and small traders lost work. In Paris perhaps 150,000 of the city's 600,000 people were unemployed by July 1789.

Against this background of poverty and political crisis, the people of Paris entered decisively onto the revolutionary stage. They believed that, to survive, they should have steady work and enough bread at fair prices. They also feared that the dismissal of the king's liberal finance minister would put them at the mercy of aristocratic landowners and grain speculators. At the beginning of July, knowledge spread of the massing of troops near Paris. On July 14, 1789, several hundred people stormed the Bastille (ba-STEEL), a royal prison, to obtain weapons for the city's defense. Faced with popular violence, Louis soon announced the reinstatement of his finance minister and the withdrawal of troops from Paris. The National Assembly was now free to continue its work.

Just as the laboring poor of Paris had been roused to a revolutionary fervor, the struggling French peasantry had also reached a boiling point. In the summer of 1789, throughout France peasants began to rise in insurrection against their lords, ransacking manor houses and burning feudal documents that recorded their obligations. In some areas peasants reoccupied common lands enclosed by landowners and seized forests. Fear of marauders and vagabonds hired by vengeful landlords—called the **Great Fear** by contemporaries—seized the rural poor and fanned the flames of rebellion.

Faced with chaos, the National Assembly responded to peasant demands with a surprise maneuver on the night of August 4, 1789. By a decree of the Assembly, all the old noble privileges—peasant serfdom where it still existed, exclusive hunting rights, fees for having legal cases judged in the lord's court, the right to make peasants work on the roads, and a host of other dues—were abolished along with the tithes paid to the church. From this point on, French peasants would seek mainly to protect and consolidate this victory.

Having granted new rights to the peasantry, the National Assembly moved forward with its reforms. On August 27, 1789, it issued the Declaration of the Rights of Man and of the Citizen. This clarion call of the liberal revolutionary ideal guaranteed equality before the law, representative government for a sovereign people, and individual freedom. This revolutionary credo, only two pages long, was disseminated throughout France, the rest of Europe, and around the world.

The National Assembly's declaration had little practical effect for the poor and hungry people of Paris. The economic crisis worsened after the fall of the Bastille, as aristocrats fled the country and the luxury market collapsed. Foreign markets also shrank, and unemployment among the working classes grew. In addition, women—the traditional managers of food and resources in poor homes—could no longer look to the church, which had been stripped of its tithes, for aid.

The Women of Paris March to Versailles   On October 5, 1789, a large group of poor Parisian women marched to Versailles to protest the price of bread. For the people of Paris, the king was the baker of last resort, responsible for feeding his people during times of scarcity. The angry women forced the royal family to return with them and to live in Paris, rather than remain isolated from their subjects at court. (Musée de la Ville de Paris, Musée Carnavalet, Paris, France/Giraudon/ The Bridgeman Art Library)

On October 5 some seven thousand women marched the twelve miles from Paris to Versailles to demand action. This great crowd, "armed with scythes, sticks and pikes," invaded the National Assembly. Interrupting a delegate's speech, an old woman defiantly shouted into the debate, "Who's that talking down there? Make the chatterbox shut up. That's not the point: the point is that we want bread."[2] Hers was the genuine voice of the people, essential to any understanding of the French Revolution. The women invaded the royal apartments, killed some of the royal bodyguards, and searched for the queen, Marie Antoinette, who was widely despised for her frivolous and supposedly immoral behavior. It seems likely that only the intervention of Lafayette and the National Guard saved the royal family. But the only way to calm the disorder was for the king to live closer to his people in Paris, as the crowd demanded.

Liberal elites brought the Revolution into being and continued to lead politics. Yet the people of France were now roused and would henceforth play a crucial role in the unfolding of events.

A Constitutional Monarchy and Its Challenges

The day after the women's march on Versailles, the National Assembly followed the king to Paris, and the next two years, until September 1791, saw the consolidation of the liberal revolution. In June 1790 the National Assembly abolished the nobility, and in July the king swore to uphold the as-yet-unwritten constitution, effectively enshrining a constitutional monarchy. The king remained the head of state, but all lawmaking power now resided in the National Assembly, elected by the wealthiest half of French males. The constitution passed in September 1791 was the first in French history. It broadened women's rights to seek divorce, to inherit property, and to obtain financial support for illegitimate children from fathers, but excluded women from political office and voting.

This decision was attacked by a small number of men and women who believed that the rights of man should be extended to all French citizens. Olympe de Gouges (1748–1793), a self-taught writer and woman of the people, protested the evils of slavery as well as the injustices done to women. In September 1791 she published her *Declaration of the Rights of Woman*. This pamphlet echoed its famous predecessor, the Declaration of the Rights of Man and of the Citizen, proclaiming, "Woman is born free and remains equal to man in rights." De Gouges's position found little sympathy among leaders of the Revolution, however.

In addition to ruling on women's rights, the National Assembly replaced the complicated patchwork of historic provinces with eighty-three departments of approximately equal size, a move toward more rational and systematic methods of administration. Guilds, workers' associations, and internal customs fees were abolished in the name of economic liberty. Thus the National Assembly applied the spirit of the Enlightenment in a thorough reform of France's laws and institutions.

The National Assembly also imposed a radical reorganization on religious life. The Assembly granted religious freedom to the small minority of French Protestants and Jews. In November 1789 it nationalized the Catholic Church's property and abolished monasteries. The government used all former church property as collateral to guarantee a new paper currency, the assignats (A-sihg-nat), and then sold the property in an attempt to put the state's finances on a solid footing.

Imbued with the rationalism and skepticism of the eighteenth-century philosophes, many delegates distrusted popular piety and "superstitious religion." Thus in July 1790, with the Civil Constitution of the Clergy, they established a national church with priests chosen by voters. The National Assembly then forced the Catholic clergy to take an oath of loyalty to the new government. The pope formally condemned these measures, and only half the priests of France swore the oath. Many sincere Christians, especially those in the countryside, were appalled by these changes in the religious order. The attempt to remake the Catholic Church, like the abolition of guilds and workers' associations, sharpened the conflict between the educated classes and the common people that had been emerging in the eighteenth century.

World War and Republican France, 1791–1799

Why and how did the French Revolution take a radical turn entailing terror at home and war with European powers?

When Louis XVI accepted the National Assembly's constitution in September 1791, a young provincial lawyer and delegate named Maximilien Robespierre (1758–1794) concluded that "the Revolution is over." Robespierre was right in the sense that the most constructive and lasting reforms were in place. Yet he was wrong in suggesting that turmoil had ended, for a much more radical stage lay ahead, one that would bring war with foreign powers, terror at home, and a transformation in France's government.

The International Response

The outbreak of revolution in France produced great excitement and a sharp division of opinion in Europe and the United States. On the one hand, liberals and radicals saw a mighty triumph of liberty over despotism. On the other hand, conservative leaders such as British statesman Edmund Burke (1729–1797) were intensely troubled. In 1790 Burke published *Reflections on the Revolution in France*, in which he defended inherited privileges. He glorified Britain's unrepresentative Parliament and predicted that reform like that occurring in France would lead only to chaos and tyranny.

One passionate rebuttal came from a young writer in London, Mary Wollstonecraft (1759–1797). Incensed by Burke's book, Wollstonecraft (WOOL-stuhn-kraft) wrote a blistering attack, *A Vindication of the Rights of Man* (1790). Two years later, she published her masterpiece, *A Vindication of the Rights of Woman* (1792). Like de Gouges in France, Wollstonecraft demanded equal rights for women. She also advocated coeducation out of the belief that it would make women better wives and mothers, good citizens, and economically independent. Considered very radical for the time, the book became a founding text of the feminist movement.

The kings and nobles of continental Europe, who had at first welcomed the Revolution in France as weakening a competing power, now feared its impact. In June 1791 the royal family was arrested and returned to Paris after trying to slip out of France. To supporters of the Revolution, the attempted flight was proof that the king was treacherously seeking foreign support for an invasion of France. To the monarchs of Austria and Prussia, the arrest of a crowned monarch was unacceptable. Two months later they issued the Declaration of Pillnitz, which professed their willingness to intervene in France to restore Louis XVI's rule if necessary. It was expected to have a sobering effect on revolutionary France without causing war.

But the crowned heads of Europe misjudged the situation. The new French representative body, called the Legislative Assembly, that convened in October 1791 had new delegates and a different character. Although the delegates were still prosperous, well-educated middle-class men, they were younger and less cautious than their predecessors. Many of them belonged to the political **Jacobin Club**. Such clubs had proliferated in Parisian neighborhoods since the beginning of the Revolution, drawing men and women to debate the political issues of the day.

Jacobins and other deputies reacted with patriotic fury to the Declaration of Pillnitz. They said that if the kings of Europe were attempting to incite war against France, then "we will incite a war of people against kings. . . . Ten million Frenchmen, kindled by the fire of liberty, armed with the sword, with reason, with eloquence would be able to change the face of the world and make the tyrants tremble on their thrones."[3] In April 1792 France declared war on Francis II, the Habsburg monarch.

France's crusade against tyranny went poorly at first. Prussia joined Austria against the French, who broke and fled at their first military encounter with this First Coalition of foreign powers united against the Revolution. The Legislative Assembly declared the country in danger, and volunteers rallied to the capital. In this wartime atmosphere, rumors of treason by the king and queen spread in Paris. On August 10, 1792, a revolutionary crowd attacked the royal palace at the Tuileries (TWEE-luh-reez), while the royal family fled to the Legislative Assembly. Rather than offering refuge, the Assembly suspended the king from all his functions, imprisoned him, and called for a constitutional assembly to be elected by universal male suffrage.

The Second Revolution and the New Republic

The fall of the monarchy marked a radicalization of the Revolution, a phase that historians often call the **second revolution**. Louis's imprisonment was followed by the September Massacres. Fearing invasion by the Prussians and riled up by rumors that counter-revolutionaries would aid the invaders, angry crowds stormed the prisons and killed jailed priests and aristocrats. In late September 1792 the new, popularly elected National Convention, which replaced the Legislative Assembly, proclaimed France a republic, a nation in which the people, instead of a monarch, held sovereign power.

As with the Legislative Assembly, many members of the new National Convention belonged to the Jacobin Club of Paris. But the Jacobins themselves were increasingly divided into two bitterly opposed groups — the **Girondists** (juh-RAHN-dihsts) and **the Mountain**, led by Robespierre and another young lawyer, Georges Jacques Danton.

This division emerged clearly after the National Convention overwhelmingly convicted Louis XVI of treason. The Girondists accepted his guilt but did not wish to put the king to death. By a narrow majority, the Mountain carried the day, and Louis was executed on January 21, 1793, by guillotine, which the French had recently perfected. Marie Antoinette suffered the same fate later that year. But both the Girondists and the Mountain were determined to continue the "war against tyranny." The Prussians had been stopped at the Battle of Valmy on September 20, 1792, one day before the republic was proclaimed. French armies then invaded Savoy and captured Nice, moved into the German Rhineland, and by November 1792 were occupying the entire Austrian Netherlands (modern Belgium).

Everywhere they went, French armies of occupation chased princes, abolished feudalism, and found support among some peasants and middle-class people. But French armies also lived off the land, requisitioning food and supplies and plundering local treasures. The liberators therefore looked increasingly like foreign invaders. Meanwhile, international tensions mounted. In February 1793 the National Convention, at war with Austria and Prussia, declared war on Britain, the Dutch Republic, and Spain as well. Republican France was now at war with almost all of Europe.

Groups within France added to the turmoil. Peasants in western France revolted against being drafted into the army, with the Vendée region of Brittany emerging as the epicenter of revolt. Devout Catholics, royalists, and foreign agents encouraged their rebellion, and the counter-revolutionaries recruited veritable armies to fight for their cause.

In March 1793 the National Convention was locked in a life-and-death political struggle between members of the Mountain and the more moderate Girondists. With the middle-class delegates so bitterly divided, the people of Paris once again emerged as the decisive political factor. The laboring poor and the petty traders were often known as the **sans-culottes** because their men wore trousers instead of the knee breeches of the aristocracy and the solid middle class. They demanded radical political action to defend the Revolution. The Mountain, sensing an opportunity to outmaneuver the Girondists, joined with sans-culottes activists to engineer a popular uprising. On June 2, 1793, armed sans-culottes invaded the Convention and forced its deputies to arrest twenty-nine Girondist deputies for treason. All power passed to the Mountain.

The Convention also formed the Committee of Public Safety in April 1793 to deal with threats from within and outside France. The committee, led by Robespierre, held dictatorial power, allowing it to use whatever force necessary to defend the Revolution. Moderates in leading provincial cities revolted against the committee's power and demanded a decentralized government. Counter-revolutionary forces in the Vendée won significant victories, and the republic's armies were driven back on all fronts. By July 1793 only the areas around Paris and on the eastern frontier were firmly held by the central government. Defeat seemed imminent.

Total War and the Terror

A year later, in July 1794, the central government had reasserted control over the provinces, and the Austrian Netherlands and the Rhineland were once again in French hands. This remarkable change of fortune was due to the revolutionary government's success in harnessing the explosive forces of a planned economy, revolutionary terror, and modern nationalism in a total war effort.

Robespierre and the Committee of Public Safety advanced on several fronts in 1793 and 1794, seeking to impose republican unity across the nation. First, they collaborated with the sans-culottes, who continued pressing the common people's case for fair prices and a moral economic order. Thus in September 1793 Robespierre and his coworkers established a planned economy with egalitarian social overtones. Rather than let supply and demand determine prices, the government set maximum prices for key products. Though the state was too weak to enforce all its price regulations, it did fix the price of bread in Paris at levels the poor could afford.

The people were also put to work, mainly producing arms and munitions for the war effort. The government told craftsmen what to produce, nationalized many small workshops, and requisitioned raw materials and grain. Through these economic reforms the second revolution produced an emergency form of socialism, which thoroughly frightened Europe's propertied classes and greatly influenced the subsequent development of socialist ideology.

Second, while radical economic measures supplied the poor with bread and the armies with weapons, the **Reign of Terror** (1793–1794) enforced compliance with republican beliefs and practices. Special revolutionary courts responsible only to Robespierre's Committee of Public Safety tried "enemies of the nation" for political crimes. Some forty thousand French men and women were executed or died in prison, making Robespierre's Reign of Terror one of the most controversial phases of the Revolution. Presented as a necessary measure to save the republic, the Terror was a weapon directed against all suspected of opposing the revolutionary government. As Robespierre himself put it, "Terror is nothing more than prompt, severe inflexible justice."[4] For many Europeans of the time, however, the Reign of Terror represented a frightening perversion of the ideals of 1789.

In their efforts to impose unity, the Jacobins took actions to suppress women's participation in political debate, which they perceived as disorderly and a distraction from women's proper place in the home. On October 30, 1793, the National Convention declared that "the clubs and popular societies of women, under whatever denomination are prohibited." Among those convicted of sedition was writer Olympe de Gouges, who was sent to the guillotine in November 1793.

The Terror also sought to bring the Revolution into all aspects of everyday life. The government sponsored revolutionary art and songs as well as a new series of secular festivals to celebrate republican virtue and patriotism. Moreover, the government attempted to rationalize French daily life by adopting the decimal system for weights and measures and a new calendar based on ten-day weeks. Another important element of this cultural revolution was the campaign of de-Christianization, which aimed to eliminate Catholic symbols and beliefs. Fearful of the hostility aroused in rural France, however, Robespierre called for a halt to de-Christianization measures in mid-1794.

The third and perhaps most decisive element in the French republic's victory over the First Coalition was its ability to draw on the power of dedication to a national state and a national mission. An essential part of modern nationalism, which would fully emerge throughout Europe in the nineteenth century, this commitment was something new in history. With a common language and a common tradition newly reinforced by the ideas of popular sovereignty and democracy, large numbers of French people were stirred by a common loyalty. They developed an intense emotional commitment to the defense of the nation, and they saw the war against foreign opponents as a life-and-death struggle between good and evil.

The all-out mobilization of French resources under the Terror combined with the fervor of nationalism to create an awesome fighting machine. After August 1793 all unmarried young men were subject to the draft, and by January 1794 French armed forces outnumbered those of their enemies almost four to one.[5] Well trained, well equipped, and constantly indoctrinated, the enormous armies of the republic were led by young, impetuous generals. These generals often had risen from the ranks, and they personified the opportunities the Revolution offered gifted sons of the people. By spring 1794 French armies were victorious on all fronts. The republic was saved.

The Thermidorian Reaction and the Directory

The success of the French armies led Robespierre and the Committee of Public Safety to relax the emergency economic controls, but they extended the political Reign of Terror. In March 1794 Robespierre's Terror wiped out many of his critics. Two weeks later Robespierre sent long-standing collaborators whom he believed had turned against him, including Danton, to the guillotine. A group of radicals and moderates in the Convention, knowing that they might be next, organized a conspiracy. They howled down Robespierre when he tried to speak to the National Convention on July 27, 1794—a date known as 9 Thermidor according to France's newly adopted republican calendar. The next day it was Robespierre's turn to be guillotined.

As Robespierre's closest supporters followed their leader to the guillotine, the respectable middle-class lawyers and professionals who had led the liberal revolution of 1789 reasserted their authority. This period of **Thermidorian reaction**, as it was called, hearkened back to the beginnings of the Revolution; the middle class rejected the radicalism of the sans-culottes in favor of moderate policies that favored property owners. In 1795 the National Convention abolished many economic controls, let prices rise sharply, and severely restricted the local political organizations through which the sans-culottes exerted their strength.

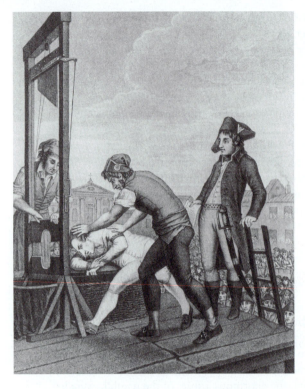

The Execution of Robespierre
Completely wooden except for the heavy iron blade, the guillotine was painted red for Robespierre's execution, a detail not captured in this black-and-white engraving of the 1794 event. Large crowds witnessed the execution in a majestic public square in central Paris, then known as the Place de la Revolution and now called the Place de la Concorde (Harmony Square). (Musée de la Ville de Paris, Musée Carnavalet, Paris, France/ Giraudon/The Bridgeman Art Library)

In 1795 the middle-class members of the National Convention wrote yet another constitution to guarantee their economic position and political supremacy. As in previous elections, the mass of the population could vote only for electors who would in turn elect the legislators, but the new constitution greatly reduced the number of men eligible to become electors by instating a substantial property requirement. It also inaugurated a bicameral legislative system for the first time in the Revolution, with a Council of 500 serving as the lower house that initiated legislation and a Council of Elders (composed of about 250 members aged forty years or older) acting as the upper house that approved new laws. To prevent a new Robespierre from monopolizing power, the new Assembly granted executive power to a five-man body, called the Directory.

The Directory continued to support French military expansion abroad. War was no longer so much a crusade as a response to economic problems. Large, victorious French armies reduced unemployment at home. However, the French people quickly grew weary of the corruption and ineffectiveness that characterized the Directory. This general dissatisfaction revealed itself clearly in the national elections of 1797, which returned a large number of conservative and even monarchist deputies who favored peace at almost any price. Two years later Napoleon Bonaparte ended the Directory in a coup d'état (koo day-TAH) and substituted a strong dictatorship for a weak one.

The Napoleonic Era, 1799–1815

Why did Napoleon Bonaparte assume control of France and much of Europe, and what factors led to his downfall?

For almost fifteen years, from 1799 to 1814, France was in the hands of a keen-minded military dictator of exceptional ability. One of history's most fascinating leaders, Napoleon Bonaparte (1769–1821) realized that he needed to put an end to civil strife in France in order to create unity and consolidate his rule. And he did. But Napoleon saw himself as a man of destiny, and the glory of war and the dream of universal empire proved irresistible. For years he spiraled from victory to victory, but in the end he was destroyed by a mighty coalition united in fear of his restless ambition.

Napoleon's Rule of France

Born in Corsica into an impoverished noble family in 1769, Napoleon left home and became a lieutenant in the French artillery in 1785. Rising rapidly in the new army, Napoleon was placed in command of French forces in Italy and won brilliant victories there in 1796 and 1797. His next campaign, in Egypt, was a failure, but Napoleon returned to France before the fiasco was generally known, and his reputation remained intact.

Napoleon soon learned that some prominent members of the legislature were plotting against the Directory. The plotters' dissatisfaction stemmed not so much from the Directory's ruling dictatorially as from the fact that it was a weak dictatorship. Ten years of upheaval and uncertainty had made firm rule much more appealing than liberty and popular politics to these disillusioned revolutionaries. The abbé Sieyès personified this evolution in thinking. In 1789 he had written that the nobility was grossly overprivileged and that the entire people should rule the French nation. Now Sieyès's motto was "Confidence from below, authority from above."

The Coronation of Napoleon, 1804   In this detail from a grandiose painting by Jacques-Louis David, Napoleon, instead of the pope, prepares to crown his wife, Josephine, in an elaborate ceremony in Notre Dame Cathedral. Napoleon, the ultimate upstart, also crowned himself. Pope Pius VII, seated glumly behind the emperor, is reduced to being a spectator. (Louvre/Paris, France/The Bridgeman Art Library)

PRIMARY SOURCE Napoleon's Proclamation to the French People

In his proclamation to the French people, Napoleon justified the coup d'état of November 10, 1799, in which he and co-conspirators overthrew the Directory government. He does not mention the two men named consul alongside him, but takes sole credit for the events, which he presents as a necessary defense of the republic against traitorous legislators.

On my return to Paris, I found division among all the authorities and agreement only on one truth, that the Constitution was half destroyed and could no longer save liberty.

Every faction came to me, confided their plans in me, and asked me for my support: I refused to be the man of one faction. . . .

The Council of Elders resolved to transfer the Legislative Body to Saint-Cloud; it gave me the responsibility of organizing the force necessary for its independence. I believed it my duty to my fellow citizens, to the soldiers perishing in our armies, and for the national glory acquired at the cost of their blood, to accept the command.

The Councils assembled at Saint-Cloud; republican troops guaranteed their safety from without, but assassins created terror from within. Several deputies from the Council of Five Hundred, armed with stilettos and firearms, circulated death threats. . . .

I took my indignation and grief to the Council of Elders. I asked it to guarantee the execution of its generous plans. I presented it with the evils besetting the fatherland which they were able to imagine. They united with me through new testimony of their steadfast will.

I then went to the Council of Five Hundred; alone, unarmed, head uncovered, just as the Elders had received and applauded me. I came to remind the majority of its wishes, and to assure it of its power.

The flamboyant thirty-year-old Napoleon, nationally revered for his heroism, was an ideal figure of authority. On November 9, 1799, Napoleon and his conspirators ousted the Directors, and the following day soldiers disbanded the legislature at bayonet point. Napoleon was named first consul of the republic, and a new constitution consolidating his position was overwhelmingly approved by a nationwide vote in December 1799. Republican appearances were maintained, but Napoleon became the real ruler of France. (See "Primary Source: Napoleon's Proclamation to the French People," above.)

Napoleon's domestic policy centered on using his popularity and charisma to maintain order and end civil strife. He did so by appeasing powerful groups in France by according them favors in return for loyal service. Napoleon's bargain with the solid middle class was codified in the famous Civil Code of March 1804, also known as the **Napoleonic Code**, which reasserted two of the fundamental principles of the Revolution of 1789: equality of all male citizens before the law, and security of wealth and private property. Napoleon and the leading bankers of Paris established the privately owned Bank of France in 1800, which served the interests of both the state and the financial oligarchy. Napoleon won over peasants by defending the gains in land and status they had won during the Revolution.

The stilettos which threatened the deputies were immediately raised against their liberator; twenty assassins threw themselves on me and aimed at my chest. The grenadiers of the Legislative Body, whom I had left at the entrance to the hall, ran to put themselves between me and the assassins. One of the brave grenadiers was struck and had his clothes torn by a stiletto. They carried me out. . . .

They crowded around the president, uttering threats, arms in hand. . . . I ordered that he be snatched from their fury, and six grenadiers of the Legislative Body carried him out. Immediately afterwards, grenadiers from the Legislative Body charged into the hall and had it evacuated.

The factions, thus intimidated, dispersed and fled. The majority, freed from their attacks, returned freely and peaceably to the meeting hall, heard the propositions which were made for public safety, deliberated, and prepared the salutary resolution which is to become the new and provisional law of the Republic.

Frenchmen, you will undoubtedly recognize in this conduct the zeal of a soldier of liberty, of a citizen devoted to the Republic.

EVALUATE THE EVIDENCE

1. How does Napoleon justify his actions on November 10, 1799, and the dismissal of the existing legislature of France?

2. In what ways does this document illustrate Napoleon's recurrent tactic of presenting his actions as a means to preserve, not destroy, the Revolution and its achievements?

Source: *The French Revolution and Napoleon: A Sourcebook*, ed. Philip G. Dwyer and Peter McPhee (London: Routledge, 2002), p. 138. Used by permission of Taylor & Francis.

At the same time, Napoleon consolidated his rule by recruiting disillusioned revolutionaries to form a network of ministers, prefects, and centrally appointed mayors. Nor were members of the old nobility slighted. In 1800 and again in 1802 Napoleon granted amnesty to one hundred thousand émigrés on the condition that they return to France and take a loyalty oath. Members of this returning elite soon ably occupied many high posts in the expanding centralized state. Napoleon also created a new imperial nobility in order to reward his most talented generals and officials.

Napoleon applied his diplomatic skills to healing the Catholic Church in France so that it could serve as a bulwark of social stability. After arduous negotiations, Napoleon and Pope Pius VII (pontificate 1800–1823) signed the Concordat (kuhn-KOHR-dat) of 1801. The pope obtained the right for French Catholics to practice their religion freely, but Napoleon gained political power: his government now nominated bishops, paid the clergy, and exerted great influence over the church.

The domestic reforms of Napoleon's early years were his greatest achievement. Much of his legal and administrative reorganization has survived in France to this day, but order and unity had a price: authoritarian rule. Women lost many of the gains they had made in the 1790s. Under the Napoleonic Code, women were dependents of either their fathers or their husbands, and they could not make contracts or have bank accounts in their own names. Napoleon and his advisers aimed at re-establishing a family monarchy, where the power of the husband and father was as absolute over the wife and the children as that of Napoleon was over his subjects. He also curtailed free speech and freedom of the press and manipulated voting in the occasional elections. After 1810 political suspects were held in state prisons, as they had been during the Terror.

Napoleon's Expansion in Europe

Napoleon was above all a great military man. After coming to power in 1799, he sent peace feelers to Austria and Great Britain, the two remaining members of the Second Coalition that had been formed against France in 1798. When they rejected his overtures, Napoleon's armies decisively defeated the Austrians. In the Treaty of Lunéville (1801), Austria accepted the loss of almost all its Italian possessions, and German territory on the west bank of the Rhine was incorporated into France. The British agreed to the Treaty of Amiens in 1802, allowing France to control the former Dutch Republic (known as the Batavian Republic since 1795), the Austrian Netherlands, the west bank of the Rhine, and most of the Italian peninsula. The Treaty of Amiens was a diplomatic triumph for Napoleon, and peace with honor and profit increased his popularity at home.

In 1802 Napoleon was secure but driven to expand his power. Aggressively redrawing the map of Germany so as to weaken Austria and encourage the secondary states of southwestern Germany to side with France, Napoleon tried to restrict British trade with all of Europe. He then plotted to attack Great Britain, but his Mediterranean fleet was destroyed by Lord Nelson at the Battle of Trafalgar on October 21, 1805. Invasion of England was henceforth impossible. Renewed fighting had its advantages, however, for the first consul used the wartime atmosphere to have himself proclaimed emperor in late 1804.

Austria, Russia, and Sweden joined with Britain to form the Third Coalition against France shortly before the Battle of Trafalgar. Actions such as Napoleon's assumption of the Italian crown had convinced both Alexander I of Russia and Francis II of Austria that Napoleon was a threat to the European balance of power. Yet they were no match for Napoleon, who scored a brilliant victory over them at the Battle of Austerlitz in December 1805. Alexander I decided to pull back, and Austria accepted large territorial losses in return for peace as the Third Coalition collapsed.

Napoleon then proceeded to reorganize the German states. In 1806 he abolished many of the tiny German states as well as the ancient Holy Roman Empire and established by decree the German Confederation of the Rhine, a union of fifteen German states minus Austria, Prussia, and Saxony. Naming himself "protector" of the confederation, Napoleon firmly controlled western Germany.

Napoleon's intervention in German affairs alarmed the Prussians, who mobilized their armies after more than a decade of peace with France. Napoleon attacked and won two more brilliant victories in October 1806 at Jena and Auerstädt, where the Prussians were outnumbered two to one. The war with Prussia, now joined by Russia, continued into the following spring. After Napoleon's larger armies won another victory, Alexander I of Russia was ready to negotiate the peace. In the subsequent treaties of Tilsit in 1807, Prussia lost half of its population, while Russia accepted Napoleon's reorganization of western and central Europe and promised to enforce Napoleon's economic blockade against British goods.

The Grand Empire and Its End

Increasingly, Napoleon saw himself as the emperor of Europe, not just of France. The so-called **Grand Empire** he built had three parts. The core, or first part, was an ever-expanding France, which by 1810 included today's Belgium and the Netherlands, parts of northern Italy, and German territories on the east bank of the Rhine. The second part consisted of a number of dependent satellite kingdoms, on the thrones of which Napoleon placed members of his large family. The third part comprised the independent but allied states of Austria, Prussia, and Russia. After 1806 Napoleon expected both satellites and allies to support his **Continental System**, a blockade in which no ship coming from Britain or her colonies could dock at a port controlled by the French. It was intended to halt all trade between Britain and continental Europe, thereby destroying the British economy and its military force.

The impact of the Grand Empire on the peoples of Europe was considerable. In the areas incorporated into France and in the satellites (Map 19.2), Napoleon abolished feudal dues and serfdom to the benefit of the peasants and middle class. Yet Napoleon had to put the prosperity and special interests of France first in order to safeguard his power base. Levying heavy taxes in money and men for his armies, he came to be regarded more as a conquering tyrant than as an enlightened liberator. Thus French rule sparked patriotic upheavals and encouraged the growth of reactive nationalism, for individuals in different lands learned to identify emotionally with their own embattled national families as the French had done earlier.

The first great revolt occurred in Spain. In 1808 a coalition of Catholics, monarchists, and patriots rebelled against Napoleon's attempts to make Spain a French satellite. French armies occupied Madrid, but the foes of Napoleon fled to the hills and waged uncompromising guerrilla warfare. Spain was a clear warning: resistance to French imperialism was growing.

Yet Napoleon pushed on. In 1810, when the Grand Empire was at its height, Britain still remained at war with France, helping the guerrillas in Spain and Portugal. The Continental System was a failure. Instead of harming Britain, the system provoked the British to set up a counter-blockade, which created hard times in France. Perhaps looking for a scapegoat, Napoleon turned on Alexander I of Russia, who in 1811 openly repudiated Napoleon's war of prohibitions against British goods.

Napoleon's invasion of Russia began in June 1812 with a force that eventually numbered 600,000, probably the largest force yet assembled in a single army. Only one-third of this army was French, however; nationals of all the satellites and allies were drafted into the operation. Originally planning to winter in the Russian city of Smolensk, Napoleon recklessly pressed on toward Moscow. The great Battle of Borodino that followed was a draw. Alexander ordered the evacuation of Moscow, which the Russians then burned in part, and he refused to negotiate. Finally, after five weeks in the scorched and abandoned city, Napoleon ordered a retreat, one of the greatest military disasters in history. The Russian army, the Russian winter, and starvation cut Napoleon's army to pieces. When the frozen remnants staggered into Poland and Prussia in December, 370,000 men had died and another 200,000 had been taken prisoner.[6]

Leaving his troops to their fate, Napoleon raced to Paris to raise yet another army. Possibly he might still have saved his throne if he had been willing to accept a France reduced to its historical size—the proposal offered by Austria's foreign minister, Prince

MAP 19.2 Napoleonic Europe in 1812

At the height of the Grand Empire in 1810, Napoleon had conquered or allied with every major European power except Britain. But in 1812, angered by Russian repudiation of his ban on trade with Britain, Napoleon invaded Russia with disastrous results.

Klemens von Metternich. But Napoleon refused. Austria and Prussia deserted Napoleon and joined Russia and Great Britain in the Treaty of Chaumont in March 1814, by which the four powers pledged allegiance to defeat the French emperor.

All across Europe patriots called for a "war of liberation" against Napoleon's oppression. Less than a month later, on April 4, 1814, a defeated Napoleon abdicated his throne. After this unconditional abdication, the victorious allies granted Napoleon the island of Elba off the coast of Italy as his own tiny state. Napoleon was allowed to keep his imperial title, and France was required to pay him a yearly income of 2 million francs.

The allies also agreed to the restoration of the Bourbon dynasty under Louis XVIII (r. 1814–1824) and promised to treat France with leniency in a peace settlement. The new monarch sought support among the people by issuing the Constitutional Charter, which accepted many of France's revolutionary changes and guaranteed civil liberties.

Yet Louis XVIII lacked the magnetism of Napoleon. Hearing of political unrest in France and diplomatic tensions in Vienna, Napoleon staged a daring escape from Elba in February 1815 and marched on Paris with a small band of followers. French officers and soldiers who had fought so long for their emperor responded to the call. Louis XVIII fled, and once more Napoleon took command. But Napoleon's gamble was a desperate long shot, for the allies were united against him. At the end of a frantic period known as the Hundred Days, they crushed his forces at Waterloo on June 18, 1815, and imprisoned him on the rocky island of St. Helena, off the western coast of Africa. Louis XVIII returned to the throne, and the allies dealt more harshly with the French. As for Napoleon, he took revenge by writing his memoirs, nurturing the myth that he had been Europe's revolutionary liberator, a romantic hero whose lofty work had been undone by oppressive reactionaries.

The Haitian Revolution, 1791–1804

How did slave revolt on colonial Saint-Domingue lead to the creation of the independent nation of Haiti in 1804?

The events that led to the creation of the independent nation of Haiti constitute the third, and perhaps most extraordinary, chapter of the revolutionary era in the late eighteenth century. Prior to 1789 Saint-Domingue, the French colony that was to become Haiti, reaped huge profits through a ruthless system of slave-based plantation agriculture. News of revolution in France lit a powder keg of contradictory aspirations among white planters, free people of color, and slaves. While revolutionary authorities debated how far to extend the rights of man on Saint-Domingue, first free people of color then enslaved people took matters into their own hands, rising up to claim their freedom. A massive slave revolt of 1791 ultimately succeeded in ending slavery and winning independence from France, despite invasion by the British and Spanish and Napoleon Bonaparte's bid to reimpose French control. In 1804 Haiti became the first nation in history to claim its freedom through slave revolt.

Revolutionary Aspirations in Saint-Domingue

On the eve of the French Revolution, Saint-Domingue — the most profitable of all Caribbean colonies — was even more rife with social tensions than France itself. The colony, which occupied the western third of the island of Hispaniola, was inhabited by

Saint-Domingue Slave Life   Although the brutal conditions of plantation slavery left little time or energy for leisure, slaves on Saint-Domingue took advantage of their day of rest on Sunday to engage in social and religious activities. The law officially prohibited slaves of different masters from mingling together, but such gatherings were often tolerated if they remained peaceful. This image depicts a fight between two slaves, precisely the type of unrest and violence feared by authorities. (Musée du Nouveau Monde, La Rochelle/Photos12.com—ARJ)

a variety of social groups who resented and mistrusted one another. The European population included French colonial officials, wealthy plantation owners and merchants, and poor immigrants. Individuals of French or European descent born in the colonies were called "Creoles," and over time they had developed their own interests, at times distinct from those of metropolitan France. Vastly outnumbering the white population were the colony's five hundred thousand enslaved people alongside a sizable population of some forty thousand free people of African and mixed African and European descent. Members of this last group referred to themselves as free people of color.

Legal and economic conditions on Saint-Domingue vastly favored the white population. Most of the island's enslaved population performed grueling toil in the island's sugar plantations. The highly outnumbered planters used extremely brutal methods, such as beating, maiming, and executing slaves, to maintain their control. The 1685 Code Noir (Black Code) that set the parameters of slavery was intended to provide minimal standards of humane treatment, but its tenets were rarely enforced. Masters calculated that they could earn more by working slaves ruthlessly and purchasing new ones when they died, than by providing the food, rest, and medical care needed to allow the enslaved population to reproduce naturally. This meant a constant inflow of newly enslaved people from Africa was necessary to work the plantations.

Despite their brutality, slaveholders on Saint-Domingue freed a surprising number of their slaves, mostly their own mixed-race children, thereby producing one of the largest populations of free people of color in any slaveholding colony. The Code Noir had originally granted free people of color the same legal status as whites: they could own property, live where they wished, and pursue any education or career they desired. From the 1760s on, however, the rising prosperity and visibility of this group provoked resentment from the white population. In response, colonial administrators began rescinding the rights of free people of color, and by the time of the French Revolution myriad aspects of their lives were subject to discriminatory laws.

The political and intellectual turmoil of the 1780s, with its growing rhetoric of liberty, equality, and fraternity, raised new challenges and possibilities for each of Saint-Domingue's social groups. For enslaved people, who constituted approximately 90 percent of the population, news of abolitionist movements in France led to hopes that the mother country might grant them freedom. Free people of color looked to reforms in Paris as a means of gaining political enfranchisement and reasserting equal status with whites. The Creole elite, not surprisingly, saw matters very differently. Infuriated by talk of abolition and determined to protect their way of life, they looked to revolutionary ideals of representative government for the chance to gain control of their own affairs, as had the American colonists before them.

The National Assembly frustrated the hopes of all these groups. Cowed by colonial representatives who claimed that support for free people of color would result in slave insurrection and independence, the Assembly refused to extend French constitutional safeguards to the colonies. After dealing this blow to the aspirations of slaves and free people of color, the Assembly also reaffirmed French monopolies over colonial trade, thereby angering Creole planters as well. Like the American settlers did earlier, the colonists chafed under the rule of the mother country.

In July 1790 Vincent Ogé (aw-ZHAY) (ca. 1750–1791), a free man of color, returned to Saint-Domingue from Paris determined to win rights for his people. He raised an army of several hundred and sent letters to the new Provincial Assembly of Saint-Domingue demanding political rights for all free citizens. But Ogé's demands were refused, so he and his followers turned to armed insurrection. After initial victories, his army was defeated, and Ogé was tortured and executed by colonial officials. Revolutionary leaders in Paris were more sympathetic to Ogé's cause. In May 1791, responding to what it perceived as partly justified grievances, the National Assembly granted political rights to free people of color born to two free parents who possessed sufficient property. When news of this legislation arrived in Saint-Domingue, the white elite was furious, and the colonial governor refused to enact it. Violence now erupted between groups of whites and free people of color in parts of the colony.

The Outbreak of Revolt

Just as the sans-culottes helped push forward more radical reforms in France, the second stage of revolution in Saint-Domingue also resulted from decisive action from below. In August 1791 slaves, who had witnessed the confrontation between whites and free people of color for over a year, took events into their own hands. Groups of slaves held a series of nighttime meetings to plan a mass insurrection. In doing so, they drew on their own considerable military experience; the majority of slaves had been born in

Africa, and many had served in the civil wars of the kingdom of Congo and other conflicts before being taken into slavery.[7] They also drew on a long tradition of slave resistance prior to 1791, which had ranged from work slowdowns, to running away, to taking part in African-derived religious rituals and dances known as *vodou* (or voodoo). According to some sources, the August 1791 pact to take up arms was sealed by such a voodoo ritual.[8]

Revolts began on a few plantations on the night of August 22. Within a few days the uprising had swept much of the northern plain, creating a slave army estimated at around 2,000 individuals. By August 27 it was described by one observer as "10,000 strong, divided into 3 armies, of whom 700 or 800 are on horseback, and tolerably well-armed."[9] During the next month enslaved combatants attacked and destroyed hundreds of sugar and coffee plantations.

On April 4, 1792, as war loomed with the European states, the National Assembly issued a decree extending full citizenship rights to free people of color, including the right to vote for men. As in France, voting rights and the ability to hold public office applied to men only. The Assembly hoped this measure would win the loyalty of free people of color and their aid in defeating the slave rebellion.

Warfare in Europe soon spread to Saint-Domingue (Map 19.3). Since the beginning of the slave insurrection, the Spanish colony of Santo Domingo, just to the east of Saint-Domingue, had supported rebel slaves. In early 1793 the Spanish began to bring slave leaders and their soldiers into the Spanish army. Toussaint L'Ouverture (TOO-sahn LOO-vair-toor) (1743–1803), a freed slave who had joined the revolt, was named a Spanish officer. In September the British navy blockaded the colony, and invading British troops captured French territory on the island. For the Spanish and British, revolutionary chaos provided a tempting opportunity to capture a profitable colony.

Desperate for forces to oppose France's enemies, commissioners sent by the newly elected National Convention promised to emancipate all those who fought for France. By October 1793 they had abolished slavery throughout the colony. On February 4, 1794, the Convention ratified the abolition of slavery and extended it to all French territories, including the Caribbean colonies of Martinique and Guadeloupe. In some ways this act merely acknowledged the achievements already won by the slave insurrection itself.

The tide of battle began to turn when Toussaint L'Ouverture switched sides, bringing his military and political skills, along with four thousand well-trained soldiers, to support the French war effort. By 1796 the French had regained control of the colony, and L'Ouverture had emerged as a key military leader. (See "Individuals in Society: Toussaint L'Ouverture," page 650.) In May 1796 he was named commander of the western province of Saint-Domingue (see Map 19.3). The increasingly conservative nature of the French government during the Thermidorian reaction, however, threatened to undo the gains made by former slaves and free people of color.

The War of Haitian Independence

With Toussaint L'Ouverture acting increasingly as an independent ruler of the western province of Saint-Domingue, another general, André Rigaud (1761–1811), set up his own government in the southern peninsula. Tensions mounted between L'Ouverture and Rigaud. While L'Ouverture was a freed slave of African descent, Rigaud belonged

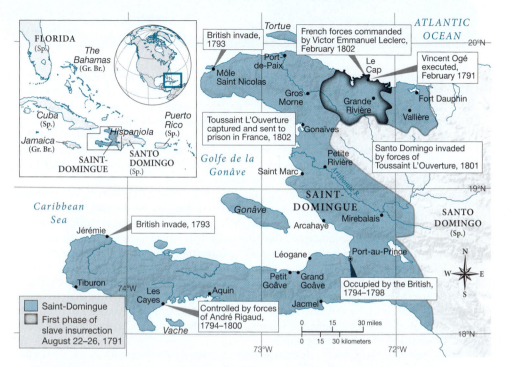

MAP 19.3 The War of Haitian Independence, 1791–1804
Neighbored by the Spanish colony of Santo Domingo, Saint-Domingue was the most profitable European colony in the Caribbean. In 1770 the French transferred the capital from Le Cap to Port-au-Prince. Slave revolts erupted in the north near Le Cap in 1791. Port-au-Prince became the capital of the newly independent Haiti in 1804.

to the free colored elite. This elite resented the growing power of former slaves like L'Ouverture, who in turn accused them of adopting the racism of white settlers. Civil war broke out between the two sides in 1799, when L'Ouverture's forces, led by his lieutenant, Jean Jacques Dessalines (1758–1806), invaded the south. Victory over Rigaud in 1800 gave L'Ouverture control of the entire colony.

This victory was soon challenged by Napoleon, who had his own plans for re-establishing slavery and using the profits as a basis for expanding French power. Napoleon ordered his brother-in-law, General Charles-Victor-Emmanuel Leclerc (1772–1802), to lead an expedition to the island to crush the new regime. In 1802 Leclerc landed in Saint-Domingue and ordered the arrest of Toussaint L'Ouverture. The rebel leader, along with his family, was deported to France, where he died in 1803.

It was left to L'Ouverture's lieutenant, Jean Jacques Dessalines, to unite the resistance, and he led it to a crushing victory over French forces. On January 1, 1804, Dessalines formally declared the independence of Saint-Domingue and the creation of the new sovereign nation of Haiti, the name used by the pre-Columbian inhabitants of the island. The Haitian constitution was ratified in 1805.

Haiti, the second independent state in the Americas and the first in Latin America, was born from the first successful large-scale slave revolt in history. This event spread

INDIVIDUALS IN SOCIETY • Toussaint L'Ouverture

L
ittle is known of the early life of Saint-Domingue's brilliant military and political leader Toussaint L'Ouverture. He was born in 1743 on a plantation outside Le Cap owned by the Count de Bréda. According to tradition, L'Ouverture was the eldest son of a captured African prince from modern-day Benin. Toussaint Bréda, as he was then called, occupied a privileged position among slaves. Instead of performing backbreaking labor in the fields, he served his master as a coachman and livestock keeper. He also learned to read and write French and some Latin, but he was always more comfortable with the Creole dialect.

During the 1770s the plantation manager emancipated L'Ouverture, who subsequently leased his own small coffee plantation and slaves. He married Suzanne Simone, who already had one son, and the couple had another son during their marriage. In 1791 he joined the slave uprisings that swept Saint-Domingue, and he took on the *nom de guerre* (war name) "L'Ouverture," meaning "the opening." L'Ouverture rose to prominence among rebel slaves allied with Spain and by early 1794 controlled his own army. A devout Catholic who led a frugal and ascetic life, L'Ouverture impressed others with his enormous physical energy, intellectual acumen, and air of mystery. In 1794 he defected to the French side and led his troops to a series of victories against the Spanish. In 1795 the National Convention promoted L'Ouverture to brigadier general.

Over the next three years L'Ouverture successively eliminated rivals for authority on the island. First he freed himself of the French commissioners sent to govern the colony. With a firm grip on power in the northern province, L'Ouverture defeated General André Rigaud in 1800 to gain control in the south. His army then marched on the capital of Spanish Santo Domingo on the eastern half of the island, meeting little resistance. The entire island of Hispaniola was now under his command.

With control of Saint-Domingue in his hands, L'Ouverture was confronted with the challenge of building a post-emancipation society, the first of its kind. The task was made even more difficult by the chaos wreaked by war, the destruction of plan-

shock and fear through slaveholding societies in the Caribbean and the United States, bringing their worst nightmares of the utter reversal of their power and privilege to life. Fearing the spread of rebellion to the United States, President Thomas Jefferson refused to recognize Haiti as an independent nation. The liberal proponents of American Revolution thus chose to protect slavery at the expense of revolutionary ideals of universal human rights. The French government imposed crushing indemnity charges on Haiti to recompense the loss of French property, dealing a harsh blow to the fledgling nation's economy.

Yet Haitian independence had fundamental repercussions for world history, helping spread the idea that liberty, equality, and fraternity must apply to all people. The next phase of Atlantic revolution soon opened in the Spanish American colonies.

tations, and bitter social and racial tensions. For L'Ouverture the most pressing concern was to re-establish the plantation economy. Without revenue to pay his army, the gains of the rebellion could be lost. He therefore encouraged white planters to return to reclaim their property. He also adopted harsh policies toward former slaves, forcing them back to their plantations and restricting their ability to acquire land. When they resisted, he sent troops across the island to enforce submission. L'Ouverture's 1801 constitution reaffirmed his draconian labor policies and named L'Ouverture governor for life, leaving Saint-Domingue as a colony in name alone. In June 1802 French forces arrested L'Ouverture and jailed him at Fort de Joux in France's Jura Mountains near the Swiss border. L'Ouverture died of pneumonia on April 7, 1803. It was left to his lieutenant, Jean Jacques Dessalines, to win independence for the new Haitian nation.

QUESTIONS FOR ANALYSIS

1. Toussaint L'Ouverture was both slave and slave owner. How did each experience shape his life and actions?

2. What did Toussaint L'Ouverture and Napoleon Bonaparte have in common? How did they differ?

ONLINE DOCUMENT ASSIGNMENT

How did slaves and free people of color from France's Caribbean colonies respond to the French Revolution? Explore documents that reveal how slaves and free people of color in the colonies and in Paris made their concerns part of the revolutionary dialogue, and then complete a writing assignment based on the evidence and details from this chapter.

bedfordstmartins.com/mckaywestvalue

Notes

1. Quoted in G. Wright, *France in Modern Times*, 4th ed. (New York: W. W. Norton, 1987), p. 34.
2. G. Pernoud and S. Flaisser, eds., *The French Revolution* (Greenwich, Conn.: Fawcett, 1960), p. 61.
3. Quoted in L. Gershoy, *The Era of the French Revolution, 1789–1799* (New York: Van Nostrand, 1957), p. 150.
4. Cited in Wim Klooster, *Revolutions in the Atlantic World: A Comprehensive History* (New York: New York University Press, 2009), p. 74.
5. T. Blanning, *The French Revolutionary Wars, 1787–1802* (London: Arnold, 1996), pp. 116–128.
6. D. Sutherland, *France, 1789–1815: Revolution and Counterrevolution* (New York: Oxford University Press, 1986), p. 420.
7. John K. Thornton, "'I Am the Subject of the King of Congo': African Political Ideology and the Haitian Revolution," *Journal of World History* 4, no. 2 (Fall 1993): 181–214.
8. Laurent Dubois, *Avengers of the New World: The Story of the Haitian Revolution* (Cambridge, Mass.: Belknap Press, 2004), pp. 43–45, 99–100.
9. Quoted ibid., p. 97.

Chapter Review

MAKE IT STICK

LearningCurve
bedfordstmartins.com/mckaywestvalue
After reading the chapter, use LearningCurve to retain what
you've read.

IDENTIFY KEY TERMS

Identify and explain the significance of each item below.

Estates General (p. 629)   the Mountain (p. 635)

estates (p. 630)   sans-culottes (p. 635)

National Assembly (p. 630)   Reign of Terror (p. 636)

Great Fear (p. 631)   Thermidorian reaction (p. 637)

Jacobin Club (p. 634)   Napoleonic Code (p. 640)

second revolution (p. 635)   Grand Empire (p. 643)

Girondists (p. 635)   Continental System (p. 643)

REVIEW THE MAIN IDEAS

Answer the focus questions from each section of the chapter.

* What were the factors behind the revolutions of the late eighteenth century? (p. 618)

* Why and how did American colonists forge a new, independent nation? (p. 621)

* How did the events of 1789 result in a constitutional monarchy in France, and what were the consequences? (p. 627)

* Why and how did the French Revolution take a radical turn entailing terror at home and war with European powers? (p. 633)

* Why did Napoleon Bonaparte assume control of France and much of Europe, and what factors led to his downfall? (p. 638)

* How did slave revolt on colonial Saint-Domingue lead to the creation of the independent nation of Haiti in 1804? (p. 645)

MAKE CONNECTIONS

Think about the larger developments and continuities within and across chapters.

1. What were major differences and similarities among the American, French, and Haitian Revolutions?

2. How did the increased circulation of goods, people, and ideas across the Atlantic in the eighteenth century (Chapter 17) contribute to the outbreak of revolution on both sides of the ocean?

ONLINE DOCUMENT ASSIGNMENT

Toussaint L'Ouverture

How did slaves and free people of color from France's Caribbean colonies respond to the French Revolution?

You encountered Toussaint L'Ouverture's story on page 650. Keeping the question above in mind, go online and explore documents that reveal how slaves and free people of color in the colonies and in Paris made their concerns part of the revolutionary dialogue, and then complete a writing assignment based on the evidence and details from this chapter.

bedfordstmartins.com/mckaywestvalue

CHRONOLOGY

1775–1783	• American Revolution
1786–1789	• Height of French monarchy's financial crisis
1789	• Ratification of U.S. Constitution; storming of the Bastille; feudalism abolished in France
1789–1799	• French Revolution
1790	• Burke publishes *Reflections on the Revolution in France*
1791	• Slave insurrection in Saint-Domingue
1792	• Wollstonecraft publishes *A Vindication of the Rights of Woman*
1793	• Execution of Louis XVI
1793–1794	• Robespierre's Reign of Terror
1794	• Robespierre deposed and executed; France abolishes slavery in all territories
1794–1799	• Thermidorian reaction
1799–1815	• Napoleonic era
1804	• Haitian republic declares independence
1812	• Napoleon invades Russia
1814–1815	• Napoleon defeated and exiled

20

LearningCurve
bedfordstmartins.com/mckaywestvalue
After reading the chapter, use
LearningCurve to retain what
you've read.

The Revolution in Energy and Industry

ca. 1780–1850

WHILE REVOLUTIONS IN FRANCE AND ACROSS THE ATLANTIC WERE
opening a new political era, another revolution was beginning to transform
economic and social life. The Industrial Revolution took off around 1780 in
Great Britain and soon began to influence continental Europe and the United
States. Quite possibly only the development of agriculture during Neolithic
times had a comparable impact and significance.

Drawing on British profits from empire and overseas trade, including the
transatlantic slave trade, industrialization profoundly modified much of human
experience. It changed patterns of work, transformed the social class structure
and the way people thought about class, and eventually altered the international balance of political power.

What was revolutionary about the Industrial Revolution was not its pace
or that it represented a sharp break with the previous period. On the contrary,
the Industrial Revolution built on earlier developments and the rate of progress was slow. What was remarkable about the Industrial Revolution was that
it inaugurated a period of sustained and continuous economic growth that
has continued to the present day. Although it took time, the Industrial Revolution eventually helped ordinary people in the West gain a higher standard
of living as the widespread poverty of preindustrial Europe gradually receded.
It also allowed for an unprecedented continuous growth in population, which
persists to this day.

Such fundamental transitions did not occur overnight. National wealth rose
much more quickly than improvements in the European standard of living until

about 1850. This was because, even in Britain, only a few key industries experienced a technological revolution. Many more industries continued to use old methods. In addition, wage increases were modest until the mid-nineteenth century, and the gradual withdrawal of children and married women from paid work meant that the household as a whole earned the same or less.

In turn, early progress in industrialization allowed Britain and other nations in western Europe and the United States to increase their economic and political dominance over other regions of the world.

The Industrial Revolution in Britain

What were the origins of the Industrial Revolution in Britain, and how did it develop between 1780 and 1850?

The Industrial Revolution began in Great Britain, the nation created in 1707 by the formal union of Scotland, Wales, and England. The transformation in industry was something new in history, and it was unplanned. With no models to copy and no idea of what to expect, Britain pioneered not only in industrial technology but also in social relations and urban living. Just as France was a trailblazer in political change, Britain was the leader in economic development, and it must therefore command special attention.

Origins of the British Industrial Revolution

Although many aspects of the origins of the British Industrial Revolution are still matters for scholarly debate, it is generally agreed that industrial changes grew out of a long process of development. The Scientific Revolution and Enlightenment fostered a new worldview that embraced progress and the role of research and experimentation in understanding and mastering the natural world. The British Royal Society of Arts, for example, sponsored prizes for innovations in machinery and agriculture and played a pivotal part in the circulation of "useful knowledge." Britain's vibrant scientific and Enlightenment culture allowed British industrialists to exploit the latest findings of scientists and technicians from other countries.

In the economic realm, the seventeenth-century expansion of English woolen cloth exports throughout Europe brought commercial profits and high wages to the detriment of traditional producers in Flanders and Italy. By the eighteenth century the expanding Atlantic economy and trade with India and China were also serving Britain well. The mercantilist colonial empire Britain aggressively built, augmented by a strong position in Latin America and in the African slave trade, provided raw materials like cotton and a growing market for British goods (see Chapter 17). Strong demand for British manufacturing meant that British workers earned high wages compared to the rest of Europe.

Agriculture also played an important role in bringing about the Industrial Revolution in Britain. English farmers were second only to the Dutch in productivity in 1700, and they were continually adopting new methods of farming. The result was a period of bountiful crops and low food prices. Because of increasing efficiency, landowners were able to produce more food with a smaller workforce. By the mid-eighteenth century, on the eve of the Industrial Revolution, less than half of Britain's population worked in agriculture. The enclosure movement had deprived many small landowners of their land, leaving the landless poor to work as hired agricultural laborers or in cottage industry. These groups created a large pool of potential laborers for the new factories.

Abundant food and high wages meant that the ordinary English family no longer had to spend almost everything it earned just to buy bread. Thus the family could spend more on manufactured goods—a razor for the man or a shawl for the woman. They could also pay to send their children to school. Britain's populace enjoyed high levels of literacy and numeracy (knowledge of mathematics) compared to the rest of Europe. Moreover, in the eighteenth century the members of the average British family were redirecting their labor away from unpaid work for household consumption and toward work for wages that they could spend on goods, a trend reflecting the increasing commercialization of the entire European economy.

Britain also benefited from rich natural resources and a well-developed infrastructure. In an age when it was much cheaper to ship goods by water than by land, no part of England was more than fifty miles from navigable water. Beginning in the 1770s a canal-building boom enhanced this advantage. Rivers and canals provided easy movement of England's and Wales's enormous deposits of iron and coal, resources that would be critical raw materials in Europe's early industrial age. The abundance of coal combined with high wages in manufacturing placed Britain in a unique position among European nations: its manufacturers had extremely strong incentives to develop technologies to draw on the power of coal to increase workmen's productivity.

A final factor favoring British industrialization was the heavy hand of the British state and its policies, especially in the formative decades of industrial change. Despite its rhetoric in favor of "liberty," Britain's parliamentary system taxed its population aggressively. The British state collected twice as much per capita as the supposedly "absolutist" French monarchy and spent the money on a navy to protect imperial commerce and on an army that could be used to quell uprisings by disgruntled workers. Starting with the Navigation Acts under Oliver Cromwell (see Chapter 15), the British state also adopted aggressive tariffs, or duties, on imported goods to protect its industries.

All these factors combined to initiate the **Industrial Revolution**, a term first coined in 1799 to describe the burst of major inventions and technical changes under way. This technical revolution went hand in hand with an impressive quickening in the annual rate of industrial growth in Britain. Whereas industry had grown at only 0.7 percent between 1700 and 1760 (before the Industrial Revolution), it grew at the much higher rate of 3 percent between 1801 and 1831 (when industrial transformation was in full swing).[1]

The great economic and political revolutions that shaped the modern world occurred almost simultaneously, though they began in different countries. The Industrial Revolution was, however, a much longer process than the political upheavals of the French Revolution. It was not complete in Britain until 1850 at the earliest, and it did not reach the continent as a whole until after 1815. It spread beyond Europe in the second half of the nineteenth century.

Technological Innovations and Early Factories

The pressure to produce more goods for a growing market and to reduce the labor costs of manufacturing was directly related to the first decisive breakthrough of the Industrial Revolution: the creation of the world's first machine-powered factories in the British cotton textile industry. Technological innovations in the manufacture of cotton cloth led to a new system of production and social relationships. This was not the first time in European history that large numbers of people were systematically put to work in a single locale; the military arsenals of late medieval Venice are one example of a much older form of "factory." The crucial innovation in Britain was the introduction of machine power into the factory and the organization of labor around the functioning of highly productive machines.

The putting-out system that developed in the seventeenth-century textile industry involved a merchant who loaned, or "put out," raw materials to cottage workers who processed the raw materials in their own homes and returned the finished products to the merchant. There was always a serious imbalance in textile production based on cottage industry: the work of four or five spinners was needed to keep one weaver steadily employed. Cloth weavers constantly had to find more thread and more spinners. During the eighteenth century the putting-out system grew across Europe, but most extensively in Britain. There, pressured by growing demand, the system's limitations began to outweigh its advantages around 1760.

Many a tinkering worker knew that a better spinning wheel promised rich rewards. It proved hard to spin the traditional raw materials—wool and flax—with improved machines, but cotton was different. Cotton textiles had first been imported into Britain from India by the East India Company as a rare and delicate luxury for the upper classes. In the eighteenth century a lively market for cotton cloth emerged in West Africa, where the English and other Europeans traded it in exchange for slaves. By 1760 a tiny domestic cotton industry had emerged in northern England, but it could not compete with cloth produced by low-paid workers in India and other parts of Asia. International competition thus drove English entrepreneurs to invent new technologies to bring down labor costs.

After many experiments over a generation, a gifted carpenter and jack-of-all-trades, James Hargreaves, invented his cotton-spinning jenny about 1765. At almost the same moment, a barber-turned-manufacturer named Richard Arkwright invented (or possibly pirated) another kind of spinning machine, the water frame. These breakthroughs produced an explosion in the infant cotton textile industry in the 1780s, when it was increasing the value of its output at an unprecedented rate of about 13 percent each year. By 1790 the new machines were producing ten times as much cotton yarn as had been made in 1770.

Hargreaves's **spinning jenny** was simple, inexpensive, and powered by hand. In early models from six to twenty-four spindles were mounted on a sliding carriage, and each spindle spun a fine, slender thread. The machines were usually worked by women, who moved the carriage back and forth with one hand and turned a wheel to supply power with the other. Now it was the male weaver who could not keep up with the vastly more efficient female spinner.

Arkwright's **water frame** employed a different principle. It quickly acquired a capacity of several hundred spindles and demanded much more power than a single operator could provide. A solution was found in waterpower. The water frame required large specialized mills to take advantage of the rushing currents of streams and rivers. The factories they powered employed as many as one thousand workers from the very beginning. The water frame did not completely replace cottage industry, however, for it could spin only a coarse, strong thread, which was then put out for respinning on

Woman Working a Spinning Jenny   The loose cotton strands on the slanted bobbins shown in this illustration of Hargreaves's spinning jenny passed up to the sliding carriage and then on to the spindles in back for fine spinning. The worker, almost always a woman, regulated the sliding carriage with one hand, and with the other she turned the crank on the wheel to supply power. By 1783 one woman could spin by hand a hundred threads at a time. (Mary Evans Picture Library/The Image Works)

hand-operated cottage jennies. Around 1790 a hybrid machine invented by Samuel Crompton proved capable of spinning very fine and strong thread in large quantities. Gradually, all cotton spinning was concentrated in large-scale water-powered factories.

These revolutionary developments in the textile industry allowed British manufacturers to compete successfully in international markets in both fine and coarse cotton thread. At first, the machines were too expensive to build and did not provide enough savings in labor to be adopted in continental Europe or elsewhere. Where wages were low and investment capital was more scarce, there was little point in adopting mechanized production until significant increases in the machines' productivity, and a drop in the cost of manufacturing them, occurred in the first decades of the nineteenth century.

Families using cotton in cottage industry were freed from their constant search for adequate yarn from scattered part-time spinners, since all the thread needed could be spun in the cottage on the jenny or obtained from a nearby factory. The income of weavers, now hard-pressed to keep up with the spinners, rose markedly until about 1792. They were among the highest-earning workers in England. As a result, large numbers of agricultural laborers became handloom weavers, while mechanics and capitalists sought to invent a power loom to save on labor costs. This Edmund Cartwright achieved in 1785. But the power looms of the factories worked poorly at first, and they did not replace handlooms until the 1820s.

Despite the significant increases in productivity, the working conditions in the early cotton factories were atrocious. Adult weavers and spinners were reluctant to leave the safety and freedom of work in their own homes to labor in noisy and dangerous factories where the air was filled with cotton fibers. Therefore, factory owners often turned to young orphans and children who had been abandoned by their parents and put in the care of local parishes. Parish officers often "apprenticed" such unfortunate foundlings to factory owners. The parish thus saved money, and the factory owners gained workers over whom they exercised almost the authority of slave owners.

Apprenticed as young as five or six years of age, boy and girl workers were forced by law to labor for their "masters" for as many as fourteen years. Housed, fed, and locked up nightly in factory dormitories, the young workers labored thirteen or fourteen hours a day for little or no pay. Harsh physical punishment maintained brutal discipline. Hours were appalling—commonly thirteen or fourteen hours a day, six days a week. To be sure, poor children typically worked long hours in many types of demanding jobs, but this wholesale coercion of orphans as factory apprentices constituted exploitation on a truly unprecedented scale.

The creation of the world's first machine-powered factories in the British cotton textile industry in the 1770s and 1780s, which grew out of the putting-out system of cottage production, was a major historical development. Both symbolically and substantially, the big new cotton mills marked the beginning of the Industrial Revolution in Britain. By 1831 the largely mechanized cotton textile industry accounted for fully 22 percent of the country's entire industrial production.

The Steam Engine Breakthrough

Human beings have long used their toolmaking abilities to construct machines that convert one form of energy into another for their own benefit. In the medieval period Europeans began to adopt water mills to grind their grain and windmills to pump water and drain swamps. More efficient use of water and wind in the sixteenth and seventeenth centuries enabled them to accomplish more. Nevertheless, even into the eighteenth century Europe, like other areas of the world, continued to rely mainly on wood for energy, and human beings and animals continued to perform most work. This dependence meant that Europe and the rest of the world remained poor in energy and power.

By the eighteenth century wood was in ever-shorter supply. Processed wood (charcoal) was the fuel that was mixed with iron ore in the blast furnace to produce pig iron. The iron industry's appetite for wood was enormous, and by 1740 the British iron industry was stagnating. Vast forests enabled Russia in the eighteenth century to become the world's leading producer of iron, much of which was exported to Britain. As wood became ever more scarce, the British looked to coal as an alternative. They had first used coal in the late Middle Ages as a source of heat. By 1640 most homes in London were heated with coal, and it was also used in industry to provide heat for making beer, glass, soap, and other products. The breakthrough came when industrialists began to use coal to produce mechanical energy and to power machinery.

To produce more coal, mines had to be dug deeper and deeper and were constantly filling with water. Mechanical pumps, usually powered by animals walking in circles at the surface, had to be installed. At one mine, fully five hundred horses were used in pumping. Such power was expensive and bothersome. In an attempt to overcome these disadvantages, Thomas Savery in 1698 and Thomas Newcomen in 1705 invented the first primitive **steam engines**. Both engines burned coal to produce steam, which was then used to operate a pump. Although both models were extremely inefficient, by the early 1770s many of the Savery engines and hundreds of the Newcomen engines were operating successfully in English and Scottish mines.

In 1763 a gifted young Scot named James Watt (1736–1819) was drawn to a critical study of the steam engine. Watt was employed at the time by the University of Glasgow as a skilled craftsman making scientific instruments. Scotland's Enlightenment emphasis on practicality and social progress had resulted in its universities becoming pioneers in technical education. In 1763 Watt was called on to repair a Newcomen engine being used in a physics course. After a series of observations, Watt saw that the Newcomen engine's waste of energy could be reduced by adding a separate condenser. This splendid invention, patented in 1769, greatly increased the efficiency of the steam engine.

To invent something is one thing; to make it a practical success is quite another. Watt needed skilled workers, precision parts, and capital, and the relatively advanced nature of the British economy proved essential. A partnership in 1775 with Matthew Boulton, a wealthy English industrialist, provided Watt with adequate capital and exceptional skills in salesmanship that equaled those of the renowned pottery king, Josiah Wedgwood. (See "Individuals in Society: Josiah Wedgwood," page 662.) Among Britain's highly skilled locksmiths, tinsmiths, and millwrights, Watt found mechanics who could install, regulate, and repair his sophisticated engines. From ingenious manufacturers such as the cannonmaker John Wilkinson, Watt was gradually able to purchase precision parts. This support allowed him to create an effective vacuum in the condenser and regulate a complex engine. In more than twenty years of constant effort, Watt made many further improvements. By the late 1780s the firm of Boulton and Watt had made the steam engine a practical and commercial success in Britain.

The coal-burning steam engine of Watt and his followers was the Industrial Revolution's most fundamental advance in technology. For the first time in history, humanity had, at least for a few generations, almost unlimited power at its disposal. For the first time, inventors and engineers could devise and implement all kinds of power equipment to aid people in their work.

The steam engine was quickly put to use in several industries in Britain. It drained mines and made possible the production of ever more coal to feed steam engines elsewhere. The steam-power plant began to replace waterpower in cotton-spinning factories during the 1780s, contributing greatly to that industry's phenomenal rise. Steam also took the place of waterpower in flour mills, in the malt mills used in breweries, in the flint mills supplying the pottery industry, and in the mills exported by Britain to the West Indies to crush sugarcane.

Coal and steam power promoted important breakthroughs in other industries. The British iron industry was radically transformed. Originally, the smoke and fumes resulting from coal burning meant that coal could not be used as a cheap substitute for expensive charcoal in smelting iron. Starting around 1710, ironmakers began to use

James Nasmyth's Mighty Steam Hammer   Nasmyth's invention was the forerunner of the modern pile driver, and its successful introduction in 1832 epitomized the rapid development of steam-power technology in Britain. In this painting by the inventor himself, workers manipulate a massive iron shaft being hammered into shape at Nasmyth's foundry near Manchester. (Science & Society Picture Library, London)

coke—a smokeless and hot-burning fuel produced by heating coal to rid it of water and other impurities—to smelt pig iron. After 1770 the adoption of steam-driven bellows in blast furnaces allowed for great increases in the quantity of pig iron produced by British ironmakers. In the 1780s Henry Cort developed the puddling furnace, which allowed pig iron to be refined in turn with coke.

Strong, skilled ironworkers—the puddlers—"cooked" molten pig iron in a great vat, raking off globs of refined iron for further processing. Cort also developed steam-powered rolling mills, which were capable of turning out finished iron in every shape and form. The economic consequence of these technical innovations was a great boom in the British iron industry. In 1740 annual British iron production was only 17,000 tons. With the spread of coke smelting and the impact of Cort's inventions, production had reached 260,000 tons by 1806. In 1844 Britain produced 3 million tons of iron. Once expensive, iron became the cheap, basic, indispensable building block of the economy.

INDIVIDUALS IN SOCIETY • Josiah Wedgwood

As the making of cloth and iron was revolutionized by technical change and factory organization, so too were the production and consumption of pottery. Acquiring beautiful tableware became a craze for eighteenth-century consumers, and continental monarchs often sought prestige in building royal china works. But the grand prize went to Josiah Wedgwood, who wanted to "astonish the world."

The twelfth child of a poor potter, Josiah Wedgwood (1730–1795) grew up in the pottery district of Staffordshire in the English Midlands, where many tiny potteries made simple earthenware utensils for sale in local markets. Growing up as an apprentice in the family business inherited by his oldest brother, Wedgwood struck off on his own in 1752. Soon manager of a small pottery, Wedgwood learned that new products recharged lagging sales. Studying chemistry and determined to succeed, Wedgwood spent his evenings experimenting with different chemicals and firing conditions.

In 1759, after five years of tireless efforts, Wedgwood perfected a beautiful new green glaze. Now established as a master potter, he opened his own factory and began manufacturing teapots and tableware finished in his green and other unique glazes, or adorned with printed scenes far superior to those being produced by competitors. Wedgwood's products caused a sensation among consumers, and his business quickly earned substantial profits. Subsequent breakthroughs, including ornamental vases imitating classical Greek models and jasperware for jewelry, contributed greatly to Wedgwood's success.

Competitors were quick to copy Wedgwood's new products and sell them at lower prices. Thus Wedgwood and his partner Thomas Bentley sought to cultivate an image of superior fashion, taste, and quality in order to develop and maintain a dominant market position. They did this by first capturing the business of the trend-setting elite. In one brilliant coup the partners first sold a very large cream-colored dinner set to Britain's queen, which they quickly christened "Queen's ware" and sold as a very expensive, must-have luxury to English aristocrats. Equally brilliant was Bentley's suave expertise in the elegant London showroom selling Wedgwood's imitation Greek vases, which became the rage after the rediscovery of the Roman towns Pompeii and Herculaneum in the mid-eighteenth century.

Above all, once Wedgwood had secured his position as the luxury market leader, he was able to successfully extend his famous brand to the growing middle class, capturing an enormous mass market for his "useful ware." Thus when sales of a

The Coming of the Railroads

The coal industry had long used plank roads and rails to move coal wagons. Rails reduced friction and allowed a horse or a human being to pull a much heavier load. Thus, once a rail capable of supporting a heavy locomotive was developed in 1816, all sorts of experiments with steam engines on rails went forward.

The first steam locomotive was built by Richard Trevithick after much experimentation. George Stephenson acquired glory for his locomotive named *Rocket*, which sped

luxury good grew "stale," Wedgwood made tasteful modifications and sold it to the middling classes for twice the price his competitors could charge. This unbeatable combination of mass appeal and high prices all across Europe brought Wedgwood great fame and enormous wealth.

A workaholic with an authoritarian streak, Wedgwood contributed substantially to the development of the factory system. In 1769 he opened a model factory on a new canal he had promoted. With two hundred workers in several departments, Wedgwood exercised tremendous control over his workforce, imposing fines for many infractions, such as being late, drinking on the job, or wasting material. He wanted, he said, to create men who would be like "machines" that "cannot err." Yet Wedgwood also recognized the value in treating workers well. He championed a division of labor that made most workers specialists who received ongoing training. He also encouraged employment of family groups, who were housed in company row houses with long, narrow backyards suitable for raising vegetables and chickens. Paying relatively high wages and providing pensions and some benefits, Wedgwood developed a high-quality labor force that learned to accept his rigorous discipline and carried out his ambitious plans.

QUESTIONS FOR ANALYSIS

1. How and why did Wedgwood succeed?
2. Was Wedgwood a good boss or a bad one? Why?
3. How did Wedgwood exemplify the new class of factory owners?

ONLINE DOCUMENT ASSIGNMENT

How did observers of early industrialization imagine the relationship between workers and their work, and between workers and their employers? Explore different views on the impact of industrial production on individual workers in light of Wedgwood's approach to industrial labor. Then complete a writing assignment based on the evidence and details from this chapter.

bedfordstmartins.com/mckaywestvalue

down the track of the just-completed Liverpool and Manchester Railway at a maximum speed of 24 miles per hour in 1829. The line from Liverpool to Manchester was a financial as well as a technical success, and many private companies quickly emerged to build more rail lines. Within twenty years they had completed the main trunk lines of Great Britain (Map 20.1). Other countries were quick to follow, with the first steam-powered trains operating in the United States in the 1830s and in Brazil, Chile, Argentina, and the British colonies of Canada, Australia, and India in the 1850s.

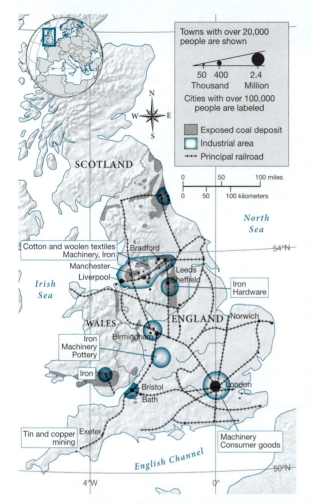

MAP 20.1 The Industrial Revolution in Great Britain, ca. 1850
Industry concentrated in the rapidly growing cities of the north and the center of England, where rich coal and iron deposits were close to one another.

The significance of the railroad was tremendous. It dramatically reduced the cost and uncertainty of shipping freight over land. This advance had many economic consequences. Previously, markets had tended to be small and local; as the barrier of high transportation costs was lowered, markets became larger and even nationwide. Larger markets encouraged larger factories with more sophisticated machinery in a growing number of industries. Such factories could make goods more cheaply and gradually subjected most cottage workers and many urban artisans to severe competitive pressures. In all countries, the construction of railroads created a strong demand for unskilled labor and contributed to the growth of a class of urban workers.

Water travel was also transformed by the steam engine. French engineers completed the first steam ships in the 1770s, and the first commercial steam ships came into use in North America several decades later. The *Clermont* began to travel the waters of the Hudson River in New York State in 1807, shortly followed by ships belonging to brewer John Molson on the St. Lawrence River.

Industry and Population

In 1851 London hosted an industrial fair called the Great Exhibition in the newly built **Crystal Palace**. The more than 6 million visitors from all over Europe marveled at the gigantic new exhibition hall set in the middle of a large, centrally located park. The building was made entirely of glass and iron, both of which were now cheap and abundant. Sponsored by the British royal family, the exhibition celebrated the new era of industrial technology and the kingdom's role as world economic leader.

Britain's claim to be the "workshop of the world" was no idle boast, for it produced two-thirds of the world's coal and more than half of all iron and cotton cloth. More generally, in 1860 Britain produced a remarkable 20 percent of the entire world's output of industrial goods, whereas it had produced only about 2 percent of the total in 1750.[2] As the British economy significantly increased its production of manufactured goods, the gross national product (GNP) rose roughly fourfold at constant prices between 1780 and 1851. At the same time, the population of Britain boomed, growing from about 9 million in 1780 to almost 21 million in 1851. Thus growing numbers consumed much of the increase in total production.

Rapid population growth in Britain was key to industrial development. More people meant a more mobile labor force, with many young workers in need of employment and ready to go where the jobs were. Sustaining the dramatic increase in population, in turn, was only possible through advances in production in agriculture and industry. Based on the lessons of history, many contemporaries feared that the rapid growth in population would inevitably lead to disaster. In his *Essay on the Principle of Population* (1798), Thomas Malthus (1766–1834) examined the dynamics of human populations. He argued:

> There are few states in which there is not a constant effort in the population to in-crease beyond the means of subsistence. This constant effort as constantly tends to subject the lower classes of society to distress, and to prevent any great permanent melioration of these conditions.[3]

Given the limited resources available, Malthus concluded that the only hope of warding off such "positive checks" to population growth as famine and disease was "prudential restraint." That is, young men and women had to limit the growth of population by marrying late in life. But Malthus was not optimistic about this possibility. The power-ful attraction of the sexes, he feared, would cause most people to marry early and have many children.

Economist David Ricardo (1772–1823) spelled out the pessimistic implications of Malthus's thought. Ricardo's depressing **iron law of wages** posited that over an extended period of time, because of the pressure of population growth, wages would always sink to subsistence level. That is, wages would be just high enough to keep workers from starving.

Malthus, Ricardo, and their followers were proved wrong in the long run, largely because industrialization improved productivity beyond what they could imagine. However, until the 1820s, or even the 1840s, contemporary observers might reasonably have concluded that the economy and the total population were racing neck and neck, with the outcome very much in doubt. There was another problem as well. Perhaps workers, farmers, and ordinary people did not get their rightful share of the new wealth. Perhaps only the rich got richer, while the poor got poorer or made no progress. We will turn to this great issue after looking at the process of industrialization beyond the British Isles.

Industrialization Beyond Britain

How did countries outside of Britain respond to the challenge of industrialization?

As new technologies and new ways of employing labor began to revolutionize produc-tion in Britain, other countries took notice and began to emulate its example. With the end of the Napoleonic Wars, the countries of the European continent quickly adopted

British inventions and achieved their own pattern of technological innovation and economic growth. By the last decades of the nineteenth century, western European countries as well as the United States and Japan had industrialized their economies to a considerable, albeit variable, degree.

Outside of western Europe industrialization proceeded more gradually, with uneven jerks and national and regional variations. Scholars are still struggling to explain these variations as well as the dramatic gap that emerged for the first time in history between Western and non-Western levels of economic production. These questions are especially important because they may offer valuable lessons for poor countries that today are seeking to improve their material condition through industrialization and economic development. The latest findings on the nineteenth-century experience are encouraging. They suggest that there were alternative paths to the industrial world and that there was and is no need to follow a rigid, predetermined British model.

National and International Variations

Comparative data on industrial production in different countries over time help give us an overview of what happened. One set of data, the work of a Swiss scholar, compares the level of industrialization on a per capita basis in several countries from 1750 to 1913. These data are far from perfect, but they reflect basic trends and are presented in Table 20.1 for closer study.

Table 20.1 presents a comparison of how much industrial product was produced, on average, for each person in a given country in a given year. All the numbers are expressed in terms of a single index number of 100, which equals the per capita level of industrial goods in Great Britain in 1900. Every number in the table is thus a percentage of the 1900 level in Britain and is directly comparable with other numbers. The countries are listed in roughly the order that they began to use large-scale, power-driven technology.

TABLE 20.1   Per Capita Levels of Industrialization, 1750–1913

	1750	1800	1830	1860	1880	1900	1913
Great Britain	10	16	25	64	87	100	115
Belgium	9	10	14	28	43	56	88
United States	4	9	14	21	38	69	126
France	9	9	12	20	28	39	59
Germany	8	8	9	15	25	52	85
Austria-Hungary	7	7	8	11	15	23	32
Italy	8	8	8	10	12	17	26
Russia	6	6	7	8	10	15	20
China	8	6	6	4	4	3	3
India	7	6	6	3	2	1	2

Note: All entries are based on an index value of 100, equal to the per capita level of industrialization in Great Britain in 1900. Data for Great Britain includes Ireland, England, Wales, and Scotland.

Source: P. Bairoch, "International Industrialization Levels from 1750 to 1980," *Journal of European Economic History* 11 (Spring 1982): 294, U.S. Journals at Cambridge University Press.

What does this overview tell us? First, one sees in the first column that in 1750 all countries were fairly close together, including non-Western nations such as China and India. Both China and India had been extremely important players in early modern world trade, earning high profits from exporting their luxury goods (see Chapter 14). However, the column headed 1800 shows that Britain had opened up a noticeable lead over all countries by 1800, and that gap progressively widened as the Industrial Revolution accelerated through 1830 and reached full maturity by 1860.

Second, the table shows that Western countries began to emulate the British model successfully over the course of the nineteenth century, with significant variations in the timing and in the extent of industrialization. Belgium, achieving independence from the Netherlands in 1831 and rich in iron and coal, led in adopting Britain's new technology, and it experienced a truly revolutionary surge between 1830 and 1860. France developed factory production more gradually, and most historians now detect no burst in French mechanization and no acceleration in the growth of overall indus-trial output that may accurately be called revolutionary. Its slow but steady growth — and continued dominance of the market in luxury goods using traditional artisanal techniques — was overshadowed by the spectacular rise of the German lands and the United States after 1860 in what has been termed the "second industrial revolution." In general, eastern and southern Europe began the process of modern industrialization later than northwestern and central Europe. Nevertheless, these regions made real progress in the late nineteenth century, as growth after 1880 in Austria-Hungary, Italy, and Russia suggests.

Finally, the late but substantial industrialization in eastern and southern Europe meant that all European states as well as the United States managed to raise per capita industrial levels in the nineteenth century. These increases stood in stark contrast to the decreases that occurred at the same time in many non-Western countries, most notably in China and India, as Table 20.1 shows. European countries industrialized to a greater or lesser extent even as most of the non-Western world stagnated. Japan, which is not included in this table, stands out as an exceptional area of non-Western industrial growth in the second half of the nineteenth century. After the forced opening of the country to the West in the 1850s, Japanese entrepreneurs began to adopt Western technology and manufacturing methods, resulting in a production boom by the late nineteenth century. Different rates of wealth- and power-creating industrial development, which heightened disparities within Europe, also greatly magnified existing inequalities between Europe and the rest of the world.

Industrialization in Continental Europe

Throughout Europe the eighteenth century was an era of agricultural improvement, population increase, expanding foreign trade, and growing cottage industry. Thus, when the pace of British industry began to accelerate in the 1780s, continental businesses began to adopt the new methods as they proved their profitability. British industry enjoyed clear superiority, but the European continent was close behind. During the period of the revolutionary and Napoleonic Wars, from 1793 to 1815, however, western Europe experienced tremendous political and social upheaval that temporarily halted economic development. With the return of peace in 1815, however, western European countries again began to play catch-up.

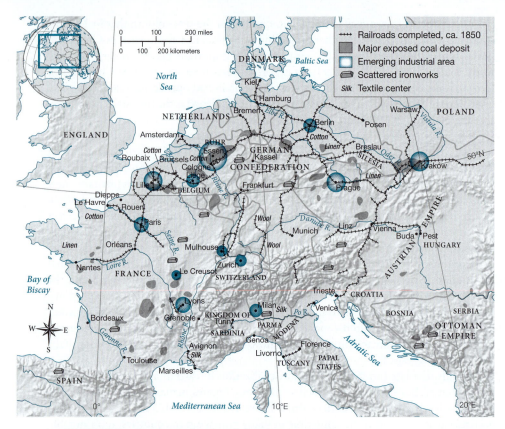

MAP 20.2 Continental Industrialization, ca. 1850
Although continental countries were beginning to make progress by 1850, they still lagged far behind Great Britain. For example, continental railroad building was still in an early stage, whereas the British rail system was essentially complete (see Map 20.1). Coal played a critical role in nineteenth-century industrialization both as a power source for steam engines and as a raw material for making iron and steel.

They faced significant challenges. In the newly mechanized industries, British goods were being produced very economically, and these goods had come to dominate world markets. In addition, British technology had become so advanced and complicated that few engineers or skilled technicians outside England understood it. Moreover, the technology of steam power had grown much more expensive. It involved large investments in the iron and coal industries and, after 1830, required the existence of railroads. Continental business people had difficulty finding the large sums of money the new methods demanded, and laborers bitterly resisted the move to working in factories. All these factors slowed the spread of machine-powered industry (Map 20.2).

Nevertheless, western European nations possessed a number of advantages that helped them respond to their challenges. Most had a rich tradition of putting-out enterprise, which endowed them with experienced merchant capitalists and skilled urban artisans. Moreover, while British inventors and entrepreneurs had to discover and implement new technologies on their own, other nations could simply "borrow" the new methods developed in Great Britain. Such a tradition gave their firms the ability to adapt and survive in the face of new market conditions. European countries also had a third asset that many non-Western areas lacked in the nineteenth century: they had strong, independent governments that did not fall under foreign political control. These governments would use the power of the state to promote industry and catch up with Britain.

Agents of Industrialization

Western European success in adopting British methods took place despite the best efforts of the British to prevent it. The British realized the great value of their technical discoveries and tried to keep their secrets to themselves. Until 1825 it was illegal for artisans and skilled mechanics to leave Britain; until 1843 the export of textile machinery and other equipment was forbidden. Many talented, ambitious workers, however, slipped out of the country illegally and introduced the new methods abroad.

One such man was William Cockerill, a Lancashire carpenter. He and his sons began building cotton-spinning equipment in French-occupied Belgium in 1799. In 1817 the most famous son, John Cockerill, built a large industrial enterprise in Liège in southern Belgium, which produced machinery, steam engines, and then railway locomotives. He also established modern ironworks and coal mines.

Cockerill's plants in the Liège area became a center for the gathering and transmitting of industrial information across Europe. Many skilled British workers came to work for Cockerill, and some went on to found their own companies throughout Europe. Newcomers brought the latest industrial plans and secrets from Britain, so Cockerill could boast that ten days after an industrial advance occurred in Britain, he knew all about it in Belgium.

Thus British technicians and skilled workers were a powerful force in the spread of early industrialization. A second agent of industrialization consisted of talented entrepreneurs such as Fritz Harkort (1793–1880), a pioneer in the German machinery industry. Serving in England as a Prussian army officer during the Napoleonic Wars, Harkort was impressed with what he saw. He contrasted British achievements with the situation in the German-speaking lands, where some territories in the west, especially Prussia, were quite advanced, but much of the east lagged behind. Harkort set up shop building steam engines in the Ruhr Valley, on the western border with France.

Lacking skilled laborers, Harkort turned to Britain for experienced, though expensive, mechanics. Getting materials was also difficult. He had to import the thick iron boilers that he needed from England at great cost. In spite of all these problems, Harkort succeeded in building and selling engines. His ambitious efforts over sixteen years also resulted in large financial losses for himself and his partners. His career illustrates both the great efforts of a few important business leaders to duplicate the British achievement and the difficulty of the task.

Entrepreneurs like Harkort were obviously exceptional. Most continental businesses adopted factory technology slowly, and handicraft methods lived on. Indeed, continental industrialization usually brought substantial but uneven expansion of handicraft industry in both rural and urban areas for a time. Artisan production of luxury items grew in France as the rising income of the international middle class created

A German Ironworks, 1845   The Borsig ironworks in Berlin mastered the new British method of smelting iron ore with coke. Germany, and especially the state of Prussia, was well endowed with both iron and coal, and the rapid exploitation of these resources after 1840 transformed a poor agricultural country into an industrial powerhouse. (akg-images)

increased foreign demand for silk scarves, embroidered needlework, perfumes, and fine wines. Many historians now emphasize that focusing on artisanal luxury production made sense for French entrepreneurs given their long history of dominance in that sector; rather than being a "backward" refusal to modernize, it represented a sound strategic choice that allowed the French to capitalize on their know-how and international reputation.

Government Support and Corporate Banking

Just as the British government provided crucial support for the growth of industrialization, so did national governments in other parts of Europe. After 1815 western European states adopted a set of largely successful policies similar to those in Britain. **Tariff protection** was one such support. The French, for example, responded to a flood of cheap British goods in 1815 after the Napoleonic Wars by laying high tariffs on imported goods.

After 1815 continental governments also bore the cost of building roads, canals, and railroads to improve transportation. Belgium led the way in the 1830s and 1840s. Built rapidly as a unified network, Belgium's state-owned railroads stimulated the development of heavy industry and made the country an early industrial leader. The Prussian government provided another kind of invaluable support for railroads. It guaranteed that the state treasury would pay the interest and principal on railroad bonds if the closely regulated private companies in Prussia were unable to do so. In France, the state shouldered all the expense of acquiring and laying roadbed, including bridges and tunnels. In short, governments helped pay for railroads, the all-important leading sector in continental industrialization.

German journalist and thinker Friedrich List (1789–1846) was a strong proponent of government support for industrialization. In the 1820s and 1830s List spent several years in the United States, where he observed the country's rapidly developing economy with great interest. He returned with the conviction that the growth of modern industry was of the utmost importance. For List, manufacturing was a primary means of increasing people's well-being and relieving their poverty. Moreover, he believed industrialization was essential to prevent the German states from falling behind the rest of the world. He wrote that the "wider the gap between the backward and advanced nations becomes, the more dangerous it is to remain behind."

The practical policies that List focused on were railroad building and the tariff. An early proponent of unifying the German lands, List supported the formation of a customs union, or *Zollverein* (TSOL-feh-rign), among the separate states. Such a tariff union came into being in 1818 and had spread to most of the German states by 1834, allowing goods to move between member states without tariffs, while erecting a single uniform tariff against other nations. List wanted a high protective tariff, which would encourage infant industries, allowing them to develop and eventually hold their own against their more advanced British counterparts.

Finally, banks also played an important role in supporting development on the continent, more so than in Britain. Previously, almost all banks in Europe had been private. Because of the possibility of unlimited financial loss, the partners of private banks tended to be conservative and were content to deal with a few rich clients and a few big merchants. They generally avoided industrial investment as being too risky.

In the 1830s two important Belgian banks pioneered in a new direction. They received permission from the growth-oriented government to establish themselves as corporations enjoying limited liability. That is, if the bank went bankrupt, stockholders could now lose only their original investments in the bank's common stock, and they could not be forced by the courts to pay for any additional losses out of other property they owned. Limited liability helped these Belgian banks attract investors. They mobilized impressive resources for investment in big companies, became industrial banks, and successfully promoted industrial development.

Similar corporate banks became important in France and the German lands in the 1850s and 1860s. Usually working in collaboration with governments, corporate banks established and developed many railroads and many companies working in heavy industry, which were also increasingly organized as limited liability corporations.

The combined efforts of governments, skilled workers, entrepreneurs, and industrial banks meshed successfully after 1850. In Belgium, France, and the German states, key indicators of modern industrial development — such as railway mileage, iron and coal production, and steam-engine capacity — increased at average annual rates of 5 to 10 percent. As a result, rail networks were completed in western and much of central Europe, and the leading continental countries mastered the industrial technologies that had first been developed by the British. In the early 1870s Britain was still Europe's most industrial nation, but a select handful of nations had closed the gap. Western European countries—along with the United States—thus became technological innovators in their own right and enjoyed sustained economic growth that made them the wealthiest nations in the world.

The Situation Outside of Europe

The Industrial Revolution did not have a transformative impact beyond Europe prior to the 1860s, with the exception of the United States and Japan, both early adopters of British practices. In many countries, national governments and pioneering entrepreneurs did make efforts to adopt the technologies and methods of production that had proved so successful in Britain, but they fell short of transitioning to an industrial economy. For example, in Russia the imperial government brought steamships to the Volga River and a railroad to the capital, St. Petersburg, in the first decades of the nineteenth century. By midcentury ambitious entrepreneurs had established steam-powered cotton factories using imported British machines. However, these advances did not lead to overall industrialization of the country, most of whose people remained mired in rural servitude. Instead, Russia confirmed its role as provider of raw materials, especially timber and grain, to the hungry West.

Egypt similarly began an ambitious program of modernization in the first decades of the nineteenth century, which included the use of imported British technology and experts in textile manufacture and other industries. These industries, however, could not compete with lower-priced European imports. Like Russia, Egypt fell back on agricultural exports to European markets, like sugar and cotton.

Such examples of faltering efforts at industrialization could be found in many other regions of the Middle East, Asia, and Latin America. Where European governments maintained direct or indirect political control, they acted to monopolize colonial markets as both sources of raw materials and consumers for their own products, rather than encouraging the spread of industrialization. Such regions could not respond to low-cost imports by raising tariffs, as the United States and western European nations had done, because they were controlled by imperial powers that did not allow them to do so. In India, millions of poor textile workers lost their livelihood because they could not compete with industrially produced British cottons. As a British trade encyclopedia boasted in 1844:

> The British manufacturer brings the cotton of India from a distance of 12,000 miles, commits it to his spinning jennies and power-looms, carries back their products to the East, making them again to travel 12,000 miles; and in spite of the loss of time, and of the enormous expense incurred by this voyage of 24,000 miles, the cotton manufactured by his machinery becomes less costly than the cotton of India spun and woven by the hand near the field that produced it.[4]

Latin American countries were distracted from economic concerns by the early-nineteenth-century wars of independence. By the mid-nineteenth century they had adopted steam power for sugar and coffee processing, but as elsewhere these developments led to increased reliance on agricultural crops for export, not a rise in industrial production. As in India, the arrival of cheap British cottons destroyed the pre-existing textile industry that had employed many Latin American men and women. The rise of industrialization in Britain, western Europe, and the United States thus resulted in other regions of the world becoming increasingly economically dependent and, in turn, ever more vulnerable to political domination. Instead of industrializing, many territories underwent a process of deindustrialization due to imperialism and economic competition.

New Patterns of Working and Living

How did work evolve during the Industrial Revolution, and how did daily life change for working people?

Having first emerged in the British countryside in the late eighteenth century, factories and industrial labor began migrating to cities by the early nineteenth century. As factories moved from rural to urban areas, their workforce evolved as well, from pauper children to families to men and women uprooted from their traditional rural communities. Many women, especially young single women and poor women, continued to work, as married women began to limit their participation in the workforce when possible. For some people, the Industrial Revolution brought improvements, but living and working conditions for the poor stagnated or even deteriorated until around 1850, especially in overcrowded industrial cities.

Work in Early Factories

The first factories of the Industrial Revolution were cotton mills, which began functioning in the 1770s along fast-running rivers and streams and were often located in sparsely populated areas. Cottage workers, accustomed to the putting-out system, were reluctant to work in the new factories even when they received relatively good wages. In a factory, workers had to keep up with the machine and follow its relentless tempo. Moreover, they had to show up every day, on time, and work long, monotonous hours under the constant supervision of demanding overseers, and they were punished systematically if they broke the work rules. For example, if a worker was late to work, or accidentally spoiled material, or nodded off late in the day, the employer imposed fines that were deducted from the weekly pay. Children and adolescents were often beaten for their infractions.

Cottage workers were not used to that way of life. In the putting-out system, all members of the family worked hard and long, but in spurts, setting their own pace. They could interrupt their work when they wished. Women and children could break up their long hours of spinning with other tasks. On Saturday afternoon the head of the family delivered the week's work to the merchant manufacturer and got paid. Saturday night was a time of relaxation and drinking, especially for the men.

Also, early factories resembled English poorhouses, where destitute people went to live at public expense. Some poorhouses were industrial prisons, where the inmates had to work in order to receive food and lodging. The similarity between large brick factories and large stone poorhouses increased the cottage workers' fear of factories and their hatred of factory discipline. It was cottage workers' reluctance to work in factories that prompted the early cotton mill owners to turn to pauper children for their labor. Mill owners contracted with local officials to employ large numbers of such children, who had no say in the matter. In the eighteenth century semi-forced child labor seemed necessary to the survival of poor families and was therefore socially accepted. Attitudes began to change in the last decade of the eighteenth century, as middle-class reformers publicized the brutal toil imposed on society's most vulnerable members.

Workers at a Large Cotton Mill   This 1833 engraving shows adult women operating power looms under the supervision of a male foreman, and it accurately reflects both the decline of family employment and the emergence of a gender-based division of labor in many British factories. The jungle of belts and shafts connecting the noisy looms to the giant steam engine on the ground floor created a constant din. (Time Life Pictures/Getty Images)

Working Families and Children

By the 1790s the early pattern had begun to change. The use of pauper apprentices was in decline, and in 1802 it was forbidden by Parliament. Many more textile factories were being built, mainly in urban areas, where they could use steam power rather than waterpower and attract a workforce more easily than in the countryside. As a result, people came from near and far to work in the cities, both as factory workers and as porters, builders, and domestic servants. Collectively, these wage laborers came to be known as the "working class," a term first used in the late 1830s.

In some cases, workers were able to accommodate to the system by carrying over familiar working traditions. Some came to the mills and the mines as family units. This was how they had labored on farms and in the putting-out system. The mill or mine owner bargained with the head of the family and paid him or her for the efforts of the whole family. In the cotton mills, children worked for their mothers or fathers, collecting scraps and "piecing" broken threads together. In the mines, children sorted coal and worked the ventilation equipment. Their mothers hauled coal in the tunnels below the surface, while their fathers hewed with pick and shovel at the face of the seam.

Ties of kinship were particularly important for newcomers, who often traveled great distances to find work. Many urban workers in Great Britain were from Ireland. They were forced out of rural Ireland by population growth and deteriorating economic conditions from 1817 on and their numbers increased dramatically in the desperate years of the potato famine, from 1845 to 1851 (see Chapter 21). As early as 1824 most of the workers in the Glasgow cotton mills were Irish; in 1851 one-sixth of the population of Liverpool was Irish. Pauper children were especially likely to be Irish, reflecting the precariousness of life for migrants. Like many other immigrant groups held together by ethnic and religious ties, however, the Irish worked together, formed their own neighborhoods, and not only survived but also thrived.

The preservation of the family as an economic unit in the factories helped people accommodate to the new surroundings during the early stages of industrialization. Parents disciplined their children and directed their upbringing. The presence of the whole family meant that children and adults worked the same long hours (twelve-hour shifts were normal in cotton mills in 1800). Adult workers were often complicit in the exploitation of their children. They were not particularly interested in limiting the minimum working age or hours of children as long as family members worked side by side and they maintained control of their young. Only when technical changes threatened to place control in the hands of impersonal managers did adult workers protest against inhuman conditions in the name of their children.

Some enlightened employers and social reformers in Parliament argued that more humane standards were necessary, and they used widely circulated parliamentary reports to influence public opinion. For example, Robert Owen (1771–1858), a successful manufacturer in Scotland, testified in 1816 before an investigating committee on the basis of his experience. He argued that employing children under ten years of age as factory workers was "injurious to the children, and not beneficial to the proprietors."[5] Workers also provided graphic testimony at such hearings as reformers pressed Parliament to pass corrective laws.

These efforts resulted in a series of **Factory Acts** from 1802 to 1833 that progressively limited the workday of child laborers and set minimum hygiene and safety requirements. The 1833 act installed a system of full-time professional inspectors to enforce the provisions of previous acts. Children between ages nine and thirteen could work a maximum of eight hours per day, not including two hours that must be devoted to education. Teenagers aged fourteen to eighteen could work up to twelve hours, while those under nine were banned from employment. The Factory Acts constituted a major victory in preventing the exploitation of children, especially those without families to protect them at the worksite. One unintended drawback of restrictions on child labor, however, was that they broke the pattern of whole families working together in the factory because efficiency required standardized shifts for all workers. After 1833 the number of children employed in industry declined rapidly.

The New Sexual Division of Labor

With the restriction of child labor and the collapse of the family work pattern in the 1830s came a new sexual division of labor. By 1850 the man was emerging as the family's primary wage earner, while the married woman found only limited job opportunities. Generally denied good jobs at high wages in the growing urban economy, wives were expected to concentrate on their duties at home.

This new pattern of **separate spheres** had several aspects. First, all studies agree that married women from the working classes were much less likely to work full-time for wages outside the house after the first child arrived, although they often earned small amounts doing putting-out handicrafts at home and taking in boarders. Second, when married women did work for wages outside the house, they usually came from the poorest families, where the husbands were poorly paid, sick, unemployed, or missing. Third, these poor married or widowed women were joined by legions of young unmarried women, who worked full-time but only in certain jobs, of which textile factory work, laundering, and domestic service were particularly important. Fourth, all women were generally confined to low-paying, dead-end jobs. Evolving gradually, but largely in place by 1850, the new sexual division of labor constituted a major development in the history of women and of the family. (See "Primary Source: Living Conditions of the Working Classes," at right.)

Several factors combined to create this new sexual division of labor. First, the new and unfamiliar discipline of the clock and the machine was especially hard on married women of the laboring classes. Relentless factory discipline conflicted with child care in a way that labor on the farm or in the cottage had not. A woman operating earsplitting spinning machinery could mind a child of seven or eight working beside her (until such work was outlawed), but she could no longer pace herself through pregnancy or breast-feed her baby on the job. Thus a working-class woman had strong incentives to concentrate on child care within her home if her family could afford it. This factor was less important in areas of continental Europe, such as northern France and Scandinavia, where women continued to rely on wet nurses instead of breast-feeding their own babies (see Chapter 18).

Second, running a household in conditions of primitive urban poverty was an extremely demanding job in its own right. There were no supermarkets or public transportation. Shopping, washing clothes, and feeding the family constituted a never-ending challenge. Taking on a brutal job outside the house—a "second shift"—had limited appeal for the average married woman from the working class. Thus many women might well have accepted the emerging division of labor as the best available strategy for family survival in the industrializing society.[6]

Third, to a large degree the young, generally unmarried women who did work for wages outside the home were segregated from men and confined to certain "women's jobs" because the new sexual division of labor replicated long-standing patterns of gender segregation and inequality. In the preindustrial economy, a small sector of the labor market had always been defined as "women's work," especially tasks involving needlework, spinning, food preparation, and child care. This traditional sexual division of labor took on new overtones, however, in response to the factory system. Previously, at least in theory, young people worked under the watchful eye of a parent or the master or mistress of a small workshop. The growth of factories and mines brought unheard-of opportunities for girls and boys to mix on the job, free of familial supervision. Such opportunities led to more unplanned pregnancies and fueled the illegitimacy explosion that had begun in the late eighteenth century and that gathered force until at least 1850. Thus segregation of jobs by gender was partly an effort by older people to control the sexuality of working-class youths.

Investigations into the British coal industry before 1842 provide a graphic example of this concern. The middle-class men leading the inquiry professed horror at the sight of girls and women working without shirts, which was a common practice because of

PRIMARY SOURCE   Living Conditions of the Working Classes

For the vast majority of European women, the realities of life still included long and hard toil for themselves and their children. As middle-class reformers began to investigate working-class living conditions, they were shocked at what they found. This excerpt comes from an 1845 interview of doctors by an economist and reformer in a German industrial city.

QUESTION: What is your usual experience regarding the cleanliness of these classes?

DR. BLUEMNER: Bad! Mother has to go out to work, and can therefore pay little attention to the domestic economy, and even if she makes an effort, she lacks time and means. A typical woman of this kind has four children, of whom she is still suckling one, she has to look after the whole household, to take food to her husband at work, perhaps a quarter of a mile away on a building site; she therefore has no time for cleaning and then it is such a small hole inhabited by so many people. The children are left to themselves, crawl about the floor or in the streets, and are always dirty; they lack the necessary clothing to change more often, and there is no time or money to wash these frequently. There are, of course, gradations; if the mother is healthy, active and clean, and if the poverty is not too great, then things are better.

QUESTION: What is the state of health among the lower class? . . .

DR. KALCKSTEIN: . . . The dwellings of the working classes mostly face the yards and courts. The small quantity of fresh air admitted by the surrounding buildings is vitiated by the emanations from stables and middens [garbage heaps]. Further, because of the higher rents, people are forced to share their dwellings and to overcrowd them. The adults escape the worst influences by leaving the dwellings during the day, but the children are exposed to it with its whole force.

EVALUATE THE EVIDENCE

1. Based on this document, what challenges confronted working-class women in their daily lives?

2. To what extent do the doctors seem to blame the women themselves for their situation? How might observations like these have affected the new sexual division of labor discussed in the text?

Source: Laura L. Frader, ed., *The Industrial Revolution: A History in Documents* (Oxford, U.K.: Oxford University Press, 2006), pp. 85–86.

the heat, and they quickly assumed the prevalence of licentious sex with the male miners, who also wore very little clothing. In fact, many girls and married women worked for related males in a family unit that provided considerable protection and restraint. Yet many witnesses from the working class also believed that the mines were inappropriate and dangerous places for women and girls. Some miners stressed particularly the danger of sexual aggression for girls working past puberty. As one explained, "I consider

Child Laborer   This illustration of a girl dragging a coal wagon was one of several that shocked the public and contributed to the Mines Act of 1842. (© British Library Board)

it a scandal for girls to work in the pits. Till they are 12 or 14 they may work very well but after that it's an abomination. . . . The work of the pit does not hurt them, it is the effect on their morals that I complain of."[7] The **Mines Act of 1842** prohibited underground work for all women and girls as well as for boys under ten.

Some women who had to support themselves protested against being excluded from coal mining, which paid higher wages than most other jobs open to working-class women. But provided they were part of families that could manage economically, the girls and the women who had worked underground were generally pleased with the law. In explaining her satisfaction in 1844, one mother of four provided real insight into why many married working women accepted the emerging sexual division of labor:

> While working in the pit I was worth to my [miner] husband seven shillings a week, out of which we had to pay 2½ shillings to a woman for looking after the younger children. I used to take them to her house at 4 o'clock in the morning, out of their own beds, to put them into hers. Then there was one shilling a week for washing; besides, there was mending to pay for, and other things. The house was not guided. The other children broke things; they did not go to school when they were sent; they would be playing about, and get ill-used by other children, and their clothes torn. Then when I came home in the evening, everything was to do after the day's labor, and I was so tired I had no heart for it; no fire lit, nothing cooked, no water fetched, the house dirty, and nothing comfortable for my husband. It is all far better now, and I wouldn't go down again.[8]

A final factor encouraging working-class women to withdraw from paid labor was the domestic ideals emanating from middle-class women, who had largely embraced the "separate spheres" ideology. Middle-class reformers published tracts and formed societies to urge poor women to devote more care and attention to their homes and families.

Relations Between Capital and Labor

How did the changes brought about by the Industrial Revolution lead to new social classes, and how did people respond to the new structure?

In Great Britain, industrial development led to the creation of new social groups and intensified long-standing problems between capital and labor. A new class of factory owners and industrial capitalists arose. These men and women and their families strengthened the wealth and size of the middle class, which had previously been made up mainly of merchants and professional people. The demands of modern industry regularly brought the interests of the middle-class industrialists into conflict with those of the people who worked for them — the working class. Individuals experienced a growing sense of **class-consciousness**, or awareness of belonging to a distinct social and economic class whose interests might conflict with those of other classes. New questions about social relationships emerged. Meanwhile, enslaved labor in European colonies contributed to the industrialization process in multiple ways.

The New Class of Factory Owners

Early industrialists operated in a highly competitive economic system. As the careers of James Watt and Fritz Harkort illustrate, there were countless production problems, and success and large profits were by no means certain. Manufacturers therefore waged a constant battle to cut their production costs and stay afloat. Much of the profit had to go back into the business for new and better machinery.

Most early industrialists drew upon their families and friends for labor and capital, but they came from a variety of backgrounds. Many, such as Harkort, were from well-established families with rich networks of contacts and support. Others, such as Watt, Wedgwood, and Cockerill, were of modest means, especially in the early days. Artisans and skilled workers of exceptional ability had unparalleled opportunities. Members of ethnic and religious groups who had been discriminated against jumped at the new chances and often helped each other. Scots, Quakers, and other Protestant dissenters were tremendously important in Britain; Protestants and Jews dominated banking in Catholic France. Many of the industrialists were newly rich, and, not surprisingly, they were very proud and self-satisfied.

As factories and firms grew larger, opportunities declined, at least in well-developed industries. It became considerably harder for a gifted but poor young mechanic to start a small enterprise and end up as a wealthy manufacturer. Formal education became more important for young men as a means of success and advancement, but studies at the advanced level were expensive. In Britain by 1830 and in France and Germany by 1860, leading industrialists were more likely to have inherited their well-established enterprises, and they were financially much more secure than their struggling parents had been. They also had a greater sense of class-consciousness; they were fully aware that ongoing industrial development had widened the gap between themselves and their workers.

Just like working-class women, the wives and daughters of successful businessmen found fewer opportunities for active participation in Europe's increasingly complex business world. Rather than contributing as vital partners in a family-owned enterprise, as so many middle-class women had done, these women were increasingly valued for

Ford Maddox Brown, *Work*   This midcentury painting provides a rich and realistic visual representation of the new concepts of social class that became common by 1850. (Birmingham Museums and Art Gallery/The Bridgeman Art Library)

their ladylike gentility. By 1850 some influential women writers and most businessmen assumed that middle-class wives and daughters should avoid work in offices and factories. Rather, a middle-class lady should concentrate on her proper role as wife and mother, preferably in an elegant residential area far removed from ruthless commerce and the volatile working class. (See "Primary Source: Advice for Middle-Class Women," at right.) As we have seen, this ideology of "separate spheres" spread to working-class men and women as well.

Debates over Industrialization

From the beginning, the British Industrial Revolution had its critics. Among the first were the romantic poets. William Blake (1757–1827) called the early factories "satanic mills" and protested against the hard life of the London poor. William Wordsworth (1770–1850) lamented the destruction of the rural way of life and the pollution of the land and water. Some handicraft workers—notably the **Luddites**, who attacked factories in northern England in 1811 and later—smashed the new machines, which they believed were putting them out of work. Doctors and reformers wrote of problems in the factories and new towns, while Malthus and Ricardo concluded that workers would earn only enough to stay alive.

PRIMARY SOURCE   Advice for Middle-Class Women

The adoption of steam-powered machines generated tremendous profits during the Industrial Revolution. Factory owners and managers enjoyed new wealth, and skilled male workers eventually began to hope for wages high enough to keep their wives and children at home. These social changes encouraged the nineteenth-century "separate spheres" ideology, which emphasized the importance of women's role as caretakers of the domestic realm. Sarah Stickney Ellis's The Women of England: Their Social Duties and Domestic Habits, *excerpted below, was one of a flood of publications offering middle-class women advice on shopping, housekeeping, and supervising servants.*

"What shall I do to gratify myself—to be admired—or to vary the tenor of my existence?" are not the questions which a woman of right feelings asks awaking to the avocations of the day. Much more congenial to the highest attributes of woman's character, are inquiries such as these: "How shall I endeavor through this day to turn the time, the health, and the means permitted me to enjoy, to the best account? Is any one sick, I must visit their chamber without delay, and try to give their apartment an air of comfort, by arranging such things as the wearied nurse may not have thought of. Is any one about to set off on a journey, I must see that the early meal is spread, to prepare it with my own hands, in order that the servant, who was working late last night, may profit by unbroken rest. Did I fail in what was kind or considerate to any of the family yesterday; I will meet her this morning with a cordial welcome, and show, in the most delicate way I can, that I am anxious to atone for the past. Was any one exhausted by the last day's exertion, I will be an hour before them this morning, and let them see that their labor is so much in advance. Or, if nothing extraordinary occurs to claim my attention, I will meet the family with a consciousness that, being the least engaged of any member of it, I am consequently the most at liberty to devote myself to the general good of the whole, by cultivating cheerful conversation, adapting myself to the prevailing tone of feeling, and leading those who are least happy, to think and speak of what will make them more so.

EVALUATE THE EVIDENCE

1. What daily tasks and duties does Sarah Stickney Ellis prescribe for the mother of the family?

2. How does this document exemplify the changes in the sexual division of labor and ideals of domesticity described in the text?

Source: Sarah Stickney Ellis, *The Women of England: Their Social Duties and Domestic Habits*, in *The Past Speaks*, 2d ed., ed. Walter Arnstein (Lexington, Mass.: D. C. Heath, 1993), 2:173.

This pessimistic view was accepted and reinforced by Friedrich Engels (1820–1895), the future revolutionary and colleague of Karl Marx (see Chapter 21). After studying conditions in northern England, this young son of a wealthy Prussian cotton manufacturer published in 1844 *The Condition of the Working Class in England*, a blistering indictment of the capitalist classes. "At the bar of world opinion," he wrote, "I charge the English middle classes with mass murder, wholesale robbery, and all the other crimes in the calendar." The new poverty of industrial workers was worse than the old poverty of cottage workers and agricultural laborers, according to Engels. The culprit was industrial capitalism, with its relentless competition and constant technical change. Engels's extremely influential charge of capitalist exploitation and increasing worker poverty was embellished by Marx and later socialists (see Chapter 21).

And if the new class interpretation was more of a deceptive simplification than a fundamental truth for some critics, it appealed to many because it seemed to explain what was happening. Therefore, conflicting classes existed, in part, because many individuals came to believe they existed and developed an appropriate sense of class feeling—what we now call class-consciousness.

Despite the criticism unleashed over industrial working conditions and the broader concerns about new class structures, some observers believed that conditions were improving for the working people. In 1835 in his study of the cotton industry, Andrew Ure (yoo-RAY) wrote that conditions in most factories were not harsh and were even quite good. Edwin Chadwick, a government official well acquainted with the problems of the working population, concluded that the "whole mass of the laboring community" was increasingly able "to buy more of the necessities and minor luxuries of life."[9] Nevertheless, those who thought—correctly—that conditions were getting worse for working people were probably in the majority.

The Early British Labor Movement

Not everyone worked in large factories and coal mines during the Industrial Revolution. In 1850 more British people still worked on farms than in any other occupation, although rural communities were suffering from outward migration. The second-largest occupation was domestic service, with more than 1 million household servants, 90 percent of whom were women. Thus many old, familiar jobs outside industry lived on and provided alternatives to industrial labor.

Within industry itself, the pattern of artisans working with hand tools in small shops remained unchanged in many trades, even as others were revolutionized by technological change. For example, the British iron industry was completely dominated by large-scale capitalist firms by 1850. Many large ironworks had more than one thousand people on their payrolls. Yet the firms that fashioned iron into small metal goods, such as tools, tableware, and toys, employed on average fewer than ten wage workers who used handicraft skills. Only gradually after 1850 did owners find ways to reorganize handicraft industries by increasing the division of labor (and thus undermining the skills and wages of workers) and also by increasing the speed and intensity of work.

Working-class solidarity and class-consciousness developed both in small workshops and in large factories. A general strike of adult cotton spinners in Manchester in 1810 testifies to the growth of anticapitalist sentiment in Britain's northern factory districts in the first decades of the nineteenth century. Commenting in 1825 on a strike in the woolen center of Bradford and the support it had gathered from other regions, one paper claimed with pride that "it is all the workers of England against a few masters of

Bradford."[10] Even in trades that did not undergo mechanization, unemployment and stagnant wages contributed to class awareness.

The classical liberal concept of economic freedom and laissez faire emerged in the late eighteenth century, and it continued to gather strength in the early nineteenth century in opposition to the rising tide of working-class anger. In 1799 Parliament passed the **Combination Acts**, which outlawed unions and strikes. In 1813 and 1814 Parliament repealed the old and often-disregarded law of 1563 regulating the wages of artisans and the conditions of apprenticeship. As a result of these and other measures, certain skilled artisan workers, such as bootmakers and high-quality tailors, found aggressive capitalists ignoring traditional work rules and trying to flood their trades with unorganized women workers and children to beat down wages.

The capitalist attack on artisan guilds and work rules was bitterly resented by many craftworkers, who subsequently played an important part in Great Britain and in other countries in gradually building a modern labor movement. The Combination Acts were widely disregarded by workers. Printers, papermakers, carpenters, tailors, and other such craftsmen continued to take collective action, and societies of skilled factory workers also organized unions in defiance of the law. Unions sought to control the number of skilled workers, to limit apprenticeship to members' own children, and to bargain with owners over wages.

In the face of such widespread union activity, Parliament repealed the Combination Acts in 1824. Unions were subsequently tolerated, though they were not fully legal until 1867. The government also kept the army in readiness to put down any worker protests deemed too unruly or threatening.

The next stage in the development of the British trade-union movement was the attempt to create a single large national union. This effort was led not so much by working people as by social reformers such as Robert Owen. Owen, a self-made cotton manufacturer (see page 675), had pioneered in industrial relations by combining firm discipline with concern for the health, safety, and hours of his workers. After 1815 he experimented with cooperative and socialist communities, including one at New Harmony, Indiana. Then in 1834 Owen was involved in the organization of one of the largest and most visionary of the early national unions, the Grand National Consolidated Trades Union.

When Owen's and other ambitious schemes collapsed, the British labor movement moved once again after 1851 in the direction of craft unions. The most famous of these was the Amalgamated Society of Engineers, which represented skilled machinists. These unions won real benefits for members by fairly conservative means and thus became an accepted part of the industrial scene.

British workers also engaged in direct political activity in defense of their own interests. After the collapse of Owen's national trade union, many working people went into the Chartist movement, which sought political democracy. The key Chartist demand—that all men be given the right to vote—became the great hope of millions of common people. Workers were also active in campaigns to limit the workday in factories to ten hours and to permit duty-free importation of wheat into Great Britain to secure cheap bread. Thus working people developed a sense of their own identity and played an active role in shaping the new industrial system. They were neither helpless victims nor passive beneficiaries.

The Impact of Slavery

Another mass labor force of the Industrial Revolution consisted of the millions of en-slaved men, women, and children who toiled in European colonies in the Caribbean and in North and South America. Historians have long debated the extent to which revenue from slavery contributed to Britain's achievements in the Industrial Revolution.

Most now agree that profits from colonial plantations and slave trading were a small portion of British national income in the eighteenth century and were probably more often invested in land than in industry. Nevertheless, the impact of slavery on Britain's economy was much broader than its direct profits alone. In the mid-eighteenth century the need for items to exchange for colonial cotton, sugar, tobacco, and slaves stimulated demand for British manufactured goods in the Caribbean, North America, and West Africa. Britain's dominance in the slave trade also led to the development of finance and credit institutions that helped early industrialists obtain capital for their businesses. Investments in canals, roads, and railroads made possible by profits from colonial trade provided the necessary infrastructure to move raw materials and products of the factory system.

The British Parliament abolished the slave trade in 1807 and freed all slaves in British territories in 1833, but by 1850 most of the cotton processed by British mills was supplied by the labor of enslaved people in the southern United States. Thus the Industrial Revolution was deeply entangled with the Atlantic world and the misery of slavery.

Notes

1. N. F. R. Crafts, *British Economic Growth During the Industrial Revolution* (Oxford, U.K.: Oxford University Press, 1985), p. 32.
2. P. Bairoch, "International Industrialization Levels from 1750 to 1980," *Journal of European Economic History* 11 (Spring 1982): 269–333.
3. Quoted in J. Bowditch and C. Ramsland, eds., *Voices of the Industrial Revolution* (Ann Arbor: University of Michigan Press, 1961), p. 55, from the fourth edition of Thomas Malthus, *Essay on the Principle of Population* (1807).
4. Quoted in Emma Griffin, *A Short History of the British Industrial Revolution* (Basingstoke, U.K.: Palgrave Macmillan, 2010), p. 126.
5. Quoted in E. R. Pike, *"Hard Times": Human Documents of the Industrial Revolution* (New York: Praeger, 1966), p. 109.
6. See especially J. Brenner and M. Rama, "Rethinking Women's Oppression," *New Left Review* 144 (March–April 1984): 33–71, and sources cited there.
7. J. Humphries, ". . . 'The Most Free from Objection' . . . The Sexual Division of Labor and Women's Work in Nineteenth-Century England," *Journal of Economic History* 47 (December 1987): 941; Pike, *"Hard Times,"* p. 266.
8. Quoted in Pike, *"Hard Times,"* p. 208.
9. Quoted in W. A. Hayek, ed., *Capitalism and the Historians* (Chicago: University of Chicago Press, 1954), p. 126.
10. Quoted in D. Geary, ed., *Labour and Socialist Movements in Europe Before 1914* (Oxford, U.K.: Berg, 1989), p. 29.

Chapter Review

MAKE IT STICK

 LearningCurve
bedfordstmartins.com/mckaywestvalue
After reading the chapter, use LearningCurve to retain what
you've read.

IDENTIFY KEY TERMS

Identify and explain the significance of each item below.

Industrial Revolution (p. 656)   **tariff protection** (p. 670)
spinning jenny (p. 657)   **Factory Acts** (p. 675)
water frame (p. 657)   **separate spheres** (p. 675)
steam engines (p. 660)   **Mines Act of 1842** (p. 678)
Rocket (p. 662)   **class-consciousness** (p. 679)
Crystal Palace (p. 664)   **Luddites** (p. 680)
iron law of wages (p. 665)   **Combination Acts** (p. 683)

REVIEW THE MAIN IDEAS

Answer the focus questions from each section of the chapter.

* What were the origins of the Industrial Revolution in Britain, and how did
  it develop between 1780 and 1850? (p. 655)

* How did countries outside of Britain respond to the challenge of industrialization? (p. 665)

* How did work evolve during the Industrial Revolution, and how did daily
  life change for working people? (p. 673)

* How did the changes brought about by the Industrial Revolution lead to
  new social classes, and how did people respond to the new structure?
  (p. 679)

MAKE CONNECTIONS

**Think about the larger developments and continuities within and
across chapters.**

1. Why did Great Britain take the lead in industrialization and when did
   other countries begin to adopt the new techniques and organization of
   production?

2. How did the achievements in agriculture and rural industry of the late
   seventeenth and eighteenth centuries (Chapter 17) pave the way for the
   Industrial Revolution of the late eighteenth century?

ONLINE DOCUMENT ASSIGNMENT

Josiah Wedgwood

How did observers of early industrialization imagine the relationship between workers and their work, and between workers and their employers?

You encountered Josiah Wedgwood's story on page 662. Keeping the question above in mind, go online and explore different views on the impact of industrial production on individual workers in light of Wedgwood's approach to industrial labor. Then complete a writing assignment based on the evidence and details from this chapter.

bedfordstmartins.com/mckaywestvalue

CHRONOLOGY

ca. 1765	• Hargreaves invents spinning jenny; Arkwright creates water frame
1769	• Watt patents modern steam engine
1775–1783	• American Revolution
ca. 1780–1850	• Industrial Revolution; population boom in Britain
1799	• Combination Acts passed
1802–1833	• Series of Factory Acts passed by British government to limit the workday of child laborers and set minimum hygiene and safety requirements
1810	• Strike of Manchester cotton spinners
ca. 1815	• Western European countries seek to adopt British industrial methods
1824	• Combination Acts repealed
1829	• Stephenson introduces the *Rocket*, an early locomotive
1830s	• Industrial banks in Belgium
1834	• *Zollverein* erected among most German states
1842	• Mines Act passed in Britain
1844	• Engels publishes *The Condition of the Working Class in England*
1850s	• Japan begins to adopt Western technologies; industrial gap widens between the West and the rest of the world
1851	• Great Exhibition held at Crystal Palace in London
1860s	• Germany and the United States begin to rapidly industrialize

21

LearningCurve
bedfordstmartins.com/mckaywestvalue
After reading the chapter, use
LearningCurve to retain what
you've read.

Ideologies and Upheavals

1815–1850

THE MOMENTOUS ECONOMIC AND POLITICAL TRANSFORMATION OF
modern times that began in the late eighteenth century with the "unfinished"
revolutions—the Industrial Revolution in England and the political revolution
in France—would play out with unpredictable consequences in the first half
of the nineteenth century. Attempts to manage the progressive forces associated with the French Revolution led first to a reassertion of conservative
political control in continental Europe. Following the leadership of Austrian
foreign minister Klemens von Metternich, the aristocratic leaders of the Great
Powers sought to stamp out the spread of liberal and democratic reforms.

The political and cultural innovations made possible by the unfinished
revolutions proved difficult to contain, however. In politics, powerful new
ideologies—liberalism, nationalism, and socialism—emerged to oppose
Metternich's revitalized conservatism. In literature, art, and music, romanticism—an intellectual and artistic movement that challenged the certainties
of the Enlightenment and fed the growth of popular nationalism—captured
the intensity of the era. A successful revolution in Greece, liberal reform in
Great Britain, and popular unrest in France gave voice to ordinary people's
desire for political and social change. All these movements helped launch the
great wave of revolutions that swept across Europe in 1848.

The Aftermath of the Napoleonic Wars

How was peace restored and maintained after 1815?

The eventual eruption of revolutionary political forces was by no means predictable as the Napoleonic era ended. Quite the contrary. After finally defeating Napoleon, the conservative, aristocratic monarchies of Russia, Prussia, Austria, and Great Britain — known as the Quadruple Alliance — reaffirmed their determination to hold France in line. Other international questions remained unresolved. Even before Napoleon's final defeat, the allies had agreed to meet to fashion a general peace accord in 1814 at the Congress of Vienna, where they faced a great challenge: how could they construct a lasting settlement that would not sow the seeds of another war? By carefully managing the balance of power and embracing conservative restoration, they brokered an agreement that contributed to fifty years of peace in Europe (Map 21.1).

The European Balance of Power

The allied powers were concerned first and foremost with the defeated enemy, France. Agreeing to the restoration of the Bourbon dynasty (see Chapter 19), the allies offered France lenient terms after Napoleon's abdication. The first Treaty of Paris, signed before Napoleon escaped from Elba and attacked the Bourbon regime, gave France the boundaries it had possessed in 1792, which were larger than those of 1789. In addition, France did not have to pay war reparations. Thus the victorious powers avoided provoking a spirit of victimization and desire for revenge in the defeated country.

Representatives of the Quadruple Alliance (plus a representative of the restored Bourbon monarch of France) fashioned the peace at the Congress of Vienna from September 1814 to June 1815, with minor assistance from a host of delegates from the smaller European states. One of the main tasks of the four allies was to raise a number of formidable barriers against renewed French aggression. The Low Countries — Belgium and Holland — were united under an enlarged Dutch monarchy capable of opposing France more effectively. Prussia received considerably more territory on France's eastern border so as to stand as the "sentinel on the Rhine" against France. In these ways, the Quadruple Alliance combined leniency toward France with strong defensive measures.

Self-interest and traditional ideas about the balance of power motivated allied moderation toward France. To Klemens von Metternich (MEH-tuhr-nihk) and Robert Castlereagh (KA-suhl-ray), the foreign ministers of Austria and Great Britain, respectively, as well as their French counterpart, Charles Talleyrand, the balance of power meant an international equilibrium of political and military forces that would discourage aggression by any combination of states or, worse, the domination of Europe by any single state.

The Great Powers — Austria, Britain, Prussia, Russia, and France — used the balance of power to settle their own dangerous disputes at the Congress of Vienna. The victors generally agreed that each of them should receive compensation in the form of territory for their successful struggle against the French. Great Britain had already won colonies and strategic outposts during the long wars. Austria gave up territories in Belgium and southern Germany but expanded greatly elsewhere, taking the rich provinces of Venetia and Lombardy in northern Italy as well as former Polish possessions and new lands on

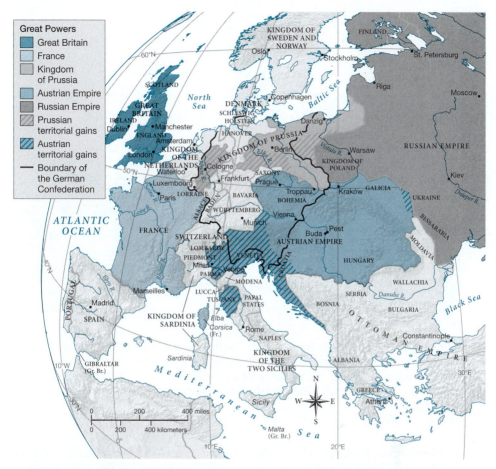

MAP 21.1   Europe in 1815
In 1815 Europe contained many different states, but after the defeat of Napoleon, international politics was dominated by the five Great Powers: Russia, Prussia, Austria, Great Britain, and France. (The number rises to six if one includes the Ottoman Empire.)

the eastern coast of the Adriatic. Russian and Prussian claims for territorial expansion were more contentious. When France, Austria, and Great Britain all argued for limited gain, Russia accepted a small Polish kingdom and Prussia took only part of Saxony in addition to its gains to the west (see Map 21.1). This compromise fell very much within the framework of balance-of-power ideology.

Unfortunately for France, Napoleon suddenly escaped from his "comic kingdom" on the island of Elba and reignited his wars of expansion for a brief time (see Chapter 19). Yet the second Treaty of Paris, concluded after Napoleon's final defeat at Waterloo in 1815, was still relatively moderate toward France. Fat, old Louis XVIII was restored to his throne for a second time. France lost only a little territory, had to pay an indemnity of 700 million francs, and had to support a large army of occupation for five years. The rest of the settlement concluded at the Congress of Vienna was left intact. The

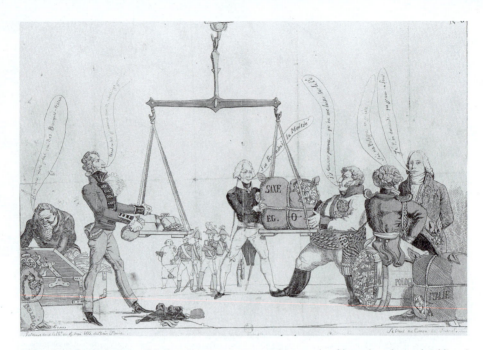

Adjusting the Balance   This French cartoon captures the essence of how the educated public thought about the balance-of-power diplomacy resulting in the Treaty of Vienna. The Englishman on the left uses his money to counterbalance the people that the Prussian and the fat Metternich are gaining in Saxony and Italy. Alexander I sits happily on his prize, Poland. (Bibliothèque nationale de France)

members of the Quadruple Alliance, however, did agree to meet periodically to discuss their common interests and to consider appropriate measures for the maintenance of peace in Europe. This agreement marked the beginning of the European "Congress System," which lasted long into the nineteenth century and settled many international crises peacefully, through international conferences or "congresses" and balance-of-power diplomacy.

Metternich and Conservatism

The political ideals of conservatism, often associated with Austrian foreign minister Prince Klemens von Metternich (1773–1859), dominated Great Power discussions at the Congress of Vienna. Metternich's determined defense of the monarchical status quo made him a villain in the eyes of most progressive, liberal thinkers of the nineteenth century. Yet rather than denounce his politics, we can try to understand the general conservatism he represented. Born into the middle ranks of the landed nobility of the Rhineland, Metternich was an internationally oriented aristocrat who made a brilliant diplomatic career. Austrian foreign minister from 1809 to 1848, the cosmopolitan and conservative Metternich had a pessimistic view of human nature, which he believed was ever prone to error, excess, and self-serving behavior. The disruptive events of the French Revolution and the Napoleonic Wars confirmed these views, and Metternich's conservatism would emerge as a powerful new political ideological force in response to the revolutionary age.

Metternich firmly believed that liberalism, as embodied in revolutionary America and France, bore the responsibility for the untold bloodshed and suffering caused by twenty-five years of war. Like Edmund Burke (see Chapter 19) and other conservatives, Metternich blamed liberal middle-class revolutionaries for stirring up the lower classes. Authoritarian governments, he concluded, were necessary to protect society from the baser elements of human behavior, which were easily released in a democratic system. Organized religion was another pillar of strong government; Metternich despised the anticlericalism of the Enlightenment and the French Revolution and maintained that Christian morality was a vital bulwark against radical change.

Metternich defended his class and its rights and privileges with a clear conscience. The church and nobility were among Europe's most ancient and valuable institutions, and conservatives regarded tradition as the basic foundation of human society.

The threat of liberalism appeared doubly dangerous to Metternich because it generally went with aspirations for national independence. Liberals believed that each people, each national group, had a right to establish its own independent government and fulfill its own destiny. The idea of national self-determination under constitutional government was repellent to Metternich because it threatened to revolutionize central Europe and destroy the Austrian Empire.

After centuries of war, royal intermarriage, and territorial expansion, the vast Austrian Empire of the Habsburgs included many peoples within its borders (Map 21.2). Germans made up about one-fourth of the population. Large numbers of Magyars (Hungarians), Czechs, Italians, Poles, and Ukrainians lived alongside each other in the imperial state, as did smaller groups of Slovenes, Croats, Serbs, and Romanians. The various Slavic groups, together with the Italians and the Romanians, were widely scattered and completely divided, yet they outnumbered the politically dominant Germans and Hungarians. Different ethnic groups mingled in the same provinces and the same villages. The peoples of the Austrian Empire spoke at least eleven different languages, observed vastly different customs, and lived with a surprising variety of regional civic and political institutions.

The multiethnic state Metternich served had strengths and weaknesses. A large population and vast territories gave the empire economic and military clout, but its potentially dissatisfied nationalities undermined political unity. In these circumstances, Metternich virtually had to oppose liberalism and nationalism—if Austria was to remain intact and powerful, it could hardly accommodate ideologies that supported national self-determination.

On Austria's borders, Russia and, to a lesser extent, the Ottoman Empire supported and echoed Metternich's efforts to hold back liberalism and nationalism. Bitter enemies, these far-flung empires were both absolutist states with powerful armies and long traditions of expansion and conquest. Because of those conquests, both were also multinational empires with many peoples, languages, and religions, but in each case most of the ruling elite came from the dominant ethnic group—the Orthodox Christian Russians of central and northern Russia and the Muslim Ottoman Turks of Anatolia (much of modern Turkey). After 1815 both of these multinational absolutist states worked to preserve their respective traditional conservative orders. Only after 1840 did each in turn experience a profound crisis and embark on a program of fundamental reform and modernization, as we shall see in Chapter 23.

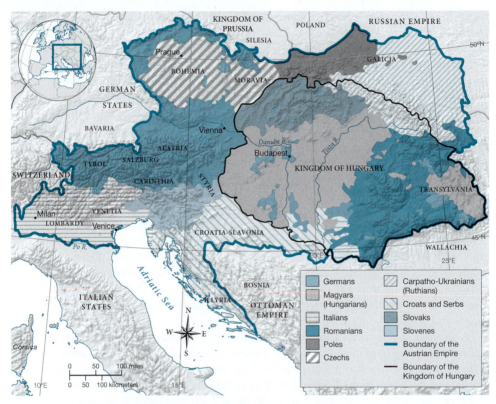

MAP 21.2   Peoples of the Habsburg Monarchy, 1815
The old dynastic state ruled by the Habsburg monarchy was a patchwork of nationalities and ethnic groups, in which territorial borders barely reflected the diversity of where different peoples actually lived. Note especially the widely scattered pockets of Germans and Hungarians. How do you think this ethnic diversity might have led to the rise of national independence movements in the Austrian Empire?

Repressing the Revolutionary Spirit

Conservative political ideologies had important practical consequences. Under Metternich's leadership, Austria, Prussia, and Russia embarked on a decades-long crusade against the liberties and civil rights associated with the French and American Revolutions. The first step was the formation in September 1815 of the **Holy Alliance** by Austria, Prussia, and Russia. First proposed by Russia's Alexander I, the alliance worked to repress reformist and revolutionary movements and stifle desires for national independence across Europe.

The conservative restoration first brought its collective power to bear on southern Europe. In 1820 revolutionaries successfully forced the monarchs of Spain and the southern Italian Kingdom of the Two Sicilies to establish constitutional monarchies, with press freedoms, universal male suffrage, and other liberal reforms. Metternich was horrified: revolution was rising once again. Calling a conference at Troppau in Austria, he and Alexander I proclaimed the principle of active intervention to maintain all autocratic regimes whenever they were threatened. Austrian forces then marched into Naples in 1821 and restored the autocratic power of Ferdinand I in the Two Sicilies. A French invasion of Spain in 1823 likewise returned power to the king there.

The conservative policies of Metternich and the Holy Alliance crushed reform not only in Austria and the Italian peninsula but also in the entire German Confederation, which the peace settlement of Vienna had called into being. The new confederation, a loose association of German-speaking states based on Napoleon's reorganization of the territory, replaced the roughly three hundred principalities, free cities, and dynastic states of the Holy Roman Empire with just thirty-eight German states, dominated by Prussia and Austria (see Map 21.1). The states in the German Confederation retained independence, and though ambassadors from each met in a Confederation Diet, or assembly, it had little real political power. When liberal reformers and university students began to protest for the national unification of the German states, the Austrian and Prussian leadership used the diet to issue and enforce the infamous **Karlsbad Decrees** in 1819. These decrees required the German states to outlaw liberal political organizations, police their universities and newspapers, and establish a permanent committee with spies and informers to clamp down on liberal or radical reformers. (See "Primary Source: Metternich: Conservative Reaction in the German Confederation," page 694.)

The forces of reaction squelched reform in Russia as well. In St. Petersburg in December 1825, a group of about three thousand army officers inspired by liberal ideals staged a protest against the new tsar, Nicholas I. Troops loyal to Nicholas I surrounded and assaulted the group with gunfire, cavalry, and cannon, leaving some sixty men dead; the surviving leaders were publicly hanged, and the rest sent to exile in Siberia. Through military might, secret police, imprisonment, and execution, conservative regimes in central Europe used the powers of the state to repress liberal reform wherever possible.

Limits to Conservative Power and Revolution in South America

Metternich liked to call himself "the chief Minister of Police in Europe," and in the following years, the members of the Holy Alliance continued to battle against liberal political change.[1] While Metternich's system proved quite effective in central Europe, at least until 1848, the monarchists failed to stop dynastic change in France in 1830 or prevent Belgium from winning independence from the Netherlands in 1831.

The most dramatic challenge to conservative power occurred not in Europe, but overseas in South America. In the 1820s South American elites rose up and broke away from the Spanish crown and established a number of new republics based at first on liberal, Enlightenment ideals. The leaders of the revolutions were primarily wealthy Creoles, direct descendants of Spanish parents born in the Americas. The well-established and powerful Creoles — only about 5 percent of the population — resented the political and economic control of an even smaller elite minority of *peninsulares*, people born in Spain who lived in and ruled the colonies. The vast majority of the population, composed of "mestizos" and "mulattos" (people of ethnically mixed heritage), enslaved and freed Africans, and native indigenous peoples, languished at the bottom of the social pyramid.

By the late 1700s the Creoles had begun to question Spanish policy and even the necessity of further colonial rule. The spark for revolt came during the Napoleonic Wars, when the French occupation of Spain in 1808 weakened the power of the autocratic

PRIMARY SOURCE   Metternich: Conservative Reaction in the German Confederation

In 1819 a member of a radical student fraternity at the German University of Jena assassinated the conservative author and diplomat August von Kotzebue. Metternich used the murder as an excuse to promulgate the repressive Karlsbad Decrees, excerpted below, which clamped down on liberal nationalists in the universities and the press throughout the German Confederation.

Law on Universities

1. A special representative of the ruler of each state shall be appointed for each university, with appropriate instructions and extended powers, and shall reside in the place where the university is situated. . . .

The function of this agent shall be to see to the strictest enforcement of existing laws and disciplinary regulations; to observe carefully the spirit which is shown by the instructors in the university in their public lectures and regular courses, and, without directly interfering in scientific matters or in the methods of teaching, to give a salutary direction to the instruction, having in view the future attitude of the students. Lastly, he shall devote unceasing attention to everything that may promote morality, good order, and outward propriety among the students. . . .

2. The confederated governments mutually pledge themselves to remove from the universities or other public educational institutions all teachers who, by obvious deviation from their duty, or by exceeding the limits of their functions, or by the abuse of their legitimate influence over the youthful minds, or by propagating harmful doctrines hostile to public order or subversive of existing governmental institutions, shall have unmistakably proved their unfitness for the important office intrusted to them. . . .

[Articles 3 and 4 ordered the universities to enforce laws against secret student societies.]

Press Law

1. So long as this decree shall remain in force no publication which appears in the form of daily issues, or as a serial not exceeding twenty sheets of printed matter,

---

Spanish crown and the Napoleonic rhetoric of rights inspired revolutionaries. Yet the Creoles hesitated, worried that open revolt might upend the social pyramid or even lead to a slave revolution as in Haiti (see Chapter 19).

The South American revolutions thus began from below, with spontaneous uprisings by subordinated peoples of color. Creole leaders quickly emerged to take control of a struggle that would prove to be more prolonged and violent than the American Revolution, with outcomes less clear. In the north, the competent general Simón Bolívar—the Latin American equivalent of George Washington—defeated Spanish forces and established a short-lived "Gran Colombia," which lasted from 1819 to 1830. Bolívar, the "people's liberator," dreamed of establishing a federation of South American states, modeled on the United States. To the south, José de San Martín, a liberal-minded military commander, successfully threw off Spanish control by 1825.

shall go to press in any state of the union without the previous knowledge and approval of the state officials. . . .

6. The Diet shall have the right, moreover, to suppress on its own authority, without being petitioned, such writings included in Article 1, in whatever German state they may appear, as, in the opinion of a commission appointed by it, are inimical to the honor of the union, the safety of individual states, or the maintenance of peace and quiet in Germany. There shall be no appeal from such decisions. . . .

Establishment of an Investigative Committee

1. Within a fortnight, reckoned from the passage of this decree, there shall convene, under the auspices of the Confederation . . . an extraordinary commission of investigation to consist of seven members, including the chairman.

2. The object of the commission shall be a joint investigation, as thorough and extensive as possible, of the facts relating to the origin and manifold ramifications of the revolutionary plots and demagogical associations directed against the existing constitution and the internal peace both of the union and of the individual states.

EVALUATE THE EVIDENCE

1. How do the regulations in the decrees express the spirit of reactionary politics after the Napoleonic Wars?

2. The decrees were periodically renewed until finally overturned during the revolutions of 1848. How effective were they in checking the growth of liberal politics?

Source: James Harvey Robinson, *Readings in European History*, vol. 2 (Boston: Ginn and Company, 1906), pp. 547–550.

Dreams of South American federation and unity proved difficult to implement. By 1830 the large northern state established by Bolívar had fractured, and by 1840 the borders of the new nations looked much like the map of Latin America today. Most of the new states initially received liberal constitutions, but these were difficult to implement in lands where the vast majority of people had no experience with constitutional rule and women and the great underclass of non-Creoles were not allowed to vote. Experiments with liberal constitutions soon gave way to a new political system controlled by *caudillos* (cow-DEE-yohs), or strong men, sometimes labeled warlords. Often former Creoles, the caudillos ruled limited territories on the basis of military strength, family patronage, and populist politics. The South American revolutions had failed to establish lasting constitutional republics, but they did demonstrate the revolutionary potential of liberal ideals and the limits on conservative control.

The Spread of Radical Ideas

What new ideologies emerged to challenge conservatism?

In the years following the peace settlement of 1815, intellectuals and social observers sought to harness the radical ideas of the revolutionary age to new political movements. Many rejected conservatism, with its stress on tradition, a hereditary monarchy, a privileged landowning aristocracy, and an official state church. Often inspired by liberties championed during the French Revolution, radical thinkers developed and refined alternative ideologies—or political philosophies—and tried to convince society to act on them. In so doing, they helped articulate the basic political ideals that continue to shape Western society today.

Liberalism and the Middle Class

The principal ideas of liberalism—liberty and equality—were by no means defeated in 1815. First realized successfully in the American Revolution and then achieved in part in the French Revolution, liberalism demanded representative government as opposed to autocratic monarchy, and equality before the law as opposed to legally separate classes. The idea of liberty also meant specific individual freedoms: freedom of the press, freedom of speech, freedom of assembly, freedom of worship, and freedom from arbitrary arrest. Such ideas are still the guiding beliefs in modern democratic states, but in Europe in 1815 only France with Louis XVIII's Constitutional Charter and Great Britain with its Parliament had realized any of the liberal program. Even in those countries, liberalism had only begun to succeed.

Although conservatives still saw liberalism as a profound threat, it had gained a group of powerful adherents: the new upper classes made wealthy through growing industrialization and global commerce. Liberal economic principles, the doctrine of laissez faire (lay-say FEHR), called for free trade (including relaxation of import/export duties), unrestricted private enterprise, and no government interference in the economy.

As we saw in Chapter 17, Adam Smith posited the idea of free-market capitalism in 1776 in opposition to mercantilism and its attempt to regulate trade. Smith argued that freely competitive private enterprise would give all citizens a fair and equal opportunity to do what they did best and would result in greater income for everyone, not just the rich. (Smith's form of liberalism is often called "classical" liberalism in the United States in order to distinguish it sharply from modern American liberalism, which usually favors more government programs to meet social needs and to regulate the economy.)

In the first half of the nineteenth century, liberal political ideals became closely associated with narrow class interests. Starting in the 1820s in Britain, business elites enthusiastically embraced laissez-faire policies because they proved immensely profitable, and used liberal ideas to defend their right to do as they wished in their factories. Labor unions were outlawed because, these elites argued, unions restricted free competition and the individual's "right to work." Early-nineteenth-century liberals favored representative government, but they generally wanted property qualifications attached to the right to vote. In practice, this meant limiting the vote to very small numbers of the well-to-do. Workers, peasants, and women, as well as middle-class shopkeepers, clerks, and artisans, did not own the necessary property and thus could not vote.

As liberalism became increasingly identified with upper-class business interests, some opponents of conservatism felt that liberalism did not go nearly far enough. Inspired by memories of the French Revolution and the example of Jacksonian democracy in the young American republic, these republicans expanded liberal ideology to include universal voting rights, at least for males. Republicans were more radical than the liberals, and they were more willing than most liberals to endorse violent upheaval to achieve goals. As a result, liberals and radical republicans could join forces against conservatives only up to a point.

The Growing Appeal of Nationalism

Nationalism—an idea destined to have an enormous influence in the modern world—was another radical idea that gained popularity in the years after 1815. The nascent power of nationalism was revealed in the success of the French armies in the revolutionary and Napoleonic Wars, when soldiers inspired by patriotic loyalty to the French nation achieved victory after victory (see Chapter 19). Early nationalists found inspiration in the vision of a people united by a common language, a common history and culture, and a common territory. In German-speaking central Europe, defeat by Napoleon's armies had made the vision of a national people united in defense of their "fatherland" particularly attractive.

In the early nineteenth century such national unity was more a dream than a reality as far as most ethnic groups or nationalities were concerned. Local dialects abounded, even in relatively cohesive countries like France, where peasants from nearby villages often failed to understand each other. Moreover, a variety of ethnic groups shared the territory of most states, not just the Austrian, Russian, and Ottoman Empires discussed earlier. Over the course of the nineteenth century, nationalism nonetheless gathered force as a political philosophy. Advancing literacy rates, the establishment of a mass press, the growth of large state bureaucracies, compulsory education, and conscription armies all created a common culture that encouraged ordinary people to take pride in their national heritage.

In multiethnic states, however, nationalism also promoted disintegration. Recognizing the power of the "national idea," European nationalists—generally educated, middle-class liberals and intellectuals—sought to turn the cultural unity that they desired into political reality. They believed that every nation, like every citizen, had the right to exist in freedom and to develop its unique character and spirit, and they hoped to make the territory of each people coincide with well-defined borders in an independent nation-state.

This political goal made nationalism explosive, particularly in central and eastern Europe, where different peoples overlapped and intermingled. As discussed, the Austrian, Russian, and Ottoman central states refused to allow national minorities independence; that suppression fomented widespread discontent among nationalists who wanted freedom from oppressive imperial rule. In the many different principalities of the Italian peninsula and the German Confederation, to the contrary, nationalists yearned for national unification across what they saw as divisive and obsolete state borders. Whether they sought independence or unification, before 1850 nationalist movements were fresh, idealistic, and progressive, if not revolutionary.

In recent years scholars have tried to understand how the nationalist vision, often fitting so poorly with existing conditions and promising so much upheaval, was so successful in the long run. Of fundamental importance in the rise of nationalism was the development of a complex industrial and urban society, which required much better communication between individuals and groups.[2] This need for improved communication promoted the use of a standardized national language in many areas, creating at least a superficial cultural unity as a standard tongue spread through mass education and the emergence of the popular press. When a minority population was large and concentrated, the nationalist campaign for a standardized language often led the minority group to push for a separate nation-state.

Many scholars also argue that nations are recent creations, the product of a new, self-conscious nationalist ideology. Thus nation-states emerged in the nineteenth century as "imagined communities" that sought to bind millions of strangers together around the abstract concept of an all-embracing national identity. This meant bringing citizens together with emotionally charged symbols and ceremonies, such as independence holidays and patriotic parades. On these occasions the imagined nation of spiritual equals might celebrate its most hallowed traditions, which were often recent inventions.[3]

Between 1815 and 1850 most people who believed in nationalism also believed in either liberalism or radical republicanism. A deep belief in the creativity and nobility of the people linked these two concepts. Liberals and especially democrats saw the people as the ultimate source of all government. Yet liberals and nationalists agreed that the benefits of self-government would be possible only if the people were united by common traditions that transcended local interests and even class differences. Thus the liberty of the individual and the love of a free nation overlapped greatly in the early nineteenth century.

Despite some confidence that a world system based on independent nations would promote global harmony, early nationalists eagerly emphasized the differences among peoples and developed a strong sense of "us" versus "them." To this "us-them" outlook, it was all too easy for nationalists to add two highly volatile ingredients: a sense of national mission and a sense of national superiority. As Europe entered an age of increased global interaction, these two underlying ideas would lead to aggression and conflict, as powerful nation-states backed by patriotic citizens competed with each other on the international stage.

The Foundations of Modern Socialism

More radical than liberalism or nationalism was **socialism**. Early socialist thinkers were a diverse group with wide-ranging ideas. Yet they shared a sense that the political revolution in France, the growth of industrialization in Britain, and the rise of laissez faire had created a profound spiritual and moral crisis. Modern capitalism, they believed, fomented a selfish individualism that encouraged inequality and split the community into isolated fragments. Society urgently required fundamental change to re-establish cooperation and a new sense of community.

Early socialists felt an intense desire to help the poor, and they preached that the rich and the poor should be more nearly equal economically. To this end, they believed that private property should be strictly regulated by the government, or abolished outright and replaced by state or community ownership. Economic planning, greater social equality, and state regulation of property were the key ideas of early socialism—and of all socialism since.

One influential group of early socialist advocates became known as the "utopian socialists" because their grand schemes for social improvement ultimately proved unworkable. The Frenchmen Count Henri de Saint-Simon (awn-REE duh san-see-MOHN) (1760–1825) and Charles Fourier (sharl FAWR-ee-ay) (1772–1837) and the British industrialist Robert Owen all founded movements intended to establish model communities that would usher in a new age of happiness and equality.

Saint-Simon optimistically proclaimed the tremendous possibilities of industrial development: "The golden age of the human species . . . is before us!"[4] The key to progress was proper social organization that required the "parasites"—the court, the aristocracy, lawyers, and churchmen—to give way, once and for all, to the "doers"—the leading scientists, engineers, and industrialists. The doers would carefully plan the economy and guide it forward by undertaking vast public works projects and establishing investment banks. Saint-Simon also stressed in highly moralistic terms that every social institution ought to have as its main goal improved conditions for the poor.

After 1830 the utopian critique of capitalism became sharper. Charles Fourier envisaged a socialist utopia of mathematically precise, self-sufficient communities called "phalanxes," each made up of 1,620 people. Fourier was also an early proponent of the total emancipation of women. According to Fourier, under capitalism young single women were shamelessly "sold" to their future husbands for dowries and other financial considerations. Therefore, he called for the abolition of marriage and for sexual freedom and free unions based only on love. The great British utopian Robert Owen, an early promoter of labor unions, likewise called for society to be reorganized into model industrial-agricultural communities. Saint-Simon, Fourier, and Owen all had followers who tried to put their ideas into practice. Though these attempts had basically collapsed by the 1850s, utopian socialist ideas remained an inspiration for future reformers and revolutionaries.

Some socialist thinkers embraced the even more radical ideas of anarchism. In his 1840 pamphlet *What Is Property?* Pierre-Joseph Proudhon (1809–1865), a self-educated printer, famously argued that "property is theft!" Property, he claimed, was profit that was stolen from the worker, the source of all wealth. Distrustful of all authority and political systems, Proudhon believed that states should be abolished and that society should be organized in loose associations of working people.

Other early socialists, like Louis Blanc (1811–1882), a sharp-eyed, intelligent journalist, focused on more practical reforms. In his *Organization of Work* (1839), he urged workers to agitate for universal voting rights and to take control of the state peacefully. Blanc believed that the state should set up government-funded workshops and factories to guarantee full employment. The right to work had to become as sacred as any other right.

As industrialization advanced in European cities, working people began to embrace the socialist message. This happened first in France, where workers cherished the memory of the radical phase of the French Revolution and became violently opposed to laissez-faire laws that denied their right to organize in guilds and unions. Developing a sense of class in the process of their protests, workers favored collective action and government intervention in economic life. Thus the aspirations of workers and radical theorists reinforced each other, and a genuine socialist movement emerged in Paris in the 1830s and 1840s.

The Birth of Marxist Socialism

In the 1840s France was the center of socialism, but in the following decades the German intellectual Karl Marx (1818–1883) would weave the diffuse strands of socialist thought into a distinctly modern ideology. Marxist socialism — or **Marxism** — would have a lasting impact on political thought and practice.

The son of a Jewish lawyer who had converted to Lutheranism, the young Marx was a brilliant student. After earning a Ph.D. in philosophy at Humboldt University in Berlin in 1841, he turned to journalism, and his critical articles about the laboring poor caught the attention of the Prussian police. Forced to flee Prussia in 1843, Marx traveled around Europe, promoting socialism and avoiding the authorities. He lived a modest, middle-class life with his wife, Jenny, and their children, often relying on his friend and colleague Friedrich Engels (see Chapter 20) for financial support. After the revolutions of 1848, Marx settled in London, where he spent the rest of his life as an advocate of working-class revolution. *Capital*, his magnum opus, appeared in 1867.

Marx was a dedicated scholar, and his work united sociology, economics, philosophy, and history in an impressive synthesis. From Scottish and English political economists like Adam Smith and David Ricardo, Marx learned to apply social-scientific analysis to economic problems, though he pushed these liberal ideas in radical directions. Deeply influenced by the utopian socialists, Marx championed ideals of social equality and community. He criticized his socialist predecessors, however, for their fanciful utopian schemes, claiming that his version of "scientific" socialism was rooted in historic law, and therefore realistic. Following German philosophies of idealism associated with Georg Hegel (1770–1831), Marx came to believe that history had patterns and purpose and moved forward in stages toward an ultimate goal.

Bringing these ideas together, Marx argued that class struggle over economic wealth was the great engine of human history. In his view, one class had always exploited the other, and with the advent of modern industry, society was split more clearly than ever before: between

Mr. and Mrs. Karl Marx Active in the revolution of 1848, Marx fled from Germany in 1849 and settled in London. There Marx and his young wife lived a respectable middle-class life while he wrote *Capital*, the weighty exposition of his socialist theories. Marx also worked to organize the working class, and he earned a modest income as a journalist and received financial support from his coauthor and lifelong friend, Friedrich Engels. (Time Life Pictures/Mansell/ Getty Images)

the upper class—the **bourgeoisie** (boor-ZHWAH-zee)—and the working class—the **proletariat**. The bourgeoisie, a tiny minority, owned the means of production and grew rich by exploiting the labor of workers. Over time, Marx argued, the proletariat would grow ever larger and ever poorer, and their increasing alienation would lead them to develop a sense of revolutionary class-consciousness. Then, just as the bourgeoisie had triumphed over the feudal aristocracy in the French Revolution, the proletariat would overthrow the bourgeoisie in a violent revolutionary cataclysm. The result would be the end of class struggle and the arrival of communism, a system of radical equality.

Fascinated by the rapid expansion of modern capitalism, Marx based his revolutionary program on an insightful yet critical analysis of economic history. Under feudalism, he wrote, labor had been organized according to long-term contracts of rights and privileges. Under capitalism, to the contrary, labor was a commodity like any other, bought and sold for wages in the free market. The goods workers produced were always worth more than what those workers were paid, and the difference—"surplus value," in Marx's terms—was pocketed by the bourgeoisie in the form of profit.

Capitalism for Marx was immensely productive but highly exploitative. In a never-ending search for profit, the bourgeoisie would squeeze workers dry and then expand across the globe, until all parts of the world were trapped in capitalist relations of production. Contemporary ideals, such as free trade, private property, and even marriage and Christian morality, were myths that masked and legitimized class exploitation. To many people, Marx's argument that the contradictions inherent in this unequal system would eventually be overcome in a working-class revolution, appeared to be the irrefutable capstone of a brilliant interpretation of historical trends.

When Marx and Engels published *The Communist Manifesto* on the eve of the revolutions of 1848, their opening claim that "a spectre is haunting Europe—the spectre of Communism" was highly exaggerated. The Communist movement was in its infancy; scattered groups of socialists, anarchists, and labor leaders were hardly united around Marxist ideas. But by the time Marx died in 1883, Marxist socialism had profoundly reshaped left-wing radicalism in ways that would inspire revolutionaries around the world for the next one hundred years.

The Romantic Movement

What were the characteristics of the romantic movement?

The early nineteenth century brought changes to literature and the other arts as well as political ideas. Followers of the new romantic movement, or romanticism, revolted against the emphasis on rationality, order, and restraint that characterized the Enlightenment and the controlled style of classicism. Forerunners appeared from about 1750 on, but the movement crystallized fully in the 1790s, primarily in England and Germany. Romanticism gained strength and swept across Europe until the 1840s, when it gradually gave way to realism.

The Tenets of Romanticism

Like other cultural movements, **romanticism** was characterized by intellectual diversity. Nonetheless, common parameters stand out. Artists inspired by romanticism repudiated the emphasis on reason associated with well-known Enlightenment philosophes like

Voltaire or Montesquieu (see Chapter 16). Romantics championed instead emotional exuberance, unrestrained imagination, and spontaneity in both art and personal life. Preoccupied with emotional excess, romantic works explored the awesome power of love and desire and of hatred, guilt, and despair.

Where Enlightenment thinkers applied the scientific method to social issues and cast rosy predictions for future progress, romantics valued intuition and nostalgia for the past. Where Enlightenment thinkers embraced secularization, romantics sought the inspiration of religious ecstasy. Where the Enlightenment valued public life and civic affairs, romantics delved into the supernatural and turned inward, to the hidden recesses of the self. As the Austrian composer Franz Schubert exclaimed in 1824:

> Oh imagination, thou supreme jewel of mankind, thou inexhaustible source from which artists and scholars drink! Oh, rest with us — despite the fact that thou art recognized only by a few — so as to preserve us from that so-called Enlightenment, that ugly skeleton without flesh or blood![5]

Nowhere was the break with Enlightenment classicism more apparent than in romanticism's general conception of nature. Classicists were not particularly interested in nature. The romantics, in contrast, were enchanted by stormy seas, untouched forests, and icy arctic wastelands. Nature could be awesome and tempestuous, a source of beauty or spiritual inspiration. Most romantics saw the growth of modern industry as an ugly, brutal attack on their beloved nature and on venerable traditions. They sought escape — in the unspoiled Lake District of northern England, in exotic North Africa, in an imaginary and idealized Middle Ages.

The study of history became a romantic obsession. History held the key to a universe now perceived to be organic and dynamic, not mechanical and static, as Enlightenment thinkers had believed. Historical novels like Sir Walter Scott's *Ivanhoe* (1820), a passionate romance set in twelfth-century England, found eager readers among the literate middle classes. Professional historians influenced by romanticism, such as Jules Michelet, went beyond the standard accounts of great men or famous battles. Michelet's many books on the history of France consciously promoted the growth of national aspirations; by fanning the embers of memory, Michelet encouraged the French people to search the past for their special national destiny.

Romanticism was a lifestyle as well as an intellectual movement. Many early-nineteenth-century romantics lived lives of tremendous emotional intensity. Obsessive love affairs, duels to the death, madness, strange illnesses, and suicide were not uncommon. Romantic artists typically led bohemian lives, wearing their hair long and uncombed in preference to donning powdered wigs, and rejecting the materialism of refined society. Great individualists, the romantics believed that the full development of one's unique human potential was the supreme purpose in life.

Literature

Romanticism found its distinctive voice in poetry, as the Enlightenment had in prose. Though romantic poetry had important forerunners in the German "Storm and Stress" movement of the 1770s and 1780s, its first great poets were English: William Blake, William Wordsworth, Samuel Taylor Coleridge, and Sir Walter Scott were all active by 1800, followed shortly by Lord Byron, Percy Bysshe Shelley, and John Keats.

A towering leader of English romanticism, William Wordsworth was deeply influenced by Rousseau and the spirit of the early French Revolution. Wordsworth settled in the rural Lake District of England with his sister, Dorothy, and Samuel Taylor Coleridge (1772–1834). In 1798 Wordsworth and Coleridge published their *Lyrical Ballads*, which abandoned flowery classical conventions for the language of ordinary speech and endowed simple subjects with the loftiest majesty. Wordsworth believed that all natural things were sacred, and his poetry often expressed a mystical appreciation of nature:

> To every natural form, rock, fruit or flower
> Even the loose stones that cover the high-way
> I gave a moral life, I saw them feel,
> Or link'd them to some feeling: the great mass
> Lay bedded in a quickening soul, and all
> That I beheld, respired with inward meaning.[6]

Here Wordsworth expressed his love of nature in commonplace forms that a variety of readers could appreciate; this stanza well illustrates his famous conception of poetry as the "spontaneous overflow of powerful feeling [which] takes its origin from emotion recollected in tranquility."[7]

In France under Napoleon, classicism remained strong and at first inhibited the growth of romanticism. An early French champion of the new movement, Germaine de Staël (duh STAHL) (1766–1817) urged the French to throw away their worn-out classical models. Her study *On Germany* (1810) extolled the spontaneity and enthusiasm of German writers and thinkers, and it had a powerful impact on the post-1815 generation in France. (See "Individuals in Society: Germaine de Staël," page 704.) Between 1820 and 1850, the romantic impulse broke through in the poetry and prose of Alphonse de Lamartine, Victor Hugo, and George Sand (pseudonym of the woman writer Armandine-Aurore-Lucile Dudevant). Of these, Victor Hugo (1802–1885) became the most well known.

Son of a Napoleonic general, Hugo achieved an amazing range of rhythm, language, and image in his lyric poetry. His powerful novels exemplified the romantic fascination with fantastic characters, exotic historical settings, and human emotions. The hero of Hugo's famous *The Hunchback of Notre Dame* (1831) is the great cathedral's deformed bell-ringer, a "human gargoyle" overlooking the teeming life of fifteenth-century Paris. Renouncing his early conservatism, Hugo equated freedom in literature with liberty in politics and society. His political evolution was thus exactly the opposite of Wordsworth's, in whom youthful radicalism gave way to middle-aged caution. As the contrast between the two artists suggests, romanticism was compatible with many political beliefs.

In central and eastern Europe, literary romanticism and early nationalism often reinforced one another. Well-educated romantics championed their own people's histories, cultures, and unique greatness. Like modern anthropologists, they studied peasant life and transcribed the folk songs, tales, and proverbs that the cosmopolitan Enlightenment had disdained. The brothers Jacob and Wilhelm Grimm were particularly successful at rescuing German fairy tales from oblivion. In the Slavic lands, romantics played a decisive role in converting spoken peasant languages into modern written languages. In the vast Austrian, Russian, and Ottoman Empires, with their many ethnic minorities, the combination of romanticism and nationalism was particularly potent. Ethnic groups dreaming of independence could find revolutionary inspiration in romantic visions of a historic national destiny.

INDIVIDUALS IN SOCIETY • Germaine de Staël

Rich, intellectual, passionate, and assertive, Germaine Necker de Staël (1766–1817) astonished contemporaries and still fascinates historians. She was strongly influenced by her parents, poor Swiss Protestants who soared to the top of prerevolutionary Parisian society. Her brilliant but rigid mother filled Germaine's head with knowledge, and each week the precocious child listened, wide-eyed and attentive, to illustrious writers and philosophers debating ideas at her mother's salon. At age twelve, she suffered a physical and mental breakdown. Only then was she allowed to have a playmate to romp about with on the family estate. Her adoring father was Jacques Necker, a banker who made an enormous fortune and became France's reform-minded minister of finance before the Revolution. Worshipping her father in adolescence, Germaine also came to love politics.

Accepting at nineteen an arranged marriage with Baron de Staël-Holstein, a womanizing Swedish diplomat bewitched by her dowry, Germaine began her life's work. She opened her own intellectual salon and began to write and publish. Her wit and exuberance attracted foreigners and liberal French aristocrats, one of whom became the first of many lovers as her marriage soured and she searched unsuccessfully for the happiness of her parents' union. Fleeing Paris in 1792 and returning after the Thermidorian reaction (see Chapter 19), she subsequently angered Napoleon by criticizing his dictatorial rule. In 1803 he permanently banished her from Paris.

Retiring again to her isolated estate in Switzerland and skillfully managing her inherited wealth, Staël fought insomnia with opium and boredom with parties that attracted luminaries from all over Europe. Always seeking stimulation for her restless mind, she traveled widely in Italy and Germany and drew upon these experiences in her novel *Corinne* (1807) and her study *On Germany* (1810). Both works summed up her romantic faith and enjoyed enormous success.

Staël urged creative individuals to abandon traditional rules and classical models. She encouraged them to embrace experimentation, emotion, and enthusiasm. Enthusiasm, which she had in abundance, was the key, the royal road to creativity, personal fulfillment, and human improvement. Thrilling to music, for example, she felt that only an enthusiastic person could really appreciate this gift of God, this wordless message that "unifies our dual nature and blends senses and spirit in a common rapture."*

*Quoted in G. R. Besser, *Germaine de Staël Revisited* (New York: Twayne Publishers, 1994), p. 106. Enhanced by a feminist perspective, this fine study is highly recommended.

Art and Music

Romantic concerns with nature, history, and the imagination extended well beyond literature into the realms of art and music. France's Eugène Delacroix (oo-ZHEHN deh-luh-KWAH) (1798–1863), one of romanticism's greatest artists, painted dramatic, colorful scenes that stirred the emotions. Delacroix was fascinated with remote and exotic subjects, whether lion hunts in Morocco or dreams of languishing, sensuous women in a sultan's harem. The famous German painter Casper David Friedrich

Yet a profound sadness runs through her writing. This sadness, so characteristic of the romantic temperament, grew in part out of disappointments in love and prolonged exile. But it also grew out of the insoluble predicament of being an enormously gifted woman in an age of intense male sexism. Little wonder that uneasy male competitors and literary critics took delight in ridiculing and defaming her as a neurotic and masculine woman, a mediocre and unnatural talent who had foolishly dared to enter the male world of serious thought and action. Even her supporters could not accept her for what she was. Poet Lord Byron recognized her genius and called her "the most eminent woman author of this, or perhaps of any century" but quickly added that "she should have been born a man."†

Buffeted and saddened by this scorn and condescension, Staël advocated equal rights for women throughout her life. Only with equal rights and duties— in education and careers, in love and marital relations—could a woman ever hope to realize her intellectual and emotional potential. Practicing what she preached as best she could, Germaine de Staël was a trailblazer in the struggle for women's rights.

QUESTIONS FOR ANALYSIS

1. In what ways did Germaine de Staël's life and thought reflect basic elements of the romantic movement?

2. Why did male critics often attack Staël? What do these criticisms tell us about gender relations in the early nineteenth century?

†Quoted ibid., p. 139.

ONLINE DOCUMENT ASSIGNMENT

How did the German landscape and the idea of enthusiasm figure into Staël's view of German romanticism? Examine excerpts from her work *On Germany* and key examples of German romantic paintings that echo Staël's ideas. Then complete a writing assignment based on the evidence and details from this chapter.

bedfordstmartins.com/mckaywestvalue

(1774–1840) preferred somber landscapes of ruined churches or remote arctic shipwrecks, which captured the divine presence in natural forces.

In England the most notable romantic painters were Joseph M. W. Turner (1775–1851) and John Constable (1776–1837). Both were fascinated by nature, but their interpretations of it contrasted sharply, aptly symbolizing the tremendous emotional range of the romantic movement. Turner depicted nature's power and terror; wild storms and sinking ships were favorite subjects. Constable painted gentle Wordsworthian landscapes in which human beings lived peacefully with their environment, the comforting

Delacroix, *Massacre at Chios* The Greek struggle for freedom and independence won the enthusiastic support of liberals, nationalists, and romantics. The Ottoman Turks were portrayed as cruel oppressors who were holding back the course of history, as in this moving masterpiece by Delacroix. (Louvre, Paris, France/Giraudon/The Bridgeman Art Library)

countryside of unspoiled rural England.

Musicians and composers likewise explored the romantic sensibility. Abandoning well-defined structures, the great romantic composers used a wide range of forms to create a thousand musical landscapes and evoke a host of powerful emotions. They transformed the small classical orchestra, tripling its size by adding wind instruments, percussion, and more brass and strings. The crashing chords evoking the surge of the masses in Chopin's "Revolutionary Etude," and the bottomless despair of the funeral march in Beethoven's Third Symphony — such were the modern orchestra's musical paintings that plumbed the depths of human feeling.

This range and intensity gave music and musicians much greater prestige than in the past. Music no longer simply complemented a church service or helped a nobleman digest his dinner. It became a sublime end in itself, most perfectly realizing the endless yearning of the soul. The unbelievable one-in-a-million performer — the great virtuoso who could transport the listener to ecstasy and hysteria — became a cultural hero. People swooned for Franz Liszt (1811–1886), the greatest pianist of his age, as they scream for rock stars today.

The first great romantic composer is also the most famous today. Ludwig van Beethoven (1770–1827) used contrasting themes and tones to produce dramatic conflict and inspiring resolutions. As one contemporary admirer wrote, "Beethoven's music sets in motion the lever of fear, of awe, of horror, of suffering, and awakens just that infinite longing which is the essence of Romanticism."[8] Beethoven's range and output were tremendous. At the peak of his fame, he began to lose his hearing. He considered suicide but eventually overcame despair: "I will take fate by the throat; it will not bend me completely to its will."[9] Beethoven continued to pour out immortal music, although his last years were silent, spent in total deafness.

Reforms and Revolutions Before 1848

How and where was conservatism challenged after 1815?

While the romantics enacted a revolution in the arts, liberal, national, and socialist forces battered against the conservative restoration of 1815. Political change could occur through gradual and peaceful reform, or through violent insurrection, but everywhere it took the determination of ordinary people standing up to prerogatives of the powerful. Between 1815 and 1848, three important countries — Greece, Great Britain, and France — experienced variations on these basic themes.

National Liberation in Greece

Though conservative statesmen had maintained the autocratic status quo despite revolts in Spain and the Two Sicilies, a national revolution succeeded in Greece in the 1820s. Since the fifteenth century the Greeks had lived under the domination of the Ottoman Turks. In spite of centuries of foreign rule, the Greeks had survived as a people, united by their language and the Greek Orthodox religion. In the early nineteenth century the general growth of national aspirations inspired a desire for independence. This rising national movement led to the formation of secret societies and then to open revolt in 1821, led by Alexander Ypsilanti (ihp-suh-LAN-tee), a Greek patriot and a general in the Russian army.

At first, the Great Powers, particularly Metternich, opposed the revolution and refused to back Ypsilanti, primarily because they sought a stable Ottoman Empire as a bulwark against Russian interests in southeast Europe. Yet the Greek cause had powerful defenders. Educated Europeans and Americans cherished the culture of classical Greece; Russians admired the piety of their Orthodox brethren. Writers and artists, moved by the romantic impulse, responded enthusiastically to the Greek national struggle. The famous English romantic poet Lord Byron even joined the Greek revolutionaries to fight (as he wrote in a famous poem) "that Greece might yet be free."

The Greeks, though often quarreling among themselves, battled the Ottomans while hoping for the eventual support of European governments. In 1827 Great Britain, France, and Russia yielded to popular demands at home and directed Ottoman leaders to accept an armistice. When they refused, the navies of these three powers trapped the Ottoman fleet at Navarino and destroyed it. Russia then declared another of its periodic wars of expansion against the Ottomans. This led to the establishment of a Russian protectorate over much of present-day Romania, which had also been under Ottoman rule. Great Britain, France, and Russia finally declared Greece independent in 1830 and installed a German prince as king of the new country in 1832. Despite this imposed regime, which left the Greek people restive, they had won their independence in a heroic war of liberation against a foreign empire.

Liberal Reform in Great Britain

Pressure from below also reshaped politics in Great Britain, but through a process of gradual reform rather than revolution. Eighteenth-century Britain had been remarkably stable. The landowning aristocracy dominated society, but that class was neither closed nor rigidly defined. Successful business and professional people could buy land and become gentlefolk, while the common people enjoyed limited civil rights. Yet the constitutional monarchy was hardly democratic. With only about 8 percent of the population allowed to vote, the British Parliament, easily manipulated by the king, remained in the hands of the upper classes. Government policies supported the aristocracy and the new industrial capitalists at the expense of the laboring classes.

By the 1780s there was growing interest in some kind of political reform, and organized union activity began to emerge in force during the Napoleonic Wars (see Chapter 19). Yet the radical aspects of the French Revolution threw the British aristocracy into a panic for a generation, making it extremely hostile to any attempts to change the status quo.

In 1815 open conflict between the ruling class and laborers emerged when the aristocracy rammed far-reaching changes in the **Corn Laws** through Parliament. Britain had been unable to import cheap grain from eastern Europe during the war years, leading to high prices and large profits for the landed aristocracy. With the war over, grain (which the British generically called "corn") could be imported again, allowing the price of wheat and bread to go down and benefiting almost everyone—except aristocratic landlords. The new Corn Laws prohibited the importation of foreign grain unless the price at home rose to improbable levels, ensuring artificially high bread prices for working people and handsome revenues for the aristocracy. Seldom has a class legislated more selfishly for its own narrow economic advantage or done more to promote a class-based view of political action.

The change in the Corn Laws, coming as it did at a time of widespread unemployment and postwar economic distress, triggered protests and demonstrations by urban laborers, who enjoyed the support of radical intellectuals. In 1817 the Tory government, controlled completely by the landed aristocracy, responded by temporarily suspending the traditional rights of peaceable assembly and habeas corpus, which gives a person under arrest the right to a trial. Two years later, Parliament passed the infamous Six Acts, which, among other things, placed controls on a heavily taxed press and practically eliminated all mass meetings. These acts followed an enormous but orderly protest, at Saint Peter's Fields in Manchester, which was savagely broken up by armed cavalry. Nicknamed the **Battle of Peterloo**, in scornful reference to the British victory at Waterloo, this incident demonstrated the government's determination to repress dissenters.

Strengthened by ongoing industrial development, the new manufacturing and commercial groups insisted on a place for their new wealth alongside the landed wealth of the aristocracy in the framework of political power and social prestige. They called for many kinds of liberal reform: changes in town government, organization of a new police force, more rights for Catholics and dissenters, and reform of the Poor Laws to provide aid to some low-paid workers. In the 1820s a less frightened Tory government moved in the direction of better urban administration, greater economic liberalism, civil equality for Catholics, and limited imports of foreign grain. These actions encouraged the middle classes to press on for reform of Parliament so they could have a larger say in government.

The Whig Party, though led like the Tories by great aristocrats, had by tradition been more responsive to middle-class commercial and manufacturing interests. In 1830 a Whig ministry introduced "an act to amend the representation of the people of England and Wales." After a series of setbacks, the Whigs' **Reform Bill of 1832** was propelled into law by a mighty surge of popular support.

Significantly, the bill moved British politics in a democratic direction and allowed the House of Commons to emerge as the all-important legislative body, at the expense of the aristocrat-dominated House of Lords. The new industrial areas of the country gained representation in the Commons, and many old "rotten boroughs"—electoral districts that had very few voters and that the landed aristocracy had bought and sold— were eliminated. The number of voters increased by about 50 percent, to include about 12 percent of adult men in Britain and Ireland. Comfortable middle-class groups in the urban population, as well as some substantial farmers who leased their land, received the vote. Thus the conflicts building in Great Britain were successfully—though only temporarily—resolved. Continued peaceful reform within the system appeared difficult but not impossible.

The "People's Charter" of 1838 and the Chartist movement it inspired pressed British elites for yet more radical reform (see Chapter 20). Inspired by the economic distress of the working class in the 1830s and 1840s, the Chartists demanded universal male (but not female) suffrage. They saw complete political democracy and rule by the common people—the great majority of the population—as the means to a good and

just society. Hundreds of thousands of people signed gigantic petitions calling on Parliament to grant all men the right to vote, first in 1839, again in 1842, and yet again in 1848. Parliament rejected all three petitions. In the short run, the working poor failed with their Chartist demands, but they learned a valuable lesson in mass politics.

While calling for universal male suffrage, many working-class people joined with middle-class manufacturers in the Anti–Corn Law League, founded in Manchester in 1839. Mass participation made possible a popular crusade led by fighting liberals, who argued that lower food prices and more jobs in industry depended on repeal of the Corn Laws. Much of the working class agreed. When Ireland's potato

The Anti–Corn Law Movement in Action This contemporary illustration focuses on the Anti–Corn Law League's remarkable ability to mobilize a broad urban coalition that was dedicated to free trade and the end of tariffs on imported grain. (The Granger Collection, New York)

crop failed in 1845 and famine prices for food seemed likely in England, Tory prime minister Robert Peel joined with the Whigs and a minority of his own party to repeal the Corn Laws in 1846 and allow free imports of grain. England escaped famine. Thereafter the liberal doctrine of free trade became almost sacred dogma in Great Britain.

The following year, the Tories passed a bill designed to help the working classes, but in a different way. The Ten Hours Act of 1847 limited the workday for women and young people in factories to ten hours. In competition with the middle class for the support of the working class, Tory legislators continued to support legislation regulating factory conditions. This competition between a still-powerful aristocracy and a strong middle class was a crucial factor in Great Britain's peaceful political evolution. The working classes could make temporary alliances with either competitor to better their own conditions.

Ireland and the Great Famine

The people of Ireland did not benefit from the political competition in Britain. In the mid-1800s Ireland was an agricultural nation, and the great majority of the rural population (outside of the northern counties of Ulster, which were partly Presbyterian) were Irish Catholics. They typically rented their land from a tiny minority of Church of England Protestant landowners, who often resided in England. Using a middleman system, these absentee landlords leased land for short periods only, set rents at will, and easily evicted their tenants. In short, landlords used their power to grab as much profit as possible.

Trapped in an exploitative tenant system driven by a pernicious combination of religion and class, Irish peasants lived in abominable conditions. Wretched one-room mud cabins dotted the Irish countryside; the typical tenant farmer could afford neither shoes nor stockings. Hundreds of shocking accounts described hopeless poverty. The novelist Sir Walter Scott wrote:

> The poverty of the Irish peasantry is on the extreme verge of human misery; their cottages would scarce serve for pig styes even in Scotland; and their rags seem the very refuse of a sheep, and are spread over their bodies with such an ingenious variety of wretchedness that you would think nothing but some sort of perverted taste could have assembled so many shreds together.[10]

A compassionate French traveler agreed, writing that Ireland was "pure misery, naked and hungry. . . . I saw the American Indian in his forests and the black slave in his chains, and I believed that I was seeing the most extreme form of human misery; but that was before I knew the lot of poor Ireland."[11]

Despite the terrible conditions, population growth sped upward, part of Europe's general growth trend begun in the early eighteenth century (see Chapter 17). Between 1780 and 1840 the Irish population doubled from 4 million to 8 million. Extensive cultivation of the humble potato was largely responsible for this rapid growth. A single acre of land planted with the nutritious potato could feed a family of six for a year, and the hardy tuber thrived on Ireland's boggy wastelands. About one-half of the Irish population subsisted on potatoes and little else. Needing only a big potato patch to survive, the rural poor married early. To be sure, a young couple faced a life of extreme poverty. They would literally live on potatoes, supplemented perhaps with a bit of grain or milk. Yet the decision to marry and have large families made sense. A couple could manage rural poverty better than someone living alone, and children meant extra hands in the fields.

As population and potato dependency grew, however, conditions became more precarious. From 1820 onward, deficiencies and diseases in the potato crop occurred with disturbing frequency. Then in 1845 and 1846, and again in 1848 and 1851, the potato crop failed in Ireland. Blight attacked the young plants, and leaves and tubers rotted. Unmitigated disaster — the **Great Famine** — followed, as already impoverished peasants experienced widespread sickness and starvation.

The British government, committed to rigid free-trade ideology, reacted slowly. Relief efforts were tragically inadequate. Moreover, the government continued to collect taxes, landlords demanded their rents, and tenants who could not pay were evicted and their homes destroyed. Famine or no, Ireland remained the conquered jewel of foreign landowners.

The Great Famine shattered the pattern of Irish population growth. Fully 1 million emigrants fled the famine between 1845 and 1851, mostly to the United States and Canada, and up to 1.5 million people died; the elderly and the very young were hardest hit. Alone among the countries of Europe, Ireland experienced a declining population in the second half of the nineteenth century, as it became a land of continuous out-migration, early death, late marriage, and widespread celibacy.

The Great Famine intensified anti-British feeling and promoted Irish nationalism, for the bitter memory of starvation, exile, and British inaction burned deeply into the popular consciousness. Patriots of the later nineteenth and early twentieth centuries could call on powerful collective emotions in their campaigns for land reform, home rule, and, eventually, Irish independence.

The Revolution of 1830 in France

The Constitutional Charter granted by Louis XVIII in the Bourbon restoration of 1814 was basically a liberal constitution (see Chapter 19). The charter protected economic and social gains made by sections of the middle class and the peasantry in the French Revolution, permitted some intellectual and artistic freedom, and created a parliament with upper and lower houses. Immediately after Napoleon's abortive Hundred Days, the moderate, worldly king refused to bow to the wishes of die-hard aristocrats who wanted to sweep away all the revolutionary changes. Instead, Louis appointed as his ministers moderate royalists, who sought and obtained the support of a majority of the representatives elected to the lower Chamber of Deputies between 1816 and Louis's death in 1824.

Louis XVIII's charter was liberal but hardly democratic. Only about 100,000 of the wealthiest males out of a total population of 30 million had the right to vote for the deputies who, with the king and his ministers, made the laws of the nation. Nonetheless, the "notable people" who did vote came from very different backgrounds. There were wealthy businessmen, war profiteers, successful professionals, ex-revolutionaries, large landowners from the old aristocracy and the middle class, Bourbons, and Bonapartists. The old aristocracy, with its pre-1789 mentality, was a minority within the voting population.

Louis's conservative successor, Charles X (r. 1824–1830), a true reactionary, wanted to re-establish the old order in France. Increasingly blocked by the opposition of the deputies, Charles's government turned in 1830 to military adventure in an effort to rally French nationalism and gain popular support. A long-standing economic and diplomatic dispute with Muslim Algeria, a vassal state of the Ottoman Empire, provided the opportunity.

In June 1830 a French force of thirty-seven thousand crossed the Mediterranean, landed to the west of Algiers, and took the capital city in three short weeks. Victory seemed complete, but in 1831 Algerians in the interior revolted and waged a fearsome war that lasted until 1847, when French armies finally subdued the country. Bringing French, Spanish, and Italian settlers to Algeria and leading to the expropriation of large tracts of Muslim land, the conquest of Algeria marked the rebirth of French colonial expansion.

Emboldened by the initial good news from Algeria, Charles repudiated the Constitutional Charter in an attempted coup in July 1830. He issued decrees stripping much of the wealthy middle class of its voting rights and censored the press. The immediate reaction, encouraged by lawyers, liberal journalists, and middle-class businessmen, was an insurrection in the capital. Printers, other artisans, and small traders rioted in the streets of Paris, and three days of vicious street fighting brought down the government. Charles fled. Then the upper middle class, which had fomented the revolt, skillfully seated Charles's cousin, Louis Philippe, duke of Orléans, on the vacant throne.

Events in Paris reverberated across Europe. In the Netherlands, Belgian Catholics revolted against the Dutch king and established the independent kingdom of Belgium. In Switzerland, regional liberal assemblies forced cantonal governments to amend their constitutions, leading to two decades of political conflict. And in partitioned Poland, an armed nationalist rebellion against the tsarist government was crushed by the Russian Imperial Army.

Despite the abdication of Charles X, in France the political situation remained fundamentally unchanged. The new king, Louis Philippe (r. 1830–1848), did accept the Constitutional Charter of 1814 and adopted the red, white, and blue flag of the French Revolution. Beyond these symbolic actions, popular demands for reform went unanswered. The upper middle class had effected a change in dynasty that maintained the status quo and the narrowly liberal institutions of 1815. Republicans, democrats, social reformers, and the poor of Paris were bitterly disappointed. They had made a revolution, but it seemed for naught.

The Revolutions of 1848

What were the main causes and results of the revolutions of 1848?

In the late 1840s Europe entered a period of tense economic and political crisis. Bad harvests across the continent caused widespread distress. Uneven industrial development failed to provide jobs or raise incomes, and revolts and insurrections rocked Europe: a rebellion in the northern part of Austria in 1846, a civil war in Switzerland in 1847, and an uprising in Naples, Italy, in January 1848.

Full-scale revolution broke out in France in February 1848, and its shock waves ripped across the continent. Only the most developed countries — Great Britain, Belgium,

and the Netherlands—and the least developed—the Ottoman and Russian Empires—
escaped untouched. Elsewhere governments toppled, as monarchs and ministers bowed
or fled. National independence, liberal democratic constitutions, and social reform: the
lofty aspirations of a generation seemed at hand. Yet in the end, the revolutions failed.

A Democratic Republic in France

By the late 1840s revolution in Europe was almost universally expected, but it took
events in Paris—once again—to turn expectations into realities. For eighteen years
Louis Philippe's reign, labeled the "bourgeois monarchy" because it served the selfish
interests of France's wealthy elites, had been characterized by stubborn inaction and
complacency. Corrupt politicians refused to approve social legislation or consider electoral reform. Frustrated desires for change, high-level financial scandals, and a general
sense of stagnation dovetailed with a severe depression that began with crop failures in
1846 to 1847. The government did little to prevent the agrarian crisis from dragging
down the entire economy.

The government's failures united a diverse group of opponents against the king.
Bourgeois merchants, opposition deputies, and liberal intellectuals shared a sense of
outrage with middle-class shopkeepers, skilled artisans, and unskilled working people.
Widespread discontent eventually touched off a popular revolt in Paris. On the night
of February 22, 1848, workers joined by some students began tearing up cobblestones
and building barricades. Armed with guns and dug in behind their makeshift fortresses,
the workers and students demanded a new government. On February 24 the National
Guard broke ranks and joined the revolutionaries. Louis Philippe refused to call in the
army and abdicated in favor of his grandson. But the common people in arms would
tolerate no more monarchy. This refusal led to the proclamation of a provisional republic, headed by a ten-man executive committee and certified by cries of approval from
the revolutionary crowd.

The revolutionaries immediately set about drafting a democratic, republican constitution for France's Second Republic. Building such a republic meant giving the right
to vote to every adult male, and this was quickly done. Bold decrees issued by the
provisional republican government further expressed sympathy for revolutionary freedoms by calling for liberty, fraternity, and equality; guaranteeing workplace reforms;
freeing all slaves in French colonies; and abolishing the death penalty. (See "Primary
Source: The Republican Spirit in Paris, 1848," page 714.)

Yet there were profound differences within the revolutionary coalition. On the one
hand, the moderate liberal republicans of the middle class viewed universal male suffrage
as the ultimate concession to dangerous popular forces, and they strongly opposed any
further radical social measures. On the other hand, radical republicans, influenced by
a generation of utopian socialists and appalled by the poverty and misery of the urban
poor, were committed to some kind of socialism. Hard-pressed urban artisans, who
hated the unrestrained competition of cutthroat capitalism, advocated a combination
of strong craft unions and worker-owned businesses.

Worsening depression and rising unemployment brought these conflicting goals
to the fore in 1848. Louis Blanc (see page 699), who along with a worker named
Albert represented the republican socialists in the provisional government, pressed for
recognition of a socialist right to work. Blanc urged the creation of the permanent

PRIMARY SOURCE The Republican Spirit in Paris, 1848

After a revolutionary mob overturned the bourgeois monarchy of Louis Philippe, the provisional republican government issued the following decrees on February 24 and 25, 1848.

Decrees of the Provisional Republican Government in Paris, February 1848

The Overthrow of the Orléanist Monarchy

In the name of the French people:

A reactionary and oligarchical government has just been overthrown by the heroism of the people of Paris. That government has fled, leaving behind it a trail of blood that forbids it ever to retrace its steps.

The blood of the people has flowed as in July [1830]; but this time this noble people shall not be deceived. It has won a national and popular government in accord with the rights, the progress, and the will of this great and generous nation.

A provisional government, the result of pressing necessity and ratified by the voice of the people and of the deputies of the departments, in the session of February 24, is for the moment invested with the task of assuring and organizing the national victory. . . .

With the capital of France on fire, the justification for the present provisional government must be sought in the public safety. All France will understand this and will lend it the support of its patriotism. Under the popular government which the provisional government proclaims, every citizen is a magistrate.

Frenchmen, it is for you to give to the world the example which Paris has given to France; prepare yourselves by order and by confidence in your destiny for the firm institutions which you are about to be called upon to establish.

The provisional government wishes to establish a republic,—subject, however, to ratification by the people, who shall be immediately consulted.

---

government-sponsored cooperative workshops he had advocated in *The Organization of Work*. Such workshops would be an alternative to capitalist employment and a decisive step toward a new, noncompetitive social order.

The moderate republicans, willing to provide only temporary relief, wanted no such thing. The resulting compromise set up national workshops—soon to become little more than a vast program of pick-and-shovel public works—and established a special commission under Blanc to "study the question." This satisfied no one. The national workshops were, however, better than nothing. An army of desperate poor from the French provinces and even from foreign countries streamed into Paris to sign up for the workshops. As the economic crisis worsened, the number enrolled in the workshops soared from 10,000 in March to 120,000 by June, and another 80,000 tried unsuccessfully to join.

While the Paris workshops grew, the French people went to the election polls in late April. The result was a bitter loss for the republicans. Voting in most cases for the

The unity of the nation (formed henceforth of all the classes of citizens who compose it); the government of the nation by itself; liberty, equality, and fraternity, for fundamental principles, and "the people" for our emblem and watchword: these constitute the democratic government which France owes to itself, and which our efforts shall secure for it. . . .

Decrees Relating to the Workingmen

The provisional government of the French republic pledges itself to guarantee the means of subsistence of the workingman by labor.

It pledges itself to guarantee labor to all citizens.

It recognizes that workingmen ought to enter into associations among themselves in order to enjoy the advantage of their labor. . . .

The provisional government of the French republic decrees that all articles pledged at the pawn shops since the first of February, consisting of linen, garments, or clothes, etc., upon which the loan does not exceed ten francs, shall be given back to those who pledged them. . . .

The provisional government of the republic decrees the immediate establishment of national workshops.

EVALUATE THE EVIDENCE

1. What kind of practical rewards did the provisional government offer to ordinary people who supported the revolution?

2. Which political ideology—liberalism, nationalism, or socialism—seems predominant in these decrees?

Source: James Harvey Robinson, *Readings in European History*, vol. 2 (Boston: Ginn and Company, 1906), pp. 559–561.

first time, the people of France elected to the new 900-person Constituent Assembly 500 monarchists and conservatives, only about 270 moderate republicans, and just 80 radicals or socialists.

One of the moderate republicans was the author of *Democracy in America*, Alexis de Tocqueville (1805–1859), who had predicted the overthrow of Louis Philippe's government. He explained the election result by observing that the socialist movement in Paris aroused the fierce hostility of France's peasants as well as the middle and upper classes. The French peasants owned land, and according to Tocqueville, "private property had become with all those who owned it a sort of bond of fraternity."[12] Tocqueville saw that a majority of the members of the new Constituent Assembly was firmly committed to centrist moderation and strongly opposed to the socialists and their artisan allies, a view he shared.

This clash of ideologies—of liberal moderation and radical socialism—became a clash of classes and arms after the elections. The new government's executive committee

The Triumph of Democratic Republics   This French illustration offers an opinion of the initial revolutionary breakthrough in 1848. The peoples of Europe, joined together around their respective national banners, are achieving republican freedom, which is symbolized by the statue, representing liberty, and the discarded crowns. The woman wearing pants at the base of the statue—very radical attire—represents feminist hopes for liberation. (Musée de la Ville, Paris/ Giraudon/The Bridgeman Art Library)

dropped Blanc and thereafter included no representative of the Parisian working class. Fearing that their socialist hopes were about to be dashed, artisans and unskilled workers invaded the Constituent Assembly on May 15 and tried to proclaim a new revolutionary state. The government used the middle-class National Guard to squelch this uprising. As the workshops continued to fill and grow more radical, the fearful but powerful propertied classes in the Assembly took the offensive. On June 22 the government dissolved the workshops in Paris, giving the workers the choice of joining the army or going to workshops in the provinces.

A spontaneous and violent uprising followed. Frustrated in their thwarted attempt to create a socialist society, masses of desperate people were now losing even their life-sustaining relief. Barricades sprang up again in the narrow streets of Paris, and a terrible class war began. Working people fought with the courage of utter desperation, but this time the government had the army and the support of peasant France. After three terrible "June Days" of street fighting and the death or injury of more than ten thousand people, the republican army under General Louis Cavaignac stood triumphant in a sea of working-class blood and hatred.

The revolution in France thus ended in spectacular failure. The February coalition of the middle and working classes had in four short months become locked in mortal combat. In place of a generous democratic republic, the Constituent Assembly completed a constitution featuring a strong executive. This allowed Louis Napoleon, nephew of

Napoleon Bonaparte, to win a landslide victory in the election of December 1848. The appeal of his great name as well as the desire of the propertied classes for order at any cost had led to what would become a semi-authoritarian regime.

Revolution and Reaction in the Austrian Empire

Throughout central Europe, the first news of the upheaval in France evoked feverish excitement and then popular revolution, lending credence to Metternich's famous quip "When France sneezes, all Europe catches cold." Liberals demanded written constitutions, representative government, and greater civil liberties from authoritarian regimes. When governments hesitated, popular revolts broke out. Urban workers and students served as the shock troops, but they were allied with middle-class liberals and peasants. In the face of this united front, monarchs made quick concessions. The revolutionary coalition, having secured great and easy victories, then broke down as it had in France. The traditional forces—the monarchy, the aristocracy, the regular army—recovered their nerve, reasserted their authority, and revoked many, though not all, of the reforms. Reaction was everywhere victorious.

The revolution in the Austrian Empire began in Hungary in March 1848, when nationalistic Hungarians demanded national autonomy, full civil liberties, and universal suffrage. When the monarchy in Vienna hesitated, Viennese students and workers took to the streets and raised barricades in defiance of the government while peasant disturbances broke out in parts of the empire. The Habsburg emperor Ferdinand I (r. 1835–1848) capitulated and promised reforms and a liberal constitution. Metternich fled to London. The old absolutist order seemed to be collapsing with unbelievable rapidity.

Yet the coalition of revolutionaries lacked stability. When the monarchy abolished serfdom, with its degrading forced labor and feudal services, the newly free peasants lost interest in the political and social questions agitating the cities. Meanwhile, the coalition of urban revolutionaries broke down along class lines over the issue of socialist workshops and universal voting rights for men.

Conflicting national aspirations further weakened and ultimately destroyed the revolutionary coalition. In March the Hungarian revolutionary leaders pushed through an extremely liberal, almost democratic, constitution. But the Hungarian revolutionaries also sought to transform the mosaic of provinces and peoples that was the kingdom of Hungary into a unified, centralized Hungarian nation. The minority groups that formed half of the population—the Croats, Serbs, and Romanians—rejected such unification. Each group felt entitled to political autonomy and cultural independence. In a similar way, Czech nationalists based in Prague and other parts of Bohemia came into conflict with German nationalists. Thus desires for national autonomy within the Austrian Empire enabled the monarchy to play off one ethnic group against the other.

Finally, the conservative aristocratic forces rallied under the leadership of the archduchess Sophia, a Bavarian princess married to the emperor's brother. Deeply ashamed of the emperor's collapse before a "mess of students," she insisted that Ferdinand, who had no heir, abdicate in favor of her son, Francis Joseph.[13] Powerful nobles organized around Sophia in a secret conspiracy to reverse and crush the revolution.

The first conservative breakthrough came when the army bombarded Prague and savagely crushed a working-class revolt there on June 17. Other Austrian officials and nobles led the minority nationalities of Hungary against the revolutionary government. At the end of October, the well-equipped, predominantly peasant troops of the regular Austrian army bombarded the student and working-class radicals dug in behind barricades in Vienna with heavy artillery. They retook the city at the cost of more than four thousand casualties. The determination of the Austrian aristocracy and the loyalty of its army sealed the triumph of reaction and the defeat of revolution.

When Francis Joseph (r. 1848–1916) was crowned emperor of Austria immediately after his eighteenth birthday in December 1848, only Hungary had yet to be brought under control. Another determined conservative, Nicholas I of Russia (r. 1825–1855), obligingly lent his iron hand. On June 6, 1849, 130,000 Russian troops poured into Hungary and subdued the country after bitter fighting. For a number of years, the Habsburgs ruled Hungary as a conquered territory.

Prussia, the German Confederation, and the Frankfurt National Parliament

After Austria, Prussia was the largest and most influential kingdom in the German Confederation. Since the Napoleonic Wars, liberal German reformers had sought to transform absolutist Prussia into a constitutional monarchy, hoping it would then lead the thirty-eight states of the German Confederation into a unified nation-state. The agitation that followed the fall of Louis Philippe, on top of several years of crop failure and economic crises, encouraged liberals to press their demands. In March 1848 excited crowds in urban centers across the German Confederation called for liberal reforms and a national parliament, and many regional rulers quickly gave in to their demands.

When artisans and factory workers rioted in Berlin, the capital of Prussia, and joined temporarily with the middle-class liberals in the struggle against the monarchy, the autocratic yet compassionate Prussian king, Frederick William IV (r. 1840–1861), vacillated and then caved in. On March 21 he promised to grant Prussia a liberal constitution and to merge Prussia into a new national German state.

But urban workers wanted much more, and the Prussian aristocracy wanted much less than the moderate constitutional liberalism the king conceded. The workers issued a series of democratic and vaguely socialist demands that troubled their middle-class allies. An elected Prussian Constituent Assembly met in Berlin to write a constitution for the Prussian state, and a conservative clique gathered around the king to urge counter-revolution.

At the same time, elections were held across the German Confederation for a national parliament, which convened to write a federal constitution that would lead to national unification. When they met in Frankfurt that May, the state officials, lawyers, professors, and businessmen elected to parliament represented the interests of the social elite. Their calls for constitutional monarchy, free speech, religious tolerance, and abolition of aristocratic privilege were typical of moderate national liberalism. The deputies essentially ignored calls for more radical action from industrial workers, peasants, republicans, and socialists.

In October 1848 the Frankfurt parliament turned to the question of national unification and borders. At first, the deputies proposed unification around a **Greater Germany** that would include the German-speaking lands of the Austrian Empire in a national state—but not non-German territories in Italy and central Europe. This proposal foundered on Austrian determination to maintain its empire, and some parliamentarians advocated a Lesser Germany that would unify Prussia and other German states without Austria. Even as the deputies debated Germany's future in the autumn of 1848, the forces of counter-revolution pushed back reformists and revolutionaries in Prussia and the other German states.

Despite Austrian intransigence, in March 1849 the national parliament finally completed its draft of a liberal constitution and elected Frederick William of Prussia emperor of a "lesser" German national state (minus Austria). By early 1849, however, reaction had rolled back liberal reforms across the German Confederation. Frederick William had already reasserted his royal authority and disbanded the Prussian Constituent Assembly, and he contemptuously refused to accept the "crown from the gutter" offered by the parliament in Frankfurt. Bogged down by their preoccupation with nationalist issues, the reluctant revolutionaries in Frankfurt had waited too long and acted too timidly. By May 1849 all but the most radical deputies had resigned from the parliament, and in June Prussian troops dissolved the remnants of the parliament.

When Frederick William, who really wanted to be emperor but only on his own authoritarian terms, tried to get the small monarchies of Germany to elect him emperor, Austria balked. Supported by Russia, Austria forced Prussia to renounce all schemes of unification in late 1850. The German Confederation was re-established in 1851, and a decade of reaction followed. In an echo of the Karlsbad Decrees, state security forces monitored universities, civic organizations, and the press throughout the confederation. Former revolutionaries fled into exile, and German liberals gave up demands for national unification. In the various German states, reactionary monarchs, aided by ever-growing state bureaucracies, granted their subjects conservative constitutions and weak parliaments that maintained aristocratic control. Attempts to unite the Germans— first in a liberal national state and then in a conservative Prussian empire—had failed completely.

Notes

1. Quoted in David Blackbourn, *The Long Nineteenth Century: A History of Germany, 1780–1918* (New York: Oxford University Press, 1998), p. 122.
2. E. Gellner, *Nations and Nationalism* (Oxford: Basil Blackwell, 1983), especially pp. 19–39.
3. This paragraph draws on the influential views of B. Anderson, *Imagined Communities: Reflections on the Origins and Spread of Nationalism*, rev. ed. (London/New York: Verso, 1991), and E. J. Hobsbawm and T. Ranger, eds., *The Invention of Tradition* (Cambridge, U.K.: Cambridge University Press, 1983).
4. Quoted in Frank E. Manuel and Fritzie P. Manuel, *Utopian Thought in the Western World* (Cambridge: Harvard University Press, 1979), p. 589.
5. Quoted in H. G. Schenk, *The Mind of the European Romantics* (New York: Oxford University Press, 1979), p. 5.
6. Quoted ibid., p. 169.
7. Quoted in Olivia Frey, *Emotions Recollected in Tranquility—Wordsworth's Concept of Poetry in "I Wandered Lonely as a Cloud"* (Munich: GRIN Verlag, 2008), p. 5.
8. Quoted in Alessandra Comini, *The Changing Image of Beethoven: A Study in Mythmaking* (Santa Fe, N.M.: Sunstone Press, 2008), p. 79.
9. Quoted in F. B. Artz, *From the Renaissance to Romanticism: Trends in Style in Art, Literature, and Music, 1300–1830* (Chicago: University of Chicago Press, 1962), pp. 276, 278.
10. Quoted in G. O'Brien, *The Economic History of Ireland from the Union to the Famine* (London: Longmans, Green, 1921), p. 21.
11. Quoted ibid., pp. 23–24.
12. A. de Tocqueville, *Recollections* (New York: Columbia University Press, 1949), p. 94.
13. W. L. Langer, *Political and Social Upheaval, 1832–1852* (New York: Harper & Row, 1969), p. 361.

Chapter Review

MAKE IT STICK

LearningCurve
bedfordstmartins.com/mckaywestvalue

After reading the chapter, use LearningCurve to retain what you've read.

IDENTIFY KEY TERMS

Identify and explain the significance of each item below.

Congress of Vienna (p. 688)	**bourgeoisie** (p. 701)
Holy Alliance (p. 692)	**proletariat** (p. 701)
Karlsbad Decrees (p. 693)	**romanticism** (p. 701)
liberalism (p. 696)	**Corn Laws** (p. 708)
laissez faire (p. 696)	**Battle of Peterloo** (p. 708)
nationalism (p. 697)	**Reform Bill of 1832** (p. 708)
socialism (p. 698)	**Great Famine** (p. 711)
Marxism (p. 700)	**Greater Germany** (p. 718)

REVIEW THE MAIN IDEAS

Answer the focus questions from each section of the chapter.

- How was peace restored and maintained after 1815? (p. 688)
- What new ideologies emerged to challenge conservatism? (p. 696)
- What were the characteristics of the romantic movement? (p. 701)
- How and where was conservatism challenged after 1815? (p. 707)
- What were the main causes and results of the revolutions of 1848? (p. 712)

MAKE CONNECTIONS

Think about the larger developments and continuities within and across chapters.

1. Why did the ideas of the romantic movement so easily support reformist and radical political ideas, including liberalism, republicanism, and nationalism? What does this reveal about the general connections between art and politics?

2. How did the spread of radical ideas and the movements for reform and revolution explored in this chapter draw on the "unfinished" political and industrial revolutions (Chapters 19 and 20) of the late 1700s?

ONLINE DOCUMENT ASSIGNMENT

Germaine de Staël

How did the German landscape and the idea of enthusiasm figure into Staël's view of German romanticism?

You encountered Germaine de Staël's story on page 704. Keeping the question above in mind, go online and examine excerpts from her work *On Germany* and key examples of German romantic paintings that echo Staël's ideas. Then complete a writing assignment based on the evidence and details from this chapter.

bedfordstmartins.com/mckaywestvalue

CHRONOLOGY

1790s–1840s	Romantic movement in literature and the arts	**1830**	Greece wins independence from Ottomans
1809–1848	Metternich serves as Austrian foreign minister		Charles X repudiates the Constitutional Charter; insurrection and collapse of the government follow
1810	Germaine de Staël publishes *On Germany*		Louis Philippe succeeds to the throne and maintains a narrowly liberal regime
1815	Holy Alliance formed; revision of Corn Laws in Britain	**1832**	Reform Bill in Britain
1819	Karlsbad Decrees issued by German Confederation	**1839**	Louis Blanc publishes *Organization of Work*
1820	Congress of Troppau proclaims the principle of intervention to maintain autocratic regimes	**1840**	Pierre-Joseph Proudhon publishes *What Is Property?*
		1845–1851	Great Famine in Ireland
1821	Austria crushes a liberal revolution in Naples and restores the Sicilian autocracy	**1847**	Ten Hours Act in Britain
		1848	Revolutions in France, Austria, and Prussia; Marx and Engels publish *The Communist Manifesto*
1823	French armies restore the Spanish regime		

22

LearningCurve
bedfordstmartins.com/mckaywestvalue
After reading the chapter, use
LearningCurve to retain what
you've read.

Life in the Emerging Urban Society

1840–1914

WHEN LONDONERS GATHERED IN 1860 AT THE CRYSTAL PALACE, TO
participate in the Grand Fete sponsored by the Royal Dramatic College, they
enjoyed the pleasures of an established industrial urban society that would
have been unthinkable just sixty years earlier. Across the nineteenth century,
as industrialization expanded exponentially, Europeans left their farms and
country villages to find work in the ever-growing towns and cities. By 1900,
in much of developed western Europe, more than 50 percent of the population lived in urban conglomerations, a trend of rural-to-urban migration that
would spread and continue across the twentieth century.

The emerging urban society brought costs as well as benefits to city dwellers. Advances in public health and urban planning brought some relief to
the squalid working-class slums. On the whole, living standards rose in the
1800s, but wages and living conditions varied greatly according to one's status, and many urban residents were still poor workers. At the same time,

ONLINE DOCUMENT ASSIGNMENT
Life in the Modern City on Film
**How did people respond to the challenges brought on by rapid
urbanization?** View film footage that captures new developments
in city life—from mass transit to waste disposal—and then complete a writing assignment based on the evidence and details from
this chapter.

bedfordstmartins.com/mckaywestvalue

differences in income, education, and occupation divided people into a welter of socially stratified groups; rather than discuss "the" working class or "the" middle class, it is more accurate to speak of "working classes" and "middle classes" and consider the blurring boundaries between the two. Major changes in family life and gender roles accompanied this more complex and diversified class system. Dramatic breakthroughs in chemistry, medicine, and electrical engineering further transformed urban society after 1880, and a new generation of professional social scientists and a changing cohort of artists and writers struggled to explain and portray the vast changes wrought by urbanization.

Taming the City

How did urban life change in the nineteenth century?

Since the Middle Ages, European cities had been centers of government, culture, and large-scale commerce. They had also been congested, dirty, and unhealthy. Beginning in the early nineteenth century, the Industrial Revolution took these unfortunate realities of urban life to unprecedented levels. While historians may debate whether the overall social impact of industrialization was generally positive or negative, there is little doubt that rapid urban growth worsened long-standing overcrowding, pollution, and unhealthy living conditions, and posed a frightening challenge for society. Only the full-scale efforts of government leaders, city planners, reformers, scientists, and reform-minded citizens would tame the ferocious savagery of the industrial city.

Industry and the Growth of Cities

The main causes of the poor quality of urban life—deadly overcrowding, pervasive poverty, and lack of medical knowledge—had existed for centuries. Because the typical city had always been a "walking city," with no public transportation, great masses of people needed to live in close proximity to shops, markets, and workplaces. Packed together almost as tightly as possible, people in cities suffered and died from the spread of infectious disease in far greater numbers than their rural counterparts. In the larger towns, more people died each year than were born, on average, and urban populations maintained their numbers only because newcomers continually arrived from rural areas.

The Industrial Revolution exacerbated these deplorable conditions. The steam engine freed industrialists from dependence on the energy of fast-flowing streams and rivers so that by 1800 there was every incentive to build new factories in urban areas, which had many advantages. Cities had better shipping facilities than the countryside and thus better supplies of coal and raw materials. Cities had many hands wanting work, for they drew people like a magnet. And it was a great advantage for a manufacturer to have other factories nearby to supply the business's needs and buy its products. Therefore, as industry grew, already overcrowded and unhealthy cities expanded rapidly.

Great Britain, the first country in the world to go through the early stages of the Industrial Revolution (see Chapter 20), was forced to face the acute challenges of a changing urban environment early on. In the 1820s and 1830s the populations of a

ONLINE DOCUMENT ASSIGNMENT

Life in the Modern City on Film

How did people respond to the challenges brought on by rapid urbanization? View film footage that captures new developments in city life—from mass transit to waste disposal—and then complete a writing assignment based on the evidence and details from this chapter.

bedfordstmartins.com/mckaywestvalue

number of British cities increased by 40 to 70 percent each decade. The number of people living in cities of 20,000 or more in England and Wales jumped from 1.5 million in 1801 to 6.3 million in 1851 and reached 15.6 million in 1891. Such cities accounted for 17 percent of the total English population in 1801, 35 percent as early as 1851, and fully 54 percent in 1891. Other countries duplicated the English pattern as they industrialized (Map 22.1). (See "Primary Source: First Impressions of the World's Biggest City," page 726.)

Except on the outskirts, early-nineteenth-century cities in Britain used every scrap of available land to the fullest extent. Parks and open areas were almost nonexistent. Developers erected buildings on the smallest possible lots in order to pack the maximum number of people into a given space. Narrow houses were built attached to one another in long rows. These row houses had neither front nor back yards, and only a narrow alley in back separated one row from the next. Other buildings were built around tiny courtyards completely enclosed on all four sides. Many people lived in extremely small, often overcrowded cellars or attics. "Six, eight, and even ten occupying one room is anything but uncommon," wrote a Scottish doctor for a government investigation in 1842.

These highly concentrated urban populations lived in extremely unsanitary and unhealthy conditions. Open drains and sewers flowed alongside or down the middle of unpaved streets. Toilet facilities were extremely primitive and inadequate. In parts of Manchester, as many as two hundred people shared a single outhouse. Such privies filled up rapidly, and since they were infrequently emptied, sewage often overflowed and seeped into cellar dwellings. Moreover, some courtyards in poorer neighborhoods became dunghills, collecting excrement that was sometimes sold as fertilizer and sometimes simply continued to accumulate. By the 1840s there was among the better-off classes a growing, shocking "realization that," as one scholar put it, "millions of English men, women, and children were living in shit."[1]

The environmental costs of rapid urbanization and industrialization were enormous as well. Black soot from coal-fired factories and train engines fouled city air, and by 1850 the River Thames was little better than an open sewer.

Who or what bore responsibility for these awful conditions? The crucial factors included the tremendous pressure of more people and the total absence of public transportation. People simply had to jam themselves together to get to shops and factories on foot. In addition, government in Great Britain, both local and national, only slowly established sanitary facilities and adequate building codes. Scientific understanding of the causes and consequences of urban crowding advanced slowly, and some elites rigidly

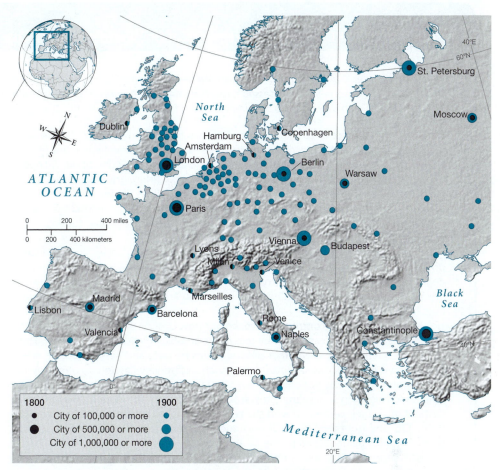

MAP 22.1   European Cities of 100,000 or More, 1800–1900
There were more large cities in Great Britain in 1900 than in all of Europe in 1800.

opposed government action. Certainly, Great Britain had no monopoly on overcrowded and unhealthy urban conditions; many continental cities were every bit as bad.

Most responsible of all was the sad legacy of rural housing conditions in preindustrial society combined with appalling ignorance of germs and basic hygiene. When ordinary people moved to the city, housing was far down on their list of priorities, and they generally took dirt for granted. One English miner told an investigator, "I do not think it usual for the lasses [in the coal mines] to wash their bodies; my sisters never wash themselves." As for the men, "their legs and bodies are as black as your hat."[2]

The Advent of the Public Health Movement

Toward the middle of the nineteenth century, people's fatalistic acceptance of their overcrowded, unsanitary surroundings began to give way to a growing interest in reform and improvement. Edwin Chadwick, one of the commissioners charged with the

PRIMARY SOURCE   First Impressions of the World's Biggest City

In 1870, with over 4 million inhabitants, London was the largest city in the world. In this anonymous, tongue-in-cheek passage, first published as a humorous sketch around 1870, a country man describes his first impressions of urban life.

A man's first residence in London is a revolution in his life and feelings. He loses at once no small part of his individuality. He was a man before, now he is a "party." No longer known as Mr. Brown, but as (say) No. XXI., he feels as one of many cogs in one of the many wheels of an incessantly wearing, tearing, grinding, system of machinery. His country notions must be modified, and all his life-long ways and takings-for-granted prove crude and questionable. He is hourly reminded "This is not the way in London; that this won't work here," or, "people always expect," and "you'll soon find the difference." . . .

Competition in London is very rife. The cheap five-shilling hatter was soon surprised by a four-and-nine-penny shop opposite. Few London men could live but by a degree of energy which the country dealer little knows. The wear and tear of nerve-power and the discharge of brain-power in London are enormous. The London man lives fast. . . .

Many other things contribute to make our new Londoner feel smaller in his own eyes. The living stream flows by him in the streets; he never saw so many utter strangers to him and to each other before; their very pace and destination are different; there is a walk and business determination distinctly London. In other towns men saunter they know not whither, but nearly every passer-by in London has his point, and is making so resolutely towards it that it seems not more his way than his destination as he is carried on with the current; and of street currents there are two, to the City and from the City, so distinct and persistent, that our friend can't get out of one without being jostled by the other. . . .

Self-dependence is another habit peculiarly of London growth. Men soon discover they have no longer the friend, the relative or the neighbour of their own small town to fall back upon. . . .

No doubt there are warm friendships and intimacies in London as well as in the country, but few and far between. People associate more at arm's length, and give their hand more readily than their heart, and hug themselves within their own domestic circles. You know too little of people to be deeply interested either in them or their fortunes, so you expect nothing and are surprised at nothing. An acquaintance may depart London life, and even this life, or be sold up and disappear, without the same surprise or making the same gap as in a village circle.

EVALUATE THE EVIDENCE

1. How does the author use humor to engage the reader?
2. Does this account of modern city life support or contradict the arguments of the new sociologists, discussed later in the chapter?

Source: Henry Mayhew et al., "Life in London," in *London Characters and the Humorous Side of London Life* (London: Chatto and Windus, 1881), pp. 277–281.

What Torrents of Filth Come from That Walbrook Sewer!!   This 1832 cartoon by renowned satirist George Cruikshank shows the director of the Southwark Water Works, a main source of London's drinking water, enthroned on an intake valve in the midst of a heavily polluted River Thames. Wearing a chamber pot for a hat and holding a trident with an impaled dog, cat, and rat, he raises a glass of foul liquid to cries of "Give Us Clean Water!" and "It Makes Me Sick!" (© Science Museum/Science & Society Picture Library)

administration of relief to paupers under Britain's revised Poor Law of 1834, emerged as a powerful voice for reform. Chadwick found inspiration in the ideas of radical philosopher Jeremy Bentham (1748–1832), whose approach to social issues, called **utilitarianism**, had taught that public problems ought to be dealt with on a rational, scientific basis to advance the "greatest good for the greatest number." Applying these principles, Chadwick soon became convinced that disease and death actually caused poverty, because a sick worker was an unemployed worker and orphaned children were poor children. Most important, Chadwick believed that government could help prevent disease by cleaning up the urban environment.

Chadwick collected detailed reports from local Poor Law officials on the "sanitary conditions of the laboring population" and published his hard-hitting findings in 1842. This mass of widely publicized evidence proved that disease was related to filthy environmental conditions, which were in turn caused largely by lack of drainage, sewers, and garbage collection.

Chadwick correctly believed that the stinking excrement of communal outhouses could be dependably carried off by water through sewers at less than one-twentieth the cost of removing it by hand. The cheap iron pipes and tile drains of the industrial age would provide running water and sewerage for all sections of town, not just the wealthy ones. In 1848, with the cause strengthened by a cholera epidemic that raged across Britain, Chadwick's report became the basis of Great Britain's first public health law, which created a national health board and gave cities broad authority to build modern sanitary systems.

The public health movement won dedicated supporters in the United States, France, and Germany from the late 1840s on. Governments accepted at least limited responsibility for the health of all citizens, and their programs broke decisively with the age-old fatalism of urban populations. By the 1860s and 1870s European cities were making real progress toward adequate water supplies and sewerage systems. Though factories and coal stoves continued to pump black smoke into the air, and pollution remained a serious problem, city dwellers started to reap the reward of better health, and death rates began to decline.

The Bacterial Revolution

Although improved sanitation in cities promoted a better quality of life and some improvements in health care, effective control of communicable disease required a great leap forward in medical knowledge and biological theory. Early reformers, including Chadwick, were seriously handicapped by their adherence to the prevailing miasmatic theory of disease—the belief that people contracted disease when they inhaled the bad odors of decay and putrefying excrement. In the 1840s and 1850s keen observation by doctors and public health officials pinpointed the role of bad drinking water in the transmission of disease and suggested that contagion was spread through physical contact with filth, not by its odors, thus weakening the miasmatic idea.

The breakthrough in understanding how bad drinking water and filth actually made people sick arrived when the French chemist Louis Pasteur developed the **germ theory** of disease. Pasteur (pas-TUHR) (1822–1895), who began studying fermentation for brewers in 1854, used a microscope to develop a simple test that brewers could use to monitor the fermentation process and avoid spoilage. He found that fermentation depended on the growth of living organisms and that the activity of these organisms could be suppressed by heating the beverage—a process that came to be called pasteurization, which he first implemented in the early 1860s. The breathtaking implication was that specific diseases were caused by specific living organisms—germs—and that those organisms could be controlled.

By 1870 the work of Pasteur and others had demonstrated the general connection between germs and disease. When, in the middle of the 1870s, German country doctor Robert Koch (kawkh) and his coworkers developed pure cultures of harmful bacteria and described their life cycles, the dam broke. Over the next twenty years, researchers—mainly Germans—identified the organisms responsible for disease after disease. These discoveries led to the development of a number of effective vaccines, though some infections resisted treatment until scientists developed antibiotics in the middle of the next century.

Acceptance of germ theory brought about dramatic improvements in the deadly environment of hospitals and operating rooms (see Chapter 18). In 1865, when Pasteur showed that the air was full of bacteria, English surgeon Joseph Lister (1827–1912) immediately grasped the connection between aerial bacteria and the problem of wound infection. He reasoned that a chemical disinfectant applied to a wound dressing would "destroy the life of the floating particles," by which he meant germs. Lister's antiseptic principle worked wonders. In the 1880s German surgeons developed the more sophisticated practice of sterilizing not only the wound but also everything—hands, instruments, clothing—that entered the operating room.

The achievements of the bacterial revolution coupled with the public health movement saved millions of lives, particularly after about 1880. Mortality rates began to decline dramatically in European countries as the awful death sentences of the past—diphtheria, typhoid, typhus, cholera, yellow fever—became vanishing diseases. City dwellers benefited especially from these developments. By 1910 a great silent revolution had occurred: the death rates for people of all ages in urban areas were generally no greater than those for people in rural areas, and sometimes they were lower.

Improvements in Urban Planning

In addition to public health improvements, more effective urban planning was a major key to a better quality of urban life in the nineteenth century. France took the lead in this area during the rule of Napoleon III (r. 1848–1870), who sought to promote the welfare of his subjects through government action. He believed that rebuilding much of Paris would provide employment, improve living conditions, limit the outbreak of cholera epidemics—and testify to the power and glory of his empire. In Baron Georges Haussmann (HOWS-muhn) (1809–1884), an aggressive, impatient Alsatian whom he placed in charge of Paris, Napoleon III found an authoritarian planner capable of bulldozing both buildings and opposition. In twenty years Paris was completely transformed (Map 22.2).

The Paris of 1850 was a labyrinth of narrow, dark streets, the results of desperate overcrowding and a lack of effective planning. More than one-third of the city's 1 million inhabitants lived in a central district not twice the size of New York's Central Park. Residents faced terrible conditions and extremely high death rates. The entire metropolis had few open spaces and only two public parks.

For two decades Haussmann and his fellow planners proceeded on many interrelated fronts. With a bold energy that often shocked their contemporaries, they razed old buildings in order to cut broad, straight, tree-lined boulevards through the center of the city as well as in new quarters rising on the outskirts (see Map 22.2). These boulevards, designed in part to prevent the easy construction and defense of barricades by revolutionary crowds, permitted traffic to flow freely and afforded impressive vistas. Their creation also demolished some of the worst slums. New streets stimulated the construction of better housing, especially for the middle classes. Planners created small neighborhood parks and open spaces throughout the city and developed two very large parks suitable for all kinds of holiday activities—one on the affluent west side and one on the poor east side of the city. The city improved its sewers, and a system of aqueducts more than doubled the city's supply of clean, fresh water.

Rebuilding Paris provided a new model for urban planning and stimulated urban reform throughout Europe, particularly after 1870. In city after city, public authorities mounted a coordinated attack on many of the interrelated problems of the urban environment. As in Paris, improvements in public health through better water supply and waste disposal often went hand in hand with new boulevard construction. Urban planners

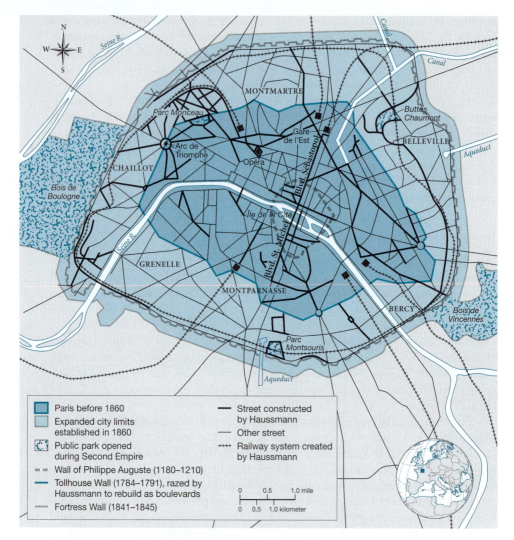

MAP 22.2   The Modernization of Paris, ca. 1850–1870
The addition of broad boulevards, large parks, and grand train stations transformed Paris. The cutting of the new north-south axis—known as the Boulevard Saint-Michel—was one of Haussmann's most controversial projects. It razed much of Paris's medieval core and filled the Île de la Cité with massive government buildings.

in cities such as Vienna and Cologne followed the Parisian example of tearing down old walled fortifications and replacing them with broad, circular boulevards on which they erected office buildings, town halls, theaters, opera houses, and museums. These ring roads and the new boulevards that radiated outward from the city center eased movement and encouraged urban expansion (see Map 22.2). Zoning expropriation laws, which allowed a majority of the owners of land in a given quarter of the city to impose major street or sanitation improvements on a reluctant minority, were an important mechanism of this new urban reform movement.

Public Transportation

The development of mass public transportation often accompanied urban planning, further enhancing living conditions. In the 1870s many European cities authorized private companies to operate horse-drawn streetcars, which had been developed in the United States, to carry riders along the growing number of major thoroughfares. Then in the 1890s the real revolution occurred: European countries adopted another American transit innovation, a streetcar that ran on the newly harnessed power of electricity (see page 748).

Electric streetcars were cheaper, faster, more dependable, cleaner, and more comfortable than their horse-drawn counterparts. Workers, shoppers, and schoolchildren hopped on board during the workweek. On weekends and holidays, streetcars carried urban dwellers on happy outings to parks and the countryside, to racetracks and music halls. In 1886 the horse-drawn streetcars of Austria-Hungary, France, Germany, and Great Britain carried about 900 million riders per year. By 1910 electric streetcar systems in those four countries were carrying 6.7 billion riders.[3]

Mass transit helped greatly in the struggle for decent housing. The new boulevards and horse-drawn streetcars facilitated a middle-class move to better and more spacious housing in the 1860s and 1870s; after 1890 electric streetcars meant people of even modest means could access new, improved housing. Though still densely populated, cities expanded and became less congested. In England in 1901, only 9 percent of the urban population was overcrowded in terms of the official definition of more than two persons per room. On the continent, many city governments in the early twentieth century built electric streetcar systems that provided transportation to new public and private housing developments for the working classes beyond the city limits. Suburban commuting was born.

Rich and Poor and Those in Between

What did the emergence of urban industrial society mean for rich and poor and those in between?

As the quality of urban life improved across Europe, the class structure became more complex and diverse. Urban society featured many distinct social groups, all of which existed in a state of constant flux and competition. The gap between rich and poor remained enormous and quite traditional, but there were numerous gradations between the extremes.

The Distribution of Income

By 1850 at the latest, real wages — that is, wages received by workers adjusted for changes in the prices they paid — were rising for the mass of the population, and they continued to do so until 1914. The real wages of British workers, for example, almost doubled between 1850 and 1906. Similar increases occurred in continental countries as industrial development quickened after 1850. Ordinary people took a major step forward in the centuries-old battle against poverty, reinforcing efforts to improve many aspects of human existence.

Greater economic rewards for the average person did not eliminate hardship and poverty, however, nor did they make the wealth and income of the rich and the poor significantly more equal, as contemporary critics argued and economic historians have clearly demonstrated. The aristocracy—with imposing wealth, unrivaled social prestige, and substantial political influence—retained its position at the very top of the social ladder, followed closely by a new rich elite, composed mainly of the most successful business families from banking, industry, and large-scale commerce. In fact, the prominent families of the commercial elite tended to marry into the old aristocracy, to form a new upper class of at most 5 percent of the population. Much of the aristocracy welcomed this development. Having experienced a sharp decline in its relative income in the course of industrialization, the landed aristocracy had met big business coming up the staircase and was often delighted to trade titles, country homes, and snobbish elegance for good, hard cash. Some of the best bargains were made through marriages to American heiresses. Correspondingly, wealthy aristocrats tended increasingly to exploit their agricultural and mineral resources as if they were business people.

Income inequality reflected social status. In almost every advanced country around 1900, the richest 5 percent of all households in the population received about a third of all national income, and the richest 20 percent of households received from 50 to 60 percent of it. As a result, the lower 80 percent received only 40 to 50 percent of all income—less than the two richest classes. Moreover, the bottom 30 percent of all households received 10 percent or less of all income.

To understand the full significance of these statistics, one must realize that the middle classes were much smaller than they are today. In the nineteenth century they accounted for less than 20 percent of the population. Moreover, in the nineteenth century (and for centuries before as well) income taxes on the wealthy were light or nonexistent. Thus the gap between rich and poor remained enormous at the beginning of the twentieth century. Indeed, it was probably almost as great as it had been in the late eighteenth century, in the age of agriculture and aristocracy.

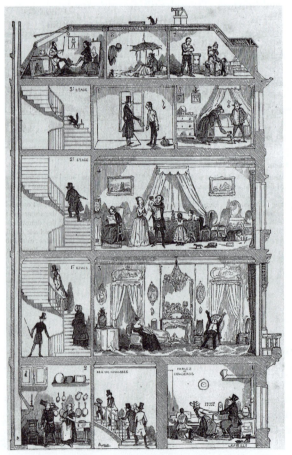

Apartment Living in Paris   This drawing shows a typical layout for a European city apartment building in about 1850. (Bibliothèque nationale de France)

The great gap between rich and poor endured, in part, because industrial and urban development made society more diverse and classes less unified. Society had not split into two sharply defined opposing classes, as Karl Marx had predicted (see Chapter 21). Instead, the economic specialization that enabled society to produce goods more effectively had created a remarkable variety of new social groups. There developed an almost unlimited range of jobs, skills, and earnings; one group or subclass blended into another in a complex, confusing hierarchy. Between the tiny elite of the very rich and the sizable mass of the dreadfully poor lived a range of subclasses, each filled with individuals struggling to rise or at least to hold their own in the social order. In this atmosphere of competition and hierarchy, neither the "middle class" nor the "working class" actually acted as a single unified force. Rather, the social and occupational hierarchy developed enormous variations, though the age-old pattern of great economic inequality remained firmly intact.

The People and Occupations of the Middle Classes

By the beginning of the twentieth century, the diversity and range within the urban middle class were striking. Indeed, it makes sense to replace the idea of a single "middle class" with a confederation of "middle classes" whose members engaged in occupations requiring mental, rather than physical, skill.

Below the wealthy top tier, the much larger, much less wealthy, and increasingly diversified middle class included moderately successful industrialists and merchants as well as professionals in law, business, and medicine. As industry and technology expanded in the nineteenth century, a growing demand developed for experts with specialized knowledge, and advanced education soared in importance among the middle classes. Engineering, for example, emerged from the world of skilled labor as a full-fledged profession with considerable prestige. Architects, chemists, accountants, and surveyors, to name only a few, first achieved professional standing in this period. They established criteria for advanced training and certification and banded together in organizations to promote and defend their interests.

Management of large public and private institutions also emerged as a kind of profession as governments provided more services and as very large corporations such as railroads managed ever-larger numbers of human and physical resources. Government officials and many private executives had specialized knowledge and the capacity to earn a good living. And they shared most of the values of the business-owning entrepreneurs and the older professionals.

Industrialization expanded and diversified the lower middle class. The number of independent, property-owning shopkeepers and small business people grew, and so did the number of white-collar employees—a mixed group of traveling salesmen, bookkeepers, store managers, and clerks who staffed the offices and branch stores of large corporations. White-collar employees owned little property and often earned no more than better-paid skilled or semiskilled workers. Yet white-collar workers were fiercely committed to the middle-class ideal of upward social mobility. The tie, the suit, the soft, clean hands that accompanied low-level retail and managerial work became important status symbols that set this group above those who earned a living through manual labor.

Relatively well educated but without complex technical skills, many white-collar occupational groups strove to achieve professional standing and higher social status.

Elementary school teachers largely succeeded in this effort. From being miserably paid part-time workers in the early nineteenth century, teachers rode the wave of mass education to respectable middle-class status and income. Nurses also rose from the lower ranks of unskilled labor to precarious middle-class standing. Dentistry was taken out of the hands of working-class barbers and placed in the hands of highly trained (and middle-class) professionals.

Middle-Class Culture and Values

Despite growing occupational diversity and conflicting interests, lifestyle preferences loosely united the European middle classes. Food, housing, clothes, and behavior all expressed middle-class values and testified to the superior social standing of this group over the working classes.

Unlike the working classes, the middle classes had the money to eat well, and spent a substantial portion of their household budget on food and entertainment. They consumed meat in abundance: a well-off family might spend 10 percent of its annual income on meat and fully 25 percent on food and drink. The dinner party—a favored social occasion—boosted spending. A wealthy middle-class family might give a lavish party for eight to twelve almost every week, but even more modest households in the lower middle class did so once a month.

The middle-class wife could cope with this endless procession of meals, courses, and dishes because she had servants as well as money at her disposal. Indeed, the employment of at least one full-time maid to cook and clean was the clearest sign that a family had crossed the cultural divide separating the working classes from what some contemporary observers called the "servant-keeping classes." The greater a family's income, the greater the number of servants it employed. Servants absorbed about another 25 percent of income at all levels of the middle class.

Well fed and well served, by 1900 the middle classes were also well housed. Many prosperous families rented, rather than owned, their homes, complete with tiny rooms for servants under the eaves of the top floor. And, just as the aristocracy had long divided the year between palatial country estates and lavish townhouses during "the season," so the upper middle class purchased country places or built beach houses for weekend and summer use.

The middle classes paid great attention to outward appearances, especially their clothes. The factory, the sewing machine, and the department store had all helped reduce the cost and expand the variety of clothing. Middle-class women were particularly attentive to the dictates of fashion, though men also wore the now-appropriate business suit. Private coaches and carriages, expensive items in the city, further testified to rising social status.

Rich Europeans could devote more time to "culture" and leisure pursuits than less wealthy or well-established families. The keystones of culture and leisure were books, music, and travel. The long realistic novel, the heroic operas of composers Wagner and Verdi, the diligent striving of the dutiful daughter at the piano, and the packaged tour to a foreign country were all sources of middle-class pleasure.

In addition to their material tastes, the middle classes generally agreed upon a strict code of behavior and morality, which stressed hard work, self-discipline, and personal achievement. Middle-class social reformers denounced drunkenness and gambling as vices and celebrated sexual purity and fidelity as virtues. Men and women who fell into crime or poverty were held responsible for their own circumstances. A stern sense of Christian morality, preached tirelessly by religious leaders, educators, and politicians, reaffirmed these values. The middle-class individual was supposed to know right from wrong and act accordingly.

The People and Occupations of the Working Classes

At the beginning of the twentieth century, about four out of five people belonged to the working classes — that is, people whose livelihoods depended primarily on physical labor and who did not employ domestic servants. Many of them were still small land-owning peasants and hired farm hands, and this was especially the case in eastern Europe. In western and central Europe, however, the typical worker had left the land. By 1900 less than 8 percent of the people in Great Britain worked in agriculture, and in rapidly industrializing Germany only 25 percent were employed in agriculture and forestry. Even in less industrialized France, less than 50 percent of the population worked the land.

The urban working classes were even less unified and homogeneous than the middle classes. First, economic development and increased specialization expanded the tradi-tional range of working-class skills, earnings, and experiences. Meanwhile, the old sharp distinction between highly skilled artisans and unskilled manual workers gradually broke down. To be sure, highly skilled printers and masons as well as unskilled dock-workers and common laborers continued to exist. But between these extremes there appeared ever more semiskilled groups, including trained factory workers. In addition, skilled, semiskilled, and unskilled workers developed divergent lifestyles and cultural values. These differences contributed to a keen sense of social status and hierarchy within the working classes, creating great diversity and undermining the class unity predicted by Marx.

Highly skilled workers — about 15 percent of the working classes — became known as the **labor aristocracy**. They earned only about two-thirds of the income of the bot-tom ranks of the servant-keeping classes, but that was fully double the earnings of unskilled workers. The most "aristocratic" of these highly skilled workers were construc-tion bosses and factory foremen, who had risen from the ranks and were fiercely proud of their achievement. The labor aristocracy also included members of the traditional highly skilled handicraft trades that had not been mechanized or placed in factories, like cabinetmakers, jewelers, and printers.

While the labor aristocracy enjoyed its exalted position, maintaining that status was by no means certain. Gradually, as factory production eliminated more and more crafts, lower-paid, semiskilled factory workers replaced many skilled artisans. Traditional wood-carvers and watchmakers virtually disappeared, for example, as the making of furniture and timepieces now took place in factories. At the same time, industrialization opened new opportunities for new kinds of highly skilled workers, such as shipbuilders and railway locomotive engineers. Thus the labor elite remained in a state of flux, as indi-viduals and whole crafts moved in and out of it.

To maintain this precarious standing, the upper working class adopted distinctive values and straitlaced, almost puritanical behavior. Like the middle classes, the labor aristocracy believed firmly in middle-class morality and economic improvement. Families in the upper working class saved money regularly, worried about their children's

The Labor Aristocracy   This group of British foremen is attending the International Exhibition in Paris in 1862. Their "Sunday best" includes the silk top hats and long morning coats of the propertied classes, but they definitely remain workers, the proud leaders of laboring people.
(© The Board of Trustees of the Victoria & Albert Museum)

education, and valued good housing. Wives seldom sought employment outside the home. Despite these similarities, skilled workers viewed themselves not as aspirants to the middle class but as the pacesetters and natural leaders of all the working classes. Well aware of the degradation not so far below them, they practiced self-discipline and stern morality and generally frowned on heavy drinking and sexual permissiveness. As one German skilled worker somberly warned, "The path to the brothel leads through the tavern" and from there to drastic decline or total ruin.[4]

Below the labor aristocracy stood the enormously complex world of hard work, composed of both semiskilled and unskilled workers. Established construction workers—carpenters, bricklayers, pipe fitters—stood near the top of the semiskilled hierarchy, often flirting with (or sliding back from) the labor elite. A large number of the semiskilled were factory workers, who earned highly variable but relatively good wages. These workers included substantial numbers of unmarried women, who began to play an increasingly important role in the industrial labor force.

Below the semiskilled workers, a larger group of unskilled workers included day laborers such as longshoremen, wagon-driving teamsters, and "helpers" of all kinds. Many of these people had real skills and performed valuable services, but they were unorganized and divided, united only by the common fate of meager earnings and poor living conditions. The same lack of unity characterized street vendors and market people—these self-employed members of the lower working classes competed savagely with each other and with established shopkeepers of the lower middle class.

One of the largest components of the unskilled group was domestic servants, whose numbers grew steadily in the nineteenth century. In Great Britain, for example, one out of every seven employed persons in 1911 was a domestic servant. The great majority were women; indeed, one out of every three girls in Britain between the ages of fifteen and twenty worked as a domestic servant. Throughout Europe, many female domestics in the cities were recent migrants from rural areas. As in earlier times, domestic service meant hard work at low pay with limited personal independence and the danger of sexual exploitation. For the full-time general maid in a lower-middle-class family, an unending routine of babysitting, shopping, cooking, and cleaning defined a lengthy working day. In the wealthiest households, the serving girl was at the bottom of a rigid hierarchy of status-conscious butlers and housekeepers.

Nonetheless, domestic service had real attractions for young women from rural areas who had few specialized skills. Marriage prospects were better, or at least more varied, in the city than back home. And though wages were low, they were higher and more regular than in hard agricultural work—which was being replaced by mechanization, at any rate. Finally, as one London observer noted, young girls and other migrants from the countryside were drawn to the city by "the contagion of numbers, the sense of something going on, the theaters and the music halls, the brightly lighted streets and busy crowds—all, in short, that makes the difference between the Mile End fair on a Saturday night, and a dark and muddy country lane, with no glimmer of gas and with nothing to do."[5]

Many young domestics made the successful transition to working-class wife and mother. Yet with an unskilled or unemployed husband, a growing family, and limited household income, many working-class wives had to join the broad ranks of working women in the **sweated industries**. These industries expanded rapidly after 1850 and resembled the old putting-out and cottage industries of earlier times (see Chapter 17). The women normally worked at home and were paid by the piece, not by the hour. They and their young children who helped them earned pitiful wages and lacked any job security. Women decorated dishes or embroidered linens, took in laundry for washing and ironing, or made clothing, especially after the advent of the sewing machine. An army of poor women, usually working at home, accounted for many of the inexpensive ready-made clothes displayed on department store racks and in tiny shops.

Working-Class Leisure and Religion

Notwithstanding hard physical labor and lack of wealth, the urban working classes sought fun and recreation, and they found both. Across the face of Europe, drinking remained unquestionably the favorite leisure-time activity of working people. For many middle-class moralists, as well as moralizing historians since, love of drink was the curse of the modern age—a sign of social dislocation and popular suffering. Certainly, drinking was deadly serious business. One English slum dweller recalled that "drunkenness was by far the commonest cause of dispute and misery in working class homes. On account of it one saw many a decent family drift down through poverty into total want."[6]

Generally, however, heavy problem drinking declined in the late nineteenth century as it became less socially acceptable. This decline reflected in part the moral leadership of the labor aristocracy. At the same time, drinking became more publicly acceptable. Cafés and pubs became increasingly bright, friendly places. Working-class political activities, both moderate and radical, were also concentrated in taverns and pubs. Moreover, social drinking in public places by married couples and sweethearts became an accepted and widespread practice for the first time. This greater participation by women undoubtedly helped civilize the world of drink and hard liquor.

The two other leisure-time passions of working-class culture were sports and music halls. "Cruel sports," such as bullbaiting and cockfighting, had greatly declined throughout Europe by the late nineteenth century. Commercialized spectator sports filled their place; horse racing and soccer were the most popular. Working people gambled on sports events, and for many a working person a desire to decipher racing forms provided a powerful incentive toward literacy. Music halls and vaudeville theaters, the working-class counterparts of middle-class opera and classical theater, were enormously popular throughout Europe. In 1900 London had more than fifty such halls and theaters. Music hall audiences included men and women, which may account for the fact that drunkenness, premarital sex, marital difficulties, and mothers-in-law were all favorite themes of broad jokes and bittersweet songs.

In more serious moments, religion continued to provide working people with solace and meaning. The eighteenth-century vitality of popular religion in Catholic countries and the Protestant rejuvenation exemplified by German Pietism and English Methodism (see Chapter 18) carried over into the nineteenth century. Indeed, many historians see the early nineteenth century as an age of religious revival. Yet historians recognize that by the last few decades of the nineteenth century, a considerable decline in both church attendance and church donations had occurred in most European countries. And it seems clear that this decline was greater for the urban working classes than for their rural counterparts or for the middle classes.

Why did working-class church attendance decline? On one hand, the construction of churches failed to keep up with the rapid growth of urban population, especially in new working-class neighborhoods. On the other, throughout the nineteenth century workers saw Catholic and Protestant churches as conservative institutions that defended status quo politics, hierarchical social order, and middle-class morality. Socialist political parties, in particular, attacked organized religion as a pillar of bourgeois society, and as the working classes became more politically conscious, they tended to see established churches as allied with their political opponents. In addition, religion underwent a process historians call "feminization": in the working and middle classes alike, women were more pious and attended service more regularly than men. Urban workingmen in particular developed vaguely antichurch attitudes, even though they remained neutral or positive toward religion.

The pattern was different in the United States, where most nineteenth-century churches also preached social conservatism. But because church and state had always been separate and because a host of denominations and even different religions competed for members, working people identified churches much less with the political and social status quo. Instead, individual churches in the United States were often closely identified with an ethnic group rather than a social class, and churches thrived, in part, as a means of asserting ethnic identity. This same process occurred in Europe if the church or synagogue had never been linked to the state and served as a focus for ethnic cohesion. Irish Catholic churches in Protestant Britain, Catholic churches in partitioned Polish lands, and Jewish synagogues in Russia were outstanding examples.

Changing Family Lifestyles

How did urbanization affect family life and gender roles?

By the 1850s the family had stabilized considerably after the disruption of the late eighteenth and early nineteenth centuries. With the consolidation caused by industrialization and urbanization, the growing middle classes created a distinctive middle-class lifestyle, which set them off from peasants, workers, and the aristocracy. New ideas about courtship and marriage, family and gender roles, homemaking and child rearing all expressed middle-class norms and values in ways that would have a profound impact on family life in the century to come. Changes in family life affected both men and women and all social classes, but to varying degrees. Leading a middle-class lifestyle was prohibitively expensive for workers and peasants, and middle-class family values at first had little relevance for their lives. Yet as the nineteenth century drew to a close, the middle-class lifestyle increasingly became the norm for all classes.

Middle-Class Marriage and Courtship Rituals

Rather than marry for convenience, or for economic or social reasons—as was still common among workers, peasants, and aristocrats—by the 1850s the middle-class couple was supposed to meet, court, fall deeply in love, and join for life because of a shared emotional bond. Of course, economic considerations in marriage by no means disappeared. But an entire culture of romantic love—popularized in advice manuals, popular fiction, and art, and practiced in courtship rituals, weddings, and married life—now surrounded the middle-class couple with a tender emotional charge. The growing popularity among all classes toward the end of the nineteenth century of what historians call **companionate marriage** underscores the way historical contexts influence human emotions and behaviors.

Strict rules for courtship and engagement enshrined in the concept of falling in love ensured that middle-class individuals would make an appropriate match. Parents, chaperones, and the general public closely guarded the boundary between courtship and sex, between the proper and the improper. Young couples were seldom alone before they became engaged, and people rarely paired off with someone from an inappropriate class background. Premarital sex was taboo for women, though men might experiment, a double standard that expressed middle-class assumptions about sexual morality and especially women's virginity before marriage.

Engagement also followed a complicated set of rules and rituals. Secret engagements led to public announcements, and then the couple could appear together, though only with chaperones when in potentially delicate situations. They might walk arm in arm, but custom placed strict limits on physical intimacy. A couple might find ways to experiment with sexual behaviors, but only in secret—which confirmed the special feelings of "true love" between the couple.

Marriage had its own set of rules. Usually a middle-class man could marry only if he could support a wife, children, and a servant. He was supposed to be fairly prosperous and well established in his career. As a result, some middle-class men never married, because they could not afford it. These customs created special difficulties for young middle-class women, who could rarely pursue an independent career or acquire a home without a husband. The system encouraged mixed-age marriages. A new husband was typically much older than his young wife, who usually had no career and entered marriage directly out of her parents' home or perhaps a girl's finishing school. She would have had little experience with the realities of adult life.

Love meant something different to men and women. Trained to fall passionately in love with "Mr. Right," young women equated marriage with emotional intensity. Men, on the other hand, were supposed to "find a wife": they took a more active but dispassionate role in courtship. Since women generally were quite young, the man was encouraged to see himself as the protector of a young and fragile creature. In short, the typical middle-class marriage was more similar to a child-parent relationship than a partnership of equals, a situation finely portrayed in Henrik Ibsen's noted play *A Doll's House* (1879). The inequality of marriage was codified in European legal systems that, with rare exceptions, placed property ownership in the hands of the husband.

Middle- and Working-Class Sexuality

A double standard in sexual relations paralleled the gender inequalities built into middle-class standards of love and marriage. Middle-class moralists of all stripes cast men as aggressively sexual creatures, while women—the "angel in the house"—were supposed to be pure and chaste and act as a brake on male desire. Contemporary science legitimized this double standard. According to late-nineteenth-century physicians, men, easily aroused by the sight of a wrist or ankle, fell prey to their raging biological drives, while respectable women were supposedly uninterested in sex by nature.

Middle-class moralists assumed that men would enter marriage with some sexual experience, though this was unthinkable for a middle-class woman. When middle-class men did seek premarital sex, middle-class women were off limits. Instead, bourgeois men took advantage of their class status and sought lower-class women, domestic servants, or prostitutes. If a young middle-class woman had experimented with or even was suspected of having had premarital sex, her chances for an acceptable marriage fell dramatically.

The sexual standards of the working classes stood in marked contrast to these norms early in the nineteenth century, but that changed over time. Premarital sex for both men and women was common and more acceptable among the working class. In the first half of the nineteenth century, among the lower classes, about one-third of the births in many large European cities occurred outside of wedlock. The second half of the century saw the reversal of this high rate of illegitimacy: in western, northern, and central Europe, more babies were born to married mothers. Young, unmarried workers were probably engaging in just as much sexual activity as their parents and grandparents who had created the illegitimacy explosion of 1750 to 1850 (see Chapter 18). But in the later part of the nineteenth century, pregnancy for a young single woman, which a couple might see as the natural consequence of a serious relationship, led increasingly to marriage and the establishment of a two-parent household. Indeed, one in three working-class women were pregnant when they married. This important development reflected the spread of middle-class ideals of family respectability among the working classes, as well as their gradual economic improvement. Romantic love held working-class families together, and marriage was less of an economic challenge. The urban working-class couple of the late nineteenth century thus became more stable, and that stability strengthened the family as an institution.

Prostitution

In the late nineteenth century prostitution was legal in much of Europe. In Italy, France, Great Britain, and much of Germany, the state licensed brothels and registered individual prostitutes. In Paris, 155,000 women were registered as prostitutes between 1871 and 1903, and 750,000 others were suspected of prostitution in the same years. In Berlin, in 1909 alone, the authorities registered over 40,000 prostitutes. The totals are probably low, since most women in the sex trade tried to avoid government registration.

In streets, dance halls, and pubs across Europe, young working-class women used prostitution as a source of second income or as a way to weather a period of unemployment. Prostitutes generally serviced lower-class men, soldiers, and sailors, though middle- and upper-class men looking to "sow wild oats" also paid for sexual encounters. Streetwalking offered women some measure of financial independence, but the work was dangerous. Violence and rape, police harassment, and venereal disease were commonplace hazards.

Prostitutes clearly transgressed middle-class ideals of feminine respectability, but among the working classes prostitution was tolerated as more-or-less acceptable work of a temporary nature. Like domestic service, prostitution was a stage of life, not permanent employment. Having practiced it for a while in their twenties, many women went on to marry (or live with) men of their own class and establish homes and families.

As middle-class family values became increasingly prominent after the 1860s, prostitution generated great concern among social reformers. The prostitute — immoral, lascivious, and unhealthy in middle-class eyes — served as the mirror image of the respectable middle-class woman. Moreover, authorities blamed prostitutes for spreading crime and disease, particularly syphilis. Before the discovery of penicillin, syphilis was indeed a terrifying and widespread affliction. Its painful symptoms led to physical and mental decline and often death, and medical treatment was embarrassing and for the most part ineffective.

As general concerns with public health gained publicity, state and city authorities across Europe subjected prostitutes — in their eyes the vector of contagious disease — to increased surveillance. The British Contagious Diseases Acts, in force between 1864 and 1886, exemplified the trend. Under these acts, special plainclothes policemen required women identified as "common prostitutes" to undergo biweekly medical exams. If they showed signs of venereal disease, they were interned in a "lock hospital" and forced to undergo treatment; when the outward signs of disease went away, they were released.

The Contagious Diseases Acts were controversial from the start. A determined middle-class feminist campaign against the policy, led by Josephine Butler and the Ladies National Association, loudly proclaimed that the acts physically abused poor women, violated their constitutional rights, and legitimized male vice. Under pressure, Parliament repealed the laws in 1886. Yet heavy-handed government regulation had devastated the informality of working-class prostitution. Now branded as "registered girls," prostitutes experienced new forms of public humiliation, and the trade was increasingly controlled by male pimps rather than by the women themselves. Prostitution had never been safe, but it had been accepted, at least among the working classes. Prostitutes were now stigmatized as social and sexual outsiders.

Separate Spheres and the Importance of Homemaking

After 1850 the work of wives became increasingly distinct and separate from that of their husbands in all classes. The preindustrial pattern among both peasants and cottage workers, in which husbands and wives both worked and shared basic household duties, became less common. In wealthier homes, this change was particularly dramatic. The good middle-class family man earned the wages to support the household; the public world of work, education, and politics was male space. Respectable middle-class women did not work outside the home and rarely even traveled alone in public. Working-class women, including servants and prostitutes, were more visible in public places, but if a middle-class woman went out without a male escort she might be accused of low morals or character. Thus many historians have stressed that the societal ideal in nineteenth-century Europe became a strict division of labor by gender within rigidly constructed **separate spheres**: the wife as mother and homemaker, the husband as wage earner and breadwinner.

For the middle classes, the single-family home, a symbol of middle-class status and a sanctuary from the callous outside world of competitive capitalism, was central to the notion of separate spheres. Middle-class floor plans grew to include separate sleeping rooms for parents and each family member—unheard of among the lower classes—as well as a special drawing room (or parlor), used to entertain guests. Plump sofas, bric-a-brac, and souvenirs graced domestic interiors; curtains of heavy red velvet and colorful silks draped doors and windows. Such ostentatious displays were too expensive for the working classes, who made up 80 percent of the population.

At the heart of the middle-class home stood the woman: notions of femininity, motherhood, and private life came together in the ideal of domestic space. Middle-class women were spared the manly burdens of the outside world, while lower-class servants ensured that they had free time to turn the private sphere into a domestic refuge of love and privacy. Numerous middle-class housekeeping manuals made the wife's responsibilities quite clear, as this Swedish handbook from 1889 suggests: "A man who spends most of his day away from the family, who has to work outside the home, counts on finding a restful and refreshing atmosphere when he returns home, and sometimes even a little merriment or a surprise. . . . It is his wife's duty to ensure that he is not disappointed in his expectation. She must do her utmost to make his stay at home as pleasant as possible; she can thus continue to keep her influence over him and retain his affection undiminished."[7]

By 1900 working-class families had adopted many middle-class values, but they did not have the means to fully realize the ideal of separate spheres. Women were the primary homemakers, and, as in the upper classes, men did little or no domestic labor. But many working-class women also made a monetary contribution to family income by taking in a boarder, doing piecework at home in the sweated industries (see page 737), or getting an outside job. While middle-class family life centered on an ample daily meal, working-class women struggled to put sufficient food on the table. Working women worked to create a homelike environment that at least resembled that of the

Christmas and the Sentimental Pleasures of the Middle-Class Home   The Victorian Christmas celebrated the family values and lifestyles of the middle classes at their most expressive, aptly portrayed in this sentimental painting by English genre artist Walter Dendy Sadler. His clichéd portrait of a wealthy middle-class family holiday — with holly adorning the walls, mistletoe hanging above the fireplace, children singing carols with their parents, and contented grandparents sitting by a warm fire — captures the intimacy and love that increasingly bound together middle-class and working-class families alike during the nineteenth century. Titled *Home Sweet Home* and released for commercial reproduction and sale around 1900, prints of this image of domestic bliss no doubt adorned the walls of many middle-class parlors like the one portrayed in the painting. (Private Collection/Photo © Christie's Images/The Bridgeman Art Library)

middle class — cleaning house, collecting trinkets, and decorating domestic interiors — but working men often preferred to spend time in the local pub with workmates, rather than come home. Indeed, alcoholism and domestic violence afflicted many working-class families, even as they worked to build a relationship based on romantic love.

Feminist historians have often criticized the middle-class ideal of separate spheres because it restricted women's educational and employment opportunities, and the women's rights movement that emerged in the late nineteenth century certainly challenged the limitations of the model. In recent years, however, some scholars have been rethinking gender roles within the long-term development of consumer behavior and household economies. In the era of industrialization, these scholars suggest, the "breadwinner-homemaker" household that developed from about 1850 onward was rational consumer behavior that improved the lives of all family members, especially in the working classes.[8]

According to this view, when husbands specialized in earning an adequate cash income — the "family wage" that labor unions demanded — and wives specialized in managing the home, the working-class wife could produce desirable goods that could not be bought in a market, such as improved health, better eating habits, and better behavior. For example, higher wages from the breadwinner could buy more raw food, but only the homemaker's careful selection, processing, and cooking would allow the family to benefit from increased spending on food. Running an urban household was a complicated, demanding, and valuable task. Twice-a-day food shopping, careful economizing, and fighting the growing crusade against dirt — not to mention child rearing — constituted a full-time occupation. Working yet another job for wages outside the home had limited appeal for most married women unless the earnings were essential for family survival. The homemaker's managerial skills, however, enabled the working-class couple to maximize their personal well-being.

The woman's guidance of the household went hand in hand with the increased pride in the home and family and the emotional importance attached to them in working- and middle-class families alike. According to one historian, by 1900 the song "Home, Sweet Home" had become "almost a second national anthem."[9] Domesticity and family ties were now central to the lives of millions of people of all classes.

Child Rearing

Another striking sign of deepening emotional ties within the family was a growing emphasis on the love and concern that mothers gave their infants. Early emotional bonding and a willingness to make real sacrifices for the welfare of the infant became increasingly important among the comfortable classes by the end of the eighteenth century, though the ordinary mother of modest means adopted new attitudes only as the nineteenth century progressed. The baby became more important, and women became better mothers.

The surge of maternal feeling was shaped by and reflected in a wave of specialized books on child rearing and infant hygiene, such as French family reformer Gustav Droz's phenomenally successful book *Papa, Mama, and Baby*, which went through 121 editions between 1866 and 1884. Droz urged fathers to become affectionate toward their children and pitied those "who do not know how to roll around on the carpet, play at being a horse and a great wolf, and undress their baby."[10] Following expert advice, mothers increasingly breast-fed their infants, rather than paying wet nurses to do so. Breast-feeding involved sacrifice — a temporary loss of freedom, if nothing else. Yet when there was no good alternative to mother's milk, it saved lives. Another sign, from France, of increased parental affection is that fewer illegitimate babies were abandoned as foundlings after about 1850. Moreover, the practice of swaddling disappeared completely. Instead, ordinary mothers allowed their babies freedom of movement and delighted in their spontaneity.

The loving care lavished on infants was matched by greater concern for older children and adolescents. They, too, were wrapped in the strong emotional ties of a more intimate and protective family. For one thing, European women began to limit the number of children they bore in order to care adequately for those they had. By the end of the nineteenth century, the birthrate was declining across Europe, and it continued to do so until after World War II. The Englishwoman who married in the 1860s, for example, had an average of about six children; her daughter marrying in the 1890s had only four; and her granddaughter marrying in the 1920s had only two or possibly three.

The most important reason for this revolutionary reduction in family size, in which the comfortable and well-educated classes took the lead, was parents' desire to improve their economic and social position and that of their children. Children were no longer an economic asset in the late nineteenth century. By having fewer youngsters, parents could give those they had valuable advantages, from music lessons and summer vacations to long, expensive university educations and suitable dowries. A young German skilled worker with only one child spoke for many in his class when he said, "We want to get ahead, and our daughter should have things better than my wife and sisters did."[11] Thus the growing tendency of couples in the late nineteenth century to use a variety of contraceptive methods — the rhythm method, the withdrawal method, and mechanical devices, including since the 1840s condoms and diaphragms made of vulcanized rubber — reflected increased concern for children.

In middle-class households, parents expended considerable effort to ensure that they raised their children according to prevailing family values. Indeed, many parents, especially in the middle classes, probably became too concerned about their children, unwittingly subjecting them to an emotional pressure cooker of almost unbearable intensity. Professional family experts, including teachers, doctors, and reformers like Droz, produced a vast popular literature on child rearing that encouraged parents to focus on developing their children's self-control, self-fulfillment, and sense of Christian morality. Family specialists recommended against corporal punishment — still common in worker and peasant households — but even though they typically escaped beatings, the children of the wealthy grew up under constant observation and discipline, a style of parenting designed to teach the self-control necessary for adult success. Parents carefully monitored their children's sexual behavior, and masturbation — according to one expert "the most shameful and terrible of all vices" — was of particular concern.[12]

Attempts to repress the child's sexuality generated unhealthy tension, often made worse by the rigid division of gender roles within the family. While family experts lauded parental love, and especially love between mother and child, they believed that relations between father and child were troubled by a lack of emotional bonding. At work all day, the father came home a stranger to his offspring; his world of business was far removed from the maternal world of spontaneous affection. Moreover, the father set demanding rules, often expecting the child to succeed where he himself had failed and making his love conditional on achievement. This kind of distance was the case among mothers as well as fathers in the wealthiest families. Domestic servants, nannies, and tutors did much of the work of child rearing; parents saw their children only over dinner, or on special occasions like birthdays or holidays.

The children of the working classes probably had more avenues of escape from such tensions than did those of the middle classes. Unlike their middle-class counterparts, who remained economically dependent on their families until a long education was finished or a proper marriage secured, working-class boys and girls went to work when they reached adolescence. Earning wages on their own, by the time they were sixteen or seventeen they could bargain with their parents for greater independence within the household. If they were unsuccessful in these negotiations, they could and did leave home to live cheaply as paying lodgers in other working-class homes. Not until the twentieth century could middle-class youths be equally free to break away from the family when emotional ties became oppressive.

The Feminist Movement

The ideal of separate spheres and the rigid gender division of labor meant that middle-class women faced great obstacles when they needed—or wanted—to move into the man's world of paid employment outside the home. Married women were subordinated to their husbands by law and lacked many basic legal rights. In England, a wife had no legal identity and hence no right to own property in her own name. Even the wages she might earn belonged to her husband. In France, the Napoleonic Code (see Chapter 19) enshrined the principle of female subordination and gave the wife few legal rights regarding property, divorce, and custody of the children.

Facing discrimination in education and employment and suffering from a lack of legal rights, some women rebelled and began the long-continuing fight for equality of the sexes and the rights of women. Their struggle proceeded on two main paths. First, following in the steps of women such as Mary Wollstonecraft (see Chapter 19), organizations founded by middle-class feminists campaigned for equal legal rights for women as well as access to higher education and professional employment. Middle-class feminists argued that unmarried women and middle-class widows with inadequate incomes simply had to have more opportunities to support themselves. Second, they also recognized that paid (as opposed to unpaid) work could relieve the monotony that some women found in their sheltered middle-class existence and add greater meaning to their lives. In the late nineteenth century these organizations scored some significant victories, such as the 1882 law giving English married women full property rights. More women gradually found professional and white-collar employment, especially after about 1880, in fields such as teaching, nursing, and social work.

Progress toward women's rights was slow and hard-won. In Britain, the women's **suffrage movement** mounted a militant struggle for the right to vote, particularly in the decade before World War I. Inspired by the slogan "Deeds Not Words," "suffragettes" marched in public demonstrations, heckled members of Parliament, and slashed paintings in London's National Gallery. Jailed for political activities, they went on highly publicized hunger strikes. Yet conservatives dismissed what they called "the shrieking sisterhood," and British women received the vote only in 1919.

In Germany before 1900, women were not admitted as fully registered students at a single university. Determined pioneers had to fight with tremendous fortitude to break through sexist barriers to advanced education and subsequent professional employment. (See "Individuals in Society: Franziska Tiburtius," page 748.) By 1913 the Federation of German Women's Association, an umbrella organization for regional feminist groups, had some 470,000 members. Their protests had a direct impact on the revised German Civil Code of 1906, which granted women substantial gains in family law and property rights.

Women inspired by utopian and especially Marxist socialism (see Chapter 21) blazed a second path. Often scorning the reform programs of middle-class feminists, socialist women leaders argued that the liberation of working-class women would come only with the liberation of the entire working class through revolution. In the meantime, they championed the cause of working women and won some practical improvements, especially in Germany, where the socialist movement was most effectively organized. In a general way, these different approaches to women's issues reflected the diversity of classes in urban society.

Science and Thought

How and why did intellectual life change in this period?

Major changes in Western science and thought accompanied the emergence of urban society. Two aspects of these complex intellectual developments stand out as especially significant. First, scientific knowledge in many areas expanded rapidly. Breakthroughs in chemistry, physics, and electricity profoundly influenced the Western worldview and spurred the creation of new products and whole industries. The natural and social sciences were also established as highly respected fields of study. Second, between about the 1840s and the 1890s European literature underwent a shift from soaring romanticism to tough-minded realism.

The Triumph of Science in Industry

As the pace of scientific advancements quickened and resulted in greater practical benefits, science exercised growing influence on human thought. The intellectual achievements of the Scientific Revolution (see Chapter 16) had resulted in few such benefits, and theoretical knowledge had also played a relatively small role in the Industrial Revolution in England (see Chapter 20). But breakthroughs in industrial technology in the late eighteenth century enormously stimulated basic scientific inquiry as researchers sought to explain theoretically how such things as steam engines and blast furnaces actually worked. The result was an explosive growth of fundamental scientific discoveries from the 1830s onward. In contrast to earlier periods, these theoretical discoveries were increasingly transformed into material improvements for the general population.

A perfect example of the translation of better scientific knowledge into practical human benefits was the work of Louis Pasteur and his followers in biology and the medical sciences (see page 728). Another was the development of the branch of physics known as **thermodynamics**. Building on Isaac Newton's laws of mechanics and on studies of steam engines, thermodynamics investigated the relationship between heat and mechanical energy. The law of conservation of energy held that different forms of energy—such as heat, electricity, and magnetism—could be converted but neither created nor destroyed. By midcentury, physicists had formulated the fundamental laws of thermodynamics, which were then applied to mechanical engineering, chemical processes, and many other fields.

Chemistry and electricity were two other fields characterized by extremely rapid scientific progress. And in both fields, "science was put in the service of industry," as the influential economist Alfred Marshall (1842–1924) argued at the time. Chemists devised ways of measuring the atomic weight of different elements, and in 1869 the Russian chemist Dmitri Mendeleev (mehn-duh-LAY-uhf) (1834–1907) codified the rules of chemistry in the periodic law and the periodic table. Chemistry was subdivided into many specialized branches, including organic chemistry—the study of the compounds of carbon. Applying theoretical insights gleaned from this new field, researchers in large German chemical companies discovered ways of transforming the dirty, useless coal tar that accumulated in coke ovens into beautiful, expensive synthetic dyes for the world of fashion. German production of synthetic dyes soared, and by 1900 German chemical companies controlled 90 percent of world production.

INDIVIDUALS IN SOCIETY ◆ Franziska Tiburtius

Why did a small number of women in the late nineteenth century brave great odds and embark on professional careers? And how did a few of them manage to reach their objectives? The career and personal reflections of Franziska Tiburtius (tigh-bur-TEE-uhs), a pioneer in German medicine, suggest that talent, determination, and economic necessity were critical ingredients to both the attempt and the success.*

Like many women of her time who studied and pursued professional careers, Franziska Tiburtius (1843–1927) was born into a property-owning family of modest means. The youngest of nine children growing up on a small estate in northeastern Germany, the sensitive child wilted under a harsh governess but flowered with a caring teacher and became an excellent student. Graduating at sixteen and needing to support herself, Tiburtius had few opportunities. A young woman from a "proper" background could work as a governess or teacher without losing her respectability and spoiling her matrimonial prospects, but that was about it. She tried both avenues. Working for six years as a governess in a noble family and no doubt learning that poverty was often one's fate in this genteel profession, she then turned to teaching. Called home from her studies in Britain in 1871 to care for her brother, who had contracted typhus as a field doctor in the Franco-Prussian War, she found her calling. She decided to become a medical doctor.

Supported by her family, Tiburtius's decision was truly audacious. In all Europe, only the University of Zurich accepted female students. Moreover, if it became known that she had studied medicine and failed, she would probably never get a job as a teacher. No parent would entrust a daughter to an emancipated radical who had carved up dead bodies. Although the male students at the university sometimes harassed the female ones with crude pranks, Tiburtius thrived. The revolution of the microscope and the discovery of microorganisms thrilled Zurich, and she was fascinated by her studies. She became close friends with a fellow female student from Germany, Emilie Lehmus, with whom she would form a lifelong partnership in

*This portrait draws on Conradine Lück, *Frauen: Neun Lebensschicksale* (Reutlingen: Ensslin & Laiblin, n.d.), pp. 153–185.

Electricity, a scientific curiosity in 1800, was totally transformed by a century of tremendous technological advancement. It became a commercial form of energy, first used in communications (the telegraph, which spurred quick international communication with the laying of underwater cables), then in electrochemistry (refining aluminum, for example), and finally in central power generation (for lighting, transportation, and industrial motors). By 1890 the internal combustion engine fueled by petroleum was an emerging competitor to steam and electricity alike.

The successful application of scientific research in the fast-growing electrical and organic chemical industries between 1880 and 1913 provided a model for other industries. Systematic "R&D"—research and development—was born in the late nineteenth century. Above all, the burst of industrial creativity and technological innovation, often

medicine. She did her internship with families of cottage workers around Zurich and loved her work.

Graduating at age thirty-three in 1876, Tiburtius went to stay with her doctor brother in Berlin. Though well qualified to practice, she was blocked by pervasive discrimination. Not permitted to take the state medical exams, she could practice only as an unregulated (and unprofessional) "natural healer." But after persistent fighting with the bureaucrats, she was able to display her diploma and practice as "Franziska Tiburtius, M.D., University of Zurich."

Soon Tiburtius and Lehmus realized their dream and opened a clinic. Subsidized by a wealthy industrialist, they focused on treating women factory workers. The clinic filled a great need and was soon treating many patients. A room with beds for extremely sick women was later expanded into a second clinic.

Tiburtius and Lehmus became famous. For fifteen years, they were the only women doctors in all of Berlin and inspired a new generation of women. Though they added the wealthy to their thriving practice, they always concentrated on the poor, providing them with subsidized and up-to-date treatment. Talented, determined, and working with her partner, Tiburtius experienced fully the joys of personal achievement and useful service. Above all, Tiburtius overcame the tremendous barriers raised up against women seeking higher education and professional careers, providing an inspiring model for those who dared to follow.

QUESTIONS FOR ANALYSIS

1. Analyze Franziska Tiburtius's life. What lessons do you draw from it? How do you account for her bold action and success?

2. In what ways was Tiburtius's career related to improvements in health in urban society and to the expansion of the professions?

called the **Second Industrial Revolution**, promoted the strong economic growth in the last third of the nineteenth century that drove the urban reforms and the rising standard of living considered in this chapter.

The triumph of science and technology had three other significant consequences. First, though ordinary citizens continued to lack detailed scientific knowledge, everyday experience and innumerable articles in newspapers and magazines impressed the importance of science on the popular mind. Second, as science became more prominent in popular thinking, the philosophical implications of science formulated in the Enlightenment spread to broad sections of the population. Natural processes appeared to be determined by rigid laws, leaving little room for either divine intervention or human will. Yet scientific and technical advances had also fed the Enlightenment's optimistic faith in human progress, which now appeared endless and automatic to growing numbers of people. Third, the methods of science acquired unrivaled prestige after 1850. For many, the union of careful experiment and abstract theory was the only reliable route to truth and objective reality. The "unscientific" intuitions of poets and the revelations of saints seemed hopelessly inferior.

Darwin and Natural Selection

Scientific research also progressed rapidly outside of the world of industry and technology, sometimes putting forth direct challenges to traditional beliefs. In geology, for example, Charles Lyell (1797–1875) effectively discredited the long-standing view that the earth's surface had been formed by short-lived cataclysms, such as biblical floods and earthquakes. Instead, according to Lyell's principle of uniformitarianism, the same geological processes that are at work today slowly formed the earth's surface over an immensely long time. The vast timescale required for the processes that Lyell described to have these effects undermined traditional beliefs about the age of the earth based on religious teachings. Similarly, the evolutionary view of biological development, first proposed by the Greek Anaximander in the sixth century B.C.E., re-emerged in a more modern form in the work of French naturalist Jean-Baptiste Lamarck (1744–1829). Lamarck asserted that all forms of life had arisen through a long process of continuous adjustment to the environment, a dramatic challenge to the belief in divine creation of species.

Lamarck's work was flawed — he believed that the characteristics parents acquired in the course of their lives could be inherited by their children — and was not accepted, but it helped prepare the way for Charles Darwin (1809–1882), the most influential of all nineteenth-century evolutionary thinkers. As the official naturalist on a five-year scientific cruise to Latin America and the South Pacific beginning in 1831, Darwin carefully collected specimens of the different animal species he encountered on the voyage. Back in England, convinced by fossil evidence and by his friend Lyell that the earth and life on it were immensely ancient, Darwin came to doubt the general belief in a special divine creation of each species of animal. Instead, he concluded, all life had gradually evolved from a common ancestral origin in an unending "struggle for survival." After long hesitation, Darwin published his research, which immediately attracted wide attention.

Darwin's great originality lay in suggesting precisely how biological evolution might have occurred. His theory of **evolution** is summarized in the title of his work *On the Origin of Species by the Means of Natural Selection* (1859). Decisively influenced by the gloomy assertions of Thomas Malthus (MAL-thuhs) that populations naturally grow faster than their food supplies (see Chapter 20), Darwin argued that chance differences among the members of a given species help some survive while others die. Thus the variations that prove useful in the struggle for survival are selected naturally, and they gradually spread to the entire species through reproduction.

Darwin's controversial theory had a powerful and many-sided influence on European thought and the European middle classes. Because his ideas seemed to suggest that evolution moved along without God's intervention, and that humans were simply one species among many others, some conservatives mocked Darwin for suggesting that humans descended from apes. Others hailed Darwin as the great scientist par excellence, the "Newton of biology," who had revealed once again the powers of objective science.

Some thinkers went a step further and applied Darwin's theory of biological evolution to human affairs. English philosopher Herbert Spencer (1820–1903) saw the human race as driven forward to ever-greater specialization and progress by a brutal economic struggle that determined the "survival of the fittest." The poor were the ill-fated weak; the prosperous were the chosen strong. **Social Darwinism** gained adherents among nationalists, who viewed global competition between countries as a grand struggle for survival, as well as among imperialists, who used Social Darwinist ideas to justify the rule of the "advanced" West over their colonial subjects and territories.

The Modern University and the Social Sciences

By the 1880s major universities across Europe had been modernized and professionalized. Education now emphasized controlled research projects in newly established clinics and laboratories; advanced students conducted independent research in seminar settings. An increasingly diversified professoriate established many of the academic departments still at work in today's universities, from anthropology to zoology. In a striking development, faculty devoted to the newly instituted human or social sciences took their place alongside the hard sciences. Using critical methods often borrowed from natural science, social scientists studied massive sets of numerical data that governments had begun to collect on everything from children to crime and from population to prostitution. Like Karl Marx, they were fascinated by the rise of capitalism and modernity; unlike Marx, they preferred to understand rather than revolutionize society.

Sociology, the critical analysis of contemporary or historical social groups, emerged as a leading social science. Perhaps the most prominent and influential late-nineteenth-century sociologist was the German Max Weber (1864–1920). In his most famous book, *The Protestant Ethic and the "Spirit" of Capitalism* (1890), Weber argued that the rise of capitalism was directly linked to Protestantism in northern Europe. Pointing to the early and successful modernization of countries like the Netherlands and England, he concluded that Protestantism gave religious approval to hard work, saving, and investing — the foundations for capitalist development — because worldly success was a sign of God's approval. This famous argument seriously challenged the basic ideas of Marxism: ideas, for Weber, were just as important as economics or class struggle in the rise of capitalism. An ambitious scholar, Weber also wrote on capitalist rationalization, modern bureaucracy, industrialization and agriculture, and the forms of political leadership. (See "Primary Source: Max Weber Critiques Industrial Capitalism," page 752.)

In France, the prolific sociologist Émile Durkheim (1858–1917) earned an international reputation for his wide-ranging work. His study of the psychic and social basis of religion, *The Elementary Forms of Religious Life* (1912), remains a classic of social-scientific thought. In his pioneering work of quantitative sociology, *Suicide* (1897), Durkheim concluded that ever-higher suicide rates were caused by widespread feelings of "anomie," or rootlessness. Because modern society had stripped life of all sense of tradition, purpose, and belonging, Durkheim believed, anomie was inescapable; only an entirely new moral order might offer some relief.

Other sociologists contributed to the critique of modern society. The German Ferdinand Tönnies (1855–1936) argued that with industrialization Western civilization had undergone a fundamental transformation from "community" to "society." Rationalized

PRIMARY SOURCE   Max Weber Critiques Industrial Capitalism

When prominent U.S. sociologist Talcott Parsons first translated Max Weber's 1905 classic work The Protestant Ethic and the "Spirit" of Capitalism and Other Writings *in 1930, his use of the term "iron cage" to describe capitalist rationality was seared into the consciousness of generations of English-speaking academics. In this more up-to-date and accurate translation, "shell as hard as steel" replaces "iron cage." Weber's scathing critique of capitalist rationality remains the same.*

A constituent part of the capitalist spirit, and not only this but of modern culture, namely, the rational conduct of life on the foundation of the *idea of the calling*, was born (as this essay shows) out of the spirit of *Christian asceticism*. One only needs to reread [Benjamin] Franklin's tract (quoted at the beginning of this essay) to see that the essential elements of the attitude which is there termed the "spirit of capitalism" are precisely those which we found to be the content of Puritan asceticism of the calling, only *without* the religious foundation, which had already ceased to exist at the time of Franklin. . . .

The Puritans *wanted* to be men of the calling—we, on the other hand, *must be*. For when asceticism moved out of the monastic cells and into working life, and began to dominate innerworldly morality, it helped to build that mighty cosmos of the modern economic order (which is bound to the technical and economic conditions of mechanical and machine production). Today this mighty cosmos determines, with overwhelming coercion, the style of life *not only* of those directly involved in business but of every individual who is born into this mechanism, and may well continue to do so until the day that the last ton of fossil fuel has been consumed.

In Baxter's* view, concern for outward possessions should sit lightly on the shoulders of his saints "like a thin cloak which can be thrown off at any time." But fate decreed that the cloak should become a shell as hard as steel [or "iron cage" in the earlier translation]. As asceticism began to change the world and endeavored

*Richard Baxter (1615–1691) was a Puritan minister famous for advocating toleration in the Church of England.

self-interest had replaced traditional values, leading to intensified alienation and a cold bureaucratic age. In *The Crowd* (1895), French sociologist Gustav Le Bon (1841–1931) wrote that the alienated masses were prone to gathering in mass crowds, in which individuals lost control over their emotions and actions. According to the deeply conservative Le Bon, a strong, charismatic leader could easily manipulate the crowd's collective psyche, and the servile crowd could become a violent and dangerous revolutionary mob.

The new sociologists cast a bleak image of urban industrial society. While they acknowledged some benefits of rationalization and modernization, they bemoaned the accompanying loss of community and tradition. In some ways, their diagnosis of the modern individual as an isolated atom suffering from anomie and desperately seeking human connection was chillingly prescient: the powerful Communist and Fascist movements that swept through Europe after World War I seemed to win popular support precisely by offering ordinary people a renewed sense of belonging.

to exercise its influence over it, the outward goods of this world gained increasing and finally inescapable power over men, as never before in history. Today its spirit has fled from this shell—whether for all time, who knows? Certainly, victorious capitalism has no further need for this support now that it rests on the foundation of the machine. Even the optimistic mood of its laughing heir, the Enlightenment, seems destined to fade away, and the idea of the "duty in a calling" haunts our lives like the ghost of once-held religious beliefs. . . .

No one yet knows who will live in that shell in the future. Perhaps new prophets will emerge, or powerful old ideas and ideals will be reborn at the end of this monstrous development. Or perhaps—if neither of these occurs—"Chinese" [or mechanized] ossification, dressed up with a kind of desperate self-importance, will set in. Then, however, it might truly be said of the "last men" in this cultural development: "specialists without spirit, hedonists without a heart, these nonentities imagine they have attained a stage of humankind never before reached."†

EVALUATE THE EVIDENCE

1. Why is Weber pessimistic about the possibility of escaping from the hardened "shell" or the "iron cage" of "outward goods"? How, according to Weber, has human consciousness changed to accommodate the growth of industrial capitalism?

2. Does Weber's argument about the rise of capitalism challenge Marx's explanation of the same?

Source: *The Protestant Ethic and the "Spirit" of Capitalism and Other Writings*, by Max Weber, translated by Peter Baehr and Gordon C. Wells, translation copyright © 2002 by Peter Baehr and Gordon C. Wells. Used by permission of Penguin, a division of Penguin Group (USA) Inc.

†Though Weber offered no citation, the ideas expressed in this quote are usually attributed to the German philosopher Friedrich Nietzsche.

Realism in Art and Literature

In art and literature, the key themes of **realism** emerged in the 1840s and continued to dominate Western culture and style until the 1890s. Realist artists and writers believed that cultural works should depict life exactly as it was. Forsaking the personal, emotional viewpoint of the romantics for strict, supposedly scientific objectivity, the realists observed and recorded the world around them—often to expose the sordid reality of modern life.

Emphatically rejecting the romantic search for the exotic and the sublime, realism (or "naturalism," as it was often called) energetically pursued the typical and the commonplace. Beginning with a dissection of the middle classes, from which most of them sprang, many realists eventually focused on the working classes, especially the urban working classes, which had been neglected in imaginative literature before this time. The realists put a microscope to many unexplored and taboo subjects, including sex, labor strikes, violence, and alcoholism, and hastened to report that slums and factories teemed with savage behavior. Shocked middle-class critics denounced realism as ugly sensationalism wrapped provocatively in pseudoscientific declarations and crude language—even as the movement attracted a growing middle-class audience, fascinated by the sensationalist view "from below."

The realist movement started in France, where romanticism had never been completely dominant. Artists like Gustave Courbet, Jean-François Millet, and Honoré Daumier painted scenes of laboring workers and peasants in somber colors and simple compositions. Daumier's art championed the simple virtues of the urban working class and lampooned the greed and ill will of the rich bourgeoisie; a caricature of King Louis Philippe earned him six months in prison.

Literary realism also began in France, where Honoré de Balzac, Gustave Flaubert, and Émile Zola became internationally famous novelists. Balzac (1799–1850) spent thirty years writing a vastly ambitious panorama of postrevolutionary French life. Known collectively as *The Human Comedy*, this series of nearly one hundred stories, novels, and essays vividly portrays more than two thousand characters from virtually all sectors of French society. Balzac pictured urban society as grasping, amoral, and brutal. In his

Realism in the Arts   Realist depictions of gritty everyday life challenged the romantic fascination with nature and the emotions, as well as the neoclassical focus on famous men and grand events. French painter Honoré Daumier's *The Third-Class Carriage*, completed in 1864, is a famous example of realism in the arts that portrays the effects of industrialization in the mid-nineteenth century. In muted colors, Daumier's painting captures the grinding poverty and weariness of the poor but also lends a sense of dignity to their humble lives. (Metropolitan Museum of Art, New York, USA/De Agostini Picture Library/The Bridgeman Art Library)

novel *Father Goriot* (1835), the hero, a poor student from the provinces, eventually surrenders his idealistic integrity to feverish ambition and society's pervasive greed.

Madame Bovary (1857), the masterpiece of Flaubert (floh-BEHR) (1821–1880), is far narrower in scope than Balzac's work but is still famous for its depth and accuracy of psychological insight. Unsuccessfully prosecuted as an outrage against public morality and religion, Flaubert's carefully crafted novel tells the ordinary, even banal, story of a frustrated middle-class housewife who has an adulterous love affair and is betrayed by her lover. Without moralizing, Flaubert portrays the provincial middle class as petty, smug, and hypocritical.

Émile Zola (1840–1902) was most famous for his seamy, animalistic view of working-class life. But he also wrote gripping, carefully researched stories featuring the stock exchange, the big department store, and the army, as well as urban slums and bloody coal strikes. Like many later realists, Zola sympathized with socialism, a view evident in his overpowering novel *Germinal* (1885).

Realism quickly spread beyond France. In England, Mary Ann Evans (1819–1880), who wrote under the pen name George Eliot, brilliantly achieved a more deeply felt, less sensational kind of realism in her great novel *Middlemarch: A Study of Provincial Life* (1871–1872). The novels of Thomas Hardy (1840–1928), such as *Tess of the D'Urbervilles* (1891) and *The Return of the Native* (1878), depict ordinary men and women frustrated and crushed by fate and bad luck. The greatest Russian realist, Count Leo Tolstoy (1828–1910), combined realism in description and character development with an atypical moralizing, especially in his later work. In *War and Peace* (1864–1869), a monumental novel set against the background of Napoleon's invasion of Russia in 1812, Tolstoy developed his fatalistic theory of human history, which regards free will as an illusion and the achievements of even the greatest leaders as only the channeling of historical necessity. Yet Tolstoy's central message is one that most of the people discussed in this chapter would have readily accepted: human love, trust, and everyday family ties are life's enduring values.

Notes

1. S. Marcus, "Reading the Illegible," in *The Victorian City: Images and Realities*, ed. H. J. Dyos and Michael Wolff, vol. 1 (London: Routledge & Kegan Paul, 1973), p. 266.
2. Quoted in E. Chadwick, *Report on the Sanitary Condition of the Labouring Population of Great Britain*, ed. M. W. Flinn (Edinburgh: University of Edinburgh Press, 1965; original publication, 1842), pp. 315–316.
3. J. McKay, *Tramways and Trolleys: The Rise of Urban Mass Transport in Europe* (Princeton, N.J.: Princeton University Press, 1976), p. 81.
4. Quoted in R. P. Neuman, "The Sexual Question and Social Democracy in Imperial Germany," *Journal of Social History* 7 (Winter 1974): 276.
5. Quoted in J. A. Banks, "The Contagion of Numbers," in *The Victorian City: Images and Realities*, ed. H. J. Dyos and Michael Wolff, vol. 1 (London: Routledge & Kegan Paul, 1973), p. 112.
6. Quoted in R. Roberts, *The Classic Slum: Salford Life in the First Quarter of the Century* (Manchester, U.K.: University of Manchester Press, 1971), p. 95.
7. Jonas Frykman and Orvar Löfgren, *Culture Builders: A Historical Anthropology of Middle-Class Life* (New Brunswick, N.J.: Rutgers University Press, 1987), p. 134.
8. See the pioneering work of J. de Vries, *The Industrious Revolution: Consumer Behavior and the Household Economy* (Cambridge, U.K.: Cambridge University Press, 2008), especially pp. 186–237.
9. Roberts, *The Classic Slum*, p. 35.
10. Quoted in T. Zeldin, *France, 1848–1945*, vol. 1 (Oxford, U.K.: Clarendon Press, 1973), p. 328.
11. Quoted in Neuman, "The Sexual Question," p. 281.
12. Frykman and Löfgren, *Culture Builders*, p. 114.

Chapter Review

MAKE IT STICK

LearningCurve
bedfordstmartins.com/mckaywestvalue
After reading the chapter, use LearningCurve to retain what you've read.

IDENTIFY KEY TERMS

Identify and explain the significance of each item below.

utilitarianism (p. 727)

germ theory (p. 728)

labor aristocracy (p. 735)

sweated industries (p. 737)

companionate marriage (p. 739)

separate spheres (p. 742)

suffrage movement (p. 746)

thermodynamics (p. 747)

Second Industrial Revolution (p. 749)

evolution (p. 750)

Social Darwinism (p. 751)

realism (p. 753)

REVIEW THE MAIN IDEAS

Answer the focus questions from each section of the chapter.

- How did urban life change in the nineteenth century? (p. 723)
- What did the emergence of urban industrial society mean for rich and poor and those in between? (p. 731)
- How did urbanization affect family life and gender roles? (p. 739)
- How and why did intellectual life change in this period? (p. 747)

MAKE CONNECTIONS

Think about the larger developments and continuities within and across chapters.

1. What were the most important changes in everyday life from the eighteenth century (Chapter 18) to the nineteenth century? What main causes or agents drove these changes?

2. Did the life of ordinary people improve, stay the same, or even deteriorate over the 1800s when compared to the previous century? What role did developments in science, medicine, and urban planning play in this process?

3. How did the emergence of a society divided into working and middle classes impact the workplace, homemaking, and family values and gender roles?

ONLINE DOCUMENT ASSIGNMENT

Life in the Modern City on Film
How did people respond to the challenges brought on by rapid urbanization?

Keeping the question above in mind, go online and view film footage that captures new developments in city life — from mass transit to waste disposal — and then complete a writing assignment based on the evidence and details from this chapter.

bedfordstmartins.com/mckaywestvalue

CHRONOLOGY

ca. 1840s–1890s	• Realism dominant in Western literature
1848	• First public health law in Britain
ca. 1850–1870	• Modernization of Paris
1850–1914	• Condition of working classes improves
1854	• Pasteur begins studying fermentation and in 1863 develops pasteurization
1854–1870	• Development of germ theory
1859	• Darwin publishes *On the Origin of Species by the Means of Natural Selection*
1869	• Mendeleev creates periodic table
1880–1913	• Second Industrial Revolution; birthrate steadily declines in Europe
1890s	• Electric streetcars introduced in Europe

23

✓ LearningCurve
bedfordstmartins.com/mckaywestvalue
After reading the chapter, use
LearningCurve to retain what
you've read.

The Age of Nationalism

1850–1914

IN THE YEARS THAT FOLLOWED THE REVOLUTIONS OF 1848, WESTERN
society progressively developed, for better or worse, an effective organizing
principle capable of coping with the many-sided challenges of the unfinished
industrial and political revolutions and the emerging urban society. That principle was nationalism—mass identification with the nation-state. Just as industrialization and urbanization had brought vast changes to class relations,
family lifestyles, and science and culture, the triumph of nationalism remade
territorial boundaries and forged new relations between the nation-state and
its citizens.

The rise of nationalism and the nation-state, enormously significant historical developments, was by no means completely predictable. Nationalism had
been a powerful force since at least 1789, but the goal of creating independent
nation-states, inhabited by people sharing a common ethnicity, language, history, and territory, had repeatedly failed, most spectacularly in the revolutions
of 1848. By 1914, however, most Europeans lived in nation-states and the ideology of nationalism had become an almost universal faith in the Western
world. The governments of the new nation-states took various forms, from
conservative authoritarianism to parliamentary monarchy to liberal republicanism. Whatever the political system, in most cases the nation-state became
increasingly responsive to the needs of its people, opening the political franchise and offering citizens at least rudimentary social and economic benefits.
At the same time, nationalism, which before 1848 appealed primarily to liberals seeking political reform or national independence, had become a widespread and ever more conservative ideology. At its worst, populists and fanat-

ics eagerly manipulated and sometimes abused the growing nationalist beliefs of ordinary people to justify exclusionary policies against Jews and other ethnic minorities, and to promote expansionary projects in overseas colonies.

Napoleon III in France

How did Napoleon III seek to reconcile popular and conservative forces in an authoritarian nation-state?

Early nationalism was generally liberal and idealistic and often democratic and radical. Yet nationalism can also flourish in authoritarian and dictatorial states, which may be conservative, fascist, or communist, and which may impose social and economic changes from above. Napoleon Bonaparte's France had already combined national feeling with authoritarian rule. Napoleon's nephew, Louis Napoleon, revived and extended this merger.

France's Second Republic

Although Louis Napoleon Bonaparte had played no part in French politics before 1848, universal male suffrage and widespread popular support gave him three times as many votes as the four other presidential candidates combined in the French presidential election of December 1848. This outcome occurred for several reasons. First, he had the great name of his uncle, whom romantics had transformed into a demigod after 1820. Second, as Karl Marx stressed at the time, middle-class and peasant property owners feared the socialist challenge of urban workers and the chaos of the revolution of 1848, and they wanted a tough ruler to protect their property and provide stability. Third, Louis Napoleon enunciated a positive program for France in pamphlets widely circulated before the election.

Above all, Louis Napoleon promoted a vision of national unity and social progress. He believed that the government should represent the people and help them economically. But how could these tasks be accomplished? Corrupt parliaments and political parties were not the answer, according to Louis Napoleon. French politicians represented special-interest groups, particularly middle-class ones. The answer was a strong, even authoritarian, national leader, like the first Napoleon, whose efforts to provide jobs and stimulate the economy would serve all people, rich and poor. This leader would be linked to each citizen by direct democracy, his sovereignty uncorrupted by politicians and legislative bodies. To the many common people who voted for him, Louis Napoleon appeared to be a strong leader and a forward-looking champion of popular interests.

Elected to a four-year term by an overwhelming majority, Louis Napoleon was required by the constitution to share power with the National Assembly, which was overwhelmingly conservative. With some misgivings, he signed conservative-sponsored bills that increased greatly the role of the Catholic Church in primary and secondary education and deprived many poor people of the right to vote. He took these steps in hopes that the Assembly would vote funds to pay his personal debts and change the constitution so he could run for a second term.

But in 1851, after the Assembly failed to cooperate with that last aim, Louis Napoleon began to conspire with key army officers. On December 2, 1851, he illegally dismissed the legislature and seized power in a coup d'état. There was some armed resistance in Paris and widespread insurrection in the countryside in southern France, but the army crushed these popular protests. Restoring universal male suffrage and claiming to stand above political bickering, Louis Napoleon called on the French people, as the first Napoleon had done, to legalize his actions. They did: 92 percent voted to make him president for ten years. A year later, 97 percent in a plebiscite made him hereditary emperor.

Napoleon III's Second Empire

Louis Napoleon — now proclaimed Emperor Napoleon III — experienced both success and failure between 1852 and 1870, when he fell from power. In the 1850s his policies led to economic growth. His government promoted the new investment banks and massive railroad construction that were at the heart of the Industrial Revolution on the continent (see Chapter 20). It also fostered general economic expansion through an ambitious program of public works, which included rebuilding Paris to improve the urban environment (see Chapter 22). The profits of business owners soared, rising wages of workers outpaced inflation, and unemployment declined greatly.

Initially, Louis Napoleon's hope that economic progress would reduce social and political tensions was at least partially realized. Until the mid-1860s he enjoyed support

Paris in the Second Empire   The flash and glitter of unprecedented prosperity in the Second Empire come alive in this vibrant contemporary painting. Writers and intellectuals chat with elegant women and trade witticisms with financiers and government officials at the Café Tortoni, a favorite rendezvous for fashionable society. Horse-drawn omnibuses with open top decks mingle with cabs and private carriages on the broad new boulevard. (Musée de la Ville de Paris, Musée Carnavalet, Paris/Giraudon/The Bridgeman Art Library)

from France's most dissatisfied group, the urban workers. Government regulation of pawnshops and support for credit unions and better working-class housing were evidence of helpful reform in the 1850s. In the 1860s Louis Napoleon granted workers the right to form unions and the right to strike—important economic rights denied by earlier governments.

At first, political power remained in the hands of the emperor. He alone chose his ministers, who had great freedom of action. At the same time, Louis Napoleon restricted but did not abolish the newly reformed Assembly. Members were elected by universal male suffrage every six years, and Louis Napoleon and his government took these elections very seriously. They tried to entice notable people, even those who had opposed the regime, to stand as government candidates in order to expand the base of support. Moreover, the government used its officials and appointed mayors to spread the word that election of the government's candidates—and defeat of the opposition—would provide roads, tax rebates, and a thousand other local benefits.

In 1857 and again in 1863, Louis Napoleon's system worked brilliantly and produced overwhelming electoral victories for government-backed candidates. In the 1860s, however, this electoral system gradually disintegrated. A sincere nationalist, Napoleon had wanted to reorganize Europe on the principle of nationality and gain influence and territory for France and himself in the process. Instead, problems in Italy and the rising power of Prussia led to increasing criticism at home from his Catholic and nationalist supporters. With increasing effectiveness, the middle-class liberals who had always wanted a less authoritarian regime denounced his rule.

Napoleon was always sensitive to the public mood. Public opinion, he once said, always wins the last victory, and he responded to critics with progressive liberalization. He gave the Assembly greater powers and opposition candidates greater freedom, which they used to good advantage. In 1869 the opposition, consisting of republicans, monarchists, and liberals, polled almost 45 percent of the vote.

The next year, a sick and weary Louis Napoleon again granted France a new constitution, which combined a basically parliamentary regime with a hereditary emperor as chief of state. In a final plebiscite on the eve of the disastrous war with Prussia (see page 769), 7.5 million Frenchmen approved the new constitution—only 1.5 million opposed it. Napoleon III's attempt to reconcile a strong national state with universal male suffrage moved in an increasingly democratic direction.

Nation Building in Italy, Germany, and the United States

How did conflict and war lead to the construction of strong nation-states in Italy, Germany, and the United States?

Louis Napoleon's triumph in 1848 and his authoritarian rule in the 1850s provided the old ruling classes of Europe with a new model in politics. Would the expanding urban middle classes and even portions of the working classes rally to a strong, conservative national state that promised economic growth, social benefits, and national unity, as in France? This was one of the great political questions in the 1850s and 1860s. In Europe, the national unification of Italy and Germany offered a resounding answer. In the United States, nation building marked by sectional differences over slavery offered another.

Italy to 1850

Before 1850 Italy had never been united. The Italian peninsula was divided in the Middle Ages into competing city-states. A battleground for the Great Powers after 1494, Italy was reorganized in 1815 at the Congress of Vienna into a hodgepodge of different states. Austrian foreign minister Prince Klemens von Metternich captured the essence of the situation when he dismissed Italy as only "a geographical expression" (see Map 23.1).

Between 1815 and 1848 the goal of a unified Italian nation captured the imaginations of many Italians. There were three basic approaches. First, the radical and idealistic patriot Giuseppe Mazzini called for a centralized democratic republic based on universal male suffrage and the will of the people. (See "Primary Source: The Struggle for the Italian Nation," at right.) Second, Vincenzo Gioberti, a Catholic priest, called for a federation of existing states under the presidency of a progressive pope. Many

MAP 23.1   The Unification of Italy, 1859–1870
The leadership of Sardinia-Piedmont, nationalist fervor, and Garibaldi's attack on the Kingdom of the Two Sicilies were decisive factors in the unification of Italy.

PRIMARY SOURCE   The Struggle for the Italian Nation

The leading prophet of Italian nationalism and unification before 1848, Giuseppe Mazzini founded a secret society called Young Italy to fight for the unification of the Italian states in a democratic republic. This selection, from the chapter "Duties Towards Your Country" in Mazzini's best-known work, The Duties of Man *(1858), was addressed to Italian workingmen.*

Your first Duties . . . are to Humanity. . . . But what can each of you, with his isolated powers, do for the moral improvement, for the progress of Humanity? . . .

God gave you the means of multiplying your forces and your powers of action indefinitely when he gave you a Country, when, like a wise overseer of labor, who distributes the different parts of the work according to the capacity of the workmen, he divided Humanity into distinct groups upon the face of our globe, and thus planted the seeds of nations. Evil governments have disfigured the design of God, which you may see clearly marked out, as far, at least, as regards Europe, by the courses of the great rivers, by the lines of the lofty mountains, and by other geographical conditions; they have disfigured it by conquest, by greed, by jealousy of the just sovereignty of others; disfigured it so much that today there is perhaps no nation except England and France whose confines correspond to this design.

[These evil governments] did not, and they do not, recognize any country except their own families and dynasties, the egoism of caste. But the divine design will infallibly be fulfilled. Natural divisions, the innate spontaneous tendencies of the peoples will replace the arbitrary divisions sanctioned by evil governments. The map of Europe will be remade. The Countries of the People will rise, defined by the voice of the free, upon the ruins of the Countries of Kings and privileged castes. Between these Countries there will be harmony and brotherhood. And then the work of Humanity for the general amelioration, for the discovery and application of the real law of life, carried on in association and distributed according to local capacities, will be accomplished by peaceful and progressive development.

Then each of you, strong in the affections and in the aid of many millions of men speaking the same language, endowed with the same tendencies, and educated by the same historic tradition, may hope by your personal effort to benefit the whole of Humanity.

Without Country you have neither name, voice, nor rights, no admission as brothers into the fellowship of the Peoples. You are the bastards of Humanity. Soldiers without a banner, . . . you will find neither faith nor protection. . . . Do not beguile yourselves with the hope of emancipation from unjust social conditions if you do not first conquer a Country for yourselves; where there is no Country there is no common agreement to which you can appeal; the egoism of self-interest rules alone, and he who has the upper hand keeps it, since there is no common safeguard for the interests of all.

EVALUATE THE EVIDENCE

1. What, according to Mazzini, are the sources of national belonging?
2. How does Mazzini express the main ideas of liberal nationalism?

Source: G. Mazzini, *The Duties of Man and Other Essays* (London: J. M. Dent and Sons, 1907), pp. 51–54.

Italians, though, looked to the autocratic kingdom of Sardinia-Piedmont for leadership, much as many Germans looked to Prussia.

This third alternative was strengthened by the failures of 1848, when Austria smashed Mazzini's republicanism. Sardinia's king, Victor Emmanuel II, crowned in 1849, retained the liberal constitution granted by his father under duress the previous year. This constitution combined a strong monarchy with a fair degree of civil liberties and parliamentary government, though deputies were elected by a limited franchise based on income. To some of the Italian middle classes, Sardinia appeared to be a liberal, progressive state ideally suited to drive Austria out of northern Italy and lead a united Italy. By contrast, Mazzini's brand of democratic republicanism seemed quixotic and too radical.

As for the papacy, the initial cautious support for unification by Pius IX (pontificate 1846–1878) had given way to hostility after he was temporarily driven from Rome during the upheavals of 1848. For a long generation, the papacy opposed not only national unification but also most modern trends. In 1864 in the *Syllabus of Errors*, Pius IX denounced rationalism, socialism, separation of church and state, and religious liberty, denying that "the Roman pontiff can and ought to reconcile and align himself with progress, liberalism, and modern civilization."

Cavour and Garibaldi in Italy

Sardinia had the good fortune of being led by a brilliant statesman, Count Camillo Benso di Cavour (kuh-VOOR), from 1850 until his death in 1861. A nobleman who made a substantial fortune in business before entering politics, Cavour had limited and realistic national goals. Until 1859 he sought unity only for the states of northern and perhaps central Italy in a greatly expanded kingdom of Sardinia.

In the 1850s Cavour worked to consolidate Sardinia as a liberal constitutional state capable of leading northern Italy. His program of building highways and railroads, expanding civil liberties, and opposing clerical privilege increased support for Sardinia throughout northern Italy. Yet Cavour realized that Sardinia could not drive Austria out of the north without the help of a powerful ally. Accordingly, he established a secret alliance with Napoleon III against Austria in July 1858.

Cavour then goaded Austria into attacking Sardinia in 1859, and Louis Napoleon came to Sardinia's defense. After the Franco-Sardinian victory, Napoleon did a sudden about-face. Worried by criticism from French Catholics for supporting the pope's declared enemy, he abandoned Cavour and made a compromise peace with the Austrians in July 1859. Sardinia would receive only Lombardy, the area around Milan, from Austria. The rest of Italy remained essentially unchanged. Cavour resigned in a rage.

Yet the skillful maneuvers of Cavour's allies in the moderate nationalist movement salvaged his plans for Italian unification. While the war against Austria raged in the north, pro-Sardinian nationalists in Tuscany and elsewhere in central Italy encouraged popular revolts that easily toppled their ruling princes. Using and controlling this popular enthusiasm, middle-class nationalist leaders in central Italy called for fusion with Sardinia. This was not at all what the Great Powers wanted, but the nationalists held firm. Returning to power in early 1860, Cavour gained Napoleon III's support by ceding Savoy and Nice to France. The people of central Italy then voted overwhelmingly to join a greatly enlarged kingdom of Sardinia under Victor Emmanuel. Cavour had achieved his original goal, a northern Italian state (see Map 23.1).

Garibaldi and Victor Emmanuel II   The historic meeting in Naples between the leader of Italy's revolutionary nationalists and the king of Sardinia sealed the unification of northern and southern Italy. With the sleeve of his red shirt showing, Garibaldi offers his hand—and his conquests—to the uniformed king and his moderate monarchical government. (Palazzo Pubblico, Siena, Italy/The Bridgeman Art Library)

For superpatriots such as Giuseppe Garibaldi (1807–1882), however, the job of unification was still only half done. The son of a poor sailor, Garibaldi personified the romantic, revolutionary nationalism and republicanism of Mazzini and 1848. Leading a corps of volunteers against Austria in 1859, Garibaldi emerged in 1860 as an independent force in Italian politics.

Partly to use him and partly to get rid of him, Cavour secretly supported Garibaldi's bold plan to "liberate" the Kingdom of the Two Sicilies. Landing in Sicily in May 1860, Garibaldi's guerrilla band of a thousand **Red Shirts** captured the imagination of the peasantry, which rose in bloody rebellion against their landlords. Outwitting the twenty-thousand-man royal army, the guerrilla leader won battles, gained volunteers, and took Palermo. Then Garibaldi and his men crossed to the mainland, marched triumphantly toward Naples, and prepared to attack Rome and the pope. The wily Cavour quickly sent Sardinian forces to occupy most of the Papal States (but not Rome) and to intercept Garibaldi.

Cavour realized that an attack on Rome would bring war with France, and he feared Garibaldi's radicalism and popular appeal. He immediately organized a plebiscite in the conquered territories. Despite the urging of some radical supporters, the patriotic Garibaldi did not oppose Cavour, and the people of the south voted to join the kingdom of Sardinia. When Garibaldi and Victor Emmanuel II rode together through Naples to cheering crowds, they symbolically sealed the union of north and south, of monarch and nation-state.

Cavour had successfully controlled Garibaldi and turned popular nationalism in a conservative direction. The new kingdom of Italy, which expanded to include Venice in 1866 and Rome in 1870, was a parliamentary monarchy under Victor Emmanuel II, neither radical nor fully democratic. Only a half million out of 22 million Italians had the right to vote, and the propertied classes and the common people remained divided. A great and growing social and cultural gap also separated the progressive, industrializing north from the stagnant, agrarian south. The new Italy was united on paper, but profound divisions remained.

Growing Austro-Prussian Rivalry

In the aftermath of 1848 the German states were locked in a political stalemate. After Austria and Russia blocked Prussian king Frederick William IV's attempt in 1850 to unify Germany, tension grew between Austria and Prussia as they struggled to dominate the German Confederation (see Chapter 21).

Economic differences exacerbated this rivalry. Austria had not been included in the German Customs Union, or *Zollverein* (TZOLE-fur-ayne), when it was founded in 1834 to stimulate trade and increase state revenues. By the end of 1853 Austria was the only state in the German Confederation outside the union. As middle-class and business groups profited from participation in the Zollverein, Prussia's leading role within the customs union gave it a valuable advantage in its struggle against Austria.

Prussia had emerged from the upheavals of 1848 with a weak parliament, which was in the hands of the wealthy liberal middle class by 1859. Longing for national unification, these middle-class representatives wanted to establish once and for all that the parliament, not the king, held ultimate political power, including control of the army. At the same time, the national uprising in Italy in 1859 made a profound impression on Prussia's tough-minded William I (r. 1861–1888). Convinced that great political change and war—perhaps with Austria, perhaps with France—were quite possible, William I and his top military advisers pushed to raise taxes and increase the defense budget in order to double the size of the army. The Prussian parliament rejected the military budget in 1862, and the liberals triumphed completely in new elections. King William then appointed Count Otto von Bismarck as Prussian prime minister and encouraged him to defy the parliament. This was a momentous choice.

Bismarck and the Austro-Prussian War

The most important figure in German history between Martin Luther and Adolf Hitler, Otto von Bismarck (1815–1898) has been the object of enormous interest and debate. A great hero to some and a great villain to others, Bismarck was above all a master of practical politics who first honed his political skills as a high-ranking diplomat for the Prussian government. Born into the Prussian landowning aristocracy and devoted to his sovereign, Bismarck had a strong personality and an unbounded desire for power. Yet in his drive to secure power for himself and for Prussia, Bismarck remained extraordinarily flexible and pragmatic. Keeping his options open, Bismarck moved with determination and cunning toward his goal.

When he took office as prime minister in 1862, in the midst of the constitutional crisis caused by the deadlock on the military budget, Bismarck made a strong but unfavorable impression. Declaring that William's government would rule without parliamentary consent, he lashed out at the liberal middle-class opposition: "The great questions of the day will not be decided by speeches and resolutions—that was the blunder of 1848 and 1849—but by blood and iron."

Denounced by liberals for his view that "might makes right," Bismarck had the Prussian bureaucracy go right on collecting taxes, even though the parliament refused to approve the budget. Bismarck also reorganized the army. And for four years, from 1862 to 1866, voters continued to express their opposition by sending large liberal majorities to the parliament.

Opposition at home spurred Bismarck to search for success abroad. The extremely complicated question of Schleswig-Holstein—two provinces that belonged to Denmark but were members of the German Confederation (Map 23.2)—provided a welcome opportunity. In 1864, when the Danish king tried, as he had in 1848, to bring these two provinces into a more centralized Danish state against the will of the German Confederation, Prussia enlisted Austria in a short and successful war against Denmark.

Bismarck, however, was convinced that Prussia had to control completely the northern, predominantly Protestant part of the confederation, which meant expelling Austria from German affairs. After the victory over Denmark, Bismarck's clever maneuvering left Prussia in a position to force Austria out by war. Recognizing that such a war would have to be localized to avoid provoking a larger European alliance against Prussia, Bismarck skillfully neutralized Russia and France.

The Austro-Prussian War of 1866 that followed lasted only seven weeks. Using railroads to quickly mobilize troops, who were armed with new and more efficient breech-loading rifles, the Prussian army defeated Austria decisively at the Battle of Sadowa (SAH-daw-vah) in Bohemia on July 3. Anticipating Prussia's future needs, Bismarck offered Austria generous peace terms. Austria paid no reparations and lost no territory to Prussia, although Venetia was ceded to Italy. But the existing German Confederation was dissolved, and Austria agreed to withdraw from German affairs. Prussia conquered and annexed several small states north of the Main River and completely dominated the remaining principalities in the newly formed North German Confederation. The mainly Catholic states of the south remained independent but allied with Prussia. Bismarck's fundamental goal of Prussian expansion was partially realized (see Map 23.2).

Taming the German Parliament

Bismarck had long been convinced that the old order he so ardently defended would have to make peace, on its own terms, with the liberal middle class and nationalists. Impressed with Napoleon III's example, he realized that nationalists were not necessarily hostile to conservative, authoritarian government. Moreover, the events of 1848 convinced Bismarck that the German middle class could be led to prefer national unity under conservative leadership rather than a long, uncertain battle for truly liberal institutions. Thus during the Austrian war, he increasingly identified Prussia's fate with the "national development of Germany."

To consolidate Prussian control, Bismarck fashioned a federal constitution for the new North German Confederation. Each state retained its own local government, but

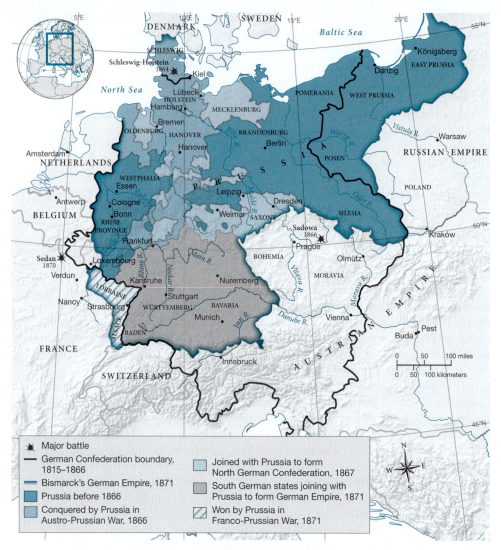

MAP 23.2 The Unification of Germany, 1864–1871
This map shows how Prussia expanded and a new German Empire was created through the Austro-Prussian War of 1866 and the Franco-Prussian War of 1870–1871.

the king of Prussia became president of the confederation, and the chancellor — Bismarck — was responsible only to the president. The federal government — William I and Bismarck — controlled the army and foreign affairs. There was also a legislature with members of the lower house elected by universal male suffrage. With this radical innovation, Bismarck opened the door to popular participation and the possibility of going over the head of the middle class directly to the people, as Napoleon III had done in France. All the while, however, ultimate power rested in the hands of the Prussian king and army.

In Prussia itself, Bismarck held out an olive branch to the parliamentary opposition. Marshaling all his diplomatic skill, Bismarck asked the parliament to pass a special indemnity bill to approve after the fact all the government's spending between 1862 and 1866. With German unity in sight, most of the liberals eagerly cooperated. The constitutional struggle in Prussia ended, and the German middle class came to accept the monarchical authority that Bismarck represented.

The Franco-Prussian War

The final act in the drama of German unification followed quickly. Bismarck calculated that a patriotic war with France would drive the south German states into his arms. Taking advantage of a diplomatic issue—whether a distant relative of Prussia's William I might become king of Spain—Bismarck pressed France. By 1870 the French leaders of the Second Empire, goaded by Bismarck and alarmed by their powerful new neighbor, declared war to teach Prussia a lesson.

As soon as war began, Bismarck had the wholehearted support of the south German states. While other governments maintained their neutrality—Bismarck's generosity to Austria in 1866 paid big dividends—German forces under Prussian leadership decisively defeated the main French army at Sedan on September 1, 1870. Louis Napoleon himself was captured and humiliated. Three days later, French patriots in Paris proclaimed yet another French republic and vowed to continue fighting. But after five months, in January 1871, a besieged and starving Paris surrendered, and France accepted Bismarck's harsh peace terms.

Proclaiming the German Empire, January 1871 This commemorative painting by Anton von Werner testifies to the nationalistic intoxication in Germany after the victory over France at Sedan. William I of Prussia stands on a platform surrounded by princes and generals in the famous Hall of Mirrors in the palace of Versailles, while officers from all the units around a besieged Paris cheer and salute him with uplifted swords as emperor of a unified Germany. Bismarck, in white (center), stands between king and army. (akg-images)

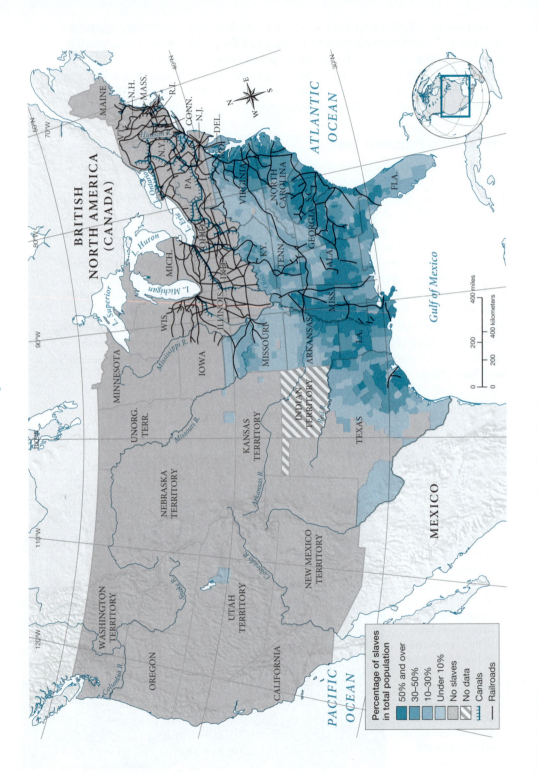

◀ **MAP 23.3** **Slavery in the United States, 1860**
This map shows the nation on the eve of the Civil War. Although many issues contributed to the developing opposition between North and South, slavery was the fundamental, enduring issue that underlay all others. Lincoln's prediction, "I believe this government cannot endure permanently half slave and half free," tragically proved correct.

By this time, the south German states had agreed to join a new German Empire. With Bismarck by his side, William I was proclaimed emperor of Germany in the Hall of Mirrors in the palace of Versailles. As in the 1866 constitution, the king of Prussia and his ministers had ultimate power in the new German Empire, and the lower house of the legislature was elected by universal male suffrage.

Bismarck imposed a severe penalty on France: payment of a colossal indemnity of 5 billion francs and loss of the rich eastern province of Alsace and part of Lorraine to Germany. French men and women of all classes viewed these territorial losses as a terrible crime. They could never forget and never forgive, poisoning relations between France and Germany after 1871.

The Franco-Prussian War, which many Europeans saw as a test of nations in a pitiless Darwinian struggle for existence, released an enormous surge of patriotic feeling in the German Empire. Bismarck's genius, the invincible Prussian army, the solidarity of king and people in a unified nation—such themes grew immensely popular with many German citizens during and after the war. The weakest of the Great Powers in 1862, Prussia with united Germany had become the most powerful state in Europe in less than a decade, and most Germans were enormously proud. Semi-authoritarian nationalism and a new conservatism, based on an alliance of the landed nobles and middle classes, had triumphed in Germany.

Slavery and Nation Building in the United States

The United States also experienced a process of bloody nation building. Nominally united, the country was divided by slavery from its birth, and economic development in the young republic carried free and slaveholding states in very different directions. Northerners extended family farms westward and began building English-model factories in the northeast. By 1850 an industrializing, urbanizing North was also building canals and railroads and attracting most of the European immigrants arriving in the nation.

In sharp contrast, industry and cities developed more slowly in the South, and European immigrants largely avoided the region. Even though three-quarters of all Southern white families were small farmers and owned no slaves, plantation owners holding twenty or more slaves dominated the economy and society. These profit-minded slave owners used gangs of black slaves to establish a vast plantation economy across the Deep South, where cotton was king (Map 23.3). By 1850, the region produced 5 million bales a year, supplying textile mills in Europe and New England.

The rise of the cotton empire greatly expanded slave-based agriculture in the South, spurred exports, and played a key role in igniting rapid U.S. economic growth. The large profits flowing from cotton led influential Southerners to defend slavery. In doing so, Southern whites developed a strong cultural identity and came to see themselves as a closely knit "we" distinct from the Northern "they." Because Northern whites viewed their free-labor system as more just, and economically and morally superior to slavery, North-South antagonisms intensified.

Tensions reached a climax after 1848 when the United States gained through war with Mexico a vast area stretching from west Texas to the Pacific Ocean. Debate over the extension of slavery in this new territory hardened attitudes on both sides. Abraham Lincoln's election as president in 1860 gave Southern secessionists the chance they had been waiting for. Determined to win independence, eleven states left the Union and formed the Confederate States of America.

The resulting Civil War (1861–1865), the bloodiest conflict in American history, ended with the South decisively defeated and the Union preserved. In the aftermath of the war, certain dominant characteristics of American life and national culture took shape. Powerful business corporations emerged, steadfastly supported by the Republican Party during and after the war. The **Homestead Act** of 1862, which gave western land to settlers, and the Thirteenth Amendment of 1865, which ended slavery, reinforced the concept of free labor taking its chances in a market economy. Finally, the success of Lincoln and the North in holding the Union together seemed to confirm that the "manifest destiny" of the United States was indeed to straddle a continent as a great world power. Thus a new American nationalism, grounded in economic and territorial expansion, grew out of a civil war.

The Modernization of Russia and the Ottoman Empire

What steps did Russia and the Ottoman Turks take toward modernization, and how successful were they?

The Russian and the Ottoman Empires experienced profound political crises in the mid-nineteenth century. These crises differed from those occurring in Italy and Germany, for both empires were vast multinational states built on long traditions of military conquest and absolutist rule by elites from the dominant Russians and Ottoman Turks. In the early nineteenth century the governing elites in both empires strongly opposed representative government and national independence for ethnic minorities, concentrating on absolutist rule and competition with other Great Powers. For both states, however, relentless power politics led to serious trouble. Their leaders recognized that they had to embrace the process of modernization, defined narrowly as the economic, military, and social-political reforms that might enable a country to compete effectively with leading European nations.

The "Great Reforms" in Russia

In the 1850s Russia was a poor agrarian society with a rapidly growing population. Almost 90 percent of the people lived off the land, and industrialization developed slowly. Bound to the lord from birth, the peasant serf was little more than a slave, and by the 1840s serfdom had become a central moral and political issue for the government. The slow pace of modernization encouraged the growth of protest movements, from radical Marxists clamoring for socialist revolution to middle-class intellectuals who sought a liberal constitutional state. Then a humiliating Russian defeat in the Crimean War underscored the need for modernizing reforms.

The **Crimean War** (1853–1856) grew out of the breakdown of the European balance of power established at the Congress of Vienna (see Chapter 21), general Great Power competition over the Middle East, and Russian desires to expand into the European territories of the Ottoman Empire. An immediate Russian-French dispute over the protection of Christian shrines in Jerusalem sparked the conflict. Famous for incompetent leadership on all sides, the war revealed the awesome power of modern weaponry, particularly artillery, in ways that anticipated the U.S. Civil War. Massive naval engagements, doomed cavalry charges, and staggering casualties — Russia alone lost about 450,000 soldiers — captured the imagination of home-front audiences, who followed events in the national press. By 1856 France and Great Britain, aided by the Ottoman Empire and Sardinia, had decisively defeated Russia.

The war convinced Russia's leaders that they had fallen behind the industrializing nations of western Europe. At the very least, Russia needed railroads, better armaments, and military reform to remain a Great Power. Moreover, the disastrous war raised the specter of massive peasant rebellion, making reform of serfdom imperative. Military disaster forced liberal-leaning Tsar Alexander II (r. 1855–1881) and his ministers along the path of rapid social change and modernization.

In a bold move, Alexander II abolished serfdom in 1861. About 22 million emancipated peasants received citizenship rights and the chance to purchase, on average, about half of the land they cultivated. Yet they had to pay fairly high prices, and because the land was to be owned collectively, each peasant village was jointly responsible for the payments of all the families in the village. Collective ownership made it difficult for individual peasants to improve agricultural methods or leave their villages. Thus old patterns of behavior predominated, limiting the effects of reform.

Most of Alexander II's later reforms were also halfway measures. In 1864 the government established a new institution of local government, the zemstvo. Members of this local assembly were elected by a three-class system of townspeople, peasant villagers, and noble landowners. A zemstvo executive council dealt with local problems. Russian liberals hoped that this reform would lead to an elected national parliament, but it did not. The zemstvos remained subordinate to the traditional bureaucracy and the local nobility. In addition, changes to the legal system established independent courts and equality before the law. The government relaxed but did not remove censorship, and somewhat liberalized policies toward Russian Jews.

Russian efforts to promote economic modernization proved more successful. Transportation and industry, both vital to the military, were transformed in two industrial surges. The first came after 1860, when the government encouraged and subsidized private railway companies. The railroads enabled Russia to export grain and thus earn money to finance further development. Industrial suburbs grew up around Moscow and St. Petersburg, and a class of modern factory workers began to take shape. Industrial development and the growing proletariat class helped spread Marxist thought and spurred the transformation of the Russian revolutionary movement after 1890.

Strengthened by industrial development, Russia began seizing territory in far eastern Siberia, on the border with China; in Central Asia, north of Afghanistan; and in the Islamic lands of the Caucasus. The rapid expansion of the Russian empire to the south and east excited ardent Russian nationalists and superpatriots, who became some of the government's most enthusiastic supporters. Alexander II also suppressed nationalist movements among Poles, Ukrainians, and Baltic peoples on the western borders of the empire.

Alexander II's political reforms outraged reactionaries but never went far enough for liberals and radicals. In 1881 a member of the "People's Will," a small anarchist group, assassinated the tsar, and the era of reform came to an abrupt end. The new tsar, Alexander III (r. 1881–1894), was a determined reactionary. Nevertheless, from 1890 to 1900 economic modernization and industrialization surged ahead for the second time, led by Sergei Witte (suhr-GAY VIH-tuh), the tough, competent finance minister from 1892 to 1903. Inspired by the writings of Friedrich List (see Chapter 20), Witte believed that industrial backwardness threatened Russia's greatness. Under his leadership, the government doubled the network of state-owned railways to thirty-five thousand miles. Witte established high protective tariffs to support Russian industry, and he put the country on the gold standard to strengthen Russian finances.

Witte's greatest innovation was to use Westerners to catch up with the West. He encouraged foreigners to build factories in Russia, believing that "the inflow of foreign capital is . . . the only way by which our industry will be able to supply our country quickly with abundant and cheap products."[1] His efforts to entice western Europeans to locate their factories in Russia were especially successful in southern Russia. There, in eastern Ukraine, foreign entrepreneurs and engineers built an enormous and very modern steel and coal industry. In 1900 peasants still constituted the great majority of the population, but Russia was catching up with the more industrialized West.

The Russian Revolution of 1905

Catching up partly meant further territorial expansion, for this was the age of Western imperialism. By 1903 Russia had established a sphere of influence in Chinese Manchuria and was eyeing northern Korea, which put Russia in conflict with the goals of an equally imperialistic Japan. When Tsar Nicholas II (r. 1894–1917), who replaced his father in 1894, ignored their diplomatic protests, the Japanese launched a surprise attack in February 1904. After Japan scored repeated victories, which included annihilating a Russian fleet, Russia surrendered in September 1905.

Once again, military disaster abroad brought political upheaval at home. The business and professional classes had long wanted a liberal, representative government. Urban factory workers were organized in a radical and still-illegal labor movement. Peasants had gained little from the era of reforms and suffered from poverty and overpopulation. At the same time, the empire's minorities and subject nationalities, such as the Poles, the Ukrainians, and the Latvians, continued to call for self-rule. With the army pinned down in Manchuria, all these currents of discontent converged in the revolution of 1905.

On a Sunday in January 1905, a massive crowd of workers and their families converged peacefully on the Winter Palace in St. Petersburg to present a petition to Nicholas II. Suddenly troops opened fire, killing and wounding hundreds. The **Bloody Sunday** massacre produced a wave of general indignation that turned many Russians against the tsar. (See "Primary Source: Eyewitness Accounts of Bloody Sunday," page 776.)

By the summer of 1905 strikes and political rallies, peasant uprisings, revolts among minority nationalities, and mutinies by troops were sweeping the country. The revolutionary surge culminated in October 1905 in a paralyzing general strike that forced the government to capitulate. The tsar issued the **October Manifesto**, which granted full civil rights and promised a popularly elected **Duma** (or parliament) with real legislative power. The manifesto split the opposition. Frightened middle-class leaders embraced it, which helped the government repress the popular uprising and survive as a constitutional monarchy.

On the eve of the opening of the first Duma in May 1906, the government issued the new constitution, the Fundamental Laws. The tsar retained great powers. The Duma, elected indirectly by universal male suffrage with a largely appointive upper house, could debate and pass laws, but the tsar had an absolute veto. As in Bismarck's Germany, the tsar appointed his ministers, who did not need to command a majority in the Duma.

The predominantly middle-class liberals, the largest group in the newly elected Duma, saw the Fundamental Laws as a step backward. Cooperation with Nicholas II's ministers soon broke down, and after months of deadlock the tsar dismissed the Duma. Thereupon he and his reactionary advisers unilaterally rewrote the electoral law, increasing greatly the weight of the conservative propertied classes. When new elections were held, the tsar could count on a loyal legislative majority. His government then pushed through important agrarian reforms designed to break down collective village ownership of land and encourage the more enterprising peasants — a "wager on the strong" meant to encourage economic growth. In 1914, on the eve of the First World War, Russia was partially modernized, a conservative constitutional monarchy with a peasant-based but industrializing economy.

Reform and Readjustment in the Ottoman Empire

By the early nineteenth century the economic and political changes reshaping Europe were also at play in the Ottoman Empire, which stretched around the northeastern, eastern, and southern shores of the Mediterranean Sea. The borderlands of this vast empire experienced constant flux and conflict. Russia had occupied Ottoman provinces on the Danube River in the last decades of the eighteenth century and grabbed more during the Napoleonic Wars. In 1816 the Ottomans were forced to grant Serbia local autonomy. In 1830 the Greeks won independence, and French armies began their long and bloody takeover of Ottoman Algeria. Yet the Ottomans achieved important victories during the same decades. Egyptian forces under the leadership of Muhammad Ali, the Ottoman governor in Egypt, restored order in the Islamic holy lands and conquered significant portions of Sudan, south of Egypt.

Muhammad Ali, a ruthless and intelligent soldier-politician, ruled Egypt in the name of the Ottoman sultan from 1805 to 1848. His modernizing reforms of agriculture, industry, and the military (see Chapter 24) helped turn Egypt into the most powerful state in the eastern Mediterranean. In time, his growing strength directly challenged the Ottoman sultan and Istanbul's ruling elite. From 1831 to 1840 Egyptian troops under the leadership of Muhammad Ali's son Ibrahim occupied and governed the Ottoman province of Syria and Palestine, and threatened to depose the Ottoman sultan Mahmud II (r. 1808–1839).

PRIMARY SOURCE   Eyewitness Accounts of Bloody Sunday

Newspaper reporters for the Times *and* Le Matin *expressed shock at the rapid outbreak of deadly violence on Bloody Sunday (January 22, 1905), one of the events that sparked the Russian Revolution of 1905. The Cossacks referred to in the* Times *account were soldiers recruited from Russia's southern steppes. Father Gapon, also mentioned in that report, was an Orthodox priest who led the march.*

From the *Times* (London)

Event has succeeded event with such bewildering rapidity that the public is staggered and shocked beyond measure. The first trouble began at 11 o'clock, when the military tried to turn back some thousands of strikers at one of the bridges . . . where the constant flow of workmen pressing forward refused to be denied access to the common rendezvous in the Palace Square. The Cossacks at first used their knouts [whips], then the flat of their sabers, and finally they fired. The strikers in the front ranks fell on their knees and implored the Cossacks to let them pass, protesting that they had no hostile intentions. They refused, however, to be intimidated by blank cartridges, and orders were given to load with ball.

   The passions of the mob broke loose like a bursting dam. The people, seeing the dead and dying carried away in all directions, the snow on the streets and pavements soaked with blood, cried aloud for vengeance. Meanwhile the situation at the Palace was becoming momentarily worse. The troops were reported to be unable to control the vast masses which were constantly surging forward. Re-enforcements were sent, and at 2 o'clock here also the order was given to fire. Men, women, and children fell at each volley, and were carried away in ambulances, sledges, and carts. The indignation and fury of every class were aroused. Students, merchants, all classes of the population alike were inflamed. At the moment of writing, firing is going on in every quarter of the city.

This conflict forced the Ottomans to seek European support. Mahmud II's dynasty survived, but only because the European powers, led by Britain, allied with the Ottomans to discipline Muhammad Ali. The European powers preferred a weak and dependent Ottoman Empire to a strong, economically independent state under a dynamic leader such as Muhammad Ali.

Faced with growing European military and economic competition, in 1839 liberal Ottoman statesmen launched an era of radical reforms known as the **Tanzimat**, or "Reorganization." The Tanzimat reforms were designed to modernize the empire and borrowed from western European models. The high point of reform came when the new liberal-minded sultan, Abdul Mejid (r. 1839–1861), issued the Imperial Rescript of 1856, just after the Crimean War. Articles in the decree called for equality before the law regardless of religious faith, a modernized administration and army, and private ownership of land. As part of the reform policy, and under economic pressure from the European powers that had paid for the empire's war against Russia in Crimea, Ottoman leaders adopted free-trade policies. New commercial laws removed tariffs on foreign imports and permitted foreign merchants to operate freely throughout the empire.

Father Gapon, marching at the head of a large body of workmen, carrying a cross and other religious emblems, was wounded in the arm and shoulder. The two forces of workmen are now separated. Those on the other side of the river are arming with swords, knives, and smiths' and carpenters' tools, and are busy erecting barricades. The troops are apparently reckless, firing right and left, with or without reason. The rioters continue to appeal to them, saying, "You are Russians! Why play the part of bloodthirsty butchers?" . . .

A night of terror is in prospect.

From *Le Matin* (Paris)

The soldiers of the Preobrazhensky regiment, without any summons to disperse, shoot down the unfortunate people as if they were playing at bloodshed. Several hundred fall; more than a hundred and fifty are killed. They are almost all children, women, and young people. It is terrible. Blood flows on all sides. At 5 o'clock the crowd is driven back, cut down and repelled on all sides. The people, terror-stricken, fly in every direction. Scared women and children slip, fall, rise to their feet, only to fall again farther on. At this moment a sharp word of command is heard and the victims fall en masse. There had been no disturbances to speak of. The whole crowd is unarmed and has not uttered a single threat.

EVALUATE THE EVIDENCE

1. Can you begin to reconstruct the events of Bloody Sunday from these reports? Who seems to be responsible for the violence?

2. Did popular protest help ordinary people win rights from the Russian state?

Source: James Harvey Robinson and Charles Beard, eds., *Readings in Modern European History*, vol. 2 (Boston: Ginn and Company, 1909), pp. 373–374.

The turn to nineteenth-century liberal capitalism had mixed effects. On one hand, with the growth of Western-style banking and insurance systems, elite Christian and Jewish businessmen in the empire prospered. Yet the bulk of the profits went to foreign investors rather than Ottoman subjects. More important, the elimination of traditional state-controlled monopolies sharply cut imperial revenues. In 1851 Sultan Mejid was forced to borrow 55 million francs from British and French bankers to cover state deficits. Other loans followed, and intractable indebtedness led to the bankruptcy of the Ottoman state two decades later.

Intended to bring revolutionary modernization, the Tanzimat permitted partial recovery but fell short of its goals. The Ottoman initiatives did not curtail the appetite of Western imperialism, which secured a stranglehold on the imperial economy via issuing loans. The reforms also failed to halt the growth of nationalism among some Christian subjects in the Balkans, which resulted in crises and increased pressure from neighboring Austria and Russia, eager to gain access to the Balkans and the eastern Mediterranean.

Finally, equality before the law for all citizens, regardless of religious affiliation, actually increased religious disputes, which were often encouraged and manipulated by the

European powers eager to seize any pretext for intervention. This development embittered relations between religious conservatives and social liberals, a struggle that ultimately distracted the government from its reform mission. Religious conservatives in both the Muslim and Greek Orthodox communities detested the religious reforms, which they viewed as an impious departure from tradition. These conservatives became dependable supporters of Sultan Abdülhamid II (ahb-dool-hah-MEED) (r. 1876–1909), who in 1876 halted the reform movement and turned away from European liberalism in his long and repressive reign.

Abdülhamid II's government failed to halt foreign efforts to fragment and ultimately take control over key Ottoman territories. By the 1890s the government's failures had encouraged a powerful resurgence of the modernizing impulse under the banner of the Committee of Union and Progress (CUP), an umbrella organization that united multiethnic reformist groups from across the empire. These fervent patriots, unofficially called the **Young Turks**, seized power in a 1908 coup and forced the sultan to implement new reforms. Although they failed to stop the rising tide of anti-Ottoman nationalism in the Balkans, the Young Turks helped prepare the way for the birth of modern secular Turkey after the defeat and collapse of the Ottoman Empire in World War I.

The Responsive National State, 1871–1914

What general domestic political trends emerged after 1871?

The decades after 1870 brought dramatic change to the structures and ideas of European politics. Despite some major differences between countries, European domestic politics had a new common framework, the nation-state. The common themes within that framework were the emergence of mass politics and growing popular loyalty toward the nation. Traditional elites hardly disappeared, but they were forced into new arrangements in order to exercise power, and a group of new, pragmatic politicians took leading roles. The major states of western Europe adopted constitutions of some sort, and universal male suffrage was granted in Britain, France, and Germany and elsewhere, at least in voting for the lower houses of parliament. New political parties representing a broad spectrum of interests and groups from workers and liberals to Catholics and conservatives engaged in hard-fought election campaigns to provide benefits to their constituencies.

Powerful bureaucracies emerged to govern growing populations and manage modern economies, and the growth of the state spurred a growth in the social responsibilities of government. The new responsive national state offered its citizens free education and some welfare and public health benefits, and for good reason many ordinary people felt increasing loyalty to their governments and their nations.

Building popular support for strong nation-states had a less positive side. Conservative and moderate leaders both found that workers who voted socialist—whose potential revolutionary power they feared—would rally around the flag in a diplomatic crisis or cheer when colonial interests seized a distant territory of doubtful value. Therefore, after 1871 governing elites frequently used antiliberal militarist and imperialist policies in attempts to unite national populations and overcome or mask intractable domestic conflicts. In the end, the manipulation of foreign policy to manage domestic issues inflamed the international tensions that erupted in the cataclysms of World War I and the Russian Revolution.

The German Empire

Politics in Germany after 1871 reflected many of these general political developments. The new German Empire was a federal union of Prussia and twenty-four smaller states. Much of the everyday business of government was conducted by the separate states, but there was a strong national government with a chancellor — until 1890, Bismarck — and a popularly elected lower house called the **Reichstag** (RIKES-tahg). Although Bismarck repeatedly ignored the wishes of the parliamentary majority, he nonetheless preferred to win the support of the Reichstag to lend legitimacy to his policy goals. This situation gave the political parties opportunities. Until 1878 Bismarck relied mainly on the National Liberals, who had rallied to him after 1866. They supported legislation useful for economic growth and unification of the country.

Less wisely, the National Liberals backed Bismarck's attack on the Catholic Church, the so-called **Kulturkampf** (kool-TOOR-kahmpf), or "culture struggle." Like Bismarck, the middle-class National Liberals were alarmed by Pius IX's declaration of papal infallibility in 1870. That dogma seemed to ask German Catholics to put loyalty to their church, a foreign power, above their loyalty to their newly unified nation. Kulturkampf initiatives aimed at making the Catholic Church subject to government control. However, only in Protestant Prussia did the Kulturkampf have even limited success, because elsewhere Catholics generally voted for the Center Party, which blocked passage of laws hostile to the church.

In 1878 Bismarck abandoned his attack on the church and instead courted the Catholic Center Party, whose supporters included many Catholic small farmers in western and southern Germany. By revoking free-trade policy and enacting high tariffs on cheap grain from the United States, Canada, and Russia, he won over both the Catholic Center and the conservative Protestant Junkers, nobles with large landholdings.

Other governments followed Bismarck's lead, and the 1880s and 1890s saw a widespread return to protectionism in Europe. France, in particular, established very high tariffs to protect agriculture and industry. By raising tariffs, European governments offered an effective response to a major domestic economic problem — foreign competition — in a way that won greater popular loyalty. At the same time, the rise of protectionism exemplified the dangers of self-centered nationalism: new tariffs led to international name-calling and nasty trade wars.

After the failure of the Kulturkampf, Bismarck's government tried to stop the growth of the **German Social Democratic Party (SPD)**, Germany's Marxist, working-class political party that was established in the 1870s. Both conservative elites and middle-class liberals genuinely feared the SPD's revolutionary language and allegiance to a Marxist movement that transcended the nation-state. In 1878 Bismarck pushed through the Reichstag the Anti-Socialist Laws, which banned Social Democratic associations, meetings, and publications. The Social Democratic Party was driven underground, but it maintained substantial influence, and Bismarck decided to try another tack.

In an attempt to win working-class support, Bismarck urged the Reichstag to enact a variety of state-supported social welfare measures. Big business and some conservatives accused him of creating "state socialism," but Bismarck ably pressed his program in many lively speeches, as the following excerpt suggests:

> Give the working-man the right to work as long as he is healthy; assure him care when he is sick; assure him maintenance when he is old. If you do that, and do not fear the [financial] sacrifice, or cry out at State Socialism as soon as the words "provision for old age" are uttered, . . . then I believe the gentlemen of the Wyden [Social Democratic] program will sound their bird-call in vain, and that the thronging toward them will cease as soon as working-men see that the Government and legislative bodies are earnestly concerned with their welfare.[2]

Bismarck and his supporters carried the day, and his essentially conservative nation-state pioneered in providing social welfare programs. In 1883 he pushed through the Reichstag the first of several social security laws to help wage earners by providing national sickness insurance. An 1884 law created accident insurance; one from 1889 established old-age pensions and retirement benefits. Henceforth sick, injured, and retired workers could look forward to some regular benefits from the state. This national social security system, paid for through compulsory contributions by wage earners and employers as well as grants from the state, was the first of its kind anywhere. Bismarck's social security system did not wean workers from voting socialist, but it did give them a small stake in the system and protect them from some of the uncertainties of the complex, modern industrial economy. This enormously significant development was a product of political competition, as well as government efforts to win popular support by defusing the SPD's radical appeal.

Increasingly, the great issues in German domestic politics were socialism and, specifically, the Social Democratic Party. In 1890 the new emperor, the young, idealistic, and unstable William II (r. 1888–1918), opposed Bismarck's attempt to renew the Anti-Socialist Laws. Eager to rule in his own right and to earn the support of the workers, William II forced Bismarck to resign. Afterwards, German foreign policy changed profoundly and mostly for the worse, but the government did pass new laws to aid workers and legalize socialist political activity.

Yet William II was no more successful than Bismarck in getting workers to renounce socialism. Indeed, Social Democrats won more and more seats in the Reichstag, becoming Germany's largest single party in 1912. Though this electoral victory shocked aristocrats and their wealthy, conservative allies, who held exaggerated fears of an impending socialist upheaval, the revolutionary socialists had actually become less radical in Germany. In the years before World War I, the SPD broadened its base by adopting a more patriotic tone, allowing for greater military spending and imperialist expansion. German socialists abandoned revolutionary aims to concentrate instead on gradual social and political reform (see page 792).

Republican France

Although Napoleon III's reign made some progress in reducing antagonisms between classes, the Franco-Prussian War undid these efforts. In 1871 France seemed hopelessly divided once again. The patriotic republicans who proclaimed the Third Republic in Paris after the military disaster at Sedan refused to admit defeat by the Germans. They defended Paris with great heroism for weeks, living off rats and zoo animals until they were starved into submission by German armies in January 1871.

When the next national elections sent a large majority of conservatives and monarchists to the National Assembly and France's new leaders decided they had no choice but to surrender Alsace (al-SAS) and Lorraine to Germany, the traumatized Parisians exploded in patriotic frustration and proclaimed the Paris Commune in March 1871. Vaguely radical, the leaders of the Commune wanted to govern Paris without interference from the conservative French countryside. The National Assembly, led by aging politician Adolphe Thiers (TEE-ehr), ordered the French army into Paris and brutally crushed the Commune. Twenty thousand people died in the fighting. As in June 1848, it was Paris against the provinces, French against French.

Out of this tragedy, France slowly formed a new national unity, achieving considerable stability before 1914. How do we account for this? Luck played a part. Until 1875 the monarchists in the ostensibly republican National Assembly had a majority but could not agree on who should be king. The compromise Bourbon candidate refused to rule except under the white flag of his absolutist ancestors — a completely unacceptable condition for many supporters of a constitutional monarchy. In the meantime, Thiers's destruction of the radical Commune and his other firm measures showed the fearful provinces and the middle classes that the Third Republic could be politically moderate and socially conservative. France therefore reluctantly retained republican government. As President Thiers cautiously said, this was "the government which divides us least."

Another stabilizing factor was the skill and determination of moderate republican leaders in the early years. The most famous was Léon Gambetta (gam-BEH-tuh), the son of an Italian grocer, a warm, easygoing, unsuccessful lawyer turned professional politician. By 1879 the great majority of members of both the upper and the lower houses of the National Assembly were republicans, and the Third Republic had firm foundations after almost a decade.

The moderate republicans sought to preserve their creation by winning the hearts and minds of the next generation. The Assembly legalized trade unions, and France worked to expand its colonial empire. More important, a series of laws between 1879 and 1886 greatly expanded the state system of public, tax-supported schools and established free compulsory elementary education for both girls and boys. In the past, most elementary and much secondary education had occurred in Catholic schools, which had long been hostile to republics and much of secular life. Free compulsory elementary education became secular republican education. Not only in France, but throughout the Western world, the expansion of public education served as a critical nation-building tool in the late nineteenth century.

Although the educational reforms of the 1880s disturbed French Catholics, many of them rallied to the republic in the 1890s. The limited acceptance of the modern world by the more liberal Pope Leo XIII (pontificate 1878–1903) eased tensions between church and state. Unfortunately, the **Dreyfus affair** changed all that.

In 1894 Alfred Dreyfus, a Jewish captain in the French army, was falsely accused and convicted of treason. His family never doubted his innocence and fought to reopen the case, enlisting the support of prominent republicans and intellectuals, including novelist Émile Zola. In 1898 and 1899 the case split France apart. On one side was the army, which had manufactured evidence against Dreyfus, joined by anti-Semites and most of the Catholic establishment. On the other side stood civil libertarians and most of the more radical republicans.

Dreyfus was eventually declared innocent, but the battle revived republican animosity toward the Catholic Church. Between 1901 and 1905 the government severed all ties between the state and the church. The government stopped paying priests' and bishops' salaries and placed committees of lay Catholics in control of all churches. Suddenly on their own financially, Catholic schools soon lost a third of their students, greatly increasing the state school system's reach and thus its power of indoctrination. In France, only the growing socialist movement, with its very different and thoroughly secular ideology, stood in opposition to republican nationalism.

Great Britain and Ireland

Historians often cast late-nineteenth-century Britain as a shining example of peaceful and successful political evolution, where an effective two-party parliament skillfully guided the country from classical liberalism to full-fledged democracy with hardly a misstep. This "Whig view" of Great Britain is not so much wrong as it is incomplete. After the right to vote was granted to males of the wealthy middle class in 1832, opinion leaders and politicians wrestled for some time with further expansion of the franchise. In 1867 the Second Reform Bill of Benjamin Disraeli and the Conservative Party extended the vote to all middle-class males and the best-paid workers in order to broaden their own base of support beyond the landowning class. After 1867 English political parties and electoral campaigns became more modern, and the "lower orders" appeared to vote as responsibly as their "betters." Hence the Third Reform Bill of 1884 gave the vote to almost every adult male.

While the House of Commons drifted toward democracy, the House of Lords was content to slumber nobly. Between 1901 and 1910, however, the Lords tried to reassert itself. Acting as supreme court of the land, it ruled against labor unions in two important decisions. And after the Liberal Party came to power in 1906, the Lords vetoed several measures passed by the Commons, including the so-called **People's Budget**, designed to increase spending on social welfare services. The Lords finally capitulated, as they had with the Reform Bill of 1832 (see Chapter 21), when the king threatened to create enough new peers to pass the bill, and aristocratic conservatism yielded to popular democracy.

Extensive social welfare measures, previously slow to come to Great Britain, were passed in a spectacular rush between 1906 and 1914. During those years the Liberal Party, inspired by the fiery Welshman David Lloyd George (1863–1945), enacted the People's Budget and substantially raised taxes on the rich. This income helped the government pay for national health insurance, unemployment benefits, old-age pensions, and a host of other social measures. The state tried to integrate the urban masses socially as well as politically, though the refusal to grant women the right to vote encouraged a determined and increasingly militant suffrage movement (see Chapter 22).

This record of accomplishment was only part of the story, however. On the eve of World War I, the unanswered question of Ireland brought Great Britain to the brink of civil war. The terrible Irish famine of the 1840s and early 1850s had fueled an Irish revolutionary movement. Thereafter, the English slowly granted concessions, such as

"No Home Rule" Posters like this one helped to incite pro-British, anti-Catholic sentiment in the northern Irish counties of Ulster before the First World War. The rifle raised defiantly and the accompanying rhyme are a thinly veiled threat of armed rebellion and civil war. (Reproduced with the kind permission of the Trustees of the National Museums & Galleries of Northern Ireland. Photograph © Ulster Museum, Belfast)

rights for Irish peasants and the abolition of the privileges of the Anglican Church. Liberal prime minister William Gladstone (1809–1898), who twenty years earlier had proclaimed, "My mission is to pacify Ireland," introduced bills to give Ireland self-government, or home rule, in 1886 and in 1893. They failed to pass, but in 1913 Irish nationalists finally gained such a bill for Ireland.

Thus Ireland, the Emerald Isle, was on the brink of achieving self-government. Yet to the same extent that the Catholic majority in the southern counties wanted home rule, the Protestants of the northern counties of Ulster came to oppose it. Motivated by the accumulated fears and hostilities of generations, the Ulster Protestants refused to submerge themselves in a majority-Catholic Ireland, just as Irish Catholics had refused to submit to a Protestant Britain.

The Ulsterites vowed to resist home rule. By December 1913 they had raised one hundred thousand armed volunteers, and much of English public opinion supported their cause. In 1914, then, the Liberals in the House of Lords introduced a compromise home-rule bill that did not apply to the northern counties. This bill, which openly betrayed promises made to Irish nationalists, was rejected in the Commons, and in September the original home-rule bill passed but with its implementation delayed. The Irish question had been overtaken by the earth-shattering world war that began in August 1914, and final resolution was suspended for the duration of the hostilities.

Irish developments illustrated once again the power of national feeling and national movements in the nineteenth century. Moreover, they demonstrated that governments could not elicit greater loyalty unless they could capture and control that elemental current of national feeling. Though Great Britain had much going for it — power, parliamentary rule, prosperity — none of these availed in the face of the conflicting nationalisms created by Irish Catholics and Protestants. Similarly, progressive Sweden was powerless to stop a Norwegian national movement, which culminated in Norway's leaving Sweden and becoming fully independent in 1905. In this light, one can also understand the difficulties faced by the Ottoman Empire in the Balkans in the late nineteenth century. It was only a matter of time before the Serbs, Bulgarians, and Romanians would break away.

The Austro-Hungarian Empire

The dilemma of conflicting nationalisms in Ireland helps one appreciate how desperate the situation in the Austro-Hungarian Empire had become by the early twentieth century as well. In 1848 Magyar nationalism had driven Hungarian patriots to declare an independent Hungarian republic, which Russian and Austrian armies savagely crushed in the summer of 1849 (see Chapter 21). Throughout the 1850s Hungary was ruled as a conquered territory, and Emperor Francis Joseph and his bureaucracy tried hard to centralize the state and Germanize the language and culture of the different ethnic groups there.

Then, in the wake of its defeat by Prussia in 1866 and loss of northern Italy, a weakened Austria agreed to a compromise and in 1867 established the so-called dual monarchy. The Austrian Empire was divided in two, and the Magyars gained virtual independence for Hungary. Henceforth each half of the empire dealt with its own ethnic minorities. The two states still shared the same monarch and common ministries for finance, defense, and foreign affairs.

In Austria, ethnic Germans were only one-third of the population, and many Germans saw their traditional dominance threatened by Czechs, Poles, and other Slavs. The language used in government and elementary education at the local level became a particularly emotional issue in the Austrian parliament. From 1900 to 1914 the legislature was so divided that ministries generally could not obtain a majority and ruled instead by decree. Efforts by both conservatives and socialists to defuse national antagonisms by stressing economic issues that cut across ethnic lines were largely unsuccessful.

In Hungary, the Magyar nobility in 1867 restored the constitution of 1848 and used it to dominate both the Magyar peasantry and the minority populations until 1914. Only the wealthiest one-fourth of adult males had the right to vote, making the parliament the creature of the Magyar elite. Laws promoting the use of the Magyar language in schools and government were bitterly resented, especially by Croatians and Romanians. While Magyar extremists campaigned loudly for total separation from Austria, the radical leaders of their subject nationalities dreamed of independence from Hungary. Unlike most major countries, which harnessed nationalism to strengthen the state after 1871, the Austro-Hungarian Empire was progressively weakened by it.

The Nation and the People

How did popular nationalism evolve in the last decades of the nineteenth century?

In the first two-thirds of the nineteenth century, nationalism convulsed the autocratic states of Europe. Liberal constitutionalists and radical republicans championed the national idea as a way to challenge authoritarian monarchs, liberate minority groups from imperial rule, and unify diverse territories into a single state. Yet in the decades after 1870 — corresponding to the rise of the responsive national state — nationalist ideology evolved in a different direction. Nationalism became increasingly populist and began to appeal more to those on the right wing of the political spectrum than the left. In these same years the "us-them" outlook associated with nationalism gained force, bolstered by modern scientific racism. Some fanatics and demagogic political leaders sought to build extreme nationalist movements by whipping up racist animosity toward imaginary enemies, especially Jews, and the growth of modern anti-Semitism after 1880 epitomized the most negative aspects of European nationalism before the First World War.

Making National Citizens

Responding to national unification, an Italian statesman famously remarked, "We have made Italy. Now we must make Italians." His comment captured the dilemma faced by political leaders in the last third of the nineteenth century. As the nation-state extended voting rights and welfare benefits to more and more people, the question of national loyalty became more and more pressing: politicians and nationalist ideologues made forceful attempts to ensure the people's conformity to their laws, but how could they ensure that national governments would win their citizens' allegiance?

The issue was pressing. The recent unification of Italy and Germany, for example, had brought together a patchwork of previously independent states with different customs, loyalties, and in some cases languages. In Italy, only about 2 percent of the population spoke the language that would become official Italian. In Germany, regional and religious differences and strong traditions of local political autonomy undermined unity. In Great Britain, deep class differences still dampened national unity, and across central and eastern Europe, overlapping ethnic groups with distinct languages and cultures challenged the logic of nation building. Even in France, where national boundaries had been fairly stable for several centuries, only about 50 percent of the people spoke correct French. The 60 percent of the population that still lived in rural areas often felt stronger allegiance to their village or region than the distant nation headquartered in Paris.

Yet by the 1890s most ordinary people had accepted if not embraced the notion of national belonging. There were various reasons for nationalism's growing popularity. For one, modern nation-states imposed centralized institutions across their entire territories, which reached even the lowliest citizen. Universal military conscription, introduced in most of Europe after the Franco-Prussian War (Britain was an exception), yanked peasants off their land and workers out of their factories and exposed young male conscripts to patriotic values. Free compulsory education leveled out language differences and taught children about glorious national traditions. In Italy and Germany, the introduction of a common currency, standard weights and measurements, and a national post office eroded regional differences. Boasting images of grand historical events or prominent leaders, even postage stamps and banknotes could impart a sense of national solidarity.

Improved transportation and communication networks broke down regional differences and reinforced the national idea as well. The extension of railroad service into hinterlands and the improvement of local roads shattered rural isolation, boosted the growth of national markets for commercial agriculture, and helped turn "peasants into Frenchmen."[3] Literacy rates and compulsory schooling advanced rapidly in the late nineteenth century, and more and more people read about national history or the latest political events in growing numbers of newspapers, magazines, and books.

A diverse group of intellectuals, politicians, and ideologues of all stripes eagerly promoted national pride. At Humboldt University in Berlin, for example, prominent historian Heinrich von Treitschke championed German superiority, especially over archrival Great Britain. Scholars uncovered the deep roots of national identity in ancient folk traditions; in shared language, customs, race, and religion; and in historic attachments to national territory. Such accounts, often based on flimsy historical evidence, were popularized in the classroom and the press. Few nationalist thinkers sympathized with French philosopher Ernest Renan, who suggested that national identity was based more on a people's current desire for a "common life" and an invented, heroic past than on actual historical experiences.

A variety of new symbols and rituals brought nationalism into the lives of ordinary people. Each nation had its own unique capital city, flag, military uniform, and national anthem. New symbols, such as Britain's doughty John Bull, France's republican Marianne, America's stern Uncle Sam, and Germany's solid Michel, supposedly embodied shared national characteristics. All citizens could participate in newly invented national holidays, such as Bastille Day in France, first held in 1880 to commemorate the French Revolution, or Sedan Day in Germany, instituted to celebrate Germany's victory over France in 1871. Royal weddings, coronations, jubilees, and funerals brought citizens into the streets to celebrate the nation's leaders; Queen Victoria's 1887 Golden Jubilee set a high standard. Public squares and parks received prominent commemorative statues and monuments, such as the grand memorial to Victor Emmanuel II in central Rome, or the ostentatious Monument to the Battle of Nations built in Leipzig to honor German victory in the Napoleonic Wars. Surrounded by these inescapable elements of everyday nationalism, most ordinary people had accepted if not embraced the notion of national belonging by the 1890s.[4]

Nationalism and Racism

Where nationalism in the first two-thirds of the 1800s had been a force for liberal reform and peaceful brotherhood, expressed in its most optimistic form by thinkers like Giuseppe Mazzini (see "Primary Source: The Struggle for the Italian Nation," page 763), it now took on more populist and exclusionary tones. The ideal of national belonging had from the start created an "us-them" outlook (see Chapter 21); after 1871 new supposedly scientific understandings of racial difference added new layers of meaning to this dichotomy. Though we now understand that there is no genetic evidence that divides humanity into distinct races, most people in the late nineteenth century believed that race was a product of heredity. Many felt pride in their own national racial characteristics—French, English, German, Jewish, Slav, and many others—that were supposedly passed down from generation to generation. Unfortunately, pride in one's own heritage easily leads to denigration of someone else's.

Modern attempts to use race to categorize distinct groups of people had their roots in Enlightenment thought (see Chapter 16). Now a new group of intellectuals, including race theorists such as Count Arthur de Gobineau and Houston Stewart Chamberlain, claimed that their ideas about racial difference were scientific, based on hard biological "facts" about bloodlines and heredity. In his early book *On the Inequality of the Human Races* (1854), Gobineau divided humanity into the white, black, and yellow races based on geographical location and championed the white "Aryan race" for its supposedly superior qualities. Social Darwinist ideas about the "survival of the fittest," when applied to the "contest" between nations and races, drew on such ideas to further popularize stereotypes about inferior and superior races.

The close links between nationalism and scientific racism helped justify imperial expansion, as we shall see in the next chapter. Nationalist racism also fostered domestic persecution and exclusion, as witnessed by Bismarck's Kulturkampf and the Dreyfus affair. According to race theorists, the nation was supposed to be racially pure, and ethnic minorities were viewed as outsiders and targets for reform, repression, and relocation. Thus the ethnic Russian leaders of the Russian empire targeted minority Poles and Czechs for "Russification," a process by which they might learn the Russian language and assimilate into Russian society. Germans likewise viewed the large number of ethnic Poles living in East Prussia as a "national threat" that required "Germanization" before they could be seen as equals to the supposedly superior Germans. For many nationalists, driven by ugly currents of race hatred, Jews were the ultimate outsiders, the stereotypical "inferior race" that posed the greatest challenge to national purity.

Jewish Emancipation and Modern Anti-Semitism

Changing political principles and the triumph of the nation-state had revolutionized Jewish life in western and central Europe. The decisive turning point came in 1848, when Jews formed part of the revolutionary vanguard in Vienna and Berlin and the Frankfurt Assembly endorsed full rights for German Jews. In 1871 the constitution of the new German Empire consolidated the process of Jewish emancipation in that nation. It abolished all restrictions on Jewish marriage, choice of occupation, place of residence, and property ownership. However, even with this change, exclusion from government employment and discrimination in social relations remained.

The ongoing process of emancipation presented Jews with challenges and opportunities. Traditional Jewish occupations, such as court financial agent, village moneylender, and peddler, were undermined by free-market reforms, but careers in business, the professions, and the arts opened. European Jews excelled in wholesale and retail trade, banking and finance, consumer industries, journalism, medicine, and law, as well as the fine arts. By 1871 a majority of Jewish people in western and central Europe had improved their economic situation enough to enter the middle classes. Most Jewish people also identified strongly with their respective nation-states and, with good reason, saw themselves as patriotic citizens.

Vicious anti-Semitism reappeared with force in central and eastern Europe after the stock market crash of 1873. Drawing on long traditions of religious intolerance, ghetto exclusion, and periodic anti-Jewish riots and expulsions, this anti-Semitism also built on the exclusionary aspects of modern popular nationalism and the pseudoscience of race. Fanatic anti-Semites whipped up resentment against Jewish achievement and Jewish "financial control" and claimed that the Jewish race or "blood" (rather than the Jewish religion) posed a biological threat to Christian peoples. Such ideas were popularized by the repeated publication of the notorious forgery "The Protocols of the Elders

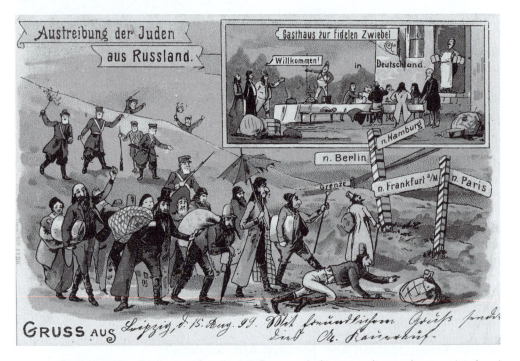

"The Expulsion of the Jews from Russia"   So reads this postcard, correctly suggesting that Russian government officials often encouraged popular anti-Semitism and helped drive many Jews out of Russia in the late nineteenth century. The road signs indicate that these poor Jews are crossing into Germany, where they will find a grudging welcome and a meager meal at the Jolly Onion Inn. Other Jews from eastern Europe settled in France and Britain, thereby creating small but significant Jewish populations in both of these countries for the first time since they had expelled most of their Jews in the Middle Ages. (Alliance Israelite Universelle, Paris/Archives Charmet/ The Bridgeman Art Library)

of Zion," a falsified account of a secret meeting supposedly held at the First Zionist Congress in Basel in 1897. The "Protocols," actually written by the Russian secret police, suggested that Jewish elders planned to dominate the globe. Such anti-Semitic beliefs were particularly popular among conservatives, extreme nationalists, and people who felt threatened by Jewish competition, such as small shopkeepers, office workers, and professionals.

Anti-Semites created nationalist political parties that attacked and degraded Jews to win popular support. Karl Lueger and his Christian Socialist Party, for example, won striking electoral victories in Vienna in the early 1890s. Lueger, mayor of Vienna from 1897 to 1910, combined fierce anti-Semitic rhetoric with municipal ownership of basic services, and he appealed especially to the German-speaking lower middle class—and an unsuccessful young artist named Adolf Hitler.

Before 1914 anti-Semitism was most oppressive in eastern Europe, where Jews suffered from terrible poverty. In the western borderlands of the Russian empire, where 4 million of Europe's 7 million Jewish people lived in 1880 with few legal rights, officials used anti-Semitism to channel popular discontent away from the government and onto the Jewish minority. Russian Jews were denounced as foreign exploiters who corrupted national traditions, and in 1881 to 1882 a wave of violent pogroms commenced in southern Russia. The police and the army stood aside for days while peasants looted and destroyed Jewish property, and official harassment continued in the following decades.

The growth of radical anti-Semitism spurred the emergence of **Zionism**, a Jewish political movement whose adherents believed that Christian Europeans would never overcome their anti-Semitic hatred. To escape the burdens of anti-Semitism, leading Zionists such as Theodor Herzl advocated the creation of a Jewish state in Palestine—a homeland where European Jews could settle and live free of social prejudice. (See "Individuals in Society: Theodor Herzl," page 790.) Zionism was particularly popular among Jews living in Russia. Many embraced self-emancipation and the vision of a Zionist settlement in Palestine, or emigrated to western or central Europe and the United States. About 2.75 million Jews left central and eastern Europe between 1881 and 1914.

Marxism and the Socialist Movement

Why did the socialist movement grow, and how revolutionary was it?

Nationalism served, for better or worse, as a new unifying principle. But what about socialism? Socialist parties, generally Marxist groups dedicated to international proletarian revolution, grew rapidly in these years. Did this mean that national states had failed to gain the support of workers?

The Socialist International

The growth of socialist parties after 1871 was phenomenal. Neither Bismarck's Anti-Socialist Laws nor his extensive social security system checked the growth of the Social Democratic Party, which espoused radical Marxism even though it sought reform through legal parliamentary politics. By 1912 the SPD had millions of followers—mostly people from the working classes—and was the largest party in the Reichstag. Socialist parties grew in other countries as well, though nowhere else with such success. In 1883 Russian exiles in Switzerland founded the Russian Social Democratic Party, and various socialist parties were unified in 1905 in the French Section of the Workers International. Belgium and Austria-Hungary also had strong socialist parties.

As the name of the French party suggests, Marxist socialist parties were eventually linked together in an international organization. Marx himself played an important role in founding the socialist International Working Men's Association, also known as the First International. In the following years, he battled successfully to control the organization and used its annual meetings as a means of spreading his doctrines of socialist revolution. Marx enthusiastically endorsed the radical patriotism of the Paris Commune and its terrible struggle against the French state as a giant step toward socialist revolution. Marx's fervent embrace of working-class violence frightened many of his early supporters, especially the more moderate British labor leaders. The First International collapsed.

INDIVIDUALS IN SOCIETY • Theodor Herzl

In September 1897, only days after his vision and energy had called into being the First Zionist Congress in Basel, Switzerland, Theodor Herzl (1860–1904) assessed the results in his diary: "If I were to sum up the Congress in a word—which I shall take care not to publish—it would be this: At Basel I founded the Jewish state. If I said this out loud today I would be greeted by universal laughter. In five years perhaps, and certainly in fifty years, everyone will perceive it."* Herzl's buoyant optimism, which so often carried him forward, was prophetic. Leading the Zionist movement until his death at age forty-four in 1904, Herzl guided the first historic steps toward modern Jewish political nationhood and the creation of Israel in 1948.

Theodor Herzl was born in Budapest, Hungary, into an upper-middle-class, German-speaking Jewish family. When he was eighteen, his family moved to Vienna, where he studied law. As a university student, he soaked up the liberal beliefs of most well-to-do Viennese Jews, which included assimilation of German culture. Wrestling with his nonreligious Jewishness and his strong pro-German feeling, Herzl embraced German nationalism and joined a German dueling fraternity. There he discovered that full acceptance required openly anti-Semitic attitudes and a repudiation of all things Jewish. Herzl resigned.

After receiving his law degree, Herzl embarked on a literary career. In 1889 he married into a wealthy Viennese Jewish family, but he and his socialite wife were mismatched and never happy together. Herzl achieved considerable success as both a journalist and a playwright. His witty comedies focused on the bourgeoisie, including Jewish millionaires trying to live like aristocrats. Accepting many German stereotypes, Herzl sometimes depicted eastern Jews as uneducated and grasping. But he believed that the Jewish shortcomings he perceived were the results of age-old persecution and would disappear through education and assimilation. Herzl also took a growing pride in Jewish steadfastness in the face of victimization and suffering.

The emergence of modern anti-Semitism (see page 787) shocked Herzl, as it did many acculturated Jewish Germans. Moving to Paris in 1891 as the correspondent for Vienna's leading liberal newspaper, Herzl studied contemporary politics and pondered recent historical developments. He came to a bold conclusion, published in 1896 as *The Jewish State: An Attempt at a Modern Solution to the Jewish Question*. According to Herzl, Jewish assimilation had failed, and attempts to combat anti-Semitism would never succeed. Only by building an independent Jewish state could the Jewish people flourish.

*Quotes are from Theodor Herzl, *The Diaries of Theodor Herzl*, trans. and ed. with an introduction by Marvin Lowenthal (New York: Grosset & Dunlap, 1962), pp. 224, 22, xxi.

Yet international proletarian solidarity remained an important objective for Marxists. In 1889, as the individual parties in different countries grew stronger, socialist leaders came together to form the Second International, which lasted until 1914. Though only a federation of national socialist parties, the International had a great psychological impact. The International had a permanent executive, and every three

Herzl developed his Zionism before the anti-Jewish agitation accompanying the Dreyfus affair, which only served to strengthen his faith in his analysis. Generally rebuffed by skeptical Jewish elites in western and central Europe, Herzl turned for support to youthful idealists and the poor Jewish masses. He became an inspiring man of action, rallying the delegates to the annual Zionist congresses, directing the growth of the worldwide Zionist organization, and working himself to death. Herzl also understood that national consciousness required powerful emotions and symbols, such as a Jewish flag. Flags build nations, he said, because people "live and die for a flag."

Putting the Zionist vision before non-Jews and world public opinion, Herzl believed in international diplomacy and political agreements. He traveled constantly to negotiate with European rulers and top officials, seeking their support in securing territory for a Jewish state, usually suggesting that it take form in Palestine, a territory in the Ottoman Empire. Aptly described by an admiring contemporary as "the first Jewish statesman since the destruction of Jerusalem," Herzl proved most successful in Britain. His work paved the way for the 1917 Balfour Declaration, which solemnly pledged British support for a "Jewish homeland" in Palestine.

QUESTIONS FOR ANALYSIS

1. Describe Theodor Herzl's background and early beliefs. Do you see a link between Herzl's early German nationalism and his later Zionism?

2. Why did Herzl believe an independent Jewish state with its own national flag was necessary?

3. How did Herzl work as a leader to turn his Zionist vision into a reality?

ONLINE DOCUMENT ASSIGNMENT

What role did popular nationalism play in the emergence of modern anti-Semitism, and how did Herzl respond to the virulent anti-Semitism of this period? Examine examples of anti-Semitic nationalist writings and Herzl's argument for the creation of a Jewish state, and then complete a writing assignment based on the evidence and details from this chapter.

bedfordstmartins.com/mckaywestvalue

years delegates from the different parties met to interpret Marxist doctrines and plan coordinated action. May 1 (May Day) was declared an annual international one-day strike, a day of marches and demonstrations. Prosperous and conservative citizens feared the growing power of socialism and the Second International, but many others rejoiced in it.

Unions and Revisionism

Was socialism really radical and revolutionary in these years? On the whole, it was not. As socialist parties grew and attracted large numbers of members, they looked more and more toward gradual change and steady improvement for the working class and less and less toward revolution. The mainstream of European socialism became militantly moderate; that is, socialists increasingly combined radical rhetoric with sober practical action.

Workers themselves grew less inclined to follow radical programs for several reasons. As they gained the right to vote and to participate politically in the nation-state, workers focused their attention more on elections than on revolutions. As workers won real, tangible benefits, this furthered the process. And workers were not immune to patriotic education and indoctrination during military service. Many responded positively to drum-beating parades and aggressive foreign policy as they loyally voted for socialists. Nor were workers a unified social group.

Perhaps most important of all, workers' standard of living rose gradually but substantially after 1850 (see Chapter 22). The quality of life in urban areas improved dramatically as well. For all these reasons, workers became more moderate: they demanded gains, but they were less likely to take to the barricades in pursuit of them.

The growth of labor unions also reinforced this trend toward moderation. In the early stages of industrialization, unions were generally prohibited by law. A famous law of the French Revolution had declared all guilds and unions illegal in the name of "liberty" in 1791. In Great Britain, attempts by workers to unite were made criminal conspiracies in 1799. Other countries had similar laws that hampered union development. Unions were considered subversive bodies to be hounded and crushed.

From this sad position workers struggled to escape. Great Britain led the way in 1824 and 1825 when it granted unions the right to exist — though generally not the right to strike. After the collapse of Robert Owen's attempt to form one big national union in the 1830s (see Chapter 20), new and more practical kinds of unions appeared. Limited primarily to highly skilled workers such as machinists and carpenters, these "new model unions" concentrated on winning better wages and hours through collective bargaining and compromise. This approach helped pave the way to the full acceptance of unions in Britain in the 1870s, and after 1890 unions for unskilled workers developed.

Developments in Germany, the most industrialized, socialized, and unionized continental country by 1914, were particularly instructive. German unions did not receive basic rights until 1869, and until the Anti-Socialist Laws were repealed in 1890, they were frequently harassed by the government as socialist fronts. As a result, in1895 Germany had only about 270,000 union members in a male industrial workforce of nearly 8 million. Then, with almost all legal harassment eliminated, union membership skyrocketed, reaching roughly 3 million in 1912.

This great expansion both reflected and influenced the changing character of German unions. Increasingly, union activists focused on bread-and-butter issues — wages, hours, working conditions — rather than on fomenting socialist revolution. Genuine collective bargaining, long opposed by socialist intellectuals as a sellout, was officially recognized as desirable by the German Trade Union Congress in 1899. When employers proved unwilling to bargain, a series of strikes forced them to change their minds. In 1913 alone, over ten thousand collective bargaining agreements benefiting 1.25 million workers were signed.

The German trade unions and their leaders were in fact, if not in name, thorough-going revisionists. **Revisionism** was an effort by various socialists to update Marx's doctrines to reflect the realities of the time. Thus the socialist Eduard Bernstein (1850–1932) argued in 1899 in his *Evolutionary Socialism* that many of Marx's predictions had been proved false.

> Social conditions have not developed to such an acute opposition of things and classes as is depicted in the Communist Manifesto. . . . The number of members of the possessing classes to-day is not smaller but larger. . . .
>
> In all advanced countries we see the privileges of the capitalist bourgeoisie yield-ing step by step to democratic organizations. Under the influence of this, and driven by the movement of the working classes which is daily becoming stronger, a social reaction has set in against the exploiting tendencies of capital.[5]

Therefore, Bernstein argued, socialists should reform their doctrines and tactics. They should combine with other progressive forces to win continued evolutionary gains for workers through legislation, unions, and further economic development. These views were denounced as heresy by the SPD and later by the Second International. Yet the revisionist, gradualist approach continued to gain the tacit acceptance of many German socialists, particularly in the trade unions.

Moderation found followers elsewhere. In France, the great socialist leader Jean Jaurès (1859–1914) formally repudiated revisionism in order to establish a unified so-cialist party, but he remained at heart a gradualist and optimistic secular humanist. Questions of revolution or revisionism also divided Russian Marxists.

By the early twentieth century socialist parties had clear-cut national characteristics. Russians and socialists in the Austro-Hungarian Empire tended to be the most radical. The German party talked revolution and practiced reformism, greatly influenced by its enormous trade-union movement. The French party talked revolution and tried to practice it, unrestrained by a trade-union movement that was both very weak and very radical. In Britain, the socialist but non-Marxist Labour Party, reflecting the well-established union movement, was formally committed to gradual reform. In Spain and Italy, Marxist socialism was very weak. There anarchism, seeking to smash the state rather than the bourgeoisie, dominated radical thought and action.

In short, socialist policies and doctrines varied from country to country. Socialism itself was to a large extent "nationalized" behind the façade of international unity. This helps explain why when war came in 1914, almost all socialist leaders and most work-ers supported their national governments and turned away from international solidarity.

Notes

1. Quoted by J. McKay in *Pioneers for Profit: Foreign Entrepreneurship and Russian Industrialization, 1885–1913* (Chicago: University of Chicago Press, 1970), p. 11.
2. W. Dawson, *Bismarck and State Socialism* (London: Swan Sonnenschen & Co., 1890), pp. 63–64.
3. Eugen Weber, *Peasants into Frenchmen: The Modernization of Rural France, 1870–1914* (Stanford: Stanford University Press, 1976).
4. See Eric Hobsbawm, "Mass Producing Traditions: Europe, 1870–1914," in *The Invention of Tradition*, Eric Hobsbawm and Terrence Ranger, eds. (New York: Cambridge University Press, 1992), pp. 263–307.
5. Eduard Bernstein, *Evolutionary Socialism: A Criticism and Affirmation*, trans. Edith Harvey (New York: B. W. Huebsch, 1909), pp. x–xvi, quoted in J. H. Hexter et al., *The Traditions of the Western World* (Chicago: Rand McNally, 1967), pp. 797–798.

Chapter Review

MAKE IT STICK

LearningCurve
bedfordstmartins.com/mckaywestvalue

After reading the chapter, use LearningCurve to retain what you've read.

IDENTIFY KEY TERMS

Identify and explain the significance of each item below.

Red Shirts (p. 765)
Homestead Act (p. 772)
Crimean War (p. 773)
Bloody Sunday (p. 774)
October Manifesto
  (p. 775)
Duma (p. 775)

Tanzimat (p. 776)
Young Turks (p. 778)
Reichstag (p. 779)
Kulturkampf (p. 779)
German Social
  Democratic Party
  (SPD) (p. 779)

Dreyfus affair (p. 781)
People's Budget (p. 782)
Zionism (p. 789)
revisionism (p. 793)

REVIEW THE MAIN IDEAS

Answer the focus questions from each section of the chapter.

* How did Napoleon III seek to reconcile popular and conservative forces in an authoritarian nation-state? (p. 759)

* How did conflict and war lead to the construction of strong nation-states in Italy, Germany, and the United States? (p. 761)

* What steps did Russia and the Ottoman Turks take toward modernization, and how successful were they? (p. 772)

* What general domestic political trends emerged after 1871? (p. 778)

* How did popular nationalism evolve in the last decades of the nineteenth century? (p. 784)

* Why did the socialist movement grow, and how revolutionary was it? (p. 789)

MAKE CONNECTIONS

Think about the larger developments and continuities within and across chapters.

1. By 1900 most countries in Europe and North America had established modern nation-states, but the road to nation building varied dramatically from place to place. Which countries were most successful in building viable nation-states? What accounts for the variation?

2. Liberalism, socialism, and nationalism first emerged as coherent ideologies in the decades around 1800 (Chapter 21). How had they changed by 1900?

ONLINE DOCUMENT ASSIGNMENT

Theodor Herzl

What role did popular nationalism play in the emergence of modern anti-Semitism, and how did Herzl respond to the virulent anti-Semitism of this period?

You encountered Herzl's story on page 790. Keeping the question above in mind, go online and examine examples of anti-Semitic nationalist writings and Herzl's argument for the creation of a Jewish state, and then complete a writing assignment based on the evidence and details from this chapter.

bedfordstmartins.com/mckaywestvalue

CHRONOLOGY

1839–1876	• Western-style Tanzimat reforms in Ottoman Empire
1852–1870	• Reign of Napoleon III in France
1859–1870	• Unification of Italy
1861	• Freeing of Russian serfs
1861–1865	• U.S. Civil War
1866	• Austro-Prussian War
1870–1871	• Franco-Prussian War
1870–1878	• Kulturkampf, Bismarck's attack on Catholic Church
1873	• Stock market crash spurs renewed anti-Semitism, beginning in central and eastern Europe
1880s	• Educational reforms in France create a secular public school system
1880s–1890s	• Widespread return to protectionism among European states
1883	• First social security laws to help workers in Germany
1890–1900	• Witte initiates second surge of Russian industrialization
1905	• Revolution in Russia
1906–1914	• Social reform in Great Britain
1908	• Young Turks seize power in Ottoman Empire

✓ LearningCurve
bedfordstmartins.com/mckaywestvalue
After reading the chapter, use
LearningCurve to retain what
you've read.

The West and the World

1815–1914

WHILE INDUSTRIALIZATION AND NATIONALISM WERE TRANSFORMING
urban and rural life throughout Europe, Western society itself was reshaping
the world. At the peak of its power and pride, the West entered the third and
most dynamic phase of the aggressive expansion that had begun with the
Crusades and continued with the rise of seaborne colonial empires. At the
same time, millions of Europeans picked up stakes and emigrated abroad,
primarily to North and South America but also to Australia, North and South
Africa, and Asiatic Russia. An ever-growing stream of people, products, and
ideas flowed into and out of Europe in the nineteenth century. Hardly any
corner of the globe was left untouched.

The most spectacular manifestations of Western expansion came in the late
nineteenth century when the leading European nations established or enlarged
their far-flung political empires. This political annexation of territory in the
1880s—the "new imperialism," as it is often called by historians—was the
capstone of Europe's underlying economic and technological transformation.
More directly, Europe's new imperialism rested on a formidable combination
of superior military might and strong authoritarian rule, and it posed a brutal
challenge to African and Asian peoples. Different societies met this Western
challenge in different ways and with changing tactics, as we shall see. Nevertheless, by 1914 non-Western elites in many lands were rallying their peoples
and leading an anti-imperialist struggle for dignity and genuine independence
that would eventually triumph after 1945.

Industrialization and the World Economy

What were some of the global consequences of European industrialization between 1815 and 1914?

The Industrial Revolution created, first in Great Britain and then in continental Europe and North America, a tremendously dynamic economic system. In the course of the nineteenth century, that system expanded across the face of the earth. Some of this extension into non-Western areas was peaceful and beneficial, for the West had many products and techniques the rest of the world desired. If peaceful methods failed, however, Europeans used their superior military power to force non-Western nations to open their doors to Western economic interests. In general, Europeans fashioned the global economic system so that the largest share of the ever-increasing gains from trade, technology, and migration flowed to the West and its propertied classes.

The Rise of Global Inequality

The Industrial Revolution in Europe marked a momentous turning point in human history. Those regions of the world that industrialized in the nineteenth century (mainly Europe and North America) increased their wealth and power enormously in comparison to those that did not. A gap between the core industrializing regions and the soon-to-be colonized or semi-colonized regions outside the European–North American core (mainly in Africa, Asia, the Middle East, and Latin America) emerged and widened throughout the nineteenth century. Moreover, this pattern of uneven global development became institutionalized, or built into the structure of the world economy. Thus a "lopsided world" evolved, a world with a rich north and a poor south.

In recent years historical economists have charted the long-term evolution of this gap, and Figure 24.1 summarizes the findings of one important study. Three main points stand out. First, in 1750 the average standard of living was no higher in Europe as a whole than in the rest of the world. Second, it was industrialization that opened the gaps in average wealth and well-being among countries and regions. Third, income per person stagnated in the colonized world before 1913, in striking contrast to the industrializing regions. Only after 1945, in the era of decolonization and political independence, did former

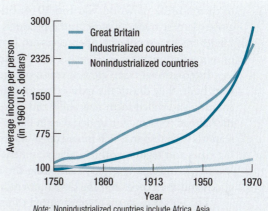

FIGURE 24.1   The Growth of Average Income per Person in Industrialized Countries, Nonindustrialized Countries, and Great Britain, 1750–1970   Growth is given in 1960 U.S. dollars and prices.

Note: Nonindustrialized countries include Africa, Asia, Latin America, and Oceania. Industrialized countries include all European countries, Canada, the United States, and Japan.

colonies make real economic progress, beginning in their turn the critical process of industrialization.

The rise of these enormous income disparities, which indicate similar and striking disparities in food and clothing, health and education, and life expectancy and general material well-being, has generated a great deal of debate. One school of interpretation stresses that the West used science, technology, capitalist organization, and even its rational worldview to create massive wealth, and then used that wealth and power to its advantage. Another school argues that the West used its political and economic power to steal much of the world's riches, continuing in the nineteenth and twentieth centuries the rapacious colonialism born of the era of expansion. Because these issues are complex and there are few simple answers, it is helpful to consider them in the context of world trade in the nineteenth century.

The World Market

Commerce between nations has always stimulated economic development. In the nineteenth century Europe directed an enormous increase in international commerce. Great Britain took the lead in cultivating export markets for its booming industrial output, as British manufacturers looked first to Europe and then around the world.

Take the case of cotton textiles. By 1820 Britain was exporting 50 percent of its production. Europe bought 50 percent of these cotton textile exports, while India bought only 6 percent and had its own well-established textile industry. Then as European nations and the United States erected protective tariff barriers to promote domestic industry, British cotton textile manufacturers aggressively sought other foreign markets in non-Western areas. By 1850 India was buying 25 percent and Europe only 16 percent of a much larger volume of production. As a British colony, India could not raise tariffs to protect its ancient, indigenous cotton textile industry, which collapsed, leaving thousands of Indian weavers unemployed.

In addition to its dominance in the export market, Britain was also the world's largest importer of goods. From the repeal of the Corn Laws in 1846 (see Chapter 21) to the outbreak of World War I in 1914, Britain remained the world's emporium, the globe's largest trader of agricultural products, raw materials, and manufactured goods. Under free-trade policies, open access to Britain's market stimulated the development of mines and plantations in many non-Western areas.

International trade grew as transportation systems improved. Wherever railroads were built, they drastically reduced transportation costs, opened new economic opportunities, and called forth new skills and attitudes. European investors funded much of the railroad construction undertaken in Latin America, Asia, and Africa, which connected seaports with resource-rich inland cities and regions, as opposed to linking and developing cities and regions within a given country. Thus railroads dovetailed effectively with Western economic interests, facilitating the inflow and sale of Western manufactured goods and the export and the development of local raw materials.

The power of steam revolutionized transportation by sea as well as by land. Steam power began to supplant sails on the oceans of the world in the late 1860s. Passenger and freight rates tumbled as ship design became more sophisticated, and the intercontinental shipment of low-priced raw materials became feasible. The time needed to cross the Atlantic dropped from three weeks in 1870 to about ten days in 1900, and the opening of the Suez and Panama Canals (in 1869 and 1914, respectively) shortened transport time to other areas of the globe considerably. In addition, improved port facilities made loading and unloading cheaper, faster, and more dependable.

The revolution in land and sea transportation encouraged European entrepreneurs to open up and exploit vast new territories around the world. Improved transportation enabled Asia, Africa, and Latin America to ship not only familiar agricultural products — spices, tea, sugar, coffee — but also new raw materials for industry, such as jute, rubber, cotton, and coconut oil. The export of raw materials supplied by these "primary producers" to Western manufacturers boosted economic growth in core countries but did little to establish independent industry in the nonindustrialized periphery.

New communications systems were used to direct the flow of goods across global networks. Transoceanic telegraph cables, firmly in place by the 1880s, enabled rapid communications among the financial centers of the world. While a British tramp freighter steamed from Calcutta to New York, a broker in London could arrange by telegram for it to carry American cargo to Australia. The same communications network conveyed world commodity prices instantaneously.

As their economies grew, Europeans began to make massive foreign investments beginning about 1840. By the outbreak of World War I in 1914, Europeans had invested more than $40 billion abroad. Great Britain, France, and Germany were the principal investing countries (Map 24.1). The great gap between rich and poor within Europe meant that the wealthy and moderately well-to-do could and did send great sums abroad in search of interest and dividends.

Most of the capital exported did not go to European colonies or protectorates in Asia and Africa. About three-quarters of total European investment went to other European countries, or to settler colonies or **neo-Europes** — a term coined by historian Alfred Crosby to describe regions that already had significant populations of ethnic Europeans, including the United States, Canada, Australia, New Zealand, Latin America, and Siberia. Europe found its most profitable opportunities for investment in construction of the railroads, ports, and utilities that were necessary to settle and develop the lands in such places as Australia and the Americas. By lending money to construct foreign railroads, Europeans enabled white settlers to buy European rails and locomotives and to develop sources of cheap food and raw materials.

Much of this investment was peaceful and mutually beneficial for lenders and borrowers. The extension of Western economic power and the construction of neo-Europes, however, were disastrous for indigenous peoples. Native Americans and Australian aborigines especially were decimated by the diseases, liquor, and weapons of an aggressively expanding Western society.

The Opening of China

Europe's development of robust offshoots in sparsely populated North America, Australia, and much of Latin America absorbed huge quantities of goods, investments, and migrants. Yet Europe's economic and cultural penetration of old, densely populated civilizations was also profoundly significant. Interaction with such civilizations increased the Europeans' trade and profit, and they were prepared to use force, if necessary, to attain their desires. This was what happened in China, a striking example of the pattern of European intrusion into non-Western lands.

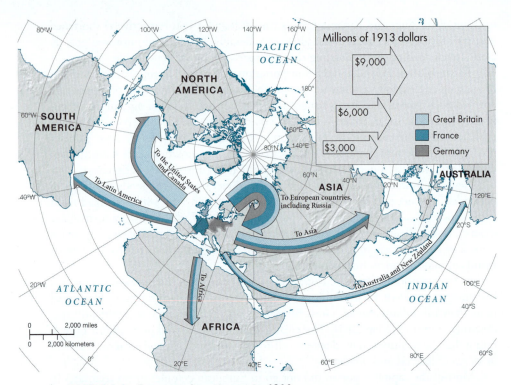

MAP 24.1 European Investment to 1914
Foreign investment grew rapidly after 1850, and Britain, France, and Germany were the major investing nations. As this map suggests, most European investment was not directed to the African and Asian areas seized in the new imperialism after 1880.

For centuries China had sent more goods and inventions to Europe than it had received, and such was still the case in the early nineteenth century. Trade with Europe was carefully regulated by the Chinese imperial government—ruled by the Qing (ching), or Manchu, Dynasty in the 1800s—which required all foreign merchants to live in the southern port of Guangzhou (Canton) and to buy and sell only to licensed Chinese merchants. Practices considered harmful to Chinese interests were strictly forbidden.

For years the little community of foreign merchants in Guangzhou had to accept this Chinese system. By the 1820s, however, the dominant group of these merchants, the British, were flexing their muscles. Moreover, in opium—that "destructive and ensnaring vice" denounced by Chinese decrees—the British found a means to break China's self-imposed isolation. British merchants smuggled opium grown legally in British-occupied India into China, where its use and sale were illegal. Huge profits and growing addiction led to a rapid increase in sales. By 1836 the British merchants in Guangzhou aggressively demanded the creation of an independent British colony in China and "safe and unrestricted liberty" in their Chinese trade. Spurred on by economic motives, they pressured the British government to take decisive action and enlisted the support of British manufacturers with visions of vast Chinese markets to be opened to their goods as well.

At the same time, the Qing government decided that the opium trade had to be stamped out. It was ruining the people and stripping the empire of its silver, which went to British merchants to pay for the drug. The government began to vigorously prosecute Chinese drug dealers. In 1839 it sent special envoy Lin Zexu to Guangzhou to deal with the crisis. Lin Zexu punished Chinese who purchased opium and seized the opium supplies of the British merchants, who then withdrew to the barren island of Hong Kong. He sent a famous letter justifying his policy to Queen Victoria in London.

The wealthy, well-connected British merchants appealed to their allies in London for support, and the British government responded. It also wanted free, unregulated trade with China, as well as the establishment of diplomatic relations on the European model, complete with ambassadors, embassies, and published treaties. Using troops from India and taking advantage of its control of the seas, Britain occupied several coastal cities and in the first of two **Opium Wars** forced China to give in to British demands. In the Treaty of Nanking in 1842, the imperial government was required to cede the island of Hong Kong to Britain forever, pay an indemnity of $100 million, and open up four large cities to unlimited foreign trade with low tariffs.

With Britain's new power over Chinese commerce, the opium trade flourished, and Hong Kong developed rapidly as an Anglo-Chinese enclave. But disputes over trade between China and the Western powers continued. Finally, the second Opium War (1856–1860) culminated in the occupation of Beijing by seventeen thousand British and French troops, who intentionally burned down the emperor's summer palace.

Britain and China at War   Britain capitalized on its overwhelming naval superiority in its war against China, as shown in this British painting celebrating a dramatic moment in a crucial 1841 battle near Guangzhou. Having received a direct hit from a steam-powered British ironclad, a Chinese sailing ship explodes into a wall of flame. The Chinese lost eleven ships and five hundred men in the two-hour engagement; the British suffered only minor damage. (© National Maritime Museum, London/The Image Works)

Another round of one-sided treaties gave European merchants and missionaries greater privileges and protection and forced the Chinese to accept trade and investment on unfavorable terms in several more cities. Thus did Europeans use opium addiction and military aggression to blow a hole in the wall of Chinese seclusion and open the country to foreign trade and foreign ideas.

Japan and the United States

China's neighbor Japan had its own highly distinctive civilization and even less use for Westerners. European traders and missionaries first arrived in Japan in the sixteenth century. By 1640 Japan had reacted quite negatively to their presence. The government decided to expel all foreigners and seal off the country from all European influences in order to preserve traditional Japanese culture and society. When American and British whaling ships began to appear off Japanese coasts almost two hundred years later, the policy of exclusion was still in effect. An order of 1825 commanded Japanese officials to "drive away foreign vessels without second thought."[1]

Japan's unbending isolation seemed hostile and barbaric to the West, particularly to the United States. It complicated the practical problems of ensuring the safety of shipwrecked American sailors and the provisioning of whaling ships and China traders sailing in the eastern Pacific. It also thwarted American business leaders' hope of trade and profit. Moreover, Americans shared the self-confidence and dynamism of expanding Western society, and they felt destined to play a great role in the Pacific. To Americans it seemed the duty of the United States to force the Japanese to open their ports and behave as a "civilized" nation.

After several unsuccessful American attempts to establish commercial relations with Japan, Commodore Matthew Perry steamed into Edo (now Tokyo) Bay in 1853. Relying on **gunboat diplomacy** by threatening to attack, Perry demanded diplomatic negotiations with the emperor. Japan entered a grave crisis. Some Japanese military leaders urged resistance, but senior officials realized how defenseless their cities were against naval bombardment. Shocked and humiliated, they reluctantly signed a treaty with the United States that opened two ports and permitted trade. Over the next five years, more treaties spelled out the rights and privileges of the Western nations and their merchants in Japan. Japan was "opened." What the British had done in China with two wars, the Americans had achieved in Japan with the threat of one.

Western Penetration of Egypt

Egypt's experience illustrates not only the explosive power of the expanding European economy and society but also their seductive appeal. European involvement in Egypt also led to a new model of formal political control, which European powers applied widely in Africa and Asia after 1882.

Of great importance in African and Middle Eastern history, the ancient land of the pharaohs had since 525 B.C.E. been ruled by a succession of foreigners, most recently by the Ottoman sultans. In 1798 French armies under young General Napoleon Bonaparte invaded the Egyptian part of the Ottoman Empire and occupied the territory for three years. Into the power vacuum left by the French withdrawal stepped an extraordinary Albanian-born, Turkish-speaking general, Muhammad Ali (1769–1849).

First appointed governor of Egypt in 1805 by the Ottoman sultan, Muhammad Ali set out to build his own state on the strength of a large, powerful army organized along European lines. He drafted for the first time the illiterate peasant masses of Egypt, and he hired French and Italian army officers to train both these raw recruits and their Turkish officers in modern military methods. He also reformed the government, cultivated new lands, and improved communication networks. By the end of his reign in 1848, Muhammad Ali had established a strong and virtually independent Egyptian state, to be ruled by his family on a hereditary basis within the Ottoman Empire (see Chapter 23).

Muhammad Ali's modernization program attracted large numbers of Europeans to the banks of the Nile. The port city of Alexandria had more than fifty thousand Europeans by 1864. Europeans served not only as army officers but also as engineers, doctors, government officials, and police officers. Others turned to trade, finance, and shipping.

To pay for his ambitious plans, Muhammad Ali encouraged the development of commercial agriculture. This development had profound implications. Egyptian peasants were poor but largely self-sufficient, growing food for their own consumption on state-owned lands allotted to them by tradition. Faced with the possibility of export agriculture, high-ranking officials and members of Muhammad Ali's family began carving large private landholdings out of the state domain. These new landlords made the peasants their tenants and forced them to grow cash crops such as cotton and rice geared to European markets. Egyptian landowners "modernized" agriculture, but to the detriment of peasant living standards.

These trends continued under Muhammad Ali's grandson Ismail (ihs-MAH-eel), who in 1863 began his sixteen-year rule as Egypt's khedive (kuh-DEEV), or prince. Educated at France's leading military academy, Ismail was a westernizing autocrat. The large irrigation networks he promoted boosted cotton production and exports to Europe, and with his support a French company completed the Suez Canal in 1869. The Arabic of the Egyptian masses replaced the Turkish spoken by Ottoman rulers as the official language; young Egyptians educated in Europe spread new skills; and Cairo acquired modern boulevards and Western hotels. As Ismail proudly declared, "My country is no longer in Africa, we now form part of Europe."[2]

Yet Ismail was too impatient and reckless. His projects were enormously expensive, and by 1876 Egypt owed foreign bondholders a colossal debt that it could not pay. France and Great Britain intervened and forced Ismail to appoint French and British commissioners to oversee Egyptian finances to ensure payment of the Egyptian debt in full. This momentous decision marked a sharp break with the past. Throughout most of the nineteenth century, Europeans had used military might and political force primarily to make sure that non-Western lands would accept European trade and investment. Now Europeans were going to effectively rule Egypt.

Foreign financial control evoked a violent nationalistic reaction among Egyptian religious leaders, young intellectuals, and army officers. In 1879, under the leadership of Colonel Ahmed Arabi, they formed the Egyptian Nationalist Party. Continuing diplomatic pressure on the government, which forced Ismail to abdicate in favor of his weak son, Tewfiq (r. 1879–1892), resulted in bloody anti-European riots in Alexandria in 1882. A number of Europeans were killed, and Tewfiq and his court had to flee to British ships for safety. When the British fleet bombarded Alexandria, more riots swept the country, and Colonel Arabi led a revolt. But a British expeditionary force put down the rebellion and occupied all of Egypt that year.

The British said their occupation was temporary, but British armies remained in Egypt until 1956. They maintained the façade of Egypt as an autonomous province of the Ottoman Empire, but the khedive was a mere puppet. British rule did result in tax reforms and somewhat better conditions for peasants, while foreign bondholders received their interest and Egyptian nationalists nursed their injured pride.

British rule in Egypt provided a new model for European expansion in densely populated lands. Such expansion was based on military force, political domination, and a self-justifying ideology of beneficial reform. This model predominated until 1914. Thus did Europe's Industrial Revolution lead to tremendous political as well as economic expansion throughout the world after 1880.

Global Migration Around 1900

How was massive migration an integral part of Western expansion?

A poignant human drama accompanied economic expansion: millions of people pulled up stakes and left their ancestral lands in the course of history's greatest migration. To millions of ordinary people for whom the opening of China and the interest on the Egyptian debt had not the slightest significance, this great movement was the central experience in the saga of Western expansion. It was, in part, because of this **global mass migration** that the West's impact on the world in the nineteenth century was so powerful and many-sided.

A note on vocabulary may be in order here: *migration* refers to general human movement; *emigrants* (or *emigration*) refers to people leaving one country for another; *immigrants* (or *immigration*) refers to people entering one country from another. People emigrate from and immigrate to.

The Pressure of Population

In the early eighteenth century European population growth entered its third and decisive stage, which continued unabated until the early twentieth century. Birthrates eventually declined in the nineteenth century, but so did death rates, mainly because of the rising standard of living and the revolution in public health (see Chapter 22). During the hundred years before 1900 the population of Europe (including Asiatic Russia) more than doubled, from approximately 188 million to roughly 432 million.

These figures actually understate Europe's population explosion, for between 1815 and 1932 more than 60 million people left Europe. These emigrants went primarily to the rapidly growing neo-Europes—North and South America, Australia, New Zealand, and Siberia. Since the population of native Africans, Asians, and Americans grew more slowly than that of Europeans in Europe and the neo-Europes, Europeans and people of predominantly European origin jumped from about 24 percent of the world's total in 1800 to about 38 percent on the eve of World War I.

The growing number of Europeans provided further impetus for Western expansion, and it drove more and more people to emigrate. As in the eighteenth century, the rapid increase in numbers in Europe proper led to land hunger and relative overpopulation in area after area. In most countries, emigration increased twenty years after a rapid growth in population, as children grew up, saw little available land and few opportunities, and departed. This pattern was especially prevalent when rapid population increase predated extensive industrial development, which offered the best long-term hope of creating jobs and reducing poverty. Thus millions of country folk in industrialized parts of Europe moved to cities in search of work, while those in more slowly industrializing regions went abroad.

Before looking at the people who emigrated, consider these three facts. First, the number of men and women who left Europe increased rapidly at the end of the nineteenth century and leading up to World War I. More than 11 million left in the first decade of the twentieth century, over five times the number departing in the 1850s. Thus large-scale emigration was a defining characteristic of European society at the turn of the century.

Second, different countries had very different patterns of migration. People left Britain and Ireland in large numbers from the 1840s on. This outflow reflected not only rural poverty but also the movement of skilled industrial technicians and the preferences shown to British migrants in the overseas British Empire. Ultimately, about one-third of all European migrants between 1840 and 1920 came from the British Isles. German emigration was quite different. It grew irregularly after about 1830, reaching a first peak in the early 1850s and another in the early 1880s. Thereafter it declined rapidly, for at that point Germany's rapid industrialization provided adequate jobs at home. This pattern contrasted sharply with that of Italy. More and more Italians left the country right up to 1914, reflecting severe problems in Italian villages and relatively slow industrial growth. In short, migration patterns mirrored social and economic conditions in the various European countries and provinces.

Third, although the United States did absorb the largest overall number of European emigrants, fewer than half of all these emigrants went to the United States. Asiatic Russia, Canada, Argentina, Brazil, Australia, and New Zealand also attracted large numbers, as Figure 24.2 shows. Moreover, immigrants accounted for a larger proportion of the total population in Argentina, Brazil, and Canada than in the United States. The common American assumption that European emigration meant immigration to the United States is quite inaccurate.

FIGURE 24.2 Origins and Destinations of European Emigrants, 1851–1960
European emigrants came from many countries; almost half of them went to the United States.

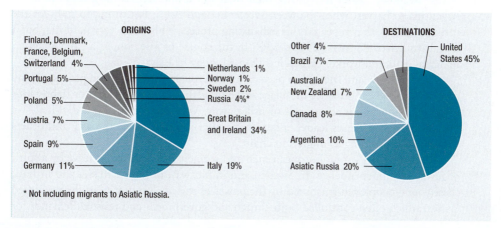

* Not including migrants to Asiatic Russia.

European Emigration

What kind of people left Europe, and what were their reasons for doing so? The European emigrant was generally an energetic small farmer or skilled artisan trying hard to stay ahead of poverty, not a desperately impoverished landless peasant or urban proletarian. These small peasant landowners and village craftsmen typically left Europe because of the lack of available land and the growing availability of cheap factory-made goods, which threatened their traditional livelihoods.

Determined to maintain or improve their status, immigrants brought great benefits to the countries that received them, in large part because the vast majority were young, typically unmarried, and ready to work hard in the new land, at least for a time. Many Europeans moved but remained within Europe, settling temporarily or permanently in another European country. Jews from central Europe and peasants from Ireland moved to Great Britain; Russians and Poles sought work in Germany; and Spaniards, Portuguese, and Italians went to France. A substantial number of Europeans were actually migrants as opposed to immigrants who settled in new lands — that is, they returned home after some time abroad. One in two immigrants to Argentina and probably one in three to the United States eventually returned to their native land.

The likelihood of repatriation varied greatly by nationality. People who emigrated from the Balkans, for instance, were much more likely to return to their countries than people from Ireland or eastern European Jews. For those who returned, the possibility of buying land in the old country was of central importance. In Ireland (as well as in England and Scotland), large, often-absentee landowners owned most land; little was up for sale. In Russia, most Jews faced discrimination and were forced to live in the Pale of Settlement (see Chapter 16), and non-Jews owned most property. Therefore, when Irish farmers and Russian Jewish artisans emigrated in search of opportunity, or, for Jews, to escape pogroms (see Chapter 23), it was basically a once-and-for-all departure.

The mass movement of Italians illustrates many of the characteristics of European emigration. As late as the 1880s, three of every four Italians worked in agriculture. With the influx of cheap North American wheat, many small landowning peasants whose standard of living was falling began to leave their country. Numerous Italians went to the United States, but before 1900 even greater numbers went to Argentina and Brazil.

Many Italians had no intention of permanently settling abroad. Some called themselves "swallows." After harvesting their own wheat and flax in Italy, they "flew" to Argentina to harvest wheat between December and April. Returning to Italy for the spring planting, they repeated this exhausting process. This was a very hard life, but a frugal worker could save $250 to $300 in the course of a season, at a time when an Italian agricultural worker earned less than $1 a day in Italy.

Ties of family and friendship played a crucial role in the emigration process. Many people from a given province or village settled together in rural enclaves or tightly knit urban neighborhoods thousands of miles away. Very often a strong individual — a businessman, a religious leader, a family member — would blaze the way and others would follow, forming a "migration chain."

Many landless young European men and women were spurred to leave by a spirit of revolt and independence. In Sweden and in Norway, in Jewish Russia and in Italy, these young people felt frustrated by the power of the small minority in the privileged classes, which often controlled both church and government and resisted demands for change and greater opportunity. Many a young Norwegian seconded the passionate cry of Norway's national poet, Martinius Bjørnson (BYURN-sawn): "Forth will I! Forth! I will be crushed and consumed if I stay."[3] Many young Jews wholeheartedly agreed with a spokesman of Kiev's Jewish community in 1882, who summed up his congregation's growing defiance in the face of brutal persecution: "Our human dignity is being trampled upon, our wives and daughters are being dishonored, we are looted and pillaged; either we get decent human rights or else let us go wherever our eyes may lead us."[4]

Thus for many, emigration was a radical way to gain basic human rights. Emigration rates slowed in countries where the people won basic political and social reforms, such as the right to vote, equality before the law, and social security.

Asian Emigration

Not all emigration was from Europe. A substantial number of Chinese, Japanese, Indians, and Filipinos — to name only four key groups — responded to rural hardship with temporary or permanent emigration. At least 3 million Asians moved abroad before 1920. Most went as indentured laborers to work under incredibly difficult conditions on the plantations or in the gold mines of Latin America, southern Asia, Africa, California, Hawaii, and Australia. White estate owners very often used Asian immigrants to replace or supplement blacks after the suppression of the slave trade.

In the 1840s, for example, the Spanish government actively recruited Chinese laborers to meet the strong demand for field hands in Cuba. Between 1853 and 1873, when such immigration was stopped, more than 130,000 Chinese laborers went to Cuba. The majority spent their lives as virtual slaves. The great landlords of Peru also brought in more than 100,000 workers from China in the nineteenth century, and there were similar movements of Asians elsewhere.

Emigration from Asia would undoubtedly have grown to much greater proportions if planters and mine owners in search of

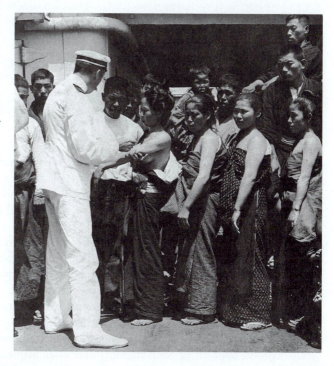

Vaccinating Migrants Bound for Hawaii, 1904
First Chinese, then Japanese, and finally Koreans and Filipinos went across the Pacific in large numbers to labor in Hawaii on American-owned sugar plantations in the late nineteenth century. The native Hawaiians had been decimated by disease, creating a severe labor shortage for Hawaii's plantation economy. (© Corbis)

PRIMARY SOURCE   Nativism in the United States

In this 1896 Senate speech, the dynamic and well-respected Republican senator Henry Cabot Lodge expressed nativist anxieties about "race mixing" in the United States and called for rigid immigration restrictions. Most Europeans who emigrated to the United States in the late nineteenth century were Roman Catholics from Italy and central Europe and Jews and Slavs from Poland and Russia—"races" that nativists considered superior to Asians and Africans but far below the Anglo-Saxon Protestants from northern Europe, who constituted the majority of U.S. immigrants until the 1870s.

Restricting Immigration

This bill is intended to amend the existing law so as to restrict still further immigration to the United States. Paupers, diseased persons, convicts, and contract laborers are now excluded. By this bill it is proposed to make a new class of excluded immigrants, and to add to those which have just been named the totally ignorant. . . .

[We propose] to exclude all immigrants who could neither read nor write, and this is the plan which was adopted by the committee. . . . In their report the committee have shown by statistics, which have been collected and tabulated with great care, the emigrants who would be affected by this illiteracy test. . . . It is found . . . that the illiteracy test will bear most heavily upon the Italians, Russians, Poles, Hungarians, Greeks, and Asiatics, and very lightly, or not at all, upon English-speaking emigrants, or Germans, Scandinavians, and French. In other words, the races most affected by the illiteracy test are those whose emigration to this country has begun within the last twenty years and swelled rapidly to enormous proportions, races with which the English-speaking people have never hitherto assimilated, and who are most alien to the great body of the people of the United States. . . .

Immigration and the Economy

There is no one thing which does so much to bring about a reduction of wages and to injure the American wage earner as the unlimited introduction of cheap foreign

cheap labor had been able to hire as many Asian workers as they wished. But they could not. Many Asians fled the plantations and gold mines as soon as possible, seeking greater opportunities in trade and towns. There they came into conflict with local populations, whether in Malaya, southern Africa, or areas settled by Europeans. When that took place in neo-Europes, European settlers demanded a halt to Asian immigration. By the 1880s the American and Australian governments had instituted exclusionary acts—discriminatory laws designed to keep Asians from entering the country.

In fact, the explosion of mass mobility in the late nineteenth century, combined with the growing appeal of nationalism and scientific racism (see Chapter 23), encouraged a variety of attempts to control immigration flows and seal off national borders. National governments established strict rules for granting citizenship and asylum to foreigners. Passports and customs posts monitored movement across increasingly tight national boundaries. Such attempts were often inspired by **nativism**, beliefs that led to

labor through unrestricted immigration. Statistics show that the change in the race character of our immigration has been accompanied by a corresponding decline in its quality. . . .

Immigration and Citizenship

When we speak of a race, . . . we mean the moral and intellectual characters, which in their association make the soul of a race, and which represent the product of all its past, the inheritance of all its ancestors. . . .

[I]t is on the moral qualities of the English-speaking race that our history, our victories, and all our future rest. There is only one way in which you can lower those qualities or weaken those characteristics, and that is by breeding them out. If a lower race mixes with a higher in sufficient numbers, history teaches us that the lower race will prevail. . . . The lowering of a great race means not only its own decline, but that of civilization. . . .

Mr. President, more precious even than forms of government are the mental and moral qualities which make what we call our race. While those stand unimpaired all is safe. When those decline all is imperiled. . . . The time has certainly come, if not to stop, at least to check, to sift, and to restrict those immigrants. . . . The gates which admit men to the United States and to citizenship in the great republic should no longer be left unguarded.

EVALUATE THE EVIDENCE

1. How does Lodge's understanding of race drive his enthusiasm for immigration restrictions?

2. Why would nativist arguments win popular support in the late nineteenth century?

Source: Henry Cabot Lodge, *Speeches and Addresses 1884–1909* (Boston: Houghton Mifflin Company, 1909), pp. 245, 247, 249–250, 262, 264–266.

policies giving preferential treatment to established inhabitants above immigrants. Thus French nativists tried to limit the influx of Italian migrant workers, German ones worked to stop Poles from crossing eastern borders, and Americans (in the 1920s) restricted immigration from southern and eastern Europe as well as banning it outright from much of Asia. (See "Primary Source: Nativism in the United States," above.)

A crucial factor in the migrations before 1914 was, therefore, immigration policies that offered preferred status to "acceptable" racial and ethnic groups in the open lands of possible permanent settlement. This, too, was part of Western dominance in the increasingly lopsided world. Largely successful in monopolizing the best overseas opportunities, Europeans and people of European ancestry reaped the main benefits from the mass migration. By 1913 people in Australia, Canada, and the United States had joined the British in having the highest average incomes in the world, while incomes in Asia and Africa lagged far behind.

Western Imperialism, 1880–1914

How did Western imperialism change after 1880?

The expansion of Western society reached its apex between about 1880 and 1914. In those years, the leading European nations not only continued to send massive streams of migrants, money, and manufactured goods around the world, but also rushed to create or enlarge vast political empires. This political empire building contrasted sharply with the economic penetration of non-Western territories between 1816 and 1880, which had left a China or a Japan "opened" but politically independent. By contrast, the empires of the late nineteenth century recalled the old European colonial empires of the sixteenth to eighteenth centuries. Because this renewed imperial push came after a long pause in European expansionism, contemporaries termed it the **new imperialism**.

Characterized by a frantic rush to plant the flag over as many people and as much territory as possible, the new imperialism had momentous consequences. By the early 1900s almost 84 percent of the globe was dominated by European nations, and Britain alone controlled one-quarter of the earth's territory and one-third of its population. The new imperialism created new tensions among competing European states and led to wars and threats of war with non-European powers. Aimed primarily at Africa and Asia, the new imperialism put millions of black, brown, and yellow peoples directly under the rule of whites.

The European Presence in Africa Before 1880

Prior to 1880, European nations controlled only 10 percent of Africa. The French had begun conquering Algeria in 1830, and by 1880 substantial numbers of French, Italian, and Spanish colonists had settled among the overwhelming Arab majority there. Yet the overall effect on Africa was minor.

At the southern tip of the continent, Britain had taken possession of the Dutch settlements in and around Cape Town during the wars with Napoleon I. This take-over of the Cape Colony had led disgruntled Dutch cattle ranchers and farmers in 1835 to make their so-called Great Trek into the interior, where they fought the Zulu and Xhosa peoples for land. After 1853 the Boers, or **Afrikaners** (a-frih-KAH-nuhrz), as the descendants of the Dutch in the Cape Colony were beginning to call themselves, proclaimed their independence and defended it against British armies. By 1880 Afrikaner and British settlers, who detested each other and lived in separate areas, had wrested control of much of South Africa from the Zulu, Xhosa, and other African peoples.

In addition to the French in the north and the British and Afrikaners in the south, European trading posts and forts dating back to the Age of Discovery and the slave trade dotted the coast of West Africa, and the Portuguese maintained a loose hold on their old possessions in Angola and Mozambique. Elsewhere, over the great mass of the continent, Europeans did not rule.

After 1880 the situation changed drastically. In a spectacular manifestation of the new imperialism, European countries jockeyed for territory in Africa, breaking sharply with previous patterns of colonization and diplomacy.

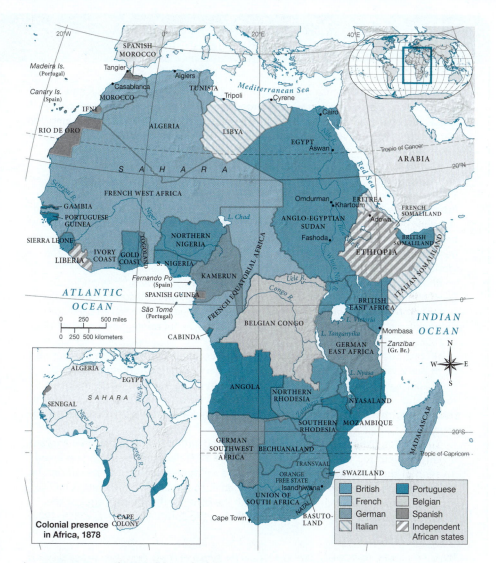

MAP 24.2 The Partition of Africa
The European powers carved up Africa after 1880 and built vast political empires. European states also seized territory in Asia in the nineteenth century, although some Asian states and peoples managed to maintain their political independence (see Map 24.3, page 816).

The Scramble for Africa After 1880

Between 1880 and 1900 Britain, France, Belgium, Germany, and Italy scrambled for African possessions as if their national livelihoods depended on it (Map 24.2). By 1900 nearly the whole continent had been carved up and placed under European rule: only Ethiopia, which fought off Italian invaders, and Liberia, which had been settled by freed slaves from the United States, remained independent. In all other African territories,

INDIVIDUALS IN SOCIETY • Cecil Rhodes

Cecil Rhodes epitomized the dynamism and the ruthlessness of the new imperialism. He built a corporate monopoly, claimed vast tracts in Africa, and established the famous Rhodes scholarships to develop colonial (and American) leaders who would love and strengthen the British Empire. But to Africans, he left a bitter legacy.

Rhodes came from a large middle-class family and at seventeen went to southern Africa to seek his fortune. He soon turned to diamonds, newly discovered at Kimberley, picked good business partners, and was wealthy by 1876. But Rhodes, often called a dreamer, wanted more. He entered Oxford University, where he studied while returning periodically to Africa. His musings crystallized in a Social Darwinist belief in progress through racial competition and territorial expansion. "I contend," he wrote, "that we [English] are the finest race in the world and the more of the world we inhabit the better it is for the human race."*

Rhodes's belief in British expansion never wavered. In 1880 he formed the De Beers Mining Company, and by 1888 his firm had monopolized southern Africa's diamond production and earned fabulous profits. Rhodes also entered the Cape Colony's legislature and became the colony's all-powerful prime minister from 1890 to 1896.

His main objective was to annex the Afrikaner republics and impose British rule on as much land as possible beyond their northern borders. Working through a state-approved private company financed in part by De Beers, Rhodes's agents forced and cajoled African kings to accept British "protection," and then put down rebellions with machine guns. Britain thus obtained a great swath of empire on the cheap.

But Rhodes, like many high achievers obsessed with power and personal aggrandizement, went too far. He backed, and then in 1896 declined to call back, a failed invasion of the Transvaal, which was designed to topple the Dutch-speaking republic. Repudiated by top British leaders who had encouraged his plan, Rhodes had to resign as prime minister. In declining health, he continued to agitate against the Afrikaner republics. He died at age forty-nine as the South African War (1899–1902) ended.

*Robert I. Rotberg, *The Founder: Cecil Rhodes and the Pursuit of Power* (New York: Oxford University Press, 1988), p. 150.

European powers tightened their control and established colonial governments in the years before 1914.

The Dutch-settler republics also succumbed to imperialism, but the final outcome was different. The British, led by Cecil Rhodes (1853–1902) in the Cape Colony, leapfrogged over the two Afrikaner states—the Orange Free State and the Transvaal—in the early 1890s and established protectorates over Bechuanaland (bech-WAH-nuh-land; now Botswana) and Rhodesia (now Zimbabwe and Zambia), named in honor of its founder. Although the British were unable to subdue the stubborn Afrikaners, English-speaking capitalists like Rhodes developed fabulously rich gold mines in the

In accounting for Rhodes's remarkable but flawed achievements, both sympathetic and critical biographers stress his imposing physical size, enormous energy, and charismatic personality. His ideas were commonplace, but he believed in them passionately, and he could persuade and inspire others to follow his lead. Rhodes the idealist was nonetheless a born negotiator, a crafty deal maker who believed that everyone could be had for a price. According to his most insightful biographer, Rhodes's homosexuality—discreet, partially repressed, but undeniable—was also "a major component of his magnetism and his success."† Never comfortable with women, he loved male companionship. He drew together a "band of brothers," both gay and straight, who shared in his pursuit of power.

Rhodes cared nothing for the rights of Africans and blacks. Both a visionary and an opportunist, he looked forward to an eventual reconciliation of Afrikaners and British in a united white front. Therefore, as prime minister of the Cape Colony, he broke with the colony's liberal tradition and supported Afrikaner demands to reduce drastically the number of black voters and limit black freedoms. This helped lay the foundation for the Union of South Africa's brutal policy of racial segregation known as apartheid after 1948.

QUESTIONS FOR ANALYSIS

1. In what ways did Rhodes's career epitomize the new imperialism in Africa?

2. How did Rhodes relate to Afrikaners and to black Africans? How do you account for the differences and the similarities?

†Ibid., p. 408.

ONLINE DOCUMENT ASSIGNMENT

What does the life of Cecil Rhodes suggest about the "great man" theory of history that was popular during this period? Examine a variety of perspectives on Rhodes's legacy. Then complete a writing assignment based on the evidence and details from this chapter.

bedfordstmartins.com/mckaywestvalue

Transvaal, and the British eventually conquered their white rivals in the bloody South African War, or Boer War (1899–1902). In 1910 the Afrikaner territories were united with the old Cape Colony and the eastern province of Natal in a new Union of South Africa, established as a largely "self-governing" colony. Gradually, though, the defeated Afrikaners used their numerical superiority over the British settlers to take political power, as even the most educated nonwhites lost the right to vote, except in the Cape Colony. (See "Individuals in Society: Cecil Rhodes," above.)

In the complex story of the European seizure of Africa, certain events and individuals stand out. Of enormous importance was the British occupation of Egypt in

1882, which established the new model of formal political control (see page 802). King Leopold II of Belgium (r. 1865–1909), an energetic, strong-willed monarch of a tiny country with a lust for distant territory, also played an important role. As early as 1861, he had laid out his vision of expansion: "The sea bathes our coast, the world lies before us. Steam and electricity have annihilated distance, and all the nonappropriated lands on the surface of the globe can become the field of our operations and of our success."[5]

By 1876 Leopold's expansionism focused on central Africa. He formed a financial syndicate under his personal control to send Henry M. Stanley, a sensation-seeking journalist and part-time explorer, to the Congo basin. Stanley established trading stations, signed unfair treaties with African chiefs, and planted the Belgian flag. Leopold's actions alarmed the French, who quickly sent out an expedition under Pierre de Brazza. In 1880 de Brazza signed a treaty of protection with the chief of the large Teke tribe and began to establish a French protectorate on the north bank of the Congo River.

Leopold's intrusion into the Congo area called attention to the possibilities of African colonization, and by 1882 Europe had caught "African fever." A gold-rush mentality led to a determined race for territory. To lay down some basic rules for this new and dangerous global competition, Jules Ferry of France and Otto von Bismarck of Germany arranged an international conference on Africa in Berlin in 1884 and 1885. The **Berlin Conference** established the principle that European claims to African territory had to rest on "effective occupation" (a strong presence on the ground) to be recognized by other states. This meant that Europeans would push relentlessly into interior regions from all sides and that no single European power would be able to claim the entire continent. The conference recognized Leopold's personal rule over a neutral Congo Free State and agreed to work to stop slavery and the slave trade in Africa.

The Berlin Conference coincided with Germany's sudden emergence as an imperial power. Prior to about 1880, Bismarck, like many other European leaders at the time, had seen little value in colonies. In 1884 and 1885, as political agitation for expansion increased, Bismarck did an abrupt about-face, and Germany established protectorates over a number of small African kingdoms and tribes in Togo, the Cameroons region, southwest Africa, and, later, East Africa. In acquiring colonies, Bismarck cooperated against the British with France's Jules Ferry, an ardent republican who also embraced imperialism. With Bismarck's tacit approval, the French pressed southward from Algeria, eastward from their old forts on the Senegal coast, and northward from their protectorate on the Congo River to take control of parts of West and Central Africa.

Meanwhile, the British began enlarging their own West African enclaves and impatiently pushed northward from the Cape Colony and westward from Zanzibar. Their thrust southward from Egypt was blocked in Sudan by fiercely independent Muslims who massacred a British force at Khartoum in 1885.

A decade later, another British force, under General Horatio H. Kitchener, moved cautiously and more successfully up the Nile River, building a railroad to supply arms and reinforcements as it went. Finally, in 1898 these British troops met their foe at Omdurman (ahm-duhr-MAHN) (see Map 24.2), where poorly armed Sudanese Muslim troops charged time and time again, only to be cut down by the recently invented Maxim machine gun. In the solemn words of one English observer, "It was not a battle but an execution. The bodies were not in heaps . . . but they spread evenly over acres and acres." In the end, about 10,000 Muslim soldiers lay dead, while only 28 Britons had been killed and 145 wounded.[6]

Continuing up the Nile after the Battle of Omdurman, Kitchener's armies found that a small French force had already occupied the village of Fashoda (fuh-SHOH-duh). Locked in imperial competition with Britain ever since the British occupation of Egypt, France had tried to be first to reach one of Africa's last unclaimed areas—the upper reaches of the Nile. The result was a serious diplomatic crisis and the threat of war between two Great Powers. Wracked by the Dreyfus affair (see Chapter 23) and unwilling to fight, France eventually backed down and withdrew its forces, allowing the British to take over.

The British conquest of Sudan exemplifies the general process of empire building in Africa. The fate of the Muslim force at Omdurman was inflicted on all native peoples who resisted European rule: they were blown away by vastly superior military force. But as the Fashoda incident showed, however much the European powers squabbled for territory around the world, they always had the sense to stop short of actually fighting each other. Imperial ambitions were not worth a great European war.

Imperialism in Asia

Although their sudden division of Africa was more spectacular, Europeans also exerted political control over much of Asia. Here the Dutch were a major player. In 1815 the Dutch ruled little more than the island of Java in the East Indies. Thereafter they gradually brought almost all of the three-thousand-mile Malay Archipelago under their political authority, though—in good imperialist fashion—they had to share some of the spoils with Britain and Germany. In the critical decade of the 1880s, the French under the leadership of Ferry took Indochina. India, Japan, and China also experienced a profound imperialist impact (Map 24.3).

Two other great imperialist powers, Russia and the United States, also acquired territories in Asia. Russia moved steadily forward on two fronts throughout the nineteenth century. Russians conquered Muslim areas to the south in the Caucasus and in Central Asia, reaching the border of Afghanistan in 1885. Russia also proceeded to nibble greedily on China's outlying provinces, especially in the 1890s.

The great conquest by the United States was the Philippines, taken from Spain in 1898 through the Spanish-American War. When it quickly became clear that the United States had no intention of granting the independence it had promised, Philippine patriots rose in revolt and were suppressed only after long, bitter fighting. Some Americans protested the taking of the Philippines, but to no avail. Thus another great Western power joined the imperialist ranks in Asia.

Causes of the New Imperialism

Many factors contributed to the late-nineteenth-century rush for empire, which was in turn one aspect of Western society's generalized expansion in the age of industry and nationalism. It is little wonder that controversies have raged over interpretation of the new imperialism, especially since authors of every persuasion have often exaggerated particular aspects in an attempt to prove their own theories. Yet despite complexity and controversy, basic causes are clearly identifiable.

Economic motives played an important role in the extension of political empires, especially in the British Empire. By the late 1870s France, Germany, and the United States were industrializing rapidly behind rising tariff barriers. Great Britain was losing

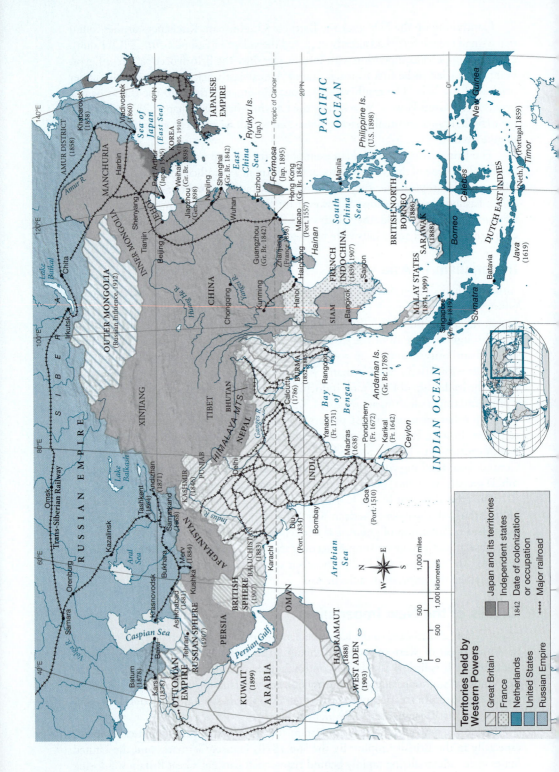

RUSSIAN EMPIRE

SIBERIA

Trans-Siberian Railway

Omsk

Kazalinsk

Orenburg

Samara

Volga R.

Batum
(1878)

Kars
(1878)

Baku

OTTOMAN
EMPIRE

RUSSIAN SPHERE
(1907)

Tehran

PERSIA

Caspian Sea

Ashkhabad
(1881)

Merv
(1884)

Kushka
(1885)

Bukhara

Samarkand
(1865)

Tashkent
(1864)

Andizhan
(1871)

Lake
Balkash

Aral
Sea

Lake
Baikal

Irkutsk

Chita

OUTER MONGOLIA
(Russian Influence, 1912)

INNER MONGOLIA

XINJIANG

AFGHANISTAN

BRITISH
SPHERE
(1907)

BALUCHISTAN
(1883)

Karachi

Diu
(Port. 1834)

OMAN

Persian Gulf

Arabian
Sea

KUWAIT
(1899)

ARABIA

HADRAMAUT
(1888)

WEST ADEN
(1903)

KASHMIR
(1846)

PUNJAB

Indus R.

Delhi

TIBET

HIMALAYA MTS.

NEPAL

BHUTAN

Ganges R.

INDIA

Bombay

Goa
(Port. 1510)

Madras
(1638)

Pondicherry
(Fr. 1672)

Karikal
(Fr. 1642)

Ceylon

Tranan
(Fr. 1731)

Calcutta
(1786)

Bay
of
Bengal

INDIAN OCEAN

Rangoon
(1853, 1885)

BURMA
(1885)

Andaman Is.
(Gr. Br. 1789)

CHINA

Chongqing

Kunming

Yangtze R.

Huang He R.

Beijing

Tianjin

Shenyang

Harbin

MANCHURIA

Amur R.

AMUR DISTRICT
(1858)

Khabarovsk
(1858)

Vladivostok
(1860)

Sea of
Japan
(East Sea)

KOREA
(Jap. 1905, 1910)

Port Arthur
(Jap. 1905)

Weihai (Gr. Br.
1898)

Jiaozhou (Ger. 1898)

Nanjing

Shanghai
(Gr. Br. 1842)

Wuhan

Guangzhou
(Gr. Br. 1842)

Zhanjiang
(France 1898)

Macao
(Port. 1557)

Hong Kong
(Gr. Br. 1842)

Hainan

Fuzhou

East
China
Sea

Formosa
(Jap. 1895)

Ryukyu Is.
(Jap.)

JAPANESE
EMPIRE

Tropic of Cancer

PACIFIC
OCEAN

40°N

20°N

Philippine Is.
(U.S. 1898)

Manila

South
China
Sea

FRENCH
INDOCHINA
(1859, 1907)

Hanoi

Haiphong

Saigon

SIAM

Bangkok

Singapore
(Gr. Br. 1819)

MALAY STATES
(1874, 1909)

Sumatra

Java
(1619)

Batavia

Borneo

SARAWAK
(1888)

BRITISH NORTH
BORNEO
(1886)

Celebes

DUTCH EAST INDIES

New Guinea

Timor
(Portugal 1859)

140°E   120°E   100°E   80°E   60°E   40°E

N
W   E
S

1,000 miles

1,000 kilometers

500

500

0

0

Territories held by Western Powers

Great Britain	Japan and its territories
France	Independent states
Netherlands	1842 Date of colonization or occupation
United States	┼┼┼┼ Major railroad
Russian Empire	

◄ **MAP 24.3** **Asia in 1914**
India remained under British rule, while China precariously preserved its political independence. The Dutch Empire in modern-day Indonesia was old, but French control of Indochina was a product of the new imperialism. Russia continued to expand to the south and also to the east.

its early economic lead and facing increasingly tough competition in foreign markets. In this new economic climate, the seizure of Asian and African territory by continental powers in the 1880s raised alarms. Fearing that France and Germany would seal off their empires with high tariffs, resulting in the permanent loss of future economic opportunities, the British followed suit and began their own push to expand empire.

Actually, the overall economic gains of the new imperialism proved quite limited before 1914. The new colonies were simply too poor to buy much, and they offered few immediately profitable investments. Nonetheless, even the poorest, most barren desert was jealously prized, and no territory was ever abandoned. This was because colonies became important for political and diplomatic reasons. Each leading country saw colonies as crucial to national security and military power. For instance, safeguarding the Suez Canal played a key role in the British occupation of Egypt, and protecting Egypt in turn led to the bloody conquest of Sudan. Far-flung possessions guaranteed ever-growing navies the safe havens and the dependable coaling stations they needed in time of crisis or war.

Along with economic motives, many people were convinced that colonies were essential to great nations. "There has never been a great power without great colonies," wrote one French publicist. The influential nationalist historian of Germany, Heinrich von Treitschke, spoke for many when he wrote: "Every virile people has established colonial power. . . . All great nations in the fullness of their strength have desired to set their mark upon barbarian lands and those who fail to participate in this great rivalry will play a pitiable role in time to come."[7]

Treitschke's harsh statement reflects not only the increasing aggressiveness of European nationalism after Bismarck's wars of German unification, but also Social Darwinian theories of brutal competition among races (see Chapter 23). As one prominent English economist argued, the "strongest nation has always been conquering the weaker . . . and the strongest tend to be best." Thus European nations, which saw themselves as racially distinct parts of the dominant white race, had to seize colonies to show they were strong and virile. Moreover, since victory of the fittest in the struggle for survival was nature's inescapable law, the conquest of "inferior" peoples was just. "The path of progress is strewn with the wreck . . . of inferior races," wrote one professor in 1900. "Yet these dead peoples are, in very truth, the stepping stones on which mankind has risen to the higher intellectual and deeper emotional life of today."[8] Social Darwinism and pseudo-scientific racial doctrines fostered imperialist expansion.

So did the industrial world's unprecedented technological and military superiority. Three aspects were particularly important. First, the rapidly firing Maxim machine gun, so lethal at Omdurman, was an ultimate weapon in many another unequal battle. Second, newly discovered quinine proved no less effective in controlling malaria, which had previously decimated whites in the tropics whenever they left breezy coastal enclaves and dared to venture into mosquito-infested interiors. Third, the combination of the steamship and the international telegraph permitted Western powers to quickly concentrate their firepower in a given area when it was needed. Never before—and never again after 1914—would the technological gap between the West and non-Western regions of the world be so great.

Social tensions and domestic political conflicts also contributed mightily to overseas expansion. In Germany and Russia, and in other countries to a lesser extent, conservative political leaders manipulated colonial issues to divert popular attention from the class struggle at home and to create a false sense of national unity. Thus imperial propagandists relentlessly stressed that colonies benefited workers as well as capitalists, providing jobs and cheap raw materials that raised workers' standard of living. Government leaders and their allies in the tabloid press successfully encouraged the masses to savor foreign triumphs and to glory in the supposed increase in national prestige. In short, conservative leaders defined imperialism as a national necessity, which they used to justify the status quo and their hold on power.

Finally, certain special-interest groups in each country were powerful agents of expansion. White settlers in the colonial areas demanded more land and greater state protection. Missionaries and humanitarians wanted to spread religion and stop the slave trade within Africa. Shipping companies wanted lucrative subsidies to protect rapidly growing global trade. Military men and colonial officials foresaw rapid advancement and highly paid positions in growing empires. The actions of such groups pushed the course of empire forward.

A "Civilizing Mission"

Western society did not rest the case for empire solely on naked conquest and a Darwinian racial struggle or on power politics and the need for naval bases on every ocean. Imperialists developed additional arguments for imperialism to satisfy their consciences and answer their critics.

A favorite idea was that Westerners could and should civilize more primitive nonwhite peoples. According to this view, Westerners shouldered the responsibility for governing and converting the supposed savages under their charge and strove to remake them on superior European models. Africans and Asians would eventually receive the benefits of industrialization and urbanization, Western education, Christianity, advanced medicine, and finally higher standards of living. In time, they might be ready for self-government and Western democracy. Thus the French repeatedly spoke of their imperial endeavors as a sacred "civilizing mission." Other imperialists agreed: as one German missionary put it, a combination of prayer and hard work under German direction would lead "the work-shy native to work of his own free will" and thus lead him to "an existence fit for human beings."[9] In 1899 Rudyard Kipling (1865–1936), who wrote masterfully of Anglo-Indian life and was perhaps the most influential British writer of the 1890s, summarized such ideas in his poem "The White Man's Burden."

Many Americans accepted the ideology of the **white man's burden**. It was an important factor in the decision to rule, rather than liberate, the Philippines after the Spanish-American War. Like their European counterparts, these Americans believed that their civilization had reached unprecedented heights and that they had unique benefits to bestow on supposedly less advanced peoples. Another argument was that imperial government protected natives from tribal warfare as well as from cruder forms of exploitation by white settlers and business people.

A Missionary School
A Swahili schoolboy leads his classmates in a reading lesson in Dar es Salaam in German East Africa before 1914, as portraits of Emperor William II and his wife look down on the classroom. Europeans argued that they were spreading the benefits of a superior civilization with schools like this one, which is unusually well built and furnished because of its strategic location in the capital city. (Ullstein Bilderdienst/The Granger Collection, New York)

Peace and stability under European control also facilitated the spread of Christianity. Catholic and Protestant missionaries competed with Islam south of the Sahara, seeking converts and building schools to spread the Gospel. Many Africans' first real contact with whites was in mission schools. Some peoples, such as the Ibo in Nigeria, became highly Christianized.

Such occasional successes in black Africa contrasted with the general failure of missionary efforts in India, China, and the Islamic world. There Christians often preached in vain to peoples with ancient, complex religious beliefs. Yet the number of Christian believers around the world did increase substantially in the nineteenth century, and missionary groups kept trying.

Orientalism

Even though many Westerners shared a sense of superiority over non-Western peoples, they were often fascinated by foreign cultures and societies. In the late 1970s the influential literary scholar Edward Said (Sigh-EED) (1935–2003) coined the term **Orientalism** to describe this fascination and the stereotypical and often racist Western understandings of non-Westerners that dominated nineteenth-century Western thought. Said originally used "Orientalism" to refer to the way Europeans viewed "the Orient," or Arab societies in North Africa and the Middle East. The term caught on, however, and is often used more broadly to refer to Western views of non-Western peoples across the globe.

As Said demonstrated, it was almost impossible for people in the West to look at or understand non-Westerners without falling into some sort of Orientalist stereotype. Politicians, scholarly experts, writers and artists, and ordinary people readily adopted "us versus them" views of foreign peoples: the West, they believed, was modern, while the non-West was primitive; the West was white, the non-West colored; the West was rational, the non-West emotional; the West was Christian, the non-West pagan or Islamic. As part of this view of the non-West as radically "other," Westerners imagined the Orient as a place of mystery and romance, populated with exotic, dark-skinned peoples, where Westerners might have remarkable experiences of foreign societies and cultures.

Such views swept through North American and European scholarship, arts, and literature in the late nineteenth century. The emergence of ethnography and anthropology as academic disciplines in the 1880s were part of the process. Inspired by a new culture of collecting, scholars and adventurers went into the field, where they studied supposedly primitive cultures and traded for, bought, or stole artifacts from non-Western peoples. The results of their work were reported in scientific studies, articles, and books, and intriguing objects filled the display cases of new public museums of ethnography and natural history. In a slew of novels published around 1900, authors portrayed romance and high adventure in the colonies and so contributed to the Orientalist worldview. Artists followed suit, and dramatic paintings of ferocious Arab warriors, Eastern slave markets, and the sultan's harem adorned museum walls and wealthy middle-class parlors. Scholars, authors, and artists were not necessarily racists or imperialists, but they found it difficult to escape Orientalist stereotypes. In the end they helped spread the notions of Western superiority and justified colonial expansion.

Critics of Imperialism

The expansion of empire aroused sharp, even bitter, critics. A forceful attack was delivered in 1902, after the unpopular South African War, by radical English economist J. A. Hobson (1858–1940) in his *Imperialism*, a work that influenced Lenin and others. Hobson contended that the rush to acquire colonies was due to the economic needs of unregulated capitalism, particularly the need of the rich to find outlets for their surplus capital. Yet, Hobson argued, imperial possessions did not pay off economically for the entire country. Only unscrupulous special-interest groups profited from them, at the expense of both European taxpayers and the natives. Moreover, Hobson argued that the quest for empire diverted popular attention away from domestic reform and the need to reduce the great gap between rich and poor.

Like Hobson, Marxist critics offered a thorough analysis and critique of Western imperialism. Rosa Luxemburg, a radical member of the German Social Democratic Party, argued that capitalism needed to expand into noncapitalist Asia and Africa to maintain high profits. The Russian Marxist and future revolutionary leader Vladimir Lenin concluded that imperialism represented the "highest stage" of advanced monopoly capitalism and predicted that its onset signaled the coming decay and collapse of capitalist society. These and similar arguments were not very persuasive, however. Most people then (and now) were sold on the idea that imperialism was economically profitable for the homeland, and the masses developed a broad and genuine enthusiasm for empire.

Hobson and many other critics struck home, however, with their moral condemnation of whites imperiously ruling nonwhites. They rebelled against crude Social Darwinian thought. "O Evolution, what crimes are committed in thy name!" cried one foe. Another sardonically coined a new beatitude: "Blessed are the strong, for they shall prey on the weak."[10] Kipling and his kind were lampooned as racist bullies whose rule rested on brutality, racial contempt, and the Maxim machine gun. Similarly, in

1902 in *Heart of Darkness*, Polish-born novelist Joseph Conrad (1857–1924) castigated the "pure selfishness" of Europeans in supposedly civilizing Africa; the main character, once a liberal scholar, turns into a savage brute.

Critics charged Europeans with applying a degrading double standard and failing to live up to their own noble ideals. At home, Europeans had won or were winning representative government, individual liberties, and a certain equality of opportunity. In their empires, Europeans imposed military dictatorships; forced Africans and Asians to work involuntarily, almost like slaves; and subjected them to shameless discrimination. Only by renouncing imperialism, its critics insisted, and giving captive peoples the freedoms Western society had struggled for since the French Revolution would Europeans be worthy of their traditions. These critics provided colonial peoples with a Western ideology of liberation.

Responding to Western Imperialism

What was the general pattern of non-Western responses to Western expansion?

To Africans and Asians, Western expansion represented a profoundly disruptive assault. Everywhere it threatened traditional ruling classes, local economies, and long-standing ways of life. Christian missionaries and European secular ideologies challenged established beliefs and values. Non-Western peoples experienced a crisis of identity, one made all the more painful by the power and arrogance of the white intruders.

The Pattern of Response

Generally, the initial response of African and Asian rulers to aggressive Western expansion was to try to drive the unwelcome foreigners away. This was the case in China, Japan, and Sudan, as we have seen. Violent antiforeign reactions exploded elsewhere again and again, as in the lengthy U.S.-Indian wars, but the superior military technology of the industrialized West almost invariably prevailed. Beaten in battle, many Africans and Asians concentrated on preserving their cultural traditions at all costs. Others found themselves forced to reconsider their initial hostility. Some (such as Ismail of Egypt) concluded that the West was indeed superior in some ways and that it was therefore necessary to copy some European achievements, especially if they wished to escape full-blown Western political rule. Thus it is possible to think of responses to the Western impact as a spectrum, with "traditionalists" at one end, "westernizers" or "modernizers" at the other, and many shades of opinion in between. Both before and after European domination, the struggle among these groups was often intense. With time, however, the modernizers tended to gain the upper hand.

When the power of both the traditionalists and the modernizers was thoroughly shattered by superior force, some Asians and Africans accepted imperial rule. Political participation in non-Western lands was historically limited to small elites, and ordinary people often did what their rulers told them to do. In these circumstances Europeans, clothed in power and convinced of their righteousness, tried to govern smoothly and effectively. At times they received considerable support from both traditionalists (local chiefs, landowners, religious leaders) and modernizers (Western-educated professional classes and civil servants).

Nevertheless, imperial rule was in many ways an imposing edifice built on sand. Support for European rule among subjugated peoples was shallow and weak. Colonized lands were primarily peasant societies, and much of the burden of colonization fell on small farmers who tenaciously fought for some measure of autonomy. When colonists demanded extra taxes or crops, peasants played dumb and hid the extent of their harvest; when colonists asked for increased labor, peasants dragged their feet. These "weapons of the weak" stopped short of open defiance but nonetheless presented a real challenge to Western rule.[11] Moreover, native people followed with greater or lesser enthusiasm the few determined personalities who came to openly oppose the Europeans. Such leaders always arose, both when Europeans ruled directly and when they manipulated native governments, for at least two basic reasons.

First, the nonconformists — the eventual anti-imperialist leaders — developed a burning desire for human dignity, economic emancipation, and political independence, all incompatible with foreign rule. Second, and somewhat ironically, potential leaders found in the Western world the ideologies underlying and justifying their protest. They discovered liberalism, with its credos of civil liberties and political self-determination. They echoed the demands of anti-imperialists in Europe and America that the West live up to its own ideals. Above all, they found themselves attracted to nationalism, which asserted that every people had the right to control its own destiny. After 1917 anti-imperialist revolt would find another European-made weapon in Lenin's version of Marxist socialism. Thus the anti-imperialist search for dignity drew strength from Western thought and culture, as is particularly apparent in the development of three major Asian countries — India, Japan, and China.

Empire in India

India was the jewel of the British Empire, and no colonial area experienced a more profound British impact. Unlike Japan and China, which maintained a real if precarious independence, and unlike African territories, which Europeans annexed only at the end of the nineteenth century, India was ruled more or less absolutely by Britain for a very long time.

Arriving in India on the heels of the Portuguese in the seventeenth century, the British East India Company had conquered the last independent native state by 1848. The last "traditional" response to European rule — an attempt by the indigenous ruling classes to drive the invaders out by military force — was broken in India in 1857 and 1858. Those were the years of the **Great Rebellion** (which the British called a "mutiny"), an insurrection by Muslim and Hindu mercenaries in the British army that spread throughout northern and central India before it was finally crushed, primarily by loyal native troops from southern India. Britain then ruled India directly until Indian independence was gained in 1947.

India was ruled by the British Parliament in London and administered by a tiny, all-white civil service in India. In 1900 this elite consisted of fewer than 3,500 top officials, who controlled a population of 300 million. The white elite, backed by white officers and native troops, was competent and generally well disposed toward the welfare of the Indian peasant masses. Yet it practiced strict job discrimination and social segregation, and most of its members quite frankly considered what they saw as the jumble of Indian peoples and castes to be racially inferior. As Lord Kitchener, one of the most distinguished top military commanders in India, stated:

> It is this consciousness of the inherent superiority of the European which has won for us India. However well educated and clever a native may be, and however brave he may prove himself, I believe that no rank we can bestow on him would cause him to be considered an equal of the British officer.[12]

British women played an important part in the imperial enterprise, especially after the opening of the Suez Canal in 1869 made it much easier for civil servants and businessmen to bring their wives and children with them to India. These British families tended to live in their own separate communities, where they occupied large houses with well-shaded porches, handsome lawns, and a multitude of servants. It was the wife's responsibility to manage this complex household. Many officials' wives learned to relish their duties, and they directed their households and servants with the same self-confident authoritarianism that characterized their husbands' political rule.

A small minority of British women — many of them feminists, social reformers, or missionaries, both married and single — sought to go further and shoulder what one historian has called the "white women's burden" in India.[13] These women tried especially to improve the lives of Indian women, both Hindu and Muslim, promoting education and legislation to move them closer to the better conditions they believed Western women had attained. Their greatest success was educating some elite Hindu women who took up the cause of reform.

With British men and women sharing a sense of mission as well as strong feelings of racial and cultural superiority, the British acted energetically and introduced many desirable changes to India. Realizing that they needed well-educated Indians to serve as skilled subordinates in both the government and the army, the British established a modern system of secondary education, with all instruction in English. Thus some Indians gained excellent opportunities for economic and social advancement. High-caste Hindus, particularly quick to respond, emerged as skillful intermediaries between the British rulers and the Indian people, and soon they formed a new elite profoundly influenced by Western thought and culture.

This new native elite joined British officials and businessmen to promote modern economic development, a second result of British rule. Examples included constructing irrigation projects for agriculture, building the world's third-largest railroad network for good communications, and forming large tea and jute plantations geared to the world economy. Unfortunately, the lot of the Indian masses improved little, for the profits from the increase in production went to native and British elites.

Finally, with a well-educated, English-speaking Indian bureaucracy and steps toward economic development, the British created a unified, powerful state. They placed under the same system of law and administration the different Hindu and Muslim peoples and the vanquished kingdoms of the entire subcontinent — groups that had fought each other for centuries and had been repeatedly conquered by Muslim and Mongol invaders. It was as if Europe, with its many states and varieties of Christianity, had been conquered and united in a single great empire.

Despite these achievements, the decisive reaction to European rule was the rise of nationalism among the Indian elite. No matter how anglicized and necessary a member of the educated classes became, he or she could never become the white ruler's equal. The top jobs, the best clubs, the modern hotels, and even certain railroad compartments were off limits to brown-skinned Indians. The peasant masses might accept such inequality as the latest version of age-old oppression, but the well-educated, English-speaking elite eventually could not. For them, racial discrimination meant injured pride and bitter injustice. It flagrantly contradicted the cherished Western concepts of human rights and equality that they had learned about in Western schools. Moreover, it was based on dictatorship, no matter how benign.

By 1885, when educated Indians came together to found the predominantly Hindu Indian National Congress, demands were increasing for the equality and self-government that Britain had already granted white-settler colonies, such as Canada and Australia. By 1907, emboldened in part by Japan's success (see the next section), a radical faction in the Indian National Congress called for Indian independence. Although there were sharp divisions between Hindus and Muslims on what shape the Indian future should take, among other issues, Indians were finding an answer to the foreign challenge. The common heritage of British rule and Western ideals, along with the reform and revitalization of the Hindu religion, had created a genuine movement for national independence.

The Example of Japan

When Commodore Matthew Perry arrived in Tokyo in 1853 with his crude but effective gunboat diplomacy, Japan was a complex feudal society. At the top stood a figurehead emperor, but real power was in the hands of a hereditary military governor, the shogun. With the help of a warrior nobility known as samurai, the shogun governed a country of hard-working, productive peasants and city dwellers. The intensely proud samurai were humiliated by the sudden American intrusion and the unequal treaties with Western countries that followed.

When foreign diplomats and merchants began to settle in Yokohama, radical samurai reacted with a wave of antiforeign terrorism and antigovernment assassinations that lasted from 1858 to 1863. In response, an allied fleet of American, British, Dutch, and French warships demolished key forts, further weakening the power and prestige of the shogun's government. Then in 1867 a coalition led by patriotic samurai seized control of the government with hardly any bloodshed and restored the political power of the emperor in the **Meiji Restoration**, a great turning point in Japanese history.

The immediate goal of the new government was to meet the foreign threat. The battle cry of the Meiji (MAY-jee) reformers was "Enrich the state and strengthen the armed forces." Yet how were these tasks to be accomplished? In a remarkable about-face, the leaders of Meiji Japan dropped their antiforeign attacks. Convinced that Western civilization was indeed superior in its military and industrial aspects, they initiated a series of measures to reform Japan along modern lines. In the broadest sense, the Meiji leaders tried to harness Western industrialization and political reform to protect their country and catch up with Europe.

In 1871 the new leaders abolished the old feudal structure of aristocratic, decentralized government and formed a strong unified state. Following the example of the French Revolution, they dismantled the four-class legal system and declared social equality. They decreed freedom of movement in a country where traveling abroad had been a serious crime. They created a free, competitive, government-stimulated economy. Japan began to build railroads and modern factories. The new generation adopted many principles of a free, liberal society, and, as in Europe, the resulting freedom resulted in a tremendously creative release of human energy.

Yet the overriding concern of Japan's political leadership was always to maintain a powerful state and a strong military. State leaders created a powerful modern navy and completely reorganized the army along European lines, forming a professional officer corps and requiring three years of military service of all males. This army of draftees effectively put down disturbances in the countryside, and in 1877 it crushed a major rebellion by feudal elements protesting the loss of their privileges. In addition, Japan skillfully adapted the West's science and technology, particularly in industry, medicine, and education, and many Japanese studied abroad. The government paid large salaries to attract foreign experts, who were replaced by trained Japanese as soon as possible.

By 1890, when the new state was firmly established, the wholesale borrowing of the early restoration had given way to a more selective emphasis on those things foreign that were in keeping with Japanese tradition. Following the model of the German Empire, Japan established an authoritarian constitution and rejected democracy. The power of the emperor and his ministers was vast, that of the legislature limited.

Japan also successfully copied the imperialism of Western society. Expansion proved that Japan was strong and cemented the nation together in a great mission. Having "opened" Korea with its own gunboat diplomacy in 1876, Japan decisively defeated China in a war over Korea in 1894 and 1895 and took Formosa (modern-day Taiwan). In the next years, Japan competed aggressively with European powers for influence and territory in China, particularly in Manchuria, where Japanese and Russian imperialism collided. In 1904 Japan attacked Russia without warning. After a bloody war, Japan emerged with a valuable foothold in China, Russia's former protectorate over Port Arthur (see Map 24.3). By 1910, with the annexation of Korea, Japan had become a major imperialist power.

Japan became the first non-Western country to use an ancient love of country to transform itself and thereby meet the many-sided challenge of Western expansion. Moreover, Japan demonstrated convincingly that a modern Asian nation could defeat and humble a great Western power. Japan's achievement fascinated many Chinese and Vietnamese nationalists and provided patriots throughout Asia and Africa with an inspiring example of national recovery and liberation.

Toward Revolution in China

In 1860 the two-hundred-year-old Qing Dynasty in China appeared on the verge of collapse. Efforts to repel foreigners had failed, and rebellion and chaos wracked the country. Yet the government drew on its traditional strengths and made a surprising comeback that lasted more than thirty years.

Two factors were crucial in this reversal. First, the traditional ruling groups temporarily produced new and effective leadership. Loyal scholar-statesmen and generals quelled disturbances such as the great Tai Ping rebellion. The remarkable empress dowager Tzu Hsi (tsoo shee) governed in the name of her young son, combining shrewd insight with vigorous action to revitalize the bureaucracy.

Second, destructive foreign aggression lessened, for the Europeans had obtained their primary goal of establishing commercial and diplomatic relations. Indeed, some

Europeans contributed to the dynasty's recovery. A talented Irishman effectively reorganized China's customs office, increasing government tax receipts, and a sympathetic American diplomat represented China in foreign lands, helping to strengthen the Chinese government. Such efforts dovetailed with the dynasty's efforts to adopt some aspects of Western government and technology while maintaining traditional Chinese values and beliefs.

The parallel movement toward domestic reform and limited cooperation with the West collapsed under the blows of Japanese imperialism. The Sino-Japanese War of 1894 to 1895 and the subsequent harsh peace treaty revealed China's helplessness in the face of aggression, triggering a rush by foreign powers for concessions and protectorates. At the high point of this rush in 1898, it appeared that the European powers might actually divide China among themselves, as they had recently divided Africa. Probably only the jealousy each nation felt toward its imperialist competitors saved China from partition. In any event, the tempo of foreign encroachment greatly accelerated after 1894.

China's precarious position after the war with Japan led to a renewed drive for fundamental reforms. Like the leaders of the Meiji Restoration, some modernizers saw salvation in Western institutions. In 1898 they convinced the young emperor to launch a desperate **hundred days of reform** in an attempt to meet the foreign challenge. More radical reformers, such as the revolutionary Sun Yatsen (1866–1925), who came from the peasantry and was educated in Hawaii by Christian missionaries, sought to overthrow the dynasty altogether and establish a republic.

The efforts at radical reform by the young emperor and his allies threatened the Qing establishment and the empress dowager Tzu Hsi, who had dominated the court for a quarter of a century. In a palace coup, she and her supporters imprisoned the emperor, rejected the reform movement, and put reactionary officials in charge. Hope for reform from above was crushed.

A violent antiforeign reaction swept the country, encouraged by the Qing court and led by a secret society that foreigners called the Boxers. The conservative, patriotic Boxers blamed China's ills on foreigners, charging foreign missionaries with undermining Chinese reverence for their ancestors and thereby threatening the Chinese family and the society as a whole. In the agony of defeat and unwanted reforms, the Boxers and other secret societies struck out at their enemies. In northeastern China, more than two hundred foreign missionaries and several thousand Chinese Christians were killed, prompting threats and demands from Western governments. The empress dowager answered by declaring war, hoping that the Boxers might relieve the foreign pressure on the government.

The imperialist response was swift and harsh. After the Boxers besieged the embassy quarter in Beijing, foreign governments organized an international force of twenty thousand soldiers to rescue their diplomats and punish China. Western armies defeated the Boxers and occupied and plundered Beijing. In 1901 China was forced to accept a long list of penalties, including a heavy financial indemnity payable over forty years.

The years after this heavy defeat were ever more troubled. Anarchy and foreign influence spread as the power and prestige of the Qing Dynasty declined still further. Antiforeign, antigovernment revolutionary groups agitated and plotted. Finally, in 1912 a spontaneous uprising toppled the Qing Dynasty. After thousands of years of emperors, a loose coalition of revolutionaries proclaimed a Western-style republic and called for

Demonizing the Boxer Rebellion
The Sunday supplement to *Le Petit Parisien*, a popular French newspaper, ran a series of gruesome front-page pictures of ferocious Boxers burning buildings, murdering priests, and slaughtering Chinese Christians. In this 1910 illustration, Boxer rebels invade a church in Mukden, Manchuria, and massacre the Christian worshippers. Whipping up European outrage about native atrocities was a prelude to harsh reprisals by the Western powers. (Mary Evans Picture Library)

ÉVÉNEMENTS DE CHINE
Massacre dans l'église de Moukden en Mandchourie

an elected parliament. The transformation of China under the impact of expanding Western society entered a new phase, and the end was not in sight.

Notes

1. Quoted in J. W. Hall, *Japan: From Prehistory to Modern Times* (New York: Delacorte Press, 1970), p. 250.
2. Quoted in Earl of Cromer, *Modern Egypt* (London, 1911), p. 48.
3. Quoted in T. Blegen, *Norwegian Migration to America*, vol. 2 (Northfield, Minn.: Norwegian-American Historical Association, 1940), p. 468.
4. Quoted in I. Howe, *World of Our Fathers* (New York: Harcourt Brace Jovanovich, 1975), p. 290.
5. Quoted in W. L. Langer, *European Alliances and Alignments, 1871–1890* (New York: Vintage Books, 1931), p. 290.
6. Quote from J. Ellis, *The Social History of the Machine Gun* (New York: Pantheon Books, 1975), pp. 86, 101. The numbers given for British casualties at the Battle of Omdurman vary; the total casualties quoted here come from an original British army report. See Lieutenant General H. M. L. Rundle, M.G., Chief of Staff, "Herewith Returns of Killed and Wounded of the Expeditionary Force at the Battle of Khartum, on September 2, 1898," Khartum, September 9, 1898, at North East Medals, http://www.britishmedals.us/kevin/other/lgomdurman.html.
7. Quoted in G. H. Nadel and P. Curtis, eds., *Imperialism and Colonialism* (New York: Macmillan, 1964), p. 94.
8. Quoted in W. L. Langer, *The Diplomacy of Imperialism*, 2d ed. (New York: Alfred A. Knopf, 1951), pp. 86, 88.
9. Quoted in Sebastian Conrad, *Globalisation and the Nation in Imperial Germany* (New York: Cambridge University Press, 2010), p. 78.
10. Quoted in Langer, *The Diplomacy of Imperialism*, p. 88.
11. James C. Scott, *Weapons of the Weak: Everyday Forms of Peasant Resistance* (New Haven: Yale University Press, 1985), p. xvi.
12. Quoted in K. M. Panikkar, *Asia and Western Dominance: A Survey of the Vasco da Gama Epoch of Asian History* (London: George Allen & Unwin, 1959), p. 116.
13. A. Burton, "The White Women's Burden: British Feminists and 'The Indian Women,' 1865–1915," in *Western Women and Imperialism: Complicity and Resistance*, ed. N. Chauduri and M. Strobel (Bloomington: Indiana University Press, 1992), pp. 137–157.

Chapter Review

MAKE IT STICK

LearningCurve
bedfordstmartins.com/mckaywestvalue
After reading the chapter, use LearningCurve to retain what you've read.

IDENTIFY KEY TERMS

Identify and explain the significance of each item below.

neo-Europes (p. 799)   Berlin Conference (p. 814)
Opium Wars (p. 801)   white man's burden (p. 818)
gunboat diplomacy (p. 802)   Orientalism (p. 819)
global mass migration (p. 804)   Great Rebellion (p. 822)
nativism (p. 808)   Meiji Restoration (p. 824)
new imperialism (p. 810)   hundred days of reform (p. 826)
Afrikaners (p. 810)

REVIEW THE MAIN IDEAS

Answer the focus questions from each section of the chapter.

* What were some of the global consequences of European industrialization between 1815 and 1914? (p. 797)

* How was massive migration an integral part of Western expansion? (p. 804)

* How did Western imperialism change after 1880? (p. 810)

* What was the general pattern of non-Western responses to Western expansion? (p. 821)

MAKE CONNECTIONS

Think about the larger developments and continuities within and across chapters.

1. How did the expansion of European empires transform everyday life around the world?

2. Historians often use the term "new imperialism" to describe the globalization of empire that began in the last decades of the nineteenth century. Was the new imperialism really that different from earlier waves of European expansion (Chapters 14 and 17)?

3. How did events and trends in European colonies connect to or reflect events and trends in the European homeland?

ONLINE DOCUMENT ASSIGNMENT

Cecil Rhodes

What does the life of Cecil Rhodes suggest about the "great man" theory of history that was popular during this period?

You encountered Cecil Rhodes's story on page 812. Keeping the question above in mind, go online and examine a variety of perspectives on Rhodes's legacy. Then complete a writing assignment based on the evidence and details from this chapter.

bedfordstmartins.com/mckaywestvalue

CHRONOLOGY

1805–1848	• Muhammad Ali modernizes Egypt
1839–1842	• First Opium War; Treaty of Nanking
1853	• Perry "opens" Japan for trade
1856–1860	• Second Opium War
1857–1858	• Britain crushes Great Rebellion in India
1863–1879	• Reign of Ismail in Egypt
1867	• Meiji Restoration in Japan
1869	• Suez Canal opens
1880–1900	• Most of Africa falls under European rule
1884–1885	• Berlin Conference
1885	• Russian expansion reaches borders of Afghanistan
1898	• United States takes over Philippines; hundred days of reform in China; Battle of Omdurman
1899	• Kipling writes "The White Man's Burden"
1899–1902	• South African War
1902	• Conrad publishes *Heart of Darkness*; Hobson publishes *Imperialism*
1912	• Western-style republic replaces China's Qing Dynasty
1914	• Panama Canal opens

25

✓ LearningCurve
bedfordstmartins.com/mckaywestvalue
After reading the chapter, use
LearningCurve to retain what
you've read.

War and Revolution

1914–1919

IN THE SUMMER OF 1914 THE NATIONS OF EUROPE WENT WILLINGLY
to war. They believed they had no other choice. Both peoples and governments confidently expected a short war leading to a decisive victory and thought that European society would be able to go on as before. These expectations were totally mistaken. The First World War was long, indecisive, and tremendously destructive. To the shell-shocked generation of survivors, it was known simply as the Great War because of its unprecedented scope and intensity.

From today's perspective, it is clear that the First World War was closely connected to the ideals and developments of the previous century. Industrialization, which promised a rising standard of living, now produced horrendous weapons that killed and maimed millions. Imperialism, which promised to civilize those the Europeans considered savages, now led to intractable international conflicts. Nationalism, which promised to bring compatriots together in a harmonious nation-state, now encouraged hateful prejudice and chauvinism. The extraordinary violence of world war shook confidence in such nineteenth-century certainties to its core.

The war would also have an enormous impact on the century that followed. The need to provide extensive supplies and countless soldiers for the war effort created mass suffering, encouraged the rise of the bureaucratic state, and brought women in increasing numbers into the workplace. Millions were killed or wounded at the front, and millions more grieved these losses. Grand states collapsed: the Russian, Austro-Hungarian, and Ottoman Empires passed into history. The trauma of war contributed to the rise of extremist politics—

in the Russian Revolution of 1917 the Bolsheviks established a radical Communist regime, and totalitarian Fascist movements gained popularity across Europe in the postwar decades. Explaining the war's causes and consequences remains one of the great challenges for historians of modern Europe.

The Road to War

What caused the outbreak of the First World War?

Historians have long debated why Europeans so readily pursued a war that was long and costly and failed to resolve the problems faced by the combatant nations. There was no single most important cause. Growing competition over colonies and world markets, a belligerent arms race, and a series of diplomatic crises sharpened international tensions. On the home front, new forms of populist nationalism strengthened people's unquestioning belief in "my country right or wrong" while ongoing domestic conflicts encouraged governments to pursue aggressive foreign policies in attempts to bolster national unity. All helped pave the road to war.

Growing International Conflict

The First World War began, in part, because European statesmen failed to resolve the diplomatic problems created by Germany's rise to Great Power status. The Franco-Prussian War and the unification of Germany opened a new era in international relations. By war's end in 1871, France was defeated, and Bismarck had made Prussia-Germany the most powerful nation in Europe (see Chapter 23). After 1871 Bismarck declared that Germany was a "satisfied" power. Within Europe, he stated, Germany had no territorial ambitions and wanted only peace.

But how was peace to be preserved? Bismarck's first concern was to keep France—bitter over its defeat and the loss of Alsace and Lorraine—diplomatically isolated and without allies. His second concern was the threat to peace posed by the enormous multinational empires of Austria-Hungary and Russia, particularly in southeastern Europe, where the waning strength of the Ottoman Empire had created a threatening power vacuum in the disputed border territories of the Balkans.

Bismarck's accomplishments in foreign policy were great, but only temporary. From 1871 to the late 1880s, he maintained German leadership in international affairs, and he signed a series of defensive alliances with Austria-Hungary and Russia designed to isolate France. Yet in 1890 the new emperor William II incautiously dismissed Bismarck, in part because he disagreed with the chancellor's friendly policy toward Russia. Under William II, Bismarck's carefully planned alliance system began to unravel. Germany refused to renew a nonaggression pact with Russia, the centerpiece of Bismarck's system, in spite of Russian willingness to do so. This fateful move prompted long-isolated republican France to court absolutist Russia, offering loans, arms, and support. In early 1894 France and Russia became military allies. As a result, continental Europe was divided into two rival blocs. The **Triple Alliance** of Austria, Germany, and Italy faced an increasingly hostile Dual Alliance of Russia and France, and the German general staff began secret preparations for a war on two fronts (Map 25.1).

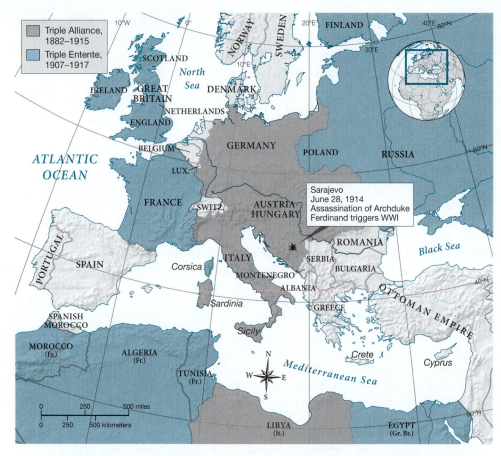

MAP 25.1 **European Alliances at the Outbreak of World War I, 1914**
At the start of World War I, Europe was divided into two hostile alliances: the Triple Entente
of Britain, France, and Russia, and the Triple Alliance of Germany, Austria-Hungary, and Italy.
Italy joined the Entente in 1915.

As rivalries deepened on the continent, Great Britain's foreign policy became in-
creasingly crucial. After 1891 Britain was the only uncommitted Great Power. Many
Germans and some Britons felt that the advanced, racially related Germanic and Anglo-
Saxon peoples were natural allies. However, the good relations that had prevailed between
Prussia and Great Britain since the mid-eighteenth century gave way to a bitter Anglo-
German rivalry.

There were several reasons for this ill-fated development. Commercial rivalry in
world markets between Germany and Great Britain increased sharply in the 1890s, as
Germany became a great industrial power. Germany's ambitious pursuit of colonies
further threatened British interests. Above all, Germany's decision in 1900 to expand
significantly its battle fleet posed a challenge to Britain's long-standing naval supremacy.
In response to German expansion, British leaders prudently shored up their exposed
global position with alliances and agreements. Britain improved its often-strained rela-

tions with the United States, concluded an alliance with Japan in 1902, and allied with France in the Anglo-French Entente of 1904, which settled all outstanding colonial disputes between Britain and France.

Alarmed by Britain's closer ties to France, Germany's leaders decided to test the strength of their alliance. In 1905 William II declared that Morocco—where France had colonial interests—was an independent, sovereign state and demanded that Germany receive the same trading rights as France. William II insisted on an international conference in hopes that his saber rattling would settle the Moroccan question to Germany's benefit. But his crude bullying only brought France and Britain closer together, and Germany left the conference empty-handed.

The result of the First Moroccan Crisis in 1905 was something of a diplomatic revolution. Britain, France, Russia, and even the United States began to see Germany as a potential threat. At the same time, German leaders began to see sinister plots to encircle Germany and block its development as a world power. In 1907 Russia, battered by its disastrous war with Japan and the revolution of 1905, agreed to settle its quarrels with Great Britain in Persia and Central Asia and signed the Anglo-Russian Agreement. This agreement laid the foundation of the **Triple Entente** (ahn-TAHNT), an alliance between Britain, Russia, and France.

Germany's decision to expand its navy with a large, enormously expensive fleet of big-gun battleships, known as "dreadnoughts" because of their great size and power, heightened international tensions. German patriots saw a large navy as the legitimate right of a great world power and as a source of national pride. But British leaders saw the German buildup as a military challenge that forced them to spend the "People's Budget" (see Chapter 23) on battleships rather than on social welfare. In 1909 the London *Daily Mail* hysterically informed its readers that "Germany is deliberately preparing to destroy the British Empire."[1] By then Britain had sided psychologically, if not officially, with France and Russia.

The leading nations of Europe were divided into two hostile camps, both ill-prepared to deal with the worsening situation in the Balkans. Britain, France, and Russia—the Triple Entente—were in direct opposition to the German-led Triple Alliance. This unfortunate treaty system only confirmed the failure of all European leaders to incorporate Bismarck's mighty empire permanently and peacefully into the international system. By 1914 many believed that war was inevitable (see Map 25.1).

The Mood of 1914

Diplomatic rivalries and international crises played key roles in the rush to war, but a complete understanding of the war's origins requires an account of the "mood of 1914"—the attitudes and convictions of Europeans around 1914.[2] Widespread militarism (the popular approval of military institutions and their values) and nationalism encouraged leaders and citizens alike to see international relations as an arena for the testing of national power, with war if necessary.

Germany was especially famous for its powerful and aggressive army, but military institutions played a prominent role in affairs of state and in the lives of ordinary people across Europe. In a period marked by diplomatic tensions, politicians relied on generals and military experts to help shape public policy. All the Great Powers built up their armed forces and designed mobilization plans to rush men and weapons to the field of battle. Universal conscription in Germany, France, Italy, Austria-Hungary, and Russia—only Britain still relied on a volunteer army—exposed hundreds of thousands of young men each year to military culture and discipline.

The continent had not experienced a major conflict since the Franco-Prussian War (1870–1871), so Europeans vastly underestimated the destructive potential of modern weapons. Encouraged by the patriotic national press, many believed that war was glorious, manly, and heroic. If they expected another conflict, they thought it would be over quickly. Leading politicians and intellectuals likewise portrayed war as a test of strength that would lead to national unity and renewal. Such ideas permeated European society. As one German volunteer wrote in his diary as he left for the front in 1914, "I believe that this war is a challenge for our time and for each individual, a test by fire, that we may ripen into manhood, become men able to cope with the coming stupendous years and events."[3]

Support for military values was closely linked to a growing sense of popular nationalism, the notion that one's country was superior to all others (see Chapters 21 and 23). Since the 1850s the spread of the idea that members of an ethnic group should live together in a homogeneous, united national state had provoked all kinds of international conflicts over borders and citizenship rights. Nationalism drove the spiraling arms race and the struggle over colonies. Broad popular commitment to national interests above all else weakened groups that thought in terms of international communities and consequences. Expressions of antiwar sentiment by socialists or women's groups were seen as a betrayal of country in time of need. Inspired by nationalist beliefs, much of the population was ready for war.

Leading statesmen had practical reasons for promoting militarism and nationalism. Political leaders had long used foreign adventurism and diplomatic posturing to distract

German Militarism   The German emperor William II reviews his troops with the Italian king Victor Emmanuel in front of the royal palace in Potsdam in 1902. Aggressive militarism and popular nationalism helped pave the road to war. (© Scherl/SV-Bilderdienst/The Image Works)

the people from domestic conflicts. In Great Britain, leaders faced civil war in Northern Ireland and a vocal and increasingly radical women's movement. In Russia, defeat in the Russo-Japanese War (1904–1905) and the revolution of 1905 had greatly weakened support for the tsarist regime. In Germany, the victory of the Marxist Social Democratic Party in the parliamentary elections of 1912 led government authorities to worry that the country was falling apart. The French likewise faced difficult labor and budget problems.

Determined to hold onto power and frightened by rising popular movements, ruling classes across Europe were willing to gamble on diplomatic brinksmanship and even war to postpone dealing with intractable social and political conflicts. Victory promised to preserve the privileged positions of elites and rally the masses behind the national cause. The patriotic nationalism bolstered by the outbreak of war did bring unity in the short run, but the wealthy governing classes underestimated the risk of war to themselves. They had forgotten that great wars and great social revolutions very often go hand in hand.

The Outbreak of War

On June 28, 1914, Archduke Francis Ferdinand, heir to the Austro-Hungarian throne, was assassinated by Serbian revolutionaries during a state visit to the Bosnian capital of Sarajevo (sar-uh-YAY-voh). After a series of failed attempts to bomb the archduke's motorcade, Gavrilo Princip, a fanatical member of the radical group the Black Hand, shot the archduke and his wife, Sophie, in their automobile. After his capture, Princip remained defiant, asserting at his trial, "I am a Yugoslav nationalist, aiming for the unification of all Yugoslavs, and I do not care what form of state, but it must be free from Austria."[4]

Princip's deed, in the crisis-ridden border between the weakened Ottoman and Austro-Hungarian Empires, led Europe into world war. In the early years of the twentieth century, war in the Balkans—"the powder keg of Europe"—seemed inevitable. The reason was simple: between 1900 and 1914 the Western powers had successfully forced the Ottoman rulers to give up their European territories. Serbs, Bulgarians, Albanians, and others now sought to establish independent nation-states, and the ethnic nationalism inspired by these changing state boundaries was destroying the Ottoman Empire and threatening Austria-Hungary. The only questions were what kinds of wars would result and where they would lead.

By the early twentieth century nationalism in southeastern Europe was on the rise. Independent Serbia was eager to build a state that would include all ethnic Serbs and was thus openly hostile to Austria-Hungary and the Ottoman Empire, since both states included substantial Serbian minorities within their borders. To block Serbian expansion, Austria in 1908 annexed the territories of Bosnia and Herzegovina (hehrt-suh-goh-VEE-nuh). The southern part of the Austro-Hungarian Empire now included an even larger Serbian population. Serbians expressed rage but could do nothing without support from Russia, their traditional ally.

The tensions in the Balkans soon erupted into regional warfare. In the First Balkan War (1912), Serbia joined Greece and Bulgaria to attack the Ottoman Empire and then quarreled with Bulgaria over the spoils of victory. In the Second Balkan War (1913), Bulgaria attacked its former allies. Austria intervened and forced Serbia to give up Albania. After centuries, nationalism had finally destroyed the Ottoman Empire in Europe. Encouraged by their success against the Ottomans, Balkan nationalists increased

PRIMARY SOURCE   German Diplomacy and the Road to War

This "top secret" diplomatic report, written a week after the assassination of Archduke Francis Ferdinand, suggests that Emperor William II (Kaiser Wilhelm in the text below) of Germany will offer Austria-Hungary unconditional support in its actions against Serbia. According to many historians, German encouragement helped push Austria-Hungary into war with Serbia despite the risk of Russian involvement.

From the Austro-Hungarian Ambassador in Berlin to the Austro-Hungarian Foreign Minister in Vienna

Berlin, July 5, 1914
Top secret

   After I informed Kaiser Wilhelm that I had a letter from His Imperial and Royal Apostolic Majesty [Emperor Franz Joseph I of Austria], which Count Hoyos delivered to me today to present to him, I received an invitation from the German Majesties to a *déjeuner* [lunch] at noon today in the Neue Palais [New Palace]. I presented His Majesty with the exalted letter and the attached memorandum. The Kaiser read both papers quite carefully in my presence.

   First, His Majesty assured me that he had expected us to take firm action against Serbia, but he had to concede that, as a result of the conflicts facing our most gracious Lord, he needed to take into account a serious complication in Europe, which is why he did not wish to give any definite answer prior to consultations with the chancellor [Bethmann-Hollweg]. When, after our *déjeuner*, I once again emphasized the gravity of the situation, His Majesty authorized me to report to our most gracious Lord that in this case, too, we could count on Germany's full support. As mentioned, he first had to consult with the chancellor, but he did not have the slightest doubt that Herr von Bethmann Hollweg would fully agree with him, particularly with regard to action on our part against Serbia. In his [Kaiser Wilhelm's] opinion, though, there was no need to wait patiently before taking action.

their demands for freedom from Austria-Hungary, dismaying the leaders of that multinational empire.

   Within this complex context, the assassination of Archduke Francis Ferdinand instigated a five-week period of intense diplomatic activity that culminated in world war. The leaders of Austria-Hungary concluded that Serbia was implicated in the assassination and deserved severe punishment. On July 23 Austria-Hungary presented Serbia with an unconditional ultimatum that would violate Serbian sovereignty. When Serbia replied moderately but evasively, Austria mobilized its armies and declared war on Serbia on July 28. Thus multinational Austria-Hungary, desperate to save its empire, deliberately chose war to stem the rising tide of hostile nationalism within its borders.

   From the beginning of the crisis, Germany pushed Austria-Hungary to confront Serbia and thus bore much responsibility for turning a little war into a world war. Emperor William II and his chancellor Theobald von Bethmann-Hollweg realized that war between Austria and Russia was likely, for a resurgent Russia would not stand by

The Kaiser said that Russia's stance would always be a hostile one, but he had been prepared for this for many years, and even if war broke out between Austria-Hungary and Russia, we could rest assured that Germany would take our side, in line with its customary loyalty. According to the Kaiser, as things stood now, Russia was not at all ready for war. It would certainly have to think hard before making a call to arms. Nevertheless, it would attempt to turn the other powers of the Triple Entente against us and to fan the flames in the Balkans.

The Kaiser said he understood full well that it would be difficult for His Imperial and Royal Apostolic Majesty [Emperor Franz Joseph] to march into Serbia, given his well-known love of peace; however, if we really deemed a military operation against Serbia necessary, he [Kaiser Wilhelm] would find it regrettable if we did not seize the present moment, which was so favorable for us.

[A short review of the German position on Romania and Bulgaria and a timetable for further diplomatic discussion followed. The next day the German chancellor sent a telegram to Vienna intended to assure the Austrian emperor that Germany "will faithfully stand by Austria-Hungary."]

EVALUATE THE EVIDENCE

1. What does this report reveal about Germany's position in the Great Power politics that led to the First World War? What is Emperor William II's attitude toward Russia?

2. Why would the German emperor encourage Austro-Hungarian aggressiveness? How much responsibility does he bear for the war that followed?

Source: German Historical Institute online archive, http://www.ghi-dc.org/index.php?option=com_content&view=article&id=151&Itemid=108. Courtesy of German History in Documents and Images.

and watch the Austrians crush the Serbs. Yet Bethmann-Hollweg hoped that, although Russia (and its ally France) would go to war, Great Britain would remain neutral, unwilling to fight in the distant Balkans. With that hope, the German chancellor sent a telegram to Austria-Hungary, which promised that Germany would "faithfully stand by" its ally in case of war. This "blank check" of unconditional support encouraged the prowar faction in Vienna to take a hard line against the Serbs at a time when moderation might still have limited the crisis. (See "Primary Source: German Diplomacy and the Road to War," above.)

The diplomatic situation quickly spiraled out of control as military plans and timetables began to dictate policy. Vast Russia required much more time to mobilize its armies than did Germany and Austria-Hungary. And since the complicated mobilization plans of the Russian general staff assumed a two-front war with both Austria and Germany, Russia could not mobilize against one without mobilizing against the other. Therefore, on July 29 Tsar Nicholas II ordered full mobilization, which in effect declared

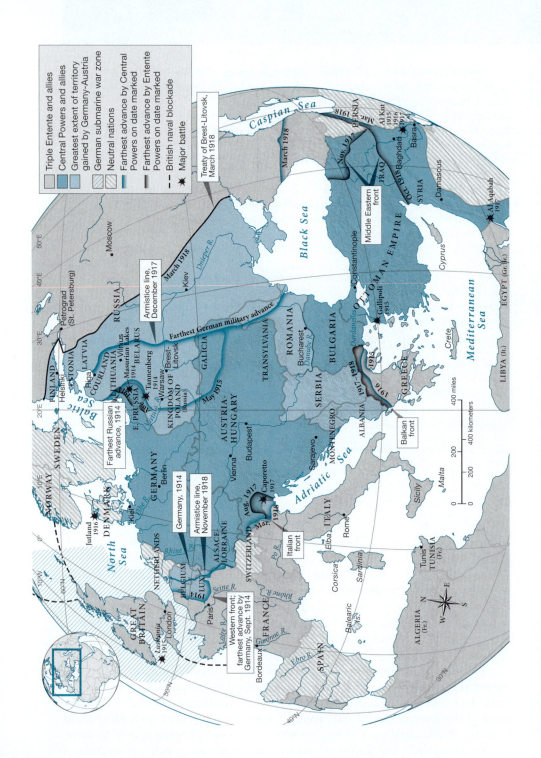

Legend:
- Triple Entente and allies
- Central Powers and allies
- Greatest extent of territory gained by Germany-Austria
- German submarine war zone
- Neutral nations
- Farthest advance by Central Powers on date marked
- Farthest advance by Entente Powers on date marked
- British naval blockade
- Major battle

Treaty of Brest-Litovsk, March 1918

Armistice line, December 1917

Farthest Russian advance, 1914

Germany, 1914

Armistice line, November 1918

Western front; farthest advance by Germany, Sept. 1914

Italian front

Balkan front

Middle Eastern front

Farthest German military advance

Caspian Sea

Black Sea

Mediterranean Sea

Baltic Sea

North Sea

Adriatic Sea

RUSSIA, Moscow, Petrograd (St. Petersburg), FINLAND, Helsinki, SWEDEN, NORWAY, DENMARK, GERMANY, Berlin, NETHERLANDS, BELGIUM, LUX., GREAT BRITAIN, London, Paris, FRANCE, Bordeaux, SWITZERLAND, ITALY, Rome, SPAIN, ALGERIA (Fr.), TUNISIA (Fr.), Tunis, LIBYA (It.), EGYPT (Br.), OTTOMAN EMPIRE, Constantinople, GREECE, ALBANIA, MONTENEGRO, SERBIA, BULGARIA, ROMANIA, Bucharest, TRANSYLVANIA, AUSTRIA-HUNGARY, Budapest, Vienna, GALICIA, KINGDOM OF POLAND (Russia), Warsaw, E. PRUSSIA, LITHUANIA, Vilnius, COURLAND, LATVIA, Riga, ESTONIA, BELARUS, Kiev, PERSIA, IRAQ, Baghdad, Basra, SYRIA, Damascus, Cyprus, Crete, Sicily, Sardinia, Corsica, Malta, Balearic Is., Elba

Jutland 1916, Lusitania 1915, Tannenberg 1914, Masurian Lakes 1914, Brest-Litovsk, Gallipoli 1915, Dardanelles, Caporetto 1917, Sarajevo, Al Kut 1915 1916 1917, Al Aqabah 1917

Dnieper R., Danube R., Elbe R., Rhine R., Seine R., Loire R., Rhône R., Garonne R., Po R., Ebro R., Vistula R.

March 1918, Nov. 1917, Mar. 1918, May 1915, Aug. 1917, Mar. 1918, 1915, 1916, 1917–1918, Oct. 1918

400 miles
400 kilometers
0 200
0 200

◀ **MAP 25.2** **World War I in Europe and the Middle East, 1914–1918**
Trench warfare on the western front was concentrated in Belgium and northern France, while the war in the east encompassed an enormous territory.

war on both the empire and Germany. The German general staff had also long thought in terms of a two-front war. Their misguided **Schlieffen Plan** called for a quick victory over France after a lightning attack through neutral Belgium — the quickest way to reach Paris — before turning on Russia. On August 3 German armies invaded Belgium. Great Britain declared war on Germany the following day.

The speed of the so-called July Crisis created shock, panic, and excitement, and a bellicose public helped propel Europe into war. In the final days of July and the first few days of August, massive crowds thronged the streets of Paris, London, St. Petersburg, Berlin, and Vienna. Shouting prowar slogans, the enthusiastic crowds pushed politicians and military leaders toward the increasingly inevitable confrontation. Events proceeded rapidly, and those who opposed the war could do little to prevent its arrival. In a little over a month, a limited Austrian-Serbian war had become a European-wide conflict, and the First World War had begun.

Waging Total War

How did the First World War differ from previous wars?

When the Germans invaded Belgium in August 1914, they and everyone else thought that the war would be short and relatively painless. Many sincerely believed that "the boys will be home by Christmas." They were wrong. On the western front in France and the eastern front in Russia, the belligerent armies bogged down in a new and extremely costly kind of war, termed **total war** by German general Erich Ludendorff. Total war meant new roles for soldiers and civilians alike. At the front, total war meant lengthy, deadly battles fought with all the destructive weapons a highly industrialized society could produce. At home, national economies were geared toward the war effort. Governments revoked civil liberties, and many civilians lost lives or livelihoods as occupying armies moved through their towns and cities. The struggle expanded outside Europe, and the Middle East, Africa, East Asia, and the United States were all brought into the maelstrom of total war.

Stalemate and Slaughter on the Western Front

In the face of the German invasion, the Belgian army heroically defended its homeland and fell back in good order to join a rapidly landed British army corps near the Franco-Belgian border. At the same time, Russian armies attacked eastern Germany, forcing the Germans to transfer much-needed troops to the east. Instead of quickly capturing Paris per the Schlieffen Plan, by the end of August dead-tired German soldiers were advancing slowly along an enormous front in the scorching summer heat.

On September 6 the French attacked a gap in the German line at the Battle of the Marne. For three days, France threw everything into the attack. At one point, the French government desperately requisitioned all the taxis of Paris to rush reserves to the front. Finally, the Germans fell back. France had been miraculously saved (Map 25.2).

Writing Home from the Front
Cramped within the tight network of trenches on the western front, a British soldier writes a letter home while his compatriots rest before the next engagement. The post was typically the only connection between soldiers and their relatives, and over 28 billion pieces of mail passed between home and front on all sides during the war. (Courtesy of the Trustees of the Imperial War Museum)

With the armies stalled, both sides began to dig trenches to protect themselves from machine-gun fire. By November 1914 an unbroken line of four hundred miles of defensive trenches extended from the Belgian coast through northern France and on to the Swiss frontier. Armies on both sides dug in behind rows of trenches, mines, and barbed wire defenses, and slaughter on the western front began in earnest. The cost in lives of **trench warfare** was staggering, the gains in territory minuscule. For ordinary soldiers, conditions in the trenches were atrocious. Recently invented weapons, the products of an industrial age, made battle impersonal, traumatic, and extremely deadly. The machine gun, hand grenades, poison gas, flamethrowers, long-range artillery, the airplane, and the tank were all used to murderous effect. All favored the defense, increased casualty rates, and revolutionized the practice of war.

The leading generals of the combatant nations, who had learned military tactics and strategy in the nineteenth century, struggled to understand trench warfare. For four years they repeated the same mistakes, mounting massive offensives designed to achieve decisive breakthroughs. Brutal frontal assaults against highly fortified trenches might overrun the enemy's frontline, but attacking soldiers rarely captured any substantial territory. The French and British offensives of 1915 never gained more than three miles of territory. In 1916 the unsuccessful German campaign against Verdun cost some 700,000 lives on both sides and ended with the combatants in their original positions. The results in 1917 were little better. In hard-fought battles on all fronts, millions of young men were wounded or died for no real gain.

The Battle of the Somme, a great British offensive undertaken in the summer of 1916 in northern France, exemplified the horrors of trench warfare. The battle began with a weeklong heavy artillery bombardment on the German line, intended to cut the barbed wire fortifications, decimate the enemy trenches, and prevent the Germans from making an effective defense. For seven days and nights, the British artillery fired nonstop on the German lines, expending 3 million shells. On July 1 the British went "over the top," climbing out of the trenches and moving into no-man's land toward the German lines, dug into a series of ridges about half a mile away.

During the bombardment, the Germans had fled to their dugouts—underground shelters dug deep into the trenches—where they suffered from lack of water, food, or sleep. But they survived. As the British soldiers neared the German lines and the shelling stopped, the Germans emerged from their bunkers, set up their machine guns, and mowed down the approaching troops. In many places, the wire had not been cut by the bombardment, so the attackers, held in place by the wire, made easy targets. About 20,000 British men were killed and 40,000 more were wounded on just the first day, a crushing loss that shook troop morale and public opinion at home. The battle lasted until November, and in the end the British did push the Germans back—a whole seven miles. Some 420,000 British, 200,000 French, and 600,000 Germans were killed or wounded defending an insignificant piece of land.

As the war ground on, exhausted soldiers found it difficult to comprehend or describe the bloody reality of their experiences at the front. As one French soldier wrote:

> I went over the top, I ran, I shouted, I hit, I can't remember where or who. I crossed the wire, jumped over holes, crawled through shell craters still stinking of explosives, men were falling, shot in two as they ran; shouts and gasps were half muffled by the sweeping surge of gunfire. But it was like a nightmare mist all around me. . . . Now my part in it is over for a few minutes. . . . Something is red over there; something is burning. Something is red at my feet: blood.[5]

The anonymous, almost unreal qualities of high-tech warfare made its way into the art and literature of the time. In each combatant nation, artists and writers sought to portray the nightmarish quality of total war. Paintings by artists like Paul Nash or the poems of the famous British "trench poets," may do more to capture the experience of the war than contemporary photos or the dry accounts of historians.

The Widening War

On the eastern front, the slaughter did not immediately degenerate into trench warfare, and the fighting was dominated by Germany. Repulsing the initial Russian attacks, the Germans won major victories at the Battles of Tannenberg and the Masurian Lakes in August and September 1914. Russia put real pressure on the relatively weak Austro-Hungarian army, but by 1915 the eastern front had stabilized in Germany's favor. A staggering 2.5 million Russian soldiers had been killed, wounded, or captured. German armies occupied huge swaths of the Russian empire in central Europe, including ethnic Polish, Belorussian, and Baltic territories. Yet Russia continued to fight, marking another failure of the Schlieffen Plan.

To govern these occupied territories, the Germans installed a vast military bureaucracy, with some 15,000 army administrators and professional specialists. Anti-Slavic prejudice dominated the mind-set of the occupiers, who viewed the local Slavs as savages and ethnic "mongrels." German military administrators used prisoners of war and refugees as forced labor. They stole animals and crops from local farmers to supply the occupying army or send home to Germany. About one-third of the civilian population was killed or became refugees under this brutal occupation. In the long run, the German state hoped to turn these territories into German possessions, a chilling forerunner of Nazi policies in World War II.[6]

The changing tides of victory and hopes for territorial gains brought neutral countries into the war (see Map 25.2). Italy, a member of the Triple Alliance since 1882, had declared its neutrality in 1914 on the grounds that Austria had launched a war of aggression. Then in May 1915 Italy switched sides to join the Triple Entente in return for promises of Austrian territory. The war along the Italian-Austrian front was bitter and deadly and cost some 600,000 Italian lives.

In October 1914 the Ottoman Empire joined Austria and Germany, by then known as the Central Powers. The following September Bulgaria followed the Ottoman Empire's lead in order to settle old scores with Serbia. The Balkans, with the exception of Greece, were occupied by the Central Powers.

The entry of the Ottomans carried the war into the Middle East. Heavy fighting between the Ottomans and the Russians enveloped the Armenians, who lived on both sides of the border and had experienced brutal repression by the Ottomans in 1909. When in 1915 some Armenians welcomed Russian armies as liberators, the Ottoman government, with German support, ordered a mass deportation of its Armenian citizens from their homeland. In this early example of modern ethnic cleansing, about 1 million Armenians died from murder, starvation, and disease.

In 1915, at the Battle of Gallipoli, British forces tried and failed to take the Dardanelles and Constantinople from the Ottoman Turks. The invasion force was pinned down on the beaches, and the ten-month-long battle cost the Ottomans 300,000 and the British 265,000 men killed, wounded, or missing.

The British were more successful at inciting the Arabs to revolt against their Ottoman rulers. They bargained with the foremost Arab leader, Hussein ibn-Ali (1856–1931), the chief magistrate (*sharif*) of Mecca, the holiest city in the Muslim world. Controlling much of the Ottoman Empire's territory along the Red Sea, an area known as the Hejaz, Hussein managed in 1915 to win vague British commitments for an independent Arab kingdom. In 1916 Hussein rebelled against the Turks, proclaiming himself king of the Arabs. Hussein was aided by the British liaison officer T. E. Lawrence, who in 1917 helped lead Arab soldiers in a successful guerrilla war against the Turks on the Arabian peninsula.

The British enjoyed similar victories in the Ottoman province of Iraq. British troops occupied the southern Iraqi city of Basra in 1914 and captured Baghdad in 1917. In September 1918 British armies and their Arab allies rolled into Syria. This offensive culminated in the triumphal entry of Hussein's son Faisal (FIGH-suhl) into Damascus. Arab patriots in Syria and Iraq now expected a large, unified Arab nation-state to rise from the dust of the Ottoman collapse—though they would later be disappointed by the Western powers (see page 861).

The war spread to East Asia and colonial Africa as well. Japan declared war on Germany in 1914, seized Germany's Pacific and East Asian colonies, and used the opportunity to expand its influence in China. In Africa, instead of rebelling as the Germans hoped, colonial subjects of the British and French generally supported the Allied powers and helped local British and French commanders take over German colonies. More than a million Africans and Asians served in the various armies of the warring powers; more than double that number served as porters to carry equipment. The French, facing a shortage of young men, made especially heavy use of colonial troops from North

Africa. Large numbers of troops came from the British Commonwealth, a voluntary association of former British colonies. Soldiers from Commonwealth members Canada, Australia, and New Zealand fought with the British; those from Australia and New Zealand fought with particular distinction in the failed allied assault on Gallipoli.

After three years of refusing to play a fighting role, the United States was finally drawn into the expanding conflict. American intervention grew out of the war at sea and general sympathy for the Triple Entente. At the beginning of the war, Britain and France established a naval blockade to strangle the Central Powers. No neutral cargo ship was permitted to sail to Germany. In early 1915 Germany retaliated with attacks on supply ships from the murderously effective new weapon, the submarine.

In May 1915 a German submarine sank the British passenger liner *Lusitania*, claiming more than 1,000 lives, among them 139 U.S. citizens. President Woodrow Wilson protested vigorously, using the tragedy to incite American public opinion against the Germans. To avoid almost-certain war with the United States, Germany halted its submarine warfare for almost two years.

Early in 1917 the German military command—hoping that improved submarines could starve Britain into submission before the United States could come to its rescue—resumed unrestricted submarine warfare. This was a reckless gamble, and the United States declared war on Germany in April of that year. Eventually the United States tipped the balance in favor of the British, French, and their allies.

The Home Front

In what ways did the war transform life on the home front?

The war's impact on civilians was no less massive than it was on the men crouched in the trenches. Total war encouraged the growth of state bureaucracies, transformed the lives of ordinary women and men, and by the end inspired mass antiwar protest movements.

Mobilizing for Total War

In August 1914 many people greeted the outbreak of hostilities enthusiastically. In every country, ordinary folk believed that their nation was right to defend itself from foreign aggression. With the exception of those on the extreme left, even socialists supported the war. Yet by mid-October generals and politicians had begun to realize that victory would require more than patriotism. Heavy casualties and the stalemate meant each combatant country experienced a desperate need for men and weapons. To keep the war machine moving, national leaders aggressively intervened in society and the economy.

By the late nineteenth century the responsive national state had already shown an eagerness to manage the welfare of its citizens (see Chapter 23). Now, confronted by the crisis of total war, the state intruded even further into people's daily lives. New government ministries mobilized soldiers and armaments, established rationing programs, and provided care for war widows and wounded veterans. Censorship offices controlled news about the course of the war. Government planning boards temporarily abandoned free-market capitalism and set mandatory production goals and limits on wages and prices. Government management of highly productive industrial economies worked: it yielded an effective and immensely destructive war effort on all sides.

Germany went furthest in developing a planned economy to wage total war. As soon as war began, the Jewish industrialist Walter Rathenau convinced the government to set up the War Raw Materials Board to ration and distribute raw materials. Under Rathenau's direction, every useful material from foreign oil to barnyard manure was inventoried and rationed. Moreover, the board launched successful attempts to produce substitutes, such as synthetic rubber and nitrates, for scarce war supplies. Food was rationed in accordance with physical need. Germany failed to tax the war profits of private firms heavily enough, however. This failure contributed to massive deficit financing, inflation, the growth of a black market, and the eventual re-emergence of class conflict.

Following the terrible Battles of Verdun and the Somme in 1916, German military leaders forced the Reichstag to accept the Auxiliary Service Law, which required all males between seventeen and sixty to work only at jobs considered critical to the war effort. Women also worked in war factories, mines, and steel mills, where they labored, like men, at heavy and dangerous jobs. While war production increased, people lived on little more than one thousand calories a day.

After 1917 Germany's leaders ruled by decree. Generals Paul von Hindenburg and Erich Ludendorff—heroes of Tannenberg—drove Chancellor Bethmann-Hollweg from office. With the support of the newly formed ultraconservative Fatherland Party, the generals established a military dictatorship. Hindenburg called for the ultimate mobilization for total war. Germany could win, he said, only "if all the treasures of our soil that agriculture and industry can produce are used exclusively for the conduct of War. . . . All other considerations must come second."[7] Thus in Germany total war led to the establishment of history's first "totalitarian" society, a model for future National Socialists, or Nazis.

Only Germany was directly ruled by a military government, yet leaders in all the belligerent nations took power from parliaments, suspended civil liberties, and ignored democratic procedures. After 1915 the British Ministry of Munitions organized private industry to produce for the war, allocated labor, set wage and price rates, and settled labor disputes. In France, a weakened parliament met without public oversight, and the courts jailed pacifists who dared criticize the state. Once the United States entered the war, new federal agencies such as the War Labor Board and the War Industries Board regulated industry, labor relations, and agricultural production, while the Espionage and Sedition Acts weakened civil liberties. The war may have been deadly for citizen armies, but it was certainly good for the growth of the bureaucratic nation-state.

The Social Impact

The social changes wrought by total war were no less profound than the economic impact, though again there were important national variations. National conscription sent millions of men to the front, exposing many to foreign lands for the first time in their lives. The insatiable needs of the military created a tremendous demand for workers, making jobs readily available. This situation—seldom, if ever, seen before 1914, when unemployment and poverty had been facts of urban life—brought momentous changes.

The need for workers meant greater power and prestige for labor unions. Unions cooperated with war governments on workplace rules, wages, and production schedules in return for real participation in important decisions. The entry of labor leaders and unions into policymaking councils paralleled the entry of socialist leaders into war

Women Factory Workers Building a Truck, London, 1917 Millions of men on all sides were drafted to fight in the war, creating a serious labor shortage. When women left home to fill jobs formerly reserved for men, they challenged traditional gender roles. (© Hulton-Deutsch Collection/ Corbis)

governments. Both reflected a new government openness to the needs of those at the bottom of society.

The role of women changed dramatically. The production of vast amounts of arms and ammunition required huge numbers of laborers, and women moved into skilled industrial jobs long considered men's work. Women became highly visible in public — as munitions workers, bank tellers, and mail carriers, and even as police officers, firefighters, and farm laborers. Women also served as auxiliaries and nurses at the front. (See "Individuals in Society: Vera Brittain," page 846.)

The war expanded the range of women's activities and helped change attitudes about proper gender roles, but the long-term results were mixed. Women gained experience in jobs previously reserved for men, but at war's end millions of demobilized soldiers demanded their jobs back, and governments forced women out of the workplace. Thus women's employment gains were mostly temporary, except in nursing and social work, already considered "women's work." The great dislocations of war loosened sexual morality, and some women bobbed their hair, shortened their skirts, and smoked in public. Yet supposedly "loose" women were often criticized for betraying their soldier-husbands away at the front. As a result of women's many-sided war effort, the United States, Britain, Germany, Poland, and other countries granted women the right to vote immediately after the war, but women's rights movements faded in the 1920s and 1930s, in large part because feminist leaders found it difficult to regain momentum after the crisis of war.

To some extent, the war promoted greater social equality, blurring class distinctions and lessening the gap between rich and poor. This blurring was most apparent in Great Britain, where the bottom third of the population generally lived better than they ever

INDIVIDUALS IN SOCIETY • Vera Brittain

Although the Great War upended millions of lives, it struck Europe's young people with the greatest force. For Vera Brittain (1893–1970), as for so many in her generation, the war became life's defining experience, which she captured forever in her famous autobiography, *Testament of Youth* (1933).

Brittain grew up in a wealthy business family in northern England, bristling at small-town conventions and discrimination against women. Very close to her brother Edward, two years her junior, Brittain read voraciously and dreamed of being a successful writer. Finishing boarding school and overcoming her father's objections, she prepared for Oxford's rigorous entry exams and won a scholarship to its women's college. Brittain also fell in love with Roland Leighton, an equally brilliant student from a literary family and her brother's best friend. All three, along with two other close friends, Victor Richardson and Geoffrey Thurlow, confidently prepared to enter Oxford in late 1914.

When war suddenly loomed in July 1914, Brittain shared with millions of Europeans a surge of patriotic support for her government, a prowar enthusiasm she later downplayed in her published writings. She wrote in her diary that her "great fear" was that England would declare its neutrality and commit the "grossest treachery" toward France.* She supported Leighton's decision to enlist, agreeing with his glamorous view of war as "very ennobling and very beautiful." Later, exchanging anxious letters with Leighton in France in 1915, Brittain began to see the conflict in personal, human terms. She wondered if any victory or defeat could be worth her fiancé's life.

Struggling to quell her doubts, Brittain redoubled her commitment to England's cause and volunteered as an army nurse. For the next three years, she served with distinction in military hospitals in London, Malta, and northern France, repeatedly torn between the vision of noble sacrifice and the reality of human tragedy. Having lost sexual inhibitions while caring for mangled male bodies, she longed to consummate her love with Leighton. Awaiting his return on leave on Christmas Day in 1915, she was greeted instead with a telegram: he had been killed two days before.

Leighton's death was the first of several devastating blows that eventually overwhelmed Brittain's idealistic patriotism. In 1917 Thurlow and then Richardson died from gruesome wounds. In early 1918, as the last great German offensive covered

*Quoted in the excellent study P. Berry and M. Bostridge, *Vera Brittain: A Life* (London: Virago Press, 2001), p. 59; additional quotations are from pp. 80 and 136.

had, for the poorest gained most from the severe shortage of labor. Elsewhere, greater equality was reflected in full employment, distribution of scarce rations according to physical needs, and a sharing of hardships. In general, despite some war profiteering, European society became more uniform and egalitarian.

Death itself had no respect for traditional social distinctions. It savagely decimated the young aristocratic officers who led the charge, and it fell heavily on the mass of drafted peasants and unskilled workers who followed, leading commentators to speak of a "lost generation." Yet death often spared highly skilled workers and foremen. Their

the floors of her war-zone hospital with maimed and dying German prisoners, the bone-weary Brittain felt a common humanity and saw only more victims. A few weeks later her brother Edward—her last hope—died in action. When the war ended, she was, she said, a "complete automaton," with her "deepest emotions paralyzed if not dead."

Returning to Oxford and finishing her studies, Brittain gradually recovered. She formed a deep, restorative friendship with another talented woman writer, Winifred Holtby; published novels and articles; and became a leader in the feminist campaign for gender equality. She also married and had children. But her wartime memories were always with her. Finally, Brittain succeeded in coming to grips with them in *Testament of Youth*, her powerful antiwar autobiography. The unflinching narrative spoke to the experiences of an entire generation and became a runaway bestseller. Above all, Brittain captured the contradictory character of the war, in which millions of young people found excitement, courage, and common purpose but succeeded only in destroying their lives with their superhuman efforts and futile sacrifices. Becoming increasingly committed to pacifism, Brittain opposed England's entry into World War II.

QUESTIONS FOR ANALYSIS

1. What were Brittain's initial feelings toward the war? How and why did they change as the conflict continued?

2. Why did Brittain volunteer as a nurse, as many women did? How might wartime nursing have influenced women of her generation?

3. In portraying the contradictory character of World War I for Europe's youth, was Brittain describing the character of all modern warfare?

ONLINE DOCUMENT ASSIGNMENT

What role did wartime propaganda play in encouraging women like Vera Brittain to get involved in the war effort? Analyze a variety of propaganda posters calling for women to serve as military nurses. Then complete a writing assignment based on the evidence and details from this chapter.

bedfordstmartins.com/mckaywestvalue

lives were too valuable to squander at the front, for they were needed to train the newly recruited women and older unskilled men laboring valiantly in war plants at home.

Growing Political Tensions

During the first two years of war, many soldiers and civilians supported their governments. Patriotic nationalism and belief in a just cause united peoples behind their national leaders. Each government used rigorous censorship and crude propaganda to bolster popular support. German propaganda pictured black soldiers from France's African empire abusing German women, while the French and British ceaselessly recounted and exaggerated German atrocities in Belgium and elsewhere. Patriotic posters and slogans, slanted news, and biased editorials inflamed national hatreds, helped control public opinion, and encouraged soldiers to keep fighting.

Political and social tensions re-emerged, however, and by the spring of 1916 ordinary people were beginning to crack under the strain of total war. Strikes and protest marches over war-related burdens and shortages flared up on every home front. On May 1, 1916, several thousand demonstrators in Berlin heard the radical socialist leader Karl Liebknecht (1871–1919) attack the costs of the war effort. Liebknecht was arrested and imprisoned, but his daring action electrified Europe's far left. In France, Georges Clemenceau (zhorzh kleh-muhn-SOH) (1841–1929) established a virtual dictatorship, arrested strikers, and jailed without trial journalists and politicians who dared to suggest a compromise peace with Germany.

In April 1916 Irish republican nationalists took advantage of the tense wartime conditions to continue their rebellion against British rule. During the great Easter Rising, armed republican militias took over parts of Dublin and proclaimed an independent Irish Republic. After a week of bitter fighting, British troops crushed the rebels and executed their leaders. Though the republicans were defeated, the punitive aftermath fueled anti-British sentiment in Ireland. The Rising set the stage for the success of the nationalist Sinn Fein Party and a full-scale civil war for Irish independence in the early 1920s.

On all sides, soldiers' morale began to decline. Numerous French units refused to fight after the disastrous French offensive of May 1917. Only tough military justice, including executions for mutiny leaders, and a tacit agreement with the troops that there would be no more grand offensives enabled the new general-in-chief, Henri-Philippe Pétain (pay-TAN), to restore order. Facing defeat, wretched conditions at the front, and growing hopelessness, Russian soldiers deserted in droves, providing fuel for the Russian Revolution of 1917. After the murderous Battle of Caporetto in northern Italy, which lasted from October to November in 1917, the Italian army collapsed in despair. In the massive battles of 1916 and 1917, the British armies had been "bled dry." Only the promised arrival of fresh troops from the United States stiffened the resolve of the allies.

The strains were even worse for the Central Powers. In October 1916 a young socialist assassinated the chief minister of Austria-Hungary. The following month, when the aging Emperor Francis Joseph died, a symbol of unity disappeared. In spite of absolute censorship, political dissatisfaction and conflicts among nationalities grew. Both Czech and Yugoslav leaders demanded independent states for their peoples. By April 1917 the Austro-Hungarian people and army were exhausted. Another winter of war would bring revolution and disintegration.

Germans likewise suffered immensely. The British naval blockade greatly limited food imports, and the scarcity of basic necessities had horrific results: some 750,000 German civilians starved to death. For the rest, heavy rationing of everyday goods such as matches, bread, cooking oil, and meat undermined morale. A growing minority of moderate socialists in the Reichstag gave voice to popular discontent when they called for a compromise "peace without annexations or reparations."

Such a peace was unthinkable for the Fatherland Party. Yet Germany's rulers faced growing unrest. When the bread ration was further reduced in April 1917, more than 200,000 workers and women struck and demonstrated for a week in Berlin, returning to work only under the threat of prison and military discipline. That same month, radicals left the Social Democratic Party to form the Independent Social Democratic Party; in 1918 they would found the German Communist Party. Thus Germany, like its ally Austria-Hungary (and its enemy France), was beginning to crack in 1917. Yet it was Russia that collapsed first and saved the Central Powers—for a time.

The Russian Revolution

Why did world war lead to revolution in Russia, and what was its outcome?

Growing out of the crisis of the First World War, the Russian Revolution of 1917 was one of modern history's most momentous events. For some, the revolution was Marx's socialist vision come true; for others, it was the triumph of a Communist dictatorship. To all, it presented a radically new prototype of state and society.

The Fall of Imperial Russia

Like its allies and enemies, Russia had embraced war with patriotic enthusiasm in 1914. At the Winter Palace, throngs of people knelt and sang "God Save the Tsar!" while Tsar Nicholas II (r. 1894–1917) repeated the oath Alexander I had sworn in 1812 during Napoleon's invasion of Russia (see Chapter 19), vowing never to make peace as long as the enemy stood on Russian soil. Russia's lower house of parliament, the Duma, voted to support the war. Conservatives anticipated expansion in the Balkans, while liberals and most socialists believed that alliance with Britain and France would bring democratic reforms. For a moment, Russia was united.

Enthusiasm for the war soon waned as better-equipped German armies inflicted terrible losses. By 1915 substantial numbers of Russian soldiers were being sent to the front without rifles; they were told to find their arms among the dead. Russia's battered peasant army nonetheless continued to fight, and Russia moved toward full mobilization on the home front. The government set up special committees to coordinate defense, industry, transportation, and agriculture. These efforts improved the military situation, but overall Russia mobilized less effectively than the other combatants.

One problem was weak leadership. Under the constitution resulting from the revolution of 1905 (see Chapter 23), the tsar had retained complete control over the bureaucracy and the army. A kindly but narrow-minded aristocrat, Nicholas II distrusted the publicly elected Duma and resisted popular involvement in government, relying instead on the old bureaucracy. Excluded from power, the Duma, the educated middle classes, and the masses became increasingly critical of the tsar's leadership. In September 1915 parties ranging from conservative to moderate socialist formed the Progressive bloc, which called for a completely new government responsible to the Duma instead of the tsar. In answer, Nicholas temporarily adjourned the Duma. The tsar then announced that he was traveling to the front in order to lead and rally Russia's armies, leaving the government in the hands of his wife, the strong-willed and autocratic Tsarina Alexandra.

His departure was a fatal turning point. In his absence, Tsarina Alexandra arbitrarily dismissed loyal political advisers. She turned to her court favorite, the disreputable and unpopular Rasputin, an uneducated Siberian preacher whose influence with the tsarina rested on his purported ability to heal Alexis—Alexandra's only son and heir to the throne — from his hemophilia. In a desperate attempt to right the situation, three members of the high aristocracy murdered Rasputin in December 1916. The ensuing scandal further undermined support for the tsarist government.

Imperial Russia had entered a terminal crisis. Tens of thousands of soldiers deserted, swelling the number of the disaffected at home. By early 1917 the cities were wracked by food shortages, heating fuel was in short supply, and the economy was breaking down. In March violent street demonstrations broke out in Petrograd (formerly St. Petersburg), spread to the factories, and then engulfed the city. From the front, the tsar ordered the army to open fire on the protesters, but the soldiers refused to shoot and joined the revolutionary crowd instead. The Duma declared a provisional government on March 12, 1917. Three days later, Nicholas abdicated.

The Provisional Government

The **February Revolution**, then, was the result of an unplanned uprising of hungry, angry people in the capital, but it was eagerly accepted throughout the country. (The name of the revolution matches the Russian calendar, which used a different dating system.) The patriotic upper and middle classes embraced the prospect of a more determined war effort, while workers anticipated better wages and more food. After generations of autocracy, the provisional government established equality before the law; freedom of religion, speech, and assembly; and the right of unions to organize and strike.

Yet both liberals and moderate socialist leaders rejected these broad political reforms. Though the Russian people were sick of fighting, the new leaders would not take Russia out of the war. A new government formed in May 1917 included the fiery agrarian socialist Alexander Kerensky, who became prime minister in July. He refused to confiscate large landholdings and give them to peasants, fearing that such drastic action would complete the disintegration of Russia's peasant army. For the patriotic Kerensky, as for other moderate socialists, the continuation of war was still a national duty. Human suffering and war-weariness grew, testing the limited strength of the provisional government.

From its first day, the provisional government had to share power with a formidable rival — the **Petrograd Soviet** (or council) of Workers' and Soldiers' Deputies. Modeled on the revolutionary soviets of 1905, the Petrograd Soviet comprised two to three thousand workers, soldiers, and socialist intellectuals. Seeing itself as a true grassroots product of revolutionary democracy, the Soviet acted as a parallel government. It issued its own radical orders, weakening the authority of the provisional government.

The most famous edict of the Petrograd Soviet was Army Order No. 1, issued in May 1917, which stripped officers of their authority and placed power in the hands of elected committees of common soldiers. Designed to protect the revolution from resistance by the aristocratic officer corps, the order led to a collapse of army discipline.

In July 1917 the provisional government ordered a poorly considered summer offensive against the Germans. The campaign was a miserable failure, and desertions mounted as peasant soldiers returned home to help their families get a share of the land, which peasants were seizing in a grassroots agrarian upheaval. By the summer of 1917 Russia was descending into anarchy. It was an unparalleled opportunity for the most radical and talented of Russia's many revolutionary leaders, Vladimir Ilyich Lenin (1870–1924).

Lenin and the Bolshevik Revolution

Born into the middle class, Lenin became an enemy of imperial Russia when his older brother was executed for plotting to kill the tsar in 1887. As a law student, Lenin eagerly studied Marxist socialism, which began to win converts among radical intellectuals during Russia's industrialization in the 1890s. A pragmatic and flexible thinker, Lenin updated Marx's revolutionary philosophy to address existing conditions in Russia.

Three interrelated concepts were central for Lenin. First, he stressed that only violent revolution could destroy capitalism. He tirelessly denounced all theories of a peaceful evolution to socialism as a betrayal of Marx's message of violent class conflict. Second, Lenin argued that under certain conditions a Communist revolution was possible even in a predominantly agrarian country like Russia. Peasants, who were numerous, poor, and exploited, could take the place of Marx's traditional working class in the coming revolutionary conflict.

Third, Lenin believed that the possibility of revolution was determined more by human leadership than by historical laws. He called for a highly disciplined workers' party strictly controlled by a small, dedicated elite of intellectuals and professional revolutionaries. This elite would not stop until revolution brought it to power. Lenin's version of Marxism had a major impact on events in Russia and ultimately changed the way future revolutionaries engaged in radical revolt around the world.

Other Russian Marxists challenged Lenin's ideas. At meetings of the Russian Social Democratic Labor Party in London in 1903, matters came to a head. Lenin demanded a small, disciplined, elitist party dedicated to Communist revolution, while his opponents wanted a more democratic, reformist party with mass membership. The Russian Marxists split into two rival factions. Lenin called his camp the **Bolsheviks**, or "majority group"; his opponents were Mensheviks, or "minority group." The Bolsheviks had only a tenuous majority of a single vote, but Lenin kept the name for propaganda reasons and they became the revolutionary party he wanted: tough, disciplined, and led from above.

Unlike other socialists, Lenin had not rallied around the national flag in 1914. Observing events from neutral Switzerland, where he lived in exile to avoid persecution by the tsar's police, Lenin viewed the war as a product of imperialist rivalries and an opportunity for socialist revolution. After the February Revolution of 1917, the German government provided Lenin with safe passage across Germany and back into Russia. The Germans hoped Lenin would undermine the sagging war effort of the provisional government. They were not disappointed.

Arriving triumphantly at Petrograd's Finland Station on April 3, Lenin attacked at once. He rejected all cooperation with what he called the "bourgeois" provisional government. His slogans were radical in the extreme: "All power to the soviets"; "All land to the peasants"; "Stop the war now." Lenin was a superb tactician. His promises of "Peace, Land, and Bread" spoke to the expectations of suffering soldiers, peasants, and workers and earned the Bolsheviks substantial popular support. The moment for revolution was at hand.

Yet Lenin and the Bolsheviks almost lost the struggle for Russia. A premature attempt to seize power in July collapsed, and Lenin went into hiding. However, this temporary setback made little difference in the long run. The army's commander in chief, General Lavr Kornilov, led a feeble coup against the provisional Kerensky government in September. In the face of this rightist counter-revolutionary threat, the Bolsheviks were rearmed. Kornilov's forces disintegrated, but Kerensky lost all credit with the army, the only force that might have saved democratic government in Russia.

Trotsky and the Seizure of Power

Throughout the summer, the Bolsheviks greatly increased their popular support. Party membership soared from 50,000 to 240,000, and in October the Bolsheviks gained a fragile majority in the Petrograd Soviet. Now Lenin's supporter Leon Trotsky (1879–1940), a spellbinding revolutionary orator and radical Marxist, brilliantly executed the Bolshevik seizure of power.

Painting a vivid but untruthful picture of German and counter-revolutionary plots, Trotsky convinced the Petrograd Soviet to form a special military-revolutionary committee in October and make him its leader. Thus military power in the capital passed into Bolshevik hands.

On the night of November 6, militants from Trotsky's committee joined with trusted Bolshevik soldiers to seize government buildings in Petrograd and arrest members of the provisional government. Then they went on to the Congress of Soviets where a Bolshevik majority—roughly 390 of 650 excited delegates—declared that all power had passed to the soviets and named Lenin head of the new government. John Reed, a sympathetic American journalist, described the enthusiasm that greeted Lenin at the congress:

> Now Lenin, gripping the edge of the reading stand . . . stood there waiting, apparently oblivious to the long-rolling ovation, which lasted several minutes. When it finished, he said simply, "We shall now proceed to construct the Socialist order!" Again that overwhelming human roar.[8]

The Bolsheviks came to power for three key reasons. First, by late 1917 democracy had given way to anarchy: power was there for those who would take it. Second, in Lenin and Trotsky the Bolsheviks had an utterly determined and superior leadership, which both the tsarist and the provisional governments lacked. Third, as Reed's comment suggests, Bolshevik policies appealed to ordinary Russians. Exhausted by war and weary of tsarist autocracy they were eager for radical changes. (See "Primary Source: Peace, Land, and Bread for the Russian People," page 854.) With time, many Russians would become bitterly disappointed with the Bolshevik regime, but for the moment they had good reason to hope for peace, better living conditions, and a more equitable society.

Dictatorship and Civil War

The Bolsheviks' truly monumental accomplishment was not taking power, but keeping it. Over the next four years, they conquered the chaos they had helped create and began to build a Communist society. How was this done?

Lenin had the genius to profit from developments over which the Bolsheviks had little control. Since summer, a peasant revolution had swept across Russia, as impoverished peasants had seized for themselves the estates of the landlords and the church. Thus when Lenin mandated land reform, he merely approved what peasants were already doing. Similarly, urban workers had established their own local soviets or committees and demanded direct control of individual factories. This, too, Lenin ratified with a decree in November 1917.

Lenin Rallies Soldiers
Lenin, known for his fiery speeches, addresses Red Army soldiers in Moscow in the midst of the Russian civil war, in May 1920. Leon Trotsky, the leader of the Red Army, stands on the podium stairs to the right. (Mansell/Time Life Images/Getty Images)

The Bolsheviks proclaimed their regime a "provisional workers' and peasants' government," promising that a freely elected Constituent Assembly would draw up a new constitution. But free elections in November produced a stunning setback: the Bolsheviks won only 23 percent of the elected delegates. The Socialist Revolutionary Party— the peasants' party—had a clear plurality with about 40 percent of the vote. After the Constituent Assembly met for one day, however, Bolshevik soldiers acting under Lenin's orders disbanded it. By January 1918 Lenin had moved to establish a one-party state.

Lenin acknowledged that Russia had effectively lost the war with Germany and that the only realistic goal was peace at any price. That price was very high. Germany demanded that the Soviet government give up all its western territories, areas inhabited primarily by Poles, Finns, Lithuanians, and other non-Russians—people who had been conquered by the tsars over three centuries and put into the "prisonhouse of nationalities," as Lenin had earlier called the Russian empire.

At first, Lenin's fellow Bolsheviks refused to accept such great territorial losses. But when German armies resumed their unopposed march into Russia in February 1918, Lenin had his way in a very close vote. A third of old Russia's population was sliced away by the **Treaty of Brest-Litovsk**, signed with Germany in March 1918. With peace, Lenin escaped the disaster of continued war and could pursue his goal of absolute power for the Bolsheviks—now also called Communists—within Russia.

The peace treaty and the abolition of the Constituent Assembly inspired armed opposition to the Bolshevik regime. People who had supported self-rule in November saw that once again they were getting dictatorship. The officers of the old army organized the so-called White opposition to the Bolsheviks in southern Russia, Ukraine, Siberia, and the area west of Petrograd. The Whites came from many social groups and were united only by their hatred of communism and the Bolsheviks—the Reds.

By the summer of 1918 Russia was in a full-fledged civil war. Eighteen self-proclaimed regional governments—several of which represented minority nationalities—challenged Lenin's government in Moscow. By the end of the year White armies were on the attack.

PRIMARY SOURCE   Peace, Land, and Bread for the Russian People

Lenin wrote this dramatic manifesto in the name of the Congress of Soviets in Petrograd, the day after Trotsky seized power in the city. The Bolsheviks boldly promised the Russian people a number of progressive reforms, including an immediate armistice, land reform, democracy in the army, and ample food for all. They also issued a call to arms. The final paragraphs warn of counter-revolutionary resistance and capture the looming descent into all-out civil war.

To Workers, Soldiers, and Peasants!

The . . . All-Russia Congress of Soviets of Workers and Soldiers' Deputies has opened. The vast majority of the Soviets are represented at the Congress. A number of delegates from the Peasants' Soviets are also present. . . . Backed by the will of the vast majority of the workers, soldiers, and peasants, backed by the victorious uprising of the workers and the garrison which has taken place in Petrograd, the Congress takes power into its own hands.

The Provisional Government has been overthrown. The majority of the members of the Provisional Government have already been arrested.

The Soviet government will propose an immediate democratic peace to all the nations and an immediate armistice on all fronts. It will secure the transfer of the land of the landed proprietors, the crown and the monasteries to the peasant committees without compensation; it will protect the rights of the soldiers by introducing complete democracy in the army; it will establish workers' control over production; it will ensure the convocation of the Constituent Assembly at the time appointed; it will see to it that bread is supplied to the cities and prime necessities to the villages; it will guarantee all the nations inhabiting Russia the genuine right to self-determination.

The Congress decrees: all power in the localities shall pass to the Soviets of Workers', Soldiers' and Peasants' Deputies, which must guarantee genuine revolutionary order.

The Congress calls upon the soldiers in the trenches to be vigilant and firm. The Congress of Soviets is convinced that the revolutionary army will be able to defend

---

In October 1919 they closed in on central Russia from three sides, and it appeared they might triumph. They did not.

Lenin and the Red Army beat back the counter-revolutionary White armies for several reasons. Most important, the Bolsheviks had quickly developed a better army. Once again, Trotsky's leadership was decisive. At first, the Bolsheviks had preached democracy in the military and had even elected officers in 1917. But beginning in March 1918, Trotsky became war commissar of the newly formed Red Army. He re-established strict discipline and the draft. Soldiers deserting or disobeying an order were summarily shot. Moreover, Trotsky made effective use of former tsarist army officers, who were actively recruited and given unprecedented powers over their troops. Trotsky's disciplined and effective fighting force repeatedly defeated the Whites in the field.

the revolution against all attacks of imperialism until such time as the new government succeeds in concluding a democratic peace, which it will propose directly to all peoples. The new government will do everything to fully supply the revolutionary army by means of a determined policy of requisitions and taxation of the propertied classes, and also will improve the condition of the soldiers' families.

The Kornilov men—Kerensky, Kaledin and others—are attempting to bring troops against Petrograd. Several detachments, whom Kerensky had moved by deceiving them, have come over to the side of the insurgent people.

Soldiers, actively resist Kerensky the Kornilovite! Be on your guard!

Railwaymen, hold up all troop trains dispatched by Kerensky against Petrograd!

Soldiers, workers in factory and office, the fate of the revolution and the fate of the democratic peace is in your hands!

Long live the revolution!

> November 7, 1917
> The All-Russia Congress of Soviets
> Of Workers' and Soldiers' Deputies
> The Delegates from the Peasants' Soviets

EVALUATE THE EVIDENCE

1. How does Lenin's manifesto embody Bolshevik political goals? Why might it appeal to ordinary Russians in the crisis of war and revolution?

2. What historical conditions made it difficult for the Bolsheviks to fulfill the ambitious promises made at the 1917 congress?

Source: Marxists Internet Archive Library, http://www.marxists.org/archive/lenin/works/1917/oct/25 -26/25b.htm.

Ironically, foreign military intervention helped the Bolsheviks. For a variety of reasons, but primarily to stop the spread of communism, the Western Allies (including the United States, Britain, France, and Japan) sent troops to support the White armies. Yet their efforts were limited and halfhearted. By 1919, with the Great War over, Westerners were sick of war, and few politicians wanted to get involved in a new military crusade. Allied intervention failed to offer effective aid, though it did permit the Bolsheviks to appeal to the patriotic nationalism of ethnic Russians, in particular former tsarist army officers who objected to foreign involvement in Russian affairs.

Other conditions favored a Bolshevik victory as well. Strategically, the Reds controlled central Russia and the crucial cities of Moscow and Petrograd. The Whites attacked from the fringes and lacked coordination. Moreover, the poorly defined political program of the Whites was a mishmash of liberal republicanism and monarchism incapable of uniting the Bolshevik's enemies. And while the Bolsheviks promised ethnic minorities in Russian-controlled territories substantial autonomy, the nationalist Whites sought to preserve the tsarist empire.

The Bolsheviks mobilized the home front for the war by establishing a system of centralized controls called **War Communism**. The leadership nationalized banks and industries and outlawed private enterprise. Bolshevik commissars introduced rationing, seized grain from peasants to feed the cities, and maintained strict workplace discipline. Although normal economic activity broke down, these measures maintained labor discipline and kept the Red Army supplied with men and material.

Revolutionary terror also contributed to the Communist victory. Lenin and the Bolsheviks set up a fearsome secret police known as the Cheka, dedicated to suppressing counter-revolutionaries. During the civil war, the Cheka imprisoned and executed without trial tens of thousands of supposed "class enemies." Victims included clergymen, aristocrats, the wealthy Russian bourgeoisie, deserters from the Red Army, and political opponents of all kinds. The tsar and his family were callously executed in July 1918. The "Red Terror" of 1918 to 1920 helped establish the secret police as a central tool of the new Communist government.

By the spring of 1920 the White armies were almost completely defeated, and the Bolsheviks had retaken much of the territory ceded to Germany under the Treaty of Brest-Litovsk. The Red Army reconquered Belarus and Ukraine, both of which had briefly gained independence. Building on this success, the Bolsheviks moved westward into Polish territory, but they were halted on the outskirts of Warsaw in August 1920 by troops under the leadership of the Polish field marshal and chief of state Jozef Pilsudski. This defeat halted Bolshevik attempts to spread communism further into Europe, though in 1921 the Red Army overran the independent national governments of the Caucasus. The Russian civil war was over, and the Bolsheviks had won an impressive victory.

The Peace Settlement

In what ways was the Allied peace settlement flawed?

Even as civil war raged in Russia and chaos engulfed much of central and eastern Europe, the war in the west came to an end in November 1918. Early in 1919 the victorious Western Allies came together in Paris, where they worked out terms for peace with Germany and created the peacekeeping League of Nations. Expectations were high; optimism was almost unlimited. Nevertheless, the peace settlement of 1919 turned out to be a disappointment for peoples and politicians alike. Rather than lasting peace, the immediate postwar years brought economic crisis and violent political conflict.

The End of the War

In early 1918 the German leadership decided that the time was ripe for a last-ditch, all-out attack on France. The defeat of Russia had released men and materials for the western front. The looming arrival of the first U.S. troops and the growth of dissent at home quickened German leaders' resolve. In the great Spring Offensive of 1918, Ludendorff launched an extensive attack on the French lines. German armies came within thirty-five miles of Paris, but Ludendorff's exhausted, overextended forces never broke through. They were stopped in July at the second Battle of the Marne, where 140,000 American soldiers saw action. The late but massive American intervention tipped the scales in favor of Allied victory.

By September British, French, and American armies were advancing steadily on all fronts. Hindenburg and Ludendorff realized that Germany had lost the war. Not wanting to shoulder the blame, they insisted that moderate politicians should take responsibility for the defeat. On October 4 the German emperor formed a new, more liberal civilian government to sue for peace.

As negotiations over an armistice dragged on, frustrated Germans rose up in revolt. On November 3 sailors in Kiel mutinied, and throughout northern Germany soldiers and workers established revolutionary councils like the Russian soviets. The same day, Austria-Hungary surrendered to the Allies and began breaking apart. Revolution erupted in Germany, and masses of workers demonstrated for peace in Berlin. With army discipline collapsing, William II abdicated and fled to Holland. Socialist leaders in Berlin proclaimed a German republic on November 9 and agreed to tough Allied terms of surrender. The armistice went into effect on November 11, 1918. The war was over.

Revolution in Austria-Hungary and Germany

Military defeat brought turmoil and revolution to Austria-Hungary and Germany, as it had to Russia. Having started the war to preserve an imperial state, the Austro-Hungarian Empire perished in the attempt. The independent states of Austria, Hungary, and Czechoslovakia, and a larger Romania, were carved out of its territory (Map 25.3). A greatly expanded Serbian monarchy gained control of the western Balkans and took the name Yugoslavia. For four months in 1919, until conservative nationalists seized power, Hungary became a Marxist republic along Bolshevik lines.

In late 1918 Germany likewise experienced a dramatic revolution that resembled the Russian Revolution of March 1917. In both cases, a genuine popular uprising welled up from below, toppled an authoritarian monarchy, and created a liberal provisional republic. In both countries, liberals and moderate socialist politicians struggled with more radical workers' and soldiers' councils (or soviets) for political dominance. In Germany, however, moderates from the Social Democratic Party and their liberal allies held on to power and established the Weimar Republic—a democratic government that would lead Germany for the next fifteen years. Their success was a deep disappointment for Russia's Bolsheviks, who had hoped that a more radical revolution in Germany would help spread communism across the European continent.

There were several reasons for the German outcome. The great majority of the Marxist politicians in the Social Democratic Party were moderates, not revolutionaries. They wanted political democracy and civil liberties and favored the gradual elimination of capitalism. They were also German nationalists, appalled by the prospect of civil war and revolutionary terror. Of crucial importance was the fact that the moderate Social Democrats quickly came to terms with the army and big business, which helped prevent total national collapse.

Yet the triumph of the Social Democrats brought violent chaos to Germany in 1918 to 1919. The new republic was attacked from both sides of the political spectrum. Radical Communists led by Karl Liebknecht and Rosa Luxemburg tried to seize control of the government in the Spartacist Uprising in Berlin in January 1919. The Social

MAP 25.3 Territorial Changes After World War I
World War I brought tremendous changes to eastern Europe. New nations and new boundaries were established, and a dangerous power vacuum was created by the relatively weak states established between Germany and Soviet Russia.

Democrats called in nationalist Free Corps militias, bands of demobilized soldiers who had kept their weapons, to crush the uprising. Liebknecht and Luxemburg were arrested and then brutally murdered by Free Corps soldiers. In Bavaria, a short-lived Bolshevik-style republic was violently overthrown on government orders by the Free Corps. Nationwide strikes by leftist workers and a short-lived, right-wing military takeover—the Kapp Putsch—were repressed by the central government.

By the summer of 1920 the situation in Germany had calmed down, but the new republican government faced deep discontent. Communists and radical socialists blamed the Social Democrats for the murders of Liebknecht and Luxemburg and the repression in Bavaria. Right-wing nationalists, including the new Nazi Party, despised the government from the start. They spread the myth that the German army had never actually lost the war—instead, the nation was "stabbed in the back" by socialists and pacifists at home. In Germany, the end of the war brought only a fragile sense of political stability.

The Treaty of Versailles

In January 1919 over seventy delegates from twenty-seven nations met in Paris to hammer out a peace accord. The conference produced several treaties, including the **Treaty of Versailles**, which laid out the terms of the postwar settlement with Germany. The peace negotiations inspired great expectations. A young British diplomat later wrote that the victors "were journeying to Paris . . . to found a new order in Europe. We were preparing not Peace only, but Eternal Peace."[9]

This idealism was greatly strengthened by U.S. president Wilson's January 1918 peace proposal, the **Fourteen Points**. The plan called for open diplomacy; a reduction in armaments; freedom of commerce and trade; and the establishment of a **League of Nations**, an international body designed to provide a place for peaceful resolution of international problems. Perhaps most important, Wilson demanded that peace be based on the principle of **national self-determination**, meaning that peoples should be able to choose their own national governments through democratic majority-rule elections and live free from outside interference in territories with clearly defined, permanent borders. Despite the general optimism inspired by these ideas, the conference and the treaty itself quickly generated disagreement.

The "Big Three"—the United States, Great Britain, and France—controlled the conference. Germany, Austria-Hungary, and Russia were excluded, though their lands were placed on the negotiating table. Italy took part, but its role was quite limited. Representatives from the Middle East, Africa, and East Asia attended as well, but their concerns were largely ignored.

Almost immediately, the Big Three began to quarrel. Wilson, who was wildly cheered by European crowds as the champion of democratic international cooperation, was almost obsessed with creating the League of Nations. He insisted that this question come first, for he passionately believed that only a permanent international organization could avert future wars. Wilson had his way—the delegates agreed to create the League, though the details would be worked out later and the final structure was too weak to achieve its grand purpose. Prime Ministers Lloyd George of Great Britain and Georges Clemenceau of France were unenthusiastic about the League. They were primarily concerned with punishing Germany.

The question of what to do with Germany dominated discussions among the Big Three. Clemenceau wanted Germany to pay for its aggression. The war in the west had been fought largely on French soil, and like most French people, Clemenceau wanted revenge, economic retribution, and lasting security for France. This, he believed, required the creation of a buffer state between France and Germany, the permanent demilitarization of Germany, and vast reparation payments. Lloyd George supported Clemenceau, but was less harsh. Wilson disagreed. Clemenceau's demands seemed vindictive, and they violated Wilson's sense of Christian morality and the principle of national self-determination. By April the conference was deadlocked, and Wilson packed his bags to go home.

In the end, Clemenceau, fearful of future German aggression, agreed to a compromise. Clemenceau gave up the French demand for a Rhineland buffer state in return for

French military occupation of the region for fifteen years and a formal defensive alliance with the United States and Great Britain. Both Wilson and Lloyd George promised that their countries would come to France's aid in the event of a German attack. The Allies moved quickly to finish the settlement, believing that further adjustments would be possible within the dual framework of a strong Western alliance and the League of Nations.

The various agreements signed at Versailles redrew the map of Europe, and the war's losers paid the price. The new independent nations carved out of the Austro-Hungarian and Russian Empires included Poland, Czechoslovakia, Finland, the Baltic States, and Yugoslavia. The Ottoman Empire was also split apart, its territories placed under the control of the victors (see page 861).

The Treaty of Versailles, signed by the Allies and Germany, was key to the settlement. Germany's African and Asian colonies were given to France, Britain, and Japan as League of Nations mandates or administered territories, though Germany's losses within Europe were relatively minor, thanks to Wilson. Alsace-Lorraine was returned to France. Ethnic Polish territories seized by Prussia during the eighteenth-century partition of Poland (see Chapter 16) were returned to a new independent Polish state. Predominantly German Danzig was also placed within the Polish border but as a self-governing city under League of Nations protection. Germany had to limit its army to one hundred thousand men, agree to build no military fortifications in the Rhineland, and accept temporary French occupation of that region.

More harshly, in Article 231, the famous **war guilt clause**, the Allies declared that Germany (with Austria) was entirely responsible for the war and thus had to pay reparations equal to all civilian damages caused by the fighting. This much-criticized clause expressed French and to some extent British demands for revenge. For the Germans, reparations were a crippling financial burden. Moreover, the clause was a cutting insult to German national pride. Many Germans believed wartime propaganda that had repeatedly claimed that Germany was an innocent victim, forced into war by a circle of barbaric enemies. When presented with these terms, the new German government protested vigorously but to no avail. On June 28, 1919, representatives of the German Social Democrats signed the treaty in Louis XIV's Hall of Mirrors at Versailles, where Bismarck's empire had been joyously proclaimed almost fifty years before (see Chapter 23).

The rapidly concluded Versailles treaties were far from perfect, but within the context of war-shattered Europe they were a beginning. Germany had been punished but not dismembered. A new world organization complemented a traditional defensive alliance of satisfied powers: Britain, France, and the United States. The remaining serious problems, the Allies hoped, could be worked out in the future. Allied leaders had seen speed as essential because they feared that the Bolshevik Revolution might spread. The best answer to Lenin's unending calls for worldwide upheaval, they believed, was peace and tranquillity.

Yet the great hopes of early 1919 had turned to ashes by the end of the year. The Western alliance had collapsed, and a grandiose plan for permanent peace had given way to a fragile truce. There were several reasons for this turn of events. First, the U.S. Senate and, to a lesser extent, the American people rejected Wilson's handiwork. Republican senators led by Henry Cabot Lodge believed that the treaty gave away Congress's constitutional right to declare war and demanded changes in the articles. In failing health, the self-righteous Wilson rejected all compromise. In doing so, he ensured that the treaty would never be ratified by the United States and that the United States would never join the League of Nations. Moreover, the Senate refused to ratify treaties forming a defensive alliance with France and Great Britain. America in effect had turned its back on Europe. The new American gospel of isolationism represented a tragic renunciation of international responsibility. Using U.S. actions as an excuse, Great Britain too refused to ratify its defensive alliance with France. Bitterly betrayed by its allies, France stood alone.

A second cause for the failure of the peace was that the principle of national self-determination, which had engendered such enthusiasm, was good in theory but flawed in practice. In Europe, the borders of new states such as Poland, Czechoslovakia, and Yugoslavia cut through a jumble of ethnic and religious groups that often despised each other. The new central European nations would prove to be economically weak and politically unstable, the source of conflict in the years to come. In the colonies, desires for self-determination were simply ignored, leading to problems particularly in the Middle East.

The Peace Settlement in the Middle East

Although Allied leaders at Versailles focused mainly on European questions, they also imposed a political settlement on what had been the Ottoman Empire. Their decisions brought radical and controversial changes to the region: the Allies dismantled the Ottoman Empire, Britain and France expanded their influence, and Arab nationalists felt cheated and betrayed.

The British government had encouraged the wartime Arab revolt against the Ottoman Turks (see page 842) and had even made vague promises of an independent Arab kingdom. However, when the fighting stopped, the British and the French chose instead to honor their own secret wartime agreements to divide and rule the Ottoman lands. Most important was the Sykes-Picot Agreement of 1916, named after British and French diplomats. In the secret accord, Britain and France agreed that former Ottoman territories would be administered by the European powers under what was later termed the **mandate system**. France would receive a mandate to govern modern-day Lebanon and Syria and much of southern Turkey, and Britain would control Palestine, Transjordan, and Iraq. Though the official goal of the mandate system was to eventually grant these regions national independence, it quickly became clear that the Allies never intended to do so. Critics labeled the system colonialism under another name, and when Britain and France set about implementing their agreements after the armistice, Arab nationalists reacted with understandable surprise and resentment.

British plans for the former Ottoman lands that would become Palestine further angered Arab nationalists. The **Balfour Declaration** of November 1917, written by British foreign secretary Arthur Balfour, had announced that Britain favored a "National Home for the Jewish People" in Palestine, but without discriminating against the civil and religious rights of the non-Jewish communities already living in the region. Some members of the British cabinet believed the declaration would appeal to German, Austrian, and American Jews and thus help the British war effort. Others sincerely supported the Zionist vision of a Jewish homeland (see Chapter 23), which they hoped would also help Britain maintain control of the Suez Canal. Whatever the motives, the declaration enraged Arabs.

In 1914 Jews accounted for about 11 percent of the population in the three Ottoman districts that the British would lump together to form Palestine; the rest of the population was predominantly Arab. Both groups understood that Balfour's National Home for the Jewish People implied the establishment of some kind of Jewish state that would violate majority rule. Moreover, a state founded on religious and ethnic exclusivity was out of keeping with Islamic and Ottoman tradition, which had historically been more tolerant of religious diversity and minorities than Christian Europe.

Though Arab leaders attended the Versailles Peace Conference, their efforts to secure autonomy in the Middle East came to nothing. Only the kingdom of Hejaz—today part of Saudi Arabia—was granted independence. In response, Arab nationalists came together in Damascus as the General Syrian Congress in 1919 and unsuccessfully called again for political independence. The congress proclaimed Syria an independent kingdom; a similar congress declared Iraqi independence.

The Western reaction was swift and decisive. A French army stationed in Lebanon attacked Syria, taking Damascus in July 1920. The Arab government fled, and the French took over. Meanwhile, the British bloodily put down an uprising in Iraq and established control there. Brushing aside Arab opposition, the British in Palestine formally incorporated the Balfour Declaration and its commitment to a Jewish national home. Western imperialism, in the form of the mandate system authorized by the League of Nations, appeared to have replaced Ottoman rule in the Middle East.

The Allies sought to impose even harsher terms on the defeated Turks than on the "liberated" Arabs. A treaty forced on the Ottoman sultan dismembered the Turkish heartland. Great Britain and France occupied parts of modern-day Turkey, and Italy and Greece claimed shares. There was a sizable Greek minority in western Turkey, and Greek nationalists wanted to build a modern Greek empire modeled on long-dead Byzantium. In 1919 Greek armies carried by British ships landed on the Turkish coast at Smyrna (SMUHR-nuh) and advanced unopposed into the interior, while French troops moved in from the south. Turkey seemed finished.

Turkey survived the postwar invasions. Led by Mustafa Kemal (1881–1938), the Turks refused to acknowledge the Allied dismemberment of their country and gradually mounted a forceful resistance. Kemal had directed the successful Turkish defense against the British at the Battle of Gallipoli, and despite staggering losses, his Turkish army repulsed the invaders. The Greeks and British sued for peace. In 1923, after long negotiations, the resulting Treaty of Lausanne (loh-ZAN) recognized the territorial integrity of Turkey and solemnly abolished the hated capitulations that the European powers had imposed over the centuries to give their citizens special privileges in the Ottoman Empire.

Kemal, a nationalist without religious faith, believed that Turkey should modernize and secularize along Western lines. He established a republic, was elected president, and created a one-party system—partly inspired by the Bolshevik example—to transform his country. The most radical reforms pertained to religion and culture. For centuries, Islamic religious authorities had regulated most of the intellectual, political, and social activities of Ottoman citizens. Profoundly influenced by the example of western Europe, Kemal set out to limit the place of religion and religious leaders in daily affairs. He decreed a controversial separation of church and state, promulgated law codes inspired by European models, and established a secular public school system. Women received rights that they never had before. By the time of his death in 1938, Kemal had implemented much of his revolutionary program and moved Turkey much closer to Europe, foretelling current efforts by Turkey to join the European Union as a full-fledged member.

The Human Costs of the War

World War I broke empires, inspired revolutions, and changed national borders on a world scale. It also had immense human costs, and ordinary people in the combatant nations struggled to deal with its legacy in the years that followed. The raw numbers are astonishing: estimates vary, but total deaths on the battlefield numbered about 8 million soldiers. Russia had the highest number of military casualties, followed by Germany. France had the highest proportionate number of losses; about one out of every ten adult males died in the war. The other belligerents paid a high price as well. Between 7 and 10 million civilians died because of the war and war-related hardships, and another 20 million people died in the worldwide influenza epidemic that followed the war in 1918.

The number of dead, the violence of their deaths, and the nature of trench warfare made proper burials difficult, if not impossible. Soldiers were typically interred where they fell, and by 1918 thousands of ad hoc military cemeteries were scattered across northern France and Flanders. When remains were gathered, the chaos and danger of the battlefield limited accurate identification. After the war, the bodies were moved to more formal cemeteries, but hundreds of thousands remained unidentified. British and German soldiers ultimately remained in foreign soil, in graveyards managed by national commissions. After some delay, the bodies of most of the French combatants were brought home to local cemeteries.

Millions of ordinary people grieved, turning to family, friends, neighbors, and the church for comfort. Towns and villages across Europe raised public memorials to honor the dead and held ceremonies on important anniversaries: on November 11, the day the war ended, and in Britain on July 1, to commemorate the Battle of the Somme. These were poignant and often tearful moments for participants. For the first time, each nation built a Tomb of the Unknown Soldier as a site for national mourning. Memorials were also built on the main battlefields of the war. All expressed the general need to recognize the great sorrow and suffering caused by so much death.

The victims of the First World War included millions of widows and orphans and huge numbers of emotionally scarred and disabled veterans. Countless soldiers suffered from what the British called "shell shock"—now termed post-traumatic stress disorder. Contemporary physicians and policymakers poorly understood this complex mental health issue, and though some soldiers received medical treatment, others were accused of cowardice and shirking, and were denied veterans' benefits after the war. In addition, some 10 million soldiers came home physically disfigured or mutilated. Governments tried to take care of the disabled and the survivor families, but there was never enough money to adequately fund pensions and job-training programs. Artificial limbs were expensive, uncomfortable, and awkward, and employers rarely wanted disabled workers. Crippled veterans were often forced to beg on the streets, a common sight for the next decade.

The German case is illustrative. Nearly 10 percent of German civilians were direct victims of the war, and the new German government struggled to take care of them. Veterans' groups organized to lobby for state support, and fully one-third of the federal budget of the Weimar Republic was tied up in war-related pensions and benefits. With the onset of the Great Depression in 1929, benefits were cut, leaving bitter veterans vulnerable to Nazi propagandists who paid homage to the sacrifices of the war while

Disabled French Veterans   The war killed millions of soldiers and left many more permanently disabled, making the sight of men missing limbs or disfigured in other ways a common one in the 1920s. (Bettmann/Corbis)

calling for the overthrow of the republican government. The human cost of the war thus had another steep price: across Europe, newly formed radical right-wing parties, including the German Nazis and the Italian Fascists, successfully manipulated popular feelings of loss and resentment to undermine fragile parliamentary governments.

Notes

1. Quoted in J. Remak, *The Origins of World War I* (New York: Holt, Rinehart & Winston, 1967), p. 84.
2. On the mood of 1914, see James Joll, *The Origins of the First World War* (New York: Longman, 1992), pp. 199–233.
3. Quoted in George L. Mosse, *Fallen Soldiers: Reshaping the Memory of the World Wars* (New York: Oxford University Press, 1990), p. 64.
4. Quoted in Noel Malcolm, *Bosnia: A Short History* (New York: New York University Press, 1996), p. 153.
5. Quoted in S. Audoin-Rouzeau, *Men at War, 1914–1918: National Sentiment and Trench Journalism in France During the First World War* (Oxford, U.K.: Berg, 1992), p. 69.
6. Vejas Gabriel Liulevicius, *War Land on the Eastern Front: Culture, National Identity, and German Occupation in World War I* (New York: Cambridge University Press, 2000), pp. 54–89; quotation on p. 71.
7. Quoted in F. P. Chambers, *The War Behind the War, 1914–1918* (London: Faber & Faber, 1939), p. 168.
8. John Reed, *Ten Days That Shook the World* (New York: International Publishers, 1967), p. 126.
9. Quoted in H. Nicolson, *Peacemaking 1919* (New York: Grosset & Dunlap Universal Library, 1965), pp. 8, 31–32.

Chapter Review

MAKE IT STICK

LearningCurve
bedfordstmartins.com/mckaywestvalue
After reading the chapter, use LearningCurve to retain what you've read.

IDENTIFY KEY TERMS

Identify and explain the significance of each item below.

Triple Alliance (p. 831)

Triple Entente (p. 833)

Schlieffen Plan (p. 839)

total war (p. 839)

trench warfare (p. 840)

February Revolution (p. 850)

Petrograd Soviet (p. 850)

Bolsheviks (p. 851)

Treaty of Brest-Litovsk (p. 853)

War Communism (p. 856)

Treaty of Versailles (p. 859)

Fourteen Points (p. 859)

League of Nations (p. 859)

national self-determination (p. 859)

war guilt clause (p. 860)

mandate system (p. 861)

Balfour Declaration (p. 861)

REVIEW THE MAIN IDEAS

Answer the focus questions from each section of the chapter.

* What caused the outbreak of the First World War? (p. 831)
* How did the First World War differ from previous wars? (p. 839)
* In what ways did the war transform life on the home front? (p. 843)
* Why did world war lead to revolution in Russia, and what was its outcome? (p. 849)
* In what ways was the Allied peace settlement flawed? (p. 856)

MAKE CONNECTIONS

Think about the larger developments and continuities within and across chapters.

1. While the war was being fought, peoples on all sides of the fighting often referred to the First World War as "the great war." Why would they find this label appropriate?

2. How did the First World War draw on long-standing political rivalries and tensions among the European powers (Chapters 19, 23, and 24)?

3. To what extent was the First World War actually a "world" war?

ONLINE DOCUMENT ASSIGNMENT

Vera Brittain

What role did wartime propaganda play in encouraging women like Vera Brittain to get involved in the war effort?

You encountered Vera Brittain's story on page 846. Keeping the question above in mind, go online and analyze a variety of propaganda posters calling for women to serve as military nurses. Then complete a writing assignment based on the evidence and details from this chapter.

bedfordstmartins.com/mckaywestvalue

CHRONOLOGY

1914–1918	• World War I
June 28, 1914	• Serbian nationalist assassinates Archduke Francis Ferdinand
August 1914	• War begins
September 1914	• Battle of the Marne; German victories on the eastern front
October 1914	• Ottoman Empire joins the Central Powers
1915	• Italy joins the Triple Entente; German submarine sinks the *Lusitania*; Germany halts unrestricted submarine warfare
1915–1918	• Armenian genocide; German armies occupy large parts of east-central Europe
1916	• Battles of Verdun and the Somme
1916–1918	• Antiwar movement spreads throughout Europe; Arab rebellion against Ottoman Empire
1917	• Germany resumes unrestricted submarine warfare
March 1917	• February Revolution in Russia
April 1917	• United States enters the war
October–November 1917	• Battle of Caporetto
November 1917	• Bolshevik Revolution in Russia; Balfour Declaration on Jewish homeland in Palestine
1918	• Treaty of Brest-Litovsk; revolution in Germany
1918–1920	• Civil war in Russia
1919	• Treaty of Versailles; Allies invade Turkey
1923	• Treaty of Lausanne recognizes Turkish independence

26

✓ LearningCurve
bedfordstmartins.com/mckaywestvalue
After reading the chapter, use LearningCurve to retain what you've read.

The Age of Anxiety

1880–1940

WHEN ALLIED DIPLOMATS MET IN PARIS IN EARLY 1919 WITH THEIR optimistic plans for building a lasting peace, most people looked forward to happier times. After the terrible trauma of total war, they hoped that life would return to normal and would make sense in the familiar prewar terms of peace, prosperity, and progress. Their hopes were in vain. The First World War and the Russian Revolution had mangled too many things beyond repair. Life would no longer fit neatly into the old molds, and great numbers of men and women felt themselves increasingly adrift in an age of anxiety and continual change.

Late-nineteenth-century thinkers had already called attention to the pessimism, uncertainty, and irrationalism that seemed to accompany modern life. By 1900 radical developments in philosophy and the sciences had substantiated and popularized such ideas. The modernist movement had begun its sweep through literature, music, and the arts, as avant-garde innovators rejected old cultural forms and began to experiment with new ones. Radical innovations in the arts and sciences dominated Western culture and intellectual life in the 1920s and 1930s and remained influential after the Second World War. At the same time, a growing consumer society, along with the new media of radio and film, transformed the habits of everyday life and leisure.

Even as modern science, art, and culture challenged received wisdom of all kinds, public affairs and international relations in the postwar years spiraled into crisis. Despite some progress in the mid-1920s, political stability remained short-lived, and the Great Depression that began in 1929 cast millions into poverty and shocked the status quo. Democratic liberalism was besieged by the rise of authoritarian and Fascist governments, and another world conflict seemed imminent. In the early 1920s the French poet and critic Paul Valéry (1871–1945) described his widespread "impression of darkness," where "almost all the affairs of men remain in a terrible uncertainty. We think of what has disappeared, and we are almost destroyed by what has been destroyed; we do not know what will be born, and we fear the future, not without reason."[1] Valéry's words captured the gloom and foreboding that dominated the decades between the world wars.

Uncertainty in Modern Thought

How did intellectual developments reflect the general crisis in Western thought?

The decades surrounding the First World War—from the 1880s to the 1930s—brought intense cultural and intellectual experimentation. As people grappled with the costs of the First World War and the difficulty of postwar recovery, philosophers and scientists questioned and even abandoned many of the cherished values and beliefs that had guided Western society since the eighteenth-century Enlightenment and the nineteenth-century triumph of industry and science. Though some intellectuals turned to Christianity, others rejected Christian teachings and dismissed the possibility that rational thought could lead to greater human understanding or social progress. Radical intellectual thought thus dovetailed with the ongoing political and social crisis, and many people felt anxious and adrift in a world without certainties.

Historians find it relatively easy to set precise dates for political events, such as the outbreak of wars or the outcome of national elections. Exact dates for the rise and fall of intellectual and cultural developments are much more difficult to define. The emergence of modern philosophy, for example, did not follow the clear-cut timelines of political history. Thus to understand the history of modern thought, we must investigate trends dating back to the last decades of the nineteenth century and follow them into the 1950s.

Modern Philosophy

Before 1914 most people still believed in Enlightenment ideals of progress, reason, and individual rights. At the turn of the century supporters of these philosophies had some cause for optimism. Women and workers were gradually gaining support in their struggles for political and social recognition, and the rising standard of living, the taming of the city, and the growth of state-supported social programs suggested that life was indeed improving. Such developments encouraged faith in the ability of a rational human mind to discover the laws of society and then wisely act on them.

Nevertheless, in the late nineteenth century a small group of serious thinkers mounted a determined attack on these optimistic beliefs. These critics rejected the general faith in progress and the rational human mind. The German philosopher Friedrich Nietzsche (NEE-chuh) (1844–1900) was particularly influential, though not until after

Friedrich Nietzsche The German philosopher's ideas posted a radical challenge to conventional Western thought and had enormous influence on later thinkers. (akg-images)

his death. Never a systematic philosopher, he wrote more as a prophet in a provocative and poetic style. In the first of his *Untimely Meditations* (1873), he argued that ever since classical Athens, the West had overemphasized rationality and stifled the authentic passions and animal instincts that drive human activity and true creativity.

Nietzsche questioned the conventional values of Western society. He believed that reason, progress, and respectability were outworn social and psychological constructs that suffocated self-realization and excellence. Though he was the son of a Lutheran minister, Nietzsche famously rejected religion. In his 1887 book, *On the Genealogy of Morals*, he claimed that Christianity embodied a "slave morality" that glorified weakness, envy, and mediocrity. In one of his most famous lines, an apparent madman proclaims that "God is dead," metaphorically murdered by lackadaisical modern Christians who no longer really believed in him. (See "Primary Source: Friedrich Nietzsche Pronounces the Death of God," page 870.)

Nietzsche painted a dark world, perhaps foreshadowing his own loss of sanity in 1889. He warned that Western society was entering a period of nihilism—the philosophical idea that human life is entirely without meaning, truth, or purpose. Nietzsche asserted that all moral systems were invented lies and that liberalism, democracy, and socialism were corrupt systems designed to promote the weak at the expense of the strong. The West was in decline; false values had triumphed. The death of God left people disoriented and depressed. According to Nietzsche, the only hope for the individual was to accept the meaninglessness of human existence and then make that very meaninglessness a source of self-defined personal integrity and hence liberation. In this way, at least a few superior individuals could free themselves from the humdrum thinking of the masses and become true heroes.

Little read during his active years, Nietzsche's works attracted growing attention in the early twentieth century. Artists and writers experimented with his ideas, which were fundamental to the rise of the philosophy of existentialism in the 1920s. Subsequent generations remade Nietzsche to suit their own needs, and his influence remains enormous to this day.

The growing dissatisfaction with established ideas before 1914 was apparent in other important thinkers as well. In the 1890s French philosophy professor Henri Bergson (1859–1941), for one, argued that immediate experience and intuition were as important as rational and scientific thinking for understanding reality. According to

PRIMARY SOURCE   Friedrich Nietzsche Pronounces the Death of God

In this selection from philosopher Friedrich Nietzsche's The Gay Science *(1882), one of the best-known passages in his entire body of work, a "madman" pronounces the death of God and describes the anxiety and despair—and the opportunities—faced by people in a world without faith.*

The Madman. Haven't you heard of that madman, who on a bright morning day lit a lantern, ran into the marketplace, and screamed incessantly: "I am looking for God! I am looking for God!" Since there were a lot of people standing around who did not believe in God, he only aroused great laughter. Is he lost? asked one person. Did he lose his way like a child? asked another. Or is he in hiding? Is he frightened of us? Has he gone on a journey? Or emigrated? And so they screamed and laughed. The madman leaped into the crowd and stared straight at them. "Where has God gone?" he cried. "I will tell you! *We have killed him.* You and I! All of us are his murderers! But how did we do this? How did we manage to drink up the sea? Who gave us the sponge to wipe away the entire horizon? What were we doing when we unchained this earth from its sun? Where is it going now? Where are we going? Away from all the suns? Aren't we ceaselessly falling? Backward, sideways, forward, in all directions? Is there an up or a down at all? Aren't we just roaming through an infinite nothing? Don't you feel the breath of this empty space? Hasn't it gotten colder? Isn't night and ever more night falling? Don't we have to light our lanterns in the morning? Do we hear anything yet of the noise of the gravediggers who are burying God? Do we smell anything yet of the rot of God's decomposition? Gods decompose too! God is dead! God will stay dead! And we have killed him! How do we console ourselves, the murderers of all murderers? The holiest and mightiest the world has ever known has bled to death against our knives—who will wipe the blood off? Where is the water to cleanse ourselves? What sort of rituals of atonement, what sort of sacred games, will we have to come up with now? Isn't the greatness of this deed too great for us? Don't we have to become gods ourselves simply to appear worthy of it? There has never been a greater deed, and whoever will be born after us will belong to a history greater than any history up to now!"

EVALUATE THE EVIDENCE

1. Does Nietzsche believe that the "death of God" is a positive experience? In what ways can people come to grips with this "great deed"?

2. How does the nihilism expressed in this passage foreshadow many of the main ideas in the philosophy of existentialism?

Source: *Nietzsche and the Death of God: Selected Writings*, trans. and ed. Peter Fritzsche (Boston: Bedford/St. Martin's, 2007), pp. 71–72. Used by permission of Bedford/St. Martin's.

Bergson, a religious experience or mystical poem was often more accessible to human comprehension than a scientific law or a mathematical equation.

The First World War accelerated the revolt against established certainties in philosophy, but that revolt went in two very different directions. In English-speaking countries, the main development was the acceptance of logical positivism in university circles. In the continental countries, the primary development in philosophy was existentialism.

Logical positivism was truly revolutionary. Adherents of this worldview argued that what we know about human life must be based on rational facts and direct observation. They concluded that theology and most traditional philosophy were meaningless because even the most cherished ideas about God, eternal truth, and ethics were impossible to prove using logic. This outlook is often associated with the Austrian philosopher Ludwig Wittgenstein (VIHT-guhn-shtine) (1889–1951), who later immigrated to England, where he trained numerous disciples.

In his pugnacious *Tractatus Logico-Philosophicus* (Essay on Logical Philosophy), published in 1922, Wittgenstein argued that philosophy is only the logical clarification of thoughts and that therefore it should concentrate on the study of language, which expresses thoughts. In his view, the great philosophical issues of the ages — God, freedom, morality, and so on — were quite literally senseless, a great waste of time, for neither scientific experiments nor mathematical logic could demonstrate their validity. Statements about such matters reflected only the personal preferences of a given individual. As Wittgenstein put it in the famous last sentence of this work, "Of what one cannot speak, of that one must keep silent." Logical positivism, which has remained dominant in England and the United States to this day, drastically reduced the scope of philosophical inquiry and offered little solace to ordinary people.

On the continent, others looked for answers in **existentialism**. This new philosophy loosely united highly diverse and even contradictory thinkers in a search for usable moral values in a world of anxiety and uncertainty. Modern existentialism had many nineteenth-century forerunners, including Nietzsche, the Danish religious philosopher Søren Kierkegaard (1813–1855), and the Russian novelist Fyodor Dostoyevsky (1821–1881). The philosophy gained recognition in Germany in the 1920s when philosophers Martin Heidegger (1889–1976) and Karl Jaspers (1883–1969) found a sympathetic audience among disillusioned postwar university students. These writers placed great emphasis on the loneliness and meaninglessness of human existence in a godless world and the individual's need to come to terms with the fear caused by this situation.

Most existential thinkers in the twentieth century were atheists. Often inspired by Nietzsche, they did not believe that a supreme being had established humanity's fundamental nature and given life its meaning. In the words of French existentialist Jean-Paul Sartre (ZHAWN-pawl SAHR-truh) (1905–1980), "existence precedes essence." By that, Sartre meant that there are no God-given, timeless truths outside or independent of individual existence. Only after they are born do people struggle to define their essence, entirely on their own. According to thinkers like Sartre and his life-long intellectual partner Simone de Beauvoir (1908–1986), existence itself is absurd. Human beings are terribly alone, for there is no God to help them. They are left to confront the inevitable arrival of death and so are hounded by despair. The crisis of the existential thinker epitomized the modern intellectual crisis — the shattering of beliefs in God, reason, and progress.

At the same time, existentialists recognized that human beings must act in the world. Indeed, in the words of Sartre, "man is condemned to be free." Because life is meaningless, existentialists believe that individuals are forced to create their own meaning and define themselves through their actions. Such radical freedom is frightening, and Sartre concluded that most people try to escape it by structuring their lives around conventional social norms. According to Sartre, to escape is to live in "bad faith," to hide from the hard truths of existence. To live authentically, individuals must become "engaged" and choose their own actions in full awareness of their inescapable responsibility for their own behavior. Existentialism thus had a powerful ethical component. It placed great stress on individual responsibility and choice, on "being in the world" in the right way.

Existentialism had important precedents in the late nineteenth and early twentieth centuries, but the philosophy really came of age in France during and immediately after World War II. The terrible conditions of that war, discussed in the next chapter, reinforced the existential view of and approach to life. After World War II, French existentialists such as Sartre and Albert Camus (1913–1960) became enormously influential. They offered powerful but unsettling answers to the profound moral issues and the crises of the first half of the twentieth century.

The Revival of Christianity

Though philosophers such as Nietzsche, Wittgenstein, and Sartre all argued that religion had little to teach people in the modern age, the decades after the First World War witnessed a tenacious revival of Christian thought. Christianity—and religion in general—had been on the defensive in intellectual circles since the Enlightenment. In the years before 1914 some theologians, especially Protestant ones, had felt the need to interpret Christian doctrine and the Bible so that they did not seem to contradict science, evolution, and common sense. They saw Christ primarily as a great moral teacher and downplayed the mysterious, spiritual aspects of his divinity. Indeed, some modern theologians were embarrassed by the miraculous, unscientific aspects of Christianity and rejected them.

Especially after World War I, a number of thinkers and theologians began to revitalize the fundamental beliefs of Christianity. Sometimes called Christian existentialists because they shared the loneliness and despair of atheistic existentialists, they stressed human beings' sinful nature, their need for faith, and the mystery of God's forgiveness. The revival of Christian belief after World War I was fed by the rediscovery of the work of the nineteenth-century Danish theologian Søren Kierkegaard (KIHR-kuh-gahrd), whose ideas became extremely influential. Kierkegaard believed it was impossible for ordinary individuals to prove the existence of God, but he rejected the notion that Christianity was an empty practice. In his classic *Sickness unto Death* (1849), Kierkegaard mastered his religious doubts by suggesting that people must take a "leap of faith" and accept the existence of an objectively unknowable but nonetheless awesome and majestic God.

In the 1920s the Swiss Protestant theologian Karl Barth (1886–1968) propounded similar ideas. In brilliant and influential writings, Barth argued that human beings were imperfect, sinful creatures whose reason and will are hopelessly flawed. Religious truth is therefore made known to human beings only through God's grace, not through reason. People have to accept God's word and the supernatural revelation of Jesus Christ with awe, trust, and obedience, not reason or logic.

Among Catholics, the leading existential Christian was Gabriel Marcel (1889–1973). Born into a cultivated French family, Marcel found in the Catholic Church an answer to what he called the postwar "broken world." Catholicism and religious belief provided the hope, humanity, honesty, and piety for which he hungered. Marcel and his countryman Jacques Maritain (1882–1973) denounced anti-Semitism and supported closer ties with non-Catholics.

After 1914 religion became much more meaningful to intellectuals than it had been before the war. Between about 1920 and 1950, in addition to Marcel and Maritain, poets T. S. Eliot and W. H. Auden, novelists Evelyn Waugh and Aldous Huxley, historian Arnold Toynbee, writer C. S. Lewis, psychoanalyst Karl Stern, and physicist Max Planck were all either converted to a faith or became attracted to religion for the first time. Religion, often of a despairing, existential variety, was one meaningful answer to uncertainty and anxiety and the horrific costs of world war. In the words of English novelist Graham Greene, a Roman Catholic convert, "One began to believe in heaven because one believed in hell."[2]

The New Physics

Ever since the Scientific Revolution of the seventeenth century, scientific advances and their implications had greatly influenced the beliefs of thinking people. By the late nineteenth century science was one of the main pillars supporting Western society's optimistic and rationalistic worldview. Progressive minds believed that science, unlike religion or philosophical speculation, was based on hard facts and controlled experiments. Unchanging natural laws seemed to determine physical processes and permit useful solutions to more and more problems. All this was comforting, especially to people no longer committed to traditional religious beliefs. And all this was challenged by the new physics.

An important first step came at the end of the nineteenth century with the discovery that atoms were not like hard, permanent little billiard balls. They were actually composed of many far-smaller, fast-moving particles, such as electrons and protons. Polish-born physicist Marie Curie (1867–1934) and her French husband, Pierre, discovered that radium constantly emits subatomic particles and thus does not have a constant atomic weight. Building on this and other work in radiation, German physicist Max Planck (1858–1947) showed in 1900 that subatomic energy is emitted in uneven little spurts, which Planck called "quanta," and not in a steady stream, as previously believed. Planck's discovery called into question the old sharp distinction between matter and energy: the implication was that matter and energy might be different forms of the same thing. The view of atoms as the stable basic building blocks of nature, with a different kind of unbreakable atom for each of the ninety-two chemical elements, was badly shaken.

In 1905 the German-Jewish genius Albert Einstein (1879–1955) went further than the Curies and Planck in undermining Newtonian physics. His **theory of special relativity** postulated that time and space are relative to the viewpoint of the observer and that only the speed of light is constant for all frames of reference in the universe. In order to make his revolutionary and paradoxical idea somewhat comprehensible to the nonmathematical layperson, Einstein used analogies involving moving trains. For example, if a woman in the middle of a moving car got up and walked forward to the door, she had gone, relative to the train, a half car length. But relative to an observer on the embankment, she had gone farther. To Einstein, this meant that time and distance were not natural universals but depended on the position and motion of the observer.

In addition, Einstein's theory stated that matter and energy are interchangeable and that even a particle of matter contains enormous levels of potential energy. These ideas unified an apparently infinite universe with the incredibly small, fast-moving subatomic world. In comparison, the closed framework of the Newtonian physics developed during the Scientific Revolution, exemplified by Newton's supposedly immutable laws of motion and mechanics, was quite limited (see Chapter 16).

The 1920s opened the "heroic age of physics," in the apt words of Ernest Rutherford (1871–1937), one of its leading pioneers. Breakthrough followed breakthrough. In 1919 Rutherford showed that the atom could be split. By 1944 seven subatomic particles had been identified, the most important of which was the neutron. Physicists realized that the neutron's capacity to shatter the nucleus of another atom could lead to chain reactions of shattered atoms that would release unbelievable force. This discovery was fundamental to the subsequent development of the nuclear bomb.

Although few nonscientists truly understood the revolution in physics, its implications, as presented by newspapers and popular writers, were disturbing to millions of men and women in the 1920s and 1930s. As unsettling as Einstein's ideas was a notion popularized by German physicist Werner Heisenberg (VER-nuhr HIGH-zuhn-buhrg) (1901–1976). In 1927 Heisenberg formulated the "uncertainty principle," which postulates that nature itself is ultimately unknowable and unpredictable. He suggested that the universe lacked any absolute objective reality. Everything was "relative," that is, dependent on the observer's frame of reference. Such ideas caught on among ordinary people, who found the unstable, relativistic world described by the new physicists strange and troubling. Instead of Newton's dependable, rational laws, there seemed to be only tendencies and probabilities in an extraordinarily complex and uncertain universe. Like modern philosophy, physics no longer provided comforting truths about natural laws or optimistic answers about humanity's place in an understandable world.

Freudian Psychology

With physics presenting an uncertain universe so unrelated to ordinary human experience, questions regarding the power and potential of the rational human mind assumed special significance. The findings and speculations of Sigmund Freud were particularly influential, yet also deeply disturbing.

Before Freud, poets and mystics had probed the unconscious and irrational aspects of human behavior. But most scientists assumed that the conscious mind processed sense experiences in a rational and logical way. Human behavior in turn was the result of rational calculation — of "thinking." Beginning in the late 1880s Freud developed a very different view of the human psyche. Basing his insights on the analysis of dreams and of hysteria, Freud concluded that human behavior was basically irrational, governed by the unconscious, a sort of mental reservoir that contained vital instinctual drives and powerful memories. Though the unconscious profoundly influenced people's behavior, it was unknowable to the conscious mind, leaving people unaware of the source or meaning of their actions.

Freud described three structures of the self — the **id**, the **ego**, and the **superego** — that were basically at war with one another. The primitive, irrational id was entirely unconscious. The source of sexual, aggressive, and pleasure-seeking instincts, the id sought immediate fulfillment of all desires and was totally amoral. Keeping the id in check was the superego, the conscience or internalized voice of parental or social control. For Freud, the superego was also irrational. Overly strict and puritanical, it was constantly in conflict with the pleasure-seeking id. The third component was the ego, the rational self that was mostly conscious and worked to negotiate between the demands of the id and the superego.

For Freud, the healthy individual possessed a strong ego that effectively balanced the id and superego. Neurosis, or mental illness, resulted when the three structures were out of balance. Since the id's instinctual drives were extremely powerful, the danger for individuals and indeed whole societies was that unacknowledged drives might overwhelm the control mechanisms of the ego in a violent, distorted way. Freud's "talking cure" — in which neurotic patients lay back on a couch and shared their innermost thoughts with the psychoanalyst — was an attempt to resolve such unconscious tensions and restore the rational ego to its predominant role.

Yet Freud, like Nietzsche, believed that the mechanisms of rational thinking and traditional moral values could be too strong. In his book *Civilization and Its Discontents* (1930), Freud argued that civilization was possible only when individuals renounced their irrational instincts in order to live peaceably in groups. Such renunciation made communal life possible, but it left basic instincts unfulfilled and so led to widespread unhappiness. Freud gloomily concluded that Western civilization was itself inescapably neurotic.

Freudian psychology and clinical psychiatry had become an international movement by 1910, but only after 1919 did they receive more attention, especially in northern Europe and the United States, where Freud's ideas attained immense popularity after the Second World War. Many opponents and even some enthusiasts interpreted Freud as saying that the first requirement for mental health was an uninhibited sex life — popular understandings of Freud thus reflected and encouraged growing sexual experimentation, particularly among middle-class women. For more serious students, the psychology of Freud and his followers contributed to the weakening of the old easy optimism about the rational and progressive nature of the human mind.

Modernism in Architecture, Art, Literature, and Music

How did modernism revolutionize Western culture?

Like the scientists and intellectuals who were part of this increasingly unsettled modern culture, creative artists rejected old forms and old values. **Modernism** in architecture, art, literature, and music meant constant experimentation and a search for new kinds of expression. Even today the modernism of the first half of the twentieth century seems strikingly fresh and original. And though many people still find the varied modern visions of the arts strange and disturbing, these decades, so dismal in many respects, stand as one of Western society's great artistic eras.

Architecture and Design

Already in the late nineteenth century, architects inspired by modernism had begun to transform the physical framework of urban society. The United States, with its rapid urban growth and lack of rigid building traditions, pioneered the new architecture. In the 1890s the Chicago School of architects, led by Louis H. Sullivan (1856–1924), used inexpensive steel, reinforced concrete, and electric elevators to build skyscrapers and office buildings lacking almost any exterior ornamentation. In the first decade of the twentieth century, Sullivan's student Frank Lloyd Wright (1867–1959) built a series of radically modern houses featuring low lines, open interiors, and mass-produced building materials. Europeans were inspired by these and other American examples of functional construction, like the massive, unadorned grain elevators of the Midwest.

Promoters of modern architecture argued that buildings and living spaces in general should be ordered according to a new principle: **functionalism**. Buildings, like industrial products, should be "functional" — that is, they should serve, as well as possible, the purpose for which they were made. According to the Franco-Swiss architect Le Corbusier (luh cowr-booz-YAY) (1887–1965), one of the great champions of modernism, "a house is a machine for living in."[3]

Le Corbusier's polemical work *Towards a New Architecture*, published in 1923, laid out guidelines meant to revolutionize building design. Le Corbusier argued that architects should affirm and adopt the latest technologies. Rejecting fancy ornamentation, they should find beauty in the clean, straight lines of practical construction and efficient machinery. The resulting buildings, fashioned according to what was soon called the "international style," were typically symmetrical rectangles made of concrete, glass, and steel.

In Europe, architectural leadership centered in German-speaking countries until Hitler took power in 1933. In 1911 twenty-eight-year-old Walter Gropius (1883–1969) broke sharply with the past in his design of the Fagus shoe factory at Alfeld, Germany — a clean, light, elegant building of glass and iron. In 1919 Gropius merged the schools of fine and applied arts at Weimar into a single interdisciplinary school, the **Bauhaus**. The Bauhaus brought together many leading modern architects, designers, and theatrical innovators. Working as an effective, inspired team, they combined the study of fine art, including painting and sculpture, with the study of applied art in the crafts of printing, weaving, and furniture making. Throughout the 1920s the Bauhaus, with its stress on functionalism and quality design for everyday goods, attracted enthusiastic students from all over the world.

Another leading modern architect, Ludwig Mies van der Rohe (1886–1969), followed Gropius as director of the Bauhaus in 1930. Like many modernist intellectuals, he emigrated to the United States to escape the repressive Nazi regime. His classic steel-frame and glass-wall Lake Shore Apartments in Chicago, built between 1948 and 1951, epitomized the spread and triumph of the modernist international style in the great building boom that followed the Second World War.

New Artistic Movements

In the decades surrounding the First World War, the visual arts also experienced radical change and experimentation. For the last several centuries, artists had tried to produce accurate representations of reality. Now a new artistic avant-garde emerged to challenge that practice. From impressionism and expressionism to Dadaism and surrealism, a sometimes bewildering array of artistic movements followed one after another. Modern painting and sculpture became increasingly abstract as artists turned their backs on figurative representation and began to break down form into its constituent parts: lines, shapes, and colors.

Berlin, Munich, Moscow, Vienna, New York, and especially Paris became famous for their radical artistic undergrounds. Commercial art galleries and exhibition halls exhibited the new work, and schools and institutions, such as the Bauhaus, emerged to train a generation in modern techniques. Young artists flocked to these cultural centers to participate in the new movements, earn a living making art, and perhaps change the world with their revolutionary ideas.

One of the earliest modernist movements was impressionism, which blossomed in Paris in the 1870s. French artists such as Claude Monet (1840–1926) and Edgar Degas (1834–1917) and the American Mary Cassatt (1844–1926), who settled in Paris in 1875, tried to portray their sensory "impressions" in their work. Impressionists looked to the world around them for subject matter, turning their backs on traditional themes such as battles, religious scenes, and wealthy elites. Monet's colorful and atmospheric paintings of farmland haystacks and Degas's many pastel drawings of ballerinas exemplify the way impressionists moved toward abstraction. Capturing a fleeting moment of color and light, in often blurry and quickly painted images, was far more important than making a heavily detailed, precise rendering of an actual object.

In the next decades an astonishing array of new artistic movements emerged one after another. Postimpressionists and expressionists, such as Vincent van Gogh (1853–1890), built on impressionist motifs of color and light but added a deep psychological element to their pictures, reflecting the attempt to search within the self and reveal (or "express") deep inner feelings on the canvas.

After 1900 avant-garde artists increasingly challenged the art world status quo. In Paris in 1907 painter Pablo Picasso (1881–1973), along with other artists, established cubism—a highly analytical approach to art concentrated on a complex geometry of zigzagging lines and sharply angled overlapping planes that exemplified the ongoing trend toward abstract, nonrepresentational art. In 1909 Italian Filippo Tommaso Marinetti (1876–1944) announced the founding of futurism, a radical art and literary movement determined to transform the mentality of an anachronistic society. According to Marinetti, traditional culture could not deal with the advances of modern technology—automobiles, radios, telephones, phonographs, ocean liners, airplanes, the cinema, the newspaper—and the way these had changed human consciousness. Marinetti embraced the future and cast away the past, calling for radically new art forms that would express the modern condition.

The shock of World War I encouraged further radicalization. In 1916 a group of artists and intellectuals in exile in Zurich, Switzerland, championed a new movement they called **Dadaism**, which attacked all the familiar standards of art and delighted in outrageous behavior. The war had shown once and for all that life was meaningless, the Dadaists argued, so art should be meaningless as well. Dadaists tried to shock their audiences with what they called "anti-art," works and public performances that were insulting and entirely nonsensical. A well-known example is a reproduction of Leonardo da Vinci's *Mona Lisa* in which the masterpiece is ridiculed with the addition of a hand-drawn mustache and an obscene inscription. Like futurists, Dadaists embraced the modern age and grappled with the horrors of modern war. "Art in its execution and direction is dependent on the time in which it lives, and artists are creatures of their epoch," wrote Richard Huelsenbeck (1892–1974), one of the movement's founders. "The highest art will be that which in its conscious content presents the thousandfold problems of the day, the art which has been visibly shattered by the explosions of last week, which is forever trying to collect its limbs after yesterday's crash."[4] After the war, Dadaism became an international movement, spreading to Paris, New York, and particularly Berlin in the early 1920s.

During the mid-1920s some Dadaists were attracted to surrealism. Surrealists such as Salvador Dalí (1904–1989) were deeply influenced by Freudian psychology and portrayed images of the unconscious in their art. They painted fantastic worlds of wild dreams and uncomfortable symbols, where watches melted and giant metronomes beat time in precisely drawn but impossible alien landscapes.

Many modern artists sincerely believed that art had a radical mission. By calling attention to the bankruptcy of mainstream society, they believed, art had the power to change the world. The sometimes-nonsensical manifestos written by members of the Dadaist, futurist, and surrealist movements were meant to spread their ideas, challenge conventional assumptions of all kinds, and foment radical social change.

By the 1920s art and culture had become increasingly politicized. Many avant-garde artists sided with the far left; some became committed Communists. Such artists and art movements had a difficult time surviving the political crises of the 1930s. Between 1933 and 1945, when the National Socialist (Nazi) Party came to power in Germany and brought a second world war to the European continent, hundreds of artists and intellectuals fled to the United States to escape the war and the repressive Nazi state. After World War II, New York greatly benefited from this transfusion of talent and replaced Paris and Berlin as the global capital of modern art.

Twentieth-Century Literature

In the decades that followed the First World War, Western literature was deeply influenced by the general intellectual climate of pessimism and alienation and the turn toward radical experimentation sweeping through the other arts. The great nineteenth-century novelists had typically written as all-knowing narrators, describing realistic characters and their relationships to an understandable, if sometimes harsh, society (see Chapter 22). Modernist writers now developed new techniques to express new realities. In the twentieth century many authors adopted the limited, often confused viewpoint of a single individual. Like Freud, they focused their attention on the complexity and irrationality of the human mind, where feelings, memories, and desires are forever scrambled. French novelist Marcel Proust (1871–1922), in his semi-autobiographical *Remembrance of Things Past* (1913–1927), recalled bittersweet memories of childhood and youthful love and tried to discover their innermost meaning. To do so, Proust lived like a hermit in a soundproof Paris apartment for ten years, withdrawing from the present to dwell on the past.

Some novelists used the **stream-of-consciousness technique**, relying on internal monologues to explore the human psyche. In *Jacob's Room* (1922), the English author Virginia Woolf (1882–1941) created a novel made up of a series of such monologues in which she tried to capture the inner voice in prose. In this and other stories, Woolf portrayed characters whose ideas and emotions from different periods of their lives bubble up as randomly as from a patient on a psychoanalyst's couch. William Faulkner (1897–1962), one of America's greatest novelists, used the same technique in *The Sound and the Fury* (1929), with much of its intense drama confusedly seen through the eyes of a man who is mentally disabled.

The most famous and perhaps most experimental stream-of-consciousness novel is *Ulysses* (1922) by Irish novelist James Joyce (1882–1941). Into an account of a single day in the life of an ordinary man, Joyce weaves an extended ironic parallel between the aimless wanderings of his hero through the streets and pubs of Dublin and the adventures of Homer's hero Ulysses on his way home from Troy. *Ulysses* was surely one of the most disturbing novels of its generation. Abandoning any sense of a conventional plot; breaking rules of grammar; and blending foreign words, puns, bits of knowledge, and scraps of memory together in bewildering confusion, *Ulysses* is intended to mirror modern life: a gigantic riddle impossible to unravel. Since Joyce included frank descriptions of the main character's sexual thoughts and encounters, the novel was considered obscene in Great Britain and the United States and was banned there until the early 1930s.

As creative writers turned their attention from society to the individual and from realism to psychological relativity, they rejected the idea of progress. Some described "anti-utopias," nightmare visions of things to come, as in the T. S. Eliot (1888–1965) poem *The Waste Land* (1922), which depicts a world of growing desolation:

> April is the cruelest month, breeding
> Lilacs out of the dead land, mixing
> Memory and desire, stirring
> Dull roots with spring rain.
> . . .
> What are the roots that clutch, what branches grow
> Out of this stony rubbish? Son of man,
> You cannot say, or guess, for you know only
> A heap of broken images, where the sun beats,
> And the dead tree gives no shelter, the cricket no relief,
> And the dry stone no sound of water.[5]

With its biblical references, images of a ruined and wasted natural world, and general human incomprehension, Eliot's poem expressed the widespread despair that followed the First World War. The Czech writer Franz Kafka (1883–1924) likewise portrayed an incomprehensible, alienating world. Kafka's novels *The Trial* (1925) and *The Castle* (1926) are stories about helpless individuals crushed by inexplicably hostile forces, as is his famous novella *The Metamorphosis* (1915), in which the main character turns into a giant insect. The German-Jewish Kafka died young, at forty-one, and was spared the horror of seeing the world of his nightmares materialize in the Nazi state. In these and many other works, authors between the wars used new literary techniques and dark imagery to capture the anxiety of the age.

Modern Music

Developments in modern music paralleled those in painting and fiction. Composers and performers expressed the emotional intensity and shock of the age in radically experimental forms. The ballet *The Rite of Spring* by Russian composer Igor Stravinsky (1882–1971), for example, practically caused a riot when it was first performed in Paris in 1913. The combination of pulsating rhythms and dissonant sounds from the orchestra pit with earthy representations of lovemaking by the strangely dressed dancers on the stage shocked audiences accustomed to traditional ballet.

Musical Modernism   Dancers in Russian composer Igor Stravinsky's avant-garde opera *The Rite of Spring* perform at the Paris premiere. The dissonant music, wild sets and costumes, and unpredictable dance movements shocked and insulted the audience, which rioted on the opening night in May 1913. (© Lebrecht/The Image Works)

After the First World War, when irrationality and violence had seemed to pervade human experience, modernism flourished in opera and ballet. One of the most powerful examples was the opera *Wozzeck*, by Alban Berg (1885–1935), first performed in Berlin in 1925. Blending a half-sung, half-spoken kind of dialogue with harsh, atonal music, *Wozzeck* is a gruesome tale of a soldier driven by Kafka-like inner terrors and vague suspicions of infidelity to murder his mistress.

Some composers turned their backs on long-established musical conventions. Just as abstract painters arranged lines and color but did not draw identifiable objects, so modern composers arranged sounds without creating recognizable harmonies. Led by Viennese composer Arnold Schönberg (SHUHN-buhrg) (1874–1951), they abandoned traditional harmony and tonality. The musical notes in a given piece were no longer united and organized by a key; instead they were independent and unrelated. Schönberg's twelve-tone music of the 1920s arranged all twelve notes of the scale in an abstract mathematical pattern, or "tone row." This pattern sounded like no pattern at all to the ordinary listener and could be detected only by a highly trained eye studying the musical score. Accustomed to the harmonies of classical and romantic music, audiences generally resisted atonal music. Only after the Second World War did it begin to win acceptance.

An Emerging Consumer Society

How did consumer society change everyday life?

Fundamental innovations in the basic provision and consumption of goods and services accompanied the radical transformation of artistic and intellectual life. After the First World War, modern business forms of credit, retail, and advertising helped sell increasing numbers of mass-produced goods—the products of a highly industrialized factory system—to ever-larger numbers of people. With the arrival of cinema and radio, commercial entertainment increasingly dominated the leisure time of ordinary people. The consumer revolution had roots in the prosperous decades before World War I and would not be fully consolidated until the 1950s and 1960s. Yet in the interwar years the outlines of a modern consumer society emerged with startling clarity.

Mass Culture

The emerging consumer society of the 1920s is a good example of the way technological developments can lead to widespread social change. The arrival of a highly industrialized manufacturing system dedicated to mass-producing inexpensive goods, the establishment of efficient transportation systems that could bring these goods to national markets, and the rise of professional advertising experts to sell them were all part of a revolution in the way consumer goods were made, marketed, and used by ordinary people.

Contemporaries viewed the new mass culture as a distinctly modern aspect of everyday life. It seemed that consumer goods themselves were modernizing society by changing so many ingrained habits. Some people embraced the new ways; others worried that these changes threatened familiar values and precious traditions.

Critics had good reason to worry. Mass-produced goods had a profound impact on the lives of ordinary people. Housework and private life were increasingly organized around an array of modern appliances, from telephones and radios to electric ovens, washing machines, and refrigerators. The aggressive marketing of fashionable clothing and personal care products, such as shampoo, perfume, and makeup, encouraged a cult of youthful "sex appeal"; individual attractiveness was increasingly determined by the use of brand-name products. The mass production and marketing of automobiles and the rise of tourist agencies opened roads to increased mobility and travel.

Commercialized mass entertainment likewise prospered and began to dominate the way people spent their leisure time. Movies and radio thrilled millions. Professional sporting events drew throngs of fans. Thriving print media brought readers an astounding variety of newspapers, inexpensive books, and glossy illustrated magazines. Flashy restaurants, theatrical revues, and nightclubs competed for evening customers.

Department stores epitomized the emergence of consumer society. Already well established across Europe and the United States by the 1890s, by the 1920s they had become veritable temples of commerce. The typical store sold an enticing variety of goods, including clothing, magazines, housewares, food, and spirits. Larger stores included travel bureaus, movie theaters, and refreshment stands. Aggressive advertising campaigns, youthful and attractive salespeople, and easy credit and return policies helped attract customers in droves.

The emergence of modern consumer culture both undermined and reinforced existing social differences. On one hand, consumerism helped democratize Western society. Since everyone with the means could purchase any good, mass culture helped break down old social barriers based on class, region, and religion. Yet it also reinforced social differences. Manufacturers soon realized they could profit by marketing goods to specific groups. Catholics, for example, could purchase their own popular literature and inexpensive devotional items, and young people eagerly bought the latest fashions

The New Woman   Images of the new woman appeared in movies, illustrated magazines, and advertisements, such as this German poster selling "this winter's perfume." (Lordprice Collection/Alamy)

marketed directly to them. The expense of many items meant that only the wealthy could purchase them. Automobiles and, in the 1920s, even vacuum cleaners cost so much that ownership became a status symbol.

The changes in women's lives were particularly striking. The new household items transformed how women performed housework. Advice literature of all kinds encouraged housewives to rush out and buy the latest appliances so they could "modernize" the home. Consumer culture brought growing public visibility to women, especially the young. Girls and young women worked behind the counters and shopped in the aisles of department stores, and they went out on the street alone in ways unthinkable in the nineteenth century. Contemporaries spoke repeatedly about the arrival of the **"modern girl,"** a surprisingly independent female who could vote and held a job, spent her salary on the latest fashions, applied makeup and smoked cigarettes, and used her sex appeal to charm any number of young men. The modern girl had precedents in the assertive, athletic, and more independent "new woman" of the 1890s, but she became a dominant global figure in the 1920s. "The woman of yesterday," wrote one German feminist in 1929, yearned for marriage and children and "honor[ed] the achievements of the 'good old days.'" The "woman of today," she continued, "refuses to be regarded as a physically weak being . . . and seeks to support herself through gainful employment. . . . Her task is to clear the way for equal rights for women in all areas of life."[6]

Despite such enthusiasm, the modern girl was in some ways a stereotype, a product of marketing campaigns dedicated to selling goods to the masses. Few young women could afford to live up to this image, even if they did have jobs. Yet the changes associated with the First World War (see Chapter 25) and the emergence of consumer society did loosen traditional limits on women's behavior.

The emerging consumer culture generated a chorus of complaint from cultural critics of all stripes. On the left, socialist writers worried that its appeal undermined working-class radicalism, creating passive consumers rather than active class-conscious revolutionaries. On the right, conservatives complained that money spent on mass-produced goods sapped the livelihood of industrious artisans and undermined proud national traditions. Religious leaders protested that modern consumerism encouraged rampant individualism and that greedy materialism was replacing spirituality. Others bemoaned the supposedly loose morals of the modern girl and fretted over the decline of traditional family values.

Despite such criticism—which continued after World War II—consumer society was here to stay. Ordinary people enjoyed the pleasures of mass consumption, and individual identities were tied ever more closely to modern mass-produced goods. Yet the Great Depression of 1929 (see page 892) soon made actual participation in the new world of goods elusive. The promise of prosperity would only truly be realized during the economic boom that followed the Second World War.

The Appeal of Cinema

Nowhere was the influence of mass culture more evident than in the rapid growth of commercial entertainment, especially cinema and radio. Both became major industries in the interwar years, and an eager public enthusiastically embraced them, spending their hard-earned money and their leisure hours watching movies or listening to radio broadcasts. These mass media overshadowed and began to replace the traditional arts and amusements of people in villages and small towns, changing familiar ways of life.

Cinema first emerged in the United States around 1880, driven in part by the inventions of Thomas Edison. By 1910 American directors and business people had set up "movie factories," at first in the New York area and then in Los Angeles. Europeans were quick to follow. By 1914 small production companies had formed in Great Britain, France, Germany, and Italy, among others. World War I quickened the pace. National leaders realized that movies offered distraction to troops and citizens and served as an effective means of spreading propaganda. Audiences lined up to see *The Battle of the Somme*, a British film released in August 1916 that was frankly intended to encourage popular support for the war. For the audience, watching this early example of cinematic propaganda could be heart wrenching. "The tears in many people's eyes and the silence that prevailed when I saw the film showed that every heart was full of love and sympathy for our soldiers," wrote one viewer to the *London Times* that September.[7]

Cinema became a true mass medium in the 1920s, the golden age of silent film. The United States was again a world leader, but European nations also established important national studios. Germany's Universal Film Company (or UFA) was particularly renowned. In the massive Babelsberg Studios just outside Berlin, talented UFA directors produced classic expressionist films such as *Nosferatu* (1922), a creepy vampire story, and *Metropolis* (1927), about a future society in the midst of a working-class revolt. Such films made use of cutting-edge production techniques, thrilling audiences with fast and slow motion, montage sequences, unsettling close-ups, and unusual dissolves.

Film making became big business on an international scale. Studios competed to place their movies on foreign screens, and European theater owners were sometimes forced to book whole blocks of American films to get the few pictures they really wanted. In response, European governments set quotas on the number of U.S. films they imported. By 1926 U.S. money was drawing German directors and stars to Hollywood and consolidating America's international domination. These practices put European producers at a disadvantage until "talkies" permitted a revival of national film industries in the 1930s, particularly in France.

Motion pictures would remain the central entertainment of the masses until after the Second World War. People flocked to the gigantic movie palaces built across Europe in the mid-1920s, splendid theaters that could seat thousands. There they viewed the latest features, which were reviewed by critics in newspapers and flashy illustrated magazines. Cinema audiences grew rapidly in the 1930s. In Great Britain in the late 1930s, one in every four adults went to the movies twice a week, and two in five went at least once a week. Other countries had similar figures.

As these numbers suggest, motion pictures could be powerful tools of indoctrination, especially in countries with dictatorial regimes. Lenin encouraged the development of Soviet film making, believing that the new medium was essential to the social and ideological transformation of the country. Beginning in the mid-1920s, a series of epic films, the most famous of which were directed by Sergei Eisenstein (1898–1948), brilliantly dramatized the Communist view of Russian history. In Nazi Germany, a young and immensely talented woman film maker, Leni Riefenstahl (REE-fuhn-shtahl) (1902–2003), directed a masterpiece of documentary propaganda, *Triumph of the Will*, based on the 1934 Nazi Party rally at Nuremberg. Riefenstahl combined stunning aerial photography with mass processions of young Nazi fanatics and images of joyful crowds welcoming Adolf Hitler. Her film, released in 1935, was a brilliant yet chilling documentary of the rise of Nazism.

The Arrival of Radio

Like film, radio became a full-blown mass medium in the 1920s. Experimental radio sets were first available in the 1880s; the work of Italian inventor Guglielmo Marconi (1874–1937) around 1900 and the development of the vacuum tube in 1904 made possible primitive transmissions of speech and music. But the first major public broadcasts of news and special events occurred only in 1920, in Great Britain and the United States.

Every major country quickly established national broadcasting networks. In the United States such networks were privately owned and were financed by advertising, but in Europe the typical pattern was direct control by the government. In Great Britain, Parliament set up an independent public corporation, the British Broadcasting Corporation (BBC), supported by licensing fees. Whatever the institutional framework, radio enjoyed a meteoric growth in popularity. By the late 1930s more than three out of every four households in both democratic Great Britain and dictatorial Germany had at least one radio.

Like the movies, radio was well suited for political propaganda and manipulation. Dictators such as Hitler and Italy's Benito Mussolini controlled the airwaves and could reach enormous national audiences with their dramatic speeches. In democratic countries, politicians such as American president Franklin Roosevelt and British prime minister Stanley Baldwin effectively used informal "fireside chats" to bolster their popularity.

The Search for Peace and Political Stability

What obstacles to lasting peace did European leaders face?

As established patterns of thought and culture were further challenged and mangled by the ferocious impact of World War I, so too was the political fabric stretched and torn. The Versailles settlement had established a shaky truce, not a solid peace. After the war, leaders faced a gigantic task as they sought to create a stable international order within the general context of intellectual crisis, slow economic growth, and political turmoil.

The pursuit of real and lasting peace proved difficult for many reasons. Germany hated the Treaty of Versailles. France was fearful and isolated. Britain was undependable, and the United States turned its back on European problems. Eastern Europe was in ferment, and Communist Russia had an unpredictable future. Moreover, the international economic situation was weak and greatly complicated by war debts and disrupted patterns of trade. Yet from 1925 to late 1929, it appeared that peace and stability were within reach. When the economic collapse of the 1930s mocked these hopes and brought the rise of brutal dictators, the disillusionment of liberals in the democracies intensified.

Germany and the Western Powers

Germany was the key to lasting stability. Yet to Germans of all political parties, the Treaty of Versailles represented a harsh dictated peace, to be revised or repudiated as soon as possible. Germany still had the potential to become the strongest country in Europe but remained a source of uncertainty. Moreover, with ominous implications, France and Great Britain did not see eye to eye on Germany.

Immediately after the war, the French wanted to stress the harsh elements in the Treaty of Versailles. Most of the war in the west had been fought on French soil, and the expected costs of reconstruction, as well as of repaying war debts to the United States, were staggering. Thus French politicians believed that massive reparations from Germany were vital for economic recovery. After having compromised with President Wilson only to be betrayed by America's failure to ratify the treaty, many French leaders saw strict implementation of all provisions of the Treaty of Versailles as France's last best hope. Large reparation payments could hold Germany down indefinitely, ensuring French security.

The British soon felt differently. Before the war Germany had been Great Britain's second-best market in the world; after the war a healthy, prosperous Germany appeared to be essential to the British economy. Many Brits agreed with the analysis of the English economist John Maynard Keynes (1883–1946), who eloquently denounced the Treaty of Versailles in his book *The Economic Consequences of the Peace* (1919). According to Keynes, astronomical reparations and harsh economic measures would impoverish Germany, encourage Bolshevism, and increase economic hardship in all countries. Only a complete revision of the treaty could save Germany—and Europe. Keynes's attack engendered much public discussion and became very influential. It created sympathy for Germany in the English-speaking world, which often paralyzed English and American leaders in their relations with Germany over the next two decades. (See "Primary Source: Keynes on German Reparations After World War I," page 886.)

British politicians were also suspicious of both France's army—the largest in Europe, and authorized at Versailles to occupy the German Rhineland until 1935—and France's expansive foreign policy. Since 1890 France had looked to Russia as a powerful ally against Germany. But with Russia hostile and Communist, and with Britain and the United States unwilling to make any firm commitments, France turned to the newly formed states of central Europe for diplomatic support. In 1921 France signed a mutual defense pact with Poland and associated itself closely with the so-called Little Entente, an alliance that joined Czechoslovakia, Romania, and Yugoslavia against defeated and bitter Hungary.

PRIMARY SOURCE   Keynes on German Reparations After World War I

Dismayed by the harsh reparations forced on Germany at the Versailles peace conference and their potential to create social and political mayhem, noted economist John Maynard Keynes issued an impassioned plea for a more moderate road to postwar recovery in his 1919 book, The Economic Consequences of the Peace, *excerpted below.*

The essential facts of the situation, as I see them, are expressed simply. Europe consists of the densest aggregation of population in the history of the world. This population is accustomed to a relatively high standard of life, in which, even now, some sections of it anticipate improvement rather than deterioration. In relation to other continents Europe is not self-sufficient; in particular it cannot feed itself. Internally the population is not evenly distributed, but much of it is crowded into a relatively small number of dense industrial centers. This population secured for itself a livelihood before the war, without much margin of surplus, by means of a delicate and immensely complicated organization, of which the foundations were supported by coal, iron, transport, and an unbroken supply of imported food and raw materials from other continents. By the destruction of this organization and the interruption of the stream of supplies, a part of this population is deprived of its means of livelihood. . . . The danger confronting us, therefore, is the rapid depression of the standard of life of the European populations to a point which will mean actual starvation for some (a point already reached in Russia and approximately reached in Austria). Men will not always die quietly. For starvation, which brings to some lethargy and a helpless despair, drives other temperaments to the nervous instability of hysteria and to a mad despair. And these in their distress may overturn the remnants of organization, and submerge civilization itself in their attempts to satisfy desperately the overwhelming needs of the individual. This is the danger against which all our resources and courage and idealism must now co-operate. . . .

I cannot leave this subject as though its just treatment wholly depended either on our own pledges or on economic facts. The policy of reducing Germany to servitude for a generation, of degrading the lives of millions of human beings, and of depriving a whole nation of happiness should be abhorrent and detestable,— abhorrent and detestable, even if it were possible, even if it enriched ourselves, even if it did not sow the decay of the whole civilized life of Europe. Some preach it in the name of Justice. In the great events of man's history, in the unwinding of the complex fates of nations Justice is not so simple. And if it were, nations are not authorized, by religion or by natural morals, to visit on the children of their enemies the misdoings of parents or of rulers.

EVALUATE THE EVIDENCE

1. What evidence does Keynes use to support his argument that reparations should be reduced? Why does he connect social despair to political turmoil?

2. What, according to Keynes, has undermined the optimism expressed in Woodrow Wilson's Fourteen Points and by diplomats at the Versailles peace conference?

Source: John Maynard Keynes, *The Economic Consequences of the Peace* (New York: Harcourt, Brace, and Howe, 1920), pp. 225, 227–228.

"German Women Protest the Colored Occupation on the Rhine" In 1923 the French army occupied the industrial district of the Ruhr in Germany in an effort to force reparations payments. The occupying forces included colonial troops from West Africa, and Germans responded with a racist propaganda campaign that cast the West African soldiers as uncivilized savages. (Stiftung Deutsches Historiches Museum, Berlin, P62/1483.2)

While French and British leaders drifted in different directions, the Allied commission created to determine German reparations completed its work. In April 1921 it announced that Germany had to pay the enormous sum of 132 billion gold marks ($33 billion) in annual installments of 2.5 billion gold marks. Facing possible occupation of more of its territory, the young German republic—generally known as the Weimar Republic—made its first payment in 1921. Then in 1922, wracked by rapid inflation and political assassinations and motivated by hostility and arrogance as well, the Weimar Republic announced its inability to pay more. It proposed a moratorium on reparations for three years, with the clear implication that thereafter reparations would be either drastically reduced or eliminated entirely.

The British were willing to accept a moratorium, but the French were not. Led by their tough-minded prime minister, Raymond Poincaré (1860–1934), they decided they had to either call Germany's bluff or see the entire peace settlement dissolve to France's great disadvantage. If the Germans refused to pay reparations, France would use occupation to paralyze Germany and force it to accept the Treaty of Versailles. So, despite strong British protests, in early January 1923 French and Belgian armies moved out of the Rhineland and began to occupy the Ruhr district, the heartland of industrial Germany, creating the most serious international crisis of the 1920s.

Strengthened by a wave of German patriotism, the German government ordered the people of the Ruhr to stop working and offer passive resistance to the occupation. The coal mines and steel mills of the Ruhr fell silent, leaving 10 percent of Germany's population out of work. The French responded by sealing off the Ruhr and the Rhineland from the rest of Germany, letting in only enough food to prevent starvation. German opinion was incensed when the French sent over forty thousand colonial troops from North and West Africa to control the territory. German propagandists labeled these troops the "black shame," warning that the African soldiers were savages, eager to brutalize civilians and assault German women. These racist accounts, though entirely unfounded, nonetheless intensified tensions.

By the summer of 1923 France and Germany were engaged in a great test of wills. French armies could not collect reparations from striking workers at gunpoint, but the

INDIVIDUALS IN SOCIETY • **Gustav Stresemann**

German foreign minister Gustav Stresemann is a controversial historical figure. Hailed in the 1920s as a hero of peace, he was denounced as a traitor by radical German nationalists and Hitler's Nazis. After World War II, revisionist historians stressed Stresemann's persistent nationalism and cast doubt on his peaceful intentions. Weimar Germany's most renowned leader is a fascinating example of the restless quest for convincing historical interpretation.

Stresemann's origins were modest. His parents were Berlin innkeepers and beer retailers, and of their five children only Gustav attended high school. Attracted first to literature and history, Stresemann later turned to economics, earned a doctoral degree, and quickly reached the top as a manager and director of German trade associations. A highly intelligent extrovert with a knack for negotiation, Stresemann became a deputy in the German Reichstag (parliament) in 1907 as a business-oriented liberal and nationalist. When World War I erupted, he believed, like most Germans, that Germany had acted defensively and was not at fault. A strident nationalist, he urged German annexation of conquered foreign territories. Germany's collapse in defeat and revolution devastated Stresemann. He seemed a prime candidate to join the hateful extremism of the far right.

Yet although Stresemann opposed the Treaty of Versailles as unjust and unrealistic, he turned toward the center. He accepted the new Weimar Republic and played a growing role in the Reichstag as the leader of his own small pro-business party. His hour came when French and Belgian troops occupied the Ruhr. Named chancellor in August 1923, he called off passive resistance and began talks with the French. His government also quelled Communist uprisings; put down rebellions in Bavaria, including Hitler's attempted coup; and ended runaway inflation with the introduction of a new currency. Stresemann fought to preserve German unity, and he succeeded.

Voted out as chancellor in November 1923, Stresemann remained as foreign minister in every German government until his death in 1929. Proclaiming a policy of peace and agreeing to pay reparations, he achieved his greatest triumph in the Locarno agreements of 1925 (see page 890). But these agreements did not lead the French to make any further concessions that might have disarmed Germany's extremists. Stresemann made little additional progress in achieving international reconciliation and true sovereignty for Germany. His premature death in office was a

occupation was paralyzing Germany and its economy. To support the striking workers and their employers, the German government began to print money to pay its bills, causing runaway inflation. Prices soared as German money rapidly lost all value. People went to the store with bags of banknotes; they returned home with handfuls of groceries. Catastrophic inflation cruelly mocked the old middle-class virtues of thrift, caution, and self-reliance as savings were wiped out. Many Germans felt betrayed. They hated and blamed the Western governments, their own government, big business, the Jews, the workers, and the Communists for their misfortune. Right-wing nationalists—including Adolf Hitler and the newly established National Socialist, or Nazi, Party—eagerly capitalized on the widespread discontent.

serious blow to German pragmatism, encouraging the turn to a more aggressive and nationalist foreign policy.

Stresemann was no fuzzy pacifist. Historians debunking his legend are right in seeing an enduring nationalism in his defense of German interests. But Stresemann, like his French counterpart Aristide Briand, was a statesman of goodwill who wanted peace through mutually advantageous compromise. A realist trained by business and politics in the art of the possible, Stresemann perceived that Germany had to be a satisfied and equal partner for peace to be secure. His un-willingness to guarantee Germany's eastern borders (see Map 25.3, page 858), which is often criticized as contributing to the coming of the Second World War, reflected his conviction that keeping some Germans under Polish and Czecho-sloakian rule created a ticking time bomb in Europe. Stresemann was also con-vinced that war on Poland would almost certainly re-create the Allied coalition that had crushed Germany in 1918.* The mighty coalition that formed after Hitler's 1939 invasion of Poland proved this view prophetic.

QUESTIONS FOR ANALYSIS

1. What did Gustav Stresemann do to promote reconciliation in Europe? How did his policy toward France differ from that toward Poland and Czechoslovakia?

2. What is your interpretation of Stresemann? Does he arouse your sympathy or your suspicion and hostility? Why?

*Robert Grathwol, "Stresemann: Reflections on His Foreign Policy," *Journal of Modern History* 45 (March 1973): 52–70.

ONLINE DOCUMENT ASSIGNMENT

What were some of the challenges leaders like Stresemann faced in building political consensus in Weimar Germany? Examine documents that illuminate the competing visions of major Wei-mar political parties during the 1920s. Then complete a writing assignment based on the evidence and details from this chapter.

bedfordstmartins.com/mckaywestvalue

In August 1923, as the mark lost value and unrest spread throughout Germany, Gustav Stresemann (GOOS-tahf SHTRAY-zuh-mahn) (1878–1929) assumed leadership of the government. Stresemann tried compromise. He called off passive resistance in the Ruhr and in October agreed in principle to pay reparations, but asked for a re-examination of Germany's ability to pay. Poincaré accepted. His hard line had become unpopular in France, and it was hated in Britain and the United States. (See "Individu-als in Society: Gustav Stresemann," above.) In addition, power in both Germany and France was passing to more moderate leaders who realized that continued confrontation was a destructive, no-win situation. Thus, after five long years of hostility and tension, culminating in a kind of undeclared war in the Ruhr in 1923, Germany and France both decided to try compromise. The British, and even the Americans, were willing to help. The first step was to reach an agreement on the reparations question.

Hope in Foreign Affairs

In 1924 an international committee of financial experts headed by American banker Charles G. Dawes met to re-examine reparations from a broad perspective. The resulting **Dawes Plan** (1924) was accepted by France, Germany, and Britain. Germany's yearly reparations were reduced and linked to the level of German economic output. Germany would also receive large loans from the United States to promote economic recovery. In short, Germany would get private loans from the United States in order to pay reparations to France and Britain, thus enabling those countries to repay the large war debts they owed the United States.

This circular flow of international payments was complicated and risky, but for a while it worked. With continual inflows of American capital, the German republic experienced a shaky economic recovery. Germany paid about $1.3 billion in reparations in 1927 and 1928, enabling France and Britain to repay the United States. In this way the Americans belatedly played a part in the general economic settlement that, though far from ideal, facilitated a worldwide recovery in the late 1920s.

A political settlement accompanied the economic accords. In 1925 the leaders of Europe signed a number of agreements at Locarno, Switzerland. Germany and France solemnly pledged to accept their common border, and both Britain and Italy agreed to fight either France or Germany if one invaded the other. Stresemann reluctantly agreed to settle boundary disputes with Poland and Czechoslovakia by peaceful means, although he did not agree to permanent borders to Germany's east. In response, France reaffirmed its pledge of military aid to those countries if Germany attacked them. The refusal to settle Germany's eastern borders angered the Poles, and though the "spirit of Locarno" lent some hope to those seeking international stability, political tensions deepened in central Europe.

Other developments suggested possibilities for international peace. In 1926 Germany joined the League of Nations, and in 1928 fifteen countries signed the Kellogg-Briand Pact, initiated by French prime minister Aristide Briand and U.S. secretary of state Frank B. Kellogg. The signing states agreed to "renounce [war] as an instrument of international policy" and to settle international disputes peacefully. The pact made no provisions for action in case war actually occurred and could not prevent the arrival of the Second World War in 1939. In the late 1920s, however, it fostered a cautious optimism and encouraged the hope that the United States would accept its responsibilities as a great world power by contributing to European stability.

Hope in Democratic Government

Domestic politics also offered reason to hope. During the occupation of the Ruhr and the great inflation, republican government in Germany had appeared on the verge of collapse. In 1923 Communists momentarily entered provincial governments, and in November an obscure politician named Adolf Hitler leaped onto a table in a beer hall in Munich and proclaimed a "national socialist revolution." But the young republican government easily crushed Hitler's plot to seize control, and he was sentenced to prison. In the late 1920s liberal democracy seemed to take root in Weimar Germany. Elections were held regularly, and republican democracy appeared to have growing support among a majority of Germans. A new currency was established, and the economy stabilized. The moderate businessmen who tended to dominate the various German coalition governments were convinced that economic prosperity demanded good relations with the Western powers, and they supported parliamentary government at home.

Sharp political divisions remained, however. Throughout the 1920s Hitler's Nazi Party attracted support from fanatical anti-Semites, ultranationalists, and disgruntled ex-servicemen. Many unrepentant nationalists and monarchists populated the right and the army. On the left, members of Germany's recently formed Communist Party were noisy and active. The Communists, directed from Moscow, reserved their greatest hatred and sharpest barbs for their cousins the Social Democrats, whom they accused of betraying the revolution. Though the working class was divided, a majority supported the nonrevolutionary Social Democrats.

The situation in France was similar to that in Germany. Communists and Socialists battled for workers' support. After 1924 the democratically elected government rested mainly in the hands of coalitions of moderates, with business interests well represented. France's great accomplishment was the rapid rebuilding of its war-torn northeastern region. The expense of this undertaking led, however, to a large deficit and substantial inflation. By early 1926 the franc had fallen to 10 percent of its prewar value, causing a severe crisis. Poincaré was recalled to office, while Briand remained minister for foreign affairs. Poincaré slashed spending and raised taxes, restoring confidence in the economy. The franc was stabilized at about one-fifth of its prewar value, and the economy remained fairly stable until 1930.

Britain, too, faced challenges after 1920. The great problem was unemployment. In June 1921 almost 2.2 million people—23 percent of the labor force—were out of work, and throughout the 1920s unemployment hovered around 12 percent, leading to a massive general strike in 1926. Yet the state provided unemployment benefits and supplemented the payments with subsidized housing, medical aid, and increased old-age pensions. These and other measures kept living standards from seriously declining, helped moderate class tensions, and pointed the way toward the welfare state Britain would establish after World War II.

Relative social harmony was accompanied by the rise of the Labour Party as a determined champion of the working class and of greater social equality. Committed to the kind of moderate revisionist socialism that had emerged before World War I (see Chapter 23), the Labour Party replaced the Liberal Party as the main opposition to the Conservatives. This shift reflected the decline of old liberal ideals of competitive capitalism, limited government control, and individual responsibility. In 1924 and from 1929 to 1931, the Labour Party under Ramsay MacDonald (1866–1937) governed the country with the support of the smaller Liberal Party. Yet Labour moved toward socialism gradually and democratically, so as not to antagonize the middle classes.

The British Conservatives showed the same compromising spirit on social issues. In 1922 Britain granted southern, Catholic, Ireland full autonomy after a bitter guerrilla war, thereby removing a key source of prewar friction. Despite conflicts such as the 1926 strike by hard-pressed coal miners, which led to an unsuccessful general strike, social unrest in Britain was limited in the 1920s and 1930s. Developments in both international relations and the domestic politics of the leading democracies across western Europe gave cause for optimism in the late 1920s.

The Great Depression, 1929–1939

What were the causes and consequences of the Great Depression?

This fragile optimism was short-lived. Beginning in 1929, a massive economic downturn struck the entire world with ever-greater intensity. Recovery was slow and uneven, and contemporaries labeled the economic crisis the **Great Depression**, to emphasize its severity and duration. Only with the Second World War did the depression disappear in much of the world.

The social and political consequences of the Great Depression were enormous. Mass unemployment and failing farms made insecurity and unemployment a reality for millions of people (Map 26.1). In Europe and the United States, governments instituted a variety of social welfare programs intended to manage the crisis. Yet the prolonged economic collapse shattered the fragile political stability of the mid-1920s and encouraged the growth of extremists on both ends of the political spectrum. Democratic government faltered, and authoritarian Fascist parties gained power across Europe.

The Economic Crisis

Though economic activity was already declining moderately in many countries by early 1929, the crash of the stock market in the United States in October of that year initiated a worldwide crisis. The American economy had prospered in the late 1920s, but there were large inequalities in income and a serious imbalance between actual business investment and stock market speculation. Thus net investment—in factories, farms, equipment, and the like—actually fell from $3.5 billion in 1925 to $3.2 billion in 1929. In the same years, as money flooded into stocks, the value of shares traded on the exchanges soared from $27 billion to $87 billion. Such inflated prices should have raised serious concerns about economic solvency, but even experts failed to predict the looming collapse.

This stock market boom—or "bubble" in today's language—was built on borrowed money. Many wealthy investors, speculators, and people of modest means bought stocks by paying only a small fraction of the total purchase price and borrowing the remainder from their stockbrokers. Such buying "on margin" was extremely dangerous. When prices started falling in 1929, the hard-pressed margin buyers either had to put up more money, which was often impossible, or sell their shares to pay off their brokers. Thousands of people started selling all at once. The result was a financial panic. Countless investors and speculators were wiped out in a matter of days or weeks.

The consequences were swift and severe. Stripped of wealth and confidence, battered investors and their fellow citizens started buying fewer goods. Prices fell, production began to slow down, and unemployment began to rise. Soon the entire American economy was caught in a spiraling decline.

The financial panic triggered an international financial crisis. Throughout the 1920s American bankers and investors had lent large amounts of capital to many countries. Once the panic broke, U.S. bankers began recalling the loans they had made to foreign businesses. Gold reserves began to flow rapidly out of European countries, particularly Germany and Austria, toward the United States. It became very hard for European businesses to borrow money, and panicky Europeans began to withdraw their savings

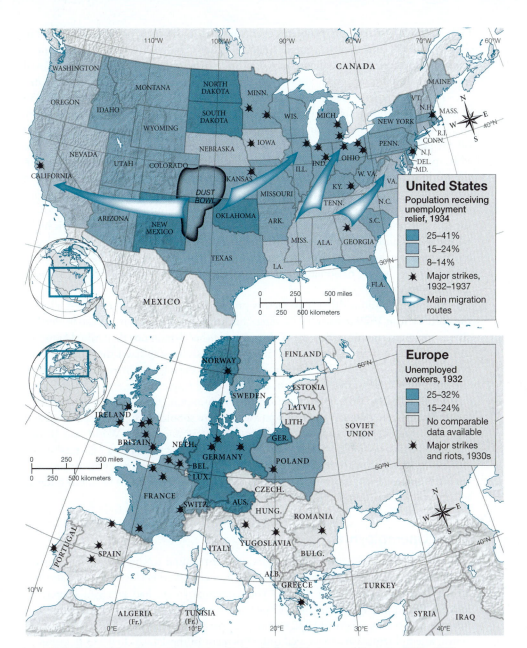

MAP 26.1   **The Great Depression in the United States and Europe, 1929–1939**
These maps show that unemployment was high almost everywhere, but that national and regional differences were also substantial.

from banks. These banking problems eventually led to the crash of the largest bank in Austria in 1931 and then to general financial chaos. The recall of loans by American bankers also accelerated a collapse in world prices when businesses dumped industrial goods and agricultural commodities in a frantic attempt to get cash to pay their loans.

The financial crisis led to a general crisis of production: between 1929 and 1933 world output of goods fell by an estimated 38 percent. As this happened, each country turned inward and tried to manage the crisis alone. In 1931, for example, Britain went off the gold standard, refusing to convert banknotes into gold, and reduced the value of its money. Britain's goal was to make its goods cheaper and therefore more salable in the world market. But more than twenty other nations, including the United States in 1934, also went off the gold standard, so few countries gained a real advantage from this step — though Britain was an exception. Similarly, country after country followed the example of the United States when in 1930 it raised protective tariffs to their highest levels ever and tried to seal off shrinking national markets for domestic producers. Such actions further limited international trade. Within this context of fragmented and destructive economic nationalism, a recovery did not begin until 1933 and it was a halting one at that.

Although opinions differ, two factors probably best explain the relentless slide to the bottom from 1929 to early 1933. First, the international economy lacked leadership able to maintain stability when the crisis came. Neither Britain nor the United States — the world's economic leaders at the time — successfully stabilized the international economic system in 1929. The American decisions to cut back on international lending and erect high tariffs, as we have seen, had damaging ripple effects.

The second factor was poor national economic policy in almost every country. Governments generally cut their budgets when they should have raised spending and accepted large deficits in order to stimulate their economies. After World War II, this "counter-cyclical policy," advocated by John Maynard Keynes, became a well-established weapon against downturn and depression. But in the 1930s Keynes's prescription was generally regarded with horror by orthodox economists who believed balanced budgets to be the key to economic growth.

Mass Unemployment

The lack of large-scale government spending contributed to the rise of mass unemployment. As the financial crisis led to production cuts, workers lost their jobs and had little money to buy goods. In Britain, where unemployment had averaged 12 percent in the 1920s, it averaged more than 18 percent between 1930 and 1935. Far worse was the case of Germany, where in 1932 one in every three workers was jobless. In the United States, unemployment had averaged only 5 percent in the 1920s. In 1933 it soared to about 30 percent: almost 13 million people were out of work (see Map 26.1).

Mass unemployment created great social problems. Poverty increased dramatically, although in most countries unemployed workers generally received some kind of meager unemployment benefits or public aid that prevented starvation. Millions of people lost their spirit, condemned to an apparently hopeless search for work. Homes and ways of life were disrupted in millions of personal tragedies. Young people postponed marriages, and birthrates fell sharply. There was an increase in suicide and mental illness. Poverty or the threat of poverty became a grinding reality. In 1932 the workers of

Manchester, England, appealed to their city officials—a typical plea echoed throughout the Western world:

> We tell you that thousands of people . . . are in desperate straits. We tell you that men, women, and children are going hungry. . . . We tell you that great numbers are being rendered distraught through the stress and worry of trying to exist without work. . . . If you do not do this—if you do not provide useful work for the unemployed—what, we ask, is your alternative? Do not imagine that this colossal tragedy of unemployment is going on endlessly without some fateful catastrophe. Hungry men are angry men.[8]

Only strong government action could deal with mass unemployment, a social powder keg preparing to explode.

The New Deal in the United States

The Great Depression and the government response to it marked a major turning point in American history. President Herbert Hoover (r. 1929–1933) and his administration initially reacted to the stock market crash and economic decline with dogged optimism but limited action. When the full force of the financial crisis struck Europe in the summer of 1931 and boomeranged back to the United States, people's worst fears became reality. Banks failed; unemployment soared. Between 1929 and 1932 industrial production fell by about 50 percent.

In these dire circumstances, Franklin Delano Roosevelt (r. 1933–1945) won a landslide presidential victory in 1932 with grand but vague promises of a "New Deal for the forgotten man." Roosevelt's goal was to reform capitalism in order to preserve it. Though Roosevelt rejected socialism and government ownership of industry, he advocated forceful government intervention in the economy and instituted a broad range of government-supported social programs designed to stimulate the economy and provide jobs.

In the United States, innovative federal programs promoted agricultural recovery, a top priority. Almost half of the American population still lived in rural areas, and the depression hit farmers hard. Roosevelt took the United States off the gold standard and devalued the dollar in an effort to raise American prices and rescue farmers. The Agricultural Adjustment Act of 1933 also aimed at raising prices—and thus farm income—by limiting agricultural production. These measures worked for a while, and in 1936 farmers repaid Roosevelt with overwhelming support in his re-election campaign.

The most ambitious attempt to control and plan the economy was the National Recovery Administration (NRA). Intended to reduce competition among industries by setting minimum prices and wages, the NRA broke with the cherished American tradition of free competition. Though participation was voluntary, the NRA aroused conflicts among business people, consumers, and bureaucrats and never worked well. The program was abandoned when declared unconstitutional by the Supreme Court in 1935.

Roosevelt and his advisers then attacked the key problem of mass unemployment. The federal government accepted the responsibility of employing as many people as financially possible. New agencies like the Works Progress Administration (WPA), set up in 1935, were created to undertake a vast range of projects. One-fifth of the entire

U.S. labor force worked for the WPA at some point in the 1930s, constructing public buildings, bridges, and highways. The WPA was enormously popular, and the opportunity of taking a government job helped check the threat of social revolution in the United States.

In 1935 the U.S. government also established a national social security system with old-age pensions and unemployment benefits. The National Labor Relations Act of 1935 gave union organizers the green light by declaring collective bargaining to be the policy of the United States. Union membership more than doubled from 4 million in 1935 to 9 million in 1940. In general, between 1935 and 1938 government rulings and social reforms chipped away at the privileges of the wealthy and tried to help ordinary people.

Programs like the WPA were part of the New Deal's fundamental commitment to use the federal government to provide relief welfare for all Americans. This commitment marked a profound shift from the traditional stress on family support and community responsibility. Embraced by a large majority in the 1930s, this shift in attitudes proved to be one of the New Deal's most enduring legacies.

Despite undeniable accomplishments in social reform, the New Deal was only partly successful in responding to the Great Depression. At the height of the recovery in May 1937, 7 million workers were still unemployed — better than the high of about 13 million in 1933 but way beyond the numbers from the 1920s. The economic situation then worsened seriously in the recession of 1937 and 1938, and unemployment had risen to a staggering 10 million when war broke out in Europe in September 1939. The New Deal never pulled the United States out of the depression; it took the Second World War to do that.

The Scandinavian Response to the Depression

Of all the Western democracies, the Scandinavian countries under Social Democratic leadership responded most successfully to the challenge of the Great Depression. Having grown steadily in the late nineteenth century, the Social Democrats became the largest political party in Sweden and then in Norway after the First World War. In the 1920s they passed important social reform legislation that benefited both peasants and workers and developed a unique kind of socialism. Flexible and nonrevolutionary, this Scandinavian socialism grew out of a strong tradition of cooperative community action. Even before 1900 Scandinavian agricultural cooperatives had shown how individual peasant families could join together for everyone's benefit. Labor leaders and capitalists were also inclined to cooperate with one another.

When the economic crisis struck in 1929, socialist governments in Scandinavia built on this pattern of cooperative social action. Sweden in particular pioneered in the use of large-scale deficits to finance public works and thereby maintain production and employment. In ways that paralleled some aspects of Roosevelt's New Deal, Scandinavian governments also increased such social welfare benefits as old-age pensions, unemployment insurance, subsidized housing, and maternity allowances. All this spending required a large bureaucracy and high taxes, first on the rich and then on practically everyone. Yet both private and cooperative enterprise thrived, as did democracy. Some observers saw Scandinavia's welfare socialism as an appealing middle way between sick capitalism and cruel communism or fascism.

OSLOFROKOSTEN

HVA DEN ER OG GIR

Oslo Breakfast   Scandinavian Social Democrats championed cooperation and practical welfare measures, playing down strident rhetoric and theories of class conflict. The "Oslo Breakfast" portrayed in this pamphlet from the mid-1930s exemplified the Scandinavian approach. It provided every schoolchild in the Norwegian capital with a good breakfast free of charge. (Courtesy, Directorate for Health and Social Affairs, Oslo)

Recovery and Reform in Britain and France

In Britain, MacDonald's Labour government and then, after 1931, the Conservative-dominated coalition government followed orthodox economic theory. The budget was balanced, spending was tightly controlled, and unemployed workers received barely enough welfare to live. Nevertheless, the economy recovered considerably after 1932. By 1937 total production was about 20 percent higher than in 1929. In fact, for Britain the years after 1932 were actually somewhat better than the 1920s had been, the opposite of the situation in the United States and France.

This good but by no means brilliant performance reflected the gradual reorientation of the British economy. After going off the gold standard in 1931 and establishing protective tariffs in 1932, Britain concentrated increasingly on the national, rather than the international, market. The old export industries of the Industrial Revolution, such as textiles and coal, continued to decline, but new industries, such as automobiles and electrical appliances, grew in response to British home demand. Moreover, low interest rates encouraged a housing boom. By the end of the decade, there were highly visible differences between the old, depressed industrial areas of the north and the new, growing areas of the south.

Because France was relatively less industrialized and thus more isolated from the world economy, the Great Depression came to it late. But once the depression hit France, it stayed and stayed. Decline was steady until 1935, and a short-lived recovery never brought production or employment back up to predepression levels. Economic stagnation both reflected and heightened an ongoing political crisis. There was no stability in government. As before 1914, the French parliament was made up of many political parties that could never cooperate for long. In 1933, for example, five coalition cabinets formed and fell in rapid succession.

The French had lost the underlying unity that had made government instability bearable before 1914, however. Fascist organizations agitated against parliamentary democracy and turned to Mussolini's Italy and Hitler's Germany for inspiration. In February 1934 French Fascists rioted and threatened to take over the republic. At the same time, the Communist Party and many workers opposed to the existing system looked to Stalin's Russia for guidance. The vital center of moderate republicanism was weakened by attacks from both sides.

Frightened by the growing strength of the Fascists at home and abroad, the Communists, Socialists, and Radicals formed an alliance — the **Popular Front** — for the national elections of May 1936. Their clear victory reflected the trend toward polarization. The number of Communists in the parliament jumped dramatically from 10 to 72, while the Socialists, led by Léon Blum, became the strongest party in France, with 146 seats. The Radicals — who were actually quite moderate — slipped badly, and the conservatives lost ground to the far right.

In the next few months, Blum's Popular Front government made the first and only real attempt to deal with the social and economic problems of the 1930s in France. Inspired by Roosevelt's New Deal, it encouraged the union movement and launched a far-reaching program of social reform, complete with paid vacations and a forty-hour workweek. Supported by workers and the lower middle class, these measures were quickly sabotaged by rapid inflation and accusations of revolution from Fascists and frightened conservatives. Wealthy people sneaked their money out of the country, labor unrest grew, and France entered a severe financial crisis. Blum was forced to announce a "breathing spell" in social reform.

Political dissension in France was encouraged by the Spanish Civil War (1936–1939), during which authoritarian Fascist rebels overthrew the democratically elected republican government. French Communists demanded that the government support the Spanish republicans, while many French conservatives would gladly have joined Hitler and Mussolini in aiding the Spanish Fascists. Extremism grew, and France itself was within sight of civil war. Blum was forced to resign in June 1937, and the Popular Front quickly collapsed. An anxious and divided France drifted aimlessly once again, preoccupied by Hitler and German rearmament.

Notes

1. P. Valéry, *Variety*, trans. M. Cowley (New York: Harcourt Brace, 1927), pp. 27–28.
2. G. Greene, *Another Mexico* (New York: Viking Press, 1939), p. 3.
3. C. E. Jeanneret-Gris (Le Corbusier), *Towards a New Architecture* (London: J. Rodker, 1931), p. 15.
4. R. Huelsenbeck, "Collective Dada Manifesto (1920)," in *The Dada Painters and Poets*, ed. Robert Motherwell and Jack D. Flam (Boston: G. K. Hall, 1981), pp. 242–246.
5. From *The Waste Land* by T. S. Eliot. Used by permission of Faber and Faber Ltd.
6. Elsa Herrmann, *This Is the New Woman* (1929), quoted in *The Weimar Republic Sourcebook*, ed. A. Kaes, M. Jay, and E. Dimendberg (Berkeley: University of California Press, 1994), pp. 206–208.
7. Quoted in R. Smither, ed., *The Battles of the Somme and Ancre* (London: Imperial War Museum, 1993), p. 67.
8. Quoted in S. B. Clough et al., eds., *Economic History of Europe: Twentieth Century* (New York: Harper & Row, 1968), pp. 243–245.

Chapter Review

MAKE IT STICK

LearningCurve
bedfordstmartins.com/mckaywestvalue

After reading the chapter, use LearningCurve to retain what you've read.

IDENTIFY KEY TERMS

Identify and explain the significance of each item below.

logical positivism (p. 871)
existentialism (p. 871)
theory of special relativity (p. 873)
id, ego, and superego (p. 874)
modernism (p. 875)
functionalism (p. 876)
Bauhaus (p. 876)

Dadaism (p. 877)
stream-of-consciousness
   technique (p. 878)
"modern girl" (p. 882)
Dawes Plan (p. 890)
Great Depression (p. 892)
Popular Front (p. 898)

REVIEW THE MAIN IDEAS

Answer the focus questions from each section of the chapter.

- How did intellectual developments reflect the general crisis in Western thought? (p. 868)
- How did modernism revolutionize Western culture? (p. 875)
- How did consumer society change everyday life? (p. 880)
- What obstacles to lasting peace did European leaders face? (p. 884)
- What were the causes and consequences of the Great Depression? (p. 892)

MAKE CONNECTIONS

Think about the larger developments and continuities within and across chapters.

1. How did trends in politics, economics, culture, and the arts and sciences come together to create a general sense of crisis in the 1920s and 1930s?
2. To what extent did the problems of the 1920s and 1930s have roots in the First World War (Chapter 25)?
3. What made modern art and intellectual thought "modern"?

ONLINE DOCUMENT ASSIGNMENT

Gustav Stresemann

What were some of the challenges leaders like Stresemann faced in building political consensus in Weimar Germany?

You encountered Gustav Stresemann's story on page 888. Keeping the question above in mind, go online and examine documents that illuminate the competing visions of major Weimar political parties during the 1920s. Then complete a writing assignment based on the evidence and details from this chapter.

bedfordstmartins.com/mckaywestvalue

CHRONOLOGY

1919	• Treaty of Versailles; Freudian psychology gains popularity; Keynes publishes *The Economic Consequences of the Peace*; Rutherford splits the atom; Bauhaus school founded
1920s	• Existentialism, Dadaism, and surrealism gain prominence
1922	• Eliot publishes *The Waste Land*; Joyce publishes *Ulysses*; Woolf publishes *Jacob's Room*; Wittgenstein writes on logical positivism
1923	• French and Belgian armies occupy the Ruhr
1924	• Dawes Plan
1925	• Berg's opera *Wozzeck* first performed; Kafka publishes *The Trial*
1926	• Germany joins the League of Nations
1927	• Heisenberg formulates the "uncertainty principle"
1928	• Kellogg-Briand Pact
1929	• Faulkner publishes *The Sound and the Fury*
1929–1939	• Great Depression
1933	• The National Socialist Party takes power in Germany
1935	• Riefenstahl's documentary film *Triumph of the Will*
1936	• Formation of Popular Front in France

27

LearningCurve
bedfordstmartins.com/mckaywestvalue
After reading the chapter, use
LearningCurve to retain what
you've read.

Dictatorships and the Second World War

1919–1945

THE INTENSE WAVE OF ARTISTIC AND CULTURAL INNOVATION IN THE
1920s and 1930s, which shook the foundations of Western thought, was paralleled by radical developments in the realm of politics. In the age of anxiety, Communist and Fascist states undertook determined assaults on democratic government and individual rights across Europe. On the eve of the Second World War, popularly elected governments survived only in Great Britain, France, Czechoslovakia, the Low Countries, Scandinavia, and Switzerland.

Totalitarian regimes in the Communist Soviet Union and Fascist Italy and Germany practiced a ruthless and dynamic tyranny. Their attempts to revolutionize state and society went far beyond traditional forms of conservative authoritarianism. Communist and Fascist states ruled with unprecedented severity. They promised to greatly improve the lives of ordinary citizens and intervened radically in those lives in pursuit of utopian schemes of social engineering. Their drive for territorial expansion threatened neighboring nations. The human costs of these policies were appalling. Millions died as Stalin forced communism on the Soviet Union in the 1930s. Attempts to build a "racially pure" New Order in Europe by Hitler's Nazi Germany led to the deaths of tens of millions more in World War II and the Holocaust, a scale of destruction far beyond that of World War I.

Such brutalities may seem a thing of the distant past that "can't happen again." Yet horrible atrocities in Rwanda, Bosnia, and Sudan show that they continue to plague the world in our time. It remains vital that we understand Europe's era of overwhelming violence in order to guard against the possibility of its recurrence in the future.

901

Authoritarian States

How were Fascist and Communist totalitarian dictatorships similar and different?

Both conservative and radical dictatorships took power in Europe in the 1920s and 1930s. Although these two types of dictatorship shared some characteristics, in essence they were quite different. Conservative authoritarian regimes, which had a long history in Europe, were limited in scope. Radical totalitarian dictatorships, based on the ideologies of communism and fascism, were a new and frightening development aimed at the radical reconstruction of society.

Conservative Authoritarianism and Radical Totalitarian Dictatorships

The traditional form of antidemocratic government in European history was conservative authoritarianism. Like Catherine the Great in Russia and Metternich in Austria, the leaders of such governments relied on obedient bureaucracies in their efforts to control society. Though political opponents were often jailed or exiled, these older authoritarian governments were limited in both power and objectives. They had neither the ability nor the desire to control many aspects of their subjects' lives. As long as the people did not try to change the system, they were typically allowed considerable personal independence.

After the First World War, authoritarianism revived, especially in eastern Europe. What emerged, however, were new kinds of radical dictatorship that went much further than conservative authoritarianism, particularly in the Soviet Union, Germany, and Italy. In addition, both Communist and Fascist political parties became well established in all major European nations and mounted challenges to democratic rule.

Some scholars use the term **totalitarianism** to describe these radical dictatorships, which made unprecedented "total claims" on the beliefs and behavior of their citizens. The totalitarian model emphasizes the characteristics that Fascist and Communist dictatorships had in common. One-party totalitarian states used violent political repression and intense propaganda to gain complete power. In addition, the state tried to dominate the economic, social, intellectual, and cultural aspects of people's lives.

Most historians agree that totalitarianism owed much to the experience of total war in 1914 to 1918 (see Chapter 25). World War I required state governments to limit individual liberties and intervene in the economy in order to achieve one supreme objective: victory. Totalitarian leaders were inspired by the example of the modern state at war. They showed a callous disregard for human life and greatly expanded the power of the state in pursuit of social control.

Communist and Fascist dictatorships shared other characteristics. Both rejected parliamentary government and liberal values. Classical liberals (see Chapter 21) sought to limit the power of the state and protect the rights of the individual. Totalitarians, on the other hand, believed that individualism undermined equality and unity, and rejected democracy in favor of one-party political systems.

A charismatic leader typically dominated the totalitarian state—Stalin in the Soviet Union, Mussolini in Italy, Hitler in Germany. All three created political parties of a new kind, dedicated to promoting idealized visions of collective harmony. They used force and terror to intimidate and destroy political opponents and pursued policies of imperial expansion to exploit other lands. They censored the mass media and instituted propaganda campaigns to advance their goals. Finally, and perhaps most important, totalitarian governments engaged in massive projects of state-controlled social engineering dedicated to replacing individualism with a unified "people" capable of exercising the collective will.

Communism and Fascism

Communism and fascism clearly shared a desire to revolutionize state and society. Yet some scholars—arguing that the differences between the two systems are more important than the similarities—have moved beyond the totalitarian model. What were the main differences between these two systems? To answer this question, it is important to consider the way ideology, or a guiding political philosophy, was linked to the use of state-sponsored repression and violence.

Following Marx, Soviet Communists strove to create an international brotherhood of workers. In the Communist utopia ruled by the revolutionary working class, economic exploitation would disappear and society would be based on radical social equality (see Chapter 21). Under Stalinism—the name given to the Communist system during Stalin's rule—the state aggressively intervened in all walks of life to pursue this social leveling. Using brute force to destroy the upper and middle classes, the Stalinist state nationalized private property, pushed rapid industrialization, and collectivized agriculture (see pages 904–911).

The Fascist vision of a new society was quite different. Leaders who embraced **fascism**, such as Mussolini and Hitler, claimed that they were striving to build a new community on a national—not an international—level. Extreme nationalists, and often racists, Fascists glorified war and the military. For them, the nation was the highest embodiment of the people, and the powerful leader was the materialization of the people's collective will.

Like Communists, Fascists promised to improve the lives of ordinary workers. Fascist governments intervened in the economy, but unlike Communist regimes they did not try to level class differences and nationalize private property. Instead, they presented a vision of a community bound together by nationalism. In the ideal Fascist state, all social strata and classes would work together to build a harmonious national community.

Communists and Fascists differed in another crucial respect: the question of race. Where Communists sought to build a new world around the destruction of class differences, Fascists typically sought to build a new national community grounded in racial homogeneity. Fascists embraced the doctrine of **eugenics**, a pseudoscience that maintained that the selective breeding of human beings could improve the general characteristics of a national population. Eugenics was popular throughout the Western world in the 1920s and 1930s and was viewed by many as a legitimate social policy. But Fascists, especially the German National Socialists, or Nazis, pushed these ideas to the extreme.

Adopting a radicalized view of eugenics, the Nazis maintained that the German nation had to be "purified" of groups of people deemed "unfit" by the regime. Such ideas ultimately led to the Holocaust, the attempt to purge Germany and Europe of all

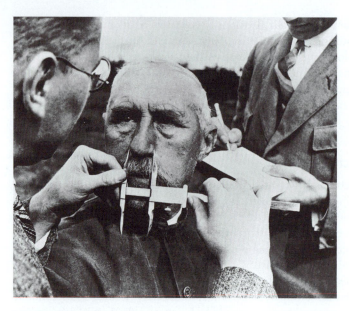

Eugenics in Nazi Germany Nazi "race scientists" believed they could use the eugenic methods of social engineering to build a powerful Aryan race. In this photograph, published in a popular magazine in 1933, a clinician measures a man's nose. Such pseudoscientific methods were used to determine an individual's supposed "racial value." (Hulton-Deutsch Collection/Corbis)

Jews and other undesirable groups by mass killing during World War II (see page 925). Though the Soviets sometimes persecuted specific ethnic groups, in general they justified these attacks using ideologies of class rather than race.

Perhaps because both championed the overthrow of existing society, Communists and Fascists were sworn enemies. The result was a clash of ideologies, which was in large part responsible for the horrific destruction and loss of life in the middle of the twentieth century. Explaining the nature of totalitarian dictatorships thus remains a crucial project for historians, even as they look more closely at the ideological differences between communism and fascism.

One important set of questions explores the way dictatorial regimes generated popular consensus. Neither Hitler nor Stalin ever achieved the total control each sought. Nor did they rule alone; modern dictators need the help of large state bureaucracies and the cooperation of large numbers of ordinary people. Which was more important for generating popular support: terror and coercion or material rewards? Under what circumstances did people resist or perpetrate totalitarian tyranny? These questions lead us toward what Holocaust survivor Primo Levi called the "gray zone" of moral compromise, which defined everyday life in totalitarian societies. (See "Individuals in Society: Primo Levi," page 930.)

Stalin's Soviet Union

How did Stalin and the Communist Party build a totalitarian state in the Soviet Union?

Lenin's harshest critics claim that he established the basic outlines of a modern totalitarian dictatorship after the Bolshevik Revolution and during the Russian civil war. If so, Joseph Stalin (1879–1953) certainly finished the job. A master of political infighting, Stalin cautiously consolidated his power and eliminated his enemies in the mid-1920s.

Then in 1928, as undisputed leader of the ruling Communist Party, Stalin launched the first **five-year plan**—the "revolution from above," as he aptly termed it—the beginning of a radical attempt to transform Soviet society into a Communist state. The ultimate goal of this immensely ambitious effort was to generate new attitudes, new loyalties, and a new socialist humanity. The means were constant propaganda, enormous sacrifice by the people, harsh repression that included purges and executions, and rewards for those who followed the party line. Thus the Soviet Union in the 1930s became a dynamic modern totalitarian state.

From Lenin to Stalin

By spring 1921 Lenin and the Bolsheviks had won the civil war, but they ruled a shattered and devastated land. Many farms were in ruins, and food supplies were exhausted. In southern Russia, drought combined with the ravages of war to produce the worst famine in generations. Industrial production had broken down completely. In the face of economic disintegration, riots by peasants and workers, and an open rebellion by previously pro-Bolshevik sailors at Kronstadt, Lenin was tough but, as ever, flexible. He repressed the Kronstadt rebels, and in March 1921 he replaced War Communism with the **New Economic Policy (NEP)**, which re-established limited economic freedom in an attempt to rebuild agriculture and industry. During the civil war, the Bolsheviks had simply seized grain without payment. Now peasant producers were permitted to sell their surpluses in free markets, and private traders and small handicraft manufacturers were allowed to reappear. Heavy industry, railroads, and banks, however, remained wholly nationalized.

The NEP was a political and economic success. Politically, it was a necessary but temporary compromise with the Soviet Union's overwhelming peasant majority. Realizing that his government was not strong enough to take land from the peasants and turn them into state workers, Lenin made a deal with the only force capable of overturning his government. The NEP brought rapid economic recovery, and by 1926 industrial output surpassed, and agricultural production almost equaled, prewar levels.

In 1924, as the economy recovered and the government partially relaxed its censorship and repression, Lenin died without a chosen successor, creating an intense struggle for power in the inner circles of the Communist Party. The principal contenders were Stalin and Trotsky. Joseph Dzhugashvili (joo-guhsh-VEEL-yih)—later known as Stalin (from the Russian for "steel")—was a good organizer but a poor speaker and writer, and he had no experience outside of Russia. Trotsky, a great and inspiring leader who had planned the 1917 Bolshevik takeover and then created the victorious Red Army, appeared to have all the advantages in the power struggle. Yet Stalin won because he was more effective at gaining the all-important support of the party. Having risen to general secretary of the party's Central Committee in 1922, he used his office to win friends and allies with jobs and promises.

Stalin also won because he was better able to relate Marxist teaching to Soviet realities in the 1920s. Stalin developed a theory of "socialism in one country" that was more appealing to the majority of party members than Trotsky's doctrine of "permanent revolution." Stalin argued that the Russian-dominated Soviet Union had the ability to build socialism on its own. Trotsky maintained that socialism in the Soviet Union could succeed only if a socialist revolution swept throughout Europe. To many Russian

Communists, this view sold their country short and promised risky conflicts with capitalist countries. Stalin's willingness to break with the NEP and "build socialism" at home also appealed to young party militants, who detested the capitalist-appearing NEP.

Stalin's ascendancy had a momentous impact on the policy of the new Soviet state toward non-Russians. The Communists had inherited the vast multiethnic territories of the former Russian empire. Lenin initially argued that these ethnic groups should have the right to self-determination even if they claimed independence from the Soviet state. In 1922, reflecting such ideas, the Union of Soviet Socialist Republics (or U.S.S.R.) was organized as a federation of four Soviet republics: the Russian Soviet Federative Socialist Republic, Ukraine, Belorussia, and a Transcaucasian republic. The last was later split into Armenia, Azerbaijan, and Georgia, and five Central Asian republics were established in the 1920s and 1930s.

In contrast to Lenin, Stalin argued for more centralized Russian control of these ethnic regions. His view would dominate state policy until the breakup of the Soviet Union in the early 1990s. The Soviet republics were granted some cultural independence but no real political autonomy. Party leaders allowed the use of non-Russian languages in regional schools and government institutions, but the right to secede was a fiction, and real authority remained in Moscow, in the hands of the Russian Communist Party. The Stalinists thus established a far-flung Communist empire on the imperial holdings of the former tsars.

With cunning skill, Stalin achieved supreme power between 1922 and 1927. First he allied with Trotsky's personal enemies to crush his rival, and then he moved against all who might challenge his ascendancy, including former allies. Stalin's final triumph came at the party congress of December 1927, which condemned all "deviation from the general party line" that he had formulated. The dictator and his followers were ready to launch the revolution from above, radically changing the lives of millions of people.

The Five-Year Plans

The party congress of 1927, which ratified Stalin's consolidation of power, marked the end of the NEP; the following year marked the beginning of the era of socialist five-year plans. The first of these plans had staggering economic objectives. In just five years, total industrial output was to increase by 250 percent, with heavy industry, the preferred sector, growing even faster. Agricultural production was slated to increase by 150 percent, and one-fifth of the peasants in the Soviet Union were to give up their private plots and join collective farms.

Stalin unleashed his "second revolution" for a variety of interrelated reasons. There were, first of all, ideological considerations. Stalin and his militant supporters were deeply committed to socialism as they understood it. They feared a gradual restoration of capitalism; wished to promote the working classes; and were eager to abolish the NEP's private traders, independent artisans, and property-owning peasants. Economic motivations were also important. A fragile economic recovery stalled in 1927 and 1928, and a new offensive seemed necessary to ensure industrial and agricultural growth. Moreover, economic development would allow the U.S.S.R. to catch up with the West and so overcome traditional Russian "backwardness."

The independent peasantry remained a major problem as well. For centuries the peasants had wanted to own the land, and finally they had it. Sooner or later, Stalinists reasoned, landowning peasants would embrace conservative capitalism and pose a threat to the regime. At the same time, the Communists—mainly urban dwellers—believed that the feared and despised "class enemy" in the villages could be squeezed to provide the enormous sums needed for all-out industrialization.

To resolve these issues, in 1929 Stalin ordered the **collectivization of agriculture**— the forced consolidation of individual peasant farms into large, state-controlled enterprises that were basically agricultural factories. Peasants across the Soviet Union were compelled to move off their small plots onto large state-run farms, where their tools, livestock, and produce would be held in common and central planners could control all work.

The increasingly repressive measures instituted by the state first focused on the **kulaks,** the class of well-off peasants who had benefited the most from the NEP. The kulaks were small in number, but they were held up as a great enemy of progress, and Stalin called for their "liquidation" and seizure of their land. Stripped of land and livestock, many starved or were deported to forced-labor camps for "re-education."

Forced collectivization led to disaster. Large numbers of peasants opposed to the change slaughtered their animals and burned their crops rather than turn them over to state commissars. Between 1929 and 1933 the number of horses, cattle, sheep, and goats in the Soviet Union fell by at least half. Nor were the state-controlled collective farms more productive. The output of grain barely increased over the first five-year plan, and collectivized agriculture was unable to make any substantial financial contribution to Soviet industrial development in the first five-year plan.

Collectivization in the fertile farmlands of the Ukraine was more rapid and violent than in other Soviet territories. The drive against peasants snowballed into an assault on Ukrainians in general, who had sought independence from Soviet rule after the First World War; Stalin and his associates viewed peasant resistance as an expression of unacceptable anti-Soviet nationalism. In 1932, as collectivization and deportations continued, party leaders set levels of grain deliveries for the Ukrainian collectives at excessively high levels and refused to relax those quotas or allow food relief when Ukrainian Communist leaders reported that starvation was occurring. The result was a terrible man-made famine in Ukraine in 1932 and 1933, which claimed 3 to 3.5 million lives.

Collectivization was a cruel but real victory for Stalinist ideologues. Though millions died, by the end of 1938 government representatives had moved 93 percent of peasant households onto collective farms, neutralizing them as a political threat. Nonetheless, peasant resistance had forced the supposedly all-powerful state to make modest concessions. Peasants secured the right to limit a family's labor on the state-run farms and to cultivate tiny family plots, which provided them with much of their food. In 1938 these family plots produced 22 percent of all Soviet agricultural produce on only 4 percent of all cultivated land.

The rapid industrialization mandated by the five-year plans was more successful— indeed, quite spectacular. A huge State Planning Commission, the "Gosplan," was created to set production goals and control deliveries of raw and finished materials. This was a complex and difficult task, and production bottlenecks and slowdowns often resulted. In addition, Stalinist planning favored heavy industry over the production of consumer goods, which led to shortages of basic necessities. Despite such problems, Soviet industry produced about four times as much in 1937 as it had in 1928. No other major country had ever achieved such rapid industrial growth.

Day Shift at Magnitogorsk   Beginning in 1928, Stalin's government issued a series of ambitious five-year plans designed to rapidly industrialize the Soviet Union. The plans focused primarily on boosting heavy industry and included the building of a gigantic steel complex at Magnitogorsk in the Ural Mountains. Here steelworkers review production goals at the Magnitogorsk foundry. (Sovfoto)

Steel was the idol of the Stalinist age. The Soviet state needed heavy machinery for rapid development, and an industrial labor force was created almost overnight as peasant men and women began working in the huge steel mills built across the country. Independent trade unions lost most of their power. The government could assign workers to any job anywhere in the country, and an internal passport system ensured that individuals could move only with permission. When factory managers needed more hands, they called on their counterparts on the collective farms, who sent them millions of "unneeded" peasants over the years. Rapid industrial growth, then, produced urban development: more than 25 million people, mostly peasants, migrated to cities during the 1930s.

Workers typically lived in deplorable conditions in hastily built industrial cities such as Magnitogorsk (Magnetic Mountain City) in the Ural Mountains. Yet they also experienced some benefits of upward mobility. In a letter published in the Magnitogorsk newspaper, an ordinary electrician described the opportunities created by rapid industrialization:

> In old tsarist Russia, we weren't even considered people. We couldn't dream about education, or getting a job in a state enterprise. And now I'm a citizen of the U.S.S.R.

> Like all citizens I have the right to a job, to education, to leisure. . . . In 1931, I came
> to Magnitogorsk. From a common laborer I have turned into a skilled worker. . . .
> I live in a country where one feels like living and learning. And if the enemy should
> attack this country, I will sacrifice my life in order to destroy the enemy and save my
> country.[1]

We should read such words with care, since they appeared in a state-censored publication. Yet the enthusiasm was at least partly authentic. The great industrialization drive
of 1928 to 1937 was an awe-inspiring achievement, purchased at enormous sacrifice on
the part of ordinary Soviet citizens.

Life and Culture in Soviet Society

Daily life was difficult in Stalin's Soviet Union. The lack of housing was a particularly
serious problem. Millions were moving into the cities, but the government built few
new apartments. A relatively lucky family received one room for all its members and
shared both a kitchen and a toilet with others living on the same floor.

There were constant shortages of goods as well. Because consumption was reduced
to pay for investment, there was little improvement in the average standard of living in
the years before World War II. The average nonfarm wage purchased only about half as
many goods in 1932 as it had in 1928. After 1932 real wages rose slowly, but by 1937
workers could still buy only about 60 percent of what they had bought in 1928 and less
than they could purchase in 1913. Collectivized peasants experienced greater hardships.

Life was by no means hopeless, however. Idealism and ideology had real appeal for
many Communists and ordinary citizens, who saw themselves heroically building the
world's first socialist society while capitalism crumbled in a worldwide depression and
degenerated into fascism in the West. This optimistic belief in the future of the Soviet
Union attracted many disillusioned Westerners to communism in the 1930s. On a more
practical level, Soviet workers received important social benefits, such as old-age pensions, free medical services, free education, and day-care centers for children. Unemployment
was almost unknown.

Communism also opened possibilities for personal advancement. Rapid industrialization required massive numbers of skilled workers, engineers, and plant managers.
In the 1930s the Stalinist state broke with the egalitarian policies of the 1920s and
provided tremendous incentives to those who could serve its needs. It paid the mass of
unskilled workers and collective farmers very low wages, but offered high salaries and
special privileges to its growing technical and managerial elite. This group joined with
the political and artistic elites in a new upper class, whose members grew rich and
powerful.

The radical transformation of Soviet society had a profound impact on women's
lives. Marxists had traditionally believed that both capitalism and middle-class husbands
exploited women, and the Russian Revolution of 1917 immediately proclaimed complete
equality for women. In the 1920s divorce and abortion were made easily available, and
women were urged to work outside the home. After Stalin came to power, he reversed
this trend. The government revoked many laws supporting women's emancipation in
order to strengthen the traditional family and build up the state's population.

At the same time, women saw lasting changes in education. The Soviets opened
higher education to women, who could now enter the ranks of the better-paid specialists

in industry and science. Medicine practically became a woman's profession. By 1950, 75 percent of all doctors in the Soviet Union were female.

Alongside such advances, however, Soviet society demanded great sacrifices from women. The vast majority of women had to work outside the home. Wages were so low that it was almost impossible for a family or couple to live only on the husband's earnings. Peasant women continued to work on farms, and millions of women toiled in factories and in heavy construction, building dams, roads, and steel mills in summer heat and winter frost. Men continued to dominate the very best jobs. Finally, rapid change and economic hardship led to many broken families, creating further physical and emotional strains for women. In any event, the massive mobilization of women was a striking characteristic of the Soviet state.

Culture was thoroughly politicized for propaganda and indoctrination purposes. Party activists lectured workers in factories and peasants on collective farms, while newspapers, films, and radio broadcasts endlessly recounted socialist achievements and capitalist plots. Whereas the 1920s had seen considerable modernist experimentation in art and theater, in the 1930s intellectuals were ordered by Stalin to become "engineers of human minds." They were instructed to exalt the lives of ordinary workers and glorify Russian nationalism. Russian history was rewritten so that early tsars such as Ivan the Terrible and Peter the Great became worthy forerunners of the greatest Russian leader of all—Stalin. Writers and artists who could effectively combine genuine creativity and political propaganda became the darlings of the regime.

Stalin seldom appeared in public, but his presence was everywhere—in portraits, statues, books, and quotations from his writings. Although the government persecuted those who practiced religion and turned churches into "museums of atheism," the state had both an earthly religion and a high priest—Marxism-Leninism and Joseph Stalin.

Stalinist Terror and the Great Purges

In the mid-1930s the great offensive to build socialism and a new society culminated in ruthless police terror and a massive purging of the Communist Party. First used by the Bolsheviks in the civil war to maintain their power, terror as state policy was revived in the collectivization drive against the peasants. Top members of the party and government publicly supported Stalin's initiatives, but there was some grumbling. At a small gathering in November 1932, even Stalin's wife complained bitterly about the misery of the people and the horrible famine in Ukraine. Stalin showered her with insults, and she committed suicide that night. In late 1934 Stalin's number-two man, Sergei Kirov, was mysteriously killed. Stalin—who probably ordered Kirov's murder—blamed the assassination on "Fascist agents" within the party. He used the incident to launch a reign of terror that purged the Communist Party of supposed traitors and solidified his own control.

Murderous repression picked up steam over the next two years. It culminated in the "great purge" of 1936 to 1938, a series of spectacular public show trials in which false evidence, often gathered using torture, was used to incriminate party administrators and Red Army leaders. In August 1936 sixteen "Old Bolsheviks"—prominent leaders who had been in the party since the Russian Revolution—confessed to all manner of contrived plots against Stalin; all were executed. In 1937 the secret police arrested a mass of lesser party officials and newer members, using torture to extract confessions and precipitating more show trials. In addition to the party faithful, union officials, managers, intellectuals, army officers, and countless ordinary citizens were accused of counter-revolutionary activities. At least 6 million people were arrested, and probably 1 to 2 million of these were executed or never returned from prisons and forced-labor camps.

Stalin's mass purges remain baffling, for most historians believe that the victims posed no threat and were innocent of their supposed crimes. Some scholars have argued that the terror was a defining characteristic of the totalitarian state, which must always fight real or imaginary enemies. Certainly the highly publicized purges sent a warning: no one was secure; everyone had to serve the party and its leader with redoubled devotion.

The long-standing interpretation that puts most of the blame for the purges on Stalin has been confirmed by recent research in newly opened Soviet archives. Apparently fearful of active resistance, Stalin and his allies used the harshest measures against their political enemies, real or imagined. Moreover, many in the general population shared such fears. Bombarded with ideology and political slogans, numerous people responded energetically to Stalin's directives. Investigations and trials snowballed into mass hysteria, resulting in a modern witch-hunt that claimed millions of victims. In this view of the 1930s, a deluded Stalin found large numbers of willing collaborators for crime as well as for achievement.[2]

The purges seriously weakened the Soviet Union in economic, intellectual, and military terms. But they left Stalin in command of a vast new state apparatus, staffed by the 1.5 million new party members enlisted to replace the purge victims. Thus more than half of all Communist Party members in 1941 had joined since the purges, and they experienced rapid social advance. Often the children of workers, they had usually studied in the new technical schools, and they soon proved capable of managing the government and large-scale production. Despite its human costs, the great purges thus brought substantial practical rewards to this new generation of committed Communists. They would serve Stalin effectively until his death in 1953, and they would govern the Soviet Union until the early 1980s.

Mussolini and Fascism in Italy

What kind of government did Mussolini establish in Italy?

Mussolini's Fascist movement and his seizure of power in 1922 were important steps in the rise of dictatorships in Europe between the two world wars. Mussolini and his supporters were the first to call themselves "Fascists" — revolutionaries determined to create a new totalitarian state based on extreme nationalism and militarism.

The Seizure of Power

In the early twentieth century, Italy was a liberal constitutional monarchy that recognized the civil rights of Italians. On the eve of World War I, the parliament granted universal male suffrage, and Italy appeared to be moving toward democracy. But there were serious problems. Much of the Italian population was still poor, and many peasants were more attached to their villages and local interests than to the national state. Moreover, the papacy, many devout Catholics, conservatives, and landowners remained strongly opposed to liberal institutions, and relations between church and state were often tense. Class differences were also extreme, leading to the development of a powerful revolutionary socialist movement.

World War I worsened the political situation. To win support for the war effort, the Italian government had promised territorial expansion as well as social and land reform, which it could not deliver. Instead, the Versailles treaty denied Italy any territorial gains, and soaring unemployment and inflation after the war created mass hardship. In response, the Italian Socialist Party followed the Bolshevik example, and radical workers and peasants began occupying factories and seizing land in 1920. These actions mobilized the property-owning classes. Moreover, after the war the pope lifted his ban on participation by Catholics in Italian politics, and a strong Catholic party quickly emerged. Thus by 1921 revolutionary socialists, conservatives, Catholics, and property owners were all opposed—though for different reasons—to the liberal government.

Into these crosscurrents of unrest and fear stepped bullying, blustering Benito Mussolini (1883–1945). Mussolini began his political career before World War I as a Socialist Party leader and radical newspaper editor. In 1914 he had urged that Italy join the Allies, a stand for which he was expelled from the Socialist Party. Returning home after being wounded at the front in 1917, Mussolini began organizing bitter war veterans like himself into a band of Fascists—from the Italian word for "a union of forces."

At first Mussolini's program was a radical combination of nationalist and socialist demands. As such, it competed directly with the well-organized Socialist Party and failed to get off the ground. When Mussolini saw that his violent verbal assaults on rival Socialists won him growing support from conservatives and the frightened middle classes, he shifted gears in 1920 and became a sworn enemy of socialism. Mussolini and his private militia of **Black Shirts** grew increasingly violent. Few people were killed, but Socialist Party newspapers, union halls, and local headquarters were destroyed, and the Black Shirts managed to push Socialists out of city governments in northern Italy.

Fascism soon became a mass movement, one which Mussolini claimed would help the little people against the established interests. In 1922, in the midst of chaos largely created by his Black Shirt militias, Mussolini stepped forward as the savior of order and property. Striking a conservative, anticommunist note in his speeches and gaining the support of army leaders, Mussolini demanded the resignation of the existing government. In October 1922 a band of armed Fascists marched on Rome to threaten the king and force him to appoint Mussolini prime minister of Italy. The threat worked. Victor Emmanuel III (r. 1900–1946)—who himself had no love for the liberal regime—asked Mussolini to take over the government and form a new cabinet. Thus, after widespread violence and a threat of armed uprising, Mussolini seized power using the legal framework of the Italian constitution.

The Regime in Action

Mussolini became prime minister in 1922, but moved cautiously in his first two years in office to establish control of the government. At first, he promised a "return to order" and consolidated his support among Italian elites. Fooled by Mussolini's apparent moderation, the Italian parliament passed a new electoral law that gave two-thirds of the representatives in the parliament to the party that won the most votes. This change allowed the Fascist Party and its allies to win an overwhelming majority in April 1924. Shortly thereafter, a group of Fascist extremists kidnapped and murdered the leading Socialist politician Giacomo Matteotti (JAHK-oh-moh mat-tee-OH-tee). Alarmed, a group of prominent parliamentary leaders demanded that Mussolini's armed squads be dissolved and all violence be banned.

Mussolini may not have ordered Matteotti's murder, but he took advantage of the resulting political crisis. Declaring his desire to "make the nation Fascist," he imposed a series of repressive measures. The government ruled by decree, abolished freedom of the press, and organized fixed elections. Mussolini arrested his political opponents, disbanded all independent labor unions, and put dedicated Fascists in control of Italy's schools. Mussolini trumpeted his goal in a famous slogan: "Everything in the state, nothing outside the state, nothing against the state." By the end of 1926 Italy was a one-party dictatorship under Mussolini's unquestioned leadership.

Mussolini's Fascist Party drew support from broad sectors of the population, in large part because he was willing to compromise with the traditional elites that controlled the army, the economy, and the state. He left big business to regulate itself, and there was no land reform. Mussolini also drew increasing support from the Catholic Church. In the **Lateran Agreement** of 1929, he recognized the Vatican as an independent state, and he agreed to give the church significant financial support in return for the pope's support. Because he was forced to compromise with these conservative elites, Mussolini never established complete totalitarian control.

Mussolini's government nonetheless proceeded with attempts to bring fascism to Italy. The state engineered popular consent by staging massive rallies and sporting events, creating Fascist youth and women's movements, and providing new welfare benefits. Newspapers, radio, and film promoted a "cult of the Duce" (leader), portraying Mussolini as a powerful strongman who embodied the best qualities of the Italian people. Like other Fascist regimes, his government was vehemently opposed to liberal feminism and promoted traditional gender roles. Mussolini also gained support by manipulating popular pride in the grand history of the ancient Roman Empire—as one propagandist put it, "Fascism, in its entirety, is the resurrection of Roman-ness."[3]

Mussolini matched his aggressive rhetoric with military action: Italian armies invaded the African nation of Ethiopia in October 1935. After surprising setbacks at the hands of the poorly armed Ethiopian army, the Italians won in 1936, and Mussolini could proudly declare that Italy again had its empire. Though it shocked international opinion, the war resulted in close ties between Italy and Nazi Germany. After a visit to Berlin in the fall of 1937, the Italian dictator pledged support for Hitler and promised that Italy and Germany would "march together right to the end."[4]

Deeply influenced by Hitler's example (see below), Mussolini's government passed a series of anti-Jewish racial laws in 1938. Though the laws were unpopular, Jews were forced out of public schools and dismissed from professional careers. Nevertheless, extreme anti-Semitic persecution did not occur in Italy until late in World War II, when Italy was under Nazi control. Though Mussolini's repressive tactics were never as ruthless as those in Nazi Germany, his government did much to turn Italy into a totalitarian police state.

Hitler and Nazism in Germany

What policies did Nazi Germany pursue, and how did they lead to World War II?

The most frightening dictatorship developed in Nazi Germany. National Socialism (or Nazism) shared some characteristics with Italian fascism, but Nazism was far more interventionist. Under Hitler, the Nazi dictatorship smashed or took over most independent organizations, established firm control over the German state and society, and violently persecuted the Jewish population and non-German peoples. Truly totalitarian in aspiration, the dynamism of Nazi Germany, based on racial aggression and territorial expansion, led to history's most destructive war.

The Roots of National Socialism

National Socialism grew out of many complex developments, of which the most influential were extreme nationalism and racism. These two ideas captured the mind of the young Adolf Hitler (1889–1945), and he dominated Nazism until the end of World War II.

The son of an Austrian customs official, Hitler spent his childhood in small towns in Austria. He was a mediocre student who dropped out of high school at age fourteen. Hitler then moved to Vienna, where he was exposed to extreme Austro-German nationalists who believed Germans to be a superior people and the natural rulers of central Europe. They advocated the union of Austria with Germany and the violent expulsion of "inferior" peoples as the means of maintaining German domination of the Austro-Hungarian Empire.

In Vienna, Hitler developed an unshakable belief in the crudest distortions of Social Darwinism (see Chapter 24), the superiority of Germanic races, and the inevitability of racial conflict. Exposure to poor eastern European Jews contributed to his anti-Semitic prejudice. Jews, Hitler now claimed, directed an international conspiracy of finance capitalism and Marxist socialism against German culture, German unity, and the German people.

Hitler was not alone. Racist anti-Semitism became wildly popular on the far right wing of European politics in the decades surrounding the First World War. Such irrational beliefs, rooted in centuries of Christian anti-Semitism, were given pseudoscientific legitimacy by nineteenth-century developments in biology and eugenics. These ideas came to define Hitler's worldview and would play an immense role in the ideology and actions of National Socialism.

Hitler greeted the outbreak of the First World War as a salvation. The struggle and discipline of war gave life meaning, and Hitler served bravely as a dispatch carrier on the western front. Germany's defeat shattered his world. Convinced that Jews and Marxists had "stabbed Germany in the back," he vowed to fight on.

In late 1919 Hitler joined a tiny extremist group in Munich called the German Workers' Party. In addition to denouncing Jews, Marxists, and democrats, the party promised a uniquely German National Socialism that would abolish the injustices of capitalism and create a mighty "people's community." By 1921 Hitler had gained control of this small but growing party, which had been renamed the National Socialist German Workers' Party, or Nazis for short. Hitler became a master of mass propaganda and political showmanship. In wild, histrionic speeches, he worked his audience into a frenzy with demagogic attacks on the Versailles treaty, Jews, war profiteers, and the Weimar Republic.

In late 1923 that republic seemed on the verge of collapse, and Hitler, inspired by Mussolini's recent victory, organized an armed uprising in Munich—the so-called Beer Hall Putsch. Despite the failure of the poorly planned coup and Hitler's arrest, National Socialism had been born.

Hitler's Road to Power

At his trial, Hitler gained enormous publicity by denouncing the Weimar Republic. He used his brief prison term to dictate his book *Mein Kampf* (My Struggle), where he laid out his basic ideas on "racial purification" and territorial expansion that would define National Socialism.

In *Mein Kampf*, Hitler claimed that Germans were a "master race" that needed to defend its "pure blood" from groups he labeled "racial degenerates," including Jews, Slavs, and others. The German race was destined to triumph and grow, and, according to Hitler, it needed *Lebensraum* (living space). This space could be found to Germany's east, which Hitler claimed was inhabited by the "subhuman" Slavs and Jews. The future dictator outlined a sweeping vision of war and conquest in which the German master race would colonize east and central Europe and ultimately replace the "subhumans" living there. He championed the idea of the leader-dictator, or *Führer* (FYOUR-uhr), whose unlimited power would embody the people's will and lead the German nation to victory. These ideas—a deadly combination of race and space—would ultimately propel the world into the Second World War.

In the years of relative prosperity and stability between 1924 and 1929, Hitler built up the Nazi Party. From the failed beer hall revolt, he had concluded that he had to come to power through electoral competition rather than armed rebellion. To appeal to middle-class voters, Hitler de-emphasized the anticapitalist elements of National Socialism and vowed to fight communism. The Nazis still remained a small splinter group in 1928, when they received only 2.6 percent of the vote in the general elections and only twelve seats in the Reichstag, the German parliament. There the Nazi deputies pursued the legal strategy of using democracy to destroy democracy.

The Great Depression of 1929 brought the ascent of National Socialism. Now Hitler promised German voters economic as well as political salvation. His appeals for "national rebirth" appealed to a broad spectrum of voters, including middle- and lower-class groups—small business owners, office workers, artisans, peasants, and skilled workers. Seized by panic as bankruptcies increased, unemployment soared, and the Communists made dramatic election gains, voters deserted conservative and moderate parties for the Nazis. In the election of 1930 the Nazis won 6.5 million votes and 107 seats, and in July 1932 they gained 14.5 million votes—38 percent of the total. They were now the largest party in the Reichstag.

The breakdown of democratic government helped the Nazis seize power. Chancellor Heinrich Brüning (BROU-nihng) tried to overcome the economic crisis by cutting back government spending and ruthlessly forcing down prices and wages. His conservative policies intensified Germany's economic collapse and convinced many voters that the country's republican leaders were stupid and corrupt, adding to Hitler's appeal.

Division on the left also contributed to Nazi success. Even though the two left-wing parties together outnumbered the Nazis in the Reichstag, the Communists refused to cooperate with the Social Democrats. Failing to resolve their differences, these parties could not mount an effective opposition to the Nazi takeover.

Finally, Hitler excelled in the dirty backroom politics of the decaying Weimar Republic. In 1932 Hitler cleverly gained the support of the conservative politicians in power, who thought they could use Hitler for their own advantage, to resolve the political crisis, but also to clamp down on leftists. They accepted Hitler's demand to be appointed chancellor in a coalition government, reasoning that he could be used and controlled. On January 30, 1933, Adolf Hitler, leader of the largest party in Germany, was appointed chancellor by President Hindenburg.

State and Society in Nazi Germany

Hitler moved rapidly and skillfully to establish an unshakable dictatorship that would pursue the Nazi program of race and space. First, Hitler and the Nazi Party worked to consolidate their power. To maintain appearances, Hitler called for new elections. In February 1933, in the midst of an electoral campaign plagued by violence — much of it caused by Nazi toughs — the Reichstag building was partly destroyed by fire. Hitler blamed the Communists and convinced Hindenburg to sign emergency acts that abolished freedom of speech and assembly as well as most personal liberties.

The façade of democratic government was soon torn asunder. When the Nazis won only 44 percent of the vote in the elections, Hitler outlawed the Communist Party and arrested its parliamentary representatives. Then on March 23, 1933, the Nazis pushed through the Reichstag the **Enabling Act**, which gave Hitler dictatorial power for four years. The Nazis' deceitful stress on legality, coupled with divide-and-conquer techniques, disarmed the opposition until it was too late for effective resistance.

Germany became a one-party Nazi state. Elections were farces. The new regime took over the government bureaucracy intact, installing Nazis in top positions. At the same time, it created a series of overlapping Nazi Party organizations responsible solely to Hitler. As recent research has shown, the resulting system of dual government was riddled with rivalries, contradictions, and inefficiencies. The Nazi state was often disorganized and lacked the all-encompassing unity that its propagandists claimed. Yet this fractured system suited Hitler and his purposes. The lack of unity encouraged competition among state personnel, who worked to outdo each other to fulfill Hitler's vaguely expressed goals. The Führer thus played the established bureaucracy against his personal party government and maintained dictatorial control.

Once the Nazis were firmly in command, Hitler and the party turned their attention to constructing a National Socialist society defined by national unity and racial exclusion. First they eliminated political enemies. Communists, Social Democrats, and trade-union leaders were forced out of their jobs or arrested and taken to hastily built concentration camps. The Nazis outlawed strikes and abolished independent labor unions, which were replaced by the Nazi-controlled German Labor Front.

Hitler then purged the Nazi Party itself of its more extremist elements. The Nazi storm troopers (the SA), the quasi-military band of 3 million toughs in brown shirts who had fought Communists and beaten up Jews before the Nazis took power, now expected top positions in the army. Some SA radicals even talked of a "second revolution" that would create equality among all Germans by sweeping away capitalism. Now that he was in power, however, Hitler was eager to win the support of the traditional military and maintain social order. He decided that the leadership of the SA had to be eliminated. On the night of June 30, 1934, Hitler's elite personal guard—the SS— arrested and executed about one hundred SA leaders and other political enemies. Afterward, the SS grew rapidly. Under its methodical, ruthless leader Heinrich Himmler (1900–1945), the SS took over the political police and the concentration camp system.

The Nazis instituted a policy it called "coordination" that forced existing institutions to conform to National Socialist ideology. Professionals—doctors and lawyers, teachers and engineers—saw their previously independent organizations swallowed up by Nazi associations. Charity and civic organizations were also put under Nazi control, and universities, publishers, and writers were quickly brought into line. Democratic, social-ist, and Jewish literature was put on ever-growing blacklists. Passionate students and radicalized professors burned forbidden books in public squares. Modern art and archi-tecture—which the Nazis considered "degenerate"—were prohibited. Life became violently anti-intellectual. By 1934 a brutal dictatorship characterized by frightening dynamism and obedience to Hitler was largely in place.

Acting on its vision of racial purity, the party began a many-faceted campaign against those deemed incapable of making positive contributions to the "master race." The Nazis persecuted a number of supposedly undesirable groups. Jews headed the list, but Slavic peoples, Sinti and Roma (Gypsies), homosexuals, Jehovah's Witnesses, and people con-sidered handicapped were also targets of ostracism and brutal repression.

In what some historians term the Nazi "racial state," barbarism and race hatred were institutionalized with the force of science and law.[5] New university academies, such as the German Society for Racial Research, wrote studies that measured and defined racial differences; prejudice was thus presented in the guise of enlightened science, a means for creating a strong national race. The ethical breakdown was exemplified in a series of sterilization laws, which led to the forced sterilization of some four hundred thousand "undesirable" citizens.

From the beginning, German Jews were a special target of Nazi persecution. By the end of 1934 most Jewish lawyers, doctors, professors, civil servants, and musicians had been banned from their professions. In 1935 the infamous Nuremberg Laws clas-sified as Jewish anyone having three or more Jewish grandparents, outlawed marriage and sexual relations between Jews and those defined as German, and deprived Jews of all rights of citizenship. Conversion to Christianity and abandonment of the Jewish faith made no difference. In their commentary on the Nuremberg Laws, two leading German legal scholars attacked German Jews and championed the close connections between "blood" and "nation" that defined citizenship in the racial state. (See "Primary Source: The 'Reich Citizenship Law' and the Nazi *Volk*," page 918.) For the vast major-ity of German citizens not targeted by such laws, the creation of a demonized outsider group may well have contributed to feelings of national unity and support for the Hitler regime.

In late 1938 the assault on the Jews accelerated. During a well-organized wave of violence known as Kristallnacht (or the Night of Broken Glass), Nazi gangs smashed windows and looted over 7,000 Jewish-owned shops, destroyed many homes, burned down over 200 synagogues, and killed dozens of Jews. German Jews were then rounded up and made to pay for the damage. By 1939 some 300,000 of Germany's 500,000

PRIMARY SOURCE   The "Reich Citizenship Law" and the Nazi *Volk*

In this excerpt from the Official Commentary on the Reich Citizenship Law, the centerpiece of the 1935 Nuremberg Laws, the high-ranking Nazi jurists Wilhelm Stuckart and Hans Globke critique the ideals of classical liberalism and link citizenship rights to the "common blood" of the national Volk, or "people."

In the individualistic-liberal conception . . . the primary element was the free and independent individual and the totality of all individuals in society. For this reason alone the state was worthy of protection because, through the "free play of forces," it supposedly achieved the greatest possible happiness for the individual as well as for the sum of individuals. . . . Exercising a strict control over society, this juristic political personality, entirely cut off from the people, had to promote the free development of the individual and had to see to it that no one's personal liberty was restricted. . . . With painstaking concern for the individual and his rights, the content of citizenship was discussed and precisely determined. . . . Above all, the principle of equality was most scrupulously guarded. Rights and duties were the same for every citizen. . . .

The revolution in the conception of the state has perforce changed the concept, essence, and content of nationality and citizenship. National Socialism has put the people directly into the center of thought, faith, and will, of creativity and life. . . .

The community of the people, sustained by a community of will and a community consciousness of [the] honor of the racially homogeneous German people, constitutes political unity. . . . The real bond is the common blood. . . .

According to the National Socialist conception . . . it is not individual human beings, but races, peoples, and nations that constitute the elements of the divinely

Jews had emigrated, sacrificing almost all their property in order to escape this persecution. Some Germans privately opposed these outrages, but most went along or looked the other way. This lack of opposition expressed anti-Semitism to a degree still being debated by historians, but it certainly revealed the strong popular support for Hitler's government.

Popular Support for National Socialism

Why did millions of ordinary Germans back a brutally repressive regime? A combination of coercion and reward enlisted popular support for the racial state. Using the secret police and the growing concentration camp system in a reign of ruthless terror, the regime persecuted its political and "racial" enemies. Yet for the large majority of ordinary German citizens who were not Jews, Communists, or members of other targeted groups, Hitler's government brought new opportunities. The German "master race" clearly benefited from Nazi ideologies of race and space.

Hitler had promised the masses economic recovery, and he delivered. The Nazi state launched a large public works program to help pull Germany out of the depression. Work began on superhighways, offices, gigantic sports stadiums, and public housing,

willed order of this world. . . . The individual human being can be conceived only as a member of a community of people to whom he is racially similar, from whom he inherits his physical and spiritual endowments. . . . National Socialism does not recognize a separate individual sphere which, apart from the community, is to be painstakingly protected from any interference from the state. . . .

The Reich Citizenship Law actualizes the Volkish ordering of the German people on the political level. . . .

[The law] elevates the bearer of German or racially kindred blood above the rest of the state's subjects by according to him alone the right to assume full Reich citizenship. All persons of alien blood—hence, especially Jews—are automatically excluded from attaining Reich citizenship.

EVALUATE THE EVIDENCE

1. What role does race play in Nazi conceptions of citizenship? How did the Nazis' ideas about race play into their persecution of European Jews?

2. What arguments do Stuckart and Globke use to challenge Enlightenment ideals about equal rights and the relationship between the individual and the state? How would their ideas be received in today's democratic societies?

Source: George L. Mosse, ed., *Nazi Culture: Intellectual, Cultural, and Social Life in the Third Reich* (Madison: University of Wisconsin Press, 2003; first published Grosset & Dunlap, 1966), pp. 327–332. © 1966 by the Board of Regents of The University of Wisconsin System. Reprinted by permission of The University of Wisconsin Press.

which created jobs and instilled pride in national recovery. By 1938 unemployment had fallen to 2 percent, and there was a shortage of workers. Between 1932 and 1938 the standard of living for the average worker increased moderately. Business profits rose sharply.

The persecution of Jews brought substantial benefits to ordinary Germans as well. As Jews were forced out of their jobs and compelled to sell their homes and businesses, Germans stepped in to take their place in a process known as Aryanization (named after the "Aryan master race" prized by the Nazis for their supposedly pure German blood). For millions of so-called Aryans, a rising standard of living—at whatever ethical price—was tangible evidence that Nazi promises were more than show and propaganda.

Economic recovery was accompanied by a wave of social and cultural innovation intended to construct what Nazi propagandists called the *Volksgemeinschaft*—a "people's community" for racially pure Germans. The party set up mass organizations to spread Nazi ideology and enlist volunteers for the Nazi cause. Millions of Germans joined the Hitler Youth, the League of German Women, and the German Labor Front. Mass rallies, such as annual May Day celebrations and Nazi Party conventions in Nuremberg, brought together thousands of participants. Glowing reports on such events in the Nazi-controlled press brought the message home to millions more.

Mothers in the Fatherland Nazi ideologues promoted strictly defined gender roles for men and women, and the Nazi state implemented a variety of social programs to encourage "racially correct" women to stay home and raise "Aryan" children. This poster portrays the joy of motherhood and calls for donations to the Mother and Child division of the National Socialist People's Welfare office. (akg-images)

As the economy recovered, the government touted a glittering array of inexpensive and enticing people's products. Items such as the Volkswagen (the "people's car") were intended to link individuals' desire for consumer goods to the collective ideology of the "people's community." Though such programs faltered as the state increasingly focused on rearmament for the approaching war, they suggested to all that the regime was working hard to improve German living standards.

Women played a special role in the Nazi state. Promising to "liberate women from women's liberation," Nazi ideologues championed a return to traditional family values. They outlawed abortion, discouraged women from holding jobs or obtaining higher education, and glorified domesticity and motherhood. Women were cast as protectors of the hearth and home and were instructed to raise young boys and girls in accordance with Nazi ideals. In the later 1930s, facing labor shortages, the Nazis had to reluctantly reverse course and encourage women to enter the labor force. Whatever the employment situation, the millions of women enrolled in Nazi mass organizations, which organized charity drives and other social programs, experienced a new sense of freedom and community in these public activities.

Few historians today believe that Hitler and the Nazis brought about a real social revolution, as an earlier generation of scholars thought. Yet Hitler's rule promoted economic growth, and Nazi propagandists continually played up the supposed accomplishments of the regime. The vision of a "people's community," national pride in recovery, and feelings of belonging created by acts of racial exclusion led many Germans to support the regime. Hitler himself remained popular with broad sections of the population well into the war.

Not all Germans supported Hitler, however, and a number of groups actively resisted him after 1933. But opponents of the Nazis were never unified, which helps explain their lack of success. In addition, the regime clamped down on dissidents: tens of thousands of political enemies were imprisoned, and thousands were executed. After Communists and Socialists were smashed by the SS system, a second group of opponents arose in the Catholic and Protestant churches. However, their efforts were directed primarily at preserving religious life, not at overthrowing Hitler. In 1938 and again during the war, a few high-ranking army officers, who feared the consequences of Hitler's reckless aggression, plotted against him, but their plans were unsuccessful.

Aggression and Appeasement

The nazification of German society fulfilled only part of the Nazi agenda. While building the "people's community," the regime aggressively pursued policies meant to achieve territorial expansion for the supposedly superior German race. At first, Hitler carefully camouflaged his expansionist goals. Germany was still militarily weak, and the Nazi leader proclaimed his peaceful intentions. Germany's withdrawal from the League of Nations in October 1933, however, indicated that Gustav Stresemann's policy of peaceful cooperation was dead (see Chapter 26). Then in March 1935 Hitler declared that Germany would no longer abide by the disarmament clauses of the Treaty of Versailles. He established a military draft and began to build up the German army. France and Great Britain protested strongly and warned against future aggressive actions.

Any hope of a united front against Hitler quickly collapsed. Britain adopted a policy of **appeasement**, granting Hitler everything he could reasonably want (and more) to avoid war. British appeasement, which practically dictated French policy, was motivated in large part by the pacifism of a population still horrified by the memory of the First World War. As in Germany, many powerful conservatives in Britain underestimated Hitler. They believed that Soviet communism was the real danger and that Hitler could be used to stop it. Such strong anticommunist feelings made an alliance between the Western powers and Stalin against Hitler unlikely.

When Hitler suddenly marched his armies into the demilitarized Rhineland in March 1936, brazenly violating the treaties of Versailles and Locarno, Britain refused to act. France could do little without British support. Emboldened, Hitler moved ever more aggressively, enlisting powerful allies in international affairs. Italy and Germany established the so-called Rome-Berlin Axis in 1936. Japan, also under the rule of a Fascist dictatorship, joined the Axis alliance that same year.

At the same time, Germany and Italy intervened in the Spanish Civil War (1936–1939), where their military aid helped General Francisco Franco's revolutionary Fascist movement defeat the democratically elected republican government. Republican Spain's only official aid in the fight against Franco came from the Soviet Union, for public opinion in Britain and especially in France was hopelessly divided on whether to intervene.

In late 1937 Hitler moved forward with plans to seize Austria and Czechoslovakia as the first step in his long-contemplated drive for living space in the east. By threatening Austria with invasion, Hitler forced the Austrian chancellor to put local Nazis in control of the government in March 1938. The next day, in the Anschluss (annexation), German armies moved in unopposed, and Austria became two provinces of Greater Germany.

Simultaneously, Hitler demanded that territories inhabited mostly by ethnic Germans in western Czechoslovakia—the Sudetenland—be ceded to Nazi Germany. Though democratic Czechoslovakia was allied with France and the Soviet Union and prepared to defend itself, appeasement triumphed again. In negotiations British prime minister Arthur Neville Chamberlain and the French agreed with Hitler that Germany should immediately take over the Sudetenland. Returning to London from the Munich Conference in September 1938, Chamberlain told cheering crowds that he had secured "peace with honor . . . peace for our time." Sold out by the Western powers, Czechoslovakia gave in.

Chamberlain's peace was short-lived. In March 1939 Hitler's armies invaded and occupied the rest of Czechoslovakia. The effect on Western public opinion was electrifying. This time, there was no possible rationale of self-determination for Nazi aggression, since Hitler was seizing ethnic Czechs and Slovaks — not Germans — as captive peoples. When Hitler next used the question of German minorities in Danzig as a pretext to confront Poland, a suddenly militant Chamberlain declared that Britain and France would fight if Hitler attacked his eastern neighbor. Hitler did not take these warnings seriously.

In August 1939, in an about-face that stunned the world, sworn enemies Hitler and Stalin signed a nonaggression pact that paved the road to war. Each dictator promised to remain neutral if the other became involved in open hostilities. An attached secret protocol ruthlessly divided Poland, the Baltic nations, Finland, and a part of Romania into German and Soviet spheres of influence. Stalin agreed to the pact because he remained distrustful of Western intentions and because Hitler offered immediate territorial gain.

For Hitler, everything was now set. On September 1, 1939, German armies and warplanes smashed into Poland from three sides. Two days later, Britain and France, finally true to their word, declared war on Germany. The Second World War had begun.

The Second World War

How did Germany and Japan conquer enormous empires during World War II, and how did the Allies defeat them?

Nazi Germany's unlimited ambition unleashed an apocalyptic cataclysm. Hitler's armies quickly conquered much of western and eastern Europe, establishing a vast empire of death and destruction based on Nazi ideas of race and space. At the same time, Japanese armies overran much of Southeast Asia and created their own racial empire. This reckless aggression brought together a coalition of unlikely but powerful allies determined to halt the advance of fascism: Britain, the United States, and the Soviet Union. After years of slaughter that decimated much of Europe and East Asia, this "Grand Alliance" decisively defeated the Axis powers.

German Victories in Europe

Using planes, tanks, and trucks in the first example of a blitzkrieg, or "lightning war," Hitler's armies crushed Poland in four weeks. While the Soviet Union quickly took its part of the booty — the eastern half of Poland and the independent Baltic states of Lithuania, Estonia, and Latvia — French and British armies prepared their defenses in the west.

In spring 1940 the Nazi lightning war struck again. After occupying Denmark, Norway, and Holland, German motorized columns broke into France through southern Belgium, split the Franco-British forces, and trapped the entire British army on the French beaches of Dunkirk. By heroic efforts, the British withdrew their troops — although equipment could not be saved. Soon after, France was taken by the Nazis. By July 1940 Hitler ruled practically all of continental Europe. Italy was a German ally; Romania, Hungary, and Bulgaria joined the Axis powers; and the Soviet Union, Spain, and Sweden were friendly neutrals. Only the Balkans and Britain, the nation led by the uncompromising Winston Churchill (1874–1965), remained unconquered.

To prepare for an amphibious invasion of Britain, Germany sought to gain control of the air. In the Battle of Britain, which began in July 1940, up to a thousand German planes a day attacked British airfields and key factories, dueling with British defenders high in the skies. Losses were heavy on both sides. In September 1940 Hitler angrily turned from military objectives to indiscriminate bombing of British cities in an attempt to break British morale. British aircraft factories increased production, and the heavily bombed people of London defiantly dug in. By October Britain was beating Germany three to one in the air war, and the Battle of Britain was over. (See "Primary Source: Everyday Life in the London Blitz," page 924.) Stymied there, the Nazi war machine invaded and occupied Greece and the Balkans.

Hitler now allowed his lifetime obsession of creating a vast eastern European empire ruled by the master race to dictate policy. In June 1941 he broke his pact with Stalin and launched German armies into the Soviet Union along a vast front (Map 27.1). By October most of Ukraine had been conquered, Leningrad was practically surrounded, and Moscow was besieged. But the Soviets did not collapse, and when a severe winter struck German armies outfitted only in summer uniforms, the invaders were stopped. Nevertheless, Hitler and his allies ruled over a vast European empire stretching from eastern Europe to the English Channel. Hitler, the Nazi leadership, and the loyal German army were positioned to greatly accelerate construction of their New Order in Europe.

Europe Under Nazi Occupation

Hitler's **New Order** was based firmly on the guiding principle of National Socialism: racial imperialism. Occupied peoples were treated according to their place in the Nazi racial hierarchy. All were subject to harsh policies dedicated to ethnic cleansing and the plunder of resources for the Nazi war effort.

Within this New Order, the so-called Nordic peoples—the Dutch, Norwegians, and Danes—received preferential treatment, for the Germans believed them related to the Aryan master race. In Holland, Norway, and Denmark, the Nazis established puppet governments of various kinds; though many people hated the conquerors, the Nazis found willing collaborators who ruled in accord with German needs. France was divided into two parts. The German army occupied the north, including Paris. The southeast remained nominally independent. There the aging First World War general Marshal Henri-Philippe Pétain formed a new French government—the Vichy (VIH-shee) regime—that adopted many aspects of National Socialist ideology and willingly placed French Jews in the hands of the Nazis.

In all conquered territories, the Nazis used a variety of techniques to enrich Germany and support the war effort. Occupied nations were forced to pay for the costs of the war and for the occupation itself, and the price was high. Nazi administrators stole goods and money from local Jews, set currency exchanges at favorable rates, and forced occupied peoples to accept worthless wartime scrip. Soldiers were encouraged to steal but also to purchase goods at cheap exchange rates and send them home. A flood of plunder thus reached Germany, helping maintain high living standards and preserving home-front morale well into the war. Nazi victory, furthermore, placed national Jewish populations across Europe under German control, easing the mass murder of Europe's Jews.

In central and eastern Europe, the war and German rule were far more ruthless and deadly than in the west. From the start, the Nazi leadership had cast the war in the east

PRIMARY SOURCE   Everyday Life in the London Blitz

In 1941 Hilde Marchant, a young English journalist, published an account of her experiences in the streets of London during the Battle of Britain the year before. Here she speaks of Mr. Smith, an air raid warden. Mr. Smith, she reported, was neither strong nor brave, but he nonetheless learned to effectively manage the destruction of the blitz.

But perhaps the greatest battle of all in those early days was a personal one. Smith had to adjust his warm, sentimental, domestic nature to the grim agonising sights of the night. He loves humanity, in all its virtue and vice, and it was a shock for him to see the pain and distortion of life around him. Yet he corseted his sentimentality with the months of training he had had and became the handyman of the blitz. . . .

Smith began to tell me about that first night, the night he fell in the road and broke his glasses. A bomb just a few yards from him had hit a block of buildings, and there were eleven people trapped on the ground floor.

"It was a noisy night, but every time we bent low we could hear the groans of the people underneath. I thought I'd be sick. I held a man's hand that was clear. It took us nine hours to get him out. An hour later we got a woman out. They were in a bad way. There was dirt and blood caked on the woman's face. We wiped it off. She must have been about thirty. They both died. We were all a bit quiet. It was the first we'd seen. We couldn't have got them out quicker—we'd torn our hands up dragging the stones away. But it was awful seeing them take the last gasps as they lifted them into the ambulance."

Smith was quiet, even retelling the story, and one of the [other wardens] said: "It was the first, you see."

Then Smith told me about the next night—the night when he was really "blooded." Incendiaries had started a fire in one of the smaller streets and high explosives began to fall into the fire. Smith approached the houses from the back and got through to the kitchen of one of the houses.

"I fell over something. I picked it up and it was a leg. I stood there with it in my hand wondering what I should do with it. I knew it was a woman's leg. I put it down and went to look for the ambulance. They had got the fire out at the front. The ambulance men brought a stretcher and I showed them the leg. Then we looked farther in and there were pieces all over. All they said was they didn't need a stretcher."

As Smith sat thinking, his whole body seemed to pause. . . .

"You see, how we look at things now is like this. If they're alive you work like the devil to keep 'em alive and get 'em out. . . . If they're dead there's nothing we can do. Getting upset hampers your work."

So Smith learned not to over-indulge his sensitivity on seeing death, or torn limb and flesh. His job was with the spark of life that survived.

EVALUATE THE EVIDENCE

1. Does Marchant's story have a political message for the British people?
2. What does this passage reveal about the resilience of human beings in times of war?

Source: James M. Brophy et al., *Perspectives from the Past: Primary Sources in Western Civilizations*, 4th ed., vol. 2 (New York: W. W. Norton, 2009), pp. 766–767.

as one of annihilation. The Nazis now set out to build a vast colonial empire where Jews would be exterminated and Poles, Ukrainians, and Russians would be enslaved and forced to die out. According to the plans, ethnic German peasants would resettle the resulting abandoned lands, a "mass settlement space." In pursuit of such goals, large parts of western Poland were incorporated into Germany. Another part of Poland was placed under the rule of a merciless civilian administration.

With the support of military commanders, German policemen, and bureaucrats in the occupied territories, Nazi administrators and Himmler's elite SS corps now implemented a program of destruction and annihilation to create a "mass settlement space" for racially pure Germans. Across the east, the Nazi armies destroyed cities and factories, stole crops and farm animals, and subjected conquered peoples to forced starvation and mass murder. The murderous sweep of Nazi occupation in the east destroyed the lives of millions.[6]

In response to such atrocities, small but determined underground resistance groups fought back. They were hardly unified. Communists and socialists often disagreed with more centrist or nationalist groups on long-term goals and short-term tactics. In Yugoslavia, for example, Communist and royalist military resistance groups attacked the Germans, but also each other. The resistance nonetheless presented a real challenge to the Nazi New Order. Poland, under German occupation longer than any other nation, had the most determined and well-organized resistance. The Nazis had closed all Polish universities and outlawed national newspapers, but the Poles organized secret classes and maintained a thriving underground press. Underground members of the Polish Home Army, led by the government in exile in London, passed intelligence about German operations to the Allies and committed sabotage. The famous French resistance undertook similar actions, as did groups in Italy, Greece, Russia, and the Netherlands.

The German response was swift and deadly. The Nazi army and the SS tortured captured resistance members and executed hostages in reprisal for attacks. Responding to actions undertaken by resistance groups, the German army murdered the male populations of Lidice (Czechoslovakia) and Oradour (France) and leveled the entire towns, brutal examples of Nazi barbarism in pursuit of a racial New Order. Despite reprisals, Nazi occupiers were never able to eradicate popular resistance to their rule.

The Holocaust

The ultimate abomination of Nazi racism was the condemnation of all European Jews and other peoples considered racially inferior to extreme racial persecution and then annihilation in the **Holocaust**, a great spasm of racially inspired mass murder.

As already described, the Nazis began to use social, legal, and economic means to persecute Jews and other "undesirable" groups immediately after taking power. Between 1938 and 1940, persecution turned deadly in the Nazi euthanasia (mercy killing) campaign, an important step toward genocide. Just as Germany began the war, some 70,000 people with physical and mental disabilities were forced into special hospitals, barracks, and camps. Deemed by Nazi administrators to be "unworthy lives" who might "pollute" the German race, they were murdered in cold blood. The victims were mostly ethnic Germans, and the euthanasia campaign was stopped after church leaders and ordinary families spoke out. The staff involved took what they learned in implementing this

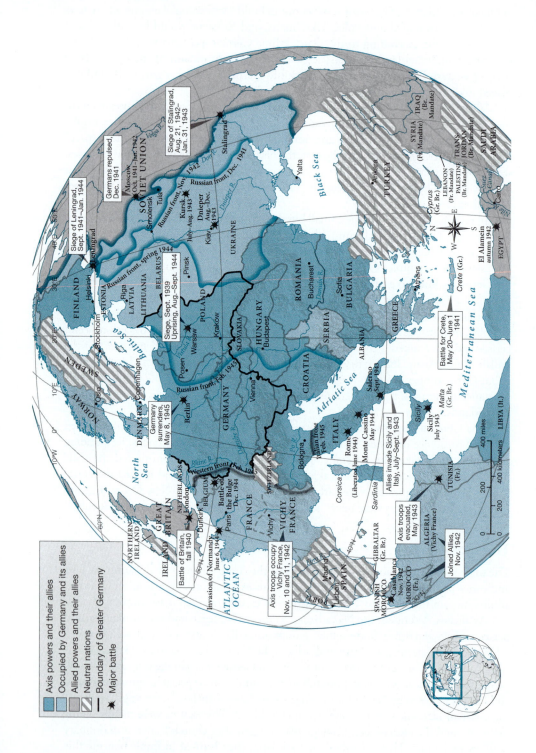

Siege of Leningrad, Sept. 1941–Jan. 1944

Germans repulsed, Dec. 1941

Siege of Stalingrad, Aug. 21, 1942–Jan. 31, 1943

Moscow Oct. 1941–Jan. 1942

Smolensk

Tula

Russian front, Nov. 1942

Kursk July–Aug. 1943

Dnieper Aug.–Dec. 1943

Kiev

Stalingrad

Yalta

Black Sea

Ankara

TURKEY

Cyprus (Gr. Br.)

SYRIA (Fr. Mandate)

IRAQ (Br. Mandate)

LEBANON (Fr. Mandate)

PALESTINE (Br. Mandate)

TRANS-JORDAN (Br. Mandate)

SAUDI ARABIA

Suez Canal

Cairo

SOVIET UNION

Volga R.

Don R.

Dnieper R.

FINLAND

Helsinki

ESTONIA

LATVIA

LITHUANIA

BELARUS

Pinsk

UKRAINE

Riga

Russian front, spring 1944

Siege, Sept. 1939 Uprising, Aug.–Sept. 1944

ROMANIA

Bucharest

Danube R.

Sofia

BULGARIA

SERBIA

GREECE

Athens

Crete (Gr.)

Battle for Crete, May 20–June 1 1941

El Alamein autumn 1942

EGYPT

Mediterranean Sea

SWEDEN

Stockholm

NORWAY

Oslo

Baltic Sea

DENMARK

Copenhagen

Germany surrenders, May 8, 1945

Berlin

POLAND

Kraków

Warsaw

Posen

Vistula R.

SLOVAKIA

HUNGARY

Budapest

Vienna

CROATIA

ALBANIA

Adriatic Sea

Salerno Sept. 1943

Sicily July 1943

Battle of Sicily and Italy, July–Sept. 1943

Sicily

Malta (Gr. Br.)

LIBYA (It.)

North Sea

Russian front, Feb. 1945

GERMANY

Rhine R.

Western front, Feb. 1945

Bologna

Po R.

Italian front Feb. 1945

Rome

Monte Cassino

Corsica (Liberated June 1944)

Sardinia

ITALY

TUNISIA (Fr.)

Axis troops evacuated, May 1943

ALGERIA (Vichy France)

400 miles

400 kilometers

200

200

0

0

NORTHERN IRELAND

GREAT BRITAIN

London

IRELAND

Dunkirk

Battle of Britain, fall 1940

NETHERLANDS

BELGIUM

Battle of the Bulge Dec. 1944

Paris

FRANCE

Invasion of Normandy, June 6, 1944

Vichy

VICHY FRANCE

SWITZERLAND

Axis troops occupy Vichy France, Nov. 10 and 11, 1942

GIBRALTAR (Gr. Br.)

Madrid

SPAIN

Lisbon

PORTUGAL

SPANISH MOROCCO

Casablanca Nov. 1942

MOROCCO (Fr.)

Ebro R.

Joined Allies, Nov. 1942

ATLANTIC OCEAN

◀ **MAP 27.1** **World War II in Europe and Africa, 1939–1945**
This map shows the extent of Hitler's empire before the Battle of Stalingrad in late 1942 and the subsequent advances of the Allies until Germany surrendered on May 8, 1945.

program with them to the extermination camps the Nazis would soon build in the east (Map 27.2).

The German victory over Poland in 1939 brought some 3 million Jews under Nazi control. Jews in German-occupied territories were soon forced to move into urban districts termed "ghettos." In walled-off ghettos in cities large and small—two of the most important were in Warsaw and Lodz—hundreds of thousands of Polish Jews lived in crowded and unsanitary conditions, without real work or adequate sustenance. Over 500,000 people died under these conditions.

The racial violence reached new extremes when Germany invaded the Soviet Union in 1941. Three military death squads known as Special Task Forces (*Einsatz-gruppen*) and other military units followed the advancing German armies. They

A "Transport" Arrives at Auschwitz Upon arrival at Auschwitz in May 1944, Jews from Subcarpathian Rus, a rural district on the border of Czechoslovakia and Ukraine, undergo a "selection" managed by Nazi officers and prisoners in striped uniforms. Camp guards will send the fittest people to the barracks, where they will probably soon die from forced labor under the most atrocious conditions. The aged, ill, very young, or otherwise infirm will be murdered immediately in the Auschwitz gas chambers. The tower over the main gate to the camp, which today opens onto a vast museum complex, is visible in the background. (Yad Vashem [Public Domain] Panstwowe Museum Auschwitz-Birkenau w Oswiecimiu)

MAP 27.2   The Holocaust, 1941–1945

The leadership of Nazi Germany established an extensive network of ghettos and concentration and extermination camps to persecute their political opponents and those people deemed "racially undesirable" by the regime. The death camps, where the Nazi SS systematically murdered millions of European Jews, Soviet prisoners of war, and others, were located primarily in Nazi-occupied territories in eastern Europe, but the conditions in the concentration camps within Germany's borders were almost as brutal.

moved systematically from town to town, shooting Jews and other target populations. The victims of these mobile killing units were often forced to dig their own graves in local woods or fields before they were shot. In this way the German armed forces murdered some 2 million civilians.

In late 1941 Hitler and the Nazi leadership, in some still-debated combination, ordered the SS to implement the mass murder of all Jews in Europe. What the Nazi leadership called the "final solution of the Jewish question" had begun. The Germans set up an industrialized killing machine that remains unparalleled, with an extensive network of concentration camps, industrial complexes, and railroad transport lines to imprison and murder Jews and other so-called undesirables, and to exploit their labor before they died. In the occupied east, the surviving residents of the ghettos were loaded onto trains and taken to camps such as Auschwitz-Birkenau, the best known of the Nazi killing centers, where over 1 million people—the vast majority of them Jews—were murdered in gas chambers. Some few were put to work as expendable laborers. The Jews of Germany and then of occupied western and central Europe were likewise rounded up, put on trains, and sent to the camps. Even after it was quite clear that Germany would lose the war, the killing continued.

The murderous attack on European Jews was the ultimate monstrosity of Nazi racism and racial imperialism. By 1945 the Nazis had killed about 6 million Jews and some 5 million other Europeans, including millions of ethnic Poles and Russian POWs. (See "Individuals in Society: Primo Levi," page 930.) Who was responsible for this terrible crime? Historians continue to debate this critical question. Some lay the guilt on Hitler and the Nazi leadership, arguing that ordinary Germans had little knowledge of the extermination camps or were forced to participate by Nazi terror and totalitarian control. Other scholars conclude that far more Germans knew about and were at best indifferent to the fate of "racial inferiors."

The question remains: what inspired those who actually worked in the killing machine—the "desk murderers" in Berlin who sent trains to the east, the soldiers who shot Jews in the Polish forests, the guards at Auschwitz? Some historians believe that widely shared anti-Semitism led "ordinary Germans" to become Hitler's "willing executioners." Others argue that heightened peer pressure, the desire to advance in the ranks, and the need to prove one's strength under the most brutalizing wartime violence turned average Germans into reluctant killers. The conditioning of racist Nazi propaganda clearly played a role. Whatever the motivation, numerous Germans were somehow prepared to join the SS ideologues and perpetrate ever-greater crimes, from mistreatment to arrest to mass murder.[7]

Japanese Empire and the War in the Pacific

The racist war of annihilation in Europe was matched by racially inspired warfare in East Asia. In response to political divisions and economic crisis, a Fascist government had taken control of Japan in the 1930s. As in Germany and Italy, the Japanese government was highly nationalistic and militaristic, and it was deeply committed to imperial expansion. According to Japanese race theory, the Asian races were far superior to Western ones. In speeches, schools, and newspapers, ultranationalists eagerly voiced the extreme anti-Western views that had risen in the 1920s and 1930s. They glorified the warrior virtues of honor and sacrifice and proclaimed that Japan would liberate East Asia from Western colonialists.

Japan soon acted on its racial-imperial ambitions. In 1931 Japanese armies invaded and occupied Manchuria, a vast territory bordering northeastern China. In 1937 Japan brutally invaded China itself. Seeking to cement ties with the Fascist regimes of Europe, in 1940 the Japanese entered into a formal alliance with Italy and Germany, and in summer 1941 Japanese armies occupied southern portions of the French colony of Indochina (now Vietnam and Cambodia).

INDIVIDUALS IN SOCIETY • Primo Levi

Most Jews deported to Auschwitz-Birkenau were murdered soon after arriving, but the Nazis made some prisoners into slave laborers, and a few of them survived. Primo Levi (1919–1987), one of these laborers, lived to become one of the most influential witnesses to the Holocaust.

Like much of Italy's small Jewish community, Levi's family belonged to the urban professional classes. Levi graduated from the University of Turin with highest honors in chemistry in 1941. Growing discrimination against Italian Jews led him to join the antifascist resistance two years later. Captured, he was deported to Auschwitz with 650 Italian Jews in February 1944. Stone-faced SS men picked 96 men, Levi among them, and 29 women from this group to work in labor camps; the rest were gassed upon arrival.

Levi and his fellow prisoners were kicked, punched, stripped, branded with tattoos, crammed into huts, and worked unmercifully. Hoping for some prisoner solidarity, Levi found only a desperate struggle of each against all and enormous status differences among prisoners. Many bewildered newcomers, beaten and demoralized by their bosses—the most privileged prisoners—collapsed and died. Others struggled to secure their own privileges, however small, because food rations and working conditions were so abominable that prisoners who were not bosses usually perished in two to three months.

Sensitive and noncombative, Levi found himself sinking into oblivion. But instead of joining the mass of the "drowned," he became one of the "saved"—a complicated surprise with moral implications that he would ponder all his life. As Levi explained in *Survival in Auschwitz* (1947), the usual road to salvation in the camps was some kind of collaboration with German power. Savage German criminals were released from prison to become brutal camp guards; non-Jewish political prisoners competed for jobs entitling them to better conditions; and, especially troubling for Levi, a few Jews plotted and struggled to gain the power of life and death over other Jewish prisoners.

Though not one of these Jewish bosses, Levi believed that he, like almost all survivors, had entered the "gray zone" of moral compromise. "Nobody can know for how long and under what trials his soul can resist before yielding or breaking," Levi wrote. "The harsher the oppression, the more widespread among the oppressed is the willingness, with all its infinite nuances and motivations, to collaborate."*

*Primo Levi, *The Drowned and the Saved* (New York: Vintage, 1989), pp. 43, 60. See also Levi, *Survival in Auschwitz: The Nazi Assault on Humanity* (London: Collier Books, 1961). These powerful testimonies are highly recommended.

The goal was to establish what the Japanese called the Greater East Asia Co-Prosperity Sphere. Under the slogan "Asia for Asians," Japanese propagandists maintained that this expansion would free Asians from hated Western imperialists. By promising to create a mutually advantageous union for long-term development, the Japanese tapped currents of nationalist sentiment, and most local populations were glad to see the Westerners go.

The camps held no saints, he believed: the Nazi system degraded its victims, forcing them to commit sometimes-bestial acts against their fellow prisoners in order to survive.

For Levi, salvation came from his education. Interviewed by a German technocrat for work in the camp's synthetic rubber program, Levi was chosen for this relatively easy labor because he spoke fluent German, including scientific terminology. Work in the warm camp laboratory offered Levi opportunities to pilfer equipment he could then trade to other prisoners for food and necessities. Levi also gained critical support from three prisoners who refused to do wicked and hateful acts. And he counted luck as essential for his survival: in the camp infirmary with scarlet fever in February 1945 as advancing Russian armies prepared to liberate the camp, Levi was not evacuated by the Nazis and shot to death like most Jewish prisoners.

After the war, Levi was haunted by the nightmare that the Holocaust would be ignored or forgotten. Ashamed that so many people whom he considered better than himself had perished, and wanting the world to understand the genocide in all its complexity so that people would never again tolerate such atrocities, he turned to writing about his experiences. Primo Levi, while revealing Nazi guilt, tirelessly grappled with his vision of individual choice and moral ambiguity in a hell designed to make the victims collaborate and persecute each other.

QUESTIONS FOR ANALYSIS

1. Describe Levi's experience at Auschwitz. How did camp prisoners treat each other? Why?

2. What does Levi mean by the "gray zone"?

3. Will a vivid historical memory of the Holocaust help to prevent future genocide?

ONLINE DOCUMENT ASSIGNMENT

Why do so many Holocaust survivors like Levi struggle with the moral implications of their experiences in the camps? Watch personal testimonies of Holocaust survivors. Then complete a writing assignment based on the evidence and details from this chapter.

bedfordstmartins.com/mckaywestvalue

But the Co-Prosperity Sphere was a sham. Real power remained in the hands of the Japanese. They exhibited great cruelty toward civilian populations and prisoners of war, and exploited local peoples for Japan's wartime needs, arousing local populations against them. Nonetheless, the ability of the Japanese to defeat the Western colonial powers set a powerful example for national liberation groups in Asia, which would become important in the decolonization movement that followed World War II.

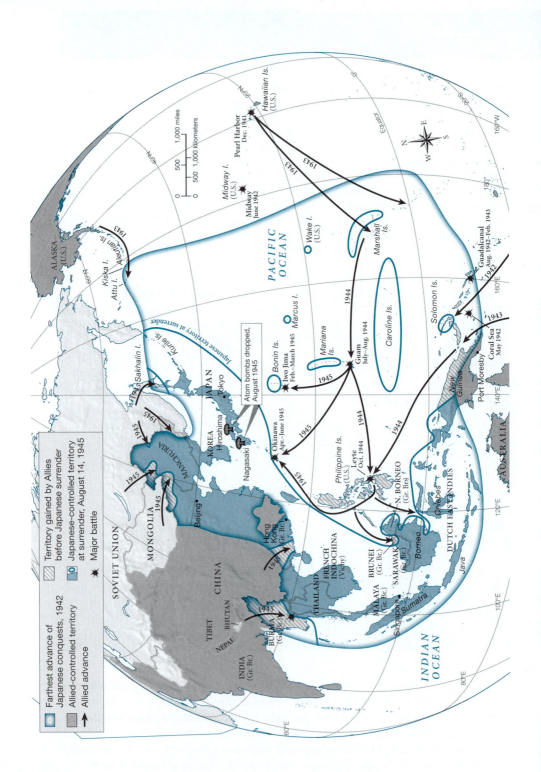

Pearl Harbor
Dec. 1941

Hawaiian Is.
(U.S.)

PACIFIC
OCEAN

Equator

Midway I.
(U.S.)

Midway
June 1942

Wake I.
(U.S.)

Marshall
Is.

1943

1943

ALASKA
(U.S.)

Kiska I.   Aleutian Is.
Attu I.

1943

1943

Caroline Is.

Guadalcanal
1942–Feb. 1943

Solomon Is.

1942

1943

Kurile Is.

Japanese territory at surrender

Sakhalin I.

Marcus I.

Mariana
Is.

Guam
July–Aug. 1944

Coral Sea
May 1942

New Guinea

Port Moresby

1944

JAPAN

Tokyo

Bonin Is.

Iwo Jima
Feb.–March 1945

1945

1944

1944

AUSTRALIA

Atom bombs dropped,
August 1945

KOREA

Hiroshima

Nagasaki

Okinawa
Apr.–June 1945

1945

1945

1944

MANCHURIA

1945

Beijing

Philippine Is.
(U.S.)

Leyte
Oct. 1944

N. BORNEO
(Gr. Br.)

Celebes

DUTCH EAST INDIES

SOVIET UNION

MONGOLIA

1945

Hong Kong
(Gr. Br.)

1945

Borneo

SARAWAK
(Gr. Br.)

BRUNEI
(Gr. Br.)

FRENCH
INDOCHINA
(Vichy)

THAILAND

CHINA

TIBET

BHUTAN

NEPAL

BURMA
(Gr. Br.)

1945

INDIA
(Gr. Br.)

MALAYA
(Gr. Br.)

Singapore

Sumatra

Java

INDIAN
OCEAN

1,000 miles
500   1,000 kilometers

N
W   E
S

Farthest advance of
Japanese conquests, 1942

Allied-controlled territory

Allied advance

Territory gained by Allies
before Japanese surrender

Japanese-controlled territory
at surrender, August 14, 1945

Major battle

◀ **MAP 27.3** **World War II in the Pacific**
In 1942 Japanese forces overran an enormous amount of territory, which the Allies slowly recaptured in a long, bitter struggle. As this map shows, Japan still held a large Asian empire in August 1945, when the unprecedented devastation of atomic warfare suddenly forced it to surrender.

Japanese expansion from 1937 to 1941 evoked a sharp response from U.S. president Franklin Roosevelt, and Japan's leaders came to believe that war with the United States was inevitable. After much debate, they decided to launch a surprise attack on the U.S. fleet based at Pearl Harbor in the Hawaiian Islands. On December 7, 1941, the Japanese sank or crippled every American battleship, but by chance all the American aircraft carriers were at sea and escaped unharmed. Pearl Harbor brought the Americans into the war in a spirit of anger and revenge.

As the Americans mobilized for war, Japanese armies overran more European and American colonies in Southeast Asia. By May 1942 Japan controlled a vast empire (Map 27.3) and was threatening Australia. The Americans pushed back and engaged the Japanese in a series of hard-fought naval battles. In July 1943 the Americans and their Australian allies opened a successful island-hopping campaign that slowly forced Japan out of its conquered territories. The war in the Pacific was extremely brutal—a "war without mercy," in the words of a leading American scholar—and atrocities were committed on both sides. A product of spiraling violence, mutual hatred, and dehumanizing racial stereotypes, the fighting intensified as the United States moved toward Japan.[8]

The "Hinge of Fate"

While the Nazis and the Japanese built their savage empires, Great Britain, the United States, and the Soviet Union joined together in a military pact Churchill termed the Grand Alliance. This was a matter of chance more than choice. It had taken the Japanese surprise attack to bring the isolationist United States into the war. Moreover, the British and Americans were determined opponents of Soviet communism, and disagreements between the Soviets and the capitalist powers during the course of the war sowed mutual distrust. Stalin repeatedly urged Britain and the United States to open a second front in France to relieve pressure on Soviet forces, but Churchill and Roosevelt refused until the summer of 1944. Despite such tensions, the overriding goal of defeating the Axis powers brought together these reluctant allies.

In one area of agreement, the Grand Alliance concurred on a policy of "Europe first." Only after Hitler was defeated would the Allies mount an all-out attack on Japan, the lesser threat. The Allies also agreed to concentrate on immediate military needs, postponing tough political questions about the eventual peace settlement that might have divided them. To further encourage mutual trust, the Allies adopted the principle of the unconditional surrender of Germany and Japan. This policy cemented the Grand Alliance because it denied Hitler any hope of dividing his foes. It also meant that Soviet and Anglo-American armies would almost certainly be forced to invade and occupy all of Germany, and that Japan would fight to the bitter end.

The military resources of the Grand Alliance were awesome. The United States harnessed its vast industrial base to wage global war and in 1943 outproduced not only Germany, Italy, and Japan, but all of the rest of the world combined. Great Britain became an impregnable floating fortress, a gigantic frontline staging area for a decisive blow to the heart of Germany. After a determined push, the Soviet Union's military strength was so great that it might well have defeated Germany without Western help. Stalin drew heavily on the heroic resolve of the Soviet people, especially those in the central Russian heartland. Broad-based Russian nationalism, as opposed to narrow communist ideology, became a powerful unifying force in what the Soviet people appropriately called the Great Patriotic War of the Fatherland.

The combined might of the Allies forced back the Nazi armies on all fronts (see Map 27.1). Through early 1942 heavy fighting between British and Axis forces had resulted in significant German advances in North Africa. At the Second Battle of El Alamein (el al-uh-MAYN) in October–November 1942, however, British forces decisively defeated combined German and Italian armies and halted Axis penetration of North Africa. Winston Churchill called the battle the "hinge of fate" that cemented Allied victory. Shortly thereafter, an Anglo-American force landed in Morocco and Algeria. These French possessions, which were under the control of Pétain's Vichy government, went over to the Allies. Fearful of an Allied invasion across the Mediterranean, German forces occupied Vichy France in November 1942, and the collaborationist French government effectively ceased to exist.

After driving the Axis powers out of North Africa, U.S. and British forces invaded Sicily in the summer of 1943 and mainland Italy that autumn. Mussolini was overthrown by a coup d'état, and the new Italian government publicly accepted unconditional surrender. In response, Nazi armies invaded and seized control of northern and central Italy, and German paratroopers rescued Mussolini in a daring raid and put him at the head of a puppet government. Facing stiff German resistance, the Allies battled their way slowly up the Italian peninsula. The Germans still held northern Italy, but they were clearly on the defensive.

The spring of 1943 brought crucial Allied victories at sea and in the air. In the first years of the war, German submarines had successfully attacked North Atlantic shipping, severely hampering the British war effort. New antisubmarine technologies favored the Allies. Soon massive convoys of hundreds of ships were streaming across the Atlantic, bringing much-needed troops and supplies from the United States to Britain.

The German air force had never really recovered from its defeat in the Battle of Britain. With almost unchallenged air superiority, the United States and Britain now mounted massive bombing raids on German cities to maim industrial production and break civilian morale. By the war's end, hardly a German city of any size remained untouched, and many—including Dresden, Hamburg, and Cologne—lay in ruins.

Great Britain and the United States had made critical advances in the western theater, but the worst German defeats came at the hands of the Red Army on the eastern front. Although the Germans had almost captured the major cities of Moscow and Leningrad in early winter 1941, they were forced back by determined Soviet counterattacks. The Germans mounted a second and initially successful invasion of the Soviet Union in the summer of 1942, but the campaign turned into a disaster. The downfall came at the Battle of Stalingrad, when in November 1942 the Soviets surrounded and systematically destroyed the entire German Sixth Army of 300,000 men. In January 1943 only 123,000 soldiers were left to surrender. Hitler, who had refused to allow a retreat, suffered a catastrophic defeat. For the first time, German public opinion turned decisively against the war. In summer 1943 the larger, better-equipped Soviet armies took the offensive and began to push the Germans back along the entire eastern front (see Map 27.1).

Allied Victory

The balance of power was now clearly in Allied hands, yet bitter fighting continued in Europe for almost two years. Germany, less fully mobilized for war in 1941 than Britain, stepped up its efforts. The German war industry, under the Nazi minister of armaments Albert Speer, put to work millions of prisoners of war and slave laborers from across occupied Europe. Between early 1942 and July 1944, German war production tripled despite heavy Anglo-American bombing.

German resistance against Hitler also failed to halt the fighting. An unsuccessful attempt by conservative army leaders to assassinate Hitler in July 1944 only brought increased repression by the fanatic Nazis who had taken over the government. Closely disciplined by the regime, frightened by the prospect of unconditional surrender, and terrorized by Nazi propaganda that portrayed the advancing Russian armies as rapacious Slavic beasts, the Germans fought on with suicidal resolve.

On June 6, 1944, American and British forces under General Dwight Eisenhower landed on the beaches of Normandy, France, in history's greatest naval invasion. In a hundred dramatic days, more than 2 million men and almost half a million vehicles broke through the German lines and pushed inland. Rejecting proposals to strike straight at Berlin in a massive attack, Eisenhower moved forward cautiously on a broad front. Not until March 1945 did American troops cross the Rhine and enter Germany. By spring of 1945 the Allies had finally forced the Germans out of the Italian peninsula. That April, Mussolini was captured in northern Italy by Communist partisans and executed, along with his mistress and other Fascist leaders.

The Soviets, who had been advancing steadily since July 1943, reached the outskirts of Warsaw by August 1944. Anticipating German defeat, the Polish underground Home Army ordered an uprising, so that the Poles might take the city on their own and establish independence from the Soviets. The Warsaw Uprising was a tragic miscalculation. Citing military pressure, the Red Army refused to enter the city. Stalin and Soviet leaders thus allowed the Germans to destroy the Polish insurgents, a cynical move that paved the way for the establishment of a postwar Communist regime. Only after the decimated Home Army surrendered did the Red Army continue its advance. Warsaw lay in ruins, and between 150,000 and 200,000 Poles—mostly civilians—had lost their lives.

Over the next six months, the Soviets moved southward into Romania, Hungary, and Yugoslavia. In January 1945 the Red Army crossed Poland into Germany, and on April 26 met American forces on the Elbe River. The Allies had overrun Europe and closed their vise on Nazi Germany. As Soviet forces fought their way into Berlin, Hitler committed suicide, and on May 8 the remaining German commanders capitulated.

The war in the Pacific also drew to a close. Despite repeated U.S. victories through the summer of 1945, Japanese troops had continued to fight with enormous courage and determination. American commanders believed the invasion and conquest of Japan itself might cost 1 million American casualties and claim 10 to 20 million Japanese lives. In fact, Japan was almost helpless, its industry and dense, fragile wooden cities largely destroyed by intense American bombing. Yet the Japanese seemed determined to fight on, ready to die for a hopeless cause.

After much discussion at the upper levels of the U.S. government, American planes dropped atomic bombs on Hiroshima and Nagasaki in Japan on August 6 and 9, 1945. The mass bombing of cities and civilians, one of the terrible new practices of World

Nuclear Wasteland at Hiroshima   Only a handful of buildings remain standing in the ruins of Hiroshima in September 1945. Fearing the costs of a prolonged ground and naval campaign against the Japanese mainland, the United States dropped atomic bombs on Hiroshima and Nagasaki in August 1945. The bombings ended the war and opened the nuclear age. (AP Images)

War II, now ended in the final nightmare—unprecedented human destruction in a single blinding flash. On August 14, 1945, the Japanese announced their surrender. The Second World War, which had claimed the lives of more than 50 million soldiers and civilians, was over.

Notes

1. Quoted in S. Kotkin, *Magnetic Mountain: Stalinism as a Civilization* (Berkeley: University of California Press, 1997), pp. 221–222.
2. R. Thurston, *Life and Terror in Stalin's Russia, 1934–1941* (New Haven, Conn.: Yale University Press, 1996), esp. pp. 16–106; also M. Malia, *The Soviet Tragedy: A History of Socialism in Russia, 1917–1991* (New York: Free Press, 1995), pp. 227–270.
3. Quoted in C. Duggan, *A Concise History of Italy* (New York: Cambridge University Press, 1994), p. 227.
4. Quoted ibid, p. 234.
5. M. Burleigh and W. Wippermann, *The Racial State: Germany 1933–1945* (New York: Cambridge University Press, 1991).
6. See, for example, the population statistics on the German occupation of Belarus in C. Gerlach, "German Economic Interests, Occupation Policy, and the Murder of the Jews in Belorussia, 1941–43," in *National Socialist Extermination Policies: Contemporary German Perspectives and Controversies*, U. Herbert, ed. (New York: Berghan Books, 2000), pp. 210–239. See also M. Allen, *The Business of Genocide: The SS, Slave Labor, and the Concentration Camps* (Chapel Hill: University of North Carolina Press, 2002), pp. 270–285.
7. D. Goldhagen, *Hitler's Willing Executioners: Ordinary Germans and the Holocaust* (New York: Vintage Books, 1997); for an alternate explanation, see C. Browning, *Ordinary Men: Reserve Police Battalion 101 and the Final Solution in Poland* (New York: Harper, 1992).
8. J. Dower, *War Without Mercy: Race and Power in the Pacific War* (New York: Pantheon, 1986).

Chapter Review

IDENTIFY KEY TERMS

Identify and explain the significance of each item below.

totalitarianism (p. 902)	**collectivization of agriculture** (p. 907)	**National Socialism** (p. 914)
fascism (p. 903)	**kulaks** (p. 907)	**Enabling Act** (p. 916)
eugenics (p. 903)	**Black Shirts** (p. 912)	**appeasement** (p. 921)
five-year plan (p. 905)	**Lateran Agreement** (p. 913)	**New Order** (p. 923)
New Economic Policy (NEP) (p. 905)		**Holocaust** (p. 925)

REVIEW THE MAIN IDEAS

Answer the focus questions from each section of the chapter.

- How were Fascist and Communist totalitarian dictatorships similar and different? (p. 902)
- How did Stalin and the Communist Party build a totalitarian state in the Soviet Union? (p. 904)
- What kind of government did Mussolini establish in Italy? (p. 911)
- What policies did Nazi Germany pursue, and how did they lead to World War II? (p. 914)
- How did Germany and Japan conquer enormous empires in World War II, and how did the Allies defeat them? (p. 922)

MAKE CONNECTIONS

Think about the larger developments and continuities within and across chapters.

1. Historians continue to disagree on whether "totalitarianism" is an appropriate way to describe Communist and Fascist dictatorships in Europe. How would you define this term? Is it a useful label to describe state and society under Stalin, Mussolini, and Hitler? Why is the debate over totalitarianism still important today?

2. Why would ordinary people support dictatorships that trampled on familiar political freedoms and civil rights?

ONLINE DOCUMENT ASSIGNMENT

Primo Levi

Why do so many Holocaust survivors like Levi struggle with the moral implications of their experiences in the camps?

You encountered Primo Levi's story on page 930. Keeping the question above in mind, go online and watch personal testimonies of Holocaust survivors. Then complete a writing assignment based on the evidence and details from this chapter.

bedfordstmartins.com/mckaywestvalue

CHRONOLOGY

1921	• New Economic Policy (NEP) in U.S.S.R.
1922	• Mussolini gains power in Italy
1924	• Mussolini seizes dictatorial powers
1924–1929	• Buildup of Nazi Party in Germany
1927	• Stalin comes to power in U.S.S.R.
1928	• Stalin's first five-year plan
1929	• Lateran Agreement; start of collectivization in Soviet Union
1929–1939	• Great Depression
1931	• Japan invades Manchuria
1932–1933	• Famine in Ukraine
1933	• Hitler appointed chancellor in Germany; Reichstag passes the Enabling Act, granting Hitler absolute dictatorial power
1935	• Nuremberg Laws deprive Jews of all rights of citizenship
1936	• Start of great purges under Stalin; Spanish Civil War begins

1937	• Japanese army invades China
1938	• Kristallnacht marks beginning of more aggressive anti-Jewish policy in Germany
1939	• Germany occupies Czech lands and invades western Poland; Britain and France declare war on Germany, starting World War II; Soviet Union occupies eastern Poland
1940	• Germany defeats and occupies France; Battle of Britain begins
1941	• Germany invades U.S.S.R.; Japan attacks Pearl Harbor; United States enters war
1941–1945	• The Holocaust
1942–1943	• Battle of Stalingrad
1944	• Allied invasion at Normandy
1945	• Soviet and U.S. forces enter Germany; United States drops atomic bombs on Japan; World War II ends

Cold War Conflict and Consensus

1945–1965

THE DEFEAT OF THE NAZIS AND THEIR ALLIES IN 1945 LEFT EUROPE in ruins. In the immediate postwar years, as Europeans struggled to overcome the effects of rampant death and destruction, the victorious Allies worked to shape an effective peace accord. Disagreements between the Soviet Union and the Western allies emerged during this process and quickly led to an apparently endless Cold War between the two new superpowers—the United States and the Soviet Union. This conflict split much of Europe into a Soviet-aligned Communist bloc and a U.S.-aligned capitalist bloc and spurred military, economic, and technological competition.

Amid these tensions, battered western European countries fashioned a remarkable recovery, building strong democratic institutions and vibrant economies. In the Soviet Union and the "East Bloc" (the label applied to central and eastern European countries governed by Soviet-backed Communist regimes), Communist leaders repressed challenges to one-party rule but also offered limited reforms, leading to stability there as well. Yet the postwar period was by no means peaceful. Anti-Soviet uprisings in East Bloc countries led to military intervention and death and imprisonment for thousands. Colonial independence movements in the developing world sometimes erupted in violence, even after liberation was achieved. Cold War hostilities had an immense impact on the decolonization process, often to the detriment of formerly colonized peoples.

Cold War conflicts notwithstanding, the postwar decades witnessed the construction of a relatively stable social and political consensus in both Communist and capitalist Europe. At the same time, changing class structures, new migration patterns, and new roles for women and youths had a profound impact on European society, laying the groundwork for major transformations in the decades to come.

Postwar Europe and the Origins of the Cold War

Why was World War II followed so quickly by the Cold War?

In 1945 the Allies faced the momentous challenges of rebuilding a shattered Europe, dealing with Nazi criminals, and creating a lasting peace. Reconstruction began and war crimes were punished, but the Allies found it difficult to cooperate in peacemaking. Motivated by different goals and hounded by misunderstandings, Great Britain and the United States on one side found themselves at loggerheads with the Soviet Union (U.S.S.R.). Though a handful of countries maintained a neutral stance, by 1949 most of Europe was divided into East and West Blocs allied with the U.S.S.R. and the United States, respectively. For the next forty years, the competing superpowers engaged in the **Cold War**, a determined competition for political and military superiority around the world.

The Legacies of the Second World War

In the summer of 1945 Europe lay in ruins. Across the continent, the fighting had destroyed cities and landscapes and obliterated buildings, factories, farms, rail tracks, roads, and bridges. Many cities—including Leningrad, Warsaw, Vienna, Budapest, Rotterdam, and Coventry—were completely devastated. Postwar observers compared the remaining piles of rubble to moonscapes. Surviving cities such as Prague and Paris were left relatively unscathed, mostly by chance.

The human costs of the Second World War are almost incalculable (Map 28.1). The death toll far exceeded the mortality figures for World War I. At least 20 million Soviets, including soldiers and civilians, died in the war. Between 9 and 11 million noncombatants lost their lives in Nazi concentration camps, including 6 million Jews and over 220,000 Sinti and Roma (Gypsies). One out of every five Poles died in the war, including 3 million of Poland's 3.25 million Jews. German deaths numbered 5 million, 2 million of them civilians. France and Britain both lost fewer soldiers than in World War I, but about 350,000 French civilians were killed in the fighting. Over 400,000 U.S. soldiers died in the European and Pacific campaigns, and other nations across Europe and the globe also lost staggering numbers. In total, about 50 million human beings perished in the conflict.

The destruction of war also left tens of millions homeless—25 million in the U.S.S.R. and 20 million in Germany alone. The wartime policies of Hitler and Stalin had forced some 30 million people from their homes in the hardest-hit war zones of central and eastern Europe. The end of the war and the start of the peace increased their numbers. Some 13 million ethnic Germans fled west before the advancing Soviet troops or were forced to leave eastern Europe under the terms of Allied agreements. Forced laborers from Poland, France, the Balkans, and other nations, brought to Germany by the Nazis, now sought to go home. A woman in Berlin described the flow of refugees passing through the city in spring 1945:

> The streets were filled with small, tired caravans of people. . . . All the vehicles looked the same: pitiful handcarts piled high with sacks, crates, and trunks. Often I saw a woman or an older child in front, harnessed to a rope, pulling the cart forward, with the smaller children or a grandpa pushing from behind. There were people perched on top, too, usually very little children or elderly relatives. The old people look terrible amid all the junk, the men as well as the women—pale, dilapidated, apathetic. Half-dead sacks of bones.[1]

These **displaced persons** or DPs—their numbers increased by concentration camp survivors, released prisoners of war, and hundreds of thousands of orphaned children— searched for food and shelter. From 1945 to 1947 the newly established United Nations Relief and Rehabilitation Administration (UNRRA) opened over 760 DP camps and spent $10 billion to house, feed, clothe, and repatriate the refugees.

For DPs, going home was not always the best option. Soviet citizens who had spent time in the West were seen as politically unreliable by political leaders in the U.S.S.R. Many DPs faced prison terms, exile to labor camps in the Siberian gulag, and even execution upon their return to Soviet territories. Jewish DPs faced unique problems. Their families and communities had been destroyed, and persistent anti-Semitism often made them unwelcome in their former homelands. Many stayed in special Jewish DP camps in Germany for years. After the creation of Israel in 1948 (see page 968), over 330,000 European Jews left for the new Jewish state. By 1952 about 100,000 Jews had also immigrated to the United States; smaller numbers moved to other western European countries, South America, and the British Commonwealth countries. When the last DP camp closed in 1957, the UNRRA had cared for and resettled many millions of refugees, Jews and non-Jews alike.

When the fighting stopped, Germany and Austria had been divided into four occupation zones, each governed by one of the Allies—the United States, the Soviet Union, Great Britain, and France. The Soviets collected substantial reparations from their zone in eastern Germany and from former German allies Hungary and Romania. In Soviet-occupied Germany, administrators seized factories and equipment, even tearing up railroad tracks and sending the rails to the U.S.S.R.

The authorities in each zone worked to punish those guilty of Nazi atrocities. Across Europe, almost 100,000 Germans and Austrians were convicted of war crimes; many more were investigated or indicted. In Soviet-dominated central and eastern Europe— where the worst crimes had taken place—retribution was particularly intense. There and in other parts of Europe, collaborators, non-Germans who had assisted the German occupiers during the war, were also punished. In the days and months immediately after the war, spontaneous acts of retribution brought some collaborators to account. In both France and Italy, unofficial groups seeking revenge summarily executed some 25,000 persons. French women accused of "horizontal collaboration"—having sexual relations with German soldiers during the occupation—were publicly humiliated by angry mobs. Newly established postwar governments also established official courts to sanction collaborators or send them to prison. A minority received the death sentence.

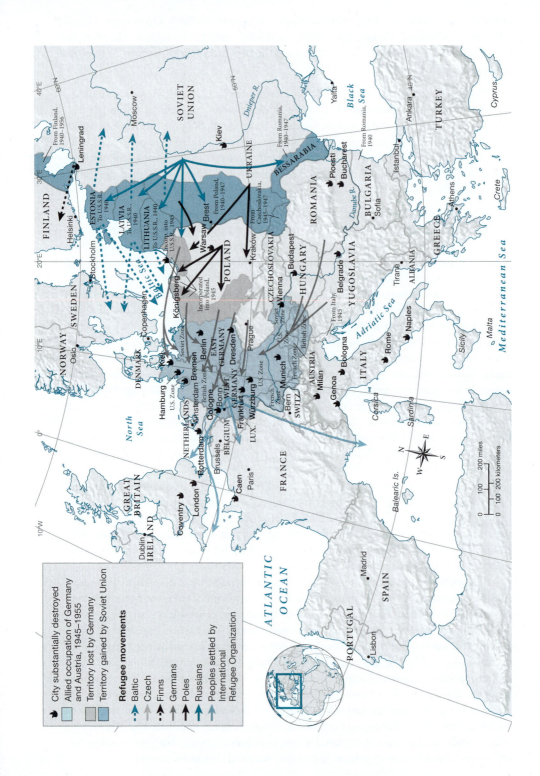

◀ **MAP 28.1** **The Aftermath of World War II in Europe, ca. 1945–1950**
By 1945 millions of people displaced by war and territorial changes were on the move. The Soviet
Union and Poland took land from Germany, which the Allies partitioned into occupation zones.
Those zones subsequently formed the basis of the East and West German states. Austria was
detached from Germany and similarly divided, but the Soviets subsequently permitted Austria
to reunify as a neutral state.

In Germany and Austria, occupation authorities set up "denazification" procedures
meant to eradicate National Socialist ideology from social and political institutions and
identify and punish former Nazi Party members responsible for the worst crimes. At
the Nuremberg trials (1945–1946), an international military tribunal organized by the
four Allied powers tried the highest-ranking Nazi military and civilian leaders who had
survived the war, charging them with war crimes and crimes against humanity. After
chilling testimony from victims of the regime, which revealed the full systematic horror
of Nazi atrocities, twelve were sentenced to death and ten more to lengthy prison terms.

The Nuremberg trials marked the last time the four Allies worked closely together
to punish former Nazis. As the Cold War developed and the Soviets and the Western
Allies drew increasingly apart, each carried out separate denazification programs in their
own zones of occupation. In the Western zones, military courts at first actively prosecuted
leading Nazis. But the huge numbers implicated in Nazi crimes, German opposition to
the proceedings, and the need for stability in the looming Cold War made thorough
denazification impractical. Except for the worst offenders, the Western authorities had
quietly shelved denazification by 1948. The process was similar in the Soviet zone. At
first, punishment was swift and harsh. About 45,000 former party officials, upper-class
industrialists, and large landowners identified as Nazis were sentenced to prison or death.
As in the West, however, former Nazis who cooperated with the Soviet authorities could
avoid prosecution. Thus, many former Nazis found leading positions in government
and industry in both the Soviet and Western zones.

The Peace Settlement and Cold War Origins

In the years immediately after the war, as ordinary people across Europe struggled to
come to terms with the war and recover from the ruin, the victorious Allies — the
U.S.S.R., the United States, and Great Britain — tried to shape a reasonable and lasting
peace. Yet the Allies began to quarrel almost as soon as the unifying threat of Nazi
Germany disappeared, and the interests of the Communist Soviet Union and the capitalist Britain and United States increasingly diverged. The hostility between the Eastern
and Western superpowers was the sad but logical outgrowth of military developments,
wartime agreements, and long-standing political and ideological differences that stretched
back to the Russian Revolution.

Once the United States entered the war in late 1941, the Americans and the British
had made military victory their highest priority. They did not try to take advantage of
the Soviet Union's precarious position in 1942, because they feared that hard bargaining
would encourage Stalin to consider making a separate peace with Hitler. Together, the
Allies avoided discussion of postwar aims and the shape of the eventual peace settlement

The Big Three In 1945 a triumphant Winston Churchill, an ailing Franklin Roosevelt, and a determined Stalin met at Yalta in southern Russia to plan for peace. Cooperation soon gave way to bitter hostility, and the decisions made by these leaders transformed the map of Europe. (Franklin D. Roosevelt Presidential Library)

and focused instead on pursuing a policy of German unconditional surrender to solidify the alliance. By late 1943 negotiations about the postwar settlement could no longer be postponed. The conference that the "Big Three" — Stalin, Roosevelt, and Churchill — held in the Iranian capital of Teheran in November 1943 proved crucial for determining the shape of the postwar world.

At Teheran, the Big Three jovially reaffirmed their determination to crush Germany, followed by tense discussions of Poland's postwar borders and a strategy to win the war. Stalin, concerned that the U.S.S.R. was bearing the brunt of the fighting, asked his allies to relieve his armies by opening a second front in German-occupied France. Churchill, fearing the military dangers of a direct attack, argued that American and British forces should follow up their Italian campaign with an indirect attack on Germany through the Balkans. Roosevelt, however, agreed with Stalin that an American-British assault through France would be better, though the date for the invasion was set later than the Soviet leader desired. This decision had momentous implications for the Cold War. While the delay in opening a second front fanned Stalin's distrust of the Allies, the agreement on a British-U.S. invasion of France also ensured that the American-British and Soviet armies would come together in defeated Germany along a north-south line, and that Soviet troops would play the predominant role in pushing the Germans out of eastern and central Europe. Thus the basic shape of postwar Europe was cast even as the fighting continued.

When the Big Three met again in February 1945 at Yalta, on the Black Sea in southern Russia, advancing Soviet armies had already occupied Poland, Bulgaria, Romania, Hungary, part of Yugoslavia, and much of Czechoslovakia, and were within a hundred miles of Berlin. The stalled American-British forces had yet to cross the Rhine into Germany. Moreover, the United States was far from defeating Japan. In short, the U.S.S.R.'s position on the ground was far stronger than that of the United States and Britain, which played to Stalin's advantage.

The Allies agreed at Yalta that each of the four victorious powers would occupy a separate zone of Germany and that the Germans would pay heavy reparations to the

Soviet Union. At American insistence, Stalin agreed to declare war on Japan after Germany's defeat. As for Poland, the Big Three agreed that the U.S.S.R. would permanently incorporate the eastern Polish territories its army had occupied in 1939 and that Poland would be compensated with German lands to the west. They also agreed in an ambiguous compromise that the new governments in Soviet-occupied Europe would be freely elected but "friendly" to the Soviet Union.

The Yalta compromise over elections in these countries broke down almost immediately. Even before the conference, Communist parties were gaining control in Bulgaria and Poland. Elsewhere, the Soviets formed coalition governments that included Social Democrats and other leftist parties but reserved key government posts for Moscow-trained Communists. At the Potsdam Conference of July 1945, the differences over elections in Soviet-occupied Europe surged to the fore. Roosevelt had died and had been succeeded by President Harry Truman (r. 1945–1953), who demanded immediate free elections throughout central and eastern Europe. Stalin refused point-blank. "A freely elected government in any of these East European countries would be anti-Soviet," he admitted simply, "and that we cannot allow."[2]

Here, then, were the keys to the much-debated origins of the Cold War. While fighting Germany, the Allies could maintain an alliance of necessity. As the war drew to a close, long-standing hostility between East and West re-emerged. Mutual distrust, security concerns, and antagonistic desires for economic, political, and territorial control began to destroy the former partnership.

Stalin, who had lived through two enormously destructive German invasions, was determined to establish a buffer zone of sympathetic states around the U.S.S.R. and at the same time expand the reach of communism and the Soviet state. Stalin believed that only Communists could be dependable allies, and that free elections would result in independent and possibly hostile governments on his western border. With Soviet armies in central and eastern Europe, there was no way short of war for the United States to control the region's political future, and war was out of the question. The United States, for its part, pushed to maintain democratic capitalism and open access to free markets in western Europe. The Americans quickly showed that they, too, were willing to use their vast political, economic, and military power to maintain predominance in their sphere of influence.

West Versus East

The Cold War took shape over the next five years, as both sides hardened their positions. After Japan's surrender in September 1945, Truman cut off aid to the ailing U.S.S.R. In October he declared that the United States would never recognize any government established by force against the will of its people. In March 1946 former British prime minister Churchill ominously informed an American audience that an "iron curtain" had fallen across the continent, dividing Europe into two antagonistic camps (Map 28.2).

The Soviet Union was indeed consolidating its hold on central and eastern Europe. In fact, the Soviets enjoyed some popular support in the region, though this varied from country to country. After all, the Red Army had thrown out the German invaders, and after the abuses of fascism the ideals of Communist equality retained some appeal. Yet the Communist parties in these areas quickly recognized that they lacked enough

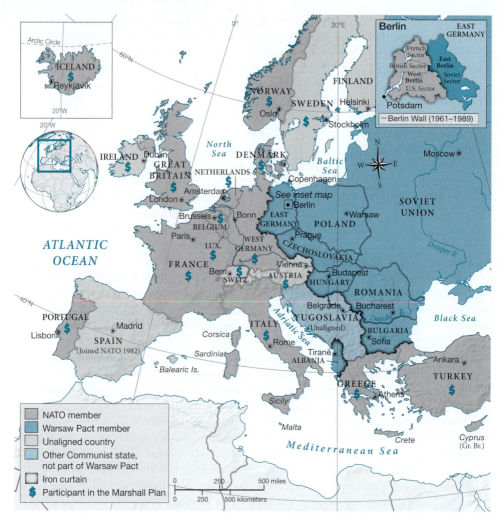

MAP 28.2   Cold War Europe in the 1950s
The Cold War divided Europe into two hostile military alliances that formed to the east and west of an "iron curtain."

support to take power in free elections. In Romania, Bulgaria, Poland, and Hungary, Communist politicians, backed by Moscow, repressed their liberal opponents and engineered phony elections that established Communist-led regimes. They purged the last remaining noncommunists from the coalition governments set up after the war and by 1948 had established Soviet-style, one-party Communist dictatorships. The pattern was somewhat different in Czechoslovakia, where Communists enjoyed success in open elections and initially formed a coalition government with other parties. When the noncommunist ministers resigned in February 1948, the Communists took over the government and began Stalinizing the country. This seizure of power in Czechoslovakia greatly contributed to Western fears of limitless Communist expansion.

In western Europe, communism also enjoyed some support. In Italy, which boasted the largest Communist Party outside of the Soviet bloc, Communists won 19 percent of the vote in 1946; French Communists earned 28 percent of the vote the same year. These large, well-organized parties criticized the growing role of the United States in western Europe and challenged their own governments with violent rhetoric and large strikes. At the same time, bitter civil wars in Greece and China pitted Communist revolutionaries against authoritarian leaders backed by the United States (see below and page 966).

By early 1947 it appeared to many Americans that the U.S.S.R. was determined to export communism by subversion throughout Europe and around the world. The United States responded with the **Truman Doctrine**, aimed at "containing" communism to areas already under Communist governments, a policy first advocated by U.S. diplomat George Kennan in 1946. The United States, President Truman promised, would use diplomatic, economic, and even military means to resist the expansion of communism anywhere on the globe. In the first examples of containment policies in action, Truman asked Congress to provide military aid to anticommunist forces in the Greek Civil War (1944–1949) and counter the threat of Soviet expansion in Turkey. With American support, both countries remained in the Western bloc. The American determination to enforce containment hardened when the Soviets exploded their own atomic bomb in 1949, raising popular fears of a looming nuclear holocaust. At home and abroad, the United States engaged in an anticommunist crusade. Emotional, moralistic denunciations of Stalin and Communist regimes became part of American public life. By the early 1950s the U.S. government was restructuring its military to meet the Soviet threat, pouring money into defense spending, and testing nuclear weapons that dwarfed the destructive power of atomic bombs.

Military aid and a defense buildup were only one aspect of Truman's policy of containment. In 1947 western Europe was still on the verge of economic collapse. Food was scarce, inflation was high, and black markets flourished. Recognizing that an economically and politically stable western Europe would be an effective block against the popular appeal of communism, U.S. secretary of state George C. Marshall offered Europe economic aid—the **Marshall Plan**—to help it rebuild. As Marshall wrote in a State Department bulletin, "Its purpose should be the revival of a working economy in the world so as to permit the emergence of political and social conditions in which free institutions can exist."[3]

The Marshall Plan was one of the most successful foreign aid programs in history. When it ended in 1951, the United States had given about $13 billion in aid (equivalent to over $200 billion in 2014 dollars) to fifteen western European nations, and Europe's economy was on the way to recovery. Marshall Plan funding was initially offered to East Bloc countries as well, but fearing Western interference in the Soviet sphere, they rejected the offer. In 1949 the Soviets established the **Council for Mutual Economic Assistance (COMECON)**, an economic organization of Communist states intended to rebuild the East Bloc independently of the West. Thus the generous aid of the Marshall Plan was limited to countries in the Western bloc, which further increased Cold War divisions.

In the late 1940s Berlin, the capital city of Germany, was on the frontline of the Cold War. Like the rest of Germany and Austria, Berlin had been divided into four zones of occupation. In June 1948 the Western allies replaced the currency in the western zones of Germany and Berlin, an early move in plans to establish a separate West

German state sympathetic to U.S. interests. The currency reform violated the peace settlement and raised Stalin's fears of the American presence in Europe. In addition, growing ties among Britain, France, Belgium, and the Netherlands convinced Stalin that a Western bloc was forming against the Soviet Union. In response, the Soviet dictator used the one card he had to play — access to Berlin — to force the allies to the bargaining table. Stalin blocked all traffic through the Soviet zone of Germany to Berlin in an attempt to win concessions and perhaps reunify the city under Soviet control. Acting firmly, the Western allies coordinated around-the-clock flights of hundreds of planes over the Soviet roadblocks, supplying provisions to West Berliners and thwarting Soviet efforts to swallow up the western half of the city. After 324 days, the Berlin airlift succeeded, and the Soviets reopened the roads.

Success in breaking the Berlin blockade had several lasting results. First, it paved the way for the creation of two separate German states in 1949: the Federal Republic of Germany (West Germany), aligned with the United States, and the German Democratic Republic (East Germany), aligned with the U.S.S.R. Germany would remain divided for the next forty-one years, a radical solution to the "German problem" that satisfied people fearful of the nation's possible military resurgence.

The Berlin crisis also seemed to show that containment worked, and thus strengthened U.S. resolve to maintain a strong European and U.S. military presence in western Europe. In 1949 the United States formed **NATO** (the North Atlantic Treaty Organization), an anti-Soviet military alliance of Western governments. As one British diplomat put it, NATO was designed "to keep the Russians out, the Americans in, and the Germans down."[4] With U.S. backing, West Germany joined NATO in 1955 and was allowed to rebuild its military to join in defense of western Europe against possible Soviet attack. That same year, the Soviets countered by organizing the **Warsaw Pact**, a military alliance among the U.S.S.R. and its Communist satellites. In both political and military terms, most of Europe was divided into two hostile blocs.

The superpower confrontation that emerged from the ruins of World War II took shape in Europe, but it quickly spread around the globe. The Cold War turned hot in East Asia. When Soviet-backed Communist North Korea invaded South Korea in 1950, President Truman swiftly sent U.S. troops. In the end, the Korean War was indecisive: the fragile truce agreed to in 1953 left Korea divided between a Communist north and a capitalist south. The war nonetheless showed that though the superpowers might maintain a fragile peace in Europe, they were perfectly willing to engage in open conflict in non-Western territories.

By 1955 the Soviet-American confrontation had become an apparently permanent feature of world affairs. For the next thirty-five years, despite intermittent periods of relaxation, the superpowers would struggle to win political influence and territorial control and to achieve technological superiority. Cold War hostilities helped foster a nuclear arms race, a space race, and the computer revolution, all made possible by stunning advances in science and technology.

Big Science in the Nuclear Age

During the Second World War, theoretical science lost its innocence when it was joined with practical technology (applied science) on a massive scale. Most leading university scientists went to work on top-secret projects to help their governments fight the war.

A Soviet View of the Arms Race   This propaganda poster from the 1950s reads, "We are a peaceful people, but our armored train stands in ready reserve." The reference to the armored train recalls the Bolshevik use of trains in combat against the White armies during the Russian civil war of the early 1920s. (Sovfoto)

The development by British scientists of radar to detect enemy aircraft was a particularly important outcome of this new kind of sharply focused research. The air war also greatly stimulated the development of rocketry and jet aircraft. The most spectacular and deadly result of directed scientific research during the war was the atomic bomb, which showed the world both the awesome power and the heavy moral responsibilities of modern science and its high priests.

The impressive results of this directed research inspired a new model for science — Big Science. By combining theoretical work with sophisticated engineering in a large bureaucratic organization, Big Science could tackle extremely difficult problems, from new and improved weapons for the military to better products for consumers. Big Science was extremely expensive, requiring large-scale financing from governments and large corporations.

After the war, scientists continued to contribute to advances in military technologies, and a large portion of all postwar scientific research supported the growing arms race. New weapons such as missiles, nuclear submarines, and spy satellites demanded breakthroughs no less remarkable than those responsible for radar and the first atomic bomb. After 1945 roughly one-quarter of all men and women trained in science and engineering in the West — and perhaps more in the Soviet Union — were employed full-time in the production of weapons to kill other humans. By the 1960s both sides had enough nuclear firepower to destroy each other and the rest of the world many times over.

Sophisticated science, lavish government spending, and military needs came together in the space race of the 1960s. In 1957 the Soviets used long-range rockets developed in their nuclear weapons program to launch Sputnik, the first man-made satellite to orbit the earth. In 1961 they sent the world's first cosmonaut circling the globe. Embarrassed by Soviet triumphs, the United States caught "Sputnikitis" and made an all-out commitment to catch up with the Soviets. The U.S. National Aeronautics and Space Administration (NASA), founded in 1958, won a symbolic victory by landing a manned spacecraft on the moon in 1969. Four more moon landings followed by 1972.

Advanced nuclear weapons and the space race were made possible by the concurrent revolution in computer technology. The search for better weaponry in World War II boosted the development of sophisticated data-processing machines, including the electronic Colossus computer used by the British to break German military codes. The massive mainframe ENIAC (Electronic Numerical Integrator and Computer), built for the U.S. Army at the University of Pennsylvania, went into operation in 1945. The invention of the transistor in 1947 further advanced computer design. From the mid-1950s on, this small, efficient electronic switching device increasingly replaced bulky vacuum tubes as the key workings of computers. By the 1960s sophisticated computers were indispensable tools for a variety of military, commercial, and scientific uses, foreshadowing the rise of personal computers in the decades to come.

Big Science had tangible benefits for ordinary people. During the postwar green revolution, directed agricultural research greatly increased the world's food supplies. Farming was industrialized and became more and more productive per acre, resulting in far fewer people being needed to grow food. The application of scientific advances to industrial processes made consumer goods less expensive and more available to larger numbers of people. The transistor, for example, was used in computers but also in portable radios, kitchen appliances, and many other consumer products. In sum, in the nuclear age, Big Science created new sources of material well-being and entertainment as well as destruction.

The Western Renaissance/Recovery in Western Europe

What were the sources of postwar recovery and stability in western Europe?

In the late 1940s the outlook for Europe appeared bleak. Ruins still covered urban areas, economic conditions were the worst in generations, and Cold War confrontations divided the continent. Yet Europe recovered, with the nations of western Europe in the vanguard. In less than a generation, many western European countries constructed democratic political institutions and entered a period of unprecedented economic growth. As a consumer revolution brought improved living standards and a sense of prosperity to ever-larger numbers of people, politicians entered collective economic agreements and established the European Economic Community, the first steps toward broader European unity.

The Search for Political and Social Consensus

In the first years after the war, economic conditions in western Europe were terrible. Infrastructure of all kinds barely functioned, and runaway inflation and a thriving black market testified to severe shortages and hardships. In 1948, as Marshall Plan dollars poured in, the battered economies of western Europe began to improve. The outbreak of the Korean War in 1950 further stimulated economic activity, and Europe entered a period of rapid economic progress that lasted into the late 1960s. Never before had the European economy grown so fast. By the late 1950s contemporaries were talking about a widespread **economic miracle** that had brought robust growth to most western European countries.

There were many reasons for this stunning economic performance. American aid got the process off to a fast start. Moreover, economic growth became a basic objective of all western European governments, for leaders and voters alike were determined to avoid a return to the dangerous and demoralizing stagnation of the 1930s.

The postwar governments in western Europe thus embraced new political and economic policies that led to a remarkably lasting social consensus. They turned to liberal democracy and generally adopted Keynesian economics (see Chapter 26) in successful attempts to stimulate their economies. In addition, whether they leaned to the left or to the right, national leaders in the core European states applied an imaginative mixture of government planning and free-market capitalism to promote economic growth. They nationalized (or established government ownership of) significant sectors of the economy, used economic regulation to encourage growth, and established generous welfare provisions, paid for with high taxes, for all citizens. This consensual framework for good government lasted until the middle of the 1970s.

In politics, the Nazi occupation and the war had discredited old ideas and old leaders, and a new team of European politicians emerged to guide the postwar recovery. Across the West, newly formed Christian Democratic parties became important power brokers. Rooted in the Catholic parties of the prewar decades (see Chapters 23 and 27), the **Christian Democrats** offered voters tired of radical politics a center-right vision of reconciliation and recovery. Socialists and Communists, active in the resistance against Hitler, also increased their power and prestige, especially in France and Italy. They, too, provided fresh leadership as they pushed for social change and economic reform.

Across much of continental Europe, the centrist Christian Democrats defeated their left-wing competition. In Italy, the Christian Democrats were the leading party in the first postwar elections in 1946, and in early 1948 they won an absolute majority in the parliament in a landslide victory. In France, the Popular Republican Movement, a Christian Democratic party, provided some of the best postwar leaders after General Charles de Gaulle (duh-GOHL) resigned from his position as head of the provisional government in January 1946. West Germans, too, elected a Christian Democratic government from 1949 until 1969.

As they provided effective leadership for their respective countries, Christian Democrats drew inspiration from a common Christian and European heritage. They steadfastly rejected authoritarianism and narrow nationalism and placed their faith in democracy and liberalism. Steadfast cold warriors, their anticommunist rhetoric was unrelenting. Rejecting the class politics of the left, they championed a return to traditional family values, a vision with great appeal after a war that left many broken families and destitute households; the Christian Democrats often received a majority of women's votes.

PRIMARY SOURCE   Western European Recovery and the Promise of Prosperity

Christian Democrat Ludwig Erhard, minister for economic affairs (1949–1963) and then chancellor (1963–1966) of West Germany, was an outspoken proponent of liberal capitalism and free markets in the years of the "economic miracle." In this newspaper article from June 16, 1953, Erhard defends the use of consumer credit and the expansion of consumption, starting with the wealthy, as an engine of postwar economic growth.

I have often pointed out that the consumption of quality goods can only be expanded provided we tolerate their use being confined initially to a relatively small number of people in the higher income brackets. If this is not accepted, and if the enjoyment of such goods is regarded as indulgence and made the subject of social obloquy and hostility, then the economy will be forced to abandon production in this sector, and there will be a corresponding loss of potential national income (and jobs) and the growth of the country's productive capacity will be forcibly curtailed. One section of the press actually challenged me to say how an old-age pensioner was to set about getting his refrigerator. To this puerile question I replied that the first motor-cars in America were presumably not run by pensioners but by millionaires, and I do not consider this reply unduly flippant. Does not the history of the world in the last hundred years afford abundant proof of the fact that every single improvement in the standard of living can only be effected step by step, spreading progressively over a gradually mounting proportion of the population? . . .

Ever since 1948 I have been propounding an economic policy which puts the consumer at the very centre of all economic processes, by ensuring freedom of choice to him and restoring him to a position of dignity and power. . . .

Responding to a critique of shoppers purchasing goods on credit, Erhard continues:

At first sight, this argument seems reasonable enough, but in the balance-sheet of the economy as a whole the picture looks different. Consumer credit enables

---

Following their U.S. allies, Christian Democrats advocated free-market economics and promised voters prosperity and ample supplies of consumer goods. (See "Primary Source: Western European Recovery and the Promise of Prosperity," above.) At the same time, they established education subsidies, family and housing allowances, public transportation, and public health insurance throughout continental Europe. When necessary, Christian Democratic leaders accepted the need for limited government planning. In France, the government established modernization commissions for key industries, and state-controlled banks funneled money into industrial development. In West Germany, the Christian Democrats broke decisively with the straitjacketed Nazi economy and promoted a "social-market economy" based on a combination of free-market liberalism, some state intervention, and an extensive social benefits network.

Though Portugal, Spain, and Greece generally supported NATO and the United States in the Cold War, they proved exceptions to the rule of democratic transformation outside the Soviet bloc. In Portugal and Spain, nationalist authoritarian regimes had

goods to be produced which could otherwise not find a market. . . . Now, consumer credit goes a step further and initiates an expansion of production (e.g. of refrigerators), and this expanded production creates new income which in its turn appears as additional purchasing power on the market. The volume of goods at the disposal of the economy has in other words been built up to a higher level, the national product and the national income have been extended. . . .

In this connection of course the question of magnitude is of vital importance. Consumer credit cannot carry, but can usefully supplement an upswing of the economy as a whole. . . . The use of consumer credit [is] one of the means capable of subserving a general policy aimed at expanded consumption. . . .

Consumer credit can be a means of increasing employment, creating additional returns, and thus enlarging the national product and the national income. The wider the choice of goods available to the consumer, the more active competition becomes, and the more prices will tend to come down, to the benefit of us all.

EVALUATE THE EVIDENCE

1. How, according to Erhard, does expanded consumption and the use of credit lead to economic growth?

2. Why would promises of looming prosperity—such as Erhard's—play an important role in Cold War rhetoric?

Source: Ludwig Erhard, *The Economics of Success*, trans. J. A. Arengo-Jones and D. J. S. Thomson (Princeton: D. Van Nostrand Co., 1963). Used by permission of Ludwig-Erhard-Stiftung e.V.

taken power in the 1930s. Portugal's authoritarian state was overthrown in a left-wing military coup only in 1974, while Spain's dictator Francisco Franco remained in power until his death in 1975. The authoritarian monarchy established in Greece when the civil war ended in 1949, bolstered by military support and kept in power in a series of army coups, was likewise replaced by democratic government only in 1975.

By contrast, the Scandinavian countries and Great Britain took decisive turns to the left. Norway, Denmark, and especially Sweden earned a global reputation for long-term Social Democratic governance, generous state-sponsored welfare benefits, tolerant lifestyles, and independent attitudes toward Cold War conflicts. In Britain, the social-democratic Labour Party took power after the war and ambitiously established a "cradle-to-grave" welfare state. Although the Labour Party suffered defeats throughout much of the 1950s and early 1960s, its Conservative opponents maintained much of the welfare state when they came to power. Many British industries were nationalized, including banks, iron and steel industries, and utilities and public transportation networks. The British government gave its citizens free medical services and hospital care, generous retirement pensions, and unemployment benefits, all subsidized by progressive taxation that pegged tax payments to income levels, with the wealthy paying significantly more than those below them. Even though wartime austerity and rationing programs were in place until the mid-1950s, Britain offered the most comprehensive state benefit programs outside Scandinavia. Economic growth and state-sponsored welfare measures meant that, by the early 1960s, western European living standards were higher than ever before.

Toward European Unity

Though there were important regional differences across much of western Europe, politicians and citizens supported policies that brought together limited state planning, strong economic growth, and democratic government, and this political and social consensus accompanied the first tentative steps on the long road toward a more unified Europe. Christian Democrats were committed to cultural and economic cooperation, and other groups shared their dedication. Many European intellectuals believed that only a new "European nation" could effectively rebuild the war-torn continent and reassert the continent's influence in world affairs.

A number of new financial arrangements and institutions encouraged slow but steady moves toward European integration, as did cooperation with the United States. The Bretton Woods agreement of 1944 had already linked Western currencies to the U.S. dollar and established the International Monetary Fund and the World Bank to facilitate free markets and world trade. To receive Marshall Plan aid, the European states were required by the Americans to cooperate with one another, leading to the creation of the Organization for European Economic Cooperation and the Council of Europe in 1948, both of which promoted commerce and cooperation among European countries.

European federalists hoped that the Council of Europe would evolve into a European parliament with sovereign rights, but this did not happen. Britain, with its still-vast empire and its close relationship with the United States, consistently opposed conceding sovereignty to the council. On the continent, many prominent nationalists and Communists agreed with the British view.

Frustrated in political consolidation, European federalists turned to economics as a way of working toward genuine unity. In 1950 two far-seeing French statesmen, the diplomat and political economist Jean Monnet and Foreign Minister Robert Schuman, called for a special international organization to control and integrate all European steel and coal production. Christian Democratic governments in West Germany, Italy, Belgium, the Netherlands, and Luxembourg accepted the French idea and founded the European Coal and Steel Community in 1951 (the British steadfastly refused to join). The founding states quickly attained their immediate economic goal—a single, transnational market for steel and coal without national tariffs or quotas. Close economic ties, advocates hoped, would eventually bind the six member nations so closely together that war among them would become unthinkable.

In 1957 the six countries of the Coal and Steel Community signed the Treaty of Rome, which created the European Economic Community, or **Common Market**. The first goal of the treaty was a gradual reduction of all tariffs among the six in order to create a single market almost as large as that of the United States. Other goals included the free movement of capital and labor and common economic policies and institutions. The Common Market encouraged trade among European states, promoted global exports, and helped build shared resources for the modernization of national industries. European integration thus increased transnational cooperation even as it bolstered economic growth on the national level.

The development of the Common Market fired imaginations and encouraged the hopes of some for rapid progress toward political as well as economic union. In the 1960s, however, these hopes were frustrated by a resurgence of nationalism. France again took the lead. French president Charles de Gaulle, re-elected to office in 1958, was at heart a romantic nationalist. De Gaulle viewed the United States as the main threat to genuine French (and European) independence. He withdrew all French military forces from what he called an "American-controlled" NATO, developed France's own nuclear weapons, and vetoed the scheduled advent of majority rule within the Common Market. Thus the 1950s and 1960s established a lasting pattern: Europeans would establish ever-closer economic ties, but the Common Market remained a union of independent, sovereign states.

The Consumer Revolution

In the late 1950s western Europe's rapidly expanding economy led to a rising standard of living and remarkable growth in the number and availability of standardized consumer goods. Modern consumer society had precedents in the decades before the Second World War (see Chapter 26), but the years of the "economic miracle" saw the arrival of a veritable consumer revolution: as the percentage of income spent on necessities such as housing and food declined dramatically, near full employment and high wages meant that more Europeans could buy more things than ever before. Shaken by war and eager to rebuild their homes and families, western Europeans eagerly embraced the new products of consumer society. Like North Americans, they filled their houses and apartments with modern appliances such as washing machines, and they eagerly purchased the latest entertainment devices of the day: radios, record players, and televisions.

The purchase of consumer goods was greatly facilitated by the increased use of installment purchasing, which allowed people to buy on credit. With the expansion of social security safeguards reducing the need to accumulate savings for hard times and old age, ordinary people were increasingly willing to take on debt, and new banks and credit unions offered loans for consumer purchases on easy terms. The consumer market became an increasingly important component of general economic growth. For example, the European automobile industry expanded phenomenally after lagging far behind that of the United States since the 1920s. In 1948 there were only 5 million cars in western Europe; by 1965 there were 44 million. Car ownership was democratized and became possible for better-paid workers — the consumer revolution brought a vast array of new items into everyday activities, changing both lifestyles and attitudes.

Visions of consumer abundance became a powerful weapon in an era of Cold War competition. Politicians in both East and West claimed that their respective systems could best provide citizens with ample consumer goods. In the competition over consumption, Western capitalism clearly surpassed Eastern planned economies in the production and distribution of inexpensive products. Western leaders boasted about the arrival of prosperity and promised new forms of social equality in which all citizens would have equal access to consumer goods — rather than relying on class leveling mandated by the state, as in the despised East Bloc. The race to provide ordinary people with higher living standards would be a central aspect of the Cold War, as the Communist East Bloc struggled to catch up to Western standards of prosperity.

Developments in the Soviet Union and the East Bloc

What was the pattern of postwar development in the Soviet bloc?

While western Europe surged ahead economically and increased its independent political power as American influence gradually waned, East Bloc countries followed a different path. The Soviet Union first tightened its grip on peoples it had "liberated" during the Second World War and then refused to let go. Though limited reforms after Stalin's death in 1953 led to some economic improvement and limited gains in freedoms, postwar recovery in Communist central and eastern Europe proceeded along Soviet lines, and political and social developments there were strongly influenced by developments in the U.S.S.R.

Postwar Life in the East Bloc

The "Great Patriotic War of the Fatherland" had fostered Russian nationalism and a relaxation of dictatorial terror. It also had produced a rare but real unity between Soviet rulers and most citizens. Having made a heroic war effort, the vast majority of the Soviet people hoped in 1945 that a grateful party and government would grant greater freedom and democracy. Such hopes were soon disappointed.

Even before the war ended, Stalin was moving the U.S.S.R. back toward rigid dictatorship. By early 1946 Stalin was arguing that war was inevitable as long as capitalism existed. Working to extend Communist influence across the globe, the Soviets established the Cominform, or Communist Information Bureau, an international organization dedicated to maintaining Russian control over Communist parties abroad, in western Europe and the East Bloc. Stalin's new superpower foe, the United States, served as an excuse for re-establishing a harsh dictatorship in the U.S.S.R. itself. Stalin reasserted the Communist Party's complete control of the government and his absolute mastery of the party. Rigid ideological indoctrination, attacks on religion, and the absence of civil liberties were soon facts of life for citizens of the Soviet empire. Millions of supposed political enemies were sent to prison, exile, or forced-labor camps.

As discussed earlier, in the satellite states of central and eastern Europe — including East Germany, Poland, Hungary, Czechoslovakia, Romania, Albania, and Bulgaria — national Communist parties remade state and society on the Soviet model. Though there were significant differences in these East Bloc countries, postwar developments followed a similar pattern. Popular Communist leaders who had led the resistance against Germany were ousted as Stalin sought to create obedient instruments. With Soviet backing, national Communist parties absorbed their Social Democratic rivals and established one-party dictatorships subservient to the Communist Party in Moscow. State security services arrested, imprisoned, and sometimes executed dissenters. Show trials of supposedly disloyal Communist Party leaders took place across the East Bloc from the late 1940s into the 1950s, but were particularly prominent in Bulgaria, Czechoslovakia, Hungary, and Romania. They testified to the influence of Soviet advisers and the unrestrained power of the domestic secret police in the satellite states, as well as Stalin's urge to establish complete control — and his increasing paranoia.

Only Josip Broz Tito (TEE-toh) (1892–1980), the resistance leader and Communist chief of Yugoslavia, was able to proclaim political independence and successfully resist Soviet domination. Tito stood up to Stalin in 1948, and because there was no Russian army in Yugoslavia, he got away with it. Though Communist led, Yugoslavia remained outside of the Soviet bloc. The country prospered as a multiethnic state until it began to break apart in 1991.

Within the East Bloc, the newly installed Communist governments moved quickly to restructure national economies along Soviet lines, introducing five-year plans to cope with the enormous task of economic reconstruction. Most industries and businesses were nationalized. These efforts transformed prewar patterns of everyday life, even as they laid the groundwork for industrial development later in the decade.

Rebellion in East Germany   In June 1953 disgruntled construction workers in East Berlin walked off the job to protest low pay and high work quotas, setting off a nationwide rebellion against the Communist regime. The protesters could do little against the Soviet tanks and troops who put down the revolt. (Deutsches Historiches Museum, Berlin, Germany/© DHM/The Bridgeman Art Library)

In their attempts to revive the economy, Communist planners gave top priority to heavy industry and the military, and neglected consumer goods and housing. In the 1950s East Bloc leaders were generally suspicious of Western-style consumer culture. A glut of consumer goods, they believed, created waste, encouraged rampant individualism, and led to social inequality. Thus, for practical and ideological reasons, the provision of consumer goods lagged in the East Bloc, leading to complaints and widespread disillusionment with the constantly deferred promise of socialist prosperity.

Communist regimes also moved aggressively to collectivize agriculture, as the Soviets had done in the 1930s (see Chapter 27). By the early 1960s independent farmers had virtually disappeared in most of the East Bloc. Poland was the exception: there the Stalinist regime tolerated the existence of private agriculture, hoping to maintain stability in the large and potentially rebellious country.

For many people in the East Bloc, everyday life was hard throughout the 1950s. Socialist planned economies often led to production problems and persistent shortages of basic household items. Party leaders encouraged workers to perform almost super-human labor to "build socialism," often for low pay and under poor conditions. In East Germany, popular discontent with this situation led to open revolt in June 1953. A strike by Berlin construction workers protesting poor wages and increased work quotas led to nationwide demonstrations that were put down with Soviet troops and tanks. At least fifty-five protesters were killed and about five thousand were arrested during the uprising. When the revolt ended, the authorities rescinded the increased work quotas, but despite this apparent concession the protest strengthened the position of hardliner Stalinists within the East German government.

Communist censors purged culture and art of independent voices in aggressive campaigns that imposed rigid anti-Western ideological conformity. In the 1950s and 1960s, the Communist states required artists and writers to conform to the dictates of **socialist realism**, which idealized the working classes and the Soviet Union. Party propagandists denounced artists who strayed from the party line, and forced many talented writers, composers, and film directors to produce works that conformed to the state's political goals. In short, the postwar East Bloc resembled the U.S.S.R. in the 1930s, although police terror was far less intense (see Chapter 27).

Reform and De-Stalinization

In 1953 the aging Stalin finally died, and the dictatorship that he had built began to change. Even as Stalin's heirs struggled for power, they realized that reforms were necessary because of the widespread fear and hatred created by Stalin's political terrorism. The power of the secret police was curbed, and many forced-labor camps were gradually closed. Change was also necessary to spur economic growth, which had sputtered in the postwar years. Moreover, Stalin's belligerent foreign policy had led directly to a strong Western alliance, which took steps to isolate the Soviet Union.

The Soviet leadership was badly split on the question of just how much change could be permitted while still preserving the system. Conservatives wanted to move slowly. Reformers, led by Nikita Khrushchev (1894–1971), argued for major innovations. Khrushchev (kroush-CHAWF), who had joined the party as a coal miner in 1918 and risen to a high-level position in the Ukraine in the 1930s, emerged as the new Soviet premier in 1955.

To strengthen his position and that of his fellow reformers, Khrushchev launched a surprising attack on Stalin and his crimes at a closed session of the Twentieth Party Congress in 1956. In his famous "secret speech," Khrushchev told Communist delegates startled by his open admission of errors that Stalin had "supported the glorification of his own person with all conceivable methods" to build a propagandistic "cult of personality." The delegates applauded when Khrushchev reported that Stalin had bungled the country's defense in World War II and unjustly imprisoned and tortured thousands of loyal Communists:

> [Stalin] discarded the Leninist method of convincing and educating . . . for that of administrative violence, mass repressions, and terror. . . . Mass arrests and deportations of many thousands of people, execution without trial and without normal investigation created conditions of insecurity, fear, and even desperation.[5]

The U.S.S.R. now entered a period of genuine liberalization—or **de-Stalinization**, as it was called in the West. Khrushchev's speech was read at Communist Party meetings held throughout the country, and it strengthened the reform movement. The party jealously maintained its monopoly on political power, but Khrushchev brought in new members. Calling for a relaxation of tensions with the West, the new premier announced a policy of "peaceful coexistence." In domestic policies, state planners shifted resources from heavy industry and the military toward consumer goods and agriculture, and relaxed Stalinist workplace controls. Leaders in other Communist countries grudgingly adopted similar reforms, and the East Bloc's generally low standard of living began to improve.

Khrushchev was proud of Soviet achievements and liked to boast that East Bloc living standards and access to consumer goods would soon surpass those of the West. Soviet and East Bloc reforms did spark a limited consumer revolution. Consumers' options were more modest than those in the West, but people in Communist countries also purchased automobiles, televisions, and other consumer goods in increasing numbers in the 1960s.

De-Stalinization created great ferment among writers and intellectuals who sought freedom from the constraints of socialist realism, such as Russian author Boris Pasternak (1890–1960), who published his great novel *Doctor Zhivago* in 1957. Appearing in the West but not in the Soviet Union until 1988, *Doctor Zhivago* is both a literary masterpiece and a powerful challenge to communism. It tells the story of a poet who rejects the violence and brutality of the October Revolution of 1917 and the Stalinist years. Mainstream Communist critics denounced Pasternak, whose book was circulated in secret—but in an era of liberalization he was neither arrested nor shot. Other talented writers followed Pasternak's lead, and courageous editors let the sparks fly. Aleksandr Solzhenitsyn (sohl-zhuh-NEET-suhn) (1918–2008) created a sensation when his *One Day in the Life of Ivan Denisovich* was published in 1962. Solzhenitsyn's novel portrays in grim detail life in a Stalinist concentration camp—a life to which Solzhenitsyn himself had been unjustly condemned—and is a damning indictment of the Stalinist past.

Foreign Policy and Domestic Rebellion

Khrushchev also de-Stalinized Soviet foreign policy. "Peaceful coexistence" with capitalism was possible, he argued, and war was not inevitable. Khrushchev negotiated with Western diplomats, agreeing in 1955, for example, to independence for a neutral Austria

PRIMARY SOURCE   The Hungarian Communist Party Calls for Reforms

Encouraged by Khrushchev's de-Stalinization policies, a group of reformist Communist leaders took power in Hungary in October 1956 in the midst of ongoing, violent demonstrations. Though the reformers never openly challenged the legitimacy of Communist rule, their call for free elections, economic reforms, and independence from the U.S.S.R. threatened Soviet authorities, who ordered the Red Army to put down the uprising. The reformers made their case to the Hungarian people in this radio announcement, originally broadcast on October 26, just one week before the Red Army invaded to end the revolt.

Since the two world wars our country has not experienced days as tragic as these. A fratricidal battle is raging in the capital city of our country. The number of injured is estimated to run into thousands, and of the dead into hundreds. An immediate end must be put to the bloodshed. The Central Committee [of the Communist Party] therefore announces the following measures:

1. A recommendation . . . for the election of a new national Government. This Government shall make good without fail the mistakes and crimes of the past. . . . The Central Committee, led by Comrade Imre Nagy, is presenting recommendations regarding members of a Government to be formed on the basis of the broadest national foundations.

2. The new Government shall start negotiations with the Soviet Government, on the basis of independence, complete equality and non-interference in internal affairs, to settle relations between our countries. As a first step towards this end, after the restoration of order, Soviet troops will immediately return to their bases. Complete equality between Hungary and the Soviet Union corresponds with the interests of both countries, because only on that basis can a truly fraternal, unbreakable Hungarian-Soviet bond be built. . . .

3. The Central Committee deems correct the election of Workers' Councils in the factories through the intermediary of the trade union organs. . . . Wage increases must be implemented. . . .

---

after ten long years of Allied occupation. As a result, Cold War tensions relaxed considerably between 1955 and 1957. At the same time, Khrushchev began wooing the new nations of Asia and Africa—even those that were not Communist—with promises of support and economic aid.

In the East Bloc states, Communist leaders responded in complex ways to de-Stalinization. In East Germany the regime stubbornly resisted reform, but in Poland and Hungary de-Stalinization stimulated rebelliousness. Poland took the lead in 1956, when extensive popular demonstrations brought a new government to power. The new First Secretary of the Polish Communist Party argued that there were "many roads to socialism." By promising to remain loyal to the Warsaw Pact, the Polish Communists managed to win greater autonomy from Soviet control. The new leadership maintained Communist control even as it tolerated a free peasantry and an independent Catholic Church.

4. The Government shall grant an amnesty to all those who have taken part in the armed battles. . . .

5. [We] leave no room for doubt regarding [our] standpoint on socialist democracy, but at the same time [we] are firmly resolved to defend the achievements of our People's Democracy and not to relinquish anything in the cause of socialism. . . .

In these fateful days great tasks await Communists. Let them meet and talk with the people sincerely. Let them talk, straight to the hearts of the truly patriotic people. Let them explain events and reassure the people. With an adult sense of responsibility let them tell the youth: what you have rightly asked for, you have attained!

The Party's top leadership is almost completely new. Just how new is this Party leadership? It suffices to say that all three Secretaries . . . have for years been prisoners of [Stalinist] Rakosi-type despotism; as victims of faked trials they spent years in prison from which they only recently have been released. If anyone knows that the old road must not be taken it is they. Let Communists explain that whoever seeks to spread distrust against these men and to set the people against them helps everybody except the people.

EVALUATE THE EVIDENCE

1. How does the Hungarian Communist Party combine a call for reform with a firm commitment to "socialist democracy"? Why would Soviet leaders see these reforms as a threat?

2. If you were a Hungarian living in Budapest in October 1956, would you accept this broadcast as sincere? Why or why not?

Source: Melvin J. Lasky, ed., *A White Book: The Hungarian Revolution: The Story of the October Uprising as Recorded in Documents, Dispatches, Eye-Witness Accounts, and World-Wide Reactions* (New York: Congress for Cultural Freedom/Frederick A. Praeger, 1957), p. 86.

Hungary experienced an ultimately tragic revolution the same year. Led by students and workers—the classic urban revolutionaries—the people of Budapest installed Imre Nagy (Im-rey nadge), a liberal Communist reformer, as the new prime minister in October 1956. Encouraged by extensive popular protests and joined by other Communist reformers, Nagy proposed to democratize Hungary. Though never renouncing communism, he demanded open, multiparty elections, the relaxation of political repression, and other reforms. Bold moves in Hungary raised widespread hopes that Communist states could undergo substantial but peaceful change, driven from within. (See "Primary Source: The Hungarian Communist Party Calls for Reforms," above.)

At first, it seemed that the Soviets might negotiate, but the breathing space was short-lived. When Nagy announced that Hungary would leave the Warsaw Pact and asked the United Nations to protect the country's neutrality, the Soviets grew alarmed about the possibility that Hungary's independent course would affect other East Bloc countries. On November 4 Soviet troops moved in on the capital city of Budapest and crushed the revolution. Around 2,700 Hungarians died in the crackdown. Fighting was bitter until the end, for the Hungarians hoped that the United Nations would come to their aid. This did not occur—in part because the Western powers were involved in the Suez crisis (see page 969) and were, in general, reluctant to directly confront the Soviets in Europe with military force. When a new, more conservative Communist regime executed Nagy and other protest leaders and sent thousands more to prison, many people in the East Bloc concluded that their best hope was to strive for internal reform without openly challenging Soviet control.

The outcome of the Hungarian uprising weakened support for Soviet-style communism in western Europe—the brutal repression deeply discouraged those who still believed in the possibility of an equitable socialist society, and tens of thousands of Communist Party members in the West resigned in disgust. At the same time, Western politicians saw that the U.S.S.R. would use military force to defend its control of the East Bloc, and that only open war between East and West had the potential to overturn Communist rule there. This price was too high, and it seemed that Communist domination of the satellite states was there to stay.

The Limits of Reform

By late 1962 opposition to Khrushchev's reformist policies had gained momentum in party circles. Khrushchev's Communist colleagues began to see de-Stalinization as a dangerous threat to the authority of the party. Moreover, Khrushchev's policy toward the West was erratic and ultimately unsuccessful. In 1958, in a failed attempt to staunch the flow of hundreds of thousands of disgruntled East German residents who used the open border between East and West Berlin to move permanently to the West, Khrushchev tightened border controls and ordered the Western allies to evacuate the city within six months. In response, the allies reaffirmed their unity in West Berlin, and Khrushchev backed down. Then, with Khrushchev's backing, in 1961 the East German authorities built a wall between East and West Berlin, sealing off West Berlin, in clear violation of existing access agreements between the Great Powers. The recently elected U.S. president, John F. Kennedy (r. 1961–1963), insisted publicly that the United States would never abandon Berlin. Privately hoping that the wall would lessen Cold War tensions by easing hostilities in Berlin, Kennedy did little to prevent its construction.

Emboldened by American acceptance of the Berlin Wall and seeing a chance to change the balance of military power decisively, Premier Khrushchev secretly ordered missiles with nuclear warheads installed in Fidel Castro's Communist Cuba in 1962. When U.S. intelligence discovered missile sites under construction, Kennedy countered with a naval blockade of Cuba. After a tense diplomatic crisis, Khrushchev agreed to remove the Soviet missiles in return for American pledges not to disturb Castro's regime. In a secret agreement, Kennedy also promised to remove U.S. nuclear missiles from Turkey.

Khrushchev's influence in the party, already slipping, declined rapidly after the Cuban missile crisis. In 1964 the reformist premier was displaced in a bloodless coup, and he spent the rest of his life under house arrest. Under his successor, Leonid Brezhnev (1906–1982), the U.S.S.R. began a period of limited re-Stalinization and economic stagnation. Almost immediately, Brezhnev (BREHZH-nehf) and his supporters started talking quietly of Stalin's "good points" and downplaying his crimes. This change informed Soviet citizens that further liberalization could not be expected at home. Soviet leaders, determined never to suffer Khrushchev's humiliation in the face of American nuclear superiority, launched a massive arms buildup. Yet Brezhnev and company proceeded cautiously in the mid-1960s and avoided direct confrontation with the United States.

Despite popular protests and changes in leadership, the U.S.S.R. and its satellite countries had achieved some stability by the late 1950s. Communist regimes addressed dissent and uprisings with an effective combination of military force, political repression, and limited economic reform. East and West traded propaganda threats, but both sides basically accepted the division of Europe into spheres of influence. Violent conflicts now took place in the developing world, where decolonization was opening new paths for Cold War confrontation.

The End of Empires

What led to decolonization after World War II, and how did the Cold War influence the process?

In the postwar era, in one of world history's great turning points, Europe's long-standing overseas expansion was dramatically reversed. The retreat from imperial control—what Europeans called **decolonization**—remade the world map. In just two decades, some one hundred new nations in Africa, Asia, and the Middle East joined the global community (Map 28.3). In some cases, decolonization proceeded relatively smoothly, with an orderly transition and little violence. In others, the European powers were determined to preserve colonial rule—long a source of profit and national pride—and colonized peoples won independence only after long and bloody struggles.

The Cold War had a profound impact on decolonization. Independence movements often had to choose sides in the struggle between the superpowers. After independence was won, both the United States and the Soviet Union struggled to exert influence in the former colonies, and economic growth and political stability remained elusive in much of Europe's former empire. Liberation from colonial domination was a proud achievement that brought fundamental gains in human freedom but left lasting problems for the former colonized and colonizers alike.

Decolonization and the Global Cold War

The most basic cause of imperial collapse was the rising demand of non-Western peoples for national self-determination, racial equality, and personal dignity. This demand spread from intellectuals to ordinary people in nearly every colonial territory after the First World War. By 1939 the colonial powers were already on the defensive; the Second World War prepared the way for the eventual triumph of independence movements.

European empires had been based on an enormous power differential between the rulers and the ruled, a difference that had greatly declined by 1945. Western Europe was economically devastated and militarily weak immediately after the war. Moreover, the Japanese had driven imperial rulers from large parts of East Asia during the war in

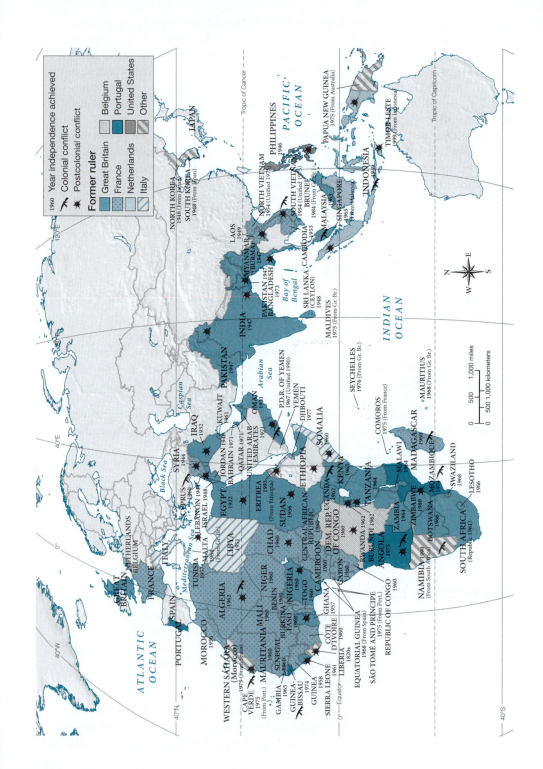

Former ruler

Great Britain	Belgium
France	Portugal
Netherlands	United States
Italy	Other

✕ Colonial conflict

✕ Postcolonial conflict

1960 Year independence achieved

NORTH KOREA 1948 (from Japan)
SOUTH KOREA 1948 (from Japan)

JAPAN

PHILIPPINES 1946

PAPUA NEW GUINEA 1975 (From Australia)

TIMOR-LESTE 1999 (From Indonesia)

PACIFIC OCEAN

Tropic of Cancer

Tropic of Capricorn

MYANMAR (BURMA) 1948

NORTH VIETNAM 1954 (Unified 1975)

SOUTH VIETNAM 1954 (Unified 1975)

BRUNEI 1984 (From U.K.)

MALAYSIA 1963

SINGAPORE 1965 (From Malaysia)

INDONESIA 1949

LAOS 1949

Bay of Bengal

PAKISTAN 1947
BANGLADESH 1971

SRI LANKA (CEYLON) 1948

INDIA 1947

MALDIVES 1965 (From Gr. Br.)

INDIAN OCEAN

SEYCHELLES 1976 (From Gr. Br.)

N
W E
S

Arabian Sea

KUWAIT 1961

OMAN 1971

P.D.R. OF YEMEN 1967 (Unified 1990)

YEMEN 1918

DJIBOUTI 1977

SOMALIA 1960

COMOROS 1975 (From France)

MAURITIUS 1968 (From Gr. Br.)

MADAGASCAR 1960

IRAQ 1932

JORDAN 1946

BAHRAIN 1971

QATAR 1971

UNITED ARAB EMIRATES 1971

Caspian Sea

Black Sea

SYRIA 1944

CYPRUS 1960

LEBANON 1943

ISRAEL 1948

EGYPT 1922

ERITREA 1993 (From Ethiopia)

SUDAN 1956

ETHIOPIA

CENTRAL AFRICAN REPUBLIC 1960

UGANDA 1962

KENYA 1963

RWANDA 1962

BURUNDI 1962

TANZANIA 1961

MALAWI 1964

MOZAMBIQUE 1975

SWAZILAND 1968

LESOTHO 1966

ZAMBIA 1964

ZIMBABWE 1980

BOTSWANA 1966

SOUTH AFRICA (Republic 1961)

NAMIBIA 1990 (From South Africa)

Mediterranean Sea

MALTA 1964 (From Gr. Br.)

LIBYA 1951

TUNISIA 1956

CHAD 1960

CAMEROON 1960

GABON 1960

DEM. REP. OF CONGO 1960

REPUBLIC OF CONGO 1960

ANGOLA 1975

GREAT BRITAIN

FRANCE

SPAIN

PORTUGAL

ITALY

NETHERLANDS

BELGIUM

MOROCCO 1956

ALGERIA 1962

NIGER 1960

NIGERIA 1960

BENIN 1960

BURKINA FASO 1960

MALI 1960

SENEGAL 1960

MAURITANIA 1960

WESTERN SAHARA (Morocco) 1975 (From Spain)

CAPE VERDE 1975 (From Port.)

GAMBIA 1965

GUINEA-BISSAU 1974

GUINEA 1958

SIERRA LEONE 1961

LIBERIA 1820s

CÔTE D'IVOIRE 1960

GHANA 1957

TOGO 1960

EQUATORIAL GUINEA 1968 (From Spain)

SÃO TOMÉ AND PRÍNCIPE 1975 (From Port.)

ATLANTIC OCEAN

Equator 0°

0 500 1,000 miles

0 500 1,000 kilometers

◀ **MAP 28.3**   **Decolonization in Africa and Asia, 1947 to the Present**
Divided primarily along religious lines into two states, British India led the way to political independence in 1947. Most African territories achieved statehood by the mid-1960s as European
empires passed away, unlamented.

the Pacific, shattering the myth of European superiority and invincibility. In Southeast
Asia, European imperialists confronted strong anticolonial nationalist movements that
re-emerged with new enthusiasm after the defeat of the Japanese.

To some degree, the Great Powers regarded their empires very differently after 1945
than before 1914, or even before 1939. Empire had rested on self-confidence and self-
righteousness; Europeans had believed their superiority to be not only technical and
military but also spiritual, racial, and moral. The horrors of the First and Second World
Wars undermined such complacent arrogance and gave opponents of imperialism much
greater influence in Europe. Increasing pressure from the United States, which had long
presented itself as an enemy of empire despite its own imperialist actions in the Philippines and the Americas, encouraged Europeans to let go of their former colonies. Indeed, Americans were eager to extend their own influence in Europe's former colonies —
except when independence movements were led by Communists, as in Vietnam.
Economically weakened, and with their political power and moral authority in tatters,
the imperial powers preferred to avoid bloody colonial wars and generally turned to
rebuilding at home.

Furthermore, the imperial powers faced dedicated anticolonial resistance. Popular
politicians, including China's Mao Zedong, India's Mohandas Gandhi, Egypt's Gamal
Abdel Nasser, and many others, provided determined leadership in the struggle against
European imperialism. A new generation of intellectuals, such as Jomo Kenyatta of
Kenya and Aimé Césaire and Frantz Fanon, both from Martinique, wrote trenchant
critiques of imperial power, often rooted in Marxist ideas. Anticolonial politicians and
intellectuals alike helped inspire colonized peoples to resist and overturn imperial rule.

Around the globe, the Cold War had an inescapable impact on decolonization.
Liberation from colonial rule had long been a central goal for proponents of Communist
world revolution. The Soviets and, after 1949, the Communist Chinese advocated rebellion in the developing world and promised to help end colonial exploitation and bring
freedom and equality in a socialist state. They supported Communist independence
movements with economic and military aid, and the guerrilla insurgent armed with a
Soviet-produced AK-47 machine gun became the new symbol of Marxist revolution.

Western Europe and particularly the United States offered a competing vision of
independence, based on free-market economics and, ostensibly, liberal democracy —
though the United States was often willing to support authoritarian regimes that voiced
staunch anticommunism. Like the U.S.S.R., the United States extended economic aid
and weaponry to decolonizing nations. The Americans promoted cautious moves toward
self-determination in the context of containment, attempting to limit the influence of
communism in newly liberated states.

After they had won independence, the leaders of the new nations often found
themselves trapped between the superpowers, compelled to voice support for one bloc
or the other. Many new leaders followed a third way, adopting a policy of **nonalignment**,
remaining neutral in the Cold War and playing both sides for what they could get.

The Struggle for Power in Asia

The first major fight for independence that followed World War II, between the Netherlands and anticolonial insurgents in the Dutch East Indies (today's Indonesia), in many ways exemplified decolonization in the Cold War world. The Dutch had been involved in Indonesia since the early seventeenth century (see Chapter 14) and had extended their colonial power over the centuries. During World War II, however, the Japanese had overrun the archipelago, encouraging hopes among the locals for independence from Western control. Following the Japanese defeat in 1945, the Dutch returned, hoping to use Indonesia's raw materials, particularly rubber, to support economic recovery at home. But Dutch imperialists faced a determined group of rebels inspired by a powerful combination of nationalism, Marxism, and Islam. Four years of deadly guerrilla war followed, and in 1949 the Netherlands reluctantly accepted Indonesian independence. The new Indonesian president became an effective advocate of nonalignment. He had close ties to the Indonesian Communist Party but received foreign aid from both the United States and the Soviet Union.

A similar combination of communism and anticolonialism inspired the independence movement in parts of French Indochina (now Vietnam, Cambodia, and Laos), though noncommunist nationalists were also involved. France desperately wished to maintain control over these prized colonies and tried its best to re-establish colonial rule after the Japanese occupation collapsed at the end of World War II. Despite substantial American aid, the French army fighting in Vietnam was defeated in 1954 by forces under the guerrilla leader Ho Chi Minh (hoh chee mihn) (1890–1969), who was supported by the U.S.S.R. and China. Vietnam was divided; as in Korea, a shaky truce established a Communist North and a pro-Western South Vietnam, which led to civil war and subsequent intervention by the United States. Cambodia and Laos also gained independence under noncommunist regimes, though Communist rebels remained active in both countries.

India, Britain's oldest, largest, and most lucrative imperial possession, played a key role in the decolonization process. Nationalist opposition to British rule coalesced after the First World War under the leadership of British-educated lawyer Mohandas (sometimes called "Mahatma," or "Great-Souled") Gandhi (1869–1948), one of the twentieth century's most significant and influential figures. In the 1920s and 1930s Gandhi (GAHN-dee) built a mass movement preaching nonviolent "noncooperation" with the British. In 1935 Gandhi wrested from the frustrated and unnerved British a new, liberal constitution that was practically a blueprint for independence. The Second World War interrupted progress toward Indian self-rule, but when the Labour Party came to power in Great Britain in 1945, it was ready to relinquish sovereignty. British socialists had long been critics of imperialism, and the heavy cost of governing India had become a large financial burden to the war-wracked country.

Britain withdrew peacefully, but conflict between India's Hindu and Muslim populations posed a lasting dilemma for South Asia. As independence neared, the Muslim minority grew increasingly anxious about their status in an India dominated by the Hindu majority. Muslim leaders called for partition — the division of India into separate Hindu and Muslim states — and the British agreed. When independence was made official on August 15, 1947, predominantly Muslim territories on India's eastern and

A Refugee Camp During the Partition of India A young Muslim man, facing an uncertain future, sits above a refugee camp established on the grounds of a medieval fortress in the northern Indian city of Dehli. In the camp, Muslim refugees wait to cross the border to the newly founded Pakistan. The chaos that accompanied the mass migration of Muslims and Hindus during the partition of India in the late summer and autumn of 1947 cost the lives of up to 1 million migrants and disrupted the livelihoods of millions more. (Time & Life Pictures/Getty Images)

western borders became Pakistan (the eastern section is today's Bangladesh). Seeking relief from ethnic conflict that erupted, some 10 million Muslim and Hindu refugees fled both ways across the new borders, an unprecedented population exchange that left mayhem and death in its wake. In just a few summer weeks, up to 1 million people (estimates vary widely) lost their lives. Then in January 1948 a radical Hindu nationalist who opposed partition assassinated Gandhi, and Jawaharlal Nehru became Indian prime minister.

As the Cold War heated up in the early 1950s, Pakistan, an Islamic republic, developed close ties with the United States. Under the leadership of Nehru, India successfully maintained a policy of nonalignment. India became a liberal, if socialist-friendly, democratic state that dealt with both the United States and the U.S.S.R. Pakistan and India both joined the British Commonwealth, a voluntary and cooperative association of former British colonies that already included Canada, Australia, and New Zealand.

Where Indian nationalism drew on Western parliamentary liberalism, Chinese nationalism developed and triumphed in the framework of Marxist-Leninist ideology. After the withdrawal of the occupying Japanese army in 1945, China erupted again in open civil war between the authoritarian Guomindang (Kuomintang, National People's Party), led by Jiang Jieshi (traditionally called Chiang Kai-shek; 1887–1975), and the Chinese Communists, led by Mao Zedong (MA-OW zuh-DOUNG) and supported by a popular grassroots uprising. The Soviets gave Mao aid, and the Americans gave Jiang much more. Winning the support of the peasantry by promising to expropriate the holdings of the big landowners, the tougher, better-organized Communists forced the Guomindang to withdraw to the island of Taiwan in 1949. Mao and the Communists united China's 550 million inhabitants in a strong centralized state. Once in power, the "Red Chinese" began building a new society that adapted Marxism to Chinese conditions. The new government promoted land reform, extended education and health-care programs to the peasantry, and introduced Soviet-style five-year plans that boosted industrial production. It also brought Stalinist-style repression — mass arrests, forced-labor camps, and ceaseless propaganda campaigns — to the Chinese people.

Independence and Conflict in the Middle East

In some areas of the Middle East, the movement toward political independence went relatively smoothly. The French League of Nations mandates in Syria and Lebanon had collapsed during the Second World War, and Saudi Arabia and Transjordan had already achieved independence from Britain. But events in the British mandate of Palestine and in Egypt showed that decolonization in the Middle East could be a dangerous and difficult process.

As part of the peace accords that followed the First World War, the British government had advocated a Jewish homeland alongside the Arab population (see Chapter 25). This tenuous compromise unraveled after World War II. Neither Jews nor Arabs were happy with British rule, and violence and terrorism mounted on both sides. In 1947 the frustrated British decided to leave Palestine, and the United Nations voted in a nonbinding resolution to divide the territory into two states — one Arab and one Jewish. The Jews accepted the plan and founded the state of Israel in 1948.

The Palestinians and the surrounding Arab nations viewed Jewish independence as a betrayal of their own interests, and they attacked the Jewish state as soon as it was proclaimed. The Israelis drove off the invaders and conquered more territory. Roughly nine hundred thousand Arab Palestinians fled or were expelled from their homes, creating a persistent refugee problem. Holocaust survivors from Europe streamed into Israel, as Theodor Herzl's Zionist dream came true (see Chapter 23). The next fifty years saw four more wars between the Israelis and the Arab states and innumerable clashes between Israelis and Palestinians.

The Arab defeat in 1948 triggered a powerful nationalist revolution in Egypt in 1952, led by the young army officer Gamal Abdel Nasser (1918–1970). The revolutionaries drove out the pro-Western king, and in 1954 Nasser became president of an Egyptian republic. A crafty politician, Nasser advocated nonalignment and expertly played the superpowers against each other, securing loans from the United States and purchasing Soviet arms.

In July 1956 Nasser abruptly nationalized the foreign-owned Suez Canal Company, the last symbol and substance of Western power in the Middle East. Infuriated, the British and the French, along with the Israelis, secretly planned a military invasion. The Israeli army invaded the Sinai Peninsula bordering the canal, and British and French bombers attacked Egyptian airfields. World opinion was outraged, and the United States feared that such a blatant show of imperialism would propel the Arab states into the Soviet bloc. The Americans joined with the Soviets to force the British, French, and Israelis to back down. Egyptian nationalism triumphed: Nasser got his canal, and Israel left the Sinai. The Suez crisis, a watershed in the history of European imperialism, showed that the European powers could no longer maintain their global empires, and it demonstrated the power and appeal of nonalignment.

Decolonization in Africa

In less than a decade, most of Africa won independence from European imperialism, a remarkable movement of world historical importance. In much of the continent south of the Sahara, decolonization proceeded relatively smoothly. Yet the new African states were quickly caught up in the struggles between the Cold War superpowers, and decolonization all too often left a lasting legacy of economic decline and political conflict (see Map 28.3).

Starting in 1957 most of Britain's African colonies achieved independence with little or no bloodshed and then entered a very loose association with Britain as members of the British Commonwealth. Ghana, Nigeria, Tanzania, and other countries gained independence in this way, but there were exceptions to this relatively smooth transfer of power. In Kenya, British forces brutally crushed the nationalist Mau Mau rebellion in the early 1950s, but nonetheless recognized Kenyan independence in 1963. In South Africa, the white-dominated government left the Commonwealth in 1961 and declared an independent republic in order to preserve apartheid—an exploitative system of racial segregation enforced by law.

The decolonization of the Belgian Congo was one of the great tragedies of the Cold War. Belgian leaders, profiting from the colony's wealth of natural resources and proud of their small nation's imperial status, maintained a system of apartheid there and dragged their feet in granting independence. These conditions sparked an anticolonial movement that grew increasingly aggressive in the late 1950s under the able leadership of the charismatic Patrice Lumumba. In January 1960 the Belgians gave in and hastily announced that the Congo would be independent six months later, a schedule that was irresponsibly fast. Lumumba was chosen prime minister in democratic elections, but when the Belgians pulled out on schedule, the new government was entirely unprepared. Chaos broke out when the Congolese army attacked Belgian military officers who remained in the country.

With substantial financial investments in the Congo, the United States and western Europe worried that the new nation might fall into Soviet hands. U.S. leaders cast Lumumba as a Soviet proxy, an oversimplification of his nonalignment policies, and American anxiety increased when Lumumba asked the U.S.S.R. for aid and protection. A cable from the CIA chief in the Congo revealed the way Cold War anxieties framed the situation:

Embassy and station believe Congo experiencing classic Communist takeover government. . . . Whether or not Lumumba actually Commie or just playing Commie game to assist solidifying his power, anti-West forces rapidly increasing power [in] Congo and there may be little time left in which to take action to avoid another Cuba.[6]

In a troubling example of containment in action, the CIA helped implement a military coup against Lumumba, who was captured and then assassinated. The military set up a U.S.-backed dictatorship under the corrupt general Joseph Mobutu. Mobutu ruled until 1997 and became one of the world's wealthiest men, while the Congo remains one of the poorest, most violent, and most politically torn countries in the world.

French colonies in Africa followed several roads to independence. Like the British, the French offered most of their African colonies the choice of a total break or independence within a kind of French commonwealth. All but one of the new states chose the latter option, largely because they identified with French culture and wanted aid from their former colonizer. The French were eager to help — provided the former colonies accepted close economic ties on French terms. As in the past, the French and their Common Market partners, who helped foot the bill, saw themselves as continuing their civilizing mission in sub-Saharan Africa (see Chapter 24). More important, they saw in Africa raw materials for their factories, markets for their industrial goods, outlets for profitable investment, and good temporary jobs for their engineers and teachers.

Things were more difficult in the French colony of Algeria, a large Muslim state on the Mediterranean Sea where some 1.2 million white European settlers, including some 800,000 French, had taken up permanent residency by the 1950s. Nicknamed Pieds-Noirs (literally "black feet"), many of these Europeans had raised families in Algeria for three or four generations, and they enforced a two-tiered system of citizenship, maintaining complete control of politics and the economy. When Algerian rebels, inspired by Islamic fundamentalism and Communist ideals, established the National Liberation Front (FLN) and revolted against French colonialism in the early 1950s, the presence of the Pieds-Noirs complicated matters. Worried about their position in the colony, the Pieds-Noirs pressured the French government to help them. In response, France sent some 400,000 troops to crush the FLN and put down the revolt.

The resulting Algerian war — long, bloody, and marred by atrocities committed on both sides — lasted from 1954 to 1962. FLN radicals repeatedly attacked civilians while the French army engaged in systematic torture and the forced relocation of Muslim civilians who supported the insurgents. News reports turned French public opinion and indeed the government against the war, but efforts to open peace talks instigated a revolt by the Algerian French and threats of a coup d'état by the French army. In 1958 the immensely popular General Charles de Gaulle was reinstated as French prime minister as part of the movement to keep Algeria French. His appointment calmed the army, the Pieds-Noirs, and the French public. Yet de Gaulle pragmatically accepted Algerian self-determination and in 1962 ended the conflict. After more than a century of French rule, Algeria became independent, and its European population quickly fled.

By the mid-1960s most African states had won independence, some through bloody insurrections. There were exceptions: Portugal waged war against independence movements in Angola and Mozambique until the 1970s. Even in liberated countries, the colonial legacy had long-term negative effects. South African blacks still longed for

A French Checkpoint in Algeria, 1962
French soldiers search a civilian in Algiers, the capital of Algeria. Inspired by a potent mix of communism and Islamic radicalism, the Algerian National Liberation Front fought a lengthy and bloody struggle against the French colonial government that finally led to Algerian independence in 1962.
(Agence France Presse/Hulton Archive/Getty Images)

liberation from apartheid, and white rulers in Rhodesia continued a bloody civil war against African insurgents until 1979. African leaders may have expressed support for socialist or democratic principles in order to win aid from the superpowers. In practice, however, corrupt and authoritarian African leaders like Mobutu in the Congo often established lasting authoritarian dictatorships and enriched themselves at the expense of their populations.

Even after decolonization, western European countries managed to increase their economic and cultural ties with their former African colonies in the 1960s and 1970s. Above all, they used the lure of special trading privileges and provided heavy investment in French- and English-language education to enhance a powerful Western presence in the new African states. This situation led a variety of leaders and scholars to charge that western Europe (and the United States) had imposed a system of **neocolonialism** on the former colonies. According to this view, neocolonialism was a system designed to perpetuate Western economic domination and undermine the promise of political independence, thereby extending to Africa (and much of Asia) the kind of economic subordination that the United States had imposed on Latin America in the nineteenth century.

Postwar Social Transformations

How did changes in social relations contribute to European stability on both sides of the iron curtain?

While Europe staged its astonishing political and economic recovery from the Nazi nightmare, the basic structures of Western society were changing no less rapidly and remarkably. A changing class structure, new patterns of global migration, and new roles for women and youths had dramatic impacts on everyday life, albeit with different effects in the East Bloc and western Europe. Yet such large-scale changes had transformative effects on both sides of the iron curtain: social and cultural trends joined political and economic recovery to build stability in the postwar decades.

Changing Class Structures

The combination of rapid economic growth, growing prosperity and mass consumption, and the implementation of generous welfare policies went a long way toward creating a new society in Europe after the Second World War. Old class barriers relaxed, and class distinctions became fuzzier.

Changes in the structure of the middle class were particularly influential in this result. In the nineteenth and early twentieth centuries, the model for the middle class had been the independent, self-employed individual who owned a business or practiced a liberal profession such as law or medicine. Ownership of property—very often inherited property—and strong family ties had often been the keys to wealth and standing within the middle class. After 1945 this pattern changed drastically in western Europe. A new breed of managers and experts—so-called white-collar workers—replaced property owners as the leaders of the middle class. Ability to serve the needs of a big organization largely replaced inherited property and family connections in determining an individual's social position in the middle and upper-middle classes. At the same time, the middle class grew massively and became harder to define.

There were several reasons for these developments. Rapid industrial and technological expansion and the consolidation of businesses created a powerful demand for technologists and managers in large corporations and government agencies. Moreover, the old propertied middle class lost control of many family-owned businesses. Numerous small businesses (including family farms) could no longer turn a profit, so their former owners regretfully joined the ranks of salaried employees.

Similar processes were at work in the Communist states of the East Bloc, where class leveling was an avowed goal of the authoritarian socialist state. The nationalization of industry, expropriation of property, and aggressive attempts to open employment opportunities to workers and equalize wage structures effectively reduced class differences. Communist Party members typically received better jobs and more pay than nonmembers, but by the 1960s the income differential between the top and bottom strata of East Bloc societies was far smaller than in the West.

In both East and West, managers and civil servants represented the model for a new middle class. Well-paid and highly trained, often with backgrounds in engineering or accounting, these pragmatic experts were primarily concerned with efficiency and with practical solutions to concrete problems.

The structure of the lower classes also became more flexible and open. Continuing trends that began in the 1800s, large numbers of people left the countryside for the city; the population of one of the most traditional and least mobile groups in European society—farmers—drastically declined. Meanwhile, the number of industrial workers in western Europe also began to fall, as new jobs for white-collar and service employees grew rapidly. This change marked a significant transition in the world of labor. The welfare benefits extended by postwar governments also helped promote greater social equality because they raised lower-class living standards and were paid for in part by higher taxes on the wealthy. In general, European workers were better educated and more specialized than before, and the new workforce bore a greater resemblance to the growing middle class of salaried specialists than to traditional industrial workers.

Patterns of Postwar Migration

The 1850s to the 1930s had been an age of global migration, as countless Europeans moved around the continent and the world seeking economic opportunity or freedom from political or religious persecution (see Chapter 24). The 1950s and 1960s witnessed new waves of migration that had a significant impact on European society.

Some postwar migration took place within countries. Declining job prospects in Europe's rural areas encouraged many peasants and small farmers to seek better prospects in cities. In the poorer countries of Spain, Portugal, and Italy, millions moved to more developed regions of their own countries. The process was similar in the East Bloc, where the forced collectivization of agriculture and state subsidies for heavy industry opened opportunities in urban areas. Before the erection of the Berlin Wall in 1961, some 3.5 million East Germans moved to the Federal Republic of Germany, seeking higher pay and a better life.

Many other Europeans moved across national borders seeking work. The general pattern was from south to north. Workers from less developed countries like Italy, Spain, and socialist Yugoslavia moved to the industrialized north, particularly to West Germany, which—having lost 5 million people during the war—was in desperate need of able-bodied workers. In the 1950s and 1960s West Germany and other prosperous countries implemented **guest worker programs** designed to recruit much-needed labor for the booming economy. West Germany signed labor agreements with Italy, Greece, Spain, Portugal, Yugoslavia, Turkey, and the North African countries of Tunisia and Morocco. By the early 1970s there were 2.8 million foreign workers in Germany and another 2.3 million in France, where they made up 11 percent of the workforce.

Most guest workers were young, unskilled single men who labored for low wages in entry-level jobs and sent much of their pay to their families at home. (See "Individuals in Society: Armando Rodrigues," page 974.) According to government plans, these guest workers were supposed to return to their home countries after a specified period. Many built new lives, however, and, to the dismay of the authorities, chose to live permanently in their adoptive countries.

Europe was also changed by **postcolonial migration**, the movement of people from the former colonies and the developing world into prosperous Europe. In contrast to guest workers, who joined formal recruitment programs, postcolonial migrants could often claim citizenship rights from their former colonizers and moved spontaneously. Immigrants from the Caribbean, India, Africa, and Asia moved to Britain; people from

INDIVIDUALS IN SOCIETY • Armando Rodrigues

Popping flashbulbs greeted Portuguese worker Armando Rodrigues when he stepped off a train in Cologne in September 1964. Celebrated in the national media as West Germany's 1 millionth guest worker, Rodrigues was met by government and business leaders—including the minister of labor—who presented him with a motorcycle and a bouquet of carnations.

In most respects, Rodrigues was hardly different from the many foreign workers recruited to work in West Germany and other northern European countries. Yet given his moment of fame, he is an apt symbol of a troubled labor program that helped turn Germany into a multiethnic society.

By the late 1950s the new Federal Republic desperately needed able-bodied men to fill the low-paying jobs created by rapid economic expansion. The West German government signed labor agreements with several Mediterranean countries to meet this demand. Rodrigues and hundreds of thousands of other young men signed up for the employment program and then submitted to an arduous application process. Rodrigues traveled from his village to the regional Federal Labor Office, where he filled out forms and took written and medical exams. Months later, after he had received an initial one-year contract from a German employer, Rodrigues and twelve hundred other Portuguese and Spanish men boarded a special train reserved for foreign workers and embarked for West Germany.

For labor migrants, life was hard in West Germany. In the first years of the guest worker program, most recruits were men between the ages of twenty and forty who were either single or willing to leave their families at home. They typically filled low-level jobs in construction, mines, and factories, and they lived apart from West Germans in special barracks close to their workplaces, with six to eight workers in a room.

West Germans gave Rodrigues and his fellow migrants a mixed reception. Though they were a welcome source of inexpensive labor, the men who emigrated from what West Germans called "the southern lands" faced discrimination and prejudice. "Order, cleanliness, and punctuality seem like the natural qualities of a respectable person to us," wrote one official in 1966. "In the south, one does

North Africa, especially Algeria, and from sub-Saharan countries such as Cameroon and the Ivory Coast moved to France; Indonesians migrated to the Netherlands. Postcolonial immigrants also moved to eastern Europe, though in far fewer numbers.

These new migration patterns had dramatic results. Immigrant labor helped fuel economic recovery. Growing ethnic diversity changed the face of Europe and enriched the cultural life of the continent. The new residents were not always welcome, however. Adaptation to European lifestyles could be difficult, and immigrants often lived in separate communities where they spoke their own languages. They faced employment and housing discrimination, and the harsh anti-immigrant rhetoric and policies of xenophobic politicians. Even prominent European intellectuals worried aloud that

not learn or know this, so it is difficult [for a person from the south] to adjust here."*

According to official plans, the so-called guest workers were supposed to return home after a specified period of time. Rodrigues, for instance, went back to Portugal in the late 1970s. Resisting government pressure, millions of temporary "guests" raised families and became permanent West German residents, building substantial ethnic minorities in the Federal Republic. Because of strict naturalization laws, however, they could not become West German citizens.

Despite the hostility they faced, foreign workers established a lasting and powerful presence in West Germany, and they were a significant factor in the country's swift economic recovery. Nearly fifty years after Rodrigues arrived in Cologne, his motorcycle is on permanent display in the House of History Museum in Bonn. The exhibit is a remarkable testament both to the contribution of migrant labor to West German economic growth and to the ongoing struggle to come to terms with ethnic difference and integration in a democratic Germany.

QUESTIONS FOR ANALYSIS

1. How did Rodrigues's welcome at his 1964 reception differ from the general attitude toward guest workers in Germany at the time?

2. What were the long-term costs and benefits of West Germany's labor recruitment policies?

*Quoted in Rita Chin, *The Guest Worker Question in Postwar Germany* (New York: Cambridge University Press, 2007), p. 43.

ONLINE DOCUMENT ASSIGNMENT

What were the social and cultural consequences of the guest worker program in postwar Germany? Examine a variety of perspectives on the guest worker program. Then complete a writing assignment based on the evidence and details from this chapter.

bedfordstmartins.com/mckaywestvalue

Muslim migrants from North Africa and Turkey would never adopt European values and customs. The tensions that surrounded changed migration patterns would pose significant challenges to social integration in the decades to come.

New Roles for Women

The postwar culmination of a one-hundred-year-long trend toward early marriage, early childbearing, and small family size in wealthy urban societies (see Chapter 22) had revolutionary implications for women. Above all, pregnancy and child care occupied a much smaller portion of a woman's life than in earlier times. The postwar baby boom did make for larger families and fairly rapid population growth of 1 to 1.5 percent per year in many European countries, but the long-term decline in birthrates resumed by the 1960s. By the early 1970s about half of Western women were having their last baby by the age of twenty-six or twenty-seven. When the youngest child trooped off to kindergarten, the average mother had more than forty years of life in front of her.

This was a momentous transition. Throughout history male-dominated society insisted on defining most women as mothers or potential mothers, and motherhood was very demanding. In the postwar years, however, motherhood no longer absorbed the energies of a lifetime, and more and more married women looked for new roles in the world of work outside the family. Three major forces helped women searching for jobs in the changing post–World War II workplace. First, the economic boom created strong demand for labor. Second, the economy continued its gradual shift away from the old male-dominated heavy industries, such as coal, steel, and shipbuilding, and toward the white-collar service industries in which some women already worked, such as government, education, trade, and health care. Third, young women shared fully in the postwar education revolution, positioning them to take advantage of the growing need for office workers and well-trained professionals. Thus more and more married women became full-time and part-time wage earners.

In the East Bloc, Communist leaders opened up numerous jobs to women, who accounted for almost half of all employed persons. Many women made their way into previously male professions, including factory work but also medicine and engineering. In western Europe and North America, the percentage of married women in the workforce rose from a range of roughly 20 to 25 percent in 1950 to anywhere from 30 to 60 percent in the 1970s.

All was not easy for women entering paid employment. Married women workers faced widespread and long-established discrimination in pay, advancement, and occupational choice in comparison to men. Moreover, many women could find only part-time work. As the divorce rate rose in the 1960s, part-time work, with its low pay and scanty benefits, often meant poverty for many women with children. Finally, married working women in both East and West still carried most of the child-rearing and housekeeping responsibilities, leaving them with an exhausting "double burden." Trying to live up to society's seemingly contradictory ideals was one reason that many women accepted part-time employment.

The injustices that married women encountered as wage earners contributed greatly to the movement for women's equality and emancipation that arose in the United States and western Europe in the 1960s. Sexism and discrimination in the workplace—and in the home—grew loathsome and evoked the sense of injustice that drives revolutions and reforms.

Youth Culture and the Generation Gap

The bulging cohort of so-called baby boomers born after World War II created a distinctive and very international youth culture, which brought remarkable changes to postwar youth roles and lifestyles. That subculture, found across western Europe and the United States, was rooted in fashions and musical tastes that set them off from their elders and fueled anxious comments about a growing "generation gap."

Youth styles in the United States often provided inspiration for movements in Europe. Groups like the British Teddy boys, the West German *Halbstarken* (half-strongs), and the French *blouson noirs* (black jackets) modeled their rebellious clothing and cynical attitudes on the bad-boy characters played by U.S. film stars such as James Dean and Marlon Brando. American jazz and rock 'n' roll spread rapidly in western Europe, aided by the invention of the long-playing record album (or LP) and the 45 rpm "single" in the late 1940s, and the growth of the corporate music industry. American musicians such as Elvis Presley, Bill Haley and His Comets, and Gene Vincent thrilled youths and worried parents, teachers, and politicians.

Youths played a key role in the consumer revolution. Marketing experts and manufacturers quickly recognized that the young people they now called "teenagers" had money to spend due to postwar prosperity. An array of advertisements and products consciously targeted the youth market. In France, for example, magazine advertising aimed at adolescents grew by 400 percent between 1959 and 1962. As the baby boomers entered their late teens, they eagerly purchased trendy clothing and the latest pop music hits, as well as record players, transistor radios, magazines, hair products, and makeup, all marketed for the "young generation."

The new youth culture became an inescapable part of Western society. One clear sign of this new presence was the rapid growth in the number of universities and college students. Before the 1960s, in North America and Europe, only a small elite received a university education. In 1950 only 3 to 4 percent of western European youths went on to higher education; numbers in the United States were only slightly higher. Then, as government subsidies made education more affordable to ordinary people, enrollments skyrocketed. By 1960 at least three times more European students attended some kind of university than they had before World War II, and the number continued to rise sharply until the 1970s.

The rapid expansion of higher education opened new opportunities for the middle and lower classes, but it also made for overcrowded classrooms. Many students felt that they were not getting the kind of education they needed for jobs in the modern world. At the same time, some reflective students feared that universities were doing nothing but turning out docile technocrats both to stock and to serve "the establishment." Thus it was no coincidence that students became leaders in a counterculture that attacked the ideals of the affluent society of the postwar world and shocked the West in the late 1960s.

Notes

1. Anonymous, *A Woman in Berlin: Eight Weeks in the Conquered City: A Diary* (New York: Metropolitan Books, 2005), pp. 239–240.
2. Quoted in N. Graebner, *Cold War Diplomacy, 1945–1960* (Princeton, N.J.: Van Nostrand, 1962), p. 17.
3. From a speech delivered by George Marshall at Harvard University on June 5, 1947, reprinted in *Department of State Bulletin* (June 15, 1947), pp. 1159–1160.
4. Quoted in T. Judt, *Postwar: A History of Europe Since 1945* (New York: Penguin, 2005), p. 150.
5. Nikita Khrushchev, "On the Cult of Personality and Its Consequences" (1956), quoted in J. M. Brophy et al., *Perspectives from the Past* (New York: W. W. Norton, 2009), pp. 804–805.
6. Quoted in M. Huband, *The Skull Beneath the Skin: Africa After the Cold War* (Boulder: Westview Press, 2001), p. 9.

Chapter Review

MAKE IT STICK

LearningCurve
bedfordstmartins.com/mckaywestvalue
After reading the chapter, use LearningCurve to retain what you've read.

IDENTIFY KEY TERMS

Identify and explain the significance of each item below.

Cold War (p. 940)

displaced persons (p. 941)

Truman Doctrine (p. 947)

Marshall Plan (p. 947)

Council for Mutual Economic
    Assistance (COMECON) (p. 947)

NATO (p. 948)

Warsaw Pact (p. 948)

economic miracle (p. 951)

Christian Democrats (p. 951)

Common Market (p. 954)

socialist realism (p. 958)

de-Stalinization (p. 959)

decolonization (p. 963)

nonalignment (p. 965)

neocolonialism (p. 971)

guest worker programs (p. 973)

postcolonial migration (p. 973)

REVIEW THE MAIN IDEAS

Answer the focus questions from each section of the chapter.

• Why was World War II followed so quickly by the Cold War? (p. 940)

• What were the sources of postwar recovery and stability in western Europe? (p. 950)

• What was the pattern of postwar development in the Soviet bloc? (p. 956)

• What led to decolonization after World War II, and how did the Cold War influence the process? (p. 963)

• How did changes in social relations contribute to European stability on both sides of the iron curtain? (p. 972)

MAKE CONNECTIONS

Think about the larger developments and continuities within and across chapters.

1. Why did the Cold War have such a powerful impact on politics, society, and everyday life in the United States and western Europe, the U.S.S.R. and the East Bloc, and the decolonizing world?

2. Compare and contrast the treaties and agreements that ended the world wars. Did those who shaped the peace accords face similar problems? Which set of agreements did a better job of resolving outstanding issues, and why?

ONLINE DOCUMENT ASSIGNMENT

Armando Rodrigues

What were the social and cultural consequences of the guest worker program in postwar Germany?

You encountered Armando Rodrigues's story on page 974. Keeping the question above in mind, go online and examine a variety of perspectives on the guest worker program. Then complete a writing assignment based on the evidence and details from this chapter.

bedfordstmartins.com/mckaywestvalue

CHRONOLOGY

1945	• Yalta Conference; end of World War II in Europe; Potsdam Conference; Nuremberg trials begin
1945–1960s	• Decolonization of Asia and Africa
1945–1965	• United States takes lead in Big Science
1947	• Truman Doctrine; Marshall Plan
1948	• Founding of Israel
1948–1949	• Berlin airlift
1949	• Creation of East and West Germany; formation of NATO; establishment of COMECON
1950–1953	• Korean War
1953	• Death of Stalin
1955–1964	• Khrushchev in power; de-Stalinization of Soviet Union
1955	• Warsaw Pact founded
1956	• Suez crisis
1957	• Formation of Common Market; Pasternak publishes *Doctor Zhivago*
1961	• Building of Berlin Wall
1962	• Cuban missile crisis; Solzhenitsyn publishes *One Day in the Life of Ivan Denisovich*
1964	• Brezhnev replaces Khrushchev as Soviet leader

29

✓ LearningCurve
bedfordstmartins.com/mckaywestvalue
After reading the chapter, use
LearningCurve to retain what
you've read.

Challenging the Postwar Order

1960–1991

AS EUROPE ENTERED THE 1960S, THE POLITICAL AND SOCIAL SYSTEMS forged in the postwar era appeared sound. Centrist politicians in western Europe agreed that managed economic expansion, abundant jobs, and state-sponsored welfare benefits would continue to improve living standards and create social consensus. In the Soviet Union and the East Bloc, although conditions varied by country, modest economic growth and limited reforms amid continued political repression likewise contributed to a sense of stability. Cold War tensions diminished, and it seemed that a remarkable age of affluence would ease political differences and lead to social harmony.

By the late 1960s, however, this hard-won sense of stability had begun to disappear as popular protest movements in East and West arose to challenge dominant certainties. In the early 1970s the astonishing postwar economic advance ground to a halt, with serious consequences. In western Europe, a new generation of conservative political leaders advanced new policies to deal with economic decline and the growth of global competition. New political groups across the political spectrum, from feminists and environmentalists to national separatists and right-wing populists, added to the atmosphere of crisis and conflict.

In the East Bloc, leaders vacillated between central economic control and liberalization and left in place tight controls on social freedom, leading to stagnation and frustration. In the 1980s popular dissident movements emerged in Poland and other satellite states, and efforts to reform the Communist system in the Soviet Union from the top down snowballed out of control. In 1989, as revolutions swept away Communist rule throughout the entire Soviet bloc, the Cold War reached a dramatic conclusion.

Reform and Protest in the 1960s

Why did the postwar consensus of the 1950s break down?

In the early 1960s politics and society in prosperous western Europe remained relatively stable. East Bloc governments, bolstered by modest economic growth and state-enforced political conformity and committed to generous welfare benefits for their citizens, maintained control. As the 1960s progressed, politics in the West shifted noticeably to the left, and Social Democratic governments worked to normalize East-West relations. Amid this more liberalized society, a youthful counterculture emerged among the children of affluence to critique the status quo. In the East Bloc, Khrushchev's limited reforms also inspired rebellions. Thus activists around the world rose in protest against the perceived inequalities of both capitalism and communism, leading to dramatic events in 1968, exemplified in Paris and Prague.

Cold War Tensions Thaw

In western Europe, the first two decades of postwar reconstruction had been overseen for the most part by center-right Christian Democrats, who successfully maintained postwar stability around Cold War politics, free-market economics with limited state intervention, and welfare provisions (see Chapter 28). In the mid- to late 1960s, buoyed by the rapidly expanding economy, much of western Europe moved politically to the left. Socialists entered the Italian government in 1963. In Britain, the Labour Party returned to power in 1964, after thirteen years in opposition. In West Germany, the aging postwar chancellor Konrad Adenauer (1876–1967) retired in 1963, and in 1969 Willy Brandt (1913–1992) became the first Social Democratic West German chancellor; his party would govern Germany until 1982. There were important exceptions to this general trend. Though the tough-minded, independent French president Charles de Gaulle resigned in 1969, the centrist Gaullists remained in power in France until 1981. And in Spain, Portugal, and Greece, authoritarian regimes maintained control until the mid-1970s.

Despite these exceptions, the general leftward drift encouraged a gradual relaxation of Cold War tensions. Though the Cold War continued to rage outside Europe and generally defined relations between the Soviet Union and the United States, western European leaders took major steps to normalize relations with the East Bloc. Willy Brandt took the lead. In December 1970 he flew to Poland for the signing of a historic treaty of reconciliation. In a dramatic moment rich in symbolism, Brandt laid a wreath at the tomb of the Polish unknown soldier and another at the monument commemorating the armed uprising of Warsaw's Jewish ghetto against occupying Nazi armies. Standing before the ghetto memorial, a somber Brandt fell to his knees as if in prayer. "I wanted," Brandt said later, "to ask pardon in the name of our people for a million-fold crime which was committed in the misused name of the Germans."[1]

Brandt's gesture at the Warsaw Ghetto memorial and the treaty with Poland were part of his broader, conciliatory foreign policy termed **Ostpolitik** (German for "Eastern policy"). Brandt aimed at nothing less than a comprehensive peace settlement for central Europe and the two postwar German states. Brandt believed that the building of the Berlin Wall in 1961 revealed the limitations of West Germany's official hard line

A West German Leader Apologizes for the Holocaust In 1970 West German chancellor Willy Brandt knelt before the Jewish Heroes' Monument in Warsaw, Poland, to ask forgiveness for the German mass murder of European Jews and other groups during the Second World War. Brandt's action, captured in photo and film by the onlooking press, symbolized the chancellor's policy of Ostpolitik, the normalization of relations between the East and West Blocs. (bpk, Berlin/ Art Resource, NY)

toward the East Bloc. Accordingly, the chancellor negotiated new treaties with the Soviet Union and Czechoslovakia, as well as Poland, that formally accepted existing state boundaries — rejected by West Germany's government since 1945 — in return for a mutual renunciation of force or the threat of force. Using the imaginative formula of "two German states within one German nation," he broke decisively with past policy and entered into direct relations with East Germany.

Brandt's Ostpolitik was part of a general relaxation of East-West tensions, termed **détente** (day-TAHNT), which began in the early 1970s. Though Cold War hostilities continued in the developing world, direct diplomatic relations between the United States and the Soviet Union grew less strained. The superpowers agreed to limit the testing and proliferation of nuclear weapons and in 1975 mounted a joint U.S.-U.S.S.R. space mission.

The move toward détente reached a high point when the United States, Canada, the Soviet Union, and all European nations (except isolationist Albania and tiny Andorra) met in Helsinki to sign the Final Act of the Conference on Security and Cooperation in Europe in 1975. Under what came to be called the Helsinki Accords, the thirty-five participating nations agreed that Europe's existing political frontiers could not be changed by force. They also accepted numerous provisions guaranteeing the civil rights and political freedoms of their citizens. The agreement was effective in diminishing Cold War conflict. Although Communist regimes would continue to curtail domestic freedoms and violate human rights guarantees, the accords encouraged East Bloc dissidents, who could now demand that their governments respect international declarations on human rights. (See "Primary Source: Human Rights Under the Helsinki Accords," page 984.)

Newly empowered Social Democrats of western Europe also engaged in reform at home. Building on the welfare systems established in the 1950s, politicians increased state spending on public services even further. These Social Democrats did not advocate "socialism" as practiced in the Soviet bloc, where strict economic planning, the nationalization of key economic sectors, and one-party dictatorships ensured rigid state control. To the contrary, they maintained a firm commitment to capitalist free markets and democratic politics. At the same time, they viewed welfare provisions as a way to ameliorate the inevitable inequalities of a competitive market economy. As a result, western European democracies spent more and more state funds on health care, education, old-age insurance, and public housing, all paid for with very high taxes.

By the early 1970s state spending on such programs hovered around 40 percent of the gross domestic product in France, West Germany, and Great Britain, and even more in Scandinavia and the Netherlands. Center-right Christian Democrats generally supported increased spending on entitlements—as long as the economy prospered. The economic slowdown of the mid-1970s undermined support for the welfare state consensus, however (see page 994).

The Affluent Society

The political shift to the left in the 1960s was accompanied by rapid social change across western Europe. A decade of economic growth and high wages meant that an expanding middle class could increasingly enjoy the benefits of the consumer revolution that began in the 1950s (see Chapter 28). However, what contemporaries called "the age of affluence" had clear limits. The living standards of workers and immigrants did not rise as fast as those of the educated middle classes, and the expanding economy did not always reach underdeveloped regions, such as southern Italy. Nonetheless the 1960s brought general prosperity to millions, and the construction of a full-blown consumer society had a profound impact on daily life.

Many Europeans now had more money to spend on leisure time and recreational pursuits, and one of the most noticeable leisure-time developments was the blossoming of mass travel and tourism. With month-long paid vacations required by law in most western European countries and with widespread automobile ownership, travel to beaches and ski resorts came within the reach of the middle class and much of the working class. By the late 1960s packaged tours with cheap group airfares and bargain hotel accommodations had made even distant lands easily accessible.

Consumerism also changed life at home. Household appliances that were still luxuries in the 1950s were now commonplace; televisions overtook radio as a popular form of domestic entertainment while vacuum cleaners, refrigerators, and washing

PRIMARY SOURCE   Human Rights Under the Helsinki Accords

At the conclusion of the two-year-long Conference on Security and Cooperation in Europe (1973–1975), the representatives of thirty-five West and East Bloc states solemnly pledged to "respect each other's sovereign equality" and to "refrain from any intervention, direct or indirect . . . in the internal or external affairs . . . of another participating state." East Bloc leaders, pleased that the West had at last officially accepted the frontiers and territorial integrity of the Communist satellite states established after World War II, agreed to recognize a lengthy list of "civil, political, economic, social, cultural and other rights and freedoms."

Principle VII on Human Rights and Freedoms, from the Final Act of the Conference on Security and Cooperation in Europe (August 1, 1975).

VII. Respect for human rights and fundamental freedoms, including the freedom of thought, conscience, religion or belief

The participating States will respect human rights and fundamental freedoms, including the freedom of thought, conscience, religion or belief, for all without distinction as to race, sex, language or religion.

They will promote and encourage the effective exercise of civil, political, economic, social, cultural and other rights and freedoms all of which derive from the inherent dignity of the human person and are essential for his free and full development.

Within this framework the participating States will recognize and respect the freedom of the individual to profess and practice, alone or in community with others, religion or belief acting in accordance with the dictates of his own conscience.

The participating States on whose territory national minorities exist will respect the right of persons belonging to such minorities to equality before the law, will afford them the full opportunity for the actual enjoyment of human rights and fundamental freedoms and will, in this manner, protect their legitimate interests in this sphere.

---

machines transformed women's housework. Studies later showed that these new "labor-saving devices" caused women to spend even more time cleaning and cooking to new exacting standards, but at the time electric appliances were considered indispensable to what contemporaries called a "modern lifestyle." The establishment of U.S.-style self-service supermarkets across western Europe changed the way food was produced, purchased, and prepared, and threatened to force independent bakers, butchers, and neighborhood grocers out of business.

Intellectuals and cultural critics greeted the age of affluence with a chorus of criticism. Some worried that rampant consumerism created a bland conformity that wiped out regional and national traditions. The great majority of ordinary people, they argued, now ate the same foods, wore the same clothes, and watched the same programs on television, sapping creativity and individualism. Others complained bitterly that these changes threatened to Americanize Europe. Neither group could do much to stop the spread of consumer culture.

The participating States recognize the universal significance of human rights and fundamental freedoms, respect for which is an essential factor for the peace, justice and well-being necessary to ensure the development of friendly relations and co-operation among themselves as among all States.

They will constantly respect these rights and freedoms in their mutual relations and will endeavor jointly and separately, including in co-operation with the United Nations, to promote universal and effective respect for them.

They confirm the right of the individual to know and act upon his rights and duties in this field.

In the field of human rights and fundamental freedoms, the participating States will act in conformity with the purposes and principles of the Charter of the United Nations and with the Universal Declaration of Human Rights. They will also fulfill their obligations as set forth in the international declarations and agreements in this field, including *inter alia* the International Covenants on Human Rights, by which they may be bound.

EVALUATE THE EVIDENCE

1. How do the Helsinki Accords express the guiding principles of liberal democracy?

2. Why would Communist representatives publicly agree to recognize a list of rights that clearly challenged many of the repressive aspects of one-party rule in the East Bloc?

Source: "The Final Act of the Conference on Security and Cooperation in Europe, Aug. 1, 1975, 14 I.L.M. 1292 (Helsinki Declaration)," University of Minnesota Civil Rights Library, http://www1.umn .edu/humanrts/osce/basics/finact75.htm.

Worries about the Americanization of Europe were overstated. European nations preserved distinctive national cultures even during the consumer revolution, but social change nonetheless occurred. The moral authority of religious doctrine lost ground before the growing materialism of consumer society. In predominantly Protestant lands — Great Britain, Scandinavia, and parts of West Germany — church membership and regular attendance both declined significantly. Even in traditionally Catholic countries, such as Italy, Ireland, and France, outward signs of popular belief seemed to falter. At the **Second Vatican Council**, convened from 1962 to 1965, Catholic leaders agreed on a number of reforms meant to democratize and renew the church and broaden its appeal. They called for new openness in Catholic theology and declared that masses would henceforth be said in local languages rather than in Latin, which few could understand. These resolutions did little to halt the slide toward secularization, however.

Family ties also weakened in the age of affluence. The number of adults living alone grew remarkably, men and women married later, the nuclear family became smaller and more mobile, and divorce rates rose rapidly. By the 1970s the baby boom of the postwar decades was over, and population growth leveled out across Europe and even began to decline in prosperous northwestern Europe.

The Counterculture Movement

One of the dramatic results of economic prosperity was the emergence of a youthful counterculture that came of age in the mid-1960s. The "sixties generation" angrily criticized the comforts of the affluent society and challenged the social and political status quo.

What accounts for the emergence of this counterculture? Simple demographics played an important role. Young soldiers returning home after World War II in 1945 eagerly established families, and the next two decades brought a dramatic increase in the number of births per year in Europe and North America. The children born during the postwar baby boom grew up in an era of political liberalism and unprecedented material abundance. They remembered the horrors of totalitarian government that caused World War II and watched as colonial peoples forged new paths to freedom during the decades of decolonization. The counterculture challenged the growing conformity that seemed to be an inherent part of consumer society and the unequal distribution of wealth that arose from market economics. In short, when the baby boomers came of age in the 1960s, they had the education to see problems like inequality and the lack of social justice, as well as the freedom from want to act on their concerns.

Counterculture movements in both Europe and the United States drew much inspiration from the American civil rights movement. In the late 1950s and early 1960s African Americans effectively challenged institutionalized inequality using the courts, public demonstrations, sit-ins, and boycotts, and thereby threw off a deeply entrenched system of segregation and repression. The landmark Civil Rights Act of 1964, which prohibited discrimination in public services and on the job, and the Voting Rights Act of 1965, which guaranteed all African Americans the right to vote, were the crowning achievements of the long struggle against racism.

If dedicated African Americans and their white supporters could successfully reform entrenched power structures, student leaders reasoned, so could they. In 1964 and 1965, at the University of California–Berkeley, students consciously adapted the tactics of the civil rights movement, including demonstrations and sit-ins, to challenge limits on free speech and academic freedom at the university. Their efforts were contagious. Soon students across the United States and western Europe, where rigid rules controlled student activities at overcrowded universities, were engaged in active protests. The youth movement had come of age, and it mounted a determined challenge to the Western consensus.

Dreaming of economic justice and freer, more tolerant societies, student activists in western Europe and the United States embraced new forms of Marxism, creating a multidimensional and heterogeneous movement that came to be known as the **New Left**. In general, adherents of the various strands of the New Left thought that Marxism in the Soviet Union had been perverted to serve the needs of a repressive totalitarian state but that Western capitalism, with its cold disregard for social equality, was little better. What was needed was a more humanitarian style of socialism that could avoid the worst excesses of both capitalism and Soviet-style communism. New Left critics also attacked what they saw as the conformity of consumer society. The "culture industry," which controlled mass culture, fulfilled only false needs and so contributed to the dehumanization they saw at the core of Western society.

Such rarefied ideas fascinated student intellectuals, but much counterculture activity revolved around a lifestyle rebellion that seemed to have broad appeal. Politics and daily life merged, a process captured in the popular 1960s slogan "the personal is political." Nowhere was this more obvious than in the so-called sexual revolution. The 1960s brought frank discussion about sexuality, a new willingness to engage in premarital sex, and a growing acceptance of homosexuality. Sexual experimentation was facilitated by the development of the birth control pill, which eliminated the risk of unwanted pregnancy for millions of women after it went on the market in most western European countries in the 1960s. Much of the new openness about sex crossed generational lines, but for the young the idea of sexual emancipation was closely linked to radical politics. Sexual openness and "free love," the sixties generation claimed, moved people beyond traditional norms and might also shape a more humane society.

The revolutionary aspects of the sexual revolution are easily exaggerated. According to a poll of West German college students taken in 1968, the overwhelming majority wished to establish permanent families on traditional middle-class models. Yet the sexual behavior of young people did change in the 1960s and 1970s. More young people engaged in premarital sex, and they did so at an earlier age than ever before. A 1973 study reported that only 4.5 percent of West German youths born in 1945 and 1946 had experienced sexual relations before their seventeenth birthday, but that 32 percent of those born in 1953 and 1954 had done so.[2] Such trends were found in other Western countries and continued in the following decades.

Along with sexual freedom, drug use and rock music inspired lifestyle rebellion. Taking drugs challenged conventional morals; users could "turn on, tune in, and drop out," in the famous words of the American cult figure Timothy Leary. The popular music of the 1960s championed these alternative lifestyles. Rock bands like the Beatles, the Rolling Stones, and many others sang songs about drugs and casual sex. Counterculture "scenes" developed in cities such as San Francisco, Paris, and West Berlin. Carnaby Street, the center of "swinging London" in the 1960s, was world famous for its clothing boutiques and record stores, revealing the inescapable connections between generational revolt and consumer culture.

The United States and Vietnam

The growth of the counterculture movement was also closely linked to the escalation of the Vietnam War. Although many student radicals at the time argued that imperialism was the main cause, American involvement in Vietnam was more clearly a product of the Cold War policy of containment (see Chapter 28). After Vietnam won independence from France in 1954, U.S. president Dwight D. Eisenhower (r. 1953–1961) refused to sign the Geneva Accords that temporarily divided the country into a Communist north and an anticommunist south. When the South Vietnamese government declined to hold free elections that would unify the two zones, Eisenhower provided the south with military aid to combat guerrilla insurgents in South Vietnam who were supported by the Communist north. President John F. Kennedy (r. 1961–1963) later increased the number of American "military advisers" to 16,000, and in 1964 President Lyndon B.

Johnson (r. 1963–1969) greatly expanded America's role in the Vietnam conflict, providing South Vietnam with massive military aid and eventually some 500,000 American troops. Though the United States bombed North Vietnam with ever-greater intensity, it did not invade the north or set up a naval blockade.

In the end, the American strategy of limited warfare backfired. The undeclared war in Vietnam, fought nightly on American television, eventually divided the nation. Initial support was strong. The politicians, the media, and the population as a whole saw the war as part of a legitimate defense against the spread of Communist totalitarianism. But an antiwar movement quickly emerged on college campuses, where the prospect of being drafted to fight savage battles in Asian jungles made male stomachs churn. In October 1965 student protesters joined forces with old-line socialists, New Left intellectuals, and pacifists in antiwar demonstrations in fifty American cities. The protests spread to western Europe. By 1967 a growing number of U.S. and European critics denounced the American presence in Vietnam as a criminal intrusion into a complex and distant civil war.

Criticism reached a crescendo after the Vietcong staged the Tet Offensive in January 1968. The Communists' first comprehensive attack on major South Vietnamese cities failed militarily. The Vietcong, an army of Communist insurgents and guerrilla fighters located in South Vietnam, suffered heavy losses, but the Tet Offensive signaled that the war was not close to ending, as Washington had claimed. The American people grew increasingly weary of the war and pressured their leaders to stop the fighting. Within months of Tet, President Johnson announced that he would not stand for re-election and called for negotiations with North Vietnam.

President Richard M. Nixon (r. 1969–1974) sought to gradually disengage America from Vietnam once he took office. Nixon intensified the bombing campaign against the north, opened peace talks, and pursued a policy of "Vietnamization" designed to give the South Vietnamese responsibility for the war and reduce the U.S. presence. He suspended the draft and cut American forces in Vietnam from 550,000 to 24,000 in four years. In 1973 Nixon finally reached a peace agreement with North Vietnam and the Vietcong that allowed the remaining American forces to complete their withdrawal and gave the United States the right to resume bombing if the accords were broken. Fighting declined markedly in South Vietnam, where the South Vietnamese army appeared to hold its own against the Vietcong.

Although the storm of criticism in the United States passed with the peace settlement, America's disillusionment with the war had far-reaching repercussions. In early 1974, when North Vietnam launched a general invasion against South Vietnamese armies, the U.S. Congress refused to permit any American military response. In 1974 the South Vietnamese were forced to accept a unified country under a Communist dictatorship, ending a conflict that had begun with the anticolonial struggle against the French at the end of World War II.

Student Revolts and 1968

While the Vietnam War had raged, American escalation had engendered worldwide opposition. New Left activists believed that the United States was fighting an immoral and imperialistic war against a small and heroic people, and the counterculture became increasingly radical. In western European and North American cities, students and sympathetic followers organized massive antiwar demonstrations and then extended their protests to support colonial independence movements, demand an end to the nuclear arms race, and call for world peace and liberation from social conventions of all kinds.

Political activism erupted in 1968 in a series of protests and riots that circled the globe. African Americans rioted across the United States after the assassination of civil rights leader Martin Luther King, Jr., and antiwar demonstrators battled police at the Democratic National Convention in Chicago. Young protesters marched for political reform in Mexico City, where police responded by shooting and killing several hundred, and students in Tokyo demonstrated against the war in Vietnam. Protesters clashed with police in the West and East Blocs as well. Berlin and London witnessed massive, sometimes-violent demonstrations, students in Warsaw marched to protest government censorship, and youths in Prague were in the forefront of the attempt to radically reform communism from within (see pages 1005–1007).

One of the most famous and perhaps far-reaching of these revolts occurred in France in May 1968, when massive student protests coincided with a general strike that brought the French economy to a standstill. The "May Events" began when a group of students dismayed by conservative university policies and inspired by New Left ideals occupied buildings at the University of Paris. Violent clashes with police followed. When police tried to clear the area around the university on the night of May 10, a pitched street battle took place. At the end of the night, 460 arrests had been made by police, 367 people were wounded, and about 200 cars had been burned by protesters.

The "May Events" might have been a typically short-lived student protest against overcrowded universities, U.S. involvement in Vietnam, and the abuses of capitalism, but the demonstrations triggered a national revolt. By May 18 some 10 million workers were out on strike, and protesters occupied factories across France. For a brief moment, it seemed as if counterculture dreams of a revolution from below would come to pass. The French Fifth Republic was on the verge of collapse, and a shaken President de Gaulle surrounded Paris with troops.

In the end, however, the goals of the radical students did not correspond to the bread-and-butter demands of the striking workers. (See "Primary Source: Counterculture Graffiti from Paris, 1968," page 990.) When the government promised workplace reforms, including immediate pay raises, the strikers returned to work. President de Gaulle dissolved the French parliament and called for new elections. His conservative party won almost 75 percent of the seats, showing that the majority of the French people supported neither general strikes nor student-led revolutions. The universities shut down for the summer, administrators enacted educational reforms, and the protests had dissipated by the time the fall semester began. The May Events marked the high point of counterculture activism in Europe; in the early 1970s the movement declined.

As the political enthusiasm of the counterculture waned, committed activists disagreed about the best way to continue to fight for social change. Some followed what West German student leader Rudi Dutschke called "the long march through the institutions" and began to work for change from within the system. They entered national politics and joined the emerging feminist, antinuclear, and environmental groups that would gain increasing prominence in the following decades (see pages 1000–1002).

Others followed a more radical path. Across Europe, but particularly in Italy and West Germany, fringe New Left groups tried to bring radical change by turning to violence and terrorism. Like the American Weather Underground, the Italian Red Brigades and the West German Red Army Faction robbed banks, bombed public buildings, and

PRIMARY SOURCE Counterculture Graffiti from Paris, 1968

The slogans that appeared as graffiti scrawled overnight on the walls in Paris in May 1968 expressed the spirit of the New Left: "Power to the imagination"; "Be realistic, demand the impossible"; "Beneath the paving stones, the beach." The critique of the dehumanization of modern society captured in these slogans reflects both the imagination and the idealistic vagueness of counterculture demands.

Boredom is counterrevolutionary.

In a society that has abolished every kind of adventure the only adventure that remains is to abolish the society.

The revolution is incredible because it's really happening.

Live in the moment.

Down with the state.

Don't liberate me—I'll take care of that.

We want structures that serve people, not people serving structures.

Politics is in the streets.

A proletarian is someone who has no power over his life and knows it.

Workers of all countries, enjoy!

We refuse to be highrised, diplomaed, licensed, inventoried, registered, indoctrinated, suburbanized, sermonized, beaten, telemanipulated, gassed, booked.

Poetry is in the streets.

I'm a Groucho Marxist.

I take my desires for reality because I believe in the reality of my desires.

kidnapped and killed business leaders and politicians. After spasms of violence in the late 1970s—in Italy, for example, the Red Brigades murdered former prime minister Aldo Moro in 1978—security forces succeeded in incarcerating most of the terrorist leaders, and the movement fizzled out.

Counterculture protests generated a great deal of excitement and trained a generation of activists. In the end, however, the protests of the sixties generation resulted only in short-term, limited political change. Lifestyle rebellions involving sex, drugs, and rock music expanded the boundaries of acceptable personal behavior, but they hardly overturned the existing system.

The 1960s in the East Bloc

The building of the Berlin Wall in 1961 suggested that communism was there to stay, and NATO's refusal to intervene showed that the United States and western Europe basically accepted the premise. In the West, the wall became a potent symbol of the

Those who lack imagination cannot imagine what is lacking.

Forget everything you've been taught. Start by dreaming.

Professors, you make us grow old.

We don't want to be the watchdogs or servants of capitalism.

Exams = servility, social promotion, hierarchical society.

When examined, answer with questions.

If God existed it would be necessary to abolish him.

Revolutionary women are more beautiful.

Make love, not war.

Down with consumer society.

You can't buy happiness. Steal it.

Only the truth is revolutionary.

No freedom for the enemies of freedom.

EVALUATE THE EVIDENCE

1. What seems to be the main target of these lines? How do they express the counterculture slogan "the personal is political"?

2. To what extent do the graffitists connect to traditional forms of Marxist thought?

Source: Michael H. Hunt, *The World Transformed, 1945 to the Present: A Documentary Reader* (Boston: Bedford/St. Martin's, 2004), pp. 172–174.

repressive nature of communism in the East Bloc, where halting experiments with economic and cultural liberalization brought only limited reform.

East Bloc economies clearly lagged behind those of the West, exposing the weaknesses of central planning. To address these problems, in the 1960s Communist governments implemented cautious forms of decentralization and limited market policies. The results were mixed. Hungary's so-called New Economic Mechanism, which broke up state monopolies, allowed some private retail stores, and encouraged private agriculture, was perhaps most successful. East Germany's New Economic System, inaugurated in 1963, also brought moderate success, though it was reversed when the government returned to centralization in the late 1960s. In other East Bloc countries, however, economic growth flagged.

Recognizing that the overwhelming emphasis on heavy industry was generating popular discontent, Communist planning commissions began to redirect resources to the consumer sector. Again, the results varied. By 1970, for example, ownership of televisions in the more developed nations of East Germany, Czechoslovakia, and Hungary approached that of the affluent nations of western Europe, and other consumer goods were also more available. In Poland, by contrast, the economy stagnated in the 1960s. In the more conservative Albania and Romania, where leaders held fast to Stalinist practices, provision of consumer goods faltered. In general, ordinary people in the East Bloc grew increasingly tired of the shortages of basic consumer goods that seemed an endemic part of Communist society.

In the 1960s Communist regimes also cautiously granted cultural freedoms. In the Soviet Union, the cultural thaw allowed dissidents like Aleksandr Solzhenitsyn to publish critical works of fiction (see Chapter 28), and this relative tolerance spread to other East Bloc countries as well. In East Germany, for example, during the Bitterfeld Movement—named after a conference of writers, officials, and workers held at Bitterfeld, an industrial city south of Berlin—the regime encouraged intellectuals to take a more critical view of life in the East Bloc, as long as they did not directly oppose communism. Author Christa Wolf's novel *Divided Heaven* (1963) is a classic example of the genre. Though the protagonist's boyfriend emigrates to West Germany in search of better work conditions and she sees very real problems in her small-town factory, she remains committed to building socialism.

Cultural openness only went so far, however. The most outspoken dissidents were harassed and often forced to emigrate to the West; other critics contributed to the rise of an underground *samizdat* (SAH-meez-daht) literature that emerged in the Soviet Union and the East Bloc. The label *samizdat*, a Russian term meaning "self-published," referred to books, periodicals, newspapers, and pamphlets published secretly and passed hand to hand by dissident readers because the works directly criticized communism and thus went far beyond the limits of criticism accepted by the state. This samizdat literature emerged in Russia, Poland, and other countries in the mid-1950s and blossomed in the 1960s. These unofficial networks of communication kept critical thought alive and built contacts among dissidents, creating the foundation for the reform movements of the 1970s and 1980s.

The citizens of East Bloc countries sought political liberty as well, and the limits on reform were sharply revealed in Czechoslovakia during the 1968 "Prague Spring" (named for the country's capital city). In January 1968 reform elements in the Czechoslovak Communist Party gained a majority and voted out the long-time Stalinist leader in favor of Alexander Dubček (1921–1992), whose new regime launched dramatic reforms. Educated in Moscow, Dubček (DOOB-chehk) was a dedicated Communist, but he and his allies believed that they could reconcile genuine socialism with personal freedom and party democracy. They called for "socialism with a human face," relaxed state censorship, and replaced rigid bureaucratic planning with local decision making by trade unions, workers' councils, and consumers. The reform program proved enormously popular.

Remembering that the Hungarian revolution had revealed the difficulty of reforming communism from within (see Chapter 28), Dubček constantly proclaimed his loyalty to the Soviet Union and the Warsaw Pact. But the determination of the Czechoslovak reformers to build a more liberal and democratic socialism nevertheless threatened hardline Communists, particularly in Poland and East Germany, where leaders knew full well that they lacked popular support. Moreover, Soviet leaders feared that a liberalized Czechoslovakia would eventually be drawn to neutrality or even to NATO. Thus the

The Invasion of Czechoslovakia   Armed with Czechoslovakian flags, courageous Czechs in downtown Prague try to stop a Soviet tank and repel the invasion and occupation of their country by the Soviet Union and its eastern European allies. Realizing that military resistance would be suicidal, the Czechs capitulated to Soviet control. (AP Photo/Libor Hajsky/CTK)

East Bloc leadership launched a concerted campaign of intimidation against the reform-ers, and five hundred thousand Soviet and East Bloc troops occupied Czechoslovakia in August 1968. The Czechoslovaks made no attempt to resist militarily, and the arrested leaders surrendered to Soviet demands. The reform program was abandoned, and the Czechoslovak experiment in humanizing communism from within came to an end.

Shortly after the invasion of Czechoslovakia, Soviet premier Leonid Brezhnev (1906–1982) announced that the Soviets would now follow the so-called **Brezhnev Doctrine**, under which the Soviet Union and its allies had the right to intervene militar-ily in any East Bloc country whenever they thought doing so necessary to preserve Communist rule. The 1968 invasion of Czechoslovakia was the crucial event of the Brezhnev era: it demonstrated the determination of the Communist elite to maintain the status quo throughout the Soviet bloc, which would last for another twenty years. At the same time, the Soviet crackdown encouraged dissidents to change their focus from "reforming" Communist regimes from within to building a civil society that might bring internal freedoms independent of the regimes (see pages 1005–1007).

Crisis and Change in Western Europe

What were the consequences of economic decline in the 1970s?

The great postwar economic boom came to a close in the early 1970s, opening a long period of economic stagnation, widespread unemployment, and social dislocation. As a result, politics in western Europe drifted to the right, and leaders cut taxes and state spending and sold off (or privatized) state-owned companies. A number of new political groups entered national politics, including feminists and environmentalists on the left and neo-nationalists on the right. By the end of the 1980s the postwar consensus based on prosperity, full employment, modest regulation, and generous welfare provisions had been deeply shaken. Led by a new generation of conservative politicians, the West had restructured its economy and entered the information age.

Economic Crisis and Hardship

Starting in the early 1970s the West entered into a long period of economic decline. One of the early causes of the downturn was the collapse of the international monetary system, which since 1945 had been based on the American dollar, valued in gold at $35 an ounce. In the postwar decades the United States spent billions of dollars on foreign aid and foreign wars, weakening the value of American currency. In 1971 President Nixon attempted to reverse this trend by abruptly stopping the exchange of U.S. currency for gold. The value of the dollar fell sharply, and inflation accelerated worldwide. Countries abandoned fixed rates of currency exchange, and great uncertainty replaced postwar predictability in international trade and finance.

Even more damaging to the global economy was the dramatic reversal in the price and availability of energy. The great postwar boom had been fueled in part by cheap oil from the Middle East. The fate of the developed world was thus increasingly linked to this turbulent region, where strains began to show in the late 1960s. In 1967, in the Six-Day War, Israel quickly defeated Egypt, Jordan, and Syria and occupied more of the former territories of Palestine, angering Arab leaders and exacerbating anti-Western feeling in the Arab states. Economics fed tension between Arab states and the West. Over the years **OPEC**, the Arab-led Organization of Petroleum Exporting Countries, had watched the price of crude oil decline consistently compared with the rising price of Western manufactured goods. OPEC decided to reverse that trend by presenting a united front against Western oil companies.

The stage was thus already set for a revolution in energy prices when Egypt and Syria launched a surprise attack on Israel in October 1973, setting off the fourth Arab-Israeli war. With the help of U.S. weapons, Israel again achieved a quick victory. OPEC then declared an embargo on oil shipments to the United States, Israel's ally, and simultaneously raised oil prices. Within a year, crude oil prices quadrupled. Western nations realized that the rapid price increase was economically destructive, but together they did nothing. Thus governments, industry, and individuals dealt piecemeal with the so-called oil shock — a "shock" that turned out to be an earthquake.

Coming on the heels of the upheaval in the international monetary system, the revolution in energy prices plunged the world into its worst economic decline since the 1930s. Energy-intensive industries that had driven the economy up in the 1950s and 1960s now dragged it down. Unemployment rose, productivity and living standards declined, and inflation soared. Economists coined a new term — **stagflation** — to describe the combination of low growth and high inflation that drove the worldwide recession. By 1976 a modest recovery was in progress, but in 1979 a fundamentalist Islamic revolution overthrew the shah of Iran. When oil production in that country collapsed, the price of crude oil doubled again, and the world economy succumbed to its second oil shock. Unemployment and inflation rose dramatically before another uneven recovery began in 1982.

Anxious observers, recalling the disastrous consequences of the Great Depression, worried that the European Common Market would disintegrate in the face of severe economic dislocation and that economic nationalism would halt steps toward European unity. Yet the Common Market continued to attract new members. In 1973 Britain finally joined, as did Denmark and Ireland. After replacing authoritarian regimes with democratic governments in the 1970s, Greece joined in 1981, and Portugal and Spain entered in 1986. The nations of the Common Market cooperated more closely in international undertakings, and the movement toward western European unity stayed alive.

The developing world was hit hard by slowed growth, and the global economic downturn widened the gap between rich and poor countries, however. Governments across South America, sub-Saharan Africa, and South Asia borrowed heavily from the United States and western Europe in attempts to restructure their economies, setting the stage for a serious international debt crisis. At the same time, the East Asian countries of Japan and then Singapore, South Korea, and Taiwan started exporting high-tech consumer goods to the West. Competition from these East Asian "tiger economies," whose labor costs were comparatively low, shifted manufacturing jobs away from the highly industrialized countries of northern Europe and North America.

Even though the world economy slowly began to recover in the 1980s, western Europe could no longer create enough jobs to replace those that were lost. By the end of the 1970s, the foundations of economic growth in the industrialized West had begun shifting to high-tech information industries, such as computing and biotechnology, and to services, including medicine, banking, and finance. Scholars spoke of the shift as the arrival of "the information age" or **postindustrial society**. Technological advances streamlined the production of many goods, making many industrial jobs superfluous. In western Europe, heavy industry, such as steel, mining, automobile manufacture, and shipbuilding, lost ground. Factory closings led to the emergence of "rust belts" — formerly prosperous industrialized areas that were now ghost lands, with vacant lots, idle machinery, and empty inner cities. The highly industrialized Ruhr district in northwest West Germany and the once-extensive factory regions around Birmingham (Great Britain) and Detroit, Michigan, were classic examples. By 1985 the unemployment rate in western Europe had risen to its highest level since the Great Depression. Nineteen million people were jobless.

The crisis struck countless ordinary people, and there were heartbreaking human tragedies — bankruptcies, homelessness, and mental breakdowns. The punk rock songs of the late 1970s captured the mood of hostility and cynicism among young people. Yet on the whole, the welfare system fashioned in the postwar era prevented mass suffering and degradation. The responsive, socially concerned national state undoubtedly contributed to the preservation of political stability and democracy in the face of economic difficulties that might have brought revolution and dictatorship in earlier times.

With the commitment of governments to supporting social needs, government spending in most European countries continued to rise sharply during the 1970s and early 1980s. In 1982 western European governments spent an average of more than 50 percent of all national income on social programs, as compared to only 37 percent fifteen years earlier. Across western Europe, people were willing to see their governments increase spending, but they resisted higher taxes. This imbalance contributed to the rapid growth of budget deficits, national debts, and inflation. While this increased spending was generally popular, a powerful reaction against government's ever-increasing role had set in by the late 1970s that would transform governance in the 1980s.

The New Conservatism

The transition to a postindustrial society was led to a great extent by a new generation of conservative political leaders, who believed they had viable solutions for restructuring the relations between the state and the economy. During the thirty years following World War II, both Social Democrats and the more conservative Christian Democrats had usually agreed that economic growth and social stability were best achieved through full employment and high wages, some government regulation, and generous welfare provisions. In the late 1970s, however, with a weakened economy and increased global competition, this consensus began to unravel. Whether politics turned to the right, as in Great Britain, the United States, and West Germany, or to the left, as in France and Spain, leaders moved to cut government spending and regulation in attempts to improve economic performance.

The new conservatives of the 1980s followed a philosophy that came to be known as **neoliberalism** because of its roots in the free market, laissez-faire policies favored by eighteenth-century liberal economists such as Adam Smith (see Chapter 21). Neoliberal theorists like U.S. economist Milton Friedman argued that governments should cut support for social services such as housing, education, and health insurance; limit business subsidies; and retreat from regulation of all kinds. (Neoliberalism should be distinguished from modern American liberalism, which supports welfare programs and some state regulation of the economy.) Neoliberals also called for **privatization**—the sale of state-managed industries to private owners. Placing government-owned industries such as transportation and communication networks and heavy industry in private hands, they argued, would both tighten government spending and lead to greater workplace efficiency. The main goal was to increase private profits, which neoliberals believed were the real engine of economic growth.

The effects of neoliberal policies are best illustrated by events in Great Britain. The broad shift toward greater conservatism, coupled with growing voter dissatisfaction with high taxes and runaway state budgets, helped elect Margaret Thatcher (1925–2013) prime minister in 1979. A member of the Conservative Party and a convinced neoliberal, Thatcher was determined to scale back the role of government, and in the 1980s—the "Thatcher years"—she pushed through a series of controversial free-market policies that transformed Britain. Thatcher's government cut spending on health care, education, and public housing; reduced taxes; and privatized or sold off government-run enterprises. In one of her most popular actions, Thatcher encouraged low- and moderate-income renters in state-owned housing projects to buy their apartments at rock-bottom prices. This initiative, part of Thatcher's broader privatization campaign, created a whole new class of property owners, thereby eroding the electoral base of Britain's socialist Labour Party. (See "Individuals in Society: Margaret Thatcher," page 998.)

Though she never eliminated all social programs, Thatcher's policies helped replace the interventionist ethos of the welfare state with a greater reliance on private enterprise and the free market. This transition involved significant human costs. In the first three years of her government, heavy industries such as steel, coal mining, and textiles shut down, and unemployment rates in Britain doubled to over 12 percent. The gap between rich and poor widened, and increasing poverty led to discontent and crime. Strikes and working-class protests sometimes led to violent riots. Street violence often had racial overtones: immigrants from former British colonies in Africa, India, and the Caribbean, dismayed with poor jobs and racial discrimination, clashed repeatedly with police. Thatcher successfully rallied support by leading a British victory over Argentina in the brief Falklands War (1982), but over time her position weakened. By 1990 Thatcher's popularity had fallen to record lows, and she was replaced by Conservative Party leader John Major.

In the United States, two-term president Ronald Reagan (r. 1981–1989) followed a similar path, though his success in cutting government was more limited. Reagan's campaign slogan — "government is not the solution to our problem, government is the problem" — summed up a movement in line with Thatcher's ideas, which was labeled the conservative movement in the United States. With widespread popular support and the agreement of most congressional Democrats as well as Republicans, Reagan pushed through major across-the-board cuts in income taxes in 1981. But Reagan and Congress failed to limit government spending, which increased as a percentage of national income in the course of his presidency. A massive military buildup was partly responsible, but spending on social programs — despite Reagan's pledges to rein them in — also grew rapidly. The harsh recession of the early 1980s required the government to spend more on unemployment benefits, welfare benefits, and medical treatment for the poor. Moreover, Reagan's antiwelfare rhetoric mobilized the liberal opposition

The Social Consequences of Thatcherism As police watch in the background, picketers outside the largest coal mine in Britain hold up a poster reading "Save the Pits" during the miners' strike of 1984 to 1985. Prime Minister Margaret Thatcher broke the strike, weakening the power of Britain's trade unions and easing the turn to free-market economic reforms. Thatcher's neoliberal policies revived economic growth but cut state subsidies for welfare benefits and heavy industries, leading to lower living standards for many working-class Britons and, as this image attests, to popular protest. (Bride Lane Library/ Pepperfoto/Getty Images)

INDIVIDUALS IN SOCIETY • Margaret Thatcher

Margaret Thatcher, the first woman elected to lead a major European state, was one of the late twentieth century's most significant leaders. The controversial "iron lady" attacked socialism, promoted capitalism, and changed the face of modern Britain.

Raised in a lower-middle-class family in a small city in southeastern England, Thatcher entered Oxford in 1943 to study chemistry and soon discovered a passion for politics and was elected president of student conservatives. Four years after her graduation, she ran for Parliament in 1950 in a solidly Labour district to gain experience. Articulate and attractive, she won the attention of Denis Thatcher, a wealthy businessman who drove her to campaign appearances in his Jaguar. Married a year later, the new Mrs. Thatcher abandoned chemistry, went to law school, gave birth to twins, and became a tax attorney. In 1959 she returned to politics and won a seat in that year's Conservative triumph.

For the next fifteen years Thatcher served in Parliament and held various ministerial posts when the Conservatives governed. In 1974, as the economy soured and the Conservatives lost two close elections, a rebellious Thatcher adroitly ran for the leadership of her party and won. Five years later, as the Labour government faced rampant inflation and crippling strikes, Thatcher promised to reduce union power, lower taxes, and promote free markets. Attracting swing votes from skilled workers, the Conservatives gained a majority, and she became prime minister.

A self-described "conviction politician," Thatcher rejected postwar Keynesian efforts to manage the economy, arguing that governments created inflation by printing too much money. Thus her government reduced the supply of money and credit and refused to retreat when interest rates and unemployment soared. Her popularity plummeted. But Thatcher remained in office, in part through an aggressive foreign policy. In 1982 the generals ruling Argentina suddenly seized the nearby Falkland Islands, home to 1,800 British citizens. A staunch nationalist, Thatcher detached a naval armada that recaptured the islands without a hitch. Britain admired Thatcher's determination and patriotism, and she was re-elected in 1983.

Thatcher's second term was the high point of her influence. Her commitment to privatization transformed British industry. More than fifty state-owned companies, ranging from the state telephone monopoly to the nationalized steel trust, were sold to private investors. Small investors were offered shares at bargain prices to promote "people's capitalism." Thatcher also curbed the power of British labor

and eventually turned many moderates against him. The budget deficit soared, and U.S. government debt tripled in a decade.

West Germany also turned to the right. After more than a decade in power, the Social Democrats foundered, and in 1982 Christian Democrat Helmut Kohl (b. 1930) became the new chancellor. Like Thatcher, Kohl cut taxes and government spending. His policies led to increasing unemployment in heavy industry but also to solid economic growth. By the mid-1980s West Germany was one of the most prosperous countries in the world. In foreign policy, Kohl drew close to President Reagan. The chancellor agreed

unions, most spectacularly in 1984, when the once-mighty coal miners rejected more mine closings and doggedly struck for a year; Thatcher stood firm and beat them. This outcome had a profound psychological impact on the public, who blamed her for growing unemployment. Thatcher was also accused of mishandling a series of protest hunger strikes undertaken by the Irish Republican Army—in 1981 ten IRA members starved themselves to death in British prisons— but she refused to compromise with those she labeled criminals. As a result, the revolt in Northern Ireland entered one of its bloodiest phases.

Despite these problems, Thatcher was elected to a third term in 1987. Afterward, she became increasingly stubborn, overconfident, and uncaring. Working with her ideological soul mate, U.S. president Ronald Reagan, she opposed greater political and economic unity within the European Community. This, coupled with rising inflation, stubborn unemployment, and an unpopular effort to assert financial control over city governments, proved her undoing. In 1990, as in 1974, party stalwarts suddenly revolted and elected a new Conservative leader. The transformational changes of the Thatcher years nonetheless endured, consolidated by her Conservative successor, John Major, and largely accepted by the new Labour prime minister, the moderate Tony Blair, who served in office from 1997 to 2007.

QUESTIONS FOR ANALYSIS

1. Why did Margaret Thatcher want to change Britain, and how did she do it?
2. How did Thatcher's policies reflect the new conservatism of the 1970s and 1980s?

ONLINE DOCUMENT ASSIGNMENT

How did Thatcher's Conservative Party adapt its message to fit the values of the majority of British people? Explore Conservative Party campaign posters from the 1979 British general election. Then complete a writing assignment based on the evidence and details from this chapter.

bedfordstmartins.com/mckaywestvalue

to deploy U.S. cruise missiles and nuclear-armed Pershing missiles on West German territory, a decision that contributed to renewed superpower tensions. In power for sixteen years, Kohl and the Christian Democrats governed during the opening of the Berlin Wall in 1989, the reunification of East and West Germany in 1990, and the end of the Cold War.

The most striking temporary exception to the general drift to the right in European politics was François Mitterrand (1916–1996) of France. After his election as president in 1981, Mitterrand and his Socialist Party led France on a lurch to the left. This marked a significant change in French politics, which had been dominated by center-right parties for some twenty-five years. Working at first in a coalition that included the French Communist Party, Mitterrand launched a vast program of nationalization and public investment designed to spend the country out of economic stagnation. By 1983 this attempt had clearly failed, and Mitterrand's Socialist government made a dramatic about-face. The Socialists were compelled to reprivatize industries they had just nationalized. They imposed a wide variety of austerity measures and maintained those policies for the rest of the decade.

Despite persistent economic crises and high social costs, by 1990 the developed nations of western Europe and North America were far more productive than they had been in the early 1970s. Western Europe was at the center of the emerging global economy, and its citizens were far richer than those in Soviet bloc countries (see pages 1004–1005). Yet the collapse of the postwar consensus and the remaking of Europe in the transitional decades of the 1970s and 1980s helped generate new forms of protest and dissent across the political spectrum.

Challenges and Victories for Women

The 1970s marked the arrival of a diverse and widespread feminist movement devoted to securing genuine gender equality and promoting the general interests of women. Three basic reasons accounted for this dramatic development. First, ongoing changes in underlying patterns of motherhood and paid work created novel conditions and new demands (see Chapter 28). Second, a vanguard of feminist intellectuals articulated a powerful critique of gender relations, which stimulated many women to rethink their assumptions and challenge the status quo. Third, taking a lesson from the civil rights movement in the United States and protests against the Vietnam War, dissatisfied women recognized that they had to band together if they were to influence politics and secure fundamental reforms.

Feminists could draw on a long heritage of protest, stretching back to the French Revolution and the women's movements of the late nineteenth century (see Chapters 19 and 22). They were also inspired by recent writings, such as the foundational book *The Second Sex* (1949) by the French writer and philosopher Simone de Beauvoir (1908–1986). Beauvoir, who worked closely with the existentialist philosopher Jean-Paul Sartre, analyzed the position of women within the framework of existential thought. Drawing on history, philosophy, psychology, biology, and literature, Beauvoir argued that women had almost always been trapped by particularly inflexible and limiting conditions. Only through courageous action and self-assertive creativity could a woman become a completely free person and escape the role of the inferior "other" that men had constructed for her gender.

The Second Sex inspired a generation of women intellectuals, and by the late 1960s and the 1970s "second-wave feminism" had spread through North America and Europe. In the United States, writer and organizer Betty Friedan's (1921–2006) pathbreaking study *The Feminine Mystique* (1963) pointed the way. Friedan called attention to the stifling aspects of women's domestic life, devoted to the service of husbands and children. Housewives lived in a "gilded cage," she concluded, because they were usually not allowed to hold professional jobs or become mature adults and genuine human beings. In 1966 Friedan helped found the National Organization for Women

(NOW) to press for women's rights. NOW flourished, growing from seven hundred members in 1967 to forty thousand in 1974.

Many other women's organizations rose in Europe and North America. The diverse groups drew inspiration from Marx, Freud, or political liberalism, but in general feminists attacked patriarchy (the domination of society by men) and sexism (the inequalities faced by women simply because they were female). Throughout the 1970s a proliferation of publications, conferences, and institutions devoted to women's issues reinforced the emerging international movement. Advocates of women's rights pushed for new statutes governing the workplace: laws against discrimination, acts requiring equal pay for equal work, and measures such as maternal leave and affordable day care designed to help women combine careers and family responsibilities.

The movement also addressed gender and family questions, including the right to divorce (in some Catholic countries), legalized abortion, the needs of single mothers, and protection from rape and physical violence. In almost every country, the effort to decriminalize abortion served as a catalyst in mobilizing an effective, self-conscious women's movement—and, as in the United States, in creating opposition to it.

In countries that had long placed women in a subordinate position, the legal changes were little less than revolutionary. In Italy, for example, new laws abolished restrictions on divorce and abortion that had been strengthened by Mussolini and defended energetically by the Catholic Church in the postwar era. By 1988 divorce and abortion were common in Italy, which had the lowest birthrate in Europe. While the women's movement of the 1970s won new rights for women, subsequently it became more diffuse, a victim of both its successes and the resurgence of an antifeminist opposition.

The Rise of the Environmental Movement

Like feminism, environmentalism had roots in the 1960s counterculture. Early environmentalists drew inspiration from writers like U.S. biologist Rachel Carson, whose book *Silent Spring*, published in 1962, was quickly translated into twelve European languages. Carson's chilling title referred to a future spring, when people in developed society would wake up and hear no birds singing, because they had all been killed by the rampant use of pesticides. The book had a striking impact on the growth of environmental movements in Europe.

By the 1970s the destructive environmental costs of industrial development in western Europe and the East Bloc were everywhere apparent. The mighty Rhine River, which flows from Switzerland, past France, and through Germany and the Netherlands, was an industrial sewer. The forests of southwestern Germany were dying from acid rain, a result of smokestack emissions. The pristine coast of Brittany, in northwest France, was fouled by oil spills from massive tanker ships. Rapid industrialization in the East Bloc, undertaken with little regard for environmental impact, severely polluted waterways, contaminated farmlands and forests, and degraded air quality. Nuclear power plants across Europe were generating toxic waste that would last for centuries; serious accidents at nuclear plants—at Three Mile Island in Pennsylvania (1979) and at Chernobyl in Soviet Ukraine (1986)—revealed nuclear power's potential to create human and environmental disaster (Map 29.1). These were just some examples of the environmental threats that inspired a growing environmental movement to challenge government and industry to clean up their acts.

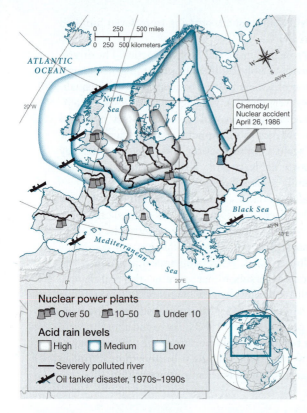

MAP 29.1   Pollution in Europe, ca. 1990
Despite attempts to remedy the negative consequences of the human impact on the environment, pollution remains a significant challenge for Europeans in the twenty-first century.

Environmentalists had two main agendas. First, they worked to lessen the ill effects of unbridled industrial development on the natural environment. Second, they argued that local environmental problems often increased human poverty, inequality, and violence around the globe. Environmental groups pursued these goals in many ways. Some used the mass media to reach potential supporters; some worked closely with politicians and public officials to change government policies. Others took a more activist stance. In Denmark in March 1969, in a dramatic example, student protesters at the University of Copenhagen took over a scientific conference on natural history. They locked the conference hall doors, sprayed the professors in attendance with polluted lake water, and held up an oil-doused duck, shouting, "Come and save it . . . you talk about pollution, why don't you do anything about it!"[3]

Environmental protesters also built new institutions, particularly in North America and western Europe. In 1971 Canadian activists established Greenpeace, a nongovernmental organization dedicated to environmental conservation and protection. Greenpeace quickly grew into an international organization, with strong support in Europe and the United States. In West Germany in 1979 environmentalists founded the Green Party, a political party to fight for environmental causes. The West German Greens met with astounding success when they elected members to parliament in 1983, the first time in sixty years that a new political party had been seated in Germany. Their success was a model for like-minded activists in Europe and North America, and Green Party members were later elected to parliaments in Belgium, Italy, and Sweden. In the East Bloc, government planners increasingly recognized and tried to ameliorate environmental problems in the 1980s, but official censorship meant that groups like the Greens would not emerge there until after the end of Communist rule.

Separatism and Right-Wing Extremism

The 1970s also saw the rise of determined separatist movements across Europe. In Ireland, Spain, Belgium, and Switzerland—and in Yugoslavia and Czechoslovakia in the East Bloc—regional ethnic groups struggled for special rights, political autonomy, and even national independence. This separatism was most violent in Spain and Northern Ireland, where well-established insurgent groups used terrorist attacks to win government concessions. In the ethnic Basque region of northern Spain, the ETA (short, in the Basque language, for Basque Homeland and Freedom) tried to use bombings and assassinations to force the government to grant independence. After the death in 1975 of Fascist dictator Francisco Franco, who had ruled Spain for almost forty years, a new constitution granted the Basque region special autonomy, but it was not enough. The ETA stepped up its terrorist campaigns, killing over four hundred people in the 1980s.

The Provisional Irish Republican Army (IRA), a paramilitary organization in Northern Ireland, used similar tactics. Though Ireland had won autonomy in 1922, Great Britain retained control of six primarily Protestant counties in the north of the island (see Chapter 26). In the late 1960s violence re-emerged as the IRA, hoping to unite these counties with Ireland, attacked British security forces, which it saw as an occupying army. On Bloody Sunday in January 1972, British soldiers shot and killed thirteen demonstrators, who had been protesting anti-Catholic discrimination, in the town of Derry, and the violence escalated. For the next thirty years the IRA attacked soldiers and civilians in Northern Ireland and in Britain itself. Over two thousand British soldiers, civilians, and IRA members were killed during "the Troubles" before negotiations between the IRA and the British government opened in the late 1990s and a settlement was reached in 1998.

Mainstream European politicians also faced challenges from newly assertive political forces on the far right. Right-wing political parties such as the National Front in France, the Northern League in Italy, the Austrian Freedom Party, and the National Democratic Party in West Germany were founded or gained popularity in the 1970s and 1980s. Populist leaders like Jean-Marie Le Pen, the founder of the French National Front, opposed European integration and called for a return to traditional national customs, often at the expense of the non-European immigrants who were a growing proportion of western Europe's working-class population (see Chapter 28). New right-wing politicians promoted themselves as the champions of ordinary (white) workers, complaining that immigrants swelled welfare rolls and stole jobs from native-born Europeans. Though their programs at times veered close to open racism, they began to win seats in national parliaments in the 1980s.

The Decline of "Developed Socialism"

What led to the decline of Soviet power in the East Bloc?

In the postwar decades the Communist states of the East Bloc had achieved a shaky social consensus based on a rising standard of living, an extensive welfare system, and political repression. When the Marxist utopia still had not arrived in the 1970s, Communist leaders told citizens that the totally egalitarian society would be realized sometime in the future. In the meantime, they would have to accept the system as it was; in the long run, leaders claimed, "developed socialism" would prove better than capitalism. Such claims were an attempt to paper over serious tensions in socialist society. Everyday life could be difficult. Limits on personal and political freedoms encouraged the growth of determined reform movements, and a revival of Cold War tensions accompanied the turn to the right in the United States and western Europe in the 1980s.

When Mikhail Gorbachev burst on the scene in 1985, the new Soviet leader opened an era of reform that was as sweeping as it was unexpected. Although many believed that Gorbachev would soon fall from power, his reforms rapidly transformed Soviet culture and politics and drastically reduced Cold War tensions. But communism, which Gorbachev wanted so desperately to revitalize, continued to stagnate and decline.

State and Society in the East Bloc

By the 1970s many of the professed goals of communism had been achieved. Communist leaders in central and eastern Europe and the Soviet Union adopted the term **developed socialism** (sometimes called "real existing socialism") to describe the accomplishments of their societies. Agriculture had been thoroughly collectivized, and though Poland was an exception, 80 to 90 percent of Soviet and East Bloc farmers worked on huge collective farms. Industry and business had been nationalized, and only a small percentage of the economy remained in private hands in most East Bloc countries. The state had also done much to level class differences. Though some people—particularly party members—clearly had greater access to better opportunities and resources, the gap between rich and poor was far smaller than in the West. An extensive system of government-supported welfare benefits included free medical care, guaranteed employment, inexpensive public transportation, and large subsidies for rent and food.

Everyday life under developed socialism was defined by an uneasy mixture of outward conformity and private disengagement—or apathy. The Communist Party dominated public life. Party-led mass organizations for youth, women, workers, and sports groups staged huge rallies, colorful festivals, and new holidays that exposed citizens to the values of the socialist state. East Bloc citizens might grudgingly participate in party-sponsored public events, but at home, and in private, they often grumbled about and sidestepped the Communist authorities.

East Bloc living standards were well above those in the developing world, but well below those in the West. Centralized economic planning continued to lead to shortages, and people complained about the poor quality and lack of choice of the most basic goods. Under these conditions, informal networks of family and friends helped people find hard-to-get goods and offered support beyond party organizations. Though the secret police persecuted those who openly challenged the system and generated mountains of files on ordinary people, they generally left alone those who demonstrated the required conformity.

Women in particular experienced the contradictions of the socialist system. Official state policy guaranteed equal rights for women and encouraged them to join the workforce in positions formerly reserved for men, while an extensive system of state-supported child care freed women to accept these employment opportunities and eased the work of parenting. Yet women rarely made it into the upper ranks of business or politics, and they faced the same double burden as those in the West (see Chapter 28). In addition, government control of the public sphere meant that the independent groups dedicated to feminist reform that emerged in the West in the 1970s never developed in the East Bloc or the Soviet Union. Women could complain to the Communist authorities about unequal or sexist conditions at work or at home, but they could not build private, nongovernmental organizations to lobby for change.

Though everyday life was fairly comfortable in the East Bloc, a number of deeply rooted structural problems undermined popular support for Soviet-style communism. These fundamental problems would contribute to the re-emergence of civic dissent and ultimately to the revolutions of 1989. East Bloc countries—like those in the West— were hard hit by the energy crisis and stagflation of the 1970s. For a time, access to inexpensive oil from the Soviet Union, which had huge resources, helped prop up faltering economies, but this cushion began to fall apart in the 1980s. For a number of reasons, East Bloc leaders refused to make the economic reforms that might have made developed socialism more effective.

First, a move toward Western-style postindustrial society would have required fundamental changes to the Communist system. As in the West, it would have hurt the already-tenuous living standard of industrial workers. But Communist East Bloc states were publicly committed to supporting the working classes, including coal miners, shipbuilders, and factory and construction workers. To pursue the neoliberal reforms undertaken in the West would have undermined popular support for the government among these basic constituencies, which was already becoming tenuous.

Second, East Bloc regimes refused to cut spending on the welfare state because that was, after all, one of the proudest achievements of socialism. Third, the state continued to provide subsidies to heavy industries such as steel and mining. High-tech industries failed to take off in Communist Europe, in part because the West maintained embargoes on technology exports. The industrial goods produced in the East Bloc became increasingly uncompetitive in the new global system. To stave off total collapse, governments borrowed massive amounts of hard currency from Western banks and governments, helping to convince ordinary people that communism was bankrupt, and setting up a cycle of indebtedness that helped bring down the entire system in 1989.

Economic decline was not the only reason people increasingly questioned one-party, Communist rule. The best career and educational opportunities were reserved for party members or handed out as political favors, leaving many talented people underemployed and resentful. Tight controls on travel continually called attention to the burdens of daily life in a repressive society. The one-party state had repeatedly quashed popular reform movements, retreated from economic liberalization, and jailed or exiled dissidents, even those who wished to reform communism from within. Though many East Bloc citizens still found the promise of Marxist egalitarian socialism appealing, they increasingly doubted the legitimacy of Soviet-style communism: the dream of distributing goods "from each according to his means, to each according to his needs" (as Marx had once put it) hardly made up for the great structural weaknesses of developed socialism.

Dissent in Czechoslovakia and Poland

Stagnation in the East Bloc encouraged small numbers of dedicated people to try to change society from below. Developments in Czechoslovakia and Poland were the most striking and significant, and determined protest movements re-emerged in both countries in the mid-1970s. Remembering a history of violent repression and Soviet invasion, dissenters carefully avoided direct challenges to government leaders. Nor did they try to reform the Communist Party itself, as Dubček and his followers had attempted in the Prague Spring of 1968. Instead, they worked to build a civil society from below—

to create a realm of freedom beyond formal politics, where civil liberties and human rights could be exercised independent of the Communist system.

In Czechoslovakia in 1977 a small group of citizens, including future Czechoslovak president Václav Havel (VAH-slahf HAH-vuhl) (1936–2011), signed a manifesto that came to be known as Charter 77. The group criticized the government for ignoring the human rights provision of the Helsinki Accords and called on Communist leaders to respect civil and political liberties. They also criticized censorship and argued for improved environmental policies. Despite immediate state repression, the group challenged passive acceptance of Communist authority and voiced public dissatisfaction with developed socialism.

In Poland, an unruly satellite from the beginning, the Communists had failed to dominate society to the extent seen elsewhere in the East Bloc. Most agricultural land remained in private hands, and the Catholic Church thrived. The Communists also failed to manage the economy effectively. The 1960s brought stagnation, and in 1970 Poland's working class rose again in angry protest. A new Communist leader came to power, and he wagered that massive inflows of Western capital and technology, especially from rich and now-friendly West Germany, could produce a Polish economic miracle. Instead, bureaucratic incompetence and the first oil shock in 1973 sent the economy into a nosedive. Workers, intellectuals, and the church became increasingly restive. Then the real Polish miracle occurred: Cardinal Karol Wojtyla (KAH-rohl voy-TIH-wah), archbishop of Kraków, was elected pope in 1978 as John Paul II. In June 1979 he returned to Poland from Rome, preaching love of Christ and country and the "inalienable rights of man." The pope drew enormous crowds and electrified the Polish nation.

In August 1980 strikes broke out across Poland; at the gigantic Lenin Shipyards in Gdansk (formerly known as Danzig) sixteen thousand workers laid down their tools and occupied the plant. As other workers joined "in solidarity," the strikers advanced the ideals of civil society, including the right to form trade unions free from state control, freedom of speech, release of political prisoners, and economic reforms. After the strikers occupied the shipyard for eighteen days, the government gave in and accepted the workers' demands in the Gdansk Agreement. In a state in which the Communist Party claimed to rule on behalf of the proletariat, a working-class revolt had won an unprecedented, even revolutionary, victory.

Led by feisty Lenin Shipyards electrician and devout Catholic Lech Wałęsa (lehk vah-WEHN-suh) (b. 1943), the workers proceeded to organize a free and democratic trade union called **Solidarity**. As had been the case in Czechoslovakia, Solidarity worked cautiously to shape an active civil society. Joined by intellectuals and supported by the Catholic Church, it became a national union with a full-time staff of 40,000 and 9.5 million members. Cultural and intellectual freedom blossomed in Poland, and Solidarity enjoyed tremendous public support. But Solidarity's leaders pursued a self-limiting revolution, meant only to defend the concessions won in the Gdansk Agreement. Solidarity thus practiced moderation, refusing to challenge directly the Communist monopoly on political power. At the same time, the ever-present threat of calling a nationwide strike gave them real leverage in ongoing negotiations with the Communist bosses.

Solidarity's combination of strength and moderation postponed a showdown, as the Soviet Union played a waiting game of threats and pressure. After a confrontation in March 1981, Wałęsa settled for minor government concessions, and Solidarity dropped plans for a massive general strike. Criticism of Wałęsa's moderate leadership gradually grew, and Solidarity lost its cohesiveness. The worsening economic crisis also encouraged radical actions among disgruntled Solidarity members, and the Polish Communist leadership shrewdly denounced the union for promoting economic collapse and provoking a possible Soviet invasion. In December 1981 Wojciech Jaruzelski (VOY-chehk yahr-oo-ZEHL-skee), the general who headed Poland's Communist government, suddenly proclaimed martial law and arrested Solidarity's leaders.

Outlawed and driven underground, Solidarity survived in part because of the government's unwillingness (and probably its inability) to impose full-scale terror. Moreover, millions of Poles decided to continue acting as if they were free—the hallmark of civil society—even though they were not. Cultural and intellectual life remained extremely vigorous as the Polish economy continued to deteriorate. Thus popular support for outlawed Solidarity remained strong under martial law in the 1980s, preparing the way for the union's political rebirth toward the end of the decade.

The rise and survival of Solidarity showed that ordinary Poles would stubbornly struggle for greater political and religious liberty, cultural freedom, trade-union rights, patriotic nationalism, and a more humane socialism. Not least, Solidarity's challenge encouraged fresh thinking in the Soviet Union, ever the key to lasting change in the East Bloc.

From Détente Back to Cold War

The Soviets and the leaders of the Soviet satellite states also faced challenges from abroad as optimistic hopes for détente in international relations gradually faded in the late 1970s. Brezhnev's Soviet Union ignored the human rights provisions of the Helsinki agreement, and East-West political competition remained very much alive outside Europe. Many Americans became convinced that the Soviet Union was taking advantage of détente, steadily building up its military might and pushing for political gains and revolutions in Africa, Asia, and Latin America. The Soviet invasion of Afghanistan in December 1979, designed to save an increasingly unpopular Marxist regime, alarmed the West. Many Americans feared that the oil-rich states of the Persian Gulf would be next, and once again they looked to the NATO alliance and military might to thwart Communist expansion.

President Jimmy Carter (r. 1977–1981) tried to lead NATO beyond verbal condemnation of the Soviet Union and urged economic sanctions against it, but only Great Britain among the European allies supported the American initiative. The alliance showed the same lack of concerted action when the Solidarity movement rose in Poland. Some observers concluded that NATO had lost the will to act decisively in dealing with the Soviet bloc.

The Atlantic alliance endured, however, and the U.S. military buildup launched by Carter in his last years in office was greatly accelerated by President Reagan, who was swept into office in 1980 by a wave of patriotism and economic discontent. The new American leadership acted as if the military balance had tipped in favor of the Soviet Union, which Reagan anathematized as the "evil empire." Increasing defense spending enormously, the Reagan administration deployed short-range nuclear missiles in western Europe and built up the navy to preserve American power in the post-Vietnam age. The broad shift toward greater conservatism in the 1980s gave Reagan invaluable allies in western Europe. Margaret Thatcher worked well with Reagan and was a forceful advocate for a revitalized Atlantic alliance, and under Helmut Kohl West Germany likewise worked with the United States to coordinate military and political policy toward the Soviet bloc.

Gorbachev's Reforms in the Soviet Union

Cold War tensions aside, the Soviet Union's Communist elite seemed safe from any challenge from below in the early 1980s. A well-established system of administrative controls stretched downward from the central ministries and state committees to provincial cities and from there to factories, neighborhoods, and villages. At each level of this massive state bureaucracy, the overlapping hierarchy of the 17.5-million-member Communist Party maintained tight state control. Organized opposition was impossible, and average people left politics to the bosses.

Although the massive state and party bureaucracy safeguarded the elite, it promoted widespread apathy and stagnation. When the ailing Brezhnev finally died in 1982, his successor, the long-time chief of the secret police, Yuri Andropov (1914–1984), tried to invigorate the system. Relatively little came of his efforts, but they combined with a sharply worsening economic situation to set the stage for the emergence in 1985 of Mikhail Gorbachev (b. 1931), the most vigorous Soviet leader in a generation.

A lawyer and experienced Communist Party official, Gorbachev was smart, charming, and tough. He believed in communism, but realized that the Soviet Union was failing to keep up with the West and was losing its superpower status. Thus Gorbachev tried to revitalize the Soviet system with fundamental reforms. An idealist who wanted to improve conditions for ordinary citizens, Gorbachev understood that the enormous expense of the Cold War arms race had had a disastrous impact on living conditions in the Soviet Union; improvement at home, he realized, required better relations with the West.

In his first year in office, Gorbachev attacked corruption and incompetence in the bureaucracy and consolidated his power. He condemned alcoholism and drunkenness, which were deadly scourges of Soviet society, and worked out an ambitious reform program designed to transform and restructure the economy in order to provide for the real needs of the Soviet population. To accomplish this economic restructuring, or **perestroika** (pehr-uh-STROY-kuh), Gorbachev and his supporters permitted an easing of government price controls on some goods, more independence for state enterprises, and the creation of profit-seeking private cooperatives to provide personal services. These timid reforms initially produced a few improvements, but shortages grew as the economy stalled at an intermediate point between central planning and free-market mechanisms. By late 1988 widespread consumer dissatisfaction posed a serious threat to Gorbachev's leadership and the entire reform program.

Gorbachev's bold and far-reaching campaign for greater freedom of expression was much more successful. Very popular in a country where censorship, dull uniformity, and outright lies had long characterized public discourse, the newfound openness, or **glasnost** (GLAZ-nohst), of the government and the media marked an astonishing break with the past. Long-banned émigré writers sold millions of copies of their works in new editions, while denunciations of Stalin and his terror became standard fare in plays and movies. In another example of glasnost in action, after several days of hesitation the usually secretive Soviet government issued daily reports on the 1986 nuclear plant acci-

Mikhail Gorbachev In his acceptance speech before the Supreme Soviet (the U.S.S.R.'s parliament), newly elected president Mikhail Gorbachev vowed to assume "all responsibility" for the success or failure of perestroika. Previous Soviet parliaments were little more than tools of the Communist Party, but this one actively debated and even opposed government programs. (AP Photo/Boris Yurchenko)

dent at Chernobyl, one of the worst environmental disasters in history. Indeed the initial openness in government pronouncements quickly went much further than Gorbachev intended and led to something approaching free speech, a veritable cultural revolution.

Democratization was a third element of reform. Beginning as an attack on corruption in the Communist Party, it led to the first free elections in the Soviet Union since 1917. Gorbachev and the party remained in control, but a minority of critical independents was elected in April 1989 to a revitalized Congress of People's Deputies. Millions of Soviets then watched the new congress for hours on television as Gorbachev and his ministers saw their proposals debated and even rejected. Thus millions of Soviet citizens took practical lessons in open discussion, critical thinking, and representative government. An active civil society was emerging—a new political culture at odds with the Communist Party's monopoly of power and control.

Democratization also ignited demands for greater political and cultural autonomy and even national independence among non-Russian minorities living in the fifteen Soviet republics. The Soviet population numbered about 145 million ethnic Russians and 140.6 million non-Russians, including 55 million Muslims in the Central Asian republics and over 44 million Ukrainians. Once Gorbachev opened the doors to greater public expression and popular desires for democracy, tensions flared between central Soviet control and national separatist movements. Independence groups were particularly active in the Baltic Soviet socialist republics of Lithuania, Latvia, and Estonia; in western Ukraine; and in the Transcaucasian republics of Armenia, Azerbaijan, and Georgia.

Finally, Gorbachev brought reforms to the field of foreign affairs. He withdrew Soviet troops from Afghanistan in February 1989 and sought to reduce East-West tensions. Of enormous importance, the Soviet leader sought to halt the arms race with the United States and convinced President Reagan of his sincerity. In a Washington summit in December 1987, the two leaders agreed to eliminate all land-based intermediate-range missiles in Europe, setting the stage for more arms reductions. Gorbachev pledged to respect the political choices of the peoples of East Bloc countries, repudiating the Brezhnev Doctrine and giving encouragement to reform movements in Poland,

Czechoslovakia, and Hungary. By early 1989 it seemed that if Gorbachev held to his word, the tragic Soviet occupation of eastern Europe might wither away, taking the long Cold War with it once and for all.

The Revolutions of 1989

Why did revolution sweep through the East Bloc in 1989, and what were the immediate consequences?

In 1989 Gorbachev's plan to reform communism from within snowballed out of control. A series of largely peaceful revolutions swept across eastern Europe, overturning existing Communist regimes (Map 29.2). The revolutions of 1989 had momentous consequences. First, the peoples of the East Bloc gained political freedom after about forty years of dictatorial Communist rule. Second, West Germany absorbed its East German rival, and a reunified Germany emerged as the most influential country in Europe. Third, as Gorbachev's reforms boomeranged, a complicated anticommunist revolution swept through the Soviet Union and the multinational empire broke into a large Russia and fourteen other independent states. The Cold War came to an end, and the United States suddenly stood as the world's only superpower.

The Collapse of Communism in the East Bloc

The collapse of Communist rule in the Soviet satellite states surprised many Western commentators, who had expected Cold War divisions to persist for many years. Yet while the revolutions of 1989 appeared to erupt quite suddenly, long-standing, structural weaknesses in the Communist system had in some ways made revolt inevitable. East Bloc economies never really recovered from the economic catastrophe of the 1970s. State spending on outdated industries and extensive welfare systems led to massive indebtedness to Western banks and undermined economic growth, while limits on personal and political freedoms fueled a growing sense of injustice (see page 1005).

In this general climate of economic stagnation and popular anger, Solidarity and the Polish people led the way to revolution. In 1988 widespread strikes, raging inflation, and the outlawed Solidarity's refusal to cooperate with the military government had brought Poland to the brink of economic collapse. Poland's frustrated Communist leaders offered to negotiate with Solidarity if the outlawed union's leaders could get the strikers back to work and resolve the political stalemate and the economic crisis. The subsequent agreement in April 1989 legalized Solidarity and declared that a large minority of representatives to the Polish parliament would be chosen by free elections that June. Still guaranteed a parliamentary majority and expecting to win many of the contested seats, the Communists believed that their rule was guaranteed for four years and that Solidarity would keep the workers in line.

Lacking access to the state-run media, Solidarity succeeded nonetheless in mobilizing the country and winning all but one of the contested seats in an overwhelming victory. Moreover, many angry voters crossed off the names of unopposed party candidates, so that the Communist Party failed to win the majority its leaders had anticipated. Solidarity members jubilantly entered the Polish parliament, and a dangerous stalemate quickly developed. But Lech Wałęsa, a gifted politician who always repudiated violence, adroitly obtained a majority by securing the allegiance of two minor pro-communist

MAP 29.2 **Democratic Movements in Eastern Europe, 1989**
Countries that had been satellites in the orbit of the Soviet Union began to set themselves free in 1989.

parties that had been part of the coalition government after World War II. In August 1989 Tadeusz Mazowiecki (Ta-DAY-ush MAH-zoe-vee-ETS-key) (b. 1927), the editor of one of Solidarity's weekly newspapers, was sworn in as Poland's new noncommunist prime minister.

In its first year and a half, the new Solidarity government cautiously introduced revolutionary political changes. It eliminated the hated secret police, the Communist ministers in the government, and finally Communist Party leader Jaruzelski himself, but it did so step-by-step in order to avoid confrontation with the army or the Soviet Union. In economics, however, the Solidarity government was radical from the beginning. It applied economic shock therapy, an intense dose of neoliberal policy designed to make a clean break with state planning and move quickly to market mechanisms and private property (see Chapter 30). Thus the government abolished controls on many prices on January 1, 1990, and reformed the monetary system with a big bang.

Hungary followed Poland. Hungary's Communist Party boss János Kádár (KAH-dahr) had permitted liberalization of the rigid planned economy after the 1956 uprising in exchange for political obedience and continued Communist control. In May 1988, in an effort to retain power by granting modest political concessions, the party replaced Kádár with a reform-minded Communist. But opposition groups rejected piecemeal progress, and in the summer of 1989 the Hungarian Communist Party agreed to hold free elections the following March. Welcoming Western investment and moving rapidly toward multiparty democracy, Hungary's Communists now enjoyed considerable popular support, and they believed, quite mistakenly, that they could defeat the opposition in the upcoming elections.

In an effort to strengthen their support at home, the Hungarians opened their border to East Germans and tore down the barbed wire curtain separating Hungary from Austria. Tens of thousands of dissatisfied East German "vacationers" then poured into Hungary, crossed into Austria as refugees, and continued on to immediate re-settlement in thriving West Germany. The flight of East Germans fed the rapid growth of a homegrown, spontaneous protest movement in East Germany. Workers joined intellectuals, environmentalists, and Protestant ministers in huge candlelight demonstrations, arguing that a democratic but still socialist East Germany was both possible and desirable. These "stayers" failed to convince the "leavers," however, who continued to depart en masse. In a desperate attempt to stabilize the situation, the East German government opened the Berlin Wall in November 1989, and people danced for joy atop that grim symbol of the prison state. A new, reformist government took power and scheduled free elections.

In Czechoslovakia, Communist rule began to dissolve peacefully in November to December 1989. This so-called **Velvet Revolution** grew out of popular demonstrations led by students and joined by intellectuals and a dissident playwright-turned-moral-revolutionary named Václav Havel (1936–2011). When the protesters took control of the streets, the Communist government resigned, leading to a power-sharing arrangement termed the "Government of National Understanding." As 1989 ended, the Czechoslovakian assembly elected Havel president.

In Romania, popular revolution turned violent and bloody. There the dictator Nicolae Ceaușescu (chow-SHESS-koo) (1918–1989) had long combined tight party control with stubborn independence from Moscow. Faced with mass protests in December 1989, Ceaușescu ordered his ruthless security forces to quell unrest, sparking an armed uprising. Perhaps 750 people were killed in the fighting; the numbers are often exaggerated. After the dictator and his wife were captured and executed by a military court, Ceaușescu's forces were defeated. A coalition government emerged, although the legacy of Ceaușescu's long and oppressive rule left a very troubled country.

German Unification and the End of the Cold War

The dissolution of communism in East Germany that began in 1989 reopened the "German question" and raised the threat of renewed Cold War conflict over Germany. Taking power in October 1989, East German reform Communists, enthusiastically sup-

The Fall of the Berlin Wall   The sudden and unanticipated opening of the Berlin Wall in 1989 dramatized the spectacular fall of communism throughout east-central Europe. Built on the orders of the Soviet leader Nikita Khrushchev in 1961, the hated barrier had stopped the flow of refugees from East Germany to West Germany. Over the twenty-eight years of its existence, the wall came to symbolize the limits on personal freedom enforced by Communist dictatorships. (© Patrick Piel/Gamma)

ported by leading intellectuals and former dissidents, wanted to preserve socialism by making it genuinely democratic and responsive to the needs of the people. They argued for a "third way" that would go beyond the failed Stalinism they had experienced and the ruthless capitalism they saw in the West. These reformers supported closer ties with West Germany but feared unification, hoping to preserve a distinct East German identity.

Over the next year, however, East Germany was absorbed into an enlarged West Germany, much as a faltering company is swallowed by a stronger rival and ceases to exist. Three factors were particularly important in this outcome. First, in the first week after the Berlin Wall was opened, almost 9 million East Germans — roughly half of the total population — poured across the border into West Germany. Almost all returned to their homes in the east, but the joy of warm welcomes from long-lost friends and relatives and the exhilaration of crossing a long-closed border aroused long-dormant hopes of unity among ordinary citizens.

Second, West German chancellor Helmut Kohl and his closest advisers skillfully exploited the historic opportunity handed them. Sure of support from the United States, whose leadership he had steadfastly followed, in November 1989 Kohl presented a ten-point plan for step-by-step unification in cooperation with both East Germany and the international community. Kohl then promised the struggling citizens of East Germany an immediate economic bonanza — a generous though limited exchange of East German marks in savings accounts and pensions into much more valuable West German marks.

This offer helped a well-financed conservative-liberal Alliance for Germany, established in East Germany with the support of Kohl's West German Christian Democrats, to overwhelm those who argued for the preservation of some kind of independent socialist society in East Germany. In March 1990 the Alliance won almost 50 percent of the votes in an East German parliamentary election, outdistancing the Party of Democratic Socialism (the renamed East German Communist party) (16 percent) and the revived Social Democratic Party (22 percent). The Alliance for Germany quickly negotiated an economic and political union on favorable terms with Kohl.

Third, in the summer of 1990 the crucial international aspect of German unification was successfully resolved. Unification would once again make Germany the strongest state in central Europe and would directly affect the security of the Soviet Union. But Gorbachev swallowed hard—Western cartoonists showed Stalin turning over in his grave—and negotiated the best deal he could. In a historic agreement signed by Gorbachev and Kohl in July 1990, Kohl solemnly affirmed Germany's peaceful intentions and pledged never to develop nuclear, biological, or chemical weapons. The Germans sweetened the deal by promising enormous loans to the hard-pressed Soviet Union. In October 1990 East Germany merged into West Germany, forming a single nation under the West German laws and constitution.

The peaceful reunification of Germany accelerated the pace of agreements to liquidate the Cold War. In November 1990 delegates from twenty-two European countries joined those from the United States and the Soviet Union in Paris and agreed to a scaling down of all their armed forces. The delegates also solemnly affirmed that all existing borders in Europe, including those of unified Germany and the emerging Baltic states, were legal and valid. The Paris Accord was for all practical purposes a general peace treaty bringing an end to both World War II and the Cold War.

Peace in Europe encouraged the United States and the Soviet Union to scrap a significant portion of their nuclear weapons in a series of agreements. In September 1991 a confident President George H. W. Bush canceled the around-the-clock alert status for American bombers outfitted with atomic bombs, and a floundering Gorbachev quickly followed suit with his own forces. For the first time in four decades, Soviet and American nuclear weapons were not standing ready for mutual destruction.

The Disintegration of the Soviet Union

As 1990 began, the tough work of dismantling some forty-five years of Communist rule had begun in all but two East Bloc states—tiny Albania and the vast Soviet Union. The great question now became whether the Soviet Union would follow its former satellites.

In February 1990, as competing Russian politicians noisily presented their programs and nationalists in the non-Russian republics demanded autonomy or independence from the Soviet Union, the Communist Party suffered a stunning defeat in local elections throughout the country. As in East Bloc countries, democrats and anticommunists won clear majorities in the leading cities of the Russian Soviet Republic (SFSR), the largest republic in the Soviet Union. Moreover, in Lithuania the people elected an uncompromising nationalist as president, and the newly chosen parliament soon after declared Lithuania an independent state.

Gorbachev responded by placing an economic embargo on Lithuania, but he refused to use the army to crush the separatist government. The result was a tense political stalemate that undermined popular support for Gorbachev. Separating himself further from Communist hardliners, Gorbachev asked Soviet citizens to ratify a new constitution that formally abolished the Communist Party's monopoly of political power and expanded the power of the Congress of People's Deputies. While retaining his post as party secretary, Gorbachev then convinced a majority of deputies to elect him president of the Soviet Union.

Despite his victory, Gorbachev's power continued to erode, and his unwillingness to risk a universal suffrage election for the presidency strengthened his great rival, Boris Yeltsin (1931–2007). A radical reform Communist, Yeltsin embraced the democratic movement, and in May 1990 he was elected parliamentary leader of the Russian Soviet Republic. He boldly announced that Russia would put its interests first and declare its independence from the Soviet Union, broadening the base of the anticommunist movement by joining the patriotism of ordinary Russians with the democratic aspirations of big-city intellectuals. Gorbachev tried to save the Soviet Union with a new treaty that would link the member republics in a looser, freely accepted confederation, but six of the fifteen Soviet republics rejected his plan.

Opposed by democrats and nationalists, Gorbachev was also challenged by the Communist old guard. In August 1991 a gang of hardliners kidnapped him and his family in the Caucasus and tried to seize the Soviet government. The attempted coup collapsed in the face of massive popular resistance that rallied around Yeltsin. As the spellbound world watched on television, Yeltsin defiantly denounced the rebels from atop a stalled tank in central Moscow and declared the "rebirth of Russia." The army supported Yeltsin, and Gorbachev was rescued and returned to power as head of the Soviet Union.

The leaders of the coup had wanted to preserve Communist power, state ownership, and the multinational Soviet Union; they succeeded in destroying all three. An anticommunist revolution swept Russia as Yeltsin and his supporters outlawed the Communist Party and confiscated its property. Locked in a personal and political duel with Gorbachev, Yeltsin and his democratic allies declared Russia independent, withdrew from the Soviet Union, and changed the country's name from the Russian Soviet Republic to the Russian Federation. All the other Soviet republics also left. Gorbachev resigned on December 25, 1991, and the next day the Supreme Soviet dissolved itself, marking the end of the Soviet Union. The independent republics of the old Soviet Union then established a loose confederation, the Commonwealth of Independent States, which played only a minor role in the 1990s.

Notes

1. Quoted in Kessing's Research Report, *Germany and East Europe Since 1945: From the Potsdam Agreement to Chancellor Brandt's "Ostpolitik"* (New York: Charles Scribner's Sons, 1973), pp. 284–285.
2. M. Mitterauer, *The History of Youth* (Oxford: Basil Blackwell, 1992), p. 40.
3. See R. Guha, *Environmentalism: A Global History* (New York: Longman, 2000), p. 79.

Chapter Review

MAKE IT STICK

LearningCurve
bedfordstmartins.com/mckaywestvalue

After reading the chapter, use LearningCurve to retain what you've read.

IDENTIFY KEY TERMS

Identify and explain the significance of each item below.

Ostpolitik (p. 981)

détente (p. 982)

Second Vatican Council (p. 985)

New Left (p. 986)

Brezhnev Doctrine (p. 993)

OPEC (p. 994)

stagflation (p. 995)

postindustrial society (p. 995)

neoliberalism (p. 996)

privatization (p. 996)

developed socialism (p. 1004)

Solidarity (p. 1006)

perestroika (p. 1008)

glasnost (p. 1008)

Velvet Revolution (p. 1012)

REVIEW THE MAIN IDEAS

Answer the focus questions from each section of the chapter.

- Why did the postwar consensus of the 1950s break down? (p. 981)
- What were the consequences of economic decline in the 1970s? (p. 994)
- What led to the decline of Soviet power in the East Bloc? (p. 1003)
- Why did revolution sweep through the East Bloc in 1989, and what were the immediate consequences? (p. 1010)

MAKE CONNECTIONS

Think about the larger developments and continuities within and across chapters.

1. How did the revolts that shook western European countries and the East Bloc develop out of issues left unresolved in the 1950s era of postwar reconstruction (Chapter 28)?

2. Both East and West Blocs faced similar economic problems in the 1970s, yet communism collapsed in the East and capitalism recovered. How do you account for the difference? Were economic problems the main basis for popular opposition to communism?

3. What were some of the basic ideas behind the neoliberal economic policies that emerged in the West in the 1970s and 1980s? Why are they still popular today?

ONLINE DOCUMENT ASSIGNMENT

Margaret Thatcher

How did Thatcher's Conservative Party adapt its message to fit the values of the majority of British people?

You encountered Margaret Thatcher's story on page 998. Keeping the question above in mind, go online and explore Conservative Party campaign posters from the 1979 British general election. Then complete a writing assignment based on the evidence and details from this chapter.

bedfordstmartins.com/mckaywestvalue

CHRONOLOGY

1961	• Building of Berlin Wall suggests permanence of the East Bloc
1962–1965	• Second Vatican Council
1963	• Wolf publishes *Divided Heaven*; Friedan publishes *The Feminine Mystique*
1964	• Civil Rights Act in the United States
1964–1973	• Peak of U.S. involvement in Vietnam War
1966	• Formation of National Organization for Women (NOW)
1968	• Soviet invasion of Czechoslovakia; "May Events" protests in France
1971	• Founding of Greenpeace
1973	• OPEC oil embargo
1975	• Helsinki Accords
1979	• Margaret Thatcher becomes British prime minister; founding of West German Green Party; Soviet invasion of Afghanistan
1985	• Mikhail Gorbachev named Soviet premier
1987	• United States and Soviet Union sign arms reduction treaty
1989	• Soviet withdrawal from Afghanistan
1989–1991	• Fall of communism in eastern Europe
December 1991	• Dissolution of the Soviet Union

30

✓ LearningCurve
bedfordstmartins.com/mckaywestvalue
After reading the chapter, use
LearningCurve to retain what
you've read.

Life in an Age of Globalization

1990 TO THE PRESENT

ON NOVEMBER 9, 2009, THE TWENTIETH ANNIVERSARY OF THE opening of the Berlin Wall, jubilant crowds filled the streets around the Brandenburg Gate at the former border between East and West Berlin. World leaders and tens of thousands of onlookers applauded as former Polish president Lech Wałęsa pushed over a line of one thousand eight-foot-tall foam dominos, symbolizing the collapse of communism.

The crowd had reason to celebrate. The revolutions of 1989 had opened a new chapter in European and world history. Capitalism spread across the former East Bloc and Soviet Union (now the Russian Federation and fourteen other republics), along with the potential for political reform. Some of these hopes were realized, but the new era also brought problems and tragedies. The process of remaking formerly Communist societies was more difficult than expected. In addition, across the West and around the world, globalization, the digital revolution, and the ongoing flow of immigrants into western Europe had impacts both positive and negative.

ONLINE DOCUMENT ASSIGNMENT
Contesting Globalization
What do the goals of major global organizations and antiglobal movements reveal about the experience of globalization in the twenty-first century? Learn more about key global organizations and movements. Then complete a writing assignment based on the evidence and details from this chapter.

bedfordstmartins.com/mckaywestvalue

As Europeans faced serious tensions and complex changes in the twenty-first century, they also came together to form a strong new European Union that would prove a formidable economic competitor to the United States. Ties between western Europe and the United States began to loosen, but Europe and North America—as well as the rest of the world—confronted common challenges. Finding solutions to problems in the Muslim world and addressing challenges regarding economic growth, energy needs, the environment, and human rights would require not only innovation but also creative cooperation.

Reshaping Russia and the Former East Bloc

How did life change in Russia and the former East Bloc countries after 1989?

Establishing liberal democratic governments in the former East Bloc countries and the Soviet Union, now divided into fifteen republics with Russia at its core, would not prove easy. While Russia initially moved toward economic reform and political openness, it returned to its authoritarian traditions in the early 2000s, and conflict undermined Russia's relations with some former Soviet republics.

The transition to democracy in the countries of the former Communist East Bloc was also difficult. After a period of tense reform, some countries, such as Poland, the Czech Republic, Hungary, and the Baltic States, established relatively prosperous democracies and joined NATO and then the European Union. Others, such as Romania and Bulgaria, lagged behind. In multiethnic Yugoslavia, the collapse of communism and the onset of a disastrous civil war broke the country apart. All these changes produced mixed results for ordinary folk.

Economic Shock Therapy in Russia

Politics and economics were closely intertwined in Russia after the dissolution of the Soviet Union (see Chapter 29). President Boris Yeltsin (r. 1991–1999), his democratic supporters, and his economic ministers wanted to create conditions that would prevent a return to communism and right the faltering economy. Following the example of Poland (see Chapter 29), and agreeing with neoliberal Western advisers who argued that a quick turn to free markets would speed economic growth, Russian reformers opted in January 1992 for liberalization at breakneck speed.

To implement the plan, the Russians abolished price controls on 90 percent of all Russian goods, with the exception of bread, vodka, oil, and public transportation. The government also launched rapid privatization—the sale of formerly state-owned industries and agricultural concerns to private investors; as a result, thousands of factories and mines were turned over to new private companies. In an attempt to share the wealth privatization was expected to generate, each citizen received a voucher worth 10,000 rubles (about $22) to buy stock in these private companies, but ownership usually remained in the hands of the old bosses—the managers and government officials from the Communist era—undermining the reformers' goal of worker ownership.

President Yeltsin and his economic reformers believed that shock therapy would revive production and bring widespread prosperity. The results were quite different.

Prices increased 250 percent on the very first day and kept on soaring, increasing by a factor of twenty-six in the course of 1992. At the same time, production fell a staggering 20 percent. Nor did the situation stabilize quickly. After 1995 inflation still raged, though at slower rates, and output continued to fall. According to most estimates, Russia produced from one-third to one-half less in 1996 than it had in 1991. The Russian economy crashed again in 1998 in the wake of Asia's financial crisis.

Rapid economic liberalization worked poorly in Russia for several reasons. Soviet industry had been highly monopolized and strongly tilted toward military goods. Production of many items had been concentrated in one or two gigantic factories or in interconnected combines. With privatization, these powerful state monopolies became powerful private monopolies that cut production and raised prices in order to maximize profits. Moreover, powerful corporate managers and bureaucrats forced Yeltsin's government to hand out enormous subsidies to reinforce faltering firms and to avoid bankruptcies. New corporate leaders included criminals who intimidated would-be rivals in attempts to prevent the formation of competing businesses.

Runaway inflation and poorly executed privatization brought a profound social revolution to Russia. The new capitalist elite — the so-called Oligarchs — acquired great

Rich and Poor in Postcommunist Russia   A woman sells knitted scarves in front of a department store window in Moscow in September 2005. The collapse of the Soviet Union and the use of shock therapy to reform the Russian economy created new poverty as well as new wealth. (TASS/Sovfoto)

wealth and power, while large numbers of people fell into abject poverty and the majority struggled to make ends meet. Managers, former Communist officials, and financiers who came out of the privatization process with large shares of the old state monopolies stood at the top. The new elite held more wealth than ever before, and the Oligarchs maintained control with corrupt business practices and rampant cronyism. By 1996 Moscow, with 5 percent of Russia's population, controlled 80 percent of its capital. At the other extreme, the vast majority of people saw their savings become practically worthless. Pensions lost much of their value, and many people sold their personal goods to survive. A telling indicator of the hardship caused by the collapse of the Soviet welfare state and growing poverty was the catastrophic decline in the life expectancy of the average Russian male from sixty-nine years in 1991 to only fifty-eight years in 1996. Under these conditions, effective representative government failed to develop, and many Russians came to equate democracy with the corruption, poverty, and national decline they experienced throughout the 1990s. Yeltsin became increasingly unpopular; only the support of the Oligarchs kept him in power.

Russian Revival Under Vladimir Putin

This widespread disillusionment set the stage for the "managed democracy" of Vladimir Putin (POO-tihn) (b. 1952). First elected president as Yeltsin's chosen successor in 2000, Putin won re-election in a landslide in March 2004, and, after a four-year stint as prime minister, returned to the presidency in 2012. An officer in the secret police in the Communist era, Putin maintained relatively liberal economic policies but re-established semi-authoritarian political rule. Proponents of liberal democracy were in retreat, while conservative Russian intellectuals were on the offensive, arguing that free markets required strong political rule to control corruption and prevent chaos. Putin clamped down on the excesses of the Oligarchs, lowered corporate and business taxes, and re-established some government control over key industries.

This combination of autocratic politics and economic reform — aided greatly by high world prices for oil and natural gas, Russia's most important exports — led to a decade of strong economic growth. Russia enjoyed over nine years of economic expansion, encouraging the growth of a new middle class. In 2008, however, the global financial crisis and a rapid drop in the price of oil caused a downturn, and the Russian stock market collapsed. The government initiated a $200 billion rescue plan, and the economy stabilized and returned to modest growth in 2010.

During his first two terms as president, Putin's domestic and foreign policies proved immensely popular with a majority of Russians. His housing, education, and health-care reforms significantly improved living standards. In foreign relations, Putin championed an assertive anti-Western Russian nationalism. He took a forceful stand against the expansion of NATO in the former East Bloc and regularly challenged U.S. and NATO foreign policy goals, as in the Syrian civil war that began in 2011 (see page 1048). Putin expressed pride in the accomplishments of the Soviet Union and downplayed the abuses of the Stalinist system. In addition, the Russian president centralized power in the Kremlin, increased military spending, and expanded the secret police. Putin's carefully crafted manly image and his forceful international diplomacy soothed the country's injured pride and symbolized its national revival.

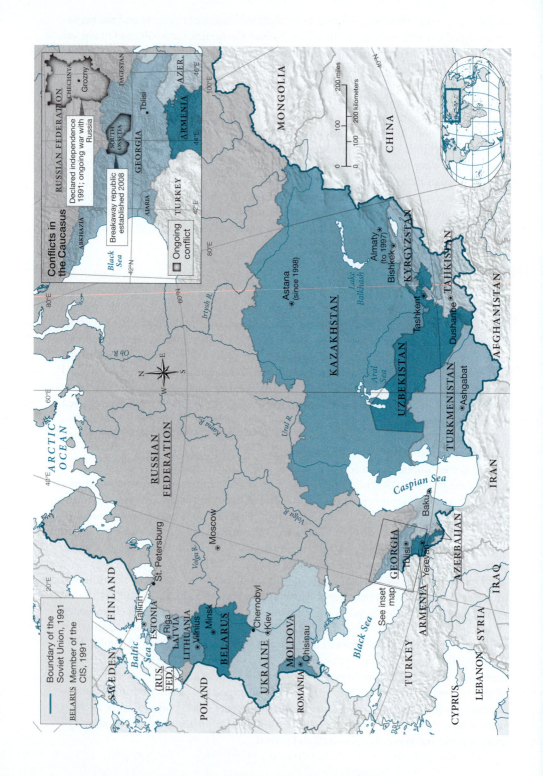

Conflicts in the Caucasus

RUSSIAN FEDERATION

Declared independence 1991; ongoing war with Russia

Breakaway republic established 2008

☐ Ongoing conflict

CHECHNYA • Grozny
DAGESTAN
SOUTH OSSETIA
ABKHAZIA
GEORGIA • Tbilisi
AJARIA
ARMENIA
AZER.
TURKEY
Black Sea

Boundary of the Soviet Union, 1991

BELARUS Member of the CIS, 1991

MONGOLIA
CHINA
200 miles
200 kilometers

ARCTIC OCEAN

RUSSIAN FEDERATION

SWEDEN
FINLAND
Tallinn
ESTONIA
Riga
LATVIA
LITHUANIA • Vilnius
(RUS. FED.)
Minsk
BELARUS
POLAND
UKRAINE • Kiev
• Chernobyl
MOLDOVA • Chişinău
ROMANIA
Baltic Sea

St. Petersburg
• Moscow
Volga R.
Ob R.
Irtysh R.
Kama R.
Ural R.

KAZAKHSTAN
Astana (since 1998)
Lake Balkhash
Almaty (to 1997)
Bishkek
KYRGYZSTAN
Tashkent
UZBEKISTAN
TAJIKISTAN
Dushanbe
TURKMENISTAN
Ashgabat
AFGHANISTAN
Aral Sea

Caspian Sea
Baku
GEORGIA • Tbilisi
ARMENIA • Yerevan
AZERBAIJAN
See inset map
Black Sea
TURKEY
IRAN
IRAQ
SYRIA
LEBANON
CYPRUS

◀ **MAP 30.1　Russia and the Successor States, 1991–2010**
After the failure of an attempt in August 1991 to depose Gorbachev, an anticommunist revolution swept the Soviet Union. The republics that formed the Soviet Union each declared their sovereignty and independence, with Russia, under President Boris Yeltsin, being the largest. Eleven of the fifteen republics then formed a loose confederation called the Commonwealth of Independent States, but the integrated economy of the Soviet Union dissolved into separate national economies, each with its own goals and policies. Conflict continues to simmer over these goals and policies, as evidenced by the ongoing civil war in Chechnya and the conflict between Russia and Georgia over South Ossetia.

Putin's government moved decisively to limit political opposition. The 2003 arrest and imprisonment for tax evasion and fraud of the corrupt oil billionaire Mikhail Khodorkovsky, an Oligarch who had openly supported opposition parties, showed early in his rule that Putin and his United Russia Party would use state powers to stifle dissent. Though the Russian constitution guarantees freedom of the press, the government cracked down on the independent media. Using a variety of tactics, officials and progovernment businessmen influenced news reports and intimidated critical journalists. The suspicious murder in 2006 of journalist Anna Politkovskaya, a prominent critic of the government's human rights abuses and its war in Chechnya, reinforced Western worries that the country was returning to Soviet-style press censorship.

Putin also took an aggressive and at times interventionist stance toward the Commonwealth of Independent States, a loose confederation of most of the former Soviet republics (Map 30.1). Conflict has been particularly intense in the oil-rich Caucasus, where an unstable combination of nationalist separatism and ethnic and religious tensions challenges Russian dominance. Since the breakup of the Soviet Union, Russian troops have repeatedly invaded Chechnya (CHEHCH-nyuh), a tiny Muslim republic with 1 million inhabitants on Russia's southern border that declared its independence in 1991.

Despite nominal Russian control over Chechnya, the cost of the conflict has been high. Thousands on both sides have lost their lives, and both sides have committed serious human rights abuses. Moscow declared an end to military operations in April 2009, but Chechen insurgents, inspired by nationalism and Islamic radicalism, continued to fight. Russia also intervened in the independent state of Georgia, which won independence when the Soviet Union collapsed in 1991. Russian troops invaded Georgia in 2008 to support a separatist movement in South Ossetia (ah-SEE-shuh), which eventually established a breakaway independent republic recognized only by Russia and a handful of small states.

Putin stepped down when his term limits expired in 2008. His handpicked successor, Dimitri Medvedev (mehd-VEHD-yehf) (b. 1965), easily won election that year and then appointed Putin prime minister, leading observers to believe that the former president was still the dominant figure. This suspicion was confirmed when Putin won the presidential election of March 2012 with over 60 percent of the vote. International observers agreed that the election itself was democratic, but reported irregularities during the vote-counting process. Some fifteen thousand protesters marched through downtown Moscow to protest election fraud and the authoritarian aspects of Putin's rule, and demonstrations also accompanied the president's inauguration that May.

Tensions between political centralization and openness continue to define Russia's difficult road away from communism. On one hand, Putin's return to the presidency seemed to reinforce Russia's system of authoritarian central control. On the other, the fact that mass assemblies and marches against the president took place with relatively little repression attests to some degree of political openness and new limits on Russian state power in the twenty-first century.

Coping with Change in the Former East Bloc

Developments in the former East Bloc paralleled those in Russia in important ways. The former satellites worked to replace state planning and socialism with market mechanisms and private property. Western-style electoral politics also took hold.

New leaders across the former East Bloc faced similar economic problems: how to restructure Communist economic systems and move state-owned businesses and property into private hands. Under Soviet-style communism, central planners determined production and distribution goals and often set wage and price controls; now former East Bloc countries would adopt market-based economic systems. In addition, industries, businesses, and farms, considered the "people's property" and managed by the state in the name of the entire population, would now be privatized.

The methods of restructuring and privatization varied from country to country. As noted earlier, Poland's new leaders turned to "shock therapy," the most rapid and comprehensive form of economic transformation, advocated by neoliberal Western institutions, including the International Monetary Fund and the World Bank. Starting in 1990, the Poles liberalized prices and trade policies, raised taxes, cut spending to reduce budget deficits, and quickly sold state-owned industries to private investors. As they would in Russia a few years later, these radical moves at first brought high inflation and a rapid decline in living standards, which generated public protests and strikes. But because the plan had the West's approval, Poland received Western financial support that eased the pain of transition. By the end of the decade, the country had one of the strongest economies in the former East Bloc.

Other countries followed alternate paths. Czechoslovakia took a more gradual approach. As in Russia, the Czechoslovak state issued vouchers to its citizens, which they could use to bid for shares in privatized companies. In Slovenia, one of the countries carved out of the former Yugoslavia, privatization included the transfer of up to 60 percent of company ownership to employees. In Estonia, reformers experimented with employee ownership, vouchers, and worker cooperatives. Compared to Poland's approach, privatization in all three countries was slower, continued more practices from the Communist past, and caused less social disruption.

Economic growth in the former Communist countries was varied, but most observers agreed that Poland, the Czech Republic, and Hungary were the most successful. Each met the critical challenge of economic reconstruction more successfully than did Russia, and each could claim to be the economic leader in the former East Bloc, depending on the criteria selected. The reasons for these successes included considerable experience with limited market reforms before 1989, flexibility and lack of dogmatism in government policy, and an enthusiastic embrace of capitalism by a new entrepreneurial class. In its first five years of reform, Poland created twice as many new businesses as did Russia in a comparable period, despite having only a quarter of Russia's population.

Poland, the Czech Republic, and Hungary also did far better than Russia in creating new civic institutions, legal systems, and independent media outlets that reinforced political freedom and national revival. Lech Wałęsa in Poland and Václav Havel in Czechoslovakia were elected presidents of their countries and proved as remarkable in power as in opposition (see Chapter 29). After Czechoslovakia's Velvet Revolution in 1989, the Czechoslovak parliament accepted a "velvet divorce" in 1993, when Slovakian nationalists wanted to break off and form their own state, creating the separate Czech and Slovak Republics. Above all, and in sharp contrast to Russia, the popular goal of adopting the liberal democratic values of western Europe reinforced political moderation and compromise. In 1999 Poland, Hungary, and the Czech Republic were accepted into NATO, and in 2004 they and Slovakia gained admission to the European Union (EU) (see page 1030).

Romania and Bulgaria lagged behind in the postcommunist transition. Western traditions were much weaker there, and both countries were much poorer than their more successful neighbors. Romania and Bulgaria did make progress after 2000, however, and joined NATO in 2004 and the EU in 2007.

The social consequences of rebuilding the former East Bloc were similar to those in Russia, though people were generally spared the widespread shortages and misery that characterized Russia in the 1990s. Ordinary citizens and the elderly were once again the big losers, while the young and former Communist Party members were the big winners. Inequalities between richer and poorer regions also increased. Capital cities such as Warsaw, Prague, and Budapest concentrated wealth, power, and opportunity as never before, while provincial centers stagnated and old industrial areas declined. Crime, corruption, and gangsterism increased in both the streets and the executive suites.

Though few former East Bloc residents wanted to return to communism, some expressed longings for the stability of the old system. They missed the guaranteed jobs and generous social benefits provided by the Communist state, and they found the individualism and competitiveness of capitalism cold and difficult. One Russian woman living on a pension of $448 a month in 2003 summed up the dilemma: "What we want is for our life to be as easy as it was in the Soviet Union, with the guarantee of a good, stable future and low prices—and at the same time this freedom that did not exist before."[1] Even the everyday consumer goods produced during the Communist years, which vanished, for the most part, after 1990, became objects of affection. Germans coined the term **Ostalgie**—a combination of the German words for "East" and "nostalgia"—to label this fondness for the lifestyles and culture of the vanished East Bloc.

At the same time, many East Bloc citizens had never fully accepted communism, primarily because they equated it with Russian imperialism and the loss of national independence. The joyous crowds that toppled Communist regimes in 1989 believed that they were liberating the nation as well as the individual. Thus, when communism died, nationalism re-emerged as a dominant force. Reflecting this new popular nationalism, conservative politicians found success in Poland, the Czech Republic, and other former East Bloc countries.

The question of whether or how to punish former Communist leaders who had committed political crimes or abused human rights emerged as a pressing issue in the former East Bloc. Germany tried major offenders and opened the records of the East German secret police (the Stasi) to the public, and by 1996 more than a million former residents had asked to see their files.[2] Other countries designed various means to deal with former Communist elites who might have committed crimes, with right-wing leaders generally taking a more punitive stand. The search for fair solutions proceeded slowly and with much controversy, an ongoing reminder of the troubling legacies of communism and the Cold War.

Tragedy in Yugoslavia

The great postcommunist tragedy was Yugoslavia, which under Josip Broz Tito had been a federation of republics under centralized Communist rule (see Chapter 28). After Tito's death in 1980, power passed increasingly to the sister republics, which encouraged a revival of centuries-old regional and ethnic conflicts that were exacerbated by charges of ethnically inspired massacres during World War II and a dramatic economic decline in the mid-1980s.

The revolutions of 1989 accelerated the breakup of Yugoslavia. Serbian president Slobodan Milošević (SLOH-buh-dayn mee-LOH-sheh-veech) (1941–2006), a former Communist bureaucrat, wished to strengthen the federation's centralized government under Serbian control. In 1989 Milošević severely limited self-rule in the Serbian province of Kosovo, where Albanian-speaking, primarily Islamic peoples constituted the over-whelming majority, but which held a medieval battleground that he claimed was sacred to Serbian identity. In 1990 Milošević supported calls to grab land from other republics and unite all Serbs, regardless of where they lived, in a "greater Serbia" (which included Kosovo). Milošević's moves strengthened the cause of national separatism in the federa-tion, and in June 1991 relatively wealthy Slovenia and Croatia declared their independence. Milošević ordered the federal army to invade both areas to assert Serbian control. The Serbs were quickly repulsed in Slovenia, but managed to take about 30 percent of Croatia.

In 1992 the civil war spread to Bosnia-Herzegovina, which had also declared its independence. Serbs—about 30 percent of that region's population—refused to live under the more numerous Bosnian Muslims, or Bosniaks. Yugoslavia had once been a tolerant and largely successful multiethnic state with different groups living side by side and often intermarrying. The new goal of the armed factions in the Bosnian civil war was **ethnic cleansing**, or genocide: the attempt to establish ethnically homogeneous territories by intimidation, forced deportation, and killing. Serbian armies and irregular militias attempted to "cleanse" the territory of its non-Serb residents, unleashing ruth-less brutality, with murder, rape, destruction, and the herding of refugees into concen-tration camps. Before the fighting in Bosnia ended, some three hundred thousand people were dead, and millions had been forced to flee their homes.

While appalling scenes of horror not seen in Europe since the Holocaust shocked the world, the Western nations had difficulty formulating an effective, unified response. The turning point came in July 1995 when Bosnian Serbs overran Srebrenica—a Muslim city previously declared a United Nations safe area. Serb forces killed about eight thou-sand of the city's Bosniak civilians, primarily men and boys. Public outrage prompted NATO to bomb Bosnian Serb military targets intensively, and the Croatian army drove all the Serbs from Croatia. In November 1995 President Bill Clinton helped the warring sides hammer out a complicated accord that gave Bosnian Serbs about 49 percent of Bosnia and Bosniaks and the Roman Catholic Bosnian Croats the rest. Troops from NATO countries patrolled Bosnia to keep the peace; by 2013 only one thousand re-mained, suggesting that the situation had significantly improved.

The Albanian Muslims of Kosovo, who hoped to establish self-rule, gained nothing from the Bosnian agreement. Frustrated Kosovar militants formed the **Kosovo Liberation Army (KLA)** and began to fight for independence. Serbian repression of the Kosovars increased, and in 1998 Serbian forces attacked both KLA guerrillas and unarmed villagers, displacing 250,000 people.

When Milošević refused to withdraw Serbian armies from Kosovo and accept self-government (but not independence) for Kosovo, NATO began bombing Serbia in March 1999. Serbian paramilitary forces responded by driving about 865,000 Albanian Kosovars into exile. NATO redoubled its destructive bombing campaign, which eventually forced Milošević to withdraw and allowed the Kosovars to regain their homeland. A United Nations and NATO peacekeeping force occupied Kosovo, ending ten years of Yugoslavian civil wars. Although U.S.-led NATO intervention finally brought an end to the conflict, the failure to take a stronger stand in the early years led to widespread and unnecessary suffering in the former Yugoslavia.

The war-weary and impoverished Serbs eventually voted the still-defiant Milošević out of office, and in July 2001 a new pro-Western Serbian government turned him over to a war crimes tribunal in the Netherlands to stand trial for crimes against humanity. After blustering his way through the initial stages of his trial, Milošević died in 2006 before the proceedings were complete. In 2008, after eight years of administration by the United Nations and NATO peacekeeping forces, the Republic of Kosovo declared its independence from Serbia. The United States and most states of the European Union recognized the declaration. Serbia and Russia did not, and the long-term status of this troubled emerging state remained uncertain.

The New Global System

How did globalization affect European life and society?

Contemporary observers often assert that the world has entered a new era of **globalization**. Though the term is difficult to define, such assertions do not mean that there were never international connections before. Europe has long had close — sometimes productive, sometimes destructive — ties to other parts of the world. Yet new global relationships and increasing interdependence did emerge in the last decades of the twentieth century.

First, the growth of multinational corporations restructured national economies on a global scale. Second, an array of international governing bodies, such as the European Union, the United Nations, the World Trade Organization, and a number of nongovernmental organizations (or NGOs) increasingly set policies that challenged the autonomy of traditional nation-states. Finally, the expansion and ready availability of highly efficient computer and media technologies led to ever-faster exchanges of information and entertainment around the world. Taken together, these global transformations had a remarkable impact — both positive and negative — on many aspects of Western society.

The Global Economy

Though large business interests had long profited from systems of international trade and investment, multinational corporations grew and flourished in a world economy increasingly organized around policies of free-market neoliberalism, which relaxed barriers to international trade (see Chapter 29). Multinational corporations built global systems of production and distribution that generated unprecedented wealth and generally escaped the control of national regulators and politicians. Conglomerates such as Siemens and Vivendi exemplified this business model. Siemens, with international headquarters in Berlin and Munich and offices around the globe, is one of the world's largest engineering companies, with vast holdings in energy, construction, health care, financial services, and industrial production. Vivendi, an extensive media and telecommunications company headquartered in Paris, controls a vast international network of producers and products, including music and film, publishing, television broadcasting, pay-TV, Internet services, and video games.

The development of sophisticated personal computer technologies and the Internet at the end of the twentieth century, coupled with the deregulation of national and international financial systems, further encouraged the growth of international trade. The ability to rapidly exchange information and capital meant that economic activity was no longer centered on national banks or stock exchanges, but rather flowed quickly across international borders. Large cities like London, Moscow, New York, and Hong Kong became global centers of banking, trade, and financial services. The influence of finance and insurance companies, communications conglomerates, and energy and legal firms headquartered in these global cities extended far beyond the borders of the traditional nation-state.

At the same time, the close connections between national economies also made the entire world vulnerable to economic panics and downturns. In 1997 a banking crisis in Thailand spread to Indonesia, South Korea, and Japan and then echoed around the world. The resulting slump in oil and gas prices hit Russia especially hard, leading to high inflation, bank failures, and the collapse of the Russian stock market. The crisis then spread to Latin America, plunging most countries there into a severe economic downturn. A decade later, a global recession triggered by a crisis in the U.S. housing market and financial system created the worst worldwide economic crisis since the Great Depression of the 1930s (see page 1049).

The New European Union

Global economic pressures encouraged the expansion and consolidation of the European Common Market, which in 1993 proudly rechristened itself the **European Union (EU)** (Map 30.2). The EU worked to add the free movement of European labor, capital, and services to the existing free trade in goods. In addition, member states sought to create a monetary union in which all EU countries would share a single currency. Membership in the monetary union required states to meet strict financial criteria defined in the 1991 **Maastricht Treaty**, which also set legal standards and anticipated the development of common policies on defense and foreign affairs.

Western European elites and opinion makers generally supported the economic integration embodied in the Maastricht Treaty. They felt that membership requirements, which imposed financial discipline on national governments, would combat Europe's ongoing economic problems and viewed the establishment of a single European currency as an irreversible historic step toward basic political unity. This unity would allow Europe as a whole to regain its place in world politics and to deal with the United States as an equal.

Support for the Maastricht Treaty was not universal, however. Ordinary people, leftist political parties, and right-wing nationalists expressed considerable opposition to

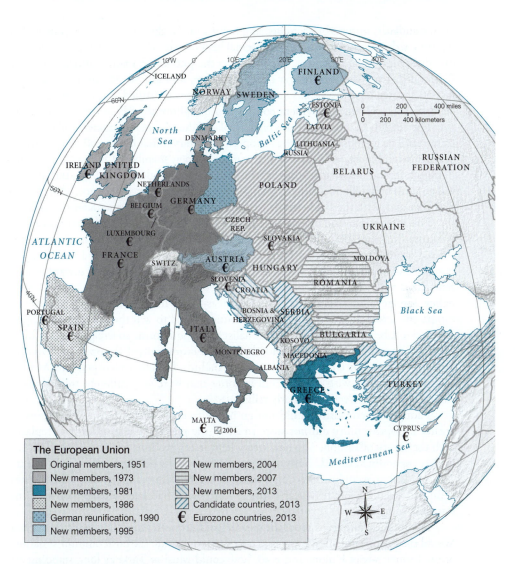

MAP 30.2   The European Union, 2013
No longer divided by ideological competition and the Cold War, much of today's Europe has banded together in a European Union that facilitates the open movement of people, jobs, and currency across borders.

the new rules. Many people resented the EU's ever-growing bureaucracy in Brussels, which imposed common standards on everything from cheese to day care, supposedly undermining national customs and local traditions. Moreover, increased unity meant yielding still more power to distant "Eurocrats" and political insiders, which limited national sovereignty and democratic control.

Above all, many citizens feared that the European Union was being created at their expense. Joining the monetary union required national governments to meet stringent fiscal standards, impose budget cuts, and contribute to the EU operating budget. The resulting reductions in health care and social benefits hit ordinary citizens and did little to reduce high unemployment. When put to the public for a vote, ratification of the Maastricht Treaty was usually very close. In France, for example, the treaty passed with just 50.1 percent of the vote. Even after the treaty was ratified, battles over budgets, benefits, and high unemployment continued throughout the EU in the 1990s.

Then in 2002, brand-new euros finally replaced the national currencies of all Eurozone countries. The establishment of the European monetary union built confidence in member nations and increased their willingness to accept new members. On May 1, 2004, the European Union began admitting its former East Bloc neighbors, and by 2007 the EU was home to 493 million citizens in twenty-seven countries. It included most of the former East Bloc and, with the Baltic republics, three territories of the former Soviet Union.

This rapid expansion underscored the need to reform the EU's unwieldy governing structure. In June 2004 a special commission presented a new EU constitution that created a president, a foreign minister, and a voting system weighted to reflect the populations of the different states. The proposed constitution moved toward a more centralized federal system, though each state retained veto power over taxation, social policy, foreign affairs, and other sensitive areas. After many contentious referendum campaigns across the continent, the constitution failed to win the unanimous support required to take effect. Ultimately, nationalist fears about losing sovereignty and cultural identity outweighed the perceived benefits of a more unified Europe. Fears that an unwieldy European Union would grow to include Ukraine, Georgia, and Muslim Turkey—countries with cultures and histories that were very different from those of western Europe—were particularly telling.

Though the constitution did not go into effect, the long postwar march toward greater European unity did not stop. In 2007 the rejected constitution was replaced with the Treaty of Lisbon. The new treaty kept many sections of the constitution, but further streamlined the EU bureaucracy and reformed its political structure. When the Treaty of Lisbon went into effect on December 1, 2009, after ratification by all EU states, it capped a remarkable fifty-year effort to unify what had been a deeply divided and war-torn continent.

Yet profound questions about the meaning of European unity and identity remained. Would the European Union expand as promised to include the postcommunist nations of the former Soviet Union, and if so, how could Muslim Turkey's long-standing application be ignored? How could a union of twenty-five to thirty diverse countries have any real cohesion and common identity? Would the EU remain closely linked with the United States in NATO, or would it develop an independent defense policy? Could members agree on an economic policy to master the stubborn recession that emerged in 2008 and still sapped economic growth five years later, and keep the seventeen-state Eurozone intact (see page 1049)? The EU struggled to shape institutions and policies to address these complicated issues.

Supranational Organizations

Beyond the European Union, the trend toward globalization empowered a variety of other supranational organizations that had tremendous reach. National governments still played the leading role in defining and implementing policy, but they increasingly had to take the policies of institutions such as the United Nations and the World Trade Organization into consideration.

The United Nations (UN), established in 1945 after World War II, remains one of the most important players on the world stage. Representatives from all independent countries meet in the UN General Assembly in New York City to try to forge international agreements. UN agencies deal with issues such as world hunger and poverty, and the International Court of Justice in The Hague, Netherlands, hears cases that violate international law. The UN also sends troops in attempts to preserve peace between warring parties — as in Yugoslavia in the 1990s. While the smaller UN Security Council has broader powers, including the ability to impose sanctions to punish uncooperative states and even to endorse military action, its five permanent members — the United States, Russia, France, Great Britain, and China — each have the power to veto resolutions introduced in that body. The predominance of the United States and western European powers on the Security Council has led some critics to accuse the UN of implementing Western neocolonial policies (see Chapter 28). Others argue that UN policies should never take precedent over national needs, and UN resolutions are at times ignored or downplayed.

A trio of nonprofit international financial institutions have also gained power in a globalizing world. Like the United Nations, the World Bank and the International Monetary Fund (IMF) were established in the years following World War II. Initially founded to help rebuild war-torn Europe, these organizations now provide loans to the developing world. Their funding comes primarily from donations from the United States and western Europe, and they typically extend loans on the condition that recipient countries adopt neoliberal economic reforms, including budget reduction, deregulation, and privatization. In the 1990s the World Bank and the IMF played especially active roles in shaping economic and social policy in the former East Bloc.

The third economic supranational, the **World Trade Organization (WTO)**, is one of the most powerful supranational financial institutions. It sets trade and tariff agreements for over 150 member countries, thus helping manage a large percentage of the world's import-export policies. Like the IMF and the World Bank, the WTO generally promotes neoliberal policies.

The rise of these institutions, which typically represent the shared interests of national governments, was paralleled by the emergence of a variety of **nongovernmental organizations (NGOs)**. Some NGOs act as lobbyists on specific issues; others conduct international programs and activities. Exemplary NGOs include Doctors Without Borders, a charitable organization of physicians headquartered in France; Greenpeace, an international environmental group; and Oxfam, a British-based group dedicated to alleviating famine, disease, and poverty in the developing world. Though financed by donations from governments and private citizens, NGOs' annual budgets can total hundreds of millions of dollars and their work can be quite extensive.

The Human Side of Globalization

Globalization transformed the lives of millions of people, as the technological changes associated with postindustrial society (see Chapter 29) remade workplaces and lifestyles around the world. Low labor costs in the industrializing world — including the former East Bloc, Latin America, and East Asia — encouraged corporations to outsource labor-intensive manufacturing jobs to these regions. Widespread adoption of neoliberal free-trade policies and low labor costs in developing countries made it less expensive to manufacture steel, automotive parts, computer components, and all manner of consumer goods in developing countries and then import them for sale in the West. In these new conditions, a car made by Volkswagen could still be sold as a product of high-quality German engineering despite being assembled in Chattanooga, Tennessee, using steel imported from South Korea and computer chips made in Taiwan. In the 1990s China, with its low wages and rapidly growing industrial infrastructure, emerged as an economic powerhouse that supplied goods across the world—even as the West's industrial heartlands continued to decline.

The outsourcing of manufacturing jobs dramatically changed the nature of work in western Europe and North America. In France in 1973, for example, some 40 percent of the employed population worked in industry—in mining, construction, manufacturing, and utilities. About 49 percent worked in services, including retail, hotels and restaurants, transportation, communications, financial and business services, and social and personal services. In 2004 only 24 percent of the French worked in industry, and a whopping 72 percent worked in services. The numbers varied country by country, yet across Europe the trend was clear: by 2005 only about one in three workers was still employed in the once-booming manufacturing sector.[3]

The deindustrialization of Europe established a multitiered society with winners and losers. At the top was a small, affluent group of experts, executives, and professionals—about one-quarter of the total population—who managed the new global enterprises. In the second, larger tier, the middle class struggled with stagnating incomes and a declining standard of living as once-well-paid industrial workers faced stubborn unemployment and cuts in both welfare and workplace benefits. Many were forced to take low-paying jobs in the retail service sector.

In the bottom tier—in some areas as much as a quarter of the population—a poorly paid underclass performed the unskilled jobs of a postindustrial economy or were chronically unemployed. In western Europe and North America, inclusion in this lowest segment of society was often linked to race, ethnicity, and a lack of educational opportunity. Recently arrived immigrants had trouble finding jobs and often lived in unpleasant, hastily built housing, teetering on the edge of poverty. In London, unemployment rates among youths and particularly young black men soared above those of their white compatriots. Frustration over these conditions, coupled with anger at a police shooting, boiled over in immigrant neighborhoods across the city in August 2011, when angry youths rioted in the streets, burning buildings and looting stores.

Geographic contrasts further revealed the unequal aspects of globalization. Regions in Europe that had successfully shifted to a postindustrial economy, such as northern Italy and southern Germany and Austria, enjoyed prosperity. Lagging behind were regions historically dependent on heavy industry, such as the former East Bloc countries and the factory districts north of London, or underdeveloped areas, such as rural sections of southern Italy and Spain. In addition, a global north-south divide increasingly separated Europe and North America—both still affluent despite their economic problems—from the industrializing nations of Africa and Latin America. Though India, China, and other East Asian nations experienced solid growth, other industrializing nations struggled to overcome decades of underdevelopment.

Antiglobalization Activism   French protesters carry the figure of Ronald McDonald through the streets to protest the trial of José Bové, a prominent leader in campaigns against the human and environmental costs associated with globalization. Bové was accused of demolishing a McDonald's franchise in a small town in southern France. With its worldwide fast-food restaurants that pay little attention to local traditions, McDonald's has often been the target of anti-globalization protests. (Witt/Haley/Sipa)

The human costs of globalization resulted in new forms of global protest. Critics accused global corporations and financial groups of doing little to address problems caused by their activities, such as social inequality, pollution, and unfair labor practices. The Slow Food movement that began in Italy, for example, criticized American-style fast-food chains that proliferated in Europe and the world in the 1990s. Cooking with local products and traditional methods, followers argued, was healthier and kept jobs and profits in local neighborhoods. (See "Primary Source: The Slow Food Manifesto," page 1034.) The fast-food giant McDonald's was often targeted as an example of the ills of corporate globalization. José Bové, a French farmer and antiglobalization activist, made world headlines by driving his truck through the windows of a McDonald's in a small French village to protest the use of hormone-fed beef and genetically modified foods as well as the reach of corporate capital.

The general tone of the antiglobalization movement was captured at the 1999 meeting of the WTO in Seattle, Washington. Tens of thousands of protesters from around the world, including environmentalists, consumer and antipoverty activists, and labor rights groups, marched in the streets and disrupted the meeting. Comparable

PRIMARY SOURCE   The Slow Food Manifesto

On December 10, 1989, delegates from fifteen countries endorsed the Slow Food Manifesto, written by Folco Portinari, officially founding the Slow Food international movement.

Born and nurtured under the sign of industrialization, this century first invented the machine and then modeled its lifestyle after it. Speed became our shackles. We fell prey to the same virus: "the fast life" that fractures our customs and assails us even in our own homes, forcing us to ingest "fast-food."

Homo sapiens must regain wisdom and liberate itself from the "velocity" that is propelling it on the road to extinction. Let us defend ourselves against the universal madness of "the fast life" with tranquil material pleasure.

Against those—or, rather, the vast majority—who confuse efficiency with frenzy, we propose the vaccine of an adequate portion of sensual gourmandise pleasures, to be taken with slow and prolonged enjoyment.

Appropriately, we will start in the kitchen, with Slow Food. To escape the tediousness of "fast-food," let us rediscover the rich varieties and aromas of local cuisines.

In the name of productivity, the "fast life" has changed our lifestyle and now threatens our environment and our land (and city) scapes. Slow Food is the alternative, the avant-garde's riposte.

Real culture is here to be found. First of all, we can begin by cultivating taste, rather than impoverishing it, by stimulating progress, by encouraging international exchange programs, by endorsing worthwhile projects, by advocating historical food culture and by defending old-fashioned food traditions.

Slow Food assures us of a better quality lifestyle. With a snail purposely chosen as its patron and symbol, it is an idea and a way of life that needs much sure but steady support.

EVALUATE THE EVIDENCE

1. How does Portinari link the production and eating of food to what he sees as the problems of life in today's industrial society?

2. To what extent does the critique expressed in the manifesto resemble forms of popular protest from the 1960s counterculture or earlier movements? How is it new or different?

Source: Slow Food Manifesto, http://www.slowfood.com/filemanager/official_docs/SF_Manifesto_ENG .pdf. Courtesy of Slow Food USA.

demonstrations took place at later meetings of the WTO, the World Bank, and other supranational groups. As one angry participant put it, "The WTO seems to be on a crusade to increase private profit at the expense of all other considerations, including the well-being and quality of life of the mass of the world's people. . . . It seems to have a relentless drive to extend its power."[4]

ONLINE DOCUMENT ASSIGNMENT

Contesting Globalization

What do the goals of major global organizations and antiglobal movements reveal about the experience of globalization in the twenty-first century? Learn more about key global organizations and movements. Then complete a writing assignment based on the evidence and details from this chapter.

bedfordstmartins.com/mckaywestvalue

Similar feelings inspired the Occupy movement, which began in the United States in 2011 and quickly spread to over eighty countries. Under the slogan "We are the 99 percent," thousands of people camped out (or "occupied") public places to protest the rapidly growing social inequality that divided a tiny wealthy elite (the "1 percent") from the vast majority of ordinary people. Though it was unclear whether the diverse groups in the Occupy movement could mount a sustained and successful challenge to the public officials and business leaders who profited from globalization, their calls for greater social equality and democracy showed that the struggle for reform continued.

Life in the Digital Age

The growing sophistication of information technologies — a hallmark of the globalizing age — has had a profound and rapidly evolving effect on patterns of communications, commerce, and politics. As tiny digital microchips replaced bulky transistors (see Chapter 28) and the Internet grew in scope and popularity, more and more people organized their everyday lives around the use of ever-smaller and more powerful high-tech devices.

Leisure-time pursuits were a case in point. The arrival of cable television, followed swiftly by DVDs and then online video streaming, enabled individuals to watch full-length movies or popular television shows on their personal computers or smartphones at any time and greatly diversified the options for home entertainment. Europe's once-powerful public broadcasting systems, such as the BBC, were forced to compete with a variety of private enterprises, including Netflix, a U.S. online video provider that announced plans to expand into Europe in 2013. Music downloads and streaming audio files replaced compact discs, which themselves had replaced vinyl records and cassettes; digital cameras eliminated the need for expensive film; e-book readers, including Kindles and iPads, offered a handheld portable library; cell phone apps provided a seemingly endless variety of distractions and conveniences.

Digitalization transformed familiar forms of communication in a few short decades. Many of these changes centered on the Internet, which began its rapid expansion around the globe in the late 1980s. In the first decade of the twenty-first century, the evolution of the cell phone into the smartphone, with its multimedia telecommunications features and more functions and power than the desktop computers of the previous decade, hastened the change. The growing popularity of Internet-based communication tools such as e-mail, text messaging, Facebook, Twitter, and other social media changed the way friends, families, and businesses kept in touch. Letter writing with pen and paper became a quaint relic of the past. Skype, first introduced in 2003, offered personal computer and smartphone users video telecommunications around the world; the old-fashioned "landline," connected to a stationary telephone, seemed ready to join the vinyl LP and the handwritten letter in the junk bin of history.

Entire industries were dramatically changed by the emergence of the Internet. With faster speeds and better online security came online shopping; people increasingly relied on the Internet to purchase goods from clothes to computers to groceries. Online file sharing of books and popular music transformed the publishing and music industries, while massive online retailers such as Amazon.com and eBay, which sell millions of goods across the globe without physical storefronts, transformed traditional distribution and retail systems.

The rapid growth of the Internet and social media raised complex questions related to personal privacy and politics. Governments and businesses can monitor personal Web use and use online tracking systems to amass an extraordinary amount of information on individuals and then use it to monitor political activities or target advertising. Privacy advocates worked with government regulators to shape laws that might preserve key elements of online privacy, and in general, rules were more stringent in Europe than the United States. Conversely, citizens could use smartphones and social media sites to organize protest campaigns. Facebook and Twitter, for example, helped mobilize demonstrators in Egypt during the Arab Spring (see page 1047) and allowed members of the Occupy movement to share news and shape strategy. A number of authoritarian states from North Korea to Iran to Cuba, recognizing the disruptive powers of the Internet, strictly limited online access.

Toward a Multicultural Continent

What are the main causes and effects of growing ethnic diversity in contemporary Europe?

As the twenty-first century opened and ongoing globalization transformed European society and politics, Europeans also saw the ethnic makeup of their communities change. On the one hand, Europe experienced a remarkable decline in birthrates that seemed to predict a shrinking and aging population in the future. On the other hand, the peaceful, wealthy European Union attracted rapidly growing numbers of refugees and immigrants from the former Soviet Union, the Middle East, Africa, and Asia. The unexpected arrival of so many newcomers raised perplexing questions about ethnic diversity and the costs and benefits of multiculturalism.

The Prospect of Population Decline

Population is still growing rapidly in many poor countries but not in the world's industrialized nations. In 2000, families in developed countries had only 1.6 children on average; only in the United States did families have, almost exactly, the 2.1 children necessary to maintain a stable population. In Europe, where birthrates had been falling since the 1950s, national fertility rates ranged from 1.2 to 1.8 children per woman of childbearing age. Italy, once renowned for large Catholic families, had achieved the world's lowest birthrate—a mere 1.2 babies per woman. By 2006 the average European fertility rate was about 1.4 children per woman.

If the current baby bust continues, the long-term consequences could be dramatic, though hardly predictable. At the least, Europe's population would decline and age. Projections for Germany are illustrative. Total German population, barring much greater immigration, would gradually decline from nearly 82 million in 2012 to just under 72 million around 2050. The number of people of working age would fall, and longer life spans mean that nearly a third of the population would be over sixty. Social security taxes paid by the shrinking labor force would need to soar to meet the skyrocketing costs of pensions and health care for seniors—a recipe for generational conflict. As the premier of Bavaria, Germany's biggest state, has warned, the prospect of demographic decline is a "ticking time bomb under our social welfare system and entire economy."[5]

Why, in times of peace, were Europeans failing to reproduce? Research has shown that European women and men in their twenties, thirties, and early forties still wanted two or even three children—as their parents had wanted. But unlike their parents, young couples did not realize their ideal family size. Many women postponed the birth of their first child into their thirties in order to finish their education and establish careers. Then, finding that balancing a child and a career was more difficult than anticipated, new mothers tended to postpone and eventually forgo having a second child. The better educated and the more economically successful a woman was, the more likely she was to have just one child or no children at all. In addition, the uneven, uninspiring European economic conditions since the mid-1970s played a role. High unemployment fell heavily on young people, especially after the recession of 2008, convincing youths to delay settling down and having children.

By 2005 some population experts believed that European women were no longer postponing having children. At the least, birthrates appeared to have stabilized. Moreover, the frightening implications of dramatic population decline had emerged as a major public issue. Opinion leaders, politicians, and the media started to press for more babies and more support for families with children. Europeans may yet respond with enough vigor to reverse their population decline and avoid societal disaster.

Changing Immigration Flows

As European demographic vitality waned in the 1990s, a surge of migrants from Africa, Asia, and the former Soviet Bloc headed for western Europe. Some migrants entered the European Union legally, with proper documentation, but increasing numbers were smuggled in past beefed-up border patrols. Large-scale immigration, both documented and undocumented, emerged as a critical and controversial issue.

Historically a source rather than a destination of immigrants, western Europe saw rising numbers of immigration in postcolonial population movements beginning in the 1950s, augmented by the influx of manual laborers in its boom years from about 1960 until about 1973 (see Chapter 28). A new and different surge of migration into western Europe began in the 1990s. The collapse of communism in the East Bloc and savage civil wars in Yugoslavia drove hundreds of thousands of refugees westward. Equally brutal conflicts in Afghanistan, Iraq, Somalia, and Rwanda—to name only four countries—brought thousands more from Central Asia and Africa. Undocumented immigration into the European Union also exploded, rising from an estimated 50,000 people in 1993 to perhaps 500,000 a decade later, far exceeding the estimated 300,000 unauthorized foreigners entering the United States each year. In 1998 most European Union states abolished all border controls, meaning that undocumented entrance into one country allowed for unimpeded travel almost anywhere—Ireland and the United Kingdom opted out of this agreement.

Though many migrants in the early twenty-first century applied for political asylum and refugee status, most were eventually rejected and classified as illegal job seekers. Even with all the economic problems of western Europe, economic opportunity undoubtedly was a major attraction for immigrants. Germans, for example, earned on average three and a half times more than neighboring Poles, who in turn earned much more than people farther east and in North Africa.

Undocumented immigration was aided by powerful criminal gangs that smuggled people for profit. These gangs contributed to the large number of young female illegal immigrants from eastern Europe, especially Russia and Ukraine. Often lured by criminals promising jobs as maids or waitresses, and sometimes simply kidnapped and sold for a few thousand dollars, these women were smuggled into the most prosperous parts of Europe and forced into prostitution.

Ethnic Diversity in Contemporary Europe

By 2010 immigration to Europe had profoundly changed the ethnic makeup of the continent, though the effects were unevenly distributed. In 2005 immigrants constituted about 10 percent of most western European nations but a far smaller share of the former East Bloc nations. One way to measure the effect of these new immigrants is to consider the rapid rise of their numbers. Since the 1960s the foreign population of western European nations has grown by two to ten times. In the Netherlands in 1960, only 1 percent of the population was foreign born. In 2006 the foreign born made up 10 percent. Over the same years the proportion of immigrants grew from 1.2 to 12.3 percent in Germany and from 4.7 to almost 11 percent in France.[6] For centuries the number of foreigners living in Europe had been relatively small. Now, permanently displaced ethnic groups, or **diasporas**, brought ethnic diversity to the continent.

The new immigrants were divided into two main groups. A small percentage were highly trained specialists who could find work in the upper ranks of education, business, and high-tech industries. Engineers from English-speaking India, for example, could find positions in international computer companies. The mass of immigrants, however, did not have access to high-quality education or language training, which limited their employment opportunities and made integration more difficult. They often lived in separate city districts marked by poor housing and crowded conditions, which set them apart from more established residents. Parts of London were home to tens of thousands of immigrants from the former colonies, and in Paris North Africans dominated some working-class *banlieues* (suburbs).

A variety of new cultural forms, ranging from sports and cuisine to music, the fine arts, and film, brought together native and foreign traditions and transformed European lifestyles. Food is a case in point. Recipes and cooks from former colonies in North Africa enlivened French cooking, while the döner kebab—the Turkish version of a gyro sandwich—became Germany's "native" fast food. Indian restaurants proliferated across

Britain, and controversy raged when the British foreign minister announced in 2001 that chicken tikka masala—a spicy Indian stew—was Great Britain's new national dish. In fact, tikka masala is a hybrid, a remarkable example of the way that peoples, recipes, and ingredients from Central Asia, Persia, and Europe had interacted for over four centuries, changing eating habits in Europe and on the Indian subcontinent alike.[7]

The **multiculturalism** and ethnic diversity associated with globalization have inspired numerous works in literature, film, and the fine arts. From rap to reggae, multiculturalism has also had a profound effect on popular music, a medium with a huge audience. Rai, which originated in the Bedouin culture of North Africa, exemplifies the new forms that emerged from cultural mixing. In the 1920s rai traveled with Algerian immigrants to France. In its current form, it blends Arab and North African folk music, U.S. rap, and French and Spanish pop styles. Lyrics range from sentimental love stories to blunt and sometimes bawdy descriptions of daily life. The Algerian Cheb Khaled, the unofficial "King of Rai," has become an international superstar. His song "To Flee, but Where?" captures Khaled's dismay with collapsing Islamic traditions in Algeria and the burdens of life in the Algerian diaspora in France.

The growth of immigration and ethnic diversity created rich social and cultural interactions but also generated intense controversy and conflict in western Europe. In most EU nations, immigrants can become full citizens if they meet certain legal qualifications; adopting the culture of the host country is not a requirement. This legal process has raised questions about who, exactly, could or should be European, and about the way these new citizens might change European society. The idea that cultural and ethnic diversity could be a force for vitality and creativity has run counter to deep-seated beliefs about national homogeneity. Some commentators have accused the newcomers of taking jobs from unemployed native Europeans and undermining national unity. Government welfare programs intended to support struggling immigrants have been criticized by some as a misuse of money, especially in times of economic downturn.

Immigration is a highly charged political issue. By the 1990s in France, some 70 percent of the population believed that there were "too many Arabs," and 30 percent supported

National Front Campaign Poster This 2009 campaign poster calls on viewers to vote for the far-right French National Front in elections to the European Parliament. It portrays the familiar French image of Lady Liberty with European Union stars circling her head. (Reuters/Handout)

right-wing politician Jean-Marie Le Pen's calls to rid France of its immigrants altogether. Even then-future president Jacques Chirac could claim in 1991 that he understood that good French workers could be driven "understandably crazy" by the "noise and smell" of foreigners in the country.[8] Le Pen's National Front and far-right political parties elsewhere, such as the Danish People's Party and Austria's Freedom Party, successfully exploited popular prejudice about what they called "foreign rabble" to make impressive gains in national elections.

Europe and Its Muslim Citizens

General concerns with migration often fused with fears of Muslim migrants and Muslim residents who have grown up in Europe. Islam is now the largest minority religion in Europe. The EU's 15 to 20 million Muslims outnumber Catholics in Europe's mainly Protestant north, and they outnumber Protestants in Europe's Catholic south. Major cities have substantial Muslim minorities. Muslim residents make up about 25 percent of the population in Marseilles and Rotterdam, 15 percent in Brussels, and about 10 percent in Paris, Copenhagen, and London.[9]

Terrorist Attack in Madrid   In March 2004 radical Islamic terrorists set bombs on commuter trains in Madrid, killing almost two hundred people. The motivation of the perpetrators remains unclear, but the bombings were probably a response to Spanish involvement in the Iraq War. A similar bombing occurred in London the next year, exacerbating anti-Muslim feeling in Europe. (Reuters/Pablo Torres/Guerrero/El Pais)

Worries increased after the September 11, 2001, al-Qaeda attack on New York's World Trade Center (see page 1045) and the subsequent war in Iraq. Terrorist attacks in Europe organized by Islamist extremists heightened anxieties. On a morning in March 2004 radical Moroccan Muslims living in Spain exploded bombs planted on trains bound for Madrid, killing 191 commuters and wounding 1,800 more. A year later an attack on the London transit system carried out by British citizens of Pakistani descent killed over 50 people.

The vast majority of Europe's Muslims clearly support democracy and reject violent extremism, but these spectacular attacks and lesser actions by Islamist militants nonetheless sharpened the European debate on immigration. Security was not the only focus of concern; critics across the political spectrum warned that Europe's rapidly growing Muslim population posed a dire threat to the West's liberal tradition, which embraced freedom of thought, representative government, toleration, separation of church and state, and, more recently, equal rights for women and gays. Islamist extremists and radical clerics living in Europe, critics proclaimed, rejected these fundamental Western values and preached the supremacy of Islamic laws for Europe's Muslims.

Secular Europeans at times had a hard time understanding the depths of Muslim spirituality. French attempts to enforce a ban on wearing the hijab (the headscarf worn by many faithful Muslim women) in public schools expressed the tension between Western secularism and Islamic religiosity on a most personal level and evoked outrage and protests in the Muslim community. As busy mosques came to outnumber dying churches in European cities, nationalist politicians exploited widespread doubts that immigrant populations from Muslim countries would ever assimilate into Western culture. A Danish-Muslim imam (spiritual leader) captured the dilemma: "The Danish shelves for faith and spirituality are empty," he reported. "They fill them instead with fear of the 'strong foreigner.'"[10] Moreover, conservative intellectuals claimed, many so-called moderate Islamic teachers were really anti-Western radicals playing for time. (See "Individuals in Society: Tariq Ramadan," page 1042.) Time was on the side of Euro-Islam, critics warned. Europe's Muslim population, estimated at 20 million in 2010, appeared likely to grow to 30 million by 2025 and to increase rapidly thereafter—even though that total would only be 4 percent of Europe's then-projected 750 million people.

Admitting that Islamic extremism could pose a serious challenge, some observers focused instead on the problem of integration. Whereas the first generation of Muslim migrants—predominantly Turks in Germany, Algerians in France, Pakistanis in Britain, and Moroccans in the Netherlands—had found jobs as unskilled workers in Europe's great postwar boom, they and their children had been hard hit after 1973 by the general economic downturn and the decline of manufacturing. Immigrants also suffered from a lack of educational opportunities. Provided for modestly by the welfare state and housed minimally in dilapidated housing projects, many second- and third-generation Muslim immigrants were outcasts in their adopted countries. To these observers, economics, inadequate job training, and discrimination had more influence on immigrant attitudes about their host communities than did religion and extremist teachings.

This argument was strengthened by widespread rioting in France in 2005 and again in 2009, which saw hundreds of Muslim youths go on a rampage. Almost always French by birth, language, and education, marauding groups labeled "Arabs" in press reports torched hundreds of automobiles night after night in Paris suburbs and other

INDIVIDUALS IN SOCIETY • Tariq Ramadan

Religious teacher, activist professor, and media star, Tariq Ramadan (b. 1962) is Europe's most famous Muslim intellectual. He is also a controversial figure, praised by many as a moderate bridge-builder and denounced by others as an Islamic militant in clever disguise.

Born in Switzerland of Egyptian ancestry, Ramadan is the grandson of Hassan al-Banna, the charismatic founder of the powerful Muslim Brotherhood. Al-Banna, who was assassinated in 1949, fought to reshape Arab nationalism within a framework of Islamic religious orthodoxy and anti-British terrorism. Tariq grew up in Geneva, where his father had sought refuge in 1954 after Egyptian president Gamal Abdel Nasser's anti-Islamic crackdown. He attended mainstream public schools, played soccer, and absorbed a wide-ranging Islamic heritage. For example, growing up fluent in French and Arabic, he learned English mainly from listening to Pakistani Muslims discuss issues with his father, who represented the Muslim Brotherhood and its ideology in Europe.

Ramadan studied philosophy and French literature as an undergraduate at the University of Geneva, and then earned a doctorate in Arabic and Islamic studies. Marrying a Swiss woman who converted to Islam, Ramadan moved his family to Cairo in 1991 to study Islamic law and philosophy. It proved to be a pivotal experience. Eagerly anticipating the return to his Muslim roots, Ramadan gradually realized that only in Europe did he feel truly at home. From this experience he concluded that Western Muslims should participate fully as active citizens and feel "at home" in their adopted countries. In developing this message, Ramadan left the classroom and became a publicly prominent intellectual, writing nonscholarly books and making audio recordings that sell tens of thousands of copies.

Slim and elegant in well-tailored suits and open collars, Ramadan is a brilliant speaker. His public lectures in French and English draw hundreds of Muslims and curious non-Muslims. He argues that Western Muslims have fundamental legal rights and can freely practice their religion, noting that they are often more secure than believers in the Muslim world, where governments are frequently repressive and arbitrary. According to Ramadan, Islamic teaching requires Western Muslims to obey Western laws, although in rare cases they may need to plead conscientious objec-

large cities. The rioters complained bitterly of high unemployment, systematic discrimination, and exclusion, and studies sparked by the rioting showed that religious ideology had almost no influence on their thinking.

A minority used such arguments to challenge anti-migrant, anti-Muslim discrimination and its racist overtones. They argued that Europe badly needed newcomers—preferably talented newcomers—to limit the impending population decline and provide valuable technical skills. Some asserted that Europe should recognize that Islam has for centuries been a European religion and a vital part of European life. This recognition might open the way to political and cultural acceptance of European Muslims and head off the resentment that can drive a tiny minority to separatism and acts of terror.

tion and disobey on religious grounds. Becoming full citizens and refusing to live as the foreign Other, Muslims should work with non-Muslims on matters of common concern, such as mutual respect, better schools, and economic justice.*

Ramadan is most effective with second- and third-generation Western Muslims who are also college graduates. He urges them to think for themselves and to distinguish the sacred revelation of Islam from the nonessential cultural aspects of Muslim life that their parents brought from Africa and Asia.

With growing fame has come growing controversy. In 2004, preparing to take up a professorship in the United States, he was denied an entry visa on the grounds that he had contributed to a Palestinian charity with ties to terrorists. Defenders disputed the facts and charged that his criticism of Israeli policies and the invasion of Iraq were the real reasons for the denial. Ramadan's critics also claim that he says different things to different groups: hard-edged criticism of the West found on recordings for Muslims belies the reasoned moderation of his books. Some critics argue that his recent condemnation of Western capitalism and globalization is an opportunistic attempt to win favor with European leftists and does not reflect his self-proclaimed Islamic passion for justice. Yet in 2010 the U.S. State Department lifted the ban that prevented Ramadan from entering the United States, and the scholar's reputation remains intact.† An innovative bridge-builder, he symbolizes the growing importance of Europe's Muslim citizens.

QUESTIONS FOR ANALYSIS

1. What is Ramadan's message to Western Muslims? How did he reach his conclusions?

2. Do you think Ramadan's ideas are realistic? Why?

*See, especially, Tariq Ramadan, *Western Muslims and the Future of Islam* (Oxford: Oxford University Press, 2004).
†See Ian Buruma, "Tariq Ramadan Has an Identity Issue," *New York Times Magazine*, February 4, 2007.

Confronting Twenty-First-Century Challenges

What challenges will Europeans face in the coming decades?

In the second decade of the twenty-first century, European societies faced a number of critical, interconnected challenges. The growing distance in international affairs between the United States and Europe revealed differences in social values and political goals, though both struggled to deal with turmoil in the Muslim world and Islamic terrorism. A persistent economic recession had a devastating impact on the lives of millions and undermined the unity of the Eurozone. Climate change and environmental degradation exposed the dangers of industrial development and the heavy dependence on fossil fuels for energy. At the same time, the relative wealth of European societies in the global context provoked serious thinking about European identity and Europe's humanitarian mission in the community of nations.

Growing Strains in U.S.-European Relations

In the fifty years after World War II, the United States and western Europe generally maintained close diplomatic relations. Though they were never in total agreement, they usually worked together to promote international consensus under U.S. guidance, as represented by the NATO alliance. For example, a U.S.-led coalition that included thousands of troops from France and the United Kingdom and smaller contributions from other NATO allies attacked Iraqi forces in Kuwait in the 1990–1991 Persian Gulf War, freeing the small nation from attempted annexation by Iraqi dictator Saddam Hussein. Over time, however, the growing power of the European Union and the new unilateral thrust of Washington's foreign policy created strains in traditional transatlantic relations.

The growing gap between the United States and Europe had several causes. For one, the European Union was now the world's largest trading block, challenging the predominance of the United States. Prosperous European businesses invested heavily in the United States, reversing a decades-long economic relationship in which investment dollars had flowed the other way. For another, under Presidents George W. Bush (r. 2001–2009) and Barack Obama (r. 2009–), the United States often ignored international opinion in pursuit of its own interests. Citing the economic impact, Washington refused to ratify the Kyoto Protocol of 1997, which was intended to limit global warming and which had been agreed to by nearly two hundred countries. Nor did the United States join the International Criminal Court, a global tribunal meant to prosecute individuals accused of crimes against humanity, which nearly 140 states agreed to join. These positions troubled EU leaders, as did unflagging U.S. support for Israel in the ongoing Palestinian-Israeli crisis.

A values gap between the United States and Europe contributed to cooler relations as well. Ever more secular Europeans had a hard time understanding the religiosity of many Americans. Relatively lax gun control laws and use of capital punishment in the United States were viewed with dismay in Europe, where most countries had outlawed private handgun ownership and abolished the death penalty. Despite Obama's health-care reforms—which evoked controversy among Americans—U.S. reluctance to establish a single-payer, state-funded program surprised Europeans, who saw their own such programs as highly advantageous.

Hardball geopolitical issues relating to NATO further widened the gap. The dissolution of the Communist Warsaw Pact left NATO without its Cold War adversaries. Yet NATO continued to expand, primarily in the territories in the former East Bloc— the defensive belt the Soviet Union had established after World War II. NATO's expansion angered Russia's leaders, particularly when President Bush moved to deploy missile defense systems in Poland and the Czech Republic in 2008. Even within the alliance there were tensions. By 2009, with twenty-eight member states, it was difficult to shape unanimous support for NATO actions. France, for example, did not support NATO's engagement in Bosnia in 1995 (see page 1026) because the alliance failed to get UN approval for the action, and in 2011 Germany and Poland refused to back NATO air strikes against the Libyan regime (see page 1047). As the EU expanded, some argued that Europe should determine its own military and defense policy without U.S. or NATO guidance.

American-led wars in Afghanistan and Iraq, undertaken in response to the September 11 terrorist attacks against the United States, further strained U.S.-European relations. On the morning of September 11, 2001, passenger planes hijacked by terrorists destroyed the World Trade Center towers in New York City and crashed into the Pentagon. Perpetrated by the radical Islamist group al-Qaeda, the attacks took the lives of more than three thousand people from many countries and put the personal safety of ordinary citizens at the top of the West's agenda.

Immediately after the September 11 attacks, the peoples and governments of Europe and the world joined Americans in heartfelt solidarity. Over time, however, tensions between Europe and the United States re-emerged and deepened markedly, particularly after President Bush declared a unilateral U.S. **war on terror**—a determined effort to fight terrorism in all its forms, around the world. The main acts in Bush's war on terror were a U.S.-led war in Afghanistan, which started in 2001, and another in Iraq, which lasted from 2003 to 2011. Both succeeded in quickly bringing down dictatorial regimes. At the same time, they fomented anti-Western sentiment in the Muslim world and failed to stop regional violence driven by ethnic and religious differences.

The U.S. invasion of Iraq and subsequent events caused some European leaders, notably in France and Germany, to question the rationale for and indeed the very effectiveness of a "war" on terror. Military victory, even over rogue states, would hardly end terrorism, since terrorist groups easily moved across national borders. Terrorism, they concluded, was better fought through police and intelligence measures. Europeans certainly shared U.S. worries about stability in the Middle East, and they faced their own problems with Islamist terrorism, especially after the Madrid and London train bombings of 2004 and 2005. But European leaders worried that the tactics used in the war, exemplified by Washington's readiness to use its military without international agreements or UN backing, violated international law.

American conduct of the war on terror also raised serious human rights concerns. The revelation of the harsh interrogation techniques used on prisoners held by American forces and abuse of prisoners in Iraq shocked many Europeans. U.S. willingness to engage in "extraordinary rendition"—secretly moving terrorism suspects to countries that allow coercive interrogation techniques—caused further concern.

The election of Barack Obama, America's first African American president, in 2008, and his re-election in 2012, brought improvement to U.S.-European foreign relations. Upon election, President Obama announced that he would halt deployment of missiles in central Europe and reduce nuclear arms, easing tensions with Russia. He took U.S. troops out of Iraq in 2011, promised to withdraw U.S. combat troops from Afghanistan in 2014, and quietly shelved the language of the "war on terror." In February 2013 the president's call for a free-trade agreement with the European Union, which would end tariffs and regulatory barriers to trade, raised hopes for closer economic and political cooperation in the future. Despite these changes, many Europeans continued to find U.S. willingness to undertake unilateral military action disturbing—American drone attacks on suspected terrorists along the Afghanistan-Pakistan border were particularly unpopular.[11] In the long run, though ties with the United States remained solid, European states increasingly responded independently to global affairs.

Turmoil in the Muslim World

Residents of North America and Europe expressed surprise and shock at the vehemence of the September 11 and other terrorist attacks, but radical Islamist hostility toward the West had a long history. Conflicts between Muslims and Christians certainly had deep roots (see Chapters 9 and 12), but modern, anti-Western Islamic militancy emerged with force only under the mandate system established by the European powers after World War I. Important factors included the legacies of European colonialism, Cold War power plays, and the Palestinian-Israeli conflict.

Radical political Islam, a mixture of traditional religious beliefs and innovative social and political reform ideas, was at first a reaction against the foreign control and secularization represented by the mandate system established in the Middle East after World War I (see Chapter 25). Groups like the **Muslim Brotherhood**, founded in Egypt in 1928, called for national liberation from European control and a return to shari'a law (based on Muslim legal codes), and demanded land reform, extensive social welfare programs, and economic independence. The appeal of such ideas crossed class lines and national borders. By the 1960s the Brotherhood had established chapters across the Middle East and North Africa, and a variety of other groups and leaders advocated similar ideas about the need for Islamic revival and national autonomy. The broad spectrum of Islamist ideas is difficult to summarize, but adherents tended to fall into two main groups: a moderate or centrist group that worked peacefully to reform society within existing institutions, and a much smaller, more militant radical minority willing to use violence to achieve their goals.

Decolonization and the Cold War sharpened anti-Western and particularly anti-U.S. sentiments among radical Islamists. As the western European powers loosened their ties to the Middle East, the Americans stepped in. Applying containment policy to limit the spread of communism, and eager to preserve steady supplies of oil, the United States supported secular, authoritarian regimes friendly to U.S. interests in Egypt, Saudi Arabia, Iran, and elsewhere. Such regimes often played on U.S. concerns about communism or the threat of radical Islam to bolster American support.

U.S. policies in the Middle East at times produced "blowback," or unforeseen and unintended consequences. One example was the Iranian revolution of 1979, when Islamist radicals antagonized by Western intervention, state corruption, and secularization overthrew the U.S.-supported shah and established an Islamic republic. The successful revolution encouraged militant Islamists elsewhere. So did the example of the mujahideen, the Muslim guerrilla fighters in Afghanistan who successfully fought off the Soviet army there from 1979 to 1989 (see Chapter 29). U.S. military aid and arms, funneled to the mujahideen during the war, also had unintended consequences. Many of the mujahideen would go on to support the Taliban, a militant Islamist faction that came to rule Afghanistan in 1996. The Taliban established a strict Islamist state based on shari'a law that denied women's right to education and banned Western movies and music—and provided a safe haven for the Saudi-born millionaire Osama bin Laden and the al-Qaeda terrorist network.

As a result of these policies, the United States, along with western Europe, became the main target for Islamist militants. During the 1990s bin Laden and al-Qaeda mounted several terrorist attacks on U.S. installations, leading up to the horrific September 11 assault. After that attack, President Bush declared with some justification that the terrorists "hate our freedoms, our freedom of religion, our freedom of speech."[12] In public calls for jihad (or struggle) against the United States and the West, however, bin Laden listed a more pragmatic list of grievances, including U.S. support for Israel in the Israeli-Palestinian crisis, the ongoing sanctions on Iraq that followed the Persian Gulf War, and the presence of U.S. military bases in Saudi Arabia—seen as an insult to the Muslim holy sites in Mecca and Medina. (See "Primary Source: Osama bin Laden Calls for Global Jihad," page 1048.)

The Bush administration hoped that the invasions of Afghanistan—a direct response to the September 11 attacks—and Iraq would end the terrorist attacks and bring peace and democracy to the Middle East, but both instead increased turmoil there. The military campaign in Afghanistan quickly achieved one of its goals, bringing down the Taliban, and the United States installed a friendly government. But U.S. troops failed to find bin Laden or disable al-Qaeda, and Taliban insurgents mounted a determined and lasting guerrilla war. Although U.S. commandos finally killed Osama bin Laden in Pakistan in May 2011, the apparently unwinnable war became increasingly unpopular in the United States and among NATO's European allies, and President Obama announced plans to withdraw American combat troops from Afghanistan by 2014.

With heavy fighting still under way in Afghanistan in late 2001, the Bush administration turned its attention to Saddam Hussein's Iraq, arguing that it was necessary to expand the war on terror to other hostile regimes in the Middle East. U.S. leaders effectively played on American fears of renewed terrorism and charged that Saddam Hussein was still developing weapons of mass destruction in flagrant disregard of his 1991 promise to end all such programs. Many Americans shared the widespread doubts held by Europeans about the legality—and wisdom—of an American attack on Iraq, especially after UN inspectors found no weapons of mass destruction in the country. Though the UN failed to approve an invasion, in March 2003 the United States and Britain, with token support from a handful of other European states, invaded Iraq.

The U.S.-led invasion quickly overwhelmed the Iraqi army, and Saddam's dictatorship collapsed in April, but America's subsequent efforts to establish a stable pro-American Iraq proved difficult. Poor postwar planning and management by administration officials was one factor, but there were others. Iraq, a creation of Western imperialism after World War I (see Chapter 25), is a fragile state with three distinct groups: non-Arab Kurds, Arab Sunni Muslims, and Arab Shi'ite Muslims. By 2006 deadly sectarian conflicts among these groups and against the United States and its Iraqi supporters had taken hold. Casualties in Iraq began to decline after President Bush sent additional troops to the country in 2007, and when President Obama took office in 2009 his administration moved forward with agreements to withdraw all U.S. forces in 2011. The shaky Iraqi government continued to struggle with ethnic divisions and terrorist violence, however.

In early 2011 an unexpected chain of events that came to be called the **Arab Spring** further destabilized the Middle East and North Africa. In a provincial town in Tunisia, a poor fruit vendor set himself on fire to protest official harassment. His death eighteen days later unleashed a series of spontaneous mass protests that brought violence, chaos, and regime change; six weeks later Tunisia's authoritarian president fled the country, opening the way for reform. Massive popular demonstrations in Egypt followed and forced the resignation of President Hosni Mubarak, a U.S.-friendly leader who had ruled for thirty years. An armed uprising in Libya, supported by NATO air strikes, brought

PRIMARY SOURCE   Osama bin Laden Calls for Global Jihad

In this interview broadcast by the Al Jazeera television network in December 1998, al-Qaeda leader Osama bin Laden called for jihad against the United States and its allies.

We demand that our land be liberated from enemies. That our lands be liberated from the Americans. . . .

Our enemies roam and meander in our seas and lands and skies, attack and assault without seeking permission from anyone. . . . The present [Arab] regimes no longer have the power. Either they are collaborators or have lost the power to do anything against this contemptible occupation. So Muslims should immigrate somewhere where they can raise the symbol of *jihad* [struggle] and protect their religion and world, otherwise they will lose everything. Are they incapable of appreciating the calamity that befell our brothers in Palestine and forgetting how the Palestinian people . . . have become a refugee people, turned into slaves of those colonialist Jews who dictate their movements? . . .

Every American man . . . is an enemy of ours whether he fights us directly or merely pays his taxes. You might have heard those who supported Clinton's [air] attacks against Iraq formed three-quarters of the American population. A people that regards its president in high favor when he kills innocent people is a decadent people with no understanding of morality. . . .

We are seeking to drive them [the Americans] out of our Islamic nations and prevent them from dominating us. We believe that this right to defend oneself is the right of all human beings. At a time when Israel stocks hundreds of nuclear warheads and when the Western crusaders control a large percentage of this [type of] weapon, we do not consider this an accusation but a right. . . . We congratulated

down the dictatorial government of Muammar Gaddafi that October. A civil war broke out in Syria in July 2011, but dragged on into 2013 as Bashar Assad hurled his army at the rebels and Western powers disagreed about what to do. Protests arose in other countries in the region as well, evoking a mixed response of reform and repression.

In summer 2013, as this was being written, it was difficult to predict the outcome of the Arab Spring. The initial protests were not organized by radical Islamists, but rather by young activists who sought greater political and social liberties from West-backed authoritarian regimes. These poorly organized groups could hardly maintain control of the changes they unleashed, which opened power to multiple players: military leaders and old elites, liberal secularists, local chieftains representing ethnic or sectarian interests, and moderate and radical Islamists. In Egypt, for example, the first open elections in decades brought to power representatives of the moderate wing of the Muslim Brotherhood; a year later, military leaders overthrew this elected government. In Egypt and other states, these diverse players continued to jockey for control.

U.S.-led campaigns against radical Islamists had weakened terrorist groups, which were for the most part disorganized and scattered in remote areas. But they could still mount deadly attacks, as in Mali, where Islamist rebels took over the northern reaches of the country and briefly occupied an Algerian natural gas refinery in January 2013.

the Pakistani people when they achieved this nuclear weapon, and we consider it the right of all Muslims to do so. . . .

Those who carried out the *jihad* [against Soviet forces] in Afghanistan did more than was expected of them because with very meager capacities they destroyed the largest military force and in doing so removed from our minds this notion of stronger nations. We believe that America is weaker than Russia, and from what we have heard from our brothers who waged *jihad* in Somalia, they found to their greatest surprise the weakness, frailty, and cowardliness of the American soldier. When only eight of them were killed[,] they packed up in the darkness of night and escaped without looking back. . . .

Finally, I advise all Muslims to adhere to the Koran. This is the way out from our present predicament. Our cure is the Koran. When one reads the Koran one wonders: Do they not read the Koran, or do they actually read but not understand as they should?

EVALUATE THE EVIDENCE

1. Why does bin Laden demand that the Islamic Middle East be "liberated"?

2. What connections does bin Laden make between jihad and the history of Muslim relations with the West?

Source: Michael H. Hunt, ed., *The World Transformed, 1945 to the Present: A Documentary Reader* (Boston: Bedford/St. Martin's), pp. 410–411.

French troops helped Mali's government push them back, underscoring once again Europe's stake in maintaining stability in the troubled but energy-rich regions of North Africa and the Middle East.

The Global Recession and the Viability of the Eurozone

While chaos and change roiled the Muslim world, economic crisis sapped growth and political unity in Europe and North America. In 2008 the United States entered a deep recession, caused by the burst of the housing boom, bank failures, and an overheated financial securities market. The U.S. government spent massive sums in attempts to recharge the economy. Banks, insurance agencies, auto companies, and financial services conglomerates received billions of dollars in federal aid. By 2013 the economy showed modest improvement, but a weak housing market and high unemployment continued to slow full recovery.

The recession quickly swept across Europe, where a housing bubble, high national deficits, and a weak bond market made the crisis particularly acute. One of the first countries affected, and one of the hardest hit, was Iceland, where in October 2008 the currency and banking system collapsed outright. Other countries followed — Ireland and Latvia made deep and painful cuts in government spending to balance national budgets. By 2010 Britain was deeply in debt, and Spain, Portugal, and especially Greece were close to bankruptcy. Greek political leaders struggled to implement a painful neoliberal austerity plan — which meant raising taxes, privatizing state-owned businesses, reforming labor markets, and drastically reducing government spending on pensions and other popular social benefits. All these measures were required before Greece could receive financial aid from the IMF, the European Common Bank, and the European Union. In the summer of 2012 Greece was still flailing, prompting speculation that it might leave the Eurozone, followed, perhaps, by Portugal or even Spain and Italy.

This sudden "euro crisis" put the very existence of the Eurozone in question. The common currency grouped together countries with vastly divergent economies. Germany and France, the zone's two strongest economies, felt pressure to provide financial support to ensure the stability of far weaker countries, including Greece and Portugal, though they did so with strings attached. As with Greece, recipients were required to reduce deficits through austerity measures. Even so, the transfer of monies within the Eurozone angered the citizens of wealthier countries, who felt they were being asked to subsidize countries in financial difficulties of their own making. Such feelings were particularly powerful in Germany, forcing Chancellor Angela Merkel (r. 2005–) — the nation's first

---

Greeks Protest Against Cuts in Public Education   In March 2013 teachers and students in Athens demonstrate against cuts in state support for public education, which threatened the integrity of the national school system and left many Greek schools without heat or food. Public protests against government austerity proposals set up to deal with the intractable economic crisis took place almost daily in hard-hit countries like Spain and Greece from fall 2012 to spring 2013. (AFP/Getty Images)

woman chancellor—to move cautiously in providing financial stimulus to troubled Eurozone economies.

If bailouts troubled wealthy Germans, deep cuts to benefits coupled with ongoing hardship from the recession infuriated the citizens of poorer countries. In Greece, unemployment hit a record 25 percent in 2012, and more than half of young adults lacked jobs. Even in Spain—the Eurozone's fourth-largest economy—one in four adults was unemployed and housing prices had dropped 25 percent since 2008.[13] As governments cut popular social programs, demonstrators took to the streets to protest declining living standards and the lack of work; in Athens, protests large and small were almost a daily occurrence in autumn 2012.

The euro crisis shook general faith in European unity, especially among conservatives. In Britain in January 2013, Conservative Party leader and prime minister David Cameron (r. 2010–) pledged to hold an "in/out" popular vote on Britain's membership in the EU within five years. On the far right, the crisis generated even stronger anti-EU sentiment and anti-immigrant extremism. In Hungary, a far-right political party demanded that the nation leave the EU immediately; in Greece, the extreme-right Golden Hand Party climbed to 12 percent in popularity polls even as party thugs carried out violent attacks on the country's undocumented immigrants. In early 2013 Europe's mainstream leaders were still committed to the euro and the EU, but more countries were heading into recession and unemployment was still rising. It remained to be seen whether economic troubles would persist and lead to political disintegration.

Dependence on Fossil Fuels

One of the most significant long-term challenges facing Europe and the world in the twenty-first century is the need for adequate energy resources. Maintaining standards of living in industrialized countries and modernizing the developing world requires extremely high levels of energy use, and current supplies are heavily dependent on fossil fuels: oil, coal, and natural gas. In 2011 Europe and Russia combined had about 12 percent of the world's population but annually consumed about 34 percent of the world's natural gas production, 22 percent of oil production, and 13 percent of coal output. Scientists warned that such high levels of usage were unsustainable over the long run. Fossil fuel supplies will eventually run out, especially as the countries of the developing world—including giants such as India and China—increase their own rates of consumption.[14]

Struggles to control and profit from these shrinking resources often resulted in tense geopolitical conflicts. The need to preserve access to oil, for example, has led to a transformation in military power in the post–Cold War world. Between 1945 and 1990 the largest areas of military buildup were along the iron curtain in Europe and in East Asia, as U.S. forces formed a bulwark against the spread of communism. Today military power is increasingly concentrated in oil-producing areas such as the Middle East, which holds about 65 percent of the world's oil reserves. One scholar labeled conflicts in the Persian Gulf and Central Asia "resource wars" because they are fought, in large part, to preserve the West's access to the region's energy supplies.[15]

The global struggle for ample energy has placed Russia, which in 2011 became the world's number-one oil producer (surpassing Saudi Arabia) and the number-two natural gas producer, in a powerful but strained position. The Russian invasions of Chechnya and Georgia were attempts to maintain political influence in these territories, but also to preserve control of the region's rich energy resources.

Beyond military action, Russian leaders readily use their control over energy to assert political influence. The Russian corporation Gazprom, one of the world's largest producers of natural gas, sells Europe 28 percent of its natural gas, and the EU treads softly with Russia to maintain this supply. Russia is willing to play hardball: it has engaged in over fifty politically motivated disruptions of natural gas supply in the former Soviet republics, including one in January 2009 when Russia shut off supplies to Ukraine for three weeks, resulting in closed factories and no heat for hundreds of thousands of people. "Yesterday tanks, today oil," a Polish politician remarked about Russia's willingness to use energy to exert influence in central Europe.[16]

Climate Change and Environmental Degradation

Even setting aside the question of the supply of fossil fuels, their use has led to serious environmental problems. Burning oil and coal releases massive amounts of carbon dioxide (CO_2) into the atmosphere, the leading cause of **climate change** or global warming. While the future effects of climate change are difficult to predict, climatologists generally agree that global warming is proceeding dramatically faster than previously predicted and that some climatic disruption is now unavoidable. Rising average temperatures were playing havoc with familiar weather patterns, melting glaciers and polar ice packs, and drying up freshwater resources across the world. Moreover, in the next fifty years rising sea levels may well flood low-lying coastal areas.

Since the 1990s the EU has spearheaded efforts to control energy consumption and contain climate change. EU leaders have imposed tight restrictions on CO_2 emissions, and Germany, the Netherlands, and Denmark have become world leaders in harnessing alternative energy sources such as solar and wind power. Some countries, hoping to combat the future effects of global warming, have also taken pre-emptive measures. The Dutch government, for example, has spent billions of dollars constructing new dykes, levees, and floodgates. These efforts provided models for U.S. urban planners after floodwaters churned up by Hurricane Sandy swamped low-lying swaths of New York City in October 2012.

Environmental degradation encompasses a number of problems beyond climate change. Overfishing and toxic waste threaten the world's oceans and freshwater lakes, which once seemed to be inexhaustible sources of food and drinking water. The disaster that resulted when an offshore oil rig exploded in the Gulf of Mexico in April 2010, spewing millions of gallons of oil into the gulf waters, underscored the close connections between energy consumption and water pollution. Deforestation, land degradation, soil erosion, and overfertilization; species extinction related to habitat loss; the accumulation of toxins in the air, land, and water; the disposal of poisonous nuclear waste—all will continue to pose serious problems in the twenty-first century.

Though North American and European governments, NGOs, and citizens have taken a number of steps to limit environmental degradation and regulate energy use, the overall effort to control energy consumption has been an especially difficult endeavor, underscoring the interconnectedness of the contemporary world. Industrializing countries such as India and China, which in 2008 surpassed the United States as the largest emitter of CO_2, have had a difficult time balancing environmental concerns and the energy use necessary for economic growth. Because of growing demand for electricity, for example, China currently accounts for about 47 percent of the world's coal consumption, causing hazardous air pollution in Chinese cities and contributing to climate change.[17]

Can international agreements and good intentions make a difference? In December 2012 representatives of 192 nations met at the annual United Nations Climate Change Conference, in Doha, Qatar. They extended the Kyoto Protocol on climate change, set ambitious goals for the reduction of CO_2 emissions by 2020, and promised to help developing countries manage the effects of climate change. Such changes would require substantial modifications in the planet's consumption of energy derived from fossil fuels, however, and the ultimate success of ambitious plans to limit the human impact on the environment remains uncertain.

Promoting Human Rights

Though regional differences persisted in the twenty-seven EU member states, Europeans entering the twenty-first century enjoyed some of the highest living standards in the world, the sweet fruit of more than fifty years of peace, security, and overall economic growth. The recent agonies of barbarism and war in the former Yugoslavia as well as the memories of the horrors of World War II and the Holocaust cast in bold relief the ever-present reality of collective violence. For some Europeans, the realization that they had so much and so many others had so little kindled a desire to help. As a result, European intellectuals and opinion makers began to envision a new historic mission for Europe: the promotion of domestic peace and human rights in lands plagued by instability, violence, and oppression.

European leaders and humanitarians believed that more global agreements and new international institutions were needed to set moral standards and to regulate countries, leaders, armies, corporations, and individuals. In practice, this meant more curbs on the sovereign rights of the world's states, just as the states of the European Union had imposed increasingly strict standards of behavior on themselves in order to secure the rights and welfare of EU citizens. As one EU official concluded, the European Union has a "historical responsibility" to make morality "a basis of policy" because "human rights are more important than states' rights."[18]

In practical terms, this mission raised questions. Europe's evolving human rights policies would require military intervention to stop civil wars and to prevent tyrannical governments from slaughtering their own people. Thus the EU joined the United States to intervene militarily to stop the killing and protect minority rights in Bosnia, Croatia, and Kosovo. The EU states vigorously supported UN initiatives to verify compliance with anti–germ warfare conventions, outlaw the use of land mines, and establish a new international court to prosecute war criminals.

Europeans also broadened definitions of individual rights. Having abolished the death penalty in the EU, they condemned its continued use in China, the United States, and other countries. At home, Europe expanded personal rights. The pacesetting Netherlands gave pensions and workers' rights to prostitutes and provided assisted suicide (euthanasia) for the terminally ill. The Dutch recognized same-sex marriage in 2001. By the time France followed suit in 2013, nine western European countries had legalized same-sex marriage and twelve others recognized alternative forms of civic union.

The countries of the former East Bloc, where people were generally less supportive of gay rights, lagged behind in this regard.

Europeans extended their broad-based concept of human rights to the world's poorer countries. Such efforts often included sharp criticism of globalization and unrestrained neoliberal capitalism. For example, Europe's moderate Social Democrats joined human rights campaigners in 2001 to secure drastic price cuts from international pharmaceutical corporations selling drugs to combat Africa's AIDS crisis. Advocating greater social equality and state-funded health care, European socialists embraced morality as a basis for the global expansion of human rights.

The record was not always perfect. Critics accused the European Union (and the United States) of selectively promoting human rights in their differential responses to the Arab Spring—the West was willing to act in some cases, as in Libya, but dragged their feet in others, as in Egypt and Syria. Attempts to extend rights to women, indigenous peoples, and immigrants remained controversial, but the general trend suggested that Europe's leaders and peoples alike took very seriously the ideals articulated in the 1948 UN Universal Declaration of Human Rights.

Notes

1. Quoted in T. Judt, *Postwar: A History of Europe Since 1945* (New York: Penguin, 2005), p. 691.
2. Ibid., pp. 698–699.
3. *Quarterly Labor Force Statistics*, vol. 2004/4 (Paris: OECD Publications, 2004), p. 64.
4. Quoted in Geoffrey Lean, "Trade Wars—The Hidden Tentacles of the World's Most Secret Body," *The Independent*, July 18, 1999.
5. Quoted in *The Economist*, January 6, 2001, p. 6.
6. Mark Mazower, *Dark Continent: Europe's Twentieth Century* (New York: Vintage, 2000), p. 415; *United Nations International Migration Report 2006* (UN Department of Economic and Social Affairs), http://www.un.org/esa/populationpublications/2006_MigrationRep/report.htm.
7. L. Collingham, *Curry: A Tale of Cooks and Conquerors* (London: Oxford University Press, 2006), pp. 2, 9.
8. J. Gross, D. McMurray, and T. Swedenborg, "Rai, Rap, and Ramadan Nights: Franco-Maghribi Cultural Identities," in *Political Islam: Essays from Middle East Report*, ed. Joel Beinin and Joe Stork (London: I. B. Tauris, 1997), p. 258.
9. J. Klausen, *The Islamic Challenge: Politics and Religion in Western Europe* (New York: Oxford University Press, 2006), p. 16; Malise Ruthven, "The Big Muslim Problem!" *New York Review*, December 17, 2009, p. 62.
10. Quoted in Klausen, *The Islamic Challenge*, p. 16.
11. "Global Opinion of Obama Slips, International Policies Faulted," *Pew Research Global Attitudes Research Project*, June 13, 2012, http://www.pewglobal.org/2012/06/13/global-opinion-of-obama-slips-international-policies-faulted/.
12. Quoted in "Text: President Bush Addresses the Nation," Sept. 20, 2001, *Washington Post Online*, http://www.washingtonpost.com/wpsrv/nation/specials/attacked/transcripts/bushaddress_092001.html.
13. Elena Becatoros, "Hit by Crisis, Greek Society in Free Fall," *Washington Times*, November 1, 2012, http://www.washingtontimes.com/news/2012/nov/1/hit-crisis-greek-society-free-fall/?page=all; "Eurozone Crisis—Spain in Numbers," *BBC News—Eurozone Crisis*, July 25, 2012, http://www.bbc.co.uk/news/world-europe-18338616.
14. Statistics in *BP Statistical Review of World Energy June 2012*, http://www.bp.com/statisticalreview.
15. M. T. Klare, *Resource Wars: The New Landscape of Global Conflict* (New York: Henry Holt, 2001), pp. 25–40.
16. A. E. Kramer, "Eastern Europe Fears New Era of Russian Sway," *New York Times*, October 13, 2009, p. A1.
17. Edward Wong, "Beijing Takes Steps to Fight Pollution as Problem Worsens," *New York Times*, January 31, 2013, p. A4.
18. Quoted in *International Herald Tribune*, June 15, 2001, p. 6.

Chapter Review

MAKE IT STICK

LearningCurve
bedfordstmartins.com/mckaywestvalue
After reading the chapter, use LearningCurve to retain what you've read.

IDENTIFY KEY TERMS

Identify and explain the significance of each item below.

Ostalgie (p. 1025)
ethnic cleansing (p. 1026)
Kosovo Liberation Army (KLA) (p. 1027)
globalization (p. 1027)
European Union (EU) (p. 1028)
Maastricht Treaty (p. 1028)
World Trade Organization (WTO) (p. 1031)

nongovernmental organizations (NGOs) (p. 1031)
diasporas (p. 1038)
multiculturalism (p. 1039)
war on terror (p. 1045)
Muslim Brotherhood (p. 1046)
Arab Spring (p. 1047)
climate change (p. 1052)

REVIEW THE MAIN IDEAS

Answer the focus questions from each section of the chapter.

* How did life change in Russia and the former East Bloc countries after 1989? (p. 1019)
* How did globalization affect European life and society? (p. 1027)
* What are the main causes and effects of growing ethnic diversity in contemporary Europe? (p. 1036)
* What challenges will Europeans face in the coming decades? (p. 1043)

MAKE CONNECTIONS

Think about the larger developments and continuities within and across chapters.

1. Did people's lives really change dramatically during the wave of globalization that emerged in the late twentieth century? How have they stayed the same?
2. The globalization of today's world seems inseparable from advances in digital technology. How are the two connected? Were there other times in the history of Western society during which technological developments drove social, political, or cultural change?

ONLINE DOCUMENT ASSIGNMENT

Contesting Globalization

What do the goals of major global organizations and antiglobal movements reveal about the experience of globalization in the twenty-first century?

Go online and learn more about key global organizations and movements. Then complete a writing assignment based on the evidence and details from this chapter.

bedfordstmartins.com/mckaywestvalue

CHRONOLOGY

1980s–1990s	• Emergence of globalization
1990s–2010s	• New waves of legal and illegal immigration to Europe
1991	• Maastricht Treaty
1991–2001	• Civil war in Yugoslavia
1992–1997	• Decline of Russian economy
1993	• Creation of the European Union
1999	• Protests against WTO in Seattle
2000–2008	• Resurgence of Russian economy under Putin
2001	• September 11 terrorist attack on the United States; war in Afghanistan begins
2002	• Euro replaces national currencies in Eurozone
2003–2011	• Iraq War
2004	• Train bombings in Madrid by Islamic extremists
2005	• Young Muslims riot in France; subway bombing in London by Islamic extremists
2008	• Worldwide financial crisis begins
2009	• Ratification of Treaty of Lisbon; young Muslims riot in France
2011	• Start of Arab Spring
2012–2013	• Mass protests against government austerity plans in Greece and Spain
2013	• France legalizes same-sex marriage

Glossary

Afrikaners Descendants of the Dutch settlers in the Cape Colony in southern Africa. (p. 810)

al-Andalus The part of the Iberian Peninsula under Muslim control in the eighth century, encompassing most of modern-day Spain. (p. 231)

anticlericalism Opposition to the clergy. (p. 402)

apostolic succession The doctrine that all bishops can trace their spiritual ancestry back to Jesus's apostles. (p. 197)

appeasement The British policy toward Germany prior to World War II that aimed at granting Hitler whatever he wanted, including western Czechoslovakia, in order to avoid war. (p. 921)

aqueducts Canals, channels, and pipes that brought freshwater into cities. (p. 174)

Arab Spring A series of popular revolts in several countries in the Middle East and North Africa that sought an end to authoritarian, often Western-supported regimes. (p. 1047)

Arianism A theological belief that originated with Arius, a priest of Alexandria, denying that Christ was co-eternal with God the Father. (p. 195)

Atlantic slave trade The forced migration of Africans across the Atlantic for slave labor on plantations and in other industries; the trade reached its peak in the eighteenth century and ultimately involved more than 12 million Africans. (p. 571)

Babylonian Captivity The period from 1309 to 1376 when the popes resided in Avignon rather than in Rome. The phrase refers to the seventy years when the Hebrews were held captive in Babylon. (p. 348)

Balfour Declaration A 1917 British statement that declared British support of a National Home for the Jewish People in Palestine. (p. 861)

barracks emperors The emperors of the middle of the third century, so called because they were military commanders. (p. 186)

Battle of Peterloo The army's violent suppression of a protest that took place at Saint Peter's Fields in Manchester in reaction to the revision of the Corn Laws. (p. 708)

Bauhaus A German interdisciplinary school of fine and applied arts that brought together many leading modern architects, designers, and theatrical innovators. (p. 876)

Berlin Conference A meeting of European leaders held in 1884 and 1885 in order to lay down some basic rules for imperialist competition in sub-Saharan Africa. (p. 814)

bishops Christian Church officials with jurisdiction over certain areas and the power to determine the correct interpretation of Christian teachings. (p. 185)

Black Death Plague that first struck Europe in 1347 and killed perhaps one-third of the population. (p. 334)

Black Shirts Mussolini's private militia that destroyed socialist newspapers, union halls, and Socialist Party headquarters, eventually pushing Socialists out of the city governments of northern Italy. (p. 912)

blood sports Events such as bullbaiting and cockfighting that involved inflicting violence and bloodshed on animals and that were popular with the eighteenth-century European masses. (p. 598)

Bloody Sunday A massacre of peaceful protesters at the Winter Palace in St. Petersburg in 1905, triggering a revolution that overturned absolute tsarist rule and made Russia into a conservative constitutional monarchy. (p. 774)

Bolsheviks Lenin's radical, revolutionary arm of the Russian party of Marxist socialism, which successfully installed a dictatorial socialist regime in Russia. (p. 851)

Book of the Dead Egyptian funerary manuscripts, written to help guide the dead through the difficulties they would encounter on the way to the afterlife. (p. 23)

bourgeoisie The middle-class minority who owned the means of production and, according to Marx, exploited the working-class proletariat. (p. 701)

boyars The highest-ranking members of the Russian nobility. (pp. 253, 497)

Brezhnev Doctrine Doctrine created by Leonid Brezhnev that held that the Soviet Union had the right to intervene in any East Bloc country when necessary to preserve Commnist rule. (p. 993)

Bronze Age The period in which the production and use of bronze implements became basic to society. (p. 10)

caliph A successor, as chosen by a group of Muhammad's closest followers. (p. 230)

cameralism View that monarchy was the best form of government, that all elements of society should serve the monarch, and that, in turn, the state should use its resources and authority to increase the public good. (p. 542)

canon law Church law, which had its own courts and procedures. (p. 276)

caravel A small, maneuverable, three-mast sailing ship developed by the Portuguese in the fifteenth century that gave the Portuguese a distinct advantage in exploration and trade. (p. 446)

carnival The few days of revelry in Catholic countries that preceded Lent and that included drinking, masquerading, dancing, and rowdy spectacles that upset the established order. (p. 598)

Cartesian dualism Descartes's view that all of reality could ultimately be reduced to mind and matter. (p. 526)

cathedral The church of a bishop and the administrative headquarters of a diocese. (p. 326)

charivari Degrading public rituals used by village communities to police personal behavior and maintain moral standards. (p. 587)

chivalry Code of conduct in which fighting to defend the Christian faith and protecting one's countrymen was declared to have a sacred purpose. (p. 270)

Christendom The term used by early medieval writers to refer to the realm of Christianity. (p. 290)

Christian Democrats Center-right political parties that rose to power in western Europe after the Second World War. (p. 951)

Christian humanists Northern humanists who interpreted Italian ideas about and attitudes toward classical antiquity and humanism in terms of their own religious traditions. (p. 381)

civilization A large-scale system of human political, economic, and social organizations; civilizations have cities, laws, states, and often writing. (p. 3)

civitas The city and surrounding territory that served as a basis of the administrative system in the Frankish kingdoms, based on Roman models. (p. 236)

class-consciousness Awareness of belonging to a distinct social and economic class whose interests might conflict with those of other classes. (p. 679)

climate change Changes in long-standing weather patterns caused primarily by carbon dioxide emissions from the burning of fossil fuels. (p. 1052)

Cold War The rivalry between the Soviet Union and the United States that divided much of Europe into a Soviet-aligned Communist bloc and a U.S.-aligned capitalist bloc between 1945 and 1989. (p. 940)

collectivization of agriculture The forcible consolidation of individual peasant farms into large state-controlled enterprises in the Soviet Union under Stalin. (p. 907)

college of cardinals A special group of high clergy with the authority and power to elect the pope and the responsibility to govern the church when the office of the pope is vacant. (p. 273)

Columbian exchange The exchange of animals, plants, and diseases between the Old and the New Worlds. (p. 462)

Combination Acts British laws passed in 1799 that outlawed unions and strikes, favoring capitalist business people over skilled artisans. Bitterly resented and widely disregarded by many craft guilds, the acts were repealed by Parliament in 1824. (p. 683)

comitatus A war band of young men in a barbarian tribe who were closely associated with the chief, swore loyalty to him, and fought with him in battle. (p. 206)

comites A senior official or royal companion, later called a count, who presided over the civitas. (p. 236)

commercial revolution The transformation of the European economy as a result of changes in business procedures and growth in trade. (p. 312)

common law A body of English law established by King Henry II's court that in the next two or three centuries became common to the entire country. (p. 267)

Common Market The European Economic Community, created by six western and central European countries in the West Bloc in 1957 as part of a larger search for European unity. (p. 954)

communes Sworn associations of free men in Italian cities led by merchant guilds that sought political and economic independence from local nobles. (p. 368)

community controls A pattern of cooperation and common action in a traditional village that sought to uphold the economic, social, and moral stability of the closely knit community. (p. 587)

companionate marriage Marriage based on romantic love and middle-class family values that became increasingly dominant in the second half of the nineteenth century. (p. 739)

conciliarists People who believed that the authority in the Roman Church should rest in a general council composed of clergy, theologians, and laypeople, rather than in the pope alone. (p. 349)

confraternities Voluntary lay groups organized by occupation, devotional preference, neighborhood, or charitable activity. (p. 350)

Congress of Vienna A meeting of the Quadruple Alliance — Russia, Prussia, Austria, and Great Britain — restoration France, and smaller European states to fashion a general peace settlement that began after the defeat of Napoleon's France in 1814. (p. 688)

conquistadors Spanish for "conquerors"; Spanish soldier-explorers, such as Hernando Cortés and Francisco Pizarro, who sought to conquer the New World for the Spanish crown. (p. 445)

constitutionalism A form of government in which power is limited by law and balanced between the authority and power of the government on the one hand, and the rights and liberties of the subjects or citizens on the other hand; could include constitutional monarchies or republics. (p. 502)

consuls Primary executives in the Roman Republic, elected for one-year terms, who commanded the army in battle, administered state business, and supervised financial affairs. (p. 129)

consumer revolution The wide-ranging growth in consumption and new attitudes toward consumer goods that emerged in the cities of northwestern Europe in the second half of the eighteenth century. (p. 601)

Continental System A blockade imposed by Napoleon to halt all trade between continental Europe and Britain, thereby weakening the British economy and military. (p. 643)

Copernican hypothesis The idea that the sun, not the earth, was the center of the universe. (p. 520)

Corn Laws British laws governing the import and export of grain, which were revised in 1815 to prohibit the importation of foreign grain unless the price at home rose to improbable levels, thus benefiting the aristocracy but making food prices high for working people. (p. 708)

Cossacks Free groups and outlaw armies originally comprising runaway peasants living on the borders of Russian territory from the fourteenth century onward. By the end of the sixteenth century they had formed an alliance with the Russian state. (p. 498)

cottage industry A stage of industrial development in which rural workers used hand tools in their homes to manufacture goods on a large scale for sale in a market. (p. 559)

Council for Mutual Economic Assistance (COMECON) An economic organization of Communist states meant to help rebuild East Bloc countries under Soviet auspices. (p. 947)

courts Magnificent households and palaces where signori and other rulers lived, conducted business, and supported the arts. (p. 369)

Covenant An agreement that the Hebrews believed to exist between themselves and Yahweh, in which he would consider them his chosen people if they worshipped him as their only god. (p. 43)

craft guild A band of producers in a town that regulated most aspects of production of a good in that town. (p. 309)

Crimean War A conflict fought between 1853 and 1856 over Russian desires to expand into Ottoman territory; Russia was defeated by France, Britain, and the Ottomans, underscoring the need for reform in the Russian empire. (p. 773)

Crusades Wars sponsored by the papacy for the recovery of Jerusalem and surrounding territories from the Muslims from the late eleventh to the late thirteenth centuries. (p. 283)

Crystal Palace The location of the Great Exhibition in 1851 in London; an architectural masterpiece made entirely of glass and iron. (p. 664)

cuneiform Sumerian form of writing; the term describes the wedge-shaped marks made by a stylus. (p. 13)

Dadaism An artistic movement of the 1920s and 1930s that attacked all accepted standards of art and behavior and delighted in outrageous conduct. (p. 877)

Dawes Plan War reparations agreement that reduced Germany's yearly payments, made payment dependent on economic prosperity, and granted large U.S. loans to promote recovery. (p. 890)

debate about women Debate among writers and thinkers in the Renaissance about women's qualities and proper role in society. (p. 391)

debt peonage A form of serfdom that allowed a planter or rancher to keep his workers or slaves in perpetual debt bondage by periodically advancing food, shelter, and a little money. (p. 571)

decolonization The postwar reversal of Europe's overseas expansion caused by the rising demand of the colonized peoples themselves, the declining power of European nations, and the freedoms promised by U.S. and Soviet ideals. (p. 963)

Delian League A military alliance led by Athens aimed at protecting the Aegean Islands, liberating Ionia from Persian rule, and keeping the Persians out of Greece. (p. 77)

democracy A type of Greek government in which all citizens administered the workings of government. (p. 70)

de-Stalinization The liberalization of the post-Stalin Soviet Union led by reformer Nikita Khrushchev. (p. 959)

détente The progressive relaxation of Cold War tensions that emerged in the early 1970s. (p. 982)

developed socialism A term used by Communist leaders to describe the socialist accomplishments of their societies, such as nationalized industry, collective agriculture, and extensive social welfare programs. (p. 1004)

diasporas Enclaves of ethnic groups settled outside of their homelands. (p. 1038)

diocese An administrative unit in the later Roman Empire; adopted by the Christian Church as the territory under the authority of a bishop. (p. 192)

displaced persons Postwar refugees, including 13 million Germans, former Nazi prisoners and forced laborers, and orphaned children. (p. 941)

Domesday Book A general inquiry about the wealth of his lands ordered by William of Normandy. (p. 261)

Dreyfus affair A divisive case in which Alfred Dreyfus, a Jewish captain in the French army, was falsely accused and convicted of treason. The Catholic Church sided with the anti-Semites against Dreyfus; after Dreyfus was declared innocent, the French government severed all ties between the state and the church. (p. 781)

Duma The Russian parliament that opened in 1906, elected indirectly by universal male suffrage but controlled after 1907 by the tsar and the conservative classes. (p. 775)

economic liberalism A belief in free trade and competition based on Adam Smith's argument that the invisible hand of free competition would benefit all individuals, rich and poor. (p. 565)

economic miracle Term contemporaries used to describe rapid economic growth, often based on the consumer sector, in post–World War II western Europe. (p. 951)

Edict of Nantes A document issued by Henry IV of France in 1598, granting liberty of conscience and of public worship to Calvinists, which helped restore peace in France. (p. 431)

empiricism A theory of inductive reasoning that calls for acquiring evidence through observation and experimentation rather than deductive reason and speculation. (p. 526)

Enabling Act An act pushed through the Reichstag by the Nazis that gave Hitler absolute dictatorial power for four years. (p. 916)

enclosure The movement to fence in fields in order to farm more effectively, at the expense of poor peasants who relied on common fields for farming and pasture. (p. 554)

encomienda system A system whereby the Spanish crown granted the conquerors the right to forcibly employ groups of Indians in exchange for providing food, shelter, and Christian teaching. (p. 458)

English Peasants' Revolt Revolt by English peasants in 1381 in response to changing economic conditions. (p. 356)

enlightened absolutism Term coined by historians to describe the rule of eighteenth-century monarchs who, without renouncing their own absolute authority, adopted Enlightenment ideals of rationalism, progress, and tolerance. (p. 541)

Enlightenment The influential intellectual and cultural movement of the late seventeenth and eighteenth centuries that introduced a new worldview based on the use of reason, the scientific method, and progress. (p. 529)

Epicureanism A system of philosophy based on the teachings of Epicurus, who viewed a life of contentment, free from fear and suffering, as the greatest good. (p. 114)

estates The three legal categories, or orders, of France's inhabitants: the clergy, the nobility, and everyone else. (p. 630)

Estates General A legislative body in prerevolutionary France made up of representatives of each of the three classes, or estates. It was called into session in 1789 for the first time since 1614. (p. 629)

ethnic cleansing The attempt to establish ethnically homogeneous territories by intimidation, forced deportation, and killing. (p. 1026)

eugenics A pseudoscientific doctrine that maintains that the selective breeding of human beings can improve the general characteristics of a national population, which helped inspire Nazi ideas about "race and space" and ultimately contributed to the Holocaust. (p. 903)

European Union (EU) The economic, cultural, and political alliance of twenty-seven European nations. (p. 1028)

evolution The idea, applied by thinkers in many fields, that stresses gradual change and continuous adjustment. (p. 750)

excommunication A penalty used by the Christian Church that meant being cut off from the sacraments and all Christian worship. (p. 273)

existentialism A philosophy that stresses the meaninglessness of existence and the importance of the individual in searching for moral values in an uncertain world. (p. 871)

experimental method The approach, pioneered by Galileo, that the proper way to explore the workings of the universe was through repeatable experiments rather than speculation. (p. 522)

Factory Acts English laws passed from 1802 to 1833 that limited the workday of child laborers and set minimum hygiene and safety requirements. (p. 675)

fascism A movement characterized by extreme, often expansionist nationalism, antisocialism, a dynamic and violent leader, and glorification of war and the military. (p. 903)

February Revolution Unplanned uprisings accompanied by violent street demonstrations begun in March 1917 (old calendar February) in Petrograd, Russia, that led to the abdication of the tsar and the establishment of a provisional government. (p. 850)

Fertile Crescent An area of mild climate and abundant wild grain where agriculture first developed, in present-day Lebanon, Israel, Jordan, Turkey, and Iraq. (p. 7)

feudalism A term devised by later scholars to describe the political system in which a vassal was generally given a piece of land in return for his loyalty. (p. 255)

fief A piece of land granted by a feudal lord to a vassal in return for service and loyalty. (p. 254)

First Triumvirate The name later given to an informal political alliance among Caesar, Crassus, and Pompey in which they agreed to advance one another's interests. (p. 152)

"five good emperors" The five Roman emperors (Nerva, Trajan, Hadrian, Antoninus Pius, and Marcus Aurelius) of the second century whose reigns were relatively prosperous and stable. (p. 169)

Five Pillars of Islam The five practices Muslims must fulfill according to the shari'a, or sacred law, including the profession of faith, prayer, fasting, giving alms to the poor, and pilgrimage to Mecca. (p. 230)

five-year plan A plan launched by Stalin in 1928, and termed the "revolution from above," aimed at modernizing the Soviet Union and creating a new Communist society with new attitudes, new loyalties, and a new socialist humanity. (p. 905)

flagellants People who believed that the plague was God's punishment for sin and sought to do penance by flagellating (whipping) themselves. (p. 339)

Fourteen Points Wilson's 1918 peace proposal calling for open diplomacy, a reduction in armaments, freedom of commerce and trade, the establishment of the League of Nations, and national self-determination. (p. 859)

friars Men belonging to certain religious orders who did not live in monasteries but out in the world. (p. 281)

Fronde A series of violent uprisings during the early reign of Louis XIV triggered by growing royal control and increased taxation. (p. 484)

functionalism The principle that buildings, like industrial products, should serve as well as possible the purpose for which they were made, without excessive ornamentation. (p. 876)

German Social Democratic Party (SPD) A German working-class political party founded in the 1870s, the SPD championed Marxism but in practice turned away from Marxist revolution and worked instead for social and workplace reforms in the German parliament. (p. 779)

germ theory The idea that disease was caused by the spread of living organisms that could be controlled. (p. 728)

Girondists A moderate group that fought for control of the French National Convention in 1793. (p. 635)

glasnost Soviet premier Mikhail Gorbachev's popular campaign for openness in government and the media. (p. 1008)

globalization The emergence of a freer, more technologically connected global economy, accompanied by a worldwide exchange of cultural, political, and religious ideas. (p. 1027)

global mass migration The mass movement of people from Europe in the nineteenth century; one reason that the West's impact on the world was so powerful and many-sided. (p. 804)

Gothic An architectural style typified by pointed arches and large stained-glass windows. (p. 326)

Grand Empire The empire over which Napoleon and his allies ruled, encompassing virtually all of Europe except Great Britain and Russia. (p. 643)

Great Depression A worldwide economic depression from 1929 through 1939, unique in its severity and duration and with slow and uneven recovery. (p. 892)

Greater Germany A liberal plan for German national unification that included the German-speaking parts of the Austrian Empire, put forth at the national parliament in 1848 but rejected by Austrian rulers. (p. 718)

Great Famine A terrible famine in 1315–1322 that hit much of Europe after a period of climate change. (p. 332)

Great Famine The result of four years of potato crop failure in the late 1840s in Ireland, a country that had grown dependent on potatoes as a dietary staple. (p. 711)

Great Fear The fear of noble reprisals against peasant uprisings that seized the French countryside and led to further revolt. (p. 631)

Great Rebellion The 1857 and 1858 insurrection by Muslim and Hindu mercenaries in the British army that spread throughout northern and central India before finally being crushed. (p. 822)

Great Schism The division, or split, in church leadership from 1378 to 1417 when there were two, then three, popes. (p. 348)

guest worker programs Government-run programs in western Europe designed to recruit labor for the booming postwar economy. (p. 973)

guild system The organization of artisanal production into trade-based associations, or guilds, each of which received a monopoly over its trade and the right to train apprentices and hire workers. (p. 563)

gunboat diplomacy The use or threat of military force to coerce a government into economic or political agreements. (p. 802)

gynaeceum Women's quarters at the back of an Athenian house where the women of the family and the female slaves worked, ate, and slept. (p. 83)

Hammurabi's law code A proclamation issued by Babylonian king Hammurabi to establish laws regulating many aspects of life. (p. 18)

Hanseatic League A mercantile association of towns begun in northern Europe that allowed for mutual protection and trading rights. (p. 311)

Haskalah The Jewish Enlightenment of the second half of the eighteenth century, led by the Prussian philosopher Moses Mendelssohn. (p. 547)

Hellenistic A term that literally means "like the Greek," used to describe the period after the death of Alexander the Great, when Greek culture spread. (p. 97)

Hellenization The spread of Greek ideas, culture, and traditions to non-Greek groups across a wide area. (p. 102)

helots Unfree residents of Sparta forced to work state lands. (p. 72)

heresy The denial of a basic doctrine of faith. (pp. 185, 195)

Holocaust The systematic effort of the Nazi state to exterminate all European Jews and other groups deemed racially inferior during the Second World War. (p. 925)

Holy Alliance An alliance formed by the conservative rulers of Austria, Prussia, and Russia in September 1815 that became a symbol of the repression of liberal and revolutionary movements all over Europe. (p. 692)

Holy Office The official Roman Catholic agency founded in 1542 to combat international doctrinal heresy. (p. 427)

Holy Roman Empire The loose confederation of principalities, duchies, cities, bishoprics, and other types of regional governments stretching from Denmark to Rome and from Burgundy to Poland. (p. 264)

Homestead Act An American law enacted during the Civil War that gave western land to settlers, reinforcing the concept of free labor in a market economy. (p. 772)

hoplites Heavily armed citizens who served as infantrymen and fought to defend the polis. (p. 70)

Huguenots French Calvinists. (p. 430)

humanism A program of study designed by Italians that emphasized the critical study of Latin and Greek literature with the goal of understanding human nature. (p. 373)

hundred days of reform A series of Western-style reforms launched in 1898 by the Chinese government in an attempt to meet the foreign challenge. (p. 826)

Hundred Years' War A war between England and France from 1337 to 1453, with political and economic causes and consequences. (p. 340)

id, ego, and superego Freudian terms to describe the three parts of the self and the basis of human behavior, which Freud saw as basically irrational. (p. 874)

illegitimacy explosion The sharp increase in out-of-wedlock births that occurred in Europe between 1750 and 1850, caused by low wages and the breakdown of community controls. (p. 587)

imperator Title given to a Roman general after a major victory that came to mean "emperor." (p. 159)

Inca Empire The vast and sophisticated Peruvian empire centered at the capital city of Cuzco that was at its peak from 1438 until 1532. (p. 455)

indulgence A document issued by the Catholic Church lessening penance or time in purgatory, widely believed to bring forgiveness of all sins. (pp. 284, 404)

Industrial Revolution A term first coined in 1799 to describe the burst of major inventions and economic expansion that began in Britain in the late eighteenth century. (p. 656)

industrious revolution The shift that occurred as families in northwestern Europe focused on earning wages instead of producing goods for household consumption; this reduced their economic self-sufficiency but increased their ability to purchase consumer goods. (p. 563)

infidel A disparaging term used for a person who does not believe in a particular religion. (p. 234)

Institutes of the Christian Religion, The Calvin's formulation of Christian doctrine, which became a systematic theology for Protestantism. (p. 422)

Iron Age Period beginning about 1100 B.C.E., when iron became the most important material for tools and weapons. (p. 36)

iron law of wages Theory proposed by English economist David Ricardo suggesting that the pressure of population growth prevents wages from rising above the subsistence level. (p. 665)

Jacobin Club A political club in revolutionary France whose members were well-educated radical republicans. (p. 634)

Jacquerie A massive uprising by French peasants in 1358 protesting heavy taxation. (p. 353)

janissary corps The core of the sultan's army, composed of slave conscripts from non-Muslim parts of the empire; after 1683 it became a volunteer force. (p. 502)

Jansenism A sect of Catholicism originating with Cornelius Jansen that emphasized the heavy weight of original sin and accepted the doctrine of predestination; it was outlawed as heresy by the pope. (p. 609)

Jesuits Members of the Society of Jesus, founded by Ignatius Loyola, whose goal was the spread of the Roman Catholic faith. (p. 429)

Junkers The nobility of Brandenburg and Prussia, they were reluctant allies of Frederick William in his consolidation of the Prussian state. (p. 494)

just price The idea that prices should be fair, protecting both consumers and producers, and that they should be imposed by government decree if necessary. (p. 599)

Karlsbad Decrees Issued in 1819, these decrees were designed to uphold Metternich's conservatism, requiring the German states to root out subversive ideas and squelch any liberal organizations. (p. 693)

Kievan Rus A confederation of Slavic territories, with its capital at Kiev, ruled by descendants of the Vikings. (p. 252)

Kosovo Liberation Army (KLA) Military organization formed in 1998 by Kosovar militants who sought independence from Serbia. (p. 1027)

kulaks The better-off peasants who were stripped of land and livestock under Stalin and were generally not permitted to join collective farms; many of them starved or were deported to forced-labor camps for "re-education." (p. 907)

Kulturkampf Bismarck's attack on the Catholic Church within Germany from 1870 to 1878, resulting from Pius IX's declaration of papal infallibility. (p. 779)

Kush Kingdom in Nubia that adopted hieroglyphics and pyramids, and later conquered Egypt. (p. 38)

labor aristocracy The highly skilled workers, such as factory foremen and construction bosses, who made up about 15 percent of the working classes from about 1850 to 1914. (p. 735)

laissez faire A doctrine of economic liberalism that calls for unrestricted private enterprise and no government interference in the economy. (p. 696)

Lateran Agreement A 1929 agreement that recognized the Vatican as an independent state, with Mussolini agreeing to give the church heavy financial support in return for public support from the pope. (p. 913)

latifundia Huge agricultural estates owned by wealthy absentee landowners and worked by slaves. (p. 147)

law of inertia A law formulated by Galileo that states that motion, not rest, is the natural state of an object, and that an object continues in motion forever unless stopped by some external force. (p. 522)

law of universal gravitation Newton's law that all objects are attracted to one another and that the force of attraction is proportional to the objects' quantity of matter and inversely proportional to the square of the distance between them. (p. 525)

League of Nations A permanent international organization, established during the 1919 Paris Peace Conference, designed to protect member states from aggression and avert future wars. (p. 859)

liberalism The principal ideas of this movement were equality and liberty; liberals demanded representative government and equality before the law as well as individual freedoms such as freedom of the press, freedom of speech, freedom of assembly, freedom of worship, and freedom from arbitrary arrest. (p. 696)

logical positivism A philosophy that sees meaning in only those beliefs that can be empirically proven, and that therefore rejects most of the concerns of traditional philosophy, from the existence of God to the meaning of happiness, as nonsense. (p. 871)

Luddites Group of handicraft workers who attacked factories in northern England in 1811 and later, smashing the new machines that they believed were putting them out of work. (p. 680)

Maastricht Treaty The basis for the formation of the European Union, which set financial and cultural standards for potential member states and defined criteria for membership in the monetary union. (p. 1028)

ma'at The Egyptian belief in a cosmic harmony that embraced truth, justice, and moral integrity; it gave the kings the right and duty to govern. (p. 22)

Magna Carta A peace treaty intended to redress the grievances that particular groups had against King John; it was later viewed as the source of English rights and liberty more generally. (p. 268)

mandate system The plan to allow Britain and France to administer former Ottoman territories, put into place after the end of the First World War. (p. 861)

manorialism A system in which peasant residents of manors, or farming villages, provided work and goods for their lord in exchange for protection. (p. 255)

manumission The freeing of individual slaves by their masters. (p. 142)

Marshall Plan American plan for providing economic aid to western Europe to help it rebuild. (p. 947)

Marxism An influential political program based on the socialist ideas of German radical Karl Marx, which called for a working-class revolution to overthrow capitalist society and establish a Communist state. (p. 700)

Meiji Restoration The restoration of the Japanese emperor to power in 1867, leading to the subsequent modernization of Japan. (p. 824)

mercantilism A system of economic regulations aimed at increasing the power of the state based on the belief that a nation's international power was based on its wealth, specifically its supply of gold and silver. (p. 488)

merchant guild A band of merchants in a town that prohibited nonmembers from trading in that town. (p. 308)

Messiah In Jewish belief, a savior who would bring a period of peace and happiness for Jews. (p. 181)

Methodists Members of a Protestant revival movement started by John Wesley, so called because they were so methodical in their devotion. (p. 607)

Mexica Empire Also known as the Aztec Empire, a large and complex Native American civilization in modern Mexico and Central America that possessed advanced mathematical, astronomical, and engineering technology. (p. 453)

millet system A system used by the Ottomans whereby subjects were divided into religious communities, with each millet (nation) enjoying autonomous self-government under its religious leaders. (p. 502)

Mines Act of 1842 English law prohibiting underground work for all women and girls as well as for boys under ten. (p. 678)

Minoan A wealthy and vibrant culture on Crete from around 1900 B.C.E. to 1450 B.C.E., ruled by a king with a large palace at Knossos. (p. 64)

"modern girl" Somewhat stereotypical image of the modern and independent working woman popular in the 1920s. (p. 882)

modernism A label given to the artistic and cultural movements of the late nineteenth and early twentieth centuries, which were typified by radical experimentation that challenged traditional forms of artistic expression. (p. 875)

Mountain, the Led by Robespierre, the French National Convention's radical faction, which seized legislative power in 1793. (p. 635)

multiculturalism The mixing of ethnic styles in daily life and in cultural works such as film, music, art, and literature. (p. 1039)

Muslim Brotherhood Islamic social and political reform group founded in Egypt in 1928 that called for national liberation from European control and a return to shari'a law (based on Muslim legal codes), and demanded land reform, extensive social welfare programs, and economic independence. (p. 1046)

Mycenaean A Bronze Age culture that flourished in Greece from about 1650 B.C.E. to 1100 B.C.E., building fortified palaces and cities. (p. 64)

mystery religions Belief systems that were characterized by secret doctrines, rituals of initiation, and sometimes the promise of rebirth or an afterlife. (p. 90)

Napoleonic Code French civil code promulgated in 1804 that reasserted the 1789 principles of the equality of all male citizens before the law and the absolute security of wealth and private property, as well as restricting rights accorded to women by previous revolutionary laws. (p. 640)

National Assembly The first French revolutionary legislature, made up primarily of representatives of the third estate and a few from the nobility and clergy, in session from 1789 to 1791. (p. 630)

nationalism The idea that each people had its own genius and specific identity that manifested itself especially in a common language and history, and often led to the desire for an independent political state. (p. 697)

national self-determination The notion that peoples should be able to choose their own national governments through democratic majority-rule elections and live free from outside interference in nation-states with clearly defined borders. (p. 859)

National Socialism A movement and political party driven by extreme nationalism and racism, led by Adolf Hitler; its adherents ruled Germany from 1933 to 1945 and forced Europe into World War II. (p. 914)

nativism Policies and beliefs, often influenced by nationalism, scientific racism, and mass migration, that give preferential treatment to established inhabitants over immigrants. (p. 808)

NATO The North Atlantic Treaty Organization, an anti-Soviet military alliance of Western governments. (p. 948)

natural law A Stoic concept that a single law that was part of the natural order of life governed all people. (p. 115)

natural philosophy An early modern term for the study of the nature of the universe, its purpose, and how it functioned; it encompassed what we would call "science" today. (p. 517)

Navigation Acts A series of English laws that controlled the import of goods to Britain and British colonies. (p. 569)

neocolonialism A postcolonial system that perpetuates Western economic exploitation in former colonial territories. (p. 971)

neo-Europes Settler colonies with established populations of Europeans, such as North America, Australia, New Zealand, and Latin America, where Europe found outlets for population growth and its most profitable investment opportunities in the nineteenth century. (p. 799)

neoliberalism Philosophy of 1980s conservatives who argued for privatization of state-run industries and decreased government spending on social services. (p. 996)

Neolithic era The period after 9000 B.C.E., when people developed agriculture, domesticated animals, and used tools made of stone and wood. (p. 4)

New Christians A term for Jews and Muslims in the Iberian Peninsula who accepted Christianity; in many cases they included Christians whose families had converted centuries earlier. (p. 397)

New Economic Policy (NEP) Lenin's 1921 policy to re-establish limited economic freedom in an attempt to rebuild agriculture and industry in the face of economic disintegration. (p. 905)

new imperialism The late-nineteenth-century drive by European countries to create vast political empires abroad. (p. 810)

New Left A 1960s counterculture movement that embraced updated forms of Marxism to challenge both Western capitalism and Soviet-style communism. (p. 986)

New Order Hitler's program based on racial imperialism, which gave preferential treatment to the Nordic peoples; the French, an "inferior" Latin people, occupied a middle position, and Slavs and Jews were treated harshly as "subhumans." (p. 923)

nonalignment Policy of postcolonial governments to remain neutral in the Cold War and play both the United States and the Soviet Union for what they could get. (p. 965)

nongovernmental organizations (NGOs) Independent organizations with specific agendas, such as humanitarian aid or environmental protection, that conduct international programs and activities. (p. 1031)

October Manifesto The result of a paralyzing general strike in October 1905, a Russian decree that granted full civil rights and promised a popularly elected Duma (parliament) with real legislative power. (p. 775)

oligarchy A type of Greek government in which citizens who owned a certain amount of property ruled. (p. 70)

OPEC The Arab-led Organization of Petroleum Exporting Countries. (p. 994)

open-field system System in which the arable land of a manor was divided into two or three fields without hedges or fences to mark individual holdings. (p. 295)

Opium Wars Two mid-nineteenth-century conflicts between China and Great Britain over the British trade in opium, which was designed to "open" China to European free trade. In defeat, China gave European traders and missionaries increased protection and concessions. (p. 801)

Orientalism A term coined by literary scholar Edward Said to describe the way Westerners misunderstood and described colonial subjects and cultures. (p. 819)

Orthodox Church Eastern Christian Church in the Byzantine Empire. (p. 220)

Ostalgie German term referring to nostalgia for the lifestyles and culture of the vanished East Bloc. (p. 1025)

Ostpolitik German for "Eastern policy"; West Germany's attempt in the 1970s to ease diplomatic tensions with East Germany, exemplifying the policies of détente. (p. 981)

pagan Originally referring to those who lived in the countryside, it came to mean those who practiced religions other than Judaism or Christianity. (p. 181)

Paleolithic era The period of human history up to about 9000 B.C.E., when tools were made from stone and bone and people gained their food through foraging. (p. 4)

pastoralism An economic system based on herding flocks of goats, sheep, cattle, or other animals beneficial to humans. (p. 8)

paterfamilias The oldest dominant male of the family, who held great power over the lives of family members. (p. 139)

patriarchy A society in which most power is held by older adult men, especially those from the elite groups. (p. 9)

patricians The Roman hereditary aristocracy, who held most of the political power in the republic. (p. 132)

patronage Financial support of writers and artists by cities, groups, and individuals, often to produce specific works or works in specific styles. (p. 367)

patron-client system An informal system of patronage in which free men promised their votes to a more powerful man in exchange for his help in legal or other matters. (p. 135)

pax Romana The "Roman peace," a period during the first and second centuries C.E. of political stability and relative peace. (p. 163)

Peace of Utrecht A series of treaties, from 1713 to 1715, that ended the War of the Spanish Succession, ended French expansion in Europe, and marked the rise of the British Empire. (p. 489)

Peace of Westphalia The name of a series of treaties that concluded the Thirty Years' War in 1648 and marked the end of large-scale religious violence in Europe. (p. 480)

People's Budget A bill proposed after the Liberal Party came to power in Britain in 1906, it was designed to increase spending on social welfare services, but was initially vetoed in the House of Lords. (p. 782)

perestroika Economic restructuring and reform implemented by Premier Mikhail Gorbachev in the Soviet Union in 1985. (p. 1008)

Petrine Doctrine A doctrine stating that the popes (the bishops of Rome) were the successors of Saint Peter and therefore heirs to his highest level of authority as chief of the apostles. (p. 197)

Petrograd Soviet A huge, fluctuating mass meeting of two to three thousand workers, soldiers, and socialist intellectuals modeled on the revolutionary soviets of 1905. (p. 850)

pharaoh The title given to the king of Egypt in the New Kingdom, from a word that meant "great house." (p. 21)

philosophes A group of French intellectuals who proclaimed that they were bringing the light of knowledge to their fellow humans in the Age of Enlightenment. (p. 531)

Phoenicians Seafaring people from Canaan who traded and founded colonies throughout the Mediterranean and spread the phonetic alphabet. (p. 39)

Pietism A Protestant revival movement in early-eighteenth-century Germany and Scandinavia that emphasized a warm and emotional religion, the priesthood of all believers, and the power of Christian rebirth in everyday affairs. (p. 606)

Platonic ideals In Plato's thought, the eternal unchanging ideal forms that are the essence of true reality. (p. 93)

plebeians The common people of Rome, who were free but had few of the patricians' advantages. (p. 132)

polis Generally translated as "city-state," it was the basic political and institutional unit of Greece in the Hellenic period. (p. 67)

politiques Catholic and Protestant moderates who held that only a strong monarchy could save France from total collapse. (p. 431)

polytheism The worship of many gods and goddesses. (p. 10)

popolo Disenfranchised common people in Italian cities who resented their exclusion from power. (p. 369)

Popular Front A short-lived New Deal–inspired alliance in France led by Léon Blum that encouraged the union movement and launched a far-reaching program of social reform. (p. 898)

postcolonial migration The postwar movement of people from former colonies and the developing world into Europe. (p. 973)

postindustrial society A society that relies on high-tech and service-oriented jobs for economic growth rather than heavy industry and manufacturing jobs. (p. 995)

Praetorians Imperial bodyguard created by Augustus. (p. 169)

predestination The teaching that God has determined the salvation or damnation of individuals based on his will and purpose, not on their merit or works. (p. 422)

primogeniture An inheritance system in which the oldest son inherits all land and noble titles. (p. 263)

principate Official title of Augustus's form of government, taken from *princeps*, meaning "first citizen." (p. 160)

privatization The sale of state-managed industries such as transportation and communication networks to private owners, a key policy of neoliberalism meant to control government spending, increase private profits, and foster economic growth, which was implemented in western Europe in response to the economic crisis of the 1970s. (p. 996)

proletarianization The transformation of large numbers of small peasant farmers into landless rural wage earners. (p. 556)

proletariat The industrial working class who, according to Marx, were unfairly exploited by the profit-seeking bourgeoisie. (p. 701)

Protectorate The English military dictatorship (1653–1658) established by Oliver Cromwell following the execution of Charles I. (p. 507)

Protestant The name originally given to followers of Luther, which came to mean all non-Catholic Western Christian groups. (p. 406)

Ptolemy's *Geography* A second-century-c.e. work that synthesized the classical knowledge of geography and introduced the concepts of longitude and latitude. Reintroduced to Europeans in about 1410 by Arab scholars, its ideas allowed cartographers to create more accurate maps. (p. 446)

public sphere An idealized intellectual space that emerged in Europe during the Enlightenment, where the public came together to discuss important issues relating to society, economics, and politics. (p. 539)

Punic Wars A series of three wars between Rome and Carthage in which Rome emerged the victor. (p. 135)

Puritans Members of a sixteenth- and seventeenth-century reform movement within the Church of England that advocated purifying it of Roman Catholic elements, like bishops, elaborate ceremonials, and wedding rings. (p. 503)

putting-out system The eighteenth-century system of rural industry in which a merchant loaned raw materials to cottage workers, who processed them and returned the finished products to the merchant. (p. 559)

Qur'an The sacred book of Islam. (p. 226)

rationalism A secular, critical way of thinking in which nothing was to be accepted on faith, and everything was to be submitted to reason. (p. 530)

reading revolution The transition in Europe from a society where literacy consisted of patriarchal and communal reading of religious texts to a society where literacy was commonplace and reading material was broad and diverse. (p. 538)

realism A literary movement that, in contrast to romanticism, stressed the depiction of life as it actually was. (p. 753)

reconquista The Christian term for the conquest of Muslim territories in the Iberian Peninsula by Christian forces. (p. 266)

Red Shirts The guerrilla army of Giuseppe Garibaldi, who invaded Sicily in 1860 in an attempt to liberate it, winning the hearts of the Sicilian peasantry. (p. 765)

Reform Bill of 1832 A major British political reform that increased the number of male voters by about 50 percent and gave political representation to new industrial areas. (p. 708)

regular clergy Men and women who lived in monastic houses and followed sets of rules, first those of Benedict and later those written by other individuals. (p. 199)

Reichstag The popularly elected lower house of government of the new German Empire after 1871. (p. 779)

Reign of Terror The period from 1793 to 1794 during which Robespierre's Committee of Public Safety tried and executed thousands suspected of treason and a new revolutionary culture was imposed. (p. 636)

relics Bones, articles of clothing, or other objects associated with the life of a saint. (p. 216)

religious orders Groups of monastic houses following a particular rule. (p. 278)

Renaissance A French word meaning "rebirth," used to describe the rebirth of the culture of classical antiquity in Italy during the fourteenth to sixteenth centuries. (p. 367)

representative assemblies Deliberative meetings of lords and wealthy urban residents that flourished in many European countries between 1250 and 1450. (p. 346)

republicanism A form of government in which there is no monarch and power rests in the hands of the people as exercised through elected representatives. (p. 503)

revisionism An effort by moderate socialists to update Marxist doctrines to reflect the realities of the time. (p. 793)

Rocket The name given to George Stephenson's effective locomotive that was first tested in 1829 on the Liverpool and Manchester Railway at 24 miles per hour. (p. 662)

rococo A popular style in Europe in the eighteenth century, known for its soft pastels, ornate interiors, sentimental portraits, and starry-eyed lovers protected by hovering cupids. (p. 538)

Roma et Augustus Patriotic cult encouraged by Augustus and later emperors in which the good of Rome and the good of the emperor were linked. (p. 161)

Romanesque An architectural style with rounded arches and small windows. (p. 326)

romanticism An artistic movement at its height from about 1790 to the 1840s that was in part a revolt against classicism and the Enlightenment, characterized by a belief in emotional exuberance, unrestrained imagination, and spontaneity in both art and personal life. (p. 701)

runic alphabet Writing system developed in some barbarian groups that helps to give a more accurate picture of barbarian society. (p. 203)

sacraments Certain rituals defined by the church in which God bestows benefits on the believer through grace. (p. 202)

salon Regular social gathering held by talented and rich Parisians in their homes, where philosophes and their followers met to discuss literature, science, and philosophy. (p. 538)

sans-culottes The laboring poor of Paris, so called because the men wore trousers instead of the knee breeches of the aristocracy and middle class; the word came to refer to the militant radicals of the city. (p. 635)

satraps Administrators in the Persian Empire who controlled local government, collected taxes, heard legal cases, and maintained order. (p. 56)

Schlieffen Plan Failed German plan calling for a lightning attack through neutral Belgium and a quick defeat of France before turning on Russia. (p. 839)

Scholastics University professors in the Middle Ages who developed a method of thinking, reasoning, and writing in which questions were raised and authorities cited on both sides of a question. (p. 321)

Second Industrial Revolution The burst of industrial creativity and technological innovation that promoted strong economic growth in the last third of the nineteenth century. (p. 749)

second revolution From 1792 to 1795, the second phase of the French Revolution, during which the fall of the French monarchy introduced a rapid radicalization of politics. (p. 635)

Second Triumvirate A formal agreement in 43 B.C.E. among Octavian, Mark Antony, and Lepidus to defeat Caesar's murderers. (p. 153)

Second Vatican Council A meeting of Catholic leaders convened from 1962 to 1965 that initiated a number of reforms, including the replacement of Latin with local languages in church services, designed to democratize the church and renew its appeal. (p. 985)

secular clergy Priests and bishops who staffed churches where people worshipped and who were not cut off from the world. (p. 199)

Senate The assembly that was the main institution of power in the Roman Republic, originally composed only of aristocrats. (p. 129)

separate spheres A gender division of labor with the wife at home as mother and homemaker and the husband as wage earner. (pp. 675, 742)

serfs Peasants bound to the land by a relationship with a manorial lord. (p. 256)

signori Government by one-man rule in Italian cities such as Milan; also refers to these rulers. (p. 369)

simony The buying and selling of church offices, a policy that was officially prohibited but often practiced. (p. 273)

Social Darwinism A body of thought drawn from the ideas of Charles Darwin that applied the theory of biological evolution to human affairs and saw the human race as driven by an unending economic struggle that would determine the survival of the fittest. (p. 751)

socialism A backlash against the emergence of individualism and the fragmentation of industrial society, and a move toward cooperation and a sense of community; the key ideas were economic planning, greater social equality, and state regulation of property. (p. 698)

socialist realism Artistic movement that followed the dictates of Communist ideals, enforced by state control in the Soviet Union and East Bloc countries in the 1950s and 1960s. (p. 958)

Socratic method A method of inquiry used by Socrates based on asking questions, through which participants developed their critical-thinking skills and explored ethical issues. (p. 92)

Solidarity Independent Polish trade union that worked for workers' rights and political reform throughout the 1980s. (p. 1006)

Sophists A group of thinkers in fifth-century-B.C.E. Athens who applied philosophical speculation to politics and language and were accused of deceit. (p. 92)

Spanish Armada The fleet sent by Philip II of Spain in 1588 against England as a religious crusade against Protestantism. Weather and the English fleet defeated it. (p. 421)

spinning jenny A simple, inexpensive, hand-powered spinning machine created by James Hargreaves in 1765. (p. 657)

stadholder The executive officer in each of the United Provinces of the Netherlands, a position often held by the princes of Orange. (p. 511)

stagflation Term coined in the early 1980s to describe the combination of low growth and high inflation that led to a worldwide recession. (p. 995)

Statute of Kilkenny Law issued in 1366 that discriminated against the Irish, forbidding marriage between the English and the Irish, requiring the use of the English language, and denying the Irish access to ecclesiastical offices. (p. 361)

steam engines A breakthrough invention by Thomas Savery in 1698 and Thomas Newcomen in 1705 that burned coal to produce steam, which was then used to operate a pump; the early models were superseded by James Watt's more efficient steam engine, patented in 1769. (p. 660)

Stoicism A philosophy, based on the ideas of Zeno, that people could be happy only when living in accordance with nature and accepting whatever happened. (p. 115)

stream-of-consciousness technique A literary technique, found in works by Virginia Woolf, James Joyce, and others, that uses interior monologue—a character's thoughts and feelings as they occur—to explore the human psyche. (p. 878)

Struggle of the Orders A conflict in which the plebeians sought political representation and safeguards against patrician domination. (p. 134)

suffrage movement A militant movement for women's right to vote led by middle-class British women around 1900. (p. 746)

sultan The ruler of the Ottoman Empire; he owned all the agricultural land of the empire and was served by an army and bureaucracy composed of highly trained slaves. (p. 501)

sumptuary laws Laws that regulated the value and style of clothing and jewelry that various social groups could wear as well as the amount they could spend on celebrations. (p. 316)

sweated industries Poorly paid handicraft production, often carried out by married women paid by the piece and working at home. (p. 737)

Tanzimat A set of reforms designed to remake the Ottoman Empire on a western European model. (p. 776)

tariff protection A government's way of supporting and aiding its own economy by laying high taxes on imported goods from other countries, as when the French responded to cheaper British goods flooding their country by imposing high tariffs on some imported products. (p. 670)

Test Act Legislation, passed by the English Parliament in 1673, to secure the position of the Anglican Church by stripping Puritans, Catholics, and other dissenters of the right to vote, preach, assemble, hold public office, and teach at or attend the universities. (p. 507)

tetrarchy Diocletian's four-part division of the Roman Empire. (p. 191)

theory of special relativity Albert Einstein's theory that time and space are relative to the observer and that only the speed of light remains constant. (p. 873)

Thermidorian reaction A reaction to the violence of the Reign of Terror in 1794, resulting in the execution of Robespierre and the loosening of economic controls. (p. 637)

thermodynamics A branch of physics built on Newton's laws of mechanics that investigated the relationship between heat and mechanical energy. (p. 747)

Torah The first five books of the Hebrew Bible, containing the most important legal and ethical Hebrew texts; later became part of the Christian Old Testament. (p. 43)

totalitarianism A radical dictatorship that exercises "total claims" over the beliefs and behavior of its citizens by taking control of the economic, social, intellectual, and cultural aspects of society. (p. 902)

total war A war in which distinctions between the soldiers on the battlefield and civilians at home are blurred, and where the government plans and controls economic and social life in order to supply the armies at the front with supplies and weapons. (p. 839)

Treaty of Brest-Litovsk Peace treaty signed in March 1918 between the Central Powers and Russia that ended Russian participation in World War I and ceded Russian territories containing a third of the Russian empire's population to the Central Powers. (p. 853)

Treaty of Paris The treaty that ended the Seven Years' War in Europe and the colonies in 1763, and ratified British victory on all colonial fronts. (p. 570)

Treaty of Tordesillas The 1494 agreement giving Spain everything to the west of an imaginary line drawn down the Atlantic and giving Portugal everything to the east. (p. 452)

Treaty of Verdun Treaty signed in 843 by Charlemagne's grandsons dividing the Carolingian Empire into three parts and setting the pattern for political boundaries in Europe still in use today. (p. 246)

Treaty of Versailles The 1919 peace settlement that ended war between Germany and the Allied powers. (p. 859)

trench warfare A type of fighting used in World War I behind rows of trenches, mines, and barbed wire; the cost in lives was staggering and the gains in territory minimal. (p. 840)

tribunes Plebeian-elected officials; tribunes brought plebeian grievances to the Senate for resolution and protected plebeians from the arbitrary conduct of patrician magistrates. (p. 134)

Triple Alliance The alliance of Austria, Germany, and Italy. Italy left the alliance when war broke out in 1914 on the grounds that Austria had launched a war of aggression. (p. 831)

Triple Entente The alliance of Great Britain, France, and Russia prior to and during the First World War. (p. 833)

troubadours Poets who wrote and sang lyric verses celebrating love, desire, beauty, and gallantry. (p. 325)

Truman Doctrine America's policy geared to containing communism to those countries already under Soviet control. (p. 947)

tyranny Rule by one man who took over an existing government, generally by using his wealth to gain a political following. (p. 70)

Union of Utrecht The alliance of seven northern provinces (led by Holland) that declared its independence from Spain and formed the United Provinces of the Netherlands. (p. 432)

utilitarianism The idea of Jeremy Bentham that social policies should promote the "greatest good for the greatest number." (p. 727)

vassal A warrior who swore loyalty and service to a noble in exchange for land, protection, and support. (p. 254)

Velvet Revolution The term given to the relatively peaceful overthrow of communism in Czechoslovakia; the label came to signify the collapse of the East Bloc in general in 1989 to 1990. (p. 1012)

vernacular literature Writings in the author's local dialect, that is, in the everyday language of the region. (p. 324)

viceroyalties The name for the four administrative units of Spanish possessions in the Americas: New Spain, Peru, New Granada, and La Plata. (p. 457)

virtù The quality of being able to shape the world according to one's own will. (p. 376)

War Communism The application of centralized state control during the Russian civil war, in which the Bolsheviks seized grain from peasants, introduced rationing, nationalized all banks and industry, and required everyone to work. (p. 856)

war guilt clause An article in the Treaty of Versailles that declared that Germany (with Austria) was solely responsible for the war and had to pay reparations equal to all civilian damages caused by the fighting. (p. 860)

war on terror American policy under President George W. Bush to fight global terrorism in all its forms. (p. 1045)

Warsaw Pact Soviet-backed military alliance of East Bloc Communist countries in Europe. (p. 948)

water frame A spinning machine created by Richard Arkwright that had a capacity of several hundred spindles and used waterpower; it therefore required a larger and more specialized mill—a factory. (p. 657)

wergeld Compensatory payment for death or injury set in many barbarian law codes. (p. 207)

wet-nursing A widespread and flourishing business in the eighteenth century in which women were paid to breast-feed other women's babies. (p. 590)

white man's burden The idea that Europeans could and should civilize more primitive nonwhite peoples and that imperialism would eventually provide nonwhites with modern achievements and higher standards of living. (p. 818)

World Trade Organization (WTO) A powerful supranational financial institution that sets trade and tariff agreements for over 150 member countries and so helps manage a large percentage of the world's import-export policies. Like the IMF and the World Bank, the WTO promotes neoliberal policies around the world. (p. 1031)

Yahweh The sole god in Hebrew monotheism. (p. 41)

Young Turks Fervent patriots who seized power in a 1908 coup in the Ottoman Empire, forcing the conservative sultan to implement reforms. (p. 778)

Zionism A movement dedicated to building a Jewish national homeland in Palestine, started by Theodor Herzl. (p. 789)

Zoroastrianism Religion based on the ideas of Zoroaster that stressed devotion to the god Ahuramazda alone, and that emphasized the individual's responsibility to choose between good and evil. (p. 57)

Index

ABOUT THE AUTHORS

John P. McKay (Ph.D., University of California, Berkeley) is professor emeritus at the University of Illinois. He has written or edited numerous works, including the Herbert Baxter Adams Prize–winning book *Pioneers for Profit: Foreign Entrepreneurship and Russian Industrialization, 1885–1913.*

Bennett D. Hill (Ph.D., Princeton), late of Georgetown University, published *Church and State in the Middle Ages* and numerous articles and reviews, and was one of the contributing editors to *The Encyclopedia of World History*. He taught for many years at the University of Illinois and was a Benedictine monk of St. Anselm's Abbey in Washington, D.C.

John Buckler (Ph.D., Harvard University), late of the University of Illinois, published numerous works, including *Theban Hegemony, 371–362 B.C.*; *Philip II and the Sacred War*; and *Aegean Greece in the Fourth Century B.C.* With Hans Beck, he published *Central Greece and the Politics of Power in the Fourth Century.*

Clare Haru Crowston (Ph.D., Cornell University) teaches at the University of Illinois, where she is currently associate professor of history. She is the author of *Credit, Fashion, Sex: Economies of Regard in Old Regime France* and *Fabricating Women: The Seamstresses of Old Regime France, 1675–1791*, which won the Berkshire and Hagley Prizes. She edited two special issues of the *Journal of Women's History*, has published numerous journal articles and reviews, and is a past president of the Society for French Historical Studies.

Merry E. Wiesner-Hanks (Ph.D., University of Wisconsin–Madison) taught first at Augustana College in Illinois, and since 1985 at the University of Wisconsin–Milwaukee, where she is currently UWM Distinguished Professor in the department of history. She is the Senior Editor of the *Sixteenth Century Journal*, one of the editors of the *Journal of Global History*, and the author or editor of more than twenty books, including *The Marvelous Hairy Girls: The Gonzales Sisters and Their Worlds* and *Gender in History* (2nd ed.). She is the former Chief Reader for Advanced Placement World History.

Joe Perry (Ph.D., University of Illinois at Urbana-Champaign) is associate professor of modern German and European history at Georgia State University. He has published numerous articles and is author of *Christmas in Germany: A Cultural History*. His current research interests focus on issues of consumption, gender, and popular culture in West Germany and Western Europe after World War II.